Historic Houses & Gardens
Castles and Heritage Sites

2002

"Apart from some form of wheels,

the other essential for anyone bent on enjoying the

United Kingdom's unrivalled range of historic houses and

gardens, is a copy of Hudson's guide"

Barbara Ballard. Travellady Magazine USA

Published by:

NORMAN HUDSON & COMPANY

High Wardington House, Upper Wardington, Banbury, Oxfordshire OX17 1SP, United Kingdom

Tel: +44 (0) 1295 750750 • Fax: +44 (0) 1295 750800 • e-mail: enquiries@hudsons.co.uk • website: www.hudsons.co.uk

THE GLOBE PEQUOT PRESS

246 Goose Lane, Guilford, Connecticut 06437, USA

GREAT BRITAIN & IRELAND
REGIONAL COLOURS

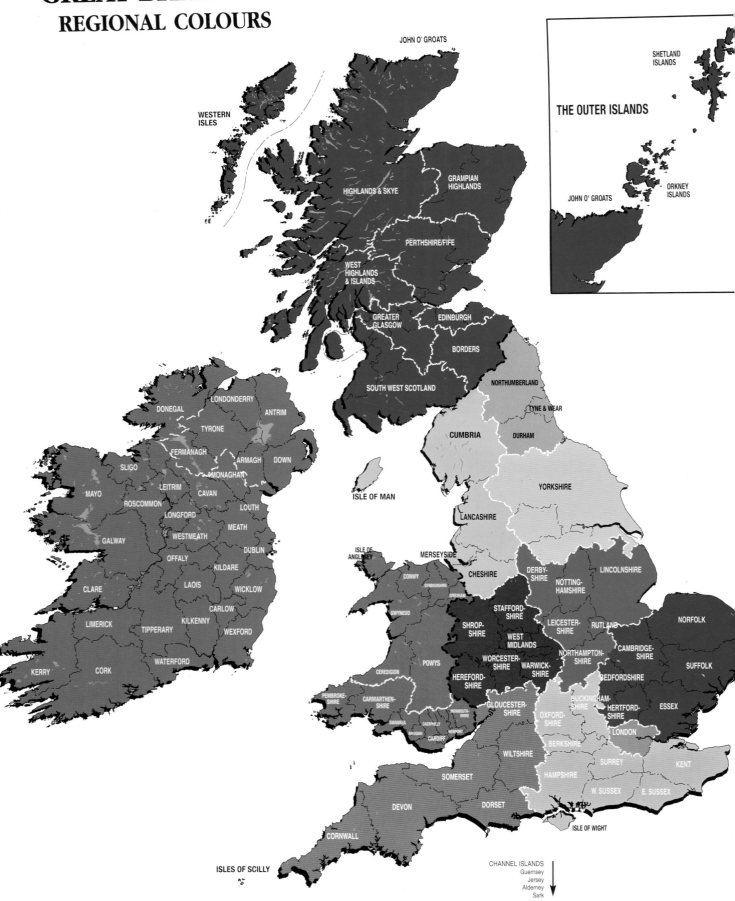

JOHN O' GROATS

WESTERN ISLES

THE OUTER ISLANDS

SHETLAND ISLANDS

JOHN O' GROATS

ORKNEY ISLANDS

HIGHLANDS & SKYE

GRAMPIAN HIGHLANDS

PERTHSHIRE/FIFE

WEST HIGHLANDS & ISLANDS

GREATER GLASGOW

EDINBURGH

BORDERS

SOUTH WEST SCOTLAND

NORTHUMBERLAND

TYNE & WEAR

CUMBRIA

DURHAM

DONEGAL

LONDONDERRY

ANTRIM

TYRONE

FERMANAGH

ARMAGH

DOWN

SLIGO

MONAGHAN

LEITRIM

CAVAN

MAYO

ROSCOMMON

LONGFORD

LOUTH

MEATH

WESTMEATH

GALWAY

OFFALY

DUBLIN

KILDARE

CLARE

LAOIS

WICKLOW

CARLOW

LIMERICK

KILKENNY

TIPPERARY

WEXFORD

KERRY

CORK

WATERFORD

YORKSHIRE

ISLE OF MAN

LANCASHIRE

ISLE OF ANGLESEY

MERSEYSIDE

CONWY

DENBIGHSHIRE

WREXHAM

CHESHIRE

DERBY-SHIRE

NOTTING-HAMSHIRE

LINCOLNSHIRE

GWYNEDD

STAFFORD-SHIRE

LEICESTER-SHIRE

RUTLAND

NORFOLK

SHROP-SHIRE

WEST MIDLANDS

CAMBRIDGE-SHIRE

POWYS

WORCESTER-SHIRE

WARWICK-SHIRE

NORTHAMPTON-SHIRE

SUFFOLK

CEREDIGION

HEREFORD-SHIRE

BEDFORDSHIRE

PEMBROKE-SHIRE

CARMARTHEN-SHIRE

MONMOUTH-SHIRE

GLOUCESTER-SHIRE

BUCKINGHAM-SHIRE

HERTFORD-SHIRE

ESSEX

SWANSEA

CAERPHILLY

BRIDGEND

NEWPORT

CARDIFF

OXFORD-SHIRE

LONDON

BERKSHIRE

WILTSHIRE

SURREY

KENT

SOMERSET

HAMPSHIRE

W. SUSSEX

E. SUSSEX

DEVON

DORSET

ISLE OF WIGHT

CORNWALL

ISLES OF SCILLY

CHANNEL ISLANDS
Guernsey
Jersey
Alderney
Sark

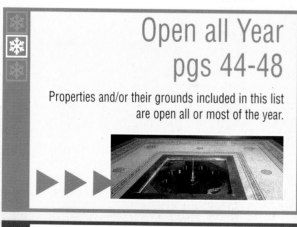

Heritage Bookshop DIRECT

Catalogue preview, see pages 606 - 608

HUDSON'S

This 2002 edition has changed in important respects. The structure and overall layout remains the same but the design and setting of individual entries has been revised to further improve readability and give a cleaner look.

Website addresses, where they exist, have been included with each property entry rather than as a separate index. Properties' individual websites can incorporate more extensive information and give details of up-to-the-minute changes. The value of this was particularly marked last year when the impact of Foot and Mouth Disease caused changes to publicised opening times.

By far the best and easiest way to access these various websites is through the portal site www.hudsons.co.uk – bookmark it for future reference.

Users of *Hudson's* frequently stress to us the importance and value of having things in print. A book has the virtue of portability, speed of access and provides the visual joy of flicking through the pages. Each year *Hudson's* has incorporated new features and many new pictures – 2002 is no exception.

Norman Hudson

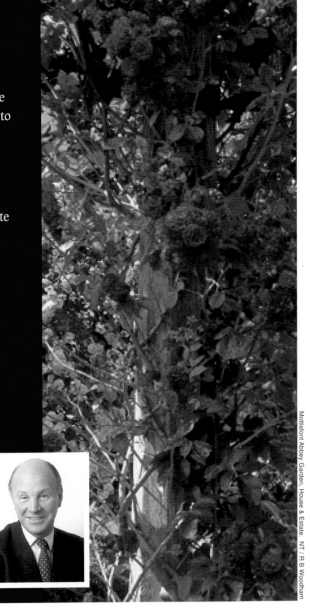

Mottisfont Abbey Garden, House & Estate. NT / R B Woodham

Hudson's Historic Houses & Gardens

Editor	Norman Hudson
Editorial/Production	Edwina Brash
Administration	Jennie Carwithen
Graphic Design	KC Graphics
Page Layout & Maps	Taurus Graphics
Scanning & Pre-press	Spot-On Reprographics
Sales	Fiona Rolt
Consultant/Maps	Patrick Lane
Printed by	E T Heron & Co Ltd
UK & European Distribution	Portfolio - tel: 020 8997 9000
USA Distribution	The Globe Pequot Press - tel: 001 203 458 4505

Published by: Norman Hudson & Company,
High Wardington House, Upper Wardington, Banbury, Oxfordshire OX17 1SP, UK
Tel: 01295 750750   Fax: 01295 750800   enquiries@hudsons.co.uk
www.hudsons.co.uk

ISBN: 0-9531426-7-1

Co-published in the USA by: The Globe Pequot Press,
246 Goose Lane, Guilford, Connecticut 06437, USA

Library of Congress Cataloging-in-Publication data is available.

ISBN: 0-7627-1210-4

British Cover: Sandringham House, Norfolk, England. © HM The Queen / Rod Edwards
US Cover: Lanhydrock, Bodmin Cornwall, England. © Andy Williams
Frontispiece: Brocade Shoes. Killerton House & Garden. NTPL / Andreas Von Einseidel

On my appointment as Director of the Victoria & Albert Museum in the autumn of 1973 an old friend, the distinguished architectural historian John Harris, urged upon me the need for a major exhibition to be mounted on the plight of Britain's historic houses. The Labour Party had promised that if they came to power they would introduce a Wealth Tax, an act which would cause yet more historic houses to be brought tumbling down. The urgent need was to reach out to the general public through the medium of an exhibition which would spell out the horrifying scale of loss to our heritage since 1900 and suggest also what needed to be done to prevent further collapse. Above all it was seen that the country house inheritance needed to be presented to the public as a shared heritage. *The Destruction of the Country House* which opened in the autumn 1974, has gone down as a landmark exhibition changing public perception and influencing government policy.

But how do I see our great houses and gardens today? What strikes me most is their ability to move on. Nothing is more stultifying than a country house and its garden frozen in time. As we enter the 21st century all around me I feel a commitment to the new and innovative. Those houses and their owners that respond to the creativity of the present (and there are already many) to me represent the future. For centuries country house owners have been at the cultural cutting edge. To appeal to today's dot.com generation they must reassert that tradition if they are to retain a place in the country's affections. A unique opportunity beckons for the historic house to occupy a central role in demonstrating that old and new are not opposites but true to this country's spirit, and compatible.

But such things are more easily said than done. Private owners are faced with the disastrous consequences of Foot and Mouth, of declining agricultural income and the effect of 11 September on world tourism. Add to that the disappearance of the 'one estate election', a principal fiscal relief since 1963, and we have all the ingredients in place to take our heritage of historic houses not forwards but backwards. Government will need to do far more than merely concede in its publicity, as it now has, that tourists come to this country as much (surely in truth more) to see the glories of our past rather than our present creativity. Ironically, from being in the vanguard in recognising the importance of giving incentives to private owners of great houses and gardens, this country is in danger of slipping behind what is being achieved now by other governments of the European Union.

Sir Roy Strong Hon D Litt PhD FSA FRSL

Cottesbrooke Hall & Gardens, Nothamptonshire

The HHA Friends scheme provides amazing value for the interested house and gardens visitor

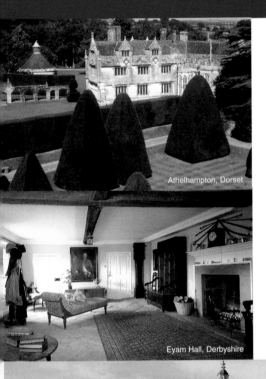
Athelhampton, Dorset

Eyam Hall, Derbyshire

The HHA is a group of highly individualistic and diverse properties most of which are still lived-in family houses. They range from the great palaces to small manor houses.

Many HHA member properties are open to the public and offer free admission to Friends of the HHA.

Southside House, London

Forde Abbey & Gardens, Dorset

Castle Howard, Yorkshire

Duart Castle, West Highlands & Islands

Minterne Gardens, Dorset

HISTORIC HOUSES ASSOCIATION

KINGSTON BAGPUIZE HOUSE, OXFORDSHIRE

HISTORIC HOUSES ASSOCIATION

join on line
www.hha.org.uk

Become a Friend of the HHA and visit nearly 300 privately owned houses and gardens for FREE.

Other benefits:

- Receive the quarterly magazine of the HHA which gives news and features about the Association, its members and our heritage

- Take advantage of organised tours in the UK and overseas

- Join the specially arranged visits to houses, some of which are not usually open to the public

LEVENS HALL GARDENS, CUMBRIA

Richard Wilkin, Director General of the HHA, explains . . .

"It is not generally realised that two-thirds of Britain's built heritage remains in private ownership. There are more privately-owned houses, castles and gardens open to the public than are opened by the National Trust, English Heritage and their equivalents in Scotland and Wales put together.

Successive Governments have recognised the private owner as the most economic and effective guardian of this heritage. But the cost of maintaining these properties is colossal, and the task is daunting. The owners work enormously hard and take a pride in preserving and presenting this element of Britain's heritage.

The HHA helps them do this by:

- *representing their interests in Government*
- *providing an advisory service for houses – taxation, conservation, security, regulations, etc.*
- *running charities assisting disabled visitors, conserving works of art and helping promote educational facilities*

There is a fascinating diversity of properties to visit free with a Friends of the HHA card – from the great treasure houses such as Blenheim and Castle Howard through to small manor houses. What makes these places so special is their individuality and the fact that they are generally still lived in – often by the same family that has owned them through centuries of British history. As well as the stunning gardens which surround the houses, there are over 60 additional wonderful gardens to visit.

We have held the subscription rate again this year, so it remains outstanding value for money at £28.00 for an individual or £40.00 for two people at the same address. If you do wish to become a Friend of the HHA, and I very much hope you will, then you can join, using your credit/debit card by calling 01462 896688 or simply fill in the form below."

HOLKHAM HALL, NORFOLK

Membership: Single £28, Double £40, £10 additional Friend at same address. Members of NADFAS, CLA and NACF are offered special rates of £25 Individual and £37 Double (at same address).

We may live without poetry, music and art;

We may live without conscience, and live without heart;

We may live without friends; we may live without books;

But civilised man cannot live without cooks!

Edward Robert Bulwer, Earl of Lytton, 'Lucile', 1860

Tour the house, amble in the garden, browse and buy a little something in the shop ..... it's all part of a day out to a National Trust property. But surely one of the highlights must be choosing that special tasty morsel at one of the Trust's restaurants. You may even find yourself making a return trip just to have lunch or tea!

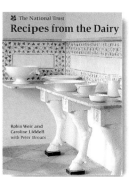

The variety of books published by the National Trust is testament to the interest people have in cooking. Simply dip into Sarah Edington's book **National Trust Recipes** (£9.99) and you will find a wonderfully varied collection of delicious recipes, some traditional, some innovative, some simple, some even elaborate, but all rewarding to cook and good to eat.

The delight of this book is the author's awareness of the importance and value of regional cooking and the need to cook, serve and write down the recipes if they

are to survive. The 28 National Trust cooks featured in this book work right across the country. Visit any of the Trust's Welsh properties, and you cannot possibly leave without trying *Bara Brith*, a traditional teabread from Wales. Travel to the Northumbrian properties and enjoy *Singin' Hinnies*, which is a term of endearment used especially for children – the 'fat' in the Hinnies making them 'sing' when they are cooking. They are ready to eat when the singing stops. Impatient children would be told to wait for their tea, "*it's still singin' Hinnie*". This book can serve as a reminder of a good day out at a National Trust property – and a chance to discover some of the gastronomic delights that are on offer in some of the most beautiful places in Britain.

Bara Brith

8oz/225g sultanas or
mixed dried fruit
6fl oz/175ml cold Earl Grey tea
8oz/225g wholemeal flour
2oz/50g baking powder
1 tsp mixed spice
6oz/175g demerara sugar
pinch salt
2 eggs, well beaten

Singin' Hinnies

8oz/225g plain flour
2oz/50g butter
2oz/50g lard
1oz/25g currants
1 tsp baking powder
1/2 tsp salt
milk and soured cream to mix

Rich Custard Pie with Dates & Prunes

for the pastry:
8oz/225g plain flour
5oz/150g unsalted butter
1/2 oz/15g icing sugar
1 egg yolk
about 3 tablespoons/45ml cold water
for the filling:
1 level tsp/5ml cornflour
about 1oz/25g caster sugar
3 large egg yolks
1pt/600ml double cream
a good pinch of saffron
2oz/50g stoned dates, chopped
2oz/50g no-soak prunes, chopped
(a recipe from Medieval & Early Tudor Food)

Welsh Cheese and Herb Scones

1lb/450g self-raising flour, sifted
1tsp salt
4oz/100g margarine, softened
1tsp mixed dried herbs
8oz/225g cheddar or other strong cheese, grated
8 tablespoons milk
8 tablespoons water

Clotted Cream Ice Cream

12fl oz/375ml whole milk
10oz/280oz granulated sugar
5 egg yolks
4fl oz/125ml clotted cream

Sara Paston-Williams' **A Book of Historical Recipes** (£8.50), provides a fascinating insight into the social history and commentary on food, the different dishes eaten, and an explanation why certain foods enjoyed favour in their day.

Forget about roast swan or stewed porpoise – Sara provides easily acquired and acceptable ingredients to adapt the original recipes for delicious meals to enjoy today.

Recipes from the Dairy (£12.99) written by Robin Weir and Caroline Liddell with Peter Brears, recaptures the tastes of the elegant country house cooking. The authors describe the work traditionally undertaken by the dairymaid, introducing some of the historic dairies that can be seen at various Trust properties. They then provide mouth-watering recipes for dishes that focus on dairy products, from supper dishes like Devonshire Chicken and Parsley Pie to sweet Yorkshire Puddings and real Rice Pudding. Try some of these out, or the ice creams – everything is deliciously moreish and wickedly fattening!

But somehow it is still the wonderfully comforting cup of afternoon tea and a piece of cake which is the vital ingredient for many when visiting a property.

Some of the very best recipes from the Trust's tea rooms are to be found in Jane Pettigrew's **Tea Time Recipes** (£12.99). Try the Derbyshire Spiced Fruit Bread, or the *Welsh Cheese and Herb*

Simple Syllabub

4oz/110g sugar
8fl oz/250ml cider
grated nutmeg, to taste
20fl oz/625ml
whipping/double cream

Scones with a cup of tea and, as Jane explains, you are perpetuating a ritual which has its origins in Britain in the 17th century, when the marriage of Charles II to the Portuguese Princess, Catherine of Braganza, estab-lished tea drinking as part of social life.

Dip into these books, pick up your pencil and jot a few ingredients down on the shopping list, and you can easily recreate that 'special tasty morsel' you first enjoyed on your day out with the Trust – the choice is just too mouth-wateringly inviting.

All these books will be available from **Heritage Bookshop Direct**. For further information see page 606.

CADW
WELSH HISTORIC MONUMENTS

The National Assembly for Wales
Cathays Park
Cardiff CF10 3NQ
Telephone: 029 2050 0200   Fax: 029 2082 6375
E-mail: cadw@wales.gsi.gov.uk

Cadw is the executive agency within the **National Assembly for Wales** that carries out the Assembly's statutory responsibilities to protect, conserve and promote an appreciation of the built heritage of Wales.

Cadw gives grant aid for the repair or restoration of outstanding historic buildings. Usually it is a condition of grant that the owner or occupier should allow some degree of public access to the property. Conditions of grant remain in force for ten years.

Details of properties grant aided by Cadw and to which the public currently enjoys a right of access can be found on Cadw's website: **www.cadw.wales.gov.uk**

This contains a wide range of information, including details of buildings and monuments in its care. If you experience any difficulty in exercising the rights of access indicated, please write to Cadw at the above address or contact us via telephone, fax or e-mail.

Cadw encourages you to visit these properties, as well as buildings and monuments in its care.

THE CHURCHES CONSERVATION TRUST

Caring for historic churches throughout England

Christ Church Waterloo is just one of the 50 outstanding churches selected by The Churches Conservation Trust to illustrate the churches in its care. Your *Starter for 50* churches all have something very special to offer – and can be visited *free* throughout the year.

The job of The Churches Conservation Trust is to repair and preserve churches in England of exceptional architectural and historic interest which are no longer needed for regular parish use.

We have over 300 churches, but why not begin your exploration by sampling the glories of our selected *Starter for 50*? Some are opened daily, others have more limited opening times and still others have nearby keyholders. See overleaf for details.

www.visitchurches.org.uk

11

LEICESTERSHIRE

Stapleford
St Mary Magdalene ▲

The best time to visit this church is in the spring, but the setting in the fine landscape of Stapleford Park is memorable at any time. Built in the 18th century by the fourth Earl of Harborough, it is an elegant example of Gothic Revival architecture. The interior is cool, spacious and light, with oak pews ranged facing each other on either side of the nave. Across the west end is an oak gallery which served as the Earl's family pew. There is pretty plasterwork on the walls and ceilings. The finest monument is by Rysbrack, and shows the first Earl in a Roman toga, reclining and gesturing to his wife, who holds their son on her knee.

3m E of Melton Mowbray, off B676
SK 812 183
Keyholder nearby

WEST SUSSEX

North Stoke
North Stoke Church ▼

In an idyllic rural setting on the South Downs, North Stoke Church is in the simple shape of a cross and remains virtually unaltered since mediaeval times. Its simplicity and elegant proportions give the impression of height and space. Light floods in through the clear glass of the beautiful mediaeval windows to illuminate the interior. Traces of wall paintings dating from the 14th century show that the church would have been a blaze of colour and decoration in the Middle Ages. Some very early and rare stained glass remains from the beginning of the 14th century. Intriguing stone carving includes a sheep's head above a recessed stone seat on the west wall and a quaint little hand. Outside is carved a mediaeval mass dial.

5m N of Arundel off B2139
TQ 019 108
Open daily

WILTSHIRE

Fisherton Delamere
St Nicholas ▼

This delightful former estate village sits on a hill overlooking the Wylye Valley, and the church seems almost to be pegged to the hillside by its tower. The outside is built in a chequerboard pattern of flint and stone. There was a church here in Norman times and the font dates from that period. The present building is 14th-century in origin but was substantially rebuilt in the 19th century, using much of the old stone and retaining the look of the mediaeval building. The elegant screen, which separates the nave and chancel, dates only from 1912. Interesting monuments include a poignant memorial to two babies of Thomas and Joan Crockford, showing one in bed and the other wrapped in a shroud.

11m NW of Salisbury off A36, 1m N of Wylye
SU 001 385
Open daily

NORTH YORKSHIRE

Skelton-cum-Newby
Christ the Consoler ▶

The extraordinary exuberance of Christ the Consoler makes an immediate impact on the visitor. Built in 1871–76 by the famous Victorian architect, William Burges, it is an extravagant memorial to a young man, Frederick Vyner, who was murdered by brigands while travelling in Greece. The outside is impressive, with its lofty spire, pinnacles and fine rose window. The design is based on mediaeval French church architecture, but with Burges' unique interpretation. The interior is wonderfully rich and colourful, with stained glass in strong and vibrant colours. Burges employed the best craftsmen of the day, and everywhere there are examples of their skill. Excellent carving in stone and wood, lovely metalwork, and the finest quality sculpture enrich the walls. Everything is on a magnificent scale.

4m SE of Ripon off B6265
SE 360 679
Open daily Apr–Sep, other times keyholder nearby

CAMBRIDGESHIRE

Cambridge
St Peter ▼

St Peter's has retained its character as a little village church despite its site near the city centre. Its history is one of repeated rebuilding, restoration and repair. The original church was built in the 11th century. Additions included the tower and spire, which still stand today. However the original nave and chancel were demolished in 1781 to make way for the present building. Two doorways from the old church, mediaeval though Norman in spirit, were then reset in the north and south walls. A charming weathervane incorporates the initials AP, said to be those of Andrew Perne, an 18th-century Dean of Ely. The most remarkable survival is the 11th-century stone font, which has extraordinary carved mermen at each corner.

Off Castle Street
TF 448 591
Key at Kettle's Yard Gallery or Office nearby
01223 352 124, open Tue–Sun 9.30–5

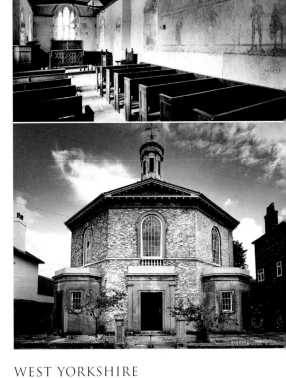

DORSET

Tarrant Crawford
St Mary the Virgin ▶▶

This simple and evocative church is all that remains of Tarrant Abbey. The chancel dates from the 12th century, while the nave, tower and porch are mostly 14th-century. The church remained largely untouched until 1911 when major restoration work was undertaken. Mediaeval paintings cover most of the nave walls still giving a vivid impression of warmth and colour. The earliest, in the chancel, is 13th-century. On the south wall, are 14th-century scenes from the life of St Margaret of Antioch, and, in the lower row, a morality tale. Over the nave is a 16th-century wagon roof. All the fittings are made of oak. Several 13th- and 14th-century coffin lids set in the floor are probably of abbesses and nuns.

3m SE of Blandford off A350
ST 924 035
Open daily

WEST SUSSEX

Chichester
St John's Chapel ◢

St John's, a severely elegant building in pale brick, is a rare and almost unchanged example of an evangelical 'preaching house', dating from the early 19th century. It was privately funded and run by trustees who were members of the evangelical movement of the Church of England. The layout reflects the importance the evangelical movement laid on sermons and reading from scripture, rather than communion. The pulpit, reading desk and clerk's desk are impressively large and placed centrally in the church. Standing high up in the pulpit, the preacher could be seen and heard by (and could himself see) everyone in the chapel. Today, the annual Chichester Festivities holds a number of its concerts at St John's.

St John's Street
SU 864 046
Open daily 10–5.30
Custodian 01243 787 674

WEST YORKSHIRE

Leeds
St John the Evangelist ▽

St John's, the oldest church in Leeds city centre, was built in 1632–34. John Harrison, a wealthy local wool merchant, bore the entire expense of the church. The glory of St John's lies in its Jacobean fittings, particularly the superb carved wooden screen, and lovely carving on the wall panels, pews and pulpit. The ceiling panels have pretty plaster reliefs, and the corbels supporting the beams have curiously carved creatures, including angels with musical instruments. The 19th-century stained glass includes a memorial window to the founder, John Harrison. Monuments commemorate citizens of Leeds, and emphasise the importance of the wool industry to the city's prosperity. A mid-19th century restoration by Norman Shaw is very much in the original style of the building.

New Briggate in central Leeds
SE 302 338
Open Tue–Sat, 9.30–5.30
Custodian 0113 244 1689

CHESHIRE

Macclesfield
Christ Church ◢

This large and impressive town church was built in 1775–76 at the expense of Charles Roe, a prominent local industrialist. It is built of brick, with cast-iron columns supporting the galleries inside. The church is very plain inside and originally had clear glass in all windows. In the 19th century some of these were replaced with fine stained glass. The east window was given in memory of Charles Roe's son, daughter-in-law and grandson. Another window commemorates David Simpson, the much-loved first minister of Christ Church. Roe's ornate monument, in marble, on the south wall lists his achievements. The original pulpit was more than 3.5 metres high. John Wesley, the founder of Methodism preached here at least 12 times. The church has a fine ring of ten bells, which are still used regularly.

Catherine Street
SJ 914 736
Open May–Sep Mon, Tue, Fri 9–4; Oct–Apr Mon, Tue, Fri 9–3 or by app. 01625 423 894

MERSEYSIDE

Waterloo
Christ Church Old Church ◢

Christ Church was built in 1891–99 to replace a much humbler building. Its majestic tower of pink sandstone became a landmark for sailors, and still dominates the neighbourhood. It is a huge and impressive building with wonderful stained glass and a strong sense of Victorian confidence and civic pride. Soaring timber vaults form the roofs and graceful arches lead your eye to the great east window. Here, in vibrantly colourful stained glass, are depicted Christ with angels, saints and Old Testament figures. The west window depicts the 12 Apostles. The glass is by Shrigley and Hunt, among the leading manufacturers of their period.

Junction of Alexandra, Victoria and Waterloo Roads, off Crosby Road South (A565), a northern suburb of Liverpool
SJ 321 976
Keyholder nearby

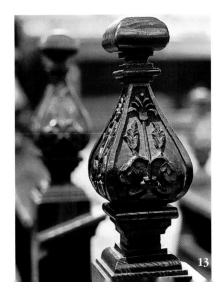

Your Starter for 50 churches in the care of The Churches Conservation Trust

All churches on the map are opened regularly or have keyholders nearby*. Further details may be obtained by ordering the booklet below.

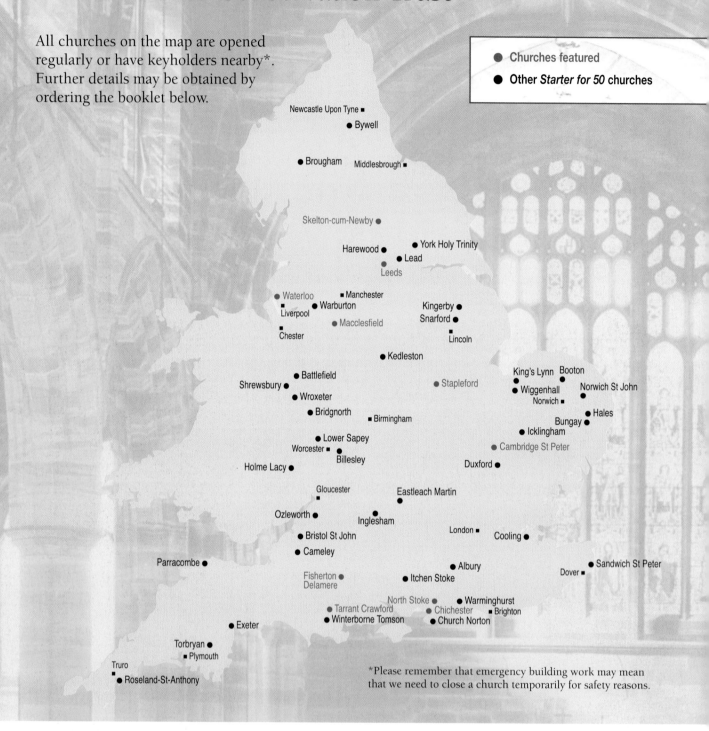

● Churches featured
● **Other *Starter for 50* churches**

Newcastle Upon Tyne ■
● Bywell
● Brougham   Middlesbrough ■
Skelton-cum-Newby ●
Harewood ●   ● York Holy Trinity
● Lead
Leeds
● Waterloo   ■ Manchester
Liverpool   ● Warburton   Kingerby ●
Chester ■   ● Macclesfield   Snarford ●
Lincoln
● Kedleston
● Battlefield   King's Lynn ● Booton ●
Shrewsbury ●   ● Stapleford   ● Wiggenhall   Norwich St John ●
● Wroxeter   Norwich ●   ● Hales
● Bridgnorth   ■ Birmingham   Bungay ●
● Lower Sapey   ● Icklingham
Worcester ■   ● Cambridge St Peter
● Billesley
Holme Lacy ●   Duxford ●
Gloucester ●   Eastleach Martin ●
Ozleworth ●   ● Inglesham
London ■
● Bristol St John   Cooling ●
● Cameley
Parracombe ●   ● Albury   Dover ■   ● Sandwich St Peter
Fisherton ●   ● Itchen Stoke
Delamere
North Stoke ●   ● Warminghurst
Tarrant Crawford ●   ● Chichester   ■ Brighton
Exeter ●   ● Winterborne Tomson   ● Church Norton
Torbryan ●
Truro ■   ■ Plymouth
● Roseland-St-Anthony

*Please remember that emergency building work may mean that we need to close a church temporarily for safety reasons.

Complete and send to The Churches Conservation Trust, 89 Fleet Street, London, EC4Y 1DH

Name .... Title ....

Address .... Postcode ....

Please send me: *Your Starter for 50* booklet. ☐

Full List of Churches in the care of The Churches Conservation Trust ☐

County leaflets, please specify county(ies) ....

Why not visit our website? www.visitchurches.org.uk

HHH3

Celebrating
H M The Queen's
Golden Jubilee

2002 will be a year of great celebration to mark the 50th Anniversary of Her Majesty The Queen's Accession to the Throne. The whole country will have a chance to extend its thanks and good wishes to Her Majesty for her years of service to the Nation and the Commonwealth at a number of national events throughout the year. The Golden Jubilee Weekend of 1 - 4 June will be the high point of these celebrations. These events will have both a public and a ceremonial nature, many revolving around The Queen's official residences at Buckingham Palace, Windsor Castle and the Palace of Holyroodhouse in Edinburgh.

Hundreds of thousands of UK and overseas visitors will no doubt visit one of these royal palaces to enjoy the celebrations. Few though may realise that even The Queen's private residences' at Sandringham in Norfolk, and Balmoral Castle on Deeside, Aberdeenshire, are also open to the general public. These are the homes where the Royal Family has a brief chance to be 'off-duty' for a few weeks of the year and they hold a very special place in their hearts.

Sandringham

'Dear old Sandringham, the place I love better than anywhere else in the world' …
George V

Sandringham Estate in Norfolk, is to be found eight miles north east of King's Lynn. The estate, which today extends to over 20,000 acres, was bought by the Prince of Wales, the future Edward VII, in 1862, so that he might have a private retreat from public life, similar to Queen Victoria's own homes at Balmoral and Osborne House on the Isle of Wight.

Sandringham may not be the most classically proportioned of houses, but the amount of time spent by The Queen and her family here testifies to the very real affection that they all have for their Norfolk home. It is the tradition of the Royal Family to spend Christmas and New Year at Sandringham to enjoy both the Christmas festivities as well as the legendary shooting parties. The estate's sandy soil and exceptionally well maintained coverts makes it an ideal environment for game birds.

The present red brick and sandstone neo-Jacobean house was designed and built on the site of an earlier house by A J Humbert and completed in 1870 to accommodate the Prince of Wales' growing family. The main reception, rooms, now full of successive generations' memorabilia, still strongly retain the mark of the Prince and Princess of Wales' tastes, both of whom throughout their lives poured immense energy and enthusiasm into improving the estate, to the extent that a friend of the Prince of Wales, Edward Carrington, was to describe Sandringham as *"the most comfortable house in England"*.

However, Sandringham is not set in an Edwardian time warp, it is very much a working estate where each succeeding generation of the Royal Family has made its mark. The immaculate gardens around the house owe much to The Queen's father, George VI who employed Sir Geoffrey Jellicoe to design a garden to the north of the house. Here you can wander through a garden of pleached limes and a long series of box edged beds filled with herbs, roses and annuals. The sweet scent in high summer is intoxicating. In the 1960s Her Majesty The Queen invited Sir Eric Savill to remodel the areas of the garden between the lawns and the garden wall. The soft sandy loamy soil, provides the perfect condition for rhododendrons, camellias and azaleas, and this area of the garden is a riot of colour in the early spring.

It was The Queen's express wish in 1977 that Sandringham was first opened to

Above: The Dining Room, Sandringham.

Right: Wisteria at the lake, Sandringham.

Below: Sir Geoffrey Jellicoe's North Garden.

the public. There is now a huge variety of ways in which the visitor can enjoy a day at Sandringham: whether having a picnic in the 600 acre woodland park, walking along one of the two nature trails, or simply taking the tractor and trailer tour. As well as the house, there are the coach houses and stable block, which house the Museum and a self-service restaurant and tearoom serving delicious homemade refreshments. The plant centre and gift shop give visitors the opportunity to take home a souvenir of their visit.

Sandringham is open daily from Easter Saturday to mid-July and early August to October. For full information on the opening arrangements at Sandringham see page 271. ■

Balmoral

'Every year I seem to become fonder of this dear place'

Queen Victoria

Balmoral Castle is the Scottish estate and holiday home of the Royal Family. The estate was purchased for Queen Victoria by Prince Albert in 1852, but the original castle was considered too small, and a new castle was built in soft white granite quarried from the nearby Glen Gelder.

Balmoral nestles in Deeside, which is the land stretching west of the coast along the River Dee running from its source high in the Cairngorms to the sea at Aberdeen. The area is spectacularly beautiful, the granite, heather clad hills, having an immense rugged and craggy charm. The ground rises very steeply in parts of the estate, 656ft at the junction of the River Dee and River Muick, and 919ft at Balmoral, up to 3,789ft at the top of the Lochnagar massif which dominates the whole area.

The original estate of Balmoral consisted of over 11,000 acres of hill, woodland and small tenant farms. Today, it has expanded to just over 50,000 acres but of this only about 500 acres is good farmland. The Queen, The Duke of Edinburgh and The Prince of Wales take a close personal interest in the running of the estate, and, as at Sandringham, it is seen by the family as much more than just a favourite holiday home - they all consider that the land is held in trust for future generations.

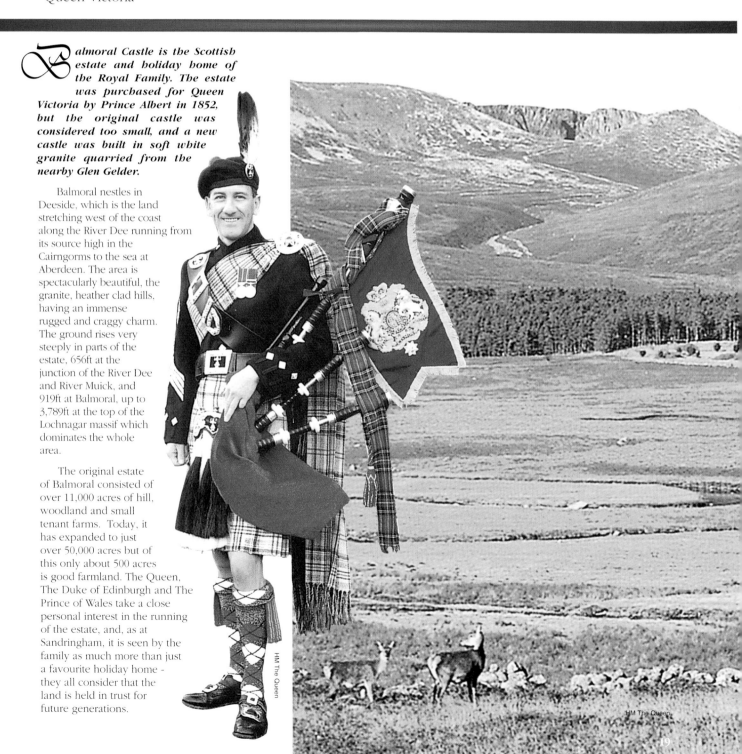

HM The Queen

HM The Queen

HM The Queen

Twenty five years ago The Duke of Edinburgh enclosed a small area of the Ballcochbuie Forest (one of the largest remnants of native Caledonian Pine forest left in Scotland) in a regeneration trial. The trial has been highly successful. Further areas have been enclosed, and are now monitored by the Institute of Terrestrial Ecology.

In addition to Ballochbuie, nearly 5,000 acres are planted with trees providing shelter for red deer. The estate has taken a lead in Scotland's programme both to manage the deer population and to restore the heather habitat. Highland, Fell and Haflinger ponies are also kept on the estate. Their main use is to recover the red deer from the hills during the stalking season, but they are also used for pony trekking from mid-April to the end of July when parties of up to 12 riders are taken out by the estate staff on half-day treks.

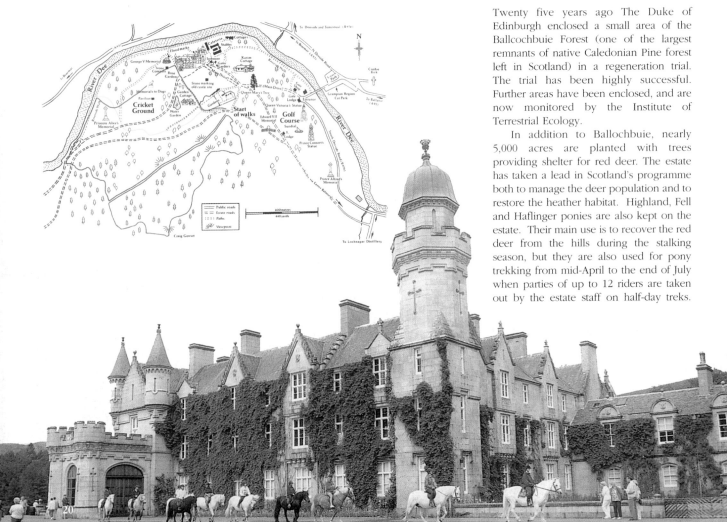

Her Majesty The Queen is also Patron of the Highland Cattle Society and founded the Balmoral Fold in 1953. A window into this idyllic world is opened to visitors between mid April and the end of July each year, when the estate grounds, gardens and exhibitions (displayed in the Ballroom) are open to members of the public.

For full information on the opening arrangements at Balmoral see page 494. ■

HM The Queen

HM The Queen

HM The Queen

Golden Jubilee Weekend Celebrations

'A chance to say thank you, and to have a good time ... a time to thank The Queen for fifty years of service to the nation'

The extended Bank Holiday Golden Jubilee Weekend of 1 - 4 June 2002
will allow the whole country to celebrate Fifty Years of The Queen's reign.

The events planned for the Jubilee Weekend are:-

SATURDAY 1 JUNE
Classical Concert in Buckingham Palace Gardens

SUNDAY 2 JUNE
Jubilee Church Services and Bell-Ringing across the UK

MONDAY 3 JUNE
Pop Concert in Buckingham Palace Gardens, followed by Beacon Lighting and Firework Display

TUESDAY 4 JUNE
Ceremonial Procession to St Paul's and the National Service of Thanksgiving and Service at St Paul's (morning)
Lord Mayor of London hosts lunch at The Guildhall
Golden Jubilee Carnival Pageant in The Mall (afternoon)

For further information contact:-
Postal enquiries: Golden Jubilee Office, 85 Buckingham Gate, London SW1E 6PD
Telephone enquiries for the public (during normal office hours): 0845 000 2002

HISTORIC TRUST CHAPELS

CHAIRMAN
Sir Hugh Rossi

DIRECTOR
Dr Jennifer M Freeman

29 Thurloe Street, London SW7 2LQ
Telephone: 020 7584 6072 Fax: 020 7225 0607

The Historic Chapels Trust has been established to take into ownership redundant chapels and other places of worship in England of outstanding architectural and historic interest. Our object is to secure for public benefit the preservation, repair and maintenance of our buildings including their contents, burial grounds and curtilages.

▲ Dissenters' Chapel, Kensal Green
Cemetery ~ London

Listed below are thirteen chapels
the trust has in its care which
can be visited on application
to the keyholder.

▲ Farfield Friends Meeting House ~
West Yorkshire

▲ Walpole Old Chapel ~ Suffolk

Biddlestone RC Chapel, Northumberland	01665 574420
Coanwood Friends Meeting House, Northumberland	01434 320256
Cote Baptist Chapel, Oxfordshire	01993 850421
Farfield Friends Meeting House, West Yorkshire	01756 710225
The Dissenters' Chapel, Kensal Green Cemetery, London	020 7402 2749
Penrose Methodist Chapel, St Ervan, Cornwall	01872 263939
Salem Chapel, East Budleigh, Devon	01395 445236
St Benet's Chapel and Presbytery, Netherton, Merseyside	0151 520 2600
St George's German Lutheran Church, Tower Hamlets, London	020 8302 3437
Todmorden Unitarian Church, West Yorkshire	01706 815648
Umbersland Baptist Church, West Yorkshire	01564 783362
Wallasey Unitarian Church, Merseyside	0151 639 5137
Walpole Old Chapel, Suffolk	01986 798308

For further information please ring the Director at the office address.

WORDSWORTH'S LAKE DISTRICT

Derwentwater and Skiddaw

"Here the rainbow comes - the cloud - And mists that spread the flying shroud..."

WORDSWORTH HOUSE
Cockermouth

Birthplace of William Wordsworth in 1770

Open April to October, Monday to Friday and selected Saturdays . Closed remaining Saturdays and all Sundays. Tearoom using local produce. Events during season. Parking in town centre car parks. National Trust.

TEL: 01900 824805

DOVE COTTAGE
Grasmere

Dove Cottage & Wordsworth Museum, Grasmere

Open Daily 9.30 to 5.30pm. Closed 24th - 26th December

Parking next to Dove Cottage Tearoom & Restaurant immediately south of Grasmere village.

TEL: 015394 35544

RYDAL MOUNT & GARDENS
Near Ambleside

Rydal Mount Home of William Wordsworth from 1813 - 1850

Open:
Summer: Mar - Oct 9.30 - 5.00pm
Winter: Nov - Feb 10.00 - 4.00pm

(Closed Tuesdays in Winter)

FREE PARKING

TEL: 015394 33002

RECIPROCAL DISCOUNT OFFER - DETAILS FROM ANY OF THE ABOVE ATTRACTIONS

www.wordsworthlakes.co.uk

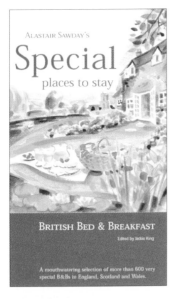
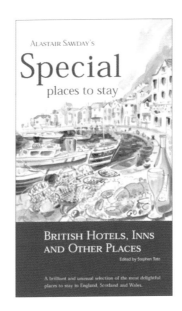
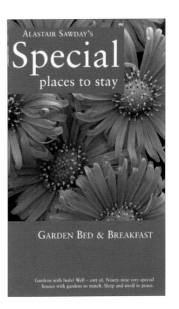

The Landmark Trust

The Landmark Trust is a preservation charity which rescues and restores historic and architecturally important buildings at risk and lets them for holidays. There are 170 Landmarks where you can become, for a short time, the owner of such a building, including follies, forts, castles, gatehouses and towers. The Landmark Handbook illustrates every building with 188 pages of plans, location maps and black and white photographs. The price, including post and packing, is refundable against a booking.

Warden Abbey

Near Biggleswade, Bedfordshire

Landmarks are chosen for their historic interest or architectural importance, and also because many are in surroundings which give unexpected pleasure. Warden Abbey is a fragment of a great Cistercian Abbey and a Tudor House, set in fruitful countryside, once farmed by monks.

Lundy: Old Light

Lundy Island, Bristol Channel

The beauty of the Landmark solution is not only that a building is saved and put to good use, but also that the restoration respects its original design. For a short time it is possible to live in surprising places. One of the light houses on Lundy Island, off the north coast of Devon, now provides unusual holiday accommodation.

Langley Gatehouse

Acton Burnell, Shropshire

Landmarks often lie off the beaten track. Langley is no exception, set in a remote valley with a view to the Wrekin. In our restorations, we prefer to repair the old, and avoid renewal, to preserve the building's texture. When the building is timber framed, this can be like trying to patch a cobweb!

Saddell

Kintyre, Argyll

Some Landmarks, like this one, are connected with great families. Saddell Castle, a fine tower house with battlements, on the long white strand of Saddell Bay, was in the hands of the Campbells for 400 years. Today the Castle and four cottages are available for holidays.

Order Form

The Landmark Trust Handbook

The Handbook costs £9.50 including postage and packing when posted to an address in the UK, otherwise it costs £12.00 to Europe; £22.00 to the Americas*, Central Asia, Middle East and Africa; £26.00 to Australasia and Far East.

*Residents of USA and Canada can order a copy for US $25.00 from Landmark USA, 707 Kipling Road, Dummerston, Vermont 05301. Tel 802-254 6868.

Payment can be made by Mastercard/Visa/Switch/Delta or £sterling cheque drawn on a UK bank.

The cost of the Handbook is refundable against your first booking.

Once you have bought a Handbook, you will be put on our mailing list to receive up-to-date price and availability lists and bi-annual Newsletters.

Payment by credit or debit card can be made by telephoning our Booking Office on (01628) 825925 or by filling in this order form and sending it to:

The Landmark Trust, Shottesbrooke, Maidenhead, Berkshire SL6 3SW, England Charity number 243312

Telephone +44 (0) 1628 825925 Fax +44 (0) 1628 825417 www.landmarktrust.co.uk

Data Protection Act We promise that any information you give will be used for the purpose of the Landmark Trust only. We will write to you about our work and will occasionally include details of products developed by third parties in association with the Landmark Trust. Should you not wish to hear about such products please tick this box ☐

Credit card details   H

My Visa/Mastercard/Switch/Delta number is

☐☐☐☐ ☐☐☐☐ ☐☐☐☐ ☐☐☐☐ ☐☐☐☐

Expires ☐☐   Switch card starts ☐☐   Issue No. ☐

Please send me _____ copies @ _____ Total £ ____

Card holder's details:

Name _____

Address _____

_____ Postcode _____

Card holder's signature _____

Delivery details if different from above:

Name _____

Address _____

_____ Postcode _____

25

A Century of Royal Wedding Dresses

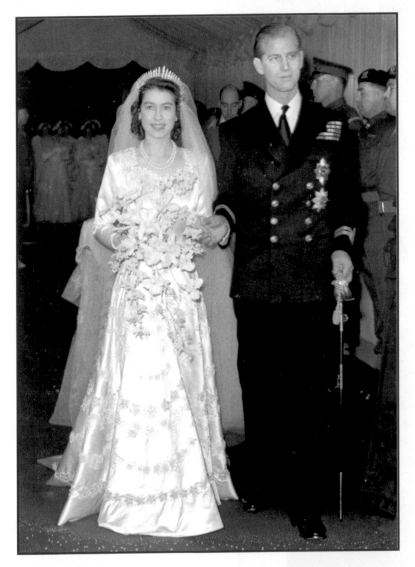

Kensington Palace is pleased to announce
that a new exhibition will open on 1 May 2002,
displaying a collection of royal wedding dresses from
Queen Victoria (1840) to HM Queen Elizabeth II (1947).

For group bookings contact: Thomas Sheaf
Kensington Palace State Apartments, London W8 4PX
Tel: 020 7937 7079

General tel no: 020 7937 9561

Places Offering Accommodation

The historic properties listed below are not hotels. Their inclusion indicates that accommodation can be arranged, often for groups only. The type and standard of rooms offered vary widely from the luxurious to the utilitarian. Full details can be obtained from each individual property.

ENGLAND

SCOTLAND

WALES

IRELAND

This list is merely intended to draw attention to some properties which offer accommodation, it is only a guide.

ENGLAND

All Wedding Photographs
© Sarah Ward-Hendry
tel: 01295 811092 or 07785 901522
e-mail: ward-hendry@msn.com
website: www.ward-hendry.com

28

Civil Wedding Venues

**Places at which the marriage ceremony itself can take place
although many will also be able to provide facilities for wedding receptions.**

Full details about each property are available in the regional listings.

There are numerous other properties included within *Hudson's* which do not have a
Civil Wedding Licence but which can accommodate wedding receptions.

The Marriage Act 1995, which has resulted in many more wedding venues in England, has not changed the
situation in Scotland. In Scotland religious wedding ceremonies can take place anywhere subject to the Minister
being prepared to perform them. Civil Weddings, however, are still confined to Registry Offices.

WALES

IRELAND

This list is merely intended to draw attention to properties which can host Civil Weddings, it is intended only as a guide.

ENGLAND

Corporate Hospitality Venues

Properties which are able to accommodate corporate functions,
wedding receptions and events.
Some properties specialise in corporate hospitality and are open only rarely,
if ever, to day visitors. Others do both. See entry for details.

This is not an exclusive list. It is intended to draw attention to some of these properties where functions
or corporate hospitality is a major part of their business.

SCOTLAND

Corporate Hospitality Venues

Properties which are able to accommodate corporate functions,
wedding receptions and events.
Some properties specialise in corporate hospitality and are open only rarely,
if ever, to day visitors. Others do both. See entry for details.

WALES

IRELAND

This is not an exclusive list. It is intended to draw attention to some of these properties where functions
or corporate hospitality is a major part of their business.

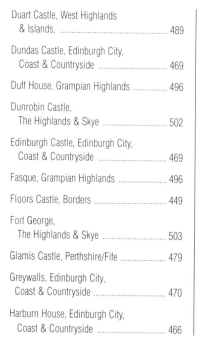

HERITAGE VENUES

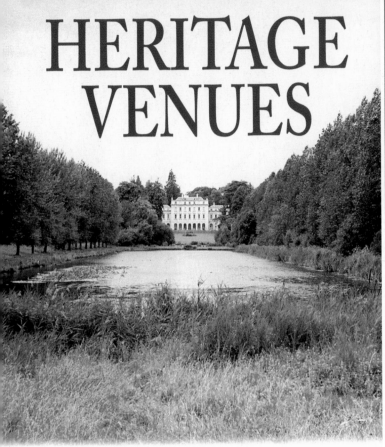

HERITAGE VENUES is the company that has access to some of the finest properties in the United Kingdom. All of them have intrinsic historical or architectural interest, most have beautiful gardens and parks but some have never been opened to the general public – they don't even appear in Hudson's!

For the finest properties Heritage Venues provides the most professional service, the best entertainment and delicious food and wine.

Heritage Venues is the sensible answer for the discerning corporate or private client who wants the top event or function, with the minimum of fuss in a unique setting.

Head Office: HERITAGE VENUES
Bagendon, Cirencester, Gloucestershire GL7 7DU
Tel/Fax: 01285 831417
e-mail: heritage.venues@virgin.net
www.heritagevenues.co.uk

34

Bed & Breakfast *for* Garden Lovers
2001 EDITION
www.bbgl.co.uk

The original garden B&B guide founded in 1994

Quality accommodation in beautiful locations.

*103 quietly situated private homes
at various prices*

*Keen gardening hosts personally chosen for their
kindness, courtesy and helpfulness and
good local knowledge of horticultural matters*

Useful tips to help plan garden visits

*Excellent reputation for
personal service built up over 8 years*

TO OBTAIN BROCHURES:
From the UK: Send ten loose first class stamps
per copy required, with a 11 x 22cm sae
From abroad: Send five international reply-paid coupons
per copy required, with a 11 x 22cm sae
*To: BBGL/HD, Handywater Farm, Sibford Gower
Banbury, Oxfordshire OX15 5AE*

VISIT
SAUSMAREZ MANOR

GUERNSEY

the home of the Seigneurs de Sausmarez since c1220
with a façade built at the bequest
of the first Governor of New York

An entrancing and entertaining half day encompassing something to interest everyone. The family have been explorers, inventors, diplomats, prelates, generals, admirals, privateers, politicians and governors etc, most of whom have left their mark on the house, garden or the furniture.

The sub-tropical woodland garden is crammed with such exotics as banana trees, tree ferns, ginger, 300+ camellias, lilies, myriads of bamboos, as well as the more commonplace hydrangeas, hostas etc.

The sculpture in the art park with its 200 or so pieces by artists from a dozen countries is the most comprehensive in Britain.

The dolls' house collection displays pieces from 1830 onwards and is the third largest dedicated collection in Britain.

The pitch and putt is a cruelly testing 500m 9 hole par 3.

The ride-on trains travel $^1/_4$ mile through part of the woodland.

The two lakes are a haven for ornamental wildfowl and some of the sculpture.

Sausmarez Manor is available for corporate hospitality functions and Civil weddings. It also offers guided tours, welcomes schools (has education programmes), and has a tearoom, café, gift shop and art gallery.

There is ample parking for cars and coaches. Partially suitable for disabled access.

For further information contact Peter de Sausmarez
Tel: 01481 235571/235655   Fax: 01481 235572

www.artparks.co.uk or www.guernsey.org/sausmarez

ENGLAND

Plant Sales

Properties where plants are offered for sale

SCOTLAND

WALES

IRELAND

This list is merely intended to draw attention to properties which have plant sales, it is intended only as a guide.

Celebrate 75 years of Garden Visiting with the
NATIONAL GARDENS SCHEME
in 2002

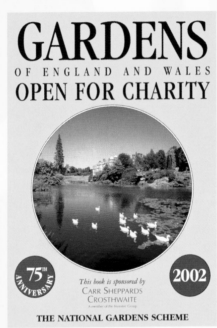

The **Gardens of England and Wales Open for Charity** Guide 2002 lists around 3500 gardens of quality and interest open to the public during the 75th Anniversary year of the National Gardens Scheme. Gardens listed in this renowned publication, known as the 'Yellow Book' range from small suburban plots packed with plants, through cottage gardens, spilling over with summer colour, to large country mansions set in picturesque parkland. Some of the gardens listed have been opening for over 50 years. All of the gardens listed are waiting to welcome visitors in 2002.

Garden Finder, a search and mapping facility on the NGS website gives detailed information, often with accompanying photographs, about the gardens. Plan your visiting using the latest opening information announced on the NGS website **www.ngs.org.uk**

Published in February 2002, the **Gardens of England and Wales Open for Charity** is for sale in all major bookstores, price £5. It is also available through the NGS website.

The National Gardens Scheme Charitable Trust, Hatchlands Park, East Clandon, Guildford, Surrey GU4 7RT
T 01483 211535   F 01483 211537   E ngs@ngs.org.uk

Website Information

Visit www.hudsons.co.uk
Your online guide to the best heritage properties in Britain

- **Live links to over 500 sites**
- Special Event Listings
- Corporate Hospitality
- Romantic properties for Civil Weddings
- Heritage Bookshop

Direct links to hundreds of properties – no need to type in long web addresses. Let Hudson's be your guide.

Useful Web Addresses

Hudson's	**www.hudsons.co.uk**
Historic Houses Association	www.hha.org.uk
National Trust	www.nationaltrust.org.uk
English Heritage	www.english-heritage.org.uk
National Trust For Scotland	www.nts.org.uk
Historic Scotland	www.historic-scotland.gov.uk
CADW	www.cadw.wales.gov.uk
Dúchas	www.heritageireland.ie
Historic Royal Palaces	www.hrp.org.uk
The Royal Collection	www.the-royal-collection.org.uk
National Gardens Scheme	www.ngs.org.uk
British Tourist Authority	www.visitbritain.com
Wordsworth's Lake District	www.wordsworthlakes.co.uk
Heritage Venues	www.heritagevenues.co.uk

PLACES TO STAY

Landmark Trust	www.landmarktrust.co.uk
Alastair Sawday Publishing	www.sawdays.co.uk
Bed & Breakfast for Garden Lovers	www.bbgl.co.uk

1
Claydon House, Buckinghamshire
New Year's Day Walk – two hour guided walk including refreshments, starts 10.30am, adult £5, child £3 (tel: 01494 755572).

1
Leeds Castle, Kent
New Year Treasure Trail.

4 – 6
Tatton Park, Cheshire
Robert Bailey Antiques Fair.

13
2 Willow Road, London
'Walk Back in Time' – architectural walk through Hampstead, including refreshments, 11am-1pm, adult £6 (tel: 01494 755572/020 7435 3471).

13
Gibside, Tyne & Wear
Guided Winter Walk, 2pm, £1 (tel: 01207 542255).

14 – 31
Tatton Park, Cheshire
Onetree Exhibition.

19 – 31
Leeds Castle, Kent
Lady Baillie Exhibition.

20
Gibside, Tyne & Wear
'The Sleeping Wood' – family walk, 2pm, £1 (tel: 01207 542255).

26
Saltram House, Devon
Burns' Night Supper in Tudor Kitchen Restaurant, 7pm, £25.95 (tel: 01752 333500).

30
Sutton House, London
Lecture lunch 'Walking in the footsteps of Samuel Pepys', 11.30am, adult £12 (tel: 01494 755572).

FEBRUARY

1 – 28
Leeds Castle, Kent
Lady Baillie Exhibition.

1 – 28
Tatton Park, Cheshire
Onetree Exhibition.

2
Sulgrave Manor, Northamptonshire
Chamber Concert – Musica Donum Dei present 'For Love of Shakespeare' settings of songs and music for his plays. 7.30pm. Tickets £17.50 inc buffet supper and wine. Booking essential.

3
Heale Gardens, Wiltshire
Snowdrop Sunday.

6
Arley Hall, Cheshire
Gardening Course.

6
Gibside, Tyne & Wear
'The Farne Islands – Europe's Finest Nature Reserve?' – a lighthearted talk by John Walton followed by lunch, booking essential (tel: 01207 542255).

9 – 17
Leeds Castle, Kent
Half Term Theatre for Children.

9 – 28
Spencer House, London
The Indian Imperial Orders: an exhibition to mark the Golden Jubilee of Her Majesty The Queen.

10
2 Willow Road, London
'Walk Back in Time' – architectural walk through Hampstead, including refreshments, 11am-1pm, adult £6 (tel: 01494 755572/020 7435 3471).

10
Gibside, Tyne & Wear
'Cold Comfort' – how do the animals, birds and insects survive in winter? 2pm, £1 (tel: 01207 542255).

10
Heale Gardens, Wiltshire
Snowdrop Sunday.

10
The Royal Pavilion, Sussex
Wedding Fair.

14
Saltram House, Devon
Valentine's Day Supper in the Tudor Kitchen Restaurant, from 7pm, £18.95 (tel: 01752 333500).

14
Sutton House, London
Silent Film Night – for Valentines, café open from 6pm, start 7.30pm, £7.50 (tel: 01494 755572).

17
Gibside, Tyne & Wear
Winter Water – a walk round the rivers and ponds showing these habitats bare of cover, 2pm, £1 (tel: 01207 542255).

20
Arley Hall, Cheshire
Gardening for Beginners.

20
Sutton House, London
Lecture lunch – 'Where Sweet Turnips Grow', start 11.30am, adult £12.

23
Castle Drogo, Devon
Literary Festival, 11am-4pm, £1.

23 – 24
Castle Drogo, Devon
Art Show, 11am-4pm, £1.

24
Gibside, Tyne & Wear
Guided Winter Walk, 2pm, £1 (tel: 01207 542255).

MARCH

1 – 3
Wilton House, Wiltshire
25th (Silver) Wilton House Antique Fair.

1 – 4
Tatton Park, Cheshire
Onetree Exhibition.

1 – 11
Spencer House, London
The Indian Imperial Orders: an exhibition to mark the Golden Jubilee of Her Majesty The Queen.

1 – 31
Wellington Arch, London
Exhibition on the Sikh contribution to the World Wars.

2
Sulgrave Manor, Northamptonshire
Orchestral Concert – The Cherwell Orchestra plays Bach's Orchestral Suite in D, Haydn's Cello Concerto and Mozart's 'Jupiter' Symphony. 7.30pm. Tickets £17.50 inc buffet supper and wine. Booking essential.

5
Saltram House, Devon
Lecture Lunch – 'Surprisingly Simple Spring Flowers', 12 noon, £9.95 (tel: 01752 333500).

6
Arley Hall, Cheshire
Gardening Course.

7 – 10
Tatton Park, Cheshire
Robert Bailey Antiques Fair.

9 – 10
Powderham Castle, Devon
Powderham Historic Motor Rally.

9 – 31
Killerton House & Garden, Devon
Special Costume Exhibition "Lace – The Ultimate Luxury".

10
Gibside, Tyne & Wear
'The Waking Wood' – a guided walk through the woodland as it comes back to life, 2pm, £1.

10
Saltram House, Devon
Mother's Day Lunch, 12 noon (tel: 01752 333500).

11 – 17
Hever Castle, Kent
Spring Garden Week.

12
Saltram House, Devon
Lecture Lunch – 'New Thoughts for a New Season', 12 noon, £9.95 (tel: 01752 333500).

15 – 17
Ripley Castle, Yorkshire
Galloway Antiques Fair.

16 – 17
Ragley Hall, Warwickshire
Craft Fair.

17
Gibside, Tyne & Wear
'Something Stirring' – a walk through the estate showing how the woodland families are preparing for Spring, 2pm, £1 (tel: 01207 542255).

19 – 20
Tatton Park, Cheshire
RHS Lecture in the Tenants' Hall.

20
Arley Hall, Cheshire
'The Herb Garden' Workshop with Julia White.

24
Cobham Hall, Kent
National Garden Scheme Day (+ House open 2-5pm).

24
Gibside, Tyne & Wear
Guided Spring Walk, 2pm, £1 (tel: 01207 542255).

29 – 31
Cobham Hall, Kent
Medway Craft Show (+ House open 1-4pm).

29 – 31
Hever Castle, Kent
Easter Weekend.

29 – 31
Leeds Castle, Kent
Easter Holiday Fun.

29 – 31
Sulgrave Manor, Northamptonshire
Easter Customs - house beautifully decorated with Spring flowers, hear from the Lord of the Manor and his Cook of

Easter customs through the ages. The Courtyard Hall will feature 'Taking in Art', an exhibition of arts and crafts by Northamptonshire craftspeople. Adults £6.50, children £3.25. 10.30am-5pm.

31
Floors Castle, Borders
Easter Eggstravaganza.

31
Lulworth Castle, Dorset
Easter Bunny Hunt.

31
Traquair, Borders
Easter Egg Hunt.

APRIL

1
Cobham Hall, Kent
Medway Craft Show (+ House open 1-4pm).

1
Hever Castle, Kent
Easter Weekend.

1
Ludlow Castle, Shropshire
Easter Egg Hunt.

1
Lulworth Castle, Dorset
Easter Bunny Hunt.

1
Sulgrave Manor, Northamptonshire
Easter Customs - house beautifully decorated with Spring flowers, hear from the Lord of the Manor and his Cook of Easter customs throughout the ages. The Courtyard Hall will feature 'Taking in Art', an exhibition of arts and crafts by Northamptonshire craftspeople. Adults £6.50, children £3.25. 10.30am-5pm.

1 – 7
Leeds Castle, Kent
Easter Holiday Fun.

1 – 30
Fairfax House, Yorkshire
James Gilray – 'The dark side'.

1 – 30
Killerton House & Garden, Devon
Special Costume Exhibition "Lace – The Ultimate Luxury".

1 – 30
Wellington Arch, London
Exhibition on the Sikh contribution to the World Wars.

2 – 30
Holburne Museum of Art, Somerset
'A Pelican in the Wilderness': Hermits and Hermitages.

3
Arley Hall, Cheshire
Gardening Course.

6
Sulgrave Manor, Northamptonshire
Chamber Concert – Martin Souter, spinet and Sara Stowe, soprano play and sing a diverse programme of 17th and 18th century songs and keyboard music. 7.30pm. Tickets £17.50 inc buffet supper and wine. Booking essential.

7
Arley Hall, Cheshire
Rare & Unusual Plant Fair (admission charged and admission to gardens extra).

12 – 14
Arley Hall, Cheshire
Whichford Pottery Sale.

12 – 14
Blair Castle, Perthshire/Fife
Needlework & Lace Exhibition.

13 – 14
Capesthorne Hall, Cheshire
Rainbow Craft Fair.

13 – 14
Ragley Hall, Warwickshire
Gardeners' Weekend (free admission for Season Ticket Holders on Saturday).

16 – 21
Leeds Castle, Kent
Spring Gardens Week & Flower Festival.

17
Arley Hall, Cheshire
Gardening for Beginners.

20 – 21
Kentwell Hall, Suffolk
Re-Creation: WWII (Landgirls).

21
Pencarrow, Cornwall
Charity Afternoon – National Gardens Scheme.

27 – 28
Sulgrave Manor, Northamptonshire
Food Festival – local, regional and British food events. Meet the producers, watch the cookery demonstrations, taste, try and buy the fine fare. Adults £6.50, children £2.25, family £17.50. 10.30am - 5pm.

28
Beaulieu, Hampshire
Boat Jumble.

28
Wartnaby Gardens, Leicestershire & Rutland
Plant Sale.

Special Events 2002

MAY

1
Arley Hall, Cheshire
Gardening Course.

1 – 4
Trelissick Garden, Cornwall
Cornwall Gardens Society Show.

1 – 7
Blair Castle, Perthshire/Fife
Quilt Exhibition.

1 – 31
Fairfax House, Yorkshire
James Gilray – 'The dark side'.

1 – 31
Holburne Museum of Art, Somerset
'A Pelican in the Wilderness': Hermits and Hermitages.

1 – 31
Killerton House & Garden, Devon
Special Costume Exhibition "Lace – The Ultimate Luxury".

1 – 31
Wellington Arch, London
Exhibition on the Sikh contribution to the World Wars.

4 – 6
Hever Castle, Kent
May Day Music and Dance.

4 – 6
Leonardslee Gardens, Sussex
Bonsai Weekend.

4 – 6
Raby Castle, Co Durham
Orchid Show.

4 – 12
Sulgrave Manor, Northamptonshire
Local History Week – guided tours of historically important sites in the Parish. May Day Festival on Monday 6 May – dancing, music, mumming and local traditional games. Adults £6, children £3. Village tours: Adults £3, children £1.50.

5 – 6
Eastnor Castle, Herefordshire
Spring Country Crafts Fair.

5 – 6
Finchcocks, Kent
Spring Garden Fair & Flower Festival.

6
Capesthorne Hall, Cheshire
Church of England Children's Society Garden Party.

9 – 12
Hatfield House, Hertfordshire
Living Crafts (adult £7.00, group £6.00, child £3.50).

11 – 12
Chatsworth, Derbyshire
International Horse Trials.

11 – 12
Leeds Castle, Kent
Festival of English Food & Wine.

11 – 12
Lulworth Castle, Dorset
Country Gardening & Food Fair.

11 – 19
Sandringham, Norfolk
The Royal Philatelic Collection will be on display.

12
Ludlow Castle, Shropshire
Vintage Vehicle Display.

12
Newby Hall, Yorkshire
Spring Plant Fair.

15
Arley Hall, Cheshire
'Gardening with shrubs' – Peter Foley.

18
Dalemain, Cumbria
Fell Pony Society Stallion Show.

18
Ragley Hall, Warwickshire
Miniature Sail Fiesta by the Lake (free admission for Season Ticket Holders).

18 – 19
Beaulieu, Hampshire
Spring Autojumble.

18 – 19
Chatsworth, Derbyshire
Angling Fair.

18 – 19
Floors Castle, Borders
Horse Trials.

18 – 19
Parham House & Gardens, Sussex
"Stitches in Time" needlework weekend (10am – 5pm).

18 – 19
Rockingham Castle, Northamptonshire
Civil War at Rockingham Castle, 11.30am-5pm. A major re-enactment by the Sealed Knot – 500 Civil War troops lay siege to the Castle (info and group bookings tel: 01536 770240).

18 – 19
Stafford Castle & Visitor Centre, Staffordshire
1000 Year Fair 2002, 11am-5pm. Historical entertainments, re-enactments and children's activities spanning 1000 years of history.

19
Capesthorne Hall, Cheshire
Rochdale Owners' Club Kit Car Show.

19
Traquair, Borders
Garden Lovers Fair.

19
Wartnaby Gardens, Leicestershire & Rutland
Plant Sale.

20 – 24
Chelsea Physic Garden, London
Chelsea Show Week, 12 noon - 5pm with lunches.

21 – 23
Goodwood House, Sussex
Race Meeting.

24 – 26
Harewood House, Yorkshire
Food Lovers' Fair.

24 – 26
Loseley Park, Surrey
Craft Fair.

24 – 26
Newby Hall, Yorkshire
Rainbow Craft Fair.

25
Blair Castle, Perthshire/Fife
Atholl Highlanders' Parade.

25 – 26
Dalemain, Cumbria
Lilliput Lane Collectors Fair.

25 – 26
Traquair, Borders
Beer Festival.

25 – 27
Ludlow Castle, Shropshire
Festival of Crafts.

26
Blair Castle, Perthshire/Fife
Atholl Gathering & Highland Games.

30
Goodwood House, Sussex
Race Meeting.

31
Holker Hall, Cumbria
Holker Garden Festival.

JUNE

1
Chatsworth, Derbyshire
Open Air Concert.

1 – 2
Cawdor Castle, The Highlands & Skye
Special Gardens Weekend: guided tours of gardens and Cawdor Big Wood.

1 – 2
Holburne Museum of Art, Somerset
'A Pelican in the Wilderness': Hermits and Hermitages.

1 – 2
Holker Hall, Cumbria
Holker Garden Festival.

1 – 2
Kentwell Hall, Suffolk
Re-Creation: WWII (Landgirls).

1 – 4
Harewood House, Yorkshire
Spring Craft Fair.

1 – 4
Hever Castle, Kent
Elizabethan Revelries.

1 – 4
Sulgrave Manor, Northamptonshire
Stuart Living History – the Guild of Gentry and Allied Skills portray a typical gentry household of about 1635. The Courtyard Hall will feature 'Taking in Art', an exhibition of work by local artists and craftspeople. Adults £6.50, children £3.25, family £17.50. 10.30am-5pm.

1 – 9
Leeds Castle, Kent
Golden Jubilee Week.

1 – 30
Fairfax House, Yorkshire
James Gilray – 'The dark side'.

1 – 30
Killerton House & Garden, Devon
Special Costume Exhibition "Lace – The Ultimate Luxury".

1 – 30
Wellington Arch, London
Exhibition on the Sikh contribution to the World Wars.

2
Blenheim Palace, Oxfordshire
Classical Concert with Fireworks (Performing Arts, Blenheim Park – separate admission, tel: 01625 560000).

2 – 3
Capesthorne Hall, Cheshire
Cheshire Classic Car and Motorcycle Event.

2 – 4
Ragley Hall, Warwickshire
Classic Car & Transport Show.

3 – 4
Eastnor Castle, Herefordshire
Steam Fair & Country Show with Fred Dibnah.

5
Arley Hall, Cheshire
Gardening Course.

7
Goodwood House, Sussex
Race Meeting (evening).

7 – 9
Hatfield House, Hertfordshire
Festival of Gardening (adult £9.50, group £7.00, child £4.00).

8 – 9
Blenheim Palace, Oxfordshire
Craft Fair (Blenheim Park – separate admission).

8 – 9
Eastnor Castle, Herefordshire
Festival of Wood.

13
Arley Hall, Cheshire
Arley Celebrity Lecture with Anna Pavord.

13 – 16
Blenheim Palace, Oxfordshire
Blenheim Palace Flower Show
(Blenheim Park – separate admission, Event Innovations Ltd, tel: 01737 379911/ www.blenheimpalaceflowershow.co.uk).

13 – 16
Ripley Castle, Yorkshire
Homes & Gardens Grand Summer Sale.

14
Goodwood House, Sussex
Race Meeting (evening).

15
Gilbert White's House & The Oates Museum, Hampshire
Picnic to 'Jazz in June'.

15 – 16
Gilbert White's House & The Oates Museum, Hampshire
Unusual Plants Fair.

16
Harewood House, Yorkshire
Classic & Vintage Vehicle Rally.

19
Arley Hall, Cheshire
Gardening for Beginners.

21
Goodwood House, Sussex
Race Meeting (evening).

21 – 27
Hever Castle, Kent
Rose Week.

22 – 23
Rockingham Castle, Northamptonshire
Rainbow Craft Fair, 10.30am-5pm (info and group bookings tel: 01536 770240/01529 414793).

22 – 23
Sulgrave Manor, Northamptonshire
The Return of the Vikings! – the Vikings of Middle England recreate life as it was in Viking Britain. A full living history encampment with much 'hands on' opportunity, combat displays and a vivid presentation of these often gruesome times. Adults £6.50, children £3.25, family £17.50. 10.30am-5pm.

22 – 30
Ludlow Castle, Shropshire
Ludlow Festival.

23
Wartnaby Gardens, Leicestershire & Rutland
Plant Fair & Sketching Clubs Exhibition.

25 – 30
Holburne Museum of Art, Somerset
'Pickpocketing the Rich': Portrait painters in Bath from 1720-1793.

28
Goodwood House, Sussex
Race Meeting (evening).

29
Burghley House, Lincolnshire
Summer concert in the park (Performing Arts Management Ltd tel: 01625 560000).

29
Leeds Castle, Kent
Open Air Classical Concert.

29 – 30
Arley Hall, Cheshire
7th Arley Garden Festival.

29 – 30
Leonardslee Gardens, Sussex
West Sussex Country Craft Fair.

29 – 30
Tatton Park, Cheshire
Stars & Stripes.

30
Goodwood House, Sussex
Race Meeting.

JULY

1 – 7
Ludlow Castle, Shropshire
Ludlow Festival.

1 – 31
Holburne Museum of Art, Somerset
'Pickpocketing the Rich': Portrait painters in Bath from 1720-1793.

1 – 31
Killerton House & Garden, Devon
Special Costume Exhibition "Lace – The Ultimate Luxury".

1 – 31
Wellington Arch, London
Exhibition on the Sikh contribution to the World Wars.

3
Arley Hall, Cheshire
Gardening Course.

3
Leeds Castle, Kent
Children's Prom Concert.

4
Blair Castle, Perthshire/Fife
Charity Day in Aid of Macmillan Cancer Research.

4
Tatton Park, Cheshire
As You Like It – performed by Theatre Set-Up.

6
Leeds Castle, Kent
Open Air Classical Concert.

6 – 7
Dyrham Park, Gloucestershire
Music Festival.

6 – 31
Petworth House, Sussex
'Turner at Petworth' exhibition of over 70 oils, watercolours and gouaches that Turner painted of Petworth House and its surrounding landscape. During the exhibition, for the first time ever, Turner's studio at Petworth House will be open to the general public.

7
Tatton Park, Cheshire
Cystic Fibrosis Bike Ride.

11
Arley Hall, Cheshire
Arley Celebrity Lecture with Roy Lancaster.

12
Ragley Hall, Warwickshire
Alcester Singers Summer Concert.

12 – 14
Tatton Park, Cheshire
Robert Bailey Antiques Fair.

13
Chartwell, Kent
BBC Big Band.

13
Wilton House, Wiltshire
Classical Firework Proms Night.

13 – 14
Powderham Castle, Devon
28th Annual Historic Vehicle Gathering.

13 – 14
Sulgrave Manor, Northamptonshire
Tudor Living History – the Tudor Group present the house exactly as it would have been in Elizabethan times. Adults £6.50, children £3.25, family £17.50. 10.30am-5pm.

14
Beaulieu, Hampshire
4 x 4 Show.

14
Cobham Hall, Kent
National Garden Scheme Day (+ House open 2-5pm).

14
Ragley Hall, Warwickshire
Caspian Horse Society (free admission for Season Ticket Holders).

14
Rockingham Castle, Northamptonshire
Open Air Shakespeare – Richard III. Gates open from 6pm, performances commence 7.30pm. Box office tel: 01536 771238.

14 – 31
Chelsea Physic Garden, London
Summer Exhibition.

19 – 21
Loseley Park, Surrey
Great Gardening Show.

20
Hever Castle, Kent
Jousting Tournament.

20 – 21
Dalemain, Cumbria
Rainbow Craft Fair.

21
Chenies Manor House, Buckinghamshire
Plant Fair, 10am-5pm, £4.

21
Gilbert White's House & The Oates Museum, Hampshire
Gilbert White Day.

21
Hever Castle, Kent
Tudor Archery.

21
Hole Park, Kent
Hardy Plant Society Plant Fair.

21
Newby Hall, Yorkshire
Historic Vehicle Rally.

21
Rockingham Castle, Northamptonshire
Open Air Shakespeare – Romeo & Juliet. Gates open from 6pm, performances commence 7.30pm. Box office tel: 01536 771238.

26 – 28
Sulgrave Manor, Northamptonshire
Moll Flanders – outdoor theatre. The Motley Crew Theatre Company present a riotous production of Daniel Defoe's famous story of low life and scandal in 18th century society. Bring your own picnic and comfortable chairs – the show will go on whatever the weather. Advance booking advisable. Adults £7.50, children/OAPs £5. 7.30pm on Fri and Sat, 3pm on Sun.

27
Burghley House, Lincolnshire
Summer concert in the park (Performing Arts Management Ltd tel: 01625 560000).

27
Hever Castle, Kent
Jousting Tournament.

27
Ragley Hall, Warwickshire
Newfoundland Dog Trials (free admission to Season Ticket Holders).

27
Tatton Park, Cheshire
Fireworks & Light Spectacular Concert with the Hallé Orchestra (tel: 01625 534400).

27 – 28
Lulworth Castle, Dorset
Lulworth Horse Trials & Country Fair.

28
Hever Castle, Kent
Tudor Archery.

30 – 31
Goodwood House, Sussex
Glorious Goodwood Race Week.

31
Cobham Hall, Kent
Summer Stroll Garden Tour, 7pm (guidebook tour and glass of wine, £5 per person). Please telephone to book.

AUGUST

1 – 3
Goodwood House, Sussex
Glorious Goodwood Race Week.

1 – 31
Chelsea Physic Garden, London
Summer Exhibition.

1 – 31
Holburne Museum of Art, Somerset
'Pickpocketing the Rich': Portrait painters in Bath from 1720-1793.

1 – 31
Killerton House & Garden, Devon
Special Costume Exhibition "Lace – The Ultimate Luxury".

1 – 31
Petworth House, Sussex
'Turner at Petworth' exhibition of over 70 oils, watercolours and gouaches that Turner painted of Petworth House and its surrounding landscape. During the exhibition, for the first time ever, Turner's studio at Petworth House will be open to the general public.

1 – 31
Wellington Arch, London
Exhibition on the Sikh contribution to the World Wars.

2
Powderham Castle, Devon
Last Night of the Powderham Proms Bournemouth Symphony Orchestra Open Air Firework Concert.

2 – 4
Hatfield House, Hertfordshire
Art in Clay – National Pottery & Ceramics Festival (adult £5.50, group £4.50, child £3.00).

3
Powderham Castle, Devon
Open Air Pop Concert.

3
Ragley Hall, Warwickshire
Firework & Light Extravaganza – outdoor concert.

3 – 4
Hever Castle, Kent
Jousting Tournament.

3 – 4
Kentwell Hall, Suffolk
Re-Creation: WWII (Landgirls).

3 – 4
Traquair, Borders
Traquair Fair.

4
Drummond Castle Gardens, Perthshire/Fife
Open Day – entertainments, teas, raffle.

6 – 11
Sulgrave Manor, Northamptonshire
Stars, Stripes and Stitches – Sulgrave's annual festival of needlework. Classes and workshops (booking essential). Phone/send for full programme. Adults £6.50, children £3.25. 10.30am - 5pm.

7
Arley Hall, Cheshire
Gardening Course.

10 – 11
Great Comp Garden, Kent
Hardy Plant Society Annual Garden Show.

10 – 11
Hever Castle, Kent
Jousting Tournament.

11
Harewood House, Yorkshire
Rolls Royce Rally.

11
Loseley Park, Surrey
Open Air Concert & Fireworks.

11
Tatton Park, Cheshire
VW North West.

12 – 16
Eastnor Castle, Herefordshire
Children's Fun Week.

17 – 18
Bosworth Battlefield, Leicestershire & Rutland
Anniversary weekend – Medieval Spectacular including battle re-enactment.

17 – 18
Hever Castle, Kent
Jousting Tournament.

17 – 18
Ragley Hall, Warwickshire
Warwickshire & West Midlands Game Fair.

17 – 18
Tatton Park, Cheshire
Vintage & Classic Sports Car Show.

18
Dalemain, Cumbria
Cumbria Classic Car Show.

21
Arley Hall, Cheshire
Gardening for Beginners.

22 – 25
Blair Castle, Perthshire/Fife
Bowmore Blair Castle International Horse Trials & Country Fair.

23 – 26
Capesthorne Hall, Cheshire
Rainbow Craft Fair.

24
Hever Castle, Kent
Jousting Tournament.

24 – 25
Goodwood House, Sussex
Race Meeting.

24 – 26
Blenheim Palace, Oxfordshire
Craft Fair (Blenheim Park – separate admission).

24 – 26
Harewood House, Yorkshire
Steam Rally.

25
Floors Castle, Borders
Massed Pipe Bands Family Day.

25 – 26
Eastnor Castle, Herefordshire
TV & Film Arms and Berkeley Household.

25 – 26
Hever Castle, Kent
Tudor Archery.

25 – 26
Rockingham Castle, Northamptonshire
Vikings! Middle England – once again the Vikings are visiting the Castle – be prepared for Battles, Horses, Pageant, Living History Camp and much more (info and group bookings 01536 770240).

25 – 26
Sulgrave Manor, Northamptonshire
Harvest Home – the Tudor Lord of the Manor and his Cook will tell of the customs and traditions of Harvest and Autumn in the countryside of early rural England. Adults £6.50, children £3.25. 10.30am-5pm.

26
Ripley Castle, Yorkshire
'Ripley Revel' – Hog Roast.

29 – 31
Burghley House, Lincolnshire
Horse Trials (enquiries tel: 01780 752131).

30
Ragley Hall, Warwickshire
Last Night of the Ragley Proms – outdoor concert.

31
Chatsworth, Derbyshire
Country Fair.

31
Harewood House, Yorkshire
Last Night of the Proms Concert.

31
Hever Castle, Kent
Jousting Tournament.

31
Ripley Castle, Yorkshire
'Last Night at the Proms' open air concert.

SEPTEMBER

1
Arley Hall, Cheshire
Autumn Plant Hunters' Fair.

1
Burghley House, Lincolnshire
Horse Trials (enquiries tel: 01780 752131).

1
Chatsworth, Derbyshire
Country Fair.

1
Hever Castle, Kent
Tudor Archery.

1 – 2
Killerton House & Garden, Devon
Special Costume Exhibition "Lace – The Ultimate Luxury".

1 – 8
Chelsea Physic Garden, London
Summer Exhibition.

1 – 15
Holburne Museum of Art, Somerset
'Pickpocketing the Rich': Portrait painters in Bath from 1720-1793.

1 – 29
Petworth House, Sussex
'Turner at Petworth' exhibition of over 70 oils, watercolours and gouaches that Turner painted of Petworth House and its surrounding landscape. During the exhibition, for the first time ever, Turner's studio at Petworth House will be open to the general public.

1 – 30
Fairfax House, Yorkshire
'Time for Tea' – the evolution of teatime, 1660 - 1860'.

1 – 30
Wellington Arch, London
Exhibition on the Sikh contribution to the World Wars.

4
Arley Hall, Cheshire
Gardening Course.

5 – 8
Blenheim Palace, Oxfordshire
The Blenheim International Horse Trials (Blenheim Park – separate admission. tel: 01993 813335).

5 – 8
Tatton Park, Cheshire
Robert Bailey Antiques Fair.

6 – 8
Hatfield House, Hertfordshire
Homes, Gardens & Flower Show (adult £6.00, group £5.00, child £3.00).

6 – 8
Ludlow Castle, Shropshire
Food & Drink Fair.

7 – 8
Beaulieu, Hampshire
International Autojumble.

7 – 8
Finchcocks, Kent
Music Festival.

7 – 8
Leeds Castle, Kent
The Great Leeds Castle Balloon & Vintage Car Weekend.

7 – 8
Ragley Hall, Warwickshire
Gardeners' Weekend (free admission for Season Ticket Holders on Saturday).

13 –14
Goodwood House, Sussex
Race Meeting.

13 – 15
Hever Castle, Kent
Patchwork & Quilting.

14 – 15
Finchcocks, Kent
Music Festival.

15
Capesthorne Hall, Cheshire
Capesthorne Vintage & Classic Car and Motorcycle Event.

15
Newby Hall, Yorkshire
Autumn Plant Fair.

18
Arley Hall, Cheshire
'Late colour in the garden' – with Peter Foley.

21 – 22
Finchcocks, Kent
Music Festival.

21 – 22
Holkham Hall, Norfolk
Holkham Country Fair.

21 – 22
Kentwell Hall, Suffolk
Re-Creation: Tudor.

21 – 29
Sulgrave Manor, Northamptonshire
Tudor Living History – Melford-hys-Companie return to take the house and gardens back to Tudor times. Adults £6.50, children £3.25, family £17.50. Sat-Sun 10.30am-5pm; weekdays 2-5pm.

25 – 26
Goodwood House, Sussex
Race Meeting.

27 – 29
Newby Hall, Yorkshire
Rainbow Craft Fair.

28 – 29
Finchcocks, Kent
Music Festival.

OCTOBER

1– 31
Fairfax House, Yorkshire
'Time for Tea' – the evolution of teatime, 1660 - 1860'.

2
Arley Hall, Cheshire
Gardening Course.

5
Sulgrave Manor, Northamptonshire
Chamber Concert – The Aurora Ensemble play a dazzling variety of highly enjoyable wind pieces including works by Arnold, Elgar, Barber, Poulenc and Janacek. 7.30pm. Tickets £17.50 inc buffet supper and wine. Booking essential.

5 – 6
Eastnor Castle, Herefordshire
Festival of Fine Food & Drink.

9 – 13
Leeds Castle, Kent
Autumn Gold Flower Festival.

14 – 20
Hever Castle, Kent
Autumn Colour Week.

16
Arley Hall, Cheshire
Gardening for Beginners.

19 – 20
Ragley Hall, Warwickshire
Craft Fair.

19 – 20
Sulgrave Manor, Northamptonshire
Apple Day – over 300 varieties of English apples on display, cookery demonstrations, fruit to buy and cider to try. Farmers Market, displays and stands. Adults £7.50, children £3.50, family £20. 10.30am-5pm.

26 – 27
Blair Castle, Perthshire/Fife
Glenfiddich Piping & Fiddling Championships.

26 – 27
Kentwell Hall, Suffolk
Re-Creation: WWII (Landgirls).

26 – 27
Stowe House, Buckinghamshire
Craft Fair.

26 – 31
Leeds Castle, Kent
Fall Fun for Families.

NOVEMBER

1
Leeds Castle, Kent
Fall Fun for Families.

1– 20
Fairfax House, Yorkshire
'Time for Tea' – the evolution of teatime, 1660 - 1860'.

2
Leeds Castle, Kent
Grand Firework Spectacular.

2
Sulgrave Manor, Northamptonshire
Chamber Concert – Stromenti playing on period instruments present an evening of Baroque music including pieces by Purcell, Corelli, Vivaldi and Telemann amongst others. 7.30pm. Tickets £17.50 inc buffet supper and wine. Booking essential.

2 – 3
Cobham Hall, Kent
The Medway Flower Festival & Craft Show (+ House open 1-4pm).

6
Arley Hall, Cheshire
Garden Floristry Day.

9 – 10
Sulgrave Manor, Northamptonshire
The Embroiderer's Casket – inspired by the Manor's project 'The New Elizabethan Embroideries'. A range of displays, stalls and demonstrations with the theme centred on embroidery and textiles. Adults £6.50, children £3.25. 10.30am-4.30pm.

20
Arley Hall, Cheshire
'The Winter Garden' – with Julia White.

23 – 24
Ludlow Castle, Shropshire
Medieval Christmas Fayre.

23 – 24
Ragley Hall, Warwickshire
Yuletide Craft Fair.

30
Finchcocks, Kent
Christmas Fair.

DECEMBER

1
Finchcocks, Kent
Christmas Fair.

1
Gilbert White's House & The Oates Museum, Hampshire
Mulled Wine & Christmas Shopping Day.

3 – 31
Fairfax House, Yorkshire
Annual Christmas Exhibition – Georgian decoration for the festive season; carol singing each day at 1.30pm.

6 – 7
Sulgrave Manor, Northamptonshire
Christmas Choral Concerts – the Cherwell Singers present two evenings of traditional Christmas songs, madrigals and carols interspersed with seasonal readings and stories. 7.30pm. Tickets £17.50 inc buffet supper and wine. Booking essential.

7 – 8
Sulgrave Manor, Northamptonshire
A Tudor Christmas – see the Great Hall bedecked with seasonal greenery, with the log fire burning and beeswax candles glowing. Hear from the Lord of the Manor of the customs and traditions of Christmas past and from his Cook of food and feasting, with music by Wynndebagge the Piper. Timed tickets issued on arrival. Adults £6.50, children £3.25. 10.30am-4.30pm.

13 – 14
Ragley Hall, Warwickshire
Alcester Singers Christmas Concert.

14 – 15
Sulgrave Manor, Northamptonshire
A Tudor Christmas – see the Great Hall bedecked with seasonal greenery, with the log fire burning and beeswax candles glowing. Hear from the Lord of the Manor of the customs and traditions of Christmas past and from his Cook of food and feasting, with music by Wynndebagge the Piper. Timed tickets issued on arrival. Adults £6.50, children £3.25. 10.30am-4.30pm.

16 – 24
Leeds Castle, Kent
Christmas at the Castle.

21 – 22
Sulgrave Manor, Northamptonshire
A Tudor Christmas – see the Great Hall bedecked with seasonal greenery, with the log fire burning and beeswax candles glowing. Hear from the Lord of the Manor of the customs and traditions of Christmas past and from his Cook of food and feasting, with music by Wynndebagge the Piper. Timed tickets issued on arrival. Adults £6.50, children £3.25. 10.30am-4.30pm.

27 – 30
Sulgrave Manor, Northamptonshire
A Tudor Christmas – see the Great Hall bedecked with seasonal greenery, with the log fire burning and beeswax candles glowing. Hear from the Lord of the Manor of the customs and traditions of Christmas past and from his Cook of food and feasting, with music by Wynndebagge the Piper. Timed tickets issued on arrival. Adults £6.50, children £3.25. 10.30am-4.30pm.

ENGLAND

Open All Year

Properties included in this list are open to some extent for all or most of the year.
See individual entries for details.

This list is merely intended to draw attention to properties which are open for most of the year, it is intended only as a guide.

Open All Year

Properties included in this list are open to some extent for all or most of the year.
See individual entries for details.

SCOTLAND

This list is merely intended to draw attention to properties which are open for most of the year, it is intended only as a guide.

WALES

IRELAND

This list is merely intended to draw attention to properties which are open for most of the year, it is intended only as a guide.

THE COUNTIES OF
ENGLAND

Oak Gallery, The Vyne © NTPL/James Mortimer

ENGLAND

Chelsea Physic Garden

London

Chelsea Physic Garden

Arms of the Worshipful Society of Apothecaries of London

"… The reputation of Chelsea Garden excels all the gardens of Europe for its amazing variety of plants of all orders and classes and from all climates as I survey with wonder and delight this 19th July 1764."

Peter Collinson, botanist

SCVLPTOR
Vitus Rodolph. Speckle.

PICTORES OPERIS,
Heinricus Füllmaurer.   Albertus Meyer.

Punica granatum

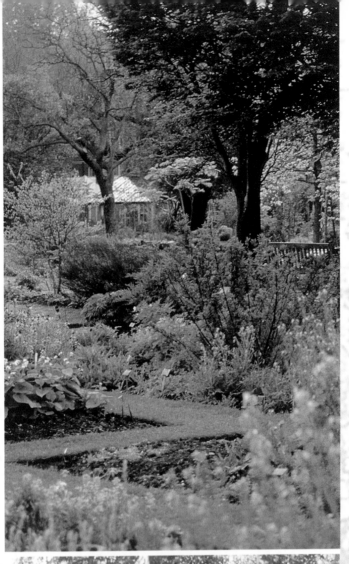

Ginkgo biloba

Chelsea Physic Garden nestles quietly at the beginning of Cheyne Walk in Chelsea, an area of London which was once the fashionable centre of writers and artists – Turner, Whistler and Rossetti were all enchanted by the Thames view from Cheyne Walk. Today though, it is the garden which is one of the main reasons for visiting this part of London.

Chelsea, the second oldest botanic garden in England, founded in 1673, resides peacefully in a four acre plot hidden from prying eyes by high protective walls. A handsome brick house forms a backdrop to the garden, which runs down towards the River Thames. The first view of the garden is seen from the original Students' Gate in Swan Walk, where a wide formal gravel walk leads into the garden. From this central path, smaller paths branch off at right-angles, those to the left lead down towards the river while those to the right pass the culinary and officinal plants *en route* to the glass house range.

As the highly informative guide to the gardens explains, a botanic garden has certain features which distinguish it from other gardens, however large they may be. It must have a comprehensive and properly labelled collection of plants which are formally arranged by their families in a taxonomic system.

There are two suggested walks for the visitor to Chelsea. The first, the Medicinal Walk, shows medical plants laid out in ordered beds. Many of these plants are important in current medical practice. There are also plants with traditional and homoeopathic remedies, American and Chinese medicine, medicinal plants of the rainforest and plants under current research. It is perhaps worth remembering that over 80% of prescribed medicine today is of plant origin.

The second, a Historical Walk, is based on plants introduced to the garden by eight prominent botanists and plant hunters associated with Chelsea. These include Philip Miller and Sir Joseph Banks, but everywhere you look are names associated with the garden which have been commemorated in plant generic names: Hermannia, Doodia, Milleria, Martynia, Banksia…the list is endless. Although the garden was founded in the 17th century to train London's apothecaries in herbal medicine and its research and educational work are as important today, a visit to the garden is not in the least bit dry or indigestible. Chelsea's atmosphere may be one of learning, but it is highly friendly and welcoming and the garden may be enjoyed on a number of intellectual levels. You can merely pick up a leaflet listing the month's most interesting flowers and shrubs and potter around at your leisure, or become a Friend of the Garden for a small annual fee which will allow you free entry (+ friend) on all public open days and at other times during office hours.

Chelsea Physic Garden has been described as London's 'secret garden' and one of its 'most fascinating cultivated spaces'. Visit it and you will appreciate why it richly deserves these titles. So on whatever level you visit this garden, you will not be disappointed by the history and medicinal stories it unfolds. ⊣

For further details about *Chelsea Physic Garden* see entry on page 71.

London - England

Owner:
Historic Royal Palaces

THE BANQUETING HOUSE

WHITEHALL

www.hrp.org.uk/bh/indexbh.htm

The magnificent Banqueting House is all that survives of the great Palace of Whitehall which was destroyed by fire in 1698. It was completed in 1622, commissioned by King James I, and designed by Inigo Jones, the noted classical architect. In 1635 the main hall was further enhanced with the installation of 9 magnificent ceiling paintings by Sir Peter Paul Rubens, which survive to this day. The Banqueting House was also the site of the only royal execution in England's history, with the beheading of Charles I in 1649.

The Banqueting House is open to visitors, as well as playing host to many of society's most glittering occasions.

▶ **CONTACT**
Irma Hay
(day visitors)
Fiona Thompson
(functions)

The Banqueting House
Whitehall
London SW1A 2ER

Tel: 020 7930 4179
or 020 7839 7569

Fax: 020 7930 8268

▶ **LOCATION**
OS Ref. TQ302 801

Underground:
Westminster,
Embankment and
Charing Cross.

Rail: Charing Cross.

▶ **OPENING TIMES**
All Year
Mon - Sat
10am - 5pm
Last admission 4.30pm.

Closed
24 December - 1 January,
Good Friday and other
public holidays.

NB. Liable to close at short
notice for Government
functions.

▶ **ADMISSION**
Adult £3.90
Child (5-15yrs) £2.30
Student £3.10
OAP/Conc £3.10
Under 5s .... Free

Groups please telephone
020 7930 4179 for details.

Concerts.
No photography in house.

Banquets.

Undercroft suitable.

Video and audio guide.

None.

Welcome.

CONFERENCE/FUNCTION

ROOM	SIZE	MAX CAPACITY
Main Hall	110' x 55'	400
Undercroft	64' x 55'	350

© HM Queen Elizabeth II

Royal Collection Enterprises

BUCKINGHAM PALACE

LONDON

www.the-royal-collection.org.uk

Owner:
HM The Queen

▶ CONTACT

The Visitor Office
Buckingham Palace
London SW1A 1AA

Tel: 020 7321 2233
Fax: 020 7930 9625

e-mail:
buckinghampalace@
royalcollection.org.uk

▶ LOCATION
OS Ref. TQ291 796

Underground:
Green Park, Victoria,
St James's Park.

Rail: Victoria.

Air: Heathrow.

Sightseeing tours
A number of tour
companies include a
visit to the State Rooms
in their sightseeing tours.
Ask your concierge or
hotel porter for details.

Buckingham Palace is the official London residence of Her Majesty The Queen Elizabeth II and serves as both home and office. Its nineteen state rooms, which open for just eight weeks a year, form the heart of the working palace. They are used extensively by The Queen and members of the Royal Family to receive and entertain their guests on State, ceremonial and official occasions. The State Rooms are lavishly furnished with some of the finest treasures from the Royal Collection – paintings by Rembrandt, Rubens and Vermeer; sculpture by Canova; exquisite examples of Sèvres porcelain, and some of the finest English and French furniture in the world. The new garden walk offers superb views of the Garden Front of the Palace and the 19th century lake.

Adjacent to Buckingham Palace are The Royal Mews and Queen's Gallery. The Royal Mews is one of the finest working stables in existence and houses both the horse-drawn carriages and motor cars used for coronations, State Visits, royal weddings and the State Opening of Parliament.

The Queen's Gallery, which has been closed for major redevelopment, will reopen in May 2002 as part of the Queen's Golden Jubilee celebrations.

© HM Queen Elizabeth II

▶ OPENING TIMES
Opening arrangements may
change at short notice.

The State Rooms
4 August - 29 September*
Daily: 9.30am - 4.30pm.

Tickets available during
Aug & Sept from the Ticket
Office in Green Park.
To pre-book your tickets
telephone the Visitor
Office 020 7321 2233.

The Queen's Gallery
The Queen's Gallery will
reopen in May 2002 to
celebrate The Queen's
Golden Jubilee.

The Royal Mews
All year: Monday -
Thursday
12 noon - 4pm
Last adm. 3.30pm.
Extra hours are added
during the summer
months.

* Further days may be added.

▶ ADMISSION
The State Rooms

Adult	£11.50
Child (up to 17yrs)	£6.00
Child (under 5yrs)	Free
OAP	£9.50
Family (2+2)	£29.00

Groups (15+)	
Per person	£10.50

Admission prices for the
Royal Mews and Queen's
Gallery are available from
the Visitor Office.

No photography inside.

None. None

Wheelchair users are required to pre-book for the summer opening. The Royal Mews is fully accessible.

Guide dogs only.

English Heritage Photo Library

CHISWICK HOUSE ⌗

CHISWICK

www.english-heritage.org.uk

Owner:
English Heritage

▶ CONTACT
Visits:
House Manager
Chiswick House
Burlington Lane
London W4 2RP

Tel: 020 8995 0508

English Heritage Hospitality:
The Hospitality Manager
Chiswick House
Burlington Lane
London W4 2RP

Tel: 020 8742 1978

▶ LOCATION
OS Ref: TQ210 775

Burlington Lane
London W4.

Rail: ¼ mile NE of Chiswick Station.

Tube: Turnham Green, ¾ mile

Bus: 190, E3.

CONFERENCE/FUNCTION

ROOM	MAX CAPACITY
Domed Saloon	100 standing 48 dining
Red Velvet Room	24 dining
Green Velvet Room	24 dining
Whole House	150 standing 80 dining

Chiswick House is internationally renowned as one of the first and finest English Palladian villas. Lord Burlington, who built the villa from 1725 - 1729, was inspired by the architecture and gardens of ancient Rome and this house is his masterpiece. His aim was to create a fit setting to show his friends his fine collection of art and his library. The opulent interior features gilded decoration, velvet walls and painted ceilings. The important 18th century gardens surrounding Chiswick House have, at every turn, something to surprise and delight the visitor from the magnificent cedar trees to the beautiful Italianate gardens with their cascade, statues, temples, urns and obelisks.

English Heritage Hospitality

English Heritage Hospitality offers the use of Chiswick House in the evenings for dinners, receptions and weddings.

English Heritage Photo Library

Summer
1 April - 30 September
Daily, 10am - 6pm.

Autumn
October
Daily, 10am - 5pm.

Winter
1 Nov - 31 March
Wed - Sun, 10am - 4pm.

Note: opening times may change in April 2001, please telephone for details before you visit.

▶ ADMISSION
Adult £3.30
Child (5-15yrs) £1.70
Conc £2.50
Groups (11+)
.... 15% discount

Tour leader and coach driver have free entry. 1 extra place for every 20 additional people.

🎥 ℹ️ Filming, plays, photographic shoots.

🍽 Private & corporate hospitality.

♿ Please call in advance.

🧍 Personal guided tours must be booked in advance. Colour guide book £2.50.

🎧 Free audio tours in English, French & German.

🍴 Free if booked in advance. Tel: 020 7973 3485.

🐕 Guide dogs in grounds.

🔔 Civil Wedding Licence.

❄️

🛡 Tel for details.

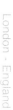

English Heritage Photo Library/Jonathan Bailey

ELTHAM PALACE

ELTHAM

www.english-heritage.org.uk

Owner:
English Heritage

▶ CONTACT

English Heritage
Hospitality:
Hospitality Manager
Eltham Palace
Court Yard
Eltham
SE9 5QE
Tel: 020 8294 2577

Visits:
Property Secretary
Eltham Palace
Court Yard
Eltham
SE9 5QE
Tel: 020 8294 2548

▶ LOCATION
OS Ref. TQ425 740

M25/J3, then A20
towards Eltham. The
Palace is signposted
from A20 and from
Eltham High Street.

Rail: Eltham or
Mottingham.

The epitome of 1930s chic, Eltham Palace dramatically demonstrates the glamour and allure of the period.

Bathe in the light flooding from a spectacular glazed dome in the Entrance Hall as it highlights beautiful blackbeam veneer and figurative marquetry. It is a *tour de force* only rivalled by the adjacent Dining Room – where an Art Deco aluminium-leafed ceiling is a perfect complement to the bird's-eye maple walls. Step into Virginia Courtauld's magnificent gold-leaf and onyx bathroom and throughout the house discover lacquered, 'ocean liner' style veneered walls and built-in furniture.

A Chinese sliding screen is all that separates chic '30s Art Deco from the medieval Great Hall. You will find concealed electric lighting, centralised vacuum cleaning and a loud-speaker system that allowed music to waft around the house. Authentic interiors have been recreated by the finest contemporary craftsmen. Their appearance was painstakingly researched from archive photographs, documents and interviews with friends and relatives of the Courtaulds.

Outside you will find a delightful mixture of formal and informal gardens including a rose garden, pergola and loggia, all nestled around the extensive remains of the medieval palace.

▶ OPENING TIMES

1 Apr - 30 September:
Wed - Fri & Sun
10am - 6pm.

1 - 31 October: Wed - Fri
& Sun, 10am - 5pm.

1 November - 31 March:
Wed - Fri & Sun,
10am - 4pm.

Open BH Mon
throughout the year.

Closed from 24 Dec -
15 Feb 2002 & from
23 Dec - 1 Feb 2003.

Groups visits must be
booked two weeks in
advance.

**English Heritage
Hospitality**
English Heritage Hospitality
offers exclusive use of the
Palace on Mon, Tue or Sat
for daytime conferences,
meetings and weddings and
in the evenings for dinners,
concerts and receptions.

English Heritage Photo Library/Jonathan Bailey

 Filming, plays
and photographic
shoots.

 Exclusive
private and
corporate
hospitality.

Free. English,
German & French.

 Coaches must
book.

Tel for details.

▶ ADMISSION

House and Grounds

Adult	£6.20
Child	£3.10
OAP	£4.70
Family (2+3)	£15.50

Grounds only

Adult	£3.60
Child	£1.80
OAP	£2.70

CONFERENCE/FUNCTION

ROOM	MAX CAPACITY
Great Hall	400 standing 200 dining
Entrance Hall	100 seated
Drawing Room	120 standing 80 theatre-style
Dining Room	50 dining

London - England

English Heritage Photo Library

KENWOOD HOUSE ⊞

HAMPSTEAD

www.english-heritage.org.uk

Owner:
English Heritage

▶ **CONTACT**

Visits:
The House Manager
Kenwood House
Hampstead Lane
London NW3 7JR
Tel: 020 8348 1286

**English Heritage
Hospitality:**
The Hospitality Manager
Kenwood House
Hampstead Lane
London NW3 7JR
Tel: 020 7973 3507

▶ **LOCATION**

OS Ref. TQ271 874

Hampstead Lane, NW3.

Bus: London
Transport 210.

Rail: Hampstead
Heath.

Underground:
Archway or Golders
Green Northern Line
then bus 210.

Kenwood, one of the treasures of London, is an idyllic country retreat close to the popular villages of Hampstead and Highgate.

The house was remodelled in the 1760s by Robert Adam, the fashionable neo-classical architect. The breathtaking library or 'Great Room' is one of his finest achievements.

Kenwood is famous for the internationally important collection of paintings bequeathed to the nation by Edward Guinness, 1st Earl of Iveagh. Some of the world's finest artists are represented by works such as a Rembrandt *Self Portrait*, Vermeer's *The Guitar Player; Mary, Countess*

Howe by Gainsborough and paintings by Turner, Reynolds and many others.

As if the house and its contents were not riches enough, Kenwood stands in 112 acres of landscaped grounds on the edge of Hampstead Heath, commanding a fine prospect towards central London. The meadow walks and ornamental lake of the park, designed by Humphry Repton, contrast with the wilder Heath below. The open air concerts held in the summer at Kenwood have become part of London life, combining the charms of music with the serenity of the lakeside setting.

▶ **OPENING TIMES**

Summer
1 April - 30 September
Daily: 10am - 6pm, open
10.30am Wed & Fri.

1 - 31 October
Daily: 10am - 5pm, open
10.30am Wed & Fri.

Winter
1 November - 31 March
Daily: 10am - 4pm, open
10.30am Wed & Fri.

Closed 24 - 26 December
& 1 January.

**English Heritage
Hospitality** offers exclusive use of Kenwood House in the evenings for dinners, concerts and receptions, and the lecture room for daytime events.

▶ **ADMISSION**

House & Grounds: Free.
Donations welcome.

English Heritage Photo Library

English Heritage Photo Library

CONFERENCE/FUNCTION	
ROOM	MAX CAPACITY
Orangery	80 dining
Music Room	40 dining
Dining Room	50 dining
Lecture Room	80 theatre-style
Whole House	150 dining

🖻

ⓘ Concerts, exhibitions, filming. No photography in house.

⊤ Exclusive private and corporate hospitality.

♿ Ground floor access.

☕ Available in the Brew House.

🚶 Available on request (in English). Please call for details.

🎧 English, French, Italian & German.

🅿 West Lodge car park on Hampstead Lane. Parking for the disabled.

🐾 Free when booked in advance on 020 7973 3485.

❄

London England

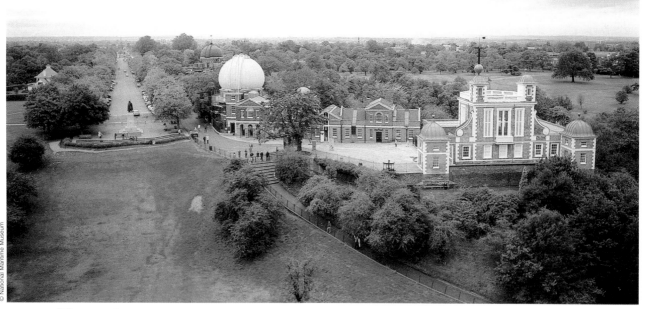

© National Maritime Museum

ROYAL OBSERVATORY GREENWICH & QUEEN'S HOUSE

GREENWICH PARK

www.nmm.ac.uk

Owner: National Maritime Museum

▶ CONTACT

Royal Observatory &
Queen's House
Robin Scates
Greenwich Park
Greenwich
London SE10 9NF

Tel: 020 8858 4422
Visit Bookings:
020 8312 6608
Functions:
020 8312 6644
Fax: 020 8312 6572
e-mail: bookings@
nmm.ac.uk

▶ LOCATION

OS Ref. TQ388 773

Within Greenwich Park
on the S bank of the
Thames at Greenwich.
Travel by river cruise or
Docklands Light Railway.
M25 (S) via A2, from
M25 (N) M11, A12 and
Blackwall Tunnel.

The Maritime Greenwich World Heritage Site encompasses Wren's imposing Royal Observatory (1675), the National Maritime Museum and the Queen's House (Inigo Jones c.1635). The Royal Observatory defines the Prime Meridian of the world – Longitude 0°. Visit the Astronomer Royal's apartments, see the 1833 time ball and admire Harrison's intricate marine timekeepers.

The National Maritime Museum's 20 modern galleries chart Britain's history of seafaring and Empire ranging from Nelson's navy to recent environmental protection. The Queen's House contains exhibitions from the extensive fine art collections of the Museum, a special room dedicated to the royal history of Greenwich and work by an artist in residence.

▶ OPENING TIMES

Daily, 10am - 5pm, last
admission 4.30pm (later
opening in summer).

Gallery talks and drama
(see notices on arrival).

Planetarium shows (not
Sundays).

Special Exhibitions
Tattooing: 21 Mar - 30 Sept
Oceans of Discovery: from
Jun 2002.

▶ ADMISSION

New from December 2001:
Free admission for
all visitors.

Planetarium Show
  Adult £2.00
  Child/Conc. £1.50

© National Maritime Museum

CONFERENCE/FUNCTION

ROOM	SIZE	MAX CAPACITY
Queen's House Great Hall	40 x 40'	120
Observatory, Octagon Room	25 x 25'	60
NMM Upper Court	140 x 70'	500
NMM Lecture Theatre		120

No photography.

Partial. WC.

Licensed.

Limited for coaches.

Guide dogs only.

Sampson Lloyd

ST PAUL'S CATHEDRAL

LONDON

www.stpauls.co.uk

Owner: Dean & Chapter of St Paul's Cathedral

▶ CONTACT

Mark McVay
The Chapter House
St Paul's Churchyard
London   EC4M 8AD

Tel: 020 7246 8346
020 7246 8348

Fax: 020 7248 3104

e-mail: chapterhouse@ stpaulscathedral.org.uk

▶ LOCATION

OS Ref. TQ321 812

Central London.

Underground:
St Paul's,
Mansion House,
Blackfriars, Bank.

Rail: Blackfriars,
City Thameslink.

Air: London Airports.

A Cathedral dedicated to St Paul has stood at the heart of the City of London for 1400 years, a constant reminder of the spiritual life in this busy commercial centre.

The present St Paul's, the fourth to occupy the site, was built between 1675 - 1710. Sir Christopher Wren's masterpiece rose from the ashes of the previous Cathedral, which had been destroyed in the Great Fire of London.

Over the centuries, the Cathedral has been the setting for royal weddings, state funerals and thanksgivings. Admiral Nelson and the Duke of Wellington are buried here, Queen Victoria celebrated her gold and diamond jubilees and Charles, Prince of Wales married Lady Diana Spencer. Most recently, St Paul's hosted the

thanksgiving service for the 100th birthday of HM Queen Elisabeth the Queen Mother. On 4 June 2002 the Cathedral will host the National Service of Thanksgiving for the Golden Jubilee of HM The Queen.

Hundreds of memorials pay tribute to famous statesmen, soldiers, artists, doctors and writers and mark the valuable contributions to national life made by many ordinary men and women.

The soaring dome, one of the largest in the world, offers panoramic views across London from the exterior galleries. Inside, a whisper in the Whispering Gallery can be heard on the opposite side.

Far more than a beautiful landmark, St Paul's Cathedral is a living symbol of the city and nation it serves.

Sampson Lloyd

🞉 ℹ No photography, video or mobile phones.

Ⱦ

♿ Partial.

☕ 🍴 Licensed.

🚶 🎧

🅿 None for cars, limited for coaches.

🐕 Guide dogs only.

❄

▶ OPENING TIMES

Mon - Sat, 8.30am - 4.30pm, last admission 4pm.

Guided tours: daily,
11.30am, 1.30pm and 2pm.

Tours of the Triforium: Mon & Thur, 11.30am & 2.30pm.

Cathedral Shop & Café:
9am - 5.30pm,
Sun, 10.30am - 5pm.

Restaurant:
11am - 5.30pm.

Service Times
Mon - Sat
7.30am Mattins (Sat 8.30am)
8am Holy Communion (said)
12.30pm Holy Communion (said)
5pm Choral Evensong

Sun: 8am Holy Communion (said)
10.15am Choral Mattins & sermon
11.30am Choral Eucharist & sermon
3.15pm Choral Evensong & sermon
6pm Evening service

The Cathedral may be closed to tourists on certain days of the year. It is advisable to phone or check our website for up-to-date information.

▶ ADMISSION

Adult	£5.00
Child	£2.50
Student	£4.00
OAP	£4.00
Groups (10+)	
Adult	£4.50
Child	£2.25
Student	£3.75
OAP	£3.75

(2001 prices)

CONFERENCE/FUNCTION

ROOM	MAX CAPACITY
Conference Suite	100 (standing)

Richard Kalina

SHAKESPEARE'S GLOBE

SOUTHWARK

www.shakespeares-globe.org

Owner: Shakespeare Globe Trust

▶ CONTACT

David Marshall
21 New Globe Walk,
Bankside, Southwark,
London SE1 9DT

Tel: 020 7902 1400

Globe Exhibition & Tour: 020 7902 1500
Fax: 020 7902 1515

Theatre Box Office
020 7401 9919

Globe Education
020 7902 1433

Entertaining
020 7902 1503

▶ LOCATION

OS Ref. TF323 805

On Bankside next to
Tate Modern & opposite
St Paul's Cathedral.
Underground:
London Bridge,
Waterloo.
Air: Heathrow,
Gatwick, City.

CONFERENCE/FUNCTION

ROOM	SIZE	MAX CAPACITY
Balcony Room	22 x 6m	dinner 70 theatre 70 drinks 120 buffet 100
Founder's Foyer	12 x 8m	dinner 40 drinks 100 buffet 80
UnderGlobe	1500m²	dinner 250 drinks 450 buffet 400

Shakespeare's Globe Exhibition is the most exciting place in which to explore Shakespeare's theatre and the London in which he lived and worked. In the vast UnderGlobe beneath the theatre, aspects of Shakespeare's work are brought imaginatively to life using a combination of modern technology and traditional crafts. Against the background of Elizabethan Bankside – the City of London's playground in Shakespeare's time – the role of actor, musician and audience is explored. Elizabethan special effects are brought to life on touch screens and the secrets of period costume designs revealed. A visit to the Exhibition includes a tour into today's working theatre. Let one of our storytellers introduce you to the Globe, recounting Sam Wanamaker's struggle to recreate the space for which Shakespeare wrote many of his plays. Hear the story of how this astonishing theatre has been built using hand tools and Elizabethan materials and techniques. During the matinées, in the theatre season, Exhibition storytellers will now be able to take visitors on a 'virtual' tour of the Globe.

The UnderGlobe (pictured) beneath the Globe Theatre is also a purpose-designed area for top quality private entertaining. This and other rooms around the site, some with stunning river views offer great flexibility for clients to tailor their individual events.

▶ OPENING TIMES

October - April: daily,
10am - 5pm. May -
September (theatre
season): 9am - 12 noon,
exhibition & guided tour
into the theatre.

12.30 - 4pm: exhibition &
'virtual tour' of the theatre.

Closed 24 & 25 December.

Group rates available on
request. Advanced
booking essential.

▶ ADMISSION

Please call for
information on prices

Nik Milner

🦽
🍽 Licensed.
🍴 Licensed.
🚶 Obligatory.
🎧
P None.

🦮 Guide dogs only.
❄
 Tel for details.

SOMERSET HOUSE
LONDON
www.somerset-house.org.uk

including

Courtauld Institute Gallery ~ www.courtauld.ac.uk
Gilbert Collection ~ www.gilbert-collection.org.uk
Hermitage Rooms ~ www.hermitagerooms.com

Somerset House
Owner: Somerset
House Trust, Strand,
London WC2R 1LA

Tel: 020 7845 4600
Fax: 020 7836 7613
e-mail: info@
somerset-house.org.uk

Courtauld Institute
Gallery
Courtauld Institute of Art
Tel: 020 7848 2526
e-mail: galleryinfo@
courtauld.ac.uk

Gilbert Collection
Tel: 020 7420 9400
e-mail: info@
gilbert-collection.org.uk

Hermitage Rooms
Tel: 020 7845 4630

▶ **LOCATION**
OS Ref. TQ308 809

Entrances Victoria
Embankment or Strand.

Underground: Temple
or Covent Garden.

Air: London airports.

Somerset House, Sir William Chambers' 18th century architectural masterpiece, is now open to the public. Situated between Covent Garden and the South Bank, it takes its place as one of Europe's great centres for art and culture, and the enjoyment of long-hidden classical interiors and architectural vistas.

The Courtauld Institute Gallery has one of the greatest small collections of paintings in the world, including world famous Old Masters and the finest Impressionist paintings in Britain.

The Gilbert Collection is London's newest museum of the decorative arts. Given to the nation by Sir

Arthur Gilbert, the magnificent collections of European silver, gold snuff boxes and Italian mosaics are pre-eminent in the world. The vaulted spaces of Somerset House provide an inspirational setting for these works of great historical and artistic importance.

The Hermitage Rooms at Somerset House recreate, in miniature, the imperial splendour of the Winter Palace and its various wings, which now make up The State Hermitage Museum in St Petersburg. The beautifully furnished galleries provide a backdrop for a programme of changing exhibitions, offering a privileged glimpse of some of the museum's magnificent treasures.

▶ **OPENING TIMES**
Courtauld Institute
Gallery, Gilbert Collection
& Hermitage Rooms
Daily, 10am - 6pm.
Last admission 5pm.
Closed 24 - 26 December.

▶ **ADMISSION**
Somerset House
Free except special exhibitions.

Courtauld Institute
Gallery
Adult £4.00
Child (under 18) ..... Free
Student (UK full)......Free
OAP £3.00
Pre-booked Groups
Adult £3.00
Disabled & Helper.... £2.00

Mon, 10am - 2pm ...... Free

Gilbert Collection
Adult £5.00
Child (under 18) ..... Free
Student (UK full)......Free
OAP £4.00
Pre-booked Groups
Adult £4.00
Disabled & Helper.... £3.00

Daily after 4.30pm .... Free

Hermitage Rooms
Adult £6.00
Child (under 5yrs) ...... Free
Conc. £4.00
Pre-booked Groups
Adult £4.00

Advance booking for
Hermitage Rooms:
Ticketmaster -
020 7413 3398

Save an extra £1 pp on
joint tickets to visit two
collections & £2 pp on
tickets to visit all three.

Peter Durant

📷 Apply at desk for permission for photography/filming.

🍴 Licensed.

♿ By arrangement.

🔊 Gilbert Collection and Hermitage Rooms.

P None.

 Guide dogs only.

❄

FUNCTION/RECEPTION

ROOM	MAX CAPACITY
Silver Gallery	350
Fine Rooms	250
Great Room	200
Fine & Gt Rm.	400
Seamen's Hall	200
Courtyard	2,700

Mark Fiennes

SPENCER HOUSE

ST JAMES'S PLACE

www.spencerhouse.co.uk

Spencer House, built 1756 - 66 for the 1st Earl Spencer, an ancestor of Diana, Princess of Wales (1961-97), is London's finest surviving 18th century town house. The magnificent private palace has regained the full splendour of its late 18th century appearance, after a painstaking ten-year restoration programme.

Designed by John Vardy and James 'Athenian' Stuart, the nine state rooms are amongst the first neo-classical interiors in Europe. Vardy's Palm Room, with its spectacular screen of gilded palm trees and arched fronds, is a unique Palladian setpiece, while the elegant mural decorations of Stuart's Painted Room reflect the

18th century passion for classical Greece and Rome. Stuart's superb gilded furniture has been returned to its original location in the Painted Room by courtesy of the V&A and English Heritage. Visitors can also see a fine collection of 18th century paintings and furniture, specially assembled for the house, including five major Benjamin West paintings, graciously lent by Her Majesty The Queen.

The state rooms are open to the public for viewing on Sundays. They are also available on a limited number of occasions each year for private and corporate entertaining during the rest of the week.

▶ CONTACT

Jane Rick
Director
Spencer House
27 St James's Place
London   SW1A 1NR

Tel: 020 7514 1964
Fax: 020 7409 2952

Info Line: 020 7499 8620

▶ LOCATION

OS Ref. TQ293 803

Central London:
off St James's Street,
overlooking
Green Park.

Underground:
Green Park.

All images are
copyright of Spencer
House Ltd and may not
be used without the
permission of
Spencer House Ltd.

▶ OPENING TIMES

All Year
(except January & August)
Suns, 10.30am - 5.30pm.

Last tour 4.45pm.

Tours begin approximately
every 20 mins and last
1hr 10 mins. Maximum
number on each tour is 20.

Mon mornings for
pre-booked groups only.

Open for corporate
hospitality except
during January & August.

▶ ADMISSION

Adult £6.00
Conc.* £5.00

* Students, Friends of V&A, Tate Gallery and Royal Academy (all with cards), children under 16 (no under 10s admitted).

Prices include guided tour.

ⓘ No photography inside House.

🍸

♿ Ramps and lifts. WC.

🚶 Obligatory. Comprehensive colour guidebook £3.50.

🅿 None. Coaches can drop off at door.

▶ SPECIAL EVENTS

SPECIFIC SUNDAYS:

The authentically restored garden of this 18th century London palace will be open to the public on specific Sundays during Spring and Summer.

For updated information telephone 020 7499 8620 or see our website.

Mark Fiennes

CONFERENCE/FUNCTION

ROOM	MAX CAPACITY
Receptions	400
Lunches & Dinners	130
Board Meetings	40
Theatre Style meetings	100

HUDSON'S

SYON PARK 🏛

BRENTFORD

www.syonpark.co.uk

Owner: The Duke of Northumberland

▶ CONTACT

Louise Page-Bailey
Syon House
Syon Park
Brentford
TW8 8JF

Tel: 020 8560 0882
Fax: 020 8568 0936

e-mail: louise@
syonpark.co.uk

▶ LOCATION
OS Ref. TQ173 767

Between Brentford and
Twickenham, off the
A4, A310 in SW London.

Rail: Kew Bridge or
Gunnersbury
Underground then
Bus 237 or 267.

Air: Heathrow 8m.

Described by John Betjeman as 'the Grand Architectural Walk', Syon House and its 200 acre park is the London home of the Duke of Northumberland, whose family, the Percys, have lived here since the late 16th century.

Originally the site of a late medieval monastery, Syon Park has a fascinating history. The present house has Tudor origins but contains some of Robert Adam's finest interiors, which were commissioned by the 1st Duke in the 1760s. The private apartments and state bedrooms are now available to view (when not in use).

Within the 'Capability' Brown landscaped park are 40 acres of gardens which contain the

spectacular Great Conservatory designed by Charles Fowler in the 1820s. The House and Great Conservatory are available for corporate and private hire.

Syon House is an excellent venue for small meetings, lunches and dinners in the Duke's private dining room (max 22). The State Apartments make a sumptuous setting for dinners, concerts, receptions, launches and wedding ceremonies (max 120). Marquees can be erected on the lawn adjacent to the house for balls and corporate events. The Great Conservatory is available for summer parties, launches and wedding receptions.

▶ OPENING TIMES
House

27 March - 3 November
Wed, Thur, Sun & BHs
11am - 5pm
(open Good Fri &
Easter Sat).

Other times by
appointment for groups.

Gardens

Daily (except 25 & 26 Dec)
10.30am - 5.30pm or dusk
if earlier.

▶ ADMISSION
House and Gardens

Adult £6.95
Child £5.95
Conc £6.50
Family (2+2) £15.00

Gardens only

Adult £3.50
Child/Conc £2.50
Family (2+2) £7.00
Groups (15 - 50 persons)

House & Gardens
(Group bookings)

Adult £6.50
Child/Conc £5.50

Gardens only

Adult £3.50
Child/Conc £2.50

 No photography in house. Indoor adventure playground.

🏠 ✸ Garden centre.

⊤

♿ Partial.

🍴 Licensed.

🚶 By arrangement. 🎧

 Ⓟ 🏛

🐕 Guide dogs only.

🔔 ❄

CONFERENCE/FUNCTION		
ROOM	SIZE	MAX CAPACITY
Great Hall	50' x 30'	120
Great Conservatory	60' x 40'	150
Marquee		1000

Crown Copyright: Historic Royal Palaces 2002

ENTRY TO THE TRAITORS' GATE

THE TOWER OF LONDON

LONDON

www.hrp.org.uk/tol/indextol.htm

Managed by:
Historic Royal Palaces

▶ CONTACT

The Tower of London
London EC3N 4AB

Tel: 020 7709 0765

▶ LOCATION
OS Ref. TQ336 806

Underground:
Tower Hill on
Circle/District Line.

Docklands Light Railway:
Tower Gateway Station.

Rail: Fenchurch Street
Station and
London Bridge Station.

Bus: 15, 25, 42,
78, 100, D1.

Riverboat: From
Charing Cross,
Westminster or
Greenwich to
Tower Pier.

William the Conqueror began building the Tower of London in 1078 as a royal residence and to control the volatile City of London. Over the ensuing 900 years the Tower has served as a royal fortress, mint, armoury and more infamously as a prison and place of execution.

The Tower of London has been home to the Crown Jewels for the last 600 years and today visitors can see them in all their glory in the magnificent new Jewel House. They are still used by HM The Queen for ceremonies such as the State Opening of Parliament and the 'Crowns and Diamonds' exhibition details the jewels' history, alongside a pile of 2,314 diamonds lent by De Beers.

Visit the White Tower, the original Tower of London, which features new displays by the Royal Armouries including the Block and Axe, Tudor arms and armour and the Instruments of Torture.

Once inside, the Yeoman Warder 'Beefeaters' give free guided tours providing an unrivalled insight into the darker secrets of over 900 years of royal history. Above the notorious Traitors' Gate, costumed guides evoke life at the court of King Edward I in the recently restored rooms of his Medieval Palace.

See the execution site where many famous prisoners such as two of Henry VIII's wives were put to death and visit the Chapel Royal where they are buried. Special events take place throughout the year, including events during every school holiday, with costumed interpreters.

▶ OPENING TIMES
Summer
1 March - 31 October
Daily
Mon - Sat: 9am - 5pm
(last admission)
Suns: 10am - 5pm.

Winter
1 November - 28 February
Tues - Sat: 9am - 5pm
(last admission)
Mons & Suns: 10am - 4pm.

Closed 24 - 26 December
and 1 January.

Buildings close 30 minutes
after last admission.
Tower closes 1 hour after
last admission.

▶ ADMISSION
Telephone Info Line for
admission prices:
020 7709 0765.

Groups are advised to book,
telephone: 020 7488 5681.

No photography in
Jewel House.

020 7488 5762.

Partial. WC.

Obligatory. Yeoman Warder
tours are free and leave front
entrance every $^1/_2$ hr.

P None.

Welcome. Group rates on
request.

Tel for details.

Crown Copyright: Historic Royal Palaces 2002

Crown Copyright: Historic Royal Palaces 2000

THE WALLACE COLLECTION

MANCHESTER SQUARE

www.wallace-collection.org.uk

Hertford House is home to the internationally renowned Wallace Collection, a national museum of fine and decorative arts principally from the 16th - 19th centuries. Originally built for the 4th Duke of Manchester between 1776 - 88, it was leased in 1797 by the 2nd Marquess of Hertford, so beginning 200 years of association between house and family. Today it still serves to display the family's treasures, which were accumulated over five generations, and then bequeathed to the nation by Sir Richard Wallace's widow in 1897.

The 5,470 works of art include some of the world's best-known paintings (among them Frans Hals's *The Laughing Cavalier*), over a thousand items of French 18th century furniture, sculpture and porcelain and the finest collection of princely arms and armour in this country. Masterpieces by Rubens, Rembrandt, Velázquez, Watteau and Boucher hang above furniture made for the kings and queens of France.

The rich interiors of the ground and first floors continue to evoke something of the domestic splendor and atmosphere of a grandiose 19th century home. This 19th century aesthetic is complemented by the internal courtyard and lower ground floor, which were redeveloped in 2000. Designed by award-winning Rick Mather, the elegant contemporary design extensively features glass, steel and oak, as illustrated by the Sculpture Garden that is crowned by a spectacular glass roof.

▶ CONTACT

Press & Marketing
Office
The Wallace Collection
Hertford House
Manchester Square
London W1U 3BN

Tel: 020 7563 9500

Fax: 020 7224 2155

e-mail: information@
wallace-
collection.org.uk

▶ LOCATION

OS Ref. TQ283 813

Central London
behind Selfridges
department store.

Underground:
Bond Street.

OPENING TIMES

All Year

Mon - Sat: 10am - 5pm
Sunday: 12 noon - 5pm

Closed
Good Friday, May Day,
24 - 26 & December and
1 January.

▶ ADMISSION

Free.

[i] No photography in house.

Full range of merchandise including catalogues, postcards, books & gifts.

Rooms are available for a range of events including formal dinners, receptions, seminars and conferences. Tel Development Office 020 7563 9545.

Ramp access is to the right of the main entrance. A parking space may be booked in advance. Lift to all floors. For full details tel. Access Co-ordinator 020 7563 9515.

Café Bagatelle: morning coffee, lunch & afternoon tea.

Free lectures on the collection are given every day. Private tours can also be arranged. Please tel. Education Department on 020 7563 9551.

[headphones icon]

[P] Coaches may set down at Hertford House, parking is at Bayswater Road, W8. Meters in Manchester Square.

A free programme of teaching sessions is available. Please tel. the Education Department on 020 7563 9551.

[snowflake icon]

Tel for details.

CONFERENCE/FUNCTION

ROOM	SIZE	MAX CAPACITY
Great Gallery	35.8x10.5m	120
Sculpture Garden	23.1x15.3m	100/250
State & Dining Rms		40
Galleries		300
Lecture Theatre		150
Meeting Rm		50

2 WILLOW ROAD ✤

HAMPSTEAD, LONDON NW3 1TH

Tel: 020 7435 6166   **e-mail:** twlgen@smtp.ntrust.org.uk

Owner: The National Trust   **Contact:** The Custodian

The former home of Erno Goldfinger, designed and built by him in 1939. A three-storey brick and concrete rectangle, it is one of Britain's most important examples of modernist architecture and is filled with furniture also designed by Goldfinger. The interesting art collection includes works by Henry Moore and Max Ernst.

Location: OS Ref. TQ270 858. Hampstead, London.

Open: 2 - 23 Mar: Sat only, 12 - 5pm, free-flow with tours at 12.30 & 3.30pm; 28 Mar - 2 Nov: Thur - Sat, 12 - 5pm. Last admission 4pm. Guided tours every 45 mins. 9 Nov - 14 Dec: Sats only.

Admission: Adult £4.40, Child £2.20. Joint ticket with Fenton House £6.30.

🚶 Small ground floor area accessible, filmed tour of whole house available.
🎫 Obligatory.

APSLEY HOUSE

HYDE PARK CORNER, LONDON W1J 7NT

www.apsleyhouse.org.uk

Tel: 020 7499 5676   **Fax:** 020 7493 6576

Owner: V & A Museum & DCMS   **Contact:** The Administrator

Apsley House (No. 1, London) was originally designed by Robert Adam in 1771-8. In 1817 it was bought by the Duke of Wellington and enlarged. His London palace houses his magnificent collection: paintings by Velazquez, Goya, Rubens, Lawrence, Wilkie, Steen, de Hooch and other masters; sculpture, silver, porcelain, furniture, caricatures, medals and memorabilia.

Location: OS Ref. TQ284 799. N side of Hyde Park Corner. Nearest tube station: Hyde Park Corner exit 1 Piccadilly Line.

Open: Tue - Sun, 11am - 5pm. Closed Mon, (except BHs), Good Fri, May Day BH, 24 - 26 Dec and New Year's Day.

Admission: Adult £4.50. Groups: £2.50pp. Under 18yrs & OAPs Free.

📷 ℹ️ No photography in house. 🚻 🚶 Partial. 🎫 By arrangement.
🅿️ In Park Lane. 🐕 Guide dogs only. ✱

---

18 FOLGATE STREET

Spitalfields, East London E1 6BX

Tel: 020 7247 4013

Owner: Spitalfields Historic Buildings Trust   **Contact:** Mick Pedroli

A time capsule furnished and decorated to tell the story of the Jervis family, Huguenot silk weavers from 1725 - 1919.

Location: OS Ref. TQ335 820. ½ m NE of Liverpool St. Station. E of Bishopsgate (A10), just N of Spitalfields Market.

Open: Mon evening: times vary, booking is required. 1st Sun every month: 2 - 5pm. 1st Mon every month: 12 noon - 2pm. Group visits can be arranged by appointment.

Admission: Contribution £7 for the house's upkeep. "Silent Night" £10.

ALBERT MEMORIAL

Princes Gate, Kensington Gore SW7

Tel: 020 7495 0916 (Booking Agency)

Managed by/Contact: The Royal Parks Agency

An elaborate memorial by George Gilbert Scott to commemorate the Prince Consort.

Location: OS Ref. TQ266 798. Victoria Station 1½ m, South Kensington Tube ½ m.

Open: All visits by booked guided tours; weather dependent so please ring for confirmation.

Admission: Adult £3.50, Child/Conc. £3.

THE BANQUETING HOUSE   *See page 56 for full page entry.*

BLEWCOAT SCHOOL ✤

23 Caxton Street, Westminster, London SW1H 0PY

Tel: 020 7222 2877

Owner: The National Trust   **Contact:** The Administrator

Built in 1709 at the expense of William Green, a local brewer, to provide an education for poor children. Used as a school until 1926, it is now the NT London Gift Shop and Information Centre.

Location: OS Ref. TQ295 794. Near the junction with Buckingham Gate.

Open: All year: Mon - Fri, 10am - 5.30pm (Thurs 7pm). Also Sat 16, 23 & 30 Nov & 7, 14, 21 Dec. Closed BHs.

BOSTON MANOR HOUSE

Boston Manor Road, Brentford TW8 9JX

Tel: 020 8560 5441

Owner: Hounslow Cultural & Community Services   **Contact:** Jerome Farrell

A fine Jacobean house built in 1623.

Location: OS Ref. TQ168 784. 10 mins walk S of Boston Manor Station (Piccadilly Line) and 250yds N of Boston Manor Road junction with A4 - Great West Road, Brentford.

Open: 6 Apr - 27 Oct: Sat, Sun & BHs, 2.30 - 5pm. Park open daily.

Admission: Free.

BRUCE CASTLE

Haringey Museum & Archive Service, Lordship Lane, London N17 8NU

Tel: 020 8808 8772   **e-mail:** museum.services@haringey.gov.uk

Owner: London Borough of Haringey

A Tudor building. Sir Rowland Hill (inventor of the Penny Post) ran a progressive school at Bruce Castle from 1827.

Location: OS Ref. TQ335 906. Corner of Bruce Grove (A10) and Lordship Lane, 600yds NW of Bruce Grove Station.

Open: All year: Wed - Sun & Summer BHs, 1 - 5pm. Organised groups by appointment.

Admission: Free.

BUCKINGHAM PALACE   *See page 57 for full page entry.*

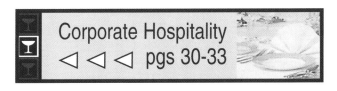

London - England

BURGH HOUSE

New End Square, Hampstead, London NW3 1LT

Tel: 020 7431 0144 **Buttery:** 020 7431 2516 **Fax:** 020 7435 8817

Owner: London Borough of Camden   **Contact:** Ms Helen Wilton

A Grade I listed building of 1703 in the heart of old Hampstead with original panelled rooms, "barley sugar" staircase bannisters and a music room. Home of the Hampstead Museum, permanent and changing exhibitions. Prize-winning terraced garden. Regular programme of concerts, art exhibitions, and meetings. Receptions, seminars and conferences. Rooms for hire. Special facilities for schools visits. Wedding receptions.

Location: OS Ref. TQ266 859. New End Square, E of Hampstead underground station.

Open: All year: Wed - Sun, 12 noon - 5pm. Sats by appointment only. BH Mons, 2 - 5pm. Closed Christmas fortnight, Good Fri & Easter Mon. Groups by arrangement. Buttery: Wed - Sun, 11am - 5.30pm. BHs, 1 - 5.00pm.

Admission: Free.

🖼 ♿Ground floor & grounds. WC. 🍽Licensed buttery. 🅿None.
🐕Guide dogs only. 🔊 ❄

CABINET WAR ROOMS   *See right for half page entry.*

CAPEL MANOR GARDENS

BULLSMOOR LANE, ENFIELD EN1 4RQ

www.capel.ac.uk

Tel: 020 8366 4442 **Fax:** 01992 717544

Owner: Capel Manor Charitable Organisation   **Contact:** Miss Julie Ryan

These extensive, richly planted gardens are delightful throughout the year offering inspiration, information and relaxation. The gardens include various themes - historical, modern, walled, rock, water, sensory and disabled and an Italianate Maze, Japanese Garden and 'Gardening Which?' demonstration and model gardens. Capel Manor is a College of Horticulture and runs a training scheme for professional gardeners originally devised in conjunction with the Historic Houses Association.

Location: OS Ref. TQ344 997. Minutes from M25/J25. Tourist Board signs posted.

Open: Daily in summer: 10am - 5.30pm. Last ticket 4.30pm. Check for winter times.

Admission: Adult £4, Conc. £3.50, Child £2, Family £10. Charges alter for special show weekends and winter months.

🖼 ♿Grounds. WC. 🍽 🐕In grounds, on leads. ❄ 🎧Tel for details.

Imperial War Museum

CABINET WAR ROOMS

CLIVE STEPS, KING CHARLES STREET, LONDON SW1A 2AQ

www.iwm.org.uk

Tel: 020 7930 6961 **Fax:** 020 7839 5897 **e-mail:** cwr@iwm.org.uk

Director: Phil Reed   **Contact:** Vanessa Rayner

Visit the hidden world of Churchill's secret underground wartime headquarters and catch a glimpse of the spartan conditions in which he and his Cabinet worked and lived during the Blitz. A former storage basement, the bunker was hurriedly converted in 1939 to become the very nerve centre of the British war effort, operating around the clock, undisturbed by the heavy bombing raids above ground. Step back in time and view the original complex just as it was left at the end of six years of war, when the lights were finally extinguished. Free personal sound guides are provided for every visitor.

Location: OS Ref. TQ301 799. Buses: 3, 11, 12, 24, 53, 77a, 88, 159, 211. Westminster Underground.

Open: All year: daily, 9.30am (1 Oct - 31 Mar: 10am) - 6pm. Last admission 5.15pm. Closed 24/25/26 Dec.

Admission: Adult £5.40, Child Free, Conc. £3.90. Booked groups (10+): Adult £3.90, Child Free, Conc. £3.40.

🖼 🎧 ♿ 🎫By arrangement. 🎧 🍽 🅿None. ❄

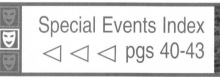
Special Events Index
◁ ◁ ◁ pgs 40-43

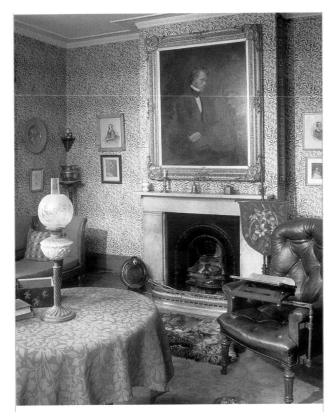

CARLYLE'S HOUSE

24 CHEYNE ROW, CHELSEA, LONDON SW3 5HL

Tel: 020 7352 7087   **Info Line:** 01494 755559   **Fax:** 020 7352 5108
e-mail: tcagen.smtp.ntrust.org.uk

Owner: The National Trust   **Contact:** The Custodian

In a quiet and beautiful residential area of London, this Queen Anne house was the home of Thomas Carlyle, the 'Sage of Chelsea', for some 47 years until his death in 1881. The skilful Scottish home-making of his wife Jane is much in evidence: the Victorian period décor, the furniture, pictures, portraits and books are all still in place. As an historian, social writer, ethical thinker and powerful public speaker, Thomas is honoured in the house, while Jane's strong belief in his genius and her own brilliant wit and gift for writing are recognised in the many existing letters. Their academic and domestic lives can be experienced today in the evocative atmosphere of the house.

NTPL / Michael Boys

Location: OS Ref. TQ272 777. Off Cheyne Walk, between Battersea and Albert Bridges on Chelsea Embankment, or off the King's Road and Oakley Street.
Open: 23 Mar - 3 Nov: Wed - Fri, 2 - 5pm; Sat, Sun & BH Mons, 11am - 5pm. Last admission 4.30pm. Closed Good Fri.
Admission: Adult £3.60, Child £1.80.
Unsuitable for wheelchairs. By arrangement for groups. Send SAE for details.

CHAPTER HOUSE, PYX CHAMBER & ABBEY MUSEUM

East Cloisters, Westminster Abbey, London SW1P 3PE
Tel: 020 7222 5897   www.english-heritage.org.uk
Owner: English Heritage   **Contact:** Head Custodian

The Chapter House, built by the Royal masons c1250 and faithfully restored in the 19th century, contains some of the finest medieval wall paintings to be seen. The building is octagonal, with a central column, and still has its original floor of glazed tiles, which have been newly conserved. Its uses have varied and in the 14th century it was used as a meeting place for the Benedictine monks of the Abbey and as well as for Members of Parliament. The 11th century Pyx Chamber now houses the Abbey treasures, reflecting its use as the strongroom of the exchequer from the 14th to 19th centuries. The Abbey museum contains medieval Royal effigies.

Location: OS Ref. TQ301 795. Approach either through the Abbey or through Dean's Yard and the cloister.
Open: 1 Apr - 30 Sept: daily, 9.30am - 5pm. 1 - 31 Oct: daily, 10am - 5pm. 1 Nov - 31 Mar: daily, 10am - 4pm. Liable to be closed at short notice on State & Holy occasions.
Admission: Adult £2.50, Child £1.30, Conc. £1.90.
Small charge. Tel for details.

CHELSEA PHYSIC GARDEN

66 ROYAL HOSPITAL ROAD, LONDON SW3 4HS

Tel: 020 7352 5646   **Fax:** 020 7376 3910
Owner: Chelsea Physic Garden Company   **Contact:** Sue Minter

The second oldest botanic garden in Britain, founded in 1673. For many years these 4 acres of peace and quiet with many rare and unusual plants were known only to a few. Specialists in medicinal plants, tender species and the history of plant introductions.

Location: OS Ref. TQ277 778. Off Embankment, between Chelsea & Albert Bridges. Entrance - Swan Walk.
Open: 7 Apr - 27 Oct: Weds, 12 noon - 5pm & Suns, 2 - 6pm. Snowdrop opening & winter festival: 3 & 10 Feb: 11am - 3pm.
Admission: Adult £4, Child £2, OAP £4, Conc. £2. Carers for disabled: Free.

CHISWICK HOUSE   *See page 58 for full page entry.*

COLLEGE OF ARMS

Queen Victoria Street, London EC4V 4BT
Tel: 020 7248 2762   **Fax:** 020 7248 6448   **e-mail:** enquiries@college-of-arms.gov.uk
Owner: Corp. of the Kings, Heralds & Pursuivants of Arms
              Contact: The Officer in Waiting

Mansion built in 1670s to house the English Officers of Arms and their records.
Location: OS Ref. TQ320 810. On N side of Queen Victoria Street, S of St Paul's Cathedral.
Open: Earl Marshal's Court only: open all year (except BHs, State and special occasions) Mon - Fri, 10am - 4pm. Group visits (up to 10) by arrangement only. Record Room: open for tours (groups of up to 20) by special arrangement in advance with the Officer in Waiting.
Admission: Free (groups by negotiation).

COURTAULD INSTITUTE GALLERY   *See page 64 for full page entry.*

THE DICKENS HOUSE MUSEUM

48 DOUGHTY STREET, LONDON WC1N 2LF

www.dickensmuseum.com

Tel: 020 7405 2127 **Fax:** 020 7831 5175 **e-mail:** dhmuseum@rmplc.co.uk

Owner: Dickens House Museum Trust　　**Contact:** Mr Andrew Xavier – Curator

House occupied by Charles Dickens and his family from 1837 - 1839 where he produced Pickwick Papers, Oliver Twist, Nicholas Nickleby and Barnaby Rudge. Contains the most comprehensive Dickens library in the world as well as portraits, illustrations and rooms laid out exactly as they were in Dickens' time.

Location: OS Ref. TQ308 822. W of Grays Inn Road.

Open: All year: Mon - Sat, 10am - 5pm (last admission 4.30pm).

Admission: Adult £4, Child £2, Conc. £3, Family £9. Booked groups (10+): Adult £3, Child £2.

By arrangement. Limited. No coaches. Guide dogs only. Tel for details.

EASTBURY MANOR HOUSE

Barking IG11 9SN

Tel: 020 8507 0119 **Fax:** 020 8507 0118

Owner: The National Trust　　**Contact:** The Administrator

Eastbury is a rare example of a medium-sized Elizabethan manor house. Leased to the Borough of Barking and Dagenham and used for a variety of arts and heritage activities.

Location: OS177, Ref. TQ457 838. In Eastbury Square, 10 mins walk S from Upney Station.

Open: Mar - Dec: first Sat every month (except Aug), 10am - 4pm. Telephone for details.

Admission: Adult £1.80, Child 60p, Conc. £1, Family £4.20. Group visits by arrangement. Rates on application. Evening tours also available.

Ground floor. Visitor days. None. Garden only.

ELTHAM PALACE　　　*See page 59 for full page entry.*

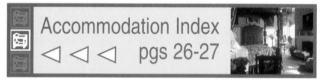

Accommodation Index ◁ ◁ ◁ pgs 26-27

FENTON HOUSE

WINDMILL HILL, HAMPSTEAD, LONDON NW3 6RT

Tel/Fax: 020 7435 3471 **Infoline:** 01494 755563 **e-mail:** tfehse@smtp.ntrust.org.uk

Owner: The National Trust　　**Contact:** The Custodian

A delightful late 17th century merchant's house, set among the winding streets of Old Hampstead. The charming interior contains an outstanding collection of Oriental and European porcelain, needlework and furniture. The Benton Fletcher Collection of beautiful early keyboard instruments is also housed at Fenton and the instruments are sometimes played by music scholars during opening hours. The walled garden has a formal lawn and walks, an orchard and vegetable garden and fine wrought-iron gates. Telephone for details of demonstrations and porcelain tours.

Location: OS Ref. TQ262 860. Visitors' entrance on W side of Hampstead Grove. Hampstead Underground station 300 yds.

Open: 2 - 17 Mar: Sat & Sun, 2 - 5pm. 23 Mar - 3 Nov: daily except Mon & Tue (open BH Mons & 4 Jun). Times: weekdays, 2 - 5pm. Weekends & BHs, 11am - 5pm. Groups at other times by appointment.

Admission: Adult £4.40, Child £2.20, Family £11. Joint ticket with 2 Willow Road, £6.30. No reduction for pre-booked groups. No picnics in grounds.

Ground floor. None. Send SAE for details.

Ham House

FREUD MUSEUM

20 MARESFIELD GARDENS, LONDON NW3 5SX

www.freud.org.uk

Tel: 020 7435 2002 **Fax:** 020 7431 5452 **e-mail:** freud@gn.apc.org

Contact: Ms E Davies

The Freud Museum was the home of Sigmund Freud after he escaped the Nazi annexation of Austria. The house retains its domestic atmosphere and has the character of turn of the century Vienna. The centrepiece is Freud's study which has been preserved intact, containing his remarkable collection of antiquities: Egyptian, Greek, Roman, Oriental and his large library. The Freuds brought all their furniture and household effects to London; fine Biedermeier and 19th century Austrian painted furniture. The most famous item is Freud's psychoanalytic couch, where his patients reclined. Fine Oriental rugs cover the floor and tables. Videos are shown of the Freud family in Vienna, Paris and London.

Location: OS Ref. TQ265 850. Between Swiss Cottage and Hampstead.

Open: Wed - Sun (inc) 12 noon - 5pm.

Admission: Adult £4, Child under 12 Free, Conc. £2. Coach groups by appointment.

🖼 ♿ Ground floor. **P** Limited. 🐕 Guide dogs only. ✳

FULHAM PALACE & MUSEUM

BISHOPS AVENUE, FULHAM, LONDON SW6 6EA

Tel: 020 7736 5821 **Museum:** 020 7736 3233

Owner: London Borough of Hammersmith & Fulham & Fulham Palace Trust

Former home of the Bishops of London (Tudor with Georgian additions and Victorian Chapel). The gardens, famous in the 17th century, now contain special specimen trees and a knot garden of herbs. The museum tells the story of this nationally important site. Education service available. Rooms and grounds are available for private functions.

Location: OS Ref. TQ240 761.

Open: Gardens: open daylight hours. Museum: Mar - Oct: Wed - Sun, 2 - 5pm. Nov - Feb: Thur - Sun, 1 - 4pm. Tours of principal rooms and gardens every 2nd Sun - contact Museum; selected other Suns contact Fulham Archaeological Rescue Group 020 7385 3723, £2. Private tours £5 each by arrangement with either organisation. Private tours with teas (50 max.).

Admission: Gardens: Free. Museum: Adult £1, Conc. 50p.

🍴 Private & wedding receptions. ♿ Partial. 🎫 Obligatory. **P** None. ■ 🐕 Guide dogs only. ✳

Reg. Charity No. 1020063

THE GEFFRYE MUSEUM

Kingsland Road, London E2 8EA

Tel: 020 7739 9893 **Fax:** 020 7729 5647 **e-mail:** info@geffrye-museum.org.uk

Owner: Independent Charitable Trust   **Contact:** Ms Nancy Loader

The Geffrye presents the changing styles of English domestic interiors through a series of period rooms from 1600 to present day.

Location: OS Ref. TQ335 833. 1m N of Liverpool St. Buses: 242, 149, 243, 67. Underground: Liverpool St. or Old St.

Open: Museum: Tue - Sat, 10am - 5pm. Sun & BH Mon, 12 noon - 5pm. Closed Mon (except BHs) Good Fri, Christmas Eve, Christmas Day, Boxing Day & New Year's Day. Gardens: Apr - Oct.

Admission: Free.

GILBERT COLLECTION   *See page 64 for full page entry.*

GUNNERSBURY PARK MUSEUM

Gunnersbury Park, London W3 8LQ

Tel: 020 8992 1612 **Fax:** 020 8752 0686 **e-mail:** gp-museum@cip.org.uk

Owner: Hounslow and Ealing Councils   **Contact:** Vanda Foster

Built in 1802 and refurbished by Sydney Smirke for the Rothschild family.

Location: OS Ref. TQ190 792. Acton Town Underground station. ¼ m N of the junction of A4, M4 North Circular.

Open: Apr - Oct: daily: 1 - 5pm. Nov - Mar: daily: 1 - 4pm. Victorian kitchens summer weekends only. Closed Christmas Day and Boxing Day. Park: open dawn - dusk.

Admission: Free. Donations welcome.

HANDEL HOUSE MUSEUM

25 BROOK STREET, LONDON W1K 4HB

www.handelhouse.org

Tel: 020 7495 1685 **Fax:** 020 7495 1759 **e-mail:** mail@handelhouse.org

Owner: The Handel House Trust Ltd   **Contact:** Emma Conway

The only composer museum in London is located in 25 Brook Street W1, where G F Handel lived for 36 years, composed masterpieces such as *Messiah*, and died in 1759. It includes refurbished interiors, fine and decorative arts and instruments, temporary exhibitions, live music and educational programmes to bring enjoyment and understanding of Handel, his time and his music to the Museum visitor.

Location: OS Ref. TQ286 809. Central London, between New Bond St and Grosvener Square. Bond Street Tube.

Open: Tue - Sat, 10am - 6pm (Thur until 8pm). Sun & BH Mons, 12 noon - 6pm. Closed Mons. Groups by arrangement.

Admission: Adult £4.50, Child £2, Conc. £3.50.

ℹ️No inside photography. 🅿️ ♿ 🅵By arrangement. 🎧 ■ ✳️

HERMITAGE ROOMS   *See page 64 for full page entry.*

HOGARTH'S HOUSE

Hogarth Lane, Great West Road, Chiswick, London W4 2QN

Tel: 020 8994 6757

Owner: Hogarth House Foundation   **Contact:** Jerome Farrell

This late 17th century house was the country home of William Hogarth, the famous painter, engraver, satirist and social reformer between 1749 and his death in 1764.

Location: OS Ref. TQ213 778. 100 yds W of Hogarth roundabout on the Great West Road - junction of Burlington Lane. Car park in named spaces in Axis Business Centre behind house and Chiswick House grounds.

Open: Feb- Oct: Tue - Sun & BH Mons, 1 - 5pm. Closed Mon (except BHs) and all Nov, Dec & Jan.

Admission: Free.

JEWEL TOWER ⌗

Abingdon Street, Westminster, London SW1P 3JY

Tel: 020 7222 2219

Owner: English Heritage   **Contact:** Head Custodian

Built c1365 to house the personal treasure of Edward III. One of two surviving parts of the original Palace of Westminster. Now houses an exhibition on 'Parliament Past and Present'.

Location: OS Ref. TQ302 794. Opposite S end of Houses of Parliament (Victoria Tower).

Open: 1 Apr - 31 Mar: daily, 10am - 6pm (closes 5pm in Oct, & 4pm Nov - Mar). Closed 24 - 26 Dec & 1 Jan.

Admission: Adult £1.60, Child 80p, Conc. £1.20.

🅿️ ✳️ ♿ Tel for details.

HAM HOUSE ❧

HAM, RICHMOND, SURREY TW10 7RS

www.nationaltrust.org.uk/regions/southern

Tel: 020 8940 1950 **Fax:** 020 8332 6903 **e-mail:** shhgen@smtp.ntrust.org.uk

Owner: The National Trust   **Contact:** The Property Manager

Ham House, set on the banks of the Thames near Richmond, is perhaps the most remarkable Stuart house in the country. Formerly the home of the influential Duke and Duchess of Lauderdale, Ham was a centre for Court intrigue throughout the 17th century. In its time, the house was at the forefront of fashion and retains much of its interior decoration from that period. The sumptuous textiles, furniture and paintings collected by the couple are shown in 26 rooms. The gardens are a remarkable survival of English formal gardening and are being gradually restored to their former glory. The 18th century dairy, decorated with cast iron cows' legs supporting marble work surfaces and hand-painted Wedgwood tiles, is now on view and the 17th century still house, used for distilling alcohol and perfumes, will open in April.

Location: OS Ref. TQ172 732. 1½ m from Richmond and 2m from Kingston. On the S bank of the River Thames, W of A307 at Petersham.

Open: 23 Mar - 3 Nov: daily except Thurs & Fris. House: 1 - 5pm, last adm. 4.30pm. Gardens: 11am - 6pm/dusk if earlier. Closed 25 - 26 Dec & 1 Jan.

Admission: House & Garden: Adult £6, Child £3, Family £15. Garden, Icehouse & Dairy: Adult £2, Child £1, Family £5. Pre-booked groups (15+): Adult £5, Child £2.50.

🅿️ ✳️ 🚆 🅱️ Partial. WC. ◼️ 🅵 🅿️ ■ 📶 Guide dogs. 🔺 ⬛ Tel for details

DR JOHNSON'S HOUSE

17 Gough Square, London EC4A 3DE

Tel: 020 7353 3745 **e-mail:** curator@drjh.dircon.co.uk

Owner: The Trustees

Fine 18th century house, once home to Dr Samuel Johnson, the celebrated literary figure, famous for his English dictionary.

Location: OS Ref. TQ314 813. N of Fleet Street.

Open: Oct - Apr: Mon - Sat, 11am - 5pm. May - Sept: Mon - Sat, 11am - 5.30pm. Closed BHs.

Admission: Adult £4, Child £1 (under 10yrs Free), Conc. £3. Family Ticket £9.00 . Groups: £3.

KEATS HOUSE

Keats Grove, Hampstead, London NW3 2RR
Tel: 020 7435 2062 **Fax:** 020 7431 9293
e-mail: keatshouse@corpoflondon.gov.uk **www**.keatshouse.org.uk
Owner: Corporation of London **Contact:** C De' Freitas
Regency home of the poet John Keats (1795 - 1821).
Location: OS Ref. TQ272 856. Hampstead, NW3. Nearest Underground: Belsize Park
& Hampstead.
Open: Summer: Apr - end Oct: General opening: Tue - Sun & BHs, 12 noon - 5pm.
Visits by appointment: Tue - Sat, 10am - 12 noon. Winter: Nov - Easter 2002: General
opening: Tue - Sun, 12 noon - 4pm. Visits by appointment, Tue - Sat, 10am - 12 noon.
Closed 24 - 26 & 31 Dec, 1 Jan & 29 Mar (Good Fri).
Admission: Adult £3, Under 16s Free, Conc. £1.50.
🔲 ♿Ground floor & garden. **P** None. 🦮 Guide dogs only. ✳

KENSINGTON PALACE
STATE APARTMENTS

See opposite for half page entry.

KENWOOD HOUSE ♯

See page 60 for full page entry.

Crown copyright: Historic Royal Palaces

RBK & C

LEIGHTON HOUSE MUSEUM

12 HOLLAND PARK ROAD, KENSINGTON, LONDON W14 8LZ

www.rbkc.gov.uk/leightonhousemuseum

Tel: 020 7602 3316 **Fax:** 020 7371 2467
e-mail: leightonhousemuseum@rbkc.gov.uk
Owner: Royal Borough of Kensington & Chelsea **Contact:** Curator
Leighton House was the home of Frederic, Lord Leighton 1830 - 1896, painter and
President of the Royal Academy, built between 1864 - 1879. It was a palace of art
designed for entertaining and to provide a magnificent working space in the studio,
with great north windows and a gilded apse. The Arab Hall is the centrepiece of
the house, containing Leighton's collection of Persian tiles, a gilt mosaic frieze and
a fountain. Victorian paintings by Leighton, Millais and Burne-Jones are on display.
Location: OS Ref. TQ247 793. N of High Street Kensington, off Melbury Rd, close
to Commonwealth Institute.
Open: Daily, except Tue. Spring & Summer BHs, 11am - 5.30pm.
Admission: Free. £3 per head for pre-booked tours.
🔲 🚻 🎨 🎧 🔳 ✖ ✳ 📺 Tel for details.

KENSINGTON PALACE
STATE APARTMENTS

LONDON W8 4PX

www.hrp.org.uk

Tel: 020 7937 9561 **Managed by/Contact:** Historic Royal Palaces
Kensington Palace dates back to 1689, and has seen such momentous events as
the death of George II and the birth of Queen Victoria. Today it provides an oasis
of tranquillity from the hustle and bustle of London.
Multi-language sound guides lead visitors round the magnificent State
Apartments, including the lavishly decorated Cupola Room, where Queen Victoria
was baptised, and the beautifully restored King's Gallery.
The Royal Court and Ceremonial Dress collection dates from the 18th century, and
audio tours allow visitors to participate in the excitement of dressing for Court,
from invitation to presentation. There are also selections of dresses owned and
worn by HM Queen Elizabeth II, and Diana, Princess of Wales, with other special
exhibitions throughout the year.

Crown copyright: Historic Royal Palaces

LINDSEY HOUSE 🏚

100 Cheyne Walk, London SW10 0DQ
Tel: 01494 528051 **Fax:** 01494 463310
Owner: The National Trust **Contact:** NT Regional Office
Part of Lindsey House was built in 1674 on the site of Sir Thomas More's garden,
overlooking the River Thames. It has one of the finest 17th century exteriors in London.
Location: OS Ref. TQ268 775. On Cheyne Walk, W of Battersea Bridge near junction
with Milman's Street on Chelsea Embankment.
Open: By written appointment only. 15 May, 12 Jun, 11 Sept & 9 Oct: 2 - 4pm.
Please write to (enc. SAE): The Secretary, 100 Cheyne Walk, London SW10 0DQ.
Admission: Free.

Location: OS Ref. TQ258 801. In Kensington Gardens. Underground: Queensway
on Central Line, High Street Kensington on Circle & District Line.
Open: Mar - Oct: Daily, 10am - 6pm. Nov - Feb: Daily, 10am - 5pm. Closed 24 - 26 Dec.
Last admission 1 hour before closing.
Admission: Adult £8.80, Child (5-15yrs) £6.30, under 5yrs Free, Conc. £6.90,
Family £26.80. Groups: Tel: 020 7937 7079.
ℹ️No photography indoors. 🔲 🚻 🍴 The Orangery serves light refreshments.
♿Partial. 🎧Sound guides for Dress Collection & State Apartments. **P**Nearby.
🔳Welcome, please book. 🦮In grounds, on leads. Guide dogs only in Palace. ✳

LINLEY SAMBOURNE HOUSE
18 Stafford Terrace, London W8 7BH
Info: 020 7602 3316 **Fax:** 020 7371 2467
Owner: The Royal Borough of Kensington & Chelsea   **Contact:** Assistant Curator
The home of Linley Sambourne (1844 - 1910) chief political cartoonist at Punch.
A unique example of a late Victorian town house.
Location: OS Ref. TQ252 794. Bus: 9, 10, 27, 28, 31, 49, 52, 70 & C1.
Underground: Kensington High Street. Parking on Sun in nearby streets.
Open: Closed for conservation work, expected to re-open Autumn 2002.

English Heritage Photo Library

MARBLE HILL HOUSE ⌗
RICHMOND ROAD, TWICKENHAM TW1 2NL

www.english-heritage.org.uk

Tel: 020 8892 5115
Owner: English Heritage   **Contact:** House Manager
This beautiful villa beside the Thames was built in 1724 - 29 for Henrietta Howard,
mistress of George II. Here she entertained many of the poets and wits of the
Augustan age including Alexander Pope and later Horace Walpole. The perfect
proportions of the villa were inspired by the work of the 16th century Italian
architect, Palladio. Today this beautifully presented house contains an important
collection of paintings and furniture, including some pieces commissioned for the
villa when it was built. Summer concerts.
Location: OS Ref. TQ174 736. A305, 600yds E of Orleans House.
Open: 1 Apr - 30 Sept: daily, 10am - 6pm. 1 Oct - 31 Oct: daily, 10am - 5pm.
1 Nov - 31 Mar, Wed - Sun, 10am - 4pm. Opening times may change in April,
please telephone for details before your visit.
Admission: Adult £3.30, Child £1.70, Conc. £2.50.
⬜ ♿Ground floor & grounds. WC. ▣Summer only. ✳ ⬛ Tel for details.

MUSEUM OF GARDEN HISTORY
LAMBETH PALACE ROAD, LONDON SE1 7LB
www.museumgardenhistory.org

Tel: 020 7401 8865 **Fax:** 020 7401 8869 **e-mail:** info@museumgardenhistory.org
Owner: The Tradescant Trust
Fascinating permanent exhibition of the history of gardens, collection of ancient
tools and recreated 17th century garden displaying flowers and shrubs of the
period – seeds of which may be purchased in the garden shop. Visit the tombs of
the Tradescants and Captain Bligh of the Bounty. They have knowledgeable staff
and lectures, concerts, courses and art exhibitions are held regularly. The Knot
Garden, part of the churchyard, is shown above.
Location: OS Ref. TQ306 791. At Lambeth Parish Church, next to Lambeth Palace,
at E end of Lambeth Bridge. Buses: 3, 77, 344, C10. Tube: Westminster or Waterloo.
Open: 1st Sun in Feb - mid Dec: daily, 10.30am - 5pm.
Admission: Voluntary: Adult £2.50, Conc. £2.
⬜ ♿ ♿Partial. ▣ 🅿None. ⬛ ✖ ✳

MORDEN HALL PARK ⚘
Morden Hall Road, Morden SM4 5JD
Tel: 020 8648 1845 **Fax:** 020 8687 0094
Owner: The National Trust   **Contact:** The Property Manager
Former deer park has an extensive network of waterways and ancient hay meadows.
Workshops now house local craftworkers.
Location: OS Ref. TQ261 684. Off A24 and A297 S of Wimbledon, N of Sutton.
Open: All year: daily.
Admission: Free.

MYDDELTON HOUSE GARDENS
Bulls Cross, Enfield, Middlesex EN2 9HG
Tel: 01992 702200
Owner: Lee Valley Regional Park Authority
Created by the famous plantsman E A Bowles.
Location: OS Ref. TQ342 992. ¼ m W of A10 via Turkey St. ¾ m S M25/J25.
Open: Mon - Fri (except Christmas), 10am - 4.30pm. Easter - Oct: Sun & BH Mons,
1 - 4pm.
Admission: Adult £2, Conc. £1.40.

THE OCTAGON, ORLEANS HOUSE GALLERY
Riverside, Twickenham, Middlesex TW1 3DJ
Tel: 020 8892 0221 **Fax:** 020 8744 0501 **e-mail:** m.denovellis@richmond.gov.uk
Owner: London Borough of Richmond-upon-Thames   **Contact:** Rachel Tranter
Outstanding example of baroque architecture built by James Gibbs c1720. Adjacent
wing now converted to an art gallery.
Location: OS Ref. TQ168 734. On N side of Riverside, 700yds E of Twickenham town
centre, 400yds S of Richmond Road, A305 via Lebanon Park Road and 500yds W of
Marble Hill House.
Open: Tue - Sat, 1 - 5.30pm (Oct - Mar closes 4.30pm). Sun & BHs, 2 - 5.30pm. Closed
Mons. Garden: open daily, 9am - sunset.
Admission: Free.

WILLIAM MORRIS GALLERY
Lloyd Park, Forest Road, Walthamstow, London E17 4PP
Tel: 020 8527 3782 **Fax:** 020 8527 7070
Owner: London Borough of Waltham Forest   **Contact:** Ms Nora Gillow
Location: OS Ref. SQ372 899. 15 mins walk from Walthamstow tube (Victoria line).
5 - 10 mins from M11/A406.
Open: Tue - Sat and first Sun each month, 10am - 1pm and 2 - 5pm.
Admission: Free for all visitors but a charge is made for guided tours which must
be booked in advance.

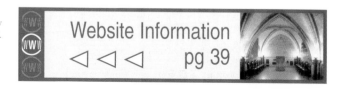

Website Information ◁ ◁ ◁ pg 39

NT Photographic Library

OSTERLEY PARK

JERSEY ROAD, ISLEWORTH TW7 4RB

Tel: 020 8232 5050 **Fax:** 020 8232 5080 **infoline:** 01494 755566
e-mail: tossms@smtp.ntrust.org.uk

Owner: The National Trust   **Contact:** The Property Manager

Osterley's four turrets look out across one of the last great landscaped parks in suburban London, its trees and lakes an unexpected haven of green. Originally built in 1575, the mansion was transformed in the 18th century into an elegant villa by architect Robert Adam. The classical interior, designed for entertaining on a grand scale, still impresses with its specially made tapestries, furniture and plasterwork.

NT Photographic Library: Dennis Gilbert

Location: OS Ref. TQ146 780. Access via Thornbury Road on N side of A4.

Open: House: 2 - 24 Mar: Sat & Sun; 27 Mar - 3 Nov; daily except Mons & Tues, 1 - 4.30pm. Closed Good Fri, open BH Mons & 4 Jun. Last admission: 4pm. Grand Stable: Sun afternoon in summer. Park & Pleasure Grounds: All year, 9am - 7.30pm or sunset if earlier. Park will be closed early during major events. Car park closed Good Fri, 25 & 26 Dec. Jersey Galleries: as house.

Admission: Adult £4.40, Child £2.20, Family £11. Group: Wed - Sat £3.80, pre-booking required. Car Park: £2.50.

Suitable, phone for details. On leads in park.

PALACE OF WESTMINSTER

London SW1A 0AA

Tel: 020 7219 3000   **Ticketmaster:** 0207344 9966   **Recorded Info:** 0207219 5532
www.parliament.uk   **Contact:** Information Office

The first Palace of Westminster was erected on this site by Edward the Confessor in 1042 and the building was a royal residence until a devastating fire in 1512. After this, the palace became the two-chamber Parliament for government - the House of Lords (largely hereditary until the reforms of the present Government) and the elected House of Commons. Following a further fire in 1834, the palace was rebuilt by Sir Charles Barry and decorated by A W Pugin.

Location: OS Ref. TQ303 795. Central London, W bank of River Thames. 1km S of Trafalgar Square. Underground: Westminster.

Open: Contact the Ticketmaster.

Admission: Ticketmaster admin charge £3.50. The 'line of route' tour: gratuity of £20 - £25 per group. Big Ben: Free.

PITSHANGER MANOR & GALLERY

Walpole Park, Mattock Lane, Ealing W5 5EQ

Tel: 020 8567 1227   **Fax:** 020 8567 0595

e-mail: pitshanger@ealing.gov.uk   **www**.ealing.gov.uk/pitshanger

Owner: London Borough of Ealing   **Contact:** Helen Walker

Set in Walpole Park, once owned by the architect Sir John Soane (1753 - 1837). He rebuilt most of the house to create a Regency villa. The later addition of a Victorian wing now houses a collection of Martinware pottery. Adjoining the Manor is Pitshanger Manor Gallery, the largest space for contemporary art in West London.

Location: OS Ref. TQ176 805. Ealing, London.

Open: All year: Tue - Sat, 11am - 6pm; May - Sept (inc): Sun, 1 - 5pm. Also closed Christmas, Easter & New Year.

Admission: Free. Adult group tours (10+): £3.

By arrangement. Limited. In grounds, on leads.

THE QUEEN'S GALLERY

Buckingham Palace, London SW1A 1AA

Tel: 020 7321 2233   **e-mail:** buckinghampalace@royalcollection.org.uk
www.the-royal-collection.org.uk

Owner: HM The Queen   **Contact:** The Visitor Office

Location: OS Ref. TQ290 795. Buckingham Palace.

Open: The Queen's Gallery opens May 2002, with a major exhibition to celebrate The Queen's Golden Jubilee.

THE ROYAL MEWS

Buckingham Palace, London SW1A 1AA

Tel: 020 7321 2233   **www**.the-royal-collection.org.uk

Owner: HM The Queen   **Contact:** The Visitor Office

The Royal Mews is one of the finest working stables in existence and provides a unique insight into the work of the Royal Household department that provides transport by road for The Queen and other members of the Royal Family. It is at the Royal Mews that State vehicles are housed, both the horse-drawn carriages and motor cars used for coronations, State Visits, royal weddings and the State Opening of Parliament.

Location: OS Ref. TQ289 794. Entrance on Buckingham Palace Road, W of The Queen's Gallery.

Open: Oct - Jul: Mon - Thur, 12 noon - 4pm. Aug & Sept: Mon - Thur, 10.30am - 4.30pm. Last admission 30mins before closing.

Admission: Prices to be confirmed.

ROYAL OBSERVATORY GREENWICH & QUEEN'S HOUSE

See page 61 for full page entry.

ROYAL SOCIETY OF ARTS
8 JOHN ADAM STREET, LONDON WC2N 6EZ

www.rsa.org.uk

Tel: 020 7839 5049　**Fax:** 020 7321 0271　**e-mail:** conference@rsa.org.uk

Owner: RSA　　　　　　　　　**Contact:** Ms Nicki Kyle

The house of the Royal Society of Arts was designed by Robert Adam specially for the Society in the early 1770s. One of the few remaining buildings from the original Adelphi development, its Georgian façade conceals many unexpected delights of both traditional and contemporary architecture. Designed as one of London's earliest debating chambers, the Great Room is one of the most spectacular theatres in the city. The Benjamin Franklin Room is spacious and elegant, featuring an antique chandelier and two Adam fireplaces. The Vaults were originally designed as river front warehouses. Now fully restored they offer a striking contrast to the splendour of the rooms above. All rooms may be hired for meetings, receptions and weddings.

Location: OS Ref. TQ305 806. Near to Charing Cross and Waterloo.

Open: All year: 8am - 8pm. Closed last 2 weeks of Aug, 24 Dec & 2 Jan.

Admission: For room hire prices, contact the RSA Conference Officer.

⊤ ⌂ ⏻ Licensed. 🎦 1st Sun in month & by arrangement. 🅿 None. ✖ ▲ ✳

ST JOHN'S GATE -
THE MUSEUM OF THE ORDER OF ST JOHN
ST JOHN'S GATE, LONDON EC1M 4DA

www.sja.org.uk/history

Tel: 020 7324 4070　**Fax:** 020 7336 0587　**e-mail:** museum@nhg.sja.org.uk

Owner: The Order of St John　　　**Contact:** Pamela Willis

Discover the rich history of the Knights Hospitaller, a monastic order dedicated to serving the sick and defending the faith, dating back to the 11th century. The Museum is in a Tudor Gatehouse, once the entrance to their English Priory and visitors can also see the 16th century church with remarkable 12th century crypt. After the Dissolution, the Gate was Hogarth's home and Dr Johnson's workplace. In Victorian times, St John Ambulance was founded here and a new interactive gallery tells its story.

Location: OS Ref. TQ317 821. St. John's Lane, Clerkenwell. Nearest underground: Farringdon.

Open: Mon - Fri: 10am - 5pm. Sat: 10am - 4pm. Closed BHs & Sat of BH weekend. Tours: Tue, Fri & Sat at 11am & 2.30pm. Reference Library: Open by appointment.

Admission: Museum Free. Tours of the building: £5, OAP £3.50 (donation).

🅾 ⌂ Ground floor. WC. 🎦 ▣ 🐕 Guide dogs only. ✳

ST GEORGE'S CATHEDRAL, SOUTHWARK
Westminster Bridge Road, London SE1 7HY
Tel: 020 7928 5256　**Fax:** 020 7202 2189　**e-mail:** stgeorges@rc.net
　　　　　　　　　　　　Contact: Canon James Cronin
Neo-Gothic rebuilt Pugin Cathedral bombed during the last war and rebuilt by Romily Craze in 1958.
Location: OS Ref. TQ315 794. Near Imperial War Museum. 1/2 m SE of Waterloo Stn.
Open: 8am - 8pm, every day, except BHs.
Admission: Free.

ST PAUL'S CATHEDRAL　　　*See page 62 for full page entry.*

SHAKESPEARE'S GLOBE　　　*See page 63 for full page entry.*

SIR JOHN SOANE'S MUSEUM
13 Lincoln's Inn Fields, London WC2A 3BP
Tel: 020 7405 2107　**Fax:** 020 7831 3957
Owner: Trustees of Sir John Soane's Museum　　**Contact:** Julie Brock
The celebrated architect Sir John Soane built this in 1812 as his own house. It now contains his collection of antiquities, sculpture and paintings.
Location: OS Ref. TQ308 816. E of Kingsway, S of High Holborn.
Open: Tue - Sat, 10am - 5pm. 6 - 9pm, first Tue of the month. Closed BHs & 24 Dec.
Admission: Free. Groups must book.

SOMERSET HOUSE including　　*See page 64 for full page entry.*
COURTAULD INSTITUTE GALLERY,
GILBERT COLLECTION
& HERMITAGE ROOMS

Plant Sales Index
◁ ◁ ◁ pgs 36-37

SOUTHSIDE HOUSE 🏛

3 WOODHAYES ROAD, WIMBLEDON, LONDON SW19 4RJ

Tel: 020 8946 7643

Owner: The Pennington-Mellor-Munthe Charity Trust   **Contact:** The Administrator

Built by Robert Pennington in 1665, the family befriended or were related to many distinguished names - among others Ann Boleyn's descendents, Nelson, Hamilton, the 'Hell Fire Duke of Wharton' and Natalie, Queen of Serbia. Family portraits and possessions on show. Bedroom prepared for Prince of Wales in 1750. In 1907 the heiress, Hilda Pennington Mellor married Axel Munthe the Swedish doctor and philanthropist. After 1945 Hilda and her sons restored the house. Malcolm, who had lived extraordinary adventures during the war, determined to make a cultural ark of the family inheritance. Guided tours give reality and excitement to the old family histories. Recently restored water gardens and orchard.

Location: OS Ref. TQ234 706. On S side of Wimbledon Common (B281), opposite Crooked Billet Inn.

Open: 2 Jan - 24 Jun: Wed, Sat, Sun & BH Mon. Guided tours on the hour, 2 - 5pm (last tour 4pm). Also open for private parties by arrangement from 1 Dec - 24 Jun.

Admission: Adult £5, Child £3 (must be accompanied by an adult).

🚫 Unsuitable. 👤 Obligatory. 🅿 Limited. ⬛ ✦

SOUTHWARK CATHEDRAL

Montague Close, Southwark, London SE1 9DA

Tel: 020 7367 6700   **Fax:** 020 7367 6725   **Welcome Desk:** 020 7367 6734

e-mail: cathedral@dswark.org.uk   **www**.dswark.org

Owner: Church of England   **Contact:** Welcome Desk

London's oldest gothic building and a place of worship for over 1,000 years, Southwark Cathedral has connections with Chaucer, Shakespeare, Dickens and John Harvard. Included in the new riverside Millennium buildings are: Interactive Exhibition 'The Long View of London', the Cathedral Shop and The Refectory.

Location: OS Ref. TQ327 803. South side of London Bridge, near Shakespeare's Globe and Tate Modern.

Open: Daily: 8.30am - 6pm. Weekday services: 8am, 12.30pm and 5.30pm. Sat services, 9am and 4pm. Sun services: 9am, 11am and 3pm. Visitor Centre: daily, 10am - 6pm, Sun, 11am - 5pm.

Admission: Recommended donation of £2.50 per person. Booked groups (min 15): Adult £2.50, Child £1, Conc. £2. Exhibition: Adult £3, Child £1.50, Conc. £2.50.

ℹ Indoor photography & video recording with permit. ⬛ ⬛ 🚻 Partial. WCs. ⬛ 🍽 Licensed. 👤 By arrangement. ⬛ 🅿 None. ⬛ 🐕 Guide dogs only. ✦

SPENCER HOUSE   *See page 65 for full page entry.*

Open All Year Index ◁ ◁ ◁ pgs 44-48

STRAWBERRY HILL

ST MARY'S, STRAWBERRY HILL, WALDEGRAVE ROAD, TWICKENHAM TW1 4SX

Tel: 020 8240 4114/020 8240 4311/020 8240 4044

Contact: The Conference Office

Horace Walpole converted a modest house at Strawberry Hill into his own version of a gothic fantasy. It is widely regarded as the first substantial building of the Gothic Revival and as such is internationally known and admired. A century later Lady Frances Waldegrave added a magnificent wing to Walpole's original structure. Lady Waldegrave's suite of rooms can be hired for weddings, corporate functions and conferences. Please telephone for details.

Location: OS Ref. TQ158 722. Off A310 between Twickenham & Teddington.

Open: Easter Sun - 20 Oct: Sun. Tours commence between 2pm & 3.30pm, please tel: 020 8240 4224 for confirmation or to make an appointment 020 8240 4114.

Admission: Adult £5, OAP £4.25. Group bookings: £4.25.

ℹ Conferences. ⬛ ⬛ 👤 ✦

London - England

NT Photographic Library: Geoffrey Frosh

English Heritage Photo Library

SUTTON HOUSE ❦

2 & 4 HOMERTON HIGH STREET, HACKNEY, LONDON E9 6JQ

Tel: 020 8986 2264   **e-mail:** tshslh@smtp.ntrust.org.uk

Owner: The National Trust   **Contact:** The Property Manager

A rare example of a Tudor red-brick house, built in 1535 by Sir Rafe Sadleir, Principal Secretary of State for Henry VIII, with 18th century alterations and later additions. Restoration revealed many 16th century details, even in rooms of later periods. Notable features include original linenfold panelling and 17th century wall paintings.

Location: OS Ref. TQ352 851. At the corner of Isabella Road and Homerton High St.

Open: 6 Feb - 22 Dec: Fri - Sun & BH Mons & 4 Jun, 2 - 5pm & from 17 Jan 2003. Café Bar: as house.

Admission: £2.10, Child 50p, Family £4.70. Group visits by prior arrangement.

🄰 🅗 Ground floor only. WC. 🄳 🄿None. 🄰 🅥 Tel for details.

WELLINGTON ARCH ⌗

HYDE PARK CORNER, LONDON W1J 7JZ

www.english-heritage.org.uk

Tel: 020 7930 2726   **Hospitality:** 020 7973 3292

Owner: English Heritage   **Contact:** The Site Manager

Newly restored and opened to the public for the first time in April 2001, Wellington Arch has had a chequered history. Originally designed in 1825 by Decimus Burton as a grand entrance to Buckingham Palace and gateway to Green Park, its lavish ornamentation was never finished. An equestrian statue of the Duke of Wellington, hoisted upon the Arch in 1846, was judged to be far too large, and caused public outcry. Plans to remove it were halted when the Duke himself announced that he would take such an action as a personal insult. The statue remained the scorn of London and beyond until 1882 when growing traffic congestion around Hyde Park Corner led to Wellington Arch being dismantled and moved to its current position. The equestrian statue was removed and the arch remained bare until 1912 when the magnificent 'Quadriga' that you see today took its place.

Location: OS Ref. TQ285 798. Hyde Park Corner Tube Station.

Open: All year: Wed - Sun & BH Mons. Apr - Sept: 10am - 6pm; Oct: 10am - 5pm; Nov - Mar: 10am - 4pm. Closed 24 - 26 Dec & 1 Jan.

Admission: Adult £2.50, Child £1.30, Conc. £1.90.

🅃 🅵 Mons. ✳ 🅦

SYON PARK 🏛   *See page 66 for full page entry.*

THE TOWER BRIDGE EXPERIENCE

Tower Bridge, London SE1 2UP

Tel: 020 7940 3985   **Fax:** 020 7357 7935

Owner: Corporation of London   **Contact:** Jo Skinner

One of London's most unusual and exciting exhibitions is situated inside Tower Bridge. Enjoy spectacular views from the high level walkways.

Location: OS Ref. TQ337 804. Adjacent to Tower of London, nearest Underground: Tower Hill.

Open: Nov - Mar: 9.30am - 6pm. Apr - Oct: 10am - 6.30pm (last entry 1¼ hrs before closing). Closed 24 - 25 Dec and 7 Jan - 15 Feb.

Admission: Adult £6.25, Child (5-15)/ Conc. £4.25, Family (2+2) £18.25 (subject to a small increase in Apr).

THE TOWER OF LONDON   *See page 67 for full page entry.*

THE WALLACE COLLECTION   *See page 68 for full page entry.*

Sutton House

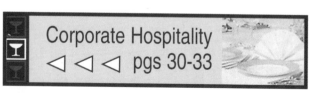

NT Photographic Library: Geoffrey Frosh

THE 'WERNHER COLLECTION' AT RANGER'S HOUSE ⊞

Chesterfield Walk, Blackheath, London SE10 8QX
Tel: 020 8853 0035 **www.**english-heritage.org.uk
Owner: English Heritage　　　**Contact:** House Manager

A handsome, red-brick house which lies between two of London's great open spaces, Greenwich Park and Blackheath. The house was built for a successful seafarer, Admiral Francis Hosier around 1700 who sited the house within view of the Thames estuary. A later owner, Lord Chesterfield, used to boast that the grand bow-windowed gallery commanded the three finest views in the world. Re-opening in Spring 2002 after a period of refurbishment, with the 'Wernher Collection', the life-time collection of self-made millionaire, Julius Wernher. A superb collection of fine and decorative art with objects dating from 3BC to the 19th century, and including a stunning display of Renaissance jewellery.

Location: OS Ref. TQ388 768. N of Shooters Hill Road.
Open: All year: Wed - Sun & BHs. Apr - Sept: 10am - 6pm (5pm in Oct); Nov - Mar: 10am - 4pm. Closed 24 Dec - 4 Mar 2003.
Admission: Adult £4.50, Child £2.30, Conc. £3.40.
🖸 ⬓ Limited, lift available. ▣ ⬙ Guide dogs only. ✳ ⬚ Tel for details.

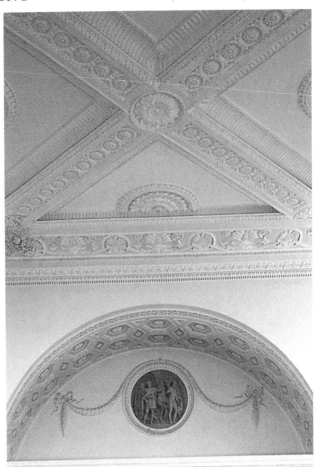

WESTMINSTER ABBEY

LONDON SW1P 3PA

www.westminster-abbey.org

Tel: 020 7222 5152 **Fax:** 020 7654 4891　**e-mail:** press@westminster-abbey.org
　　　　　　　　　　　　　　　Contact: The Press Officer

Westminster Abbey is a living church as well as an architectural masterpiece of the 13th - 16th centuries. Founded as a Benedictine monastery over 1,000 years ago, the Church was rebuilt by Edward the Confessor in 1065 and again by Henry III in the 13th century in the Gothic style we see today.

Location: OS Ref. TQ301 795. Westminster.
Open: Mon - Fri, 9am - 4.45pm (last admission 3.45pm), Sats, 9am - 2.45pm (last admission 1.45pm).
Admission: Adult £6, Child under 11yrs Free, Under 16yrs/Student/OAP £3, Family (2+2) £12 (prices from Feb 2001).

WESTMINSTER CATHEDRAL

Victoria, London SW1P 1QW
Tel: 020 7798 9055 **Fax:** 020 7798 9090 **www.**westminstercathedral.org.uk
Owner: Diocese of Westminster　　　**Contact:** Fr Mark Langham

The Roman Catholic Cathedral of the Archbishop of Westminster. Spectacular building in the Byzantine style, designed by J F Bentley, opened in 1903, famous for its mosaics, marble and music. Westminster Cathedral celebrated the Centenary of its foundation in 1995.

Location: OS Ref. TQ293 791. On Victoria Street, between Victoria Station and Westminster Abbey.
Open: All year: 7am - 7pm. Please telephone for times at Easter & Christmas.
Admission: Free. Lift charge: Adult £2. Child £1. Family (2+4) £5.
🖸 ⬓ Ground floor. ⓕ Prior booking required. ▣ None. ▣ Worksheets & tours.
⬙ Guide dogs only. ✳

Right: Syon Park

The Vyne

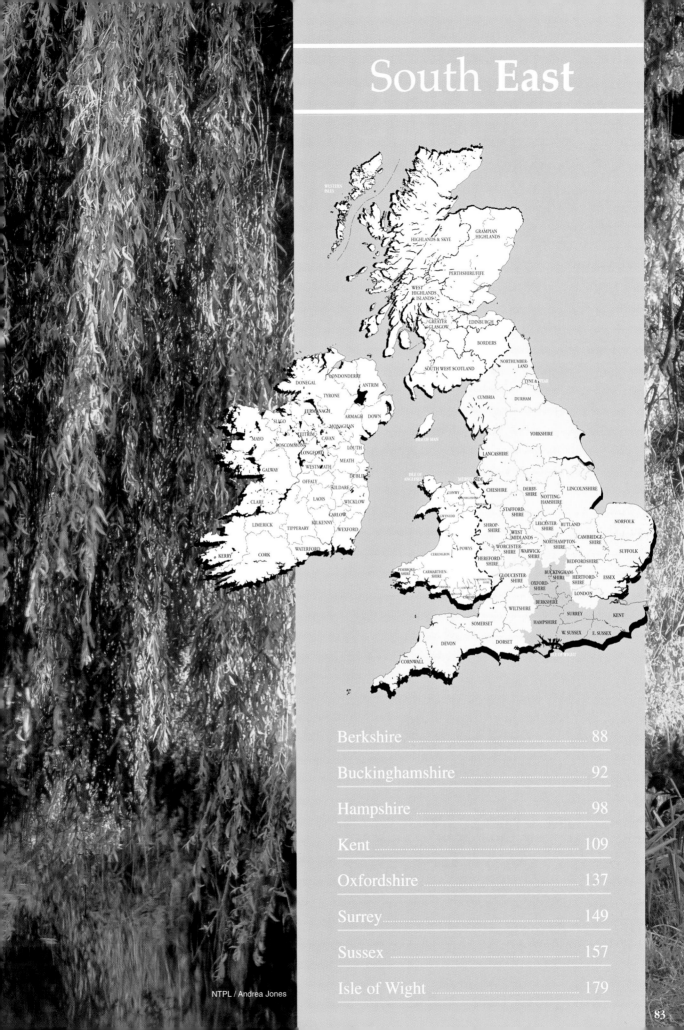

South East

NTPL / Andrea Jones

The Vyne

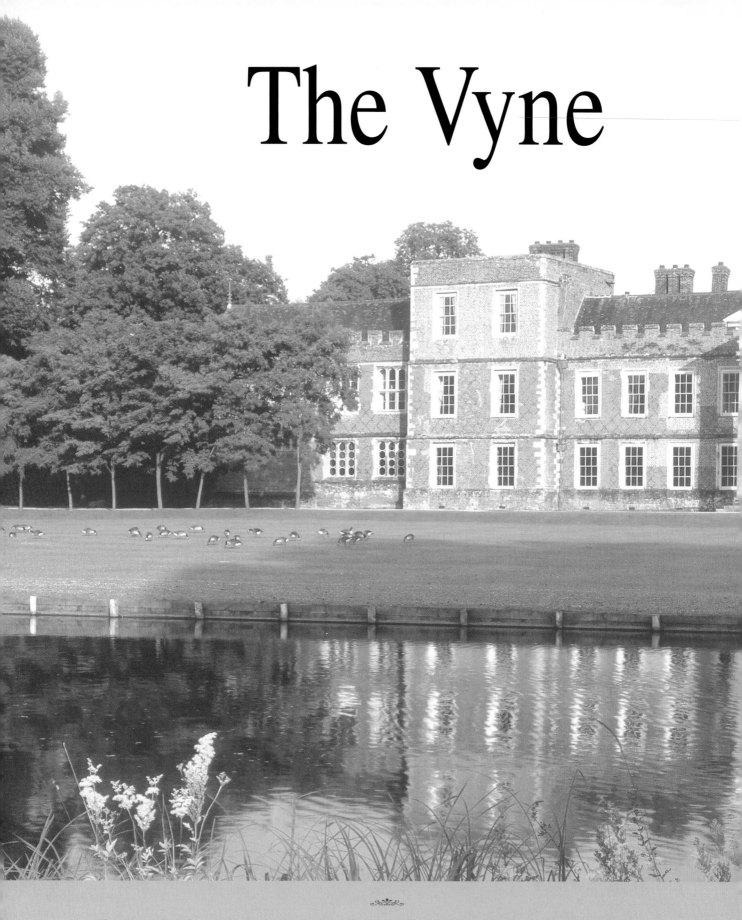

The Vyne has been described as one of the best advertisements for the National Trust: a really well kept house in a beautiful setting, with first-rate furniture and rare textiles.

Margaret Nichol, Marchioness of Carnarvon. Pastel by Rosalba Carriera.

This beautiful 16th century house outside Basingstoke, Hampshire, was once the home of William Lord Sandys, Lord Chamberlain to Henry VIII. Like many Tudor houses, it stands on low-lying ground and near water – the Shir brook, which was transformed into a spectacular lake setting for the north front in the 18th century.

The Vyne is a house with a long history which has, over the last five centuries, been respected and imaginatively reinterpreted by a succession of owners. A wide and welcoming building of soft rose-red brick, dressed in stone and decorated with purple header-bricks in diamond pattern, the long red brick entrance front still clearly shows Lord Sandys' initial building work of 1520. During the 1650s Chaloner Chute, Speaker of the House of Commons, employed John Webb to improve the old house. The white Palladian portico is thought to be the earliest known to adorn an English country house and is the first thing visitors see. Webb also provided several of the chimney pieces inside the house.

Much of the best work in The Vyne dates from the 1760s when John Chute made more improvements, which he designed himself. In the history of 18th century English architecture and interior design, The Vyne holds an important place as John Chute was a close friend of Horace Walpole, the owner of Strawberry Hill and founder of the Gothic Revival. However, whilst Chute helped to design the influential Gothic Revival interiors of Strawberry Hill in Twickenham, he rejected much of Walpole's advice when it came to his own property. Though the Tudor chapel was later enhanced with John Chute's 'Gothick' embellishments, the Staircase Hall is Neo-Classical and a good example of his sensitivity to place and versatile talent.

Since 1994 the National Trust has been re-ordering the house on the basis of research into the family papers. The aim has been to restore a sense of continuity and domesticity to the house. Visitors will soon be able to discover something of the lives of the prep school boys evacuated from Deal to The Vyne during the Second World War.

But don't visit The Vyne purely to enjoy the house. The low-lying position of the site provides a wonderfully lush and green setting for the gardens and park. Towering limes on the north east side of the property lead to the Summerhouse and the 100 Guinea Oak. You can take a circular walk across bridges at either end of the lake and wander through the wild garden and woodland walk, which is full of bluebells in the spring. In summer the most colourful area of the garden is the huge, beautifully planted herbaceous border beside the house's west front. Opposite, beds of pink 'Comte de Chambord' roses lead to a door, which is flanked by a pair of purple vines grown on frames.

The Vyne is a serene spot. It should be visited more – its mixture of styles and stories only enhance its charms. ✢

For further details about *The Vyne* see entry on page 107.

The Library. NTPL / James Mortimer

South East - England

Paul Procter, Chorley Handford

WINDSOR CASTLE

WINDSOR

www.the-royal-collection.org.uk

Owner:
HM The Queen

▶ **CONTACT**

The Visitor Office
Windsor Castle
Windsor
Berkshire SL4 1NJ

Tel: 01753 869898
01753 831118

Fax: 01753 832290

e-mail: windsorcastle@
royalcollection.org.uk

▶ **LOCATION**

OS Ref. SU969 770

M4/J6, M3/J3.
20m from central
London.

Rail: Regular service
from London Waterloo.

Coach: Victoria Coach
Station - regular service.

Sightseeing tours:
Tour companies
operate a daily service
with collection from
many London hotels.
Ask your hotel
concierge or porter
for information.

Windsor Castle, the largest and oldest occupied castle in the world, is the home of Her Majesty Queen Elizabeth II. The Castle's dramatic site encapsulates 900 years of British history, and its magnificent State Apartments and works of art reflect the tastes of successive kings and queens.

The State Apartments are the heart of the working palace and regularly used for ceremonial and official occasions. They are lavishly furnished with some of the finest treasures from the Royal Collection – paintings by Rubens, Canaletto, Van Dyck; carvings by Grinling Gibbons; collection of arms and armour (including the bullet which killed Admiral Nelson). A visit to Windsor Castle also includes Queen Mary's Dolls' House and St George's Chapel, the spiritual home of the Order of the Garter and the burial place of ten sovereigns.

Frogmore House and Mausoleum is open to visitors on a limited number of days during the year. Please contact the Visitor Office for details.

HM Queen Elizabeth II

▶ **OPENING TIMES**

March - October:
Daily except 29 March
9.45am - 5.15pm
(last admission 4pm).

November - February:
Daily except 25/26 Dec
9.45am - 4.15pm
(last admission 3pm).

St George's Chapel is
closed to visitors on
Sundays as services are
held throughout the day.
Worshippers are welcome.

The State Rooms
are closed during
Royal and State visits.

**Opening arrangements
may change at
short notice.**

▶ **ADMISSION**

Adult £11.50
Child (up to 17yrs).... £6.00
Child (under 5yrs) ...... Free
OAP £9.50
Family (2+2) £29.00

Groups (15+)
Discounts available.

 No photography.   None. Guide dogs only. ❄

SPECIAL EVENTS

With the exception of
Sundays, the Changing of
the Guard takes place at 11am
daily from April to the end of
June and on alternate days at
other times of the year.

BASILDON PARK ✤
LOWER BASILDON, READING RG8 9NR

Tel: 0118 984 3040   **Infoline:** 01494 755558   **Fax:** 0118 984 1267

e-mail: tbdgen@smtp.ntrust.org.uk

Owner: The National Trust   **Contact:** The Property Manager

An elegant, classical house designed in the 18th century by Carr of York and set in rolling parkland in the Thames Valley. The house has rich interiors with fine plasterwork, pictures and furniture, and includes an unusual Octagon Room and a decorative Shell Room. Basildon Park has connections with the East through its builder and was the home of a wealthy industrialist in the 19th century. It was rescued from dereliction in the mid 20th century. Small flower garden, pleasure grounds (currently being restored) and woodland walk.

Location: OS Ref. SU611 782. 2¹/₂ m NW of Pangbourne on the west side of the A329, 7m from M4/J12.

Open: House: 23 Mar - 3 Nov: daily except Mon & Tue (open BH Mons & 4 Jun), 1 - 5.30pm. Park, Garden & Woodland Walk: as house 12 noon - 5.30pm. Property closes at 5pm on 16/17 Aug.

Admission: House, Park & Garden: Adult £4.40, Child £2.20, Family £11. Park & Garden only: Adult £2, Child £1. Family £5. Groups (15+) by appointment: £3.

⬚ ⬚ ⬚ P In grounds. 🐕 On leads, in grounds only.

DONNINGTON CASTLE ⌗
Newbury, Berkshire

Tel: 02392 581059   **www.**english-heritage.org.uk

Owner: English Heritage   **Contact:** Area Manager

Built in the late 14th century, the twin towered gatehouse of this heroic castle survives amidst some impressive earthworks.

Location: OS Ref. SU463 691. 1m NW of Newbury off B4494.

Open: Any reasonable time.

Admission: Free.

DORNEY COURT 🏠
WINDSOR, BERKSHIRE SL4 6QP
www.dorneycourt.co.uk

Tel: 01628 604638   **Fax:** 01628 665772   **e-mail:** palmer@dorneycourt.co.uk

Owner/Contact: Mrs Peregrine Palmer

Just a few miles from the heart of bustling Windsor lies "one of the finest Tudor Manor Houses in England", *Country Life*. Grade I listed with the added accolade of being of outstanding architectural and historical importance, the visitor can get a rare insight into the lifestyle of the squirearchy through 550 years, with the Palmer family, who still live there today, owning the house for 450 of these years. The house boasts a magnificent Great Hall, family portraits, oak and lacquer furniture, needlework and panelled rooms. A private tour on a 'non-open day' takes around 1¹/₂ hours, but when open to the public this is reduced to around 40 mins. The adjacent 13th century Church of St James, with Norman font and Tudor tower can also be visited, as well as the adjoining Blooms of Bressingham Plant Centre in our walled garden where light lunches and full English cream teas are served in a tranquil setting throughout the day.

Location: OS Ref. SU926 791. 5 mins off M4/J7, 10mins from Windsor, 2m W of Eton.

Open: May: BH Sun & Mon, 1.30 - 4.30pm. Aug: daily except Sat, 1.30 - 4.30pm. Last admission 4pm.

Admission: Adult: £5, Child (10yrs +) £3. Groups: By arrangement throughout the year.

ℹ️ Film & photographic shoots. Pick your own: Jun - Sept. 🌿 Garden centre. 📺 ♿ Garden centre. ⬚ 🎞 P 🅿 🐕 Guide dogs only. ❄

Open All Year Index
◁ ◁ ◁ pgs 44-48

Graham Potlock

ENGLEFIELD HOUSE

ENGLEFIELD, THEALE, READING, BERKSHIRE RG7 5EN

www.englefield.co.uk

Tel: 01189 302221 **Fax:** 01189 303226 **e-mail:** benyon@netcomuk.co.uk

Owner: Sir William & Lady Benyon   **Contact:** Mrs Gloria Sleep

This Elizabethan house with later additions is open for groups (minimum 20) by appointment. Its formal terraces with water features, topiary and mixed borders are enclosed by stone walls and balustrades. The woodland and water garden planting includes magnolia, rhododendron, azalea, acer, camellia, cornus and other magnificent trees including davidia and gingko.

Location: OS Ref. SU622 720. 6m W of Reading on A340. Theale 1m.

Open: Garden only: All year: Mons, 10am - 6pm. 1 Apr - 1 Nov: Mon - Thur incl. 10am - 6pm.

Admission: £3.

ⓘNo photography in house. 🎈 🚽 ♿Partial.WC. 🎦By arrangement. 🅿Ample for cars, limited for coaches. ▣ ✖ ❋

SAVILL GARDEN

WINDSOR GREAT PARK, BERKSHIRE SL4 2HT

www.savillgarden.co.uk

Tel: 01753 847518 **Fax:** 01753 847536 **e-mail:** savillgarden@crownestate.org.uk

Owner: Crown Estate Commissioners   **Contact:** Jan Bartholomew

World-renowned 35 acre woodland garden, providing a wealth of beauty and interest in all seasons. Spring is heralded by hosts of daffodils, masses of rhododendrons, azaleas, camellias, magnolias and much more. Roses, herbaceous borders and countless alpines are the great features of summer, and the leaf colours and fruits of autumn rival the other seasons with a great display.

Location: OS Ref. SU977 706. Wick Lane, Englefield Green. Clearly signposted from Ascot, Bagshot, Egham and Windsor. Nearest station: Egham.

Open: Mar - Oct: 10am - 6pm. Nov - Feb: 10am - 4pm.

Admission: Apr - May: Adult £5, Child (6-16) £2, Conc. £4.50. Jun - Oct: Adult £4, Child (6-16) £1, Conc. £3.50. Nov - Mar: Adult £3, Child (6-16) £1, Conc. £2.50. Child under 6 Free. Prices subject to change in 2003.

▣ 🍽Plant centre. ♿Grounds. WC. 🍴Licensed. 🎦 🐕Guide dogs only. ❋

ETON COLLEGE

Windsor, Berkshire SL4 6DW

Tel: 01753 671177 **Fax:** 01753 671265 **e-mail:** visits@etoncollege.org.uk

Owner: Eton College   **Contact:** Rebecca Hunkin

Eton College, founded in 1440 by Henry VI, is one of the oldest and best known schools in the country. The original and subsequent historic buildings of the Foundation are a part of the heritage of the British Isles and visitors are invited to experience and share the beauty of the ancient precinct which includes the magnificent College Chapel, a masterpiece of the perpendicular style.

Location: OS Ref. SU967 779. Off M4/J5. Access from Windsor by footbridge only. Vehicle access from Slough 2m N.

Open: Mar - early Oct: Times vary, best to check with the Visits Office.

Admission: Ordinary admissions and daily guided tours. Groups by appointment only. Rates vary according to type of tour.

▣ 🚽 ♿Ground floor. WC. 🎦 🅿Limited. 🐕Guide dogs only.

FROGMORE HOUSE

Home Park, Windsor SL4 1NJ

Tel: 01753 869898 **Fax:** 01753 832290 (Windsor Castle)

Frogmore House, set in the private Home Park, is renowned for its beautiful landscaped garden and 18th century lake. Queen Victoria was inspired to write of it, 'All is peace and quiet and you only hear the hum of the bees, the singing of the birds'.

Location: OS Ref. SU977 760. In Windsor House Park, ¼ m SE of the Castle. Public access through gate on East side of the Long Walk.

Open: Frogmore House & Mausoleum open on a limited number of days during the year. Private tours of the house for groups during Aug & Sept.

Admission: Please contact the Visitor Office, Windsor Castle.

ST GEORGE'S CHAPEL WINDSOR

Tel: 01753 868286

Fine example of perpendicular architecture. Open only in conjunction with Windsor Castle.

Location: OS Ref. SU968 770.

Open: As Windsor Castle, but opening times subject to change at short notice.

Admission: Admission as part of Windsor Castle ticket.

CHA

SWALLOWFIELD PARK

SWALLOWFIELD, READING, BERKSHIRE RG7 1TG

Tel: 0118 9883815 **Fax:** 0118 9883930

Owner: Country Houses Association   **Contact:** The Administrator

Built in 1678 by the second Earl of Clarendon. The arms of the Clarendons form part of the decorative plaster in the oval vestibule. The Talman Gate has been restored. Set in 25 acres, including a beautiful walled garden. Swallowfield Park has been converted into apartments for active retired people.

Location: OS Ref. SU730 655. In Swallowfield, 6 m SE of Reading. 4m S of M4/J11. Then via Spencers Wood.

Open: 1 May - 30 Sept: Wed & Thurs, 2 - 5pm.

Admission: Adult £3, Child £1.50. Groups by arrangement.

✖ 🛏1 single & 1 double with bathroom. CHA members only.

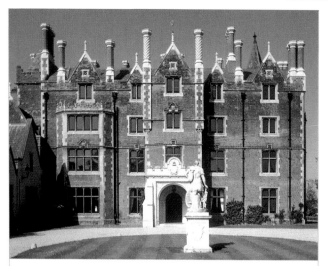

TAPLOW COURT

BERRY HILL, TAPLOW, Nr MAIDENHEAD, BERKS SL6 0ER

www.sgi-uk.org

Tel: 01628 591209 **Fax:** 01628 773055

Owner: SGI-UK   **Contact:** Michael Yeadon

Set high above the Thames, affording spectacular views. Remodelled mid-19th century by William Burn. Earlier neo-Norman Hall. 18th century home of Earls of Orkney and more recently of Lord and Lady Desborough who entertained 'The Souls' here. Tranquil gardens & grounds. Anglo-Saxon burial mound. Permanent and temporary exhibitions.

Location: OS Ref. SU907 822. M4/J7 off Bath Road towards Maidenhead. 6m off M40/J2.

Open: House & Grounds: Easter Sun & Mon, Suns & BH Mons up to mid Aug: 2 - 6pm. Please telephone to confirm.

Admission: No charge. Free parking.

Guide dogs only.

WELFORD PARK

Newbury, Berkshire RG20 8HU

Tel: 01488 608203

Owner/Contact: Mr J Puxley

A Queen Anne house, with attractive gardens and grounds. Riverside walks.

Location: OS Ref. SU409 731. On Lambourn Valley Road. 6m NW of Newbury.

Open: 2 - 28 Jun, 26 Aug: 11am - 5pm. Cream teas available for groups (10+), must book 14 days in advance.

Admission: House by prior arrangement. Adult £5, Child Free, Conc. £2. Grounds Free.

Grounds. On leads, in grounds.

WINDSOR CASTLE   *See page 88 for full page entry.*

Civil Wedding Venues
◁ ◁ ◁ pgs 28-29

Englefield House

STOWE HOUSE 🏛

BUCKINGHAM

www.stowe.co.uk

Owner:
Stowe House
Preservation Trust

▶ **CONTACT**

The Commercial Director
Stowe School
Buckingham
MK18 5EH

Tel: 01280 818282
House only
or 01280 822850
Gardens

Fax: 01280 818186

e-mail:
sses@stowe.co.uk

▶ **LOCATION**
OS Ref. SP666 366

From London, M1 to
Milton Keynes, 1½ hrs
or Banbury 1¼ hrs,
3m NW of Buckingham.

Bus: from
Buckingham 3m.

Rail: Milton Keynes 15m.

Air: Heathrow 50m.

CONFERENCE/FUNCTION

ROOM	MAX CAPACITY
Roxburgh Hall	460
Music Room	120
Marble Hall	150
State Dining Rm	160
Garter Room	180
Memorial Theatre	120

Stowe owes its pre-eminence to the vision and wealth of two owners. From 1715 to 1749 Viscount Cobham, one of Marlborough's Generals, continuously improved his estate, calling in the leading designers of the day to lay out the gardens, and commissioning several leading architects – Vanbrugh, Gibbs, Kent and Leoni – to decorate them with garden temples. From 1750 to 1779 Earl Temple, his nephew and successor continued to expand and embellish both Gardens and House. The House is now a major public school. Restoration of North Front and Colonnades is taking place until October 2002.

Around the mansion is one of Britain's most magnificent landscape gardens now in the ownership of the National Trust. Covering 325 acres and containing no fewer than 6 lakes and 32 garden temples, it is of the greatest historic importance. During the 1730s William Kent laid out in the Elysian Fields at Stowe, one of the first 'natural' landscapes and initiated the style known as 'the English Garden'. 'Capability' Brown worked there for 10 years, not as a consultant but as head gardener, and in 1744 was married in the little church hidden between the trees.

ℹ️ Indoor swimming pool, sports hall, tennis court, squash courts, parkland, cricket pitches and golf course. No photography in house.

📷 Call for opening times.

Ⓣ International conferences, private functions, weddings, and prestige exhibitions. Catering on request.

♿ Visitors may alight at entrance. Allocated parking areas. WC in garden area. 'Batricars' available.

☕ 🍴 Morning coffee, lunch and afternoon tea available by pre-arrangement only, for up to 100.

👥 For parties of 30 at additional cost. Tour time: house and garden 2½ hrs, house only 45 mins.

🅿️ Ample.

🐕 In grounds on leads.

🔔 Civil Wedding Licence.

♿ Available. ❄️

▶ **OPENING TIMES**
Summer

House
21 Mar - 14 Apr
10 Jul - 8 Sept:
daily except Mon & Tue
(open BH Mon),
12 noon - 5pm.
Last admission 4pm.
18 - 22 Dec: daily except
Mon & Tue, 11am - 3pm.
Last admission 2pm.

Guided tours by arrangement. Group visits to the house by arrangement throughout the year.

NB: It may be necessary to close the house at times when it is being used for private functions. Please telephone first to check.

▶ **ADMISSION**

Adult £3.00
Child (under 16yrs) ... £1.50

🎭 **SPECIAL EVENTS**
• **Oct 26/27:**
Craft Fair

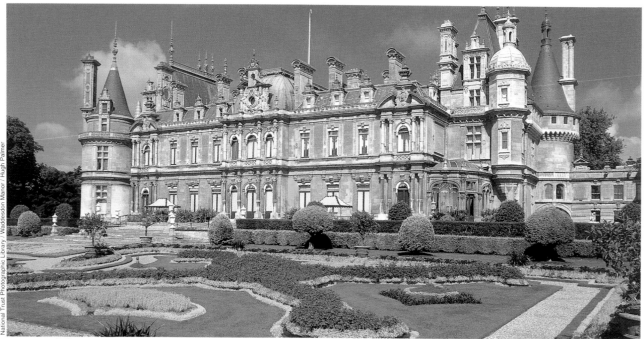

National Trust Photographic Library / Waddesdon Manor / Hugh Palmer

WADDESDON MANOR ❧

NR AYLESBURY

www.waddesdon.org.uk

▶ CONTACT

Waddesdon
Nr Aylesbury
Buckinghamshire
HP18 0JH

Tel (24-hour recorded info):
01296 653211

Booking: 01296 653226

Fax: 01296 653208

▶ LOCATION

OS Ref. SP740 169

Between Aylesbury &
Bicester, off A41.

Rail: Aylesbury 6m.

Waddesdon Manor was built (1874-89), in the style of a 16th century French château, for Baron Ferdinand de Rothschild to entertain his guests and display his vast collection of art treasures. It houses one of the finest collections of French 18th century decorative arts in the world. The furniture, Savonnerie carpets, and Sèvres porcelain ranks in importance with the Metropolitan Museum in New York and the Louvre in Paris. There is also a fine collection of portraits by Gainsborough and Reynolds and works by Dutch and Flemish Masters of the 17th century.

Waddesdon has one of the finest Victorian gardens in Britain, renowned for its seasonal displays, colourful shrubs, mature trees and parterre. Carpet bedding displays are newly created each year, and there is a rose garden and children's garden to visit. The rococo-style aviary houses a splendid collection of exotic birds; and thousands of bottles of vintage Rothschild wines are found in the wine cellars.

There is an award-winning gift shop, a wine shop with a full selection of Rothschild wines and a licensed restaurant. A full programme of events is organised throughout the year including special interest days, wine tastings and garden workshops.

▶ OPENING TIMES

House
(including wine cellars)
27 Mar - 3 Nov: Wed - Sun,
BH Mons & 4 Jun, 11am -
4pm. Last recommended
admission 2.30pm.

Bachelors' Wing
Wed - Fri, 11am - 4pm
(space is limited and entry
cannot therefore be
guaranteed).

Grounds
(including garden, aviary,
restaurant and shops)
27 Feb - 22 Dec: Wed - Sun,
BH Mons & 4 Jun,
10am - 5pm.

▶ ADMISSION

House & Grounds
Adult £10.00
Child (5-16 yrs) £7.50
Groups (15+)
Adult £8.00
Child £6.00

Grounds only
Adult £3.00
Child (5-16 yrs) £1.50
6 Nov - 22 Dec........ Free
Groups (15+)
Adult £2.40
Child £1.20

Bachelors' Wing..... £1.00

NT members free. HHA
Members free entry to grounds.
RHS members free to grounds in
Mar, Sept & Oct.

A timed ticket system to the
House is in operation. Tickets
can be purchased in advance for
a fee of £3 per transaction from
the Booking Office.

Children welcomed under
parental supervision. Babies
must be carried in a front-sling.

National Trust Photographic Library / Waddesdon Manor / John Bigelow Taylor

ℹ️ No photography in house.

🏠 Gift and Wine Shops.

🍽️ Conferences, corporate hospitality.

♿ WCs.

🍷 Licensed. 🍴 Licensed.

🚶 By arrangement.

🎧

🅿️ Ample for coaches and cars.

🐕 Guide dogs only.

🔔 Civil Wedding Licence.

🎭 **SPECIAL EVENTS**
Wine Tasting, Special Interest Days,
Family Events, Floodlit Evenings:
please telephone 01296 653226
for details.

South East - England

ASCOTT ⚜

Wing, Leighton Buzzard, Bucks LU7 0PS

Tel: 01296 688242 **Fax:** 01296 681904 **e-mail:** info@ascottestate.co.uk

Owner: The National Trust   **Contact:** The Administrator

Originally a half-timbered Jacobean farmhouse, Ascott was bought in 1876 by the de Rothschild family and considerably transformed and enlarged. It now houses a quite exceptional collection of fine paintings, Oriental porcelain and English and French furniture. The extensive gardens are a mixture of the formal and natural, containing specimen trees and shrubs, as well as an herbaceous walk, lily pond, Dutch garden and remarkable topiary sundial.

Location: OS Ref. SP891 230. ½ m E of Wing, 2m SW of Leighton Buzzard, on A418.

Open: House & Garden: 2 - 30 Apr & 6 Aug - 13 Sept: daily except Mons, 2 - 6pm, last admission 5pm. Garden only: 1 May - 1 Aug: every Wed & last Sun in each month, also 18 & 25 Sept, 2 - 6pm, last admission 5pm.

Admission: House & Garden: £5.60. Garden: £4. Child half price. No reduction for groups which must book.

♿Ground floor & grounds. 3 wheelchairs available. WCs. 🅿 220 metres. 🐕In car park only, on leads.

BLETCHLEY PARK

The Mansion, Wilton Avenue, Bletchley, Milton Keynes MK3 6EB

Tel: 01908 640404 **Fax:** 01908 274381 **e-mail:** majenkins@bletchleypark.org.uk **www.**bletchleypark.org.uk

Owner: Bletchley Park Trust   **Contact:** Merryl Jenkins

Centre of World War II Enigma code breaking operations.

Location: OS Ref. SP858 340. 200yds from Bletchley railway station. Just off the B4034 Bletchley to Buckingham road.

Open: Weekends from 3 Mar: 10.30am - 5pm, last admission 3.30pm. Last tour begins at 3pm.

Admission: Adult £6, Child/Conc. £5. Accompanied Child (under 8yrs) Free.

BOARSTALL DUCK DECOY ⚜

Boarstall, Aylesbury, Buckinghamshire HP18 9UX

Tel: 01844 237488 **e-mail:** tcdgen@smtp.ntrust.org.uk

Owner: The National Trust   **Contact:** The Administrator

A rare survival of a 17th century decoy in working order, set on a tree-fringed lake, with nature trail and exhibition hall.

Location: OS Ref. SP624 151. Midway between Bicester and Thame, 2m W of Brill.

Open: 23 Mar - 25 Aug: Weds, 5 - 8pm, Sats, Suns & BH Mons, 10am - 5pm. Talk/demonstration: Sats, Suns & BH Mons if Warden available, tel for details.

Admission: Adult £2.10, Family £5. Groups (6+) must book: £1.

♿Partial. ⬛By arrangement. 🐕In car park only, on leads.

BOARSTALL TOWER ⚜

Boarstall, Aylesbury, Buckinghamshire HP18 9UX

Tel: 01844 239339 **e-mail:** rob.dixon@boarstall.com

Owner: The National Trust   **Contact:** The Tenant

The stone gatehouse of a fortified house long since demolished. It dates from the 14th century, and was altered in the 16th and 17th centuries, but retains its crossloops for bows. The gardens are surrounded by a moat on three sides.

Location: OS Ref. SP624 141. Midway between Bicester and Thame, 2m W of Brill.

Open: 27 Mar - 30 Oct: Wed, BH Mons & 4 Jun, 2 - 6pm. Also Sats by prior arrangement with tenant.

Admission: Adult £2.10, Child £1.05.

ℹNo WC. ♿Ground floor & garden. 🐕In car park only.

BUCKINGHAM CHANTRY CHAPEL ⚜

Market Hill, Buckingham

Tel: 01280 823020/01494 528051 **Fax:** 01494 463310

Owner: The National Trust   **Contact:** Buckingham Heritage Trust

Rebuilt in 1475 and retaining a fine Norman doorway. The chapel was restored by Gilbert Scott in 1875, at which time it was used as a Latin or Grammar School.

Location: OS Ref. SP693 340. In narrow lane, NW of Market Hill.

Open: Daily by written appointment with the Buckingham Heritage Trust, c/o Old Gaol Museum, Market Hill, Buckingham MK18 1JX.

Admission: Free.

ℹNo WCs. ♿

CHENIES MANOR HOUSE 🏛
CHENIES, RICKMANSWORTH, HERTS WD3 6ER

Tel/Fax: 01494 762888

Owners: Mr Charles & Mrs MacLeod Matthews   **Contact:** Sue Brock

15th & 16th century Manor House with fortified tower. Original home of the Earls of Bedford, visited by Henry VIII and Elizabeth I. Home of the MacLeod Matthews family. Contains contemporary tapestries and furniture, hiding places, collection of antique dolls, medieval undercroft and well. Surrounded by beautiful gardens which have featured in many publications and on TV, a Tudor sunken garden, a white garden, herbaceous borders, a fountain court, a physic garden containing a very wide selection of medicinal and culinary herbs, a parterre and two mazes. The kitchen garden is in the Victorian style with unusual vegetables and fruit. Special exhibitions, flower drying and arrangements. Many specialist and rare plants in a charming setting.

Location: OS Ref. TQ016 984. N of A404 between Amersham & Rickmansworth. M25/J18, 3m.

Open: 1 Apr - 31 Oct: Wed, Thur & BH Mons & 3 Jun, 2 - 5pm. Last entry to house 4.15pm. Groups by arrangement at other times.

Admission: House & Garden: Adult £5, Child £3. Garden only: Adult £3, Child £1.

🌱 Unusual plants for sale. 🍽 ♿Grounds. 📷 🅿 Free nearby. 🐕 ❋ ♿

CHICHELEY HALL 🏛

Newport Pagnell, Buckinghamshire MK16 9JJ

Tel: 01234 391252 **Fax:** 01234 391388 **www.**chicheleyhall.co.uk

Owner: The Hon Nicholas Beatty   **Contact:** Mrs V Child

Fine 18th century house. Naval museum, English sea paintings and furniture. Suitable for residential conferences up to 15 delegates.

Location: OS Ref. SP906 458. 2m from Milton Keynes, 5 mins from M1/J14. 10m W of Bedford.

Open: All year: By appointment only

Admission: Groups (20+): Adult £7 with guided tour.

ℹConferences. 🍽By arrangement. ♿Unsuitable. 📷 📹Obligatory. 🐕 ❋

CHILTERN OPEN AIR MUSEUM

Newland Park, Gorelands Lane, Chalfont St Giles, Buckinghamshire HB8 4AB

Tel: 01494 871117 **Fax:** 01494 872774

Owner: Chiltern Open Air Museum Ltd   **Contact:** Joanna Milford

A museum of historic buildings showing their original uses including a blacksmith's forge, stables, barns etc.

Location: OS Ref. TQ011 938. At Newland Park 1½ m E of Chalfont St Giles, 4½ m from Amersham. 3m from M25/J17.

Open: Apr - Oct: daily. Telephone 01494 872163 for details.

Admission: Adult £5.50, Child under 5yrs Free, Child (5-16yrs) £3, Over 60s £4.50, Family £15. 10% discount for groups (10+).

Special Events Index
◁ ◁ ◁ pgs 40-43

South East - England

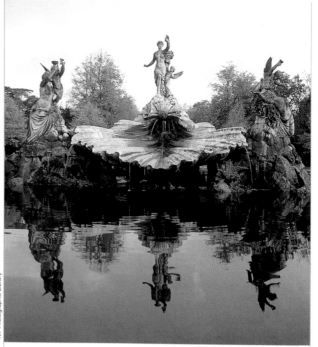

NT Photographic Library

CLAYDON HOUSE ❦

MIDDLE CLAYDON, Nr BUCKINGHAM MK18 2EY

Tel: 01296 730349 **Fax:** 01296 738511 **Infoline:** 01494 755561
e-mail: tcdgen@smtp.ntrust.org.uk

Owner: The National Trust   **Contact:** The Custodian

A fine 18th century house with some of the most perfect rococo decoration in England. A series of great rooms have wood carvings in Chinese and Gothic styles, and tall windows look out over parkland and a lake. The house has relics of the exploits of the Verney family in the English Civil War and also on show is the bedroom of Florence Nightingale, a relative of the Verneys and a regular visitor to this tranquil place.

CLIVEDEN ❦

TAPLOW, MAIDENHEAD SL6 0JA

Tel: 01628 605069 **Infoline:** 01494 755562 **Fax:** 01628 669461
e-mail: tclmrg@smtp.ntrust.org.uk

Owner: The National Trust   **Contact:** Property Manager

152 hectares of gardens and woodland. A water garden, 'secret' garden, herbaceous borders, topiary, a great formal parterre, and informal vistas provide endless variety. The garden statuary is one of the most important collections in the care of The National Trust and includes many Roman antiquities collected by 1st Viscount Astor. The Octagonal Temple (Chapel) with its rich mosaic interior is open on certain days, as are three of the principal rooms of the house (see below).

NT Photographic Library: Andrew Butler

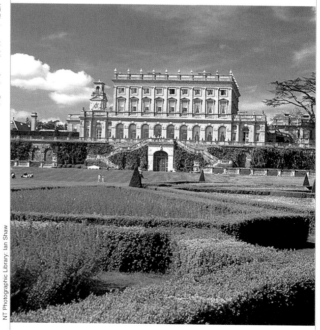

NT Photographic Library: Ian Shaw

Location: OS Ref. SP720 253. In Middle Claydon, 13m NW of Aylesbury, signposted from A413 and A41. 3¹/₂ m SW of Winslow.

Open: 23 Mar - 3 Nov: daily except Thur & Fri; House, 1 - 5pm (closes 1hr early on event days); Grounds, 12 noon - 6pm; Second-hand bookshop, 1 - 5pm.

Admission: Adult £4.40, Child £2.20, Family £11. Groups 15+ (must book): Mon - Wed & Sat. £3.60. Garden only: £1.

▢ ♿Ground floor & grounds. Braille guide. WC. ▣ 🐕In park, on leads.
▣ Tel for details.

Location: OS Ref. SU915 851. 3m N of Maidenhead, M4/J7 onto A4 or M40/J4 onto A404 to Marlow and follow signs. From London by train take Thames Train service from Paddington to Burnham (taxi rank and office adjacent to station).

Open: Estate & Garden: 13 Mar - 31 Dec, daily, 11am - 6pm (closes at 4pm from 1 Nov). House (3 rooms): Apr - Oct: Thurs & Sun, 3 - 5.30pm. Entry by timed ticket from information kiosk. Otagonal Temple: as house. Woodlands car park: all year: daily, 11am - 5.30pm (closed at 4pm Nov - Mar). Shop: 13 Mar - 15 Dec: Wed - Sun.

Admission: Grounds: Adult £6, Child £3, Family £15. House: £1 extra, Child 50p. Groups (must book): Adult £5.50. Woodlands car park: Adult £3, Child £1.50, Family £7.50. Note: Mooring charge on Cliveden Reach.

▢ ♿Partial. WC. 🍴Licensed. 🐕Specified woodlands only. ✳ ▣ Tel for details.

COWPER & NEWTON MUSEUM

Home of Olney's Heritage, Orchard Side, Market Place, Olney MK46 4AJ

Tel: 01234 711516   **e-mail:** cnm@mkheritage.co.uk

www.cowperandnewtonmuseum.org

Owner: Board of Trustees   **Contact:** Mrs J McKillop

Once the home of 18th century poet and letter writer William Cowper and now containing furniture, paintings and belongings of both Cowper and his ex-slave trader friend, Rev John Newton (author of "Amazing Grace"). Attractions include re-creations of a Victorian country kitchen and wash-house, two peaceful gardens and Cowper's restored summerhouse. Costume gallery, important collections of dinosaur bones and bobbin lace, and local history displays.

Location: OS Ref. SP890 512. On A509, 6m N of Newport Pagnell, M1/J14.

Open: 1 Mar - 23 Dec: Tue - Sat & BH Mons, 10am - 1pm & 2 - 5pm. Closed on Good Fri. Open on Sundays in June, July & August, 2 - 5pm.

Admission: Adult £3, Conc. £2, Child & Students (with card) £1.50, Family £7.50.

ℹ️No photography. 📷 ♿Gardens. 🎦By arrangement. 🦮Guide dogs only.

DORNEYWOOD GARDEN ❧

Dorneywood, Burnham, Buckinghamshire SL1 8PY

Tel: 01494 528051 (NT Regional Office)   **Fax:** 01494 463310

e-mail: tdwgen@smtp.ntrust.org.uk

Owner: The National Trust   **Contact:** The Secretary

The house was given to the National Trust as an official residence for either a Secretary of State or Minister of the Crown. Garden only open.

Location: OS Ref. SU938 848. SW of Burnham Beeches. 2m E of Cliveden.

Open: By written appointment only - one week in advance – 26 Jun, 17 Jul & 3 Aug: 2 - 5pm. Write to The Secretary, Dorneywood Trust at above address.

Admission: £3.

♿Partial. 🅿️

FORD END WATERMILL

Station Road, Ivinghoe, Buckinghamshire

Tel: 01582 600391

Contact: David Lindsey

The Watermill, a listed building, was recorded in 1767 but is probably much older.

Location: OS Ref. SP941 166. 600 metres from Ivinghoe Church along B488 (Station Road) to Leighton Buzzard.

Open: Please telephone for opening dates and milling times.

Admission: Adult £1.20, Child 40p. School Groups: 50p each adult and child.

JOHN MILTON'S COTTAGE

21 Deanway, Chalfont St. Giles, Buckinghamshire HP8 4JH

Tel: 01494 872313   **e-mail:** pbirger@clara.net   **http:**/home.clara.net/pbirger

Owner: Milton Cottage Trust   **Contact:** Mr E A Dawson

Grade I listed 16th century cottage where John Milton lived and completed 'Paradise Lost' and started 'Paradise Regained'. Four ground floor museum rooms contain important 1st editions of John Milton's 17th century poetry and prose works. Amongst many unique items on display is the portrait of John Milton by Sir Godfrey Kneller. Well stocked, attractive cottage garden, listed by English Heritage.

Location: OS Ref. SU987 933. ½ m W of A413. 3m N of M40/J2. S side of street.

Open: 1 Mar - 31 Oct: Tue - Sun, 10am - 1pm & 2 - 6pm. Closed Mons (open BH Mons). Coach parking by prior arrangement only.

Admission: Adult £2.50, under 15s £1, Groups (20+) £2.

📷 ♿Ground floor. 🎦Talk followed by free tour. 🅿️ 🦮

NETHER WINCHENDON HOUSE 🏠

Aylesbury, Buckinghamshire HP18 0DY

Tel: 01844 290199/292257   **Owner/Contact:** Mr Robert Spencer Bernard

Medieval and Tudor manor house. There is a fine 16th century frieze, ceiling and original linenfold panelling. Altered in late 18th century in the Strawberry Hill Gothick style. Fine furniture and family portraits. Continuous family occupation since mid-16th century. Home of the last British Governor of Massachusetts Bay. Interesting garden and specimen trees.

Location: OS Ref. SP734 121. 2m N of A418 equidistant between Thame & Aylesbury.

Open: 4 - 31 May & 25/26 Aug: 2.30 - 5.30pm (last group at about 4.45pm).

Admission: Adult £5 (HHA members free), Child (under 12)/OAP £2.50 (not weekends or BHs). Groups: any time by written appointment, min charge £50.

♿ ▶️By arrangement. ✳️

PITSTONE WINDMILL ❧

Ivinghoe, Buckinghamshire

Tel: 01494 528051   **Fax:** 01494 463310

Owner: The National Trust   **Contact:** The Administrator

One of the oldest post mills in Britain; in view from Ivinghoe Beacon.

Location: OS Ref. SP946 158. ½ m S of Ivinghoe, 3m NE of Tring. Just W of B488.

Open: Jun - end Aug: Sun & BHs. 2.30 - 6pm.

Admission: Adult £1, Child 30p.

ℹ️No WC. ♿Difficult access.

HUGHENDEN MANOR ❧

HIGH WYCOMBE HP14 4LA

Tel: 01494 755573   **Fax:** 01494 463310   **e-mail:** thdrxl@smtp.ntrust.org.uk

Owner: The National Trust   **Contact:** The Property Manager

Home of Prime Minister Benjamin Disraeli from 1847 - 1881, Hughenden has a red brick, 'gothic' exterior. The interior is a comfortable Victorian home and still holds many of Disraeli's pictures, books and furniture, as well as other fascinating mementoes of the life of the great statesman and writer. The surrounding park and woodland have lovely walks, and the formal garden has been recreated in the spirit of Mary Anne Disraeli's colourful designs.

Location: OS165 Ref. SU866 955. 1½ m N of High Wycombe on the W side of the A4128.

Open: House: 2 - 31 Mar: Sats & Suns. 3 Apr - 3 Nov: Wed - Sun, BH Mons & 4 Jun, 1 - 5pm (last admission 4.30pm). Closed Good Fri. On BHs and busy days entry is by timed ticket. Gardens open same days as house, 12 noon - 5pm. Park & Woodland: All year. Closed 10 May to all visitors until 2.30pm.

Admission: House & Garden: Adult £4.40, Child £2.20, Family £11. Garden only: Adult £1.50, Child 75p. Park & Woodland Free. Groups must book, no groups on Sat, Sun or BH Mons.

📷 ♿Limited. WC. ▶️

🦮In grounds, on leads. Guide dogs in house & formal gardens.

✳️ 🎦Tel for details.

PRINCES RISBOROUGH MANOR HOUSE ✕

Princes Risborough, Aylesbury, Buckinghamshire HP17 9AW
Tel: 01494 528051 **Fax:** 01494 463310
Owner/Contact: The National Trust
A 17th century red-brick house with Jacobean oak staircase.
Location: OS Ref. SP806 035. Opposite church, off market square.
Open: House (hall, drawing room & staircase) and front garden by written appointment only with the owner. Apr - Oct: Weds, 2.30 - 4.30pm.
Admission: £1.20.

NT Photographic Library: Jerry Harpur

STOWE GARDENS & PARK ✕

Nr BUCKINGHAM MK18 5EH

www.nationaltrust.org.uk

Tel: 01280 822850 **Infoline:** 01494 755568 **Fax:** 01280 822437
Owner: The National Trust   **Contact:** The Property Manager
One of the finest Georgian landscape gardens, made up of valleys and vistas, narrow lakes and rivers, with more than 30 temples and monuments designed by many of the leading architects of the 18th century. At the centre is Stowe House, occupied by Stowe School, and all around is Stowe Gardens & Park.

The creation of the Temple family, Stowe has been described as a 'work to wonder at' in its size, splendour and variety. Many of the garden buildings have now been conserved, and thousands of new trees and shrubs have been planted in recent years. Work continues on this as well as on the Mansion itself. What's new in 2002: Four newly restored monuments: the Fane of Pastoral Poetry and Lord Cobham's

Monument in the garden, and the Conduit House and Wolfe's Obelisk in the Park.
Location: OS Ref. SP665 366. Off A422 Buckingham - Banbury Rd. 3m NW of Buckingham.
Open: Gardens: 2 Mar - 22 Dec (closed 25 May): Wed - Sun (open BH Mons), 10am - 5.30pm, last admission 4pm. Nov & Dec: 10am - 4pm, last admission 3pm. Gardens may close in bad weather. House: 21 Mar - 14 Apr & 10 Jul - 6 Sept: Wed - Sun, 12 noon - 5pm, last admission 4pm. 30 Oct - 3 Nov & 18 - 22 Dec: Wed - Sun, 11am - 3pm.
Admission: Gardens: £4.80. Family £12. House: Adult £3. Groups by arrangement.
📷 ♿Pre-booked self-drive powered chairs available. WC. ▣Licensed.
🅵By arrangement. ▣ ♿In grounds, on leads. ▲ ♒Send SAE for details.

STOWE HOUSE 🏠   *See page 92 for full page entry.*

WADDESDON MANOR ✕   *See page 93 for full page entry.*

WEST WYCOMBE PARK ✕

West Wycombe, High Wycombe, Buckinghamshire HP14 3AJ
Tel: 01494 513569
Owner: The National Trust   **Contact:** The Head Guide
A perfectly preserved rococo landscape garden, created in the mid-18th century by Sir Francis Dashwood, founder of the Dilettanti Society and the Hellfire Club. The house is among the most theatrical and Italiante in England, its façades formed as classical temples. The interior has Palmyrene ceilings and decoration, with pictures, furniture and sculpture dating from the time of Sir Francis.
Location: OS Ref. SU828 947. At W end of West Wycombe S of the A40.
Open: Grounds only: 1 Apr - 31 May: Sun - Thur & BHs, 2 - 6pm. House & Grounds: 1 Jun - 31 Aug: daily except Fris & Sats, 2 - 6pm. Weekday entry by timed tour. Last admission 5.15pm.
Admission: House & Grounds: Adult £4.80, Child £2.40, Family £12. Grounds only: £2.60. Note: The West Wycombe Caves and adjacent café are privately owned and NT members must pay admission fees. Groups by arrangement.
♿Grounds partly suitable. ♒In car park only, on leads.

WYCOMBE MUSEUM

Priory Avenue, High Wycombe, Buckinghamshire HP13 6PX
Tel: 01494 421895 **Fax:** 01494 421897
e-mail: enquiries@wycombemuseum.demon.co.uk
Owner: Wycombe District Council   **Contact:** Vicki Wood (Museums Officer)
Set in historic Castle Hill House and surrounded by peaceful and attractive gardens.
Location: OS Ref. SU867 933. Signposted off the A404 High Wycombe/Amersham road. The Museum is about 5mins walk from the town centre and railway station.
Open: Mon - Sat, 10am - 5pm. Open Suns, 2 - 5pm. Closed BHs.
Admission: Free.

Open All Year Index
◁ ◁ ◁ pgs 44-48

BEAULIEU 🏛

BEAULIEU

www.beaulieu.co.uk

Owner:
Lord Montagu

▶ CONTACT

Conference Office
John Montagu Building
Beaulieu
Brockenhurst
Hampshire SO42 7ZN

Tel: 01590 614604
Fax: 01590 612624

e-mail: conference@
beaulieu.co.uk

▶ LOCATION

OS Ref. SU387 025

From London, M3,
M27 W to J2,
A326, B3054 follow
brown signs.

Bus: Bus stops
within complex.

Rail: Stations at
Brockenhurst and
Beaulieu Rd
both 7m away.

Beaulieu is set in the heart of the New Forest and is a place that gives enormous pleasure to people with an interest in seeing history of all kinds.

Overlooking the Beaulieu River, Palace House has been the ancestral home of the Montagus since 1538. The House was once the Great Gatehouse of Beaulieu Abbey and its monastic origins are reflected in such features as the fan vaulted ceilings. Many treasures, which are reminders of travels all round the world by past generations of the Montagu family, can also be seen. Walks amongst the gardens and by the Beaulieu River can also be enjoyed.

Beaulieu Abbey was founded in 1204 and although most of the buildings have now been destroyed, much of the beauty and interest remains. The

former Monks' Refectory is now the local Parish Church. The Domus, which houses an exhibition of monastic life, is home to beautiful wall hangings and 15th century beamed ceilings.

Beaulieu also houses the world famous National Motor Museum which traces the story of motoring from 1894 to the present day. 250 vehicles are on display including legendary world record breakers plus veteran, vintage and classic cars and motorcycles.

The modern Beaulieu is very much a family destination where there are various free and unlimited rides and drives on a transportation theme to be enjoyed by everyone, including a mile long monorail and replica 1912 London open-topped bus.

▶ OPENING TIMES

Summer
May - September
Daily, 10am - 6pm.

Winter
October - April
Daily, 10am - 5pm.

Closed Christmas Day.

▶ ADMISSION

All Year

Individual rates upon application.

Groups (15+)
Rates upon application.

🎭 SPECIAL EVENTS

Apr 28
Boat Jumble

May 18/19
Spring Autojumble

Jul 14
4x4 Show

Sept 7/8
International Autojumble

All enquiries should be made to our Special Events Booking Office where advance tickets can be purchased. The contact telephone is 01590 614645.

Other Event dates yet to be confirmed to include Motorcycle World.

CONFERENCE/FUNCTION

ROOM	SIZE	MAX CAPACITY
Brabazon (x3)	40'x40'	120 (x3)
Domus	69'x27'	140
Theatre		200
Hartford Suite	39'x17'	50
Palace House		60
Motor Museum		300

BEAULIEU...

CATERING AND FUNCTIONS

Beaulieu also offers a comprehensive range of facilities for conferences, company days out, product launches, management training, corporate hospitality, promotions, film locations, exhibitions and outdoor events.

The National Motor Museum is a unique venue for drinks receptions, evening product launches and dinners or the perfect complement to a conference as a relaxing visit.

The charming 13th century Domus banqueting hall with its beautiful wooden beams, stone walls and magnificent wall hangings, is the perfect setting for conferences, dinners, buffets or themed evenings.

Palace House, the ancestral home of Lord Montagu is an exclusive setting for smaller dinners, buffets and receptions. With a welcoming log fire in the winter and the coolness of the courtyard fountain in the summer, it offers a relaxing yet truly 'stately' atmosphere to ensure a memorable experience for your guests whatever the time of year

A purpose-built theatre, with tiered seating, can accommodate 200 people whilst additional meeting and syndicate rooms can accommodate from 5 to 200 delegates. With the nearby Beaulieu River offering waterborne activities and the Beaulieu Estate, with its purpose built off road course, giving you the opportunity of indulging in a variety of country pursuits and outdoor management training, Beaulieu provides a unique venue for your conference and corporate hospitality needs.

i Allow 3 hrs or more for visits. Last adm. 40 mins before closing. Helicopter landing point. When visiting Beaulieu arrangements can be made to view the Estate's vineyards. Visits, which can be arranged between Apr - Oct, must be pre-booked at least one week in advance with Beaulieu Estate Office.

Palace House Shop and Kitchen Shop plus Main Reception Shop.

Disabled visitors may be dropped off outside Visitor Reception before parking. WC. Wheelchairs can be provided free of charge in Visitor Reception by prior booking.

The self-service Brabazon restaurant seats 300. Prices range to £7 for lunch. Groups can book in advance. Further details and menus from Catering Manager 01590 612102.

Attendants on duty. Guided tours by prior arrangement for groups.

P 1,500 cars and 30 coaches. During the season the busy period is from 11.30am to 1.30pm. Coach drivers should sign in at Information Desk. Free admission for coach drivers plus voucher which can be exchanged for food, drink and souvenirs.

Professional staff available to assist in planning of visits. Services include introductory talks, films, guided tours, rôle play and extended projects. In general, educational services incur no additional charges and publications are sold at cost. Information available from Education at Beaulieu, John Montagu Building, Beaulieu, Hants SO42 7ZN.

In grounds, on leads only.

HIGHCLERE CASTLE & GARDENS

NEWBURY

www.highclerecastle.co.uk

Designed by Charles Barry in the 1830s at the same time as he was building the Houses of Parliament, this soaring pinnacled mansion provided a perfect setting for the 3rd Earl of Carnarvon, one of the great hosts of Queen Victoria's reign. The extravagant interiors range from church Gothic through Moorish flamboyance and rococo revival to the solid masculinity in the long Library. Old master paintings mix with portraits by Van Dyck and 18th century painters. Napoleon's desk and chair rescued from St. Helena sits with other 18th and 19th century furniture.

The 5th Earl of Carnarvon discovered the Tomb of Tutankhamun with Howard Carter. The castle houses a unique exhibition of some of his discoveries which were only rediscovered in the castle in 1988. The 7th Earl was the Queen's Horseracing Manager. In 1993 to celebrate his 50th year as a leading owner and breeder 'The Lord Carnarvon Racing Exhibition' was opened to the public, and offers a fascinating insight into a racing history that dates back three generations.

GARDENS

The magnificent parkland with its massive cedars was designed by 'Capability' Brown. The walled gardens also date from an earlier house at Highclere but the dark yew walks are entirely Victorian in character. The glass Orangery and Fernery add an exotic flavour. The Secret Garden has a romance of its own with a beautiful curving lawn surrounded by densely planted herbaceous gardens. A place for poets and romantics.

Owner:
Earl of Carnarvon

▶ CONTACT

Jacky Lessware
Highclere Castle
Newbury
Berkshire RG20 9RN

Tel: 01635 253210
Fax: 01635 255315
e-mail: theoffice@
highclerecastle.co.uk

▶ LOCATION

OS Ref. SU445 587

Approx 7m out
of Newbury on A34
towards Winchester.
From London: M4/J13,
A34 Bypass Newbury-
Winchester 20 mins.
M3/J5 approx 15m.

Air: Heathrow M4
45 mins.

Rail: Paddington -
Newbury 45 mins.

Taxi: 4$^{1}/_{2}$ m
01635 40829.

Conferences, exhibitions, filming, fairs, and concerts (cap. 8000). No photography in the house.

Receptions, dinners, corporate hospitality.

Visitors may alight at the entrance. WC.

Tearooms, licensed. Lunches for 20+ can be booked.

Ample.

Egyptian Exhibition: £3 per child. 1 adult free for every 10 children – includes playgroups, Brownie packs, Guides etc. Nature walks, beautiful old follies, Secret Garden.

In grounds, on leads.

Civil Wedding Licence.

Please telephone 01635 253204 for details.

▶ OPENING TIMES

2 July - 1 September:
Tue - Sun, 11am - 5pm.
Sats: 11am - 3.30pm. Also
BHs: 30/31 Mar & 1 Apr;
5/6 May & 1 - 4 Jun.
Last admission 1 hour
before closing.

The house is occasionally
closed during this
period – please call our
information line.

▶ ADMISSION

Adult £6.50
Child (4-15yrs) £3.00
Conc. £5.00
Wheelchair Pusher . FOC
Family (2+2/1+3).... £15.00

Grounds & Gardens only
Adult £3.00
Child (5-15yrs)....... £1.00
Groups (15+)
Adult £5.00
Child (4-15yrs)....... £3.00
Conc. £4.00
Private guided tour by
arrangement.

School Groups (to visit
Egyptian Exhibition only)
Child ... £3.00 (plus VAT)
1 adult Free for every
10 children

VIP Season Ticket*
(2+3) or (1+4) £25.00

*Runs for one year from date of joining, Free admission for 2 adults & 3 children to the House, Exhibitions & Gardens: 2 Jul - 1 Sept & when special events are taking place. 10% off shop, tearooms, free admission to daytime events. Discounted rate for evening concerts, free admission to 'Shakespeare in the Park', £2 off Newbury Racecourse Members' Enclosure badges when pre-booked, Newbury Hilton - Fri, Sat, Sun evenings - dinner for two for the price of one from chef's hot or cold table, 10% off the price of lunch or dinner at The Restaurant, Newbury Manor Hotel.

CONFERENCE/FUNCTION

ROOM	SIZE	MAX CAPACITY
Library	43' x 21'	120
Saloon	42' x 29'	150
Dining Rm	37' x 18'	70
Library, Saloon, Drawing Rm, Music Rm, Smoking Rm		400

NT Photographic Library: Nick Carter

HINTON AMPNER GARDEN

BRAMDEAN

www.nationaltrust.org.uk/regions/southern

'I have learned during the past years what above all I want from a garden: this is tranquillity'. so said Ralph Dutton, 8th and last Lord Sherborne, of his garden at Hinton Ampner. He created one of the great gardens of the 20th century, a masterpiece of design based upon the bones of a Victorian garden, in which he united a formal layout with varied and informal planting in pastel shades. It is a garden of all year round interest with scented plants and magnificent vistas over the park and surrounding countryside.

The garden forms the link between the woodland and parkland planting, which he began in 1930, and the house, which he remodelled into a small neo-Georgian manor house in 1936. He made further alterations when the house was reconstructed after a fire in 1960. Today it contains his very fine collection of English furniture, Italian paintings and hard-stones. Both his collection and every aspect of the decoration at Hinton Ampner reflects Ralph Dutton's sure eye and fine aesthetic judgement.

He placed the whole within the rolling Hampshire landscape that he loved and understood so well.

Owner:
The National Trust

▶ CONTACT

The Property Manager
Hinton Ampner Garden
Bramdean
Alresford
Hampshire   SO24 0LA

Tel: 01962 771305
Fax: 01962 793101

e-mail: shigen@
smtp.ntrust.org.uk

▶ LOCATION

OS Ref. SU597 275

On A272, 1m W of Bramdean village, 8m E of Winchester.

▶ OPENING TIMES

House
2 Apr - end Sept:
Tues & Weds,
also Sats & Suns in Aug,
1.30 - 5pm.

Garden
17 & 24 Mar,
30 Mar - end Sept:
daily except Thur & Fri,
11am - 5pm.

▶ ADMISSION

House & Garden
Adult £5.00
Child (5-16yrs) £2.50

Garden only
Adult £4.00
Child (5-16yrs) £2.00
Child under 5yrs ......Free
Groups (min 15, max 60)
Adult £4.50
Child £2.25

NT Members free.

NT Photographic Library: Stephen Robson

Limited for coaches.

SOMERLEY

RINGWOOD

www.somerley.com

Owner:
The Earl of Normanton

▶ **CONTACT**

Richard Horridge
Somerley
Ringwood
Hampshire BH24 3PL

Tel: 01425 480819
Fax: 01425 478613
e-mail:
info@somerley.com

▶ **LOCATION**

OS Ref. SU134 080

Off the A31 to
Bournemouth 2m.
London 1¾ hrs via
M3, M27, A31.
2m NW of Ringwood.

Air: Bournemouth
International
Airport 5m.

Rail: Bournemouth
Station 12m.

Taxi: A car can be
arranged from the
House if applicable.

Sitting on the edge of the New Forest in the heart of Hampshire, Somerley, home of the 6th Earl of Normanton and his three children, is situated in 7,000 acres of meadows, woods and rolling parkland. Designed by Samuel Wyatt in the mid 1700s, the house became the property of the Normanton family in 1825 and has remained in the same family through the years. Housing a magnificent art and porcelain collection, the house itself, albeit impressively splendid, still retains the warmth and character of a family home.

Although never open to the public, Somerley is available for corporate events and its location, along with its seclusion and privacy, provide the perfect environment for conferences and meetings, product launches, lunches and dinners, activity and team building days (the estate boasts a hugely challenging off-road driving course) and film and photographic work. It is also available for a limited number of wedding receptions every year.

Somerley only ever hosts one event at a time so exclusivity in an outstanding setting is always guaranteed. From groups as small as eight to perhaps a large dinner for 150, the style of attention and personal service go hand in hand with the splendour of the house and the estate itself.

▶ **OPENING TIMES**
Privately booked functions only.

▶ **ADMISSION**
Privately booked functions only.

ℹ️ No individual visits, ideal for all corporate events, activity days and filmwork.

 Dining Room and picture gallery available for private parties.

🅿️ Unlimited.

 1 single & 9 double rooms (8 en-suite).

❄️

CONFERENCE/FUNCTION

ROOM	SIZE	MAX CAPACITY
Picture Gall.	80' x 30'	200
Drawing Rm	38' x 30'	50
Dining Rm	39' x 19'	50
East Library	26' x 21'	30

JANE AUSTEN'S HOUSE
CHAWTON, ALTON, HAMPSHIRE GU34 1SD

www.janeaustenmuseum.org.uk

Tel/Fax: 01420 83262   **e-mail:** museum@janeausten.demon.co.uk

Owner: Jane Austen Memorial Trust   **Contact:** The Curator

17th century house where Jane Austen wrote or revised her six great novels. Contains many items associated with her and her family, documents and letters, first editions of the novels, pictures, portraits and furniture. Pleasant garden, suitable for picnics, bakehouse with brick oven and wash tub, houses Jane's donkey carriage.

Location: OS Ref. SU708 376. Just S of A31, 1m SW of Alton, signposted Chawton.

Open: 1 Mar - 30 Nov: daily, 11am - 4.30pm; Dec, Jan & Feb: weekends only. Also open 27 Dec - 2 Jan. Closed 25 - 26 Dec.

Admission: Fee charged.

🅱 Bookshop. 🅰 Ground floor & grounds. WC. 💟 Opposite house. 🅿 Opposite house. 🐕 Guide dogs only. ✳

BASING HOUSE
Redbridge Lane, Basing, Basingstoke RG24 7HB

Tel: 01256 467294

Owner: Hampshire County Council   **Contact:** Alan Turton

Ruins, covering 10 acres, of huge Tudor palace. Recent recreation of Tudor formal garden.

Location: OS Ref. SU665 526. 2m E from Basingstoke town centre. Signposted car parks are about 5 or 10 mins walk from entrance.

Open: 3 Apr - 29 Sept: Wed - Sun & BHs, 2 - 6pm.

Admission: Adult £1.50, Child 70p.

BEAULIEU 🏠   *See pages 98/99 for double page entry.*

BISHOP'S WALTHAM PALACE ⊞
Bishop's Waltham, Hampshire SO32 1DH

Tel: 01489 892460   **www**.english-heritage.org.uk

Owner: English Heritage   **Contact:** The Custodian

This medieval seat of the Bishops of Winchester once stood in an enormous park. There are still wooded grounds and the remains of the Great Hall and the three storey tower can still be seen. Dower House furnished as a 19th century farmhouse.

Location: OS Ref. SU552 173. In Bishop's Waltham, 5m NE from M27/J8.

Open: 29 Mar - 30 Sept: daily, 10am - 6pm. 1 Oct - 31 Oct: 10am - 5pm.

Admission: Adult £2.30, Child £1.20, Conc. £1.70.

ℹ Exhibition. 📷 🅰 Grounds. 🐕 Grounds only, on leads. 💷 Tel for details.

BOHUNT MANOR GARDENS
Liphook, Hampshire GU30 7DL

Tel: 01428 722208   **Fax:** 01428 727936

Owner/Contact: Lady Holman

Woodland gardens with lakeside walk, collection of ornamental waterfowl, herbaceous borders and unusual trees and shrubs.

Location: OS Ref. SU839 310. W side of B2070 at S end of village.

Open: All year: daily, 10am - 6pm.

Admission: Adult £1.50, Child under 14yrs Free, Conc. £1. Group: 10% off.

AVINGTON PARK 🏠
WINCHESTER, HAMPSHIRE SO21 1DB

www.avingtonpark.co.uk

Tel: 01962 779260   **Fax:** 01962 779864   **e-mail:** sarah@avingtonpark.co.uk

Owner/Contact: Mrs S L Bullen

Avington Park, where Charles II and George IV both stayed at various times, dates back to the 11th century. The house was enlarged in 1670 by the addition of two wings and a classical Portico surmounted by three statues. The State rooms are magnificently painted and lead onto the unique pair of conservatories flanking the South Lawn. The Georgian church, St. Mary's, is in the grounds.

Avington Park is a privately owned stately home and is a most prestigious venue in peaceful surroundings. It is perfect for any event from seminars, conferences and exhibitions to wedding ceremonies and receptions, dinner dances and private parties. The Conservatories and the Orangery offer a unique location for summer functions, whilst log fires offer a welcome during the winter. Excellent caterers provide for all types of occasion entirely to the client's wishes, ranging from breakfasts or snacks to sumptuous dinners. All bookings at Avington are individually tailor-made and only exclusive use is offered.

Location: OS Ref. SU534 324. 4m NE of Winchester ½ m S of the B3047 in Itchen Abbas.

Open: May - Sept: Suns & BH Mons, 2.30 - 5.30pm. Last tour 5pm. Other times by arrangement, coach parties welcome by appointment all year.

Admission: Adult £3.75, Child £2.

ℹ Conferences. 🍴 🅰 Partial. WC. 💟 🅵 Obligatory. 🅿 🐕 In grounds, on leads. Guide dogs only in house. 🔔 ✳

BREAMORE HOUSE & MUSEUM 🏛

BREAMORE, FORDINGBRIDGE, HAMPSHIRE SP6 2DF

Tel: 01725 512233 **Fax:** 01725 512858 **e-mail:** breamore@estate.fsnet.co.uk

Owner/Contact: Sir Edward Hulse Bt

Elizabethan manor with fine collections of pictures and furniture. Countryside Museum takes visitors back to the time when a village was self-sufficient.

Location: OS Ref. SU152 191. W Off the A338, between Salisbury and Ringwood.

Open: Easter. Apr: Tue, Wed & Sun. May, Jun, Jul & Sept: Tue, Wed, Thur, Sat & Sun & all hols. Aug: daily. House: 2 - 5.30pm. Countryside Museum: 1 - 5.30pm.

Admission: Combined ticket for house and museum: Adult £5, Child £3.50.

🖻 🔄 Ground floor & grounds. WC. 🔲 🔀

BROADLANDS

ROMSEY, HAMPSHIRE SO51 9ZD

www.broadlands.net

Tel: 01794 505010 **Event Enquiry Line:** 01794 505020
e-mail: admin@broadlands.net

Owner: Lord & Lady Romsey   **Contact:** Mrs S Armitage

Famous as the home of the late Lord Mountbatten, and equally well known as the country residence of Lord Palmerston, the great Victorian Prime Minister. Broadlands is an elegant Palladian mansion in a beautiful landscaped setting on the banks of the River Test. Visitors may view the House with its art treasures and mementoes of the famous, enjoy the superb views from the Riverside Lawns or relive Lord Mountbatten's life and times in the Mountbatten Exhibition and spectacular Mountbatten audio-visual presentation.

Location: OS Ref. SU355 204. On A31 at Romsey.

Open: 10 Jun - 1 Sept: daily, 12 noon - 5.30pm. Last admission 4pm.

Admission: Adult £5.95, Child (12-16) £3.95, Conc. £4.95. Groups (10+): Adult £4.95, Child (12-16) £3.85, Conc. £4.65. All inclusive admission charges. Accompanied child under 12, Free.

🖻 🔲 🔄 Ground floor & grounds.WC. 🔲 🔀 Obligatory. 🔀 Guide dogs only.

© Lord Romsey

CALSHOT CASTLE ⌘

Calshot, Fawley, Hampshire SO45 1BR

Tel: 023 8089 2023 www.english-heritage.org.uk

Owner: English Heritage   **Contact:** Hampshire County Council

Henry VIII built this coastal fort in an excellent position, commanding the sea passage to Southampton. The fort houses an exhibition and recreated pre-World War I barrack room.

Location: OS Ref. SU488 025. On spit 2m SE of Fawley off B3053.

Open: 29 Mar - 30 Sept: daily, 10am - 6pm. 1 Oct - 31 Oct: 10am - 5pm.

Admission: Adult £2, Child £1, Conc. £1.50, Family £5.

ELING TIDE MILL

The Toll Bridge, Eling, Totton, Southampton, Hampshire SO40 9HF

Tel: 023 8086 9575 **e-mail:** eling.tidemill@argonet.co.uk

Owner: Eling Tide Mill Trust Ltd & New Forest District Council

          Contact: Mr David Blackwell-Eaton

Location: OS Ref. SU365 126. 4m W of Southampton. 1/2 m S of the A35.

Open: Wed - Sun and BH Mons, 10am - 4pm.

Admission: Adult £1.75, Child 95p, OAP £1.30, Family £4.75. Discounts for groups. Prices subject to change 1 Jan 2002.

EXBURY GARDENS & STEAM RAILWAY 🏛

Exbury, Southampton, Hampshire SO45 1AZ

Tel: 023 8089 1203 **Fax:** 023 8089 9940 www.exbury.co.uk

Owner: Edmund de Rothschild Esq   **Contact:** Gardens Office

A 200-acre woodland garden with the world famous Rothschild collection of rhododendrons, azaleas and camellias. The Rock Garden, Rose Garden, Herbaceous Grasses Garden, ponds and cascades ensure year round interest. Steam Railway and Summer Lane Garden (summer flowering) newly opened. Features include a bridge, tunnel, viaduct and causeway across a pond.

Location: OS Ref. SU425 005. 11m SE of Totton (A35) via A326 & B3054 & minor road.

Open: 2 Mar - 3 Nov: daily, 10am - 5.30pm or dusk if earlier.

Admission: Please telephone for details.

🖻 🔄Grounds. WC. 🔲 🔳 🔀In grounds, on leads. 🔳Tel for details.

FORT BROCKHURST ⌘

Gunner's Way, Gosport, Hampshire PO12 4DS

Tel: 023 9258 1059 www.english-heritage.org.uk

Owner: English Heritage   **Contact:** The Head Custodian

This 19th century fort was built to protect Portsmouth, today its parade ground, moated keep and sergeants' mess are available to hire as an exciting setting for functions and events of all types. The fort is also open to visitors at weekends when tours will explain the exciting history of the site and the legend behind the ghostly activity in cell no. 3.

Location: OS196, Ref. SU596 020. Off A32, in Gunner's Way, Elson on N side of Gosport.

Open: 29 Mar - 30 Sept: 10am - 6pm. 1 Oct - 31 Oct: 10am - 5pm. Weekends only.

Admission: Adult £2.20, Child £1.10, Conc. £1.70.

FURZEY GARDENS

Minstead, Lyndhurst, Hampshire SO43 7GL

Tel: 023 8081 2464 **Fax:** 023 8081 2297

Owner: Furzey Gardens Charitable Trust   **Contact:** Maureen Cole

Location: OS Ref. SU273 114. Minstead village 1/2 m N of M27/A31 junction off A337 to Lyndhurst.

Open: Please contact property for details.

GREAT HALL & QUEEN ELEANOR'S GARDEN

Winchester Castle, Winchester, Hampshire SO23 8PJ

Tel: 01962 846476 **Fax:** for bookings 01962 841326

Owner: Hampshire County Council   **Contact:** Mrs Murphy

The only surviving part of Henry III's medieval castle at Winchester, this 13th century hall was the centre of court and government life. The Round Table closely associated with the legend of King Arthur has hung here for over 700 years. Queen Eleanor's garden is a faithful representation of the medieval garden visited by Kings and Queens of England.

Location: OS Ref. SU477 295. Central Winchester. SE of Westgate archway.

Open: All year: daily, 10am - 5pm (except weekends Nov - Feb, 10am - 4pm). Closed Christmas Day and Boxing Day.

Admission: Free.

🔀By arrangement. 🔳

GUILDHALL GALLERY

The Broadway, Winchester SO23 9LJ
Tel: 01962 848289 (gallery) 01962 848269 (office) **Fax:** 01962 848299
e-mail: museums@winchester.gov.uk **www**.winchester.gov.uk
Owner: Winchester City Council **Contact:** Mr C Wardman Bradbury
A constantly changing programme of contemporary exhibitions including painting, sculpture, craft, photography and ceramics.
Location: OS Ref. SU485 293. Winchester - city centre. Situated above the Tourist Office in Winchester's 19th century Guildhall.
Open: Apr - Oct: Mon - Sat, 10am - 5pm. Sun, 2 - 5pm. Nov - Mar: Tue - Sat, 10am - 4pm, Sun, 2 - 4pm.
Admission: Free.
♿ ✳

HIGHCLERE CASTLE 🏛 & GARDENS

See page 100 for full page entry.

THE SIR HAROLD HILLIER GARDENS & ARBORETUM

JERMYNS LANE, AMPFIELD, ROMSEY SO51 0QA

www.hillier.hants.gov.uk/

Tel: 01794 368787 **Fax:** 01794 368027
Managed by: Hampshire County Council **Contact:** Administration - Judith Drysdale
Marketing - Tim Brooks
Enrich your knowledge of the natural world and seek inspiration for your own garden on a journey of discovery through the landscaped features, woodlands and walkways of The Sir Harold Hillier Gardens & Arboretum. Established in 1953, by the distinguished plantsman Sir Harold Hillier, the magnificent collection of over 40,000 plants from temperate regions around the world, grow in a mixture of formal and informal landscapes set in 180 acres of rolling Hampshire countryside. Open throughout the year, the Gardens display stunning seasonal variations and include 11 National Plant Collections, Champion Trees, the Gurkha Memorial Garden and the largest Winter Garden in Europe.
Location: OS Ref. SU380 236. 3m NE of Romsey. Follow brown tourist signs from the town centre on A3090 (formerly A31) towards Winchester.
Open: Daily, 10.30am - 6pm or dusk if earlier. Closed Christmas Day & Boxing Day.
Admission: Adult £4.25, Conc. £3.75, under 16s Free.
♿ 🚻 ♿Partial. WC. ♿ 🍴 Licensed. 🎦By arrangement. 🅿 ■
🐕Guide dogs only. ✳ 🔊Tel for details.

HINTON AMPNER GARDEN 🌿

See page 101 for full page entry.

Plant Sales Index
◁ ◁ ◁ pgs 36-37

Justyn Willsmore

HOUGHTON LODGE 🏛

STOCKBRIDGE, HAMPSHIRE, SO20 6LQ

www.hydroponicum.co.uk

Tel: 01264 810502/810912 **Fax:** 01264 810177 **e-mail:** info@hydroponicum.co.uk
Owner/Contact: Captain M W Busk
A haven of peace beside the tranquil beauty of the River Test. Restoration to Shrubbery reveals wonderful views from higher ground over the informal landscape (Grade II*) surrounding the 18th century Cottage Ornée. Rare chalk cob walls enclose ancient espaliers, greenhouses and herb garden. Formal topiary 'Peacock' Garden. Wild flowers, Children's puffing topiary dragon. Popular TV/film location. Indoor hydroponicum: learn how to garden without soil or toil and control greenhouse pests with natural predators. New orchid collection.
Location: OS Ref. SU344 332. 1¹/₂ m S of Stockbridge (A30) on minor road to Houghton village. For evening open times please telephone or visit website.
Open: Garden: 1 Mar - 30 Sept: Sat, Sun & BHs, 10am - 5pm also Mon, Tue, Thur & Fri, 2 - 5pm. House: by appointment.
Admission: Adult £5, Child Free. Groups (min 25, max 50) (booked): Adult £4.50.
📷 ♿ 🚻 ♿Free tea or coffee. ♿WCs. 🎦By arrangement. 🅿 ■
🐕 In grounds, on leads. ♿

HURST CASTLE ⊞

Keyhaven, Lymington, Hampshire PO41 0PB
Tel: 01590 642344 **www**.english-heritage.org.uk
Owner: English Heritage **Contact:** (Managed by) Hurst Castle Services
This was one of the most sophisticated fortresses built by Henry VIII, and later strengthened in the 19th and 20th centuries, to command the narrow entrance to the Solent. There is an exhibition in the Castle, and two huge 38-ton guns form the fort's armaments.
Location: OS196 Ref. SZ319 898. On Pebble Spit S of Keyhaven. Best approach by ferry from Keyhaven. 4m SW of Lymington.
Open: 29 Mar - 31 Oct: daily, 10am - 5.30pm. Café: open Apr - May weekends & Jun - Sept: daily.
Admission: Adult £2.80, Child £1.60, Conc. £2.30
📷 ♿Unsuitable. ■

MEDIEVAL MERCHANTS HOUSE ⊞

58 French Street, Southampton, Hampshire SO1 0AT
Tel: 023 8022 4854
Owner: English Heritage **Contact:** The Custodian
The life of the prosperous merchant in the Middle Ages is vividly evoked in this recreated, faithfully restored 13th century townhouse.
Location: OS Ref. SU419 112. 58 French Street. ¹/₄ m S of Bargate off Castle Way. 150yds SE of Tudor House.
Open: 29 Mar - 30 Sept: daily, 10am - 6pm. 1 - 31 Oct: daily, 10am - 5pm.
Admission: Adult £2.30, Child £1.20, Conc. £1.70.

MOTTISFONT ABBEY GARDEN, HOUSE & ESTATE

MOTTISFONT, Nr ROMSEY, HAMPSHIRE SO51 0LP

www.nationaltrust.org.uk/regions/southern

Tel: 01794 340757   **Fax:** 01794 341492   **Recorded Message:** 01794 341220

Owner: The National Trust   **Contact:** The Property Manager

The Abbey and Garden form the central point of an 809 ha estate including most of the village of Mottisfont, farmland and woods. A tributary of the River Test flows through the garden forming a superb and tranquil setting for a 12th century Augustinian priory which, after the Dissolution, became a house. It contains the spring or "font" from which the place name is derived. The magnificent trees, walled gardens and the National Collection of Old-fashioned Roses combine to provide interest throughout the seasons. The Abbey contains a drawing room decorated by Rex Whistler and the cellarium of the old Priory. In 1996 the Trust acquired Derek Hill's 20th century picture collection.

Location: OS Ref. SU327 270. 4^1/$_2$ m NW of Romsey, 1m W of A3057.

Open: House, Garden & Grounds: 23 Mar - 26 May & 2 Sept - 3 Nov: Sat - Wed, 11am - 6pm (open Good Fri); 27 May - 7 Jun & 24 Jun - 1 Sept: daily except Fri, 11am - 6pm; 8 - 23 Jun: daily, 11am - 8.30pm. Last admission to house 5.30pm, to garden 5pm.

Admission: Adult £6, Child (5-18yrs) £3, Family £15. No reduction for groups. Coaches must book.

⬜ ⬛ 🔳 Guide dogs only. ▲ 📺 Tel for details.

SANDHAM MEMORIAL CHAPEL

BURGHCLERE, Nr NEWBURY, HAMPSHIRE RG20 9JT

www.nationaltrust.org.uk/regions/southern

Tel/Fax: 01635 278394   **e-mail:** ssagen@smtp.ntrust.org.uk

Owner: The National Trust   **Contact:** The Custodian

This red brick chapel was built in the 1920s for the artist Stanley Spencer to fill with murals inspired by his experiences of the First World War. Influenced by Giotto's Arena Chapel in Padua, Spencer took five years to complete what is arguably his finest achievement. The chapel is set amidst lawns and orchards with views across Watership Down. Pictures best viewed on a bright day.

Location: OS Ref. SU463 608. 4m S of Newbury, ^{1}/$_2$m E of A34, W end of Burghclere.

Open: Mar & Nov: Sats & Suns, 23 Mar - 3 Nov: daily except Mons & Tues (open BH Mons); Dec - Feb 2003: by appointment only. Times: Mar & Nov: 11am - 4pm; Apr - end Oct: 11am - 5pm.

Admission: Adult £2.80, Child £1.40. Groups by prior arrangement, no reduction.

🔳 Ramped steps. 🔳 In grounds, on leads. ✳

NETLEY ABBEY ⚏

Netley, Southampton, Hampshire

Tel: 023 9258 1059

Owner: English Heritage   **Contact:** Area Manager

A peaceful and beautiful setting for the extensive ruins of this 13th century Cistercian abbey converted in Tudor times for use as a house.

Location: OS Ref. SU453 089. In Netley, 4m SE of Southampton, facing Southhampton Water.

Open: Any reasonable time.

Admission: Free.

OLD PORTSMOUTH CATHEDRAL

Portsmouth, Hampshire PO1 2HH

Tel: 023 9282 3300   **Fax:** 023 9229 5480   **Contact:** Rosemary Fairfax

Maritime Cathedral founded in 12th century and finally completed in 1991. A member of the ship's crew of Henry VIII's flagship Mary Rose is buried in Navy Aisle.

Location: OS Ref. SZ633 994. 1^1/$_2$ m from end of M275. Follow signs to Historic Ship and Old Portsmouth.

Open: 7.45am - 6pm all year. Sun service: 8am, 9.30am, 11am, 6pm. Weekday: 6pm (Choral on Tues and Fris in term time).

Admission: Donation appreciated.

PORTCHESTER CASTLE ⚏

Portsmouth, Hampshire PO16 9QW

Tel: 023 9237 8291   **Fax:** 023 9237 8291   **www.**english-heritage.org.uk

Owner: English Heritage   **Contact:** The Custodian

The rallying point of Henry V's expedition to Agincourt and the ruined palace of King Richard II. This grand castle has a history going back nearly 2,000 years including the most complete Roman walls in Europe. Interactive exhibition telling the story of the castle and new interactive audio tour.

Location: OS196, Ref. SU625 046. On S side of Portchester off A27, M27/J11.

Open: 29 Mar - 30 Sept: daily, 10am - 6pm. 1 - 31 Oct: 10am - 5pm. 1 Nov - 31 Mar: daily, 10am - 4pm. Closed 24 - 26 Dec & 1 Jan.

Admission: Adult £3.20, Child £1.60, Conc. £2.40. 15% discount for groups (11+). One extra place free for every additional 20.

ℹ Exhibition. ⬜ 🔳 Partial. 🔲 🔳 In grounds, on leads. ✳ 📺 Tel for details.

SOMERLEY   *See page 102 for full page entry.*

STRATFIELD SAYE HOUSE 🏛

Stratfield Saye, Basingstoke RG27 0AS

Tel: 01256 882882   **www.**stratfield-saye.co.uk

Owner: The Duke of Wellington   **Contact:** The Administrator

Family home of the Dukes of Wellington since 1817.

Location: OS Ref. SU700 615. Equidistant from Reading (M4/J11) & Basingstoke (M3/J6) 1^1/$_2$ m W of the A33.

Open: Stratfield Saye House will be closed in 2002 for essential renovation work. Re-opening in 2003.

TITCHFIELD ABBEY ⚏

Titchfield, Southampton, Hampshire

Tel: 01329 842133

Owner: English Heritage   **Contact:** Mr K E Groves

Remains of a 13th century abbey overshadowed by the grand Tudor gatehouse. Reputedly some of Shakespeare's plays were performed here for the first time. Under local management of Titchfield Abbey Society.

Location: OS Ref. SU544 067. ^{1}/$_2$ m N of Titchfield off A27.

Open: 29 Mar - 30 Sept: daily, 10am - 6pm. 1 - 31 Oct: daily, 10am - 5pm. 1 Nov - 31 Mar: daily, 10am - 4pm.

Admission: Free.

TUDOR HOUSE MUSEUM

Bugle Street, Southampton, Hampshire

Tel: 023 8063 5904   **Fax:** 023 8033 9601

Owner: Southampton City Council   **Contact:** Caroline Blott

Late 15th century half timbered house. Tudor knot garden.

Location: OS Ref. SU418 113. Follow signs to Old Town and waterfront from M27/M3. 150yds NW of Merchants House.

Open: End Oct - Mar: Tue - Fri, 10am - 12 noon & 1 - 5pm. Sat, 10am - 12 noon & 1 - 4pm. Sun, 2 - 5pm. Closed Mon. End Mar - Oct: Tue - Fri, 10am - 12 noon & 1 - 5pm. Sat, 10am - 12 noon & 1 - 4pm. Sun, 2 - 5pm. Closed Mons.

Admission: Free.

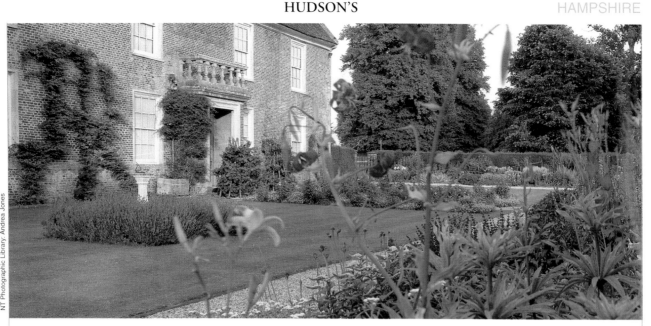

NT Photographic Library: Andrea Jones

THE VYNE ❧
SHERBORNE ST JOHN, BASINGSTOKE RG24 9HL

www.nationaltrust.org.uk/regions/southern

Tel: 01256 881337   **Fax:** 01256 881720   **e-mail:** svygen@smtp.ntrust.org.uk

Owner: The National Trust   **Contact:** The Property Manager

Built in the early 16th century for Lord Sandys, Henry VIII's Lord Chamberlain, the house acquired a classical portico in the mid-17th century (the first of its kind in England) and contains a fascinating Tudor chapel with Renaissance glass, a Palladian staircase and a wealth of old panelling and fine furniture. The attractive grounds feature herbaceous borders and a wild garden, with lawns, lakes and woodland walks. Wedding & Functions: Stone Gallery licensed for Civil Weddings. Receptions and private/corporate functions in Walled Garden or Brewhouse restaurant.

Location: OS Ref. SU637 566. 4m N of Basingstoke between Bramley and Sherborne St John.

Open: House: 23 Mar - 3 Nov: daily except Thurs & Fris, 11am - 5pm (open Good Fri). Grounds: weekends in Feb & Mar: 11am - 5pm; 23 Mar - 3 Nov: daily except Thurs & Fris, 11am - 5pm (open Good Fri).

Admission: House & Grounds: Adult £6.50, Child £3.25, Family £16.25. Grounds only: Adult £3, Child £1.50. Groups: £5 (Mon - Wed only).

ⓘ No photography in house. 🖾 ♿ 🌳 ♿ ♿ 🍴 🅿 🚫 ⬆ ♿ Tel for details.

WHITCHURCH SILK MILL
28 WINCHESTER STREET, WHITCHURCH, HAMPSHIRE RG28 7AL

www.whitchurchsilkmill.org.uk

Tel: 01256 892065   **e-mail:** silkmill@btinternet.com

Owner: Hampshire Buildings Preservation Trust   **Contact:** The Administrator

Picturesque Georgian watermill on the River Test making silk since 1825. Now a working museum, the Victorian machinery produces traditional silks for film costume, historic houses and fashion. Varied programme of temporary exhibitions and children's holiday activities. Waterwheel, delightful riverside garden, shop selling affordable silk gifts, tearoom serving home cooking.

Location: OS Ref. SU463 479. In centre of Whitchurch, just off A34 between Winchester and Newbury.

Open: All year: Tue - Sun & BH Mons, 10.30am - 5pm, last admission 4.15pm. Closed 24 Dec - 2 Jan.

Admission: Adult £3.50, Child £1.75, Conc. £3. Booked groups (10+): Adult £3, Child £1.50, Conc. £2.50.

🖾 ♿ Partial. ♿ 🅕 By arrangement. 🅿 Limited for coaches. ■ 🐕 Guide dogs only. ✻

GILBERT WHITE'S HOUSE & THE OATES MUSEUM
THE WAKES, HIGH STREET, SELBORNE, ALTON GU34 3JH

Tel: 01420 511275

Owner: Oates Memorial Trust   **Contact:** Mrs Anna Jackson

Charming 18th century house in heart of old Selborne, home of Rev Gilbert White, author of The Natural History of Selborne. Lovely garden with many plants of the 18th century. Museum devoted to Captain Oates of Antarctic fame. Tea parlour with 18th century fare and excellent shop.

Location: OS Ref. SU741 336. On W side of B3006, in village of Selborne 4m NW of the A3.

Open: 1 Jan - 24 Dec: daily, 11am - 5pm. Evenings also for groups.

Admission: Adult £4, Child £1, OAP £3.50.

ⓘ No photography in house. 🖾 ♿ ♿ Partial. ♿ 🅕 By arrangement. 🅿 🐕 Guide dogs only. ✻ ♿

WINCHESTER CATHEDRAL

Winchester, Hants SO23 9LS

Tel: 01962 857200 **Fax:** 01962 857201

e-mail: cathedral.office@winchester-cathedral.org.uk

The Cathedral was founded in 1079.

Location: OS Ref. SU483 293. Winchester city centre.

Open: 8.30am - 6pm. East end closes 5pm. Access may be restricted during services. Weekday services:7.40am, 8am, 5.30pm. Sun services: 8am, 10am, 11.15am, 3.30pm.

Admission: Recommended donations. Adult £3.50, Child 50p, Conc. £2.50, Family (2+2) £7. Photo permits £1, Video permits £2. Library & Triforium Gallery: £1, Tower & Roof tours: £1.50 (age restrictions 12 - 70). Groups of 10+ must book, tel: 01962 857225.

WINCHESTER COLLEGE

73 Kingsgate Street, Winchester, Hampshire SO23 9PE

Tel: 01962 621209 **Fax:** 01962 621166 **e-mail:** enterprises@wincoll.ac.uk

www.wincoll.ac.uk

Owner: Winchester College   **Contact:** Marcus Van Hagen

Founded in 1382 Winchester College is believed to be the oldest continuously running school in the country. Concentrating on the medieval heart of the College, the tour takes approximately 1 hour and covers Chamber Court, College Hall, Chapel, Cloisters and School. Cornflowers gift shop has a large range of quality items and souvenirs and can be found at the corner of College Street and Kingsgate Street.

Location: OS Ref. SU483 290. S of the Cathedral.

Open: All year: Mon - Sat, 10.45am, 12 noon, 2.15pm, 3.30pm. Sun, 2.15pm, 3.30pm. No tours Tues & Thurs afternoons.

Admission: Adult £2.50, Child/Conc. £2. Guided tours may be booked for groups (10+): Adult £3, Child/Conc. £2.50.

i Stone & cobbled paths may be slippery. No smoking. ⬜ T ♿ Partially. 🐕 Obligatory. ⬛ Guide dogs only. ✳

WOLVESEY CASTLE ⌗

College Street, Wolvesey, Winchester, Hampshire SO23 8NB

Tel: 01962 854766 **www.**english-heritage.org.uk

Owner: English Heritage   **Contact:** The Custodian

The fortified palace of Wolvesey was the chief residence of the Bishops of Winchester and one of the greatest of all medieval buildings in England. Its extensive ruins still reflect the importance and immense wealth of the Bishops of Winchester, occupants of the richest seat in medieval England. Wolvesey was frequently visited by medieval and Tudor monarchs and was the scene of the wedding feast of Philip of Spain and Mary Tudor in 1554.

Location: OS Ref. SU484 291. ³/4 m SE of Winchester Cathedral, next to the Bishop's Palace; access from College Street.

Open: 29 Mar - 30 Sept: 10am - 6pm. 1 - 31 Oct: 10am - 5pm.

Admission: Adult £2, Child £1, Conc. £1.50.

♿ Grounds. 🐕 In grounds, on leads.

Hinton Ampner

BOUGHTON MONCHELSEA PLACE

NR MAIDSTONE

www.boughtonmonchelseaplace.co.uk

Owner:
Mr & Mrs D Kendrick

▶ CONTACT

Mrs M Kendrick
Boughton
Monchelsea Place
Boughton Monchelsea
Nr Maidstone
Kent ME17 4BU

Tel: 01622 743120
Fax: 01622 741168

e-mail: mk@
boughtonmonchelsea
place.co.uk

▶ LOCATION
OS Ref. TQ772 499

On B2163, 5^1/$_2$ m from
M20/J8 or 4^1/$_2$ m from
Maidstone via A229.

Boughton Monchelsea Place is a battlemented manor house dating from the 16th century, set in its own country estate just outside Maidstone, within easy reach of London and the channel ports. This Grade I listed building has always been privately owned and is still lived in as a family home.

From the lawns surrounding the property there are spectacular views over unspoilt Kent countryside, with the historic deer park in the foreground. These views are shared by the 20 acre event site set back a little way from the house. A wicket gate leads from the grounds to the medieval church of St Peter, with its rose garden and ancient lych gate. At the rear of the house are to be found a pretty courtyard and walled gardens, together with an extensive range of Tudor barns and outbuildings.

Inside the house, rooms vary in character from Tudor through to Georgian Gothic; worthy of note are the fine Jacobean staircase and sundry examples of heraldic stained glass. Furnishings and paintings are mainly Victorian, with a few earlier pieces; the atmosphere is friendly and welcoming throughout.

The premises are licensed for Civil marriage ceremonies, although wedding receptions may only be held on weekdays. In addition we welcome conferences, group visits, location work and all types of corporate, private and public functions, but please note times of availability. Use outside these hours is sometimes possible, subject to negotiation. All clients are guaranteed exclusive use of this prestigious venue.

▶ OPENING TIMES

By prior
arrangement only.

House & Garden
Not open to
individual visitors.

Private functions:
Mon - Fri, 9am - 9pm.

Group visits/ house tours:
(15-50 pax), Mon - Thur,
9am - 4pm.

Outdoor Event Site
365 days a year:
8am - 11.30pm.

▶ ADMISSION
**Gardens &
Guided House Tour**
Adult £5.00

Gardens only
Adult £2.75

Venue Hire
Prices on application.

Day Delegate Rate
From £40.

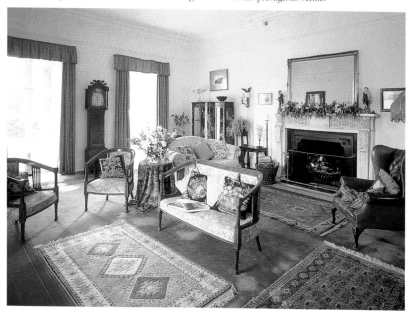

CONFERENCE/FUNCTION

ROOM	SIZE	MAX CAPACITY
Entrance Hall	25' x 19'	50 Theatre
Dining Room	31' x 19'	50 Dining
Drawing Room	28' x 19'	40 Reception
Courtyard Room	37' x 13'	70 Theatre

 By arrangement.
 By arrangement.
 By arrangement.

South East - England

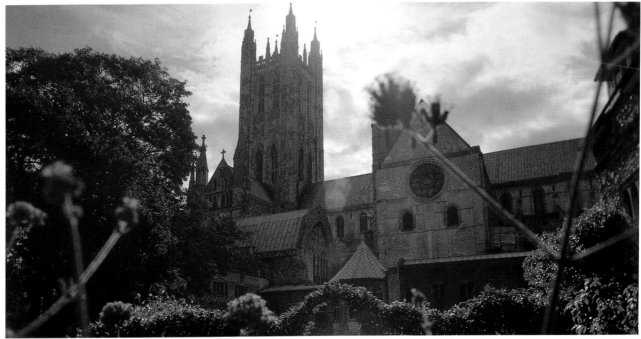

CANTERBURY CATHEDRAL

CANTERBURY

www.canterbury-cathedral.org

▶ CONTACT

Visits Office
Canterbury Cathedral
The Precincts
Canterbury
Kent CT1 2EH

Tel: 01227 762862
Fax: 01227
865222/865250
e-mail: visits@
canterbury-
cathedral.org

▶ LOCATION
OS Ref. TR151 579

Canterbury city centre.
M2/M20, then A2.

Bus: Victoria Station
coach – regular service.

Rail: London
Victoria/Bridge/Charing
Cross to Canterbury
East or West.

Sightseeing Tours:
Tour operators operate a
daily service with
collection from most
London hotels. Ask
your hotel concierge or
porter for information.

Canterbury Cathedral has a tradition of visitor welcome that reaches back to the days of medieval pilgrimages. St Augustine, sent by Pope Gregory the Great, arrived in 597 AD and became the first Archbishop, establishing his seat (or 'Cathedra') in Canterbury. In 1170 Archbishop Thomas Becket was murdered in the Cathedral and ever since, the Cathedral has attracted thousands of pilgrims.

The saint is said to have worked miracles, and the Cathedral contains some rare stained glass depicting those events. The Cathedral is also noteworthy for its medieval tombs of royal personages, such as King Henry IV and Edward the Black Prince, as well as numerous archbishops.

The Cathedral, together with St Augustine's Abbey and St Martin's Church, is a World Heritage Site.

The Cathedral Education Centre, immediately beside the Cathedral, offers purpose-built, state-of-the-art conference facilities of the highest quality. Facilities range from small seminar rooms to a 250-seat auditorium, equipped with the latest audio-visual technology and full theatre lighting. From March 2002, the Centre will offer accommodation for 40 people.

▶ OPENING TIMES
Summer
Mon - Sat, 9am - 7pm.

Winter
Mon - Sat, 9am - 5pm.

Crypt (all year):
10am - 7pm
(5pm in winter)

Sundays (all year):
12.30 - 2.30pm,
4.30 - 5.30pm.

Restrictions during services
or special events.
Arrangements may vary
at short notice, always
check opening times
before visiting.

Main Services
Evensong:
Mon - Fri, 5.30pm.
Sats & Suns, 3.15pm.

Eucharist:
Suns, 11am.

▶ ADMISSION
Adult £3.50
Conc. £2.50

Pre-booked school
  groups £2.00
(2001 prices)

 By arrangement.

CONFERENCE/FUNCTION

ROOM	SIZE	MAX CAPACITY
Clagett Auditorium	10.5 x 15m	250
'The Barn'	14 x 5m	92
Lecture Theatre (x2)	7 x 7m	60
Seminar rms	vary	12 - 50

NTPL / Rupert Truman

Owner:
The National Trust

CONTACT

The Property Manager
Chartwell
Westerham
Kent TN16 1PS

Tel: 01732 866368
01732 868381

Fax: 01732 868193

e-mail: kchxxx@
smtp.ntrust.org.uk

LOCATION
OS Ref. TQ455 515

2m S of Westerham,
forking left off B2026.

Bus: Metro bus 246
hourly service from
Bromley South.

CHARTWELL

WESTERHAM

The family home of Sir Winston Churchill from 1924 until the end of his life. He said of Chartwell, simply *'I love the place - a day away from Chartwell is a day wasted'*. With magnificent views over the Weald of Kent it is not difficult to see why.

The rooms are left as they were in Sir Winston & Lady Churchill's lifetime with daily papers, fresh flowers grown from the garden and his famous cigars. Photographs and books evoke his career, interests and happy family life. Museum and exhibition rooms contain displays and sound recordings and superb collections of memorabilia from Sir Winston's political career, including uniforms and a 'siren-suit'.

The garden studio contains Sir Winston's easel and paintbox, as well as many of his paintings. Terraced and water gardens descend to the lake, the gardens also include a golden rose walk, planted by Sir Winston and Lady Churchill's children on the occasion of their golden wedding anniversary, and the Marlborough Pavilion decorated with frescoes depicting the battle of Blenheim. Visitors can see the garden walls that Churchill built with his own hands, as well as the pond stocked with the golden orfe he loved to feed.

The Mulberry Room and/or Cabinet Room at the restaurant can be booked for meetings, conferences, lunches and dinners. Please telephone for details.

OPENING TIMES

23 March - 30 June and
1 Sept - 3 November
Wed - Sun & BHs
11am - 5pm.

2 July - 31 August
Tue - Sun & BHs
11am - 5pm.

Last admission 4.15pm.

ADMISSION

Adult £5.80
Child £2.90
Family £14.50

NTPL / Andreas von Einsiedel

NTPL / Ian Shaw

SPECIAL EVENTS

Jul 13
BBC Big Band.

[⬛] [i] Conference facilities. [♿] Partial. WC. Please telephone before visit. [¶] Licensed.
[👤] By arrangement. **P** [🐕] In grounds, on leads.

South East - England

Courtesy Ron Vernon

Owner:
Denys Eyre Bower
Bequest
Reg. Charity Trust

▶ **CONTACT**

Mrs R Vernon
Chiddingstone Castle
Edenbridge
Kent TN8 7AD

Tel: 01892 870347

▶ **LOCATION**
OS Ref. TQ497 452

B2027, turn to
Chiddingstone at Bough
Beech, 1m further on
to crossroads, then
straight to castle.

10m from Tonbridge,
Tunbridge Wells and
Sevenoaks.
4m Edenbridge.
Accessible from A21
and M25/J5.

London 35m.

Bus: Enquiries:
Tunbridge Wells TIC
01892 515675.

Rail: Tonbridge,
Tunbridge Wells,
Edenbridge then taxi.
Penshurst then 2m walk.

Air: Gatwick 15m.

CONFERENCE/FUNCTION

ROOM	SIZE	MAX CAPACITY
Assembly Rm	14' x 35'	50
Seminar Rms	15' x 15'	
Stable Block	36' x 29'	

CHIDDINGSTONE CASTLE 🏛

EDENBRIDGE

www.chiddingstone-castle.org.uk

Chiddingstone Castle ushered in a century whose pictorial art, architecture and literature was inspired by romantic medieval chivalry. In 1803 Henry Streatfeild commissioned William Atkinson to remodel his family seat in Chiddingstone village in the Castle style. His first major work, it was exhibited at the Royal Academy in 1805. He ingeniously re-oriented the mansion on its site, so that it was approached by the new mile-long drive. Visitors were entertained by a panorama in glowing sandstone of mansion and garden-houses, integrated to form a contemporary interpretation of a medieval castle. Work stopped in 1808, the plan

uncompleted, perhaps owing to expense. Ignominiously the place lapsed into obscurity despite titivation in the 1830s. The estate was sold in 1938. The Castle suffered years of disastrous military and scholastic occupation until rescued in 1955 by Denys Bower, a visionary collector without means to rehabilitate it. He died in 1977 leaving the mansion and fabulous collections to the nation, but no money. By a High Court direction, a Trust (educational) was established to manage the bequest. After lonely years of desperate struggle the Castle is a fitting home for enthralling treasures from Japan, Ancient Egypt, the Orient and our own past.

Great Hall

📷 ℹ️ Conferences, receptions, concerts. No photography in house; no smoking, prams/buggies, large bags or mobile phones.

🍽 Available for special events. Wedding receptions.

♿ Partial. WC.

🍴 Licensed. 🍴 By arrangement.

🧍 By arrangement.

🅿 Ample for cars. Limited for coaches, please book.

🎒 Teachers' pack. Educational programme.

🐕 In grounds, on leads.

🔔 ❄️

▶ **OPENING TIMES**
Summer
Easter Hol, All BHs.

June - September
Wed - Fri & Sun

Weekdays: 2 - 5.30pm.

Sun & BHs
11.30am - 5.30pm
Last admission 5pm.

Winter
Open only for specially booked groups (20+).
Last Sun in Dec: Christmas Fair - please enquire.

▶ **ADMISSION**

Adult £4.00
Child* £2.50

Groups** (pre-booked 20+)
Adult £3.50
Child* £2.00

* Child under 16yrs accompanied by adult.
Under 5 yrs Free.

** Usual hours, other times by appointment. School groups only by appointment.

Chiddingstone may be closed without notice for Special Events.

CHIDDINGSTONE CASTLE...

Stable Lecture Room

The Assembly Room

The Seminar Room

SMALL CONFERENCES AND FUNCTIONS:

The old domestic quarters, grouped around the courtyard, have been converted into a unique and elegant centre for various events. The self-contained Goodhugh Wing offers Assembly Room (capacity 50), three seminar rooms, and tea-kitchen. Meals can be provided in the refectory by our approved caterers. Additional lecture/meeting accommodation in the adjoining stable block, recently restored.

CIVIL MARRIAGES:

The Great Hall is licensed by Kent County Council, and is specially attractive to those who desire the dignity of a church ceremony without the religious aspect. We offer all features of wedding celebrations, including reception of guests and refreshments.

EDUCATION:

We welcome visits from schools who wish to use the collections in connection with classroom work. No anxiety for the teachers (admitted free). The children are safe here, can picnic and play in the grounds. We may have some exciting developments with adult education in the restored stable block. Please enquire.

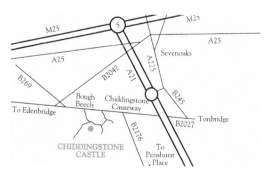

COBHAM HALL

COBHAM

www.cobhamhall.com

Owner:
Cobham Hall
School

▶ CONTACT

Mr N Powell
Bursar
Cobham Hall, Cobham
Kent DA12 3BL

Tel: 01474 823371
Fax: 01474 825904
e-mail:
cobhamhall@aol.com

▶ LOCATION

OS Ref. TQ683 689

Situated adjacent to the
A2/M2. ¹/₂ m S of A2 4m
W of Strood. 8m E of
M25/J2 between
Gravesend & Rochester.

London 25m
Rochester 5m
Canterbury 30m

Rail: Meopham 3m
Gravesend 5m
Taxis at both stations.

Air: Gatwick 45 mins.
Heathrow 60 mins,
Stansted 50 mins.

CONFERENCE/FUNCTION

ROOM	SIZE	MAX CAPACITY
Gilt Hall	41' x 34'	180
Wyatt Dining Rm	49' x 23'	135
Clifton Dining Rm	24' x 23'	75
Activities Centre	119' x 106'	300

'One of the largest, finest and most important houses in Kent', Cobham Hall is an outstandingly beautiful, red brick mansion in Elizabethan, Jacobean, Carolean and 18th century styles.

It yields much of interest to the student of art, architecture and history. The Elizabethan wings were begun in 1584 whilst the central section contains the Gilt Hall, wonderfully decorated by John Webb, Inigo Jones' most celebrated pupil, 1654. Further rooms were decorated by James Wyatt in the 18th century.

Cobham Hall, now a leading girls' boarding and day school, has been visited by several of the English monarchs from Elizabeth I to Edward VIII, later Duke of Windsor. Charles Dickens used to

walk through the grounds from his house in Higham to the Leather Bottle pub in Cobham Village. In 1883, the Hon Ivo Bligh, later the 8th Earl of Darnley, led the victorious English cricket team against Australia bringing home the 'Ashes' to Cobham.

GARDENS

The gardens, landscaped for the 4th Earl by Humphry Repton, are gradually being restored. The Gothic Dairy and some of the classical garden buildings are being renovated. The gardens are particularly delightful in Spring, when they are resplendent with daffodils and a myriad of rare bulbs.

ℹ️ Conferences, business or social functions, 150 acres of parkland for sports, corporate events, open air concerts, sports centre, indoor swimming pool, art studios, music wing, tennis courts, helicopter landing area. Filming and photography. No smoking.

🍽️ In-house catering team for private, corporate hospitality and wedding receptions. (cap. 200).

♿ House tour involves 2 staircases, ground floor access for w/chairs.

☕ Afternoon teas, other meals by arrangement.

🚶 Obligatory guided tours; tour time 1¹/₂ hrs. Garden tours arranged outside standard opening times.

🅿️ Ample. Pre-booked coach groups are welcome any time.

🖼️ Guide provided, Adult £3.50, Child / OAP £2.75.

🐕 In grounds, on leads.

🛏️ 18 single and 18 double with bathroom. 22 single and 22 double without bathroom. Dormitory. Groups only.

▶ OPENING TIMES

Summer
March:
24, 27, 29, 30, 31.

April:
1, 3, 7, 10, 14, 17.

July:
10, 14, 17, 21, 24, 28, 31.

August:
4, 7, 11, 14, 18, 21, 25, 26, 28.

November:
2, 3.

▶ ADMISSION

Adult £3.50
Child (4-14yrs.) £2.75
OAP £2.75

Gardens & Parkland
Self-guided tour
and booklet £1.50

Historical/Conservation tour of Grounds
(by arrangement)

Per person £3.50

🎭 SPECIAL EVENTS

MAR 24:
National Garden Scheme Day
(+ House open 2 - 5pm).

MAR 29 - APR 1:
The Medway Craft Show.
(+ House open 1 - 4pm).

JUL 14:
National Garden Scheme Day
(+ House open 2 - 5pm).

JUL 31:
Summer Stroll Garden Tour, 7pm.
Guidebook tour & glass of wine
£5 per person. Tel to book.

Nov 2 - 3
The Medway Flower Festival
& Craft Show.
(+ House open 1 - 4pm).

English Heritage Photo Library

DOVER CASTLE ⊞
AND THE SECRET WARTIME TUNNELS
DOVER
www.english-heritage.org.uk

Journey deep into the White Cliffs of Dover and discover the top secret World War II tunnels. Through sight, sound and smells relive the wartime drama of the underground hospital as a wounded Battle of Britain pilot is taken to the operating theatre in a bid to save his life. Discover how life would have been during the planning days of the Dunkirk evacuation and Operation Dynamo as you are led around the network of tunnels and casements housing the communications centre.

Above ground you can explore the magnificent mediaeval keep and inner bailey of King Henry II. Visit the evocative Princess of Wales' Royal Regiment Museum. There is also the Roman Lighthouse and Anglo-Saxon church to see or take an audio tour of the intriguing 13th century underground fortifications and medieval battlements. Enjoy magnificent views of the White Cliffs from Admiralty lookout.

See the exciting 'Life Under Siege' exhibition, and discover, through a dramatic light and sound presentation, how it must have felt to be a garrison soldier defending Dover Castle against the French King in 1216. In the Keep, see a reconstruction of the Castle in preparation for a visit from Henry VIII and visit the hands-on exhibition explaining the travelling Tudor court. The land train will help you around this huge site.

Throughout the summer there are many fun events taking place, bringing the Castle alive through colourful enactments and living history.

Owner:
English Heritage

▶ CONTACT

Ms Tracey Maguire
Dover Castle
Dover
Kent CT16 1HU

Tel: 01304 211067

Info Line: 01304 201628

▶ LOCATION
OS Ref. TR326 416

Easy access from A2 and M20. Well signed from Dover centre and east side of Dover.
2 hrs from central London.

Rail: London Charing Cross or Victoria
1¹/₂ hrs.

Bus: Freephone 0800 696996.

🏠 Two.

🍷 Functions catered for including themed evenings within the Keep. For private functions tel: 01304 205830.

♿ Lift for access to tunnels. Courtyard and grounds, some very steep slopes.

🍴 3 restaurants, hot and cold food and drinks.

🚶 Tour of tunnels approx. every 20 mins, more at peak times when a 30 min. wait can occur.

Ⓟ Ample. Groups welcome, discounts available. Free entry for drivers. One extra place for each additional group of 20.

🎒 Free visits available for schools. Education centre. Pre-booking essential.

❄ 🎭 Tel for details.

English Heritage Photo Library

▶ OPENING TIMES

Summer
29 Mar - 30 Sept
Daily: 10am - 6pm.

1 - 31 Oct:
Daily: 10am - 5pm.

Winter
1 November - 31 March
Daily: 10am - 4pm.

Closed 24 - 26 Dec &
1 Jan.

▶ ADMISSION

Adult £7.50
Child £3.80
Conc. £5.60
Family (2+3) £18.80

Groups: 15% discount for groups (11+).

South East - England

DOWN HOUSE ⌗

DOWNE

www.english-heritage.org.uk

A visit to Down House is a fascinating journey of discovery for all the family. This was the family home of Charles Darwin for over 40 years and now you can explore it to the full.

See the actual armchair in which Darwin wrote 'On the Origin of Species', which shocked and then revolutionised the way we think about the origins of mankind. His study is much the same as it was in his lifetime and is filled with belongings that give you an intimate glimpse into both his studies and everyday life.

At Down House you will discover both sides of Darwin - the great thinker and the family man.

Explore the family rooms where the furnishings have been painstakingly restored. An audio tour narrated by Sir David Attenborough will bring the house to life and increase your understanding of Darwin's revolutionary theory. Upstairs you will find state-of-the-art interpretation of the scientific significance of the house – especially designed to inspire a younger audience.

Outside, take the Sandwalk which he paced daily in search of inspiration, then stroll in lovely gardens. Complete your day by sampling the delicious selection of home-made cakes in the tea room.

Owner:
English Heritage

▶ **CONTACT**

The House Manager
Down House
Luxted Road
Downe
Kent   BR6 7JT

Tel: 01689 859119

▶ **LOCATION**

OS Ref, TQ431 611

In Luxted Road, Downe, off A21 near Biggin Hill.

Rail: From London Victoria or Charing Cross.

Bus: Orpington (& Bus R2) or Bromley South (& Bus 146). Buses R2 & 146 do not run on Sunday.

▶ **OPENING TIMES**

Apr - Sept:
Wed - Sun & BHs,
10am - 6pm.
Oct: 10am - 5pm.
Nov - Mar: 10am - 4pm.

Closed 24 Dec - 5 Feb 2002 & 23 Dec - 4 Feb 2003.

On BHs and throughout August visits to Down House must be booked in advance. It is not necessary to book if you travel by public transport.

▶ **ADMISSION**

Adult £6.00
Child £3.00
Conc. £4.50
Family (2+3) £15.00

Groups (11+)
.... 15% discount

Tour leader and coach driver have free entry. 1 extra place for every 20 additional people.

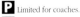 Free. English, French, German, Japanese & for visually impaired.

P Limited for coaches.

 Guide dogs only.

Tel for details.

Patrick Lane

South East England

FINCHCOCKS
GOUDHURST
www.argonet.co.uk/finchcocks

Owner:
Mr Richard Burnett

▶ **CONTACT**

Mrs Katrina Burnett
Finchcocks
Goudhurst
Kent TN17 1HH

Tel: 01580 211702

Fax: 01580 211007

e-mail: katrina@
finchcocks.co.uk

▶ **LOCATION**

OS Ref. TQ700 365

1m S of A262, 2m W of
village of Goudhurst.
5m from Cranbrook,
10m from Tunbridge
Wells, 45m from
London (1¹/₂ hrs)

Rail: Marden 6m
(no taxi), Paddock
Wood 8m (taxi),
Tunbridge Wells
10m (taxi).

Air: Gatwick 1 hr.

In 1970 Finchcocks was acquired by Richard Burnett, leading exponent of the early piano, and it now contains his magnificent collection of some eighty historical keyboard instruments: chamber organs, harpsichords, virginals, spinets and early pianos. About half of these are restored to full concert condition and are played whenever the house is open to the public. The house, with its high ceilings and oak panelling, provides the perfect setting for music performed on period instruments, and Finchcocks is now a music centre of international repute. Many musical events take place here.

There is also a fascinating collection of pictures and prints, mainly on musical themes, and there is a special exhibition on display on the theme of the 18th century pleasure gardens, such as Vauxhall and Ranelagh, which includes costumes and tableaux.

Finchcocks is a fine Georgian baroque manor noted for its outstanding brickwork, with a dramatic front elevation attributed to Thomas Archer. Named after the family who lived on the site in the 13th century, the present house was built in 1725 for barrister Edward Bathurst, kinsman to Earl Bathurst. Despite having changed hands many times, it has undergone remarkably little alteration and retains most of its original features. The beautiful grounds, with their extensive views over parkland and hop gardens, include the newly restored walled garden, which provides a dramatic setting for special events.

📷 🎪 ℹ️ Music events, conferences, seminars, promotions, archery, ballooning, filming, television. Keyboard instruments and musical furniture for hire, marquees erected for large functions. No videos in house, photography by permission only.

🍽️ Private and corporate entertaining, weddings. Full catering by arrangement. Fully licensed.

♿ Limited. WC. Suitable for visually handicapped.

☕ 🍴 Licensed. Teas and light refreshments. Picnics permitted in grounds.

🚶 🎧 Musical tours / recitals on instruments whenever required. Tour time: 2 ¹/₂ - 4 hrs.

🅿️ Ample. Pre-booked groups (25 - 100) welcome from Apr - Oct. Free meals for couriers and drivers.

🖼️ Opportunity to play instruments. Can be linked to special projects and National Curriculum syllabus.

🐕

🔔 Music a speciality, and musicians can be provided.

▶ **OPENING TIMES**

Summer

Easter Sun - end Sept
Sun & BH Mons, plus Wed
& Thur in August,
2 - 6pm.

Pre-booked groups and individuals welcome most days April to October mornings, afternoons and evenings and in some circumstances up to Christmas.

Winter

Closed
January - mid-March
Available for private
functions October,
November & December.

▶ **ADMISSION**

Open Days

House, Garden & Music

Adult £7.50
Child £4.00
Student £5.00

Garden Only

Adult £2.50
Child £0.50

Groups*

Adult £7.50
Child £4.00
Student £5.00

* Min. of 25 to open house.

🎭 **SPECIAL EVENTS**

MAY 5/6:
Spring Garden Fair & Flower Festival.

SEPT WEEKENDS:
Music Festival.

NOV 30/DEC 1:
Christmas Fair.

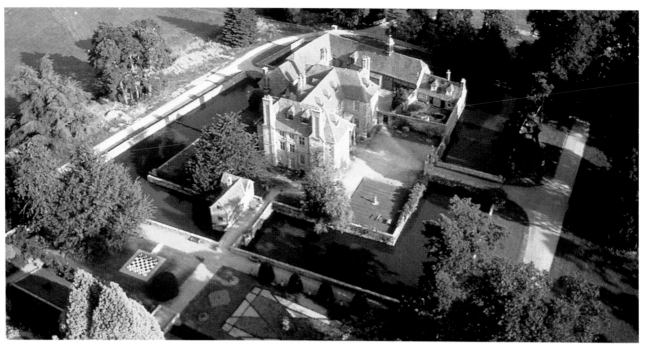

GROOMBRIDGE PLACE GARDENS

TUNBRIDGE WELLS

www.groombridge.co.uk

Owner:
Groombridge Asset
Management

▶ **CONTACT**

The Estate Office
Groombridge Place
Groombridge
Tunbridge Wells
Kent TN3 9QG

Tel: 01892 863999
01892 861444

Fax: 01892 863996

e-mail: office@
groombridge.co.uk

Surrounded by acres of magnificent parkland, Groombridge Place has a breathtaking beauty. Exquisite 17th century walled gardens with extensive herbaceous borders flank a medieval moat surrounding a classical Restoration manor house (not open to the public). With an intriguing history going back over 700 years, Groombridge Place has a timeless and magical charm.

On a high hillside above the walled gardens and estate vineyard is the Enchanted Forest, where hours of pleasure await discovery. Deep in the woodland glades are the Serpents' Lair and the Mystic Pool, Mossy Bottom and the

Double Spiral intriguing contemporary gardens, to challenge and delight your imagination and reward your mind's ingenuity.

Four major awards in three years prove what our visitors say: 'Groombridge Place is wonderful because it's so different!'. Watch the birds of prey flying, see the pigs racing, enjoy a canal boat ride. There is a tearoom serving delicious snacks, a picnic area and a gift shop. We offer a regular schedule of popular events appealing to all ages. You can enjoy the happiest day of your life at Groombridge Place, which is also licensed for Civil wedding ceremonies.

▶ **OPENING TIMES**

Summer
Gardens
29 March - 27 October
Daily, 9am - 6pm.

The house is not open to visitors.

▶ **LOCATION**
OS Ref. TQ534 375

Groombridge Place Gardens are located on the B2110 just off the A264. 4m SW of Tunbridge Wells and 9m E of East Grinstead.

Rail: London Charing Cross to Tunbridge Wells 55mins.

Air: Gatwick.

▶ **ADMISSION**

Adult £8.00
Child (3-12) £6.50
OAP £7.00
Groups(20+)
Adult £6.50
Child (3-12) £4.50
Student/OAP £5.50

Children under 3yrs Free.

Partial. WCs.
Tearoom.
By arrangement.
Limited for coaches.

Guide dogs only.

Tel for details.

HEVER CASTLE & GARDENS

EDENBRIDGE

www.hevercastle.co.uk

Hever Castle dates back to 1270, when the gatehouse, outer walls and the inner moat were first built. 200 years later the Bullen (or Boleyn) family added the comfortable Tudor manor house constructed within the walls. This was the childhood home of Anne Boleyn, Henry VIII's second wife and mother of Elizabeth I. There are many items relating to the Tudors, including two books of hours (prayer books) signed and inscribed by Anne Boleyn. The Castle was later given to Henry VIII's fourth wife, Anne of Cleves.

In 1903, the estate was bought by the American millionaire William Waldorf Astor, who became a British subject and the first Lord Astor of Hever. He invested an immense amount of time, money and imagination in restoring the castle and grounds. Master craftsmen were employed and the castle was filled with a magnificent collection of furniture, tapestries and other works of art.

'From Castles to Country Houses' the Miniature Model Houses exhibition, a collection of 1/12 scale model houses, room views and gardens, depicts life in English Country Houses.

GARDENS

Between 1904-8 over 30 acres of formal gardens were laid out and planted, these have now matured into one of the most beautiful gardens in England. The unique Italian garden is a four acre walled garden containing a superb collection of statuary and sculpture. The award-winning gardens include the Rose garden and Tudor garden, a traditional yew maze and a 110 metre herbaceous border. A water maze has been added to the other water features in the gardens. The Sunday Walk Garden has a stream meandering through a mature woodland with borders filled with specimen plants.

Owner:
Hever Castle Ltd

▶ CONTACT

Anne-Marie
Critchley-Salmonson
Hever Castle
Hever, Edenbridge
Kent TN8 7NG

Infoline: 01732 865224
Fax: 01732 866796
e-mail:
mail@HeverCastle.co.uk

▶ LOCATION

OS Ref. TQ476 450

Exit M25/J5 & J6
M23/J10,
1½ m S of B2027 at
Bough Beech,
3m SE of Edenbridge.

Rail: Hever Station
1m (no taxis),
Edenbridge Town
3m (taxis).

CONFERENCE/FUNCTION

ROOM	SIZE	MAX CAPACITY
Dining Hall	35' x 20'	70
Breakfast Rm	22' x 15'	12
Sitting Rm	24' x 20'	20
Pavilion	96' x 40'	250
Moat Restaurant	25' x 60'	75

ℹ️ 🎬 Suitable for filming, conferences, corporate hospitality, product launches. Outdoor heated pool, tennis court and billiard room. No photography in house.

🛍️ Gift, garden & book.

🍽️ 250 seat restaurant available for functions wedding receptions, etc.

♿ Access to gardens, ground floor only (no ramps into castle), restaurants, gift shop, book shop and water maze. Wheelchairs available. WC.

🍴 Two licensed restaurants. Supper provided during open air theatre season. Pre-booked lunches and teas for groups.

🚶 Pre-booked tours in mornings. 1 Mar - 30 Nov. Tour time 1 hr. Tours in French, German, Dutch, Italian and Spanish (min 20). Garden tours in English only (min 15).

🅿️ Free admission and refreshment voucher for driver and courier. Please book, group rates for 15+.

🎒 Welcome (min 15). Guide provided for groups of 20. 1:6 ratio (up to 8 year olds: 1:10 9yrs+). Free preparatory visits for teachers during opening hours. Please book.

🐕 In grounds, on leads.

❄️ Tudor Village.

[map showing M25, SEVENOAKS, WESTERHAM, EDENBORO, B2027, HEVER, B2176, TONBRIDGE, TUNBRIDGE WELLS, A264]

▶ OPENING TIMES

Summer
1 March - 30 November
Daily:
Grounds: 11am - 6pm.
Castle: 12 noon - 6pm.
Last admission 5pm.

Winter
March & November
Grounds: 11am - 4pm.

Castle: 12 noon - 4pm.

▶ ADMISSION

Castle & Gardens
 Adult £8.20
 Child (5-14 yrs) £4.50
 OAP £7.00
 Family (2+2) £20.90

Please ring for
group* prices.

Gardens only
 Adult £6.50
 Child (5-16 yrs) £4.30
 OAP £5.60
 Family (2+2) £17.30

Please ring for group (15+) prices.

Pre-booked private guided tours are available before opening, during season.

HEVER CASTLE...

Hever Castle Tudor Village was built in 1903 for William Waldorf Astor in the style of the Tudor period, to include every modern day comfort.

There are twenty individually designed rooms all with private bathroom, direct dial telephone, colour television, hair dryer, and tea and coffee making facilities. The billiard room, outdoor heated swimming pool, tennis court and croquet lawn are all available for guests to use. Hever Castle Estate includes Stables House, an imposing property with five bedrooms, overlooking the river Eden, providing additional accommodation.

The Tudor Village is a unique and unusual venue available only on an 'exclusive use' basis all year round for groups of 10 or more requiring the very highest standards of accommodation, dining and meeting facilities. There are three interconnecting reception rooms all available for private dining, receptions, product launches, private meetings or corporate hospitality.

The magnificent private dining rooms are able to seat up to 70 people for Tudor Banquets, lunches and dinners. Guests are able to enjoy a private guided tour of the Castle followed by a Tudor Banquet with Minstrels playing Tudor Music.

The Dining Hall, Sitting Room and Breakfast Room (which together form the Tudor Suite) provide formal meeting facilities for up to 30 people and 70 people 'theatre style'. Overhead projector, screen and flip charts can be provided and specialist audiovisual equipment hired. Additional arrangements can be made for laser clay pigeon shooting, archery, fishing, riding, golf and other pursuits on or near by the estate.

Hever Castle Tudor Village offers the following accommodation

- 4 single, 12 double, 4 twin bedded rooms in Tudor Village
- 4 twin, 1 double in Stables House

⚜ SPECIAL EVENTS

MAR 11 - 17 Spring Garden Week	**JUN 21 - 27** Rose Week	**SEPT 13 - 15** Patchwork & Quilting
MAR 29, 30, 31 - APR 1 Easter Weekend	**JUL 20 & 27. AUG 3, 4, 10, 11, 17, 18, 24, 31** Jousting Tournaments	**OCT 14 - 20** Autumn Colour Week
MAY 4 - 6 May Day Music & Dance	**JUL 21, 28.** **AUG 25/26. SEPT 1** Tudor Archery	
JUN 1 - 4 Elizabethan Revelries		

Tulip Bedroom in Tudor Village

Tudor Suite Dining Room in Tudor Village

Panelled Bedroom

NTPL / Nadia MacKenzie

IGHTHAM MOTE

SEVENOAKS

Owner:
The National Trust

The Property Manager
Ightham Mote
Ivy Hatch
Sevenoaks
Kent   TN15 0NT

Tel: 01732 810378
Info: 01732 811145
Fax: 01732 811029

e-mail: kimxxx@
smtp.ntrust.org.uk

▶ **LOCATION**
OS Ref. TQ584 535

6m E of Sevenoaks off
A25. 2¹/₂ m S of
Ightham off A227.

Beautiful moated manor house covering 650 years of history from medieval times to the 1960s. Discover the stories and characters associated with the house from the first owners in 1340 to Charles Henry Robinson, the American businessman who bequeathed Ightham Mote to the National Trust in 1985.

The visitor route includes the newly refurbished Great Hall and Jacobean staircase, along with the old chapel, crypt, Tudor chapel with painted ceiling, drawing room with Jacobean fireplace, frieze and 18th century hand-painted Chinese wallpaper and Victorian billiards room.

Conservation programme continues during 2002 which gives visitors a unique opportunity to see work in progress on the largest conservation project ever undertaken by the National Trust on a house of this age and fragility. Interpretation displays and a special exhibition 'Conservation in action' charts the progress of the project and gives insights into the techniques and skills used.

Extensive gardens with lakes and woodland walk. Surrounding 550 acre estate also provides many country walks including way-marked routes.

Free introductory talks and garden tours. Varied event programme including open air concerts and children's events throughout the season, for details please ring 01732 810378.

▶ **OPENING TIMES**

24 March - 3 November:
daily except Tues & Sats,
10am - 5.30pm.
Open BHs.

Last admission 5pm.

▶ **ADMISSION**

Adult	£5.40
Child	£2.70
Family	£13.50
Groups (pre-booked)	
Adult	£4.70

 Ground floor. WC.
Tea Pavilion.
On leads, Estate only.
Tel for details.

NTPL / Nadia MacKenzie

NT Photographic Library / Rupert Truman.

NT Photographic Library / Andreas Von Einsiedel.

KNOLE ❧

SEVENOAKS

Set in an extensive deer park owned by Lord Sackville, Knole is one of the great 'treasure houses' of England. It has been the home of the Sackville family since 1603, including four Dukes of Dorset, and houses an extensive collection of furnishings and paintings, many in the house since the 17th century.

The largest private house in England, Knole is a spectacular example of late medieval architecture overlaid with extensive Jacobean embellishments, including remarkable carving and plasterwork. The Sackville family crest of the leopard rampant recurs throughout.

An internationally renowned collection of Royal Stuart furnishings, including three state beds, celebrated silver furniture, and the prototype of the 'Knole' settee. Thirteen years were spent restoring the fabrics on the bed in the Kings' room.

The 6th Earl of Dorset played host to poets Pope and Dryden. Knole was the birthplace of the writer, Vita Sackville-West, and the setting for Virginia Woolf's novel *Orlando*.

Important collection of paintings, including works by Van Dyck, Lely, Kneller, Gainsborough, Hoppner, Wootton, and a room devoted to the works of Sir Joshua Reynolds, commissioned for the house by the 3rd Duke of Dorset, including portraits of Dr Johnson, David Garrick and Oliver Goldsmith.

The experience of visiting the house, which has been little altered since the 18th century, is like stepping back in time.

Owner:
The National Trust

▶ CONTACT
Property Manager
Knole
Sevenoaks
Kent TN15 0RP

Tel: 01732 462100

Info: 01732 450608

Fax: 01732 465528

e-mail: kknxxx@ smtp.ntrust.org.uk

▶ LOCATION
OS Ref. TQ532 543

25m SE of London. Just off A225 at S end of High Street, Sevenoaks.

Rail: 1/2 hr from London Charing Cross to Sevenoaks.

Bus: Chartwell Explorer 'green transport' bus link with Sevenoaks. Tel: 01732 462100

NT Photographic Library / D Sellman

NT Photographic Library / Andreas Von Einsiedel

▶ OPENING TIMES

House
23 March - 3 November:
Wed - Sun & BHs,
11am - 4pm.
Last admission 3.30pm.

Garden
May - September
1st Wed of month only
11am - 4pm.
Last admission 3pm.

Shop & Tearoom
Core season dates as above.

Christmas Shop
November - December:
Wed - Sun, 11am - 4pm.

▶ ADMISSION

House
Adult	£5.00
Child	£2.50
Family	£12.50
Groups (pre-booked)	
Adult	£4.25
Parking	£2.50
Garden	£2.00

NT members Free.

🛍️ ℹ️ Full range of NT goods and souvenirs of Knole.

♿ Wheelchair access to Green Court, Stone Court and Great Hall.

🍴 Brewhouse Restaurant serving morning coffee, lunch and teas. Also ice-creams and snacks in courtyard.

🧍 Guided tours for pre-booked groups. By arrangement.

🅿️ Ample.

🖼️ Welcome. Contact Education Officer.

LEEDS CASTLE & GARDENS

MAIDSTONE

www.leeds-castle.com

This "loveliest castle in the world", surrounded by 500 acres of magnificent parkland and gardens and set in the middle of a natural lake, is one of the country's finest historic properties. Leeds is also proud to be one of the Treasure Houses of England.

The site of a Saxon royal manor, a Norman fortress and a royal palace to the Kings and Queens of England, the chequered history of Leeds Castle continues well into the 20th century. The last private owner, the Honourable Olive, Lady Baillie, purchased the Castle in 1926. Her inheritance helped to restore the Castle and, prior to her death, she established the Leeds Castle Foundation which now preserves the Castle for the nation, hosts important

international conferences and supports the arts.

The Castle has a fine collection of paintings, tapestries and furnishings and is also home to a unique collection of antique dog collars. The Park and Grounds include the colourful and quintessentially English Culpeper Garden, the delightful Wood Garden, and the terraced Lady Baillie Garden with its views over the tranquil Great Water. An Aviary houses rare and endangered species from around the world and, next to the traditional Greenhouses can be found a Maze with its secret underground grotto.

A highly popular and successful programme of Special Events is arranged throughout the year, details of which can be found opposite.

Owner:

Leeds Castle Foundation

▶ CONTACT

Sandra Barrett
Leeds Castle
Maidstone
Kent   ME17 1PL

Tel: 01622 765400
Fax: 01622 735616

▶ LOCATION
OS Ref. TQ835 533

From London to A20/M20/J8, 40m, 1 hr. 6m E of Maidstone, ¼ m S of A20.

Rail: BR Connex train and admission. London - Bearsted.

Coach: Nat Express/ Invictaway coach and admission from Victoria.

Air: Gatwick 45m. Heathrow 65m.

Channel Tunnel: 25m.

Channel Ports: 38m.

Culpeper Garden

CONFERENCE/FUNCTION

ROOM	SIZE	MAX CAPACITY
Fairfax Hall	19.8 x 1m	200
Gate Tower	9.8 x 5.2m	50
Culpeper	7.65 x 7.34m	40
Terrace	8.9 x 15.4m	80

▶ OPENING TIMES

Summer

1 March - 31 October
Daily: 10am - 5pm (last adm).

Winter

1 November - 28 February
Daily: 10am - 3pm (last adm.)
(closed Christmas Day).

Also special private tours for pre-booked groups at any other time by appointment.

Castle & Grounds closed 29 Jun & 6 July prior to the Open Air Concerts.

▶ ADMISSION

Valid 1 Mar - 31 Oct 2002
Castle, Park & Gardens
Adult £11.00
Child (4 -15yrs) £7.50
OAP/Student £9.50
Family (2+3) £32.00
Disabled Visitors
Adult £6.00
Child (4 -15yrs) £5.50
Groups (15+)
Adult £8.50
Child (4 -15yrs) £6.50
OAP/Student £7.50

Valid 1 Nov - 28 Feb 2003
Castle, Park & Gardens
Adult £9.50
Child (4 -15yrs) £6.00
OAP/Student £8.00
Family (2+3) £27.00
Disabled Visitors
Adult £5.50
Child (4 -15yrs) £5.00
Groups (15+)
Adult £7.00
Child (4 -15yrs) £6.00
OAP/Student £6.50

A guidebook is published in English, French, German, Dutch, Spanish, Italian and Japanese.

Residential conferences, exhibitions, sporting days, clay shooting, falconry, field archery, golf, croquet and heli-pad. Talks can be arranged for horticultural, viticultural, historical and cultural groups. No radios.

Corporate hospitality, large scale marquee events, wedding receptions, buffets and dinners.

Land train for elderly/disabled, wheelchairs, wheelchair lift, special rates. WC.

Two restaurants and a tearoom, group lunch menus. Refreshment kiosks.

Guides in rooms. French, Spanish, Dutch, German, Italian and Russian speaking guides.

Free parking.

Welcome, outside normal opening hours, private tours. Teacher's resource pack.

LEEDS CASTLE...

Open Air Concerts

Fall Fun for Families

Lady Baillie Exhibition

Autumn Gold

Grand Firework Spectacular

Festival of English Food & Wine

Christmas at the Castle

Balloon & Vintage Car Weekend

SPECIAL EVENTS

DEC 27 2001 - JAN 1 2002
New Year Treasure Trail

JAN 19 - FEB 28
Lady Baillie Exhibition

FEB 9 - 17
Half Term Theatre for Children

MAR 29 - APR 7
Easter Holiday Fun

APR 16 - 21
Spring Gardens Week & Flower Festival

MAY 11/12
Festival of English Food & Wine

JUN 1 - 9
Golden Jubilee Week

JUN 29 & JUL 6
Open Air Classical Concerts

JUL 3
Children's Prom Concert

SEPT 7/8
The Great Leeds Castle Balloon & Vintage Car Weekend

OCT 9 - 13
Autumn Gold Flower Festival

OCT 26 - NOV 1
Fall Fun for Families

NOV 2
Grand Firework Spectacular

DEC 16 - 24
Christmas at the Castle

Spring Gardens Week

Easter Holiday Fun

Children's Prom

PENSHURST PLACE & GARDENS

NR TONBRIDGE

www.penshurstplace.com

Penshurst Place is one of England's greatest family-owned stately homes with a history going back six and a half centuries.

In some ways time has stood still at Penshurst; the great House is still very much a medieval building with improvements and additions made over the centuries but without any substantial rebuilding. Its highlight is undoubtedly the medieval Barons' Hall, built in 1341, with its impressive 60ft-high chestnut-beamed roof.

A marvellous mix of paintings, tapestries and furniture from the 15th, 16th and 17th centuries can be seen throughout the House, including the helm carried in the state funeral procession to St Paul's Cathedral for the Elizabethan courtier and poet, Sir Philip Sidney, in 1587. This is now the family crest.

GARDENS

The Gardens, first laid out in the 14th century, have been developed over successive years by the Sidney family who first came to Penshurst in 1552. A twenty-year restoration and re-planting programme undertaken by the late Viscount De L'Isle has ensured that they retain their historic splendour. He is commemorated with a new Arboretum, planted in 1991. The gardens are divided by a mile of yew hedges into "rooms", each planted to give a succession of colour as the seasons change. There is also a Venture Playground, Woodland Trail and Toy Museum together with a Gift Shop and Plant Centre. A special exhibition in 2002 commemorates 450 years of the Sidney family at Penshurst Place.

Owner:
Viscount De L'Isle

CONTACT

Bonnie Vernon
Penshurst Place
Penshurst
Nr Tonbridge
Kent TN11 8DG

Tel: 01892 870307
Fax: 01892 870866

e-mail: enquiries
@penshurstplace.com

LOCATION

OS Ref. TQ527 438

From London M25/J5
then A21 to
Hildenborough,
B2027 via Leigh;
from Tunbridge Wells
A26, B2176.

Visitors entrance at SE
end of village,
S of the church.

Bus: Maidstone &
District 231, 232, 233
from Tunbridge Wells.

Rail: Charing Cross/
Waterloo - Hildenborough,
Tonbridge or Tunbridge
Wells; then taxi.

Product launches, garden parties, photography, filming, fashion shows, receptions, archery, clay pigeon shooting, falconry, parkland for hire, lectures on property, its contents and history. Conference facilities. Adventure playground & parkland & riverside walks. No photography in house.

Private banqueting, wedding receptions.

Limited, disabled and elderly may alight at entrance. WC.

Licensed tearoom (waitress service can be booked by groups of 20+).

Mornings only by arrangement, lunch/dinner can be arranged. Out of season tours by appointment. Guided tours of the gardens.

Ample. Double decker buses to park from village.

All year by appointment, discount rates, education room and packs.

Guide dogs only

OPENING TIMES

Summer
From 2 March
weekends only.
23 March - 3 November

House
Daily, 12 noon - 5.30pm
Last entry 5pm.

Grounds
Daily, 10.30am - 6pm.

Shop & Plant Centre
10.30am - 6pm.

Winter
Open to Groups by
appointment only
(see Guided Tours).

ADMISSION

House & Grounds
Adult £6.50
Child* £4.50
Conc. £6.00
Family (2+2) £18.00
Groups (20+)
Adult £6.00

Garden only
Adult £5.00
Child* £4.00
OAP £4.50
Family (2+2) £15.00

Garden Season
Ticket £30.00

House Tours (pre-booked)
Adult £7.00
Child £4.00

Garden Tours (pre-booked)
Adult £8.00
Child £5.00

House & Garden £10.00

* Aged 5-16yrs; under 5s Free.

CONFERENCE/FUNCTION

ROOM	SIZE	MAX CAPACITY
Sunderland Room	45' x 18'	100
Barons' Hall	64' x 39'	250
Buttery	20' x 23'	50

SQUERRYES COURT & GARDENS 🏛

WESTERHAM

www.squerryes.co.uk

Squerryes Court is a beautiful 17th century manor house which has been the Warde family home since 1731. It is surrounded by 10 acres of attractive and historic gardens which include a lake, restored parterres and an 18th century dovecote. Squerryes is 22 miles from London and easily accessible from the M25. There are lovely views and peaceful surroundings. Visitors from far and wide come to enjoy the atmosphere of a house which is still lived in as a family home.

There is a fine collection of Old Master paintings from the Italian, 17th century Dutch and 18th century English schools, furniture, porcelain and tapestries all acquired or commissioned by the family in the 18th century. General Wolfe of Quebec was a friend of the family and there are items connected with him in the Wolfe Room.

GARDENS

These were laid out in the formal style but were re-landscaped in the mid 18th century. Some of the original features in the 1719 Badeslade print survive. The family have restored the formal garden using this print as a guide. The garden is lovely all year round with bulbs, wild flowers and woodland walks, azaleas, summer flowering herbaceous borders and roses.

Owner:
John St A Warde Esq

▶ CONTACT

Mrs Vale or Mrs Warde
Squerryes Court
Westerham
Kent TN16 1SJ

Tel: 01959 562345
or 01959 563118

Fax: 01959 565949

e-mail: squerryes.court
@squerryes.co.uk

▶ LOCATION

OS Ref. TQ440 535

Off the M25/J6, 6m,
E along A25 ¹/₂ m SW
of Westerham

London 1-1¹/₂ hrs.

Rail: Oxted Station 4m.
Sevenoaks 6m.

Air: Gatwick,
30 mins.

© Clive Boursnell

▶ OPENING TIMES

Summer
30 March - 29 September
Wed, Sat, Sun & BH Mon.

Closed: Mon (except BH Mon), Tue, Thur & Fri.

Grounds:
12 noon - 5.30pm
House: 1.30 - 5.30pm
Last admission 5pm.

NB. Pre-booked groups welcome any day except Mondays.

Winter
October - 29 March
Closed.

▶ ADMISSION

House & Garden
Adult	£4.60
Child (under 14yrs)	£2.50
OAP	£4.10
Family (2+2)	£12.00
Groups (20+)	
Adult	£3.90
Child (under 14yrs)	£2.50
OAP	£3.90

House only
Adult	£4.60
Child (under 14yrs)	£2.50
OAP	£4.10
Groups (20+)	
Adult	£3.90
Child (under 14yrs)	£2.50
OAP	£3.90

Garden only
Adult	£3.00
Child (under 14yrs)	£1.50
OAP	£2.90
Family (2+2)	£7.00
Groups (20+, booked)	
Adult	£2.50
Child (under 14yrs)	£1.50
OAP	£2.50

CONFERENCE/FUNCTION
ROOM	SIZE	MAX CAPACITY
Hall	32' x 32'	60
Old Library	20' x 25' 6"	40

🗐 Small. ℹ️ Suitable for conferences, product launches, filming, photography, outside events, garden parties. No photography in house.

🍷 Exclusive entertaining & weddingreceptions(marquee).

♿ Limited access in house and garden, please telephone before visiting.

☕ Teas on open days. Groups must book for lunch or tea. Menus upon request.

🚶 For pre-booked groups (max 55), small additional charge. Owner will meet groups by prior arrangement. Tour time 1 hr.

🅿 Ample. Free teas for drivers and couriers.

🎒 Welcome, cost £1.50 per child, guide provided. Areas of interest: nature walk, ducks and geese.

🐕 On leads, in grounds.

South East - England

THE ARCHBISHOPS' PALACE
Mill Street, Maidstone, Kent ME15 6YE
Tel: 01622 663006   **Fax:** 01622 682451
Owner: Maidstone Borough Council   **Contact:** Operations Manager
Refurbished 14th century Palace used as a resting place for Archbishops travelling from London to Canterbury.
Location: OS Ref. TQ760 555. On the banks of River Medway SW of the centre of Maidstone.
Open: Daily: 10am - 4.30pm.
Admission: Entrance to 1st floor rooms is free.

BEDGEBURY NATIONAL PINETUM
Goudhurst, Cranbrook, Kent TN17 2SL
Tel: 01580 211044   **Fax:** 01580 212423   **e-mail:** bedgebury@forestry.gsi.gov.uk
Owner: Forestry Commission   **Contact:** Mr Colin Morgan
Location: OS Ref. TQ714 337 (gate on B2079). 7m E of Tunbridge Wells on A21, turn N on B2079 for 1m.
Open: All year: daily, 10am - dusk or 7pm.
Admission: Adult £3, Child £1.50, OAP £2.50.

BELMONT 🏛
BELMONT PARK, THROWLEY, FAVERSHAM ME13 0HH
www.faversham.org/attractions/belmont.html

Tel: 01795 890202   **Fax:** 01795 890042   **e-mail:** belmontadmin@btconnect.com
Owner: Harris (Belmont) Charity   **Contact:** Mr J R Farmer
Belmont is a charming late 18th century country mansion by Samuel Wyatt, set in delightful grounds, including a recently restored 2 acre kitchen garden and a greenhouse. The seat of the Harris family since 1801 it is beautifully furnished and contains interesting items from India and Trinidad as well as the unique clock collection formed by the 5th Lord.
Location: OS Ref. TQ986 564. 4½ m SSW of Faversham, off A251.
Open: 1 Apr - 30 Sept: Sats, Suns & BHs, 2 - 5pm. Last admission to house 4.30pm. Groups (20+) on other days by appointment.
Admission: House & Garden: Adult £5.25, Child £2.50, Conc. £4.75. Groups (20+): Adult £4.75, Child £2.50. Garden: Adult £2.75, Child £1. No discount for groups.
ℹ️ No photography in house. 📷 🎁 ♿ Partial. WC. 🐕 🗝 Obligatory. 🅿 🚫

English Heritage Photo Library: Skyscan Balloon Photography

DEAL CASTLE ⌗
VICTORIA ROAD, DEAL, KENT CT14 7BA
www.english-heritage.org.uk

Tel: 01304 372762
Owner: English Heritage   **Contact:** The Custodian
Crouching low and menacing, the huge, rounded bastions of this austere fort, built by Henry VIII, once carried 119 guns. A fascinating castle to explore, with long, dark passages, battlements and a huge basement. The interactive displays and exhibition give a fascinating insight into the Castle's history.
Location: OS Ref. TR378 521. SE of Deal town centre.
Open: 29 Mar - 30 Sept: daily, 10am - 6pm. 1 - 31 Oct: 10am - 5pm. 1 Nov - 31 Mar: Wed - Sun only, 10am - 4pm. Closed 24 - 26 Dec & 1 Jan.
Admission: Adult £3.20, Child £1.60, Conc. £2.40.
📷 ♿ Restricted. 🎧 🅿 Coach parking on main road. 🐕 Guide dogs only. ✳ 🎁 Tel for details.

DICKENS CENTRE - EASTGATE HOUSE
High Street, Rochester, Medway ME1 1EW
Tel: 01634 844176   **Fax:** 01634 844676
Owner: Medway Council   **Contact:** Head Custodian
Much altered late 16th century brick house, now containing the Dickens Centre, with exhibits of his life and works, including his best known characters. At the rear is Dickens' prefabricated chalet, brought from Switzerland.
Location: OS Ref. TQ746 683. N side of Rochester High Street, close to the Eastern Road. 400yds SE of the Cathedral.
Open: 1 Apr - 30 Sept: 10am - 6pm (last admission 5.15pm). 1 Oct - 31 Mar: 10am - 4pm (last admission 3.15pm). Advisable for groups to book.
Admission: Adult £3.70, Child/Student £2.60, OAP £2.70, Family (2+2) £10. Groups (20+): Adult £3.10, Conc. £2.10. Prices valid until 31 Mar 2002.

DODDINGTON PLACE GARDENS 🏛
Doddington, Sittingbourne, Kent ME9 0BB
Tel: 01795 886101
Owner: Mr & Mrs Richard Oldfield   **Contact:** Mrs Richard Oldfield
10 acres of landscaped gardens in an area of outstanding natural beauty.
Location: OS Ref. TQ944 575. 4m N from A20 at Lenham or 5m SW from A2 at Ospringe, W of Faversham. Signposted.
Open: From Easter - Sept: Sun 2 - 5pm. Tues, Wed, Thurs & BHs 10.30am - 5pm. Groups at other times by appointment.
Admission: Adult £3.50, Child 75p. Groups: £3. Coaches by prior arrangement.

DYMCHURCH MARTELLO TOWER ⌗

Dymchurch, Kent
Tel: 01304 211067 **www.**english-heritage.org.uk
Owner: English Heritage **Contact:** Dover Castle Site Manager
Built as one of 74 such towers to counter the threat of invasion by Napoleon, Dymchurch is perhaps the best example in the country. Fully restored. You can climb to the roof which is dominated by an original 24-pounder gun complete with traversing carriage.
Location: OS189, Ref. TR102 294. In Dymchurch, access from High Street.
Open: Please telephone 01304 211067 for details.
Admission: Adult £1.20, Child 50p, Conc. 90p.

EASTBRIDGE HOSPITAL OF ST THOMAS

High Street, Canterbury, Kent CT1 2BD
Tel: 01227 471688 **Fax:** 01227 781641 **e-mail:** eastbridge@freeuk.com
www.eastbridgehospital.co.uk **Contact:** Louise Fittall
Medieval pilgrims' hospital with 12th century undercroft, refectory and chapel.
Location: OS189, Ref. TR148 579. S side of Canterbury High Street.
Open: Easter - Sept: Mon - Sat, 10am - 5pm, includes Greyfriars Franciscan Chapel House and Garden.
Admission: Adult £1, Child 50p, Conc. 75p.

Goodnestone Park Gardens

NT Photographic Library / Jerry Harpur

EMMETTS GARDEN ❀

IDE HILL, SEVENOAKS, KENT TN14 6AY

Tel: 01732 868381 (office) **info:** 01732 866368 **e-mail:** kchxxx@smtp.ntrust.org.uk
Owner: The National Trust **Contact:** The Property Manager
(Chartwell & Emmetts Garden, Mapleton Road, Westerham, Kent TN16 1PS)
Influenced by William Robinson, this charming and informal garden was laid out in the late 19th century, with many exotic and rare trees and shrubs from across the world. Wonderful views across the Weald of Kent – with the highest treetop in Kent. There are glorious shows of daffodils, carpets of bluebells, azaleas and rhododendrons, then acers and cornus in autumn, also a rose garden and rock garden.

Location: OS Ref. TQ477 524. 1½ m N of Ide Hill off B2042. M25/J5, then 4m.
Open: 23 Mar - 30 Jun: Wed - Sun, Good Fri & BH Mons. 3 Jul - 3 Nov: Sats, Suns & Weds, 11am - 5pm. Last admission 4.15pm.
Admission: Adult £3.50, Child £1.75, Family £8.75.

⬜ ♿ Steep in places. WC. Buggy from car park to garden entrance.
🖼 🐕 In grounds, on leads. 🏨 Tel: 01892 891001.

FINCHCOCKS

See page 118 for full page entry.

THE FRIARS - RETREAT HOUSE

Aylesford Priory, Aylesford, Kent ME20 7BX
Tel: 01622 717272 **Fax:** 01622 715575
e-mail: friarsreception@hotmail.com **www.**carmelite.org
Owner: Carmelite Friars **Contact:** Margaret Larcombe
A peaceful, tranquil retreat house with 100 beds, set in 42 acres of lovingly tended grounds. Outstanding ceramic works of art by Adam Kossowski. Visitors are invited to picnic in the grounds, visit the tearooms situated in the restored 17th century Barn, which also houses the gift and bookshops. While you are there do call into the pottery and the upholsterers' workshops.
Location: OS Ref. TQ724 588. W end of Aylesford village. 3m NW of Maidstone.
Open: Grounds open Summer & Winter, 24 hrs, 365 days.
Admission: No charge.
⬜ 🍽 ♿ Partial. 🖼 👶 By arrangement. 🅿 🖼 🐕 Guide dogs only. 🎫 ❄

Website Information
◁ ◁ ◁ pg 39

GODINTON HOUSE & GARDENS

GODINTON PARK, ASHFORD, KENT TN23 3BP

Tel: 01233 620773 **Fax:** 01233 632652 **e-mail:** ghpt@godinton.fsnet.co.uk

Owner: Godinton House Preservation Trust   **Contact:** Mr D Bickle

Jacobean House incorporating medieval hall, Tudor staircase and later additions, the carving, furniture, porcelain and contrasting decoration reflect its fascinating history. Topiary, terraces, ponds, herbaceous borders, new greenhouse, delphinium border, clematis collection, massed daffodils, wildflowers, fine trees, Italian, walled and formal gardens are surrounded by the famous yew hedge.

Location: OS Ref. TQ981 438. Godinton Lane, 2m NW of Ashford, off A20 (opposite Hare & Hounds public house).

Open: Gardens: 16 Mar - 6 Oct: Thur - Mon, 2 - 5.30pm (dusk if earlier). House: 29 Mar - 6 Oct: Fris, Sats & Suns, 2 - 5.30pm. Last tour of house 4.30pm. Booked groups at other times.

Admission: House & Gardens: Adult £5, Child £2. Garden only: Adult £2, Child £1.

ℹ️No photography in house. Groups must book. 👥 ♿Partial. WC.
🖥️When house open. 🚶Obligatory (house only). 🅿️ 🏠 Guide dogs only.

GREAT COMP GARDEN

COMP LANE, PLATT, BOROUGH GREEN, KENT TN15 8QS

www.greatcomp.co.uk

Tel: 01732 886154

Owner: R Cameron Esq   **Contact:** Mr W Dyson

One of the finest gardens in the country, comprising ruins, terraces, tranquil woodland walks and sweeping lawns with a breathtaking collection of trees, shrubs, heathers and perennials, many rarely seen elsewhere. The truly unique atmosphere of Great Comp is further complemented by its Festival of Chamber Music held in July/September.

Location: OS Ref. TQ635 567. 2m E of Borough Green, B2016 off A20. First right at Comp crossroads. 1/2 m on left.

Open: 1 Apr - 31 Oct: daily, 11am - 6pm.

Admission: Adult £3.50, Child £1. Groups (20+) £3, Annual ticket: Adult £10, OAP £7.

👥 ♿ 🖥️Teas daily. 🏠Guide dogs only. ⬛

GOODNESTONE PARK GARDENS 🏛️

GOODNESTONE PARK, Nr WINGHAM, CANTERBURY, KENT CT3 1PL

Tel/Fax: 01304 840107

Owner: The Lord & Lady FitzWalter   **Contact:** Lady FitzWalter

The garden is approximately 14 acres, set in 18th century parkland. There are many fine trees, a woodland area and a large walled garden with a collection of old-fashioned roses, clematis and herbaceous plants. Jane Austen was a frequent visitor, her brother Edward having married a daughter of the house.

Location: OS Ref. TR254 544. 8m ESE of Canterbury, 1 1/2 m E of B2046, at S end of village. The B2046 runs from the A2 to Wingham, the gardens are signposted from this road.

Open: 25 Mar - 25 Oct: Suns, 12 noon - 6pm. Weekdays (except Tue & Sat), 11am - 5pm. Closed Tues & Sats. House open by appointment, at any time, to groups (20+) at £1.80.

Admission: Adult £3.30, Child (under 12yrs) 50p, OAP £2.80, Student £1.50, Family (2+2) £5. Wheelchair users £1. Groups (20+): Adult £3. Guided groups: House £2, Garden £4.50.

👥 ♿ 🖥️ 🏠

GREAT MAYTHAM HALL

ROLVENDEN, CRANBROOK, KENT TN17 4NG

www.cha.org.uk

Tel: 01580 241346 **Fax:** 01580 241038

Managed by: Country Houses Association   **Contact:** The Administrators

Built in 1910 by Lutyens and set in 18 acres, the house has some fine features including an arched clock-house that frames the entrance. The walled garden inspired Frances Hodgson Burnett to write her children's classic 'The Secret Garden'. The house has been converted into apartments for active retired people.

Location: OS Ref. TQ848 306. 1/2 m S of Rolvenden village, on road to Rolvenden Layne. Stations: Headcorn 10m, Staplehurst 10m.

Open: 1 May - 30 Sept: Wed & Thur, 2 - 5pm.

Admission: Adult £4 Child £2. Groups by arrangement.

🍽️ ❌ 🛏️2 single & 1 double with bathroom. CHA members only.

GROOMBRIDGE PLACE GARDENS

See page 119 for full page entry.

HALL PLACE & GARDENS

Bourne Road, Bexley, Kent DA5 1PQ

www.hallplaceandgardens.com

Tel: 01322 526574 **Fax:** 01322 522921 **e-mail:** martin@hallplaceandgardens.com

Managed by: Bexley Heritage Trust **Contact:** Mr Martin Purslow

A fine Grade I listed country house built c1537 for Lord Mayor of London Sir John Champneis. The house stands at the centre of award winning gardens with magnificent topiary and herbaceous borders, on the banks of the River Cray at Bexley. The house boasts a Tudor Great Hall and minstrels gallery and many period rooms including vaulted long gallery and magnificent drawing room with a fine 17th century plaster ceiling. The house is open to the public with free exhibitions year round.

Location: OS Ref. TQ502 743. On the A2 less than 5m from the M25/J2 (London bound).

Open: Daily. Mon - Sat, 10am - 5pm, Sun, 11am - 5pm. Closed Sun from 1 Nov - end Feb.

Admission: Free. Pre-arranged groups(10+): Adult £3.50, Child £1.50.

House, lift & WC. Licensed. Licensed. By arrangement. Guide dogs only. Tel for details.

HEVER CASTLE & GARDENS

See pages 120/121 for double page entry.

HIGHAM PARK, HOUSE & GARDENS

Bridge, Canterbury, Kent CT4 5BE

Tel/Fax: 01227 830830 **e-mail:** highampark@aol.com

Owner/Contact: Patricia P Gibb

Passionately restored classical stately home and landscape. Original home of the famous Chitty Chitty Bang Bang racing cars.

Location: OS Ref. TR193 538. Off A2 at SE end of Bridge, 3m SE of Canterbury.

Open: 31 Mar - end Sept: Sun - Thur. Garden: 11am - 5pm. House: Tours at 12.30pm, 2.30pm (times may vary). Groups by arrangement.

Admission: Garden: Adult £3, Child £1, OAP £2.50. Groups (20+): Adult £2.50. Guided groups (20+): £3.50. House Tours: £2.

HOLE PARK

Rolvenden, Cranbrook, Kent TN17 4JB

Tel: 01580 241251/241344 (answer phone) **Fax:** 01580 241882

Owner/Contact: D G W Barham

A 15 acre garden with all year round interest, set in beautiful parkland with fine views. Trees, lawns and extensive yew hedges precisely cut are a feature. Walled garden with mixed borders, pools and water garden. Natural garden with bulbs, azaleas, rhododendrons and flowering shrubs. Bluebell walk and autumn colours a speciality.

Location: OS Ref. TQ830 325. 1m W of Rolvenden on B2086 Cranbrook road.

Open: 14 & 28 Apr; 5 & 19 May; 2 & 16 Jun; 21 Jul; 13 & 20 Oct for NGS. Also Mon & Wed in Apr - end Jun & Oct. 2 - 6pm.

Admission: Adult £3.50, Child 50p. Booked groups (15+): £3.

21 Jul. Groups only. By arrangement.

IGHTAM MOTE

See page 122 for full page entry.

KNOLE

See page 123 for full page entry.

LEEDS CASTLE & GARDENS

See pages 124/125 for double page entry.

LESNES ABBEY

Abbey Road, Abbey Wood, London DA17 5DL

Tel: 01322 526574

Owner: Bexley Council **Contact:** Mr Martin Purslow

The Abbey was founded in 1178 by Richard de Lucy as penance for his involvement in events leading to the murder of Thomas à Becket. Today only the ruins remain.

Location: OS Ref. TQ479 788. In public park on S side of Abbey Road (B213), 500yds E of Abbey Wood Station, ³/₄ m N of A206 Woolwich - Erith Road.

Open: Any reasonable time.

Admission: Free.

LULLINGSTONE CASTLE

Lullingstone Castle, Eynsford, Kent DA4 0JA

Tel: 01322 862114 **Fax:** 01322 862115 **Owner/Contact:** Guy Hart Dyke Esq

Fine state rooms, family portraits and armour in beautiful grounds. The 15th century gatehouse was one of the first ever to be made of bricks.

Location: OS Ref. TQ530 644. 1m S Eynsford W side of A225. 600yds S of Roman Villa.

Open: May - Aug: Sats, Suns & BHs, 2 - 6pm. Booked groups by arrangement.

Admission: Adult £5, Child £2, Conc. £4, Family £10. Groups (25+) 10% discount.

No interior photography. Partial. Teas at visitor centre, 1km. By arrangement. Limited.

Accommodation Index ◁ ◁ ◁ pg 27

English Heritage Photo Library

LULLINGSTONE ROMAN VILLA

LULLINGSTONE LANE, EYNSFORD, KENT DA4 0JA

www.english-heritage.org.uk

Tel: 01322 863467

Owner: English Heritage **Contact:** The Custodian

Recognised as one of the most exciting archaeological finds of the century, the villa has splendid mosaic floors and one of the earliest private Christian chapels. Take the free audio tour and discover how the middle-class owners lived, worked and entertained themselves.

Location: OS Ref. TQ529 651. ¹/₂ m SW of Eynsford off A225, M25/J3. Follow A20 towards Brands Hatch. 600yds N of Castle.

Open: 29 Mar - 30 Sept: daily, 10am - 6pm. 1 - 31 Oct: 10am - 5pm. 1 Nov - 31 Mar: 10am - 4pm. Closed 24 - 26 Dec & 1 Jan.

Admission: Adult £2.80, Child £1.40, Conc. £2.10.

Ground floor & grounds. WC. Tel for details.

South East - England

MAISON DIEU ⌗
Ospringe, Faversham, Kent
Tel: 01795 534542   www.english-heritage.org.uk
Owner: English Heritage   **Contact:** The Faversham Society
This forerunner of today's hospitals remains largely as it was in the 16th century with exposed beams and an overhanging upper storey.
Location: OS Ref. TR002 608. In Ospringe on A2, ¹/₂ m W of Faversham.
Open: 3 Apr - 31 Oct: Weekends & BHs, 2 - 5pm. Keykeeper in Winter.
Admission: Adult £1, Child 50p, OAP 80p.

MILTON CHANTRY ⌗
New Tavern Fort Gardens, Gravesend, Kent
Tel: 01474 321520   www.english-heritage.org.uk
Owner: English Heritage   **Contact:** Gravesend Borough Council
A small 14th century building which housed the chapel of the leper hospital and the chantry of the de Valence and Montechais families and later became a tavern and in 1780 part of a fort.
Location: OS Ref.TQ652 743. In New Tavern Fort Gardens ¹/₄ m E of Gravesend off A226.
Open: 1 Mar - 23 Dec: Wed - Sun & BH Mons, 10am - 4pm. Closed Jan & Feb.
Admission: Adult £1.50, Child 75p, Conc. 75p.

MOUNT EPHRAIM GARDENS 🏛
Hernhill, Faversham, Kent ME13 9TX
Tel: 01227 751496 **Fax:** 01227 750940
Owner: Mr & Mrs E S Dawes & Mrs M N Dawes   **Contact:** Mrs L Dawes
8 acres of superb gardens set in the heart of family run orchards.
Location: OS Ref.TR065 598. In Hernhill village, 1m from end of M2. Signed from A2 & A299.
Open: Apr: Suns only. May - end Sept: Mons, Weds, Thurs, Sats & Suns, 1 - 6pm. Groups at all times Mar - end Oct, by arrangement.
Admission: Adult £3, Child £1. Groups: £2.50.

OLD SOAR MANOR ✥
Plaxtol, Borough Green, Kent TN15 0QX
Tel: 01732 810378 **Info Line:** 01732 811145
Owner: The National Trust   **Contact:** The Property Manager
Location: OS Ref.TQ619 541. Plaxtol, Borough Green, Kent.
Open: 6 Apr - 29 Sept: daily except Fri, including BHs & Good Fri, 10am - 6pm.
Admission: Free.

OWL HOUSE GARDENS
Lamberhurst, Kent TN3 8LY

Tel: 01892 890230 **Fax:** 01892 891222   **Contact:** Angela Kelso
The Owl House is a small timber-framed cottage, a former haunt of wool smugglers (not open to the public). Surrounding it are 13 acres of gardens, with spring flowers, azaleas, rhododendrons, roses, shrubs and ornamental fruit trees. The sweeping lawns lead to lovely woodlands of oak, elm and beech and sunken water gardens.
Location: OS Ref. TQ665 372. 8m SE of Tunbridge Wells; 1m from Lamberhurst off A21.
Open: Gardens only: All year, daily, 11am - 6pm, except 25 Dec & 1 Jan.
Admission: Adult £4, Child £1. Coach parties welcome.
▣ ▤ 🔲 ▤ P Free. 🐕On leads. ❋

OWLETTS ✥
The Street, Cobham, Gravesend, Kent DA12 3AP
Tel: 01892 890651 (Regional Office)
Owner: The National Trust   **Contact:** The Property Manager
Location: OS Ref.TQ665 687. 1m S of A2 at W end of village.
Open: Owletts is closed during 2002.

PENSHURST PLACE & GARDENS   *See page 126 for full page entry.*

QUEBEC HOUSE ✥
Westerham, Kent TN16 1TD
Tel: 01892 890651
Owner: The National Trust   **Contact:** Regional Office
General Wolfe spent his early years in this gabled, red-brick 17th century house. Four rooms containing portraits, prints and memorabilia relating to Wolfe's family and career are on view. In the Tudor stable block is an exhibition about the Battle of Quebec (1759) and the parts played by Wolfe and his adversary, the Marquis de Montcalm.
Location: OS Ref. TQ449 541. At E end of village, on N side of A25, facing junction with B2026, Edenbridge Road.
Open: 2 Apr - 29 Oct: Suns & Tues, 2 - 6pm, last admission 5.30pm.
Admission: Adult £2.60, Child £1.30, Family (2+3) £6.50. Groups £2.20.

QUEX HOUSE & GARDEN & POWELL COTTON MUSEUM 🏛
Quex Park, Birchington, Kent CT7 0BH
Tel: 01843 842168 **e-mail:** powell-cotton-museum@virgin.net
Owner: Trustees of Powell Cotton Museum   **Contact:** John Harrison
Regency/Victorian country residence, walled gardens and Victorian explorers' museum.
Location: OS Ref. TR308 683. ¹/₂ m from Birchington Church via Park Lane.
Open: Please contact Museum for details.
Admission: Summer: Adult £4, Child, OAP, Disabled & Carer £3, Student £2.50, Family (2+3) £12. Winter: Adult £3, Child, OAP, Disabled & Carer £2.50, Family (2+3) £8.

RECULVER TOWERS & ROMAN FORT ⌗
Reculver, Herne Bay, Kent
Tel: 01227 740676 www.english-heritage.org.uk
Owner: English Heritage   **Contact:** Reculver Country Park
This 12th century landmark of twin towers has guided sailors into the Thames estuary for seven centuries. Walls of a Roman fort, which were erected nearly 2,000 years ago.
Location: OS Ref. TR228 694. At Reculver 3m E of Herne Bay by the seashore.
Open: Any reasonable time. External viewing only.
Admission: Free.

Hole Park Garden

David Winston, Period Piano Company

RESTORATION HOUSE 🏛
17 - 19 CROW LANE, ROCHESTER, KENT ME1 1RF

Tel: 01634 848520 **Fax:** 01634 880058

Owner: R Tucker & J Wilmot **Contact:** Robert Tucker

Unique survival of an ancient city mansion deriving its name from the stay or Charles II on the eve of The Restoration. Beautiful interiors with exceptional early paintwork related to decorative scheme 'run up' for Charles' visit. The house also inspired Dickens to situate Miss Havisham here.

Poetic old rooms contain fine English furniture and pictures (Mytens, Kneller, Dahl, Reynolds and several Gainsboroughs). Charming interlinked walled gardens of ingenious plan in a classic English style. A private gem.

'There is no finer pre-civil war town house in England than this' - Simon Jenkins, _The Times_.

Location: OS Ref. TQ744 683. Historic centre of Rochester, off High Street, opposite the Vines Park.

Open: 6 Jun - 27 Sept: Thurs & Fris, 10am - 5pm.

Admission: Adult £4.50 (includes 24 page illustrated guidebook), Child £2. Booked groups (12+): Adult £4, Child £2.

ℹ No stiletto heels. No photography in house. ♿Unsuitable. 🎨By arrangement. 🅿 None. ⓗ Guide dogs only.

RICHBOROUGH ROMAN FORT ⚜
Richborough, Sandwich, Kent CT13 9JW
Tel: 01304 612013 **www**.english-heritage.org.uk

Owner: English Heritage **Contact:** The Custodian

This fort and township date back to the Roman landing in AD43. The fortified walls and the massive foundations of a triumphal arch which stood 80 feet high still survive. The inclusive audio tour and the museum give an insight into life in Richborough's heyday as a busy township.

Location: OS Ref. TR324 602. $1^{1}/_{2}$ m NW of Sandwich off A257.

Open: 29 Mar - 30 Sept: daily, 10am - 6pm. 1 - 31 Oct: 10am - 5pm. 1 - 31 Nov: Wed - Sun only, 10am - 4pm. Weekends only in Dec, Jan & Feb, 10am - 4pm. 1 - 31 Mar: Wed - Sun, 10am - 4pm. Closed 24 - 26 Dec & 1 Jan.

Admission: Adult £2.80, Child £1.40, Conc. £2.10.

ℹ Museum. 📷 ♿ Ground floor. 🔊 🅿 ⓗ Guide dogs only. ❋ ⓥ Tel for details.

RIVERHILL HOUSE 🏛
Sevenoaks, Kent TN15 0RR
Tel: 01732 458802/452557 **Fax:** 01732 458802

Owner: The Rogers Family **Contact:** Mrs Rogers

Small country house built in 1714, home of the Rogers family since 1840. Panelled rooms, portraits and interesting memorabilia. Historic hillside garden with extensive views, rare trees and shrubs. Sheltered terraces and rhododendrons and azaleas in a woodland setting. Bluebells.

Location: OS Ref. TQ541 522. 2m S of Sevenoaks on E side of A225.

Open: Garden: Easter - end Jun: Weds, Suns, BH weekends & 4 Jun, 12 noon - 6pm. Coaches by arrangement. House: open only to pre-booked groups of adults (20+) on any day: Apr, May & Jun.

Admission: Adult £3, Child 50p. Pre-booked groups: £4.

ℹ Conferences. 📷 ♿Unsuitable. ● 🎨By arrangement. 🐕

ROCHESTER CASTLE ⚜
The Lodge, Rochester-upon-Medway, Medway ME1 1SX
Tel: 01634 402276

Owner: English Heritage (Managed by Medway Council) **Contact:** Head Custodian

Built in the 11th century. The keep is over 100 feet high and with walls 12 feet thick.

Location: OS Ref. TQ743 685. By Rochester Bridge (follow A2 eastwards), M2/J1 & M25/J2.

Open: 29 Mar - 30 Sept: daily, 10am - 6pm. 1 - 31 Oct: daily, 10am - 5pm. 1 Nov - 31 Mar: daily, 10am - 4pm. Closed 24 - 26 Dec & 1 Jan.

Admission: Please telephone for details.

ROCHESTER CATHEDRAL
Garth House, The Precinct, Rochester, Kent ME1 1SX
Tel: 01634 401301 **Fax:** 01634 401410

e-mail: rochester_cathedral@yahoo.co.uk **www**.rochester.anglican.org

Founded in 604AD, Rochester Cathedral has been a place of Christian worship for nearly 1,400 years. The present building is a blend of Norman and gothic architecture with a fine medieval crypt. In the cloister are the remains of the 12th century chapter house and priory. A focal point is the Doubleday statue.

Location: OS Ref. TQ742 686. Signposted from M20/J6 and on the A2/M2/J3. Best access from M2/J3.

Open: All year: 8.30am - 5pm. Visiting may be restricted during services.

Admission: Donation up to £3/Adult. Guided groups: £3, please book on above number. Separate prices for schools.

ℹ Photography permit £1. 📷 ♿ ● 🎨By arrangement. 🔊 🅿 ▣ 🐕 ❋

ROMAN PAINTED HOUSE
New Street, Dover, Kent CT17 9AJ
Tel: 01304 203279

Owner: Dover Roman Painted House Trust **Contact:** Mr B Philp

Discovered in 1970. Built around 200AD as a hotel for official travellers. Impressive wall paintings, central heating systems and the Roman fort wall built through the house.

Location: OS Ref. TR318 414. Dover town centre. E of York St.

Open: Apr - Sept: 10am - 5pm, except Mons.

Admission: Adult £2, Child/OAP 80p.

ROYDON HALL
Nr Tonbridge, Kent TN12 5NH
Tel: 01622 812121 **Fax:** 01622 813959 **e-mail:** roydonhall@btinternet.com

Owner: Maharishi Foundation **Contact:** The Events Manager

Roydon Hall is a very fine Tudor manor house which was 'modified' by the Victorians.

Location: OS Ref. TQ664 518. From M20/J2 or M26/J2A, follow B2016 SSE towards Paddock Wood. 600m beyond A26 roundabout, turn left into narrow lane. 500m beyond church.

Open: Available for film location work and corporate events. Bed and breakfast accommodation also.

ST AUGUSTINE'S ABBEY ⊞

Longport, Canterbury, Kent CT1 1TF

Tel: 01227 767345   **www**.english-heritage.org.uk

Owner: English Heritage   **Contact:** The Custodian

The Abbey, founded by St Augustine in 598, is a World Heritage Site. Take the free interactive audio tour which gives a fascinating insight into the Abbey's history and visit the museum displaying artifacts uncovered during archaeological excavations of the site.

Location: OS Ref. TR154 578. In Canterbury 1/2 m E of Cathedral Close.

Open: 29 Mar - 30 Sept: daily, 10am - 6pm. 1 - 31 Oct: 10am - 5pm. 1 Nov - 31 Mar: daily, 10am - 4pm. Closed 24 - 26 Dec & 1 Jan.

Admission: Adult £3, Child £1.50, Conc. £2.30. 15% discount for groups (11+). One extra place for every additional 20.

⊡ ⅃ Grounds. WC. ⬛ ⌂ Free. ⬛ Guide dogs only. ❋ ⊡ Tel for details.

ST JOHN'S COMMANDERY ⊞

Densole, Swingfield, Kent

Tel: 01483 252000

Owner: English Heritage   **Contact:** The South East Regional Office

A medieval chapel built by the Knights Hospitallers. It has a moulded plaster ceiling and a remarkable timber roof and was converted into a farmhouse in the 16th century.

Location: OS Ref. TR232 440. 2m NE of Densole on minor road off A260.

Open: Any reasonable time for exterior viewing. Internal viewing by appointment only.

Admission: Free.

Civil Wedding Venues
◁ ◁ ◁ pgs 28-29

Doddington Place Gardens

NT Photographic Library / Jenny Harpur

SCOTNEY CASTLE GARDEN ❧

LAMBERHURST, TUNBRIDGE WELLS, KENT TN3 8JN

Tel: 01892 891081   **Fax:** 01892 890110   **e-mail:** kscxxx@smtp.ntrust.org.uk

Owner: The National Trust   **Contact:** Administrative Assistant

One of England's most romantic gardens designed by Edward Hussey in the picturesque style. Dramatic vistas from the terrace of the new Scotney Castle, built in the 1830s, lead down to the ruins of a 14th century moated castle. Rhododendrons, kalmia, azaleas and wisteria flower in profusion. Roses and clematis scramble over the remains of the Old Castle, which is open for the summer. In autumn the garden's glowing colours merge with the surrounding woodlands where there are many country walks to be explored.

Location: OS Ref. TQ688 353. Signed off A21 1m S of Lamberhurst village.

Open: 23 Mar - 3 Nov: Wed - Sun & BHs (closed Good Fri), 11am - 6pm. Last admission 5pm or dusk. Car park: All year for estate walks.

Admission: Adult £4.40, Child £2.20, Family (2+3) £11. Pre-booked groups weekdays £3.80.

⊡ ⅃ Grounds (but steep parts). ⬛ Outside garden only, on leads. ❋

© NT Photographic Library / Eric Crichton

SISSINGHURST CASTLE GARDEN ❧

SISSINGHURST, CRANBROOK, KENT TN17 2AB

Tel: 01580 710700 **Infoline:** 01580 710701 **e-mail:** ksixxx@smtp.ntrust.org.uk
Owner: The National Trust   **Contact:** The Administration Assistant
One of the world's most celebrated gardens, the creation of Vita Sackville-West and her husband Sir Harold Nicolson. Developed around the surviving parts of an Elizabethan mansion with a central red-brick prospect tower, a series of small, enclosed compartments, intimate in scale and romantic in atmosphere, provide outstanding design and colour throughout the season. The study, where Vita worked, and library are also open to visitors.
Location: OS Ref. TQ807 383. 2m NE of Cranbrook, 1m E of Sissinghurst village (A262).
Open: 23 Mar - 3 Nov: Mon, Tue & Fri, 11am - 6.30pm; Sat, Sun, BHs & Good Fri, 10am - 6.30pm. Last admission 1 hour before closing or ¹/₂ hr before dusk if earlier.
Admission: Adult £6.50, Child £3, Family (2+3) £16, NT members Free.

© NT Photographic Library / David Sellman

SMALLHYTHE PLACE ❧

TENTERDEN, KENT TN30 7NG

Tel: 01580 762334 **Fax:** 01580 762334 **e-mail:** ksmxxx@smtp.ntrust.org.uk
Owner: The National Trust   **Contact:** The Custodian
This early 16th century half-timbered house was home to Shakespearean actress Ellen Terry from 1899 to 1928. The house contains many personal and theatrical mementoes including many of her lavish costumes. The charming cottage grounds include her rose garden and the Barn Theatre, which is open most days by courtesy of the Barn Theatre Society.
Location: OS Ref. TQ893 300. 2m S of Tenterden on E side of the Rye road B2082.
Open: 23 Mar - 3 Nov: daily except Thurs & Fris (open Good Fri), 11am - 5pm, last admission 4.30pm.
Admission: Adult £3.20, Child £1.60, Family £8.
ℹ️No photography in house. ♿Unsuitable. 🅿 Limited. ❧

SOUTH FORELAND LIGHTHOUSE ❧
& GATEWAY TO THE WHITE CLIFFS
Langdon Cliffs, Nr Dover, Kent CT16 1HJ
Tel: 01304 202756 **Fax:** 01304 207326 **e-mail:** kwcxxx@smtp.ntrust.org.uk
Owner: The National Trust   **Contact:** Countryside Manager
The Gateway to the White Cliffs is a visitor centre with spectacular views across the English Channel.
Location: OS138 Ref. TR336 422. Follow White Cliffs brown signs from roundabout 1m NE of Dover at junction of A2/A258.
Open: Gateway: 1 Mar - 31 Oct: daily 10am - 5pm. 1 Nov - 28 Feb: daily 11am - 4pm. Lighthouse: 1 Mar - 31 Oct: daily except Tues & Weds, 11am - 5.30pm (last adm. 5pm).
Admission: Adult £1.80, Child 90p. Groups: Adult £1.50, Child 75p.

SPRIVERS GARDEN ❧
Horsmonden, Kent TN12 8DR
Tel: 01892 890651 (Regional Office)
Owner: The National Trust   **Contact:** The Property Manager
A small formal garden with walled and hedged compartments, herbaceous borders and a rose garden.
Location: OS Ref. TQ6940. 3m N of Lamberhurst on B2162.
Open: 25 May, 1 & 22 Jun, 2 - 5pm, last admission 4.30pm.
Admission: Adult £2, Child £1, Family £5. Groups £1.50.

SQUERRYES COURT 🏛
& GARDENS   *See page 127 for full page entry.*

STONEACRE ❧
Otham, Maidstone, Kent ME15 8RS
Tel: 01622 862871 **Fax:** 01622 862157
Owner: The National Trust   **Contact:** The Tenant
A half-timbered mainly late 15th century yeoman's house, with great hall and crownpost, and restored cottage-style garden.
Location: OS Ref. TQ800 535. In narrow lane at N end of Otham village, 3m SE of Maidstone, 1m S of A20.
Open: 23 Mar - 16 Oct: Weds, Sats & BHs, 2 - 6pm. Last admission 5pm.
Admission: Adult £2.60, Child £1.30, Family (2+3) £6.50. Groups £2.20.

TEMPLE MANOR ⚏
Strood, Rochester, Kent
Tel: 01634 827980 **www**.english-heritage.org.uk
Owner: English Heritage   **Contact:** Medway Council
The 13th century manor house of the Knights Templar which mainly provided accommodation for members of the order travelling between London and the Continent.
Location: OS Ref. TQ733 686. In Strood (Rochester) off A228.
Open: 29 Mar - 30 Sept: weekends & BHs, 10am - 6pm.
Admission: Free.

THE THEATRE ROYAL, CHATHAM
102 High Street, Chatham, Kent ME4 4BY
Tel: 01634 831028
Owner: Chatham Theatre Royal Trust Ltd   **Contact:** The Administrator
Built in 1899, it is Kent's finest surviving Victorian Theatre.
Location: OS Ref. TQ755 679. In Chatham High Street.
Open: Mon - Sat, 10am - 3pm. Guided tours most weekdays. Groups welcome by appointment.
Admission: Donation.

TONBRIDGE CASTLE
Castle Street, Tonbridge, Kent TN9 1BG
Tel: 01732 770929
Owner: Tonbridge & Malling Borough Council   **Contact:** The Administrator
Location: OS Ref. TQ588 466. 300 yds NW of the Medway Bridge at town centre.
Open: All year: Mon - Sat, 9am - 4pm. Suns & BHs, 10.30am - 4pm.
Admission: Gatehouse - Adult £4, Conc £2. Family £9. Admission includes audio tour. Last tour 1 hour before closing.

TUDOR YEOMAN'S HOUSE ❧
Sole Street, Cobham, Kent DA12 3AX
Tel: 01892 890651
Owner: The National Trust   **Contact:** The Property Manager
Location: OS Ref. TQ657 677. Sole Street, Cobham, Kent.
Open: Tudor Yeoman's House is closed for 2002.

South East - England

Open All Year Index
◁ ◁ ◁ pgs 44-48

UPNOR CASTLE ⊞

Upnor, Kent

Tel: 01634 718742

Owner: English Heritage   **Contact:** Medway Council

Well-preserved 16th century gun fort built to protect Queen Elizabeth I's warships. However in 1667 it failed to prevent the Dutch Navy which stormed up the Medway destroying half the English fleet.

Location: OS Ref. TQ758 706. At Upnor, on unclassified road off A228. 2m NE of Strood.

Open: 29 Mar - 30 Sept: daily, 10am - 6pm.

Admission: Please telephone for details.

English Heritage Photo Library

WALMER CASTLE & GARDENS ⊞

WALMER, DEAL, KENT CT14 7LJ

www.english-heritage.org.uk

Tel: 01304 364288

Owner: English Heritage   **Contact:** The Custodian

A Tudor fort transformed into an elegant stately home. The residence of the Lords Warden of the Cinque Ports and still used by HM The Queen Mother today. Take the new free audio tour and see the Duke of Wellington's rooms where he died 150 years ago. Beautiful gardens including the Queen Mother's Garden, The Broadwalk with its famous yew tree hedge, Kitchen Garden and Moat Garden. Lunches and cream teas available in the delightful Lord Warden's tearooms.

Location: OS Ref. TR378 501. S of Walmer on A258, M20/J13 or M2 to Deal.

Open: 29 Mar - 30 Sept: daily, 10am - 6pm. 1 - 31 Oct: daily, 10am - 5pm. 1 Nov - 31 Dec & 1 - 31 Mar: Wed - Sun only, 10am - 4pm. Jan & Feb: Sats & Suns, 10am - 4pm. Closed 24 - 26 Dec & 1 Jan and when Lord Warden is in residence.

Admission: Adult £5, Child £2.50, Conc. £3.80, Family £12.50. 15% discount for groups (11+). One extra place for each additional 20. EH members free.

⬛ ♿ Grounds. 🖼 🎧 🐕 Guide dogs only. ❋ 🛏 Tel for details.

Stoneacre

WILLESBOROUGH WINDMILL

Mill Lane, Willesborough, Ashford, Kent

Tel: 01233 661866

130 year old restored smock mill.

Location: OS Ref. TR031 421. Off A292 close to M20/J10. At E end of Ashford.

Open: Apr - end Sept; Sats, Suns and BH Mons, 2 - 5pm or dusk if earlier.

Admission: Adult £1, Child/Conc. 50p. Groups 10% reduction by arrangement only.

YALDING ORGANIC GARDENS

Benover Road, Yalding, Maidstone, Kent ME18 6EX

Tel: 01622 814650 **Fax:** 01622 814 650

Owner: HDRA - the organic organisation   **Contact:** Christopher Madge

Fourteen newly created gardens reflecting mankind's experience of gardening over the centuries.

Location: OS Ref. TQ698 492. 6m SW of Maidstone, 1/2 m S of village at Yalding on B2162.

Open: Apr: w/ends only, 10am - 5pm. May - Sept: Wed - Sun, 10am - 5pm. Oct: w/ends only.

Admission: Adult £3 (no concessions), accompanied Child (up to 16yrs) Free. Groups (14+) £2.50 plus 50p for guided tour.

Patrick Lane

ARDINGTON HOUSE

WANTAGE

www.ardingtonhouse.com

Owner:
The Baring Family

▶ **CONTACT**

Sharon Stader
Ardington House
Wantage
Oxfordshire OX12 8QA

Tel: 01235 821566
Fax: 01235 821151
e-mail: info@
ardingtonhouse.com

▶ **LOCATION**

OS Ref. SU432 883

12m S of Oxford, 12m
N of Newbury,
2½ m E of Wantage.

Just a few miles south of Oxford stands the hauntingly beautiful, gracefully symmetric Ardington House. Surrounded by well-kept lawns, terraced gardens and peaceful paddocks this baroque house is still the private home of the Baring family. You'll find it in the village of Ardington in the lee of the Berkshire Downs close to the Ridgeway, the historic path that runs along the top of the Downs linking the Thames Valley to the Kennet. Its rooms to the south look across the garden and grazing horses to the river, well known to enthusiastic fly fisherman. To the front is an immaculately tended lawn, ideal for croquet and enjoyed by different generations of the Baring family as they grew up in this beautiful setting. Sir John Betjeman, one of the best loved poets of recent times, thought highly of this gracious home. But it doesn't end there because one of the greatest joys in this impressive home is the wood panelled dining room with its large oil painting of the father of the founder of this famous banking family.

The astonishing mixture of history, warmth and style you'll find at Ardington truly does place it in a class of its own.

▶ **OPENING TIMES**

Summer

1 - 3, 6 - 10, 13 - 17, 18,
21 May: 1 - 2, 5 - 9,
12 - 16 Aug & BH Mons,
2.30 - 4.30pm.

▶ **ADMISSION**

House & Gardens

Adult £3.50

ℹ Conferences, product launches, films.

⊤

⬤ Lunches and teas by arrangement for groups.

⚘ By members of the family.

P Free.

♿

⊠ Guide dogs only.

▦

▲

☺ Tel for details.

CONFERENCE/FUNCTION

ROOM	MAX CAPACITY
Imperial Hall	
Theatre Style	80
U shape	30
Cabaret	40
Oak Room	
Theatre Style	40
U shape	20
Cabaret	30
Music Room	
Theatre Style	40
U shape	20
Cabaret	30

BLENHEIM PALACE 🏛

WOODSTOCK

www.blenheimpalace.com

Owner:
The Duke of Marlborough

▶ **CONTACT**

The Administrator
Blenheim Palace
Woodstock OX20 1PX

Tel: 01993 811091
Fax: 01993 813527
e-mail: administration
@blenheimpalace.com

▶ **LOCATION**

OS Ref. SP441 161

From London, M40, A44
(1¹/₂ hrs), 8m NW of
Oxford. London 63m
Birmingham 54.
Air: Heathrow 60m.
Birmingham 54m.
Coach: From London
(Victoria) to Oxford.
Rail: Oxford Station.
Bus: Oxford
(Cornmarket) -
Woodstock.

BLenheim Palace, home of the 11th Duke of Marlborough and birthplace of Sir Winston Churchill, was built between 1705-1722 for John Churchill, 1st Duke of Marlborough, in grateful recognition of his magnificent victory at the Battle of Blenheim in 1704. One of England's largest private houses, it was built in the baroque style by Sir John Vanbrugh and is considered his masterpiece. The land and £240,000 were given by Queen Anne and a grateful nation.

Blenheim's wonderful interior reveals striking contrasts – from the lofty Great Hall to gilded state rooms and the majestic Long Library. The superb collection includes fine paintings, furniture, bronzes and the famous Marlborough Victories tapestries. The five-room Churchill Exhibition includes his birth room.

GARDENS

The Palace grounds reflect the evolution of grand garden design. Of the original work by Queen Anne's gardener, Henry Wise, only the Walled Garden remains; but dominating all is the superb landscaping of 'Capability' Brown. Dating from 1764, his work includes the lake, park and gardens. Achille Duchêne, employed by the 9th Duke, subsequently recreated the Great Court and built the Italian Garden on the east and the Water Terraces on the west of the Palace. Recently the Pleasure Gardens complex has been developed. This includes the Marlborough Maze, Herb Garden, Adventure Playground, Butterfly House and Putting Greens.

▶ **OPENING TIMES**

Summer - Palace
Mid March - 31 October
Daily: 10.30am-5.30pm
Last admission 4.45pm.

Winter - Park only
1 November - Mid March

The Duke of Marlborough reserves the right to close the Palace or Park or to amend admission prices without notice.

▶ **ADMISSION**

- Palace Tour and
  Churchill Exhibition
- Park
- Garden
- Butterfly House
- Herb & Lavender Garden
- Train
- Car or coach parking
- Maze & Adventure Play
  Area optional extras
  Adult £10.00
  Child (5 - 15 yrs.) £5.00
  Child (16 & 17 yrs.) .. £7.50
  OAP £7.50
  Family £26.00
Groups
  Adult £7.70
  OAP/Student £6.70
  Child (5 - 15 yrs.) £4.20
  Child (16 & 17 yrs.) £6.70

- Blenheim Park, Butterfly
  House, Train, Parking,
  (Maze & Adventure Play
  Area optional extras).
  Coaches* £35.00
  Cars* £6.50
  Adult** £2.00
  Child** £1.00

- Winter Rate Park only
  Coaches* £30.00
  Cars* £5.00
  Adult** £1.00
  Child** £0.50

- Private visits† £15.00

* Including occupants.
** Pedestrians.
† By appointment only.
  Min. charge of £375 (mornings
  and £525 (evenings).

CONFERENCE/FUNCTION

ROOM	SIZE	MAX CAPACITY
Orangery		200
Great Hall	70' x 40'	150
Saloon	50' x 30'	72
with Great Hall		450
with Great Hall & Library		750
Library	180' x 30'	300

BLENHEIM PALACE...

📷 Five Shops. ℹ️ Filming, Equestrian Events, Craft Fairs. Will consider any proposals (contact Admin Office). Lake, Golf Buggy rides, Train rides. Photography outside only.

🍸 Corporate hospitality, including dinners and receptions. For the Palace contact the Administrator, & for the Orangery contact Sodexho Prestige tel: 01993 813874/811274.

♿ Visitors may alight at the Palace entrance then park in allocated area. WCs.

🍽️ 2 Restaurants, 2 Cafeterias. Group capacity 150. Groups can book for afternoon tea, buffets and luncheon. Menus on request. Contact Sodexho Prestige for further info: 01993 813874/811274.

🚶 Included in the cost of entry. Private and language tours may be pre-booked.

🅿️ Unlimited for cars and coaches. Advise Administrator's office for groups of over 100. Coaches/groups welcome, without pre-booking. Group organisers guide available by post.

📖 Blenheim has held the Sandford Award for an outstanding contribution to Heritage Education since 1982. Operated by a very experienced headmaster, education groups may study virtually all subjects at all four stages of the National Curriculum as well as have general interest or leisure visits. Tourism Studies (all levels) available.

🐕 Dogs on leads in Park. Guide dogs for the blind & hearing dogs for the deaf only in house and garden.

The Water Terrace

BROUGHTON CASTLE

BANBURY

www.broughtoncastle.demon.co.uk

Owner:
Lord Saye & Sele

▶ **CONTACT**

Mrs J Moorhouse
Broughton Castle
Banbury OX15 5EB

Tel/Fax: 01295 276070
Tel: 01295 722547

e-mail:
admin@broughton
castle.demon.co.uk

▶ **LOCATION**

OS Ref. SP418 382

Broughton Castle is
2¹/₂ m SW of Banbury
Cross on the B4035,
Shipston-on-Stour -
Banbury Road.
Easily accessible from
Stratford-on-Avon,
Warwick, Oxford,
Burford and the
Cotswolds. M40/J11.

Rail: From London/
Birmingham to Banbury.

Broughton Castle is essentially a family home lived in by Lord and Lady Saye & Sele and their family.

The original medieval Manor House, of which much remains today, was built in about 1300 by Sir John de Broughton. It stands on an island site surrounded by a 3-acre moat. The Castle was greatly enlarged between 1550 and 1600, at which time it was embellished with magnificent plaster ceilings, splendid panelling and fine fireplaces.

In the 17th century William, 8th Lord Saye & Sele, played a leading role in national affairs. He opposed Charles I's efforts to rule without Parliament and Broughton became a secret meeting place for the King's opponents.

During the Civil War William raised a regiment and he and his four sons all fought at the nearby Battle of Edgehill. After the battle the Castle was besieged and captured.

Arms and armour for the Civil War and from other periods are displayed in the Great Hall. Visitors may also see the gatehouse, gardens and park together with the nearby 14th century Church of St Mary, in which there are many family tombs, memorials and hatchments.

GARDENS

The garden area consists of mixed herbaceous and shrub borders containing many old roses. In addition, there is a formal walled garden with beds of roses surrounded by box hedging and lined by more mixed borders.

▶ **OPENING TIMES**

Summer

19 May - 11 September
Weds & Suns
2 - 5pm.

Also Thurs in July and
August and all Bank
Holiday Suns and Bank
Holiday Mons
(including Easter)
2 - 5pm.

Groups welcome on
any day and at any time
throughout the year
by appointment.

▶ **ADMISSION**

Adult £5.00
Child (5-15yrs)....... £2.00
OAP/Student £4.00
Groups*
Adult £4.00
Child (5-15yrs)....... £2.00
OAP/Student £4.00

* Min payment: adults £80,
children £50.

  Filming, product launches, advertising features, corporate events in park. Photography permitted for personal use. Brief guidance notes available in French, Spanish, Dutch, Italian, Japanese, German, Polish, Greek & Russian.

Visitors allowed vehicle access to main entrance.

Guided groups should book. Tea, coffee or light lunches available.

Available to pre-booked groups at no extra charge. Not available on open days.

P 300 yards from the castle.

Welcome.

No dogs inside House.

STONOR 🏛

HENLEY-ON-THAMES

www.stonor.com

Stonor, family home of Lord and Lady Camoys and the Stonor family for over 800 years, is set in a valley in the beautiful woods of the Chiltern Hills and surrounded by an extensive deer park.

The earliest part of the house dates from the 12th century, whilst most of the house was built in the 14th century. Early use of brick in Tudor times resulted in a more uniform façade concealing the earlier buildings, and changes to the windows and the roof in the 18th century reflect the Georgian appearance still apparent today.

Inside, the house shows strong Gothic decoration, also from the 18th century, and contains many items of rare furniture, sculptures, bronzes, tapestries, paintings and portraits of the family from Britain, Europe and America.

The Catholic Chapel used continuously through the Reformation is sited close by a pagan stone circle. In 1581 Stonor served as a sanctuary for St Edmund Campion, and an exhibition at the house features his life and work.

John Steane says of Stonor – *'If I had to suggest to a visitor who had only one day to sample the beauties of Oxfordshire I would suggest a visit to Stonor and a walk through its delectable park'.*

GARDENS

Extensive gardens enclosed at the rear of the house face south and have fine views over the park. The springtime display of daffodils is particularly outstanding. Fine irises and roses.

Owner:
Lord & Lady Camoys

▶ CONTACT

The Administrator
Stonor Park
Henley-on-Thames
Oxfordshire RG9 6HF

Tel: 01491 638587

Fax: 01491 639348

e-mail: info@stonor.com

▶ LOCATION

OS Ref. SU743 893

1 hr from London,
M4/J8/9. A4130 to
Henley-on-Thames.
On B480 NW of
Henley. A4130/B480 to
Stonor.

Rail: Henley-on-Thames Station 5m.

▶ OPENING TIMES

Suns & Bank Holiday
Mons: April - September,
2 - 5.30pm

Weds: July & August only:
2 - 5.30pm.

Private groups by
arrangement:
April - September,
Tue - Thur.

▶ ADMISSION

**House, Garden
& Chapel**

Adult £5.50
Child (under 14yrs) .... Free
Groups* (12+)........... £5.00

Garden & Chapel

Adult £3.50

School groups £2.50 per
head, 1 teacher for every
10 children admitted free.

* Min. 12 persons by a single
payment. Private guided tours
£6pp, min. 20 persons and by a
single payment.

School groups £3 per head,
1 teacher for every 10 children
admitted free.

📷 ℹ️ Filming, craft fairs, photo shoots, car displays, product promotion. Evening tours and buffet suppers by prior arrangement. Lectures can be given on the property, its contents and history. No smoking and no photography in house.

♿ Visitors may alight at the entrance before parking. Ramp access to gardens, tearoom & shop. House not suitable.

☕ Open as house. Lunches, teas & suppers by arrangement for groups (20+). Licensed.

🚶 Outside normal hours for 20 - 60 people per tour. Tour time: 1¼ hrs. Single payments for group bookings.

🅿 100 yds away.

🐕 In grounds, on leads.

🛡 Tel for details.

South East - England

26A EAST ST HELEN STREET
Abingdon, Oxfordshire
Tel: 01865 242918
Owner: Oxford Preservation Trust   **Contact:** Ms Debbie Dance
One of best preserved examples of a 15th century dwelling in the area. Originally a Merchant's Hall House with later alterations, features include a remarkable domestic wall painting, an early oak ceiling, traceried windows and fireplaces. The remains of a 17th century boy's doublet found in the roof during restoration works is on display.
Location: OS Ref. SU497 969. 300 yards SSW of the market place and Town Hall.
Open: By prior appointment.
Admission: Free.

ARDINGTON HOUSE 🏛
See page 137 for full page entry.

ASHDOWN HOUSE ⚜
Lambourn, Newbury RG16 7RE
Tel: 01488 72584   **e-mail:** tadgen@smtp.ntrust.org.uk   **www.**nationaltrust.org.uk
Owner: The National Trust   **Contact:** Ashdown Estate Office
An extraordinary Dutch-style 17th century house, perched on the Berkshire Downs and famous for its association with Elizabeth of Bohemia (The Winter Queen), Charles I's sister, to whom the house was 'consecrated'. The interior has an impressive great staircase rising from hall to attic, and important paintings contemporary with the house. There are spectacular views from the roof over the formal parterre, lawns and surrounding countryside, as well as beautiful walks in neighbouring Ashdown Woods.
Location: OS Ref. SU282 820. 3½ m N of Lambourn, on W side of B4000.
Open: Hall, Stairway, Roof & Garden: Apr - end Oct: Weds & Sats. Guided tours of house only at 2.15pm, 3.15pm & 4.15pm from front door. Gardens: 2 - 5pm. Woodland: All year: daily except Fris, dawn - dusk.
Admission: Adult £2.10, Woodland Free. No reduction for groups which must book in writing.
ℹ No WCs. ♿ Garden. 📷 Obligatory. 🅿 250 metres from house.
🐕 Woodland only, on leads. ✳

BLENHEIM PALACE 🏛
See pages 138/139 for double page entry.

BROOK COTTAGE
Well Lane, Alkerton, Nr Banbury OX15 6NL
Tel: 01295 670303/670590
Owner/Contact: Mrs David Hodges
4 acre hillside garden. Roses, clematis, water gardens, colour co-ordinated borders, trees, shrubs.
Location: OS Ref. SP378 428. 6m NW of Banbury, ½m off A422 Banbury to Stratford-upon-Avon road.
Open: 1 Apr - 31 Oct: Mon - Fri, 9am - 6pm. Evenings, weekends and all group visits by appointment.
Admission: Adult £3, OAP £2, Child Free. In aid of National Gardens Scheme.

BROUGHTON CASTLE 🏛
See page 140 for full page entry.

BUSCOT OLD PARSONAGE ⚜
Buscot, Faringdon, Oxfordshire SN7 8DQ
Tel: 01793 762209   **e-mail:** tbcjap@smtp.ntrust.org.uk
Owner: The National Trust   **Contact:** Coleshill Estate Office
An early 18th century house of Cotswold stone on the bank of the Thames with a small garden. No WCs.
Location: OS Ref. SU231 973. 2m from Lechlade, 4m N of Faringdon on A417.
Open: Apr - end Oct, Weds, 2 - 6pm by written appointment with tenant.
Admission: £1.20. Not suitable for groups.
ℹ No WCs.

NTPL / Thames and Chiltern

BUSCOT PARK ⚜
BUSCOT, FARINGDON, OXFORDSHIRE SN7 8BU

www.faringdon-coll.com

Tel: 01367 240786   **Fax:** 01367 241794   **Infoline:** 0845 3453387
e-mail: estbuscot@aol.com
Owner: The National Trust   **Contact:** Lord Faringdon
A late 18th century house with pleasure gardens, set within a park of long avenues and fine Italianate water gardens. Contains the Faringdon collection of fine paintings and furniture.
Location: OS Ref. SU239 973. Between Lechlade and Faringdon on A417.
Open: House & Grounds: 29 Mar - 29 Sept: Wed - Fri. Easter Sat & Sun, plus weekends of 30/31 Mar; 13/14 & 27/28 Apr; 11/12 & 25/26 May; 8/9 & 22/23 Jun; 13/14 & 27/28 Jul; 10/11 & 24/25 Aug; 14/15 & 28/29 Sept. Grounds only: 29 Mar - 29 Sept: Mon (including BH Mon) & Tue, 2 - 6pm.
Admission: House & Grounds Adult £5, Child £2.50. Grounds only: Adult £4, Child £2. Groups must book in writing, or by fax or e-mail.
♿ Unsuitable. ☕ 🐕

CHASTLETON HOUSE ⚜
Chastleton, Moreton-in-Marsh, Gloucestershire GL56 0SU
Tel/Fax: 01608 674355   **Infoline:** 01494 755560   **e-mail:** tchgen@smtp.ntrust.org.uk
Owner: The National Trust   **Contact:** The Custodian
One of England's finest and most complete Jacobean houses, dating from 1612. It is filled with a mixture of rare and everyday objects and the atmosphere of four hundred years of continuous occupation by one family. The gardens have a Jacobean layout and the rules of modern croquet were codified here.
Location: OS Ref. SP248 291. 6m ENE of Stow-on-the-Wold. 1½ m NW of A436. Approach only from A436 between the A44 (W of Chipping Norton) and Stow.
Open: 23 Mar - 2 Nov: Wed - Sat, 1 - 5pm, last admission 4pm. Oct - Nov: Wed - Sat, 1 - 4pm, last admission 3pm. Admission for all visitors (including NT members) by timed tickets booked in advance. Bookings can be made by telephone (01494 755585) on weekdays between 10am - 4pm.
Admission: Adult £5.40, Child £2.70. Family £13.50. Groups (11-25) by appointment.
♿ Unsuitable. 🅿 Coaches limited to 25 seat minibuses. 🐕 Guide dogs only.

CHRIST CHURCH CATHEDRAL
The Sacristy, The Cathedral, Oxford OX1 1DP
Tel: 01865 276154   **Contact:** Mr Jim Godfrey
12th century Norman Church, formerly an Augustinian monastery, given Cathedral status in 16th century by Henry VIII.
Location: OS Ref. SP515 059. Just S of city centre, off St Aldates. Entry via Meadow Gate visitors' entrance on S side of college.
Open: Mon - Sat: 9am - 5pm. Suns: 1 - 5pm, closed Christmas Day. Services: weekdays 7.20am, 6pm. Suns: 8am, 10am, 11.15am & 6pm.
Admission: Adult £4, Child under 5 Free, Conc. £3, Family £6.

COGGES MANOR FARM MUSEUM
Church Lane, Witney, Oxfordshire OX28 3LA

Tel: 01993 772602 **Fax:** 01993 703056

Administered by: West Oxfordshire District Council **Contact:** Clare Pope

The Manor House dates from the 13th century, rooms are furnished to show life at the end of the 19th century. Daily cooking on the Victorian range. On the first floor, samples of original wallpapers and finds from under the floorboards accompany the story of the history of the house. In one of the rooms, rare 17th century painted panelling survives. Farm buildings including two 18th century barns, stables and a thatched ox byre, display farm implements. Traditional breeds of farm animals, hand-milking demonstration each day. Seasonal produce from the walled kitchen garden sold in the museum shop.

Location: OS Ref. SP362 097. Off A40 Oxford - Burford Road. Access by footbridge from centre of Witney, 600 yds. Vehicle access from S side of B4022 near E end of Witney.

Open: Apr - end-Oct: Tue - Fri & BH Mons, 10.30am - 5.30pm; Sat & Sun, 12 - 5.30pm. Closed Good Fri. Early closing in Oct. Limited opening in Nov & Mar.

Admission: Adult £4.20, Child £2.10, Conc. £2.65, Family (2+2) £11.55.

🖬 ⚹ Ground floor. WCs. 🖭 🅿 🖬 In grounds, on leads.

DEDDINGTON CASTLE ⌗
Deddington, Oxfordshire

Tel: 023 9258 1059

Owner: English Heritage **Contact:** Area Manager

Extensive earthworks concealing the remains of a 12th century castle which was ruined as early as the 14th century.

Location: OS Ref. SP471 316. S of B4031 on E side of Deddington, 17m N of Oxford on A423. 5m S of Banbury.

Open: Any reasonable time.

Admission: Free.

DITCHLEY PARK
Enstone, Oxfordshire OX7 4ER

Tel: 01608 677346

Owner: Ditchley Foundation **Contact:** Brigadier Christopher Galloway

The most important house by James Gibbs with most distinguished interiors by Henry Flitcroft and William Kent.

Location: OS Ref. SP391 214. 2m NE from Charlbury. 13m NW of Oxford.

Open: Visits only by prior arrangement with the Bursar.

Admission: £5 per person (minimum charge £40).

Cogges Manor Farm Museum

FAWLEY COURT
HISTORIC HOUSE & MUSEUM, HENLEY-ON-THAMES RG9 3AE

Tel: 01491 574917 **Fax:** 01491 411587

Owner: Marian Fathers **Contact:** The Secretary

Designed by Christopher Wren, built in 1684 for Col W Freeman, decorated by Grinling Gibbons and by James Wyatt. The Museum consists of a library, various documents of the Polish Kings, a very well-preserved collection of historical sabres and many memorable military objects of the Polish army. Paintings, early books, numismatic collections, arms and armour.

Location: OS Ref. SU765 842. 1m N of Henley-on-Thames E to A4155 to Marlow.

Open: May - Oct: Weds, Thurs & Suns, 2 - 5pm. Other dates by arrangement. Closed Whitsuntide and Nov - Apr inclusive.

Admission: House, Museum & Gardens: Adult £4, Child £1.50, Conc. £3. Groups (15+) £3.

🖬 ⚹ Ground floor & grounds. WC 🖭 🖬 Guide dogs only.

GREAT COXWELL BARN

Great Coxwell, Faringdon, Oxfordshire

Tel: 01793 762209   **e-mail:** tbcjap@smtp.ntrust.org.uk

Owner: The National Trust   **Contact:** Coleshill Estate Office

A 13th century monastic barn, stone built with stone tiled roof, which has an interesting timber construction.

Location: OS Ref. SU269 940. 2m SW of Faringdon between A420 and B4019.

Open: All year: daily at reasonable hours.

Admission: 50p.

GREYS COURT

ROTHERFIELD GREYS, HENLEY-ON-THAMES, OXFORDSHIRE RG9 4PG

Infoline: 01494 755564   **Tel:** 01491 628529   **e-mail:** tgrgen@smtp.ntrust.org.uk

Owner: The National Trust   **Contact:** The Property Manager

Rebuilt in the 16th century and added to in the 17th, 18th and 19th centuries, the house is set amid the remains of the courtyard walls and towers of a 14th century fortified house. A Tudor donkey wheel, well-house and an ice house are still intact, and the garden contains Archbishop's Maze, inspired by Archbishop Runcie's enthronement speech in 1980.

Location: OS Ref. SU725 834. 3m W of Henley-on-Thames, E of B481.

Open: 22 Mar - 27 Sept: House; Wed - Fri, BH Mons & 4 Jun, 2 - 6pm (closed Good Fri) Garden: daily Tue - Sat, BH Mons & 4 Jun, 2 - 6pm (closed Good Fri). Last admission 5.30pm.

Admission: House & Garden: Adult £4.80, Child £2.40, Family £12. Garden only: £3.20, Family £8. Coach parties must book in advance.

Grounds partially. WCs. In car park only, on leads. Contact Custodian.

Open All Year Index
◁ ◁ ◁ pgs 44-48

KINGSTON BAGPUIZE HOUSE

ABINGDON, OXFORDSHIRE OX13 5AX

www.kingstonbagpuizehouse.org.uk

Tel: 01865 820259   **Fax:** 01865 821659

Owner: Mr & Mrs Francis Grant   **Contact:** Mrs Francis Grant

A family home, this beautiful house originally built in the 1660s was remodelled in the early 1700s in red brick with stone facings. It has a cantilevered staircase and panelled rooms with some good furniture and pictures. Set in mature parkland, the gardens, including shrub border and woodland garden, contain a notable collection of trees, shrubs, perennials and bulbs planted for year round interest. A raised terrace walk leads to an 18th century panelled gazebo with views of the house and gardens, including a large herbaceous border and parkland. Available for special events, wedding receptions and filming. Facilities for small conferences.

Location: OS Ref. SU408 981. In Kingston Bagpuize village, off A415 Abingdon to Witney road S of A415/A420 intersection. Abingdon 5m, Oxford 9m.

Open: Feb 17,24; Mar 3, 17, 31; Apr 1, 7, 20, 21; May 5, 6, 19; Jun 3, 4, 9, 16, 30; Jul 7, 20, 21, 28; Aug 4, 25, 26, 28; Sept 7, 8, 11, 22; Oct 13; Nov 10. 2 - 5.30pm (tours of the house: 2.30 - 4.30pm). House: guided tours only. Last entry to garden 5pm.

Admission: House & Garden: Adult £4, Child £2.50, (children under 5yrs not admitted to house), OAP £3.50. Gardens: £2. (child under 5yrs Free, not admitted to house). Groups (20-100) by appointment throughout the year, prices on request.

No photography in house. Grounds. WC.

Light meals for groups by appointment. Obligatory tours of house.

Norman Hudson

KINGSTONE LISLE PARK

WANTAGE, OXON OX12 9QG

Tel: 01367 820599   **Fax:** 01367 820749

Owner: Mr James Lonsdale   **Contact:** The Secretary

A sensational Palladian house, set in 140 acres of parkland. Superb views up to the Lambourn Downs. Three lakes beside the house complete this very attractive landscape. The hall, in the style of Sir John Soane, gives a strong impression of entering an Italian palazzo with beautiful ornate plaster ceilings, columns and figurines. In complete contrast the inner hall becomes the classical English country house, the most exciting feature being the Flying Staircase winding its way up, totally unsupported. A fine collection of art, furniture, clocks, glass and needlework, together with the architecture, evoke admiration for the craftsmanship that has existed in Britain over the centuries. 12 acres of gardens. Suitable for films.

Location: OS Ref. SU326 876. M4/J14.

Open: Coach parties only, strictly by appointment.

Admission: Telephone for details.

♿ 🐕 In grounds, on leads. ✳

MAPLEDURHAM HOUSE & WATERMILL

MAPLEDURHAM, READING RG4 7TR

www.mapledurham.co.uk

Tel: 01189 723350   **Fax:** 01189 724016   **e-mail:** mtrust1997@aol.com

Owner: The Mapledurham Trust   **Contact:** Mrs Lola Andrews

Late 16th century Elizabethan home of the Blount family. Original plaster ceilings, great oak staircase, fine collection of paintings and a private chapel in Strawberry Hill Gothick added in 1797. Interesting literary connections with Alexander Pope, Galsworthy's Forsyte Saga and Kenneth Grahame's Wind in the Willows. 15th century watermill fully restored producing flour and bran which is sold in the giftshop.

Location: OS Ref. SU670 767. N of River Thames. 4m NW of Reading, 1½ m W of A4074.

Open: Easter - Sept: Sats, Suns & BHs, 2 - 5.30. Last admission 5pm. Midweek parties by arrangement only (Tue - Thur).

Admission: Please call 01189 723350 for details.

📷 ♿ Grounds. WCs. ▣ 🐕 Guide dogs only. 🏠 11 holiday cottages (all year).

MILTON MANOR HOUSE

MILTON, ABINGDON, OXFORDSHIRE OX14 4EN

Tel: 01235 862321   **Fax:** 01235 831287

Owner: Anthony Mockler-Barrett Esq   **Contact:** Gwendoline Marsh

Dreamily beautiful mellow brick house, traditionally designed by Inigo Jones, with a celebrated Gothick library (pictured on right) and a startling Catholic chapel. Lived in by the family; pleasant, relaxed and informal atmosphere. Park with fine old trees, stables (pony rides usually available); Treehouse in the garden, Stockade in the woods. Walled garden, woodland walk, two lakes, variety of charming annuals and unusual ornaments. Plenty to see and enjoy for all ages.

Location: OS Ref. SU485 924. Just off A34, village and house signposted, 9m S of Oxford, 15m N of Newbury. 3m from Abingdon and Didcot.

Open: 1 - 15 May & 1 - 15 Aug: 2 - 5pm. Guided tours of house: 2pm, 3pm, 4pm. Also all BH weekends: Easter - end Aug: open 12 noon - 5pm. For weddings etc. please write to the Administrator.

Admission: House & Gardens: Adult £4, Child £2. House: Guided tours only. Grounds only: Adult £2.50, Child £1. Special Events will take place on Easter & Aug Bank Holiday weekends (prices up £1 & 50p). Groups by arrangement throughout the year. For group bookings only please write or phone 01235 831871.

🍽 Available. ♿ Grounds. ▣ 🅿 Free. 🐕 Guide dogs only. ✳

MINSTER LOVELL HALL & DOVECOTE ⌗

Witney, Oxfordshire

Tel: 023 9258 1059

Owner: English Heritage   **Contact:** Area Manager

The ruins of Lord Lovell's 15th century manor house stand in a lovely setting on the banks of the River Windrush.

Location: OS Ref. SP324 114. Adjacent to Minster Lovell Church, ½ m NE of village. 3m W of Witney off A40.

Open: Any reasonable time.

Admission: Free.

PRIORY COTTAGES ✄

1 Mill Street, Steventon, Abingdon, Oxfordshire OX13 6SP

Tel: 01793 762209 **e-mail:** tbcjap@smtp.ntrust.org.uk

Owner: The National Trust   **Contact:** Coleshill Estate Office

Former monastic buildings, converted into two houses. South Cottage contains the Great Hall of the original priory.

Location: OS Ref. SU466 914. 4m S of Abingdon, on B4017 off A34 at Abingdon West or Milton interchange on corner of The Causeway and Mill Street, entrance in Mill Street.

Open: The Great Hall in South Cottage only: Apr - end Sept: Weds, 2 - 6pm by written appointment.

Admission: £1.

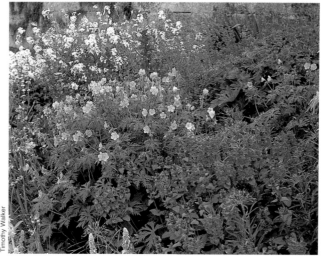

Timothy Walker

University of Oxford Botanic Garden

Plant Sales Index
◁ ◁ ◁ pgs 36-37

ROUSHAM HOUSE

Nr STEEPLE ASTON, BICESTER, OXFORDSHIRE OX25 4QX

www.rousham.org

Tel: 01869 347110/07860 360407

Owner/Contact: Charles Cottrell-Dormer Esq

Rousham represents the first stage of English landscape design and remains almost as William Kent (1685 - 1748) left it. One of the few gardens of this date to have escaped alteration. Includes Venus' Vale, Townesend's Building, seven-arched Praeneste, the Temple of the Mill and a sham ruin known as the 'Eyecatcher'. The house was built in 1635 by Sir Robert Dormer.

Location: OS Ref. SP477 242. E of A4260, 12m N of Oxford, S of B4030, 7m W of Bicester.

Open: House: Apr - Sept: Wed, Sun and BH Mon 2 - 4.30pm. Garden: All year: daily, 10am - 4.30pm.

Admission: House: £3. Garden: Adult £3. No children under 15yrs.

♿ Partial. 🅵Obligatory. 🅿 ✄ ❄

Timothy Walker

RYCOTE CHAPEL ♯
Rycote, Oxfordshire

Tel: 023 9258 1059 **www.**english-heritage.org.uk

Owner: English Heritage   **Contact:** Area Manager

A 15th century chapel with exquisitely carved and painted woodwork. It has many intriguing features, including two roofed pews and a musicians' gallery.

Location: OS165 Ref. SP667 046. 3m SW of Thame, off A329. 1½ m NE of M40/J7.

Open: 29 Mar - 30 Sept: Fri - Sun & BHs, 2 - 6pm.

Admission: Adult £2, Child £1, Conc. £1.30. 15% discount for groups (11+).

Timothy Walker

UNIVERSITY OF OXFORD BOTANIC GARDEN
ROSE LANE, OXFORD OX1 4AZ

Tel/Fax: 01865 286690 **e-mail:** postmaster@botanic-garden.ox.ac.uk

Owner: University of Oxford   **Contact:** Timothy Walker

Founded in 1621; oldest botanic garden in Britain; 8,000 plants from all over the world; original walled garden; many trees over 200 years old; herbaceous borders, recently renovated rock and bog gardens; national collection of euphorbias, tropical glasshouses including a 100 year old cacti and waterlillies; a peaceful oasis in the city centre.

Location: OS Ref. SP520 061. E end of High Street, on the banks of the River Cherwell.

Open: Apr - Sept: 9am - 5pm (glasshouses: 10am - 4.30pm). Oct - Mar: 9am - 4.30pm (glasshouses: 10am - 4pm). Closed 25 Dec & Good Fri. Last admission 4.15pm.

Admission: Adult £2, Child (under 12ys) Free.

ⓘ WCs for disabled only. 🚻 📖 By arrangement. 🅿 None. ◼
🐕 Guide dogs only. ✳

STANTON HARCOURT MANOR 🏛
STANTON HARCOURT, Nr WITNEY, OXFORDSHIRE OX29 5RJ

Tel: 01865 881928 **Answerphone/Fax:** 01865 880117

Owner/Contact: The Hon Mrs Gascoigne

12 acres of garden with Great Fish Pond and Stew Ponds provide tranquil surroundings for the unique mediaeval buildings, Old Kitchen (Alexander) Pope's Tower and Domestic Chapel. The house, a fine example of a very early unfortified Manor House built to house the Harcourt family and its retainers, is still maintained as the family home.

Location: OS Ref. SP416 056. 9m W of Oxford, 5m SE of Witney off B4449 between Eynsham and Standlake.

Open: Mar 31; Apr 1, 11, 14, 25, 28; May 2, 5, 6, 16, 19, 30; Jun 2, 3, 13, 16, 27, 30; Jul 11, 14, 25, 28; Aug 8, 11, 22, 25, 26; Sept 5, 8, 19, 22: 2 - 6pm.

Admission: House & Garden: Adult £5, Child (under 12yrs)/OAP £3. Garden: Adult £3, Child (under 12yrs) /OAP £2. Group visits and access to the upper floors of Popes Tower by prior arrangement.

🚻 ◼ 🅿 Limited. 🐕 Guide dogs in grounds.

STONOR 🏛   *See page 141 for full page entry.*

See page 141 for full page entry.

SWALCLIFFE BARN
Swalcliffe Village, Banbury, Oxfordshire

Tel: 01295 788278   **Contact:** Jeffrey Demmar

15th century half cruck barn, houses agricultural and trade vehicles.

Location: OS Ref. SP378 378. 6m W of Banbury Cross on B4035.

Open: Easter - end Oct: Suns & BHs, 2 - 5pm.

Admission: Free.

WATERPERRY GARDENS
WATERPERRY, Nr WHEATLEY, OXFORDSHIRE OX33 1LB

Tel: 01844 339226 **Fax:** 01844 339883

e-mail: office@waterperrygardens.f.s.net.co.uk **www.**waterperrygardens.co.uk

Owner: School of Economic Science   **Contact:** P Maxwell

Here is the chance to enjoy the order of careful cultivation. See one of Britain's finest herbaceous borders which flowers continually from May to October. Rose garden; alpine gardens, formal garden, shrub borders, perennial borders and river walk.

Location: OS Ref. SP630 063. Oxford 9m, London 52m M40/J8, Birmingham M40/J8A 42m. Well signposted locally.

Open: Apr - Oct: 9am - 5.30pm. Nov - Mar: 9am - 5pm. Closed during Art in Action Festival.

Admission: Adult £3.50, Child £2 (under 10yrs Free), OAP £3. Groups (20+) £2.90, Child £1.50.

🔲 ✳ 🚻 Partial. ◼ 📖 By arrangement. 🅿 Limited for coaches. ◼
🐕 In grounds, on leads. ✳

Website Information
◁ ◁ ◁   pg 39

Website Information pg 39

THE COLLEGES OF OXFORD & CAMBRIDGE UNIVERSITIES

OXFORD

All Souls College (founded 1438)
Porter's Lodge, High Street OX1 4AL
tel: 01865 279379
Mon - Fri, 2 - 4pm (winter), 2 - 4.30pm (summer).
Free. Only one group of 6 (max) at any one time

Balliol College (founded 1263)
Porter's Lodge, Broad Street
tel: 01865 277777
Daily, 2 - 5pm. £1.

Brasenose College (founded 1509)
Radcliffe Square
tel: 01865 277830
Daily, 10 - 11.30am, 2 - 5pm. Commercial
groups only, dependent on the size of the party,
please contact the college for details.
Charge to individual visitors £1 at Easter only.

Christ Church (founded 1546)
St Aldate's, enter via Meadow Gate OX1 1DP
tel: 01865 276150
Daily, 8am - 6pm. £3 adult, £2 senior /student/
child (under 7 yrs free); family (2 adults +
children) £6. Large groups must book in advance.

Corpus Christi College (founded 1517)
Porter's Lodge, Merton Street
tel: 01865 276700
Afternoons only. Free.

Exeter College (founded 1314)
Porter's Lodge, Turl Street OX1 3DP
tel: 01865 279600; fax: 01865 279630
Daily, 2 - 5pm. Free.
Large groups must book in advance.

Harris Manchester College
Mansfield Road
tel: 01865 241514
Chapel only open, 5.30am - 5.30pm. Free.

Hertford College (founded 1284, 1740 & 1874)
Porter's Lodge, Catte Street OX1 3BW
tel: 01865 279400; fax: 01865 279437
Daily, 9am - 5pm (not over lunch). Free.
Maximum 10 per group.

Jesus College (founded 1571)
Turl Street
tel: 01865 279700
Daily, 10.30am (for pre-booked groups),
2 - 4.30pm (groups and individuals). Free.

Keble College (founded 1868)
Porter's Lodge, Parks Road
tel: 01865 272727
Daily, 2 - 5pm. Free. Groups of 20+ must book.

Kellogg College
Wellington Square
tel: 01865 270360
Mon - Fri, 9am - 5pm. Free

Lady Margaret Hall (founded 1878)
Porter's Lodge, Norham Gardens
tel: 01865 274300
Daylight hours. Free. Large groups should notify
Porter's Lodge in advance.

Lincoln College (founded 1427)
Porter's Lodge, Turl Street
tel: 01865 279800
Daily, 2 - 5pm. Free. Tour groups by prior
application to the Steward.

Magdalen College (founded 1458)
High Street OX1 4AU
tel: 01865 276000; fax: 01865 276103
Daily, 2 - 6pm (until 25 June), 12 - 6pm
(25 June - 30 Sept). Adults £2.50, others £1.25,
pre-booked groups £1 per person.

Mansfield College (founded 1886)
Porter's Lodge, Mansfield Road
tel: 01865 270999
Daily, 9am - 5pm. Free. Please notify the Porter's
Lodge in advance of your visit.

Merton (founded 1264)
Merton Street OX1 4JD
tel: 01865 276310; fax: 01865 276361
Mon - Fri, 2 - 4pm, Sat - Sun, 10am - 4pm. Free.
Groups of 5+ must book in advance and be
accompanied by a Blue Badge Guide

New College (founded 1379)
New College Lane

Nuffield College (founded 1937)
Porter's Lodge, New Road
tel: 01865 278500
Daily, 9am - 5pm. Free. No large groups.

Oriel College (founded 1326)
Oriel Square OX1 4EW
tel: 01865 276555; fax: 01865 276532
Daily, 2 - 5pm. Free

Pembroke College (founded 1624)
Porter's Lodge, St Aldate's
tel: 01865 276444
Daylight hours, by prior appointment with Head
Porter only. Free.

The Queen's College (founded 1340)
High Street OX1 4AW
tel: 01865 279120; fax: 01865 790819

Daily, 2 - 5pm. £3.50 (Set by Tourist Information
rather than the college, by appointment only and
only if accompanied by an official guide from the
TIC, Gloucester Green).

St Catherine's College
Manor Road
tel: 01865 271700
Daily, 8am - 5pm. Free

St Edmund Hall (founded 1270)
Queen's Lane OX1 4AR
tel: 01865 279000
Daily, 11am - 6pm. Free. Groups must either
book in advance or be acommpanied by an
accredited guide. No groups admitted before
noon during Trinity Term.

St Hilda's College
Cowley Place
tel: 01865 276884
Daily, 2 - 5pm. Free.

St John's College (founded 1555)
St Giles' OX1 3JP
tel: 01865 277300; fax: 01865 277435
Daily, 1pm-5pm. Free

St Peter's College
New Inn Hall Street
tel: 01865 278900
Daily, 2 - 5pm. Free. No large groups

Somerville College
Woodstock Road
tel: 01865 270600
Daily, 2 - 5.30pm. Free. Advance booking
required for groups, who may also visit in the
morning by prior appointment.

Trinity College (founded 1554)
Main Gate, Broad Street OX1 3BH
tel: 01865 277300; fax: 01865 279898
10.30am - 12pm, 2 - 5pm (Apr - Oct), 10.30am -
12pm, 2 - 4pm (Nov - Mar). £2 (adults), special
rates for groups (approx 80p pp), £1 senior
citizens/students/children; no charge to citizens of
Oxford.

University College founded (1249)
Porter's Lodge, High Street OX1 4BH

Wadham College (founded 1610)
Parks Road
tel: 01865 277900
Term time: 10am - 11.45am, 1 - 4.30pm (last entry
4.15pm). Vacation: 1 - 4.30pm. Free. Groups of
4+ may only enter if accompanied by a Blue
Badge Guide and by pre-arranged appointment.
No group to exceed 20 people. Tours every 15
minutes.

Wolfson College
Linton Road
tel: 01865 274100
Daily, 9am - 5pm. Free. Advance booking
required for groups of 10 or more (contact the
Domestic Bursar on 01865 274071).

Worcester College (1714)
Porter's Lodge, Worcester Street OX1 2HB
tel: 01865 278300; fax: 01865 278387
Daily, 2 - 5pm. Free. Max 6 people in a group,
unless by prior arrangement in writing, with the
Bursar.

For further details contact: Oxford Information Centre, The Old School, Gloucester Green, Oxford OX1 2DA. Tel: 01865 726871 Fax: 01865 240261

CAMBRIDGE

Christ's College (founded 1505)
Porter's Lodge, St Andrew's Street CB2 3BU
tel: 01223 334900; fax: 01223 334967

Clare College (founded 1326)
Trinity Lane

Corpus Christi College (founded 1352)
Porter's Lodge, Trumpington Street CB2 1RH
tel: 01223 338000; fax: 01223 338061

Downing College (founded 1800)
Regent Street CB2 1DQ
tel: 01223 334800; fax: 01223 467934

Emmanuel College (founded 1584)
Porter's Lodge, St Andrew's Street CB2 3AP
tel: 01223 334200; fax: 01223 334426
Gonville & Caius College (founded 1348)
Porter's Lodge, Trinity Street CB2 1TA
tel: 01223 332400

Jesus College (founded 1496)
Porter's Lodge, Jesus Lane CB5 8BL
tel: 01223 339339

King's College (founded 1441)
Porter's Lodge, King's Parade CB2 1ST
tel: 01223 331212; fax: 01223 331315

Magdalene College (founded 1542)
Porter's Lodge, Magdalene Street

Newnham College (founded 1871)
Sidgewick Avenue
Pembroke College (founded 1347)
Trumpington Street

Peterhouse (founded 1284)
Porter's Lodge, Trumpington Street CB2 1RD
tel: 01223 338200; fax: 01223 337578

Queen's College (founded 1448)
Porter's Lodge, Silver Street CB3 9ET
tel: 01223 335511; fax: 01223 335566

Sidney Sussex College (founded 1596)
Porter's Lodge, Sidney Street CB2 3HU
tel: 01223 338800; fax: 01223 338884

St Catharine's College (founded 1473)
Porter's Lodge, Trumpington Street

St John's College (founded 1511)
Tourist Liaison Office, St John Street CB2 1TP

Trinity College (founded 1546)
Porter's Lodge, Trinity Street

For further details contact: Cambridge TIC, The Old Library, Wheeler Street, Cambridge CB2 3QB. Tel: 01223 322640 Fax: 01223 457549

Visitors, whether indivually or as a group, wishing to gain admittance to the Colleges (meaning the Courts, not to the staircases & students' rooms) are advised to contact the relevant city's Tourist Offices for further information. It should be noted that Halls normally close for lunch (12 - 2pm) and many are not open during the afternoon. Chapels may be closed during services. Libraries are not normally open, and Gardens do not usually include the Fellows' garden. Visitors, and especially guided groups, should always call on the Porters Lodge first.

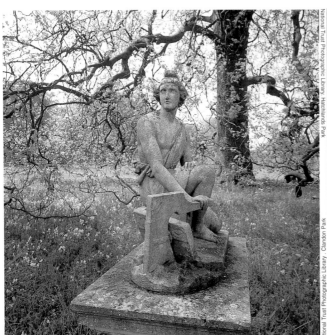

National Trust Photographic Library, Hatchlands Park

National Trust Photographic Library, Clandon Park

CLANDON PARK/ 🌳 HATCHLANDS PARK

GUILDFORD

www.nationaltrust.org.uk/regions/southern

Owner:
The National Trust

▶ **CONTACT**

The Property Manager
Clandon Park/
Hatchlands Park
East Clandon
Guildford
Surrey GU4 7RT

Tel: 01483 222482
Fax: 01483 223176
e-mail: shagen@
smtp.ntrust.org.uk

Clandon Park & Hatchlands Park were built during the 18th century and are set amidst beautiful grounds. They are two of England's most outstanding country houses and are only five minutes' drive apart.

Clandon Park is a grand Palladian mansion, built c1730 by the Venetian architect, Leoni and notable for its magnificent two-storey marble hall. The house is rightly acclaimed for its remarkable collection of 18th century porcelain, textiles and furniture, which includes the Ivo Forde Meissen collection of Italian comedy figures and a series of Mortlake tapestries. The attractive gardens feature a parterre, grotto, Dutch garden and a Maori house with a fascinating history. Clandon is also

home to the Queen's Royal Surrey Regiment Museum. The excellent restaurant is renowned for its Sunday lunches - booking is advisable.

Hatchlands Park was built in 1758 for Admiral Boscawen and is set in a beautiful 430 acre Repton park offering a variety of park and woodland walks. Hatchlands contains splendid interiors by Robert Adam, decorated in appropriately nautical style. It houses the Cobbe Collection, the world's largest group of early keyboard instruments associated with famous composers, eg Purcell, J C Bach, Chopin, Mahler, Elgar and Marie Antoinette. There is also a small garden by Gertrude Jekyll flowering from late May to early July.

The Cobbe Collection of historic keyboard instruments can be seen at Hatchlands Park. Concerts and tours take place throughout the season. Both Beethoven and Schubert owned pianos made by Graf, the maker of the piano shown on the right, and many instruments in the collection were owned or played by great composers, including Chopin, Mahler and Elgar.

The Cobbe Collection Trust
Hatchlands Park

Tel: 01483 211474
Fax: 01483 225922
www.cobbecollection.co.uk

Piano by Conrad Graf, Vienna, c.1820.

Clive Barda, London

▶ **LOCATION**

Clandon
OS Ref. TQ042 512
At West Clandon
on the A247,
3m E of Guildford.

Rail: Clandon BR 1m.

Hatchlands
OS Ref. TQ063 516
E of East Clandon
on the A246 Guildford -
Leatherhead road.

Rail: Clandon BR
2¹/₂ m, Horsley 3m.

▶ **OPENING TIMES**

Clandon - House
24 March - 3 November
Tue - Thur, Suns &
BH Mons, Good Fri
& Easter Sat
11am - 5pm.

Garden
As house: 9am - dusk.

Museum
April - October
Tue - Thur & Suns,
BH Mons, Good Fri
& Easter Sat
12 noon - 5pm.

Hatchlands - House
1 April - 31 October
Tue - Thur,
Suns & BH Mon,
Fris in August only.
2 - 5.30pm.

Park Walks
Daily (April - October)
11am - 6pm. Trail leaflets.

▶ **ADMISSION**

Clandon
Adult £6.00
Child £3.00
Family £15.00
Groups (Tue - Thur only)
Adult £5.00

Hatchlands
Adult £6.00
Park Walks £2.50
Child £3.00
Park Walks £1.25
Family £15.00
Groups (Tue - Thur only)
Adult £5.00

Combined ticket
Clandon/Hatchlands . £9.00
Child £4.50
Family £22.50

CONFERENCE/FUNCTION

ROOM	SIZE	MAX CAPACITY
Marble Hall Clandon Pk	40' x 40'	160 seated 200 standing

ℹ️ Clandon Park. Tel: 01483 222482. No photography.

🍽 For Clandon wedding receptions Tel: 01483 224912.

♿ Hatchlands suitable. Clandon partially suitable. WCs.

☕ Hatchlands: 01483 211120.

🍴 Licensed. Clandon: 01483 222502. H'lands 01483 211120.

🐾 Clandon - by arrangement.

🎧 Hatchlands only.

Children's quizzes available.

🅿️ 🐕 Guide dogs only.

🔔 Clandon only.   🎭 01483 225804.

South East - England

Crown Copyright: Historic Royal Palaces

HAMPTON COURT PALACE

SURREY

www.hrp.org.uk

Managed by:
Historic Royal Palaces

▶ **CONTACT**

Hampton Court Palace
Surrey
KT8 9AU

For all enquiries
please telephone:
020 8781 9500

▶ **LOCATION**

OS Ref. TQ155 686

From M25/J15 and
A312, or M25/J12 and
A308, or M25/J10 and
A307.

Rail: From London
Waterloo direct to
Hampton Court
(32 mins).

Hampton Court Palace was built by Cardinal Wolsey and has been a favoured home to royalty from Henry VIII to George II. Today, with complimentary costumed guided tours and audio guides, and an exciting programme of special events, it promises a magical journey back through 500 years of royal history.

The palace's vast Tudor kitchens offer an insight into domestic life at the Palace, and are laid out as if a feast were being prepared, and at Christmas, are brought to life, as dishes are created by historic chefs using authentic techniques.

The State Apartments of Henry VIII feature some of the most magnificent rooms in the Palace, including the Chapel Royal, and the Great Hall,

which is still adorned with Henry VIII's priceless tapestries.

The King's Apartments reveal the ceremonial life of William III, from the spectacular King's Staircase to the King's Guard Chamber decorated with a magnificent display of over 3000 weapons.

There are many other features to be enjoyed including some of the most important works of art in the Royal Collection.

Hampton Court Palace is set in 60 acres of immaculately restored riverside gardens, including the largest and oldest grapevine in Europe, William III's Privy Garden, and the world famous maze.

Crown Copyright: Historic Royal Palaces

▶ **OPENING TIMES**

Summer
March - October
Tue - Sun:
9.30am - 6pm
Mon: 10.15am - 6pm.

Winter
November - February
Tue - Sun:
9.30am - 4.30pm
Mon: 10.15am - 4.30pm

Closed 24 - 26 December.

Last admission 60 mins before closing.

▶ **ADMISSION**

Adult £10.80
Child (under 16yrs)... £7.20
Child (under 5yrs)...... Free
OAP/Conc. £8.30
Family (2+3) £32.20

🗄️ ℹ️ Information
Centre. No photography
indoors.

🍽️ Available by
arrangement.

♿ Motorised buggies
available at main
entrance. WCs.

🍷 🍴 Licensed.

🅿️ Ample for cars,
coach parking nearby.

🐾 Rates on request.

🐕 In grounds, on
leads. Guide dogs only
in Palace.

❄️

🛡️ For a full list of
special events please
telephone for details.

CONFERENCE/FUNCTION

ROOM	SIZE	MAX CAPACITY
Great Hall	88'6" x 35'6"	280/400
Cartoon Gallery	22'6" x 116'	220/350
Gt Watching Chamber	66'6" x 25'	120
Painted Room	33'3" x 21'3"	60/100
Ante Room	22' x 21'6"	60/100
King's Award Chamber	60'3" x 36'4"	120/150
Public Dining Room	31'6" x 55'6"	80/150

LOSELEY PARK 🏛

GUILDFORD

www.loseley-park.com

Owner:
Mr Michael
More-Molyneux

▶ **CONTACT**

Michelle Cronin
Loseley Park
Guildford
Surrey GU3 1HS

Tel: 01483 304440
Fax: 01483 302036

e-mail: enquiries@
loseley-park.com

▶ **LOCATION**
OS Ref. SU975 471

30m S of London, leave
A3 S of Guildford on to
B3000. Signposted.

Bus: 1¼ m
from House.

Rail: Farncombe 1½ m,
Guildford 2m,
Godalming 3m.

Air: Heathrow 30m,
Gatwick 30m.

Loseley Park, built in 1562 by Sir William More, is a fine example of Elizabethan architecture, its mellow stone brought from the ruins of Waverley Abbey now over 850 years old. The house is set amid magnificent parkland grazed by the Loseley Jersey herd. Many visitors comment on the very friendly atmosphere of the house, it is a country house, the family home of descendants of the builder.

Furniture has been acquired by the family and includes an early 16th century Wrangelschrank beautifully inlaid with many different woods, a Queen Anne cabinet, Georgian armchairs and settee, a Hepplewhite four-poster bed and King George IV's coronation chair. The King's bedroom has Oudenarde tapestry and a carpet commemorating James I's visit.

The Christian pictures include the Henri Met de Bles triptych of the Nativity and modern mystical pictures of the living Christ, St Francis and St Bernadette. A Christian Cancer Help Centre meets twice monthly. Loseley House is available for dinners, functions and Civil weddings.

GARDEN

A magnificent Cedar of Lebanon presides over the front lawn. Parkland adjoins the lawn and a small lake adds to the beauty of Front Park. In the Walled Garden are mulberry trees, yew hedges, a grass terrace and a moat walk with herbaceous borders. Other features include an award-winning rose garden, a herb garden, flower garden, vegetable garden and idyllic fountain garden.

🔲 ✴ ℹ️ Chapel. New lakeside walk. Business launches & promotions. 10 - 12 acre field can be hired in addition to the lawns. Fashion shows, archery, garden parties, shows, rallies, filming, parkland, moat walk & terrace. Lectures can be arranged on the property, its contents, gardens & history. Loseley Christian Trust Exhibition, children's play area, picnic area, nature trail, home to Jersey herd since 1916; No un-accompanied children, no photo-graphy in house, no videos on estate. All group visits must be booked in advance.

🍽 Special functions, banquets and conference catering. Additional marquees for hire. Wedding receptions.

♿ May alight at entrance to property. Access to all areas except house first floor. WCs.

☕ Courtyard Tea Room.

🍴 Lunchtime restaurant.

🚶 Obligatory. Tour time for house, 40 mins.

🅿 150 cars, 6 coaches. Summer overflow car park.

🐕 Guide dogs only.

🔔 ❄

▶ **OPENING TIMES**

Summer

Garden, Shop, Tea Room & Lunchtime Restaurant
6 May - 29 September
Wed - Sun & BH Mons in May, Jun & Aug,
11am - 5pm.

Loseley House
3 Jun - 26 Aug:
Wed - Sun & BH Mons in May, Jun & Aug (guided tours), 1 - 5pm.

All Year
Tithe Barn, Chestnut Lodge, House, Walled Garden and Grounds available for private/business functions, Civil weddings and receptions.

▶ **ADMISSION**

House & Gardens
Adult	£6.00
Child (5-16yrs)	£3.00
Conc.	£5.00
Child (under 5yrs)	Free

Booked Groups (10+)
Adult	£5.50
Child (5-16yrs)	£2.50
Conc.	£4.50

Garden only
Adult	£3.00
Child (5-16)	£1.50
Conc.	£2.50

Booked Groups (10+)
Adult	£2.75
Child (5-16)	£1.25
Conc.	£2.25

▶ **SPECIAL EVENTS**

MAY 24 - 26
Craft Fair.

JUL 19 - 21
Great Gardening Show.

AUG 11
Open Air Concert & Fireworks.

CONFERENCE/FUNCTION

ROOM	SIZE	MAX CAPACITY
Tithe Barn	100' x 18'	200
Marquee	sites available	
Great Hall	70' x 40'	100
Drawing Rm	40' x 30'	50
Walled Gdn	Marquee	sites

CHA

ALBURY PARK

ALBURY, GUILDFORD, SURREY GU5 9BB

www.cha.org.uk

Tel: 01483 202964 **Fax:** 01483 205023

Owner: Country Houses Association **Contact:** The Administrators

Former home of the Percy family, dukes of Northumberland. Pugin was largely responsible for the outside including the unique chimneys. Inside the house there is a beautiful staircase and drawing room designed by Sir John Soane. Albury Park has been converted into apartments for active retired people.

Location: OS Ref. TQ058 479. 1^1/$_2$ m E of Albury off A25 Guildford to Dorking road. Stations: Chilworth Clandon 3m, Gomshall 2m. Bus route: Tillingbourne No. 25 Guildford - Cranley 2m.

Open: 1 May - 30 Sept: Wed & Thur, 2 - 5pm.

Admission: Adult £2.50, Child £1.50. Groups by arrangement.

⊤ ⊠ ⊞ 1 single & 1 double with bathroom. CHA members only.

BOX HILL ✸

The Old Fort, Box Hill Road, Box Hill, Tadworth KT20 7LB

Tel: 01306 885502 **Fax:** 01306 875030 **e-mail:** sbxgen@smtp.ntrust.org.uk

www.nationaltrust.org.uk/regions/southern

Owner: The National Trust **Contact:** The Property Manager

An outstanding area of woodland and chalk downland, long famous as a destination for day-trippers from London.

Location: OS Ref. TQ171 519. 1m N of Dorking, 1^1/$_2$ m S of Leatherhead on A24.

Open: All year.

Admission: Countryside: Free. Car/coach park £1.50, NT members Free.

CARSHALTON HOUSE

Pound Street, Carshalton, Surrey SM5 3PN

Tel: 020 8770 4781 **Fax:** 020 8770 4777 **e-mail:** valary.murphy@sutton.gov.uk

Owner: St Philomena's Catholic High School for Girls **Contact:** Ms V Murphy

A Queen Anne mansion built c1707, now in use as a school, with grounds originally laid out by Charles Bridgeman.

Location: OS Ref. TQ275 644. On A232 just S of junction with B278.

Open: 1 Apr, 2 - 5pm.

Admission: Adult £3, Child under 16/Full-time students £1.50.

CLANDON PARK/ ✸ HATCHLANDS PARK

See page 149 for full page entry.

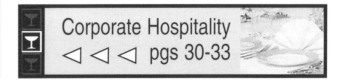

NTPL / John Bethall

NT Photographic Library

CLAREMONT LANDSCAPE GARDEN ✸

PORTSMOUTH ROAD, ESHER, SURREY KT10 9JG

www.nationaltrust.org.uk/regions/southern

Tel: 01372 467806 **Fax:** 01372 464394 **e-mail:** sclgen@smtp.ntrust.org.uk

Owner: The National Trust **Contact:** The Property Manager

One of the earliest surviving English landscape gardens, restored to its former glory. Begun by Sir John Vanbrugh and Charles Bridgeman before 1720, the garden was extended and naturalised by William Kent. 'Capability' Brown also made improvements. Features include a lake, island with pavilion, grotto, turf amphitheatre, viewpoints and avenues.

Location: OS Ref. TQ128 632. On S edge of Esher, on E side of A307 (no access from Esher bypass).

Open: Jan - end Mar, Nov - end Dec: daily except Mons: 10am - 5pm or sunset if earlier. Apr - end Oct: daily: Mon - Fri, 10am - 6pm, Sats, Suns & BHs, 10am - 7pm. NB: closed 18, 19 & 22 Jul and at 2pm on 20, 21 Jul and all day 25 Dec & 1 Jan.

Admission: Adult £3.70, Child £1.85. Coach groups must book; no coach groups on Suns. Family (2+2) £9.75. Groups (15+), £3.20. Discount if using public transport.

⬚ ♿ Limited. WC. ☻ ⌧ No dogs (Apr - Oct). ♨ Tel for details.

CROYDON PALACE

OLD PALACE ROAD, CROYDON, SURREY CR0 1AX

www.friendsofoldpalace.org

Tel: 020 8688 2027

Owner/Contact: The Whitgift Foundation

A residence of the Archbishops of Canterbury between the 12th and 18th centuries and now home of Old Palace School of John Whitgift which is a Whitgift Foundation School for girls from 4 - 18. 15th century Banqueting Hall (one of the outstanding great medieval halls of London); Norman Undercroft; 15th century Guard Room and Chapel; Tudor Long Gallery; Elizabeth I's bedroom. West wing contains some of the earliest medieval brickwork in England.

Location: OS Ref. TQ320 654. 200 yds S of Croydon parish church, 400 yds W of Croydon High St.

Open: 2 - 6 Apr, 5 - 8 Jun, 12 - 13 and 15 - 20 Jul.

Admission: Adult £4, Child/OAP £3.

NT Photographic Library: Geoff Hamilton

DAPDUNE WHARF

RIVER WEY NAVIGATIONS, WHARF ROAD, GUILDFORD GU1 4RR

www.nationaltrust.org.uk/regions/southern

Tel: 01483 561389 **Fax:** 01483 531667 **e-mail:** swybeb@smtp.ntrust.org.uk

Owner: The National Trust   **Contact:** Andrea Selley

Dapdune Wharf is the centrepiece of one of The National Trust's most unusual properties, the River Wey Navigations. Restored wharf buildings and a Wey barge can be seen. Interactive exhibits and displays tell the fascinating story of Surrey's secret waterway, one of the first British rivers to be made navigable.

Location: OS Ref. SU993 502. On Wharf Road to rear of Surrey County Cricket Ground, ¹/₂ m N of Guildford town centre off Woodbridge Road (A322).

Open: 23 Mar - 3 Nov: Thur - Mon, 11am - 5pm. River trips as for Wharf.

Admission: Adult £2.50, Child £1.50, Family £6.50. Groups (booked, min 15): Adult £2.

☐ ☐ ☐ 🄵 By arrangement. ☐ 🄿 Limited. 🄼 In grounds, on leads.

FARNHAM CASTLE

Farnham, Surrey GU9 0AG

Tel: 01252 721194 **Fax:** 01252 711283 **e-mail:** info@farnhamcastle.com

Owner: The Church Commissioners   **Contact:** Farnham Castle

Bishop's Palace built in Norman times by Henry of Blois. Tudor and Jacobean additions.

Location: OS Ref. SU839 474. ¹/₂ m N of Farnham town centre on A287.

Open: All year: Weds, 2 - 4pm except Christmas & New Year.

Admission: Adult £2, Child, £1, Conc. £1.50.

FARNHAM CASTLE KEEP ⌗

Castle Hill, Farnham, Surrey GU6 0AG

Tel: 01252 713393 www.english-heritage.org.uk

Owner: English Heritage   **Contact:** The Head Custodian

Used as a fortified manor by the medieval Bishops of Winchester, this motte and bailey castle has been in continuous occupation since the 12th century. You can visit the large shell-keep enclosing a mound in which are massive foundations of a Norman tower.

Location: OS Ref. SU839 474. ¹/₂ m N of Farnham town centre on A287.

Open: 29 Mar - 30 Sept: 10am - 6pm. 1 - 31 Oct, 10am - 5pm.

Admission: Adult £2.30, Child, £1.20, Conc. £1.70.

🄳 Ground floor & grounds. 🄰 Free. 🄼 In grounds, on leads.

GODDARDS

Abinger Common, Dorking, Surrey RH5 6TH

Tel: 01628 825920 or 01628 825925 (bookings) www.landmarktrust.co.uk

Owner: The Lutyens Trust, leased to The Landmark Trust **Contact:** The Landmark Trust

Built by Sir Edwin Lutyens in 1898 - 1900 and enlarged by him in 1910. Garden by Gertrude Jekyll. Given to the Lutyens Trust in 1991 and now managed and maintained by the Landmark Trust, which let buildings for self-catering holidays. The whole house, apart from the library, is available for up to 12 people. Full details of Goddards and 170 other historic buildings available for holidays are featured in The Landmark Handbook (price £9.50 refundable against booking), from The Landmark Trust, Shottesbrooke, Maidenhead, Berkshire SL6 3SW.

Location: OS Ref. TQ120 450. 4¹/₂ m SW of Dorking on the village green in Abinger Common. Signposted Abinger Common, Friday Street and Leith Hill from A25.

Open: Strictly by appointment. Must be booked in advance, including parking, which is very limited. Visits booked for Weds afternoons from the Wed after Easter until the last Wed of Oct, between 2.30 - 5pm. Only those with pre-booked tickets will be admitted.

Admission: £3. Tickets available from Mrs Baker on 01306 730871, Mon - Fri, 9am & 6pm. Visitors will have access to part of the garden and house only.

🄿

GUILDFORD HOUSE GALLERY

155 High Street, Guildford, Surrey Gu1 3AJ

Tel: 01483 444740 **Fax:** 01483 444742 (Guildford Borough Council)

www.guildfordhouse.co.uk

Owner/Contact: Guildford Borough Council

A beautifully restored 18th century town house with a number of original features including a finely carved staircase, panelled rooms and decorative plaster ceilings. A varied temporary exhibition programme including paintings, photography and craft work. Exhibition and events leaflet available. Lecture and workshop programme. Details on application.

Location: OS Ref. SU996 494. Central Guildford on High Street.

Open: Tue - Sat, 10am - 4.45pm.

Admission: Free.

☐ ☐ 🄵 🄵 Public car park nearby. 🄿 🄼 Guide dogs only. ✳ ☐ Tel for details.

HAMPTON COURT PALACE   *See page 150 for full page entry.*

HATCHLANDS PARK/ ⌘   *See page 149 for full page entry.*
CLANDON PARK

HONEYWOOD HERITAGE CENTRE

Honeywood Walk, Carshalton, Surrey SM5 3NX

Tel: 020 8770 4297 **Fax:** 020 8770 4777

e-mail: lbshoneywood@netscapeonline.co.uk

www.sutton.gov.uk/lfl/heritage/honeywood

Owner: London Borough of Sutton   **Contact:** The Curator

A 17th century listed building next to the picturesque Carshalton Ponds, containing displays on many aspects of the history of the London Borough of Sutton plus a changing programme of exhibitions and events on a wide range of subjects. Attractive garden at rear.

Location: OS Ref. TQ279 646. On A232 approximately 4m W of Croydon.

Open: Wed - Fri, 11am - 5pm. Sat, Suns & BH Mons, 10am - 5pm. Tearooms open Tue - Sun, 10am - 5pm.

Admission: Adult £1.20, Child 60p, under 5 Free. Groups by arrangement.

☐ 🄳 Ground floor. WC. ☐ 🄵 🄿 Limited. ☐ 🄼 Guide dogs only. ✳ ☐ Tel for details.

KEW GARDENS

Kew, Richmond, Surrey TW9 3AB

Tel: 020 8332 5655   **Fax:** 020 8332 5197   **Contact:** Enquiry Unit

Kew's 300 acres offer many special attractions: including the 65ft high Palm House.

Location: OS Ref. TQ188 776. A307. Junc. A307 & A205 (1m Chiswick roundabout M4).

Open: 9.30am, daily except Christmas Day and New Year's Day. Closing time varies according to the season. Please telephone for further information.

Admission: Adult £6.50, Child (under 16yrs & accompanied by an adult) Free, Conc. £4.50, Family £13. Groups 20% discount when pre-booked and paid.

LEITH HILL ※

Coldharbour, Surrey

Tel: 01306 711777   **Fax:** 01306 712153   www.nationaltrust.org.uk/regions/southern

Owner: The National Trust   **Contact:** The Property Manager

The highest point in south-east England, crowned by an 18th century Gothic tower, from which there are magnificent views. The surrounding woodland contains ancient stands of hazel and oak, and there is a colourful display of rhododendrons in May - Jun.

Location: OS Ref. TQ139 432. 1m SW of Coldharbour A29/B2126.

Open: Tower: 29 Mar (Good Fri) - end Sept: Wed; Sat, Sun & BHs; 10am - 5pm. Oct - Mar: Sat, Sun & BHs (closed 25 Dec), 10am - 3.30pm. Rhododendron Wood & Estate: All year: daily.

Admission: Tower: £1.50, Child 75p. Rhododendron Wood: £1.50 per car.

ⓘNo vehicular access to summit. ⅃Partial. ◗When Tower open. ⨍Guided walks. ℙParking at foot of hill, ¹/₂m walk from Tower. ⊠Not in picnic area or Tower. ❋

LITTLE HOLLAND HOUSE

40 Beeches Avenue, Carshalton, Surrey SM5 3LW

Tel: 020 8770 4781   **Fax:** 020 8770 4777

e-mail: valary.murphy@sutton.gov.uk   **www**.sutton.gov.uk/lfl/heritage/lhh

Owner: London Borough of Sutton   **Contact:** Ms V Murphy

The home of Frank Dickinson (1874 - 1961) artist, designer and craftsman, who dreamt of a house that would follow the philosophy and theories of William Morris and John Ruskin. Dickinson designed, built and furnished the house himself from 1902 onwards. The Grade II* listed interior features handmade furniture, metal work, carvings and paintings produced by Dickinson in the Arts and Crafts style.

Location: OS Ref. TQ275 634. On B278 1m S of junction with A232.

Open: First Sun of each month & BH Suns & Mons (excluding Christmas & New Year, 1.30 - 5.30pm.

Admission: Free. Groups by arrangement, £2.50pp (includes talk and guided tour).

ⓘNo photography in house. ⅃Ground floor. ⨍By arrangement. ℙNone. ⊠Guide dogs only. ❋

LOSELEY PARK 🏛

See page 151 for full page entry.

OAKHURST COTTAGE ※

Hambledon, Godalming, Surrey GU8 4HF

Tel: 01428 684090   **e-mail:** swwgen@smtp.ntrust.org.uk

Owner: The National Trust   **Contact:** The Witley Centre

A small 16th century timber-framed cottage, painted by both Helen Allingham and Myles Birket Foster, containing furniture and artefacts reflecting two or more centuries of continuing occupation. There is a delightful cottage garden and a small barn containing agricultural implements.

Location: OS Ref. SU965 385. Hambledon, Surrey.

Open: 23 Mar - 3 Nov: Weds, Thurs, Sats, Suns & BH Mons, 2 - 5pm. Strictly by appointment only.

Admission: Adult £3, Child £1.50 (including guided tour). No reduction for groups.

⅃Unsuitable. ⨍Obligatory, by arrangement. ℙLimited. ⊠

❋ Open All Year Index ◁ ◁ ◁ pgs 44-48

PAINSHILL LANDSCAPE GARDEN

PORTSMOUTH ROAD, COBHAM, SURREY KT11 1JE

www.painshill.co.uk

Tel: 01932 868113   **Fax:** 01932 868001   **e-mail:** info@painshill.co.uk

Owner: Painshill Park Trust   **Contact:** Visitor Management

One of Europe's finest 18th century landscape gardens, contemporary with Stourhead and Stowe, created by the Hon Charles Hamilton between 1738 - 1773. Europa Nostra Medal winner for 'exemplary restoration'. Situated in 158 acres, visitors can take a circuit walk through a series of emerging scenes, each one more surprising than the last. A 14-acre lake fed by a massive waterwheel gives a breathtaking setting for a variety of spectacular features including a Gothic temple, ruined abbey, Turkish tent, crystal grotto, Chinese bridge, magnificent Cedars of Lebanon, replanted 18th century shrubberies and vineyard. Available for corporate and private hire, location filming, wedding receptions, etc.

Location: OS Ref. TQ099 605. M25/J10 to London. W of Cobham on A245. Entrance 200 yds E of A245/A307 roundabout.

Open: Apr - Oct: Tue - Sun and BH Mons, 10.30am - 6pm (last admission 4.30pm). Gates close 6pm. Nov - Mar: daily except Mons & Fris (open BHs), 11am - 4pm or dusk if earlier (last admission 3pm). Closed Christmas and Boxing Day.

Admission: Adult £4.50, Child (5-16) £2, under 5 Free, Conc. £4. Groups (10+) £3.60.

▣ ⊤Marquee site. ⅃ ◗Licensed. ⨍By arrangement. ℙ ⊠Guide dogs only. ❋

POLESDEN LACEY ✻

GREAT BOOKHAM, Nr DORKING, SURREY RH5 6BD

www.nationaltrust.org.uk/regions/southern

Tel: 01372 452048 **Infoline:** 01372 458203 **Fax:** 01372 452023
e-mail: spljmg@smtp.ntrust.org.uk

Owner: The National Trust   **Contact:** The Property Manager

Originally an elegant 1820s Regency villa in magnificent landscape setting. The house was remodelled after 1906 by the Hon Mrs Ronald Greville, a well-known Edwardian hostess. Her collection of fine paintings, furniture, porcelain and silver are still displayed in the reception rooms and galleries, which surround an inner courtyard. Extensive grounds, walled rose garden, lawns and landscaped walks. King George VI and Queen Elizabeth, The Queen Mother spent part of their honeymoon here.

Location: OS Ref. TQ136 522. 5m NW of Dorking, 2m S of Great Bookham, off A246.

Open: House: 23 Mar - 3 Nov: Wed - Sun, 11am - 5pm also BH Mons starting with Easter. Grounds: All year: daily, 11am - 6pm/dusk. Last admission to house ½ hr before closing.

Admission: Garden, grounds & landscape walks: Adult £4, Family £10. House: £3 extra. Family £7.50 extra. All year, booked groups £6 (house, garden & walks).

☐ ✻ ⊤ ⅃ ⊞ Licensed. **P** Limited for coaches. ☒ In grounds on leads. ▲ ✱
☎ Tel: 01372 452048 for info.

RHS GARDEN WISLEY

Nr WOKING, SURREY GU23 6QB

www.rhs.org.uk

Tel: 01483 224234 **Fax:** 01483 211750

Owner/Contact: The Royal Horticultural Society

A garden to enjoy all year round with something to see for everyone. Wisley provides the visitor with ideas and inspiration and the benefit of experience from experts. The Wisley Plant Centre with plants for sale, The Wisley Shop with books and gifts and for refreshments the Café and Restaurant.

Location: OS Ref. TQ066 583. NW side of A3 ½ m SW of M25/J10. Brown Signs.

Open: All year: daily (except Christmas Day), Mon - Fri, 10am - 6pm (4.30pm Nov - Feb). Sat & Sun, 9am - 6pm (4.30pm Nov - Feb). RHS members only on Suns.

Admission: Adult £6, Child (up to 6) Free, Child (6-16yrs) £2. Groups (10+): Adult £5, Child £1.60. Companion for disabled or blind visitors, Free. (2001 prices).

☐ ✻ ⅃ Wheelchairs available tel: 01483 211113 & special map. WC. ☒
⊞ Licensed. ⨍ By arrangement. **P** ■ ☒ Guide dogs only. ✱

RAMSTER GARDENS

Ramster, Chiddingfold, Surrey GU8 4SN

Tel: 01428 654167 **Fax:** 01428 658345

Owner/Contact: Mrs M Gunn

20 acres of woodland and shrub garden.

Location: OS Ref. SU950 333. 1½ m S of Chiddingfold on A283.

Open: 13 Apr - 7 Jul: 11am - 5pm.

Admission: £3, Child Free.

RUNNYMEDE ✻

Egham, Surrey

Tel: 01784 432891 **Fax:** 01784 479007 **e-mail:** srygen@smtp.ntrust.org.uk
www.nationaltrust.org.uk/regions/southern

Owner: The National Trust   **Contact:** The Property Manager

Runnymede is an attractive area of riverside meadows, grassland and broadleaf woodland, rich in diversity of flora and fauna, and part-designated a Site of Special Scientific Interest. It was on this site, in 1215, that King John sealed Magna Carta.

Location: OS Ref. TQ007 720. 2m W of Runnymede Bridge, on S side of A308, M25/J13.

Open: All year. Riverside Car park (grass): Apr - 30 Sept: daily, 9am - 7pm. Tearoom Car park (hard standing): daily, all year, 8.30am - 5pm (later in Summer).

Admission: Fees payable for parking (NT members Free), fishing & mooring.

☐ ⅃ Partial. Braille guide. ☒ ⨍ **P** ✱ ☎ Tel for details.

SHALFORD MILL ✻

Shalford, Guildford, Surrey GU4 8BS

Tel: 01483 561389 **www**.nationaltrust.org.uk/regions/southern

Owner: The National Trust

18th century watermill on the Tillingbourne, given in 1932 by "Ferguson's Gang".

Location: OS Ref. TQ000 476. 1½ m S of Guildford on A281, opposite Sea Horse Inn.

Open: Daily, 10am - 5pm.

Admission: Free. No unaccompanied children.

South East - England

TITSEY PLACE

TITSEY, OXTED, SURREY RH8 0SD

www.titsey.com

Tel: 01273 407056   **Fax:** 01273 478995
e-mail: kate.moisson@struttandparker.co.uk
Owner: Trustees of the Titsey Foundation   **Contact:** Kate Moisson

Stunning mansion house. Situated outside Limpsfield. Extensive formal and informal gardens containing Victorian walled garden, lakes, fountains and rose gardens. Outstanding features of this house include important paintings and *objets d'art*. Home of the Gresham and Leveson Gower family since the 15th century. Infinite capacity in this magnificent garden, numbers unavoidably restricted on house tours.

Location: OS Ref. TQ406 553. A25 Oxted - Westerham, through Limpsfield and into Bluehouse Lane and Water Lane, follow blue signs.
Open: 15 May - 29 Sept: Wed & Sun, 1 - 5pm including Easter Mon (garden only) and all Summer BHs.
Admission: House & Garden: Adult/Child £4.50. Garden only: £2.50. Groups (20+): Adult £5.50.

🛈 No photography in house. No barbecues. ♿ Unsuitable. 🚶 Obligatory.
🅿 Limited for coaches. ✖

WHITEHALL

1 Malden Road, Cheam, Surrey SM3 8QD

Tel: 020 8643 1236   **Fax:** 020 8770 4777
e-mail: curators@whitehallcheam.fsnet.co.uk
www.sutton.gov.uk/lfl/heritage/whitehall
Owner: London Borough of Sutton   **Contact:** The Curator

A Tudor timber-framed house, c1500 with later additions, in the heart of Cheam village conservation area. Twelve rooms open to view with displays on Nonsuch Palace, timber-framed buildings, Cheam pottery, Cheam school and William Gilpin. Changing exhibition programme and special event days throughout the year. Attractive rear garden features medieval well from c1400.

Location: OS Ref. TQ242 638. Approx. 2m S of A3 on A2043 just N of junction with A232.
Open: Wed - Fri, 2 - 5pm; Sat, 10am - 5pm; Sun & BH Mons, 2 - 5pm.
Admission: Adult £1.20, Child (under 16yrs) 60p, Child under 5yrs Free. Groups by arrangement.

📷 ♿ Ground floor. 🖥 🚶 🏛 🐕 Guide dogs only. ❄ 🐾 Tel for details.

Farnham Castle

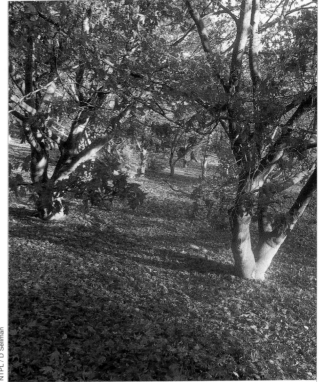

NTPL / D Sellman

WINKWORTH ARBORETUM 🌿

HASCOMBE ROAD, GODALMING, SURREY GU8 4AD

www.nationaltrust.org.uk/regions/southern

Tel: 01483 208477   **Fax:** 01483 208252   **e-mail:** swagen@smtp.ntrust.org.uk
Owner: The National Trust   **Contact:** The Head of Arboretum

Hillside woodland with two lakes, many rare trees and shrubs and fine views. The most impressive displays are in spring for bluebells and azaleas, autumn for colour and wildlife. Delightful 100 year old boathouse on Rowes Flashe lake. Seasonal opening.

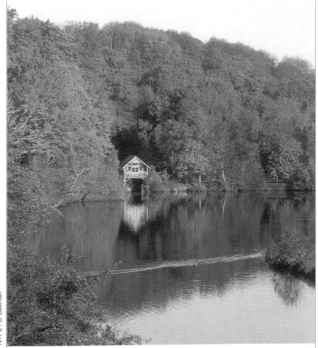

NTPL / D Sellman

Location: OS Ref. SU990 412. Near Hascombe, 2m SE of Godalming on E side of B2130.
Open: All year round: daily during daylight hours. May be closed due to high winds. Boathouse: 1 Apr - 31 Oct.
Admission: Adult £3.50, Child (5-16yrs) £1.75, Family (2+2) £8.75, additional family member £1.75. Discounts for 10 or more.

📷 ♿ Limited. WC. 🖥 🐕 In grounds, on leads. ❄

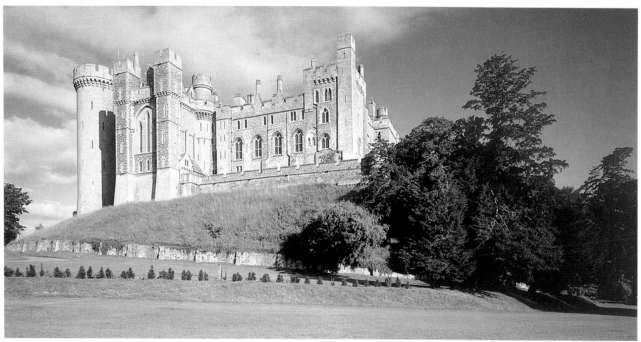

ARUNDEL CASTLE

ARUNDEL

www.arundelcastle.org

This great castle, home of the Dukes of Norfolk, dates from the Norman Conquest. Containing a very fine collection of furniture and paintings, Arundel Castle is still a family home, reflecting the changes of nearly a thousand years.

In 1643, during the Civil War, the original castle was very badly damaged and it was later restored by the 8th, 11th and 15th Dukes in the 18th and 19th centuries. Amongst its treasures are personal possessions of Mary Queen of Scots and a selection of historical, religious and heraldic items from the Duke of Norfolk's collection.

The Duke of Norfolk is the Premier Duke, the title having been conferred on Sir John Howard in 1483 by his friend King Richard III. The Dukedom also carries with it the hereditary office of Earl Marshal of England. Among the historically famous members of the Howard family are Lord Howard of Effingham who, with Drake, repelled the Spanish Armada; the Earl of Surrey, the Tudor poet and courtier and the 3rd Duke of Norfolk, uncle of Anne Boleyn and Catherine Howard, both of whom became wives of King Henry VIII.

Owner:

Arundel Castle
Trustees Ltd

▶ CONTACT

The Comptroller
Arundel Castle
Arundel
West Sussex BN18
9AB

Tel: 01903 883136
or 01903 882173

Fax: 01903 884581

e-mail: arundelcastle@
compuserve.com

▶ LOCATION

OS Ref. TQ018 072

Central Arundel, N of A27
Brighton 40 mins,
Worthing 15 mins,
Chichester 15 mins.
From London A3 or
A24, 1¹/₂ hrs.
M25 motorway, 30m.

Bus: Bus stop 100 yds.

Rail: Station ¹/₂ m.

Air: Gatwick 25m.

▶ OPENING TIMES

Summer

31 March - 31 October
Daily (except Sats)
12 noon - 5pm
Last admission 4pm.

Winter

1 November - 30 March
Pre-booked groups only.

▶ ADMISSION

Summer

Adult	£8.50
Child (5-16)	£5.50
Conc.	£7.00
Family (2+2)	£24.50
Family (2+3)	£24.50

Groups (20+)

Adult	£8.00
Child (5-16)	£4.50
Conc.	£6.00

Pre-booked Groups
(subject to minimum fee)

Mornings	£6.00
Evenings	£12.00
Saturdays	£12.00

Winter

Pre-booked groups
(subject to minimum fee)

All entries	£12.00

No photography inside the Castle. Guidebooks in French & German.

Most areas accessible. Visitors may alight at the entrance, before parking in the allocated areas. WCs.

Restaurant seats 140. Special rates for booked groups. Self-service restaurant in Castle serves home-made food. Groups must book in advance for afternoon tea, lunch or dinner.

Pre-booked groups only, £9. Tour time 1¹/₂ hrs. Tours available in French, Italian & Japanese.

Ample. Coaches can park free in town coach park.

Items of particular interest include a Norman Motte & Keep, Armoury & Victorian bedrooms. Special rates for schoolchildren (aged 5-15) and teachers.

NTPL: Rupert Truman

BATEMAN'S

BURWASH

Owner:
The National Trust

► CONTACT

The Property Manager
Bateman's
Burwash
Etchingham
East Sussex TN19 7DS

Tel: 01435 882302

Fax: 01435 882811

e-mail: kbaxxx@
smtp.ntrust.org.uk

► LOCATION

OS Ref. TQ671 238

¹/₂ m S of Burwash
off A265.

Rail: Etchingham 3m,
then bus (twice daily).

Air: Gatwick 40m.

Built in 1634 and home to Rudyard Kipling for over 30 years, Bateman's lies in the richly wooded landscape of the Sussex Weald. Visit this Sussex sandstone manor house, built by a local ironmaster, where the famous writer lived from 1902 to 1936. See the rooms as they were in Kipling's day, including the study where the view inspired him to write some of his well-loved works including *Puck of Pook's Hill* and *Rewards and Fairies*. Find the mementoes of Kipling's time in India and illustrations from his famous *Jungle Book* tales of *Mowgli, Baloo and Shere Khan*.

Wander through the delightful Rose Garden with its pond and statues, with Mulberry and Herb gardens and discover the wild garden, through which flows the River Dudwell. Through the wild garden, you will find the Mill where you can watch corn being ground on most Saturday afternoons and one of the world's first water-driven turbines installed by Kipling to generate electricity for the house. In the garage, see a 1928 Rolls Royce, one of several owned by Kipling who was a keen early motorist.

Savour the peace and tranquillity of this beautiful property which Kipling described as *'A good and peaceable place' and of which he said 'we have loved it, ever since our first sight of it...'.*

There is a picnic glade next to the car park, or you can enjoy morning coffee, a delicious lunch or afternoon tea in the licensed tearoom where there is special emphasis on using local produce. The well-stocked gift shop offers the largest collection of Kipling books in the area.

► OPENING TIMES

23 Mar - 29 Sept:
Sat - Wed, Good Fri &
BH Mons, 11am - 5.30pm.
Last admission 4.30pm.

Wild Garden:
Also open 2 - 17 Mar:
Sat & Sun, 11am - 4pm.

► ADMISSION

House & Garden

Adult	£5.20
Child	£2.60
Family (2+3)	£13.00
Groups	£4.40

Mar only

Adult	£2.60
Child	£1.30
Family	£6.50
Groups	£2.20

NTPL: Geoffrey Frosh

 Ground floor & grounds.
WC.

Licensed.

Tel for details.

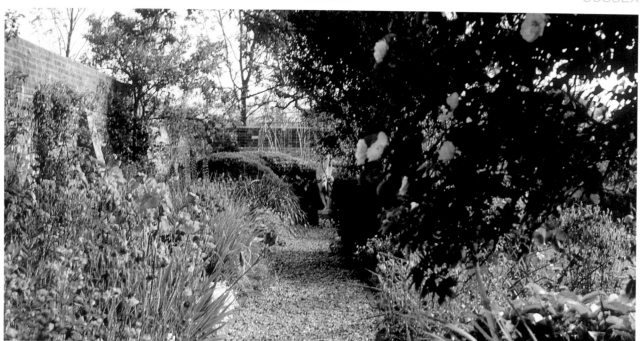

CHARLESTON

LEWES

www.charleston.org.uk

Owner:
The Charleston Trust

▶ CONTACT

Visitor Manager
Charleston
Nr Firle, Lewes
East Sussex   BN8 6LL

Tel: 01323 811265
(Visitor information)
01323 811626 (Admin)
Fax: 01323 811628
e-mail: info@
charleston.co.uk

▶ LOCATION
OS Ref. TQ490 069

6m E of Lewes on A27
between Firle &
Selmeston. The lane to
Charleston leads off the
A27, 2m beyond the
Firle turning.

London 60m. Brighton
15m. Monk's House,
Rodmell (Leonard and
Virginia Woolf's house)
11m.

Rail: London (Victoria)
hourly to Lewes (65
mins). Occasional train
to Berwick.

Bus: Rider 125
Charleston Rambler
Suns & BHs Route on
A27.
Taxi: George &
Graham, Lewes 473692.

Air: Gatwick 35m.

A mile or so from Firle village, near the end of a track leading to the foot of the Downs, lies Charleston. It was discovered in 1916 by Virginia and Leonard Woolf when Virginia's sister, the painter Vanessa Bell, was looking for a place in the country. Vanessa moved here with fellow artist Duncan Grant, the writer David Garnett, her two young sons and an assortment of animals. It was an unconventional and creative household which became the focal point for artists and intellectuals later to be known as the Bloomsbury set, among them Roger Fry, Lytton Strachey and Maynard Keynes.

Over the years the artists decorated the walls, furniture and ceramics with their own designs, influenced by Italian fresco painting and post-impressionist art. Creativity extended to the garden too. Mosaics were made in the piazza, sculpture was cleverly positioned to intrigue and subtle masses of colour were used in the planting.

After Duncan Grant's death in 1978, the Charleston Trust was formed to save and restore the house to its former glory. The task has been described as "one of the most difficult and imaginative feats of restoration current in Britain".

⬜ ✳ ℹ Filming and photography contact Wendy Hitchmough: 01323 811626. Small lecture room available by special arrangement. No filming, video or photography in house.

🚻

♿ Visitors may alight at entrance. Wheelchair visitors by prior arrangement. Ground floor only suitable. WCs.

▦ Wed - Sun, 2 - 5pm.

🚶 Obligatory.

🅿 50 spaces. Mini coaches and cars only. Mini coaches may use the lane to the property. It is essential to arrange group visits (up to 50) in advance and out of public hours. All group visits to the house are guided. Large coaches may set down at the start of the lane, 10 mins walk.

▪ Student pack and a teacher's guide suitable for KS I & II.

🐕 Guide dogs only.

🎭 See website.

▶ OPENING TIMES
1 April - 31 October
Wed - Sun: 2 - 5pm.

Extra Summer Opening
Times: July & August
Wed - Sat: 11.30am - 5pm
Sun: 2 - 5pm.

November - December
Christmas shopping
Sat & Sun, 1 - 4pm.

Guided visits
Wed - Sat,
unguided on Suns.

House closed Mon & Tue
except BH Mons.

Connoisseur Fridays
April - June, September and
October, in-depth tour of
the house, including
Vanessa Bell's studio and
the kitchen.

▶ ADMISSION
House & Garden

Adult	£6.00
Child (5+)/Conc*	£4.50
Child (under 5yrs)	Free
Disabled	£4.50
Groups (10+)	
Adult	£5.00
Child/Student	£4.00
OAP	£5.00

Connoisseur Fridays

Adult	£7.00

* OAPs, Students &
UB40 Wed & Thur
only throughout season.

Organised tours should
telephone for group rates.

South East - England

GOODWOOD HOUSE 🏛

CHICHESTER

www.goodwood.co.uk

Owner:
The Earl of March

▶ **CONTACT**

Kathryn Bellamy
Goodwood House
Goodwood
Chichester
West Sussex PO18 0PX

Tel: 01243 755048
01243 755042
(weddings)
Fax: 01243 755005
Recorded info:
01243 755040
e-mail: curator
@goodwood.co.uk
or weddings@
goodwood.co.uk

▶ **LOCATION**

OS Ref. SU888 088

3¹/2m NE of Chichester.
A3 from London then
A286 or A285. M27/A27
from Portsmouth or
Brighton.

Rail: Chichester 3¹/2m
Arundel 9m.

Air: Heathrow 1¹/2 hrs
Gatwick ¹/4 hr.

200 years ago, the 3rd Duke of Richmond laid out a racecourse on his estate for the Sussex Militia Officers' annual horse races. The Duke was so delighted with the success of that day's racing that in 1802 he organised a three day public meeting and glorious racing has continued here ever since. Today Goodwood encapsulates the flamboyance, innovation and style that have been the signature of the Richmond family ever since the time of the 1st Duke. The natural son of King Charles II and his beautiful French mistress, Louise de Keroualle, he was renowned for his love of life and brilliance at entertaining –

a tradition which continues to this day. The French interest was pursued by the 3rd Duke who, as British Ambassador to Paris, collected wonderful French furniture which now sets off the newly restored Tapestry Drawing Room; and Sèvres porcelain, which can still be seen. Still owned and lived in by the Earl and Countess of March, Goodwood effortlessly exudes the glamour of a ducal seat and is not only a beautiful house to visit, but has also established a worldwide reputation for excellence as the location for corporate, private and incentive entertainment requirements.

Goodwood Photo Collection

▶ **OPENING TIMES**

Summer

31 Mar - 30 Sept:
Most Suns & Mons.

4 Aug - 5 Sept:
Sun - Thur, 1 - 5pm.

The house is occasionally closed for Special Events on Sundays. Please ring Recorded Information on 01243 755040 or visit the website.

Connoisseurs' Days

Group visits with special guided tours can be booked.

▶ **ADMISSION**

House

Adult £6.50
Child (12 - 18yrs) £3.00
Child (under 12 yrs) ... Free
OAP £6.00
Groups (20 - 200)
Economy £5.50
Connoisseur £8.50

▶ **SPECIAL EVENTS**

MAY 21 - 23 & 30
Race Meetings.
**JUN 7, 14, 21, 28
& 30 (evenings)
AUG 24 - 25,
SEPT 13/14 & 25/26**
Race Meetings.

JUL 30 - AUG 3
Glorious Goodwood
Race Week.

Goodwood Festival of Speed & Historic Motor Sport Event: Please visit the website.

CONFERENCE/FUNCTION

ROOM	SIZE	MAX CAPACITY
Ballroom	79' x 23'	200
11 other rooms also available		

Conference facilities. No photography. Highly trained guides in every room. Shell House optional extra on Connoisseurs' Days only.

By appointment: open mornings & on Connoisseurs' Days.

Ample.

In grounds, on leads. Guide dogs only in house.

Civil Wedding Licence.

LEONARDSLEE GARDENS

HORSHAM

www.leonardslee.com

Owner:
R Loder Esq

▶ **CONTACT**

R Loder Esq
Leonardslee Gardens
Lower Beeding
Horsham
West Sussex RH13 6PP

Tel: 01403 891212
Fax: 01403 891305

▶ **LOCATION**

OS Ref. TQ222 260

M23 to Handcross then
B2110 (signposted
Cowfold) for 4m.
From London:
1 hr 15 mins.

Rail: Horsham
Station 4^1/$_2$ m

Bus: No. 107 from
Horsham and Brighton

Leonardslee Gardens represent one of the largest and most spectacular woodland gardens in England with one of the finest collections of mature rhododendrons, azaleas, choice trees and shrubs to be seen anywhere. It is doubly fortunate in having one of the most magnificent settings, within easy reach of London, only a few miles from the M23. Laid out by Sir Edmund Loder since 1889, the gardens are still maintained by the Loder family today. The 240 acre (100 hectare) valley is world famous for its spring display of azaleas and rhododendrons around the 7 lakes, giving superb views and reflections.

The delightful Rock Garden, a photographer's paradise, is a kaleidoscope of colour in May. The superb exhibition of Bonsai in a walled courtyard shows the fascinating living art-form of

Bonsai to perfection. The Alpine House has 400 different alpine plants growing in a natural rocky setting. Wallabies (used as mowing machines!) have lived wild in part of the garden for over 100 years, and deer (Sika, Fallow & Axis) may be seen in the parklands.

Many superb rhododendrons have been raised at Leonardslee. The most famous is *rhododendron loderi* raised by Sir Edmund Loder in 1901. The original plants can still be seen in the garden. In May the fragrance of their huge blooms pervades the air throughout the valley.

The Loder family collection of Victorian motorcars (1895 - 1900) provides a fascinating view of the different designs adopted on the first auto-mobile constructors.

▶ **OPENING TIMES**

Summer
1 April - 31 October
Daily 9.30am - 6pm

Winter
1 November - 31 March
Closed to the general
public.

Available for functions.

▶ **ADMISSION**

April, June - October
Adult £5.00

May (Mon - Fri)
Adult £6.00

May (Sats, Suns & BH Mons)
Adult £7.00
Child (anytime) £3.00

Groups

April, June - October
Adult £4.00

May: (Mon - Fri) £5.00
Sat, Sun &
BH Mons: £6.00
Child (anytime) £2.50

SPECIAL EVENTS

MAY 4 - 6
Bonsai Weekend.

JUN 29 - 30
West Sussex Country Craft
Fair.

CONFERENCE/FUNCTION

ROOM	MAX CAPACITY
Clock Tower	100

📷 ❄ ℹ Photography - landscape & fashion, film location.

🍽 Restaurant available for private and corporate function in the evenings and out of season.

♿ Unsuitable.

☕🍴 Restaurant & café. Morning coffee, lunch and teas.

🅿 Ample. Refreshments free to coach drivers. Average length of visit 2 - 4 hours.

Oliver Benn

Owner:
The National Trust

▶ **CONTACT**

The Administration
Office
Petworth House
Petworth
West Sussex   GU28 0AE

Tel: 01798 342207

Info Line: 01798 343929

Fax: 01798 342963

e-mail: spesht@
smtp.ntrust.org.uk

▶ **LOCATION**

OS Ref. SU976 218

In the centre of
Petworth town
(approach roads
A272/A283/A285)
Car park signposted.

Rail: Pulborough
BR 5¼ m.

PETWORTH HOUSE ❧

PETWORTH

www.nationaltrust.org.uk/regions/southern   www.turneratpetworth.com

Petworth House is one of the finest houses in the care of the National Trust and is home to an art collection that rivals many London galleries. Assembled by one family over 350 years, it includes works by Turner, Van Dyck, Titian, Claude, Gainsborough, Bosch, Reynolds and William Blake.

The state rooms contain sculpture, furniture and porcelain of the highest quality and are complemented by the old kitchens in the Servants' Quarters.

Petworth House is also the home of Lord and Lady Egremont and extra family rooms are open on weekdays by kind permission of the family (not Bank Holidays).

Petworth Park is a 700 acre park landscaped by 'Capability' Brown and is open to the public all year free of charge. Spring and autumn are particularly breathtaking and the summer sunsets over the lake are spectacular.

New for 2002: Visitors can enjoy the Carved Room, containing some of Grinling Gibbons' finest limewood carvings, fully restored to its 19th century appearance. 6 Jul - 29 Sept: 'Turner at Petworth' exhibition of over 70 oils, watercolours and gouaches that Turner painted of Petworth House and its surrounding landscape. During the exhibition, for the first-time ever, Turner's studio at Petworth House will be open to the general public.

NTPL: Andreas Von Einsiedel

▣ ⓘ Events throughout the year. Large musical concerts in the park. Baby feeding and changing facilities, highchairs. Pushchairs admitted in house but no prams, please. No photography in house.

☎ Contact Retail & Catering Manager on 01798 344975.

♿ Car park is 800 yards from house; there is a vehicle available to take less able visitors to House.

🍴 Licensed. 11am-5pm.

🏃 By arrangement with the Administration Office on variety of subjects.

🅿 800 yards from house. Coach parties alight at Church Lodge entrance, coaches then park in NT car park. Coaches must book in advance.

▦ Welcome. Must book. Teachers' pack available.

🐕 Guide dogs only in house. Dogs in park only.

❈   ⬡

▶ **OPENING TIMES**

**House &
Servants' Quarters**
23 March - 3 November
Daily except Thurs & Fris
but open Good Fri,
11am - 5.30pm.

Last admission to House &
Servants' Quarters 5pm.

Extra rooms shown on
Mons, Tues & Weds,
not BH Mons.

**Pleasure Grounds
and Car Park**
9/10 & 16/17 March
for spring bulbs, 12 noon -
4pm. Dates as House,
11am - 6pm.

Park
All year: Daily, 8am - sunset.

**Servants' Quarters,
Shop & Restaurant:**
20 Nov - 14 Dec, Wed -
Sat, 11am - 3pm.
Full programme of events
including lecture lunches,
family workshops and
Christmas lunches.

▶ **ADMISSION**

**House, Servants'
Quarters &
Pleasure Grounds**

Adult £7.00
Child (5-17yrs) £4.00
Child (under 5 yrs) ..... Free
Family (2+2) £18.00

Groups (pre-booked 15+)
Adult £6.50

Park Only .... Free

Pleasure Grounds
Adult £1.50
Children .... Free

NT Members Free.

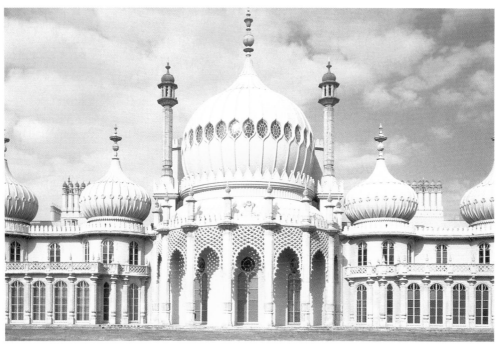

THE ROYAL PAVILION

BRIGHTON

www.royalpavilion.brighton.co.uk

Owner:
Brighton & Hove
Council

▶ **CONTACT**

Visitor Services
The Royal Pavilion
Brighton
East Sussex BN1 1EE

Tel: 01273 290900

Fax: 01273 292871

▶ **LOCATION**

OS Ref. TQ313 043

The Royal Pavilion is in the
centre of Brighton easily
reached by road and rail.
From London M25, M23, A23
- 1 hr 30 mins.

Rail: Victoria to
Brighton station
50 mins.
15 mins walk from
Brighton station.

Air: Gatwick 20 mins.

CONFERENCE/FUNCTION

ROOM	MAX CAPACITY
Banqueting Room	200
Great Kitchen	90
Music Rm	180
Queen Adelaide Suite	100
Small Adelaide	40
William IV	80

Universally acclaimed as one of the most
exotically beautiful buildings in the British
Isles, the Royal Pavilion is the former seaside
residence of King George IV.

Originally a simple farmhouse, in 1787 architect
Henry Holland created a neo-classical villa on the
site. It was later transformed into its current Indian
style by John Nash between 1815 and 1822. With
interiors decorated in the Chinese style and an
astonishingly exotic exterior, this Regency Palace
is quite breathtaking.

Magnificent decorations and fantastic furnishings
have been re-created in the recent extensive
restoration programme. From the opulence
of the main state rooms to the charm of the first floor
bedroom suites, the Royal Pavilion is filled with
astonishing colours and superb craftsmanship.

Witness the magnificence of the Music Room with
its domed ceiling of gilded scallop-shaped shells
and hand-knotted carpet, and promenade
through the Chinese bamboo grove of the
Long Gallery.

Lavish menus were created in the Great Kitchen,
with its cast iron palm trees and dazzling
collection of copperware, and then served in the
dramatic setting of the Banqueting Room, lit by a
huge crystal chandelier held by a silvered dragon.

Set in restored Regency gardens replanted to John
Nash's elegant 1820s design, the Royal Pavilion is
an unforgettable experience.

Visitors can discover more about life behind the
scenes at the Palace during the last 200 years with
a new specially commissioned interactive
multimedia presentation. Public guided tours take
place daily at 11.30am and 2.30pm for a small
additional charge.

ℹ️ Location filming and photography, including
feature films, fashion shoots and corporate videos.

🛍️ Gift shop with souvenirs unique to the Royal
Pavilion.

🍸 Spectacular rooms available for prestigious
corporate and private entertaining and wedding
receptions.

♿ Access to ground floor only. Tactile and signed
tours can be booked in advance with Visitor Services
Tel: 01273 292820/2.

☕ Tearooms with a balcony providing sweeping
views across the restored Regency gardens.

🚶 Tours in English, French and German and other
languages by prior arrangement. General introduction
and specialist tours provided.

🅿️ Close to NCP car parks, town centre voucher
parking. Coach drop-off point in Church Street, parking
in Madeira Drive. Free entry for coach drivers.

Specialist tours relating to all levels of National
Curriculum, must be booked in advance with Visitor
Services. Special winter student rates. Slide lecture
presentations by arrangement.

🔔 Civil Wedding Licence.

❄️

▶ **OPENING TIMES**

Summer
June - September
Daily: 10am - 6pm
Last admission at 6pm.

Winter
October - May
Daily: 10am - 5pm
Last admission at 5pm.

Closed 25/26 December.

▶ **ADMISSION**

Adult	£5.20
Child	£3.20
Conc.	£3.75
Groups (20+)	
Adult	£4.40

Prices valid until 31.3.2002

▶ **SPECIAL EVENTS**

**SPRING & AUTUMN
HALF TERM:**
Children's Events.

DEC 15 2001
Christmas Events Day.

OCT - FEB
Living History Family Days -
1st Sun in every month.

OCT - FEB
Specialist Talks & Tours -
3rd Sun in every month.

OCT - FEB
Winter programme of events –
call for details.

FEB 10
Wedding Fair.

163

SAINT HILL MANOR

EAST GRINSTEAD

Owner:
Church of Scientology

▶ **CONTACT**

Mrs Liz Nyegaard
Saint Hill Manor
Saint Hill Road
East Grinstead
West Sussex   RH19 4JY

Tel: 01342 326711

Fax: 01342 317057

▶ **LOCATION**

2m SW of East
Grinstead. At Felbridge,
turn off A22, down
Imberhorne Lane and
over crossroads into
Saint Hill Road,
200yds on right.

Rail: East Grinstead
station.

Air: 15 mins drive from
Gatwick airport.

Built 1792 by Gibbs Crawfurd. One of the finest Sussex sandstone buildings in existence and situated near the breathtaking Ashdown Forest. Subsequent owners included Edgar March Crookshank and the Maharajah of Jaipur. In 1959, Saint Hill Manor's final owner, acclaimed author and humanitarian L Ron Hubbard, acquired the Manor, where he lived for many years with his family. As a result of the work carried out under Mr Hubbard's direction, the Manor has been restored to its original beauty, including the uncovering of fine oak wood panelling, marble fireplaces and plasterwork ceilings. Other outstanding features of this lovely house include an impressive library of Mr Hubbard's works, elegant winter garden, and delightful Monkey Mural painted in 1945 by Winston Churchill's nephew John Spencer Churchill. This 100-foot mural depicts many famous personalities as monkeys, including Winston Churchill. Also open to the public are 59 acres of landscaped gardens, lake and woodlands. Ideal for corporate functions and also available as a film location. Annual events include open-air theatre, arts festivals, classical and jazz concerts.

▶ **OPENING TIMES**

All year
daily, 2 - 5pm,
on the hour.

Groups welcome
throughout the year.

▶ **ADMISSION**

Free.

 Ground floor.

Teas available.

Obligatory.

P

SPECIAL EVENTS

Open Air Theatre in summer –
please telephone for details.

STANSTED PARK 🏛

ROWLANDS CASTLE

www.stanstedpark.co.uk

Owner: Trustees of Stansted Park Foundation

▶ **CONTACT**

The House Manager
Stansted Park
Rowlands Castle
Hampshire PO9 6DX

Tel: 023 9241 2265

Fax: 023 9241 3773

e-mail: enquiry@
stanstedpark.co.uk

▶ **LOCATION**

OS Ref. SU761 103

Follow brown heritage signs from A3 (Rowlands Castle) or A27 (Havant)

Rail: Rowlands Castle is 3m from Stansted Park (London Waterloo 1¹/₂ hrs). No taxis from Rowlands Castle station.

Air: Eastleigh, Southampton.

Set amongst 1750 acres of glorious park and woodland, Stansted Park is a prime example of the Caroline revival, rich in wildlife and famous for its tranquillity. Not only is Stansted one of the South's most beautiful stately homes, it is also one of Sussex's best kept secrets.

The contrast between the magnificent State Rooms and the purpose-built Servants' Quarters gives an insight into the social history of an English Country House in its heyday. The Bessborough family collection includes paintings of the famous Georgiana, Duchess of Devonshire and her sister Henrietta Frances, wife to the 3rd Earl and mother of the equally famous Lady Caroline Lamb. The visionary stained glass windows in the exquisitely decorated Ancient Chapel inspired some of Keats' finest poetry.

Ivan Hicks' famous 'Garden in Mind', the restored Dutch Garden and Circular Well-head Garden, not forgetting the Arboretum and Garden Centre, are a must for people who love plants. There is also an on-site glass blower, potter, giftshop and Pavilion Tea Room.

We specialise in traditional country pursuits including on site falconry, clay pigeon shooting, gun dog displays and archery as well as being an excellent location for product launches, initiative training, team building games or action theme days, including 4-wheel driving and quad bikes.

Stansted Park is an exceptional setting for Civil wedding ceremonies of up to 80 guests whilst the Main Hall and Music Room are perfect for receptions when used in conjunction with other Staterooms or a Marquee on the lawn. Every function is tailored to individual requirements to ensure that your special day is unique.

▶ **OPENING TIMES**

House

31 March - 30 October: Sun - Wed, 1 - 5pm (last entry 3.30pm). Guided tours/free flow in operation. Please ring to confirm before visiting.

Grounds, including Ivan Hicks' 'Garden in Mind':

All year: daily (closed 25/26 & 31 Dec & 1 Jan). Open Easter Sun from 1pm. Restricted access on Sat due to weddings.

Falconry:

All year: daily except Thurs, 9am - 5pm. Flying times: 11am, 1pm & 3pm (weather permitting).

Garden Centre:

All year:
Mon - Sat, 9am - 5pm.
Suns, 10.30am - 4.30pm.

▶ **ADMISSION**

House & Grounds

Adult	£5.50
Child (5-17yrs)	£3.50
OAP	£4.50
Family (2+3)	£14.50

Grounds

Adult	£3.50
Child (5-17yrs)	£2.00
OAP	£3.00
Family (2+3)	£9.00

Stansted Falconry

Adult	£3.00
Child	£2.00
OAP	£2.50

Groups (30-50)
By arrangement.
10% discount off the above prices.

CONFERENCE/FUNCTION

ROOM	MAX CAPACITY
Mail Hall	40
Music Room	80
Blue Drawing Room	50

ℹ️ A variety of activities for Corporate Hospitality, including clay shooting, off-road driving, team-building games, action-theme days, even murder mystery evenings. Excellent film location. Childrens' play area, picnic area, woodland walk, arboretum, Garden Centre & Falconry.

🐕 In woods, on leads.

🔖 A wide variety of facilities to suit parties of all sizes. A complete package with both ceremony and reception is just one of the options offered. Every function is tailored to individual requirements and we guarantee a special day.

♿ Partial.. WC. ☕

🚶 By arrangement. 🅿️

❄️ Tel for details.

NT Photographic Library: David Sellman

UPPARK 🌿

SOUTH HARTING

www.nationaltrust.org.uk/regions/southern

Owner:
The National Trust

▶ **CONTACT**

The Property Manager
Uppark
South Harting
Petersfield GU31 5QR

Tel: 01730 825415

Info Line: 01730 825857

Fax: 01730 825873

e-mail: supgen@
smtp.ntrust.org.uk

▶ **LOCATION**

OS Ref. 197 SU781 181

5m SE of Petersfield
on B2146, 1¹/₂ m S of
South Harting.

Bus: Stagecoach Sussex
Bus 54 (not Sun).

Rail: Petersfield 5¹/₂ m.

A fine late 17th century house set high on the South Downs with magnificent sweeping views to the sea. An extensive, award-winning exhibition tells the dramatic story of the 1989 fire and restoration of the house and its collections.

The elegant Georgian interior houses a famous Grand Tour collection that includes paintings by Pompeo Batoni, Luca Giordano, and Joseph Vernet, with furniture and ceramics of superb quality. The famous 18th century dolls' house with original contents is one of the star items in the collection, and provides a rare insight into life in a great house 300 years ago.

The restaurant in the Georgian kitchen in the East Pavilion serves a Georgian themed menu using local produce. The West Pavilion houses the beautiful stables and the atmospheric and romantic Dairy. The complete servants' quarters in the basement are shown as they were in Victorian days when H G Wells' mother was housekeeper. From the basement visitors leave the house via the atmospheric subterranean passages.

The fine, peaceful, historic garden is now fully restored in the early 19th century 'Picturesque' style, with flowering shrubs and under-plantings of bulbs, perennials and herbaceous plants in a magical woodland and downland setting.

NT Photographic Library: Nadia MacKenzie

▶ **OPENING TIMES**

24 March - 31 October:
Daily except Fris & Sats.

House: 1 - 5pm
(opens 12 noon on Suns
in Aug).

Last admission 4.15pm.

Print room open on 1st
Mon of each month.

**Grounds, exhibition,
garden, shop &
restaurant:**
11am - 5pm.

▶ **ADMISSION**

**House, Garden &
Exhibition**

Adult	£5.50
Child	£2.75
Family	£13.75
Groups (15+, weekdays only, must book)	£4.50

Booked group guided
tours: mornings by
arrangement.

Special group catering
arrangements: please
telephone for details.

NT members Free.

ⓘ Pushchairs on weekdays
only. No photography, large
bags or sharp heeled shoes in
the house.

🛍 Tel for Xmas opening.

♿ Partial. WC. Wheelchairs
available.

🍽 Licensed.

🅿 Coaches must pre-book.

🐕 On leads, in Car Park (no
shade) & woodland only.

▣ Tel for details.

CONFERENCE/FUNCTION

ROOM	MAX CAPACITY
Restaurant	50
Lower Servants Hall	50

NTPL / Andrew Butler

ALFRISTON CLERGY HOUSE ❧

THE TYE, ALFRISTON, POLEGATE, EAST SUSSEX BN26 5TL

Tel: 01323 870001 **Fax:** 01323 871318 **e-mail:** ksdxxx@smtp.ntrust.org.uk
Owner: The National Trust **Contact:** The Property Manager
Step back into the Middle Ages with a visit to this 14th century thatched Wealden 'Hall House'. Trace the history of this building which in 1896 was the first to be acquired by the National Trust. Discover what is used to make the floor in the Great Hall and visit the excellent shop with its local crafts. Explore the delightful cottage garden and savour the idyllic setting beside Alfriston's parish church, with stunning views across the meandering River Cuckmere. An intriguing variety of shops, pubs and restaurants in Alfriston village make this a wonderful day out.
Location: OS Ref. TQ521 029. 4m NE of Seaford, just E of B2108.
Open: 2 - 17 Mar: Sats & Suns. 11am - 4pm. 23 Mar - 3 Nov: daily except Tues & Fris, 10am - 5pm. 6 Nov - 22 Dec: Wed - Sun, 11am - 4pm.
Admission: Adult £2.80, Child £1.40, Family (2+3) £7. Pre-booked groups £2.40.
🖼 ♿Unsuitable. 🅿Parking in village car parks.

ANNE OF CLEVES HOUSE
52 Southover High Street, Lewes, Sussex BN7 1JA
Tel: 01273 474610 **Fax:** 01273 486990 **e-mail:** anne@sussexpast.co.uk
www.sussexpast.co.uk
Owner: Sussex Past **Contact:** Mr Stephen Watts
This 16th century timber-frame Wealden hall-house was given to Anne of Cleves as part of her divorce settlement from Henry VIII in 1541, and contains wide-ranging collections of Sussex interest. Furnished rooms give an impression of life in the 17th and 18th centuries. Artefacts from Lewes Priory, Sussex pottery and Wealden ironwork.
Location: OS198 Ref. TQ410 096. S of Lewes town centre, off A27/A275/A26.
Open: 1 Jan - 28 Feb: Tue - Sat, 10am - 5pm. 1 Mar - 31 Oct: Mon - Sat, 10am - 5pm; Sun, 12 noon - 5pm. 1 Nov - 31 Dec: Tue - Sat, 10am - 5pm. Closed 24 - 26 Dec.
Admission: Adult £2.80, Child £1.40, Conc. £2.50, Family (2+2) £7 or (1+4) £5.50. Combined ticket with Lewes Castle is also available. Groups (15+): Adult £2.50, Child £1.20, Conc. £2.30.
🖼 ♿Unsuitable. 🅿Limited. 🖼 🐕Guide dogs only. 🔺 ✳ 📺Tel for details.

ARUNDEL CASTLE
See page 157 for full page entry.

ARUNDEL CATHEDRAL
Parsons Hill, Arundel, Sussex BN18 9AY
Tel: 01903 882297 **Fax:** 01903 885335
e-mail: aruncath1@aol.com **Contact:** Rev A Whale
French Gothic Cathedral, church of the RC Diocese of Arundel and Brighton built by Henry, 15th Duke of Norfolk and opened 1873.
Location: OS Ref. TQ015 072. Above junction of A27 and A284.
Open: Summer: 9am - 6pm. Winter: 9am - dusk. Mass at 10am each day. Sun Masses: 8am, 9.30am & 11am, Vigil Sat evening: 6.30pm. Shop opened after services and on special occasions and otherwise at request.
Admission: Free.

English Heritage Photo Library

English Heritage Photo Library / Jonathan Bailey

1066 BATTLE OF HASTINGS ⊞
BATTLEFIELD & ABBEY

BATTLE, SUSSEX TN33 0AD

www.english-heritage.org.uk

Tel: 01424 773792 **Fax:** 01424 775059
Owner: English Heritage **Contact:** The Custodian
Visit the site of the 1066 Battle of Hastings. A free interactive audio tour will lead you around the battlefield and to the exact spot where Harold fell. Explore the magnificent Abbey ruins and see the fascinating exhibition in the gate house and '1066 Prelude to Battle' exhibition. Children's themed play area.
Location: OS Ref. TQ749 157. Top of Battle High Street. Turn off A2100 to Battle.

Open: 29 Mar - 30 Sept: daily, 10am - 6pm. 1 - 31 Oct: 10am - 5pm. 1 Nov - 31 Mar: daily 10am - 4pm. Closed 24 - 26 Dec & 1 Jan.
Admission: Adult £4.50, Child £2.30, Conc. £3.40, Family £11.30. 15% discount for groups (11+). EH members Free.

🖼 ♿Ground floor & grounds. 🖼Free. 🐕In grounds, on leads. ✳
📺Tel for details.

South East - England

BATEMAN'S ☙

See page 158 for full page entry.

BAYHAM OLD ABBEY ⌗

Lamberhurst, Sussex

Tel/Fax: 01892 890381 **www**.english-heritage.org.uk

Owner: English Heritage **Contact:** The Custodian

These riverside ruins are of a house of 'White' Canons, founded c1208 and preserved in the 18th century, when its surroundings were landscaped to create its delightful setting.

Location: OS Ref. TQ651 366. 13/4 m W of Lamberhurst off B2169.

Open: 29 Mar - 30 Sept: daily, 10am - 6pm. 1 - 31 Oct: 10am - 5pm. 1 Nov - 31 Mar: w/ends only 10am - 4pm. Closed 24 - 26 Dec & 1 Jan.

Admission: Adult £2.30, Child £1.20, Conc. £1.70.

🄰 ♿Grounds. WC. 🐕In grounds, on leads. ❋

BENTLEY HOUSE & MOTOR MUSEUM

Halland, Lewes, East Sussex BN8 5AF

Tel: 01825 840573 **Fax:** 01825 841322

e-mail: barrysutherland@pavilion.co.uk **www**.bentley.org.uk

Owner: East Sussex County Council **Contact:** Mr Barry Sutherland - Manager

Early 18th century farmhouse with a large reception room of Palladian proportions added on either end in the 1960s by the architect Raymond Erith, each lit by large Venetian windows. Furnished to form a grand 20th century evocation of a mid-Georgian house.

Location: OS Ref. TQ485 160. 7m NE from Lewes, signposted off A22, A26 & B2192.

Open: Estate: 18 Mar - 31 Oct: daily, 10.30am - 4.30pm (last adm.). Nov, Feb - Mar: weekends only, 10.30am - 4pm (last adm.). House: 1 Apr - 31 Oct: daily 12 noon - 5pm. Estate closed Dec & Jan.

Admission: Adult £5 (£4 in winter), Child (4-15) £3.20, Conc. £4, Family (2+4) £14.80. Coach drivers free admission & refreshment ticket. 10% discount for groups of 11+. Special rates for the disabled. Call to verify prices (2001 rates).

🄰 🅃Wedding receptions. ♿ 🄻Licensed. 🄹By arrangement. 🅿 🄼

🐕Guide dogs only. 🄰

Petworth House

BODIAM CASTLE ☙

BODIAM, Nr ROBERTSBRIDGE, EAST SUSSEX TN32 5UA

Tel: 01580 830436 **Fax:** 01580 830398 **e-mail:** kboxxx@smtp.ntrust.org.uk

Owner: The National Trust **Contact:** The Administrator

Built in 1385 to defend the surrounding countryside and as a comfortable dwelling for a rich nobleman, Bodiam Castle is one of the finest examples of medieval architecture. The virtual completeness of its exterior makes it popular with adults, children and film crews alike. Inside, although a ruin, floors have been replaced in some of the towers and visitors can climb the spiral staircase to enjoy superb views from the battlements. Discover more of its intriguing past in the museum and video room, and wander in the romantic Castle grounds peacefully set on the banks of the River Rother.

Location: OS Ref. TQ782 256. 3m S of Hawkhurst, 2m E of A21 Hurst Green.

Open: 1 Jan, 10 - 4pm. 5 Jan - 9 Feb: Sats & Suns, 10am - 4pm. 10 Feb - 1 Nov: daily, 10am - 6pm. 2 Nov - mid Feb 2003: Sats & Suns, 10am - 4pm. Last admission 1 hour before closing.

Admission: Adult £3.90, Child £1.95, Family ticket (2+3) £9.75. Groups £3.30. Car parking £2 per car.

ℹSmall museum. 🄰 ♿Ground floor & grounds. 🍴 🅿

🄼Teacher and student packs and education base. ❋

BORDE HILL GARDEN, PARK & WOODLAND

HAYWARDS HEATH, WEST SUSSEX RH16 1XP

www.bordehill.co.uk

Tel: 01444 450326   **Fax:** 01444 440427   **e-mail:** info@bordehill.co.uk

Owner: Mr & Mrs A P Stephenson Clarke   **Contact:** Sarah Brook

Winner of two prestigious awards. You can find a real haven of peace and tranquillity at Borde Hill Garden, created in 1890s, where botanical interest as well as garden design and renaissance play equally important roles. 'Linked' gardens, each with their own unique style, offer a rich variety of seasonal colours. Marvel at the spring flowering bulbs and award winning camellias, rhododendrons and azaleas in May and June. In summer, the exuberant herbaceous borders and fragrant English roses give way to a vivid blaze of autumnal colour. Extensive walks to the woods with rare trees and shrubs. Borde Hill Tudor House open for conferences and product launches.

Location: OS Ref. TQ324 265. 1¹/₂ m N of Haywards Heath on Balcombe Road, 3m from A23. 45mins from Victoria Station.

Open: All year, daily (including Christmas Day), 10am - 6pm (dusk if earlier). Also Tues & Thurs for pre-booked groups (20+).

Admission: Adult £5.50, Child £3, OAP £5, Family (2+3) £15. Pre-booked groups (20+): £5.

🖼 🛉 🍴 ⚒ ●Licensed. 🛏Licensed. 🅕By arrangement. 🎧 🅿 ▣
🐾In grounds, on leads. ❊ ⚥ Tel for details.

BOXGROVE PRIORY ⚏

Boxgrove, Chichester, Sussex

Tel: 01424 775705

Owner: English Heritage   **Contact:** Area Manager

Remains of the Guest House, Chapter House and Church of this 12th century priory, which was the cell of a French abbey until Richard II confirmed its independence in 1383.

Location: OS Ref. SU909 076. N of Boxgrove, 4m E of Chichester on minor road N of A27.

Open: Any reasonable time.

Admission: Free.

BRAMBER CASTLE ⚏

Bramber, Sussex

Tel: 01424 775705

Owner: English Heritage   **Contact:** Area Manager

The remains of a Norman castle gatehouse, walls and earthworks in a splendid setting overlooking the Adur valley.

Location: OS Ref. TQ187 107. On W side of Bramber village NE of A283.

Open: Any reasonable time.

Admission: Free.

BRICKWALL HOUSE & GARDENS

Northiam, Rye, Sussex TN31 6NL

Tel: 01797 253388   **Fax:** 01797 252567

Owner: Frewen Educational Trust   **Contact:** The Curator

Impressive timber-framed house. 17th century drawing room with magnificent plaster ceilings and good portraits including by Lely, Kneller and Vereist. Topiary, chess garden.

Location: OS Ref. TQ831 241. S side of Northiam village at junction of A28 and B2088.

Open: Coaches by appointment only.

Admission: £4.

CAMBER CASTLE ⚏

Camber, Nr Rye, East Sussex

Tel: 01797 223862   **www.**english-heritage.org.uk

Owner: English Heritage   **Contact:** Rye Harbour Nature Reserve

A fine example of one of many coastal fortresses built by Henry VIII to counter the threat of invasion during the 16th century. Monthly guided walks of Rye Nature Reserve including Camber Castle, telephone for details.

Location: OS189, Ref. TQ922 185. Across fields off A259, 1m S of Rye off harbour road.

Open: 1 Jul - 30 Sept: Sat & Sun, 2 - 5pm. Last admission 4.30pm.

Admission: Adult £2, Child Free, Conc. £1.50.

⚒Unsuitable. 🅕By arrangement. 🅿None. 🐾Guide dogs only.

CHARLESTON   *See page 159 for full page entry.*

CHICHESTER CATHEDRAL

Chichester, Sussex PO19 1PX

Tel: 01243 782595   **Fax:** 01243 536190   **e-mail:** vo@chicath.freeserve.co.uk

Contact: Mrs J Thom

In the heart of the city, this fine Cathedral has been a centre of Christian worship and community life for 900 years.

Location: OS Ref. SU860 047. West Street, Chichester.

Open: Summer: 7.30am - 7pm, Winter: 7.30am - 5pm. Choral Evensong daily (except Wed) during term time.

Admission: Donation.

Special Events Index
◁ ◁ ◁ pgs 40-43

South East - England

CHA

DANNY

HURSTPIERPOINT, SUSSEX BN6 9BB

www.cha.org.uk

Tel: 01273 833000   **Fax:** 01273 832436

Owner: Country Houses Association   **Contact:** The Administrators

Built in 1595, Danny has many typical Elizabethan features and the house forms an 'E' shape. During WWI Danny was rented by Prime Minister Lloyd George as a secure location for Cabinet meetings. The Great Hall was their meeting place. Danny has been converted into apartments for active retired people.

Location: OS Ref. TQ285 149. 1m SE of Hurstpierpoint S of the Hassocks road.

Open: May - Sept: Wed & Thur, 2 - 5pm.

Admission: Adult £3.50, Child £1.50. Groups by arrangement.

T ✕ ♨ 1 single & 1 double with bathroom, CHA members only.

Peter Stiles

Goodwood House

Jeremy Whitaker

FIRLE PLACE 🏛

FIRLE, LEWES, EAST SUSSEX BN8 6LP

Tel: 01273 858307 (enquiries) **Info:** 01273 858335 **Events:** 01273 858567

Fax: 01273 858188   **Restaurant:** 01273 858307   **e-mail:** gage@firleplace.co.uk

Owner: The Rt Hon Viscount Gage

Firle Place is the home of the Gage family and has been for over 500 years. Set at the foot of the Sussex Downs within its own parkland, this unique house originally Tudor, was built of Caen stone, possibly from a monastery dissolved by Sir John Gage, friend of Henry VIII. Remodelled in the 18th century it is similar in appearance to that of a French chateau. The house contains a magnificent collection of Old Master paintings, fine English and European furniture and an impressive collection of Sèvres porcelain collected mainly by the 3rd Earl Cowper from Panshanger House, Hertfordshire.

Events: The Great Tudor Hall can, on occasion, be used for private dinners, with

drinks on the Terrace or in the Billiard Room. A private tour of the house can be arranged. The paddock area is an ideal site for a marquee. The park can be used for larger events, using the house as a backdrop.

Restaurant: Enjoy the licensed restaurant and tea terrace with views over the garden for luncheon and cream teas.

Location: OS Ref. TQ473 071. 4m S of Lewes on A27 Brighton/Eastbourne Road.

Open: 31 Mar/ 1 Apr; 5/6 & 26/27 May. 12 May - 29 Sept: Wed, Thur, Sun & BHs, 1.45 - 4.15pm. Guided tours.

Admission: Adult £5, Child £2.50, Conc. £4.50 Connoisseurs' Day (1st Thurs each month, Jun - Sept) £6.

ℹ️ No photography in house. ◻ T ♿ Ground floor & restaurant.
🍴 Licensed. ☕ Tea Terrace. ♿ P ✕ In grounds on leads.

FISHBOURNE ROMAN PALACE

SALTHILL ROAD, FISHBOURNE, CHICHESTER, SUSSEX PO19 3QR

www.sussexpast.co.uk

Tel: 01243 785859   **Fax:** 01243 539266   **e-mail:** adminfish@sussexpast.co.uk
Owner: Sussex Past   **Contact:** David Rudkin

A Roman site built around AD75. A modern building houses part of the extensive remains including a large number of Britain's finest in-situ mosaics. The museum displays many objects discovered during excavations and an audio-visual programme tells Fishbourne's remarkable story. Roman gardens have been reconstructed and include a museum of Roman gardening.

Location: OS Ref. SU837 057. 1¹/₂ m W of Chichester in Fishbourne village off A27/A259.

Open: 1 Feb - 15 Dec: daily. Feb, Nov - Dec: 10am - 4pm. Mar - Jul & Sept - Oct: 10am - 5pm. Aug: 10am - 6pm. 16 Dec - 31 Jan (excluding Christmas): Sats & Suns, 10am - 4pm.

Admission: Adult £4.70, Child £2.50, Conc. £4, Family (2+2): £12.20, Registered disabled £3.80. Groups (20+): Adult £4.10, Child £2.35, Conc. £3.80.

⬛ 🅸 ⬛ ⬛ 🅸 By arrangement. 🅿 ⬛ 🖾Guide dogs only. ✳ 🆅 Tel for details.

GLYNDE PLACE 🏛

GLYNDE, LEWES, SUSSEX BN8 6SX

www.glyndeplace.com

Tel: 01273 858224   **Fax:** 01273 858224   **e-mail:** hampden@glyndeplace.co.uk
Owners: Viscount & Viscountess Hampden   **Contact:** Viscount Hampden

Glynde Place is a magnificent example of Elizabethan architecture commanding exceptionally fine views of the South Downs. Amongst the collections of 400 years of family living can be seen a fine collection of 17th and 18th century portraits of the Trevors and a room dedicated to Sir Henry Brand, Speaker of the House of Commons 1872 - 1884 and an exhibition of 'Harbert Morley and the Great Rebellion 1638 - 1660' the story of the part played by the owner of Glynde Place in the Civil War. Plus a collection of 18th century Italian masterpieces.

Location: OS Ref. TQ457 093. In Glynde village 4m SE of Lewes on A27.

Open: House & Garden: Jun & Sept: Weds & Suns. Jul & Aug: Weds, Thus & Suns, 2 - 5pm. Last adm. 4.45pm.

Admission: Adult £5, Child £2.50.

⬛ 🅸 🅲WC. ⬛ 🅸 🅿 Free. 🅰

GOODWOOD HOUSE 🏛   *See page 160 for full page entry.*

Jonathan Buckley

GREAT DIXTER HOUSE & GARDENS 🏛

NORTHIAM, RYE, EAST SUSSEX TN31 6PH

www.greatdixter.co.uk

Tel: 01797 252878   **Fax:** 01797 252879   **e-mail:** office@greatdixter.co.uk
Owner: Christopher Lloyd   **Contact:** Perry Rodriguez

Great Dixter, built c1450 is the birthplace of Christopher Lloyd, gardening author. The house boasts the largest surviving timber-framed hall in the country. The gardens feature a variety of topiary, pools, wild meadow areas and the famous Long Border and Exotic Garden.

Location: OS Ref. TQ817 251. Signposted off the A28 in Northiam.

Open: Apr - Oct: Tue - Sun, 2 - 5pm.

Admission: House & Garden: Adult £6, Child £1.50. Garden only: Adult £4.50, Child £1. Groups (25+) by appointment. House & garden: Adult £5, Child £1.50.

🅸No photography in House. ⬛ 🅸 🅸Obligatory. 🅿 Limited for coaches. 🖾Guide dogs only.

Merriments Garden

Plant Sales Index
◁ ◁ ◁ pgs 36-37

HAMMERWOOD PARK

EAST GRINSTEAD, SUSSEX RH19 3QE

www.hammerwoodpark.com

Tel: 01342 850594 **Fax:** 01342 850864 **e-mail:** latrobe@mistral.co.uk
Owner/Contact: David Pinnegar

Built in 1792 as an Apollo's hunting lodge by Benjamin Latrobe, architect of the Capitol and the White House, Washington DC. Owned by Led Zepplin in the 1970s, rescued from dereliction in 1982. Teas in the Organ Room; mural by French artists in the hall; and a derelict dining room still shocks the unwary. Guided tours (said by many to be the most interesting in Sussex) by the family.

Location: OS Ref. TQ442 390. 3¹/2 m E of East Grinstead on A264 to Tunbridge Wells, 1m W of Holtye.

Open: 1 June - end Sept: Wed, Sat & BH Mon, 2 - 5pm. Guided tour starts 2.05pm. Private groups: Easter - Jun. Coaches strictly by appointment. Small groups any time throughout the year by appointment.

Admission: House & Park: Adult £5, Child £2. Private viewing by arrangement.
⒤Conferences. Ⓣ ⒠ ⒡Obligatory. ▣ ⊞In grounds. ⊡B&B. ✻
⒲ Tel for details.

HIGH BEECHES GARDENS ⌂

HIGH BEECHES, HANDCROSS, SUSSEX RH17 6HQ

www.highbeeches.com

Tel: 01444 400589 **Fax:** 01444 401543 **e-mail:** office@highbeeches.com
Owner: High Beeches Gardens Conservation Trust (Reg. Charity)
Contact: Sarah Bray

Explore 25 acres of magically beautiful, peaceful woodland and water gardens. Daffodils, bluebells, azaleas, naturalised gentians, autumn colours. Rippling streams, enchanting vistas. Four acres of natural wildflower meadows. Rare plants. Marked trails. Recommended by Christopher Lloyd. Enjoy lunches and teas in the new tearoom and tea lawn in restored Victorian farm building.

Location: OS Ref. TQ275 308. S side of B2110. 1m NE of Handcross.

Open: 28 Mar - 30 Jun & 1 Sept - 31 Oct: Thur - Tue, 1 - 5pm (last admission). Jul & Aug: Sun - Tue, 1 - 5pm. Coaches and guided tours by appointment only.

Admission: Adult £4.50, Child (under 14) Free. Season ticket (admits 2): £20. Groups (30+) anytime by appointment: £3.50pp. Guided tours for groups £5pp.
⒡On Event Days. ⒧Unsuitable. ⒯ ⒡By arrangement. ⒫ ⊞
⒲ Tel for details.

HERSTMONCEUX CASTLE GARDENS

Hailsham, Sussex BN27 1RN
Tel: 01323 833816 **Fax:** 01323 834499 **e-mail:** c_dennett@isc.queensu.ac.uk
www.herstmonceux-castle.com
Owner: Queen's University, Canada **Contact:** C Dennett
This breathtaking 15th century moated Castle is within 500 acres of parkland and gardens (including Elizabethan Garden) and is ideal for picnics and woodland walks. At Herstmonceux there is something for all the family. For information on our attractions or forthcoming events tel: 01323 834457.
Location: OS Ref. TQ646 104. 2m S of Herstmonceux village (A271) by minor road. 10m WNW of Bexhill.
Open: 29 Mar - 27 Oct: daily, 10am - 6pm (last adm. 5pm) Closes 5pm from Oct.
Admission: Grounds and Gardens: Adults £4, Child under 5yrs Free, Conc. £3. Castle Tour: Adult £2.50, Child £1 (under 5yrs Free). Group rates/bookings available.
⒤Visitor Centre. ⒧Limited for Castle Tour. ⒠ ⒡ ⒫ ⊞On leads. ▲
⒲ Tel for details.

HIGHDOWN GARDENS

Littlehampton Road, Goring-by-Sea, Worthing, Sussex BN12 6PE
Tel: 01903 501054
Owner: Worthing Borough Council **Contact:** C Beardsley Esq
Unique gardens in disused chalk pit, begun in 1909.
Location: OS Ref. TQ098 040. 3m WNW of Worthing on N side of A259, just W of the Goring roundabout.
Open: 1 Apr - 30 Sept: Mon - Fri, 10am - 6pm. W/ends & BHs, 10am - 6pm. 1 Oct - 30 Nov: Mon - Fri, 10am - 4.30pm. 1 Dec - 31 Jan: 10am - 4pm. 1 Feb - 31 Mar: Mon - Fri, 10am - 4.30pm.
Admission: Free.

LAMB HOUSE ⌘

West Street, Rye, Sussex TN31 7ES
Tel: 01892 890651 **Fax:** 01892 890110
Owner: The National Trust **Contact:** Regional Office
The home of the writer Henry James from 1898 to 1916 where he wrote the best novels of his later period.
Location: OS Ref. TQ920 202. In West Street, facing W end of church.
Open: 3 Apr - 2 Nov: Weds & Sats only, 2 - 6pm. Last admission 5.30pm.
Admission: Adult £2.60, Child £1.30, Family (2+3) £6.50. Group: £2.10.

LEONARDSLEE GARDENS

See page 161 for full page entry.

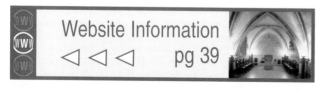

Website Information
◁ ◁ ◁ pg 39

LEWES CASTLE & BARBICAN HOUSE MUSEUM

169 HIGH STREET, LEWES, SUSSEX BN7 1YE

www.sussexpast.co.uk

Tel: 01273 486290 **Fax:** 01273 486990 **e-mail:** castle@sussexpast.co.uk

Owner: Sussex Past **Contact:** Mrs Jill Allen

Lewes's imposing Norman castle offers magnificent views across the town and surrounding downland. Barbican House, towered over by the Barbican Gate, is home to the Museum of Sussex Archaeology. A superb scale model of Victorian Lewes provides the centrepiece of a 25 minute audio-visual presentation telling the story of the county town of Sussex.

Location: OS198 Ref. TQ412 101. Lewes town centre off A27/A26/A275.

Open: Daily (except Mons in Jan & 24 - 26 Dec). Mon - Sat: 10am - 5.30pm; Suns & BHs, 11am - 5.30pm. Castle closes at dusk in winter.

Admission: Adult £4.20, Child £2.10, Conc. £3.70 Family (2+2) £11.40 or (1+4) £8.40. Groups (15+): Adult £3.70, Child £1.70, Conc. £3.10. Combined ticket with Anne of Cleves House available.

▢ ♿ Unsuitable. ✗ By arrangement. ▣ ✱ ♿ Tel for details.

MARLIPINS MUSEUM

High Street, Shoreham-by-Sea, Sussex BN43 5DA

Tel: 01273 462994 or 01323 441279 **e-mail:** pro@sussexpast.co.uk

Owner: Sussex Past **Contact:** Helen Poole

Shoreham's local and especially maritime history is explored at Marlipins, an important historic building of Norman origin.

Location: OS198 Ref. TQ214 051. Shoreham town centre on A259, W of Brighton.

Open: Due to major rebuilding work Marlipins Museum's opening times during 2002 are uncertain. Please telephone 01273 487188 for details.

Admission: Adult £1.50, Child 75p, Conc. £1.

Bodiam Castle, inner court

Patrick Lane

MERRIMENTS GARDENS

HAWKHURST ROAD, HURST GREEN, EAST SUSSEX TN19 7RA

www.merriments.co.uk

Tel: 01580 860666 **Fax:** 01580 860324 **e-mail:** markbuchele@beeb.net

Owner: Family owned **Contact:** Mark Buchele

'A unique experiment in colour composition'.

Set in 4 acres of gently sloping Weald farmland, a naturalistic garden which never fails to delight. Deep curved borders richly planted and colour themed. An abundance of rare plants will startle the visitor with sheer originality. The garden is planted according to prevailing conditions and only using plants suited for naturalising and colonising their environment. This natural approach to gardening harks back to the days of William Robinson and is growing in popularity, especially in Northern Europe. Alternatively many borders are colour themed and planted in the great tradition of English gardening. These borders use a rich mix of trees, shrubs, perennials and grasses and give an arresting display from spring to autumn.

Location: OS198, Ref. TQ412 101. Signposted off A21 London - Hastings road, at Hurst Green.

Open: Apr - Sept: Mon - Sat, 10am - 5pm, Suns, 10.30am - 5pm.

Admission: Adult £3.50, Child £2. Groups (5+) by arrangement.

▢ ✗ ♿ Partial. ▣ Licensed. ✗ By arrangement. ℗ 🐕 In grounds, on leads.

South East - England

NT Photographic Library: Stephen Robson

MICHELHAM PRIORY 🏛

UPPER DICKER, HAILSHAM, SUSSEX BN27 3QS

www.sussexpast.co.uk

Tel: 01323 844224 **Fax:** 01323 844030 **e-mail:** adminmich@sussexpast.co.uk

Owner: Sussex Past **Contact:** Mr Henry Warner

Set on a medieval moated island surrounded by superb gardens, the Priory was founded in 1229. The remains after the Dissolution were incorporated into a Tudor farm and country house that now contains a fascinating array of exhibits. Grounds include a 14th century gatehouse, watermill, physic and cloister gardens and Elizabethan great barn.

Location: OS Ref. TQ557 093. 8m NW of Eastbourne off A22/A27. 2m W of Hailsham.

Open: 1 Mar - 31 Oct: Wed - Sun & BH Mons & daily in Aug. Mar & Oct: 10.30am - 4pm. Apr - Jul & Sept: 10.30am - 5pm. Aug: 10.30am - 5.30pm.

Admission: Adult £4.80, Child £2.50, Conc. £4.20, Family (2+2) £12.20, Registered disabled & carer £2.40 each. Groups (15+): Adult/Conc. £4, Child £2.35.

🖻 🎋 🖵 🕭 🖙 🏠 Licensed. 🖅 By arrangement. 🅿 ▣ 🦮 Guide dogs only. ▲ 🐾 Tel for details.

NYMANS GARDEN ❀

HANDCROSS, HAYWARDS HEATH, SUSSEX RH17 6EB

www.nationaltrust.org.uk/regions/southern

Tel: 01444 400321/405250 **Fax:** 01444 400253 **e-mail:** snygen@smtp.ntrust.org.uk

Owner: The National Trust **Contact:** The Property Manager

One of the great gardens of the Sussex Weald, with rare and beautiful plants, shrubs and trees from all over the world. Wall garden, hidden sunken garden, pinetum, laurel walk and romantic ruins. Lady Rosse's library, drawing room and forecourt garden also open. Woodland walks and Wild Garden.

Location: OS Ref. TQ265 294. On B2114 at Handcross, 4¹/₂ m S of Crawley, just off London - Brighton M23/A23.

Open: 1 Mar - 3 Nov: daily except Mon & Tue but open BHs, 11am - 6pm or sunset if earlier. House: 23 Mar - 3 Nov: same days as garden, last entry at 4.30pm. Garden, tearoom & shop: Nov - Mar: Sats & Suns, 11am - 4pm. Closed 28 & 29 Dec 2002.

Admission: Adult £6, Child £3, Family £15. Pre-booked Groups (15+) £5. Joint group ticket which includes same day entry to Standen £9, available Wed - Fri only. Winter weekends: Adult £3, Child £1.50, Family £7.50. Booked groups: £2.50.

🖻 🎋 🖇 Grounds. WC. 🖙 🏠 Licensed. 🐾

MONK'S HOUSE ❀

Rodmell, Lewes BN7 3HF

Tel: 01892 890651 **Fax:** 01892 890110

Owner: The National Trust **Contact:** Regional Office

A small weather-boarded house, the home of Leonard and Virgina Woolf until Leonard's death in 1969.

Location: OS Ref. TQ421 064. 4 m E of Lewes, off former A275 in Rodmell village, near church.

Open: 3 Apr - 2 Nov: Weds & Sats, 2 - 5.30pm. Last admission 5pm. Groups: Thurs only, 2 - 5.30pm, by arrangement with tenant.

Admission: Adult £2.60, Child £1.30, Family £6.50.

MOORLANDS

Friar's Gate, Crowborough, East Sussex TN6 1XF

Tel: 01892 652474

Owner: Dr & Mrs Steven Smith **Contact:** Dr Steven Smith

Four acre garden set in a lush valley adjoining Ashdown Forest. Primulas, azaleas and rhododendrons flourish by streams and a small lake. New river walk with views over garden. Many unusual trees and shrubs. Good autumn colour. Featured in Meridien TV programme.

Location: OS Ref. TQ498 329. 2m NW of Crowborough. From B2188 at Friar's Gate, take left fork signposted 'Crowborough Narrow Road', entrance 100yds on left. From Crowborough crossroads take St John's Road to Friar's Gate.

Open: 1 Apr - 1 Oct: Weds, 11am - 5pm. 14 May & 19 Jul: Suns, 2 - 6pm. Other times by appointment only.

Admission: Adult £3, Child Free.

🖙 🐾

PALLANT HOUSE GALLERY

9 North Pallant, Chichester, West Sussex PO19 1TJ

Tel: 01243 774557 **Fax:** 01243 536038

Owner: Pallant House Gallery Trust **Contact:** Reception

Lovingly restored Queen Anne townhouse with historic rooms in Georgian style, fine antique furniture and formal garden. Highly important collection of Bow porcelain and displays of modern British art (Nicholson, Nash, Moore, Sutherland, Piper etc). Georgian style walled garden.

Location: OS Ref. SU861 047. City centre, SE of the Cross.

Open: All year: Tue - Sat ,10am - 5pm. Suns & BHs 12.30 - 5pm. Last admission 4.45pm. Closed Mons.

Admission: Adult £4, OAP £3, Student/Unemployed £2.50. West Sussex students and child under 16 Free.

South East · England

PARHAM HOUSE & GARDENS 🏛

PARHAM PARK, Nr PULBOROUGH, WEST SUSSEX RH20 4HS

www.parhaminsussex.co.uk

Tel: 01903 744888/742021 **Fax:** 01903 746557

e-mail: enquiries@parhaminsussex.co.uk

Owner: Parham Park Trust   **Contact:** Patricia Kennedy

Friendly staff give a warm welcome to this stunning Elizabethan house with award-winning gardens, set in the heart of a medieval deer park below the South Downs. The light, panelled rooms, from Great Hall to magnificent Long Gallery house an important collection of contemporary paintings, furniture, working clocks and needlework, all complemented by informal arrangements of flowers, freshly cut twice a week from the four acre walled garden. Light lunches and cream teas are served in the 15th century Big Kitchen (licensed), and souvenirs and gifts can be purchased from the shop, with plants and herbs on sale from the garden shop.

STITCHES IN TIME

A needlework weekend 18 - 19 May 2002

postponed from 19 - 20 May 2001 due to Foot & Mouth precautions
Official opening by Kaffe Fassett

Parham is home to perhaps the finest and most important collection of 17th century embroidery to be found anywhere in the United Kingdom. During this weekend there will be a display of 18th and 19th century Samplers never before seen by visitors to Parham, demonstrations of needleworking techniques, lectures and sales tables.

John Bushell

Location: OS Ref. TQ060 143. Midway between Pulborough & Storrington on A283.

Open: 31 Mar - 31 Oct: Weds, Thurs, Suns & BH Mons. Also Sats 18 May, 13 Jul & 7 Sept (special events). Private groups by arrangement at other times. Picnic area, Big Kitchen, and Gardens, 12 noon - 6pm. House: 2 - 6pm. Last entry 5pm.

Admission House & Gardens: Adult £5.50, Child £1, OAP £4.50, Family (2+2) £11. Unguided booked groups (20+) £4.50. Garden only: Adult/OAP £4, Child 50p.

ℹ No photography in house. 📷 ♿ 🚻 Partial. 🍴 Licensed. 🎦 🎧 🅿 🔲
🐕 In grounds, on leads. 🏨

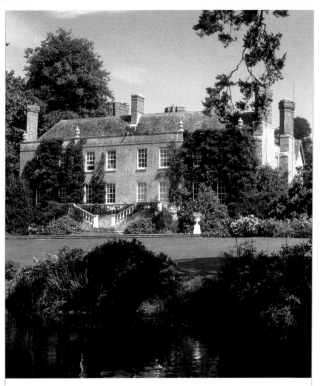

PASHLEY MANOR GARDENS 🏛

TICEHURST, WADHURST, EAST SUSSEX TN5 7HE

Tel: 01580 200888 **Fax:** 01580 200102 **e-mail:** pashleymanor@email.msn.com

Owner: Mr & Mrs James A Sellick   **Contact:** Caroline Foster

HHA/Christie's Garden of the Year 1999. The gardens offer a sumptuous blend of romantic landscaping, imaginative plantings and fine old trees, fountains, springs and large ponds. This is a quintessentially English garden of a very individual character with exceptional views to the surrounding valleyed fields. Many eras of English history are reflected here, typifying the tradition of the English Country House and its garden.

Pashley prides itself on its delicious food. Home-made soups, ploughman's lunches with pickles and patés, fresh salad from the garden (whenever possible), home-made scones and delicious cakes, filter coffee, specialist teas, fine wines - served on the Terrace Restaurant or in the Old Stables Tearoom. The gift shop caters for every taste… from postcards and local honey to traditional hand-painted ceramics and tapestry cushions. A wide selection of plants and shrubs, many of which grow at Pashley, are available for purchase.

Location: OS Ref. TQ 707 291. On B2099 between A21 and Ticehurst village.

Open: Apr - Sept: Tues, Weds, Thurs, Sats & all BH Mons, 11am - 5pm. 1 - 31 Oct: Mon - Fri, 10am - 4pm Garden only (restaurant & shop closed).

Admission: Adult £6, Child/OAP £5. Groups (20+): £5. Coaches must book.

📷 🚻 ♿ Partial. 🍴 Licensed. 🎦 By arrangement. 🅿 🐕 Guide dogs only.
🏨 Tel for details.

PETWORTH HOUSE ✤

See page 162 for full page entry.

PEVENSEY CASTLE ⊞

Pevensey, Sussex BN24 5LE

Tel: 01323 762604 www.english-heritage.org.uk

Owner: English Heritage   **Contact:** The Custodian

Originally a 4th century Roman Fort, Pevensey was the place where William the Conqueror landed in 1066 and established his first stronghold. The Norman castle included the remains of an unusual keep within the massive walls. Free audio tour tells the story of the Castle's 2,000 year history.

Location: OS Ref. TQ645 048. In Pevensey off A259.

Open: 29 Mar - 30 Sept: daily, 10am - 6pm. 1 - 31 Oct: 10am - 5pm. 1 Nov - 31 Mar: Wed - Sun only, 10am - 4pm. Closed 24 - 26 Dec & 1 Jan.

Admission: Adult £2.80, Child £1.40, Conc. £2.10. 15% discount for groups of 11+.

⬥Grounds. ▣ ⬥Free. ⬛In grounds, on leads. ✳ ⬛Tel for details.

PRESTON MANOR

PRESTON DROVE, BRIGHTON, EAST SUSSEX BN1 6SD

www.museums.brighton-hove.gov.uk

Tel: 01273 292770 **Fax:** 01273 292771

Owner: Brighton & Hove Council   **Contact:** David Beevers

A delightful Manor House which powerfully evokes the atmosphere of an Edwardian gentry home both 'upstairs' and 'downstairs'. Explore more than twenty rooms over four floors – from the servants' quarters, kitchens and butler's pantry in the basement to the attic bedrooms and nursery on the top floor. Plus charming walled gardens, pets' cemetery and 13th century parish church.

Location: OS Ref. TQ303 064. 2m N of Brighton on the A23 London road.

Open: All year: Tue - Sat 10am - 5pm, Suns 2 - 5pm, Mons 1 - 5pm (BHs 10am - 5pm). Closed Good Fri, 25/26 Dec.

Admission: Adult £3.30, Child £2.05, Conc. £2.80. Groups (20+) £2.80. Prices valid until 31 Mar 2002.

ⓘNo photography. ▣ Gift kiosk. ⊤ ⬥Unsuitable. ⓕBy arrangement. ▪ ⓟFor coaches. ✖ ✳ ⬛Spring, Summer & Autumn half-term. Easter, Summer & Christmas. Children's activities all year round.

THE PRIEST HOUSE

North Lane, West Hoathly, Sussex RH19 4PP

Tel: 01342 810479 **e-mail:** priest@sussexpast.co.uk **www.**sussexpast.co.uk

Owner: Sussex Past   **Contact:** Antony Smith

Standing in the beautiful surroundings of a traditional cottage garden on the edge of Ashdown Forest, the Priest House is an early 15th century timber-framed hall-house. In Elizabethan times it was modernised into a substantial yeoman's dwelling. Its furnished rooms contain 17th and 18th century furniture, kitchen equipment, needlework and household items. A formal herb garden contains over 150 different herbs.

Location: OS187 Ref. TQ362 325. In triangle formed by Crawley, East Grinstead and Haywards Heath, 4m off A22, 6m off M23.

Open: 1 Mar - 31 Oct: Mon - Sat, 11am - 5.30pm, Suns, 2 - 5.30pm.

Admission: Adults £2.60, Child £1.30, Conc. £2.30. Groups (15+): Adult £2.40, Child £1.20.

▣ ▦ ⬥Partial. ⓕBy arrangement. ⓟLimited (on street). ▪ ⬛In grounds, on leads.

THE ROYAL PAVILION

See page 163 for full page entry.

ST MARY'S HOUSE & GARDENS 🏠

BRAMBER, WEST SUSSEX BN44 3WE

Tel/Fax: 01903 816205 **e-mail:** stmaryshouse@btinternet.com

Owner/Contact: Mr Peter Thorogood

This enchanting, medieval timber-framed house is situated in the downland village of Bramber. The fine panelled interiors of St Mary's, which include the famous 'King's Room' associated with the escape of Charles II in 1651, and the unique Elizabethan 'Painted Room' with its intriguing trompe l'oeil murals, give an air of tranquillity and timelessness. Fact and legend tell our history from Knights Templar origins to the present day. Once the home of the real Algernon and Gwendolen brilliantly portrayed in Oscar Wilde's comedy, *The Importance of Being Earnest*, St Mary's was more than likely the setting for the Sherlock Holmes story, *The Musgrave Ritual*, and has served as a location for a number of television series including the world-famous *Dr Who*. The formal gardens with amusing animal topiary include an exceptional example of the 'Living Fossil' tree, Gingko biloba, and a mysterious ivy-clad 'Monk's Walk'. In the 'Secret Garden' can still be seen the Victorian original fruit-wall, potting shed, circular orchard, and woodland walk. St Mary's is a house of fascination and mystery. Many thousands of visitors have admired its picturesque charm and enjoyed its atmosphere of friendliness and welcome, qualities which make it a visit to remember.

Location: OS Ref. TQ189 105. Bramber village off A283. From London 56m via M23/A23 or A24. Bus from Shoreham to Steyning, alight St Mary's, Bramber.

Open: Easter - Sept: Suns, Thurs & BH Mons, 2 - 6pm. Groups at other times by arrangement. Secret Garden (3½ acres): May - Sept, 1st Sunday in every month.

Admission: House & Garden: Adult £5, Child £2, OAP £4.50. Groups (25+) £4.50. Secret Garden: Adult £2, Child Free.

ⓘNo photography in house. ▣ ⊤ ⬥Unsuitable. ▪ ⓕObligatory for Groups (max 60). Visit time 2½ hrs. ⓟ30 cars, 2 coaches. ✖ ▦ ⬛Tel for details.

SHEFFIELD PARK GARDEN ❦

SHEFFIELD PARK, EAST SUSSEX TN22 3QX

www.nationaltrust.org.uk

Tel: 01825 790231 **Fax:** 01825 791264 **e-mail:** kshxxx@smtp.ntrust.org.uk
Owner: The National Trust   **Contact:** The Property Manager

A magnificent tranquil 120 acre landscape garden, with 4 lakes, laid out in the 18th century by 'Capability' Brown. A garden for all seasons. Daffodils, snowdrops and bluebells in spring, its rhododendrons, azaleas and stream garden are spectacular in early summer. Cool tree-lined paths and lake reflections make it perfect for a stroll in high summer and the garden is ablaze with colour from its rare trees and shrubs in autumn. The mists and frosts in wintertime create a mystical mood and give the garden a unique atmosphere.

Location: OS Ref. TQ415 240. Midway between East Grinstead and Lewes, 5m NW of Uckfield on E side of A275.

Open: Jan & Feb: Sats & Suns only, 10.30am - 4pm or dusk. Mar - end Oct: Tue - Sun, BH Mons & Good Fri, 10.30am - 6pm, last admission 5pm or dusk. Nov & Dec: Tue - Sun, 10.30am - 4pm or dusk.

Admission: Adult £4.80, Child £2.40, Family (2+3) £12. Pre-booked groups £4. Joint ticket available with Bluebell Railway.

📷 ♿ Grounds. WC. ◖ Licensed (not NT). 🐕 Guide dogs only. ✳

NT Photographic Library, Jonathan Gibson

STANDEN ❦

EAST GRINSTEAD, WEST SUSSEX RH19 4NE

www.nationaltrust.org.uk/regions/southern

Tel: 01342 323029 **Fax:** 01342 316424 **e-mail:** sstpro@smtp.ntrust.org.uk
Owner: The National Trust   **Contact:** The Property Manager

Dating from the 1890s and containing original Morris & Co furnishings and decorations, Standen survives today as a remarkable testimony to the ideals of the Arts and Crafts Movement. The property was built as a family home by the influential architect Philip Webb and retains a warm, welcoming atmosphere. Details of Webb's designs can be found everywhere from the fireplaces to the original electric light fittings.

Location: OS Ref. TQ389 356. 2m S of East Grinstead, signposted from B2110.

Open: 23 Mar - 3 Nov: Wed - Sun & BHs. House: 11am - 5pm (last admission 4.30pm). Garden: As house, 11am - 6pm. Garden only: 8 Nov - 15 Dec: Fri - Sun, 11am - 3pm.

Admission: House & Garden: £5.50, Family £13.75. Garden only: £3. Joint ticket with same day entry to Nymans Garden £9, available Wed - Fri. Groups: £4.50, Wed - Fri only, if booked in advance.

📷 ♿ Partial. WC. ⊞ Licensed. ◼ 🐕 In grounds on leads, not in garden.

SAINT HILL MANOR	*See page 164 for full page entry.*

STANSTED PARK 🏛	*See page 165 for full page entry.*

UPPARK ❦	*See page 166 for full page entry.*

WAKEHURST PLACE ❦

Ardingly, Haywards Heath, Sussex RH17 6TN

Tel: 01444 894066 **Fax:** 01444 894069 **e-mail:** wakehurst@kew.org **www.**kew.org
Owner: The National Trust (managed by Royal Botanic Gdns) **Contact:** The Administrator

A superb collection of exotic trees, shrubs and other plants, many displayed in a geographic manner. Extensive water gardens, a winter garden, a rock walk and many other features. The Loder Valley Nature Reserve can be visited by prior arrangement.

Location: OS Ref. TQ339 314. 1¹/₂ m N of Ardingly, on B2028.

Open: Daily (not 25 Dec & 1 Jan). Feb & Oct: 10am - 5pm. Mar: 10am - 6pm. Apr - end Sept: 10am - 7pm. Nov - end Jan 2003: 10am - 4pm. Mansion closed 1hr before gardens.

Admission: Adult £6.50, Child (under 17) Free, Conc. £4.50.

📷 ♿ Ground floor & grounds. ⊞ ◖ Tel for details.

WEALD & DOWNLAND OPEN AIR MUSEUM

Singleton, Chichester, Sussex PO18 0EU

Tel: 01243 811348

40 original historic buildings. Interiors and gardens through the ages.

Location: OS Ref. SU876 127. 6m N of Chichester. S side of A286. S of Singleton.

Open: 1 Mar - 31 Oct: daily, 10.30am - 6pm. Nov - Feb: Weds & w/ends only. 10.30am - 4pm. 26 Dec - 3 Jan: daily, 10.30am - 4pm.

Admission: Adult £7, Child/Student £4, OAP £6.50, Family (2+3) £19. Prices from 1 Mar 2002. Group rates on request.

Carl Pendle

WEST DEAN GARDENS

WEST DEAN, CHICHESTER, WEST SUSSEX PO18 0QZ

www.westdean.org.uk

Tel: 01243 818210 **Fax:** 01243 811342 **e-mail:** gardens@westdean.org.uk

Owner: The Edward James Foundation **Contact:** Jim Buckland, Gardens Manager

Visiting the Gardens you are immersed in a classic 19th century designed landscape with its $2^{1}/_{2}$ acre walled kitchen garden, 13 original glasshouses dating from the 1890s, 35 acres of ornamental grounds, 240 acre landscaped park and the 49 acre St Roche's arboretum, all linked by a scenic 21/4 mile parkland walk. Features of the grounds are a lavishly planted 300ft long Edwardian pergola terminated by a flint and stone gazebo and sunken garden. The Visitor Centre (free entry) houses a licensed restaurant and an imaginative garden shop.

Location: OS Ref. SU863 128. SE side of A286 Midhurst Road, 6m N of Chichester.

Open: 1 Mar - 31 October: daily. Mar, Apr & Oct: 11am - 5pm. May - Sept: 10.30am - 5pm.

Admission: Adult £4.50, Child £2, OAP £4. Groups (20+): Adult £4, Child £2.

ⓘ No photography in house. 🄯 🄯 🄯 🄯 🄯 🄯 Licensed. 🅿 Limited for coaches. 🄯 By arrangement. 🄯 🄯 Guide dogs only. 🄯 Tel for details.

WILMINGTON PRIORY

Wilmington, Nr Eastbourne, East Sussex BN26 5SW

Tel: 01628 825920 or 825925 (bookings)   **www.**landmarktrust.co.uk

Owner: Leased to the Landmark Trust by Sussex Archaeological Society

Contact: The Landmark Trust

Founded by the Benedictines in the 11th century, the surviving, much altered buildings date largely from the 14th century. Managed and maintained by the Landmark Trust, which lets buildings for self-catering holidays. Full details of Wilmington Priory and 170 other historic buildings available for holidays are featured in The Landmark Handbook (price £9.50 refundable against booking), from The Landmark Trust, Shottesbrooke, Maidenhead, Berkshire, SL6 3SW.

Location: OS Ref. TQ543 042. 600yds S of A27. 6m NW of Eastbourne.

Open: Grounds, Ruins, Porch & Crypt: on 30 days between Apr - Oct. Whole property including interiors on 8 of these days, 28 - 31 May & 13 - 16 Sept 2002. Telephone for details. Accommodation is available for up to 6 people for self-catering holidays.

Admission: Please contact Landmark Trust for details.

🄯

Open All Year Index
◁ ◁ ◁ pgs 44-48

The Summerhouse, West Dean Gardens

Jim Buckland

English Heritage Photo Library

OSBORNE HOUSE ⊞

EAST COWES

Osborne House was the peaceful, rural retreat of Queen Victoria, Prince Albert and their family; they spent some of their happiest times here.

Many of the apartments have a very intimate association with the Queen who died here in 1901 and have been preserved almost unaltered ever since. The nursery bedroom remains just as it was in the 1870s when Queen Victoria's first grandchildren came to stay. Children were a constant feature of life at Osborne (Victoria and Albert had nine). Don't miss the Swiss Cottage, a charming chalet in the grounds built for the Royal children to play and entertain their parents in.

Enjoy the beautiful gardens with their stunning views over the Solent and the newly opened fruit and flower Victorian walled garden. In commemoration of the 100th anniversary of Queen Victoria's death the Durbar Wing has been refurbished. See the display of exquisite Indian gifts given by the Indian people to Queen Victoria.

Owner:
English Heritage

▶ CONTACT

The House
Administrator
Osborne House
Royal Apartments
East Cowes
Isle of Wight
PO32 6JY

Tel: 01983 200022

Fax: 01983 297281

▶ LOCATION
OS Ref. SZ516 948

1m SE of East Cowes.

Ferry: Isle of Wight ferry terminals .

East Cowes 1¹/2 m
Tel: 02380 334010.

Fishbourne 4m
Tel: 0870 58277441.

English Heritage Photo Library

▶ OPENING TIMES
House
29 March - 30 September
Daily: 10am - 6pm.
Last admission 4pm.

1 - 31 Oct
Daily: 10am - 5pm
Last admission 4pm.

May close earlier on concert days, please telephone for details.

Winter & Spring:
Telephone for details:
01983 200022.

▶ ADMISSION
House & Grounds

Adult	£7.50
Child* (5-15yrs)	£3.80
Conc.	£5.60
Family	£18.80

Grounds only

Adult	£4.00
Child* (5-15yrs)	£2.00
Conc.	£3.00
Family	£10.00

Plus normal 15% discount for groups.

* Under 5yrs Free.

⬛ ⓘ Suitable for filming, concerts, drama. No photo-graphy in the House. Children's play area.

🍽 Durbar Room available for functions.

♿ Wheelchairs available, access to house via ramp, ground floor access only. WC.

☕ Teas, coffees and light snacks. Waitress service in Swiss Cottage tearoom.

🅿 Ample. Coach drivers and tour leaders free, one extra place for every additional 20. Group rates.

📖 Visits free, please book. Education room available.

❄

APPULDURCOMBE HOUSE ⚑

Wroxall, Shanklin, Isle of Wight

Tel: 01983 852484 **www.english-heritage.org.uk**

Owner: English Heritage **Contact:** Mr & Mrs Owen

The bleached shell of a fine 18th century Baroque style house standing in grounds landscaped by 'Capability' Brown. Falconry Centre.

Location: OS Ref. SZ543 800. ¹/₂ m W of Wroxall off B3327.

Open: 1 Mar - 31 Mar: Sat & Sun, 10am - 4pm. 1 Apr - 30 Sept, daily, 10am - 6pm (last entry 5pm). 1 Oct - 31 Oct, daily, 10am - 4pm. 1 Nov - 19 Dec, Sat & Sun, 10am - 4pm.

Admission: Adult £2.50, Child £1.50, Conc. £2.25. Separate price for Falconry Centre.

⬜ ♿ 🅿 Limited. 🐕 In grounds, on leads. 🎫 Tel. for details.

BARTON MANOR GARDENS

Whippingham, East Cowes, Isle of Wight PO32 6LB

Tel: 01983 280676 **Fax:** 01983 293923

Owner: Robert Stigwood **Contact:** Julia Richards

Location: OS Ref. SZ519 944. Whippingham, East Cowes, Isle of Wight.

Open: 1st Sun, Jun - Sept.

Admission: Please telephone for details.

BEMBRIDGE WINDMILL ⚜

Enquiries to: NT Office, Strawberry Lane, Mottistone, Isle of Wight PO30 4EA

Tel: 01983 873945 **www.nationaltrust.org.uk/regions/southern**

Owner: The National Trust **Contact:** The Custodian

Dating from around 1700, this is the only windmill to survive on the Island. Much of its original wooden machinery is still intact and there are spectacular views from the top.

Location: OS Ref. SZ639 874. ¹/₂ m W of Bembridge off B3395.

Open: 28 Mar - end Jun, Sept - 25 Oct: Sun - Fri, but open Easter Sat. Jul & Aug: daily, 10am - 5pm (last admission 4.30pm).

Admission: Adult £1.70. Special charge for guided tours.

⬜ ♿ Unsuitable. 🐕 By arrangement. 🐕

DIMBOLA LODGE

TERRACE LANE, FRESHWATER BAY PO40 9QE

www.dimbola.co.uk

Tel: 01983 756814 **Fax:** 01983 755578 **e-mail:** administrator@dimbola.co.uk

Owner: Julia Margaret Cameron Trust **Contact:** Ron Smith

Historic house, former home of internationally known 19th century photographer Julia Margaret Cameron, with museum and galleries. Permanent display of Cameron images. Contemporary revolving photographic exhibitions, lectures, photographic courses, and musical performances. Available for hire, book launches, etc.

Location: OS Ref. SZ348 858. From Lymington to Yarmouth and Portsmouth to Fishbourne, Wight Link Ferries. Then A3054 to Totland and then A3055. From Southampton, Red Funnel Ferries to Cowes then A3021 to A3054.

Open: All year: Tue - Sun inclusive & BH Mons, 10am - 5pm. Closed for 5 days at Christmas.

Admission: Adult £3.50 (Jan £3), Child (under 16yrs) Free. Groups (5-45) 10% discount.

ℹ No photography in house. ⬜ 🍴 ♿ 🎫 Vegetarian restaurant. 🐕 By arrangement. 🅿 Limited. 🐕 Guide dogs only. ✳

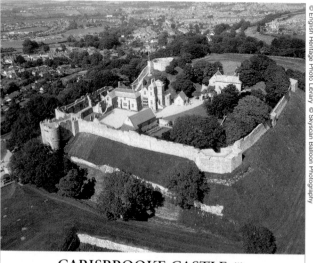

© English Heritage Photo Library © Skyscan Balloon Photography

CARISBROOKE CASTLE ⚑

NEWPORT, ISLE OF WIGHT PO30 1XY

www.english-heritage.org.uk

Tel: 01983 522107 **Fax:** 01983 528632

Owner: English Heritage **Contact:** The Custodian

The Island's Royal fortress and prison of King Charles I before his execution in London in 1648. See the famous Carisbrooke donkeys treading the wheel in the Well House or meet them in the donkey centre. Don't miss the castle story in the gatehouse, the museum in the great hall and the interactive coach house museum. Costumed guided tours available in summer.

Location: OS196 Ref. SZ486 877. Off the B3401, 1¹/₄ m SW of Newport.

Open: 29 Mar - 30 Sept: daily, 10am - 6pm. 1 - 31 Oct: daily, 10am - 5pm. 1 Nov - 31 Mar: daily, 10am - 4pm. Closed 24 - 26 Dec & 1 Jan.

Admission: Adult £4.60, Child £2.30, Conc. £3.50, Family (2+3) £11.50. 15% discount for groups (11+), extra place for additional groups of 20.

⬜ ♿ 🎫 🐕 In grounds, on leads. ✳ 🎫 Tel. for details.

MORTON MANOR

Brading, Isle of Wight PO36 0EP

Tel/Fax: 01983 406168

Owner/Contact: Mr J B Trzebski

Refurbished in the Georgian period. Magnificent gardens and vineyard.

Location: OS Ref. SZ603 863 (approx.). ¹/₄ m W of A3055 in Brading.

Open: Easter - end Oct: daily except Sats, 10am - 5.30pm.

Admission: Adult £4.25, Child £1.75, Conc. £3.75, Group £3.25 (subject to review).

MOTTISTONE MANOR GARDEN ⚜

Mottistone, Isle of Wight

Tel: 01983 741302 **www.nationaltrust.org.uk/regions/southern**

Owner: The National Trust **Contact:** The Gardener

A haven of peace and tranquillity with colourful herbaceous borders and a backdrop of the sea making a perfect setting for the historic Manor House. An annual open air Jazz Concert is held in the grounds during Jul/Aug.

Location: OS Ref. SZ406 838. 2m W of Brightstone on B3399.

Open: 24 Mar - 30 Oct: Sun, Tue, Wed & BH Mons, 11am - 5.30pm; Sun, 2 - 5.30pm. House: Aug BH Mon only, 2 - 5.30pm.

Admission: Adult £2.60.

♿ Limited access for wheelchair users. 🐕 🐕 In grounds, on leads.

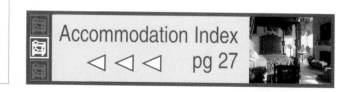

Accommodation Index
◁ ◁ ◁ pg 27

NEEDLES OLD BATTERY ❧

West High Down, Isle of Wight PO39 0JH

Tel: 01983 754772   **www**.nationaltrust.org.uk/regions/southern

Owner: The National Trust   **Contact:** The Administrator

High above the sea, the Old Battery was built in the 1860s against the threat of French invasion. New exhibition of History of Battery. Stunning views.

Location: OS Ref. SZ300 848. Needles Headland W of Freshwater Bay & Alum Bay (B3322).

Open: 28 Mar - 28 Jun, 2 Sept - 31 Oct: Sun - Thur (open Easter weekend) & Jul & Aug: daily, 10.30am - 5pm (last admission 4.30pm).

Admission: Adult £3, Child £1.50, Family £7.50. Special charge for guided tours.
🅖Grounds. 🔲 🔛In grounds, on leads.

NUNWELL HOUSE & GARDENS

Brading, Isle of Wight PO36 0JQ

Tel: 01983 407240

Owner: Col & Mrs J A Aylmer   **Contact:** Mrs J A Aylme

A lived in family home with fine furniture, attractive gardens and historic connections with Charles I.

Location: OS Ref. SZ595 874. 1m NW of Brading. 3m S of Ryde signed off A3055.

Open: 26/27 May, 1 Jul - 4 Sept: Mon - Wed, 1 - 5pm. House tours: 1.30, 2.30 & 3.30pm.

Admission: Adult £4, Pair of Adults £7.50 (inc guide book), OAP/Student £3, Child (up to 10yrs) £1. Garden only: Adult £2.50.

OLD TOWN HALL ❧

Newtown, Isle of Wight

Tel: 01983 531785   **www**.nationaltrust.org.uk/regions/southern

Owner: The National Trust   **Contact:** The Custodian

A charming small 18th century building that was once the focal point of the 'rotten borough' of Newtown.

Location: OS Ref. SZ424 905. Between Newport and Yarmouth, 1m N of A3054.

Open: 27 Mar - end Jun, Sept - 30 Oct: Mons, Weds & Suns (open Good Fri & Easter Sat) & Jul & Aug: daily except Fri & Sat, 2 - 5pm last admission 4.30pm.

Admission: Adult £1.50, Child 75p. Special charge for guided tours (written application).
🅖Unsuitable. 🅟Limited. 🔛Guide dogs only.

OSBORNE HOUSE ⌗

See page 179 for full page entry.

YARMOUTH CASTLE ⌗

Quay Street, Yarmouth, Isle of Wight PO41 0PB

Tel: 01983 760678   **www**.english-heritage.org.uk

Owner: English Heritage   **Contact:** The Custodian

This last addition to Henry VIII's coastal defences was completed in 1547 and is, unusually for its kind, square with a fine example of an angle bastion. It was garrisoned well into the 19th century. It houses exhibitions of paintings of the Isle of Wight and photographs of old Yarmouth.

Location: OS Ref. SZ354 898. In Yarmouth adjacent to car ferry terminal.

Open: 29 Mar - 30 Sept: daily, 10am - 6pm. 1 - 31 Oct: 10am - 5pm.

Admission: Adult £2.30, Child £1.20, Conc. £1.70.
📷 🅖Ground floor. 🅟None. 🔛In grounds, on leads.

Open All Year Index
◁ ◁ ◁ pgs 44-48

Website Information
◁ ◁ ◁   pg 39

Appuldurcombe House

Patrick Lane

Bourton House Garden

South West

Marianne Majerus

Bourton House Garden

"To visit Bourton House garden is like reading a favourite book. Read it
once to discover the overall plot and then revisit it on many occasions to
uncover the hidden depths, the subtle nuances, and the attention to detail."

Melanie Colver on visiting Bourton in 1999

Marianne Majerus

Marianne Majerus

Marianne Majerus

Marianne Majerus

Marianne Majerus

Marianne Majerus

Marianne Majerus

Marianne Majerus

Marianne Majerus

The exquisite garden of Bourton House, owned by Richard and Monique Paice, sits in the Gloucestershire countryside less than half-an-hour away from its nearby acclaimed neighbours – Sezincote, Batsford, Hidcote and Kiftsgate. Yet this three acre garden, tiny by comparison and created only in the last 20 years under the present energetic and passionate owners, possesses all the ingredients to rank high amongst its more famous companions.

For like all great gardens, Bourton contains secrets and surprises around every corner. The Paices' master stroke is to have taken full advantage of the position of their fine 18th century Cotswold village house which sits on the side of a hill with land sloping away across the back of the house. Wherever possible walks, terraces, borders and paths lead the eye not only to their own focal point – a pond, urn or gate – but to the beautiful countryside beyond.

This is a garden where you need to take your notebook: there is something for everyone to study, whether it is the diminutive box-edged structure of the vegetable garden, or the purity and serenity of the Knot garden, surrounded by yew topiary and ivy clad arbours and dominated by a huge oval basin, originally made for the Great Exhibition of 1851. For quiet contemplation visit the wooden shade house which provides dappled light for a collection of acid woodlanders – *Meconopsis x sheldonii* 'Lingholm' and *M chelidoniifolia*, as well as various trilliums, *Dicentra macranta* and *Rhododendron aurreum*.

However, the charm of Bourton is that it does not rely solely on dark green structure and form to create its most dramatic effects. There are also areas in the garden, planted with large herbaceous borders, which provide an abundance of colour. The main lawn is framed by two such borders. Here you can enjoy the heady scent of roses such as the spectacular 'Perle Drift', clustered with a variety of paeonies, allium *christophii* and Clematis *intergrifolia*.

Monique Paice admits that Bourton is a 'high maintenance' garden, 'to a degree that is frightening', and she gratefully acknowledges the hard work of her intrepid and well-informed team of gardeners.

Make an annual visit to this garden and you will not be disappointed. There will be something new to see and inspire, and a chance also to study the latest fashions in garden design. Bourton is a mouthwatering must if on a garden tour of Gloucestershire. ✢

For further details about *Bourton House Garden* see page 223.

Marianne Majerus

National Trust/Peter Cade

ANTONY HOUSE & GDN.
& ANTONY WOODLAND GDN.

TORPOINT

Antony House and Garden: A superb example of an early 18th century mansion. The main block is faced in lustrous silver-grey stone, flanked by mellow brick pavilions. The ancestral home of the Carew family for nearly 600 years, the house contains a wealth of paintings, tapestries, furniture and embroideries, many linking the great families of Cornwall – set in parkland and fine gardens (including the National Collection of day lilies), overlooking the Lynher river. An 18th century Bath House can be viewed by arrangement.

Antony Woodland Garden: The woodland garden was established in the late 18th century with the assistance of Humphrey Repton. It features numerous varieties of camellias, together with magnolias, rhododendrons, azaleas and other flowering shrubs, interspersed with many fine species of indigenous and exotic trees. A further 50 acres of natural woods bordering the tidal waters of the Lynher provide a number of delightful walks. The Woodland Garden is at its finest in the spring and autumn months.

**Antony House -
Owner:**
The National Trust

**Antony Woodland
Garden - Owner:**
Carew Pole
Garden Trust

▶ CONTACT
Antony House
The Administrator
Antony House & Gdn
Torpoint
Cornwall PL11 2QA

Tel: 01752 812191

**Antony Woodland
Garden**
Mrs Valerie Anderson
Antony
Torpoint
Cornwall PL11 2QA

Tel: 01752 812364

▶ LOCATION
OS Ref. SX418 564

Antony House and
Antony Woodland
Garden
5m W of Plymouth via
Torpoint car ferry,
2m NW of Torpoint.

National Trust/ Dan Flunder

🖼️ ♿ Braille guide. 💺 🐾

▶ OPENING TIMES
**Antony House
& Garden**
26 Mar - 31 May &
4 Sept - 1 Nov:
Tue - Thur & BH Mons.

1 Jun - 3 Sept: Tue - Thurs
& Suns, 1.30 - 5.30pm.
Last admission 4.45pm.

The Bath Pond House
can be seen by written
application.

Guided tours at
less busy times.

**Antony Woodland
Garden**
1 March - 31 October
Daily except Mons & Fris
but open BHs
11am - 5.30pm.

National Trust Tearoom
On open days,
12.30 - 5.30pm.

▶ ADMISSION
**Antony House
& Garden**
Adult £4.40
Groups................. £3.60
Family £10.75

NT Garden only £2.20
Groups................... £1.80

**Antony Woodland
Garden**
Adult £3.00

Joint Gardens-only ticket
to NT-owned garden and
Antony Woodland Garden
Adult £3.70
Child £1.50
Groups £3.00

NB. Entrance to the
Woodland Garden is free to NT
members on days when the
house is open.

National Trust/Andrew Besley

COTEHELE

SALTASH

www.nationaltrust.org.uk

Cotehele, owned by the Edgcumbe family for nearly 600 years, is a fascinating and enchanting estate set on the steep wooded slopes of the River Tamar. Exploring Cotehele's many and various charms provides a full day out for the family and leaves everyone longing to return.

The steep valley garden contains exotic and tender plants which thrive in the mild climate. Remnants of an earlier age include a mediaeval stewpond and domed dovecote, a 15th century chapel and 18th century tower with fine views over the surrounding countryside. A series of more formal gardens, terraces, an orchard and a daffodil meadow surround Cotehele House.

One of the least altered medieval houses in the country, Cotehele is built in local granite, slate and sandstone. Inside the ancient rooms, unlit by electricity, is a fine collection of textiles, tapestries, armour and early dark oak furniture.

The chapel contains the oldest working domestic clock in England, still in its original position.

A walk through the garden and along the river leads to the quay, a busy river port in Victorian times. The National Maritime Museum worked with the National Trust to set up a museum here which explains the vital role that the Tamar played in the local economy. As a living reminder, the restored Tamar sailing barge Shamrock (owned jointly by the Trust and the National Maritime Museum) is moored here.

A further walk through woodland along the Morden stream leads to the old estate corn mill which has been restored to working order.

This large estate with many footpaths offers a variety of woodland and countryside walks, opening up new views and hidden places. The Danescombe Valley, with its history of mining and milling, is of particular interest.

National Trust /Tymn Lintell

i No photography in house. *NPI National Heritage Award winners 1996 & 1999.*

Cotehele Quay Gallery offers a wide range of local hand-made arts and crafts.

Available for up to 90 people.

2 wheelchairs at Reception. Hall & kitchen accessible. Ramps at house, restaurant and shop. Most of garden is very steep with loose gravel. Riverside walks are flatter (from Cotehele Quay) & Edgcumbe Arms is accessible. WCs near house and at Quay. Parking near house & mill by arrangement.

In Barn restaurant (can be booked) daily (except Fri), Apr - Oct. At the Quay, Edgcumbe Arms offers lighter meals daily, Apr - Oct (plus weekends in March). Both licensed.

P Near house and garden and at Cotehele Quay. No parking at mill.

Groups (15+) must book with Property Manager and receive a coach route (limited to two per day). No groups Suns & BH weekends. Visitors to house limited to 80 at any one time. Please arrive early and be prepared to queue. Avoid dull days early and late in the season. Allow a full day to see estate.

Under control welcome only on woodland walks. **❄**

Owner:
The National Trust

▶ CONTACT

Lewis Eynon
Property Manager
Cotehele
St Dominick
Saltash, Cornwall
PL12 6TA

Tel: 01579 351346
Fax: 01579 351222
e-mail:
cctlce@smtp.ntrust.
org.uk

▶ LOCATION

OS Ref. SX422 685
1m SW of Calstock by foot. 8m S of Tavistock, 4m E of Callington, 15m from Plymouth via the Tamar bridge at Saltash

Trains: Limited service from Plymouth to Calstock (1¼ m uphill)

Boats: Limited (tidal) service from Plymouth to Calstock Quay (Plymouth Boat Cruises)
Tel: 01752 822797

River ferry: Privately run from Calstock to Cotehele Quay.
Tel: 01579 351346

Buses: Western National (seasonal variations)
Tel: 01752 222666

▶ OPENING TIMES

House & Restaurant
23 Mar - 3 Nov: Daily except Fris (but open Good Fri), 11am - 5pm (Oct & Nov: 11am - 4.30pm). Last admission 30 mins before closing time.

Mill
23 Mar - 30 June & 1 Sept - 3 Nov: Daily except Fris (but open Good Fri) 1 - 5.30pm (4.30 during Oct & Nov) Jul & Aug: Daily, 1 - 6pm

Garden
All year: daily, 10.30am - dusk.

Gallery & Tearoom on Quay
23 Mar - 3 Nov: Daily, 11am - 5pm or dusk. Gallery: 12 noon - 5pm or dusk. Nov & Dec: Christmas openings, telephone 01579 351346.

▶ ADMISSION

House, Garden & Mill
Adult £6.40
Family Tickets £16.00
Pre-booked Groups .. £5.40

Garden & Mill only
Adult £3.60
Family £9.00

*Groups must book in advance with the Property Manager. No groups Suns or BHs.

NT members free. You may join here.

NTPL / R Truman

LANHYDROCK 🌿

BODMIN

Owner:
The National Trust

▶ **CONTACT**

Property Manager
Lanhydrock
Bodmin
Cornwall PL30 5AD

Tel: 01208 73320
Fax: 01208 74084

e-mail:
clhlan@smtp.ntrust.
org.uk

▶ **LOCATION**

OS Ref. SX085 636

2¹/₂ m SE of Bodmin,
follow signposts from
either A30,
A38 or B3268.

Lanhydrock is the grandest and most welcoming house in Cornwall, set in a glorious landscape of gardens, parkland and woods overlooking the valley of the River Fowey.

The house dates back to the 17th century but much of it had to be rebuilt after a disastrous fire in 1881 destroyed all but the entrance porch and the north wing, which includes the magnificent Long Gallery with its extraordinary plaster ceiling depicting scenes from the Old Testament. A total of 50 rooms are on show today and together they reflect the entire spectrum of life in a rich and splendid Victorian household, from the many servants' bedrooms and the fascinating complex

of kitchens, sculleries and larders to the nursery suite where the Agar-Robartes children lived, learned and played, and the grandeur of the dining room with its table laid and ready.

Surrounding the house on all sides are gardens ranging from formal Victorian parterres to the wooded higher garden where magnificent displays of magnolias, rhododendrons and camellias climb the hillside to merge with the oak and beech woods all around. A famous avenue of ancient beech and sycamore trees, the original entrance drive to the house, runs from the pinnacled 17th century gatehouse down towards the medieval bridge across the Fowey at Respryn.

▶ **OPENING TIMES**

House:
23 Mar - 3 Nov:
Daily except Mons
(but open BH Mons)
23 Mar - 30 Sept:
11am - 5.30pm.
Oct - 3 Nov: 11am - 5pm.

Last admission ¹/₂ hr
before closing.

Garden:
All year: Daily.
Mid-Feb - 3 Nov
10am - 6pm.
4 Nov - mid-Feb: during
daylight hours.

Refreshments available
16 Feb - 3 Nov: Daily.
Nov - mid-Feb: limited
opening (tel for details).

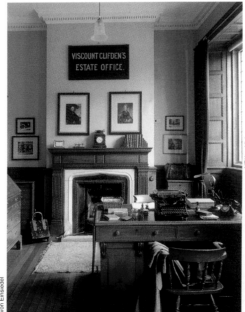

NTPL / Andreas von Einsiedel

NT/Jon Hicks

▶ **ADMISSION**

**House, Garden &
Grounds**
　Adult £7.00
　Family £17.50
　Groups................. £6.00

**Garden &
Grounds only** £3.80

📷🚼ℹ️ No photography in house.

🍽 By arrangement.

♿ Suitable. Braille guide. WC.

☕

🍴 Licensed restaurant

🐕 In park, on leads. Guide dogs only in house.

🅿 Limited for coaches.

❄

🛡 Please telephone for details.

South West - England

ANTONY HOUSE & GARDEN
ANTONY WOODLAND GARDEN
See page 188 for full page entry.

BOSVIGO
Bosvigo Lane, Truro, Cornwall TR1 3NH
Tel/Fax: 01872 275774 **e-mail**: bosvigo.plants@virgin.net **www**.bosvigo.com
Owner: Michael & Wendy Perry **Contact**: Michael Perry
A series of small, densely planted 'rooms', each with its own colour theme, surround the Georgian house (not open). The mainly herbaceous plantings give non-stop colour from June to the end of September. The Hot Garden will 'blow your socks off' in August. Small specialist nursery attached.
Location: OS Ref. SW815 452. ¼ m W of Truro city centre. Turn off A390 down Dobbs Lane just W of Sainsbury foodstore.
Open: Mar - end Sept: Thur - Sat, 11am - 6pm.
Admission: Adult £3, Child (5-15yrs) £1. No group concessions.

BURNCOOSE NURSERIES & GARDEN
Gwennap, Redruth, Cornwall TR16 6BJ
Tel: 01209 860316 **Fax**: 01209 860011 **e-mail**: burncoose@eclipse.co.uk
www.burncoose.co.uk
Owner/Contact: C H Williams
The Nurseries are set in the 30 acre woodland gardens of Burncoose.
Location: OS Ref. SW742 395. 2m SE of Redruth on main A393 Redruth to Falmouth road between the villages of Lanner and Ponsanooth.
Open: Mon – Sat: 9am - 5pm, Suns, 11am - 5pm. Gardens and Tearooms open all year (except Christmas Day).
Admission: Nurseries: Free. Gardens: Adult/Conc. £2. Child Free. Group conducted tours: £2.50 by arrangement.

CHYSAUSTER ANCIENT VILLAGE
Nr Newmill, Penzance, Cornwall TR20 8XA
Tel: 07831 757934 **e-mail**: customers@english-heritage.org.uk
www.english-heritage.org.uk
Owner: English Heritage **Contact**: The Custodian
On a windy hillside, overlooking the wild and spectacular coast, is this deserted Romano-Cornish village with a 'street' of eight well preserved houses, each comprising a number of rooms around an open court.
Location: OS203 Ref. SW473 350. 2½ m NW of Gulval off B3311.
Open: 29 Mar - 31 Oct: daily, 10am - 6pm (5pm in Oct). Winter: closed.
Admission: Adult £1.80, Child 90p, Conc. £1.40. 15% discount for groups (11+).
No coaches. On leads. Tel for details.

COTEHELE
See page 189 for full page entry.

National Trust/David Hastilow

GLENDURGAN GARDEN
Mawnan Smith, Falmouth, Cornwall TR11 5JZ
Tel: 01326 250906 (opening hours) or 01872 862090 **Fax**: 01872 865808
Owner: The National Trust **Contact**: Reception
A valley garden of great beauty with fine trees, shrubs and water gardens. The laurel maze, recently restored, is an unusual and popular feature. The garden runs down to the tiny village of Durgan and its beach on the Helford River. New this year: School Room, rebuilt in traditional cob and thatch, to replace the original built around 1876.
Location: OS Ref. SW772 277. 4m SW of Falmouth, ½ m SW of Mawnan Smith, on road to Helford Passage. 1m E of Trebah Garden.
Open: 16 Feb - 3 Nov: Tue - Sat & BH Mons (closed Good Fri), 10.30am - 5.30pm. Last admission 4.30pm.
Admission: £3.90, Family £9.75. Pre-arranged groups: £3.20.
Limited access. Braille guide.

CAERHAYS CASTLE & GARDEN
Caerhays, Gorran, St Austell, Cornwall PL26 6LY
www.caerhays.co.uk
Tel: 01872 501310 **Fax**: 01872 501870 **e-mail**: estateoffice@caerhays.co.uk
Owner: F J Williams Esq **Contact**: Miss A B Mayes
One of the very few Nash built castles still left standing – situated within approximately 60 acres of informal woodland gardens created by J C Williams, who sponsored plant hunting expeditions to China at the turn of the century. Noted for its camellias, magnolias, rhododendrons and oaks. English Heritage listing - Grade I: Outstanding.
Location: OS Ref. SW972 415. S coast of Cornwall – between Mevagissey and Portloe. 9m SW of St Austell.
Open: House: 18 Mar - 26 Apr: Mon - Fri (excluding BHs), 1 - 4pm, booking recommended. Gardens: 11 Mar - 31 May: daily, 10am - 5.30pm (last admission 4.30pm). Charity openings (gardens only): 31 Mar, 14 Apr & 6 May: 10am - 4pm.
Admission: House: £4.50. Gardens: £4.50. House & Gardens: £8. Guided group tours (15+) by Head Gardener, £5.50 - by arrangement.
Unsuitable. By arrangement. In grounds, on leads.

Godolphin, Cornwall

Patrick Lane

South West - England

GODOLPHIN 🏠

GODOLPHIN CROSS, HELSTON, CORNWALL TR13 9RE

www.godolphin-house.co.uk

Tel/Fax: 01736 763194 **e-mail:** godo@euphony.net

Owner: Mrs L M P Schofield   **Contact:** Mrs Joanne Schofield

A romantic Tudor and Stuart mansion commenced c1475. The development of the Godolphin family's courtly ambition and taste is beautifully expressed in the evolving architecture of the house. Exploitation of tin provided the wealth for this family of soldiers, entrepreneurs, poets and government officials. Birthplace of Queen Anne's Lord Treasurer. The large, compartmented Side Garden dates from the late 15th century, though it grew out of an early 14th century Castle garden (still gardened). Good 16th and 17th century English Oak furniture. 1731 painting of the Godolphin Arabian by John Wooton and pictures by American impressionist Elmer Schofield. Godolphin is undergoing a programme of English Heritage funded repairs until Spring of 2003. Adjacent walks on the National Trust estate.

Location: OS Ref. SW602 318. Breage, Helston. On minor road from Godolphin Cross to Townshend.

Open: May, Jun & Sept: Thur & Fri, 10am - 5pm, Sun, 2 - 5pm. Jul & Aug: Tue, Thurs & Fri, 10am - 5pm, Sun, 2 - 5pm. Easter - end Sept: BH Mons, 10am - 5pm. Group bookings & tours all year by arrangement.

Admission: Adult £4, Child £1. Garden: £2.

⬜ 🚻 ♿ ▣ 🔊By arrangement. 🅿 🐕Guide dogs only. ✳

THE JAPANESE GARDEN & BONSAI NURSERY

St Mawgan, Nr Newquay, Cornwall TR8 4ET

Tel: 01637 860116   **Fax:** 01637 860887   **e-mail:** rob@thebonsainursery.com

Owner/Contact: Mr & Mrs Hore

Authentic Japanese Garden set in 1½ acres.

Location: OS Ref. SW873 660. Follow road signs from A3059 & B3276.

Open: Summer: Daily 10am - 6pm. WInter: 10am - 5.30pm. Closed Christmas Day - New Year's Day.

Admission: Adult £2.50, Child £1. Groups (10+): £2.

KEN CARO

Bicton, Liskeard PL14 5RF

Tel: 01579 362446

Owner/Contact: Mr and Mrs K R Willcock

4 acre plantsman's garden.

Location: OS Ref. SX313 692. 5m NE of of Liskeard.

Open: 14 Apr - 29 Aug, Sun - Thur, 10am - 6pm.

Admission: Adult £3, Child £1.

LANHYDROCK 🌿   *See page 190 for full page entry.*

LAUNCESTON CASTLE ⚜

Castle Lodge, Launceston, Cornwall PL15 7DR

Tel: 01566 772365 **Fax:** 01566 772396

e-mail: customers@english-heritage.org.uk **www.**english-heritage.org.uk

Owner: English Heritage   **Contact:** The Custodian

Set on the motte of the original Norman castle and commanding the town and surrounding countryside. The shell keep and tower survive of this medieval castle which controlled the main route into Cornwall. An exhibition shows the early history.

Location: OS201 Ref. SX330 846. In Launceston.

Open: 29 Mar - 31 Oct: daily, 10am - 6pm (5pm in Oct). Winter: Fri - Sun, 10am - 4pm. Closed 24 - 26 Dec & 1 Jan.

Admission: Adult £2, Child £1, Conc. £1.50. 15% discount for groups (11+).

⬜ ♿Grounds. 🅿 NCP adjacent. Limited. 🐕In grounds, on leads. 📞Tel for details.

LAWRENCE HOUSE 🌿

9 Castle Street, Launceston, Cornwall PL15 8BA

Tel: 01566 773277

Owner: The National Trust   **Contact:** The Property Manager

A Georgian house given to the Trust to help preserve the character of the street, and now leased to Launceton Town Council as a museum and civic centre.

Location: OS Ref. SX330 848. Launceston.

Open: Apr - Oct, daily, except Sat & Sun, 10.30am - 4.30pm. Other times by appointment.

Admission: Free, but contributions welcome.

THE LOST GARDENS OF HELIGAN

PENTEWAN, ST AUSTELL, CORNWALL PL26 6EN

www.heligan.com

Tel: 01726 845100   **Fax:** 01726 845101   **e-mail:** info@heligan.com

Owner: Mr T Smit   **Contact:** Mr C A Howlett

These award-winning Gardens are 80 acres of superb pleasure grounds together with a magnificent complex of four walled gardens and kitchen garden, all being restored to their former glory as a living museum of 19th century horticulture. An Italian Garden, Alpine Ravine, Crystal Grotto, Summerhouses, Rides, Lawns and a 20 acre sub-tropical "Jungle Garden" are just some of the delights of this "Sleeping Beauty".

Location: OS Ref. SX000 465. 5m SW of St Austell. 2m NW of Mevagissey. Take the B3273 to Mevagissey – follow tourist signs.

Open: Daily except 24 & 25 Dec: 10am - 6pm. Last adm. 4.30pm.

Admission: Adult £6. Child (5-15yrs) £3, OAP £5.50. Family £17. Groups (20+): Adult £5.50, Child (5-15) £3, OAP £5. Under 5's Free. Groups/tours by arrangement.

⬜ 🚻 ♿ ▣ 🅿 🔊By arrangement. 🐕On leads only. ✳

Truro Cathedral

West Country Tourist Board

MOUNT EDGCUMBE HOUSE & COUNTRY PARK

CREMYLL, TORPOINT, CORNWALL PL10 IHZ

Tel: 01752 822236   **Fax:** 01752 822199

Owner: Cornwall County & Plymouth City Councils   **Contact:** Secretary

Tudor home of Earls of Mount Edgcumbe, set in historic 18th century gardens on the dramatic sea-girt Rame peninsula. Wild fallow deer, follies, forts; National camellia collection. Grade I listed.

Location: OS Ref. SX452 527. 10m W of Plymouth via Torpoint.

Open: House and Earls' Garden: 29 Mar - 29 Sept: Wed - Sun & BH Mons, 11am - 4.30pm. Country Park: All year, daily 8am - dusk.

Admission: House: Adult £4.50, Child (5-15) £2.25, Conc. £3.50, Family (2+2 or 1+3) £10. Groups: £3.50. Park: Free.

Licensed. P Grounds only. Tel for details.

PENCARROW

BODMIN, CORNWALL PL30 3AG

www.pencarrow.co.uk

Tel: 01208 841369   **Fax:** 01208 841722   **e-mail:** pencarrow@aol.com

Owner: Molesworth-St Aubyn family   **Contact:** J Reynolds

Still owned and lived in by the family. Georgian house and listed gardens. Superb collection of pictures, furniture and porcelain. Marked walks through 50 acres of beautiful formal and woodland gardens, Victorian rockery, Italian garden, over 700 different varieties of rhododendrons, lake and ice house.

Location: OS Ref. SX040 711. Between Bodmin and Wadebridge. 4m NW of Bodmin off A389 & B3266 at Washaway.

Open: 31 Mar - 31 Oct: Sun - Thur, 11am - 4pm (last tour).

Admission: House & Garden: Adult £6, Child £3. Garden only: Adult £3, Child Free. Groups (throughout year by arrangement): House & Garden: £4.50, Child £2.25.

Craft centre, small childrens' play area, self-pick soft fruit. By arrangement. Licensed. Obligatory. P Grounds only.

PENDENNIS CASTLE

FALMOUTH, CORNWALL TR11 4LP

www.english-heritage.org.uk

Tel: 01326 316594   **Fax:** 01326 319911   **e-mail:** customers@english-heritage.org.uk

Owner: English Heritage   **Contact:** The Head Custodian

Pendennis and its neighbour, St Mawes Castle, face each other across the mouth of the estuary of the River Fal. Built by Henry VIII in 16th century as protection against threat of attack and invasion from France. Extended and adapted over the years to meet the changing threats to national security from the French and Spanish and continued right through to World War II. It withstood five months of siege during the Civil War before becoming the penultimate Royalist Garrison to surrender on the mainland. Pendennis today stands as a landmark, with fine sea views and excellent site facilities including a hands-on discovery centre, exhibitions, a museum, guardhouse, shop and tearoom. Excellent special events venue.

Location: OS204, Ref SW824 318. On Pendennis Head.

Open: 29 Mar - 31 Oct: daily, 10am - 6pm (5pm in Oct). 1 Nov - 31 Mar: daily, 10am - 4pm. Closed 24 - 26 Dec & 1 Jan.

Admission: Adult £4, Child £2, Conc. £3. 15% discount for groups of 11+.

Partial. By arrangement. P In grounds only.
Tel for details.

PINE LODGE GARDENS & NURSERY
Cuddra, St Austell, Cornwall PL25 3RQ

Tel/Fax: 01726 73500

Owner/Contact: Mr & Mrs R H J Clemo

30 acre estate with a wide range of 5,500 plants.

Location: OS Ref. SX044 527. Signposted on A390.

Open: 25 Mar - 31 Oct: daily, 10am - 6pm, last ticket 5pm.

Admission: Adult £4, Child £2.

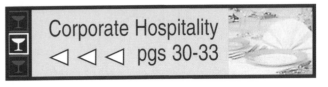

Corporate Hospitality
◁ ◁ ◁ pgs 30-33

PRIDEAUX PLACE
PADSTOW, CORNWALL PL28 8RP

Tel: 01841 532411   **Fax:** 01841 532945   **e-mail:** office@prideauxplace.fsnet.co.uk

Owner/Contact: Peter Prideaux-Brune Esq

Tucked away above the busy port of Padstow, the home of the Prideaux family for over 400 years, is surrounded by gardens and wooded grounds overlooking a deer park and the Camel estuary to the moors beyond. The house still retains its 'E' shape Elizabethan front and contains fine paintings and furniture as well as an exhibition reflecting its emergence as a major international film location. The impressive outbuildings have been restored in recent years and the 16th century plaster ceiling in the great chamber has been uncovered for the first time since 1760.

Location: OS Ref. SW913 756. 5m from A39 Newquay/Wadebridge link road. Signposted by Historic House signs.

Open: Easter Sun 31 Mar - 11 Apr & 12 May - 3 Oct: Sun - Thur, 1.30 - 4pm (last tour). Tearoom & Grounds: 12.30 - 5pm. Open all year for groups 15+ by arrangement.

Admission: Adult £6, accompanied Child £2. Grounds only: Adult £2, Child £1. Groups from £4.

By arrangement. Ground floor & grounds. By arrangement. In grounds, on leads.

RESTORMEL CASTLE
Lostwithiel, Cornwall PL22 0BD

Tel: 01208 872687   **e-mail:** customers@english-heritage.org.uk

www.english-heritage.org.uk

Owner: English Heritage   **Contact:** The Custodian

Perched on a high mound, surrounded by a deep moat, the huge circular keep of this splendid Norman castle survives in remarkably good condition. It is still possible to make out the ruins of Restormel's Keep Gate, Great Hall and even the kitchens and private rooms.

Location: OS200 Ref. SX104 614. 1¹/2 m N of Lostwithiel off A390.

Open: 29 Mar - 31 Oct: daily, 10am - 6pm (5pm in Oct). Winter: closed.

Admission: Adult £1.90, Child £1, Conc. £1.40. 15% discount for groups (11+).

Grounds. P Limited for coaches. In grounds, on leads. Tel for details.

ST CATHERINE'S CASTLE
Fowey, Cornwall

Tel: 0117 9750700

Owner: English Heritage   **Contact:** The South West Regional Office

A small fort built by Henry VIII to defend Fowey harbour, with fine views of the coastline and river estuary.

Location: OS200 Ref. SX118 508. ³/4 m SW of Fowey along footpath off A3082.

Open: Any reasonable time, daylight only.

Admission: Free.

Trewithen

© English Heritage Photo Library

ST MAWES CASTLE ⌗

ST MAWES, CORNWALL TR2 3AA

www.english-heritage.org.uk

Tel: 01326 270526 **e-mail:** customers@english-heritage.org.uk

Owner: English Heritage **Contact:** The Head Custodian

The pretty fishing village of St Mawes is home to this castle. On the opposite headland to Pendennis Castle, St Mawes shares the task of watching over the mouth of the River Fal as it has done since Henry VIII built it as a defence against the French. With three huge circular bastions shaped like clover leaves, St Mawes was designed to cover every possible angle of approach. It is the finest example of Tudor military architecture. The castle offers views of St Mawes' little boat-filled harbour, the passenger ferry tracking across the Fal, and the splendid coastline which featured in the Poldark TV series. Also the start of some delightful walks along the coastal path.

Location: OS204 Ref. SW842 328. W of St Mawes on A3078.

Open: 29 Mar - 31 Oct: daily, 10am - 6pm (5pm in Oct). Winter: 1 Nov - 31 Mar: Wed - Sun, 10am - 4pm. Closed 1 - 2pm & 24 - 26 Dec & 1 Jan.

Admission: Adult £2.90, Child £1.50, Conc. £2.30. 15% discount for groups (11+).

🖾 🖾 Grounds. WC. 🖾 🖾 Limited. 🖾 Guide dogs only. ✳ 🖾 Tel for details.

National Trust/ Peter Cade

ST MICHAEL'S MOUNT ※

MARAZION, Nr PENZANCE, CORNWALL TR17 0EF

Tel: 01736 710507 (710265 tide & ferry information) **Fax:** 01736 711544

e-mail: godolphin@manor-office.co.uk

Owner: The National Trust **Contact:** The Manor Office

This magical island is the jewel in Cornwall's crown. The great granite crag which rises from the waters of Mount's Bay is surmounted by an embattled medieval castle, home of the St Aubyn family for over 300 years. The Mount's flanks are softened by lush sub-tropical vegetation and on the water's edge there is a harbourside community which features shops and restaurants.

Location: OS Ref. SW515 300. At Marazion there is access on foot over causeway at low tide. In summer months there is a ferry at high tide. 4m E of Penzance.

Open: 25 Mar - 1 Nov: Mon - Fri, 10.30am - 5.30pm. Last admission 4.45pm on the island. 3 Nov - end Mar: guided tours as tide, weather and circumstances permit. Please telephone. Shops & restaurants: 25 Mar - 1 Nov: daily. The castle & grounds are open most week-ends during the season. These are special charity open days when NT members are asked to pay admission. Private Gardens (not NT): Apr - May: daily (weather permitting).

Admission: Adult £4.60, Family £13. Pre-arranged groups £4.20. Gardens: £2.50.

🖾 🖾 🖾 Guide dogs only. ✳

TATE ST IVES

Porthmeor Beach, St Ives, Cornwall TR26 1TG

Tel: 01736 796226 **Fax:** 01736 794480 **www**.tate.org.uk

Owner: Tate Gallery **Contact:** Ina Cole

Changing displays from the Tate Collection of British and modern art, focusing on the modern movement that St Ives is famous for. Also displays of new work by contemporary artists. Events programme, guided tours, gallery shop, rooftop café, with spectacular views over the beach. The Tate also manages the Barbara Hepworth Museum and Sculpture Garden in St Ives.

Location: OS Ref. SW515 407. Situated by Porthmeor Beach.

Open: Mar - Oct: daily, 10am - 5.30pm. Nov - Feb: Tue - Sun, 10am - 4.30pm.

Admission: Adult £3.95, Conc £2.50. Groups (10 - 30): Adult £2.50, Conc. £1.50.

🖾 🖾 🖾 Licensed. 🖾 Daily. 🅿 Nearby. 🖾 🖾 Guide dogs only. ✳ 🖾 Tel for details.

© English Heritage Photo Library

TINTAGEL CASTLE ⌗

TINTAGEL, CORNWALL PL34 0HE

www.english-heritage.org.uk

Tel/Fax: 01840 770328 **e-mail:** customers@english-heritage.org.uk

Owner: English Heritage **Contact:** The Head Custodian

The spectacular setting for the legendary castle of King Arthur is the wild and windswept Cornish coast. Clinging precariously to the edge of the cliff face are the extensive ruins of a medieval royal castle, built by Richard, Earl of Cornwall, younger brother of Henry III. Also used as a Cornish stronghold by subsequent Earls of Cornwall. Despite extensive excavations since the 1930s, Tintagel Castle remains one of the most spectacular and romantic spots in the entire British Isles. Destined to remain a place of mystery and romance, Tintagel will always jealously guard its marvellous secrets.

Location: OS200 Ref. SX048 891. On Tintagel Head, ½ m along uneven track from Tintagel.

Open: 29 Mar - 31 Oct: daily, 11am - 6pm (5pm in Oct). 1 Nov - 31 Mar: daily, 10am - 4pm. Closed 24 - 26 Dec & 1 Jan.

Admission: Adult £3, Child £1.50, Conc. £2.30. 15% discount for groups (11+).

ℹ No vehicles. 🖾 🖾 ✳ 🖾 Tel for details.

TINTAGEL OLD POST OFFICE ※

Tintagel, Cornwall PL34 0DB

Tel: 01840 770024 or 01208 74281

Owner: The National Trust **Contact:** The Custodian

One of the most characterful buildings in Cornwall, and a house of great antiquity, this small 14th century manor is full of charm and interest.

Location: OS Ref. SX056 884. In the centre of Tintagel.

Open: 23 Mar - 3 Nov: daily, 11am - 5.30pm (closes 4pm from Oct - 3 Nov).

Admission: Adult £2.30, Child £1.10. Family £5.70. Pre-arranged groups £1.80.

Website Information
◁ ◁ ◁   pg 39

TREBAH GARDEN

MAWNAN SMITH, Nr FALMOUTH, CORNWALL TR11 5JZ

www.trebah-garden.co.uk

Tel: 01326 250448 **Fax:** 01326 250781 **e-mail:** mail@trebah-garden.co.uk

Owner: Trebah Garden Trust **Contact:** Vera Woodcroft

Steeply wooded 25 acre sub-tropical ravine garden falls 200 feet from 18th century house to private beach on Helford River. Stream cascading over waterfalls through ponds full of Koi Carp and exotic water plants winds through 2 acres of blue and white hydrangeas and spills out over beach. Huge Australian tree ferns and palms mingle with shrubs of ever-changing colours and scent beneath over-arching canopy of 100 year old rhododendrons and magnolias. A paradise for plantsmen, artists and families.

Location: OS Ref. SW768 275. 4m SW of Falmouth, 1m SW of Mawnan Smith. Follow brown and white tourism signs from Treliever Cross roundabout at A39/A394 junction through Mawnan Smith to Trebah.

Open: All year: daily, 10.30am - 5pm (last admission).

Admission: Adult £4.50, Child (5-15yrs)/Disabled £2.50, OAP £4. Child under 5yrs Free, Groups (12 - 50): Adult £4, Child £2. RHS members have free entry all year, NT members have free entry 1 Nov - end Feb.

⬚ ⬚ ⬚ Partial. ⬚ ⬚ By arrangement. ⬚ ⬚ ⬚ In grounds, on leads. ⬚

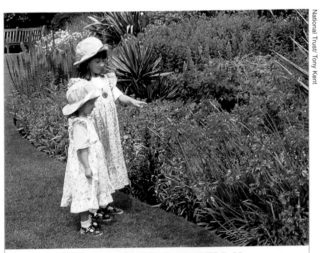

National Trust/ Tony Kent

TRELISSICK GARDEN ❧

FEOCK, TRURO, CORNWALL TR3 6QL

Tel: 01872 862090 **Fax:** 01872 865808 **e-mail:** ctlpmo@smtp.ntrust.org.uk

Owner: The National Trust **Contact:** The Property Manager

A garden and estate of rare tranquil beauty with glorious maritime views over Carrick Roads to Falmouth Harbour. The tender and exotic shrubs make this garden attractive in all seasons. Extensive park and woodland walks beside the river. There is an Art and Craft Gallery.

Location: OS Ref. SW837 396. 4m S of Truro by road, on both sides of B3289 above King Harry Ferry.

Open: 16 Feb - 3 Nov: daily; Mon - Sat, 10.30am - 5.30pm (dusk if earlier), Suns, 12.30 - 5.30pm (dusk if earlier). Restaurant, Shop, Plant Sales, Art & Crafts Gallery: as above, in addition: 4 Nov - 23 Dec: 11am - 4pm. 1 - 4 May admission to site by Park & Ride, Cornwall Gardens Society Show on site.

Admission: Adult £4.50, Family £11.25. Pre-arranged group £3.70. £1.60 car park fee (refundable on admission to garden).

⬚ ⬚ ⬚ By arrangement. ⬚ ⬚ ⬚ By arrangement. ⬚ In park on leads; only guide dogs in garden. ⬚ ⬚

TRELOWARREN HOUSE & CHAPEL

Mawgan-in-Meneage, Helston, Cornwall TR12 6AD

Tel: 01326 221366

Owner: Sir Ferrers Vyvyan Bt **Contact:** The Warden

Tudor and 17th century house. Chapel and main rooms of house are open to the public on a limited basis.

Location: OS Ref. SW721 238. 6m S of Helston, off B3293 to St Keverne.

Open: Please telephone for details.

Admission: Please telephone for details.

NTPL / Giles Clotworthy

TRENGWAINTON GARDEN ❧

PENZANCE, CORNWALL TR20 8RZ

Tel/Fax: 01736 362297

Owner: The National Trust **Contact:** The Property Manager

This large shrub garden, with many plants brought back from 1920s' plant-gathering expeditions, is a beautiful place throughout the year and a plantsman's delight. Splendid views over Mount's Bay can be gained from summer-houses at either end of the restored terrace. The walled gardens have many tender plants which cannot be grown in the open anywhere else in England and restoration of the kitchen gardens is underway. The new tea-house serves a full range of snacks and meals.

Location: OS Ref. SW445 315. 2m NW of Penzance, $^1/_2$ m W of Heamoor on Penzance - Morvah road (B3312), $^1/_2$ m off St. Just road (A3071).

Open: 17 Feb - 3 Nov: Sun - Thur & Good Fri, 10am - 5.30pm. NB: Closes 5pm in Feb, Mar, Oct & Nov. Last admission $^1/_2$ hr before closing.

Admission: Adult £3.90, Family £9.75. Pre-booked groups: £3.20.

⬚ ⬚ ⬚ Partial. ⬚ Tea-house. ⬚ On leads.

❄ Open All Year Index ◁ ◁ ◁ pgs 44-48

National Trust/Marcus Way

TRERICE 🏵

NEWQUAY, CORNWALL TR8 4PG

Tel: 01637 875404 **Fax:** 01637 879300 **e-mail:** ctrjpw@smtp.ntrust.org.uk

Owner: The National Trust **Contact:** The Property Manager

Trerice is an architectural gem and something of a rarity – a small Elizabethan manor house hidden away in a web of narrow lanes and still somehow caught in the spirit of its age. An old Arundell house, it contains much fine furniture, ceramics, glasses and a wonderful clock collection. A small barn museum traces the development of the lawn mower.

Location: OS Ref. SW841 585. 3m SE of Newquay via the A392 & A3058 (right at Kestle Mill).

Open: 24 Mar - 15 Jul & 11 Sept - 3 Nov: daily except Tues & Sats. 16 Jul - 10 Sept: daily (except Sats), 11am - 5.30pm (closes 5pm in Mar, Oct & Nov).

Admission: £4.40, Family £11. Pre-arranged groups £3.60.

⬚ 🏛 ♿ Braille & taped guides. WC. 🍽 Licensed. 🐕 Guide dogs only. ⬆

TREVARNO ESTATE GARDENS & 🏛 THE NATIONAL MUSEUM OF GARDENING

HELSTON, CORNWALL TR13 0RU

Tel: 01326 574274 **Fax:** 01326 574282 **Contact:** Garden Co-ordinator

An unforgettable gardening experience combining beautiful Victorian and Georgian gardens with the splendid fountain garden conservatory, unique range of crafts and the amazing National Museum of Gardening. Relax in the tranquil gardens and grounds, follow the progress of major restoration projects, visit the craft areas including handmade soap workshop, explore Britain's largest and most comprehensive collection of antique tools, implements, memorabilia and ephemera, creatively displayed to illustrate how gardens and gardening influence most peoples' lives.

Location: OS Ref. SW642 302. Leave Helston on Penzance road, signed from B3302 junction and N of Crowntown village. Follow brown & white tourism signs.

Open: All year, 10.30am - 5pm, except 25/26 Dec. Groups by prior arrangement.

Admission: Adult £4.50, Child (5-14yrs) £1.50. Under 5s Free, Disabled £2.50, OAP £3.95.

⬚ ♿ Partial. 🍽 🅿 🏛 🐕 On leads. ⬆ ❄

TRESCO ABBEY GARDENS 🏛

ISLES OF SCILLY, CORNWALL TR24 0QQ

Tel: 01720 424105 **Tel/Fax:** 01720 422868 **e-mail:** mikenelhams@tresco.co.net

Owner: Mr R A and Mrs L A Dorrien-Smith **Contact:** Mr M.A Nelhams

Tresco Abbey, built by Augustus Smith, has been the family home since 1834. The garden here flourishes on the small island. Nowhere else in the British Isles does such an exotic collection of plants grow in the open. Agaves, aloes, proteas and acacias from such places as Australia, South Africa, Mexico and the Mediterranean grow within the secure embrace of massive Holm Oak hedges. Valhalla Ships Figurehead Museum.

Location: OS Ref. SV895 143. Isles of Scilly. Isles of Scilly Steamship 0345 105555. BIH Helicopters 01736 363871. Details of day trips on application.

Open: All year: 10am - 4pm.

Admission: Adult £7.50, (under 14yrs free). Weekly ticket £10. Guided group tours available.

⬚ ♿ Grounds. 🍽 🍴 🐕 In grounds, on leads. ❄

Trebah Garden

Hugh Palmer

TREWITHEN 🏛

GRAMPOUND ROAD, TRURO, CORNWALL TR2 4DD

www.trewithengardens.co.uk

Tel: 01726 883647   **Fax:** 01726 882301
e-mail: gardens@trewithen-estate.demon.co.uk

Owner: A M J Galsworthy   **Contact:** The Estate Office

Trewithen means 'house of the trees' and the name truly describes this fine early Georgian House in its splendid setting of wood and parkland. Country Life described the house as *'one of the outstanding West Country houses of the 18th century'*.

The gardens at Trewithen are outstanding and of international fame. Created since the beginning of the century by George Johnstone, they contain a wide and rare collection of flowering shrubs. Some of the magnolias and rhododendron species in the garden are known throughout the world. They are one of two attractions in this country awarded three stars by Michelin.

Location: OS Ref. SW914 476. S of A390 between Grampound and Probus villages. 7m WSW of St Austell.

Open: Gardens: 1 Mar - 30 Sept: Mon - Sat, 10am - 4.30pm. Suns in Apr & May only. Walled Garden: Mons & Tues in June & 1/2 July only. House: Apr - Jul & Aug: BH Mons, Mons & Tues, 2 - 4pm.

Admission: Adult £4, Child £2. Pre booked groups (20+): Adult £3.75, Child £2. Combined gardens & house £6.

ℹ️ No photography in house. 🚻 ♿ Partial. WC. 🐕 ⓕ By arrangement. 🅿️ Limited for coaches. 🐾 In grounds, on leads.

TRURO CATHEDRAL

Cathedral Office, 14 St Mary's Street, Truro, Cornwall TR1 2AF

Tel: 01872 276782   **Fax:** 01872 277788   **e-mail:** colin@trurocathedral.org.uk
www.trurocathedral.org.uk

Owner: Church of England   **Contact:** The Visitor Officer

Beautifully designed neo-gothic Cathedral by J L Pearson. First Cathedral to be built in England since Salisbury in 1220. Possibly the finest Victorian stained glass in Europe. Inspiring Nathaniel Hitch reredos. The only Cathedral with a parish church physically incorporated within its walls. Father Willis organ recitals. Guided group tours.

Location: SW826 449. Truro city centre.

Open: 7.30am - 6.30pm. Sun services: 8am, 9am, 10am & 6pm. Weekday services: 7.30am, 8am & 5.30pm.

Admission: Free. Suggested donation £3. Booked groups: Adult £2.50, Child £1.25.

ℹ️ Photographic & video permit required. 🅾️ ⊤ ♿ 🐕 Licensed. 🍴 Licensed. ⓕ By arrangement. 🎧 🅿️ None. ◼️ ❋ 📺 Tel for details.

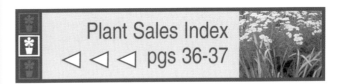

Plant Sales Index
◁ ◁ ◁ pgs 36-37

Bosvigo

BICTON PARK BOTANICAL GARDENS

BUDLEIGH SALTERTON

www.bictongardens.co.uk

Owner:
Mr & Mrs S E Lister

▶ **CONTACT**

Mr Simon Lister
Bicton Park
Botanical Gardens
East Budleigh
Budleigh Salterton
Devon EX9 7BJ

Tel: 01395 568465

Fax: 01395 568374

e-mail: info@
bictongardens.co.uk

▶ **LOCATION**

OS Ref. SY074 856

2m N of Budleigh
Salterton on B3178.

Follow the brown signs
to Bicton Park from
M5/J30 at Exeter.

Rail: Exmouth 5mins,
Exeter St Davids 12m.

Air: Exeter Airport 5m.

Spanning three centuries of horticultural history, Bicton Park Botanical Gardens are set in the picturesque Otter Valley, near the coastal town of Budleigh Salterton and 10 miles south of Exeter.

The 63-acre park's oldest ornamental area is the Italian Garden, created in the axial style of Versailles landscaper Andre le Notre, c1735. By that time formal designs were becoming unfashionable in England, which may explain why the garden was located out of view of the manor house. Today, the full grandeur of the Italian Garden can be seen from the spacious restaurant in the classically styled Orangery, built at the beginning of the 19th century.

Bicton's high-domed Palm House, one of the world's most beautiful garden buildings, was the first of many developments between 1820 and 1850. Others included an important collection of conifers in the Pinetum, now the subject of a rare species conservation project, and St Mary's Church, where Queen Victoria worshipped.

A large museum reflects changes in agriculture and rural life generally over the past 200 years. The Grade I listed gardens, which are open all year, also feature a narrow-gauge railway which meanders through the garden on its 1½ mile track. Gift shop, garden centre, children's inside and outdoor play areas.

▶ **OPENING TIMES**

Summer
10am - 6pm.

Winter
10am - 5pm.
Closed Christmas Day.

▶ **ADMISSION**

Adult	£4.75
Child	£2.75
Conc	£3.75
Family (2+2)	£12.75

Groups (16-200)

Adult	£3.40
Child	£2.50
Conc.	£3.40

Children under 3yrs Free

ℹ Children's inside & outdoor play areas.

🌸 Garden Centre.

♿

🍽 Licensed.

🍴

🚶 By arrangement.

🅿

🐕 In grounds, on leads.

South West - England

Owner:
The Earl of Devon

▶ **CONTACT**

Mr Tim Faulkner
General Manager
The Estate Office
Powderham Castle
Kenton, Exeter
Devon EX6 8JQ

Tel: 01626 890243
Functions:
01626 890243
(Virginia Salter)
Fax: 01626 890729
e-mail: castle@
powderham.co.uk

▶ **LOCATION**

OS Ref. SX965 832

6m SW of Exeter,
4m S M5/J30.
Access from A379 in
Kenton village.

Air: Exeter Airport 9m.

Rail: Starcross
Station 2m.

Bus: Devon General
No: 85, 85A, 85B to
Castle Gate.

CONFERENCE/FUNCTION

ROOM	SIZE	MAX CAPACITY
Music Room	56' x 25'	170
Dining Room	42' x 22'	100
Ante Room	28' x 18'	25
Library 1	32' x 18'	85
Library 2	31"x18'	85

POWDERHAM CASTLE

EXETER

www.powderham.co.uk

The gardens and grounds now have masses to occupy visitors of all ages. As well as informal areas, walks and the springtime Woodland Garden, there is a terraced Rose Garden overlooking an ancient deer park, home to a large herd of fallow deer. The Rose Garden is home to Timothy Tortoise, at 150+ the world's most senior family pet. A delightful steam railway links the castle to the old estate yard where visitors will find a working blacksmith and wheelwright. The train stops at the Victorian walled garden. Known as the Children's Secret Garden it now houses a collection of friendly animals.

Powderham Country Store, comprising a Food Hall, butchers, delicatessen, Plant Centre and large licensed restaurant, specialises in the finest food and drink from the West Country and is open seven days a week, all year round. This makes Powderham a great destination in any season.

Winship's Medieval Jousting Tournament takes place in the grounds of Powderham. From mid July to mid September, The Knights of Powderham joust daily (except Saturday) at 3pm. Their fantastic displays make for great family entertainment and children and grown-ups alike will love the excitement, thrills and spills, action and comedy. From thundering hooves to tumbling knights and hilarious jesters there are two packed hours of entertainment for which a separate charge applies.

Filming, car launches including 4WD, vehicle rallies, open air concerts, etc. Grand piano in Music Room, 3800 acre estate, cricket pitch, horse trials course. Deer park.

Conferences, dinners, corporate entertainment.

Limited facilities. Some ramps. WC.

Fully licensed restaurant and coach room access.

Fully inclusive. Tour time: 1 hr.

Unlimited free parking. Commission and complimentary drinks/meals for drivers. Advance warning of group bookings preferred but not essential.

Welcome. Fascinating tour and useful insight into the life of one of England's Great Houses over the centuries.

In part of grounds, on leads.

Civil Wedding Licence.

❄

▶ **OPENING TIMES**

Summer
24 March - 3 November

Daily*: 10am - 5.30pm
*Except Sat: closed to public, but available for private hire. Gardens only open Suns in March.

Powderham Country Store: daily, 9am - 6pm, (Suns, 10.30am - 4.30pm).

Winter
Available for hire for conferences, receptions and functions and private tours.

▶ **ADMISSION**

Adult	£5.85
OAP	£5.35
Child	£2.95

Group Rates

Adult	£5.15
OAP	£4.65
Child	£2.45
Family (2+2 /1+3)	£14.65

▶ **SPECIAL EVENTS**

MAR 9 - 10
Powderham Historic Motor Rally.

JUL 13/14
The 28th Annual Historic Vehicle Gathering.

AUG 2
'Last Night of the Powderham Proms' Bournemouth Symphony Orchestra Open Air Firework Concert.

AUG 3
Open Air Pop Concert.

NTPL / David Garner

A LA RONDE
SUMMER LANE, EXMOUTH, DEVON EX8 5BD
www.nationaltrust.org.uk

Tel: 01395 265514

Owner: The National Trust   **Contact:** John Rolfe – Custodian

A unique 16-sided house built on the instructions of two spinster cousins, Jane and Mary Parminter, on their return from a grand tour of Europe. Completed c1796, the house contains many 18th century contents and collections brought back by the Parminters. The fascinating interior decoration includes a feather frieze and shell-encrusted gallery which, due to its fragility, can only be viewed on closed circuit television.

Location: OS Ref. SY004 834. 2m N of Exmouth on A376.

Open: 21 Mar - 3 Nov: daily except Fri & Sat, 11am - 5.30pm. Last admission ½ hr before closing.

Admission: Adult £3.50, Child £1.70. No reduction for groups.

BAYARD'S COVE FORT ⌗
Dartmouth, Devon
Tel: 0117 9750700

Owner: English Heritage   **Contact:** South West Regional Office

Set among the picturesque gabled houses of Dartmouth, on the waterfront at the end of the quay, this is a small artillery fort built 1509 - 10 to defend the harbour entrance.

Location: OS Ref. SX879 510. In Dartmouth, on riverfront 200 yds, S of South ferry.

Open: Any reasonable time, daylight hours.

Admission: Free.

BERRY POMEROY CASTLE ⌗
Totnes, Devon TQ9 6NJ
Tel: 01803 866618   **e-mail:** customers@english-heritage.org.uk

www.english-heritage.org.uk

Owner: The Duke of Somerset   **Contact:** English Heritage

A romantic late medieval castle, dramatically sited half-way up a wooded hillside, looking out over a deep ravine and stream. It is unusual in combining the remains of a large castle with a flamboyant courtier's mansion. Reputed to be one of the most haunted castles in the country.

Location: OS202 Ref. SX839 623. 2½ m E of Totnes off A385. Entrance gate ½ m NE of Berry Pomeroy village, then ½ m drive. Narrow approach, unsuitable for coaches.

Open: 29 Mar - 31 Oct: daily, 10am - 6pm (5pm in Oct). Winter: closed.

Admission: Adult £2.80, Child £1.40, Conc £2.10. 15% discount for groups (11+). ♿Ground floor & grounds. ▣ Not EH. 🄯 🅿 No access for coaches. ⬛ ♨ Tel for details.

Website Information
◁ ◁ ◁ pg 39

National Trust / Andreas Von Einsiedel

NTPL / John Melville

ARLINGTON COURT
Nr BARNSTAPLE, NORTH DEVON EX31 4LP
www.nationaltrust.org.uk

Tel: 01271 850296   **Fax:** 01271 850711

Owner: The National Trust   **Contact:** Susie Mercer - Property Manager

Nestling in the thickly wooded valley of the River Yeo, stands the 3000 acre Arlington estate. It comprises a delightful and intimate Victorian house full of treasures including collections of model ships, pewter and shells, extensive informal gardens noted for their spring colour, a formal terraced Victorian garden with conservatory and pond and a partially restored walled garden. The working stable yard houses the National Trust's museum of horse-drawn vehicles and offers carriage rides around the gardens. Jacob sheep and Shetland ponies graze the historic parkland, beyond which lie miles of breathtaking woodland and lakeside walks. Sculpture trail, children's quiz and bat education room.

Location: OS180 Ref. SS611 405. 7m NE of Barnstaple on A39.

Open: 23 Mar - 3 Nov: daily except Tues, 10.30am - 5pm. House & Carriage Collection open at 11am. Last admission 4.30pm. Gardens, shop, tearooms, sculpture trail & bat education room: 4 Jun - 3 Sept: Tues, 10.30am - 4.30pm. 4 Nov - 22 Mar 2003: grounds open during daylight hours.

Admission: House, Gardens & Carriage Collection: Adult £5.60, Child £2.80, Family £13.90. Gardens & Carriage Collection only: Adult £3.50, Child £1.70. Tues: Adult £2.40, Child £1.20.

🄯 ♿Ground floor & grounds. WC. 🍴 Licensed. 🅿 ▣Teachers' pack. 🐾In grounds, on leads. ♨

BICKLEIGH CASTLE 🏰
BICKLEIGH, Nr TIVERTON, DEVON EX16 8RP

Tel: 01884 855363

Owner/Contact: M J Boxall Esq

Royalist stronghold: 900 years of history and architecture. 11th century detached Chapel; 14th century Gatehouse – Armoury (Cromwellian), Guard Room – Tudor furniture and fine oil paintings, Great Hall – 52' long and 'Tudor' Bedroom, massive fourposter. 17th century Farmhouse: inglenook fireplaces, bread ovens, oak beams. The Spooky Tower, Great Hall and picturesque moated garden make Bickleigh a favoured venue for functions, particularly wedding receptions. The Exe-cargot – fine French restaurant, reservations only: 01884 855680.

Location: OS Ref. SS936 068. Off the A396 Exeter-Tiverton road. Follow signs SW from Bickleigh Bridge 1m.

Open: Easter - end Sept: Wed & Sun, 2 - 5pm. Last admission 4.30pm. Coaches & groups welcome any time by prior appointment. Weekday weddings & events, please telephone for details.

Admission: Adult £4, Child (5-15yrs) £2, Family £10.

ⓘConferences. ♿Ground floor. Licensed. Obligatory. ▨ ▲ ✳

BICTON PARK BOTANICAL GARDENS
See page 199 for full page entry.

BRADLEY MANOR ✻
Newton Abbot, Devon TQ12 6BN

Tel: 01626 354513 www.nationaltrust.org.uk

Owner: The National Trust   **Contact:** Miss F Woolner

A small medieval manor house set in woodland and meadows.

Location: OS Ref. SX848 709. On Totnes road A381. ³/4 m SW of Newton Abbot.

Open: 3 Apr - 26 Sept: Weds & Thurs, 2 - 5 pm. Last admission 4.30pm.

Admission: £2.80, no reduction for groups.

BRANSCOMBE MANOR MILL, THE OLD BAKERY & FORGE ✻
Branscombe, Seaton, Devon EX12 3DB

Tel: Manor Mill - 01392 881691   Old Bakery - 01297 680333   Forge - 01297 680481 www.nationaltrust.org.uk

Owner: The National Trust   **Contact:** NT Devon Regional Office

Manor Mill, still in working order and recently restored, is a water-powered mill which probably supplied the flour for the bakery, regular working demonstrations. The Old Bakery was, until 1987, the last traditional working bakery in Devon. The old baking equipment has been preserved in the baking room and the rest of the building is now a tearoom. Information display in the outbuildings. The Forge opens regularly and ironwork is on sale - please telephone to check opening times (01297 680481).

Location: OS Ref. SY198 887. In Branscombe ¹/2 m S off A3052 by steep, narrow lane.

Open: Manor Mill: 24 Mar - 3 Nov: Suns, 2 - 5pm; also Weds in Jul & Aug. The Old Bakery: Easter - Oct, daily, weekends in winter months, 11am - 5pm.

Admission: £1 Manor Mill only.

BUCKFAST ABBEY
Buckfastleigh, Devon TQ11 0EE

Tel: 01364 645500   **Fax:** 01364 643891   **e-mail:** education@buckfast.org.uk

Owner: Buckfast Abbey Trust   **Contact:** The Warden

Location: OS Ref. SX741 674. ¹/2 m from A38 Plymouth - Exeter route.

Open: Church & Grounds: All year: 5.30am - 7pm.

Admission: Free.

BUCKLAND ABBEY ✻
YELVERTON, DEVON PL20 6EY

www.nationaltrust.org.uk

Tel: 01822 853607   **Fax:** 01822 855448

Owner: The National Trust   **Contact:** Michael Coxson - Property Manager

The spirit of Sir Francis Drake is rekindled at his home with exhibitions of his courageous adventures and achievements throughout the world. One of the Trust's most interesting historical buildings and originally a 13th century monastery, the abbey was transformed into a family residence before Sir Francis bought it in 1581. Fascinating decorated plaster ceiling in Tudor Drake Chamber. Outside there are monastic farm buildings, herb garden, craft workshops and country walks. Introductory video presentation. Beautiful new Elizabethan garden now open.

Location: OS201 Ref. SX487 667. 6m S of Tavistock; 11m N of Plymouth off A386.

Open: 22 Mar - 3 Nov: daily except Thur, 10.30am - 5.30pm (last adm. 4.45pm). 4 Nov - Mar 2002: Sat & Sun only. Closed 23 Dec - 21 Feb 2003. It may be necessary to close the Abbey, or significant parts of it, during exhibition refurbishment Nov 2002 to Spring 2003. Please telephone for details.

Admission: Abbey & Grounds: Adult £4.70, Child £2.30, Family £11.70. Group: £3.90. Grounds only: Adult £2.50, Child £1.20. Winter: half price Abbey admission.

♿Ground floor & grounds. Wheelchair stairclimber may be available. WC. Guide dogs only. ✳

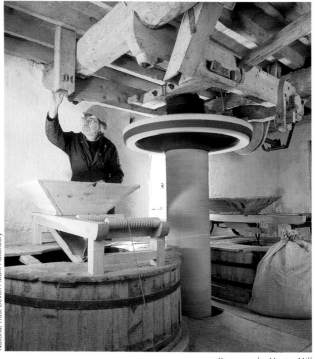

National Trust Devon / Mark Rattenbury

Branscombe Manor Mill

CADHAY 🏠
OTTERY ST MARY, DEVON EX11 1QT
www.eastdevon.net/cadhay

Tel/Fax: 01404 812432 **e-mail:** cadhay@eastdevon.net

Owner/Contact: Mr O N W William-Powlett

Cadhay is approached by an avenue of lime-trees, and stands in a pleasant listed garden, with herbaceous borders and yew hedges, with excellent views over the original medieval fish ponds. The main part of the house was built about 1550 by John Haydon who had married the de Cadhay heiress. He retained the Great Hall of an earlier house, of which the fine timber roof (about 1420) can be seen. An Elizabethan Long Gallery was added by John's successor at the end of the 16th century, thereby forming a unique and lovely courtyard.

Location: OS Ref. SY090 962. 1m NW of Ottery St Mary. From W take A30 and exit at Pattersons Cross, follow signs for Fairmile and then Cadhay. From E, exit at the Iron Bridge and follow signs as above.

Open: Jul & Aug: Tues, Weds & Thurs, also Suns & Mons in late Spring & Summer BHs, 2 - 6pm, last admission 5pm. Groups by appointment only.

Admission: Adult £4.50, Child £2.

♿Ground floor & grounds. ⟁Gardens available. ♿Guide dogs only. ▲

David Cripps

NTPL / David Garner

CASTLE DROGO ❦
DREWSTEIGNTON, EXETER EX6 6PB
www.nationaltrust.org.uk

Tel: 01647 433306 **Fax:** 01647 433186

Owner: The National Trust   **Contact:** Peter Jennings, Property Manager

Extraordinary granite and oak castle, designed by Sir Edwin Lutyens, which combines the comforts of the 20th century with the grandeur of a Baronial castle. Elegant dining and drawing rooms and fascinating kitchen and scullery. Terraced formal garden with colourful herbaceous borders and rose beds. Panoramic views over Dartmoor and delightful walks in the 300ft Teign Gorge.

Location: OS191 Ref. SX721 900. 5m S of A30 Exeter – Okehampton road.

Open: Castle: 23 Mar - 3 Nov: daily except Fri (open Good Fri), 11am - 5.30pm (last admission 5pm). 2 - 22 Mar: pre-season guided tours daily except Mon & Tue. Garden: All year: daily, 10.30am - dusk. Shop & tearoom open as Castle.

Admission: House & Garden: Adult £5.70, Child £2.80, Family £14.20. Group: £4.80. Garden only: Adult £2.90, Child £1.40.

📷 ♿Ground floor & grounds. WCs. ⟁Licensed. ⟁By arrangement. ♿Guide dogs only in certain areas. ❋

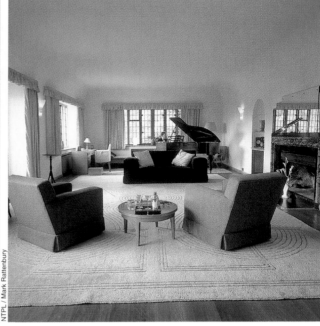

NTPL / Mark Rattenbury

COLETON FISHACRE HOUSE & GARDEN ❧

BROWNSTONE ROAD, KINGSWEAR, DARTMOUTH TQ6 0EQ

www.nationaltrust.org.uk

Tel/Fax: 01803 752466   **e-mail:** dcfdmx@smtp.ntrust.org.uk

Owner: The National Trust   **Contact:** David Mason, Property Manager

A 9 hectare property set in a stream-fed valley within the spectacular scenery of the South Devon coast. The Lutyenesque style house with art deco interior was built in the 1920s for Rupert and Lady Dorothy D'Oyly Carte who created the delightful garden, planted with a wide range of rare and exotic plants giving year round interest.

Location: OS202 Ref. SX910 508. 3m E of Kingswear, follow brown tourist signs.

Open: Garden: Mar: Sats & Suns only, 11am - 5pm. House & Garden: 23 Mar - 3 Nov: Wed - Sun & BH Mons. House: 11am - 4.30pm, Garden: 10.30am - 5.30pm.

Admission: Adult £4.90, Child £2.40. Family £12.20. Booked groups (15+) £4.20. Garden only: Adult £3.80, Child £1.90, Booked groups (15+) £3.20.

ℹ No photography in house. 📷 🚻 ♿Limited access to grounds. WC. 🅿Limited. Coaches must book. 🐕Guide dogs only in garden.

COMPTON CASTLE ❧

Marldon, Paignton TQ3 1TA

Tel: 01803 875740 (answerphone) **www**.nationaltrust.org.uk

Owner/Contact: The National Trust

A fortified manor house with curtain wall, built at three periods: 1340, 1450 and 1520 by the Gilbert family.

Location: OS Ref. SX865 648. At Compton, 3m W of Torquay.

Open: 1 Apr - 31 Oct: Mons, Weds & Thurs, 10am - 12.15pm & 2 - 5pm. The courtyard, restored great hall, solar, chapel, rose garden and old kitchen are shown. Last admission ½ hr before closing.

Admission: £2.90, pre-arranged groups £2.30.

Buckland Abbey

NT Photographic Library

CROWNHILL FORT

CROWNHILL FORT ROAD, PLYMOUTH, DEVON PL6 5BX

www.crownhillfort.co.uk

Tel: 01752 793754 **Fax:** 01752 770065 **e-mail:** info@crownhillfort.co.uk

Owner: Landmark Trust   **Contact:** James Breslin

At Crownhill Fort you are free to explore the 16 acre site, honeycombed with tunnels, surrounded by massive ramparts, protected by a deep dry moat and guarded by many cannon. After a long restoration the Fort now stands proud as one of the largest and best preserved of Britain's great Victorian forts, and in particular boasts the Moncrieff Disappearing Gun, the only example in the world.

Location: OS Ref. SX487 593. 4m from Plymouth City Centre and less than 1m from A38, signposted from A386 Tavistock Road.

Open: 3 Jan - 28 Mar & 4 Nov - 22 Dec: Schools & Groups by appointment. 16 - 24 Feb & 29 Mar - 3 Nov: daily, 10am - 5pm.

Admission: Adult £4.50, Child £2.75, Conc. £4, Family (2+2) £12. Groups (15+) 10% discount.

📷 🚻 ♿Partial. WC. 🍽 🎫By arrangement. 🅿Limited for coaches. 🔲 🐕 ❄

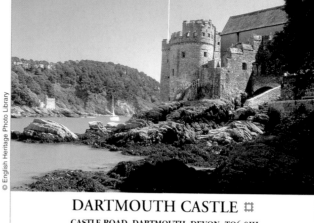

© English Heritage Photo Library

CULVER HOUSE

LONGDOWN, EXETER, DEVON EX6 7BD

www.culver.biz

Tel: 01392 811885 **Fax:** 01392 811817 **e-mail:** culverestate@aol.com

Owner/Contact: Charles Eden Esq

Culver was built in 1836, but redesigned by the great Victorian architect, Alfred Waterhouse in a mock Tudor style. the distinctive interior of the house makes it a favoured location for functions and Culver was featured in BBC1's 'Down to Earth' series in 2001.

Location: OS Ref. SX848 901. 5m W of Exeter on B3212.

Open: Not open to the public. Available for corporate hospitality.

Admission: Please telephone for booking details.

DARTMOUTH CASTLE ⌗

CASTLE ROAD, DARTMOUTH, DEVON TQ6 0JH

www.english-heritage.org.uk

Tel: 01803 833588 **Fax:** 01803 834445 **e-mail:** customers@english-heritage.org.uk

Owner: English Heritage **Contact:** The Custodian

This brilliantly positioned defensive castle juts out into the narrow entrance to the Dart estuary, with the sea lapping at its foot. When begun in 1480s it was one of the most advanced fortifications in England, and was the first castle designed specifically with artillery in mind. For nearly 500 years it kept its defences up-to-date in preparation for war. Today the castle is in a remarkably good state of repair, along with excellent exhibitions, the history of the castle comes to life. A picnic spot of exceptional beauty.

Location: OS202 Ref. SX887 503. 1m SE of Dartmouth off B3205, narrow approach road.

Open: 29 Mar - 31 Oct: daily, 10am - 6pm (5pm in Oct). 1 Nov - 31 Mar: Wed - Sun, 10am - 4pm. Closed 24 - 26 Dec & 1 Jan.

Admission: Adult £3.20, Child £1.60, Conc. £2.40. 15% discount for groups (11+).

Ground floor. P Limited. Tel. for details.

DARTINGTON HALL GARDENS

Dartington, Totnes, Devon TQ9 6EL

Tel/Fax: 01803 862367 **e-mail:** graham@dartingtonhall.org.uk

Owner: Dartington Hall Trust **Contact:** Mr G Gammin

28 acre gardens surrounds 14th century Hall.

Location: OS Ref. SX798 628. 30 mins from M5 at Exeter (off A38 at Buckfastleigh).

Open: All year. Groups by appointment only. Guided tours by arrangement £4.

Admission: £2 donation welcome.

DOCTON MILL & GARDEN

Spekes Valley, Hartland, Devon EX39 6EA

Tel/Fax: 01237 441369 **e-mail:** john@doctonmill.freeserve.co.uk

www.doctonmill.co.uk

Owner/Contact: John Borrett

Garden for all seasons in 8 acres of sheltered wooded valley, plus working mill.

Location: OS Ref. SS235 226. 3m Hartland Quay. 15m N of Bude. 3m W of A39, 3m S of Hartland.

Open: 1 Mar - 31 Oct: 10am - 6pm. Coaches by appointment.

Admission: Adult £3.50, Child (under 14 yrs) £1, OAP £3.

THE ELIZABETHAN GARDENS

Plymouth Barbican Assoc. Ltd, New St, The Barbican, Plymouth

Tel: 01752 301010 **Fax:** 01752 312430 **e-mail:** apg@plymouth.francisclark.co.uk

Owner: Plymouth Barbican Association Limited **Contact:** Tony Golding Esq

Very small series of four enclosed gardens laid out in Elizabethan style in 1970.

Location: OS Ref. SX477 544. 3 mins walk from Dartington Glass (a landmark building) on the Barbican.

Open: Mon - Sat, 9am - 5pm. Closed Christmas.

Admission: Free.

ESCOT COUNTRY PARK & GARDENS

Escot, Ottery St Mary, Devon EX11 1LU

Tel: 01404 822188 **Fax:** 01404 822903 **e-mail:** escot@eclipse.co.uk

www.escot-devon.co.uk

Owner/Contact: Mr J-M Kennaway

House: an idyllic setting for weddings, conferences and product launches. Gardens: Otters, wild boar, birds of prey displays within 25 acres of gardens, including 'Ivan Hicks at Escot' – a unique visit experience being created by BBC Gardeners' World's acclaimed gardener-artist (new for 2002). Estate: 1200 privately owned acres of glorious East Devon – an ideal film location.

Location: OS Ref. SY080 977 (gate). 9m E of Exeter on A30 at Fairmile.

Open: Easter - 31 Oct: Gardens, Aquatic Centre & Restaurant, daily, 10am - 6pm. 1 Nov - Easter: Gardens closed except by prior arrangement. Aquatic Centre & Restaurant: daily, 10am - 5pm except 25, 26 Dec & Mons in Jan, Feb & Mar.

Admission: Adult £3.95, Child £3, Child (under 4yrs) Free, OAP £3, Family (2+2) £12. Booked groups(10+): Adult £3.25, Child/Conc. £2.75.

Partial. Licensed. Licensed. By arrangement. P In grounds, on leads. Tel for details.

Compton Castle

NT Photographic Library. Nicholas Toyne

EXETER CATHEDRAL

Exeter, Devon EX1 1HS

Tel: 01392 255573   **Fax:** 01392 498769   **e-mail:** admin@exeter-cathedral.org.uk

Owner: Dean & Chapter of Exeter   **Contact:** Mrs Juliet Dymoke-Marr

Fine example of decorated gothic architecture. Longest unbroken stretch of gothic vaulting in the world.

Location: OS Ref. SX921 925. Central to the City - between High Street and Southernhay. Groups may be set down in South Street.

Open: All year: Mon - Fri 7.30am - 6.30pm, Sats, 7.30am - 5pm, Suns, 8am - 7.30pm.

Admission: No entry charge – donation requested of £3 per person.

FLETE

ERMINGTON, IVYBRIDGE, DEVON PL21 9NZ

www.cha.org.uk

Tel: 01752 830308   **Fax:** 01752 830309

Owner: Country Houses Association   **Contact:** The Administrators

First mentioned in the Domesday Book, Flete became a manor house in Elizabethan times. A wing was added in 1800 and in 1876 Norman Shaw was appointed, adding the entire north front in Gothic style. Magnificent timber panelling and floors. Flete has been converted into apartments for active retired people.

Location: OS Ref. SX631 519. 11m E of Plymouth at junction of A379 & B3121. Stations: Plymouth 12m, Totnes 14m. Bus route: No 93 Plymouth - Dartmouth.

Open: 1 May - 30 Sept: Wed & Thur, 2 - 5pm. Groups by arrangement.

Admission: Adult £3.50, Child Free. Groups by arrangement.

🇹 🗙 📱 1 single & 1 double with bathroom, CHA members only.

FURSDON HOUSE 🏛

Cadbury, Thorverton, Exeter, Devon EX5 5JS

Tel: 01392 860860   **Fax:** 01392 860126   **e-mail:** enquiries@fursdon.co.uk

www.fursdon.co.uk

Owner: E D Fursdon Esq   **Contact:** Mrs C Fursdon

The home of the Fursdon family is in beautiful hilly countryside above the Exe valley. The architecture reflects changes made throughout the centuries. Family memorabilia is displayed including scrap books, fine examples of 18th century costume and textiles and a letter from King Charles I during the Civil War.

Location: OS Ref. SS922 046. 1½ m S of A3072 between Tiverton & Crediton, 9m N of Exeter. 2m N of Thorverton by narrow lane.

Open: 30 Mar - 6 Apr; 4 - 10 May; 1 - 7 Jun; 24 - 31 Aug: guided house tours at 2.30pm & 3.30pm. Groups by arrangement: Mar - Sept.

Admission: Adult £4, Child (11-16yrs) £2, (under 10yrs Free). Groups (20+) £3.50. Gardens only: £2.

ℹ️ Conferences. 🇹 🗙 Partial. 🇫 Obligatory. 🅿 🗙 📱 Self-catering

THE GARDEN HOUSE

Buckland Monachorum, Yelverton, Devon PL20 7LQ

Tel: 01822 854769   **Fax:** 01822 855358   **e-mail:** office@thegardenhouse.org.uk

www.thegardenhouse.org.uk

Owner: Fortescue Garden Trust   **Contact:** Stuart Fraser

'Is this the best garden in Britain?' *Sunday Express*: eight acres offer year-round colour and interest centred on an enchanting walled garden surrounding the medieval ruins of a 16th century vicarage. Modern garden planted in pioneering naturalistic style. Over 6,000 varieties feature in an idyllic valley on the edge of Dartmoor. 'You'd be mad to miss it' – Alan Titchmarsh.

Location: OS Ref. SX490 682. Signposted W off A386 near Yelverton, 10m N of Plymouth.

Open: 1 Mar - 31 Oct: daily, 10.30am - 5pm. Last admission 4.30pm.

Admission: Adult £4, Child (5-16) £1, OAP £3.50, pre-booked groups (15+) £3 (if deposit paid).

🇹 🗙 Partial. 🖥 🇫 By arrangement. 🅿 🗙

HALDON BELVEDERE/LAWRENCE CASTLE

Higher Ashton, Nr Dunchideock, Exeter, Devon EX6 7QY

Tel/Fax: 01392 833668   **e-mail:** turner@haldonbelvedere.co.uk

www.haldonbelvedere.co.uk

Owner: Devon Historic Building Trust   **Contact:** Ian Turner

18th century Grade II* listed triangular tower with circular turrets on each corner. Built in memory of Major General Stringer Lawrence, founder of the Indian Army. Recently restored to illustrate the magnificence of its fine plasterwork, gothic windows, mahogany flooring and marble fireplaces. Breathtaking views of the surrounding Devon countryside.

Location: OS Ref. SX875 861. 7m SW of Exeter. Exit A38 at Exeter racecourse for 2½m.

Open: Feb - Oct: Suns & BHs, 2 - 5pm.

Admission: Adult £1.50, Child 75p. No discount for groups (20-50).

🇹 🗙 Unsuitable. 🇫 By arrangement. 🅿 Limited. 🖥 🗙 In grounds, on leads. 🔲 🔺

Lady Stucley, Hartland Abbey

CHA

HARTLAND ABBEY 🏛

HARTLAND, BIDEFORD, DEVON EX39 6DT

www.hartlandabbey.com

Tel: 01237 441264/441234   **Fax:** 01237 441264/01884 861134

e-mail: stucley@care4free.net

Owner: Sir Hugh Stucley Bt   **Contact:** The Administrator

Founded as an Augustinian Monastery in 1157 in a beautiful valley only 1 mile's walk from a spectacular Atlantic Cove, the Abbey was given by Henry VIII in 1539 to the Sergeant of his Wine Cellar, whose descendants live here today. Remodelled in the 18th & 19th century, it contains spectacular architecture and murals. Important paintings, furniture, porcelain collected over generations. Documents from 1160. Victorian and Edwardian photographs. Museum. Dairy. Recently discovered Victorian fernery and paths by Jekyll. Extensive woodland gardens of camellias, rhododendrons etc. Bog Garden. 18th century Walled gardens of vegetables, summer borders, tender and rare plants including echium pininana. Peacocks, donkeys and Welsh Mountain sheep in the park. NPI Heritage Award winner 1998.

Location: OS Ref. SS240 249. 15m W of Bideford, 15m N of Bude off A39 between Hartland and Hartland Quay.

Open: 1 Apr - 6 Oct: Wed, Thur, Sun & BHs, plus Tues in Jul & Aug, 2 - 5.30pm. Gardens: 1 Apr - 6 Oct: daily except Sats, 2 - 5.30pm.

Admission: House, Gardens & Grounds: Adult £5, Child (9-15yrs) £1.50, OAP £4.50. Groups (20+): Adult £4.25, Child £1.50. Gardens & Grounds: Adult £3, Child 50p. Groups: £2.75.

🗙 🇹 Wedding receptions. 🗙 Partial. WC. 🖥 🇫 By arrangement. 🅿 🗙 In grounds, on leads. 🔺

HEMERDON HOUSE

Sparkwell, Plympton, Plymouth, Devon PL7 5BZ

Tel: Business hours 01752 841410; other times 01752 337350   **Fax:** 01752 331477
e-mail: jim.woollcombe@connexions-cd.org.uk

Owner: J H G Woollcombe Esq   **Contact:** Paul Williams & Partners

Late 18th century family house, rich in local history.

Location: OS Ref. SX564 575. 3m E of Plympton off A38.

Open: 1 May - 30 Sept: for 30 days including May & Aug BHs, 2 - 5.30pm. Last admission 5pm. Please contact the Administrator for opening dates.

Admission: £3.

 Ground floor. Obligatory. **P**

HEMYOCK CASTLE

Hemyock, Cullompton, Devon EX15 3RJ

Tel: 01823 680745

Owner/Contact: Mrs Sheppard

Former medieval moated castle, displays show site's history as fortified manor house, castle and farm.

Location: OS Ref. ST135 134. M5/J26, Wellington then 5m S over the Blackdown Hills.

Open: BH Mons 2 - 5pm. Other times by appointment. Groups and private parties welcome.

Admission: Adult £1, Child 50p. Group rates available.

HOUND TOR DESERTED MEDIEVAL VILLAGE

Ashburton Road, Manaton, Dartmoor, Devon

Tel: 01626 832093

Owner: English Heritage   **Contact:** Dartmoor National Park Authority

The remains of four bronze age to medieval dwellings.

Location: OS191 Ref. SX746 788. 1^1/$_2$ m S of Manaton off Ashburton road. 6m N of Ashburton.

Open: Any reasonable time, daylight only.

Admission: Free.

National Trust / Chris Vile

Markers Cottage

NTPL / Chris Vile

NTPL / Andreas von Einsiedel

KILLERTON HOUSE & GARDEN

BROADCLYST, EXETER EX5 3LE

www.nationaltrust.org.uk

Tel: 01392 881345

Owner: The National Trust   **Contact:** Denise Melhuish - Property Manager

The spectacular hillside garden is beautiful throughout the year with spring flowering bulbs and shrubs, colourful herbaceous borders and fine trees. The garden is surrounded by parkland and woods offering lovely walks. The house is furnished as a family home and includes a costume collection dating from the 18th century in a series of period rooms and a Victorian laundry. Special costume exhibition for 2002 'Lace – The Ultimate Luxury'.

Location: OS Ref. SS977 001. Off Exeter – Cullompton Rd (B3181). M5 N'bound J30, M5 S'bound J28.

Open: House: 9 - 31 Mar, daily except Mon & Tue. 1 Apr - 2 Sept, daily except Tues. Aug: daily, 11am - 5.30pm, last entry ^{1}/$_2$ hr before closing. House: closed 3 Sept 2002 - Easter 2003 for essential building work. Garden: all year, daily.

Admission: House & Garden: Adult £5.40, Child £2.70, Family £13.50, Group £4.50. Garden only: Adult £3.90, Child £1.90.

    Guide dogs only in house.

KNIGHTSHAYES ❦

BOLHAM, TIVERTON, DEVON EX16 7RQ

www.nationaltrust.org.uk

Tel: 01884 254665 **Fax:** 01884 243050

Owner: The National Trust **Contact:** Penny Woollams – Property Manager
The striking Victorian gothic house is a rare survival of the work of William Burges with ornate patterns in many rooms. One of the finest gardens in Devon, mainly woodland and shrubs with something of interest throughout the seasons. Drifts of spring bulbs, summer flowering shrubs, pool garden and amusing animal topiary.

Location: OS Ref. SS960 151. 2m N of Tiverton (A396) at Bolham.

Open: House: 23 Mar - 3 Nov, daily except Fri (open Good Fri), 11am - 5.30pm (Oct 4pm) last adm. ¹/₂ hr before closing. Gardens: 23 Mar - 3 Nov, daily, 11am - 5.30pm.

Admission: House & Garden: Adult £5.50, Child £2.70, Family £13.70. Group £4.80. Garden only: Adult £3.90, Child £1.90.

⬚ ♿ ☂ ♿ Ground floor & grounds. WC. 🍴 ⌂ Guide dogs in park.

LYDFORD CASTLES & SAXON TOWN ⌂
Lydford, Okehampton, Devon

Tel: 01822 820320

Owner: English Heritage **Contact:** The National Trust – 01822 820320
Standing above the lovely gorge of the River Lyd, this 12th century tower was notorious as a prison. The earthworks of the original Norman fort are to the south. A Saxon town once stood nearby and its layout is still discernible.

Location: OS191 Castle Ref. SX510 848, Fort Ref. SX509 847. In Lydford off A386 8m SW of Okehampton.

Open: Any reasonable time, daylight hours.

Admission: Free.

MARKERS COTTAGE ❦
Broadclyst, Exeter, Devon EX5 3HR

Tel: 01392 461546

Owner: The National Trust **Contact:** The Custodian
Medieval cob house containing a cross-passage screen decorated with a painting of St Andrew and his attributes.

Location: OS Ref. SX985 973. ¹/₄ E of B3181 in village of Broadclyst.

Open: 31 Mar - 29 Oct: Sun - Tue, 2 - 5pm.

Admission: £1.50.

MARWOOD HILL
Barnstaple, Devon EX31 4EB

Tel: 01271 342528 **Owner/Contact:** Dr J A Smart
20 acre garden with 3 small lakes. Extensive collection of camellias, bog garden. National collection of astilbes.

Location: OS Ref. SS545 375. 4m N of Barnstaple. ¹/₂ m W of B3230. Signs off A361 Barnstaple - Braunton road.

Open: Dawn to dusk throughout the year.

Admission: Adult £3, Child (under 12yrs) Free.

MORWELLHAM QUAY
Morwellham, Tavistock, Devon PL19 8JL

Tel: 01822 832766 **Fax:** 01822 833808

Owner: The Morwellham & Tamar Valley Trust **Contact:** Peter Kenwright
Award-winning visitor centre at historic river port.

Location: OS Ref. SX446 697. Off A390 about 15 mins drive from Tavistock, Devon. 5m SW of Tavistock. 3m S of A390 at Gulworthy.

Open: Summer: daily, 10am - 5.30pm, last adm. 3.30pm. Winter: daily, 10am - 4.30pm, last adm. 2.30pm.

Admission: Adult £8.90, Child £6. Family (2+2) £25. Group rate please apply for details. Usual concessions.

OKEHAMPTON CASTLE ⌂
Okehampton, Devon EX20 1JB

Tel: 01837 52844 **e-mail:** customers@english-heritage.org.uk
www.english-heritage.org.uk

Owner: English Heritage **Contact:** The Custodian
The ruins of the largest castle in Devon stand above a river surrounded by splendid woodland. There is still plenty to see, including the Norman motte and the jagged remains of the Keep. There is a picnic area and lovely woodland walks.

Location: OS191 Ref. SX584 942. 1m SW of Okehampton town centre off A30 bypass.

Open: 29 Mar - 31 Oct: daily, 10am - 6pm (5pm in Oct). Winter: Closed.

Admission: Adult £2.50, Child £1.30, Conc. £1.80. 15% discount for groups (11+).

⬚ ♿ Grounds. WC. ⬚ ⬚ 🅿 ⌂ In grounds, on leads. ☎ Tel. for details.

OLDWAY MANSION
Paignton, Devon

Tel: 01803 201201 **Fax:** 01803 292866 **e-mail:** webmaster@torbay.gov.org
Owner: Torbay Council **Contact:** Peter Carpenter
Built by sewing machine entrepreneur I M Singer in the 1870s.

Location: OS Ref. SX888 615. Off W side of A3022.

Open: All year: Mon - Sat, 9am - 5pm (except Christmas & New Year). Easter - Oct: Suns, 2 - 5pm. Visitors should note that not all rooms will always be open, access depends on other activities.

Admission: Free.

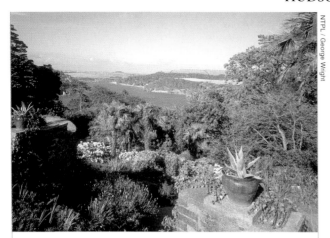

NTPL / George Wright

OVERBECKS MUSEUM & GDN

SHARPITOR, SALCOMBE, SOUTH DEVON TQ8 8LW

www.nationaltrust.org.uk

Tel: 01548 842893

Owner: The National Trust **Contact:** Roy Chandler - Property Manager

A sub-tropical garden with rare and tender plants thriving in the mild climate and spectacular views over the Salcombe Estuary. In the Edwardian house are curios such as a polyphon and rejuvenating machine and displays on the maritime history and wildlife of the area. There is also a secret room for children, with dolls, tin soldiers, other toys and a ghost hunt.

Location: OS202 Ref. SX728 374. 1¹/₂ m SW of Salcombe. Signposted from Salcombe (single track lanes).

Open: Museum: 24 Mar - 31 July, Sept: Sun - Fri (open Easter Sat), 11am - 5.30pm. August, daily, 11am - 5.30pm. October, Sun - Thur, 11am - 5pm. Garden: All year: daily.

Admission: House & Garden: Adult £4.20, Child £2.10, Family £10.50. Garden only: Adult £3, Child £1.50.

ⓘNo photography in house. 🔲 ⚿ ♿Partial. 🔳 🎬 By arrangement. 🅿Limited. ▣ ✖ ✻

PUSLINCH

YEALMPTON, PLYMOUTH, DEVON PL8 2NN

Tel: 01752 880555 **Fax:** 01752 880909

Owner/Contact: Sebastian Fenwick

A perfect example of a medium sized early Georgian house in the Queen Anne tradition with fine contemporary interiors. Built in 1720 by the Yonge family.

Location: OS Ref. SX570 509. Yealmpton.

Open: Groups only (8-60). All year except Christmas & Boxing Day by prior appointment only.

Admission: Adult £5.

ⓘNo photography. 🎬Obligatory. 🅿 ✖ ✻

POWDERHAM CASTLE 📷 *See page 200 for full page entry.*

Fursdon House

RHS GARDEN ROSEMOOR

GREAT TORRINGTON, DEVON EX38 8PH

www.rhs.org.uk

Tel: 01805 624067 **Fax:** 01805 624717

Owner/Contact: The Royal Horticultural Society

A beautiful garden mixing new gardens with Lady Anne's original garden. Something for all interests and tastes whatever the season, from formal gardens to a lake and Arboretum. The Rosemoor Plant Centre stocks a variety of hardy plants. The shop with books and gifts and for refreshments the café and restaurant.

Location: OS Ref. SS500 183. 1m S of Great Torrington on A3124.

Open: All year except Christmas Day; Apr - Sept: 10am - 6pm. Oct - Mar: 10am - 5pm.

Admission: Adult £5, Child (6 - 16yrs) £1. Child (under 6yrs) Free. Groups (10+) £4. Companion for disabled visitor Free.

🔲 ⚿ ♿ 🔳 🍴Licensed. 🎬By arrangement. 🅿 🐕Guide dogs only. ✻

The National Trust

SALTRAM HOUSE ✤
PLYMPTON, PLYMOUTH, DEVON PL7 1UH

www.nationaltrust.org.uk

Tel: 01752 333500   **Fax:** 01752 336474

Owner: The National Trust   **Contact:** Kevan Timms - Property Manager

A magnificent George II mansion set in beautiful gardens and surrounded by landscaped park overlooking the Plym estuary. Visitors can see the original contents including important work by Robert Adam, Chippendale, Wedgwood and Sir Joshua Reynolds. You can explore the garden follies including Fanny's Bower and the Castle, follow the tree trail in the garden and enjoy fascinating walks beside the river, through the parkland and in the woods. Saltram starred as Norland Park in the award winning film *Sense & Sensibility*.

Location: OS Ref. SX520 557. 3^1/$_2$ m E of Plymouth city centre. ^{1}/$_4$ m S of A38.

Open: House: 24 Mar - 3 Nov: daily, except Fri, 12 noon - 4pm, last admission 3.30pm. (1 Oct - 3 Nov: 11.30am - 3.30pm). House closed in winter. Garden, Chapel Art Gallery, Shop & Tearoom: 11am - 5pm. Also 4 Nov - 19 Dec: daily except Fri, 11am - 4pm.

Admission: House & Garden: Adult £6, Child £3, Family £15. Groups £5.20. Garden only: Adult £3, Child £1.50.

ℹ Conferences. ⬛ ♿WC. Braille guide. Audio-visual tape. 🍴 Licensed.
🐕 In grounds, on leads. Guide dogs in house.

SAND 🏛
SIDBURY, SIDMOUTH EX10 0QN

Tel: 01395 597230

Owner/Contact: Lt Col P Huyshe

Lived-in manor house owned by the Huyshe family since 1560 rebuilt 1592-4, lying in unspoilt valley. Mixed 4-acre garden with something for everyone. Screens passage, panelling, family documents and heraldry. Also Sand Lodge, roof structure of late 15th century hall house.

Location: OS Ref. SY146 925. ^{1}/$_4$ m off A375, ^{1}/$_2$ m N of Sidbury. Well signed.

Open: House: 31 Mar & 1 Apr; 5, 6 May; 2, 3, 4 Jun; 14 & 28 Jul; 11, 25 & 26 Aug, 8 Sept. Garden: 31 Mar - 1 Oct: Sun - Tue, 2 - 6pm. Last house & garden admission 5pm.

Admission: House & Garden: Adult £4, Child/Student £1. Garden only: Adult £2.50, accompanied Child (under 16) Free.

ℹ No photography in house. ♿Partial. ⬛ 🎧Obligatory. 🅿 Limited for coaches.
⬛ 🐕In grounds, on leads. 📞 Tel. for details.

SHOBROOKE PARK
Crediton, Devon EX17 1DG

Tel: 01363 775153   **Fax:** 01363 775153   **e-mail:** admin@shobrookepark.com

Owner: Dr J R Shelley   **Contact:** Clare Shelley

A classical English 180-acre park. The lime avenue dates from about 1800 and the cascade of four lakes was completed in the 1840s. Millennium amphitheatre built in the year 2000. The southern third of the Park is open to the public under the Countryside Commission Access Scheme. The 15 acre garden, created c1845 with Portland stone terraces, roses and rhododendrons is being restored.

Location: OS Ref. SS848 010. 1m E of Crediton. Access to park by kissing gate at SW end of park, just S of A3072. Garden access on A3072.

Open: South Park: daylight hours. Gardens: 27 Apr, 18 May & 15 Jun, 2 - 5pm.

Admission: Park: No charge. Gardens: NGS £2, accompanied child under 14 Free.

♿Partial, wheelchairs in garden only. 🐕Guide dogs only in garden. ✳

SHUTE BARTON ✤
Shute, Axminster, Devon EX13 7PT

Tel: 01297 34692   **www.**nationaltrust.org.uk

Owner: The National Trust

One of the most important surviving non-fortified manor houses of the Middle Ages.

Location: OS Ref. SY253 974. 3m SW of Axminster, 2m N of Colyton, 1m S of A35.

Open: 3 Apr - 30 Oct: Weds & Sats, 2 - 5.30pm. Last admission 5pm.

Admission: £1.80, No group reductions.

TAPELEY PARK 🏛
Instow, Bideford, Devon EX39 4NT

Tel: 01271 342558   **Fax:** 01271 342371

Owner: Tapeley Park Trust

Much altered Queen Anne building with extensive gardens and park.

Location: OS Ref. SS478 291. Between Bideford and Barnstaple near Instow. Follow brown tourist signs from the A39 onto B3233.

Open: Good Fri - end Oct: daily except Sats, 10am - 5pm.

Admission: Adult £3.50, Child £2, OAP £3. House only open to pre-booked groups, extra £2 admission.

TIVERTON CASTLE 🏛

Tiverton, Devon EX16 6RP

Tel: 01884 253200/255200 **Fax:** 01884 254200 **e-mail:** tiverton.castle@ukf.net

www.tivertoncastle.com

Owner: Mr and Mrs A K Gordon   **Contact:** Mrs A Gordon

After nearly 900 years few buildings evoke such an immediate feeling of history as Tiverton Castle. Many ages of architecture can be seen, from medieval to modern. With continuing conservation there is always something new and interesting to see. Old walls, new gardens. Civil War Armoury – try some on.

Location: OS Ref. SS954 130. Just N of Tiverton town centre.

Open: Easter - end of Jun, Sept: Sun, Thur, BH Mon, Jul & Aug, Sun - Thur, 2.30 - 5.30pm. Open to groups (12+) by prior arrangement at any time.

Admission: Adult £4, Child (7-16yrs) £2, Child under 7 Free. Garden only: £1.50. Groups (12+): Adult £5, Child £2.

▢ 🌳Plant centre. 🍴 🚻 🄿 Limited for coaches. ⬛ 🦮In grounds, on leads. ⬛ 🏨 ❄

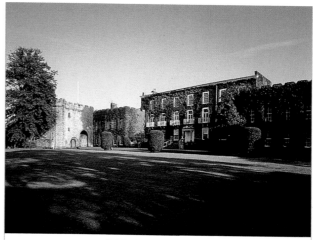

Buckfast Abbey

TORRE ABBEY

THE KINGS DRIVE, TORQUAY, DEVON TQ2 5JE

www.torre-abbey.org.uk

Tel: 01803 293593 **Fax:** 01803 215948 **e-mail:** torre-abbey@torbay.gov.uk

Owner: Torbay Council   **Contact:** L Retallick

Torre Abbey was founded as a monastery in 1196. Later adapted as a country house and in 1741-3 remodelled by the Cary family. Bought by the Council in 1930 for an art gallery. Visitors can see monastic remains, historic rooms, family chapel, mementoes of Agatha Christie, Victorian paintings including Holman Hunt & Burne-Jones & Torquay terracotta. Torre Abbey overlooks the sea and is surrounded by parkland and gardens. Teas served in Victorian Kitchen.

Location: OS Ref. SX907 638. On Torquay sea front. Between station and town centre.

Open: Apr - 1 Nov: daily, 9.30am - 6pm, last adm. 5pm. Free access to members of the National Art Collections Fund.

Admission: Adult £3, Child £1.50, Conc. £2.50, Family £7.25. Groups (pre-booked, 10+): Adult £2.25, Child £1.30.

ℹ️Conferences. ▢ ♿Unsuitable. 📷 🎞By arrangement.

⬛ Schools' programme, apply for details. 🦮 Guide dogs only.

TOTNES CASTLE ⛶

Castle Street, Totnes, Devon TQ9 5NU

Tel/Fax: 01803 864406 **e-mail:** customers@english-heritage.org.uk

www.english-heritage.org.uk

Owner: English Heritage   **Contact:** The Custodian

By the North Gate of the hill town of Totnes you will find a superb motte and bailey castle, with splendid views across the roof tops and down to the River Dart. It is a symbol of lordly feudal life and a fine example of Norman fortification.

Location: OS202 Ref. SX800 605. In Totnes, on hill overlooking the town. Access in Castle St off W end of High St.

Open: 29 Mar - 31 Oct: daily 10am - 6pm (5pm in Oct). Closed in winter.

Admission: Adult £1.80, Child 90p, Conc. £1.40. 15% discount for groups (11+).

▢ ♿Unsuitable. 📷 🦮In grounds, on leads. 🄫Tel. for details.

Knightshayes

South West - England

ATHELHAMPTON 🏛 HOUSE & GARDENS

DORCHESTER

www.athelhampton.co.uk

Owner:
Patrick Cooke Esq

▶ **CONTACT**

Owen Davies
Athelhampton House
Dorchester DT2 7LG

Tel: 01305 848363
Fax: 01305 848135

e-mail: enquiries@
athelhampton.co.uk

▶ **LOCATION**
OS Ref. SY771 942

Off A35 (T) at
Puddletown
Northbrook junction,
5m E of Dorchester.

Rail: Dorchester.

Athelhampton is one of the finest 15th century manor houses and is surrounded by one of the great architectural gardens of England. The Great Hall was built by Sir William Martyn in 1485. The West wing is Elizabethan in period and contains the Great Chamber, Library and Wine Cellar. On the East side of the house are the Green Parlour, Dining Room and three bedrooms opening off the Landing. Athelhampton houses a fine collection of English furniture starting in the Jacobean period leading on to late Victorian. There is also a collection relating to A W Pugin and The Palace of Westminster.

The glorious Grade I gardens, dating from 1891, contain the world-famous topiary pyramids, fountains and the River Piddle. Collections of tulips, magnolias, roses, clematis and lilies can be seen in season. Located in the gardens are a number of small buildings each with their own unique history. The two garden pavilions were used as water towers for the original fountain system. The Toll house was a collection point for the Wimborne turnpike trust between 1842 and 1878 and has now been restored along with its garden. The dovecote is one of the earliest in Dorset and with a capacity for 1200 birds would have supported a large household.

The Coach House contains all the facilities required for the comfort of daily visitors with private rooms available for visiting groups. The House and Gardens can be opened by appointment for evening visits and dinners. Friday late afternoons and Saturdays are available for wedding ceremonies and/or receptions.

▶ **OPENING TIMES**

March - October:
Daily (closed Saturdays).

Open Saturdays at Easter
& August BH weekends.

November - February:
Sundays only,
10.30am - 5pm/dusk. Last
admission 4pm or 3.30pm
Fridays if we have a
wedding.

Coach House Restaurant
open as house & gardens.
Carvery on Suns.
Please book.

All facilities at Athelhampton are
available for private hire outside
our normal opening hours.
We specialise in weddings on
Fridays and Saturdays and
dinners on any evening. Please
contact Owen Davies, Manager.

▶ **ADMISSION**

House & Gardens

Adult	£5.75
Child	Free
Student	£3.95
Disabled	£3.95
OAP	£5.50
Groups (12+)	
Adult	£4.40

Gardens only

Adult	£4.40
Child	Free

Left: Great Hall   *Below: Conservatory*

 By arrangement.

 Partial. WC.

 Licensed. Licensed.

 By arrangement.

 Guide dogs only.

CONFERENCE/FUNCTION

ROOM	SIZE	MAX CAPACITY
Coach House* Long Hall	11 x 9m	80
Conservatory*	16 x 11m	130
Main House* Great Hall	12 x 8m	70
Great* Chamber	10 x 6m	40
Garden Pavilions (2)	3 x 3m	6

*Licensed for Civil wedding ceremonies.

South West - England

LULWORTH CASTLE 🏛 ▦

DORSET

www.lulworth.com

A 17th century hunting lodge restored by English Heritage after the fire of 1929. Features include a gallery devoted to the Weld family, owners of the Castle and Estate since 1641. The kitchen and wine cellar have been furnished and the history of the building is brought to life through a video presentation. The Chapel of St Mary in the Castle grounds is reputed to be one of the finest pieces of architecture in Dorset. It is the first free standing Roman Catholic church to be built in England since the Reformation and contains an exhibition of 18th and 19th century vestments, church and recusant silver. A short walk from the Castle and Chapel is the Animal Farm, Play Area and Woodland Walk. The stables have been converted to house the licensed café serving morning coffee, light lunches and traditional cream teas. The Courtyard Shop offers a wide range of unusual gift items. Coach and car parking and access to the shop and café is free.

LULWORTH CASTLE HOUSE

Modern house of the Weld family containing the Blundell collection of pictures and 18th century sculptures as well as portraits and furniture from Lulworth Castle. Walled garden and grounds.

Owner:
The Weld Estate

▶ **CONTACT**
East Lulworth
Wareham
Dorset BH20 5QS

Tel: 01929 400352

Fax: 01929 400563

▶ **LOCATION**
OS194 Ref. SY853 822

In E Lulworth off B3070, 3m NE of Lulworth Cove.

▶ **OPENING TIMES**
Lulworth Castle
27 Oct - 24 Mar 2002:
10.30am - 4pm or dusk if earlier.
25 Mar - 25 Oct
10.30am - 6pm. 27 Oct - end Mar 2003: 10.30am - 4pm or dusk if earlier.
Sun - Fri, plus Easter Sat.

Closed Sats & 24 Dec - 9 Feb. Lulworth Leisure reserves the right to close the Castle without notice.

Lulworth Castle House
12 Jun - 25 Sept: Weds, 2 - 5pm. Groups: Mon - Fri by appointment only.

▶ **ADMISSION**
Lulworth Castle
Adult £5.50
Child (5-16yrs) £3.50
Conc £5.00
Family (2+3).......... £15.00
Groups (10-200)
Adult £4.95
Child (5-16yrs) £3.15
Conc £4.50

Lulworth Castle House
Adult £4.00
Child (5-16yrs) £1.50
OAP £3.50
Family (2+3).......... £10.00

Joint ticket available.

Child under 5yrs Free.

 SPECIAL EVENTS

MAR 31/APR 1
Easter Bunny Hunt.

MAY 11/12
Country Gardening & Food Fair.

JUL 27/28
Lulworth Horse Trials & Country Fair.

By kind permission of Dorset Life

Lulworth Castle House

🏛 🍷 Corporate hospitality, conferences, receptions etc.   ♿ Partial. WC.   ☕ 🍽 Licensed.   🚶 By arrangement.
🅿 📷 🐕 In grounds, on leads.   🏠 5 holiday cottages, tel: 01929 400100 (Mrs Weld).   🔔 ❄

South West - England

ABBOTSBURY SUB-TROPICAL GARDENS
ABBOTSBURY, WEYMOUTH, DORSET DT3 4JT

www.abbotsbury-tourism.co.uk

Tel: 01305 871387 **e-mail:** info@abbotsbury-tourism.co.uk

Owner: The Hon Mrs Townshend DL   **Contact:** Shop Manager

Over 20 acres of exotic and rare plants. Established in 1765. Superb colonial-style Teahouse. Extensively stocked plant centre. Quality gift shop.

Location: OS Ref. SY564 851. On B3157. Off the A35 between Weymouth & Bridport.

Open: Mar - Nov, daily 10am - 6pm. Winter, daily 10am - 4pm. Last admission 1 hr before closing.

Admission: Adult £5.50, Child £3.50, OAP £4.90.

Partial. Licensed. By arrangement. Free. In grounds, on leads.

ATHELHAMPTON HOUSE   *See page 212 for full page entry.*
& GARDENS

BROWNSEA ISLAND
Poole Harbour, Dorset BH13 7EE

Tel: 01202 707744 **Fax:** 01202 701635 **e-mail:** office@brownseaisland.fsnet.co.uk www.nationaltrust.org.uk/brownsea

Owner: National Trust   **Contact:** The Property Manager

A wonderfully atmospheric island of heath and woodland. A haven for a rich variety of wildlife, including red squirrels and many species of bird. There are many fine walks and spectacular views of Poole Harbour. Visitors may land from own boats at Pottery Pier at west end of island, accessible at all stages of the tide. Please note that the island's paths are uneven in places.

Location: OS Ref. SZ032 878. In Poole Harbour. Boats run from Poole Quay and Sandbanks.

Open: 23 Mar - 13 Oct: daily, 10am - 5pm (6pm in Jul & Aug).

Admission: Landing fee £3.50, Child £1.50, Family (2+3) £8.50 (1+3) £5. Groups £3.20, Child £1.20 by written appointment with the Property Manager.

Partial. Tel for details.

CHETTLE HOUSE
Chettle, Blandford Forum, Dorset DT11 8DB

Tel: 01258 830209 **Fax:** 01258 830380

Owner/Contact: Patrick Bourke Esq

A fine Queen Anne manor house designed by Thomas Archer and a fine example of English baroque architecture. The house features a basement with the typical north-south passage set just off centre with barrel-vaulted ceilings and a magnificent stone staircase. The house is set in 5 acres of peaceful gardens.

Location: OS Ref. ST952 132. 6m NE of Blandford NW of A354.

Open: Easter Sun - end Sept: Suns only. Groups: by appointment any time. For additional times see Tourist Information Centre pamphlet.

Admission: Adult £3, Child Free (under 16yrs).

Grounds.

CHRISTCHURCH CASTLE & NORMAN HOUSE
Christchurch, Dorset

Tel: 0117 9750700

Owner: English Heritage   **Contact:** The South West Office

Early 12th century Norman keep and Constable's house, built c1160.

Location: OS195. Ref. SZ160 927. In Christchurch, near the Priory.

Open: Any reasonable time, daylight hours.

Admission: Free.

CLOUDS HILL
Wareham, Dorset BH20 7NQ

Tel: 01929 405616 www.nationaltrust.org.uk

Owner: The National Trust   **Contact:** The Custodian

A tiny isolated brick and tile cottage, bought in 1925 by T E Lawrence (Lawrence of Arabia) as a retreat. The austere rooms inside are much as he left them and reflect his complex personality and close links with the Middle East. New guidebook.

Location: OS Ref. SY824 909. 9m E of Dorchester, 1½ m E of Waddock crossroads B3390.

Open: 31 Mar - 27 Oct: Thurs - Sun (open BH Mon & BH Tues 4 Jun), 12 noon - 5pm or dusk if earlier; no electric light. Groups wishing to visit at other times must telephone in advance.

Admission: £2.80, no reduction for children or groups.

No WC. Braille guide. No coaches.

NTPL/Joe Cornish

CORFE CASTLE
WAREHAM, DORSET BH20 5EZ

www.nationaltrust.org

Tel: 01929 481294 **e-mail:** wcfgen@smtp.ntrust.org.uk

Owner: The National Trust   **Contact:** The Property Manager

One of Britain's most majestic ruins, the Castle controlled the gateway through the Purbeck Hills and had been an important stronghold since the time of William the Conqueror. Defended during the Civil War by the redoubtable Lady Bankes, the Castle fell to treachery from within and was heavily slighted afterwards by the Parliamentarians. Many fine Norman and early English features remain. Visitor Centre at Castle View. What's new in 2002: Seasonal regular Castle tours. New family guidebook. Improved on-sight interpretation.

Location: OS Ref. SY959 824. On A351 Wareham - Swanage Rd. NW of the village.

Open: All year: daily. Mar: 10am - 5pm; Apr - Oct: 10am - 6pm; Nov - Feb 2003, 10am - 4pm. Closed 25, 26 Dec & 1 day mid-Mar (tel for details).

Admission: Adult £4.30, Child £2.15, Family (2+3) £10.80, (1+3) £6.50. Groups: Adult £3.70, Child £1.85.

Limited. Braille guide. WC. On leads. Tel for details.

CRANBORNE MANOR GARDEN
Cranborne, Wimborne, Dorset BH21 5PP

Tel: 01725 517248 **Fax:** 01725 517862 www.cranborne.co.uk

Owner: The Viscount & Viscountess Cranborne   **Contact:** The Manor Garden Centre

The beautiful and historic gardens of yew hedges, walled, herb, mount and wild gardens originate from the 17th century – originally laid out by Mounten Jennings with John Tradescant supplying many of the original plants. Spring time is particularly good with displays of spring bulbs and crab apple orchard in the wild garden.

Location: OS Ref. SU054 133. On B3078 N of Bournemouth (18m), S of Salisbury (16m).

Open: Mar - Sept: Weds, 9am - 5pm. Occasional weekends, phone for details. Entrance, parking and tearoom via the Garden Centre.

Admission: Adult £3, Child 50p, OAP £2.50.

Garden centre. Partial. By arrangement.

DEANS COURT

Wimborne, Dorset BH21 1EE

Tel: 01202 886116

Owner: Sir Michael & Lady Hanham   **Contact:** Wimborne Tourist Info Centre
13 peaceful acres a few minutes walk south of the Minster. Specimen trees, lawns, borders, herb garden, kitchen garden with long serpentine wall and rose garden. Chemical-free produce usually for sale, also interesting herbaceous plants. Wholefood teas in garden or in Housekeeper's room (down steps).

Location: OS Ref. SZ010 997. 2 mins walk S from centre of Wimborne Minster.

Open: 31 Mar; 1 Apr; 5/6 & 26/27 May; 2/3, 9 & 23 Jun; 21 Jul; 25/26 Aug; 15 Sept. Organic Gardening Weekend: 3/4 Aug. Sats & Suns: 2 - 6pm, Mons: 10am - 6pm.

Admission: Adult £2, Child (5-15yrs) 50p, OAP £1.50. Groups by arrangement. Exhibition: Adult £3.50, Child (5-16yrs)/Student £1.50, Child (under 5yrs) Free, OAP £3. Family (2+2) £6.

Garden produce sales. Guide dogs only.

EDMONDSHAM HOUSE & GARDENS

Cranborne, Wimborne, Dorset BH21 5RE

Tel: 01725 517207

Owner/Contact: Mrs Julia E Smith

Charming blend of Tudor and Georgian architecture with interesting contents. Organic walled garden, dower house garden, 6 acre garden with unusual trees and spring bulbs. 12th century church nearby.

Location: OS Ref. SU062 116. Off B3081 between Cranborne and Verwood, NW from Ringwood 9m, Wimborne 9m.

Open: House & Gardens: All BH Mons & Weds in Apr & Oct 2 - 5pm. Gardens: Apr - Oct, Suns & Weds 2 - 5pm.

Admission: House & Garden: Adult £3, Child £1 (under 5yrs Free). Garden only: Adult £1.50, Child 50p. Groups by arrangement, teas for groups.

Pre-booked (max 50). Obligatory. Car park only. (max 50).

FIDDLEFORD MANOR

Sturminster Newton, Dorset

Tel: 0117 9750700

Owner: English Heritage   **Contact:** The South West Regional Office
Part of a medieval manor house, with a remarkable interior. The splendid roof structures in the hall and upper living room are the best in Dorset. (Adjacent buildings are private dwellings and not open for visits.)

Location: OS194 ST801 136. 1m E of Sturminster Newton off A357. No coach access.

Open: 29 Mar - 30 Sept: daily, 10am - 6pm. 1 Nov - 31 Mar: daily 10am - 4pm. Closed 24 - 26 Dec & 1 Jan.

Admission: Free.

DORSET COUNTY MUSEUM

HIGH WEST STREET, DORCHESTER, DORSET DT1 1XA

www.dorsetcountymuseum.com

Tel: 01305 262735   **Fax:** 01305 257180

Owner: The Dorset Natural History & Archaeological Society

Contact: Richard De Peyer
Sixteen exhibition rooms in a distinguished high Victorian museum building. Brand new 'Dorchester History Gallery' for Easter 2002, prize winning 'Dorset Writer's Gallery' includes a reconstruction of Thomas Hardy's study, displays on William Barnes, author of Lyndon Lea and many others. Evocative Victorian Hall paved with Roman mosaics; Archaeology Gallery, Geology, Natural History and local history displays; fine temporary exhibitions gallery. Interpret Britain commendation 1997. Best Social History Museum Award 1998.

Location: OS Ref. SY688 906. In the centre of Dorchester.

Open: 1 Nov - 30 Apr: Mon - Sat, 10am - 5pm. May - Oct: daily, 10am - 5pm.

Admission: Adult £3.50, Child £1.70, Conc. £2.35, Family £18.70. Groups (15+): Adult £3 (2001 prices).

Partial. None - set down bay for coaches. Guide dogs only.

Brownsea Island

NTPL / Joe Cornish

Civil Wedding Venues ◁ ◁ ◁ pgs 28-29

FORDE ABBEY & GARDENS 🏛

Nr CHARD, SOMERSET TA20 4LU

www.fordeabbey.co.uk

Tel: 01460 221290　**e-mail:** forde.abbey@virgin.net

Owner/Contact: Mark Roper Esq

One of the top ten gardens in England. 30 acres of timeless elegance, old walls, colourful borders, wide lawns, ponds, cascades, statuary, a walled working kitchen garden and huge mature trees surround a unique former Cistercian monastery that has been a private home since 1649. The medieval abbey was founded in 1140 and survives externally almost as the monks left it in 1539. Home to the Roper family and the world famous Mortlake tapestries and a host of outstanding pictures and furniture.

Location: OS Ref. ST358 041. Just off the B3167 4m SE of Chard.

Open: House: 26 Mar - 31 Oct, Suns, Tue - Fri & BHs, 1 - 4.30pm. Gardens: All year: daily, 10am - 4.30pm.

Admission: Please contact for details.

ℹ️Conferences. No photography in house. 📷 ✴ ⊤Wedding receptions. ♿ Ground floor & gardens. WC. Wheelchair available, please telephone. 🍽 Licensed. 🅵 By arrangement. 🅿 🐕In grounds, on leads. ✳

HARDY'S COTTAGE 🌿

Higher Bockhampton, Dorchester, Dorset DT2 8QJ

Tel: 01305 262366　**www.**nationaltrust.org.uk

Owner/Contact: The National Trust

A small thatched cottage where the novelist and poet Thomas Hardy was born in 1840, and from where he would walk to school every day in Dorchester, six miles away. It was built by his great-grandfather and is little altered since. The interior has been furnished by the Trust (see also Max Gate).

Location: OS Ref. SY728 925. 3m NE of Dorchester, 1/2 m S of A35. 10 mins walk through the woods from car park.

Open: 1 Apr - 4 Nov: daily except Fri & Sat (open Good Fri), 11am - 5pm or dusk if earlier.

Admission: £2.80. No reduction for children or groups. School groups and coaches by arrangement only.

ℹ️No WC. ♿Garden. 🅿No coach parking. 🐕

HIGHCLIFFE CASTLE 🏛　　　*See next page for half page entry.*

HIGHER MELCOMBE 🏛

Melcombe Bingham, Dorchester, Dorset DT2 7PB

Tel: 01258 881310

Owner: Mr M C Woodhouse　　　　**Contact:** Claire Hundley

Consists of the surviving wing of a 16th century house with its attached domestic chapel. A fine plaster ceiling and linenfold panelling. Conducted tours by owner.

Location: OS Ref. ST749 024. 1km W of Melcombe Bingham.

Open: May - Sept by appointment.

Admission: Adult £2 (takings go to charity).

♿Unsuitable. 🅵By written appointment only. 🅿 Limited. 🐕 Guide dogs only.

THE KEEP MILITARY MUSEUM OF DEVON & DORSET

Bridport Rd, Dorchester, Dorset DT1 1RN

Tel: 01305 264066　**Fax:** 01305 250373　**e-mail:** keep.museum@talk21.com

Owner: Ministry of Defence (Museums Trustees)　　　**Contact:** The Curator

The courage, humour, tradition and sacrifice of those who served in the Regiments of Devon and Dorset for over 300 years are brought to life using touch screen computers and creative displays in this modern museum situated in a Grade II listed building. View Hardy country from the battlements.

Location: OS Ref. SY687 906. In Dorchester at the top of High West Street.

Open: All year: Apr - Sept: Mon - Sat 9.30am - 5pm (last admission 4.15pm). Jul & Aug: Suns also, 10am - 4pm. Oct - Mar: Tue - Sat, 9.30am - 5pm.

Admission: Adult £4, Conc. £3. Groups (10-50): Adult £3, Conc. £2.

ℹ️No flash photography. 📷 ⊤ ♿ 🅵By arrangement. 🅿 Limited. 🔲 🐕Guide dogs only. ✳ 🎦 Tel for details.

Plant Sales Index
◁ ◁ ◁ pgs 36-37

HIGHCLIFFE CASTLE 🏛

ROTHESAY DRIVE, HIGHCLIFFE-ON-SEA, CHRISTCHURCH BH23 4LE

www.highcliffecastle.co.uk

Tel: 01425 278807 **Fax:** 01425 280423 **e-mail:** m.allen@christchurch.gov.uk

Owner: Christchurch Borough Council **Contact:** Mike Allen, Manager

Built in 1830 in the Romantic and Picturesque style of architecture for Lord Stuart de Rothesay using his unique collection of French medieval stonework and stained glass. Recently repaired externally, it remains mostly unrepaired inside. Five rooms house a visitor centre, exhibitions, events and gift shop. Coastal grounds, village trail and nearby St Mark's church. Tea rooms in the Claretian's Wing.

Location: OS Ref. SZ200 930. Off the A337 Lymington Road, between Christchurch and Highcliffe-on-Sea.

Open: Apr - Oct: daily, 11am - 5pm. Nov - Christmas: 11am - 4pm. Grounds/Tearooms: All year. Please ring to confirm exact dates.

Admission: Adult £1.50, Child Free. Group guided tour (12+): Adult £3, Child £1. Grounds: Free.

⬚ ⊤ ⬤Partial. WC. ⬛10am - 5pm. ⓍBy arrangement. ℙLimited. Parking charge. ⬛ By arrangement. ⬛ In grounds, on leads. ▣ ❋ ⬛ Tel for details.

Rupert Truman

KINGSTON LACY 🌿

WIMBORNE MINSTER, DORSET BH21 4EA

www.nationaltrust.org.uk

Tel: 01202 883402 (Mon - Fri, 9am - 5pm) 01202 842913 (Sat & Sun 11am - 5pm)

Infoline: 01202 880413 **Fax:** 01202 882402 **e-mail:** wklgen@smtp.ntrust.org.uk

Owner: The National Trust **Contact:** The Property Manager

A 17th century house altered by Sir Charles Barry in the 19th Century. The house contains an outstanding collection of paintings and other works of art and includes the famous and dramatic Spanish room, with walls hung in magnificent gilded leather. The house and garden are set in a wooded park with a find herd of Red Devon cattle. The surrounding estate is crossed by many paths and dominated by the Iron Age hill fort of Badbury Rings. Walk leaflets available from shop.

Location: OS Ref. ST978 013. On B3082 - Blandford / Wimborne road, 1½ m NW of Wimborne.

Open: House: 23 Mar - 3 Nov: daily except Mons & Tues (open BH Mons & 4 Jun), 12 noon - 5.30pm (last admission 4.30pm). Garden & Park: 2 Feb - 17 Mar: Sat & Sun only. 11am - 4pm. 23 Mar - 3 Nov: daily, 11am - 6pm; 8 Nov - 22 Dec: Fri - Sun, 11am - 4pm. Special Snowdrop Days early 2003, telephone infoline. House may be partially scaffolded in 2002.

Admission: Adult £6.50, Child £3, Family £17. Park & garden only: Adult £3, Child £1.50. Pre-booked groups (15+): £5.

⬚ ⬤Garden only. Braille guide. WC. 🍴 ⓍBy arrangement. ℙ ⬛ ⬛In park only. ⬛Tel for details.

KINGSTON MAURWARD GARDENS

DORCHESTER, DORSET DT2 8PY

www.kmc.ac.uk

Tel: 01305 215003 **Fax:** 01305 215001 **e-mail:** mike.hancock@kmc.ac.uk

Contact: Mike Hancock

Classical Georgian mansion set in 35 acres of 18th century gardens and 5 acre lake, surrounding classical Georgian mansion. Restored Edwardian gardens with dividing hedges, stone balustrading features. Walled demonstration garden, National collections of Penstemons and Salvias. Animal park, Nature and Tree Trails. Visitors' Centre and restaurant.

Location: OS Ref. SY713 911. 1m E of Dorchester. Roundabout off A35 by-pass.

Open: 6 Jan - 23 Dec: daily, 10am - 5.30pm or dusk if earlier.

Admission: Adult £4, Child £2.50 (under 3yrs Free). Groups (10+): Adult £3.50. Guided tours (by arrangement) (12+): £4.

ⓘConferences. ⬚ ❋ ⊤Wedding receptions. 🍴 ⓍBy arrangement. ℙ ⬛ ⬛Guide dogs only. ▣ ▣ ❋

KNOLL GARDENS & NURSERY
Stapehill Road, Hampreston, Wimborne BH21 7ND
Tel: 01202 873931 **Fax:** 01202 870842 **e-mail:** enquiries@knollgardens.co.uk
Owner: J & J Flude & N R Lucas   **Contact:** Mr John Flude
Nationally acclaimed 6 acre gardens, with 6000+ named plants from the world over.
Location: OS Ref. SU059 001. Between Wimborne & Ferndown. Exit A31 Canford Bottom roundabout, B3073 Hampreston. Signposted 1½ m.
Open: Apr - Sept: daily 10am - 5pm. Oct - Mar: Sun - Thur, 10am - 5pm (or dusk if earlier) excluding Christmas & New Year holidays.
Admission: Adult £4, Child (5-15yrs) £2, OAP £3.50, Student £3. Groups: Adult £3, Child £1.75, Student £2.50. Family (2+2) £9.75.

LULWORTH CASTLE 🏛 ⌗   *See page 213 for full page entry.*

MAPPERTON 🏛
BEAMINSTER, DORSET DT8 3NR
www.mapperton.com

Tel: 01308 862645 **Fax:** 01308 863348 **e-mail:** office@mapperton.com
Owner/Contact: The Earl & Countess of Sandwich
Jacobean 1660s manor with Tudor features and classical north front. Italianate upper garden with orangery, topiary and formal borders descending to fish ponds and shrub gardens. All Saints Church forms south wing opening to courtyard and stables. Area of outstanding natural beauty with fine views of Dorset hills and woodlands. House and Gardens featured in Restoration, Emma and Tom Jones.
Location: OS Ref. SY503 997. 1m S of B3163, 2m NE of B3066, 2m SE Beaminster, 5m NE Bridport.
Open: House: 1 Jun - 10 Jul: weekdays & Spring & Summer BHs, 2 - 5pm, last admission 4.30pm. Other times by appointment. Garden & All Saints Church: 1 Mar - 31 Oct: daily, 2 - 6pm. Café: Wed, Thur & Sun & house open days, 12 noon - 6pm, other days, 3 - 6pm.
Admission: Gardens: £3.50, House: £3.50. Child (under 18yrs) £1.50, under 5 Free. Groups tours by appointment.
📷 ⊞ 🚻 Partial. 🍽 Licensed. 🎥 By arrangement. 🅿 Limited for coaches. 🐕 Guide dogs only.

MAX GATE 🦋
Alington Avenue, Dorchester, Dorset DT1 2AA
Tel: 01305 262538 **Fax:** 01305 250978 **e-mail:** max.gate@btinternet.com
www.maxgate.co.uk
Owner: The National Trust   **Contact:** The Tenant
Poet and novelist Thomas Hardy designed and lived in the house from 1885 until his death in 1928. The house is leased to tenants and contains several pieces of Hardy's furniture.
Location: OS Ref. SY704 897. 1m E of Dorchester just N of the A352 to Wareham. From Dorchester follow A352 signs to the roundabout named Max Gate (at Jct. of A35 Dorchester bypass). Turn left and left again into cul-de-sac outside Max Gate.
Open: 1 Apr - 30 Sept: Mons, Weds & Suns, 2 - 5pm. Only dining & drawing rooms open.
Admission: Adult £2.30, Child £1.20.
🚻 Limited access to ground floor for wheelchairs. Braille guide. 🅿 Limited. 🐕

MILTON ABBEY CHURCH
Milton Abbas, Blandford, Dorset DT11 0BZ
Tel: 01258 880489
Owner: Diocese of Salisbury   **Contact:** Chris Fookes
Abbey church dating from 14th century.
Location: OS117 ST798 024. 3½ m N of A354. Between Dorchester/Blandford Road.
Open: Abbey Church: daily 10am - 6pm. Groups by arrangement please.
Admission: By donation except Easter & mid-Jul - end Aug. Adult £2, Child Free.

MINTERNE GARDENS 🏛
Minterne Magna, Nr Dorchester, Dorset DT2 7AU
Tel: 01300 341370 **Fax:** 01300 341747
Owner/Contact: The Lord Digby
If you want to visit a formal garden, do not go to Minterne, but if you want to wander peacefully through 20 wild woodland acres, where magnolias, rhododendrons, eucryphias, hydrangeas, water plants and water lilies, provide a new vista at each turn and where ducks enhance the small lakes and cascades, then you will be welcome at Minterne, the home of the Churchill and Digby families for 350 years. The house which contains magnificent Churchill tapestries and naval and other historical pictures is open for Special Interest groups only which may be arranged by prior appointment.
Location: OS Ref. ST660 042. On A352 Dorchester/Sherborne Rd, 2m N of Cerne Abbas.
Open: 1 Mar - 10 Nov: daily, 10am - 7pm.
Admission: Adult £3, accompanied children Free.
🚻 Unsuitable. 🐕 In grounds on leads.

PORTLAND CASTLE ⌗
CASTLETOWN, PORTLAND, WEYMOUTH, DORSET DT5 1AZ
www.english-heritage.org.uk

Tel: 01305 820539 **Fax:** 01305 860853 **e-mail:** customers@english-heritage.org.uk
Owner: English Heritage   **Contact:** The Custodian
Discover one of Henry VIII's finest coastal fortresses. Perfectly preserved in a waterfront location overlooking Portland harbour, it is a marvellous place to visit for all the family whatever the weather. You can try on armour, explore the Tudor kitchen and gun platform, see ghostly sculptured figures from the past, enjoy the superb battlement views or picnic on the lawn in front of the Captain's House. An excellent new audio tour, included in the admission charge, brings the castle's history and characters to life. Why not visit the Captain's Tearoom?
Location: OS194 Ref. SY684 743. Overlooking Portland harbour.
Open: 29 Mar - 31 Oct: daily, 10am - 6pm (5pm in Oct). From Nov 2002 - Mar 2003: Fri - Sun, 10am - 4pm. Closed 24/26 Dec & 1 Jan.
Admission: Adult £3.50, Child £1.80, Conc. £2.70. 15% discount for groups (11+).
📷 🚻 Ground floor. WCs. 🍽 📷 🅿 🐕 🔔 ✳ ☎ Tel for details.

ST CATHERINE'S CHAPEL ⌗
Abbotsbury, Dorset
Tel: 0117 9750700
Owner: English Heritage   **Contact:** The South West Regional Office
A small stone chapel, set on a hilltop, with an unusual roof and small turret used as a lighthouse.
Location: OS194 Ref. SY572 848. ½ m S of Abbotsbury by pedestrian track to the hilltop.
Open: Any reasonable time, daylight hours.
Admission: Free.

SANDFORD ORCAS MANOR HOUSE
Sandford Orcas, Sherborne, Dorset DT9 4SB
Tel: 01963 220206
Owner/Contact: Sir Mervyn Medlycott Bt
Tudor manor house with gatehouse, fine panelling, furniture, pictures. Terraced gardens with topiary and herb garden. Personal conducted tour by owner.
Location: OS Ref. ST623 210. 2½ m N of Sherborne, Dorset 4m S of A303 at Sparkford. Entrance next to church.
Open: Easter Mon, 10am - 5pm. May & Jul - Sept: Suns & Mons, 2 - 5pm.
Admission: Adult £3, Child £1.50. Groups (10+): Adult £2.50, Child £1.
🚻 Unsuitable. 🎥 Obligatory. 🐕 In grounds, on leads.

SHERBORNE CASTLE 🏠

SHERBORNE, DORSET DT9 5NR

www.sherbornecastle.com

Tel: 01935 813182   **Fax:** 01935 816727   **e-mail:** enquiries@sherbornecastle.com

Owner: Mr & Mrs John Wingfield Digby   **Contact:** Castle & Events Manager

Built by Sir Walter Raleigh in 1594, Sherborne Castle has been the home of the Digby family since 1617. Prince William of Orange was entertained here in 1688, and George III visited in 1789. Splendid collections of art, furniture and porcelain are on view in the Castle. Lancelot 'Capability' Brown created the lake in 1753 and gave Sherborne the very latest in landscape gardening.

Location: OS Ref. ST649 164. 3/4 m SE of Sherborne town centre. Follow brown signs from A30 or A352. 1/2 m S of the Old Castle.

Open: 1 Apr - 31 Oct: Castle, Gardens, Shop & Tearoom: daily except Mon & Fri (open BH Mons) 11am - 4.30pm (last admission). Castle open Sats, 2.30 - 4.30pm (last admission). Groups (15+) by arrangement during normal opening hours. Other days if possible.

Admission: Castle & Gardens: Adult £5.75, Child (0-15yrs) Free (max. 4 accompanied by adult), OAP £5.25. Groups (15+): Adult £5, Child (0-15) Free (accompanied by adult). Private Views: Adult £8.50, Child £4.25 (min. 15 people). Gardens only: Adult £3, Child (0-15) Free (max 4 accompanied by adult). No concessions or group rates for gardens only.

🅿 🚽 ♿Partial. 🍴 🚹By arrangement. 🐕In grounds, on leads. 🔔 ♿Tel for details.

SHERBORNE OLD CASTLE ⚏

Castleton, Sherborne, Dorset DT9 3SA

Tel/Fax: 01935 812730   **e-mail:** customers@english-heritage.org.uk

www.english-heritage.org.uk

Owner: English Heritage   **Contact:** The Custodian

The ruins of this early 12th century Castle are a testament to the 16 days it took Cromwell to capture it during the Civil War, after which it was abandoned. A gatehouse, some graceful arcading and decorative windows survive.

Location: OS183 Ref ST647 167. 1/2 m E of Sherborne off B3145. 1/2 m N of the 1594 Castle.

Open: 29 Mar - 31 Oct: daily, 10am - 6pm (5pm in Oct). 1 Nov - 31 Mar: Wed - Sun, 10am - 4pm. Closed 24 - 26 Dec & 1 Jan.

Admission: Adult £1.80, Child 90p, Conc. £1.40. 15% discount for groups of 11+.

🅿 ♿Grounds. 🍴 🅿Limited for cars. No coach parking. 🐕 ❄

SMEDMORE HOUSE

Smedmore, Kimmeridge, Wareham BH20 5BG

Tel/Fax: 01929 480702

Owner: Dr Philip Mansel   **Contact:** Mr B Belsten

The home of the Mansel family for nearly 400 years nestles at the foot of the Purbeck hills looking across Kimmeridge Bay to Portland Bill.

Location: OS Ref. SY924 787. 15m SW of Poole.

Open: 2 Jun & 8 Sept: 2 - 5pm.

Admission: Adult £3.50, under 16s Free.

WHITE MILL 🌿

Sturminster Marshall, Nr Wimborne, Dorset

Tel: 01258 858051   **www.**nationaltrust.org.uk

Owner: The National Trust   **Contact:** The Custodian

Rebuilt in 1776 on a site marked as a mill in the Domesday Book, this corn mill was extensively repaired in 1994 and still retains its original elm and applewood machinery (now too fragile to be operative). Peaceful setting with nearby riverside picnic area.

Location: OS Ref. ST958 007. On River Stour 1/2 m NE of Sturminster Marshall from the B3082 Blandford to Wareham Rd, take road to SW signposted Sturminster Marshall. Mill is 1m on right. Car park nearby.

Open: 23 Mar - 27 Oct: Weekends & BH Mons including 4 Jun, 12 noon - 5pm.

Admission: Adult £2.50, Child £1.50.

ℹNo WC. ♿Ground floor. Large print guide. 🚹Obligatory. 🐕

WOLFETON HOUSE 🏠

Nr Dorchester, Dorset DT2 9QN

Tel: 01305 263500   **Fax:** 01305 265090   **e-mail:** kthimbleby@wolfeton.freeserve.co.uk

Owner: Capt N T L L Thimbleby   **Contact:** The Steward

A fine mediaeval and Elizabethan manor house lying in the water-meadows near the confluence of the rivers Cerne and Frome. It was much embellished around 1580 and has splendid plaster ceilings, fireplaces and panelling of that date. To be seen are the Great Hall, Stairs and Chamber, Parlour, Dining Room, Chapel and Cyder House. The mediaeval Gatehouse has two unmatched and older towers. There are good pictures and furniture.

Location: OS Ref. SY678 921. 1 1/2 m from Dorchester on the A37 towards Yeovil. Indicated by Historic House signs.

Open: 15 Jul - 15 Sept: Mons, Weds & Thurs. 2 - 6pm. Groups by appointment throughout the year.

Admission: Adult £4, Child £2.

🚽By arrangement. ♿Ground floor. 🍴By arrangement. 🚹By arrangement. 🅿 🐕 ❄

Owner:
Mr R J G Berkeley

▶ CONTACT

The Custodian
Berkeley Castle
Gloucestershire
GL13 9BQ

Tel: 01453 810332

▶ LOCATION

OS Ref. ST685 990

SE side of Berkeley
village. Midway
between
Bristol & Gloucester,
2m W off the A38.

From motorway
M5/J14 (5m) or
J13 (9m).

BERKELEY CASTLE 🏛

BERKELEY

Not many can boast of having their private house celebrated by Shakespeare nor of having held it in the possession of their family for nearly 850 years, nor having a King of England murdered within its walls, nor of having welcomed at their table the local vicar and Castle Chaplain, John Trevisa (1342-1402), reputed as one of the earliest translators of the Bible, nor of having a breach battered by Oliver Cromwell, which to this day it is forbidden by law to repair even if it was wished to do so. But such is the story of Berkeley.

This beautiful and historic Castle, begun in 1117, still remains the home of the famous family who gave their name to numerous locations all over the world, notably Berkeley Square in London, Berkeley Hundred in Virginia and Berkeley University in California. Scene of the brutal murder of Edward II in 1327 (visitors can see his cell and

nearby the dungeon) and besieged by Cromwell's troops in 1645, the Castle is steeped in history but twenty-four generations of Berkeleys have gradually transformed a Norman fortress into the lovely home it is today.

The State Apartments contain magnificent collections of furniture, rare paintings by primarily English and Dutch masters, and tapestries. Part of the world-famous Berkeley silver is on display in the Dining Room. Many other rooms are equally interesting including the Great Hall upon which site the Barons of the West Country met in 1215 before going to Runnymede to force King John to put his seal to the Magna Carta.

The Castle is surrounded by lovely terraced Elizabethan Gardens with a lily pond, Elizabeth I's bowling green, and sweeping lawns.

▶ OPENING TIMES

April & May
Tue - Sun, 2 - 5pm.

June & September
Tue - Sat, 11am - 5pm.
Suns, 2 - 5pm.

July & August
Mon - Sat, 11am - 5pm
Suns, 2 - 5pm

October
Suns only, 2 - 5pm

BH Mons, 11am - 5pm

NB. Groups must book.

▶ ADMISSION

Castle & Garden

Adult	£5.70
Child	£3.10
OAP	£4.70
Family (2+2)	£15.50

Groups (25+ pre-booked)

Adult	£5.20
Child	£2.80
OAP	£4.30

Gardens only

Adult	£2.00
Child	£1.00

Butterfly Farm

Adult	£2.00
Child/OAP	£1.00
Family (2+2)	£5.00
School Groups	£0.80

CONFERENCE/FUNCTION

ROOM	MAX CAPACITY
Great Hall	150
Long Drawing Rm	100

📷🧸ℹ️ Fashion shows and filming. Butterfly farm. No photography inside the Castle.

🍽 Wedding receptions and corporate entertainment.

♿ Visitors may alight in the Outer Bailey.

☕ Licensed. Serving lunches and home-made teas.

🚶 Free. Max. 120 people. Tour time: One hour. Evening groups by arrangement. Group visits must be booked.

🅿 Cars 150yds from Castle and 15 coaches 250yds away.

🎓 Welcome. General and social history and architecture.

🚫

CHAVENAGE 🏛

TETBURY

www.chavenage.com

Chavenage is a wonderful Elizabethan house of mellow grey Cotswold stone and tiles which contains much of interest for the discerning visitor.

The approach aspect of Chavenage is virtually as it was left by Edward Stephens in 1576. Only two families have owned Chavenage; the present owners since 1891 and the Stephens family before them. A Colonel Nathaniel Stephens, MP for Gloucestershire during the Civil War was cursed for supporting Cromwell, giving rise to legends of weird happenings at Chavenage since that time.

Inside Chavenage there are many interesting rooms housing tapestries, fine furniture, pictures and many relics of the Cromwellian period. Of particular note are the Main Hall, where a contemporary screen forms a minstrels' gallery and two tapestry rooms where it is said Cromwell was lodged.

Recently Chavenage has been used as a location for TV and film productions including a Hercule Poirot story *The Mysterious Affair at Styles*, many episodes of the sequel to *Are you Being Served* now called *Grace & Favour, a Gotcha for The Noel Edmonds' House Party*, episodes of *The House of Elliot* and *Casualty* and in 1997/98 *Berkeley Square* and *Cider with Rosie*.

Chavenage is especially suitable for those wishing an intimate, personal tour, usually conducted by the owner, or for groups wanting a change from large establishments. Meals for pre-arranged groups have proved hugely popular. It also provides a charming venue for small conferences and functions.

Owner:
Mr David Lowsley-Williams

▶ CONTACT

D Lowsley-Williams
Chavenage
Tetbury
Gloucestershire
GL8 8XP

Tel: 01666 502329
Fax: 01453 836778
e-mail: info@chavenage.com

▶ LOCATION
OS Ref. ST872 952

Less than 20m from M4/J16/17 or 18. 1¾ m NW of Tetbury between the B4104 & A4135. Signed from Tetbury. Less than 15m from M5/J13 or 14. Signed from A46 (Stroud -Bath road)

Rail: Kemble Station 7m.

Taxi: Martin Cars 01666 503611.

Air: Bristol 35m. Birmingham 70m. Grass airstrip on farm.

CONFERENCE/FUNCTION

ROOM	SIZE	MAX CAPACITY
Ballroom	70' x 30'	120
Oak Room	25 'x 20'	30

▶ OPENING TIMES

Summer

May - September
Easter Sun, Mon & BHs, 2 - 5pm.

Thurs & Suns
2 - 5pm.

NB. Will open at other times by prior arrangement for groups.

Winter

October - March
By appointment only for groups.

▶ ADMISSION

Tours are inclusive in the following prices.

Summer

Adult £5.00
Child (5 - 16 yrs) £2.50

CONCESSIONS

By prior arrangement, concessions may be given to groups of 40+ and also to disabled and to exceptional cases.

Winter

Groups only:
Rates by arrangement.

ℹ️ Clay pigeon shooting, archery, cross-bows, pistol shooting, ATV driving, small fashion shows, concerts, plays, seminars, filming, product launching, photography. No casual photography in house.

🍽 Corporate entertaining. In-house catering for drinks parties, dinners, wedding receptions. Telephone for details.

♿ Partial. WC.

🍴 Lunches, teas, dinners and picnics by arrangement.

👤 By owner. Large groups given a talk prior to viewing. Couriers and group leaders should arrange tour format prior to visit.

🅿 Up to 100 cars and 2 - 3 coaches. Coaches only by appointment; stop at gates for parking instructions.

🎓 Chairs can be arranged for lecturing. Tour of working farm, modern dairy and corn facilities can be arranged.

🐕 In grounds on leads. Guide dogs only in house. ❄️

South West - England

Derek Harris

SUDELEY CASTLE 🏛

WINCHCOMBE

www.stratford.co.uk/sudeley

Owner:
Lady Ashcombe

CONTACT

The Secretary
Sudeley Castle
Winchcombe
Nr Cheltenham
Gloucestershire
GL54 5JD

Tel: 01242 602308
Fax: 01242 602959

e-mail: marketing@
sudeley.org.uk

LOCATION

OS Ref. SP032 277

8m NE of Cheltenham,
at Winchcombe
off B4632.

From Bristol or
Birmingham M5/J9.
Take A46 then B4077
towards Stow-on-the-Wold.

Bus: Castleways to
Winchcombe.

Rail: Cheltenham
Station 8m.

Air: Birmingham or
Bristol 45m.

Sudeley Castle, home of Lord and Lady Ashcombe, is one of England's great historic houses with royal connections stretching back 1000 years. Once the property of King Ethelred the Unready, Sudeley was later the magnificent palace of Queen Katherine Parr, Henry VIII's sixth wife, who is buried in St Mary's church, in the grounds. Henry VIII, Anne Boleyn, Lady Jane Grey and Elizabeth I all visited Sudeley. King Charles I stayed here and his nephew, Prince Rupert established it as his headquarters during the Civil War.

During the 19th century a programme of reconstruction, under the aegis of Sir Giles Gilbert Scott, restored Sudeley for its new owners, the Dent brothers. The interiors were largely furnished with pieces bought by the Dents at the famous Strawberry Hill sale, when the contents of Horace Walpole's house were sold.

Surrounding the Castle are the enchanting and award-winning gardens that have gained international recognition. Famous for its topiary and fine collection of old-fashioned roses, the Queen's Garden is sited on the original Tudor parterre. The visitor must also see the Knot Garden, the Heritage Seed Library Garden and the recently replanted Secret Garden.

The Castle contains some interesting pieces of Civil War memorabilia, as well as pictures by Turner, Van Dyck and Rubens. The Emma Dent exhibition illustrates, at a personal level, the values and interests of the Victorian age. A licensed restaurant, gift shop and plant centre, specialising in old-fashioned roses, complete a perfect day.

CONFERENCE/FUNCTION

ROOM	MAX CAPACITY
Chandos Hall	80
North Hall	40
Library	80
Banquet Hall & Pavilion	150

Photography and filming, concerts, corporate events and conferences. Product launches, garden parties, craft fairs and activity days. Sudeley reserves the right to close part or all of the castle, gardens and grounds and to amend information as necessary.

Private dining, banquets, and medieval dinners.

Unsuitable.

Licensed restaurant and tearooms. Groups should book.

Special interest tours can be arranged.

1,000 cars. Meal vouchers, free access for coach drivers.

14 holiday cottages for 2 - 5 occupants.

 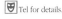 Tel for details.

▶ OPENING TIMES

Summer

**Gardens, Exhibition
Centre, Shop &
Plant Centre**
2 March - 27 October
Daily: 10.30am - 5.30pm.

**Castle Apartments
& Church**
23 March - 27 October
Daily: 11am - 5pm.

Restaurant
23 March - 27 October
Daily: 10.30am - 5pm.

Winter
Groups by appointment.

▶ ADMISSION

Castle & Gardens
Adult £6.50
Child (5-15 yrs.) £3.50
Conc £5.50
Family (2+2).......... £18.00
Groups (20+)
Adult £5.50
Child (5-15 yrs.) £3.50
Conc £4.50

Gardens & Exhibitions
Adult £5.00
Child (5-15 yrs.) £2.75
OAP £4.00

Audio tour £2.00

Adventure Playground
Child (5-15 yrs.)........... £1.50

ASHLEWORTH TITHE BARN ⚘
Ashleworth, Gloucestershire

Tel: 01684 855300 www.nationaltrust.org.uk

Owner: The National Trust   **Contact:** NT Regional Office

A C15th tithe barn with two projecting porch bays and fine roof timbers with queenposts.

Location: OS Ref. SO818 252. 6m NW of Gloucester, 1¼ m E of Hartpury A417.

Open: 1 Apr - 31 Oct: daily, 9am - 6pm or sunset if earlier. Closed Good Fri (may be closed during part of 2002 for major repairs, please contact for details).

Admission: £1.

BARNSLEY HOUSE GARDEN 🏛
Barnsley House, Cirencester GL7 5EE

Tel: 01285 740561 **Fax:** 01285 740628 www.barnsleyhouse.com

Owner: Mr & Mrs Charles Verey   **Contact:** Charles Verey

Mature 4½ acre garden designed by the late Rosemary Verey. Bulbs, mixed borders, autumn colours, knot of herb garden, laburnum walk (late May, early June). Decorative vegetable garden, garden furniture by Charles Verey. Fountain and statues by Simon Verity. Two 18th century summer houses. Winner of the HHA/Christie's Garden of the Year award, 1988.

Location: OS Ref. SP076 049. In Barnsley village, 4m NE of Cirencester on B4425.

Open: 1 Feb - mid Dec: Mons, Wed - Sat, 10am - 5.30pm. Closed Good Fri.

Admission: Adult £4, Child under 16 Free, OAP £3.50. No charge for group tour leader.

🖼 🚻 ♿Partial. 🖥 🚹By arrangement. 🅿Limited for coaches. 🐾 ❄

BATSFORD ARBORETUM
Batsford Park, Moreton-in-Marsh, Gloucestershire GL56 9QB

www.batsford-arboretum.co.uk

Tel: 01386 701441 **Fax:** 01386 701829 **e-mail:** batsarb@batsfound.freeserve.co.uk

Owner: The Batsford Foundation   **Contact:** Mr Chris Pilling

Batsford Arboretum's unique setting offers magnificent vantage points to view rare and beautiful trees. Fine collections of maple, magnolia, Japanese cherries, bamboo and many other well established shrubs and spring bulbs. Explore the grounds to find oriental statues, a Japanese rest house and hermit's cave – the Cotswold's secret garden.

Location: OS Ref. SP185 335. Off A44 Moreton-in-Marsh, Evesham road. ¼m from Moreton.

Open: Mid Feb - mid Nov: daily, 10am - 5pm; mid Nov - mid Feb: weekends only, 10am - 4pm. Boxing Day: 11am - 3pm.

Admission: Adult £4, Child £1, Conc £3. Groups (15+): less 10%.

🖼 🚻 ♿Partial.WC. 🖥Licensed. 🚹By arrangement. 🅿 🖥
🐾In grounds, on leads. ❄ 🖥Tel for details.

BERKELEY CASTLE 🏛   *See page 220 for full page entry.*

BLACKFRIARS PRIORY ⌗
Ladybellegate Street, Gloucester

Tel: 0117 9750700

Owner: English Heritage   **Contact:** The South West Regional Office

A small Dominican priory church converted into a rich merchant's house at the Dissolution. Most of the original 13th century church remains, including a rare scissor-braced roof.

Location: OS Ref. SO830 186. In Ladybellegate St, Gloucester, off Southgate Street and Blackfriars Walk.

Open: Restricted, access by guided tour only (Jul & Aug: weekends). Please contact the South West Regional Office.

Admission: Free.

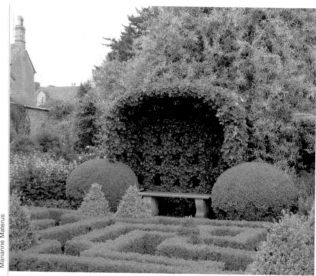

Marianne Majerus

BOURTON HOUSE GARDEN 🏛
BOURTON-ON-THE-HILL GL56 9AE

Tel: 01386 700754 **Fax:** 01386 701081 **e-mail:** cd@bourtonhouse.com

Owner/Contact: Mr & Mrs Richard Paice

Exciting 3 acre garden surrounding a delightful 18th century Cotswold manor house and 16th century tithe barn. Featuring flamboyant borders, imaginative topiary, a unique shade house, a profusion of herbaceous and exotic plants and, not least, a myriad of magically planted pots.The mood is friendly and welcoming, the atmosphere tranquil yet inspiring. The garden... "positively fizzes with ideas". New: 'The Gallery' – contemporary art and craft design in the tithe barn.

Location: OS Ref. SP180 324. 1¼ m W of Moreton-in-Marsh on A44.

Open: 22 May - 31 Aug: Wed - Fri; Oct: Thur & Fri only. Also open 2 - 4 Jun (Jubilee BH), August BH, Sun & Mon, 10am - 5pm.

Admission: Adult £3.50, Child Free.

🖼 🚻 ♿Partial. 🖥 🚹By arrangement. 🅿Limited for coaches. 🐾

CHAVENAGE 🏛   *See page 221 for full page entry.*

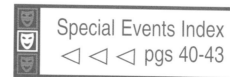

Special Events Index
◁ ◁ ◁ pgs 40-43

CHEDWORTH ROMAN VILLA ✻

YANWORTH, CHELTENHAM, GLOS GL54 3JL

www.nationaltrust.org.uk

Tel: 01242 890256 **Fax:** 01242 890544 **e-mail:** chedworth@smtp.ntrust.org.uk

Owner: The National Trust   **Contact:** The Property Manager

The remains of a Romano-British villa, excavated 1864. Set in beautiful wooded combe. Includes fine 4th century mosaics, two bath houses, spring with temple. A museum houses the smaller finds.

Location: OS163 Ref. SP053 135. 3m NW of Fossebridge on Cirencester - Northleach road A429. Coaches must avoid Withington.

Open: 26 Feb - 31 Mar: 11am - 4pm. 2 Apr - 27 Oct: 10am - 5pm; 29 Oct - 17 Nov: 11am - 4pm; daily except Mons (open BH Mons)

Admission: Adult £3.80, Child £1.90, Family £9.50. (Increased charge on special event days, including NT members).

🎧 ♿Partial. WC. 🎫By arrangement. 🎧 ▣Limited. ■By arrangement. ✖ ♨Tel for details.

FRAMPTON COURT

Frampton-on-Severn, Gloucestershire GL2 7EU

Tel: 01452 740267 **Fax:** 01452 740698

Owner/Contact: Mrs Peter Clifford

Listed Grade I, by Vanburgh. 1732. Stately family home of the Cliffords who have lived at Frampton since granted land by William the Conqueror, 1066. Fine collection of original period furniture, tapestries, needlework and porcelain. Panelled throughout. The famous botanical paintings of The Frampton Flora are all on show. Fine views over parkland to extensive lake. A famous gothic orangery stands in the garden reflected in a Dutch ornamental canal. The Orangery is available for self-catering holidays.

Location: OS Ref. SO750 078. In Frampton, ¼ m SW of B4071, 3m NW of M5/J13.

Open: By arrangement.

Admission: House & Garden: £4.50.

ℹ️No photography in house. ♿Unsuitable. ▣ 🎫Obligatory. ▣Limited for coaches. ♨In grounds, on leads. ♨Ensuite. Bed & Breakfast £45. Tel for details. ✱

FRAMPTON MANOR

Frampton-on-Severn, Gloucestershire GL2 7EU

Fax: 01452 740698

Owner: Mr & Mrs P R H Clifford   **Contact:** Mrs P R H Clifford

Medieval/Elizabethan timber-framed manor house with walled garden. Reputed 12th century birthplace of 'Fair Rosamund' Clifford, mistress of King Henry II. Wool barn c1500 and c1800 granary with dovecote.

Location: OS Ref. SO748 080. 3m M5/J13.

Open: House & Garden: open throughout the year by written appointment. Garden: 1 May - 17 Jul: Mons, 2 - 5pm.

Admission: House & Garden: £3.50. Garden only: £2.

✱

DYRHAM PARK ✻

Nr CHIPPENHAM, WILTSHIRE SN14 8ER

www.nationaltrust.org.uk

Tel/Fax: 0117 9372501 **e-mail:** wdymxa@smtp.ntrust.org.uk

Owner: The National Trust   **Contact:** The Property Manager

Crowned with a balustrade and with fine views over its ancient deer park, Dyrham was built between 1691 and 1702 for William Blathwayt, William III's Secretary at War and Secretary of State. The rooms have changed little since they were furnished by Blathwayt and their contents are recorded in his housekeeper's inventory. There are many fine textiles and paintings, as well as items of blue-and-white Delftware, reflecting the contemporary taste for Dutch fashions. Restored Victorian domestic rooms open (and for extended period, see below), including kitchen, bells passage, bakehouse, larders, tenants' hall and Delft-tiled dairy. Car park has been relocated to the East Lodge and a free bus now takes visitors to and from the house, thereby restored to its original, car-free, setting.

Location: OS Ref. ST743 757. 8m N of Bath, 12m E of Bristol. Approached from Bath - Stroud road (A46), 2m S of Tormarton interchange with M4/J18.

Open: House: 23 Mar - 3 Nov: Fri - Tue, 12 noon - 5.30pm, last admission 4.45pm. Garden: as house, 11am - 5.30pm (dusk if earlier). Park: daily (closed 25 Dec), 11am - 5.30pm (dusk if earlier). Winter opening for domestic rooms: 9 Nov - 15 Dec: Sats & Suns, 12 noon - 4pm. Note: Property closed 5 - 8 Jul for concerts. Coaches by arrangement.

Admission: Adult £7.90, Child £3.90, Family £19.50. Grounds only: Adult £3, Child £1.50, Family £7. Park only (on days when house & garden closed): Adult £2, Child £1. Winter: Park & Domestic Rooms: Adult £4, Child £2. Group rate weekdays only: contact the Property Manager.

🎧Colour guidebook & CD-ROM for sale. ♿ 🍴Licensed. 🎧 House. ▣ ■ ✖ ✱ ♨Tel for details.

GLOUCESTER CATHEDRAL

Chapter Office, College Green, Gloucester GL1 2LR

Tel: 01452 528095 **Fax:** 01452 300469

e-mail: lin@gloucester2001.demon.co.uk **www**.gloucestercathedral.uk.com

Contact: Mrs L Henderson

Daily worship and rich musical tradition continue in this abbey church founded 1300 years ago. It has a Norman nave with massive cylindrical pillars, a magnificent east window with medieval glass and glorious fan-vaulted cloisters. You can also find the tombs of King Edward II and Robert of Normandy.

Location: OS Ref. SO832 188. Off Westgate Street in central Gloucester.

Open: Daily, 8am until after Evensong. Groups must book via the Chapter Office.

Admission: £2.50 donation requested.

◻ ⊤ ⬦Partial. WC. ⊞ Licensed. 𝕀 By arrangement. ■ **P** None. ⬦In grounds, on leads.

HAILES ABBEY ⌗ ⋈

Nr Winchcombe, Cheltenham, Gloucestershire GL54 5PB

Tel: 01242 602398 **e-mail:** customers@english-heritage.org.uk
www.english-heritage.org.uk

Owner: English Heritage & The National Trust   **Contact:** The Custodian

Seventeen cloister arches and extensive excavated remains in lovely surroundings of an abbey founded by Richard, Earl of Cornwall, in 1246. There is a small museum and covered display area.

Location: OS150, Ref. SP050 300. 2m NE of Winchcombe off B4632. ½ m SE of B4632.

Open: 29 Mar - 31 Oct: daily, 10am - 6pm (5pm in Oct). Closed in winter.

Admission: Adult £2.80, Child £1.40, Conc. £2.10.

◻ ⬦Partial. WC. ■ ◻ ⬦In grounds, on leads. ⬦Tel for details.

HARDWICKE COURT ⬛

Gloucester GL2 4RS

Tel: 01452 720212 **Fax:** 01452 724465

Owner/Contact: C G M Lloyd Baker Esq

Early 19th century small country house designed by Robert Smirke.

Location: OS150, Ref. SO787 118. 6m S of Gloucester on A38.

Open: Easter - end Sept: Mons, 2 - 4pm.

Admission: Please contact property for details.

Woodley & Quick

HOLST BIRTHPLACE MUSEUM

4 CLARENCE ROAD, PITTVILLE, CHELTENHAM GL52 2AY

www.holstmuseum.org.uk

Tel: 01242 524846 **e-mail:** holstmuseum@btconnect.com

Owner: Holst Birthplace Trust   **Contact:** Dr Joanna Archibald

Birthplace of Gustav Holst (1874 - 1934), composer of The Planets, containing his piano and personal memorabilia. Holst's music is played. The museum is also a fine period house showing the 'upstairs – downstairs' way of life in Regency and Victorian times, including a working kitchen, elegant drawing room and charming nursery.

Location: OS163 Ref. SO955 237. 5mins walk from town centre, opposite Pittville Gates.

Open: All year: Tue - Sat, 10am - 4pm. Closed BHs. Closed Dec 2002 & Jan 2003 (except for booked groups). Guided tours for groups welcome by appointment.

Admission: Adult £2.50, Child/Conc. £2. Groups pay same prices unless having a guided tour (6-15): Adult £3.50, Conc. £2.50. Special rate for school groups: 75p.

ⓘPhotography by prior permission only. ◻ ⊤ ⬦Partial. 𝕀By arrangement. ■ **P** None. ⬦Guide dogs only. ✱ ▣ Tel for details.

NTPL / Nick Meers

HIDCOTE MANOR GARDEN ⋈

CHIPPING CAMPDEN, GLOUCESTERSHIRE GL55 6LR

www.nationaltrust.org.uk/hidcote

Tel: 01386 438333 **Fax:** 01386 438817 **e-mail:** hidcote_manor@smtp.ntrust.org.uk

Owner: The National Trust   **Contact:** The Property Manager

One of the most delightful gardens in England, created this century by the great horticulturist Major Lawrence Johnston; a series of small gardens within the whole, separated by walls and hedges of different species; famous for rare shrubs, trees, herbaceous borders, 'old' roses and interesting plant species.

Location: OS151 Ref. SP176 429. 4m NE of Chipping Campden, 1m E of B4632 off B4081. At Mickleton ¼ m E of Kiftsgate Court.

Open: 23 Mar - end May & Aug - 3 Nov: daily except Thur & Fri (open Good Fri). Jun & Jul: daily except Fris. Times: Mar - end Sept: 10.30am - 6.30pm; Oct - 3 Nov: 10.30am - 5.30pm. Last admission 1 hour before closing or dusk if earlier.

Admission: Adult £5.80, Child £2.90, Family £14.50.

◻ ⬦ ⬦Grounds, but limited. WC. ⊞ Licensed. ▣ ⬦Send SAE for details.

HORTON COURT ⋈

Horton, Nr Chipping Sodbury B17 6QR

Tel: 01249 730141 **www**.nationaltrust.org.uk

Owner: The National Trust   **Contact:** Lacock Estate Office

A Norman Hall and an exceptionally fine detached ambulatory are all that remain of what is probably the oldest rectory in England. House not open to the public.

Location: OS Ref. NT766 849. 3m NE of Chipping Sodbury, ¾ m N of Horton, 1m W of A46.

Open: 3 Apr - 2 Nov: Wed & Sat, 2 - 6pm or dusk if earlier.

Admission: Adult £2, Child £1.

ⓘNo WC.

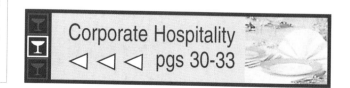

KELMSCOTT MANOR 🏛

KELMSCOTT, Nr LECHLADE, GLOUCESTERSHIRE GL7 3HJ

www.kelmscottmanor.co.uk

Tel: 01367 252486   **Fax:** 01367 253754   **e-mail:** admin@kelmscottmanor.co.uk

Owner: Society of Antiquaries   **Contact:** Helen Webb

Kelmscott Manor, a grade I listed Tudor farmhouse adjacent to the River Thames, was the summer house of William Morris from 1871 until his death in 1896. Morris loved the house as a work of true craftsmanship, totally unspoilt and unaltered, and in harmony with the village and the surrounding countryside. He considered it so natural in its setting as to be almost organic, it looked to him as if it had 'grown up out of the soil', and with 'quaint garrets amongst great timbers of the roof where of old times the tillers and herdsmen slept'. The house contains an outstanding collection of the possessions and work of Morris and his associates, including furniture, original textiles, carpets and ceramics. The Manor is surrounded by beautiful gardens with barns, dovecote, a meadow and a stream. The garden was a constant source of inspiration for Morris and the images are reflected in his textile and wallpaper designs. William Morris called the village of Kelmscott: 'a heaven on earth'. His delight in its discovery can still be felt by the visitor today. The Manor is the most evocative of all the houses associated with William Morris.

Location: OS Ref. SU252 988. At SE end of the village, 2m due E of Lechlade, off the Lechlade - Faringdon Road.

Open: Apr - Sept: Weds, 11am - 5pm. 3rd Sat in Apr, May, Jun & Sept, also 1st & 3rd Sat in July & Aug, 2 - 5pm. Private visits for groups on Thurs & Fris. Please note house only closed on Weds, 1 - 2pm.

Admission: Adult £7, Child/Student £3.50.

◻ ⊤ ♿Grounds. WCs. ◕Licensed. 🎦By arrangement. 🅿Limited for coaches. ✖

KIFTSGATE COURT GARDENS

CHIPPING CAMPDEN, GLOUCESTERSHIRE GL55 6LN

www.kiftsgate.co.uk

Tel/Fax: 01386 438777   **e-mail:** kiftsgte@aol.com

Owner: Mr and Mrs J G Chambers   **Contact:** Mr J G Chambers

Magnificently situated garden on the edge of the Cotswold escarpment with views towards the Malvern Hills. Many unusual shrubs and plants including tree peonies, abutilons, specie and old-fashioned roses.

Location: OS Ref. SP173 430. 4m NE of Chipping Campden. ¼ m W of Hidcote Garden.

Open: Apr, May, Aug, Sept: Weds, Thurs & Suns, 2 - 6pm. Jun & Jul: Weds, Thurs, Sats & Suns, 12 noon - 6pm. BH Mons, 2 - 6pm. Coaches by appointment.

Admission: Adult: £4.30, Child £1.

🌳 ♿

LITTLEDEAN HALL

Littledean, Gloucestershire GL14 3NR

Tel: 01594 824213

Owner/Contact: Mrs S Christopher

'Reputedly England's oldest inhabited house', Guinness Book of Records. Site of Roman temple.

Location: OS Ref. SO673 131. 2m E of Cinderford, 500 yds S of A4151.

Open: 1 Apr - 31 Oct: daily, 11am - 5pm.

Admission: Adult £3.50, Child £1.50, OAP £2.50. Groups £2.25 (by appointment).

Newark Park

NTPL / Nadia MacKenzie

LODGE PARK

ALDSWORTH, Nr CHELTENHAM, GLOUCESTERSHIRE GL54 3PP

www.nationaltrust.org.uk/lodgepark

Tel: 01451 844130 **Fax:** 01451 844131 **e-mail:** lodgepark@smtp.ntrust.org.uk

Owner: The National Trust **Contact:** The Visitor Services Manager

Situated on the picturesque Sherborne Estate in the Cotswolds, Lodge Park was created in 1634 by John 'Crump' Dutton. Inspired by his passion for gambling and banqueting, it is a unique survival of a Grandstand, Deer Course and Park.

Location: OS163 Ref. SP146 123. 3m E of Northleach, approach only from A40.

Open: 1 Mar - 4 Nov: Fri - Mon, 11am - 4pm. Slide talks at regular intervals.

Admission: Adult £4, Child £2, Family £10.

LYDNEY PARK GARDENS & ROMAN TEMPLE SITE

Lydney, Gloucestershire GL15 6BU

Tel: 01594 845497 **Fax:** 01594 842027 **e-mail:** lydneypark@agriplus.net

Owner: The Viscount Bledisloe **Contact:** Mrs Sylvia Jones

Eight acres of extensive valley gardens with trees and lakes. Roman temple site and museum.

Location: OS Ref. SO620 022. On A48 between Lydney and Aylburton.

Open: 24 Mar - 9 Jun: Suns, Weds & BH Mons. 6 - 10 May & 3 - 7 Jun: daily.

Admission: Adult £3 (Wed £2), Child 50p. Groups of (25+) by arrangement.

Andrea Jones / Location Photography

MISARDEN PARK GARDENS

Stroud, Gloucestershire GL6 7JA

Tel: 01285 821303 **Fax:** 01285 821530

Owner/Contact: Major M T N H Wills

Noted in the spring for its bulbs and flowering trees and in mid-summer for the large double herbaceous borders. Fine topiary throughout and a new parterre of hebes, aliums and lavender within the rose garden. Outstanding position, standing high overlooking the 'Golden Valley'.

Location: OS Ref. SO940 089. 6m NW Cirencester. Follow signs westward from A417 from Gloucester or Cirencester or B4070 from Stroud.

Open: 2 Apr - 26 Sept: Tue - Thur, 10am - 5pm.

Admission: Adult £3.50 (guided tours extra), Child Free. 10% reduction for pre-arranged groups (20+).

Nurseries: daily except Mons. Grounds. Guide dogs only.

David Brown/National Trust

NEWARK PARK

OZLEWORTH, WOTTON-UNDER-EDGE, GLOUCESTERSHIRE GL12 7PZ

www.nationaltrust.org.uk

Tel: 01453 842644 **e-mail:** michael@newark98.freeserve.co.uk

Owner: The National Trust **Contact:** Michael Claydon

A Tudor hunting lodge converted into a castellated country house by James Wyatt. An atmospheric house, set in spectacular countryside.

Location: OS Ref. GR078 932. 1½m E of Wotton-under-Edge, 1¾ m S of Junction of A4135 & B4058.

Open: Apr - May: Wed & Thur; Jun - Sept: Wed, Thur, Sat, Sun & BH Mons (except Easter): 11am - 5pm, last entry 4.30pm. Controlled access, maximum of 50 in house at any one time.

Admission: Adult £3, Child £1.50. No reduction for groups.

No photography in house. Unsuitable. By arrangement. Limited. In grounds, on leads.

Civil Wedding Venues ◁ ◁ ◁ pgs 28-29

OWLPEN MANOR 🏠

Nr ULEY, GLOUCESTERSHIRE GL11 5BZ

www.owlpen.com

Tel: 01453 860261   **Fax:** 01453 860819   **Restaurant:** 01453 860816

e-mail: sales@owlpen.com

Owner: Mr & Mrs Nicholas Mander   **Contact:** Julia Webb

Romantic Tudor manor house, 1450-1616, with Cotswold Arts & Crafts associations. Remote wooded valley setting, with 16th and 17th century formal terraced gardens and magnificent yews. Contains unique painted cloth wall hangings, family and Arts & Crafts collections. Mill (1726), Court House (1620); licensed restaurant in medieval Cyder House. Victorian church. "Owlpen - ah, what a dream is there!" - Vita Sackville-West.

Location: OS Ref. ST801 984. 3m E of Dursley, 1m E of Uley, off B4066, by Old Crown pub.

Open: Apr - Sept: Tue - Sun & BH Mons, 2 - 5pm. Restaurant 12 noon - 5pm.

Admission: Adult £4.50, Child (5-14yrs) £2, Family (2+4) £12.50. Gardens and Grounds: Adult £2.50, Child £1. Group rates available.

🔲 ⬛ 🔲 Unsuitable. 🍴 Licensed. 🅿 ⬛ Holiday cottages, sleep 2 - 9.

RODMARTON MANOR

CIRENCESTER, GLOUCESTERSHIRE GL7 6PF

www.rodmarton-manor.co.uk

Tel: 01285 841253   **Fax:** 01285 841298   **e-mail:** simon.biddulph@farming.co.uk

Owner: Mr & Mrs Simon Biddulph   **Contact:** Simon Biddulph

One of the last great country houses to be built in the traditional way and containing beautiful furniture, ironwork, china and needlework specially made for the house. The large garden complements the house and contains many areas of great beauty and character including the magnificent herbaceous borders, topiary, roses, rockery and kitchen garden.

Location: OS Ref. ST943 977. Off A433 between Cirencester and Tetbury.

Open: House & Garden: 6 May - 31 Aug: Weds, Sats & BH Mons, 2 - 5pm. Groups please book. Guided house tours (20+) can be booked at other times by appointment. Guided tours of garden can also be booked.

Admission: House & Garden: £6, Child (under 14yrs) £3. Min. group charge £120. Garden only: £3, accompanied children Free.

🎦 By arrangement.

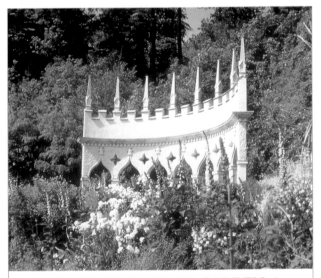

PAINSWICK ROCOCO GARDEN 🏠

PAINSWICK, GLOUCESTERSHIRE GL6 6TH

www.rococogarden.co.uk

Tel: 01452 813204   **Fax:** 01452 814888   **e-mail:** paulmoir@rococogarden.co.uk

Owner: Painswick Rococo Garden Trust   **Contact:** P R Moir

Unique 18th century garden restoration situated in a hidden 6 acre Cotswold combe. Charming contemporary buildings are juxtaposed with winding woodland walks and formal vistas. Famous for its early spring show of snowdrops. Newly planted maze.

Location: OS Ref. SO864 106. ½ m NW of village of Painswick on B4073.

Open: Jan - Apr, Oct & Nov: Wed - Sun, 11am - 5pm. May - Sept: daily, 11am - 5pm.

Admission: Adult £3.60, Child £1.80, OAP £3.30. Family (2+2) £9.50. Free introductory talk for pre-booked groups (20+).

🔲 ⬛ 🔲 Partial. WC. ⬛ Licensed. 🍴 🅿 🔲 In grounds, on leads. ⬛ ✳ 🔲 Tel for details.

ST MARY'S CHURCH ⛪

Kempley, Gloucestershire

Tel: 0117 9750700

Owner: English Heritage   **Contact:** The South West Regional Office

A delightful Norman church with superb wall paintings from the 12th - 14th centuries which were only discovered beneath whitewash in 1871.

Location: OS149 SO670 313. On minor road. 1½ m SE of Much Marcle, A449.

Open: 1 Apr - 31 Oct: daily, 10am - 6pm.

Admission: Free.

SEZINCOTE 🏠

Moreton-in-Marsh, Gloucestershire GL56 9AW

Owner: Mr and Mrs D Peake   **Contact:** Mrs D Peake

Exotic oriental water garden by Repton and Daniell. Large semi-circular orangery. House by S P Cockerell in Indian style was the inspiration for Brighton Pavilion.

Location: OS Ref. SP183 324. 2½ m SW of Moreton-in-Marsh. Turn W along A44 to Broadway and left into gateway just before Bourton-on-the-Hill (opposite the gate to Batsford Park), then 1m drive.

Open: Garden: Thurs, Fris & BH Mons, 2 - 6pm (dusk if earlier) throughout the year except Dec. House: May, Jun, Jul & Sept, Thurs & Fris, 2.30 - 6pm. Groups by written appointment.

Admission: House & Garden £5 (no children in house). Garden: Adult £3.50, Child £1 (under 5yrs Free).

🔲 Unsuitable. 🐕 Guide dogs only. ✳

Open All Year Index ◁ ◁ ◁ pgs 44-48

SNOWSHILL MANOR ✤

SNOWSHILL, Nr BROADWAY WR12 7JU

www.nationaltrust.org.uk

Tel/Fax: 01386 852410 **e-mail:** snowshill@smtp.ntrust.org.uk

Owner: The National Trust **Contact:** The Property Manager

A Tudor house with a c1700 façade, 21 rooms containing Charles Paget Wade's collection of craftsmanship, including musical instruments, clocks, toys, bicycles, weavers' and spinners' tools, Japanese armour, small formal garden and Charles Wade's cottage. The Manor is a 10 minute walk (500 yds) along an undulating countryside path.

Location: OS150 Ref. SP096 339. 3m SW of Broadway, turning off the A44, by Broadway Green.

Open: 29 Mar - 3 Nov: daily except Mons & Tues, 12 noon - 5pm (open BH Mons, & Mons in Jul & Aug). Open Jubilee Mon & Tue. Last entry to Manor 4.30pm, last entry to the property 5pm. Timed tickets issued for Manor. Grounds: as house, 11am - 5.30pm. Note: Entry to Manor may be restricted 4 Sept - 3 Nov due to essential building work. Please telephone to confirm opening.

Admission: Adult £6, Child £3, Family £15. Grounds, shop & restaurant £3.50.

📷 ♿Partial. 🍴Licensed. ✖ ♿Tel for details.

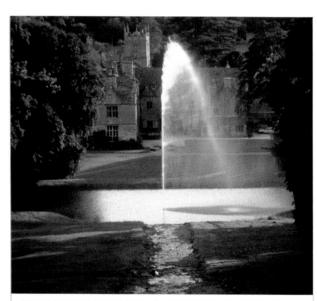

STANWAY HOUSE & WATER GARDEN 🏛

STANWAY, CHELTENHAM, GLOS GL54 5PQ

Tel: 01386 584469 **Fax:** 01386 584688 **e-mail:** stanwayhouse@btinternet.com

Owner: Lord Neidpath **Contact:** Debbie Lewis

"As perfect and pretty a Cotswold manor house as anyone is likely to see" (Fodor's 'Great Britain '98' guidebook), Stanway's peaceful Jacobethan architecture and the beauty of its surrounding villages and parkland are now complemented by its magnificent, newly restored baroque water garden, with pyramid, cascade, upper pond, waterfall, grand canal and 70 ft high fountain.

Location: OS Ref. SP061 323. N of Winchcombe, just off B4077.

Open: Gardens: Jul & Aug: Tues & Thurs, 2 - 5pm. Private tours by arrangement at other times.

Admission: Adult £3.50, Child £1, OAP £2.50.

ℹ️Film & photographic location. 🎬By arrangement. 🅿 ✖In grounds on leads. ✖

SUDELEY CASTLE 🏛

See page 222 for full page entry.

WESTBURY COURT GARDEN ✤

WESTBURY-ON-SEVERN, GLOUCESTERSHIRE GL14 1PD

www.nationaltrust.org.uk

Tel: 01452 760461 **e-mail:** westbury@smtp.ntrust.org.uk

Owner: The National Trust **Contact:** The Head Gardener

A formal water garden with canals and yew hedges, laid out between 1696 and 1705; the earliest of its kind remaining in England. Restored in 1971 and planted with species dating from pre-1700 including apple, pear and plum trees.

Location: OS162 SO718 138. 9m SW of Gloucester on A48.

Open: 1 Mar - 30 Jun: Wed - Sun, BH Mons & Jubilee BH Mon & Tue, 10am - 5pm. 1 Jul - 31 Aug: daily, 10am - 5pm. 1 Sept - 27 Oct: Wed - Sun, 10am - 5pm. Other times by appointment.

Admission: Adult £3, Child £1.50.

♿Access to most parts of the garden. WC. ✖Guide dogs only.

WESTONBIRT ARBORETUM

Tetbury, Gloucestershire GL8 8QS

Tel: 01666 880220 **Fax:** 01666 880559

Owner: The Forestry Commission **Contact:** Mr A Russell

600 acres arboretum begun in 1829, now with 18,000 catalogued trees.

Location: OS Ref. ST856 896. 3m S of Tetbury on the A433.

Open: 365 days a year, 10am - 8pm (or dusk if earlier).

Admission: Adult £4.50, Child £1, OAP £3.50.

WHITTINGTON COURT 🏛

Whittington, Cheltenham, Gloucestershire GL54 4HF

Tel: 01242 820556 **Fax:** 01242 820218

Owner: Mr & Mrs Jack Stringer **Contact:** Mrs J Stringer

Elizabethan manor house. Family possessions.

Location: OS Ref. SP014 206. 4m E of Cheltenham on N side of A40.

Open: 30 Mar - 14 Apr & 10 - 26 Aug inclusive: 2 - 5pm.

Admission: Adult £3, Child £1, OAP £2.50.

WOODCHESTER MANSION

Stroud, Gloucestershire GL10 3TS

Tel: 01453 750455 **Fax:** 01453 750457 **e-mail:** visitor@the-mansion.co.uk **www**.the-mansion.co.uk

Owner: Woodchester Mansion Trust **Contact:** David Price

Hidden in a wooded valley near Stroud is one of the most intriguing houses in the country. Woodchester Mansion was started in 1856 but abandoned incomplete in 1870. It offers a unique insight into traditional building techniques. The Trust's repair programme includes courses in stone masonry and building conservation.

Location: OS Ref. SO795 015 (gateway on B4066). 5m S of Stroud on B4066. NW of the village of Nympsfield, then 1m path E from gate.

Open: Easter - Oct: Suns & 1st Sat of every month & BH weekends including Mon. Jul & Aug: Sat.

Admission: Adult £4, Child (under 12yrs) £2, Student £2. Groups (min 10 people or £50): Adult £5. Minibus service is provided.

📷 ♿Unsuitable. ✖ 🎬 🅿 ✖Guide dogs only in Mansion.

National Trust Photographic Library: Andreas von Einsiedel

MUSEUM OF COSTUME ❧ & ASSEMBLY ROOMS

BATH

www.museumofcostume.co.uk

Owner:
The National Trust

▶ **CONTACT**

For Room Hire:
Mr Tom Deller
Room Hire Manager
Stall Street
Bath BA1 1LZ

Tel: 01225 477734
Fax: 01225 477476

e-mail: tom_deller@
bathnes.gov.uk

Museum Enquiries:
Tel: 01225 477785
Fax: 01225 477743

▶ **LOCATION**

OS Ref. ST750 648

Near centre of Bath,
10m from M4/J18.
Park & Ride or
public car park.

Rail: Great Western
from London Paddington
(regular service)
1 hr 17mins duration.

Air: Bristol airport
40 mins.

THE ASSEMBLY ROOMS in Bath are open to the public daily (free of charge) and are also popular for dinners, dances, concerts, conferences and Civil weddings.

Originally known as the Upper Rooms, they were designed by John Wood the Younger and opened in 1771. The magnificent interior consists of a splendid Ball Room, Tea Room and Card Room, connected by two fine octagonal rooms. This plan was perfect for 'assemblies', evening entertainments popular in the 18th century, which included dancing, music, card-playing and tea drinking. They are now owned by The National Trust and managed by Bath & North East Somerset Council, which runs a full conference service.

The building also houses one of the largest and most comprehensive collections of fashionable dress in the world, the Museum of Costume. Its extensive displays cover the history of fashion from the late 16th century to the present day. Hand-held audioguides allow visitors to learn about the fashions on display while the lighting is kept to levels suitable for fragile garments. The 'Dress of the Year' collection traces significant moments in modern fashion history from 1963. Special exhibition for 2002. *"Jubilee!" Dresses from Her Majesty The Queen's Collection* – celebration of The Queen's Golden Jubilee, 12 Dec 2001 - 3 Nov 2002. For the serious student of fashion, the reference library and study facilities of the nearby Fashion Research Centre are available by appointment.

The museum shop sells publications and gifts associated with the history of costume and is open daily to all visitors.

▶ **OPENING TIMES**

All Year
10am - 4.30pm
Closed 25 & 26 December

Last exit 30 mins after closing.

▶ **ADMISSION**

Assembly Rooms ... Free

Museum of Costume:
Adult	£5.00
Child*	£3.50
OAP	£4.00

Groups (20+)
Adult	£4.00
Child* (summer)	£2.70
Child* (winter)	£2.20

Combined ticket with Roman Baths
Adult	£10.50
Child*	£5.90
OAP	£9.00
Family (2+4)	£27.00

Groups (20+)
Adult	£7.50
Child* (summer)	£4.60
Child* (winter)	£3.80

* Age 6 - 16yrs.
Child under 6yrs Free

ℹ️ Conference facilities.

📖 Extensive book & gift shop.

🍽️ Corporate hospitality. Function facilities.

♿ Suitable. WC.

🚶 Hourly. Individual guided tours by arrangement.

🎧 English, Dutch, French, German, Italian, Japanese, Spanish.

🅿️ Charlotte Street car park.

🎒 Teachers' pack.

🐕 Guide dogs only.

💒 Civil Weddings/ Receptions.

❄️

CONFERENCE/FUNCTION

ROOM	SIZE	MAX CAPACITY
Ballroom	103' x 40'	450
Octagon	47' x 47'	200
Tea Room	58' x 40'	250
Card Room	59' x 18'	70

Museum of Costume

Museum of Costume

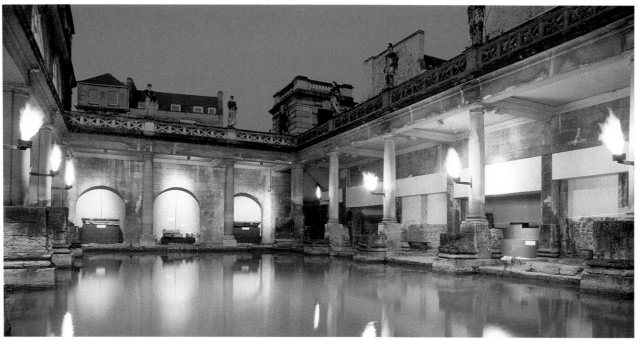

B & NES Council: Simon Mc Bride

THE ROMAN BATHS & PUMP ROOM

BATH

www.romanbaths.co.uk

Owner:
Bath & North East
Somerset Council

▶ **CONTACT**

For Room Hire:
Mr Tom Deller
Room Hire Manager
Stall Street
Bath BA1 1LZ
Tel: 01225 477734
Fax: 01225 477476
e-mail: tom_deller@
bathnes.gov.uk

**For visits to
Roman Baths:**
Tel: 01225 477785
Fax: 01225 477743

▶ **LOCATION**

OS Ref. ST750 648

Centre of Bath,
10m from M4/J18. Park
& Ride recommended.

Rail: Great Western
from London
Paddington, half hourly
service, 1 hr 17 mins
duration. Good
connection to
other UK cities.

The first stop for any visitor to Bath is the Roman Baths surrounding the hot springs where the city began and which are still its heart. Here you'll see one of the country's finest ancient monuments – the great Roman temple and bathing complex built almost 2000 years ago. Discover the everyday life of the Roman spa and see ancient treasures from the Temple of Sulis Minerva. A host of new interpretive methods bring these spectacular buildings vividly to life and help visitors to understand the extensive remains.

The Grand Pump Room, overlooking the Spring, is the social heart of Bath. The elegant interior of 1795 is something every visitor to Bath should see. You can enjoy a glass of spa water drawn from the fountain, perhaps as an appetiser to a traditional Pump Room tea, morning coffee or lunch. The Pump Room Trio and resident pianists provide live music daily. The Roman Baths shop sells publications and gifts related to the site.

In the evening, the Pump Room is available for banquets, dances and concerts. Nothing could be more magical than a meal on the terrace which overlooks the Great Bath, or a pre-dinner drinks reception by torchlight around the Great Bath itself.

▶ **OPENING TIMES**

January - February:
9.30am - 4.30pm.
March - June: 9am - 5pm.
July - August: 9am - 9pm.
September - October:
9am - 5pm.
November - December:
9.30am - 4.30pm.
Last exit 1 hour after
closing.

Closed 25 & 26 December.

The Pump Room Trio
plays 10am - 12 noon Mon
- Sat and 3 - 5pm Sunday.
During the summer it also
plays from 3 - 5pm, Mon -
Sat. Resident pianists play
at lunch-time.

▶ **ADMISSION**

Adult	£8.00
Child*	£4.60
Family (2+4)	£20.50
OAP	£7.00
Groups (20+)	
Adult	£5.90
Child* (summer)...	£3.30
Child* (winter)	£2.80

**Combined ticket with
Museum of Costume,
Bath**

Adult	£10.50
Child*	£5.90
OAP	£9.00
Family (2 + 4)	£27.00
Groups (20+)	
Adult	£7.50
Child* (summer)....	£4.60
Child* (winter).......	£3.80

* Age 6 - 17 yrs.

CONFERENCE/FUNCTION

ROOM	SIZE	MAX CAPACITY
Great Roman Bath	400 summer 200 winter	
Pump Rm.	57' x 41'	180
Terrace overlooking Great Bath	83' x 11'	70
Concert Rm	56' x 44'	100
Smoking Rm & Drawing Rm	28' x 16'	40

Extensive gift shop.

Award-winning guide book in English, French and German. The Historic Buildings of Bath include the Assembly Rooms, Guildhall, and Victoria Art Gallery.

Comprehensive service for private and corporate entertainment. The Assembly Rooms, Guildhall, Victoria Art Gallery and Pump Room are all available for private hire, contact the Pump Room.

Free access to terrace. Restricted access to the Museum, special visits for disabled groups by appointment. People with special needs welcome, teaching sessions available.

Pump Room coffees, lunches and teas, no reservation needed. Music by Pump Room Trio or pianist.

Hourly. Private tours by appointment.

English, French, German, Italian, Japanese, Spanish, Dutch.

Teaching sessions available. Pre-booking necessary.

Civil Weddings in two private rooms with photographs around the Great Bath.

Rick Godley

NT Photographic Library: Magnus Rew

Dunster Castle

NO 1 ROYAL CRESCENT

BATH BA1 2LR

www.bath-preservation-trust.org.uk

Tel: 01225 428126 **Fax:** 01225 481850 **e-mail:** admin@bptrust.demon.co.uk

Owner: Bath Preservation Trust   **Contact:** Sue Duncan – Administrator

Number 1 was the first house to be built in the Royal Crescent. The house was given to the Bath Preservation Trust in 1968 and both the exterior and interior have been accurately restored. Visitors can see a grand town-house of the late 18th century with authentic furniture, paintings and carpets. In the basement there is a period kitchen and Museum shop.

Location: OS Ref. ST746 653. M4/J18. A46 to Bath. ¹/₄ m NW of city centre.

Open: Mid Feb - end Oct: daily except Mons, 10.30am - 5pm. Closed Good Fri. Open BHs & Festival Mons. Nov: daily (except Mons), 10.30am - 4pm. Last admission 30 mins before closing. Tours at other times by arrangement.

Admission: Adult £4, Child (5 - 16)/Student £3.50, Family £10. Groups: Adult £2.50.

◻ ⬚ Unsuitable. 🅕 🅿 The Royal Crescent & Bath centre. ◼

THE AMERICAN MUSEUM & GARDENS

CLAVERTON MANOR, BATH BA2 7BD

www.americanmuseum.org

Tel: 01225 460503 **Fax:** 01225 480726 **e-mail:** amibbath@aol.com

Owner: The Trustees of the American Museum in Britain **Contact:** R Hornshaw

Claverton Manor was built in 1820 by Jeffry Wyattville. In the late 1950s it became the home of the American Museum in Britain. Inside the Manor there are 18 period rooms which show the development of American decorative arts from the 1680s to the 1860s. In addition there are galleries devoted to Folk Art, Native American Art, and our large collection of quilts and other textiles. The extensive grounds contain a replica of part of the garden at Mount Vernon, George Washington's house in Virginia, and an Arboretum of North American trees and shrubs. Light lunches and teas are available.

Location: OS Ref. ST784 640. 2m SE of Bath city centre.

Open: 23 Mar - 3 Nov: Tue - Sun, 2 - 5pm.

Admission: Adult £6, Child £3, Conc. £5.50. Groups (20-60): Adult £5, OAP £4.50.

◻ ⏀ ⬚ Partial. WC. ⬛ 🅕 By arrangement. 🅿 ◼ 🐕 In grounds, on leads.

▣ Tel for details.

NTPL, Neil Campbell-Sharp

NTPL, Alan North

BARRINGTON COURT ❦

BARRINGTON, ILMINSTER, SOMERSET TA19 0NQ

www.nationaltrust.org.uk

Tel: 01460 241938 **e-mail:** wbagen@smtp.ntrust.org.uk

Owner: The National Trust   **Contact:** Visitor Services Manager

A beautiful garden influenced by Gertrude Jekyll and laid out in a series of walled rooms, including the white garden, the rose and iris garden and the lily garden. The working kitchen garden has apple, pear and plum trees trained along high stone walls. The Tudor Manor house was restored in the 1920s by the Lyle family. It is let to Stuart Interiors as showrooms with antique furniture for sale and is also open to NT visitors. An innovative garden information area is now open to visitors which

incorporates plant sales. Access to the Long Gallery in the Court House is now fully accessible via a staircase built by Stuart Interiors.

Location: OS Ref. ST395 181. In Barrington village, 5m NE of Ilminster, on B3168.

Open: Mar & Oct - 3 Nov: Thur - Sun, 11am - 4.30pm. 1 Apr - 30 Jun & Sept: daily except Fri, 11am - 5.30pm. Jul & Aug: daily (Fri: garden only), 11am - 5.30pm. Coach parties by appointment only.

Admission: Adult £5.20, Child £2.50, Family £13. Groups: Adult £4.50.

🖼 ♿ ♿ Grounds. WC. 🍽 Licensed.

BECKFORD'S TOWER & MUSEUM

Lansdown Road, Bath BA1 9BH

Tel: 01225 422212 **Fax:** 01225 481850

Owner: Bath Preservation Trust   **Contact:** The Administrator

Built in 1827 for eccentric William Beckford. The tower is a striking feature of the Bath skyline.

Location: OS Ref. ST735 676. Lansdown Road, 2m NNW of city centre.

Open: Easter weekend - end of October: Sats, Suns & BH Mons, 10.30am - 5pm.

Admission: Adult £2.50, Child/OAP £2, Family £6. BPT & NACF members: Free. Groups by arrangement – Tel: 01225 460705.

THE BISHOP'S PALACE 🏛

Wells, Somerset BA5 2PD

Tel/Fax: 01749 678691

Owner: Church Commissioners   **Contact:** Mrs K J Scarisbrick

Fortified and moated medieval palace which is today the private residence of the Bishop of Bath and Wells. Extensive grounds and arboretum. Available for functions.

Location: OS Ref. ST552 457. 20m S of Bristol and Bath on A39.

Open: 1 Apr - 31 Oct: Tue - Fri & BHs & daily in Aug, 10.30am - 5pm. Suns: 2 - 5pm.

Admission: Adult £3.50, Child (12 - 18) £1, OAP £2.50, Conc. £1.50. Groups (10+) £2.50. Guided tour £30 plus £2.50 per person.

🍸 Wedding receptions. ♿ Partial. 🖼 🍴 🅵 By arrangement. 🐕 In grounds on leads.

THE BUILDING OF BATH MUSEUM

The Countess of Huntingdon's Chapel, The Vineyards,
The Paragon, Bath BA1 5NA

Tel: 01225 333895 / 01225 445473

Owner: Bath Preservation Trust   **Contact:** The Administrator

Discover the essence of life in Georgian Bath.

Location: OS Ref. ST751 655, 5 mins walk from city centre. Bath M4/J18.

Open: 15 Feb - 30 Nov: Tue - Sun and BH Mons, 10.30am - 5pm.

Admission: Adult £4, Child £1.50, Conc. £3. Groups: £2.50.

THE CHALICE WELL & GARDENS

CHILKWELL STREET, GLASTONBURY, SOMERSET BA6 8DD

www.chalicewell.org.uk

Tel: 01458 831154 **Fax:** 01458 835528 **e-mail:** info@chalicewell.org.uk

Owner: Chalice Well Trust   **Contact:** Michael Orchard

A jewel of a garden, nestling around one of Britain's oldest Holy Wells. Legend tells of the Well being visited by Joseph of Arimethea, bearing the Chalice of the Last Supper, and of King Arthur on his Grail Quest. Today, the beautifully landscaped grounds with the iron-rich waters are a haven of peace and tranquillity.

Location: OS Ref. ST507 384. On the A361 Glastonbury - Shepton Mallet road, at the foot of Glastonbury Tor.

Open: All year: 1 Apr - 31 Oct: 10am - 6pm; Nov, Feb & Mar: 11am - 5pm; Dec & Jan: 12 noon - 4pm.

Admission: Adult £2.20, Child £1.20, OAP £1.60, Student £2.20.

ℹ No smoking in gardens. 🖼 ♿ 🅵 By arrangement.

🅿 Limited. At nearby Rural Life Museum. 🖼 🐕 Guide dogs only. ✳

📺 Tel for details.

CLEEVE ABBEY ⊞

Tel: 01984 640377   **e-mail:** customers@english-heritage.org.uk
www.english-heritage.org.uk

Washford, Nr Watchet, Somerset TA23 0PS

Owner: English Heritage   **Contact:** The Custodian

There are few monastic sites where you will see such a complete set of cloister buildings, including the refectory with its magnificent timber roof. Built in the 13th century, this Cistercian abbey was saved from destruction at the Dissolution by being turned into a house and then a farm.

Location: OS181 Ref. ST047 407. In Washford, ¼ m S of A39.

Open: 29 Mar - 31 Oct: daily 10am - 6pm (5pm in Oct). 1 Nov - 31 Mar: daily 10am - 4pm (closed lunch 1 - 2pm). Closed 24 - 26 Dec & 1 Jan.

Admission: Adult £2.80, Child £1.40, Conc. £2.10. 15% discount for groups (11+).

▢ ⓚ Partial. ▣ P ✉ In grounds, on leads. ✳ ⓦ Tel for details.

CLEVEDON COURT ✿

Tickenham Road, Clevedon, North Somerset BS21 6QU

Tel: 01275 872257   **www**.nationaltrust.org.uk

Owner: The National Trust   **Contact:** The Administrator

Home of the Elton family since 1709, this 14th century manor house, once partly fortified, has a 12th century tower and 13th century hall. Collection of Nailsea glass and Eltonware. Beautiful terraced garden.

Location: OS Ref. ST423 716. 1½ m E of Clevedon, on B3130, signposted from M5/J20.

Open: 31 Mar - 29 Sept: Wed, Thur, Sun & BH Mons, 2 - 5pm. Also 4 Jun: 2 - 5pm.

Admission: Adult £4.50, Child £2. Groups & coaches by arrangement.

ⓚ Ground floor. P Limited. ▣ ✉

COLERIDGE COTTAGE ✿

35 Lime Street, Nether Stowey, Bridgwater, Somerset TA5 1NQ

Tel: 01278 732662   **www**.nationaltrust.org.uk

Owner: The National Trust   **Contact:** The Custodian

The home of Samuel Taylor Coleridge for three years from 1797, with mementoes of the poet on display. It was here that he wrote *The Rime of the Ancient Mariner*, part of *Christabel* and *Frost at Midnight*.

Location: OS Ref. ST191 399. At W end of Nether Stowey, on S side of A39, 8m W of Bridgwater.

Open: 24 Mar - 29 Sept: Tue - Thur & Suns, 2 - 5pm.

Admission: Adult £3, Child £1.50, no reduction for groups, which must book.

✉

COMBE SYDENHAM COUNTRY PARK 🏠

Monksilver, Taunton, Somerset TA4 4JG

Tel: 01984 656284

Owner: Theed Estates   **Contact:** Mr A Hudson

Built in 1580 on the site of a monastic settlement. Deer Park and woodland walks.

Location: OS Ref. ST075 366. Monksilver.

Open: 28 Mar - 31 Aug: guided tours by appointment.

Admission: £4 per vehicle. Guided tours £5pp. Tel 0800 7838572 for details.

Milton Lodge Gardens

The Gatehouse at Cothay Manor / Andrew Lawson

COTHAY MANOR 🏠

GREENHAM, WELLINGTON, SOMERSET TA21 0JR

Tel: 01823 672283   **Fax:** 01823 672345

Owner/Contact: Mr & Mrs Alastair Robb

It has been said that Cothay Manor (of which the gatehouse is shown above) is the finest example of a small classic, medieval manor house in England. The manor has remained virtually untouched since it was built in 1480. The gardens, laid out in the 1920s have been completely re-designed and replanted within the original framework of yew hedges. A white garden, scarlet and purple garden, herbaceous borders and bog garden are but a few of the delights to be found in this magical place.

Location: OS Ref. ST721 214. From M5 W J/27, take A38 dir Wellington. 3½ m left to Greenham. From N take A38 dir. Exeter. 3½ m right to Greenham (1½ m). On LH corner at bottom of hill turn right. Cothay 1½m, always keeping left.

Open: May - Sept: Weds, Thurs, Suns & BHs, 2 - 6pm.

Admission: Garden: Adult £3.50, Child (under 12yrs) Free. House: Groups (20+): by arrangement throughout the year, £4.50.

ⓘ No photography in house. ✳ ⓚ ▣ 𝒇 By arrangement. P ✉ ✳

CROWE HALL

Widcombe Hill, Bath, Somerset BA2 6AR

Tel: 01225 310322

Owner/Contact: John Barratt Esq

Ten acres of romantic hillside gardens. Victorian grotto, classical Bath villa with good 18th century furniture and paintings.

Location: OS Ref. ST760 640. In Bath, 1m SE of city centre.

Open: Gardens only open 7 Apr, 12 May, 9 Jun, 14 Jul, 2 - 6pm. House and Gardens by appointment.

Admission: House & Gardens: Adult £5. Gardens only: Adult £2.50, Child £1.

DODINGTON HALL

Nr Nether Stowey, Bridgwater, Somerset TA5 1LF

Tel: 01278 741400

Owner: Lady Gass   **Contact:** P Quinn (occupier)

Small Tudor manor house on the lower slopes of the Quantocks. Great Hall with oak roof. Semi-formal garden with roses and shrubs.

Location: OS Ref. ST172 405. ½ m from A39, 11m N of Bridgwater, 7m E of Williton.

Open: 8 - 17 Jun, 2 - 5pm.

Admission: Donations for charity.

ⓘ No inside photography. ⓚ Unsuitable. P Limited. No coach parking.

Accommodation Index
◁ ◁ ◁   pg 27

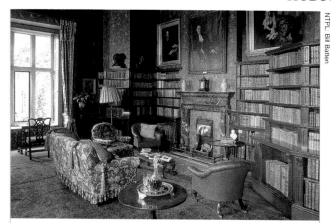

NTPL: Bill Batten

DUNSTER CASTLE

DUNSTER, NR MINEHEAD, SOMERSET TA24 6SL

www.nationaltrust.org.uk

Tel: 01643 821314 **Fax:** 01643 823000 **e-mail:** wdugen@smtp.ntrust.org.uk

Owner: The National Trust   **Contact:** The Property Manager

Dramatically sited atop a wooded hill. There has been a castle here since at least Norman times. The 13th century gatehouse survives, but the present building was re-modelled in 1868-72 by Anthony Salvin for the Luttrell family who lived here for 600 years. The fine oak staircase and plasterwork of the 17th century house he adapted can still be seen. There is a sheltered terrace to the south on which tender plants and shrubs grow, and beautiful parkland in which to walk.

Location: OS Ref. SS992 436. In Dunster, 3m SE of Minehead.

Open: Castle: 23 Mar - 3 Nov: daily except Thur & Fri (open Good Fri). 23 March - 25 Sept, 11am - 5pm; 28 Sept - 3 Nov: 11am - 4pm. Garden & Park: Daily (closed 25/26 Dec). 1 Jan - 22 Mar & 28 Sept - 31 Dec, 11am - 4pm. 23 Mar - 27 Sept: 10am - 5pm. Varied events programme, please telephone for full details.

Admission: Castle: 23 Mar - 3 Nov: Sat - Wed (open Good Fri). 23 Mar - 25 Sept: 11am - 5pm; 28 Sept - 3 Nov: 11am - 4pm. Garden & Park: daily (closed 25/26 Dec); Jan - Mar, 28 Sept - 31 Dec: 11am - 4pm; 23 Mar - 27 Sept: 10am - 5pm.

◻ ♿Braille Guide. ▣ ⬚Guide dogs only. ♨ Tel for details (01985 843601).

DUNSTER WORKING WATERMILL

Mill Lane, Dunster, Minehead, Somerset TA24 6SW

Tel: 01643 821759 **www.**nationaltrust.org.uk

Owner: The National Trust   **Contact:** The Tenant

Built on the site of a mill mentioned in the Domesday Survey of 1086, the present mill dates from the 18th century and was restored to working order in 1979. Note: the mill is a private business and all visitors, including NT members are asked to pay the admission charge.

Location: OS Ref. SS991 434. On River Avill, beneath Castle Tor, approach via Mill Lane or Castle gardens on foot.

Open: 23 Mar - 3 Nov: daily, 10.30am - 5pm.

Admission: £2.20. Family tickets available. Group rates by prior arrangement.

◻ ♿Ground floor. ▣ 🅿

ENGLISHCOMBE TITHE BARN

Rectory Farmhouse, Englishcombe, Bath BA2 9DU

Tel: 01225 425073 **e-mail:** jennie@barnhire.com

Owner/Contact: Mrs Jennie Walker

An early 14th century cruck-framed Tithe Barn built by Bath Abbey.

Location: OS172 Ref. ST716 628. Adjacent to Englishcombe Village Church. 1m SW of Bath.

Open: BHs, 2 - 6pm. Other times by appointment or please knock at house. Closed 1 Dec - 7 Jan.

Admission: Free.

FAIRFIELD

Stogursey, Bridgwater, Somerset TA5 1PU

Tel: 01278 732251 **Fax:** 01278 732277

Owner/Contact: Lady Gass

Elizabethan house of medieval origin, undergoing extensive repairs. Woodland garden. Views of Quantocks.

Location: OS Ref. ST187 430. 11m W of Bridgwater, 8m E of Williton. From A39 Bridgwater/Minehead turn North. House 1m W of Stogursey.

Open: House: open in Summer (as repairs allow). Groups: by appointment only. Garden: open for NGS & other charities on dates advertised in Spring.

Admission: Donation for charity.

ⓘNo inside photography. ♿ ⓕObligatory. 🅿Limited for coaches. ⬚Guide dogs only.

FARLEIGH HUNGERFORD CASTLE ♯

Farleigh Hungerford, Bath, Somerset BA3 6RS

Tel/Fax: 01225 754026 **e-mail:** customers@english-heritage.org.uk

www.english-heritage.org.uk

Owner: English Heritage   **Contact:** The Custodian

Extensive ruins of 14th century castle with a splendid chapel containing wall paintings, stained glass and the fine tomb of Sir Thomas Hungerford, builder of the castle.

Location: OS173 Ref. ST801 577. In Farleigh Hungerford 3¹/₂ m W of Trowbridge on A366.

Open: 29 Mar - 31 Oct: daily 10am - 6pm (5pm in Oct). Nov - Mar: Wed - Sun, 10am - 4pm (closed for lunch 1 - 2 pm). Closed 24 - 26 Dec & 1 Jan.

Admission: Adult £2.30, Child £1.20, Conc. £1.70. 15% discount for groups of 11+.

◻ ♿Grounds. ▣ 🅿 ⬚ Guide dogs only. ❋ Tel for details.

GANTS MILL & GARDEN

Bruton, Somerset BA10 0DB

Tel: 01749 812393

Owner/Contact: Brian and Alison Shingler

4-storey working watermill with beautiful colour-themed designer garden.

Location: OS Ref. ST674 342. Off A359 ¹/₂ m SW of Bruton.

Open: Mill: Easter - end of May, Thur & BH Mons. Mill & Garden: June - end Sept, Thurs, Suns & BH Mons, 2 - 5pm.

Admission: Adult £3.50, Child £1. Groups by arrangement.

GATCOMBE COURT

Flax Bourton, Somerset BS48 3QT

Tel: 01275 393141 **Fax:** 01275 394274

Owner: Mr & Mrs Charles Clarke   **Contact:** Mr Charles Clarke

A Somerset manor house, dating from early 13th century, which has evolved over the centuries since. It is on the site of a large Roman village, traces of which are apparent.

Location: OS Ref. ST525 698. 5m W of Bristol, N of the A370, between the villages of Long Ashton and Flax Bourton.

Open: By written appointment only.

♿Unsuitable. ⓕBy arrangement. 🅿 ❎ ❋

GAULDEN MANOR

Tolland, Lydeard St Lawrence, Nr Taunton, Somerset TA4 3PN

Tel: 01984 667213

Owner/Contact: James Le Gendre Starkie

Small historic manor of great charm. A real lived-in family home, guided tours by owner. Past seat of the Turberville family, immortalised by Thomas Hardy. Magnificent early plasterwork, fine furniture, many examples of embroidery by owner's wife. Interesting gardens include herb garden, old fashioned roses, bog garden and secret garden beyond monks fish pond.

Location: OS Ref. ST111 314. 9m NW of Taunton off A358 and B3224.

Open: Garden: 2 Jun - 26 Aug. Thurs, Suns & BHs, 2 - 5pm. House & Garden: groups (15+): Jun, Jul & Aug: by written appointment at any time.

Admission: House & Garden: Adult £5, Child £1. Garden only: Adult £3.50, Child £1.

◻ ♿Ground floor & grounds. ⓕObligatory. 🅿 ❎ ❋

THE GEORGIAN HOUSE

7 Great George Street, Bristol, Somerset BS1 5RR

Tel: 0117 921 1362

Owner: City of Bristol Museums & Art Gallery   **Contact:** Karin Walton

Location: OS172 ST582 730. Bristol.

Open: 1 Apr - 31 Oct: Sat - Wed, 10am - 5pm.

Admission: Free.

GLASTONBURY ABBEY

Abbey Gatehouse, Magdalene Street, Glastonbury BA6 9EL

Tel/Fax: 01458 832267 **e-mail:** glastonbury.abbey@dial.pipex.com

Owner: Glastonbury Abbey Estate   **Contact:** F C Thyer - Deputy Custodian

Traditionally the first Christian sanctuary in Britain and legendary burial place of King Arthur. Award-winning museum with model of pre-Reformation Abbey.

Location: OS Ref. ST499 388. 50 yds from the Market Cross, in the centre of Glastonbury. M5/J23, then A39.

Open: Daily (except Christmas Day), 9.30am - 6pm or dusk if earlier. Jun, Jul & Aug: opens 9am. Dec, Jan & Feb: opens 10am. (2001 times & prices.)

Admission: Adult £3.50, Child £1.50, Conc. £3. Groups (booked, 10+): Adult £3.

GLASTONBURY TRIBUNAL ♯

Glastonbury High Street, Glastonbury, Somerset

Tel: 01458 832954 **e-mail:** glastonbury.tic@ukonline.co.uk

Owner: English Heritage   **Contact:** The TIC Manager

A well preserved medieval town house, reputedly once used as the courthouse of Glastonbury Abbey. Now houses Glastonbury Tourist Information Centre.

Location: OS182 Ref. ST499 390. In Glastonbury High Street.

Open: Apr - Sept: Sun - Thur 10am - 5pm (Fri & Sat to 5.30pm). Oct - Apr: Sun - Thur, 10am - 4pm (Fri & Sat, 4.30pm). Closed 25 - 26 Dec & 1 Jan.

Admission: TIC Free. Display areas: Adult £2, Child £1.50.

THE WILLIAM HERSCHEL MUSEUM
19 New King Street, Bath BA1 2BL

Tel: 01225 311342 **Fax:** 01225 446865

Owner: The Herschel House Trust   **Contact:** The Curator

The astronomer and musician William Herschel lived here with his sister Caroline during the latter part of the 18th century. Audio tour.

Location: OS Ref. ST750 648. Bath, Somerset.

Open: 1 Mar - 31 Oct: daily, 2 - 5pm, weekends 11am - 5pm. Weekends throughout the winter, 11am - 5pm.

Admission: Adult £3.50, Child £2, Family £7.50. Educational events: £2.50. Free entry to Herschel Society & Museums Association members. Member of Bath Pass Scheme.

Special Events Index ◁ ◁ ◁ pgs 40-43

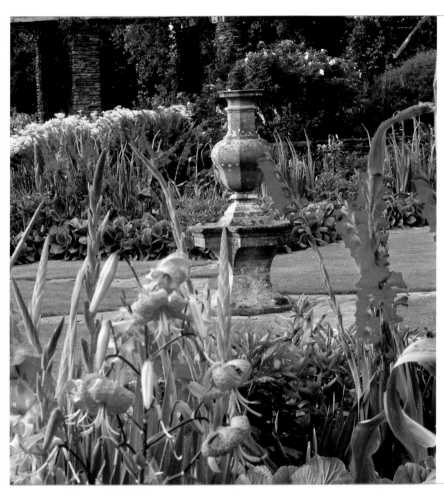

HESTERCOMBE GARDENS
CHEDDON FITZPAINE, TAUNTON, SOMERSET TA2 8LG

www.hestercombegardens.com

Tel: 01823 413923 **Fax:** 01823 413747

Owner: Somerset County Council & Hestercombe Gardens Project

Contact: Mr P White

Hestercombe's 50 acres of gardens are listed Grade I on the English Heritage Register of Parks and Gardens and encompass over three centuries of garden history. The formal gardens, designed by Sir Edwin Lutyens and planted by Gertrude Jekyll, were completed in 1906. With terraces, pools and an orangery, they are the supreme example of their famous partnership. These gardens are now reunited with Hestercombe's secret Landscape Garden, which opened in the Spring of 1997 for the first time in 125 years. Created by Coplestone Warre Bampfylde in the 1750s, these Georgian pleasure grounds comprise 40 acres of lakes, temples and delightful woodland walks. Our tearoom, shop and plant sales area are open daily from 10am to 5pm.

Location: OS Ref. ST241 287. 4m NE from Taunton, 1m NW of Cheddon Fitzpaine.

Open: All year: daily, 10am - 6pm (last admission 5pm). Groups & coach parties by arrangement.

Admission: Adult £4.30. Child (5-15yrs) £1, Child under 5 Free, Conc. £4. Guided tour: £6.50 (min. charge £100).

Partial. WC. Licensed. Licensed. By arrangement. Limited for coaches. On short leads.

HOLBURNE MUSEUM OF ART
Great Pulteney Street, Bath BA2 4DB

Tel: 01225 466669 **Fax:** 01225 333121 **e-mail:** holburne@bath.ac.uk

www.bath.ac.uk/holburne

Owner: Trustees   **Contact:** Polly Iddon

This jewel in Bath's crown, once the Georgian Sydney Hotel, houses the treasures collected by Sir William Holburne: superb English and continental silver, porcelain, majolica, glass and Renaissance bronzes. The picture gallery contains works by Turner, Guardi, Stubbs and others plus portraits of Bath society by Thomas Gainsborough.

Location: OS Ref. ST431 545. Via A4 or A431, follow brown signs.

Open: Mid Feb - mid Dec: Tue - Sat, 10am - 5pm, Sun, 2.30 - 5.30pm. Closed Mons except for group bookings by appointment.

Admission: Adult £3.50, Child £1.50, OAP £3, Students Free. Groups (10+): Adult £3, Child £1.

Licensed. Licensed. By arrangement. Guide dogs only.

KENTSFORD
Washford, Watchet, Somerset TA23 0JD

Tel: 01984 631307

Owner: Wyndham Estate   **Contact:** Mr R Dibble

Location: OS Ref. ST058 426.

Open: House open only by appointment with Mr R Dibble. Gardens: 5 Mar - 26 Aug: Tues & BHs.

Admission: House: £2, Gardens: Free.

Gardens only. Limited. In grounds, on leads.

KING JOHN'S HUNTING LODGE
The Square, Axbridge, Somerset BS26 2AP

Tel: 01934 732012 **www.**nationaltrust.org.uk

Owner/Contact: The National Trust

An early Tudor merchant's house, extensively restored in 1971. Note: the property is run as a local history museum by Axbridge & District Museum Trust in co-operation with County Museum's Service and Axbridge Archaeological & Local History Society.

Location: OS Ref. ST431 545. In the Square, on corner of High Street, off A371.

Open: 29 Mar - 30 Sept: daily, 1 - 4pm.

Admission: Free.

Ground floor. By arrangement.

LOWER SEVERALLS
Crewkerne, Somerset TA18 7NX

Tel: 01460 73234 **Fax:** 01460 76105 **e-mail:** mary@lowerseveralls.fsnet.co.uk

Owner: Mrs Howard Pring   **Contact:** Mary Cooper

2½ acre garden, developed over the last 25 years including herb garden, mixed borders and island beds with innovative features, ie a giant living dogwood basket and a wadi.

Location: OS Ref. ST457 112. 1½ m NE of Crewkerne, between A30 & A356.

Open: 2 Mar - 20 Oct: daily (except Thurs), 10am - 5pm (Suns, 2 - 5pm in May/Jun only).

Admission: Adult £2.50, Child (under 16yrs) Free.

LYTES CARY MANOR

Nr Charlton Mackrell, Somerset TA11 7HU

Tel: 01985 843600 **e-mail:** wlysxl@smtp.ntrust.org.uk **www.**nationaltrust.org.uk

Owner: The National Trust **Contact:** The Regional Office

A charming manor house with a 14th century chapel and Tudor Great Hall, much added to in the 16th century. Once the home of Henry Lyte, translator of Niewe Herball (1578). Attractive hedged garden. There is a new section to the waymarked river walk, open as the house and garden. New property guidebook.

Location: OS Ref. ST534 265. 1m N of Ilchester bypass A303, signposted from roundabout at junction of A303. A37 take A372.

Open: 23 Mar - 30 Oct: Mon, Wed & Sat, 2 - 6pm or dusk if earlier. Also Fri in Jun, Jul & Aug: 2 - 6pm (open BH Tue, 4 Jun, 2 - 6pm). Last admission 5.30pm.

Admission: £4.60, Child £2.

♿ Grounds. Braille guide. 🅿 Limited. ✴

NT Photographic Library: Rupert Truman

MONTACUTE HOUSE

MONTACUTE, SOMERSET TA15 6XP

www.nationaltrust.org.uk

Tel/Fax: 01935 823289 **e-mail:** wmogen@smtp.ntrust.org.uk

Owner: The National Trust **Contact:** The Property Manager

A magnificent Elizabethan house, with an H-shaped ground plan and many Renaissance features, including contemporary plasterwork, chimneypieces and heraldic glass. The house contains fine 17th and 18th century furniture, an exhibition of samplers dating from the 17th century and Elizabethan and Jacobean portraits from the National Portrait Gallery displayed in the Long Gallery and adjoining rooms. The formal garden includes mixed borders and old roses, also a landscaped park. Montacute featured in the award-winning film Sense & Sensibility.

Location: OS Ref. ST499 172. In Montacute village, 4m W of Yeovil, on S side of A3088, 3m E of A303.

Open: House: 23 Mar - 3 Nov: daily except Tue (open BH Tue, 4 June), 11am - 5pm. Garden & Park: 23 Mar - 3 Nov: daily except Tue, 11am - 5.30pm. 6 Nov - Mar 2003: daily except Mon & Tue, 11.30am - 4pm.

Admission: House, Park & Garden: Adult £6.20, Child £3, Family £15. Groups (15+) (must book): Adult £5.50, Child £2.80. Garden & Park only (23 Mar - 3 Nov): Adult £3.40, Child £1.50. 6 Nov - Mar 2003: Adult £2, Child £1.

📷 ♿ Grounds. WC. 🍴 Licensed. 🅿 ✴ In park only. ▣ ✳

MAUNSEL HOUSE

NORTH NEWTON, Nr BRIDGWATER, SOMERSET TA7 0BU

www.sirbenslade.co.uk

Tel: 0207 352 1132 **Fax:** 0207 352 6441

Owner: Sir Benjamin Slade **Contact:** Lou Lou Lack

This imposing 13th century manor house offers the ideal location for wedding receptions, corporate events, private and garden parties, filming and family celebrations. The ancestral seat of the Slade family and home of the 7th baronet Sir Benjamin Slade; the house can boast such visitors as Geoffrey Chaucer, who wrote part of the Canterbury Tales whilst staying there. The beautiful grounds and spacious rooms provide both privacy and a unique atmosphere for any special event.

Location: OS Ref. ST302 303. Bridgwater 4m, Bristol 20m, Taunton 7m, M5/J24, A38 to North Petherton. 2¹/₂ m SE of A38 at North Petherton via North Newton.

Open: Coach parties and groups welcome by appointment. Caravan rally field available.

🍴 Functions. ♿ Partial. ✴ In grounds, on leads.

MUCHELNEY ABBEY

Muchelney, Langport, Somerset TA10 0DQ

Tel: 01458 250664 **Fax:** 01458 253842 **e-mail:** customers@english-heritage.org.uk **www.**english-heritage.org.uk

Owner: English Heritage **Contact:** The Custodian

Well-preserved ruins of the cloisters, with windows carved in golden stone, and abbot's lodging of the Benedictine abbey, which survived by being used as a farmhouse after the Dissolution.

Location: OS193 Ref. ST428 248. In Muchelney 2m S of Langport.

Open: 29 Mar - 31 Oct: daily 10am - 6pm (5pm in Oct). Winter: closed.

Admission: Adult £2, Child £1, Conc. £1.50. 15% discount for groups (11+).

📷 ♿ Ground floor & grounds. ▣ 🅿 ✴ ☎ Tel for details.

MUSEUM OF COSTUME & ASSEMBLY ROOMS

See page 230 for full page entry.

ORCHARD WYNDHAM

Williton, Taunton, Somerset TA4 4HH

Tel: 01984 632309 **Fax:** 01984 633526

Owner: Wyndham Estate **Contact:** Wyndham Estate Office

English manor house. Family home for 700 years encapsulating continuous building and alteration from the 14th to the 20th century.

Location: OS Ref. ST072 400. 1m from A39 at Williton.

Open: Aug: Thur & Fri, 2 - 5pm & Aug BH Mon, 11am - 5pm. Guided tours only. Last tour at 4pm. Limited showing space within the house. To avoid disappointment please advance book places on tour by telephone or fax. Access only suitable for cars.

Admission: Adult £5, Child (under 12) £1.

📷 Obligatory & pre-booked. 🅿 Limited. No coach parking. ✴ In grounds, on leads.

MILTON LODGE GARDENS

Old Bristol Road, Wells, Somerset BA5 3AQ

Tel: 01749 672168

Owner/Contact: D Tudway Quilter Esq

"The great glory of the gardens of Milton Lodge is their position high up on the slopes of the Mendip Hills to the north of Wells ... with broad panoramas of Wells Cathedral and the Vale of Avalon", (Lanning Roper). Charming, mature, Grade II listed terraced garden dating from 1909. Replanned 1962 with mixed shrubs, herbaceous plants, old fashioned roses and ground cover; numerous climbers; old established yew hedges. Fine trees in garden and in 7-acre arboretum.

Location: OS Ref. ST549 470. ¹/₂ m N of Wells from A39. N up Old Bristol Road. Free car park first gate on left.

Open: Garden & Arboretum: Easter - end Oct: Tues, Weds, Suns & BHs, 2 - 5pm Parties & coaches by prior arrangement.

Admission: Adult £2.50, Child (under 14yrs) Free. Open certain Suns in aid of National Gardens Scheme.

📷 ♿ Unsuitable. ▣ 🅿 ✴

South West - England

PRIEST'S HOUSE ⚜

Muchelney, Langport, Somerset TA10 0DQ

Tel: 01458 252621 **www**.nationaltrust.org.uk

Owner: The National Trust   **Contact:** The Administrator

A late medieval hall house with large gothic windows, originally the residence of priests serving the parish church across the road. Lived-in and recently repaired.

Location: OS Ref. ST429 250. 1m S of Langport.

Open: 24 Mar - 30 Sept: Sun & Mon, 2.30 - 5.30pm, last admission 5.15pm.

Admission: £2, no reduction for groups or children.

ℹ️ No WC. ✖

PRIOR PARK LANDSCAPE GARDEN ⚜

RALPH ALLEN DRIVE, BATH BA2 5AH

www.nationaltrust.org.uk

Tel: 01225 833422 **e-mail:** wppalp@smtp.ntrust.org.uk

Owner: The National Trust   **Contact:** Gardener-in-Charge

Beautiful and intimate 18th century landscape garden created by Bath entrepreneur Ralph Allen (1693 - 1764) with advice from the poet Alexander Pope and Lancelot 'Capability' Brown. Sweeping valley with magnificent views of the City of Bath, Palladian bridge and lakes. Restoration of the garden continues. New interpretation panels detailing the history and ongoing restoration of Prior Park. All visitors must use public transport as there is no car park. For further details 01225 833422 or 24 hour information line 09001 335242 (60p per minute). Prior Park College, a co-educational school, operates from the mansion (not NT).

Location: OS Ref. ST760 632. Frequent bus service from City Centre. Badgerline 2 & 4.

Open: Feb - Nov: daily except Tues (open BH Tue, 4 Jun); Dec & Jan 2003: Fri - Sun (closed 25/26 Dec & 1 Jan 2003). Times: 11am - 5.30pm or dusk if earlier.

Admission: Adult: £4, Child £2. All visitors who produce a valid bus or train ticket will receive £1 off admission. NT members will receive a £1 voucher.

♿ Grounds. WC. Braille guide. 🅿 None. ▣ ✖ ❄ ▽ Tel for details.

THE ROMAN BATHS & PUMP ROOM

See page 231 for full page entry.

STEMBRIDGE TOWER MILL ⚜

High Ham, Somerset TA10 9DJ

Tel: 01458 250818 **www**.nationaltrust.org.uk

Owner: The National Trust   **Contact:** The Administrator

The last thatched windmill in England, dating from 1822 and in use until 1910.

Location: OS Ref. ST432 305. 2m N of Langport, ½ m E of High Ham.

Open: 24 Mar - 30 Sept: Sun, Mon & Wed, 2 - 5pm.

Admission: Adult £2, Child £1. Arrangements may be made for coach/school groups.

ℹ️ No WC. 🅿 Limited. ✖

STOKE-SUB-HAMDON PRIORY ⚜

North Street, Stoke-sub-Hamdon Somerset TA4 6QP

Tel: 01985 843600 **www**.nationaltrust.org.uk

Owner/Contact: The National Trust

A complex of buildings, begun in the 14th century for the priests of the chantry chapel of St Nicholas, which is now destroyed.

Location: OS Ref. ST473 174. ½ m S of A303. 2m W of Montacute between Yeovil and Ilminster.

Open: 23 Mar - 3 Nov: daily, 10am - 6pm or dusk if earlier. Only Great Hall open.

Admission: Free.

ℹ️ No WC. 🅿 Limited. ✖

TINTINHULL GARDEN ⚜

FARM STREET, TINTINHULL, SOMERSET BA22 9PZ

www.nationaltrust.org.uk

Tel: 01935 822545 **e-mail:** wtifxs@smtp.ntrust.org.uk

Owner: The National Trust   **Contact:** The Head Gardener

A delightful formal garden, created in the 20th century around a 17th century manor house. Small pools, varied borders and secluded lawns are neatly enclosed within walls and clipped hedges and there is also an attractive kitchen garden.

Location: OS Ref. ST503 198. 5m NW of Yeovil, ½ m S of A303, on E outskirts of Tintinhull.

Open: 23 Mar - 29 Sept: Wed - Sun, 12 noon - 6pm (open BH Mon & Tue 4 Jun).

Admission: Adult £3.80, Child £1.80. No reduction for groups.

♿ Grounds. Braille guide. ▣ 🅵 By arrangement. 🅿 Limited. ✖

TREASURER'S HOUSE ⚜

Martock, Somerset TA12 6JL

Tel: 01935 825801 **www**.nationaltrust.org.uk

Owner/Contact: The National Trust

A small medieval house, recently refurbished by The Trust. The two-storey hall was completed in 1293 and the solar block is even earlier.

Location: OS Ref. ST462 191. 1m NW of A303 between Ilminster and Ilchester.

Open: 24 Mar - 30 Sept: Sun - Tue, 2 - 5pm. Only medieval hall, wall paintings and kitchen are shown.

Admission: Adult £2, Child £1. Groups by prior appointment.

ℹ️ No WC. 🅿 Limited for cars. None for coaches & trailer caravans.

WELLS CATHEDRAL

Cathedral Green, Wells, Somerset BA5 2UE

Tel: 01749 674483 **Fax:** 01749 677360

Owner: The Chapter of Wells   **Contact:** Mr John Roberts

Fine medieval Cathedral. The West front with its splendid array of statuary, the Quire with colourful embroideries and stained glass, Chapter House and astronomical clock should not be missed.

Location: OS Ref. ST552 458. In Wells, 20m S from both Bath & Bristol.

Open: Apr - Sept: 10am - 7pm; Oct - Mar: 10am - 6.15pm; Jul & Aug: 10am - 8.30pm.

Admission: Suggested donation: Adult £4.50, Child/Student £1.50, OAP £3. Photo permit £2.

WESTBURY COLLEGE GATEHOUSE ⚜

College Road, Westbury-on-Trym, Bristol

Tel: 01985 843600 **www**.nationaltrust.org.uk

Owner: The National Trust   **Contact:** Rev G M Collins

The 15th century gatehouse of the College of Priests (founded in the 13th century) of which John Wyclif was a prebend.

Location: OS Ref. ST572 775. 3m N of the centre of Bristol. Just E of main street.

Open: Access by key only, to be collected by prior written or telephone appointment (0117 962 1536). Rev. G M Collins, The Vicarage, 44 Eastfield Road, Westbury-on-Trym, Bristol BS9 4AG.

Admission: Adult £1.10, Child 50p.

🅿 Limited. ✖ ❄

BOWOOD HOUSE & GARDENS 🏛

CALNE

www.bowood.org.co.uk

Bowood is the family home of the Marquis and Marchioness of Lansdowne. Begun c1720 for the Bridgeman family, the house was purchased by the 2nd Earl of Shelburne in 1754 and completed soon afterwards. Part of the house was demolished in 1955, leaving a perfectly proportioned Georgian home, over half of which is open to visitors. Robert Adam's magnificent Diocletian wing contains a splendid library, the laboratory where Joseph Priestley discovered oxygen gas in 1774, the orangery, now a picture gallery, the Chapel and a sculpture gallery in which some of the famous Lansdowne Marbles are displayed.

Among the family treasures shown in the numerous exhibition rooms are Georgian costumes, including Lord Byron's Albanian dress; Victoriana; Indiana (the 5th Marquess was Viceroy 1888-94); and superb collections of watercolours, miniatures and jewellery.

The House is set in one of the most beautiful parks in England. Over 2,000 acres of gardens and grounds were landscaped by 'Capability' Brown between 1762 and 1768, and are embellished with a Doric temple, a cascade, a pinetum and an arboretum. The Rhododendron Gardens are open for six weeks from late April to early June. All the walks have seats.

Owner:
The Marquis of
Lansdowne

▶ **CONTACT**

The Administrator
Bowood House and
Gardens
Calne
Wiltshire SN11 0LZ

Tel: 01249 812102

Fax: 01249 821757

e-mail:
houseandgardens@
bowood.org

▶ **LOCATION**

OS Ref. ST974 700

From London M4/J17,
off the A4 between
Chippenham and
Calne.
Swindon 17m,
Bristol 26m,
Bath 16m.

Bus: to the gate,
1¹⁄₂ m through
park to House.

Rail: Chippenham
Station 5m.

Taxi: AA Taxis,
Chippenham 657777.

▶ **OPENING TIMES**

House & Garden
23 Mar - 3 Nov:
Daily
11am - 6pm or
dusk if earlier.

Rhododendron Walks
Late April to early June
(depending on flowering
season) for 6 weeks
11am - 6pm.

▶ **ADMISSION**

House & Garden

Adult	£6.05
Child (2-4yrs)	£3.00
Child (5-15yrs)	£3.85
OAP	£5.00
Groups (20+)	
Adult	£5.10
Child (2-4yrs)	£2.80
Child (5-15)	£3.35
OAP	£4.35

Rhododendron Walks

Adult	£3.30
Child (0-15yrs)	Free
OAP	£3.30

The charge for
Rhododendron Walks is
£2.30 if combined on same
day with a visit to Bowood
House & Gardens.

🎁 ℹ️ Receptions, film location, 2,000 acre park, 40 acre lake, 18-hole golf course and Country Club, open to all players holding a current handicap.

♿ Visitors may alight at the House before parking. WCs.

☕ Self-service snacks, teas etc.

🍴 The Restaurant (waitress-service, capacity 85). Parties that require lunch or tea should book in advance.

🚶 On request, groups can be given introductory talk, or for an extra charge, a guided tour. Tour time 1¹⁄₄ hrs. Guide sheets in French, German, Dutch, Spanish & Japanese.

🅿 1,000 cars, unlimited for coaches, 400 yds from house. Allow 2-3 hrs to visit house, gardens and grounds.

🖼 Welcome. Special guide books. Picnic areas. Adventure playground.

🚫

CORSHAM COURT

CORSHAM

www.touristnetuk.com/S0/corsham/index.htm

Owner:

J Methuen-
Campbell Esq

▶ CONTACT

Corsham Court
Corsham
Wiltshire SN13 0BZ

Tel/Fax: 01249 701610

▶ LOCATION

OS Ref. ST874 706

Corsham Court
is signposted
from the A4, approx.
4m W of Chippenham.
From Edinburgh, A1,
M62, M6, M5, M4,
8 hrs.
From London, M4,
2¹/₄ hrs.
From Chester,
M6, M5, M4, 4 hrs.

Motorway: M4/J17 9m.

Rail: Chippenham
Station 6m.

Taxi: 01249 715959.

Corsham Court is an Elizabethan house of 1582 and was bought by Paul Methuen in the mid-18th century, to house a collection of 16th and 17th century Italian and Flemish master paintings and statuary. In the middle of the 19th century, the house was enlarged to receive a second collection, purchased in Florence, principally of fashionable Italian masters and stone-inlaid furniture.

Paul Methuen (1723-95) was a great-grandson of Paul Methuen of Bradford-on-Avon and cousin of John Methuen, ambassador and negotiator of the Methuen Treaty of 1703 with Portugal which permitted export of British woollens to Portugal and allowed a preferential 33¹/₃ percent duty discount on Portuguese wines, bringing about a major change in British drinking habits.

The architects involved in the alterations to the house and park were Lancelot 'Capability' Brown in the 1760s, John Nash in 1800 and Thomas Bellamy in 1845-9. Brown set the style by retaining the Elizabethan Stables and Riding School, but

rebuilding the Gateway, retaining the gabled Elizabethan stone front and doubling the gabled wings at either end and inside, by designing the East Wing as Stateroom Picture Galleries. Nash's work has now largely disappeared, but Bellamy's stands fast, notably in the Hall and Staircase.

The State Rooms, including the Music Room and Dining Room, provide the setting for the outstanding collection of over 150 paintings, statuary, bronzes and furniture. The collection includes work by such names as Chippendale, the Adam brothers, Van Dyck, Reni, Rosa, Rubens, Lippi, Reynolds, Romney and a pianoforte by Clementi.

GARDENS

'Capability' Brown planned to include a lake, avenues and specimen trees such as the Oriental Plane now with a 200-yard perimeter. The gardens, designed not only by Brown but also by Repton, contain a ha-ha, herbaceous borders, secluded gardens, lawns, a rose garden, a lily pool, a stone bath house and the Bradford Porch.

▶ OPENING TIMES

Summer

20 March - 30 September
Daily except Mons but
including BH Mons
2 - 5.30pm
Last admission 5pm.

Winter

1 October - 19 March
Weekends only
2 - 4.30pm
Last admission 4pm.

Closed December.

NB: Open throughout the
year by appointment only
for groups of 15+.

▶ ADMISSION

House & Garden

Adult £5.00
Child (5-15yrs)....... £2.50
OAP £4.50

Groups
(includes guided tour - 1 hr)
Adult £4.50

Garden only

Adult £2.00
Child (5-15yrs)....... £1.00
OAP £1.50

ℹ️ Souvenir desk. No umbrellas, no photography.

🚗 Visitors may alight at the entrance to the property, before parking in the allocated areas.

☕ Refreshments organised by prior arrangement for groups (15+).

🚶 For up to 55. If requested the owner may meet the group. Tour time 1hr.

🅿️ 400 cars, 120 yards from the house. Coaches may park in Church Square. Coach parties must book in advance.

🐾 Available: rate negotiable. A guide will be provided.

🐕 Must be kept on leads in the garden.

❄️

LONGLEAT

WARMINSTER

www.longleat.co.uk

Owner:
Marquess of Bath

▶ **CONTACT**

Estate Office
Longleat
Warminster
Wiltshire BA12 7NW

Tel: 01985 844400
Fax: 01985 844885
e-mail: enquiries@
longleat.co.uk

▶ **LOCATION**

OS Ref. ST809 430

Just off the A36
between Bath &
Salisbury (A362
Warminster - Frome).
Just 2hrs from London
following M3, A303,
A36, A362 or
M4/J18/A46-A36.

Rail: Warminster Station
(5m) on the
Cardiff/Portsmouth line.
Westbury Station (12m)
on the Paddington/
Penzance line.
Taxi rank at Warminster
& Westbury Stations.

Air: Bristol Airport 30m.

The first glimpse of Longleat House nestling at the foot of rolling 'Capability' Brown landscaped grounds and alongside the lakes is a view that must not be missed. Widely regarded as one of the most beautiful stately homes open to the public and the best example of Elizabethan architecture in Britain, Longleat House is home to the 7th Marquess of Bath. Built by Sir John Thynne and substantially completed by 1580, Longleat House has been the home of the same family ever since. Many treasures are included within: paintings by Tintoretto and Wootton, exquisite Flemish tapestries, fine French furniture and elaborate ceilings by John Dibblee Crace incorporating paintings from the 'School of Titian'.

The Murals in the private apartments in the West Wing have been painted by the present Marquess and are fascinating and unique additions to the House. Incorporating a mixture of oil paints and sawdust these private works of art offer a unique insight into Lord Bath's personality and beliefs.

Apart from the ancestral home, Longleat has a wonderland of attractions to suit all ages… discover lions and tigers, monkeys and giraffe within their magnificent Safari Park parkland setting; get lost in the World's Longest Hedge Maze; voyage on the Safari Boats; solve the riddle of King Arthur's Mirror Maze and much, much more!

But Longleat doesn't stop there!… the House and grounds are used for gala dinners; product launches; car ride 'n' drives and company fun days or how about the special events programme with concerts, balloon festivals and equestrian events. Longleat regularly acts as a film location, whilst the Orangery is licensed for Civil wedding ceremonies.

LONGLEAT PASSPORT - includes all the following attractions:
Safari Park, Longleat House, Safari Boats, World's Longest Hedge Maze, King Arthur's Mirror Maze, Pets' Corner, Adventure Castle (including Blue Peter Maze NEW for 2002), Longleat Railway, VirtuaScope Motion Ride, Butterfly Garden, Postman Pat Village, Doctor Who Exhibition, Grounds & Gardens.

Rooms in Longleat House can be hired for conferences, gala dinners and product launches. Extensive parkland for car launches, ride n' drives, company fun days, marquee based events, concerts, balloon festivals, equestrian events, caravan rallies & fishing. Film location.

Licensed.

Cellar Café (capacity 80). Groups must book. From 3 course meals to cream teas, sandwiches & snacks. Traditional Wiltshire Fare. Not open all year.

Individuals & Groups (max 20; 15 for Murals). Booking essential for Murals.

Ample.

Welcome with 1 teacher free entry per 8 children. GNVQ talks and packs available on request. Booking essential. Education sheets.

In grounds, on leads.

Orangery. ❄

Tel for details.

▶ **OPENING TIMES**

House: 1 January -
15 March: Weekends &
school holidays only.
16 March - 31 December:
daily (except Christmas).
Easter - September: 10am -
5.30pm. Rest of year
guided tours at set times
between 11am - 3.30pm.

Safari Park: 16 March -
3 November: 10am - 4pm
(10am - 5pm on
weekends, BHs & school
holidays).

Other attractions:
16 March - 3 November:
11am - 5.30pm.

Note: last admission times
my be earlier in Mar, Sept,
Oct & Nov.

▶ **ADMISSION**

House & Grounds
Adult £9.00
Child (4 -16yrs) £6.00
OAP £6.00

Longleat Passport
(see left above photo)
Adult £15.00
Child (4 -14yrs).... £11.00
OAP £11.00
Groups (12+)
Adult £11.25
Child (4 -16yrs) £8.25
OAP £8.25

Special discounted rates for
groups of 12+.

CONFERENCE/FUNCTION

ROOM	SIZE	MAX CAPACITY
Great Hall	8m x 13m	150
Banqueting Suite	2 x (10m x 7m)	50
Green Library	7m x 13m	80

NTPL / Nick Meers

STOURHEAD

STOURTON

www.nationaltrust.org.uk

An outstanding example of the English landscape style of garden. Designed by Henry Hoare II and laid out between 1741 and 1780. Classical temples, including the Pantheon and Temple of Apollo, are set around the central lake at the end of a series of vistas, which change as the visitor moves around the paths and through the magnificent mature woodland with its extensive collection of exotic trees. The house, begun in 1721 by Colen Campbell, contains furniture by the younger Chippendale and fine paintings. King Alfred's Tower, an intriguing red-brick folly built in 1772 by Henry Flitcroft, is almost 50m high and gives breathtaking views over the estate. What's new in 2002: New restaurant, shop and plant centre, specialist guided tours of house on Thursdays from 28 Mar - 31 Oct, please book in advance. Education room open summer 2002. New colour souvenir guide to garden. New farm walk in walks leaflet.

Owner:
The National Trust

▶ **CONTACT**

The Estate Office
Stourton
Nr Warminster
BA12 6QD

Tel: 01747 841152

Fax: 01747 842005
(office hours only)

e-mail: wstest@
smtp.ntrust.org.uk

▶ **LOCATION**

OS Ref. ST778 341

At Stourton off the
B3092, 3m N of A303
(Mere)

NTPL / Nick Meers

 Exhibition in
Reception Buildings

♿ Wheelchair
accessible. Braille guide.

☕

🧍 Tour guides, by
arrangement.

🅿

🎭

❄

Tel for details.

▶ **OPENING TIMES**

Garden:
All year, daily, 9am - 7pm
or sunset if earlier.

House:
23 Mar - 3 Nov: daily,
except Thur & Fri (open
Good Fri), 12 noon -
5.30pm or dusk.

King Alfred's Tower:
23 Mar - 3 Nov: daily
except Mon (open BH
Mons). Times: Tue - Fri,
2 - 5.30pm; Sat, Sun & BH
Mons: 11.30am - 5.30pm
or dusk.

▶ **ADMISSION**

House & Garden:
Adult £8.70
Child £4.10
Family £20.50
Booked groups (15+)
by appointment: £8.20

House or Garden:
Mar - 3 Nov:
Adult £4.90
Child £2.70
Family £12.30
Booked groups £4.40

Garden only:
4 Nov - end Feb:
Adult £3.80
Child £1.85
Family £9.20
Booked groups: £3.60

King Alfred's Tower:
Adult £1.65
Child 85p
Family £4.10

WILTON HOUSE 🏛

NR SALISBURY

www.wiltonhouse.com

The 17th Earl of Pembroke and his family live in Wilton House which has been their ancestral home for 450 years. In 1544 Henry VIII gave the Abbey and lands of Wilton to Sir William Herbert who had married Anne Parr, sister of Katherine, sixth wife of King Henry.

The Clock Tower, in the centre of the east front, is reminiscent of this part of the Tudor building which survived a fire in 1647. Inigo Jones and John Webb were responsible for the rebuilding of the house in the Palladian style, whilst further alterations were made by James Wyatt from 1801.

The chief architectural features are the magnificent 17th century state apartments (including the famous Single and Double Cube rooms) and the 19th century cloisters.

The house contains one of the finest art collections in Europe, with over 230 original paintings on display, including works by Van Dyck, Rubens, Joshua Reynolds and Brueghel. Also on show are Greek and Italian statuary, a lock of Queen Elizabeth I's hair, Napoleon's despatch case, and Florence Nightingale's sash.

The visitor centre houses a dynamic introductory film (narrated by Anna Massey), the reconstructed Tudor kitchen and the Estate's Victorian laundry. The house is set in magnificent landscaped parkland, bordered by the River Nadder which is the setting for the majestic Palladian Bridge. The current Earl of Pembroke is a keen gardener who has created four new gardens since succeeding to the title in 1969 including the North Forecourt Garden, Old English Rose Garden, Water and Cloister Gardens.

Owner:
The Earl of Pembroke

▶ CONTACT

Sally Salmon
The Estate Office
Wilton House
Wilton
Salisbury   SP2 0BJ

Tel: 01722 746720
Fax: 01722 744447
e-mail:
tourism@
wiltonhouse.com

▶ LOCATION

OS Ref. SU099 311

3m W of Salisbury on the A30.

Rail: Salisbury Station 3m.

Bus: Every 10 mins from Salisbury, Mon - Sat.

Taxi: Sarum Taxi 01722 334477.

CONFERENCE/FUNCTION

ROOM	SIZE	MAX CAPACITY
Double cube	60' x 30'	150
Exhibition Centre	50' x 40'	140
Film Theatre	34' x 20'	67

📷 ℹ️ Film location, fashion shows, product launches, equestrian events, garden parties, antiques fairs, concerts, vehicle rallies. No photography in house. French, German, Spanish, Italian, Japanese and Dutch information.

🍽 Exclusive banquets.

♿ Excellent access. Visitors may alight at the entrance. WCs.

🍴 Licensed. Self-service restaurant open 10.30am - 5pm. Groups must book. Hot lunches 12 noon - 2pm.

🚶 By arrangement.

🅿️ 200 cars and 12 coaches. Free coach parking. Group rates (min 15), meal vouchers, drivers' lounge.

👤 Teachers' handbook for National Curriculum. EFL students welcome. Free preparatory visit for group leaders.

🐕 Guide dogs only. ❄️

▶ OPENING TIMES

Summer
27 Mar - 27 October
Daily: 10.30am - 5.30pm

Last admission 4.30pm.

Winter
Closed, except for private parties by prior arrangement.

▶ ADMISSION

Summer

House, Grounds & Exhibition

Adult	£9.25
Child (5 - 15yrs)	£5.00
Child (2 - 5yrs)	£1.00
OAP/Student	£7.50
Family (2+2)	£22.00

Groups (15+)

Adult	£6.00
Child	£4.00
School group	£4.00

Grounds only

Adult	£4.00
Child	£3.00

Season Tickets

Grounds only
.... (from) £24.00

Inclusive... (from) £44.00

Winter
Prices on application.

🎭 **SPECIAL EVENTS**

MAR 1 - 3
25th Annual Antiques Fair.

JUL 13
Classical Firework Proms Night.

NTPL / David Norton

NT/Wessex region

AVEBURY MANOR & GARDEN, AVEBURY STONE CIRCLE ✄ ♯
& ALEXANDER KEILLER MUSEUM
AVEBURY, Nr MARLBOROUGH, WILTSHIRE SN8 1RF

Tel: 01672 539250 **e-mail:** wavgen@smtp.ntrust.org.uk

Owner: The National Trust   **Contact:** The Property Manager

Avebury Manor & Garden: A much-altered house of monastic origin, the present buildings date from the early 16th century, with notable Queen Anne alterations and Edwardian renovation by Col Jenner. The topiary and flower gardens contain medieval walls, ancient box and numerous 'rooms'. The Manor House is occupied and furnished by private tenants, who open a part of it to visitors. Owing to restricted space, timed tickets may be in operation at busy times. Following periods of prolonged wet weather it may be necessary to close the garden.

Avebury Stone Circle (above left): One of the most important Megalithic monuments in Europe, this 28 1/2 acre site with stone circles enclosed by a ditch and external bank, is approached by an avenue of stones.

Alexander Keiller Museum: The investigation of Avebury Stone Circle was largely the work of Alexander Keiller in the 1930s. He put together one of the most important prehistoric archaeological collections in Britain which can be seen at the Museum. The New Barn Gallery Exhibition – Avebury 6000 Years of Mystery, opened in Spring 2001. The development of the Avebury landscape and the story of

the people who discovered it is told, using interactive displays and CD ROMs, housed in the spectacular 17th century thatched barn.

Location: OS Ref. SU101 701 (Avebury Manor). OS Ref. SU102 699 (Stone Circle). OS Ref. SU100 699 (Alexander Keiller Museum). 6m W of Marlborough, 1m N of the A4 on A4361 & B4003.

Open: Avebury Manor: House: 31 Mar - 30 Oct: Tue, Wed, Sun & BH Mons, 2 - 5.30pm, last admission 5pm or dusk. Garden: 29 Mar - 6 Nov: daily except Mon & Thur (open BH Mons), 11am - 5.30pm or dusk. **Stone Circle:** all year, daily. **Alexander Keiller Museum & Barn Gallery Exhibition** (above right): 1 Apr - 31 Oct: daily, 10am - 6pm or dusk; 1 Nov - 31 Mar: 10am - 4pm. Closed 24/25 Dec.

Admission: Avebury Manor: House & Garden: Adult £3.60, Child £1.80. Groups: Adult £3.30, Child £1.60. Garden only: Adult £2.70, Child £1.30. Groups: Adult £2.40, Child £1.10. **Stone Circle:** Free. **Alexander Keiller Museum:** (including Barn Gallery): Adult £4, Child £2, Family (2+3) £10, Family (1+3) £7. EH members Free. ⓘNo WC. ▢Alexander Keiller Musuem. ▣Avebury Manor. ℙLimited. ✖No dogs in house, guide dogs only in garden (Avebury Manor). ✻ Stone Circle & Avebury Manor.

BOWOOD HOUSE & GARDENS ⬛   *See page 239 for full page entry.*

BRADFORD-ON-AVON TITHE BARN ♯
Bradford-on-Avon, Wiltshire

Tel: 0117 975 0700

Owner: English Heritage   **Contact:** South West Regional Office

A magnificent medieval stone-built barn with a slate roof and wooden beamed interior.

Location: OS173 Ref. ST824 604. 1/4 m S of town centre, off B3109.

Open: Daily, 10.30am - 4pm. Closed 25 Dec.

Admission: Free.

BROADLEAS GARDENS
Devizes, Wiltshire SN10 5JQ

Tel: 01380 722035

Owner: Broadleas Gardens Charitable Trust   **Contact:** Lady Anne Cowdray

10 acres full of interest, notably The Dell, where the sheltered site allows plantings of magnolias, camellias, rhododendrons and azaleas.

Location: OS Ref. SU001 601. Signposted SW from town centre at S end of housing estate, (coaches must use this entrance) or 1m S of Devizes on W side of A360.

Open: Apr - Oct: Sun, Weds & Thurs, 2 - 6pm or by arrangement for groups.

Admission: Adult £3, Child (under 12yrs) £1, Groups (10+) £2.50.

CORSHAM COURT ⬛   *See page 240 for full page entry.*

NT Photographic Library: George Wright

THE COURTS ✄
HOLT, TROWBRIDGE, WILTSHIRE BA14 6RR
www.nationaltrust.org.uk

Tel: 01225 782340 **e-mail:** wcoaxh@smtp.ntrust.org.uk

Owner: The National Trust   **Contact:** Head Gardener

One of Wiltshire's best-kept secrets, the English garden style at its best, full of charm and variety. There are many interesting plants and an imaginative use of colour surrounding water features, topiary and herbaceous borders. Complemented by an arboretum with natural planting of spring bulbs. What's new in 2002: tearoom and garden exhibition in the house to open during season, please telephone for details.

Location: OS Ref. ST861 618. 3m SW of Melksham, 3m N of Trowbridge, 2 1/2 m E of Bradford-on-Avon, on S side of B3107.

Open: 24 Mar - 13 Oct: daily except Sats, 12 noon - 5.30pm. Out of season by appointment only.

Admission: Adult £4, Child £2. Groups by arrangement with Head Gardener.

ⓘNo WC. ℙLimited. ✖

✻ Open All Year Index
◁ ◁ ◁ pgs 44-48

GREAT CHALFIELD MANOR

Melksham, Wiltshire SN12 8NJ

Tel: 01225 782239 **Fax:** 01225 783379 **www**.nationaltrust.org.uk

Owner: The National Trust   **Contact:** The Tenant

A charming manor house enhanced by a moat and gatehouse and with beautiful oriel windows and a great hall. Completed in 1480, the manor and gardens were restored earlier last century (c1905 - 1911) by Major R Fuller, whose family live here and manage the property. The garden, designed by Alfred Parsons, to compliment the Manor, has been replanted.

Location: OS Ref. ST860 633. 3m SW of Melksham via Broughton Gifford Common.

Open: 2 Apr - 31 Oct: Tue - Thur, guided tours only at 12.15, 2.15, 3, 3.45 & 4.30pm. The tours take 45 mins and numbers are limited to 25. Visitors arriving during a tour can visit the adjoining parish church and garden first. Note: Group visits are welcome on Fris & Sats (not BHs) by written arrangement with Mrs Robert Floyd. Organisers of coach parties should allow 2 hours because of limits on numbers in the house.

Admission: £4, no reductions for children and groups.

Grounds. Obligatory. Limited.

HEALE GARDENS

HEALE HOUSE, MIDDLE WOODFORD, SALISBURY, WILTSHIRE SP4 6NT

Tel: 01722 782504

Owner: Mr & Mrs Guy Rasch   **Contact:** Mrs Maureen Taylor

First winner of Christie's/HHA Garden of the Year award. Grade I Carolean Manor House where King Charles II hid during his escape in 1651. In January great drifts of snowdrops and aconites bring early colour and the promise of spring. the garden provides a wonderfully varied collection of plants, shrub, musk and other roses, growing in the formal setting of clipped hedges and mellow stonework. Particularly lovely in spring and autumn is the water garden surrounding an authentic Japanese Tea House and Nikko Bridge which create an exciting focus in this part of the garden. The specialist Plant Centre has unusual and rare plants, many propagated here, also old garden tools, old garden books, baskets, etc.

Location: OS Ref. SU125 365. 4m N of Salisbury on Woodford Valley road between A345 and A360.

Open: All year: daily except Mon (open BH Mons). Snowdrop Suns: 3 & 10 Feb.

Admission: Adult £3.25, Child (5-15) £1.50 (under 5s Free). Booked groups (20-60): Adult £3, Child £1.50.

Partial. Guide dogs only.

HAMPTWORTH LODGE

HAMPTWORTH, LANDFORD, SALISBURY, WILTSHIRE SP5 2EA

Tel: 01794 390215 **Fax:** 01794 390700

Owner/Contact: Mr N J M Anderson

Rebuilt Jacobean manor house standing in woodlands on the edge of the New Forest. Grade II* family house with period furniture including clocks. The Great Hall has an unusual roof construction. There is a collection of prentice pieces and the Moffatt collection of contemporary copies. Garden also open.

Location: OS Ref. SU227 195. 10m SE of Salisbury on road linking Downton on Salisbury/Bournemouth Road (A338) to Landford on A36, Salisbury - Southampton.

Open: 28 Mar - 30 Apr: 2.15 - 5pm except Suns. Coaches, by appointment only, 1 Apr - 30 Oct: except Suns.

Admission: £3.50, Child (under 11yrs) Free. Groups by arrangement.

Ground floor & grounds.

THE KING'S HOUSE

Salisbury & South Wiltshire Museum

65 The Close, Salisbury, Wiltshire SP1 2EN

Tel: 01722 332151 **Fax:** 01722 325611 **www**.salisburymuseum.org.uk

e-mail: museum@salisburymuseum.freeserve.co.uk

Owner: Occupied by Salisbury & South Wiltshire Museum Trust

    Contact: P R Saunders

Location: OS Ref. SU141 295. In Salisbury Cathedral Close, W side, facing cathedral.

Open: All year: Mon - Sat: 10am - 5pm. Suns in Jul & Aug: 2 - 5pm.

Admission: Adult £3.50, Child £1, Conc. £2.30, Groups £2.30.

Stourhead

NTPL / Nick Meers

Website Information ◁ ◁ ◁ pg 39

NT Photographic Library

LACOCK ABBEY, FOX TALBOT MUSEUM & VILLAGE ✻

LACOCK, CHIPPENHAM, WILTSHIRE SN15 2LG

www.nationaltrust.org.uk

Tel: 01249 730227 (Abbey) 01249 730459 (Museum) **Fax:** 01249 730501

Owner: The National Trust   **Contact:** The Property Manager

Founded in 1232 and converted into a country house c1540, the fine medieval cloisters, sacristy, chapter house and monastic rooms of the abbey have survived largely intact. The handsome stable courtyard has half-timbered gables, a clockhouse, brewery and bakehouse. Victorian rose garden and a woodland garden boasting a fine display of spring flowers and magnificent trees. The Fox Talbot Museum commemorates the achievements of William Fox Talbot, a previous resident of the Abbey and inventor of the modern photographic negative. The village, which dates from the 13th century and has many limewashed half-timbered and stone houses, featured in the TV and film productions of *Pride & Prejudice*, *Moll Flanders* and *Emma*. The Abbey was featured in *Harry Potter*.

Location: OS Ref. ST919 684. In the village of Lacock, 3m N of Melksham, 3m S of Chippenham just E of A350.

Open: Museum, Cloisters & Garden: 16 Mar - 3 Nov: daily, 11am - 5.30pm (closed Good Fri). Abbey: 30 Mar - 3 Nov: daily 1 - 5.30pm (closed Tues & Good Fri, open BH 4 Jun). Museum: winter weekends, closed 21 - 29 Dec. Tel for details.

Admission: Abbey, Museum, Cloisters & Garden: Adult £6.20, Child £3.40, Family £16.80. Groups: Adult £5.70, Child £2.90. Garden, Cloisters & Museum only: Adult £4, Child £2.40, Family £11.30. Abbey & Garden only: Adult £5, Child £2.80, Family £12.70.

🖸 ♿ Braille guides. ⬛ ✖ ✱ ⬜ Tel for details.

LITTLE CLARENDON ✻

Dinton, Salisbury, Wiltshire SP3 5DZ

Tel: 01985 843600 (Regional Office)   www.nationaltrust.org.uk

Owner: The National Trust   **Contact:** The Regional Office

A Tudor house, altered in the 17th century and with a 20th century Catholic chapel. The three principal rooms on the ground floor are open to visitors and furnished with vernacular oak furniture.

Location: OS Ref. SU015 316. ¼ m E of Dinton Church. 9m W of Salisbury.

Open: 1 Apr - 28 Oct:, Sat, 10am - 1pm, Mon, 1 - 5pm.

Admission: £2, no reductions.

ℹ️No WC, no pushchairs or prams, no coaches. ♿Unsuitable. 🅿️At Dinton Post Office.

LONG HALL GARDENS

Stockton, Warminster, Wiltshire BA12 0SE

Tel: 01985 850424   **Owner/Contact:** N H Yeatman-Biggs Esq

4 acres of gardens. Long Hall Nursery is adjacent.

Location: OS Ref. ST982 381. Stockton 7m SE of Warminster, off A36, W of A303 Wylye interchange.

Open: The gardens will be closed during 2002 except to groups by appointment, Mar - Aug.

Admission: Please contact for details.

LONGLEAT 🏛   *See page 241 for full page entry.*

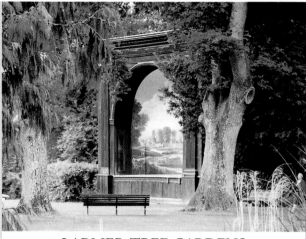

LARMER TREE GARDENS

RUSHMORE ESTATE, TOLLARD ROYAL, SALISBURY, WILTSHIRE SP5 5PT

www.rushmore-estate.co.uk

Tel: 01725 516228 **Fax:** 01725 516449 **e-mail:** larmer.tree@rushmore-estate.co.uk

Owner: Pitt-Rivers Trustees   **Contact:** Emma Chambers

General Augustus Pitt Rivers created these extraordinary 11-acre pleasure grounds in 1880. They contain a unique collection of buildings including a Roman temple, open-air theatre, colonial style tea pavilion and Nepalese rooms. Beautifully laid out gardens with mature trees, laurel hedges rides and stunning views of the Cranborne Chase. Concerts every Sunday throughout the summer.

Location: OS Ref. ST943 169. 2m S Tollard Royal.

Open: Garden only: 31 Mar - 31 Oct: daily except Sats and July, 11am - 6pm. Tearoom & Shop: 31 Mar - 31 Oct: Sun & BH Mon, also Wed - Fri, 1 May - 30 Sept. Closed Sats and July.

Admission: Adult £3.75, Child £2.50 (under 5yrs Free), Conc./Groups £3, Family (2+4) £12.50.

🖸 ✱ ⬜ ⬛Licensed. ℹ️By arrangement. 🅿️ ⬛By arrangement. ✖ ▲ ⬜ Tel for details.

LYDIARD PARK

LYDIARD TREGOZE, SWINDON, WILTSHIRE SN5 3PA

www.swindon.gov.uk

Tel: 01793 770401 **Fax:** 01793 877909

Owner: Swindon Borough Council   **Contact:** The Keeper

Lydiard Park, ancestral home of the Bolingbrokes, is Swindon's treasure. Set in rolling lawns and woodland this beautifully restored Georgian mansion contains the family's furnishings and portraits, exceptional plasterwork, rare 17th century window and room devoted to 18th century society artist Lady Diana Spencer. Exceptional monuments such as the 'Golden Cavalier' in adjacent church.

Location: OS Ref. SU104 848. 4m W of Swindon, 1½ m N of M4/J16.

Open: House: Mon - Fri, 10am - 1pm, 2 - 5pm, Sat & school summer holidays, 10am - 5pm, Sun, 2 - 5pm. Nov - Feb: early closing at 4pm. Grounds: all day, closing at dusk. Victorian Christmas decorations throughout December.

Admission: Adult £1.40, Child 70p (reviewed April 2002). Groups by appointment.

ℹ️No photography in house. 🖸 ♿ ⬛ ℹ️By arrangement. 🎧 🅿️ ⬛ ✖In grounds on leads. ✱ ⬜ Tel for details.

THE MERCHANT'S HOUSE 🏠
132 HIGH STREET, MARLBOROUGH, WILTSHIRE SN8 1HN

www.themerchantshouse.co.uk

Tel: 01672 511491 **Fax:** 01672 511491 **e-mail:** manager@themerchantshouse.co.uk

Owner: Marlborough Town Council **Contact:** Michael Gray

Situated in Marlborough's world-famous High Street, The Merchant's House is one of the finest middle-class houses in England. Its well-preserved Panelled Chamber was completed in 1656. Both the Dining Room and Great Staircase display recently uncovered 17th century wall paintings which have aroused much expert interest. Leased to the Merchant's House (Marlborough) Trust.

Location: OS Ref. SU188 691. N side of High Street, near Town Hall.

Open: Easter - Sept: Fri - Sun, 11am - 4pm.

Admission: Adult £2, Child 50p. Booked groups (10-30): Adult £3, Child £1.

ℹ️ Photography only by arrangement. 📷 🎦 By arrangement.
🅿️ Outside house, also in Hillier's Yard. 🦮 Guide dogs only. ⬛ Tel for details.

NT Photographic Library

NEWHOUSE 🏛️
REDLYNCH, SALISBURY, WILTSHIRE SP5 2NX

Tel: 01725 510055 **Fax:** 01725 510284

Owner: George & June Jeffreys **Contact:** Mrs Jeffreys

A brick, Jacobean 'Trinity' House, c1609, with two Georgian wings and a basically Georgian interior. Home of the Eyre family since 1633.

Location: OS184 Ref. SU218 214. 9m S of Salisbury between A36 & A338.

Open: 1 - 28 Mar, 1 - 4 Apr & 8 - 12 Apr: Mon - Fri, 2 - 5.30pm.

Admission: Adult £3.50, Child £2.50, Conc. £3.50. Groups (15+): Adult £3, Child £2.50, Conc. £3.

ℹ️ No photography in house, except at weddings. 🎦 ♿ Unsuitable.
🎦 By arrangement. 🅿️ Limited for coaches. 🦮 Guide dogs only. ⬛

MOMPESSON HOUSE 🌿
THE CLOSE, SALISBURY, WILTSHIRE SP1 2EL

www.nationaltrust.org.uk

Tel: 01722 335659 **e-mail:** wmpkxr@smtp.ntrust.org.uk

Owner: The National Trust **Contact:** The Property Manager

Fine Queen Anne town house containing high quality 18th century furniture, ceramics and textiles. Also the renowned Turnbull Collection of 18th century drinking glasses. Tranquil walled garden with many perfumed plants. Garden tea room serves home-made cakes. Featured in *Sense and Sensibility*. New short guide to house available.

Location: OS Ref. SU142 295. On N side of Choristers' Green in Cathedral Close, near High Street Gate.

Open: 23 Mar - 29 Sept: Sat - Wed (open Good Fri), 12 noon - 5.30pm.

Admission: Adult £3.90, Child £1.95. Groups: £3.40. Garden only: 80p.

📷 ♿ Ground floor & grounds. Braille guide. WC. ⬛ 🎦 By arrangement. 🦮

NORRINGTON MANOR
Alvediston, Salisbury, Wiltshire SP5 5LL

Tel: 01722 780367 **Fax:** 01722 780667

Owner/Contact: T Sykes

Built in 1377 it has been altered and added to in every century since, with the exception of the 18th century. Only the hall and the 'undercroft' remain of the original. It is currently a family home and the Sykes are only the third family to own it.

Location: OS Ref. ST966 237. Signposted to N of Berwick St John and Alvediston road (half way between the two villages)

Open: By appointment in writing.

Admission: A donation to the local churches is asked for.

♿ Unsuitable. 🎦 By arrangement. 🅿️ Limited for cars, none for coaches. 🦮 ❄️

OLD SARUM ⚜️
Castle Road, Salisbury, Wiltshire SP1 3SD

Tel: 01722 335398 **Fax:** 01722 416037 **e-mail:** customers@english-heritage.org.uk

www.english-heritage.org.uk

Owner: English Heritage **Contact:** The Head Custodian

Built around 500BC by the Iron Age peoples, Old Sarum is the former site of the first cathedral and ancient city of Salisbury. A prehistoric hillfort in origin, Old Sarum was occupied by the Romans, the Saxons, and eventually the Normans who made it into one of their major strongholds, with a motte-and-bailey castle built at its centre. Old Sarum eventually grew into one of the most dramatic settlements in medieval England as castle, cathedral, bishop's palace and thriving township. When the new city we know as Salisbury was founded in the early 13th century the settlement faded away. With fine views of the surrounding countryside, Old Sarum is an excellent special events venue.

Location: OS184 Ref. SU138 327. 2m N of Salisbury off A345.

Open: 29 Mar - 31 Oct: daily, 10am - 6pm (5pm in Oct). 1 Nov - 31 Mar: daily 10am - 4pm. Closed 24 - 26 Dec & 1 Jan.

Admission: Adult £2, Child £1, Conc. £1.50. 15% discount for groups (11+).

📷 ♿ Grounds. ⬛ 🅿️ 🦮 In grounds, on leads. ❄️ ⬛ Tel for details.

OLD WARDOUR CASTLE

Nr TISBURY, WILTSHIRE SP3 6RR

www.english-heritage.org.uk

Tel/Fax: 01747 870487 **e-mail:** customers@english-heritage.org.uk

Owner: English Heritage **Contact:** The Custodian

In a picture-book setting, the unusual hexagonal ruins of this 14th century castle stand on the edge of a beautiful lake, surrounded by landscaped grounds which include an elaborate rockwork grotto.

Location: OS184 Ref. ST939 263. Off A30 2m SW of Tisbury.

Open: 29 Mar - 31 Oct: daily, 10am - 6pm (5pm in Oct). 1 Nov - 31 Mar: Wed - Sun, 10am - 4pm. Closed for lunch 1 - 2pm. Closed 24 - 26 Dec & 1 Jan.

Admission: Adult £2.50, Child £1.30, Conc. £1.90. 15% discount for groups (11+).

⬚ ♿ Grounds. ▣ ⌂ **P** ⬚ In grounds, on leads. ✳ ▣ Tel for details.

PHILIPPS HOUSE & DINTON PARK ✤

Dinton, Salisbury, Wiltshire SP3 5HJ

Tel: 01985 843600 **www.**nationaltrust.org.uk

Owner: The National Trust **Contact:** The Regional Office

A neo-Grecian house by Jeffry Wyatville, completed in 1820. Principal rooms on ground floor are open and possess fine Regency furniture. Lovely walks in surrounding parkland.

Location: OS Ref. SU004 319. 9m W of Salisbury, N side of B3089, 1/2 m W of Little Clarendon. Car park off St Mary's Road next to church.

Open: House: 1 Apr - 28 Oct: Mons, 1 - 5pm, Sats, 10am - 1pm. Park: All year: daily (may be closed for one day in Aug for music event).

Admission: House £3. Dinton Park Free.

ℹ️ No WC. ♿ House suitable, Park limited. Braille guide.

PYTHOUSE

TISBURY, WILTSHIRE SP3 6PB

www.cha.org.uk

Tel: 01747 870210 **Fax:** 01747 871786

Owner: Country Houses Association **Contact:** The Administrators

Set under a well-wooded hill with panoramic views of the south Wilshire countryside. Pythouse dates from 1725 and boasts an Ice-House and attractive 18th century orangery. The stone elevation was added in 1805 and two wings in 1891. Pythouse has been converted into apartments for active retired people.

Location: OS Ref. SJ909 285. 2 1/2 m W of Tisbury, 4 1/2 m N of Shaftesbury. Rail: Tisbury 2 1/2 m.

Open: 1 May - 30 Sept: Wed & Thur, 2 - 5pm.

Admission: Adult £3, Child Free. Groups by arrangement.

☐ ⬚ ▣ 1 single & 1 double with bathroom, CHA members only.

THE PETO GARDEN AT IFORD MANOR 🏛

BRADFORD-ON-AVON, WILTSHIRE BA15 2BA

www.ifordmanor.co.uk

Tel: 01225 863146 **Fax:** 01225 862364

Owner/Contact: Mrs E A J Cartwright-Hignett

This unique Grade I Italian-style garden is set on a romantic hillside beside the River Frome. Designed by the Edwardian architect Harold A Peto, who lived at Iford Manor from 1899 - 1933, the garden has terraces, a colonnade, cloister, casita, statuary, evergreen planting and magnificent rural views. Renowned for its tranquillity and peace, the Peto Garden won the 1998 HHA/Christie's Garden of the Year Award.

Location: OS Ref. ST800 589. 7m SE of Bath via A36, signposted Iford. 2m SW of Bradford-on-Avon via Westwood.

Open: Apr & Oct: Suns only & Easter Mon, 2 - 5pm. May - Sept: Tue - Thur, Sats, Suns & BH Mons, 2 - 5pm. Coaches by appointment at other times. Children under 10yrs not admitted at weekends.

Admission: Adult £3, Child (10-16yrs)/OAP £2.50. Picnic area by River Frome.

▣ Teas (May-Aug: Sats & Suns, 2 - 5pm). **P** Coaches by appointment. ✳

Steve Day

SALISBURY CATHEDRAL

33 THE CLOSE, SALISBURY SP1 2EJ

www.salisburycathedral.org.uk

Tel: 01722 555120 **Fax:** 01722 555116 **e-mail:** visitors@salcath.co.uk

Owner: The Dean & Chapter   **Contact:** Visitor Services

Salisbury Cathedral is a building of world importance. Set within the elegant splendour of the Cathedral Close it is probably the finest medieval building in Britain. Built in one phase from about 1220 to 1258 Britain's highest spire (123m/404ft) was added a generation later. Also, the best preserved Magna Carta, Europe's oldest working clock and a unique 13th century frieze of bible stories in the octagonal Chapter House. Boy and girl choristers sing daily services which follow a tradition of worship that goes back over 750 years. Join a tower tour climbing 332 steps to the base of the spire, and marvel at the medieval craftsmanship and the magnificent views.

Location: OS Ref. SU143 295. S of City. M3, A303, A30 from London or A36.

Open: All year: Every Sunday 7.15am - 6.15pm. 1 Jan - 9 Jun/1 Sept - 31 Dec: 7.15am - 6.15pm. 10 Jun - 31 Aug (excluding Sun): 7.15am - 8.15pm.

Admission: Donation: Adult £3.50, Child £2, Conc. £2.50, Family (2+2) £8.

⬚ ⬚ ⬚ ⬚ Licensed. ⬚ ⬚ By arrangement. **P** In city centre. ⬚
⬚ In grounds, on leads. ⬚ ⬚ Tel for details.

STOURHEAD ⬚   *See page 242 for full page entry.*

STOURTON HOUSE FLOWER GARDEN

Stourton, Warminster, Wiltshire BA12 6QF

Tel: 01747 840417

Owner/Contact: Mrs E Bullivant

Four acres of peaceful, romantic garden.

Location: OS Ref. ST780 340. A303, 2m NW of Mere next to Stourhead car park. Follow blue signs.

Open: Apr - end Nov: Weds, Thurs, Suns, and BH Mons, 11am - 6pm. Plants & dried flowers for sale during the winter on weekdays.

Admission: Please contact property for details. Group guided tours by appointment.

WESTWOOD MANOR ⬚

Bradford-on-Avon, Wiltshire BA15 2AF

Tel: 01225 863374 **www**.nationaltrust.org.uk

Owner: The National Trust   **Contact:** The Tenant

A 15th century stone manor house, altered in the early 17th century, with late gothic and Jacobean windows and fine plasterwork. There is a modern topiary garden. Note: Westwood Manor is administered for The National Trust by the tenant.

Location: OS Ref. ST813 589. 1½ m SW of Bradford-on-Avon, in Westwood village, beside the church.

Open: 31 Mar - 29 Sept: Suns, Tues & Weds, 2 - 5pm.

Admission: £4. No reduction for groups or children.

⬚No WC. ⬚Unsuitable. **P** Limited. ⬚

WILTON HOUSE ⬚   *See page 243 for full page entry.*

STONEHENGE ⬚

AMESBURY, WILTSHIRE SP4 7DE

www.english-heritage.org.uk

Tel: 01980 624715 (Information Line)

Owner: English Heritage

The mystical and awe-inspiring stone circle at Stonehenge is one of the most famous prehistoric monuments in the world, designated by UNESCO as a World Heritage Site. Stonehenge's orientation on the rising and setting sun has always been one of its most remarkable features. Whether this was simply because the builders came from a sun-worshipping culture, or because – as some scholars have believed – the circle and its banks were part of a huge astronomical calendar, remains a mystery. Visitors to Stonehenge can discover the history and legends which surround this unique stone circle, which began over 5,000 years ago, with a complimentary three part audio tour available in 9 languages (subject to availability).

Location: OS Ref. SU123 422. 2m W of Amesbury on junction of A303 and A344/A360.

Open: 16 - 23 Oct: 9.30am - 5pm, 24 Oct - 15 Mar: 9.30am - 4pm, 16 Mar - 31 May & 1 Sept - 15 Oct: 9.30am - 6pm. 1 Jun - 31 Aug: 9am - 7pm. Closed 24 - 26 Dec & 1 Jan. Last recommended adm. is ½ hr before advertised closing times and the site will be closed promptly 20mins after the advertised closing times.

Admission: Adult £4.40, Child £2.20, Conc. £3.30. Family (2+3) £11. Groups (11+) 10% discount.

⬚ ⬚ Tel for details.

Audley End House

Eastern Region

English Heritage Photo Library / Jeremy Richards

Audley End

"…A house of the Earl of Suffolk, which makes a noble appearance like a town, so many towers and buildings of stone within a park which is walled round. It's built round three courts, there are 30 great and little towers on the top of a great cupilow in the middle, there are 750 rooms in the house … it's altogether a stately palace…"

Celia Fiennes on visiting Audley End in 1697

English Heritage Photo Library
Jonathan Bailey

English Heritage Photo Library

On seeing Audley End today a visitor could easily be forgiven for thinking that this magnificent Jacobean mansion appears untouched by time – however looks can be deceptive. Now in the care of English Heritage, Audley End's history is a chequered one. The many turrets and great mullioned windows are only the remaining third part of the Jacobean 'prodigy' palace built by Thomas Howard, 1st Earl of Suffolk, between 1603 and 1616.

Still a spectacularly lavish building, it was built with the express intention of providing accommodation for the visiting King, James I. As Lord Chamberlain of the Royal Household and later Lord Treasurer, Suffolk regarded it as vital that he possess a suitable residence by which to promote his personal power. Within four years of its completion the 1st Earl had fallen from favour, accused of corruption, but the house still remained the talk of the aristocracy, so much so that Charles II purchased it in 1668 from the 3rd Earl and stayed there whenever he went to the races at Newmarket.

Returned to the Suffolks after the King's death, Audley End was modified on several later occasions, most notably in 1753 when one of the Suffolks pulled down the east wing to reduce his overheads. In the second half of the 18th century the interiors were given a new lease of life by Robert Adam, who redecorated the principal living rooms. There is also a splendid sequence of first floor reception rooms, decorated in the 1820s in the romantic 'Jacobean' character for the 3rd Lord Braybrooke. The house is a treasure trove of beautiful paintings, furniture and silver, acquired through inheritance or marriage, all with an interesting history.

Audley End has always been a gem, but over the last 10 years English Heritage have put enormous energy and imagination into restoring the garden. With the beautiful surround parkland by 'Capability' Brown acting as a backdrop, the visitor can now wander through the parterre garden inspired by the 17th century French parterres, with the shrubberies relating to contemporary (1830) interiors. The flower garden, with 170 beds, is a mass of colour throughout the season – roses paeonies, astrantias, violas and hypericums all vie for compliments. The walled kitchen garden, known as Lady Portsmouth's garden, has just been restored and is run as a working organic kitchen garden. The 170 foot long vine house is worth a special visit.

Somehow English Heritage's work on the gardens at Audley End – a 21st Century Garden opened this year – has put heart and life back into this house. So enjoy your visit to Audley End for both its mixture of styles and history, and for its beautiful garden which enhances the sheer swagger of its wonder Jacobean façade. ⊹

For further details about *Audley End* see entry on page 261.

English Heritage Photo Library / Anne Hyde

WOBURN ABBEY

WOBURN

www.woburnabbey.co.uk

Owner:
Trustees of Bedford Estates

▶ CONTACT

William Lash
Woburn Abbey
Woburn
Bedfordshire MK17 9WA

Tel: 01525 290666
Fax: 01525 290271

e-mail: enquiries@
woburnabbey.co.uk

▶ LOCATION

OS Ref. SP965 325

On A4012, midway between M1/J13, 3m, J14, 6m and the A5 (turn off at Hockliffe). London approx. 1hr by road (43m).

Rail: London Euston to Leighton Buzzard, Bletchley/Milton Keynes. Kings Cross Thameslink to Flitwick.

Air: Luton 14m. Heathrow 39m.

Set in a beautiful 3,000 acre deer park, Woburn Abbey has been the home of the Dukes of Bedford for nearly 400 years. It is now lived in by the present Duke's heir, the Marquess of Tavistock and his family. One of the most important private art collections in the world can be seen here, including paintings by Van Dyck, Cuyp, Gainsborough, Reynolds and Velazquez. In the Venetian Room there are 21 views of Venice by Canaletto. The collection also features French and English 18th century furniture and silver. The tour of the Abbey covers three floors, including vaults, where the fabulous Sèvres dinner service presented to the 4th Duke by Louis XV of France is on display.

The deer park has nine species of deer, roaming freely. One of these, the Père David, descended from the Imperial Herd of China, was saved from extinction at Woburn and is now the largest breeding herd of this species in the world. In 1985 22 Père David were given by the Family to the People's Republic of China and these are now successfully re-established in their natural habitat and number several hundred.

We carry out catering ourselves with banqueting, conferences, receptions and company days out our specialities in the beautiful setting of the Sculpture Gallery, overlooking the Private Gardens. It is also a popular choice for wedding receptions and we hold a Civil Wedding Licence.

There are extensive picnic areas. Events are held in the Park throughout the summer including the Woburn Garden Show, Craft Fair and the annual fly-in of the de Havilland Moth Club. The 40-shop Antique Centre is probably the most unusual such centre outside London.

| 🖼 | Suitable for fashion shows, product launches, filming & company 'days out'. Use of parkland and garden. No photography in House. |

🛍 Two shops.

🍴 Conferences, exhibitions, banqueting, luncheons, dinners in the Sculpture Gallery, Lantern & Long Harness rooms.

♿ Wheelchairs in the Abbey by prior arrangement (max. 8 per group).

☕ Group bookings in Sculpture Gallery. Flying Duchess Pavilion Coffee Shop.

🍽 Licensed.

🎧 🚶 By arrangement, max 15. Tours in French, German & Dutch at an additional charge of £10.00 per guide. Audio tape tour available – £1pp. Lectures on the property, its contents, gardens and history can be arranged.

🅿 Ample. Free.

🏫 Welcome. Special programme on request. Cost: £2.50pp (group rate).

🐕 In park on leads, and guide dogs in house.

🔔 Civil Wedding Licence. ❄

🎭 Tel for details.

▶ OPENING TIMES

1 January - 23 March
Abbey: weekends only
11am - 4pm*
Deer Park:
Daily, 10.30am - 4pm

24 March - 29 September
Abbey:
Mon - Sat: 11am - 4pm*
Sun & BHs: 11am - 5pm
Deer Park:
Mon - Sat: 10am - 4.30pm
Sun & BHs: 10am - 4.45pm

5 - 27 Oct
Abbey: weekends only
11am - 5pm*
Deer Park:
10.30am - 5pm

Abbey: closed
28 Oct - end Dec

Antiques Centre:
All year, daily
(except 24 - 26,
31 Dec 2000 & 1 Jan,
24 - 26 Dec 2001).

*last entry time

▶ ADMISSION

Woburn Abbey
(Prices incl. Private Apts)
Adult £8.00
Child (12 - 16yrs)...... £3.50
OAP £7.00
Group rates & family tickets available.

**Grounds &
Deer Park only**
Car £6.00
Motorcycle............. £2.00
Coaches.................. Free
Other £1.00

Reduced rates apply when Private Apartments are in use by the family.

CONFERENCE/FUNCTION

ROOM	SIZE	MAX CAPACITY
Sculpture Gallery	130' x 25'	400
		220 (sit-down)
Lantern Rm	24' x 21'	100

BROMHAM MILL & GALLERY
Bromham, Bedfordshire MK43 8LP
Tel: 01234 824330
Owner: Bedfordshire County Council   **Contact:** Sally Wileman
Working water mill on River Ouse. Flour milling.
Location: OS Ref. TL010 506. Location beside the River Ouse bridge on N side of the former A428, 2½ m W of Bedford.
Open: Wed - Sat, 1 - 5pm. Suns, 10.30am - 5pm. Last entry 30 mins before closing.
Admission: Adult £2.50, Conc. £1.50, Family £5. Wed - Sat: half price.

BUSHMEAD PRIORY ⚌
Colmworth, Bedford, Bedfordshire MK44 2LD
Tel: 01234 376614   **Regional Office:** 01223 582700
Owner: English Heritage   **Contact:** The Custodian
A rare survival of the medieval refectory of an Augustinian priory, with its original timber-framed roof almost intact and containing interesting wall paintings and stained glass.
Location: OS Ref. TL115 607. On unclassified road near Colmworth; off B660, 2m S of Bolnhurst. 5m W of St. Neots (A1).
Open: Jul - Aug weekends & BHs only: 10am - 6pm. Closed 1 - 2pm.
Admission: Free.

🅿 ✖

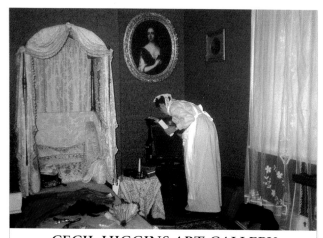

CECIL HIGGINS ART GALLERY
CASTLE LANE, BEDFORD MK40 3RP
www.cecilhigginsartgallery.org

Tel: 01234 211222   **Fax:** 01234 327149   **e-mail:** chag@bedford.gov.uk
Owner: Bedford Borough Council & Trustees of Gallery   **Contact:** The Gallery
A recreation of an 1880s home, with superb examples of 19th century decorative arts. Room settings include items from the Handley-Read collection and the famous Gothic bedroom containing works by William Burges. Adjoining gallery housing renowned collections of watercolours, prints and drawings (exhibitions changed regularly), ceramics, glass and lace. Situated in pleasant gardens near the river embankment.
Location: OS Ref. TL052 497. Centre of Bedford, just off The Embankment. E of High St.
Open: Tue - Sat, 11am - 5pm (last admission 4.45pm). Sun & BH Mons, 2 - 5pm. Closed Mons, Good Fri & 25/26 Dec.
Admission: Adults £2.10, Conc. Free (includes visit to Bedford Museum).
ℹ Photography in house by arrangement. 📷 🍵 By arrangement. ♿
🍽 Self-service coffee bar. 🐕 By arrangement. 🅿 None. ◼
✖ Guide dogs only. ✳ 🎫 Tel for details.

HOUGHTON HOUSE ⚌
Ampthill, Bedford, Bedfordshire
Tel: 01223 582700 (Regional Office)
Owner: English Heritage   **Contact:** The East of England Regional Office

Reputedly the inspiration for "House Beautiful" in Bunyan's "Pilgrim's Progress", the remains of this early 17th century mansion still convey elements which justify the description, including work attributed to Inigo Jones.
Location: OS Ref. TL039 394. 1m NE of Ampthill off A421, 8m S of Bedford, then by footpath to NE.
Open: Any reasonable time.
Admission: Free.

MOOT HALL
Elstow Green, Church View, Elstow, Bedford
Tel: 01234 266889
Owner: Bedfordshire County Council
Timber framed market hall.
Location: OS Ref. TL048 475. 1m from Bedford, signposted from A6.
Open: Apr - Oct: Tue, Wed, Thur, Sat, Sun & BHs: 2 - 5pm.
Admission: Adult £1, Conc. 50p.

STOCKWOOD PERIOD GARDENS
Farley Hill, Luton, Bedfordshire
Tel: 01582 546721
Owner: Luton Borough Council   **Contact:** Siobhan Kirrane
Includes Knot, Medieval, Victorian and Italian gardens.
Location: OS Ref. TL085 200. 1¼ m SW of Luton town centre by Farley Road B4546.
Open: Apr - Oct: Tue - Sun & BHs, 10am - 5pm. Nov - Mar: Sat - Sun, 10am - 4pm.
Admission: Free.

SWISS GARDEN
Old Warden Park, Bedfordshire
Tel: 01767 627666   **Fax:** 01767 627443   **e-mail:** swiss.garden@dial.pipex.co.uk
Operated By: Bedfordshire County Council
Laid out in the early 1800s and steeped in the indulgent romanticism of the time, Swiss Garden combines all the elements of high fashion: formal walks and vistas, classical proportions, tiny thatched buildings, woodland glades and, hidden away, a fairytale grotto with a brilliant glazed fernery, magnificent trees and a network of ponds and bridges. Shuttleworth Mansion, home of the family that owned Swiss Garden, is open on a number of days during the year.
Location: OS Ref. TL150 447. 1½ m W of Biggleswade A1 roundabout, signposted from A1 and A600. Approached from Shuttleworth Mansion, Old Warden Park.
Open: Mar - Sept: Sun & BHs, 10am - 6pm. Weekdays & Sat: 1 - 6pm. Jan, Feb & Oct: Suns & New Year's Day, 11am - 3pm. Last admission ¼ hr before closing. Groups at any time on request.
Admission: Adult £3, Conc. £2, Family £8. Season ticket available. Special rates for groups and guided tours.
🎫 ♿ 🍵 Catering. 🍽 Refreshments adjacent. 🅿 ✖ 🏠 ✳

WOBURN ABBEY
See page 256 for full page entry.

WREST PARK GARDENS ⚌
SILSOE, LUTON, BEDFORDSHIRE MK45 4HS
www.english-heritage.org.uk

Tel: 01525 860152
Owner: English Heritage   **Contact:** The Custodian
Over 90 acres of wonderful gardens originally laid out in the early 18th century, including the Great Garden. During the 18th and 19th centuries the formal parterre was introduced together with marble fountains, the Bath House and the vast Orangery, built by the Earl de Grey. The gardens form a delightful backdrop to the house, built in the style of an 18th century French chateau.
Location: OS153, Ref. TL093 356. ¾ m E of Silsoe off A6, 10m S of Bedford.
Open: 1 Apr - 31 Oct: Weekends and BHs only, 10am - 6pm (5pm in Oct). Last admission 1hr before closing time.
Admission: Adult £3.80, Child £1.90, Conc. £2.90. 15% discount for groups (11+). Family Ticket £9.50.
♿ ◼ 🎫 Tel for details.

ANGLESEY ABBEY ✹

LODE, CAMBRIDGE, CAMBRIDGESHIRE CB5 9EJ

www.nationaltrust.org.uk/angleseyabbey

Tel/Fax: 01223 811200 **email:** aayusr@smtp.ntrust.org.uk

Owner: The National Trust   **Contact:** The Property Manager

Dating from 1600, the house, built on the site of an Augustinian priory, contains the famous Fairhaven collection of paintings and furniture. Surrounded by an outstanding 100 acre garden and arboretum, with a wonderful display of hyacinths in spring and magnificent herbaceous borders and a dahlia garden in summer. A watermill in full working order is demonstrated on the first Saturday in each month.

Location: OS Ref 154. TL533 622. 6m NE of Cambridge on B1102, signs from A14.

Open: House: 27 Mar - 27 Oct: Wed - Sun & BH Mons (also open 4 Jun): 1 - 5pm. Garden: 27 Mar - 30 Jun: Wed - Sun (also open 4 Jun); 1 Jul - 1 Sept: daily (late opening Thurs to 8pm); 4 Sept - 27 Oct: Wed - Sun, 10.30am - 5.30pm. Winter Season: 30 Oct - 22 Dec, 1 Jan - 23 Mar 2003: Wed - Sun, 10.30am - 4.30pm or dusk if earlier. Lode Mill: As garden except 1 - 4.30pm; Winter Season: Sats & Suns only, 11am - 4pm. Note: closed Good Fri. Mar - Oct last admission to House & Mill 4.30pm (3.30pm in winter season). Timed entry to house on Suns & BH Mons.

Admission: House & garden: £6.25, Family discounts. Groups: £5.25. Garden & Mill only: £3.85 (groups £3.35). Group visit information pack (no groups Suns & BH Mons).

🄾 ♿Partial. 🍴 Licensed. 🐕 In park, on leads. ✱ 🖳 Tel for details.

OLIVER CROMWELL'S HOUSE

29 St Mary's Street, Ely, Cambridgeshire CB7 4HF

Tel: 01353 662062 **Fax:** 01353 668518 **e-mail:** tic@eastcambs.gov.uk

Owner: East Cambridgeshire District Council   **Contact:** Mrs A Smith

The former home of the Lord Protector.

Location: OS Ref. TL538 803. N of Cambridge, ¼ m W of Ely Cathedral.

Open: 1 Oct - 31 Mar, Mon - Sat, 10am - 5pm, Suns, 12 noon - 4pm. 1 Apr -30 Sept: daily, 10am - 5.30pm.

Admission: Adult £3.50. Joint ticket: Adult £9, Conc. £8. (2001 prices.)

DENNY ABBEY & THE FARMLAND MUSEUM ⌘

Ely Road, Chittering, Waterbeach, Cambridgeshire CB5 9TQ

Tel: 01223 860489

Owner: English Heritage/Managed by the Farmland Museum Trust

                                    Contact: The Custodian

What at first appears to be an attractive stone-built farmhouse is actually the remains of a 12th century Benedictine abbey which, at different times, also housed the Knights Templar and Franciscan nuns. Founded by the Countess of Pembroke.

Location: OS Ref. TL495 684. 6m N of Cambridge on the E side of the A10.

Open: 1 Apr - 31 Oct: daily, 12 noon - 5pm..

Admission: Adult £3.60, Child £1.40, Conc. £2.60, Family £8.50.

DOCWRA'S MANOR GARDEN ⌂

Shepreth, Royston, Hertfordshire SG8 6PS

Tel: 01763 261473 **Fax:** 01763 260677

Owner: Mrs Faith Raven   **Contact:** Peter Rocket

Extensive garden around building dating from the 18th century.

Location: OS Ref. TL393 479. In Shepreth via A10 from Royston.

Open: All year: Weds & Fris, 10am - 4pm & 1st Sun in month from Apr - Oct: 2 - 5pm.

Admission: £3.

CAMBRIDGE UNIVERSITY BOTANIC GARDEN

BATEMAN STREET, CAMBRIDGE CB2 1JF

www.botanic.cam.ac.uk

Tel: 01223 336265 Fax: 01223 336278 **e-mail:** enquiries@botanic.cam.ac.uk

Owner: University of Cambridge   **Contact:** Mrs B Stacey, Admin. Secretary

40 acres of outstanding gardens with lake and glasshouses, near the centre of Cambridge, incorporating nine National collections, including Geranium and Fritillaria. Café and shop in the Gilmour building.

Location: OS Ref. TL453 573. 1m S of Cambridge city centre, off A1309 (Trumpington Rd).

Open: Daily (except Christmas & New Year holiday), 10am - 6pm (Summer), 10am - 5pm (Spring & Autumn) 10am - 4pm (Winter). Glasshouses: daily, 10am - 3.45pm. Tours by arrangement.

Admission: Admission charged weekdays Mar - Oct inclusive, plus weekends & BHs all year.

🄾 ♿Grounds. WCs. 🖳 🅿 Street/Pay & Display. 🐕 Guide dogs only. ✱

H Rice

ELTON HALL

Nr PETERBOROUGH PE8 6SH

Tel: 01832 280468 **Fax:** 01832 280584 **e-mail:** office@eltonhall.com

Owner: Mr & Mrs W Proby   **Contact:** The Administrator

Elton Hall, the home of the Proby family for over 350 years is a fascinating mixture of styles. Every room contains treasures, magnificent furniture and fine paintings from the early 15th century. The library is one of the finest in private hands and includes Henry VIII's prayer book. The beautiful gardens have been carefully restored, with the addition of a new gothic Orangery to celebrate the Millennium.

Location: OS Ref. TL091 930. Close to A1 in the village of Elton, off A605 Peterborough - Oundle road.

Open: 3/4 Jun: Weds. Jul & Aug: Wed, Thur & Sun and 26 Aug (BH Mon). 2 - 5pm. Private groups by arrangement on weekdays Apr - Sept.

Admission: Hall & Gardens: Adult £5, Child (accompanied) Free. Gardens only: Adult £3, Child (under 16, accompanied) Free.

ℹNo photography in house. 🄾 ✱ 🍴 ♿Garden suitable. 🖳 🎥Obligatory. 🅿 🖳 🐕Guide dogs in gardens only. 🖳 Tel for details.

ISLAND HALL

GODMANCHESTER, CAMBRIDGESHIRE PE29 2BA

Tel: 020 7491 3724   **Fax:** 020 7355 4006   **e-mail:** cvp@cvpdesigns.com

Owner: Mr Christopher & Lady Linda Vane Percy   **Contact:** Mr C Vane Percy

An important mid 18th century mansion of great charm, owned and restored by an award-winning interior designer. This family home has lovely Georgian rooms, with fine period detail, and interesting possessions relating to the owners' ancestors since their first occupation of the house in 1800. A tranquil riverside setting with formal gardens and ornamental island forming part of the grounds in an area of Best Landscape. Octavia Hill wrote *"This is the loveliest, dearest old house, I never was in such a one before."*

Location: OS Ref. TL244 706. Centre of Godmanchester, Post Street next to car park. 1m S of Huntingdon, 15m NW of Cambridge A14.

Open: Groups only, by arrangement: May - Jul & Sept.

Admission: (30+) Adult £3.50, (15-30 persons) Adult £4. Under 15 persons, min charge £60 per group (sorry but no children under 13).

♻Unsuitable. ■ Home made teas. ❊

THE COLLEGES OF OXFORD & CAMBRIDGE UNIVERSITIES

see page 148 for listing

KIMBOLTON CASTLE

Kimbolton, Huntingdon, Cambridgeshire PE28 0EA

Tel: 01480 860505   **Fax:** 01480 861763   **e-mail:** domb@kimboltonschool.demon.co.uk
www.kimbolton.cambs.sch.uk

Owner: Governors of Kimbolton School   **Contact:** Mrs A Janes

A late Stuart house, an adaptation of a 13th century fortified manor house, with evidence of Tudor modifications. The seat of the Earls and Dukes of Manchester 1615 - 1950, now a school. Katharine of Aragon died in the Queen's Room - the setting for a scene in Shakespeare's Henry VIII. A minor example of the work of Vanbrugh and Hawksmoor; Gatehouse by Robert Adam; the Pellegrini mural paintings on the Staircase, in the Chapel and in the Boudoir are the best examples in England of this gifted Venetian decorator.

Location: OS Ref. TL101 676. 7m NW of St Neots on B645.

Open: 31 Mar/1 Apr, 2/3 Jun, 25/26 Aug, 2 - 5pm.

Admission: Adult £2.50, Child/Conc. £1.50. Groups by arrangement throughout the year, including evenings.

▣ ♻Unsuitable. ■ ⓘBy arrangement. Ⓞ ■ 🐕On leads in grounds. ▲❊

KING'S COLLEGE

KING'S PARADE, CAMBRIDGE CB2 1ST

www.kings.cam.ac.uk

Tel/Fax: 01223 331212   **e-mail:** derek.buxton@kings.cam.ac.uk

Owner: Provost and Fellows   **Contact:** Mr D Buxton

Visitors are welcome, but remember that this is a working college. Please respect the privacy of those who work, live and study here. The Chapel is often used for services, recordings, broadcasts, etc, and ideally visitors should check before arriving. Recorded message for services, concerts and visiting times: 01223 331155.

Location: OS Ref. TL447 584.

Open: Out of term: Mon - Sat, 9.30am - 4.30pm. Sun, 10am - 5pm. In term: Mon - Fri: 9.30am - 3.30pm. Sat: 9.30am - 3.15pm. Sun: 1.15 - 2.15pm, 5 - 5.30pm.

Admission: Adult £3.50, Child (12-17yrs)/Student (ID required)/OAP £2.50. Child (under 12 & accompanied) Free (only as part of family unit).

ⓘNo photography inside Chapel. Conferences. ☐ ▣By arrangement. ♻ ⓘBy arrangement. ⓄNone. 🐕Guide dogs only. ❊

LONGTHORPE TOWER ♯

Thorpe Rd, Longthorpe, Cambridgeshire PE1 1HA

Tel: 01733 268482

Owner: English Heritage   **Contact:** The Custodian

The finest example of 14th century domestic wall paintings in northern Europe showing a variety of secular and sacred objects. The tower, with the Great Chamber that contains the paintings, is part of a fortified manor house. Special exhibitions are held on the upper floor.

Location: OS Ref. TL163 983. 2m W of Peterborough just off A47.

Open: 1 Apr - 31 Oct: weekends & BHs only: 12 noon - 5pm.

Admission: Adult £1.70, Child 90p, Conc. £1.30.

❊

THE MANOR, HEMINGFORD GREY

HUNTINGDON, CAMBRIDGESHIRE PE28 9BN

www.greenknowe.co.uk

Tel: 01480 463134 **Fax:** 01480 465026 **e-mail:** diana_boston@hotmail.com

Owner: Mrs D S Boston   **Contact:** Diana Boston

Built about 1130 and reputedly the oldest continuously inhabited house in Britain. Made famous as 'Green Knowe' by the author Lucy Boston. Her patchwork collection is also shown. Four acre garden with topiary, old roses and herbaceous borders.

Location: OS Ref. TL290 706. Off A14, 3m SE of Huntingdon. 12m NW of Cambridge. Access is by a small gate on the riverside footpath.

Open: House: All year (except May), to individuals or groups by prior arrangement. May: guided tours at 11am & 2pm (booking advisable). Garden: All year, daily, 10am - 6pm (4pm in winter).

Admission: Adult £4, Child £1.50, OAP £3.50. Garden only: Adult £2, Child 50p.

ℹ️No photography in house. 📷 🚻 🛍️Locally, by arrangement. 🎫Obligatory. ■ 🅿️Disabled only. 🐕In garden, on leads. ✱

PETERBOROUGH CATHEDRAL

Chapter Office, Minster Precincts, Peterborough PE1 1XS

Tel: 01733 343342 **Fax:** 01733 552465 **www.peterborough-cathedral.org.uk**

Contact: Andrew Watson

'An undiscovered gem.' With magnificent Norman architecture a unique 13th century nave ceiling, the awe-inspiring West Front and burial places of two Queens to make your visit an unforgettable experience. Exhibitions tell the Cathedral's story. Tours by appointment of the cathedral, tower and roof, Deanery Garden or Precincts. Freshly prepared meals and snacks at Beckets Restaurant (advance bookings possible). Cathedral gift shop and Tourist Information Centre in Precincts.

Location: OS Ref. TL194 986. 4m E of A1, in City Centre.

Open: All year: Mon - Sat, 8.30am - 5.15pm. Suns, Services from 7.30am; visitors: 12 noon - 5.15pm.

Admission: No fixed charge – donations are requested.

ℹ️Visitors' Centre. 📷 ♿ 🍴 Mon - Sat. 🎫 By arrangement. 🅿️None. ■ 🐕 Guide dogs only. ✱

RAMSEY ABBEY GATEHOUSE ✤

Abbey School, Ramsey, Cambridgeshire PE17 1DH

Tel: 01263 738000 (Regional office) **www.**nationaltrust.org.uk/eastanglia

Owner: The National Trust   **Contact:** The Curator (in writing)

The remnants of a former Benedictine monastery, built on an island in the Fens. The late 15th century gatehouse is richly carved and contains an ornate oriel window.

Location: OS Ref. TL291 851. At SE edge of Ramsey at point where Chatteris road leaves B1096, 10m SE of Peterborough.

Open: 1 Apr - end Oct: daily, 10am - 5pm, other times by written application to curator.

Admission: Donation.

🅿️Limited. 🐕Guide dogs only.

PECKOVER HOUSE & GARDEN ✤

NORTH BRINK, WISBECH, CAMBRIDGESHIRE PE13 1JR

www.nationaltrust.org.uk/eastanglia

Tel/Fax: 01945 583463 **e-mail:** aprigx@smtp.ntrust.org.uk

Owner: The National Trust   **Contact:** The Property Manager

A town house, built c1722 and renowned for its very fine plaster and wood rococo decoration. The outstanding Victorian garden includes an orangery, summer-houses, roses, herbaceous borders, fernery, croquet lawn and Reed Barn tearoom.

Location: OS Ref. TF458 097. On N bank of River Nene, in Wisbech B1441.

Open: House: 23 Mar - 3 Nov & 4 Jun: Weds, Sats, Suns, Good Fri & BH Mons (also open Thurs in May, Jun, Jul & Aug), 1.30 - 4.30pm. Garden: 23 Mar - 3 Nov: Sat - Thur, 12.30 - 5pm. Groups welcome when house open & at other times by appointment.

Admission: Adult £4. Garden days: £2.50. Groups: £3.

🍴 ♿ Partial. 🛍️ 🎫 By arrangement. 🅿️Signposted. 🐕 ■ 📞 Tel for details.

WIMPOLE HALL & HOME FARM ✤

ARRINGTON, ROYSTON, CAMBRIDGESHIRE SG8 0BW

www.wimpole.org

Tel: 01223 207257 **Fax:** 01223 207838 **e-mail:** aweusr@smtp.ntrust.org.uk

Owner: The National Trust   **Contact:** The Property Manager

Wimpole is a magnificent country house built in 18th century style with a colourful history of owners. The Hall is set in recently restored formal gardens including parterres and a rose garden. Home Farm is a working farm and is the largest rare breeds centre in East Anglia.

Location: OS154. TL336 510. 8m SW of Cambridge (A603), 6m N of Royston (A1198).

Open: Hall: 23 Mar - 31 Jul & 3 Sept - 3 Nov: daily except Mon & Fri (open Good Fri & BH Mon); Aug: Tue - Sun (open BH Mons);10, 17 & 24 Nov, Sun only; 1 - 5pm, BH Mon, 11am - 5pm, closes 4pm after 27 Oct. Garden: as Farm. Park: dawn - dusk. Farm: 23 Mar - 30 Jun; 3 Sept - 3 Nov: daily except Mon & Fri (open Good Fri & BH Mon); Jul & Aug: Tue - Sun & BH Mon; Nov - Mar 2003: Sat & Sun (open Feb half-term week); 23 Mar - 3 Nov: 10.30am - 5pm; 5 Nov - Mar 2003, 11am - 4pm.

Admission: Hall: Adult £6.20, Child £2.80. Joint ticket with Home Farm: Adult £9, Child £4.50, Family £22. Garden: £2.50. Group rates (not Suns or BH Mons). Farm: Adult £4.90, Child (3yrs & up) £2.80. Discount for NT members (not Suns or BH Mons). Car park £2.

📷 ♿Partial. 🛍️ 🍴Licensed. 🎫 By arrangement. 🅿️ Limited & charged, NT members Free. ■ 🐕In park, on leads. 📞 Tel for details.

English Heritage Photographic Library

Owner:
English Heritage

▶ CONTACT

The General Manager
Audley End House
Audley End
Saffron Walden
Essex CB11 4JF

Tel: 01799 522842
Fax: 01799 521276

▶ LOCATION
OS Ref. TL525 382

1m W of Saffron
Walden on B1383,
M11/J8 & 9 northbound
only & J10.

Rail: Audley End 1¼ m.

AUDLEY END HOUSE & GDNS ⊞

SAFFRON WALDEN

Audley End was a palace in all but name. Built by Thomas Howard, Earl of Suffolk, to entertain King James I. The King may have had his suspicions, for he never stayed there; in 1618 Howard was imprisoned and fined for embezzlement.

Charles II bought the property in 1668 for £50,000, but within a generation the house was gradually demolished, and by the 1750s it was about the size you see today. There are still over 30 rooms to see, each with period furnishings.

The house and its gardens, including a 19th century parterre and rose garden, are surrounded by an 18th century landscaped park laid out by 'Capability' Brown.

Visitors can now also visit the working organic walled garden and purchase produce from its shop. Extending to nearly 10 acres the garden includes a 170ft long, five-bay vine house, built in 1802.

English Heritage Photographic Library

▶ OPENING TIMES

House

29 March - 30 September
Wed - Sun and BHs
12 noon - 5pm.
Last admission 4pm.

Grounds

29 March - 30 September
Wed - Sun and BHs
11am - 6pm.
Last admission 5pm.

House & Grounds

1 - 31 October
House: Wed - Sun,
(site closes 4pm), 11am -
3pm. Grounds: Wed - Fri,
11am - 4pm, last
admission 3pm.
Sat & Sun, 11am - 5pm.
Last admission 4pm.

House by pre-booked
guided tour:
29 Mar - 30 Sept:
Wed - Fri,
10am - 12 noon (extra
charge).

▶ ADMISSION
House & Grounds

Adult £6.95
Child (5 - 15yrs) *......£3.50
Conc.......................£5.20
Family (2+3)...........£17.40

Grounds only

Adult £4.00
Child(5 - 15yrs) *.......£2.00
Concessions............£3.00
Family (2+3)...........£10.00

* Under 5yrs Free.

Groups (11+)
15% discount.

ⓘ Open air concerts and other events.

♿ Ground floor and grounds.

🍴 Restaurant (max 50).

🏃 By arrangement for groups.

🅿 Coaches to book in advance, £5 per coach. Free entry for coach drivers and tour guides. One additional place for every extra 20 people.

🚌 School visits free if booked in advance. Contact the Administrator or tel 01223 582700 for bookings.

🐕 On leads only. 🎭 Tel for details.

Eastern - England

AUDLEY END HOUSE ⌗ & GARDENS

See page 261 for full page entry.

BOURNE MILL ✄

Colchester, Essex CO2 8RT

Tel: 01206 572422   **www.**nationaltrust.org.uk/eastanglia

Owner: The National Trust   **Contact:** The Custodian

Originally a fishing lodge built in 1591. It was later converted into a mill with a 4 acre mill pond. Much of the machinery, including the waterwheel, is intact.

Location: OS Ref. TM006 238. 1m S of Colchester centre, in Bourne Road, off the Mersea Road B1025.

Open: BH Suns & Mons only; also Suns & Tues in Jun, Jul & Aug, 2 - 5pm.

Admission: Adult £2. No reduction for groups.

🐕 Guide dogs only.

CHELMSFORD CATHEDRAL

New Street, Chelmsford, Essex CM1 1AT

Tel: 01245 294480   **Contact:** Mrs Bobby Harrington

15th century building became a Cathedral in 1914. Extended in 1920s, major refurbishment in 1980s with contemporary works of distinction and splendid new organs in 1994 and 1996.

Location: OS Ref. TL708 070. In Chelmsford.

Open: Daily: 8am - 5.30pm. Sun services: 8am, 9.30am, 11.15am and 6pm. Weekday services: 8.15am and 5.15pm daily. Holy Communion: Wed, 12.35pm & Thur, 10am. Tours by prior arrangement.

Admission: No charge but donation invited.

COLCHESTER CASTLE MUSEUM

14 Ryegate Road, Colchester, Essex CO1 1YG

Tel: 01206 282931/2   **Fax:** 01206 282925

Owner: Colchester Borough Council   **Contact:** Museum Resource Centre

The largest Norman Castle Keep in Europe with fine archaeological collections on show. May only be visited on an accompanied tour.

Location: OS Ref. TL999 253. In Colchester town centre, off A12.

Open: All year: Mon - Sat, 10am - 5pm, also Suns, 11am - 5pm.

Admission: Adult £3.90, Child/Conc. £2.60. Saver ticket: £10.50. Booked groups (20+): £3.40. Prices may increase from 1 Apr 2002.

CRESSING TEMPLE BARNS

Witham Road, Braintree, Essex CM7 8PD

Tel: 01376 584903   **Fax:** 01376 584864

Owner: Essex County Council   **Contact:** Mark Sweeting

Built by the Knights Templar in the 13th century, Cressing Temple has the finest remaining pair of medieval barns in Europe. Also an Elizabethan Granary, thatched cart lodge and Tudor walled garden featuring knot gardens, flowery mead, nosegay garden and physic plant area. Full Summer Events Programme.

Location: OS Ref. TL798 187. Signposted off B1018 between Witham and Braintree.

Open: Mar - Oct: Suns; May - Sept: Wed - Fri, 10.30am - 4.30pm.

Admission: Adult £3, Conc. £2. Groups (booked, 15+): Adult £2.70, Conc. £1.80.

📷 🍴 🧺 🍽 🎦 By arrangement. 🅿 🚫 🐕 In grounds, on leads. ▲

📺 Tel for details.

ESSEX SECRET BUNKER

Crown Building, Shrubland Road, Mistley, Manningtree, Essex CO11 1HS

Tel: 01206 392271   **Fax:** 01206 393847

e-mail: info@essexsecretbunker.com   **www.**essexsecretbunker.com

Owner: The Bunker Preservation Trust   **Contact:** The Curator

The huge concrete bunker half above and half below ground, gives a chilling insight into how 'Essex' stood ready for nuclear attack throughout the 40 years of the 'Cold War'. Cinemas, sound effects and historically accurate displays help you to explore the maze of passageways and rooms. Suitable for all the family.

Location: OS Ref. TM120 315. In Mistley near Manningtree on the B1352. Follow brown tourist signs from A120.

Open: 5 Jan - 24 Feb: Sat & Sun, 10.30am - 4.30pm. 2 Mar - 29 Sept: daily, 10.30am - 5pm (6pm Aug). Please telephone for Oct, Nov & Dec dates.

Admission: Adult £4.95, Child £3.75, OAP £4.45. Family (2+3) £15, 4 Adult/Senior Saver £16.50. Group discounts available (telephone for details). Booking required for: Curator's in-depth tours, schools/young persons visits (available all year).

ℹ️ Photography & video welcomed. 📷 🍴 🧺 Partial. WC. 🍽

🎦 Day & evening tours by arrangement. 🎧 🅿 🚫 🐕 Guide dogs only. ✳

FEERINGBURY MANOR

Coggeshall Road, Feering, Colchester, Essex CO5 9RB

Tel: 01376 561946

Owner/Contact: Mrs Giles Coode-Adams

Location: OS Ref. TL864 215. 1½ m N of A12 between Feering & Coggeshall.

Open: From 1st Thur in Apr to last Fri in Jul, Thur & Fri only, 8am - 4pm.

Admission: Adult £2.50, Child Free. In aid of National Gardens Scheme.

COPPED HALL

CROWN HILL, EPPING, ESSEX CM16 5HH

Tel: 020 7267 1679   **Fax:** 020 7482 0557

Owner: Copped Hall Trust   **Contact:** Alan Cox

Burnt-out 18th century Palladian mansion situated on ridge overlooking excellent landscaped park. Built adjacent to site of 16th century mansion where *'A Midsummer's Night Dream'* was first performed. Former elaborate gardens gradually being rescued from abandonment. Victorian ancillary building including stables and small racquets court. Very large early 18th century walled garden.

Location: OS Ref. TL433 016. 4m SW of Epping, N of M25.

Open: By appointment only.

Admission: Pre-arranged groups (20+) only: Adult £3, Child £1.

Partial. 🎦 Obligatory. 🅿 🚫 🐕 In grounds on leads. ✳

GARDENS OF EASTON LODGE 🏛

WARWICK HOUSE, EASTON LODGE, LITTLE EASTON, GT DUNMOW CM6 2BB

www.eastonlodge.co.uk

Tel/Fax: 01371 876979   **e-mail:** enquiries@eastonlodge.co.uk

Owner/Contact: Mr Brian Creasey

Beautiful gardens set in 25 acres. Horticultural associations from the 16th century to date. Visit the Italian gardens, currently undergoing restoration, designed by Harold Peto for 'Daisy' Countess of Warwick (Edward VII's mistress). In the dovecote, study the history of the house, garden and owners over 400 years. A peaceful and atmospheric haven! Millennium Project: Living yew and box sundial and Shakespeare border.

Location: OS Ref. TL593 240. 4m NW of Great Dunmow, off the B184 Dunmow to Thaxted road.

Open: Feb/Mar (snowdrops): daily. Easter - 31 Oct: Fri - Sun & BHs, 12 noon - 6pm or dusk if earlier. Groups at other times by appointment.

Admission: Adult £3.80, Child (3-12yrs) £1.50, Conc. £3.50. Group (20+) £3.50. Schools (20+) £1.50 per child, 1 teacher free per 10 children.

ℹ️ Exhibition & Study Centre in Dovecote. 🍴 🧺 Partial. WC. 🍽 Picnics.

🎦 By arrangement. 🅿 Limited for coaches. 🚫 🐕 In grounds on leads. ✳

📺 Tel for details.

GOSFIELD HALL

GOSFIELD, HALSTEAD, ESSEX CO9 1SF

www.cha.org.uk

Tel: 01787 472914 **Fax:** 01787 479551

Owner: Country Houses Association   **Contact:** The Administrators

Built in 1545, Gosfield Hall is steeped in history. Elizabeth I really slept here and Lady Catherine Grey arrived from the Tower of London! The house looks out onto a large lake and is shaped around a Tudor courtyard. Gosfield Hall has been converted into apartments for active retired people.

Location: OS Ref. TL788 297. On the A1037 between Braintree and Sible Hedingham. 2¹/₂ m SW of Halstead.

Open: 1 May - 30 Sept: Wed & Thurs, 2 - 5pm.

Admission: Adult £3, Child £1.50. Groups by arrangement.

⊤ ✖ 🏠1 single & 1 double with bathroom, CHA members only. ▲

HEDINGHAM CASTLE 🏰

CASTLE HEDINGHAM, Nr HALSTEAD, ESSEX CO9 3DJ

www.hedinghamcastle.co.uk

Tel: 01787 460261 **Fax:** 01787 461473 **e-mail:** hedinghamcastle@aspects.net

Owner: The Hon Thomas Lindsay   **Contact:** Mrs Diana Donoghue

Splendid Norman keep built in 1140 by the famous de Veres, Earls of Oxford. Visited by Kings Henry VII and VIII and Queen Elizabeth I and besieged by King John. Magnificent banqueting hall with minstrel's gallery and finest Norman arch in England. Beautiful grounds, peaceful woodland and lakeside walks. Beside medieval village with fine Norman church.

Location: OS Ref. TL787 358. On B1058, 1m off A1017 between Cambridge and Colchester.

Open: Week before Easter - end Oct: daily, 10am - 5pm.

Admission: Adult £4, Child £3, Conc. £3.50, Family (2+3) £14. Groups (20+): £3.50.

🔲 ⊤ 🚹Partial. 🖼 🎦By arrangement. 🅿 🔲 🐾In grounds, on leads. ▲ 🛡Tel for details.

GRANGE BARN, COGGESHALL 🍂

Coggeshall, Colchester, Essex CO6 1RE

Tel: 01376 562226 **www**.nationaltrust.org.uk/eastanglia

Owner: The National Trust   **Contact:** The Custodian

One of the oldest surviving timber-framed barns in Europe, dating from around 1140, and originally part of a Cistercian Monastery. It was restored in the 1980s by the Coggeshall Grange Barn Trust, Braintree District Council and Essex County Council. Features a small collection of farm carts and wagons.

Location: OS Ref. TL848 223. Signposted off A120 Coggeshall bypass. West side of the road southwards to Kelvedon.

Open: 31 Mar - 13 Oct: Tues, Thurs, Suns & BH Mons, 2 - 5pm.

Admission: £1.70. Joint ticket with Paycocke's £3.40.

🚹 🅿Coaches must book. 🐾Guide dogs only.

HARWICH MARITIME & LIFEBOAT MUSEUMS

Harwich Green, Harwich, Essex

Tel/Fax: 01255 503429 **e-mail:** theharwichsociety@quista.net

www.harwich-society.com

Owner: The Harwich Society   **Contact:** Mr Sheard

One housed in a disused lighthouse and the other in the nearby disused Victorian Lifeboat House, complete with full size lifeboat.

Location: OS Ref. TM263 325. On Harwich Green.

Open: 1 May - 31 Aug: daily, 10am - 1pm & 2 - 5pm. Groups by appointment at any time.

Admission: Adult 50p, Child Free (no unaccompanied children).

✳

HARWICH REDOUBT FORT

Main Road, Harwich, Essex

Tel/Fax: 01255 503429 **e-mail:** theharwichsociety@quista.net

www.harwich-society.com

Owner: The Harwich Society   **Contact:** Mr Sheard

180ft diameter circular fort built in 1808 to defend the port against Napoleonic invasion. Being restored by Harwich Society and part is a museum. Eleven guns on battlements.

Location: OS Ref. TM263 325. Rear of 29 Main Road.

Open: 1 May - 31 Aug: daily, 10am - 5pm. Sept - Apr: Suns only, 10am - 4pm. Groups by appointment at any time.

Admission: Adult £1, Child Free (no unaccompanied children).

✳

HYLANDS HOUSE

HYLANDS PARK, LONDON ROAD, CHELMSFORD CM2 8WQ

www.hylandshouse.gov.uk

Tel: 01245 355455/606812 **Fax:** 01245 250783/606970

Owner: Chelmsford Borough Council   **Contact:** Ceri Lowen

This beautiful Grade II listed villa, with its neo-classical exterior is surrounded by over 500 acres of parkland, including formal gardens. The house re-opened at Easter 1999 after a period of restoration work. The Library, Drawing Room and Saloon have been restored to their appearance in the early Victorian period. The Entrance Hall was restored to its Georgian origins in the 1995 restoration. It is possible to view the Victorian staircase, as yet unrestored. Restoration work is currently underway in the West Wing and Basement. There is an exhibition detailing the restoration work and the history of the house.

Location: OS Ref. TL681 054. 2m SW of Chelmsford. Signposted on A1016 near Chelmsford.

Open: All year: Suns, Mons & BHs, 11am - 6pm, except Christmas Day.

Admission: Adults £3, Child (12-16 yrs) £2, (under 12yrs) Free, Conc. £2. Groups: £3pp or £75 (whichever greater).

ℹNo photography in house. 🔲 ⊤ 🚹 🖼 Sun & Mon. 🎦By arrangement. 🅿Limited for coaches. 🔲 🐾In grounds. Guide dogs only in house. ▲ ✳ 🛡

INGATESTONE HALL 🏛

HALL LANE, INGATESTONE, ESSEX CM4 9NR

Tel: 01277 353010   **Fax:** 01245 248979

Owner: The Lord Petre   **Contact:** The Administrator

16th century mansion, set in 11 acres of grounds (formal garden and wild walk), built by Sir William Petre, Secretary of State to four Tudor monarchs, which has remained in the hands of his family ever since. The two Priests' hiding places can be seen, as well as the furniture, portraits and family memorabilia accumulated over the centuries.

Location: OS Ref. TQ653 986. Off A12 between Brentwood & Chelmsford. Take Station Lane at London end of Ingatestone High Street, cross level-crossing and continue for 1/2 m to SE.

Open: 30 Mar - 29 Sept: Sats, Suns & BH Mons, plus 24 Jul - 8 Sept: Wed - Fri, 1 - 6pm.

Admission: Adult £4, Child £2 (under 5yrs Free), Conc. £3.50. 50p per head discount for groups (20+).

ℹ️ No photography in house. 🔲 🚻 🚫Partial. 📷 🕤By arrangement. 🅿️ 🔲 🐕 Guide dogs only. 🚾Tel for details.

LAYER MARNEY TOWER 🏛

Nr COLCHESTER, ESSEX CO5 9US

www.layermarneytower.co.uk

Tel/Fax: 01206 330784   **e-mail:** info@layermarneytower.co.uk

Owner/Contact: Mr Nicholas Charrington

Built in the reign of Henry VIII, the tallest Tudor gatehouse in Great Britain. Lord Henry Marney clearly intended to rival Wolsey's building at Hampton Court, but he died before his masterpiece was finished. His son John died two years later, in 1525, and building work stopped. Layer Marney Tower has some of the finest terracotta work in the country, most probably executed by Flemish craftsmen trained by Italian masters. The terracotta is used on the battlements, windows, and most lavishly of all, on the tombs of Henry and John Marney. Visitors may climb the Tower, passing through the History Room, and enjoy the marvellous views of the Essex countryside. There are fine outbuildings, including the Long Gallery with its magnificent oak roof and the medieval barn which now houses some of the Home Farm's collection of Rare Breed farm animals. Function room available for receptions, etc.

Location: OS Ref. TL929 175. 5m SW of Colchester, signed off B1022.

Open: 24 Mar - 6 Oct: Sun - Fri, 12 noon - 5pm. Group visits/guided tours throughout the year by arrangement.

Admission: Adult £3.50, Child £2, Family £10. Groups (15+): Adult £3.25, Child £1.75. Guided tours (pre-booked) £4.75, min. charge £120. Schools by arrangement.

🔲 🚻 🅃 🚫Partial. WC. 📷 🅿️ 🕤By arrangement. 🔲 🐕In grounds, on leads. 🛏1 dble, 2 single. 🔲 ❋ 🚾 On BHs. Tel for details.

MISTLEY TOWERS ⌗

Colchester, Essex

Tel: 01206 393884   01223 582700 (Regional Office)

Owner: English Heritage   **Contact:** The Keykeeper (Mistley Quay Workshops)

The remains of one of only two churches designed by the great architect Robert Adam. Built in 1776. It was unusual in having towers at both the east and west ends.

Location: OS Ref. TM116 320. On B1352, 1 1/2 m E of A137 at Lawford, 9m E of Colchester.

Open: Telephone for opening times.

Admission: Key available from Mistley Quay Workshops - 01206 393884.

SIR ALFRED MUNNINGS ART MUSEUM

Castle House, Dedham, Essex CO7 6AZ

Tel/Fax: 01206 322127

Owner: Castle House Trust   **Contact:** Mrs C Woodage

The home, studios and grounds where Sir Alfred Munnings, KCVO, 1878 – 1959 (PRA 1944 – 1949) lived and painted for 40 years. Castle House, part Tudor part Georgian, restored and with original Munnings' furniture, exhibits over 200 Munnings' works representing his life's work and is augmented by private loans each season. Annual Special Exhibition.

Location: OS Ref. TM060 328. 3/4 m from Dedham centre. 8m from Colchester, 12m from Ipswich.

Open: Easter Sun - first Sun in Oct: Weds, Suns & BH Mons, 2 - 5pm. Additionally Thurs & Sats in Aug, 2 - 5pm.

Admission: Adult £3, Child 50p, Conc. £2. Groups (25+): min. price £75, larger groups per admission prices.

ℹ️ No photography in house. 🔲 🚫Partial. 🅿️ Limited for coaches. 🐕 In grounds, on leads.

PAYCOCKE'S ❀

West Street, Coggeshall, Colchester, Essex CO6 1NS

Tel: 01376 561305   www.nationaltrust.org.uk/eastanglia

Owner: The National Trust   **Contact:** The Tenant

A merchant's house, dating from about 1500, with unusually rich panelling and wood carving. A display of lace, for which Coggeshall was famous, is on show. Delightful cottage garden leading down to small river.

Location: OS Ref. TL848 225. Signposted off A120.

Open: 31 Mar - 13 Oct: Tues, Thurs, Suns & BH Mons, 2 - 5.30pm, last adm: 5pm.

Admission: £2.30, groups (10+) by prior arrangement, no reduction for groups. Joint ticket with Coggeshall Grange Barn £3.40.

🚫Access to ground floor and garden. 🅿️NT's at the Coggeshall Grange Barn.

PRIORS HALL BARN ⌗

Widdington, Newport, Essex

Tel: 01799 522842

Owner/Contact: Audley End House

One of the finest surviving medieval barns in south-east England and representative of the group of aisled barns centred on north-west Essex.

Location: OS Ref. TL538 319. In Widdington, on unclassified road 2m SE of Newport, off B1383.

Open: 29 Mar - 30 Sept: Sats & Suns, 10am - 6pm.

Admission: Telephone for further details.

Special Events Index ◁ ◁ ◁ pgs 40-43

RHS GARDEN HYDE HALL

RETTENDON, Nr CHELMSFORD, ESSEX CM3 8ET

www.rhs.org.uk

Tel: 01245 400256 **Fax:** 01245 402100 **e-mail:** hydehall@rhs.org.uk

Owner: The Royal Horticultural Society   **Contact:** Pat Everitt

The new Dry Garden demonstrates the use of drought tolerant plants from around the world to provide ideas and inspiration for the visitor, while other highlights include the colour themed herbaceous borders and the Rose Garden. The thatched barn offers refreshments and plants and gifts can be bought in the Plant Centre and Shop.

Location: OS Ref. TQ782 995. 2m E of Rettendon, 6m SE of Chelmsford. Signed off the A130.

Open: 18 Mar - 10 Nov: daily. Mar - Aug: 10am - 6pm; Sept - Nov: 10am - 5pm. Last entry 1 hour before closing.

Admission: Adult £4, Child (6 - 16yrs) £1. Groups (10+): special rates available. Companion/carer of disabled person Free.

🄾 🄰 🅃 Evenings only. 🄰 🄲 Licensed. 🄸 Licensed. 🄺 By arrangement. 🄼
🄿 Limited for coaches. 🄼 Guide dogs only.

SALING HALL GARDEN

Great Saling, Braintree, Essex CM7 5DT

Tel: 01371 850 243 **Fax:** 01371 850 274

Owner/Contact: Hugh Johnson Esq

Twelve acres including a walled garden dated 1698. Water gardens and landscaped arboretum.

Location: OS Ref. TL700 258. 6m NW of Braintree, 2m N of A120.

Open: May, Jun & Jul: Weds, 2 - 5pm.

Admission: Adult £2.50, Child Free.

TILBURY FORT ⊞

No. 2 Office Block, The Fort, Tilbury, Essex RM18 7NR

Tel: 01375 858489

Owner: English Heritage   **Contact:** The Custodian

The best and largest example of 17th century military engineering in England, commanding the Thames. The fort shows the development of fortifications over the following 200 years. Exhibitions, the powder magazine and the bunker-like 'casemates' demonstrate how the fort protected London from seaborne attack. Elizabeth I gave a speech near here on the eve of the Spanish Armada.

Location: OS Ref. TQ651 754. ½ m E of Tilbury off A126.

Open: 29 Mar - 31 Oct: daily, 10am - 6pm (5pm in Oct). 1 Nov - 31 Mar: Wed - Sun, 10am - 4pm. Closed 1 - 2pm in winter. Closed 24 - 26 Dec & 1 Jan.

Admission: Adult £2.90, Child £1.50, Conc. £2.20, Family £7.30.

🄾 🄰 🅅 Tel for details.

VALENCE HOUSE MUSEUM & ART GALLERY

Becontree Avenue, Dagenham, Essex RM8 3HT

Tel: 020 8227 5293 **Fax:** 020 8227 5295 **e-mail:** valencehousemuseum@hotmail.com

Owner: Barking & Dagenham Council   **Contact:** Ms Cherry Buckley

The only remaining manor house in Dagenham, partially surrounded by a moat. Dates from 15th century. There is an attractive herb garden to the west of the house.

Location: OS Ref. TQ481 865. S side of Becontree Ave, ½ m W of A1112 at Becontree Heath.

Open: Tue - Fri, 9am - 4.30pm. Sats, 10am - 4pm.

Admission: Free.

WALTHAM ABBEY GATEHOUSE & BRIDGE ⊞

Waltham Abbey, Essex

Tel: 01992 702200

Owner: English Heritage **Contact:** East of England Regional Office (01223 582700)

The late 14th century abbey gatehouse, part of the north range of the cloister and the medieval 'Harold's Bridge' of one of the great monastic foundations of the Middle Ages.

Location: OS Ref. TL381 008. In Waltham Abbey off A112. Just NE of the Abbey church.

Open: Any reasonable time.

Admission: Free.

The herb garden, Cressing Temple Barns

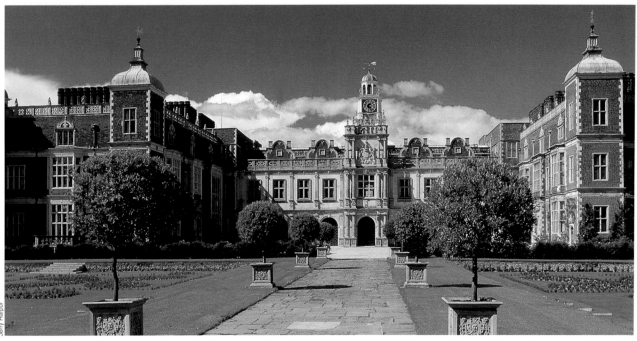

Jerry Harpur

HATFIELD HOUSE & GARDENS

HATFIELD

www.hatfield-house.co.uk

This celebrated Jacobean house, which stands in its own great park, was built between 1607 and 1611 by Robert Cecil, 1st Earl of Salisbury and Chief Minister to King James I. It has been the family home of the Cecils ever since.

The main designer was Robert Lyminge helped, it is thought, by the young Inigo Jones. The interior decoration was the work of English, Flemish and French craftsmen, notably Maximilian Colt.

The State Rooms are rich in world-famous paintings including The Rainbow Portrait of Queen Elizabeth I and The Ermine Portrait by Nicholas Hilliard. Other paintings include works by Hoefnagel, Mytens, John de Critz the Elder and Sir Joshua Reynolds. Fine furniture from the 16th, 17th and 18th centuries, rare tapestries and historic armour can be found in the State Rooms.

Within the delightful gardens stands the surviving wing of The Royal Palace of Hatfield (1485) where Elizabeth I spent much of her girlhood and held her first Council of State in November 1558. Some of her possessions can be seen in the House.

GARDENS

John Tradescant the Elder, the celebrated plant hunter, was employed to plant and lay out the gardens after the completion of the house in 1611. During the 18th century, when landscape gardening became more fashionable, much of his work was neglected or swept away. The present Marchioness has continued with the work of restoration and redevelopment, started in the mid 19th century, so that the 42 acres of gardens now include formal, knot, scented and wilderness areas which reflects their Jacobean origin. The gardens are managed entirely organically.

Jerry Harpur

Owner:
The Marquess
of Salisbury

▶ CONTACT

The Curator
Hatfield House
Hatfield
Hertfordshire AL9 5NQ

Tel: 01707 287010

Fax: 01707 287033

e-mail:
curator@hatfield-
house.demon.co.uk

▶ LOCATION

OS Ref. TL 237 084

21m N of London,
M25/J23 7m,
A1(M)/J4, 2m.

Bus: Local bus services
from St Albans and
Hertford.

Rail: From Kings Cross
every 30 mins.
Hatfield Station is
immediately opposite
entrance to Park.

Air: Luton (30 mins).
Stansted (45 mins).

FUNCTION

ROOM	SIZE	MAX CAPACITY
The Old Palace	112' x 33'	280

▶ OPENING TIMES

Easter Sat - 30 September

House
Daily, 12 noon - 4pm.
Guided tours only on weekdays.

Park, West Gardens, Restaurant & Shops
Daily, 11am - 5.30pm.

East Gardens
Open only on Fridays (Connoisseurs' Day) – except during major events.

▶ ADMISSION

House, Park & Gardens
Adult £7.00
Child (5 - 15yrs) £3.50
Groups (20+)*
Adult £6.00
Park & Gardens
Adult £4.50
Child £3.50
Park only
Adult £2.00
Child (5 - 15yrs) £1.00
Connoisseurs' Day (Fri)
House, Park & Gardens £10.50
Park & Gardens £6.50

▶ SPECIAL EVENTS

MAY 9 - 12
Living Crafts.

JUN 7-9
Festival of Gardening.

AUG 2 - 4
Art in Clay.

SEPT 6 - 8
Homes, Gardens & Flower Show.

ℹ No photography in house. National Collection of model soldiers, 5m of marked trails, children's play area.

🖼️ ✂ 🍽 Wedding receptions, functions. Elizabethan Banquets held in Old Palace throughout year: 01707 262055.

♿ WCs. Parking next to house. Lift.

☕🍽 Seats 120. Pre-booked lunch and tea for groups 10+. Tel: 01707 262030.

🚶 Mon - Fri, no extra charge. Group tours available in French, German, Italian, Spanish or Japanese by prior arrangement. Garden tour for groups £15.

🅿 Ample. Hardstanding for coaches.

📖 1:10 ratio. Teacher free. Guide provided. Resource books, play area & nature trails.

🐕 In park.

KNEBWORTH HOUSE 🏛

NR STEVENAGE

www.knebworthhouse.com

Owner: The Hon Henry Lytton Cobbold

▶ **CONTACT**

The Estate Office
Knebworth House
Knebworth
Hertfordshire SG3 6PY

Tel: 01438 812661
Fax: 01438 811908
e-mail: info@
knebworthhouse.com

▶ **LOCATION**

OS Ref. TL230 208

Direct access off the
A1(M) J7 (Stevenage
South A602).
28m N of London.
15m N of M25 J23.

Rail: Stevenage Station
2m (from Kings Cross).

Air: Luton Airport 15m
Landing facilities.

Taxi: 01438 811122.

Home of the Lytton family since 1490, and still a lived-in family house. Transformed in early Victorian times by Edward Bulwer-Lytton, the author, poet, dramatist and statesman, into the unique high gothic fantasy house of today, complete with turrets, griffins and gargoyles.

Historically home to Constance Lytton, the Suffragette, and her father, Robert Lytton, the Viceroy of India who proclaimed Queen Victoria Empress of India at the Great Delhi Durbar of 1877. Visited by Queen Elizabeth I, Charles Dickens and Sir Winston Churchill.

The interior contains various styles including the magnificent Jacobean Banqueting Hall, a unique example of the 17th century change in fashion

from traditional English to Italian Palladian. The high gothic State Drawing Room by John Crace contrasts with the Regency elegance of Mrs Bulwer-Lytton's bedroom and the 20th century designs of Sir Edwin Lutyens in the Entrance Hall, Dining Parlour and Library.

25 acres of beautiful gardens, simplified by Lutyens, including pollarded lime avenues, formal rose garden, maze, Gertrude Jekyll herb garden and newly designed Walled Garden. 250 acres of gracious parkland, with herds of red and sika deer, includes children's giant adventure playground and miniature railway. World famous for its huge open-air rock concerts, and used as a film location for *Batman*, *The Shooting Party*, *Wilde*, *Jane Eyre* and *The Canterville Ghost*, amongst others.

The Jacobean Banqueting Hall

🗄 ♟ ℹ Suitable for fashion shows, air displays, archery, shooting, equestrian events, cricket pitch, garden parties, shows, rallies, filming, helicopter landing. No pushchairs, photography, smoking or drinking in House.

🍽 Indian Raj Evenings and Elizabethan Banquets with jousting. Full catering service.

♿ Disabled parking. Ground floor accessible.

☕ Licensed tearoom. Special rates for advance bookings, menus on request.

🅿 Unlimited parking. Group visits must be booked in advance with Estate Office.

🚶 Daily at 30 min intervals or at booked times including evenings. Tour time 1hr. Shorter tours by arrangement. Room Wardens on duty on busy weekends. Themed tours available.

🖼 National Curriculum based school activity days.

🐕 Guide dogs only in House. In Park, on leads.

▶ **OPENING TIMES**

Park, Gardens,
Fort Knebworth
Adventure Playground
& Miniature Railway

23 Mar - 7 Apr; 1 - 9 Jun;
6 Jul - 3 Sept: daily.

13 Apr - 26 May;
15 - 30 Jun; 7 - 29 Sept:
weekends & BHs.

Park, Gardens &
Playground

11am - 5.30pm.

House

12 noon - 5pm (last adm.
4.15pm)

Please telephone for details
of pre-booked house tours
for groups outside of
normal opening times.

▶ **ADMISSION**

House, Gardens,
Park, Playground
& Railway

Adult £7.00
Child*/OAP £6.50
Family (2+2) £23.50
Groups (20+)
Adult £6.00
Child*/OAP............ £5.50
(subject to special events)

Gardens, Park,
Playground & Railway

All persons £5.50
Family (2+2)......... £19.00
Groups (20+)
All persons £4.75
(subject to special events)

* 4 - 16yrs. Under 4s Free.

Season Tickets available.

CONFERENCE/FUNCTION

ROOM	SIZE	MAX CAPACITY
Banqueting Hall	26' x 41'	80
Dining Parlour	21' x 38'	50
Library	32' x 21'	40
Manor Barn	70' x 25'	250
Lodge Barn	75' x 30'	150

ASHRIDGE ✼

RINGSHALL, BERKHAMSTED, HERTFORDSHIRE HP4 1LT

Tel: 01442 851227 **Fax:** 01442 842062 **e-mail:** tasgsc@smtp.ntrust.org.uk

Owner: The National Trust   **Contact:** The Property Manager

The Ashridge Estate comprises over 1800ha of woodlands, commons and downland. At the northerly end of the Estate the Ivinghoe Hills are an outstanding area of chalk downland which supports a rich variety of plants and insects. The Ivinghoe Beacon itself offers splendid views. This area may be reached from a car park at Steps Hill. The rest of Ashridge is an almost level plateau with many fine walks through woods and open commons.

Location: OS Ref. SP970 131. Between Northchurch & Ringshall, just off B4506.

Open: Visitor Centre, Shop & Tearoom: 29 Mar - 3 Nov: daily except Fris (open Good Fri). Mon - Thur & Good Fri, 2 - 5pm, Sats, Suns, BH Mon & Tue & 4 Jun, 12 noon - 5pm. Monument: Sats & Suns, 12 noon - 5pm, Mon - Thur, by arrangement. Please telephone 01442 851227 for details on winter openings. Shop only: 2 Nov - 7 Dec: Sat & Sun, 12 noon - 4pm.

Admission: Monument: £1, Child 50p.

ⓘVisitor Centre. ⬛ ⬛ Vehicles available. ⬛ ⬛ ⬛ Tel for details.

BERKHAMSTED CASTLE ⬚
Berkhamsted, St Albans, Hertfordshire

Tel: 01223 582700 (Regional Office)

Owner: English Heritage   **Contact:** Mr Stevens - The Key Keeper

The extensive remains of a large 11th century motte and bailey castle which held a strategic position on the road to London.

Location: OS165 Ref. SP996 083. Adjacent to Berkhamsted rail station.

Open: All year: daily, 10am - 6pm; Winter: 10am - 4pm. Closed 24 - 26 Dec & 1 Jan.

Admission: Free.

CATHEDRAL & ABBEY CHURCH OF ST ALBAN
St Albans, Hertfordshire AL1 1BY

Tel: 01727 860780 **Fax:** 01727 850944 **e-mail:** mail@stalbanscathedral.org.uk

Contact: Deputy Administrator

Abbey church of Benedictine Monastery founded 793AD commemorating Britain's first martyr.

Location: OS Ref. TL145 071. Centre of St Albans.

Open: All year: 9am - 5.45pm. Tel for details of services, concerts and special events Mon - Sat, 11am - 4pm.

Admission: Free of charge. (AV show, Adult £1.50, Child £1).

CROMER WINDMILL
Ardeley, Stevenage, Hertfordshire SG2 7QA

Tel: 01279 843301

Owner: Hertfordshire Building Preservation Trust   **Contact:** Cristina Harrison

17th century Post Windmill restored to working order.

Location: OS165, Ref. TL305 286. 4m NE of Stevenage on B1037. 1m SW of Cottered.

Open: Mid-May - mid-Sept: Sun, 2nd & 4th Sat & BHs, 2.30 - 5pm.

Admission: Adult £1.50, Child 25p. Groups by arrangement.

FORGE MUSEUM & VICTORIAN COTTAGE GARDEN
High Street, Much Hadham, Hertfordshire SG10 6BS

Tel/Fax: 01279 843301 **e-mail:** cristinaharrison@hotmail.com

Owner: The Hertfordshire Building Preservation Trust   **Contact:** The Curator

The garden reflects plants that would have been grown in 19th century, also houses an unusual 19th century bee shelter.

Location: OS Ref. TL428 195. Village centre.

Open: Fri, Sat, Sun & BHs, 11am - 5pm (dusk in winter).

Admission: Adult £1, Child/Conc. 50p.

BENINGTON LORDSHIP GARDENS ⬚

STEVENAGE, HERTFORDSHIRE SG2 7BS

www.beningtonlordship.co.uk

Tel: 01438 869668 **Fax:** 01438 869622 **e-mail:** rhbott@beningtonlordship.co.uk

Owner: Mr C H A Bott   **Contact:** Mr or Mrs C H A Bott

A hilltop garden which appeals to everyone with its intimate atmosphere, ruins, Queen Anne Manor, herbaceous borders, old roses, lakes and vegetable garden. For films, fashion shoots etc. the gardens and estate offer excellent facilities. Mediaeval barns, cottages and other unique countryside features.

Location: OS Ref. TL296 236. In village of Benington next to the church. 4m E of Stevenage.

Open: Gardens only: Spring & Summer BH weekends. Suns, 2 - 5pm. Mons, 12 noon - 5pm. Herbaceous Border week: 1 - 7 Jul, 2 - 5pm. By appointment all year, coaches must book. Snowdrops in Feb, telephone for details end Jan.

Admission: Adult £3.50, Child Free.

ⓘAir-strip. Suitable for filming & fashion shoots. ⬛Unsuitable. ⬛ ⬛ ⬛

THE GARDENS OF THE ROSE

CHISWELL GREEN, ST ALBANS, HERTFORDSHIRE AL2 3NR

www.roses.org.uk

Tel: 01727 850461 **Fax:** 01727 850360 **e-mail:** mail@rnrs.org.uk

Owner: The Royal National Rose Society   **Contact:** Director General

The Royal National Rose Society Gardens provide a wonderful display of one of the best and most important collections of roses in the world. There are some 30,000 roses in 1800 different varieties. The Society has introduced many companion plants which harmonise well with roses including over 100 varieties of clematis. The garden, named for the Society's Patron Her Majesty The Queen Mother, contains a fascinating collection of old garden roses. Various cultivation trials show just how easy roses are to grow and new varieties can be seen in the International Trial Ground. There are excellent facilities for films and fashion photography.

Location: OS Ref. TL124 045. 2m S of St Albans, M1/J6, M25/J21A. ¹/₂m W of B4630.

Open: 1 Jun - 29 Sept: Mon - Sat, 9am - 5pm, Sun & Aug BHs: 10am - 6pm.

Admission: Adult £4, Child (5-15yrs) £1.50, OAP £3.50.

Pre-arranged groups (20-100): Adult £3.50.

⬛ ⬛ ⬛ ⬛ ⬛Licensed. ⬛In grounds, on leads.

GORHAMBURY 🏛

St Albans, Hertfordshire AL3 6AH

Tel: 01727 854051 **Fax:** 01727 843675

Owner: The Earl Of Verulam   **Contact:** The Administrator

Late 18th century house by Sir Robert Taylor. Family portraits from 15th - 20th centuries.

Location: OS Ref. TL114 078. 2m W of St Albans. Accessible via private drive from A4147 at St Albans.

Open: May - Sept: Thur, 2 - 5pm.

Admission: House & Gardens: Adult £6, Child £3, OAP £4. Guided tour only. Groups by arrangement: Thursdays £5, other days £6.

HATFIELD HOUSE & GARDENS   *See page 266 for full page entry.*

HITCHIN BRITISH SCHOOLS

41 - 42 Queen Street, Hitchin, Hertfordshire SG4 9TS

Tel/Fax: 01462 420144 **e-mail:** brsch@britishschools.freeserve.co.uk

www.hitchinbritishschools.org.uk

Owner: Hitchin British Schools Trust   **Contact:** Mrs Judy Lee

Unique complex of school buildings dating from 1837 to 1905. Incorporates 1837 Lancasterian Schoolroom, believed to be the only surviving example, a rare 1853 galleried classroom (both Grade II*), Girls and Infants School 1857 and two Edwardian classrooms. Related displays, small museum and Family Trail with activities.

Location: OS Ref. TL186 289. Hitchin town centre.

Open: Feb - Nov: Tue, 10am - 4pm. Apr - Oct: Sun, 2.30 - 5pm. Feb - Nov: School visits, Wed & Thur, 9.45am - 12.45pm.

Admission: Adult £2, Child £1. Education programme with teaching session £2.75 plus VAT per child.

📷 ♿ Partial. WC. ⬛ 🛈 Obligatory. 🅿 ⬛ 🐕 Guide dogs only. ❋

KNEBWORTH HOUSE 🏛   *See page 267 for full page entry.*

OLD GORHAMBURY HOUSE ♯

St Albans, Hertfordshire

Tel: 01223 582700 (Regional Office)

Owner: English Heritage   **Contact:** The East of England Regional Office

The remains of this Elizabethan mansion, particularly the porch of the Great Hall, illustrate the impact of the Renaissance on English architecture.

Location: OS166, Ref. TL110 077. ¼ m W of Gorhambury House and accessible only through private drive from A4147 at St Albans (2m).

Open: Any reasonable time.

Admission: Free.

THE WALTER ROTHSCHILD ZOOLOGICAL MUSEUM

Akeman Street, Tring, Hertfordshire HP23 6AP

Tel: 020 7942 6171 **Fax:** 020 7942 6150

Owner: The Natural History Museum   **Contact:** General Organiser

The museum was opened to the public by Lord Rothschild in 1892. It houses his private natural history collection. More than 4,000 species of animal in a unique Victorian setting.

Location: OS Ref. SP924 111. S end of Akeman Street, ¼ m S of High Street.

Open: Mon - Sat, 10am - 5pm, Suns, 2 - 5pm. Closed 24 - 26 Dec.

Admission: Free.

ST PAULS WALDEN BURY

Hitchin, Hertfordshire SG4 8BP

Tel/Fax: 01438 871218/871229 **e-mail:** boweslyon@aol.com

Owner: S Bowes Lyon   **Contact:** S or C Bowes Lyon

Formal landscape garden, laid out in 1730. Avenues and allées lead to temples, statues, lake and ponds. Also more recent flower gardens. Grade I listed. Covers 60 acres. The childhood home of Queen Elizabeth, The Queen Mother.

Location: OS Ref. TL186 216. 30m N of London. 5m S of Hitchin on B651.

Open: Sundays 21 Apr, 12 May, 9 Jun: 2 - 7pm. Other times by appointment.

Admission: Adult £2.50, Child 50p. Other times £5.

SCOTT'S GROTTO

Ware, Hertfordshire

Tel: 01920 464131

Owner: East Hertfordshire District Council   **Contact:** J Watson

One of the finest grottos in England built in the 1760s by Quaker Poet John Scott.

Location: OS Ref. TL355 137. In Scotts Rd, S of the A119 Hertford Road.

Open: 1 Apr - 30 Sept: Sat & BH Mon, 2 - 4.30pm. Also by appointment.

Admission: Suggested donation of £1 for adults. Children Free. Please bring a torch.

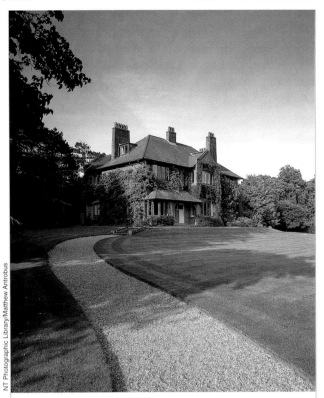

NT Photographic Library/Matthew Antrobus

SHAW'S CORNER 🌿

AYOT ST LAWRENCE, WELWYN, HERTFORDSHIRE AL6 9BX

Tel/Fax: 01438 820307 **e-mail:** tscgen@smtp.ntrust.org.uk

Owner: The National Trust   **Contact:** The Custodian

The fascinating home of playwright George Bernard Shaw until his death in 1950. The modest Edwardian villa contains many literary and personal relics, and the interior is still set out as it was in Shaw's lifetime. The garden, with its richly planted borders and views over the Hertfordshire countryside, contains the revolving summerhouse where Shaw retreated to write.

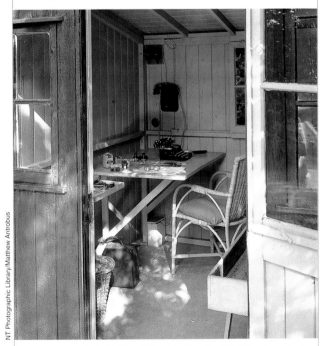

NT Photographic Library/Matthew Antrobus

Location: OS Ref. TL194 167. At SW end of village, 2m NE of Wheathampstead, approximately 2m N from B653. A1(M)/J4, M1/J10.

Open: 27 Mar - 3 Nov: Wed - Sun & BH Mons, 1 - 5pm (open Good Fri). Parties by written appointment, Mar - Nov. Last admission 4.30pm. On busy days admission by timed ticket. On event days closes at 3.30pm. No large hand luggage inside property.

Admission: Adult £3.60, Family £9.

♿ House & garden but some steps. 🚗 Car park only. 🛈 Tel for details.

HOLKHAM HALL 🏛

WELLS-NEXT-THE-SEA

www.holkham.co.uk

Owner:
The Earl of Leicester

▶ **CONTACT**

The Administrator
Holkham Hall
Estate Office
Wells-next-the-Sea
Norfolk NR23 1AB

Tel: 01328 710227
Fax: 01328 711707
e-mail: p.minchin@
holkham.co.uk

▶ **LOCATION**

OS Ref. TF885 428

From London 120m
Norwich 35m
King's Lynn 30m.

Rail: Norwich
Station 35m
King's Lynn
Station 30m.

Air: Norwich
Airport 32m.

Holkham Hall has been the home of the Coke family and the Earls of Leicester for almost 250 years. Built between 1734 and 1764 by Thomas Coke, 1st Earl of Leicester and based on a design by William Kent, this fine example of 18th century Palladian style mansion reflects Thomas Coke's natural appreciation of classical art developed during the Grand Tour. It is constructed mainly of local yellow brick with a magnificent Entrance Hall of English alabaster.

The State Rooms occupy the first floor and contain Greek and Roman statuary, paintings by Rubens, Van Dyck, Claude, Poussin and Gainsborough and original furniture.

On leaving the House visitors pass Holkham Pottery and its adjacent shop, both under the

supervision of the Countess of Leicester. Fine examples of local craftsmanship are for sale including the famous Holkham Florist Ware.

Beyond are the 19th century stables now housing the Holkham Bygones Collection; some 4,000 items range from working steam engines, vintage cars and tractors to craft tools and kitchenware. A History of Farming exhibition is in the former Porter's Lodge.

The House is set in a 3,000-acre park with 600 head of fallow deer. On the lake, 1 mile long, are many species of wildfowl. Two walks encircle either the lake or agricultural buildings.

Holkham Nursery Gardens occupy the 18th century walled Kitchen Garden and a large range of stock is on sale to the public.

▶ **OPENING TIMES**

Summer
26 May - 30 Sept, Sun - Thur (inclusive), 1 - 5pm.
Plus 31 Mar, 1 Apr, 5/6 May, 2 - 4 Jun, 25/26 Aug, 11.30am - 5pm.
Last admission 4.45pm.

Restaurant, shop and Holkham Nursery Gardens from 10am.

21 & 22 Sept: Hall & Museum closed for Holkham Country Fair.

Winter
October - May
By appointment for groups.

▶ **ADMISSION**

Summer
Hall
　Adult £5.00
　Child (5-15yrs) £2.50
Bygones
　Adult £5.00
　Child (5-15yrs) £2.50
Combined Ticket
　Adult £8.00
　Child (5-15yrs) £4.00

Groups (20+)
Hall
　Adult £4.50
　Child (5-15yrs) £2.25
Bygones
　Adult £4.50
　Child (5-15yrs) £2.25
Combined Ticket
　Adult £7.20
　Child (5-15yrs) £3.60

Private guided tours by arrangement. Rates on application.

Winter
By arrangement.

Visitors may walk in the Park without charge every day of the year.

🛡 **SPECIAL EVENTS**
SEPT 21/22
Holkham Country Fair.

📷 ℹ️ Grounds for shows, rallies and filming. No smoking or flash photography in the Hall.

♿ Visitors may alight at entrance, stairs in Hall. WC.

🍴 Menus for pre-booked groups on request.

🎧 Guides are posted in each room. Audio tour £2, other times guided tours by arrangement.

🅿 Unlimited for cars, 20+ coaches. Parking, admission, refreshments free to coach drivers, coach drivers' rest room.

Welcome. Areas of interest: Bygones Collection, History of Farming, two nature walks, deer park, lake and wildfowl.

🐕 No dogs in Hall, on leads in grounds.

❄️ Park only.

HM Queen Elizabeth II

SANDRINGHAM

NORFOLK

www.sandringhamestate.co.uk

Owner:
H M The Queen

▶ **CONTACT**

Mrs Gill Pattinson
The Estate Office
Sandringham
Norfolk   PE35 6EN

Tel: 01553 772675
Fax: 01485 541571

▶ **LOCATION**
OS Ref. TF695 287

8m NE of King's Lynn
on B1440 off A148.

Rail: King's Lynn.

Air: Norwich.

Sandringham House is the charming country retreat of Her Majesty The Queen, hidden in the heart of 60 acres of beautiful wooded gardens. Still maintained in the style of Edward and Alexandra, Prince and Princess of Wales (later King Edward VII and Queen Alexandra), all the main ground floor rooms used by The Royal Family, full of their treasured ornaments, portraits and furniture, are open to the public. A special Golden Jubilee Exhibition in the Ballroom during 2002 will display The Queen's Christmas cards, a collection of the family photographs which have been used on the personal greeting cards sent by HM The Queen and HRH The Duke of Edinburgh to their friends and employees over the years since her accession to the throne in 1952.

More family possessions are displayed in the Museum housed in the old stable and coach houses including vehicles ranging in date from the first car owned by a British monarch, a 1900 Daimler, to a half-scale Aston Martin used by Princes William and Harry. A display tells the mysterious tale of the Sandringham Company who fought and died at Gallipolli in 1915, recently made into a TV film *'All the King's Men'*. The Royal Philatelic Collection will be on display here from 11 - 19 May.

A free Land Train from within the entrance will carry passengers less able to walk through the grounds to the House and back.

▶ **OPENING TIMES**
House, Museum & Gardens

30 Mar - 27 Oct
(House and Gardens closed on 18 Jul & 24 Jul - 6 Aug inclusive).

▶ **ADMISSION**
House, Museum & Gardens

Adult	£6.00
Child (5-15yrs)	£3.50
Conc.	£4.50

Groups (20+)
10% discount for payment one month in advance.

HM Queen Elizabeth II

No photography in house.

Plant centre.

Visitor Centre only.

Licensed. Licensed.

By arrangement. Private evening tours.

Ample.

Guide dogs only.

Tel for details.

CONFERENCE/FUNCTION

ROOM	MAX CAPACITY
Restaurant	200
Tearoom	60

BERNEY ARMS WINDMILL ⌗

c/o 8 Manor Road, Southtown, Gt Yarmouth NR31 0QA

Tel: 01493 700605   01223 582700 (Regional Office)

Owner: English Heritage   **Contact:** The Custodian

A wonderfully situated marsh mill, one of the best and largest remaining in Norfolk, with seven floors, making it a landmark for miles around. It was in use until 1951.

Location: OS134 Ref. TG465 051. 3¹/₂ m NE of Reedham on N bank of River Yare, 5m from Gt. Yarmouth. Accessible by boat or by footpath, from Halvergate (3¹/₂ m).

Open: 29 Mar - 31 Oct: daily, 9am - 5pm (closed 1 - 2pm). Subject to closure at times of essential maintenance. Please check with Regional Office.

Admission: Adult £1.60, Child 80p, Conc. £1.20.

BINHAM PRIORY ⌗

Binham-on-Wells, Norfolk

Tel: 01328 830434   01223 582700 (Regional Office)

Owner: English Heritage   **Contact:** The East of England Regional Office

Extensive remains of a Benedictine priory, of which the original nave of the church is still in use as the parish church.

Location: OS132 Ref. TF982 399. ¹/₄ m NW of village of Binham-on-Wells, on road off B1388.

Open: Any reasonable time.

Admission: Free.

BIRCHAM WINDMILL

Snettisham Road, Great Bircham, Norfolk PE31 6SJ

Tel: 01485 578393

Owner/Contact: Miss E Wagg/Mr S Chalmers

One of the last remaining complete windmills.

Location: OS Ref. TF760 326. ¹/₂ m W of Bircham. N of the road to Snettisham.

Open: Easter - end Sept.

Admission: Adult £2.75, Child £1.50, Retired £2.50.

BLICKLING HALL ✹

BLICKLING, NORWICH, NORFOLK NR11 6NF

www.nationaltrust.org.uk/eastanglia

Tel: 01263 738030 **Fax:** 01263 731660 **e-mail:** abgusr@smtp.ntrust.org.uk

Owner: The National Trust   **Contact:** The Property Manager

Built in the early 17th century and one of England's great Jacobean houses. Blickling is famed for its spectacular long gallery, superb library and fine collections of furniture, pictures and tapestries.

Location: OS133 Ref. TG178 286. 1¹/₂ m NW of Aylsham on B1354. Signposted off A140 Norwich (15m) to Cromer.

Open: House: 23 Mar - 3 Nov: Wed - Sun (open BH Mons & 4 Jun), 1 - 4.30pm (last admission, house closes at 5pm). Oct & Nov: 1 - 3.30pm (last admission, house closes at 4pm). Garden: Same days as house, also Tues in Aug. 7 Nov - 22 Dec: Thur - Sun. 4 Jan - end Mar 2003: Sats & Suns, 23 Mar - 3 Nov: 10.15am - 5.15pm. Nov - Mar 2003: 11am - 4pm. Park & Woods: daily, dawn - dusk.

Admission: Hall & Gardens: £6.70. Garden only: £3.80. Family & groups discounts. Groups must book.

Open as garden. Mostly suitable. Licensed. By arrangement. Charge. NT members Free. In park, on leads. Tel for details.

BURGH CASTLE ⌗

Breydon Water, Great Yarmouth, Norfolk

Tel: 01223 582700 (Regional Office)

Owner: English Heritage   **Contact:** The East of England Regional Office

Impressive walls, with projecting bastions, of a Roman fort built in the late 3rd century as one of a chain to defend the coast against Saxon raiders.

Location: OS134 Ref. TG475 046. At far W end of Breydon Water, on unclassified road 3m W of Great Yarmouth. SW of the church.

Open: Any reasonable time.

Admission: Free.

CASTLE ACRE PRIORY ⌗

Stocks Green, Castle Acre, King's Lynn, Norfolk PE32 2XD

Tel: 01760 755394

Owner: English Heritage   **Contact:** The Custodian

The great west front of the 12th century church of this Cluniac priory still rises to its full height and is elaborately decorated. Other substantial remains include the splendid prior's lodgings and chapel and the delightful modern herb garden should not be missed.

Location: OS Ref. TF814 148. ¹/₄ m W of village of Castle Acre, 5m N of Swaffham.

Open: 29 Mar - 31 Oct: daily, 10am - 6pm (5pm in Oct). 1 Nov - 31 Mar: Wed - Sun, 10am - 4pm. Closed 24 - 26 Dec & 1 Jan.

Admission: Adult £3.70, Child £1.90, Conc. £2.80, Family £9.30.

Ground floor & grounds. Tel for details.

CASTLE RISING CASTLE

Castle Rising, King's Lynn, Norfolk PE31 6AH

Tel: 01553 631330 **Fax:** 01553 631724

Owner: Greville Howard   **Contact:** The Custodian

Possibly the finest mid-12th century Keep left in England: it was built as a grand and elaborate palace. It was home to Queen Isabella, grandmother of the Black Prince. Still in surprisingly good condition, the Keep is surrounded by massive ramparts up to 120 feet high. Picnic area adjacent tearoom. Free audio tour.

Open: 1 Apr - 31 Oct: daily, 10am - 6pm, (5pm in Oct). 1 Nov - 31 Mar: Wed - Sun, 10am - 4pm. Closed 24 - 26 Dec & 1 Jan.

Admission: Adult £3.25, Child £1.50, Conc. £2.50. 15% discount for groups (11+). Prices include VAT.

Picnic area. Grounds. WC.

DRAGON HALL

115 - 123 King Street, Norwich, Norfolk NR1 1QE

Tel: 01603 663922 **e-mail:** dragon.hall@virgin.net

Owner: Norfolk & Norwich Heritage Trust Ltd   **Contact:** Mr Neil Sigsworth

Magnificent medieval merchants' hall described as "one of the most exciting 15th century buildings in England". A wealth of outstanding features include living hall, screens passage, vaulted undercroft, superb timber-framed Great Hall, crown-post roof and intricately carved and painted dragon. Built by Robert Toppes, a wealthy and influential merchant. Dragon Hall is a unique legacy of medieval life, craftsmanship and trade.

Location: OS Ref. TG235 084. SE of Norwich city centre.

Open: Apr - Oct: Mon - Sat, 10am - 4pm. Nov - Mar: Mon - Fri, 10am - 4pm. Closed 23 Dec - 2 Jan & BHs.

Admission: Adult £2.50, Child £1, Conc. £2.

House. Obligatory. Guide dogs only.

FAIRHAVEN WOODLAND & WATER GARDEN

School Road, South Walsham NR13 6DZ

Tel: 01603 270449

Owner: The Fairhaven Garden Trust   **Contact:** George Debbage, Manager

180 acre woodland & water garden with private broad in the beautiful Norfolk Broads.

Location: OS Ref. TG368 134. 9m NE of Norwich. Follow brown tourist signs on A47 at junction with B114.

Open: Daily (except 25 Dec), 10am - 5pm, also May - Aug: Wed & Thurs evenings until 9pm.

Admission: Adult £3.50, Child £1.25 (under 5yrs Free), OAP £3. Group reductions.

NTPL / Nick Meers

NTPL / Rupert Truman

FELBRIGG HALL ✿

FELBRIGG, NORWICH, NORFOLK NR11 8PR

www.nationaltrust.org.uk/eastanglia

Tel: 01263 837444 **Fax:** 01263 837032 **e-mail:** afgusr@smtp.ntrust.org.uk

Owner: The National Trust   **Contact:** The Property Manager

One of the finest 17th century houses in East Anglia, the hall contains its original 18th century furniture and Grand Tour paintings, as well as an outstanding library. The walled garden has been restored and features a dovecote and small orchard.

Location: OS133 Ref. TG193 394. Nr Felbrigg village, 2m SW of Cromer, entrance off B1436, signposted from A148 and A140.

Open: House: 23 Mar - 3 Nov: daily except Thur & Fri, 1 - 5pm; BH Suns & Mons, 11am - 5pm. House will close at 4pm on and after 27 Oct. Garden: As house, 11am - 5.30pm. Walled Garden: 18 Jul - 30 Aug, Thur & Fri, 12 noon - 4pm.

Admission: House & Garden: Adult £5.90, Child £2.90, Family £14.70. Garden only: £2.30. Groups: (except BHs), £4.90. Groups please book with SAE to the Property Manager.

📷 01263 837040. ☎ 01263 838237. ♿ Partial. ⬛ Licensed. 🍴 Licensed.
🎓 By arrangement. **P** Charge. NT members Free. 🐕 In park, on leads. ❋ Park.
📞 01263 838297 for details.

GRIME'S GRAVES ⌗

Lynford, Thetford, Norfolk IP26 5DE

Tel: 01842 810656

Owner: English Heritage   **Contact:** The Custodian

These remarkable Neolithic flint mines, unique in England, comprise over 300 pits and shafts. The visitor can descend some 30 feet by ladder into one excavated shaft, and look along the radiating galleries, from where the flint used for making axes and knives was extracted. Special flint-knapping days are advertised throughout the year.

Location: OS144 Ref. TL818 898. 7m NW of Thetford off A134.

Open: 29 Mar - 31 Oct, daily, 10am - 6pm, (5pm in Oct). 1 Nov - 31 Mar: Wed - Sun, 10am - 4pm (closed 1 - 2pm) Closed 24 - 26 Dec & 1 Jan. Last visit to site 30 mins before close. NB: Visits to pit for children under 5yrs are at the discretion of the custodian.

Admission: Adult £2.30, Child £1.20, Conc. £1.70.

P ❋ 📞 Tel for details.

HOLKHAM HALL 🏛

See page 270 for full page entry.

Open All Year Index
◁ ◁ ◁ pgs 44-48

HOUGHTON HALL 🏛

HOUGHTON, KING'S LYNN, NORFOLK PE31 6UE

Tel: 01485 528569 **Fax:** 01485 528167 **e-mail:** enquiries@houghtonhall.com

Owner: The Marquess of Cholmondeley   **Contact:** Susan Cleaver

Houghton Hall was built in the 18th century by Sir Robert Walpole. Original designs were by Colen Campbell and revised by Thomas Ripley with interior decoration by William Kent. It is regarded as one of the finest examples of Palladian architecture in England. Houghton was later inherited by the 1st Marquess of Cholmondeley through his grandmother, Sir Robert's daughter. Situated in beautiful parkland, the house contains magnificent furniture, pictures and china. A private collection of 20,000 model soldiers and militaria. 5-acre walled garden.

Location: OS Ref. TF792 287. 13m E of King's Lynn, 10m W of Fakenham 1½ m N of A148.

Open: 31 Mar - 29 Sept: Suns, Thurs & BH Mons, 1 - 5.30pm. House: 2 - 5.30pm. Last admission 5pm.

Admission: Adult £6, Child (5-16) £3, Groups (20+): Adult £5.50, Child £2.50. Excluding house: Adult £3.50, Child £2, Groups (20+) Adult £3, Child £1.50. (2001 prices.)

📷 ♿ ⬛ 🐕

HOVETON HALL GARDENS

Wroxham, Norwich, Norfolk NR12 8RJ

Tel: 01603 782798 **Fax:** 01603 784564

Owner: Mr & Mrs Andrew Buxton   **Contact:** Mrs Buxton

10 acres of rhododendrons, azaleas, woodland and lakeside walks, walled herbaceous and vegetable gardens. Traditional tearooms and plant sales. The Hall (which is not open to the public) was built 1809 - 1812. Designs attributed to Humphry Repton.

Location: OS Ref. TG314 202. 8m N of Norwich. 1¹/₂ m NNE of Wroxham on A1151. Follow brown tourist signs.

Open: Easter Sun - mid-Sept: Weds, Fris, Suns & BH Mons, 11am - 5.30pm. Also open Thurs in May.

Admission: Adult £3.50, Child £1, Wheelchairs users £2. Family Season Ticket £20, Single Adult Season Ticket £9.50. Groups: £3 (if booked in advance).

LETHERINGSETT WATERMILL

Riverside Road, Letheringsett, Holt, Norfolk NR25 7YD

Tel: 01263 713153 **e-mail:** watermill@ic24.net

Owner/Contact: M D Thurlow

Water-powered mill producing wholewheat flour from locally grown wheat. Built in 1802.

Location: OS Ref. TG062 387. Riverside Road, Letheringsett, Holt, Norfolk.

Open: Whitsun - Oct: Mon - Fri, 10am - 5pm, Sat 9am - 1pm. Working demonstration, Tue - Fri, 2 - 4.30pm. Viewing may take place at any other time. Oct - Whitsun: Mon - Fri, 9am - 4pm. Sat, 9am - 1pm. Working demonstration, Tue - Thur, 1.30 - 3.30pm. BH Suns & Mons, 2 - 5pm.

Admission: Adult £2.50, Child £1.50. When demonstrating: Adult £3.50, Child £2.50, OAP £3, Family (2+2) £10.

KIMBERLEY HALL

WYMONDHAM, NORFOLK NR18 0RT

www.kimberleyhall.co.uk

Tel/Fax: 01603 759447 **e-mail:** events@kimberleyhall.co.uk

Owner/Contact: R Buxton

Magnificent Queen Anne house built in 1712 by William Talman for Sir John Wodehouse, an ancestor of P G Wodehouse. Towers added after 1754 and wings connected to the main block by curved colonnades in 1835. Internal embellishments in 1770s include some very fine plasterwork by John Sanderson and a 'flying' spiral staircase beneath a coffered dome. The park, with its picturesque lake, ancient oak trees and walled gardens was laid out in 1762 by 'Capability' Brown.

Location: OS Ref. TG091 048. 10m SW of Norwich, 3m from A11.

Open: House & Park not open to the public. Grounds, certain rooms and extensive cellars available for corporate hospitality & weddings (soon to be licenced for Civil ceremonies) as well as product launches, film and fashion shoots.

Admission: Please telephone for details.

T ▲Applied for.

MANNINGTON GARDENS & COUNTRYSIDE

MANNINGTON HALL, NORWICH NR11 7BB

Tel: 01263 584175 **Fax:** 01263 761214

Owner: The Lord & Lady Walpole   **Contact:** Lady Walpole

The gardens around this medieval moated manor house feature a wide variety of plants, trees and shrubs in many different settings. Throughout the gardens are thousands of roses especially classic varieties. The Heritage Rose and 20 century Rose Gardens have roses in areas with designs reflecting their date of origin from the 15th century to the present day.

Location: OS Ref. TG144 320. Signposted from Saxthorpe crossroads on the Norwich - Holt road B1149. 1¹/₂ m W of Wolterton Hall.

Open: Gardens: May - Sept: Suns 12 - 5pm. Jun - Aug: Wed - Fri, 11am - 5pm. Walks: daily from 9am. Medieval Hall open by appointment.

Admission: Adult £3, Child (under 16yrs) Free, Conc. £2.50. Groups by arrangement.

i No photography. Grounds. WCs. Licensed. By arrangement. P Guide dogs only.

Wild Flowers at Houghton Hall

NORWICH CASTLE MUSEUM & ART GALLERY
Norwich, Norfolk NR1 3JU
Tel: 01603 493625 **Fax:** 01603 493623 **e-mail:** museums@norfolk.gov.uk
Norman Castle Keep, housing displays of art, archaeology and natural history.
Location: OS Ref. TG233 085. City centre.
Open: Mon - Sat, 10.30am - 5pm. Sun, 2 - 5pm.
Admission: Single zone: Adult £2.90, Child £2.25, Conc. £2.55. Whole museum: Adult £4.70, Child £3.50, Conc. £4.10.

NT Photographic Library: Matthew Antrobus

OXBURGH HALL, GDNS & ESTATE ☙
OXBOROUGH, KING'S LYNN, NORFOLK PE33 9PS
www.nationaltrust.org.uk/eastanglia

Tel: 01366 328258 **Fax:** 01366 328066 **e-mail:** aohusr@smtp.ntrust.org.uk
Owner: The National Trust   **Contact:** The Property Manager
A moated manor house built in 1482 by the Bedingfeld family, who still live here. The rooms show the development from medieval austerity to Victorian comfort and include an outstanding display of embroidery done by Mary Queen of Scots. The attractive gardens include a French parterre, kitchen garden and orchard.
Location: OS143 Ref. TF742 012. At Oxborough, 7m SW of Swaffham on S side of Stoke Ferry road.
Open: House: 23 Mar - 3 Nov: Sat - Wed, 1 - 5pm; BH Mons, 11am - 5pm, last admission 4.30pm. Garden: 2 - 17 Mar: Sat & Sun, 11am - 4pm; 23 Mar - 3 Nov: Sat - Wed & Aug: daily, 11am - 5.30pm. Shop & Restaurant: As garden 11am - 5pm; also 9 Nov - 22 Dec: weekends only, 11am - 4pm.
Admission: House & Garden: Adult £5.50, Child £2.80, Family £14.50. Garden & Estate only: Adult £2.80, Child £1.40. Booked Groups (15+): £4.50 (except BHs). Groups must book with SAE to the Property Manager.
🖰 🍴 Licensed. ⟨ᴋ⟩ Partial. 🖈 By arrangement. ◾ 🅿 🐾 🐕 Send SAE for details.

PLANTATION GARDEN
4 Earlham Road, Norwich
Tel: 01603 621868 **Fax:** 0870 1692343
e-mail: chair@plantationgarden.co.uk **www.**plantationgarden.co.uk
Owner: Plantation Garden Preservation Trust   **Contact:** Chairperson
The Plantation Garden is a Grade II English Heritage registered garden created in the middle of the 19th century in a former chalk quarry some 600 yards from the city centre. It comprises nearly 3 acres in all, and includes a gothic fountain, flower beds, lawns, Italianate terrace, 'medieval' terrace wall, woodland walkways and rustic bridge.
Location: OS Ref. TG223 085. Leave inner ring road on B1108 Earlham Road, on left immediately after St John's Roman Catholic Cathedral (entry shared with Beeches Hotel driveway). (Reg. Charity No. 801095)
Open: Apr - mid-October: daily, 9am - 6pm and other times 10am - 4pm.
Admission: Normally £1.50 (honesty box if garden unattended). Child (accompanied) Free.
🖰 On summer Suns, pm only. 🖈 🅃 ⟨ᴋ⟩ Partial. ◾ On summer Suns, pm only. 🖈 By arrangement. 🅿 300 metres. ◾ By arrangement. 🐾 🐕 🐕 Tel for details.

RAVENINGHAM GARDENS 🏛
Raveningham, Norwich, Norfolk NR14 6NS
Tel: 01508 548480 **Fax:** 01508 548958 **e-mail:** info@raveningham.com
www.raveningham.com
Owner: Sir Nicholas Bacon Bt   **Contact:** Mrs J Woodard
Superb herbaceous borders, 18th century walled kitchen garden, Victorian glass house and much more.
Location: OS Ref. TM399 965. Between Beccles and Loddon off B1136/B1140.
Open: 31 Mar - 30 Sept: Suns, Weds & BH Mons, 2 - 5.30pm.
Admission: Adult £2.50, Child (under 16yrs) Free, OAP £2. Groups by prior arrangement.
◾ Teas on Suns.

ROW 111 HOUSE, OLD MERCHANT'S HOUSE, ⌗
& GREYFRIARS' CLOISTERS
South Quay, Great Yarmouth, Norfolk NR30 2RQ
Tel: 01493 857900
Owner: English Heritage   **Contact:** The Custodian
Two 17th century Row Houses, rows 111 and 113, a type of building unique to Great Yarmouth, containing original fixtures and displays of local architectural fittings and early wall paintings.
Location: OS134 Ref. TG525 072. In Great Yarmouth, make for South Quay, by riverside and dock, ½ m inland from beach. Follow signs to dock and south quay.
Open: 29 Mar - 31 Oct: daily, 10am - 5pm. Closed 1 - 2pm. Guided tours depart from Row 111 house at 10am, 11am, 12 noon, 2pm, 3pm, 4pm & 5pm (no 5pm in Oct).
Admission: Adult £2.50, Child £1.30, Conc. £1.90. 15% discount for groups of 11+.

ST GEORGE'S GUILDHALL ☙
27-29 King Street, Kings Lynn, Norfolk PE30 1HA
Tel: 01553 765565 **www.**west-norfolk.gov.uk
Owner: The National Trust   **Contact:** The Administrator
The largest surviving English medieval guildhall and now converted into an arts centre, but with many interesting surviving features.
Location: OS132 Ref. TF616 202. On W side of King Street close to the Tuesday Market Place.
Open: All year: Mon - Fri (closed Good Fri, BHs & 24 Dec - 1st Mon in Jan), 10am - 2pm. Times may vary in Jul & Aug. The Guildhall is not usually open on days when there are performances in the theatre, tel box office 01553 764864 for details.
Admission: Free.
🖰 ⟨ᴋ⟩ Access to galleries. ◾ 🍴 Licensed. 🐕

SANDRINGHAM
See page 271 for full page entry.

WALSINGHAM ABBEY GROUNDS & SHIREHALL MUSEUM 🏛
Little Walsingham, Norfolk NR22 6BP
Tel: 01328 820259 **Fax:** 01328 820098 **e-mail:** walsingham.estate@farmline.com
Owner: Walsingham Estate Company   **Contact:** The Agent
Set in the picturesque medieval village of Little Walsingham, a place of pilgrimage since the 11th century, the grounds contain the remains of the famous Augustinian Priory with attractive, gardens and river walks. The Shirehall Museum includes a Georgian magistrates' court and displays on the history of Walsingham.
Location: OS Ref. TF934 367. B1105 N from Fakenham - 5m.
Open: Please contact for details. Grounds also open during snowdrop season for snowdrop walks - ring for details.
Admission: Please telephone for details.
🖰 🖈 ⟨ᴋ⟩ Partial. 🖈 By arrangement. ◾ 🐾 In grounds, on leads. 🐕

WOLTERTON PARK 🏛
Norwich, Norfolk NR11 7BB
Tel: 01263 584175 **Fax:** 01263 761214
Owner: The Lord and Lady Walpole   **Contact:** The Lady Walpole
18th century Hall. Historic park with lake.
Location: OS Ref. TG164 317. Situated near Erpingham village, signposted from Norwich - Cromer Rd A140.
Open: Park: daily from 9am. Hall: Fridays 26 Apr - 25 Oct: 2 - 5pm and by appointment.
Admission: £2 car park fee only for walkers. Groups by application. Hall tours: See local press, from £4 groups, £5 individuals.
🅃 ⟨ᴋ⟩ Partial. WC. 🖈 🅿 ◾ 🐾 In park, on leads. 🐕 🐕 Tel for details.

THE ANCIENT HOUSE

Clare, Suffolk CO10 8NY

Tel: 01628 825920 or 825925 (bookings) www.landmarktrust.co.uk

Owner: Leased to the Landmark Trust by Clare PC   **Contact:** The Landmark Trust
A 14th century house extended in the 15th and 17th centuries, decorated with high relief pargetting. Half of the building is managed by the Landmark Trust, which lets buildings for self-catering holidays. The other half of the house is run as a museum. Full details of The Ancient House and 170 other historic buildings available for holidays are featured in The Landmark Handbook (price £9.50 refundable against booking), from The Landmark Trust, Shottesbrooke, Maidenhead, Berkshire SL6 3SW.

Location: OS Ref. TL769 454. Village centre, on A1092 8m WNW of Sudbury.

Open: By appointment only and, 15 - 20 Jun.

Admission: Museum: Contact 01787 277662 for details.

BELCHAMP HALL

BELCHAMP WALTER, SUDBURY, SUFFOLK CO10 7AT

www.belchamphall.com

Tel: 01787 881961 **Fax:** 01787 880729

Owner/Contact: Mr C F V Raymond

Superb Queen Anne house on a site belonging to the Raymond family since 1611. Historic portraits and period furniture. Suitable for receptions and an ideal film location, often seen as 'Lady Jane's house' in 'Lovejoy'. Gardens including a cherry avenue, follies, a sunken garden, walled garden and lake. Medieval church with 15th century wall paintings.

Location: OS Ref. TL827 407. 5m SW of Sudbury, opposite Belchamp Walter Church.

Open: By appointment only: May - Sept: Tues, Thurs & BHs, 2.30 - 6pm.

Admission: Adult £4.50, Child £2. No reduction for groups.

ℹ️No photography in house. Conference facilities. 🚽 ▣ By arrangement. 🎫Obligatory. 🅿️ 🐕Guide dogs only.

CHRISTCHURCH MANSION

Christchurch Park, Ipswich, Suffolk IP4 2BE

Tel: 01473 433554 **Fax:** 01473 433564

Owner/Contact: Ipswich Borough Council

A fine Tudor house set in beautiful parkland.

Location: OS Ref. TM165 450. Christchurch Park, near centre of Ipswich.

Open: All year: Tue - Sat, 10am - 5pm (dusk in winter). Suns, 2.30 - 4.30pm (dusk in winter). Also open BH Mons. Closed 24 - 26 Dec, 1/2 Jan & Good Fri.

Admission: Free.

EAST BERGHOLT PLACE GARDEN

East Bergholt, Suffolk CO7 6UP

Tel/Fax: 01206 299224

Owner: Mr & Mrs R L C Eley   **Contact:** Sara Eley
Fifteen acres of garden and arboretum originally laid out at the beginning of the century by the present owner's great-grandfather. A wonderful collection of fine trees and shrubs, many of which are rarely seen growing in East Anglia and originate from the famous plant hunter George Forrest. Particularly beautiful in the spring when the rhododendrons, magnolias and camellias are in flower.

Location: OS Ref. TM084 343. 2m E of A12 on B1070, Manningtree Rd, on the edge of East Bergholt.

Open: Mar - Sept: daily, 10am - 5pm. Closed Easter Sun.

Admission: Adult £2.50, Child Free. (Proceeds to garden up-keep).

🌿Specialist Plant Centre in the Victorian walled garden. 🎫By arrangement. 🐕

EUSTON HALL 🏛️

Estate Office, Euston, Thetford, Norfolk IP24 2QP

Tel: 01842 766366 **Fax:** 01842 766764 **e-mail:** lcampbell@euston-estate.co.uk
www.suffolktopattractions.com

Owner: The Duke of Grafton   **Contact:** Mrs L Campbell
18th century house contains a famous collection of paintings including works by Stubbs, Van Dyck, Lely and Kneller. The Pleasure Grounds were were laid out by John Evelyn and William Kent. 17th century parish church in Wren style. River walk, watermill and picnic area.

Location: OS Ref. TL897 786. 12m N of Bury St Edmunds, on A1088. 2m E of A134.

Open: 6 Jun - 26 Sept: Thurs 2.30 - 5pm. Also Suns 30 Jun & 1 Sept: 2.30 - 5pm.

Admission: Adult £4, Child £1, OAP £3. Groups (12+): £3pp.

🅿️ ♿Grounds. ▣ 🐕

FLATFORD BRIDGE COTTAGE 🍃

Flatford, East Bergholt, Colchester, Essex CO7 6OL

Tel: 01206 298260 **Fax:** 01206 299193 www.nationaltrust.org.uk/eastanglia

Owner: The National Trust   **Contact:** The Property Manager
Just upstream from Flatford Mill, the restored thatched cottage houses a display about John Constable, several of whose paintings depict this property. Facilities include a tea garden, shop, boat hire, an Information Centre and countryside walks.

Location: OS Ref. TM077 332. On N bank of Stour, 1m S of East Bergholt B1070.

Open: Mar & Apr: Wed - Sun, 11am - 5.30pm. May - end Sept: daily, 10am - 5.30pm. Oct: daily, 11am - 5.30pm. Nov & Dec: Wed - Sun, 11am - 3.30pm. Jan & Feb 2003: Sats & Suns only, 11am - 3.30pm. Closed Christmas & New Year.

Admission: Guided walks £1.90, accompanied child Free.

🅿️ ♿Tea garden & shop. WC. ▣ 🎫 🔲 🅿️Charge applies. 🐕Guide dogs only.

© English Heritage Photo Library

FRAMLINGHAM CASTLE ⊞

FRAMLINGHAM, SUFFOLK IP8 9BT

Tel: 01728 724189

Owner: English Heritage   **Contact:** The Custodian
A superb 12th century castle which, from the outside, looks almost the same as when it was built. From the continuous curtain wall linking 13 towers, there are excellent views of Framlingham and the charming reed-fringed mere. At different times the castle has been a fortress, an Elizabethan prison, a poor house and a school. The many alterations over the years have led to a pleasing mixture of historic styles.

Location: OS Ref. TM287 637. In Framlingham on B1116. NE of town centre.

Open: 29 Mar - 31 Oct: daily 10am - 6pm (5pm in Oct). 1 Nov - 31 Mar: daily 10am - 4pm. Closed 24 - 26 Dec & 1 Jan.

Admission: Adult £3.90, Child £2, Conc. £2.90, Family £9.70. 15% discount for groups (11+).

♿Ground floor & grounds. WCs. 🅿️ 🐕 ⊞ 📷 Tel for details.

GAINSBOROUGH'S HOUSE
46 GAINSBOROUGH ST, SUDBURY, SUFFOLK CO10 2EU

www.gainsborough.org

Tel: 01787 372958 **Fax:** 01787 376991 **e-mail:** mail@gainsborough.org

Owner: Gainsborough's House Society   **Contact:** Rosemary Woodward
Birthplace of Thomas Gainsborough RA (1727-88). Georgian-fronted town house, with attractive walled garden, displays more of the artist's work than any other gallery. The collection is shown together with 18th century furniture and memorabilia. Varied programme of contemporary exhibitions organised throughout the year includes: fine art, craft, photography, printmaking, sculpture and highlights the work of East Anglian artists.

Location: OS Ref. TL872 413. 46 Gainsborough Street, Sudbury town centre.

Open: All year: Tue - Sat, 10am - 5pm, Suns & BH Mons, 2 - 5pm. Closes at 4pm Nov - Mar. Closed: Mons, Good Fri and Christmas to New Year.

Admission: Adult £3, Child/Student £1.50, OAP £2.50.

ⓘNo photography. 🅰🅱Ground floor. WCs. 🅿None. ▉ ❉

HELMINGHAM HALL GARDENS 🏛
STOWMARKET, SUFFOLK IP14 6EF

www.helmingham.com

Tel: 01473 890363 **Fax:** 01473 890776

Owner: The Lord & Lady Tollemache   **Contact:** Ms Jane Tresidder
The Tudor Hall surrounded by its wide moat is set in a 400 acre deer park. Two superb gardens, one surrounded by its own moat and walls extends to several acres and has wide herbaceous borders and an immaculate kitchen garden. The second enclosed within yew hedges, has a special rose garden with a herb and knot garden containing plants grown in England before 1750.

Location: OS Ref. TM190 578. B1077, 9m N of Ipswich, 5m S of Debenham.

Open: Gardens only: 5 May - 22 Sept: Suns, 2 - 6pm. Groups: by appointment only on Weds, 2 - 5pm. (We can also accept individual bookings on a Wed if a group is booked.)

Admission: Adult £3.75, Child (5-15yrs) £2. Groups (30+) £3.25. Weds: £3.75pp.

🅰🅱🅲Grounds. WCs. ▉ 🅵By arrangement. 🅿🅼In grounds, on leads.

HADLEIGH GUILDHALL
Hadleigh, Suffolk IP7 5DT

Tel: 01473 827752

Owner: Hadleigh Market Feoffment Charity   **Contact:** Jane Haylock
Fine timber framed guildhall, one of the least known medieval buildings in Suffolk.

Location: OS Ref. TM025 425. S side of churchyard.

Open: Jun - end Sept: Building: Thurs & Suns; Garden: daily (except Sats), 2 - 5pm

Admission: £1.50, Conc. £1. Garden only: Free.

HAUGHLEY PARK 🏛
Stowmarket, Suffolk IP14 3JY

Tel: 01359 240701

Owner/Contact: Mr & Mrs Robert Williams
Mellow red brick manor house of 1620 set in gardens, park and woodland. Original five-gabled east front, north wing re-built in Georgian style, 1820. 6 acres of well tended gardens including walled kitchen garden. 17th century brick and timber barn restored as meeting rooms. Woodland walks with bluebells (special Sun opening), lily-of-the-valley (May), rhododendrons and azaleas (Jun).

Location: OS Ref. TM005 618. 4m W of Stowmarket signed off A14.

Open: Garden only: May - Sept: Tues & last Sun in Apr & 1st Sun in May, 2 - 5.30pm. House visits and groups by appointment (even outside normal times). Barn bookable for special lunches, teas, dinners, lectures etc. (capacity 120).

Admission: House: £2. Garden: £3. Child under 16 Free.

ⓘPicnics allowed. ⚇Bluebell Sun. ▉Bluebell Sun. 🅰 🅵By arrangement. 🅿
🅼On leads only. ❉

Right: Hengrave Hall

NT Photographic Library: Rupert Truman

HENGRAVE HALL

BURY ST EDMUNDS, SUFFOLK IP28 6LZ

www.hengravehallcentre.org.uk

Tel: 01284 701561 **Fax:** 01284 702950 **e-mail:** warden@hengravehallcentre.org.uk
Owner: Religious of the Assumption   **Contact:** Mr J H Crowe

Hengrave Hall is a unique Tudor house of stone and brick, built between 1525 and 1538 by Sir Thomas Kytson, Warden of the Mercers' Company. Former home to the Kytson and Gage families, it was visited by Elizabeth I on her Suffolk Progress in 1578. Set in 45 acres of cultivated grounds, the Hall is now run as a Conference and Retreat Centre by the Hengrave Community of Reconciliation. The Hall has many important and distinctive features, including beautiful stained glass and the magnificent Oriel Window and Frieze incorporating the Garter Arms and other Coats of Arms which were comprehensively restored in summer 2000. The ancient church with Saxon tower adjoins the Hall and continues to be used for daily prayer.

Location: OS Ref. TL824 686. 3¹/₂ m NW of Bury St Edmunds on the A1101.

Open: Please apply to the Warden (quoting ref. HHG) for conference facilities (day and residential); tours (by appointment); retreats; programme of events; schools' programme. Special group rates.

[i] Children's playground. [symbols] By arrangement. [symbols] Tel for details.

ICKWORTH HOUSE & PARK

THE ROTUNDA, HORRINGER, BURY ST EDMUNDS IP29 5QE

www.nationaltrust.org.uk/eastanglia

Tel: 01284 735270 **Fax:** 01284 735175 **e-mail:** aihusr@smtp.ntrust.org.uk
Owner: The National Trust   **Contact:** The Property Manager

One of the most unusual houses in East Anglia. The huge Rotunda of this 18th century Italianate house dominates the landscape. Inside are collections of Georgian silver, Regency furniture, Old Master paintings and family portraits.

Location: OS155 Ref. TL816 611. In Horringer, 3m SW of Bury St Edmunds on W side of A143.

Open: House: 23 Mar - 3 Nov: daily except Mons & Thurs (open BH Mons), 1 - 5pm, last admission 4.30pm (closes 4.30pm in Oct). Garden: 23 Mar - 3 Nov: daily; 10am - 5pm. 4 Nov - end Mar 2003: Mon - Fri, 10am - 4pm. Park: daily, 7am - 7pm. Note: Garden & Park closed 25 Dec.

Admission: Adult £5.95, Child £2.60. Family discounts. Park & Garden only (includes access to shop & restaurant): Adult £2.70, Child 80p. All Groups must pre-book: Adult £4.95, Child £2.10. No group discounts on Suns & BH Mons.

[symbols] Partial. [symbol] Licensed. [symbols] By arrangement. [symbols] In park, on leads. [symbol] Tel for details.

KENTWELL HALL   *See opposite for half page entry.*

LANDGUARD FORT

Felixstowe, Suffolk

Tel: 01394 277767

Owner: English Heritage   **Contact:** The Custodian

Impressive 18th century fort with later additions built on a site originally fortified by Henry VIII and in use until after World War II. There is also a museum (not EH).

Location: OS Ref. TM284 318. 1m S of Felixstowe at extreme S end of dock area.

Open: 23 Apr - 29 Oct: Suns & BHs, 10.30am - 5pm. 6 Jun - 16 Sept: Tues, Weds & Sats, 1 - 5pm (2000/2001 openings). Please telephone for 2001 - 2002 details.

Admission: Adult £2, Child £1, Conc. £1.50. EH members Free.

LAVENHAM: THE GUILDHALL OF CORPUS CHRISTI

The Market Place, Lavenham, Sudbury CO10 9QZ

Tel: 01787 247646 **e-mail:** almjtg@smtp.ntrust.org.uk
www.nationaltrust.org.uk/eastanglia

Owner: The National Trust   **Contact:** The Property Manager

This splendid 16th century timber-framed building dominates the Market Place of the picturesque town of Lavenham with its many historic houses and wonderful church. Inside are exhibitions on local history, farming and industry, as well as the story of the medieval woollen cloth trade. There is also a walled garden with dye plants.

Location: OS155 Ref. TL915 942. 6m NNE of Sudbury. Village centre. A1141 & B1071.

Open: 2 - 24 Mar: Sat & Sun, 11am - 4pm. 25 Mar - 31 May: Wed - Sun, 11am - 5pm (open BH Mon, closed Good Fri). Jun - end Sept: daily, 11am - 5pm. Oct: Wed - Sun, 11am - 5pm. Nov: Sat & Sun, 11am - 4pm. Parts of the building may be closed occasionally for community use.

Admission: Adult £3, accompanied child Free. Groups: £2.50. School parties (by arrangement) 60p per child.

[symbols] Shop & tearoom. [symbol]

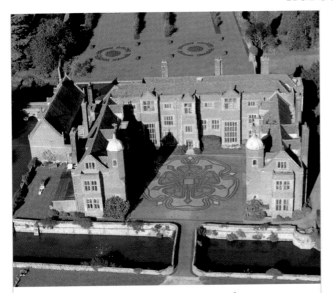

KENTWELL HALL

LONG MELFORD, SUFFOLK CO10 9BA

www.kentwell.co.uk

Tel: 01787 310207 **Fax:** 01787 379318 **e-mail:** info@kentwell.co.uk

Owner: Patrick Phillips Esq **Contact:** Mrs J G Phillips

Heritage Building of the Year 2001. Atmospheric moated Tudor House with intact service building of 1500 having dairy, bakehouse, brewhouse and solar. House illustrates the important change by which a medieval hall house was extended during the 16th century to become 'the epitome of an Elizabethan House'. Interior later re-modelled by Thomas Hopper. Still an obviously lived-in family home.

Re-creations: Kentwell is renowned for its award-winning re-creations of Everyday Tudor Life and now also for its WWII events. Re-Creations take place on selected weekends throughout the year.

Gardens: Magnificent lime avenue, tranquil moated gardens, pavement maze, camera obscura, ice house, rare breeds farm.

Corporate: Any sort of function including authentic Tudor Banquets and Tudor style activity days.

Filming: Much used for film, TV and documentaries for internal and external 16th century locations with the benefit of Kentwell's vast range of 16th century know-how, artefacts and set-ups.

Location: OS Ref. TL864 479. Off the A134. 4m N of Sudbury, 14m S of Bury St. Edmunds 1m NNW of Long Melford off A134.

Open: BHs: Sat - Mon, (+ Fri, Easter & Aug), 11am - 6pm. Mid Feb - Easter: Suns, 10am - 4pm (lambing & spring bulbs). Easter - 22 Jun: Sun, Wed, Thur & school half term: 12 noon - 5pm. 23 Jun - 14 Jul: Annual Re-Creation of Tudor Life: booked schools on weekdays, public on Sats, Suns & last Fri, 11am - 5pm. 17 Jul - 8 Sept: daily, 12 noon - 5pm. 9 - 30 Sept: Wed, Thur & Sun, 12 noon - 5pm. Oct: Sun & half term 12 noon - 5pm.

Admission: House, Gardens & Farm: Adult £6.50, Child (5-15yrs) £4, OAP £5.50. Gardens & Farm only: Adult £4.50, Child (5-15yrs) £3, OAP £4. Special prices apply for BHs & Re-Creation days.

ⓘ No photography in house. □ □ ⛓ Home-made food. **P** ▣ ✻ ▲ ▥

MANOR HOUSE MUSEUM

Honey Hill, Bury St Edmunds, Suffolk IP33 1RT

Tel: 01284 757076 **Fax:** 01284 757079 **www**.stedmundsbury.gov.uk

e-mail: stedmundsbury@buryho.stedsbc.gov.uk

Owner: St Edmundsbury Borough Council **Contact:** The Manager

A Georgian town house, built by the Earl of Bristol for his wife Elizabeth between 1736 and 1737 as her town house in which she would entertain her friends during the day and into the evening, before returning to Ickworth House, the family seat. Extensively restored in the '80s it now houses a collection of clocks, watches and wooden time pieces, a collection of costume, local and international artists. Also a friendly ghost.

Location: OS Ref. TL858 640. Bury town centre off A14. Just S of Abbey grounds.

Open: All year: Sat, Sun, Tue & Wed, 10am - 5pm.

Admission: Please telephone for details.

▢ ▣ ✻ ▥ Tel for details.

MELFORD HALL ❧

Long Melford, Sudbury, Suffolk CO10 9AA

Tel: 01787 880286 **e-mail:** amdklx@smtp.ntrust.org.uk

www.nationaltrust.org.uk/eastanglia

Owner: The National Trust **Contact:** The Senior Visitor Receptionist

A turreted brick Tudor mansion, little changed since 1578 with the original panelled banqueting hall, an 18th century drawing room, a Regency library and Victorian bedrooms, showing fine furniture and Chinese porcelain. Small collection of Beatrix Potter memorabilia.

Location: OS Ref. TL867 462. In Long Melford off A134, 14m S of Bury St Edmunds, 3m N of Sudbury.

Open: 23 Mar - 30 Apr, 1 Oct - 3 Nov: Sat, Sun & BH Mon, 2 - 5.30pm. May - Sept: Wed - Sun, BH & 4 Jun Mon, 2 - 5.30pm. Last admission 5pm.

Admission: Adult £4.50, Child (under 16) £2.25. Groups (12+): Adult £3.40, write with SAE to Senior Visitor Reception Assistant.

♿ Ramp at main door, stairlift to 1st floor. WC. 🐕 In car park & park walk only, on leads.

© English Heritage Photo Library. © Skyscan Balloon Photography

ORFORD CASTLE ⌗

ORFORD, WOODBRIDGE, SUFFOLK IP12 2ND

Tel: 01394 450472

Owner: English Heritage **Contact:** The Custodian

A royal castle built by Henry II for coastal defence in the 12th century. A magnificent keep survives almost intact with three immense towers reaching to 30m (90ft). Fine views over Orford Ness and the surrounding countryside.

Location: OS169 Ref. TM419 499. In Orford on B1084, 20m NE of Ipswich.

Open: 29 Mar - 31 Oct: daily 10am - 6pm (5pm in Oct). 1 Nov - 31 Mar: Wed - Sun, 10am - 4pm. Closed 1 - 2pm. Closed 24 - 26 Dec & 1 Jan.

Admission: Adult £3.20, Child £1.60, Conc. £2.40, Family £8. 15% discount for groups (11+).

🐕 ✻ ▥ Tel for details.

OTLEY HALL 🏛

OTLEY, IPSWICH, SUFFOLK IP6 9PA

www.otleyhall.co.uk

Tel: 01473 890264   **Fax:** 01473 890803   **e-mail:** enquiries@otleyhall.co.uk

Owner: Mr Nicholas & Mrs Ann Hagger   **Contact:** The Administrator

A stunning medieval Moated Hall (Grade I) frequently described as "one of England's loveliest houses". Noted for its richly carved beams, superb linenfold panelling and 16th century wall paintings, Otley Hall was once the home of the Gosnold family from c1401. Bartholomew Gosnold voyaged to the New World in 1602 and named Cape Cod and Martha's Vineyard, (an account of the voyage is believed to have inspired Shakespeare's *Tempest*). Gosnold returned in 1607 and founded the Jamestown colony, the first English-speaking settlement in the US. The unique 10 acre gardens include historically accurate Tudor re-creations designed by Sylvia Landsberg (author of *The Medieval Garden*).

Location: OS Ref. TM207 563. 7m N of Ipswich, off the B1079.

Open: BH Suns & Mons, 12.30 - 6pm. Jun - Sept: First two Suns in month, 11.30am - 5pm. Garden Days: 3 Apr - 25 Sept: Weds, 2 - 5pm. Coach parties welcome all year by appointment for private guided tours.

Admission: BHs: Adult £4.50, Child £2.50. Summer Suns: lunches available, tel for details. Garden days: Adult £3, Child £1, OAP £2.60.

⊤ ⅃ Partial. ▣ 🕇 By arrangement. 🄿 ✳

ST EDMUNDSBURY CATHEDRAL

Angel Hill, Bury St Edmunds, Suffolk IP33 1LS

Tel: 01284 754933   **Fax:** 01284 768655   **e-mail:** cathedral@burycathedral.fsnet.co.uk
www.stedscathedral.co.uk

Owner: The Church of England   **Contact:** Sarah Friswell

At the heart of Christian worship since Saxon times, evidence of previous churches is visible. The elegant, English Perpendicular 16th century Nave of St James' survived its patron, the once great, now ruined Abbey of St Edmund, to become the Cathedral of Suffolk in 1914. It was skilfully extended with Quire and Crossing in the 1960s and a magnificent gothic-style lantern tower, Transept and Apostles' Chapel, will complete the Cathedral to mark the millennium. Dedicated to St James, Patron Saint of Pilgrims, is subtly reflected in architectural hints of Spain.

Location: OS Ref. TL857 642. Bury St Edmunds town centre.

Open: All year: daily 8.30am - 6pm, Jun - Aug: 8.30am - 7pm.

Admission: Donation invited.

SAXTEAD GREEN POST MILL ⌗

Post Mill Bungalow, Saxtead Green, Woodbridge, Suffolk IP13 9QQ

Tel: 01728 685789

Owner: English Heritage   **Contact:** The Custodian

The finest example of a Suffolk Post Mill. Still in working order, you can climb the wooden stairs to the various floors, full of fascinating mill machinery. Ceased production in 1947.

Location: OS Ref. TM253 645. $2^{1}/_{2}$ m NW of Framlingham on A1120.

Open: 29 Mar - 31 Oct: Mon - Sat, 10am - 6pm (5pm in Oct). Closed 1 - 2pm.

Admission: Adult £2.30, Child £1.20, Conc. £1.70.

SHRUBLAND PARK GARDENS

Ipswich, Suffolk IP6 9QQ

Tel: 01473 830221   **Fax:** 01473 832202

Owner/Contact: Lord de Saumarez

One of the finest examples of an Italianate garden in England, designed by Sir Charles Barry.

Location: OS Ref. TM125 525. 6m N of Ipswich to the E of A14/A140.

Open: 31 Mar - 1 Sept: Suns & BH Mons, 2 - 5pm.

Admission: Adult £3, Child/OAP £2.

Skyscan

SOMERLEYTON HALL & GARDENS 🏛

SOMERLEYTON, LOWESTOFT, SUFFOLK NR32 5QQ

www.somerleyton.co.uk

Tel: 01502 730224 office or 01502 732950 (Entrance Gate) **Fax:** 01502 732143

Owner: The Rt Hon Lord Somerleyton GCVO   **Contact:** Ian Pollard

Splendid early Victorian mansion built in Anglo-Italian style by Sir Morton Peto, with lavish architectural features, magnificent carved stonework and fine state rooms. Paintings by Landseer, Wright of Derby and Stanfield, wood carvings by Willcox of Warwick and Grinling Gibbons. Somerleyton's 12-acre gardens are justly renowned with beautiful borders, magnificent specimen trees and the 1846 yew hedge maze which ranks amongst the finest in the country. Special features include glasshouses by Paxton, 300ft pergola, walled garden, Vulliamy tower clock, Victorian ornamentation.

Location: OS134 Ref. TM493 977. 5m NW of Lowestoft on B1074, 7m SW of Great Yarmouth off A143.

Open: Easter Sun - end Sept: Thurs, Suns, BHs. Jul & Aug: Tue - Thur, Suns & BHs. Gardens: 12.30 - 5.30pm. Hall: 1 - 5pm. Closed all other dates except by appointment. Call for details of Oct open days. Private group tours welcomed by arrangement.

Admission: Adult £5.40, Child £2.70, OAP £5.10, Family (2+2) £15.20. Groups: Adult £4.90, Child/Student £2.50. Prices and opening times subject to review.

ℹ No photography in house. ◨ ✳ ⊤ Receptions/functions/conferences. ⅃ ▣
🕇 By arrangement. 🄿 ◨ ⊠ ▲ ✳

SOUTH ELMHAM HALL

ST CROSS, HARLESTON, NORFOLK IP20 0PZ

www.southelmham.co.uk

Tel: 01986 782526 **Fax:** 01986 782203 **e-mail:** enquiries@southelmham.co.uk
Owner: John Sanderson **Contact:** Jo & John Sanderson
A Grade I listed medieval manor house set inside moated enclosure. Originally built by the Bishop of Norwich around 1270. Much altered in the 16th century. Self guided trail through former deer park to South Elmham Minster, a ruined Norman chapel with Saxon origins.
Location: OS30 Ref. TM778 324. Between Harleston and Bungay from the A143 take the B1062.
Open: Minster, Walks (free) & Café: Easter - 31 Oct: Suns, Thurs, Fris & BH Mons. 1 Nov - Easter: Suns only, 10.30am - 5pm. Hall: Thurs, BH Mons. 1 May - 30 Sept: Guided tours only, 2pm.
Admission: House: Adult £6, Child £3. Groups (12 - 50): Adult £4, Child £2.50.
🖻 ⊤ 🗟WC. ⬛ 🗷Obligatory. ⬛ 🅿 🗷In grounds, on leads. ⬛ ✳

WINGFIELD OLD COLLEGE & GARDENS 🏛

WINGFIELD, Nr STRADBROKE, SUFFOLK IP21 5RA

Tel: 01379 384888 **Fax:** 01379 388082
Owner: Mr & Mrs Ian Chance **Contact:** Mrs H Chance
Delightful family home with walled gardens. Lovely old Suffolk house with spectacular medieval great hall, contemporary art in the new College Yard Visual Arts Visitor Centre, garden sculpture, collections of ceramics and textiles, 4 acres of gardens with topiary, ponds and old roses, in unspoilt Suffolk countryside. Steeped in history, this "oasis of arts and heritage" offers an afternoon of discovery and relaxation. Children's play garden. Teas in College Yard. New Walled Arts Garden.
Location: OS Ref. TM230 767. Signposted off B1118 (2m N of Stradbroke) and B1116 at Fressingfield.
Open: Easter Sat - 29 Sept: Sats & Suns, 2 - 6pm.
Admission: Adult £3.60, Child/Student £1.50, OAP £3, Family £8.50 (2001 prices). 🛉 ⊤Wedding receptions. 🗟 ⬛ 🗷By arrangement for groups. 🅿 🕮 🗷Guide dogs only.

THE TIDE MILL

Woodbridge, Ipswich, Suffolk
Tel: 01473 626618
Owner/Contact: Geoff Gostling
First recorded in 1170, now fully restored, machinery demonstrated at low tide. Ring for wheel turning times.
Location: OS Ref. TM275 487. By riverside ¼ m SE of Woodbridge town centre. 1¼ m off A12.
Open: Easter, then May - Sept: daily. Apr & Oct: Sats & Suns only, 11am - 5pm.
Admission: Adult £1.50, Child Free, Conc. £1.

Ickworth House and Park

NT Photographic Library: Rupert Truman

WYKEN HALL GARDENS

STANTON, BURY ST EDMUNDS, SUFFOLK IP31 2DW

Tel: 01359 250287 **Fax:** 01359 252256
Owner: Sir Kenneth & Lady Carlisle **Contact:** Mrs Barbara Hurn
The Elizabethan manor house is surrounded by a romantic, plant-lover's garden with maze, knot and herb garden and rose garden featuring old roses. A walk through ancient woodlands leads to Wyken Vineyards, winner of EVA Wine of the Year. In the 16th century barn, the Vineyard Restaurant serves our wines along with a varied menu from fresh local produce. It is a 'Bib Gourmand' in the Michelin Guide and features also in The Good Food Guide.
Location: OS Ref. TL963 717. 9m NE of Bury St. Edmunds 1m E of A143. Follow brown tourist signs to Wyken Vineyards from Ixworth.
Open: 7 Jan - 24 Dec: daily, 10am - 6pm. Garden: 1 Apr - 1 Oct: daily except Sat, 2 - 6pm. Open for dinner from 7pm Fri & Sat.
Admission: Gardens: Adult £2.50, Child (under 12yrs) Free, Conc. £2. Groups by appointment.
🖻 🗟Grounds. WC. 🍴 Licensed. 🗷In grounds, on leads. ✳

East Midlands

Heritage House Group Ltd

Burghley House

"… the door you enter is of iron carv'd the finest I ever saw, all sorts of leaves flowers figures birds beast wheate in the Carving ….. the hall is a noble roome painted finely, ….. you go thence into parlours dineing rooms drawing roomes and bedchambers, one leading out of another at least 20 ….. the great variety of the roomes and fine works tooke me up 2 full hours to go from one roome to another over the house; it is esteemed the finest house and scituation that is in England …"

Celia Fiennes on visiting Burghley House in 1697

Burghley House is a house fit for royalty, indeed this is how Burghley was first envisaged, built, and subsequently added to. Today its palatial and exuberant Elizabethan exterior with profusion of Renaissance motifs creates a dramatic and breathtaking relief against the Lincolnshire skyline. The softening effect of 'Capability' Brown's beautiful deer park sloping gently towards the lake only enhances the visitor's first impressions of this magnificent house.

Built by William Cecil, one of Queen Elizabeth I's most trusted and shrewdest statesmen – her Lord High Treasurer and Chief Minister – the fascinating fact is that there can be little doubt that William (later Lord Burghley) actually designed most of this extraordinary building himself. Family papers show that whilst he worked with an Antwerp mason named Henryk, Cecil himself collected, through agents, all available new works on architecture and supplied a 'tryke' (drawing) of some detail at the request of his master mason.

The actual building period of the house extended over 32 years. State papers report that Cecil was building from 1556 and during the next 10 years he raised the east side of the house. As Lord Burghley, he completed the vast rectangular courtyard block about 1577-87 and it seems the hall and kitchen were rebuilt during this time. Today it is the kitchen with its fan-vaulted roof, which best shows the house's Tudor origins.

The shimmering and flamboyant Baroque interiors seen today are the creation of John, 5th Earl of Exeter and his Countess, Anne (a daughter of the extremely wealthy 3rd Earl of Devonshire). Among the first 'Grand Tourists', they travelled to Europe on four separate occasions, buying over 300 tapestries, sculptures and objects to adorn the newly refurbished interiors of the house. Luckily, a large part of their collection survives and can be enjoyed by visitors as a unique example of the tastes of a 17th century nobleman and his Countess. Finally, in the State Rooms, visitors can enjoy the neo-classicism of Burghley's other great moderniser, Brownlow, 9th Earl of Exeter.

Mr Simon and Lady Victoria Leatham, who welcome visitors to their home today, stress in their guidebook that Burghley is very much a 'living house', the centre of a 10,000 acre agricultural estate. Restoration and cleaning projects are an ongoing process to revive both the structure and contents of the house and, whilst the sheer opulence of the Verrio's *trompe l'oeil* ceilings in the five grandest state rooms may not be to the taste of 21st century eyes, you still leave with the impression that these are rooms with a heart.

Burghley is not a museum, it is quite simply a magnificent example of one family's legacy over the past 400 years, and is one of the greatest houses in England to visit. ⊹

For further details about *Burghley House* see entry on page 300.

William Cecil, Lord Burghley

Gary Rogers Hamburg

CHATSWORTH

BAKEWELL

www.chatsworth.org

Owner: Trustees of the Chatsworth Settlement. Home of the Duke & Duchess of Devonshire

▶ **CONTACT**

Mr John Oliver
Chatsworth
Bakewell
Derbyshire DE45 1PP

Tel: 01246 582204
01246 565300
Fax: 01246 583536

e-mail: visit@
chatsworth.org

▶ **LOCATION**

OS Ref. SK260 703

From London
3 hrs M1/J29,
signposted via
Chesterfield.

3m E of Bakewell,
off B6012,
10m W of Chesterfield.

Rail: Chesterfield
Station, 11m.

Bus: Chesterfield -
Baslow, 1½ m.

The great Treasure House of Chatsworth was first built by Bess of Hardwick in 1552 and has been lived in by the Cavendish family, the Dukes of Devonshire, ever since. The House today owes its appearance to the 1st Duke who remodelled the building at the end of the 17th century, while the 6th Duke added a wing 130 years later. Visitors can see 26 rooms including the run of 5 virtually unaltered 17th century State Rooms and Chapel. There are painted ceilings by Verrio, Thornhill and Laguerre, furniture by William Kent and Boulle, tapestries from Mortlake and Brussels, a library of over 17,000 volumes, sculpture by Cibber and Canova, old master paintings by Rembrandt, Hals, Van Dyck, Tintoretto, Veronese, Landseer and Sargent; the collection of neo-classical sculpture, Oriental and European porcelain and the dazzling silver collection, including an early English silver chandelier. The present Duke has added to the collection. The 2002 exhibition is 'A Royal Miscellany', a display of paintings, drawings, photographs and sculpture to celebrate Her Majesty Queen Elizabeth II's Golden Jubilee Year. In 1996 and 1999 Chatsworth was voted the public's favourite house winning the NPI National Heritage Gold Award.

GARDEN

The 105 acre garden was created during three great eras in garden and landscape design. The 200 metre Cascade, the Willow Tree fountain and the Canal survive from the 1st Duke's formal garden. 'Capability' Brown landscaped the garden and park in the 1760s. The 6th Duke's gardener, Sir Joseph Paxton, built rockeries and designed a series of glasshouses. He also created the Emperor fountain, the tallest gravity-fed fountain in the world. More recent additions include the Rose, Cottage and Kitchen gardens, the Serpentine Hedge and the Maze. In 1999, a new water sculpture, Revelation, was unveiled.

Farmyard and Adventure Playground. Guide book translations and audio guides in French, German, Italian, Spanish and Japanese.

No wheelchairs in house, but welcome in garden (3 electric, 7 standard available). WCs. Special leaflet.

New rooms available for conferences and private functions. Contact Head of Catering.

Restaurant (max 300); home-made food. Menus on request.

Private tours of house or Greenhouses and Behind the Scenes Days, by arrangement only (extra charges apply). Tape recorded tour may be hired at entrance. Groups please pre-book.

Cars 100 yds, Coaches 25 yds from house.

Guided tours, packs, trails and school room. Free preliminary visit recommended.

❄

CONFERENCE/FUNCTION

ROOM	MAX CAPACITY
Hartington Rm.	70
Coffee Rm.	24

▶ **OPENING TIMES**

Summer
20 March - 27 October.

Daily: 11am - 4.30pm.

Winter
Closed.

The Park is open free throughout the year.

▶ **ADMISSION**

House & Garden
Adult £8.00
Child £3.00
OAP/Student £6.50
Family £19.25
Pre-booked groups
Adult £7.00
School (no tour).... £3.00
School (w/tour)..... £3.50
OAP/Student £5.50
Garden only
Adult £4.50
Child £2.00
OAP/Student £3.50
Family £11.00
Scots Suite
Adult £1.50
Child £0.50

Car Park £1.00

**Farmyard &
Adventure Playground**
All £3.60
Groups (5+).......... £3.10
OAP/School £3.00

🎭 **SPECIAL EVENTS**

MAY 11/12
International Horse Trials.
MAY 18/19
Angling Fair.
JUN 1
Open Air Concert.
AUG 31 & SEPT 1
Country Fair.

HADDON HALL

BAKEWELL

www.haddonhall.co.uk

Haddon Hall sits on a rocky outcrop above the River Wye close to the market town of Bakewell, looking much as is would have done in Tudor times. There has been a dwelling here since the 11th century but the house we see today dates mainly from the late 14th century with major additions in the following 200 years and some alterations in the early 17th century including the creation of the Long Gallery.

William the Conqueror's illegitimate son Peverel, and his descendants, held Haddon for 100 years before it passed to the Vernon family. In the late 16th century the estate passed through marriage to the Manners family, in whose possession it has remained ever since.

When the Dukedom of Rutland was conferred on the Manners family in 1703 they moved to Belvoir Castle, and Haddon was left deserted for 200 years. This was Haddon's saving grace as the Hall thus escaped the major architectural changes of the 18th and 19th centuries ready for the great restoration at the beginning of the 20th century by the 9th Duke of Rutland. Henry VIII's elder brother Arthur, who was a frequent guest of the Vernons, would be quite familiar with the house as it stands today.

Haddon Hall is a popular location for film and television productions. Recent films include *Jane Eyre* and *Elizabeth*.

GARDENS

Magnificent terraced gardens with over 150 varieties of rose and clematis, many over 70 years old, provide colour and scent throughout the summer.

Owner:
Lord Edward Manners

▶ CONTACT

Janet O'Sullivan
Estate Office
Haddon Hall
Bakewell
Derbyshire
DE45 1LA

Tel: 01629 812855
Fax: 01629 814379

e-mail: info@
haddonhall.co.uk

▶ LOCATION

OS Ref. SK234 663

From London 3 hrs
Sheffield ½ hr
Manchester 1 hr
Haddon is on the
E side of A6 1½ m
S of Bakewell.
M1/J30.

Rail: Chesterfield
Station, 12m.

Bus: Chesterfield
Bakewell.

▶ OPENING TIMES

Summer
28 March - 30 September
(closed Sun 14 July).

Daily: 10.30am - 5.45pm
Last admission 5pm.

October: Mon - Thur
10.30am - 4.30pm
Last admission 4pm.

Winter
November - 27 March
Closed.

▶ ADMISSION

Summer

Adult	£6.75
Child (5 -15yrs)	£3.50
Conc	£5.75
Family (2+3)	£18.00

Groups (20+)

Adult	£5.75
Child (5 -15yrs)	£3.25
Conc	£5.00

Haddon Hall is ideal as a film location due to its authentic and genuine architecture requiring little alteration. Suitable locations are also available on the Estate.

Unsuitable, steep approach, varying levels of house.

Self-service, licensed (max 75). Home-made food.

Special tours £25 extra for groups of 15, 7 days' notice.

Ample, 450 yds from house, £1 per car.

Tours of the house bring alive Haddon Hall of old. Costume room also available, very popular!

Guide dogs only. Tel for details.

East Midlands - England

English Heritage Photo Library/Jonathan Bailey

BOLSOVER CASTLE ⌗
CASTLE STREET, BOLSOVER, DERBYSHIRE S44 6PR

Tel: 01246 822844

Owner: English Heritage   **Contact:** The Custodian

An enchanting and romantic spectacle, situated high on a wooded hilltop dominating the surrounding landscape. Built on the site of a Norman castle, this is largely an early 17th century mansion. Most delightful is the 'Little Castle', a bewitching folly with intricate carvings, panelling and wall painting. See the restored interiors of the Little Castle and the working Venus Fountain and statuary. There is also an impressive 17th century indoor Riding House built by the Duke of Newcastle.

Enjoy the Visitor and Discovery Centre. Bolsover is now available for Civil weddings, receptions and corporate hospitality.

Location: OS120, Ref. SK471 707. Off M1/J29, 6m from Mansfield. In Bolsover 6m E of Chesterfield on A632.

Open: 29 Mar - 31 Oct: daily, 10am - 6pm (5pm in Oct). 1 Nov - 31 Mar: Wed - Sun, 10am - 4pm. Closed 24 - 26 Dec & 1 Jan.

Admission: Adult £6, Child £3, Conc. £4.50, Family £15. 15% discount for groups (11+). ⊤ 🔲 Grounds. WC. 🅿 ⊠ ▲ ✳ 🔽 Tel for details.

NT Photographic Library: Andreas von Einsiedel

NT Photographic Library: Rupert Truman

CALKE ABBEY ✿
TICKNALL, DERBYSHIRE DE73 1LE
www.nationaltrust.org.uk

Tel: 01332 863822 **Fax:** 01332 865272 **e-mail:** eckxxx@smtp.ntrust.org.uk

Owner: The National Trust   **Contact:** The Property Manager

The house that time forgot, this baroque mansion, built 1701 - 3 for Sir John Harpur is set in a landscaped park. Little restored, Calke is preserved by a programme of conservation as a graphic illustration of the English country house in decline; it contains the family's collection of natural history, a magnificent 18th century state bed and interiors that are virtually unchanged since the 1880s. Walled garden, pleasure grounds and recently restored orangery. Early 19th century Church. Historic parkland with Portland sheep and deer. Staunton Harold Church is nearby.

Location: OS128 Ref. SK356 239. 10m S of Derby, on A514 at Ticknall between Swadlincote and Melbourne.

Open: House, Garden & Church: 23 Mar - 3 Nov: Sat - Wed; House: 1 - 5.30pm (ticket office opens 11am); Garden & Church: 11am - 5.30pm; 11am - 7pm Tues & Wed in Jul & Aug. Park: most days until 9pm or dusk. Closed 17 Aug for concert. Shop & Restaurant: 23 Mar - 3 Nov: as house, 10.30am - 5.30pm (shop) & 10.30am - 5pm (restaurant). 9 Nov - 22 Dec & Jan - Mar 2003: Sat & Sun, 11am - 4pm; also 2 - 18 Dec: Mon - Wed, 11am - 4pm.

Admission: All sites: Adult £5.40, Child £2.70, Family £13.50. Garden only: Adult £3, Child £1.50. Discount for pre-booked groups.

⌾ 🔲 House. Braille guide. Wheelchairs. WCs. 🍴 Licensed. 🅵 By arrangement. 🐾 In park, on leads only. ✳

CARNFIELD HALL

South Normanton, Nr Alfreton, Derbyshire DE55 2BE
Tel: 01773 520084
Owner/Contact: J B Cartland
Unspoilt Elizabethan 'Mansion House'. Panelled rooms, two 17th century staircases, great chamber. From 1502 the seat of the Revell, Wilmot and Cartland families. Atmospheric interior with three centuries of portraits, furniture, china, needlework, costumes, royal relics and manorial documents. Guided tours by the owner. Old walled garden.
Location: OS Ref. SK425 561. $1^{1}/_{2}$ m W of M1/J28 on B6019. Alfreton Station 5 mins walk.
Open: Easter - 30 Sept: Most Suns, Good Fri & BH Sats & Mons, 2 - 5pm; Jul & Aug: Most Tues, Thurs & Fris, 2 - 5pm. Guided tours only at 2pm & 3.30pm for 4 or more. Groups by appointment including evening visits.
Admission: £4. Evening visits £5.
No photography in Hall. Grounds. WCs. Licensed. Obligatory. In grounds, on leads only.

CATTON HALL

CATTON, WALTON-ON-TRENT, SOUTH DERBYSHIRE DE12 8LN
www.catton-hall.com

Tel: 01283 716311 **Fax:** 01283 712876 **e-mail:** kneilson@catton-hall.com
Owner/Contact: Robin & Katie Neilson
Catton, built in 1745, has been in the hands of the same family since 1405 and is still lived in by the Neilsons as their private home. This gives the house, with its original collection of 17th and 18th century portraits, pictures and antique furniture, a unique, relaxed and friendly atmosphere. Catton is available for corporate entertaining throughout the year. With its spacious reception rooms and luxurious bedrooms, Catton is centrally located for business meetings/conferences, product launches, lunches and dinners, as well as for groups visiting Birmingham, the NEC, the Belfry, the Potteries and Dukeries. The acres of parkland alongside the River Trent are ideal for all types of corporate and public events, including motorised activities.
Location: OS Ref. SK206 154. 2m E of A38 at Alrewas between Lichfield & Burton-on-Trent (8m from each). Birmingham NEC 20m.
Open: By arrangement all year for corporate hospitality, shooting parties, wedding receptions, residential and non-residential tour groups. Guided tours: Apr - Oct: Mon, 1.30pm & 3pm.
Conference facilities. By arrangement. By arrangement. 3 x four posters, 5 twin, all en-suite. Tel for details.

CHATSWORTH
See page 288 for full page entry.

CROMFORD MILL (SIR RICHARD ARKWRIGHT'S)

Cromford, Nr Matlock, Derbyshire DE4 3RQ
Tel/Fax: 01629 823256 **Contact:** The Visitor Services Dept.
Built in 1771, Cromford Mill is the world's first successful water powered cotton spinning mill, set in the beautiful Derwent Valley surrounded by limestone tors and rolling hills. There is a wholefood restaurant on site with shops, free car parking and friendly staff. A tour guide will explain the story of this important historic site and describe the development plans for the future.
Location: OS Ref. SK296 569. 3m S of Matlock, 17m N of Derby just off A6.
Open: All year except Christmas Day, 9am - 5pm.
Admission: Free entry. Guided tours: Adult £2, Conc. £1.50.
Partial. WCs. In grounds, on leads.

ELVASTON CASTLE COUNTRY PARK

Borrowash Road, Elvaston, Derbyshire DE72 3EP
Tel: 01332 571342 **Fax:** 01332 758751
Owner: Derbyshire County Council **Contact:** The Park Manager
200 acre park landscaped in 19th century. Walled garden. Estate museum with exhibitions of traditional crafts.
Location: OS Ref. SK407 330. 5m SE of Derby, 2m from A6 or A52.
Open: Please contact park for details.
Admission: Museum: Adult £1.20, Child 60p, Family (2+2) £3. Park and Gardens Free. Car park: Midweek 70p, weekends/BHs £1.30, Coaches £7.50.
Ground floor & grounds. WCs. By arrangement. In grounds, under close control.

EYAM HALL

EYAM, HOPE VALLEY, DERBYSHIRE S32 5QW
www.eyamhall.co.uk

Tel: 01433 631976 **Fax:** 01433 631603 **e-mail:** nicwri@eyamhall.co.uk
Owner: Mr R H V Wright **Contact:** Mrs Nicola Wright
This small but charming manor house in the famous plague village of Eyam has been the home of the Wright family since 1671. The present family opened the house to the public in 1992, but it retains the intimate atmosphere of a much-loved private home. A Jacobean staircase, fine tapestries and family portraits are among its interior treasures. Craft Centre in the historic farmyard with crafts people at work and genuinely local products for sale.
Location: OS119 Ref. SK216 765. Approx 10m from Sheffield, Chesterfield and Buxton. Eyam is off A623 between Stockport and Chesterfield. Eyam Hall is in the centre of the village, past the church.
Open: Jun, Jul & Aug: Wed, Thur, Sun & BH Mon, 11am - 4pm. Christmas tours, school tours (booked groups only). Craft Centre: All year: Wed - Sun, 11am - 5pm.
Admission: Adult £4.25, Child £3.25, Conc. £3.75. Family (2+4) £13.50. Group rates available. Craft Centre: Free.
Craft Centre. Partial. Obligatory. Limited. In grounds, on leads. Guide dogs only in house. Tel for details.

HADDON HALL
See page 289 for full page entry.

HARDSTOFT HERB GARDEN

Hall View Cottage, Hardstoft, Chesterfield, Derbyshire S45 8AH
Tel: 01246 854268
Owner: Mr Stephen Raynor/L M Raynor **Contact:** Mr Stephen Raynor
Consists of four display gardens with information boards and well labelled plants.
Location: OS Ref. SK436 633. On B6039 between Holmewood & Tibshelf, 3m from J29 on M1.
Open: 15 Mar - 15 Sept: daily (except Tue) 10am - 5pm. Tearoom: closed Mon & Tue. Garden & Tearoom open all week during BHs. Closed Sunday following Aug BH weekend.
Admission: Adult £1, Child Free.

HARDWICK HALL, GARDENS, PARK & STAINSBY MILL

DOE LEA, CHESTERFIELD, DERBYSHIRE S44 5QJ

www.nationaltrust.org.uk

Tel: 01246 850430 **Fax:** 01246 854200 **Shop/Restaurant:** 01246 854088
e-mail: ehwxxx@smtp.ntrust.org.uk

Owner: The National Trust   **Contact:** The Property Manager

Hardwick Hall: A late 16th century 'prodigy house' designed by Robert Smythson for Bess of Hardwick. The house contains outstanding contemporary furniture, tapestries and needlework including pieces identified in an inventory of 1601; a needlework exhibition is on permanent display. Walled courtyards enclose fine gardens, orchards and a herb garden. The country park contains Whiteface Woodland sheep and Longhorn cattle.

Location: OS120 Ref. SK456 651. 7^1/$_2$ m NW of Mansfield, 9^1/$_2$ m SE of Chesterfield: approach from M1/J29 via A6175.

Open: Hall: 27 Mar - 27 Oct: Weds, Thurs, Sats, Suns & BH Mons, Good Fri & 4 Jun: 12.30 - 5pm (Oct: 12.30 - 4pm). Gardens: 27 Mar - 27 Oct: daily except Tue, 11am - 5.30pm. Parkland: daily.

Admission: Hall & Garden: Adult £6.40, Child £3.20, Family £16. Garden only: Adult £3.40, Child £1.70, Family £8.50. Joint ticket for Hall (NT) and Old Hall (EH): Adult £8.50, Child £4.25, Family £21.25 (NT members Free). Pre-booking for groups essential, discount for groups of 15+. Timed tickets on busy days.

Hardwick Estate - Stainsby Mill is an 18th century water-powered corn mill in working order.

Location: OS120 Ref. SK455 653. From M1/J29 take A6175, signposted to Clay Cross then first left and left again to Stainsby Mill.

Open: 23 Mar - 31 May, 1 Oct - 3 Nov: Weds, Thurs, Sats, Suns & BH Mons, Good Fri & 4 Jun plus Mons in Jul & Aug; 1 Jun - 30 Sept: Wed - Sun & BH Mons, 11am - 4.30pm.

Admission: Adult £2.10, Child £1, Family £5.20. No discounts for groups. School Groups: Weds & Thurs (plus Fri: Jun - Sept), for information send SAE to Property Manager at Hardwick Hall.

Garden, Hall: 3 display rooms only. Licensed. In park, on leads.

HARDWICK OLD HALL

DOE LEA, Nr CHESTERFIELD, DERBYSHIRE S44 5QJ

Tel: 01246 850431

Owner: National Trust, managed by English Heritage   **Contact:** The Custodian
This large ruined house, finished in 1591, still displays Bess of Hardwick's innovative planning and interesting decorative plasterwork. The views from the top floor over the country park and 'New' Hall are spectacular.

Location: OS120 Ref. SK463 638. 7^1/$_2$ m NW of Mansfield, 9^1/$_2$ m SE of Chesterfield, off A6175, from M1/J29.

Open: 29 Mar - 31 Oct: Wed, Thur, Sat & Sun (also open Mons in Aug), 10am - 6pm (5pm in Oct)

Admission: Adult £3, Child £1.50, Conc. £2.30, Family £7.50. 15% discount for groups (11+).

On leads.

Chatsworth

NT Photographic Library / Oliver Benn

KEDLESTON HALL 🌿

DERBY DE22 5JH

www.nationaltrust.org.uk

Tel: 01332 842191 **Fax:** 01332 841972 **e-mail:** ekdxxx@smtp.ntrust.org.uk

Owner: The National Trust **Contact:** The Property Manager

Experience the age of elegance in this neo-classical house built between 1759 and 1765 for the Curzon family and little altered since. Set in 800 acres of parkland with an 18th century pleasure ground, garden and woodland walks – a day at Kedleston is truly an experience to remember. The influence of the architect Robert Adam is everywhere, from the Park buildings to the decoration of the magnificent state rooms. Groups are welcome and an introductory talk can be arranged.

Location: OS Ref. SK312 403. 5m NW of Derby, signposted from roundabout where A38 crosses A52 Derby ring road.

Open: House: 23 Mar - 3 Nov: Sat - Wed (open Good Fri); Garden: as house: 10am - 6pm. Park: 23 Mar - 22 Dec: daily; 5 Jan - 17 Mar 2003: Sat & Sun. Times: 23 Mar - 3 Nov: 10am - 6pm; Nov - Mar 2003: 10am - 4pm. Shop: 23 Mar - 3 Nov, 11.30am - 5pm, Nov - 22 Dec: Sat & Sun, 12 noon - 4pm. Restaurant: 23 Mar - 3 Nov, 11am - 5pm, Nov - 22 Dec: Sat & Sun, 12 noon - 4pm.

Admission: Adult £5.30, Child £2.60, Family £13.20. Garden & Park: Adult £2.40, Child £1.10. Thur & Fri: £2 per vehicle for park only.

⬜ ♿ Stairclimber & Batricar. 🍴 Licensed. 🐕 In grounds, on leads. ⬛
♿ Tel for details.

MELBOURNE HALL & GARDENS 🏛

MELBOURNE, DERBYSHIRE DE73 1EN

Tel: 01332 862502 **Fax:** 01332 862263

Owner: Lord & Lady Ralph Kerr **Contact:** Mrs Gill Weston

This beautiful house of history, in its picturesque poolside setting, was once the home of Victorian Prime Minister William Lamb. The fine gardens, in the French formal style, contain Robert Bakewell's intricate wrought iron arbour and a fascinating yew tunnel.

Location: OS Ref. SK389 249. 8m S of Derby. From London, exit M1/J24.

Open: Hall: Aug only (not first 3 Mons) 2 - 5pm. Last admission 4.15pm. Gardens: 1 Apr - 30 Sept: Weds, Sats, Suns, BH Mons. 1.30 - 5.30pm.

Admission: Hall: Adult £3, Child £1.50, OAP £2.50. Gardens: Adult £3, Child/OAP £2. Hall & Gardens: Adult £5, Child £3, OAP £4.

ℹ Crafts. No photography in house. ⬜ ♿ Partial. 🐕 ⬛ Obligatory.
Ⓟ Limited. No coach parking. 🐕 Guide dogs only.

PEVERIL CASTLE ♯

Market Place, Castleton, Hope Valley S33 8WQ

Tel: 01433 620613

Owner: English Heritage **Contact:** The Custodian

There are breathtaking views of the Peak District from this castle, perched high above the pretty village of Castleton. The great square tower stands almost to its original height. Formerly known as Peak Castle.

Location: OS110 Ref. SK150 827. S side of Castleton, 15m W of Sheffield on A6187.

Open: 29 Mar - 31 Oct: daily, 10am - 6pm (5pm in Oct). 1 Nov - 31 Mar, Wed - Sun, 10am - 4pm. Closed 24 - 26 Dec & 1 Jan.

Admission: Adult £2.40, Child £1.80, Conc. £1.20. 15% discount for groups (11+).
✱ ♿ Tel for details.

Accommodation Index
◁ ◁ ◁   pg 27

RENISHAW HALL
SHEFFIELD, DERBYSHIRE S31 3WB
www.sitwell.co.uk

Tel: 01246 432310   **Fax:** 01246 430760   **e-mail:** info@renishawhall.free-online.co.uk
Owner: Sir Reresby Sitwell Bt DL   **Contact:** The Administrator
Home of Sir Reresby and Lady Sitwell. Seven acres of Italian style formal gardens stand in 300 acres of mature parkland, encompassing statues, shaped yew hedges, herbaceous borders, a water garden and lakes. The Sitwell museum, art galleries (display of Fiori de Henriques sculptures and paintings by John Piper) are located in Georgian stables alongside craft workshops and Gallery café, furnished with contemporary art.
Location: OS Ref. SK435 786. 3m from M1/J30, equidistant from Sheffield and Chesterfield.
Open: 29 Mar - 29 Sept: Fri - Sun & BHs, 10.30am - 4.30pm. Also Thurs in Jul & Aug.
Admission: Garden only: Adult £3, Conc. £2.50. Museum & Art Exhibition: Adult £3, Conc. £2.50. Garden, Museum & Art Exhibition: Adult £5, Conc. £4. House: group tours (20+) by prior booking.
ⓘConferences. By arrangement. P
In grounds, on leads.

REVOLUTION HOUSE
High Street, Old Whittington, Chesterfield, Derbyshire S41 9LA
Tel: 01246 345727   **Contact:** Ms A M Knowles
Originally the Cock and Pynot ale house, now furnished in 17th century style.
Location: OS Ref. SK384 749. 3m N of Chesterfield on B6052 off A61.
Open: Good Fri - end Sept: daily, 10am - 4pm. Special opening over Christmas period.
Admission: Free.

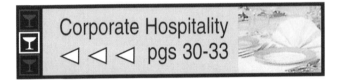

NT Photographic Library: Andreas von Einsiedel

SUDBURY HALL & NATIONAL TRUST MUSEUM OF CHILDHOOD
ASHBOURNE, DERBYSHIRE DE6 5HT
www.nationaltrust.org.uk

Tel: 01283 585305   **Fax:** 01283 585139   **e-mail:** esuxxx@smtp.ntrust.org.uk
Owner: The National Trust   **Contact:** The Property Manager
One of the most individual of late 17th century houses, begun by George Vernon c1660. The rich decoration includes wood carvings by Gibbons and Pierce, superb plasterwork, mythological decorative paintings by Laguerre. The great staircase is one of the finest of its kind in an English house. Also National Trust Museum of Childhood in 19th century service wing of the Hall. The museum contains fascinating and innovative displays about children from the 18th century onwards. There are chimney climbs for adventurous 'sweep-sized' youngsters, and Betty Cadbury's fine collection of toys and dolls is on show.
Location: OS128 Ref. SK160 323. 6m E of Uttoxeter at the junction of A50 Derby - Stoke & A515 Ashbourne.
Open: 16 Mar - 3 Nov: Wed - Sun, BH Mons, Good Fri & 4 Jun, 1 - 5pm (dusk if earlier). Grounds: as Hall, 10am - 5pm. Museum: As house.
Admission: Hall: Adult £3.90, Child £2, Family £9.80. Museum: As house. Joint Ticket for Hall & Museum: Adult £6.30, Child £3.10, Family £15.60. Groups by prior arrangement.
Limited, braille guide. WC. Licensed. Car park only.

SUTTON SCARSDALE HALL ⌗
Chesterfield, Derbyshire
Tel: 01604 735400 (Regional Office)
Owner: English Heritage   **Contact:** The East Midlands Regional Office

The dramatic hilltop shell of a great early 18th century baroque mansion.
Location: OS Ref. SK441 690. Between Chesterfield & Bolsover, 1¹/₂ m S of Arkwright Town.
Open: Daily in summer: 10am - 6pm (5pm Oct - Mar).
Admission: Free.

Derbyshire Countryside Ltd

TISSINGTON HALL ☎
ASHBOURNE, DERBYSHIRE DE6 1RA
www.tissington-hall.com

Tel: 01335 352200   **Fax:** 01335 352201   **e-mail:** tisshall@dircon.co.uk
Owner/Contact: Sir Richard FitzHerbert Bt
Home of the FitzHerbert family for over 500 years. The Hall stands in a superbly maintained estate village, and contains wonderful panelling and fine old masters. A 10 acre garden and arboretum. Schools very welcome. Award-winning Old Coach House Tearoom, open daily 11am - 5pm for lunch and tea.
Location: OS Ref. SK175 524. 4m N of Ashbourne off A515 towards Buxton.

Open: 1 - 5 Apr, 3 - 7 Jun: Mon - Fri. 16 Jul - 30 Aug: Tue - Fri, 1.30 - 4.30pm. Groups and societies welcome by appointment throughout the year. Corporate days and events also available, contact: The Estate Office on 01335 352200
Admission: Hall & Gardens: Adult £5.50, Child (10-16yrs) £2.50, Conc. £4.50, Gardens only: Adult £2, Child £1.

ⓘ No photography in house. ⏲ ♿ Partial. WCs at tearooms.
◗ Tearoom adjacent to Hall. 🅵 Obligatory. 🅿 Limited. ▣ ♿ Guide dogs only. ✳

Eyam Hall

WINGFIELD MANOR ⌗
Garner Lane, South Wingfield, Derbyshire DE5 7NH
Tel: 01773 832060
Owner: Mr S Critchlow (managed by English Heritage)   **Contact:** The Custodian
Huge, ruined, country mansion built in the mid-15th century. Mary Queen of Scots was imprisoned here in 1569, 1584 and 1585.
Location: OS Ref. SK374 548. S side of B5035, ¹/₂ m S of South Wingfield village. Access by 600yd drive (no vehicles). From M1 J28, W on A38, A615 (Matlock road) at Alfreton and turn onto B5035 after 1¹/₂ m.
Open: 29 Mar - 30 Sept: Wed - Sun, 10am - 6pm. 1 - 31 Oct: Wed - Sun, 10am - 5pm. 1 Nov - 31 Mar: 10am - 4pm. Closed 24 - 26 Dec & 1 Jan. Closed 1 - 2pm in winter. The Manor incorporates a working farm. Visitors are requested to respect the privacy of the owners, to keep to visitor routes and refrain from visiting outside official opening times.
Admission: Adult £3, Child £1.50, Conc. £2.30.

East Midlands - England

BELVOIR CASTLE 🏰

GRANTHAM

www.belvoircastle.com

Belvoir Castle, home of the Duke and Duchess of Rutland, commands a magnificent view over the Vale of Belvoir. The name Belvoir, meaning beautiful view, dates back to Norman times, when Robert de Todeni, Standard Bearer to William the Conqueror, built the first castle on this superb site. Destruction caused by two Civil Wars and by a catastrophic fire in 1816 have breached the continuity of Belvoir's history. The present building owes much to the inspiration and taste of Elizabeth, 5th Duchess of Rutland and was built after the fire.

Inside the Castle are notable art treasures including works by Poussin, Holbein, Rubens, and Reynolds, Gobelin and Mortlake tapestries, Chinese silks, furniture, fine porcelain and sculpture.

The Queen's Royal Lancers' Museum at Belvoir has a fascinating exhibition of the history of the Regiment, as well as a fine collection of weapons, uniforms and medals.

GARDENS

The Statue Gardens are built into the hillside below the castle and take their name from the collection of 17th century sculptures on view. The sculpture collection has been enhanced with the introduction of a large collection of contemporary statuary which can be viewed and is for sale. The garden is planted so that there is nearly always something in flower. The Duchess' private Spring Gardens are available for viewing throughout the year by pre-booked groups of 15 persons or more. Details from the Estate Office.

Owner:
His Grace The Duke
of Rutland

▶ CONTACT

Andrew Norman
Castle Estate Office
Belvoir Castle
Grantham
Leicestershire NG32 1PD

Tel: 01476 870262
Fax: 01476 870443
e-mail: info@
belvoircastle.com

▶ LOCATION

OS Ref. SK820 337

A1 from London 110m
York 100m
Grantham 7m.
A607 Grantham-Melton
Mowbray.

Air: East Midlands
International.

Rail: Grantham Stn 7m

Bus: Melton Mowbray -
Vale of Belvoir via
Castle Car Park.

Taxi: Grantham Taxis
01476 563944 / 563988.

CONFERENCE/FUNCTION

ROOM	SIZE	MAX CAPACITY
State Dining Room	52' x 31'	130
Regents Gallery	131' x 16'	300
Old Kitchen	45' x 22'	100

🎭🛈 Suitable for exhibitions, product launches, conferences, filming, photography welcomed (permit £2).

🍽 Banquets, private room available.

♿ Ground floor and restaurant accessible. Please telephone for advice. WC.

🍴 Licensed restaurant. Groups catered for.

🚶 By prior arrangement Additional charge of £1.50pp. Tour time: 1¼ hrs.

🅿 Ample. Coaches can take passengers to entrance by arrangement but should report to the main car park and ticket office on arrival.

📖 Guided tours. Teacher's pack. Education room. Picnic area and adventure playground.

🐕 Guide dogs only.

🔔 ❄

🎭 Tel for details.

▶ OPENING TIMES

Summer
28 - 31 March
1 - 7 & 14, 21 & 28 April
May - Sept: Daily
October: Suns only
11am - 5pm.

Winter
Groups welcome by appointment.

▶ ADMISSION

Adult	£7.00
Child (5-16yrs)	£4.50
OAP/Student	£6.50
Family (2+2)	£19.00

Groups (20-200)
Adult	£6.00
Child (5-16yrs)	£3.50
OAP/Student	£5.00

Spring Garden Tours (15+)
Adult	£5.00
OAP/Student	£4.50

STANFORD HALL 🏛

NR RUGBY

www.stanfordhall.co.uk

Owner:
The Lady Braye

▶ CONTACT

Lt Col E Aubrey-Fletcher
Stanford Hall
Lutterworth
Leicestershire
LE17 6DH

Tel: 01788 860250
Fax: 01788 860870

e-mail: enquiries@
stanfordhall.co.uk

▶ LOCATION

OS Ref. SP587 793

M1/J18 6m,
M1/J19 (from/to
the N only) 2m,
M6 exit/access at
A14/M1(N)J 2m,
A14 2m.
Follow Historic
House signs.

Rail: Rugby Stn 7¹/₂ m.

Air: Birmingham
Airport 27m.

Taxi: Fone-A-Car.
01788 543333.

Stanford has been the home of the Cave family, ancestors of the present owner, Lady Braye, since 1430. In the 1690s, Sir Roger Cave commissioned the Smiths of Warwick to pull down the old Manor House and build the present Hall, which is an excellent example of their work and of the William and Mary period.

As well as over 5000 books, the handsome Library contains many interesting manuscripts, the oldest dating from 1150. The splendid pink and gold Ballroom has a fine coved ceiling with four trompe l'oeil shell corners. Throughout the house are portraits of the family and examples of

furniture and objects which they collected over the centuries. There is also a collection of Royal Stuart portraits, previously belonging to the Cardinal Duke of York, the last of the male Royal Stuarts. An unusual collection of family costumes is displayed in the Old Dining Room, which also houses some early Tudor portraits and a fine Empire chandelier.

The Hall and Stables are set in an attractive Park on the banks of Shakespeare's Avon. There is a walled Rose Garden behind the Stables. An early ha-ha separates the North Lawn from the mile-long North Avenue.

▶ OPENING TIMES

Summer

Easter - 29 September:

Sats & Tues after BHs
House: 1.30 - 5.30pm.
Museum closed.

Suns & BH Mons:
House & Museum:
1.30 - 5.30pm

Last admissions 5pm.

NB. On BH Mons & Event days: grounds open at 12 noon.

House open any day or evening for pre-booked groups.

Winter

30 Sept - 18 Apr 2003
Closed to public. Available during October for corporate events.

▶ ADMISSION

House & Grounds
Adult £4.50
Child (4-15yrs) £2.00
Groups (20+)
Adult £4.20
Child (4-15yrs) £1.80

Grounds only
Adult £2.50
Child (4-15yrs) £1.00

Motorcycle Museum
Adult £1.00
Child (4-15yrs) £0.35
School Group
Adult .... FREE
Child (4-15yrs)....... £0.20

CONFERENCE/FUNCTION

ROOM	SIZE	MAX CAPACITY
Ballroom	39' x 26'	100
Old Dining Rm	30' x 20'	70
Crocodile Room	39' x 20'	60

📷 ℹ Craft centre (most Suns). No photography in house. Corporate days, clay pigeon shoots, filming, photography, small conferences and fashion shows. Parkland, helicopter landing area, lecture room, Blüthner piano.

🍽 Lunches, dinners & wedding receptions (outside caterers).

♿ Visitors may alight at the entrance. WC.

☕ Teas, lunch & supper. Groups must book (70 max.)

🚶 Tour time: ³/₄ hr in groups of approx 25.

🅿 1,000 cars and 6 - 8 coaches. Free meals for coach drivers, coach parking on gravel in front of house.

👶 £1.80 per child. Guide provided by prior arrangement, nature trail with guide book & map, motorcycle museum.

🐕 In park, on leads.

🎭 Tel for details.

East Midlands - England

ABBEY PUMPING STATION
Corporation Road, Leicester LE4 5PX
Tel: 0116 2995111 **Fax:** 0116 2995125 **www.**leicestermuseums.ac.uk
Owner: Leicester City Council   **Contact:** Stuart Warburton
A Victorian sewage pumping station with four massive beam engines still working by
steam. Exhibitions include: 'Flushed with Pride' which explores the history, science
and technology of public health and 'Transport of Delight'. Series of special events
and steam rallies/days throughout the year.
Location: OS Ref. SK589 067. 2m N of city centre situated on River Soar riverside
walk and 400m E of A6. 5 mins from Belgrave Hall.
Open: Please contact Abbey Pumping Station for details.
Admission: Free except for special events.
🎥 🎭 ♿Partial. 🍴On event days. 🅵 By arrangement. 🅿 ⬛ 🐕Guide dogs only.
❄ 💺 Tel for details.

ASHBY-DE-LA-ZOUCH CASTLE ♯
South Street, Ashby-de-la-Zouch, Leicestershire LE65 1BR
Tel: 01530 413343
Owner: English Heritage   **Contact:** The Custodian
The impressive ruins of this late medieval castle are dominated by a magnificent tower,
over 80 feet high, which was split in two during the Civil War. Panoramic views.
Location: OS Ref. SK363 167. In Ashby de la Zouch, 12m S of Derby on A511. SE of
town centre.
Open: 29 Mar - 31 Oct: daily, 10am - 6pm (5pm in Oct). 1 Nov - 31 Mar: Wed - Sun,
10am - 4pm. Closed 24 - 26 Dec & 1 Jan.
Admission: Adult £3, Child £1.50, Conc. £2.30, Family £7.50.
♿Grounds. 🅿 🐕On leads. ❄ 💺 Tel for details.

BELGRAVE HALL & GARDENS
Church Road, off Thurcaston Road, Leicester LE4 5PE
Tel: 0116 2666590 **Fax:** 0116 2613063 **www.**leicestermuseums.ac.uk
Owner: Leicester City Council   **Contact:** Emma Martin
Belgrave Hall and Gardens, famed for its ghost story, is a period house with period
decoration ranging from 1750 - 1900. The three story house is open throughout, and
a series of special events is organised throughout the year using themes and living
interpretation. Includes period Victorian formal gardens. Displays include the
Gimson Collection.
Location: OS Ref. SK593 072. 2m N of city centre, on riverside walk and off the
A6/A46 Loughborough Road.
Open: Please contact Belgrave Hall for details.
Admission: Free.
🎥 🎭 ♿Partial. WC. Staff with sign language skills. 🅵 By arrangement.
🅿Limited (on street). ⬛ 🐕Guide dogs only. ❄ 💺 Tel for details.

BELVOIR CASTLE 🏰   *See page 296 for full page entry.*

BOSWORTH BATTLEFIELD
VISITOR CENTRE & COUNTRY PARK, SUTTON CHENEY, MARKET BOSWORTH CV13 0AD
www.leics.gov.uk

Tel: 01455 290429 **Fax:** 01455 292841 **e-mail:** bosworth@leics.gov.uk
Owner: Leicestershire County Council   **Contact:** Ranger
Historic site of the Battle of Bosworth Field 1485, where King Richard III lost his
crown and his life to the future Henry VII. Visitor Centre, film theatre, battle trail,
picnic areas and car parks. Summer event programme: Medieval Spectacular 17th
and 18th Aug 2002 (including battle re-enactment). Living history displays.
Location: OS Ref. SK404 001. Bounded by A5, A444, A447, B585. Clearly
signposted from all these roads.
Open: 1 Apr - 31 Oct: Mon - Sat, 11am - 5pm. Sun & BHs, 11am - 6pm. Nov &
Dec: Suns, 11am - dusk. Mar: Sats & Suns, 11am - 5pm.
Admission: Adult £3, Child/Conc. £1.90, Family (2+3) £7.95. Groups (20+): Adult
£2.30, Child/Conc. £1.60. (Opening times and charges subject to review.)
🎥 🎭 ♿Partial. 🍴Licensed. 🅵 By arrangement. 🅿 ⬛ ❄ 💺

Stanford Hall

BRADGATE PARK & SWITHLAND WOOD COUNTRY PARK
Bradgate Park, Newtown Linford, Leics
Tel: 0116 2362713
Owner: Bradgate Park Trust   **Contact:** M H Harrison
Includes the ruins of the brick medieval home of the Grey family and childhood
home of Lady Jane Grey. Also has a medieval deer park.
Location: OS Ref. SK534 102. 7m NW of Leicester, via Anstey & Newtown Linford.
Country Park gates in Newtown Linford. 1¼ m walk to the ruins.
Open: All year during daylight hours.
Admission: No charge. Car parking charges.

DONINGTON-LE-HEATH MANOR HOUSE
Manor Road, Donington-le-Heath, Leicestershire LE67 2FW
Tel: 01530 831259
Owner/Contact: Leicestershire County Council
Medieval manor c1280 with 16th-17th century alterations.
Location: OS Ref. SK421 126. ½ m SSW of Coalville. 4¼ m W of M1/J22, by A511.
Open: Apr - Sept: daily, 11am - 5pm. Oct - Mar: daily 11am - 3pm.
Admission: Free.

THE GUILDHALL
Guildhall Lane, Leicester LE1 5FQ
Tel: 0116 2532569 **Fax:** 0116 2539626 **www.**leicestermuseums.ac.uk
Owner: Leicester City Council   **Contact:** Nicholas Ladlow
Magnificent timber-framed medieval building c1390. First used by the Corpus Christi
Guild. Became town hall until 1876, includes 17th century town library and Victorian
police cells. The great hall provides a unique setting for a varied programme of music,
storytelling and theatre.
Location: OS Ref. SK584 044. Adjacent to High Street, Cathedral and St Nicholas Place.
Open: Please contact The Guildhall for details.
Admission: Free.
🎥 ♿Partial. 🅵Obligatory. 🅿None. ⬛ 🐕Guide dogs only. ❄
💺Tel for details.

JEWRY WALL MUSEUM & SITE

St Nicholas Circle, Leicester LE1 4LB

Tel: 0116 2473021   **Fax:** 0116 2512257   **www**.leicestermuseums.ac.uk

Owner: Leicester City Council   **Contact:** John Lucas

Jewry Wall Museum focuses on the archaeology and history of Leicestershire from prehistoric times to 1485. Inside you can see the skeleton of the Saxon 'Glen Parva Lady' alongside fine mosaics, wall paintings and other legacies of the Roman settlement. The 'Making of Leicester' exhibition uncovers the secrets of Leicester's past. After visiting the museum, explore the site of the Roman baths and the massive 2nd century Jewry Wall.

Location: OS Ref. SK581 044. On St Nicholas Circle, at W end of High Street, opposite the Holiday Inn, next to St Nicholas Church.

Open: Please contact Jewry Wall Museum for details.

Admission: Free.

⬛ ⬛Partial. WC. 🛈By arrangement. 🅿 No parking. ⬛ 🐕Guide dogs only. ✳

KIRBY MUXLOE CASTLE ⌗

Kirby Muxloe, Leicestershire LE9 9MD

Tel: 01162 386886

Owner: English Heritage   **Contact:** East Midlands Regional Office (01604 735400)

Picturesque, moated, brick built castle begun in 1480 by William Lord Hastings. It was left unfinished after Hastings was executed in 1483.

Location: OS Ref. SK524 046. 4m W of Leicester off B5380.

Open: 29 Mar - 31 Oct: weekends & BH Mons only, 12 noon - 5pm.

Admission: Adult £2.10, Child £1.10, Conc. £1.60.

LYDDINGTON BEDE HOUSE ⌗

Blue Coat Lane, Lyddington, Uppingham, Rutland LE15 9LZ

Tel: 01572 822438

Owner: English Heritage   **Contact:** The Custodian

Set among golden-stone cottages, the Bede House was originally a medieval palace of the Bishops of Lincoln. It was later converted into an alms house.

Location: OS Ref. SP875 970. In Lyddington, 6m N of Corby, 1m E of A6003.

Open: 29 Mar - 31 Oct: daily, 10am - 6pm (5pm in Oct).

Admission: Adult £3, Child £1.50, Conc. £2.30, Family £7.50.

NEW WALK MUSEUM

New Walk, Leicester LE1 7EA

Tel: 0116 2554100   **Fax:** 0116 2473005   **www**.leicestermuseums.ac.uk

Owner: Leicester City Council   **Contact:** Operations Manager

Leicester's first public museum, opened in 1849, houses six permanent exhibitions: The Ancient Egypt Gallery, Natural History (including dinosaurs), German Expressionist, Victorian and European Art Galleries, Decorative Art Gallery and The Royal Leicestershire Regiment Gallery. 'Wild Space' the new exhibition about wildlife and the the natural world.

Location: OS Ref. SK591 039. Museum Sq, 150m W of Waterloo Way, 250m SW of station.

Open: Please contact New Walk Museum for details.

Admission: Free.

⬛ 🅃 ⬛ 🛈By arrangement. 🅿 Limited. ⬛ 🐕Guide dogs only. ⬛ ✳

NEWARKE HOUSES MUSEUM

The Newarke, Leicester LE2 7BY

Tel: 0116 2473222   **Fax:** 0116 2470403   **www**.leicestermuseums.ac.uk

Owner: Leicester City Council   **Contact:** Philip French

Over 500 years of Leicester's social history can be traced through a visit to Newarke Houses. Everyday life at home and at work is represented in displays of domestic equipment, clocks, toys and furniture. Visit the 1940s village grocer's shop, the reconstructed Victorian street scene and workshops of various local trades. Items belonging to Daniel Lambert, Leicester's largest man, can be seen in the museum. Don't forget to visit the beautiful gardens to the rear of the museum.

Location: OS Ref. SK584 041. Just SW of city centre ring road.

Open: Please contact Newarke Houses Museum for details.

Admission: Free.

🛈Photography in house by permission only. ⬛ ⬛Unsuitable. 🛈By arrangement. 🅿 None. ⬛ 🐕Guide dogs only. ✳

OAKHAM CASTLE

Rutland County Museum, Catmos St, Oakham, Rutland LE15 6HW

Tel: 01572 758440   **www**.rutnet.co.uk/rcc/rutlandmuseums

Owner: Rutland County Council   **Contact:** Mr T Clough

Exceptionally fine Norman Great Hall of a late 12th century fortified manor house, with contemporary musician sculptures. Bailey earthworks and remains of earlier motte. The hall contains over 200 unique horseshoes forfeited by royalty and peers of the realm to the Lord of the Manor from Edward IV onwards.

Location: OS Ref. SK862 088. Near town centre, E of the church.

Open: Late Mar - late Oct (BST): Mon - Sat, 10am - 1pm, 1.30 - 5pm. Sun, 1 - 5pm. Late Oct - Late Mar (GMT): As above, but closing at 4pm. Closed on Good Fri and at Christmas.

Admission: Free.

⬛ ⬛Great Hall. 🅿 For disabled, on request. ⬛ ⬛ ✳

PRESTWOLD HALL

LOUGHBOROUGH, LEICESTERSHIRE LE12 5SQ

Tel: 01509 880236   **Fax:** 01509 889060   **e-mail:** enquiries@prestwold-hall.com

Owner: E J Packe-Drury-Lowe   **Contact:** Henry Weldon

A magnificent private house, largely remodelled in 1843 by William Burn. For the past 350 years it has been the home of the Packe family and contains fine Italian plasterwork, 18th century English and European furniture and a collection of family portraits. The house is not open to the general public but offers excellent facilities as a conference centre, corporate entertainment and wedding venue. Up to 150 guests can be seated and the 20 acres of gardens provide a perfect setting for larger events using marquees. Excellent chefs provide a selection of varied menus complemented by a well stocked wine cellar. Activity days, clay pigeon shooting, motor sports and archery can also be organised on request.

Location: OS Ref. SK578 215. At the heart of the Midlands, 3m E of Loughborough on B675. 5m W of A46 via B676.

Admission: Corporate entertaining venue, conference centre and function venue by arrangement only.

🛈Conferences. 🅃 ⬛Ground floor & grounds. WC. ⬛ ✳

STANFORD HALL 🏛   *See page 297 for full page entry.*

STAUNTON HAROLD CHURCH ⚜

Staunton Harold Church, Ashby-de-la-Zouch, Leicestershire

Tel: 01332 863822   **Fax:** 01332 865272

One of the very few churches to be built during the Commonwealth, erected by Sir Robert Shirley, an ardent Royalist. The interior retains its original 17th century cushions and hangings and includes fine panelling and painted ceilings.

Location: OS Ref. SK379 208. 5m NE of Ashby-de-la-Zouch, W of B587.

Open: 23 Mar - 29 Sept: Wed - Sun & BH Mons (closed Good Fri), 1 - 5pm or sunset if earlier. Oct: Sats & Suns only, 1 - 5pm.

Admission: £1 donation.

⬛Partial. ⬛At hall.

WARTNABY GARDENS

Melton Mowbray, Leicestershire LE14 3HY

Tel: 01664 822296   **Fax:** 01664 822231

Owner: Lord and Lady King

This garden has delightful little gardens within it, including a white garden, a sunken garden and a purple border of shrubs and roses, and there are good herbaceous borders, climbers and old-fashioned roses. A large pool has an adjacent bog garden with primulas, ferns, astilbes and several varieties of willow. There is an arboretum with a good collection of trees and shrub roses, and alongside the drive is a beech hedge in a Grecian pattern. Greenhouses, a fruit and vegetable garden with rose arches and cordon fruit.

Location: OS Ref. SK709 228. 4m NW of Melton Mowbray. From A606 turn W in Ab Kettleby for Wartnaby.

Open: Suns; 28 Apr: plant sale; 19 May: plant sale; 23 Jun: plant fair & sketching clubs exhibition. Groups by appointment at other times (except Weds).

Admission: Adult £2.50, Child Free.

⬛ ⬛ 🛈By arrangement. 🅿 Limited for coaches. 🐕In grounds on leads. ✳ ⬛

East Midlands - England

BURGHLEY HOUSE

STAMFORD

www.burghley.co.uk

Owner:
Burghley House
Preservation Trust Ltd

▶ **CONTACT**

The House Manager
Burghley House
Stamford
Lincolnshire PE9 3JY

Tel: 01780 752451
Fax: 01780 480125

e-mail: burghley@
burghley.co.uk

▶ **LOCATION**

OS Ref. TF048 062

Burghley House
is 1m SE of Stamford.
From London, A1 2hrs.

Visitors entrance
is on B1443.

Rail: London -
Peterborough 1hr
(GNER).
Stamford Station
1¹⁄₂ m, regular service
to Peterborough.

Taxi: Direct Line:
01780 481481.

Burghley House, home of the Cecil family for over 400 years, was built as a country seat during the latter part of the 16th century by Sir William Cecil, later Lord Burghley, principal adviser and Lord Treasurer to Queen Elizabeth.

The House was completed in 1587 and there have been few alterations to the architecture since that date thus making Burghley one of the finest examples of late Elizabethan design in England. The interior was remodelled in the late 17th century by John, 5th Earl of Exeter who was a collector of fine art on a huge scale, establishing the immense collection of art treasures at Burghley. Burghley is truly a 'Treasure House', containing one of the largest private collections of Italian art, unique examples of Chinese and Japanese porcelain and superb items of 18th century furniture. The remodelling work of the 17th century means that examples of the work of

the principal artists and craftsmen of the period are to be found at Burghley: Antonio Verrio, Grinling Gibbons and Louis Laguerre all made major contributions to the beautiful interiors.

PARK AND GARDENS

The house is set in a 300-acre deer park landscaped by 'Capability' Brown. A lake was created by him and delightful avenues of mature trees feature largely in his design. The park is home to a large herd of Fallow deer, established in the 16th century. The Sculpture Garden contains many specimen trees and shrubs and is a display area for a number of dramatic art works by contemporary sculptors. The sculptures are varied in style, but their placement is designed to provoke thought and accentuate the beauty of the surroundings. The private gardens around the house are open in April for the display of spring bulbs. Please telephone for details.

▶ **OPENING TIMES**

Summer
29 March - 27 October
(closed 31 August).
Daily: 11am - 4.30pm
(last admission).

NB. The house is viewed
by guided tour except on
Sat and Sun afternoons
and BHs when there are
guides in each room.

**Gift Shop & Orangery
Restaurant**
Daily, 11am - 5pm.

The South Garden
Good Fri - end April:
daily, 11am - 4pm.

Winter
28 October - 1 April
closed to the
general public.

The Park and Sculpture
Gardens are open all year
and entry is free of charge.

▶ **ADMISSION**

Adult £7.10
Child* £3.50
OAP £6.50
Groups (20+)
Adult £6.20
School groups
(up to 14 yrs)......... £3.20

* (5 - 12 years) one child
Free with every paying
adult, otherwise £3.50.

| Suitable for a variety of events, large park, golf course, helicopter landing area, cricket pitch. No photography in house. | Obligatory, except Sats & Suns after 1pm. Tour time: 1¹⁄₂ hrs at ¹⁄₂ hr intervals. Max. 25. |

Visitors may alight at entrance. WC. Chair lift to Orangery Coffee Shop, house tour has two staircases one with chairlift.

Restaurant/tearoom. Groups can book in advance.

Ample. Free refreshments for coach drivers.

Welcome. Guide provided.

No dogs in house.

CONFERENCE/FUNCTION

ROOM	SIZE	MAX CAPACITY
Great Hall	70' x 30'	150
Orangery	100' x 20'	120

AUBOURN HALL

Lincoln LN5 9DZ

Tel: 01522 788270 **Fax:** 01522 788199

Owner/Contact: Lady Nevile

Late 16th century house with important staircase and panelled rooms. Garden.

Location: OS Ref. SK928 628. 6m SW of Lincoln. 2m SE of A46.

Open: Aubourn Hall will not be opened on a regular basis during 2001. The garden will be opened on occasional Sundays.

Admission: Adult £3, OAP £2.50.

BURGHLEY HOUSE ⛪   *See page 300 for full page entry*

AYSCOUGHFEE HALL MUSEUM & GARDENS

CHURCHGATE, SPALDING, LINCOLNSHIRE PE11 2RA

www.sholland.gov.uk

Tel: 01775 725468 **Fax:** 01775 762715

Owner: South Holland District Council   **Contact:** Mrs S Sladen

A late-Medieval wool merchant's house surrounded by five acres of walled gardens. The Hall contains the Museum of South Holland Life and has galleries on local villages, the history of Spalding, agriculture and horticulture. There is also a gallery dedicated to Matthew Flinders, the district's most famous son. Many specimens from the Ashley Maples bird collections are on display.

Location: OS Ref. TF240 230. E bank of the River Welland, 5 mins walk from Spalding town centre.

Open: All year: Mon - Fri, 9am - 5pm, Sats, 10am - 5pm. Suns & BHs, 11am - 5pm. Closed weekends in Nov - Feb.

Admission: Free.

ℹ TIC located in Hall. 📷 ♿ Partial. 🍴 Apr - Sept only. ✗ By arrangement. 🅿 Limited for coaches. 🚫 🐕 In grounds, on leads. Guide dogs only in Hall ❄

Burghley House

National Trust Photographic Library/Nick Meers

BELTON HOUSE ✻

GRANTHAM, LINCOLNSHIRE NG32 2LS

www.nationaltrust.org.uk

Tel: 01476 566116 / 592900 **Fax:** 01476 579071 **e-mail:** ebehah@smtp.ntrust.org.uk

Owner: The National Trust   **Contact:** The Property Manager

The crowning achievement of Restoration country house architecture, built 1685 - 88 for Sir John Brownlow, and altered by James Wyatt in the 1770s. Plasterwork ceilings by Edward Goudge and fine wood carvings of the Grinling Gibbons school. The rooms contain portraits, furniture, tapestries, oriental porcelain, silver and silver gilt. Gardens with orangery, landscaped park with lakeside walk, woodland adventure playground, and Bellmount Tower. Fine church with family monuments.

Location: OS Ref. SK929 395. 3m NE of Grantham on A607. Signed off the A1.

Open: House: 23 Mar - 3 Nov: Wed - Sun (open BH Mons, Good Fri & 4 Jun), 12.30 - 5pm. Garden & Park: as house, 11am - 5.30pm (Aug: 10.30am - 5.30pm). Garden only: 9 Nov - 22 Dec: Sat & Sun, 12 noon - 4pm. Park only: on foot only. Shop & Restaurant: as house.

Admission: Adult £5.60, Child £2.80, Family £14. Discount for groups.

📷 ♿ Partial. Please telephone for arrangements. 🍴 Licensed. 🅿 🚫 ▲

DODDINGTON HALL ⛪

LINCOLN LN6 4RU

www.doddingtonhall.free-online.co.uk

Tel: 01522 694308 **Fax:** 01522 685259

e-mail: estateoffice@doddingtonhall.free-online.co.uk

Owner: Mr & Mrs A Jarvis   **Contact:** The House Manager

Magnificent Smythson mansion was completed in 1600 and stands today with its contemporary walled gardens and gatehouse. The Hall is still very much the home of the Jarvis family and has an elegant Georgian interior with a fine collection of porcelain, furniture, paintings and textiles representing 400 years of unbroken family occupation. The beautiful gardens contain a superb layout of box-edged parterres, sumptuous borders that provide colour all seasons, and a wild garden with a marvellous succession of spring bulbs and flowering shrubs set among mature trees. Sandford Award winning schools project, and a nature trail into the nearby countryside.

Location: OS Ref. SK900 701. 5m W of Lincoln on the B1190, signposted off the A46 Lincoln bypass.

Open: Gardens only: 24 Feb - 28 Apr: Suns, 2 - 6pm. House & Garden: 1 May - 29 Sept: Weds, Suns & BH Mons, 2 - 6pm.

Admission: Gardens only: Adult £3.10, Child £1.55. House & Garden: Adult £4.60, Child £2.30, Family £12.75 (2+2). 10% discount for groups (20+) on open days.

ℹ No photography. No stilettos. 📷 🍴 Occasional. ♿ Gardens. WC. 🚫 ✗ By arrangement. 🚫 🅿 🐕 Guide dogs only. 🚫 Tel for details.

East Midlands - England

GAINSBOROUGH OLD HALL ⌗
Parnell Street, Gainsborough, Lincolnshire DN21 2NB
Tel: 01427 612669
Owner: English Heritage   **Contact:** The Custodian
A large medieval house with a magnificent Great Hall and suites of rooms.
A collection of historic furniture and a re-created medieval kitchen are on display.
Location: OS Ref. SK815 895. In centre of Gainsborough, opposite library.
Open: Easter Sun - 31 Oct: Mon - Sat, 10am - 5pm. Suns, 2 - 5.30pm. 1 Nov - Easter
Sat: Mon - Sat, 10am - 5pm (closed Good Fri, Suns Nov - Mar, 24 - 26 Dec & 1 Jan).
Admission: Adult £2.50, Child £1, Conc. £1.50 (2001/2002 prices).

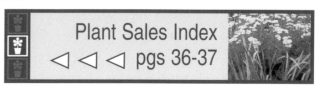

Plant Sales Index
◁ ◁ ◁ pgs 36-37

GRIMSTHORPE CASTLE, PARK & GARDENS 🏛
GRIMSTHORPE, BOURNE, LINCOLNSHIRE PE10 0NB
www.grimsthorpe.co.uk

Tel: 01778 591205 **Fax:** 01778 591259 **e-mail:** ray@grimsthorpe.co.uk
Owner: Grimsthorpe and Drummond Castle Trust Ltd   **Contact:** Ray Biggs
Home of the Willoughby de Eresby family since 1516. Examples of 13th century
architecture, Tudor period and Sir John Vanbrugh's last major work. State Rooms and
picture galleries contain magnificent contents and paintings. 3,000 acre landscaped
park, with lakes, ancient woods, nature trail, woodland adventure playground, red
deer herd, formal and woodland gardens, unusual ornamental vegetable garden,
family cycle trail, events programme. Landrover tours with park ranger.
Location: OS Ref. TF040 230. 4m NW of Bourne on A151, 8m E of Colsterworth
roundabout off A1.

Open: 31 Mar - 29 Sept: Suns, Thurs & BHs. Aug: Sun - Thur. Park & Gardens: 11am -
6pm. Castle: 1 - 4.30pm (last admission). Tearoom: 11am - 5.15pm(last orders).
Groups: Apr - Sept: anytime by arrangement. Also evening candlelight supper tours.
Admission: Park & Garden: Adult £3, Child £2, Conc. £2.50, Family (2+2) £8. Castle,
Park & Garden: Adult £6.50, Child £3.50, Conc. £5.50, Family (2+2) £16.50. Special
charges may be made for special events. Group rates on application.

ℹ No photography in house. 📷 ☎ Conferences (up to 70), inc catering ♿ Partial. WC.
♿ Licensed. 🎦 Obligatory except Suns. 🅿 Limited for coaches.🔲
🐕 In grounds, on leads. 📞 Tel for details.

GUNBY HALL 🌿
Gunby, Spilsby, Lincolnshire PE23 5SS
Tel: 01909 486411 **Fax:** 01909 486377 **www.**nationaltrust.org.uk
Owner: The National Trust   **Contact:** Regional Office
A red brick house with stone dressings, built in 1700 and extended in 1870s. Within
the house, there is good early 18th century wainscoting and a fine oak staircase, also
English furniture and portraits by Reynolds. Also of interest is the contemporary
stable block, a walled kitchen and flower garden, sweeping lawns and borders and
an exhibition of Field Marshal Sir Archibald Montgomery-Massingberd's memorabilia.
Gunby was reputedly Tennyson's 'haunt of ancient peace'.
Location: OS122 Ref. TF466 672. 2¹/₂ m NW of Burgh Le Marsh, 7m W of Skegness.
On S side of A158 (access off roundabout).
Open: Ground floor of house & garden: 27 Mar - end Sept: Weds, 2 - 6pm. Last
admission 5.30pm. Closed BHs. Garden also open Thurs, 2 - 6pm. House & garden
also open Tues, Thurs & Fris by written appointment to J D Wrisdale at above
address.
Admission: House & Garden: Adult £3.70, Child £1.80, Family £9.20. Garden only:
Adult £2.60, Child £1.30, Family £6.50. No reduction for groups. Access roads
unsuitable for coaches which must park in layby at gates ¹/₂ m from Hall.
♿ Grounds.   🐕 In grounds, on leads.

HARLAXTON MANOR
Harlaxton, Grantham, Lincolnshire NG32 1AG
Tel: 01476 403000 **Fax:** 01476 403030
Owner: University of Evansville   **Contact:** Mrs A Clark
Neo-Elizabethan house. Grandiose and imposing exterior by Anthony Salvin.
Internally an architectural tour de force with various styles and an unparalleled
Cedar Staircase.
Location: OS Ref. SK895 323. 3m W of Grantham (10 mins from A1) A607. SE of
the village.
Open: House: Sun 7 Jun & Sun 8 Aug: 11am - 5pm. House open at other times for
group tours by appointment only.
Admission: House open days: Adult £5, Child £2, OAP £4.

HECKINGTON WINDMILL
Heckington, Sleaford, Lincolnshire
Tel: 01529 461919   **Contact:** Derek James
Britain's last surviving eight sail windmill.
Location: OS Ref. TF145 436. W side of B1394, S side of Heckington village.
Open: Nov - Easter: Suns only, 2 - 5pm. Easter - 15 Jul: Thur - Sun & BH Mons, 12 noon
- 5pm. 16 Jul - 2 Sept: daily, 12 noon - 5pm. 8 Sept - 28 Oct: Sats & Suns only,
2 - 5pm. Closed 23 & 30 Dec.
Admission: Ground floor: Free. Mill: Adult £1.50, Child 75p.

LEADENHAM HOUSE

Leadenham House, Lincolnshire LN5 0PU

Tel: 01400 273256 **Fax:** 01400 272237

Owner: Mr P Reeve   **Contact:** Mr and Mrs P Reeve

Late eighteenth century house in park setting.

Location: OS Ref. SK949 518. Entrance on A17 Leadenham bypass (between Newark and Sleaford).

Open: 15 - 19 Apr; 7 - 10 & 28 - 30 May; 10 - 14, 17 - 20 & 24 - 28 Jun. Also Spring & Aug BHs: 2 - 5pm.

Admission: £3. Groups by prior arrangement only.

[i] No photography. 🔍 🖼

LINCOLN CASTLE

Castle Hill, Lincoln LN1 3AA

Tel: 01522 511068   **Contact:** The Manager

Built by William the Conqueror in 1068. Informative exhibition of the 1215 Magna Carta.

Location: OS Ref. SK975 718. Opposite west front of Lincoln Cathedral.

Open: BST: Sats, 9.30am - 5.30pm, Suns, 11am - 5.30pm. GMT: Mon - Sat: 9.30am - 4pm, Suns, 11am - 4pm. Closed Christmas Day, Boxing Day & New Year's Day.

Admission: Adult £2.50, Child £1, Family (2+3) £6.50.

LINCOLN CATHEDRAL

Lincoln LN2 1PZ

Tel: 01522 544544 **e-mail:** chiefexecutive@lincolncathedral.com

www.lincolncathedral.com   **Contact:** Communications Office

Medieval Gothic Cathedral of outstanding historical and architectural merit. Schools centre.

Location: OS Ref. SK978 718. At the centre of Uphill, Lincoln.

Open: All year: May - Aug: 7.15am - 8pm, Suns, 7.15am - 6pm. Sept - May: 7.15am - 6pm, Suns, 7.15am - 5pm. Tours daily: Jan - Apr & Oct - Dec: 11am & 2pm. May - Sept: 11am, 1pm & 3pm. Roof tours available. Booked tours throughout the year.

Admission: £3.50, Child up to 14yrs Free, Conc. £3.

LINCOLN MEDIEVAL BISHOPS' PALACE ⌗

Minster Yard, Lincoln LN2 1PU

Tel: 01522 527468

Owner: English Heritage   **Contact:** The Custodian

In the shadow of Lincoln Cathedral are the remains of this medieval palace of the Bishops of Lincoln. Climb the stairs to the Alnwick Tower, explore the undercroft and see one of the most northerly vineyards in Europe.

Location: OS121 Ref. SK981 717. S side of Lincoln Cathedral, in Lincoln.

Open: 29 Mar - 31 Oct: daily, 10am - 6pm (5pm in Oct). 1 Nov - 31 Mar: weekends only, 10am - 4pm. Closed 24 - 26 Dec & 1 Jan. Open daily for Lincoln Christmas Market.

Admission: Adult £3, Child £1.50, Conc. £2.30, Family £7.50. 15% discount for groups (11+).

✳ 🏛 Tel for details.

MARSTON HALL

Marston, Grantham NG32 2HQ

Tel/Fax: 01400 250225 **e-mail:** jthorold@aol.com

Owner/Contact: J R Thorold

The ancient home of the Thorold family. The building contains Norman, Plantagenet Tudor and Georgian elements through to the modern day.

Location: OS Ref. SK893 437. 5m N of Grantham and about 1m E of A1.

Open: 4 - 6 & 25 - 27 May, 6 - 9 & 22 - 24 Jun, 24 - 26 Aug, 14 - 16 & 21-23 Sept & 5 - 7 & 19 - 21 Oct.

Admission: Adult £3.50, Child £1.50. Groups must book.

[i] No photography. 🔍 Partial. WC.

SIBSEY TRADER WINDMILL ⌗

Sibsey, Boston, Lincolnshire

Tel: 01205 460647

Owner: English Heritage   **Contact:** The East Midlands Regional Office

An impressive old mill built in 1877, with its machinery and six sails still intact. Flour milled on the spot can be bought here.

Location: OS Ref. TF345 511. ^{1}/$_2$ m W of village of Sibsey, off A16, 5m N of Boston.

Open: Mill can be seen in action during the year, please telephone for details.

Admission: Adult £1.80, Child 90p, Conc. £1.40 (2001/2002 prices).

NTPL / Andrew Butler

TATTERSHALL CASTLE 🌿

Tattershall, Lincoln, Lincolnshire LN4 4LR

www.nationaltrust.org.uk

Tel/Fax: 01526 342543 **e-mail:** etcxxx@smtp.ntrust.org.uk

Owner: The National Trust   **Contact:** The Custodian

A vast fortified tower built c1440 for Ralph Cromwell, Lord Treasurer of England. The Castle is an important example of an early brick building, with a tower containing state apartments, rescued from dereliction and restored by Lord Curzon 1911-14. Four great chambers, with ancillary rooms, contain late gothic fireplaces and brick vaulting. There are tapestries and information displays in turret rooms.

Location: OS122 Ref. TF209 575. On S side of A153, 15m NE of Sleaford, 10m SW of Horncastle.

Open: 23 Mar - 3 Nov: daily except Thur & Fri, 11am - 5.30pm (Oct: 11am - 4pm). Also open Thur in Aug. 9 Nov - 15 Dec: Sat & Sun, 12 noon - 4pm.

Admission: Adult £3.20, Child £1.60, Family £8. Group discounts.

🔍 Ground floor. WC. 🖼 Car park only. 🔔 Free. 🔺

WOOLSTHORPE MANOR 🌿

23 Newton Way, Woolsthorpe-by-Colsterworth, Grantham NG33 5NR

Tel/Fax: 01476 860338 **e-mail:** ewmxxx@smtp.ntrust.org.uk

www.nationaltrust.org.uk

Owner: The National Trust   **Contact:** The Custodian

This small 17th century farmhouse was the birthplace and family home of Sir Isaac Newton. Some of his major work was formulated here, during the Plague years (1665 - 67); an early edition of the Principia is on display. The orchard has a descendant of the famous apple tree. Science Discovery Centre and exhibition of Sir Isaac Newton's work.

Location: OS130 Ref. SK924 244. 7m S of Grantham, ^{1}/$_2$ m NW of Colsterworth, 1m W of A1.

Open: House & Science Discovery Centre: 1 - 22 Mar: Sat & Sun, 1 - 5pm; 23 Mar - 29 Sept: Wed - Sun (open BH Mons, Good Fri & 4 Jun), 1 - 5pm (Jul & Aug: 1 - 6pm). 5 Oct - 3 Nov: Sat & Sun, 1 - 5pm, also Wed - Sun, 1 - 5pm half term week. 'The Science of Christmas' 14/15 & 21/22 Dec.

Admission: Adult £3.50, Child £1.70, Family £8.70, no reduction for groups which must book in advance.

🔍 Ground floor. 🅿 Limited. 🖼 Car park only.

Website Information
◁ ◁ ◁   pg 39

The Stable Block

ALTHORP
NORTHAMPTON
www.althorp.com

Owner:
The Earl Spencer

▶ CONTACT
Visitor Manager
Althorp
Northampton NN7 4HQ

Tel: 01604 770107
Fax: 01604 770042

**Dedicated booking
line:** 0870 1679000

e-mail:
mail@althorp.com

▶ LOCATION
OS Ref. SP682 652

From the M1/J16, 7m
J18, 10m.
Situated on A428
Northampton - Rugby.
London on average 85
mins away.

Rail: 5m from
Northampton station.
14m from Rugby
station.

The history of Althorp is the history of a family. The Spencers have lived and died here for nearly five centuries and twenty generations.

Since the death of Diana, Princess of Wales, Althorp has become known across the world, but before that tragic event, connoisseurs had heard of this most classic of English stately homes on account of the magnificence of its contents and the beauty of its setting.

Next to the mansion at Althorp lies the honey-coloured stable block, a truly breathtaking building which at one time accommodated up to 100 horses and 40 grooms. The stables are now the setting for the Exhibition celebrating the life of Diana, Princess of Wales and honouring her memory after her death. The freshness and modernity of the facilities are a unique tribute to a woman who captivated the world in her all-too-brief existence.

All visitors are invited to view the House, Exhibition and Grounds as well as the Island in the Round Oval where Diana, Princess of Wales is laid to rest.

Please contact the dedicated booking line (24 hour service) Tel: 0870 1679000 or book on-line at www.althorp.com

The Picture Gallery

▶ OPENING TIMES
Summer

1 July - 30 September
(closed 31 August)
Daily, 10am - 5pm.

Last admission 4pm.

At the time of booking visitors will be asked to state a preference for a morning or an afternoon visit.

**Pre-booking
recommended.**

Winter
Closed.

▶ ADMISSION
House & Garden
(Pre-booked)
Adult £10.50
Child* (5-17yrs)........ £5.50
OAP £8.50
Family (2+3) £26.50

(Paying at gate
subject to availability)
Adult £11.50
Child* (5-17yrs).........£5.50
OAP £9.50
Family (2+3) £28.50

* under 5yrs Free.
Carers accompanying visitors with disabilities are admitted free.

There is a supplement to view the upstairs rooms of the House of £2.50pp.

Group visits by arrangement only, Tel 01604 772110.

All the profits from visitor activity at Althorp are donated to the **Diana, Princess of Wales Memorial Fund**, a registered charity, subject to a minimum annual donation of £10,000.

Numbers are limited each day. Advance booking is recommended.

Information leaflet issued to all ticket holders who book in advance. No indoor photography with still or video cameras.

Visitor Centre & ground floor of house accessible. WCs.

Café.

Limited for coaches.

Guide dogs only.

BOUGHTON HOUSE 🏛

KETTERING

www.boughtonhouse.org.uk

Owner:
His Grace The Duke
of Buccleuch &
Queensberry KT

▶ **CONTACT**

Gareth Fitzpatrick
The Living
Landscape Trust
Boughton House
Kettering
Northamptonshire
NN14 1BJ

Tel: 01536 515731
Fax: 01536 417255

e-mail:
llt@boughtonhouse.
org.uk

▶ **LOCATION**

OS Ref. SP900 815

3m N of
Kettering on
A43 - junction
from A14.

Signposted through
Geddington.

Boughton House is the Northamptonshire home of the Duke of Buccleuch and Queensberry KT, and his Montagu ancestors since 1528. A 500 year old Tudor monastic building gradually enlarged around seven courtyards until the French style addition of 1695, which has lead to Boughton House being described as 'England's Versailles'.

The house contains an outstanding collection of 17th and 18th century French and English furniture, tapestries, 16th century carpets, porcelain, painted ceilings and notable works by El Greco, Murillo, Caracci and 40 Van Dyck sketches. There is an incomparable Armoury and Ceremonial Coach.

Beautiful parkland with historic avenues, lakes, picnic area, gift shop, adventure woodland play area, plant centre and tearoom. Boughton House is administered by The Living Landscape Trust, which was created by the present Duke of Buccleuch to show the relationship between the historic Boughton House and its surrounding, traditional, working estate.

For information on the group visits programme and educational services, including fine arts courses run in conjunction with Sotheby's Institute, please contact The Living Landscape Trust. Our newly developed Internet website gives information on Boughton House and The Living Landscape Trust, including a 'virtual' tour, together with full details of our schools' educational facilities (Sandford Award winner 1988, 1993 and 1998).

Silver award winner of the 1st Historic House Awards, given by AA and NPI, in co-operation with the Historic Houses Association, for the privately-owned historic house open to the public which has best preserved its integrity, character of its architecture and furniture, while remaining a lived-in family home.

▶ **OPENING TIMES**
Summer

House
1 August - 1 September
Daily, 2 - 4.30pm.

Grounds
1 May - 1 September
Daily:
(except Fris, May - July)
1 - 5pm.

During August opening staterooms also on view but strictly by prior appointment which can be made by telephone, fax or e-mail. For conservation reasons, numbers are restricted.

Opening of the Woodland Adventure Play Area is subject to weather conditions for reasons of health and safety.

Winter

Daily by appointment throughout the year for educational groups - contact for details.

▶ **ADMISSION**
Summer
House & Grounds
Adult £6.00
Child/Conc. £5.00

Grounds
Adult £1.50
Child/Conc. £1.00

Wheelchair visitors free. HHA Friends are admitted Free in August.

Winter

Group rates available – contact for further details.

Parkland available for film location and other events. Stable block contains 100 seats and lecture theatre. No inside photography. No unaccompanied children. Browse our web site for a 'virtual' tour of the house

Access and facilities, no charge for wheelchair visitors. WCs.

Tearoom seats 80, groups must book. Licensed.

By arrangement.

Heritage Education Trust Sandford Award winner 1988, 1993 & 1998. School groups free, teachers' pack.

No dogs in house and garden, welcome in Park on leads.

By arrangement.

CONFERENCE/FUNCTION

ROOM	MAX CAPACITY
Lecture	100
Seminar Rm	25

Conference facilities available in stable block adjacent to House

DEENE PARK

CORBY

www.deenepark.com

A very interesting house which developed over six centuries from a typical medieval manor around a courtyard into a Tudor and Georgian mansion. Many rooms of different periods are seen by visitors who enjoy the impressive yet intimate ambience of the family home of the Brudenells, seven of whom were Earls of Cardigan. The most flamboyant of them was the 7th Earl who led the Light Brigade charge at Balaklava and of whom there are some historic relics and pictures.

The present owner is Mr Edmund Brudenell who has carefully restored the house from its dilapidated condition at the end of the last war and also added considerably to the furniture and picture collection.

The gardens have been made over the last thirty years, with long, mixed borders of shrubs, old fashioned roses and flowers, a parterre designed by David Hicks and long walks under fine old trees by the water.

The car park beside the big lake is a good place for picnics.

Owner:
F. Brudenell Esq

▶ CONTACT

The House Keeper
Deene Park
Corby
Northamptonshire
NN17 3EW

Tel: 01780 450278
or 01780 450223

Fax: 01780 450282

e-mail: admin@
deenepark.com

▶ LOCATION
OS Ref. SP950 929

6m NE of
Corby off A43.
From London via
M1/J15 then A43.
or via A1, A14,
A43 - 2 hrs.

From Birmingham
via M6, A14, A43, 90
mins.

Rail: Kettering
Station
20 mins.

CONFERENCE/FUNCTION

ROOM	MAX CAPACITY
Great Hall	150
Tapestry Rm	75
East Room	18

[icon] [i] Suitable for indoor and outdoor events, filming, specialist lectures on house, its contents, gardens and history. No photography in house.

[icon] Including buffets, lunches and dinners.

[icon] Partial. Visitors may alight at the entrance, access to ground floor and garden. WC.

[icon] Special rates for groups, bookings can be made in advance, menus on request.

[icon] By arrangement.

[icon] Tours inclusive of admittance, tour time 90 mins. Owner will meet groups if requested.

[P] Unlimited for cars, space for 3 coaches 10 yards from house.

[icon] In car park only.

[icon] Residential conference facilities by arrangement.

[icon]

 Tel for details.

▶ OPENING TIMES
Summer

Open Suns & Mons of
Easter - August BH
weekends.
Also, June - August
Suns, 2 - 5pm

Open at all other times
by arrangement,
including pre-booked
parties.

Winter
House and Gardens
closed to casual visitors.
Open at all other times by
arrangement for groups.

▶ ADMISSION
Summer
House & Gardens

Adult	£5.50
Child (10-14yrs)	£2.50
Child (under 10yrs)	Free*
Conc.	£5.00

Gardens only

Adult	£3.00
Child (10-14yrs)	£1.50
Child (under 10yrs)	Free*

Groups (20+)

Weekdays	£4.50
(Min £90)	
Weekends & BHs	£5.00
(Min £100)	

* Child up to 10yrs free with
an accompanying adult.

Winter
Groups visits only by prior
arrangement.

LAMPORT HALL & GARDENS

NORTHAMPTON

www.lamporthall.co.uk

Owner:
Lamport Hall Trust

▶ **CONTACT**

George Drye
Executive Director
Lamport Hall
Northampton NN6 9HD

Tel: 01604 686272

Fax: 01604 686224

e-mail: admin@
lamporthall.co.uk

▶ **LOCATION**
OS Ref. SP759 745

From London via
M1/J15, 1¼ hours.
Entrance on A508,
8m N of Northampton
at junction with B576.
3½ m S of A14
(A1/M1 link).

Rail: Kettering
Station 9m.
Northampton 8m.

Bus: From
Northampton
and Market
Harborough.

Home of the Isham family from 1560 to 1976. The 17th and 18th century façade is by John Webb and the Smiths of Warwick and the North Wing of 1861 by William Burn.

The Hall contains a wealth of outstanding furniture, books and paintings including portraits by Van Dyck, Kneller, Lely and others. The fine rooms include the High Room of 1655 with magnificent plasterwork, the 18th century library with books from the 16th century, the early 19th century Cabinet Room containing rare Venetian cabinets with mythological paintings on glass and the Victorian Dining Room where refreshments are served.

The first floor has undergone lengthy restoration allowing further paintings and furniture to be displayed as well as a photographic record of Sir Gyles Isham, a Hollywood actor, who initiated the restoration.

The tranquil gardens were laid out in 1655 although they owe much to Sir Charles Isham, the eccentric 10th Baronet who, in the mid-19th century, created the Italian Garden and the Rockery where he introduced the first garden gnomes to England. There are also box bowers, a rose garden and lily pond and extensive walks, borders and lawns all surrounded by a spacious park.

▶ **OPENING TIMES**

Summer

Easter - 6 October
Suns and BH Mons
2.15 - 5.15pm.
Last admission/tour 4pm.

August: Mon - Sat
open for only one
tour at 2.30pm.

19 & 20 October
2.15 - 5.15pm.

Tours on other days by
prior arrangement.

Winter

Group visits only by
arrangement.

🏛 ⓘ Conferences, garden parties, activity days, clay pigeon shoots, equestrian events, fashion shows, air displays, archery, rallies, filming, parkland, grand piano, 2 exhibition rooms. Lectures on history of property and gardens. Lecture/meeting rooms. No unaccompanied children. No photography in house.

🍴 Special functions, buffets, lunches and dinners, wedding receptions.

♿ Visitors may alight at the entrance, access to ground floor and gardens.

🍽 Dining/tearoom. Groups can book in advance. Licensed.

🚶 At no additional cost, by prior arrangement, max 70 people, tour time 1¼ hours. On non-fair days.

🅿 100 cars & 3 coaches, 20 yds from property. Use main entrance only (on A508).

📚 Work room, specialist advisory teacher study packs. Further information contact Education Officer or the Trust Office.

🐕 In grounds, on leads.

🔔 ❄ 🎭 Tel for details.

▶ **ADMISSION**

Summer
House & Garden

Adult	£4.30
Child (5-16yrs)	£2.00
OAP	£3.80
Group*	
Adult	£4.30

* Min. payment £135.00
excluding refreshments

Winter

Group visits only by
prior arrangement.

CONFERENCE/FUNCTION

ROOM	SIZE	MAX CAPACITY
Dining Rm	31' x 24' 6"	70

ALTHORP

See page 304 for full page entry.

CHA

AYNHOE PARK

AYNHO, BANBURY, OXFORDSHIRE OX17 3BQ

www.cha.org.uk

Owner: Country Houses Association   **Contact:** The Administrator

Tel: 01869 810636   **Fax:** 01869 811054

Former home of the Cartwright family until 1960. The house was burned by the royalist troops in the Civil War, then rebuilt in rectangular form. Various alterations were made by Thomas Archer and later additions by Sir John Soane. Aynhoe Park has been converted into apartments for active retired people.

Location: OS Ref. SP513 331. M40/J10 then 3m W of B4100. Stations: Banbury 6m, Bicester 8m.

Open: 1 May - 30 Sept: Wed & Thur, 2 - 5pm.

Admission: Adult £3, Child/Conc. £1.50. Groups by arrangement.

⊤ ⚡ ⊠ ⊞ 1 single, 1 double with bathroom, CHA members only.

COTON MANOR GARDEN

GUILSBOROUGH, NORTHAMPTONSHIRE NN6 8RQ

www.cotonmanor.co.uk

Tel: 01604 740219   **Fax:** 01604 740838

e-mail: pasleytyler@cotonmanor.fsnet.co.uk

Owner: Ian & Susie Pasley-Tyler   **Contact:** Sarah Ball

Traditional English garden laid out on different levels surrounding a 17th century stone manor house. Many herbaceous borders, with extensive range of plants, old yew and holly hedges, rose garden, water garden and fine lawns set in 10 acres. Also wild flower meadow and bluebell wood.

Location: OS Ref. SP675 716. 9m NW of Northampton, between A5199 (formerly A50) and A428.

Open: Easter - 30 Sept: Tue - Sat & BHs; Also Suns Apr - May: 12 noon - 5.30pm.

Admission: Adult £4, Child £2, Conc. £3.50. Groups: £3.50.

▢ ⚡ ♿ Grounds. WC. ⊞ ⬛ ⚡ By arrangement. **P** ⊠

Cottesbrooke Hall & Gardens

BOUGHTON HOUSE 🏠

See page 305 for full page entry.

CANONS ASHBY ❧

Canons Ashby, Daventry, Northamptonshire NN11 3SD

Tel: 01327 860044   **Fax:** 01327 860168   **e-mail:** ecaxxx@smtp.ntrust.org.uk

www.nationaltrust.org.uk

Owner: The National Trust   **Contact:** The Property Manager

Home of the Dryden family since the 16th century, this Elizabethan manor house was built c1550, added to in the 1590s, and altered in the 1630s and c1710; largely unaltered since. Within the house, Elizabethan wall paintings and outstanding Jacobean plasterwork are of particular interest. A formal garden includes terraces, walls and gate piers of 1710. There is also a medieval priory church and a 70 acre park.

Location: OS152 Ref. SP577 506. Access from M40/J11, or M1/J16. Signposted from A5 2m S of Weedon crossroads. Then 7m to SW.

Open: House: 23 Mar - 3 Nov: Sat - Wed. Times: House: 1 - 5.30pm (Oct & Nov: 12 noon - 4.30pm). Gardens, Park & Church: 11am - 5.30pm (Oct & Nov: 11am - 4.30pm); access through garden. 9 Nov - 22 Dec: Sat & Sun, 11am - 3pm. Shop & Tearoom: as house, 12 noon - 5pm (Oct & Nov: 12 noon - 4.30pm). 9 Nov - 22 Dec: Sat & Sun, 11am - 3pm.

Admission: Adult £5.20, Child £2.60, Family £13. Garden: £1. Discount for booked groups, contact Property Manager.

▢ ♿ Some steps. WC. ⬛ ⊠ In Home Paddock, on leads.

Captain John Macdonald-Buchanan

COTTESBROOKE HALL & GDNS 🏛

COTTESBROOKE, NORTHAMPTONSHIRE NN6 8PF

www.cottesbrookehall.co.uk

Tel: 01604 505808 **Fax:** 01604 505619 **e-mail:** hall@cottesbrooke.co.uk

Owner: Capt & Mrs John Macdonald-Buchanan **Contact:** The Administrator

Architecturally magnificent house built in the reign of Queen Anne. The identity of the original architect remains a mystery but the house has stayed essentially the same since that time. Renowned picture collection, particularly of sporting and equestrian subjects. Fine English and Continental furniture and porcelain. House reputed to be the pattern for Jane Austen's *Mansfield Park*.

Winner of the *HHA/Christie's Garden of the Year* award (2000). Celebrated gardens of great variety including herbaceous borders, water and wild gardens, fine old cedars and specimen trees. Magnolia, cherry and acer collections and several fine vistas across the Park. Notable planting of containers. A number of distinguished landscape designers have been involved including Rober Weir Schultz, the late Sir Geoffrey Jellicoe and the late Dame Sylvia Crowe.

Location: OS Ref. SP711 739. 10m N of Northampton near Creaton on A5199 (formerly A50), near Brixworth on A508 or Kelmarsh on A14.

Open: House & Gardens: Easter - end Sept: Thurs & BH Suns & Mons & May - Sept: 1st Sun in each month, 2 - 5.30pm. Gardens only: 1 May - end Sept: Tue - Fri & BH Suns & Mons & May - Sept: 1st Sun in each month, 2 - 5.30pm.

Admission: House & Gardens: Adult £4.50. Gardens only: Adult £3, Child half price. RHS members Free access to gardens. Private groups welcome (except weekends) by prior arrangement.

ℹ️ No photography in house. Filming & outside events. Unusual plants. Banqueting facilities, corporate hospitality & catering for functions. Gardens. WC. Obligatory. 🅿️

DEENE PARK 🏛   *See page 306 for full page entry.*

EDGCOTE HOUSE

Edgcote, Banbury, Oxfordshire OX17 1AG

Owner/Contact: Christopher Courage

Early Georgian house with good rococo plasterwork.

Location: OS Ref. SP505 480. 6m NE of Banbury off A361.

Open: By written appointment only.

ELEANOR CROSS ♯

Geddington, Kettering, Northamptonshire

Tel: 01604 735400 (Regional Office)

Owner: English Heritage   **Contact:** The East Midlands Regional Office

One of a series of famous crosses, of elegant sculpted design, erected by Edward I to mark the resting places of the body of his wife, Eleanor, when brought for burial from Harby in Nottinghamshire to Westminster Abbey in 1290.

Location: OS Ref. SP896 830. In Geddington, off A43 between Kettering and Corby.

Open: Any reasonable time.

HADDONSTONE SHOW GARDEN

The Forge House, East Haddon, Northampton NN6 8DB

Tel: 01604 770711 **Fax:** 01604 770027

e-mail: info@haddonstone.co.uk **www.**haddonstone.co.uk

Owner: Haddonstone Ltd   **Contact:** Marketing Director

See Haddonstone's classic garden ornaments in the beautiful setting of the walled manor gardens – including urns, troughs, fountains, statuary, bird baths, sundials and balustrading. The garden is on different levels with shrub roses, conifers, clematis and climbers. The newly opened Jubilee garden features a pavilion, temple and Gothic grotto.

Location: OS Ref. SP667 682. 7m NW of Northampton off A428. Signposted.

Open: Mon - Fri, 9am - 5.30pm. Closed weekends, BHs & Christmas period.

Admission: Free. Groups by appointment only. Not suitable for coach groups.

By arrangement. Limited. Guide dogs only.

The Third Earl of Cardigan

With the kind permission of Mr & Mrs E Brudenell

HOLDENBY HOUSE GARDENS & FALCONRY CENTRE 🏠
HOLDENBY, NORTHAMPTONSHIRE NN6 8DJ

www.holdenby.com

Tel: 01604 770074 **Fax:** 01604 770962 **e-mail:** sarah@holdenby.com

Owner: James Lowther Esq   **Contact:** Mrs Sarah Maughan

Just across the fields from Althorp stands Holdenby, a house whose royal connections go back over 400 years. Built by Sir Christopher Hatton to entertain Elizabeth I, this once largest house in England became the palace of James I and the prison of his son Charles I. Today the house is a family home and a splendid backdrop to a beautiful garden and Falconry Centre. Wander through Rosemary Verey's Elizabethan Garden and Rupert Golby's Fragrant Walk. Evoke the feeling of the 17th century by visiting the 17th century farmstead. Then sit back to watch our magnificent birds of prey soar over this pastoral scene of so much history.

Location: OS Ref. SP693 681. M1/J15a. 7m NW of Northampton off A428 and A5199.

Open: 30 Mar - end Sept. Garden & Falconry Centre: Suns, 1 - 5pm, BH Suns & Mons, 1 - 6pm. Jul & Aug: daily except Sat, 1 - 5pm. House: 1 Apr, 3 Jun & 26 Aug, 1 - 6pm or by appointment.

Admission: Garden & Falconry: Adult £3, Child (3-15yrs) £1.75, OAP £2.50. House: Adult £5, Child £3, OAP £4.50. Events: Adult £4, Child £2, OAP £3.50.

ℹ️ Children's play area. 🏠 👶 🚻 ♿ Partial. WC.
🍴 Home-made teas. Groups must book. 🐕 By arrangement. 🅿
▪️ Sandford Award-winner. 🐾 In grounds, on leads. ▲ 🖤 Tel for details.

KELMARSH HALL
KELMARSH, NORTHAMPTONSHIRE NN6 9LY

www.kelmarsh.com

Tel/Fax: 01604 686543 **Infoline:** 01604 686550

Owner: The Kelmarsh Trust   **Contact:** General Manager

Built in 1732 to a James Gibbs design, Kelmarsh Hall is surrounded by its working estate, grazed parkland and beautiful gardens. In 1928 Ronald and Nancy Tree rented the Palladian house from the Lancaster family and decorated the rooms in the manner that has become the English country house look. In the 1950s she returned to Kelmarsh as Nancy Lancaster and continued to imprint develop her style both in the house and in the gardens. Additional schemes and designs by Geoffrey Jellicoe and Norah Lindsay have created a remarkable garden. Gifted to the Kelmarsh Trust by the Lancaster family the house, gardens and estate are now available for study, group and general visits.

Location: OS Ref. SP736 795. 500 metres N of A14 - A508 junction.

Open: House & Garden: 31 Mar - 1 Sept: Suns & BH Mons & Thurs in Aug, 2.30 - 5pm. Garden: 31 Mar - 26 Sept: Mon - Thur, 2.30 - 5pm.

Admission: House & Garden: Adult £3.50, Child (5-16) £2, Conc. £3. Guided tours of house at 3pm & 4pm. Garden only: £2, Child under 16 Free.

ℹ️ No photography in house. ♿ Partial. WC. 🍴 Suns only. 🐕 Obligatory.
🅿 Limited for coaches. ▪️ 🐾 In grounds, on leads.

English Heritage Photo Library

KIRBY HALL

Deene, Corby, Northamptonshire NN17 5EN

Tel: 01536 203230

Owner: English Heritage   **Contact:** The Custodian

Outstanding example of a large, stone-built Elizabethan mansion, begun in 1570 with 17th century alterations. There are fine gardens with topiary, home to peacocks. Jane Austen's *Mansfield Park* was filmed at Kirby Hall in 1998. Venue for *History in Action*, Europe's largest multi-period historical festival.

Location: OS141 Ref. SP926 927. On unclassified road off A43, Corby to Stamford road, 4m NE of Corby. 2m W of Deene Park.

Open: 29 Mar - 31 Oct: daily 10am - 6pm (5pm in Oct). 1 Nov - 31 Mar: Sats & Suns, 10am - 4pm. Closed 24 - 26 Dec & 1 Jan.

Admission: Adult £3.30, Child £1.70, Conc. £2.50, Family £8.30.

♿ **P** ✵ ⛳ Tel for details.

LAMPORT HALL & GARDENS   *See page 307 for full page entry.*

LYVEDEN NEW BIELD

Nr Oundle, Peterborough PE8 5AT

Tel: 01832 205358   **e-mail:** elnbxx@smtp.ntrust.org.uk   **www**.nationaltrust.org.uk

Owner: The National Trust   **Contact:** The Custodian

An incomplete Elizabethan garden house and moated garden. Begun in 1595 by Sir Thomas Tresham to symbolise his Catholic faith, Lyveden remains virtually unaltered since work stopped when Tresham died in 1605.

Location: OS141 Ref. SP983 853. 4m SW of Oundle via A427, 3m E of Brigstock, off Harley Way. Access by foot along a $^1/_2$ m farm track.

Open: House, Elizabethan water garden & visitor information room: 23 Mar - 3 Nov: Wed - Sun (open BH Mons & 4 Jun), 10.30am - 5pm; 4 Nov - end Mar 2003: Sat & Sun, 10.30am - 4pm. Groups by arrangement with custodian.

Admission: £2.

P Limited. ⛳ On leads. ✵

NORTHAMPTON CATHEDRAL

Cathedral House, Kingsthorpe Road, Northampton NN2 6AG

Tel: 01604 714556

     Contact: Canon D McSweeney

Partly 19th century Pugin.

Location: OS Ref. SP753 617. 3/4 m N of town centre.

Open: Daily, 10am - 7pm. Sun Service: 7pm (Sat) 8.30am, 10.30am 5.15pm. Weekday services: 9.30am and 7pm.

Admission: Guided visit by prior application.

THE PREBENDAL MANOR HOUSE

Nassington, Peterborough PE8 6QG

Tel: 01780 782575   **e-mail:** info@prebendal-manor.demon.co.uk

www.prebendal-manor.co.uk

Owner/Contact: Mrs J Baile

Grade I listed, dating from the early 13th century, it retains many fine original medieval features and included in the visit are the 15th century dovecote, tithe barn museum and medieval fish ponds. Designed by Michael Brown and encompassing 5 acres are the 14th century re-created medieval gardens.

Location: OS Ref. TL063 962. 6m N of Oundle, 9m W of Peterborough, 7m S of Stamford.

Open: May - end Sept: Sun & Wed, also BH Mons, 1 - 5.30pm. Closed Christmas.

Admission: Adult £4, Child £1.20. Groups (20 - 50) outside normal opening times by arrangement: Adult £3.50, Child £1.

ⓘ No photography. **T** ♿ Partial. ⛳ Home-made teas. **P** Limited. ✳ ◻ Free. ⛳ Guide dogs only.

ROCKINGHAM CASTLE

MARKET HARBOROUGH, LEICESTERSHIRE LE16 8TH

www.rockinghamcastle.com

Tel: 01536 770240   **Fax:** 01536 771692   **e-mail:** rockinghamcastle@lineone.net

Owner: James Saunders Watson   **Contact:** The Administrator

Built by William the Conqueror. A Royal Castle for 450 years and 450 years a family home. The predominantly Tudor building, within Norman walls, has architecture, furniture and works of art from practically every century. 12 acres of formal and wild garden command a splendid view of five counties. A new 'Castle under siege' audio visual.

Location: OS Ref. SP867 913. 1m N of Corby. 9m E of Market Harborough. 14m SW of Stamford on A427. 8m from Kettering.

Open: 31 Mar - 29 Sept: Suns & BH Mons (plus Tue & Thur in Jul & Aug): 1 - 5pm. Grounds: 11.30am on Suns & BHs, 1pm on other open days. Groups any time by appointment.

Admission: House & Garden: Adult £5.50, Child (5 - 16yrs) £3.50, Conc. £5. Groups (20+): Adult £5, Child £3.50, Schools £2.50.

◻ ⓘ Functions, Fairs & Filming. No photography in Castle. **T** ◻ Licensed. ♿ Partial. WC. ✳ By arrangement (except on open days). **P** ◻ ⛳ In grounds, on leads. ▲ ✵ ⛳

RUSHTON TRIANGULAR LODGE

Rushton, Kettering, Northamptonshire NN14 1RP

Tel: 01536 710761

Owner: English Heritage   **Contact:** The Custodian

This extraordinary building, completed in 1597, symbolises the Holy Trinity. It has three sides, 33 ft wide, three floors, trefoil windows and three triangular gables on each side.

Location: OS Ref. SP830 831. 1m W of Rushton, on unclassified road 3m from Desborough on A6.

Open: 29 Mar - 31 Oct: daily, 10am - 6pm (5pm in Oct).

Admission: Adult £1.95, Child £1, Conc. £1.50.

Website Information   ◁ ◁ ◁   **pg 39**

SOUTHWICK HALL 🏛

Nr Oundle, Peterborough PE8 5BL
Tel: 01832 274064

Owner: Christopher Capron Esq   **Contact:** G & C Bucknill

A family home since 1300, retaining medieval building dating from 1300, with Tudor rebuilding and 18th century additions. Exhibitions: Victorian and Edwardian Life, collections of agricultural and carpentry tools and local archaeological finds.

Location: OS152 Ref. TL022 921. 3m N of Oundle, 4m E of Bulwick.

Open: 31 Mar, 1 - 3 Apr, 5/6 May, 25/26 Aug, also Jul - Sept: Suns, 2 - 5pm, last admission 4.30pm. Groups at other times by arrangement.

Admission: House & Grounds: Adult £4, Child £2.

🚸 Partial. WC. ⬛ 𝒇 By arrangement. 🅿 🐕 In grounds on leads.

STOKE PARK PAVILIONS

Stoke Bruerne, Towcester, Northamptonshire NN12 7RZ
Tel: 01604 862172

Owner: A S Chancellor Esq   **Contact:** Mrs C Cook

The two Pavilions, dated c1630 and attributed to Inigo Jones, formed part of the first Palladian country house built in England by Sir Francis Crane. The central block, to which the Pavilions were linked by quadrant colonnades, was destroyed by fire in 1886. The grounds include extensive gardens and overlook the former park, now farmland.

Location: OS Ref. SP740 488. 7m S of Northampton.

Open: Aug: daily, 3 - 6pm. Other times by appointment only.

Admission: Adult £3, Child £1.

🚸 Grounds. 🅿 Limited. 🐕 In grounds, on leads. ✳

WAKEFIELD LODGE

Potterspury, Northamptonshire NN12 7QX
Tel: 01327 811218

Owner/Contact: Mrs J Richmond-Watson

Georgian Hunting Lodge with deer park.

Location: OS Ref. SP739 425. 4m S of Towcester on A5. Take signs to farm shop for advice on tour times.

Open: House: 22 Apr - 31 May: Mon - Fri (closed BHs), 12 noon - 4pm.

Admission: £5.

ℹ No photography. 🖼 🚸 Unsuitable. ⬛ 🍴 𝒇 Obligatory. 🅿 🐕 Guide dogs only.

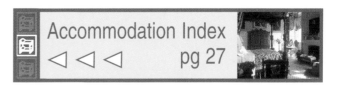

Accommodation Index
◁ ◁ ◁   pg 27

SULGRAVE MANOR

MANOR ROAD, SULGRAVE, BANBURY, OXON OX17 2SD

www.stratford.co.uk/sulgrave

Tel: 01295 760205 **Fax:** 01295 768056 **e-mail:** sulgrave-manor@talk21.com

A delightful 16th century Manor House that was the home of George Washington's ancestors. Today it presents a typical wealthy man's home and gardens of Elizabethan times. Restored with scholarly care and attention to detail that makes a visit both a pleasure and an education. *'A perfect illustration of how a house should be shown to the public'* – Nigel Nicolson, *Great Houses of Britain*. New Courtyard development with fine visitor/education facilities.

Location: OS152 Ref. SP561 457. Off Banbury - Northampton road (B4525) 5m from M40/J11. 15m from M1/J15A.

Open: 29 Mar - 31 Oct: 2 - 5pm. Closed Mon & Fri except BHs & event days. Last admission 1 hour before closing. Open for booked groups on any day or evening throughout the year (except Jan). Access to house may be restricted during private wedding ceremonies. Closed 16 Jun, 28 Jul, 25, 26 & 31 Dec & all of January.

Admission: Adult £5, Child (5-16) £2.50. Garden only: £2.50. Groups: Adult £4.50, Child £2.25. Special Events: All visitors on non-event days are taken round the Manor House on regularly organized guided tours.

ℹ No photography in house. 🖼 🎎 🍴 🚸 Partial. ⬛ 𝒇 Obligatory. 🅿 🖼
🐕 In grounds, on leads. 🔺 ✳ ♨ Various. Send for details.

BREWHOUSE YARD MUSEUM
THE MUSEUM OF NOTTINGHAM LIFE
Castle Boulevard, Nottingham NG7 1FB
Tel: 0115 9153600 **Fax:** 0115 9153601 **e-mail:** bhyoffice@notmusbhy.demon.co.uk
Owner/Contact: Ann Insker
Set in a group of 18th century cottages, the museum presents a realistic glimpse of life in Nottingham over the past 200 years.
Location: OS Ref. SK570 393. 500yds SW of City Centre.
Open: Daily, 10am - 4.30pm.
Admission: Weekdays: Free. Weekends & BHs: Adult £1.50, Conc. 80p, Family £3.80.

CARLTON HALL
Carlton-on-Trent, Nottinghamshire NG23 6LP
Tel: 01636 821421 **Fax:** 01636 821554
Owner/Contact: Lt Col & Mrs Vere-Laurie
Mid 18th century house by Joseph Pocklington of Newark. Stables attributed to Carr of York. Family home occupied by the same family since 1832.
Location: OS Ref. SK799 640. 7m N of Newark off A1. Opposite the church.
Open: By appointment only.
Admission: Hall and Garden £3.50. Minimum charge for a group £35.
Conferences. Unsuitable. In grounds, on leads. Guide dogs in house.

CASTLE MUSEUM & ART GALLERY
Nottingham NG1 6EL
Tel: 0115 9153700 **Fax:** 0115 9153653 **e-mail:** marketing@notmusbhy.demon.co.uk
Contact: Janet Owen
17th century ducal mansion, home to a museum and art gallery.
Location: OS Ref. SK569 395. SW of the city centre on hilltop.
Open: Daily, 10am - 5pm. Closed 24, 25 Dec & 1 Jan.
Admission: Weekdays Free. Weekends: Adult £2, Child/Conc. £1, Family £5.

CLUMBER PARK
Clumber Park, Worksop, Nottinghamshire S80 3AZ
Tel: 01909 476592 **Fax:** 01909 500721 **www.**nationaltrust.org.uk
Owner: The National Trust   **Contact:** Claire Herring, Property Manager
Historic parkland with peaceful woods, open heath and rolling farmland around a serpentine lake.
Location: OS120 Ref SK626 746. 4¹/₂ m SE of Worksop, 6¹/₂ m SW of Retford, just off A1/A57 via A614. 11m from M1/J30.
Open: Park: All year except 13 Jul & 10 Aug & 25 Dec. Apr - Sept: last vehicle admission 7pm, Park closes 9pm. Oct - Mar: last vehicle admission 5pm, park closes 7pm. Walled Kitchen Garden: Apr - end Sept: Weds & Thurs, 10.30am - 5.30pm, Sats, Suns & BH Mons, 10.30am - 6pm. Chapel: Apr - end Sept: Mon - Fri, 10.30am - 5.30pm, Sats & Suns, 10.30am - 6pm. Oct - 12 Jan 2003: daily, 10.30am - 4pm. Closed 13 Jan - end Mar for conservation cleaning.
Admission: Pedestrians, Cyclists & Coaches: Free, NT Members Free, Cars & Motorbikes £3.50, Minibuses & caravans £4.50. Walled kitchen garden 70p.
Partial. Wheelchairs available. In grounds on leads.

GREEN'S MILL
Windmill Lane, Sneinton, Nottingham NG2 4QB
Tel: 0115 9156878
Owner/Contact: Graham Armitage
This fully operational windmill was once owned and operated by George Green, mathematician and physicist.
Location: OS Ref. SK585 398. ¹/₂ m due E of City Centre, between A612 and B686.
Open: Wed - Sun & BH Mons, 10am - 4pm.
Admission: Free.

HODSOCK PRIORY GARDEN
Blyth, Nr Worksop, Nottinghamshire S81 0TY
Tel: 01909 591204 **Fax:** 01909 591578
Owner: Sir Andrew & Lady Buchanan   **Contact:** Lady Buchanan
Sensational snowdrops, winter flowering plants and shrubs, woodland walk.
Location: OS Ref. SK612 853. W of B6045 Worksop/Blyth road, 1m SW of Blyth, less than 2m from A1.
Open: 2 Feb - 10 Mar: Sat only, 10am - 4pm. Please telephone for details.
Admission: Adult £3.50, accompanied Child (6-16yrs) 50p.

HOLME PIERREPONT HALL
HOLME PIERREPONT, Nr NOTTINGHAM NG12 2LD
www.holmepierreponthall.com
Tel: 0115 933 2371
Owner: Mr & Mrs Robin Brackenbury   **Contact:** Robert Brackenbury
This charming late medieval manor house is set in 30 acres of Park and Gardens with regional furniture and family portraits. The Ball Room, Drawing Room and Long Gallery are available on an exclusive basis. Filming welcome.
Location: OS Ref. SK628 392. 5m ESE of central Nottingham. Follow signs to the National Water Sports Centre and continue for 1¹/₂ m.
Open: Easter, Spring & Summer BHs (Suns & Mons). Jun: Thurs, Jul: Weds & Thurs. Aug: Tue - Thurs, 2 - 5.30pm. Corporate/private and wedding venue. Functions at other times by arrangement.
Admission: Adult £4, Child £1.50. Gardens only £2.
Partial. WC. Business & charity functions, wedding receptions. In grounds on leads. Tel for details.

MUSEUM OF COSTUME & TEXTILES
Castle Gate, Nottingham NG1 6AF
Tel: 0115 9153500 **e-mail:** jeremyf@notmusbhy.demon.co.uk
Costume displays from 1790 to the mid-20th century are beautifully presented in period settings.
Location: OS Ref. SK570 395. Just SW of City Centre.
Open: Wed - Sun & BH Mons, 10am - 4pm.
Admission: Free.

NEWARK TOWN HALL
Market Place, Newark, Nottinghamshire NG24 1DU
Tel: 01636 680333 **Fax:** 01636 680350
Owner: Newark Town Council   **Contact:** The Curator
A fine Georgian Grade I listed Town Hall containing a museum of the town's treasures. Disabled access – lift and WC.
Location: OS Ref. SK570 395. Close to A46 and A1.
Open: Mon - Fri, 10.30am - 1pm & 2 - 4.30pm. Sats, 1 - 4pm (Apr - Oct). Closed BHs.
Admission: Free.

NEWSTEAD ABBEY
Newstead Abbey Park, Nottinghamshire NG15 8GE
Tel: 01623 455900 **Fax:** 01623 455904   **Contact:** Julie DeLong
Historic home of the poet, Lord Byron, set in grounds of over 300 acres. Mementoes of Byron and period rooms from medieval to Victorian times.
Location: OS Ref. SK540 639. 12m N of Nottingham 1m W of the A60 Mansfield Rd.
Open: 1 Apr - 30 Sept: 12 noon - 5pm, last adm. 4pm. Grounds: All year except last Fri in Nov. Apr - Sept: 9am - 7.30pm. Oct - Mar: 9am - 5pm.
Admission: House & Grounds: Adult £4, Child £1.50, Conc. £2. Grounds only: Adult £2, Conc. £1.50 (2000 prices).

East Midlands - England

NORWOOD PARK

SOUTHWELL, NOTTINGHAMSHIRE NG25 0PF

www.norwoodpark.org.uk

Tel: 01636 815649 **Fax:** 01636 815702 **e-mail:** events@norwoodpark.org.uk

Owner: Sir John & Lady Starkey **Contact:** Sarah Dodd, Events Manager

Delightful Georgian country house venue set in a medieval deer park, with ancient oaks, fishponds and eyecatcher Temple, overlooking apple orchards and cricket ground. Perfect venue for all manner of business or social occasion. Combination of reception/meeting/dining rooms available in the house for smaller groups. Unique Stables Gallery complex, adjacent to the house, ideal for wedding receptions, corporate dances and promotions for larger groups. Impeccable event management from experienced team. Versatile grounds for activity days, promotional work and filming. USA designed 9-hole golf course and practice area in the magnificent parkland. Second 9-holes open 2002.

Location: OS Ref. SK688 545. ¾ m W of Southwell.

Open: All year by appointment only.

Admission: Please telephone for information.

ⓘ Outdoor activity days. ⓣ Events/weddings. ⓖ Partial. ● By arrangement. ⓕ By arrangement. ⓟ Limited for coaches. ⓜ In grounds, on leads. ⓗ Honeymoon suite only. ▲ ✳

SUTTON BONINGTON HALL

Nr LOUGHBOROUGH, NOTTINGHAM LE12 5PF

Tel: 01509 672355 **Fax:** 01509 674357 **e-mail:** henryweldon@hotmail.com

Owner: Lady Anne Elton **Contact:** Mr & Mrs Henry Weldon

Sutton Bonington Hall, home of the Paget family since 1750, is a magnificent example of Queen Anne architecture, with an early conservatory (1810), and fine Queen Anne furniture. Sutton Bonington is not open to the general public, but offers excellent facilities for small conferences, corporate dinners and weddings. Extensive formally laid-out gardens can accommodate marquees for larger events. Seven luxurious bedrooms (all en-suite) can accommodate up to 14 guests in style.

Location: SK505 255. 1m E of A6, 5m N of Loughborough. In the heart of the Midlands, a short distance from Nottingham, Derby, Leicester, M1 and East Midlands airport.

Open: By arrangement.

Admission: Corporate/private entertainment and wedding venue by arrangement only. Residential rooms by prior reservation only.

ⓣ ⓖ Partial. ⓟ Ample for cars. ⓜ In grounds, on leads. ⓗ 7 doubles. ▲ ✳

PAPPLEWICK HALL

Papplewick, Nottinghamshire NG15 8FE

Tel: 0115 963 3491 **Fax:** 0115 964 2767

Owner/Contact: Dr R Godwin-Austen

A beautiful stone built classical house set in a park with woodland garden laid out in the 18th century. The house is notable for its very fine plasterwork and elegant staircase. Grade I listed.

Location: OS Ref. SK548 518. Halfway between Nottingham & Mansfield, 3m E of M1/J27 on B683.

Open: By appointment and 1st, 3rd & 5th Wed in each month, 2 -5pm.

Admission: Adult £5. Groups (10+): £4.

ⓘ No photography. ⓕ Obligatory. ⓟ Limited for coaches. ⓜ In grounds on leads. ✳

RUFFORD ABBEY ⌗

Ollerton, Nottinghamshire NG22 9DF

Tel: 01623 822944

Owner: English Heritage **Contact:** Nottinghamshire County Council

The remains of a 17th century country house; displaying the ruins of a 12th century Cistercian Abbey. It is set in what is now Rufford Country Park.

Location: OS Ref. SK645 646. 2m S of Ollerton off A614.

Open: 29 Mar - 31 Oct: Daily, 10am - 5pm. 1 Nov - 31 Mar: daily, 10am - 4pm. (Closed 24 - 26 Dec & 1 Jan).

Admission: Free - parking charge applies.

THRUMPTON HALL

THRUMPTON, NOTTINGHAM NG11 0AX

www.thrumptonhall.co.uk

Tel: 01159 830333 **Fax:** 01159 831309

Owner: Miranda Seymour **Contact:** The Hon Mrs R Seymour

Fine Jacobean house, built in 1607 incorporating an earlier manor house. Priest's hiding hole, magnificent carved Charles II staircase, carved and panelled saloon. Other fine rooms containing beautiful 17th and 18th century furniture and many fine portraits. Large lawns separated from landscaped park by ha-ha and by lake in front of the house. The house is still lived in as a home and Mrs Seymour will show parties around when possible. Dining room with capacity for 52 with silver service or buffet. Free access and meal for coach drivers.

Location: OS Ref. SK508 312. 7m S of Nottingham, 3m E M1/J24, 1m from A453.

Open: By appointment. Parties of 20+ 10.30am - 7.30pm.

Admission: Adult £5, Child £2.50.

📷 ⓣ Wedding receptions. ⓖ Ground floor & grounds. WC. ⓗ ⓜ In grounds on leads. ✳

Plant Sales Index
◁ ◁ ◁ pgs 36-37

UPTON HALL 🏛

Upton, Newark, Nottinghamshire NG23 5TE

Tel: 01636 813795 **Fax:** 01636 812258 **www.**bhi.co.uk

Owner: British Horological Institute **Contact:** The Museum Manager

A fine country house dating from the 16th century, but extensively altered in the 19th century, set within its own grounds. Since 1970, it has been the headquarters of the British Horological Institute and its fascinating museum containing a large historic collection of public and domestic clocks and watches.

Location: OS Ref. SK735 544. A612 between Newark and Southwell.

Open: Tue - Sat & BHs, 11am - 5pm, Sun, 2 - 5pm, closed Mon.

Admission: Adult £3.50, Child £1, (under 11yrs free), OAP £3. Members free.

WINKBURN HALL

Winkburn, Newark, Nottinghamshire NG22 8PQ

Tel: 01636 636465 **Fax:** 01636 636717 **e-mail:** any@alderton.co.uk

Owner/Contact: Richard Craven-Smith-Milnes Esq

A fine William and Mary house.

Location: OS Ref. SK711 584. 8m W of Newark 1m N of A617.

Open: Throughout the year by appointment only.

Admission: £4.50.

WOLLATON HALL NATURAL HISTORY MUSEUM

Wollaton Park, Nottingham NG8 2AE

Tel: 0115 915 3900

Owner: Nottingham City Council **Contact:** Phil Hackett

Tudor building set in 500 acres of parkland and home to the Natural History Museum.

Location: OS Ref. SK532 392. Wollaton Park, Nottingham. 3m W of city centre.

Open: Summer: 11am - 5pm. Winter: 11am - 4pm.

Admission: Weekdays Free. Weekends & BHs Adult: £1.50, Child 80p. Joint ticket for Wollaton Hall & Industrial Museum. Grounds £1/car (free for orange badge holders).

Holme Pierrepont Hall

Hugh Palmer

Honington Hall

West Midlands

Mr Benjamin Wiggin

Honington Hall

"Honington is different ..... it has a slightly off-beat humanity that is wholly engaging and makes it among the most desirable of English country houses."

John Cornforth, Country Life, 1978

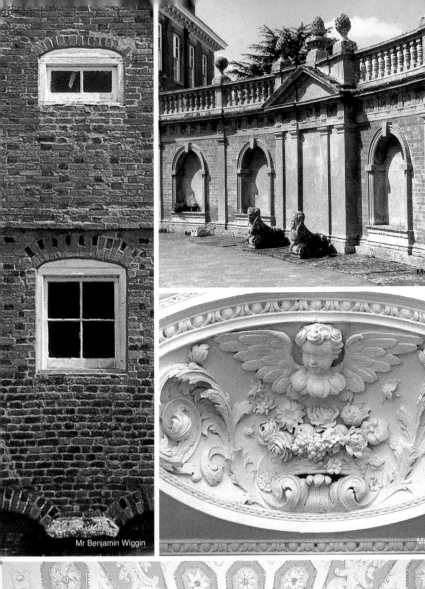

Mr Benjamin Wiggin

Mr Benjamin Wiggin

Mr Benjamin Wiggin

The sleepy and tranquil village of Honington in Warwickshire lies about a mile to the east of the A3400, the main road from Shipston-on-Stour to Stratford-upon-Avon. The Manor of Honington, or 'Hunitone' as it is referred to in the Doomsday Book, was among the endowments of the Benedictine Priory of Coventry founded in 1043 by Earl Leofric, husband of the famous Lady Godiva.

For many people visiting Honington for the first time it will seem to be the 'perfect' English country house: dignified and measured in style, comfortable in scale, nestling in a secluded park with a river at the bottom of the garden and the village church almost at the door.

Honington is a pretty house, Caroline in style with tall elegant chimneys, built of mellow red brick with stone quoins and window dressings. It was built in 1682 for the rich London merchant Sir Henry Parker, on the site of an earlier house. The stables and dovecote from this earlier building survive and are found on the north side of the house. A visit to Honington is not complete without looking at the church. Remodelled about the same time as the house, it is a fine example of a 'Wren' City church placed in a country setting. Spare some time to look at the Parker Monument at the west end of the nave. It commemorates Sir Henry Parker, the builder of the house and rebuilder of the church, who died in 1713, and his son Hugh, who died in 1712. The pair appear to be in animated conversation. It is a pity that no records now exist to tell us who the architect was of both the house and the church, because this is extremely skilled craftsmanship.

In 1737 Honington was sold to Joseph Townsend who remodelled both the house and surrounding park. Warwickshire in the middle of the 18th century was in a particular flurry of building activity and it appears from other estate records in the area that there was much 'one-upmanship' among patrons to employ the best architects and craftsmen to create the latest Rococo decoration. Indeed, it is the Rococo plasterwork schemes at Honington which make the interiors such a rich and interesting surprise. It is thought that Townsend employed Charles Stanley to decorate the hall – representations of the *Elements* swirl above.

However, the *tour de force* of the interiors is the Saloon. Believed to have been designed by John Freeman, an amateur architect and friend of Townsend and William Jones, the original great staircase of the 1680s house was removed and replaced by a great octagonal saloon with a high domed ceiling and heavily carved wall decoration. Whilst all the basic forms in this room are Palladian, Jones could not resist adding the Rococo looking glasses and corner 'drops'. It is these elements which give the room such charm.

A visit to Honington and is grounds reaches back to a quieter, gentler and elegant age. That we can enjoy it is thanks though to Major Sir John Wiggin, who during the 1970s boldly carried out major restoration work to save the house from dry rot. Had it not been for his vision the house could very easily have been lost. A journey to Warwickshire for the country house enthusiast would certainly have been very much the poorer. ⁂

For further details about *Honington Hall* see entry on page 349.

Mr Benjamin Wiggin

Mr Benjamin Wiggin

NT Photographic Library

BERRINGTON HALL

NR LEOMINSTER

www.nationaltrust.org.uk/berrington

Berrington Hall is the creation of Thomas Harley, the 3rd Earl of Oxford's remarkable son, who made a fortune from supplying pay and clothing to the British Army in America and became Lord Mayor of London in 1767 at the age of thirty-seven. The architect was the fashionable Henry Holland. The house is beautifully set above the wide valley of a tributary of the River Lugg, with views west and south to the Black Mountains and Brecon Beacons. This was the site advised by 'Capability' Brown who created the lake with its artificial island. The rather plain neo-classical exterior with a central portico gives no clue to the lavishness of the interior. Plaster ceilings now decorated in muted pastel colours adorn the principal rooms. Holland's masterpiece is the staircase hall rising to a central dome. The rooms are set off with a collection of French furniture, including pieces which belonged to the Comte de Flahault, natural son of Talleyrand, and Napoleon's step-daughter Hortense.

In the dining room, vast panoramic paintings of battles at sea, three of them by Thomas Luny, are a tribute to the distinguished Admiral Rodney.

Owner:
The National Trust

▶ CONTACT

The Property
Manager
Berrington Hall
Nr Leominster
Herefordshire
HR6 0DW

Tel: 01568 615721
Fax: 01568 613263

Information Line:
01684 855367

Restaurant:
01568 610134

e-mail: berrington
@smtp.ntrust.org.uk

▶ LOCATION
OS137 SP510 637

3m N of Leominster,
7m S of Ludlow on
W side of A49.

Rail: Leominster 4m.

NT Photographic Library

▶ OPENING TIMES

House
23 Mar - 3 Nov:
Daily except Thurs & Fris.
(open Good Fri)
1 - 5pm (4.30pm in Oct
& Nov).

Garden
23 Mar - 3 Nov:
Daily except Thurs & Fris.
(open Good Fri)
12 noon - 5pm.
(4.30pm in Oct & Nov).

Park Walk
1 Jul - 3 Nov:
Daily except Thurs & Fris.
1 - 5pm (4.30pm in Oct
& Nov).

Shop
As house: 12 noon - 5pm
(4.30pm in Oct & Nov).

Last admission to House,
Shop and Restaurant
30 minutes before stated
closing time.

▶ ADMISSION

Adult	£4.40
Child (5-12yrs)	£2.20
Family (2+3)	£11.00
Groups (15-25)*	
Adult	£3.90
Child	£1.95
Garden Ticket	£3.00

Groups must pre-book.
Two groups can visit at
a time.

[icon] [i] No photography in the house. Groups by arrangement only.

[icon] Single seater batricar, stairclimber; pre-booking essential. Audio tours for the visually impaired.

[icon] Licensed restaurant: open as house: 12 noon - 5pm (4.30pm in Oct & Nov).

[icon] By arrangement only. Tour time: 1 hr.

[P] Ample for cars. Parking for coaches limited; instructions given when booking is made.

[icon] Children's quizzes. Play area in walled garden.

[icon] Guide dogs only.　[icon] Tel for details.

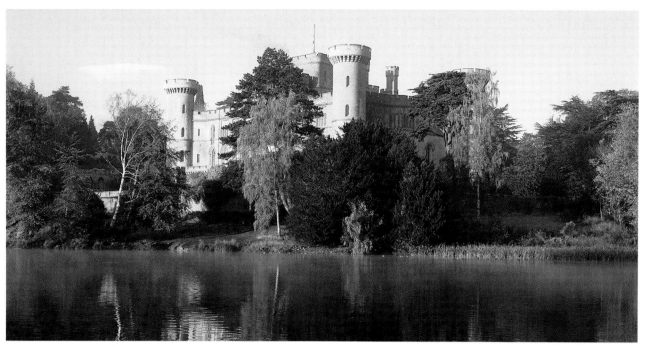

EASTNOR CASTLE

LEDBURY

www.eastnorcastle.com

Encircled by the Malvern Hills and surrounded by a famous arboretum and lake, this fairytale castle looks as dramatic inside as it does outside.

The atmosphere Everyone is struck by it. The vitality of a young family brings the past to life and the sense of warmth and optimism is tangible. Eastnor, however grand, is a home.

'Sleeping' for the past fifty years, the Castle has undergone a triumphant renaissance – 'looking better than it probably ever has', Country Life 1993.

Hidden away in attics and cellars since 1939, many of the castle's treasures are now displayed for the first time – early Italian Fine Art, 17th century Venetian furniture and Flemish tapestries, mediaeval armour and paintings by Van Dyck, Romney, Wootton and Watts, photographs by Julia Margaret Cameron. Drawing Room by Pugin.

'The princely and imposing pile' as it was described in 1812 when it was being built to pitch the owner into the aristocracy, remains the home of his descendants. The castle contains letters diaries, clothes and furnishings belonging to friends and relations who include: Horace Walpole, Elizabeth Barrett Browning, Tennyson, Watts, Julia Margaret Cameron and Virginia Woolf.

Encircled by the Malvern Hills, the medieval beauty of the estate remains unchanged.

GARDENS

Castellated terraces descend to a 21 acre lake with a restored lakeside walk. The arboretum holds a famous collection of mature specimen trees. There are spectacular views of the Malvern hills across a 300 acre deer park, once part of a mediaeval chase and now designated a Site of Special Scientific Interest.

Owner:
Mr J & The Hon Mrs Hervey-Bathurst

▶ CONTACT
Simon Foster
Portcullis Office
Eastnor Castle
Nr Ledbury
Herefordshire HR8 1RL

Tel: 01531 633160
Fax: 01531 631776
e-mail: enquiries@ eastnorcastle.com

▶ LOCATION
OS Ref. SO735 368

2m SE of Ledbury on the A438 Tewkesbury road. Alternatively M50/J2 & from Ledbury take the A449/A438.

Tewkesbury 20 mins, Malvern 20 mins, Gloucester 25 mins Hereford 25 mins, Worcester 30mins, Cheltenham 30 mins B'ham 1 hr, London 2½ hrs.

Taxi: Richard James 07836 777196.

CONFERENCE/FUNCTION

ROOM	SIZE	MAX CAPACITY
Library	18 x 8m	120
Great Hall	16 x 8m	150
Dining Rm	11 x 7m	80
Gothic Rm	11 x 7m	80
Octagon Rm	9 x 9m	50

▶ **OPENING TIMES**

Summer
31 March - 6 October:
Suns & BH Mons.
July - August: Sun - Fri
11am - 5pm.

▶ **ADMISSION**

Summer
Castle & Grounds
Adult £5.50
Child (5-15yrs) £3.00
OAP £4.75
Family (2+2)............£14.00
Groups* (with guide)
Adult £8.00
Groups* (without guide)
Adult £4.50
* Min. payment for 20 people.

Grounds only
Adult £3.50
Child (5-15yrs) £2.00
OAP £2.75

Season Ticket
Adult £16.50
Child (5-15yrs) £9.00
OAP £14.25
Family £42.00

Please telephone for admission prices for special events.

Winter
By appointment.

🦌 **SPECIAL EVENTS**

MAY 5/6
Spring Crafts Fair.

JUNE 3/4
Steam Fair & Country Show with Fred Dibnah.

JUN 8/9
Festival of Wood.

AUG 12 - 16
Children's Fun Week

AUG 25/26
TV & Film Arms & Berkeley Household.

OCT 5/6
Festival of Fine Food & Drink.

🏭 Plant Centre.

ℹ️ Maze, off-road driving, clay-pigeon shooting, quad bikes, archery and falconry. Survival training, team building activity days. Product launches, fashion shows, concerts, charity events, craft fairs, television and feature films.
No photography in castle.

🍽 Wedding receptions. Catering for booked events.

♿ Partially suitable. Visitors may alight at the castle. Priority parking.

☕ 🍴 Home-made food, menus on request, groups must book.

🧍 By arrangement.

🅿 Ample 10 - 200 yds from castle. Coaches phone in advance to arrange parking & catering. Free meal for drivers.

▪ Welcome. Guides available if required. Children's fun worksheets.

🐕 On leads in Castle and grounds.

🛏 Luxury accommodation within castle for small groups (min. 8 guests). 1 single room, 10 double. Ensuite available.

🔔 ❄

ABBEY DORE GARDEN

Abbey Dore, Herefordshire HR2 0AD

Tel/Fax: 01981 240419

Owner/Contact: Mrs C L Ward

6 acres of new and established garden with a wild river walk leading to a meadow planted with a variety of interesting trees.

Location: OS Ref. SO387 309. 3 m W of A465 midway Hereford - Abergavenny.

Open: Apr - Sept: Sat, Sun, Tue, Thur, Fri & BHs, 11am - 5.30pm. Other times by appointment.

Admission: Adult £2.50, Child 50p.

BERRINGTON HALL

See page 322 for full page entry.

NT Severn Region: R Anderson

BROCKHAMPTON ESTATE & LOWER BROCKHAMPTON

BRINGSTY, WORCESTERSHIRE WR6 5UH

www.nationaltrust.org.uk/brockhampton

Tel: 01885 488099/482077

Owner: The National Trust **Contact:** The Property Manager

A late 14th century moated manor house, with an attractive detached half-timbered 15th century gatehouse, a rare example of this type of structure. Also, the ruins of a 12th century chapel. Woodland walks including sculpture trail. Access for all, long and short waymarked walks.

Location: OS149, Ref. SO682 546. 2m E of Bromyard N side of A44, reached by narrow road through 1½ m of woods and farmland.

Open: Medieval Hall, parlour, minstrel gallery, information room, gatehouse and chapel: 29 Mar - 3 Nov: Wed - Sun & BHs, 12 noon - 5pm (Oct & Nov: 4pm). Last admission ½ hr before closing. Estate Walks: All year: daily during daylight hours. Tearoom (at Estate car park): as house.

Admission: Adult £3, Child £1.50, Family £7.50. Car park £2 (refundable on entry to house.

Partial. In woodland walks, on leads.

Berrington Hall

NT Photographic Library

CONINGSBY HOSPITAL, MUSEUM & GARDENS

Widemarsh Street, Hereford HR4 9HN

Tel: 01432 267821

Contact: Mr D G Harding

Built in 1614 on the site of a Knights-Hospitallers Place.

Location: OS Ref. SO512 404. East side of Widemarsh Street. 500 yards N of City Centre.

Open: Tue - Thur only, 2 - 5pm.

Admission: Adult £2, Child/Conc. £1. Groups rates for educational visits.

CROFT CASTLE

Leominster, Herefordshire HR6 9PW

Tel: 01568 780246 **e-mail:** croft@smtp.ntrust.org.uk **www**.nationaltrust.org.uk

Owner: The National Trust **Contact:** The House Manager

Location: OS137 Ref. SO455 655. 5m NW of Leominster, 9m SW of Ludlow, approach from B4362.

Open: Croft Castle is closed for major structural repairs during the 2002 season. Castle grounds, parkland & Croft Ambrey will remain open, please telephone for opening arrangements.

Admission: Grounds only: Car park £2 per car, £10 per coach.

EASTNOR CASTLE

See page 323 for full page entry.

English Heritage Photo Library

GOODRICH CASTLE

ROSS-ON-WYE, HEREFORDSHIRE HR9 6HY

Tel: 01600 890538

Owner: English Heritage **Contact:** The Custodian

This magnificent red sandstone castle is remarkably complete with a 12th century keep and extensive remains from 13th & 14th centuries. From the battlements there are fine views over the Wye Valley to Symonds Yat. Marvel at the maze of small rooms and the 'murder holes'.

Location: OS162, Ref. SO579 199. 5m S of Ross-on-Wye, off A40.

Open: 29 Mar - 31 Oct: daily, 10am - 6pm (5pm in Oct). 1 Nov - 31 Mar: Wed - Sun, 10am - 1pm & 2 - 4pm. Closed 24 - 26 Dec & 1 Jan.

Admission: Adult £3.60, Child £1.80, Conc. £2.70. Family ticket £9. 15% discount for groups (11+).

Tel for details.

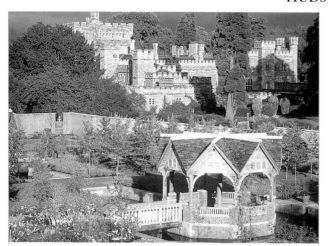

HAMPTON COURT

HOPE UNDER DINMORE, LEOMINSTER, HEREFORDSHIRE HR6 0PN

www.hamptoncourt.org.uk

Tel: 01568 797777 **Fax:** 01568 797472 **e-mail:** office@hamptoncourt.org.uk

Owner: Charity   **Contact:** Ed Waghorn

15th century fortified manor house available for private functions (24 bedrooms) set within 1,000 acres of grounds with woodland and river walks. Extensive new gardens include a walled organic kitchen garden, flower gardens, canals, pavilions, a maze and a secret tunnel to a waterfall and flooded sunken garden.

Location: OS Ref. SO520 525. On the A417 near to the junction with the A49.

Open: Gardens & Grounds: 5 Jan - 23 Dec: daily, 11am - 5pm (winter 4pm). Restaurant & Shop: daily (weekends only in winter).

Admission: Summer: Gardens & Walks: Adult £5, Child £3, OAP £4.75. Gardens only: Adult £4, Child £2, OAP £3.75. Winter: Gardens & Walks: Adult £3, Child £1.50. Walks only: Adult £2, Child £1. Groups rates by arrangement. Family & season tickets available. Variations on event days.

⬜ 🚼 🇹🇴 🎯 🍴 ♿Partial. WC. 🎬By arrangement. 🅿 ⬛ ✖ 🎫24 doubles. 🛏 ✳ 🐾Tel for details.

HEREFORD CATHEDRAL

Hereford HR1 2NG

Tel: 01432 374202 **Fax:** 01432 374220 **e-mail:** visits@herefordcathedral.co.uk

Contact: Mrs C Quinto - The Visits Manager

Location: OS Ref. SO510 398. Hereford city centre on A49.

Open: 7.30am - 5pm. Sun services: 8am, 10am, 11.30am & 3.30pm. Weekday services: 8am and 5.30pm.

Admission: Admission only for Mappa Mundi and Chained Library Exhibition: Adult £4, OAP/Student/Unemployed £3.50, Child under 5yrs Free. Family ticket (2+3) £10.00.

HERGEST COURT 🏚

c/o Hergest Estate Office, Kington HR5 3EG

Tel/Fax: 01544 230160 **e-mail:** banks@hergest.kc3.co.uk

Owner/Contact: W L Banks

The ancient home of the Vaughans of Hergest, dating from the 13th century.

Location: OS Ref. SO283 554. 1m W of Kington on unclassified road to Brilley.

Open: Strictly by appointment only through Estate Office.

Admission: Adult £4, Child £1.50. Groups: Adult £3.50, Child £1.

♿Unsuitable. 🅿Limited. 🐾Guide dogs only. ✳

Civil Wedding Venues
◁ ◁ ◁ pgs 28-29

HELLENS 🏚

MUCH MARCLE, LEDBURY, HEREFORDSHIRE HR8 2LY

Tel: 01531 660504

Owner: Pennington-Mellor-Munthe Charity Trust   **Contact:** The Administrator

Built as a monastery and then a stone fortress in 1292 by Morhimes, Earl of March, with Tudor, Jacobean and Stuart additions and lived in ever since by descendants of the original builder. Visited by the Black Prince, Bloody Mary and the 'family ghost'. Family paintings, relics and heirlooms from the Civil War and possessions of the Audleys, Walwyns and Whartons as well as Anne Boleyn. Also beautiful 17th century woodwork carved by the 'King's Carpenter', John Abel. All those historical stories incorporated into guided tours, revealing the loves and lives of those who lived and died here. Goods and chattels virtually unchanged.

Location: OS149 Ref. SO661 332. Off A449 at Much Marcle. Ledbury 4m, Ross-on-Wye 4m.

Open: Good Fri - 2 Oct: Weds, Sats, Suns & BH Mons. Guided tours only at 2pm, 3pm & 4pm. Other times only by arrangement with the Administrator.

Admission: Adult £4, Child £2.

ℹ️No photography inside house. 🎬 ♿Partial. 🎬Obligatory. ⬛ 🅿 🐾In grounds, on leads. 🐾Tel for details.

HERGEST CROFT GARDENS 🏠

KINGTON, HEREFORDSHIRE HR5 3EG

www.hergest.co.uk

Tel/Fax: 01544 230160 **e-mail:** banks@hergest.kc3.co.uk

Owner: W L Banks **Contact:** Gill Wilson

From spring bulbs to autumn colour, this is a garden for all seasons. An old-fashioned kitchen garden has spring and summer borders and roses. Over 59 Champion trees and shrubs grow in one of the finest collections in the British Isles. Holds National Collection of birches, maples and zelkovas. Park Wood is a hidden valley with rhododendrons up to 30 ft tall.

Location: OS Ref. SO281 565. On W side of Kington. 1/2 m off A44, left at Rhayader end of bypass. Turn right and gardens are 1/4 m on left. Signposted from bypass.

Open: 30 Mar - 31 Oct: 12.30pm - 5.30pm except May & June 12pm - 6pm. Season tickets and groups by arrangement throughout the year. Winter by appointment.

Admission: Adult £4, Child (under 16yrs) Free. Groups (20+) £3.50. Guided groups (20+) £5.50 (must book). Season ticket £15.

ⓘ Gift sales.🌿Rare plants. 🐕 🐾 In grounds, on leads. ❄ 🎟 Tel for details.

LANGSTONE COURT

Llangarron, Ross on Wye, Herefordshire

Tel: 01989 770254

Owner/Contact: R M C Jones Esq

Mostly late 17th century house with older parts. Interesting staircases, panelling and ceilings.

Location: OS Ref. SO534 221. Ross on Wye 5m, Llangarron 1m.

Open: 20 May - 31 Aug: Wed & Thur, 11am - 3pm, also spring & summer BHs.

Admission: Free.

LONGTOWN CASTLE ⌗

Abbey Dore, Herefordshire

Tel: 0121 625 6820 (Regional Office)

Owner: English Heritage **Contact:** The West Midlands Regional Office

An unusual cylindrical keep built c1200 with walls 15ft thick. There are magnificent views of the nearby Black Mountains.

Location: OS Ref. SO321 291. 4m WSW of Abbey Dore.

Open: Any reasonable time.

Admission: Free.

MOCCAS COURT 🏠

Moccas, Herefordshire HR2 9LH

Tel: 01981 500381

Owner: Trustees of the Baunton Trust **Contact:** Ivor Saunders

18th century Adam interiors, 'Capability' Brown park.

Location: OS149 Ref. SO359 434. 1m N of B4352, 3 1/2 m SE of Bredwardine.

Open: Apr - Sept: Thurs, 2 - 6pm.

Admission: £2.

OLD SUFTON 🏠

Mordiford, Hereford HR1 4EJ

Tel: 01432 870268/850328 **Fax:** 01432 850381 **e-mail:** jameshereford@aol.com

Owner: Trustees of Sufton Heritage Trust **Contact:** Mr & Mrs J N Hereford

A 16th century manor house which was altered and remodelled in the 18th and 19th centuries and again in this century. The original home of the Hereford family (see Sufton Court) who have held the manor since the 12th century.

Location: OS Ref. SO575 384. Mordiford, off B4224 Mordiford - Dormington road.

Open: By written appointment to Sufton Court or by fax.

Admission: Adult £2, Child 50p.

♿ Partial. 📷 Obligatory. 🅿 ■ 🐕 ❄

ROTHERWAS CHAPEL ⌗

Hereford, Herefordshire

Tel: 0121 625 6820 (Regional Office)

Owner: English Heritage **Contact:** The West Midlands Regional Office

This Roman Catholic chapel, dating from the 14th and 16th centuries, is testament to the past grandeur of the Bodenham family and features an interesting mid-Victorian side chapel and High Altar.

Location: OS Ref. SO537 383. 1 1/2 m SE of Hereford 500yds N of B4399.

Open: Any reasonable time. Keykeeper at nearby filling station.

Admission: Free.

SUFTON COURT 🏠

Mordiford, Hereford HR1 4LU

Tel: 01432 870268/850328 **Fax:** 01432 850381 **e-mail:** jameshereford@aol.com

Owner: J N Hereford **Contact:** Mr & Mrs J N Hereford

Sufton Court is a small Palladian mansion house. Built in 1788 by James Wyatt for James Hereford. The park was laid out by Humphrey Repton whose 'red book' still survives. The house stands above the rivers Wye and Lugg giving impressive views towards the mountains of Wales.

Location: OS Ref. SO574 379. Mordiford, off B4224 on Mordiford to Dormington road.

Open: 14 - 27 May & 15 - 26 Aug: 2 - 5pm.

Admission: Adult £2, Child 50p.

♿ Partial. 📷 Obligatory. 🅿 Only small coaches. ■ 🐕 In grounds, on leads.

THE WEIR 🌿

Swainshill, Hereford, Herefordshire

Tel: 01981 590509 **www**.nationaltrust.org.uk

Owner: The National Trust **Contact:** Gardener-in-Charge

Delightful riverside garden particularly spectacular in early spring, with fine view over the River Wye and Black Mountains.

Location: OS Ref. SO435 421. 5m W of Hereford on S side of A438.

Open: 19 Jan - 10 Feb: Sats & Suns, 11am - 4pm. 13 Feb - 3 Nov: Wed - Sun, Good Fri, BH Mons & 3/4 June, 11am - 6pm.

Admission: £3, Family £7.50.

♿ Unsuitable. 🅿 Unsuitable for coaches. 🐕

The Dining Room at Eastnor Castle

OAKLEY HALL
MARKET DRAYTON

Owner:
Mr & Mrs F Fisher

▶ **CONTACT**

Mrs Ann E Fisher
Oakley Hall
Market Drayton
Shropshire TF9 4AG

Tel: 01630 653472
Fax: 01630 653282

Wedding Enquiries:
Mrs D Hastie
Tel: 01244 572021

▶ **LOCATION**
OS Ref. SJ701 367

From London 3hrs:
M1, M6/J14, then A5013
to Eccleshall, turn right
at T-junction, 200 yards,
then left onto B5026.
Mucklestone is 1¾ m
from Loggerheads on
B5026. 3m NE of
Market Drayton
N of the A53,
1½ m W of
Mucklestone,
off B5145.

Oakley Hall is situated in magnificent countryside on the boundary of Shropshire and Staffordshire. The present Hall is a fine example of a Queen Anne mansion house and was built on the site of an older dwelling mentioned in the Domesday Survey of 1085. Oakley Hall was the home of the Chetwode family until it was finally sold in 1919.

GARDENS
Set in 100 acres of rolling parkland, the Hall commands superb views over the surrounding countryside and the gardens include wild areas in addition to the more formal parts.

Oakley Hall is a privately owned family house and since it is not open to the general public it provides a perfect location for exclusive private or corporate functions. The main hall can accommodate 120 people comfortably and has excellent acoustics for concerts. The secluded location and unspoilt landscape make Oakley an ideal setting for filming and photography.

The surrounding countryside is rich in historical associations. St Mary's Church at Mucklestone, in which parish the Hall stands, was erected in the 13th century and it was from the tower of this Church that Queen Margaret of Anjou observed the Battle of Blore Heath in 1459. This was a brilliant victory for the Yorkist faction in the Wars of the Roses and the blacksmith at Mucklestone was reputed to have shod the Queen's horse back to front in order to disguise her escape.

▶ **OPENING TIMES**

All Year
Not open to the public. The house is available all year round for private or corporate events.

▶ **ADMISSION**

Please telephone for details.

ℹ️ Concerts, conferences (see left for rooms available). Slide projector, word processor, fax and secretarial assistance are all available by prior arrangement, fashion shows, product launches, seminars, clay pigeon shooting, garden parties and filming. Grand piano, hard tennis court, croquet lawn, horse riding. No stiletto heels.

🍽️ Wedding receptions, buffets, lunches and dinners can be arranged for large or small groups, using high quality local caterers.

♿ Visitors may alight at the entrance to the Hall, before parking in allocated areas. WCs.

🚶 By prior arrangement groups will be met and entertained by members of the Fisher family.

🅿️ 100 cars, 100/200 yds from the Hall.

 3 double with baths.

CONFERENCE/FUNCTION

ROOM	SIZE	MAX CAPACITY
Hall	50' x 30'	100
Dining Rm	40' x 27'	60
Ballroom	40' x 27'	60

WESTON PARK 🏛

NR SHIFNAL

www.weston-park.com

Owner:
The Weston Park
Foundation

▶ CONTACT

Tricia Martin
Weston Park
Weston-under-Lizard
Nr Shifnal
Shropshire TF11 8LE

Tel: 01952 852100
Fax: 01952 850430
e-mail: enquiries@
weston-park.com

▶ LOCATION

OS Ref. SJ808 107

Birmingham 40 mins.
Manchester 1 hr.
Motorway access
M6/J12 or M54/J3.
House situated on A5 at
Weston-under-Lizard.

Rail: Nearest Railway
Stations: Wolverhampton,
Stafford or Telford.

Air: Birmingham,
West Midlands,
Manchester.

Weston Park is a magnificent Stately Home and Parkland situated on the Staffordshire/ Shropshire border. The former home of the Earls of Bradford, the Park is now held in trust for the nation by The Weston Park Foundation.

Built in 1671 by Lady Elizabeth Wilbraham, this warm and welcoming house boasts a superb collection of paintings, including work by Van Dyck, Gainsborough and Stubbs, furniture and *objets d'art*, providing continued interest and enjoyment for all of its visitors.

Step outside to enjoy the 1,000 acres of glorious Parkland, take one of a variety of woodland and wildlife walks, all landscaped by the legendary 'Capability' Brown in the 18th century. Then browse through the Gift Shop before relaxing in The Stables Restaurant and Bar.

With the exciting Woodland Adventure Playground, Pets Corner and Deer Park, as well as the Miniature Railway, there is so much for children to do.

Weston Park has a long-standing reputation for staging outstanding events. The exciting and varied programme of entertainment includes Balloon Festivals, Music Festivals, Opera Evenings and Battle Re-enactments.

▶ OPENING TIMES

Easter weekend:
30 March - 1 April

6 April - 30 June:
weekends.

1 July - 31 August:
Daily (closed 13 July, and
3, 15 - 21 August).

Every weekend in
September until
15 September,
then closed.

House: 1 - 5pm
Last admission 4.30pm.

Park: 11am - 7pm
Last admission 5pm.

NB. Visitors are advised to telephone first to check this information.

▶ ADMISSION

Park & Gardens
Adult £2.50
Child (3 - 16yrs) £2.00
OAP £1.50
Family (2+3) £6.00

House
Adult £2.00
Child (3 - 16yrs) £1.50
OAP £1.00

CONFERENCE/FUNCTION

ROOM	SIZE	MAX CAPACITY
Dining Rm	52' x 23'	120
Orangery	51' x 20'	120
Music Rm	50' x 20'	80
The Old Stables	58' x 20'	60
Conference Room	40' x 7'6"	60

ACTON BURNELL CASTLE ⊞

Acton Burnell, Shrewsbury, Shropshire

Tel: 0121 625 6820 (Regional Office)

Owner: English Heritage   **Contact:** The West Midlands Regional Office

The warm red sandstone shell of a fortified 13th century manor house.

Location: OS Ref. SJ534 019. In Acton Burnell, on unclassified road 8m S of Shrewsbury.

Open: Any reasonable time.

Admission: Free.

ADCOTE SCHOOL

Little Ness, Shrewsbury, Shropshire SY4 2JY

Tel: 01939 260202 **Fax:** 01939 261300

Owner: Adcote School Educational Trust Ltd   **Contact:** Mrs A Read

Adcote is a Grade I listed building designed by Norman Shaw, and built to a Tudor design in 1879. Its features include a Great Hall, Minstrels' Gallery, William De Morgan tiled fireplaces and stained glass windows. Landscaped gardens include many fine trees.

Location: OS Ref. SJ418 294. 7m NW of Shrewsbury. 2m NE of A5.

Open: By appointment only.

Admission: Free, but the Governors reserve the right to make a charge.

🔊 ❋

Walcot Hall

ATTINGHAM PARK ✿

SHREWSBURY, SHROPSHIRE SY4 4TP

Infoline: 01743 708123   **Tel:** 01743 708162 **Fax:** 01743 708175

Owner: The National Trust   **Contact:** The Property Manager

Late 18th century house, sitting in 500 acres of wonderful parkland. Built for the 1st Lord Berwick, the Georgian house contains some beautiful Italian furniture and a large silver collection. Lord Berwick, and subsequently his two elder sons, had a passion for art and music and this is seen in the Picture Gallery with fine paintings and a Samuel Green organ, which is often played for visitors' enjoyment during the season. Woodland walks along the River Tern and through the Deer Park take in picturesque views of the Wrekin and Shropshire Hills. Costumed guided tours of the House are on offer every day the house is open. Events planned for 2002 include Easter Egg Trail, Spring Plant Fair, Teddy Bears' Picnic, Food Fayre and Apple Weekend.

Location: OS127 Ref. SJ837 083. 4m SE of Shrewsbury on N side of B4380 in Atcham village.

Open: 23 Mar - 3 Nov: daily (closed Wed & Thur), 1 - 4.30pm, last admission to house 4pm. Deer Park & Grounds: daily, closed 25 Dec. Mar - end Oct: 9am - 8pm. Nov - Feb 2002: 9am - 5pm.

Admission: House & Grounds: Adult £4.60, Child £2.30, Family £11.50. Grounds only: Adult £2.20, Child £1.10. Booked groups (15+): Adult £4, Child £2.

ℹ️No photography in house. 📷 ♿ 📹Licensed. 🎦 By arrangement. 🅿 ▪
🐕 In grounds on leads. ❋ 🚻 Tel for details.

BENTHALL HALL ✿

Benthall, Nr Broseley, Shropshire TF12 5RX

Tel: 01952 882159

Owner: The National Trust   **Contact:** Mr R Benthall

A 16th century stone house with mullioned windows and moulded brick chimneys.

Location: OS Ref. SJ658 025. 1m NW of Broseley (B4375), 4m NE of Much Wenlock, 1m SW of Ironbridge.

Open: 31 Mar - 29 Sept: Weds, Suns, BH Mons & 4 Jun, 1.30 - 5.30pm. Last adm. 5pm. Groups at other times by prior arrangement.

Admission: Adult: £3.60, Child: £1.80. Garden: £2.30.

♿ Ground floor. WC. 🎦 By arrangement. 🅿 Limited.

Plant Sales Index
◁ ◁ ◁ pgs 36-37

BOSCOBEL HOUSE & THE ROYAL OAK ⌗

BREWOOD, BISHOP'S WOOD, SHROPSHIRE ST19 9AR

Tel: 01902 850244

Owner: English Heritage   **Contact:** The Custodian

This 17th century hunting lodge was destined to play a part in Charles II's escape from the Roundheads. A descendant of the Royal Oak, which sheltered the fugitive King from Cromwell's troops after the Battle of Worcester in 1651, still stands in the fields near Boscobel House. The timber-framed house where the King slept in a tiny 'sacred hole' has been fully restored and furnished in Victorian period and there are panelled rooms and secret hiding places. There is an exhibition in the house as well as the farmyard and smithy.

Location: OS127 Ref. SJ837 083. On unclassified road between A41 & A5. 8m NW of Wolverhampton.

Open: 1 Mar - 30 Nov: daily: 11am - 6pm (5pm in Oct & 4pm in Nov). Last tours ¹/₂ hour before closing. Closed 1 Dec - 28 Feb.

Admission: Adult £4.40, Child £2.20, Conc. £3.30, Family £11. 15% discount on groups (11+).

🔲Grounds. WC. 🔲 🔲Obligatory. 🔲 🔲 🔲 Tel for details.

BUILDWAS ABBEY ⌗

Iron Bridge, Telford, Shropshire TF8 7BW

Tel: 01952 433274

Owner: English Heritage   **Contact:** The Custodian

Extensive remains of a Cistercian abbey built in 1135, set beside the River Severn against a backdrop of wooded grounds. The remains include the church which is almost complete except for the roof.

Location: OS Ref. SJ642 044. On S bank of River Severn on A4169, 2m W of Ironbridge.

Open: 29 Mar - 30 Sept: daily, 11am - 5pm.

Admission: Adult £2.10, Child £1, Conc. £1.60.

CLUN CASTLE ⌗

Clun, Ludlow, Shropshire

Tel: 0121 625 6820 (Regional Office)

Owner: English Heritage   **Contact:** The West Midlands Regional Office

Remains of a four-storey keep and other buildings of this border castle are set in outstanding countryside. Built in the 11th century.

Location: OS Ref. SO299 809. In Clun, off A488, 18m W of Ludlow. 9m W of Craven Arms.

Open: Any reasonable time.

Admission: Free.

COLEHAM PUMPING STATION

Longden Coleham, Shrewsbury, Shropshire SY3 7DN

Tel: 01743 361196   **Fax:** 01743 358411

e-mail: museums@shrewsbury-atcham.gov.uk   **www**.shrewsburymuseums.com

Owner: Shrewsbury & Atcham Borough Council   **Contact:** Mary White

Two Renshaw beam engines of 1901 are being restored to steam by members of Shrewsbury Steam Trust.

Location: OS Ref. SJ497 122. Shrewsbury town centre, near the River Severn.

Open: Apr - Sept: 4th Sun in each month, 10am - 4pm. Plus occasional other days. Details: 01743 361196.

Admission: Adult £1, Child 50p, Student £1.

🔲Partial. 🔲By arrangement. 🔲 No parking. 🔲 🔲 Guide dogs only.

COMBERMERE ABBEY

Whitchurch, Shropshire SY13 4AJ

Tel: 01948 662880 **Fax:** 01948 660940

e-mail: cottages@combermereabbey.co.uk **www**.combermereabbey.co.uk

Owner: Mrs S Callander Beckett   **Contact:** Mrs Carol Sheard

Combermere Abbey, originally a Cistercian Monastery, and remodelled as a Gothic house in 1820 sits in a magnificent 1000 acre private parkland setting. Host to many remarkable historical personalities, the splendid 17th century Library and elegant Porter's Hall are licensed for weddings, receptions, concerts and lectures. Excellent accommodation is available on the Estate.

Location: OS Ref. SJ590 440. 5m E of Whitchurch, off A530.

Open: By arrangement for groups.

Admission: Groups: £7 per person inclusive of refreshments.

ℹ️No photography. 🔲 🔲Unsuitable. 🔲By arrangement. 🔲By arrangement. 🔲Limited. 🔲 🔲 🔲

Civil Wedding Venues
◁ ◁ ◁ pgs 28-29

DAVENPORT HOUSE

WORFIELD, Nr BRIDGNORTH, SHROPSHIRE WV15 5LE

www.davenporthouse.co.uk

Tel: 01746 716221 / 716345 **Fax:** 01746 716021

e-mail: murphy@davenporthouse.co.uk

Owner/Contact: Roger Murphy

A Grade I listed country house of 1726 by the architect Francis Smith of Warwick. The house sits within an extensive estate and is a popular regional venue for wedding receptions, civil marriage ceremonies and corporate and social group entertainment. Open to the public as a restaurant Wednesday evenings, advance booking only.

Location: OS Ref. SO756 955. Worfield village, drive entrance by war memorial.

Open: Available for weddings and other functions throughout the year.

Admission: Please telephone for details.

🔲 🔲 🔲Licensed. 🔲 🔲 🔲 🔲

Michael Caldwell

DUDMASTON ✹

QUATT, BRIDGNORTH, SHROPSHIRE WV15 6QN

Tel: 01746 780866 **Fax:** 01746 780744 **e-mail:** mduefe@smtp.ntrust.org.uk

Owner: The National Trust **Contact:** The Administrator

Late 17th century manor house. Contains furniture and china, Dutch flower paintings, watercolours, botanical art and modern pictures and sculpture, family and natural history. 9 acres of lakeside gardens and Dingle walk. Two estate walks 5¹/₂ m and 3¹/₂m starting from Hampton Loade car park.

Location: OS Ref. SO748 888. 4m SE of Bridgnorth on A442.

Open: 31 Mar - 29 Sept: House; Tues, Weds, Suns & BH Mons, 2 - 5.30pm. Mons booked groups by arrangement. Garden; Mon - Wed & Suns, 12 noon - 6pm. Tearoom: 11.30am - 5.30pm. Last admission to house 5pm.

Admission: House & Garden: Adult £3.95, Child £2, Family £9. Groups £3.30. Garden only: £2.90, free tours Mon afternoons.

ℹ️Countryside walks. 🖾 🔄 🖵 🖾In grounds, on leads.

HAUGHMOND ABBEY ♯

Upton Magna, Uffington, Shrewsbury, Shropshire SY4 4RW

Tel: 01743 709661

Owner: English Heritage **Contact:** The Custodian

Extensive remains of a 12th century Augustinian abbey, including the Chapter House which retains its late medieval timber ceiling, and including some fine medieval sculpture.

Location: OS Ref. SJ542 152. 3m NE of Shrewsbury off B5062.

Open: 29 Mar - 30 Sept: daily, 11am - 5pm.

Admission: Adult £2.10, Child £1, Conc. £1.60.

🔄 🅿 🖵 Tel for details.

HAWKSTONE HALL & GARDENS

Marchamley, Shrewsbury SY4 5LG

Tel: 01630 685242 **Fax:** 01630 685565

Owner: The Redemptorists **Contact:** Guest Mistress

Grade I Georgian mansion and restored gardens set in spacious parkland.

Location: OS Ref. SJ581 299. Entrance 1m N of Hodnet on A442.

Open: Please contact for details.

Admission: Adult £4, Child £1.

Open All Year Index
◁ ◁ ◁ pgs 44-48

HODNET HALL GARDENS 🏛

HODNET, MARKET DRAYTON, SHROPSHIRE TF9 3NN

Tel: 01630 685202 **Fax:** 01630 685853

Owner: Mr and the Hon Mrs A Heber-Percy **Contact:** Mrs M A Taylor

There have been gardens at Hodnet since the 11th century when the Heber-Percy family constructed their first house in the parkland. Their serious development began in 1921 by the late Brigadier Heber-Percy. Today, the 60+ acres are renowned as amongst the finest in the country. Forest trees provide a wonderful backdrop for formal gardens planted to give delight during every season, and for woodland walks amongst flowering shrubs. There is a daisy chain of ornamental pools and lakes.

Tearooms serve light lunches and afternoon teas and adjacent is a gift shop.. The walled kitchen garden sells plants and produce in their season.

Location: OS Ref. SJ613 286. 12m NE of Shrewsbury on A53; M6/J15, M54/J3.

Open: 29 Mar (Good Fri) - 30 Sept: Tue - Sun & BH Mons, 12 noon - 5pm.

Admission: Adult £3.50, Child £1.50, OAP £3. Reduced rates for groups.

🖾 Gift Shop. 🌱 Kitchen garden plants & produce. 🍵 For groups. 🖵 🅿
■ Educational package linked to Key stages I & 2 of National Curriculum.
🖾 On leads.

West Midlands - England

IRONBRIDGE GORGE MUSEUMS

IRONBRIDGE, TELFORD, SHROPSHIRE TF8 7AW

www.ironbridge.org.uk

Tel: 01952 432166 (7 day line) or 433522 **Fax:** 01952 432204

Owner: Independent Museum   **Contact:** Visitor Information

Freephone: 0800 590258 for a free colour guide.

Scene of pioneering events which led to the Industrial Revolution. The Ironbridge Gorge is home to nine unique museums set in six square miles of stunning scenery.   These include Jackfield Tile Museum, Coalport China Museum and a recreated Victorian Town where you can chat to locals as they go about their daily business. You'll need two days here.

Location: OS Ref. SJ666 037. Telford, Shropshire via M6/M54.

Open: All year: daily from 10am - 5pm (closed 24/25 Dec & 1 Jan). Please telephone for winter details before visit.

Admission: Passport ticket which allows admission to all museums; Adult £10, Child/Student £6, OAP £9, Family £30. Prices valid until 22 March 2002. Group discounts available.

▣ Ⓣ ☻ ⧉ Licensed. Ⓟ Ⓧ By arrangement. ▦ ▨ Guide dogs only. ▲ ✳ ▨ Tel for details.

LANGLEY CHAPEL ⌗

Acton Burnell, Shrewsbury, Shropshire

Tel: 0121 625 6820 (Regional Office)

Owner: English Heritage   **Contact:** The West Midlands Regional Office

A delightful medieval chapel, standing alone in a field, with a complete set of early 17th century wooden fittings and furniture.

Location: OS Ref. SJ538 001. 1½ m S of Acton Burnell, on unclassified road 4m E of the A49, 9½ m S of Shrewsbury.

Open: Open any reasonable time. Closed 24- 26 Dec & 1 Jan.

Admission: Free.

LILLESHALL ABBEY ⌗

Oakengates, Shropshire

Tel: 0121 625 6820 (Regional Office)

Owner: English Heritage   **Contact:** The West Midlands Regional Office

Extensive ruins of an abbey of Augustinian canons including remains of the 12th and 13th century church and the cloister buildings. Surrounded by green lawns and ancient yew trees.

Location: OS Ref. SJ738 142. On unclassified road off the A518, 4m N of Oakengates.

Open: Any reasonable time.

Admission: Free.

LONGNER HALL 🏛

Uffington, Shrewsbury, Shropshire SY4 4TG

Tel: 01743 709215

Owner: Mr R L Burton   **Contact:** Mrs R L Burton

Designed by John Nash in 1803, Longner Hall is a Tudor Gothic style house set in a park landscaped by Humphry Repton. The home of one family for over 700 years. Longner's principal rooms are adorned with plaster fan vaulting and stained glass.

Location: OS Ref. SJ529 110. 4m SE of Shrewsbury on Uffington road, ¼ m off B4380, Atcham.

Open: Apr - Oct: Tues & BH Mons, 2 - 5pm. Tours at 2pm & 3.30pm. Groups at any time by arrangement.

Admission: Adult £5, Child/OAP £3.

ⓘ No photography in house. ✳ ⬠ Partial. ☻ By arrangement for groups. Ⓧ Obligatory. Ⓟ Limited for coaches. ▦ By arrangement. ▨ Guide dogs only. ✳

LUDLOW CASTLE

CASTLE SQUARE, LUDLOW, SHROPSHIRE SY8 1AY

www.ludlowcastle.com

Tel: 01584 873355

Owner: The Earl of Powis & The Trustees of the Powis Estate

                    Contact: Helen J Duce

900 year old castle of the Marches, dates from 1086 and greatly extended over the centuries to a fortified Royal Palace. Ludlow Castle became a seat of government with the establishment of the Council for Wales and the Marches. Privately owned by the Earls of Powis since 1811. A magnificent ruin set in the heart of Ludlow and surrounding countryside.

Location: OS Ref. SO509 745. Shrewsbury 28m, Hereford 26m. A49 centre of Ludlow.

Open: Jan: weekends only, 10am - 4pm, Feb - Mar & Oct - Dec: 10am - 4pm. Apr - Jul & Sept: 10am - 5pm. Aug: 10am - 7pm. Last adm. 30mins before closing. Closed 25 Dec.

Admission: Adult £3.50, Child £1.50, Conc. £3, Family £9.50. 10% reduction for groups (10+).

▣ ⬠ Partial. WC. Ⓧ By arrangement. ⌂ Ⓟ None. ▦ ▨ In grounds on leads. ✳ ▨

MAWLEY HALL
CLEOBURY MORTIMER, DY14 8PN

www.mawley.com

Tel: 01299 270869 **Fax:** 01299 270022 **e-mail:** administration@mawley.com

Owner: R Galliers-Pratt Esq **Contact:** Mrs R Sharp
Built in 1730 and attributed to Francis Smith of Warwick, Mawley is set in 18th century landscaped parkland with extensive gardens and walks down to the River Rea. Magnificent plasterwork and a fine collection of English and Continental furniture and porcelain.

Location: OS137 Ref. SO688 753. 1m N of Cleobury Mortimer on the A4117 and 7m W of Bewdley.

Open: 15 Apr - 18 Jul: Mons & Thurs, 3 - 5pm and throughout the year by appointment.

Admission: Adult £5, Child/OAP £3.

ⓘ Lunches, dinners & functions in association with Sean Hill of the Michelin starred restaurant, The Merchant House, in Ludlow.
🅣 🅕 By arrangement. 🅟 ▣ 🅗 In grounds, on leads. ✳

MORETON CORBET CASTLE ♯
Moreton Corbet, Shrewsbury, Shropshire
Tel: 0121 625 6820 (Regional Office)

Owner: English Heritage **Contact:** The West Midlands Regional Office
A ruined medieval castle with the substantial remains of a splendid Elizabethan mansion, captured in 1644 from Charles I's supporters by Parliamentary forces.

Location: OS Ref. SJ562 232. In Moreton Corbet off B5063, 7m NE of Shrewsbury.

Open: Any reasonable time.

Admission: Free.

MORVILLE HALL 🌿
Bridgnorth, Shropshire WV16 5NB
Tel: 01743 708100

Owner: The National Trust **Contact:** Dr & Mrs C Douglas
An Elizabethan house of mellow stone, converted in the 18th century and set in attractive gardens.

Location: OS Ref. SO668 940. Morville, on A458 3m W of Bridgnorth.

Open: By written appointment only with the tenants.

OAKLEY HALL
See page 327 for full page entry.

PREEN MANOR GARDENS
Church Preen, Church Stretton, Shropshire SY6 7LQ
Tel: 01694 771207

Owner: Mr & Mrs P Trevor-Jones **Contact:** Mrs P Trevor-Jones
Six acre garden on site of Cluniac monastery, with walled, terraced, wild, water, kitchen and chess gardens. 12th century monastic church.

Location: OS Ref. SO544 981. 10m SSE of Shrewsbury. 7m NE of Church Stretton, 6m SW of Much Wenlock.

Open: Please contact for details.

Admission: Adult £3, Child 50p.

SHIPTON HALL 🏠
Much Wenlock, Shropshire TF13 6JZ
Tel: 01746 785225 **Fax:** 01746 785125

Owner: Mr J N R Bishop **Contact:** Mrs M J Bishop
Built around 1587 by Richard Lutwyche who gave the house to his daughter Elizabeth on her marriage to Thomas Mytton. Shipton remained in the Mytton family for the next 300 years. The house has been described as 'an exquisite specimen of Elizabethan architecture set in a quaint old fashioned garden, the whole forming a picture which as regards both form and colour, satisfies the artistic sense of even the most fastidious'. The Georgian additions by Thomas F Pritchard include some elegant rococo interior decorations. There is some noteworthy Tudor and Jacobean panelling. Family home. In addition to the house visitors are welcome to explore the gardens, the dovecote and the parish church which dates back to Saxon times.

Location: OS Ref. SO563 918. 7m SW of Much Wenlock on B4378. 10m W of Bridgnorth.

Open: Easter - end Sept: Thurs, 2.30 - 5.30pm. Also Suns and Mons of BH, 2.30 - 5.30pm. Groups of 20+ at any time of day or year by prior arrangement.

Admission: Adult £4, Child £2. Discount of 10% for groups (20+).
♿ Unsuitable. ▣ By arrangement for groups (20+). 🅕 Obligatory. 🅗 Guide dogs only. ✳

SHREWSBURY ABBEY
Shrewsbury, Shropshire SY2 6BS
Tel: 01743 232723 **Fax:** 01743 240172 **e-mail:** shrewsburyabbey@netscape.online.co.uk
www.virtual-shropshire.co.uk/shrewsbury-abb

Contact: Mr Terence Hyde
Benedictine Abbey founded in 1083, tomb of Roger de Montgomerie and remains of tomb of St Winefride, 7th century Welsh saint. The Abbey was part of the monastery and has also been a parish church since the 12th century. Now made popular by Ellis Peters author of 'Brother Cadfael' novels. Historical exhibition from Saxon times to present. Restored and re-sited tomb of Richard and Catherine Onslow now in the South Aisle.

Location: OS Ref. SJ499 125. Signposted from Shrewsbury bypass (A5 and A49). 500yds E of town centre, across English Bridge.

Open: 24 Mar - 26 Oct: 9.30am - 5.30pm. 27 Oct - 22 Mar 2003: 10.30am - 3pm.

Admission: Donation. Guided tours £15 per pre-arranged group.

SHREWSBURY CASTLE &
THE SHROPSHIRE REGIMENTAL MUSEUM
Castle Street, Shrewsbury SY1 2AT
Tel: 01743 358516 **Fax:** 01743 358411 **e-mail:** museums@shrewsbury-atcham.gov.uk
www.shrewsburymuseums.com

Owner: Shrewsbury & Atcham Borough Council **Contact:** Steve Martin
Norman Castle with 18th century work by Thomas Telford. Free admission to attractive floral grounds. The main hall houses The Shropshire Regimental Museum and displays on the history of the castle. Open-air theatre and concert during the summer.

Location: OS Ref. SJ495 128. Town centre, adjacent BR and bus stations.

Open: Main building & Museum: 13 Feb - 25 May: Wed - Sat, 10am - 4pm. 26 May - 29 Sept: Tue - Sat, 10am - 5pm, Sun & Mon, 10am - 4pm. Winter: Please call for details. Grounds: Mon - Sat, 10am - 5pm & Suns as above.

Admission: Museum: Adult £2, OAP £1, Shrewsbury residents, under 18s, Students & members of the regiments Free. Grounds: Free.
ⓘ No photography. 📷 ♿ 🅟 None. ▣ 🅗 Guide dogs only. ▲ ☏ Tel for details.

SHREWSBURY MUSEUM & ART GALLERY (ROWLEY'S HOUSE)
Barker Street, Shrewsbury, Shropshire SY1 1QH
Tel: 01743 361196 **Fax:** 01743 358411
e-mail: museums@shrewsbury-atcham.gov.uk **www.**shrewsburymuseums.com

Owner: Shrewsbury and Atcham Borough Council **Contact:** Mrs M White
Impressive timber-framed building and attached 17th century brick mansion with costume, archaeology and natural history, geology, local history and special exhibitions, including contemporary art.

Location: OS Ref. SJ490 126. Barker Street.

Open: 1 Jan - 25 May & 1 Oct - 31 Dec: Tue - Sat, 10am - 4pm. Closed 23 Dec 2001 - 7 Jan. 26 May - 29 Sept: Tue - Sat, 10am - 5pm, Sun & Mon, 10am - 4pm.

Admission: Free.
ⓘ No photography. 📷 ♿ Ground floor only. 🅟 None. ▣ 🅗 Guide dogs only. ✳

Special Events Index ◁ ◁ ◁ pgs 40-43

English Heritage Photo Library

Ironbridge Gorge Museums

STOKESAY CASTLE ⌗

Nr CRAVEN ARMS, SHROPSHIRE SY7 9AH

Tel: 01588 672544

Owner: English Heritage   **Contact:** The Custodian

This perfectly preserved example of a 13th century fortified manor house gives us a glimpse of the life and ambitions of a rich medieval merchant. Lawrence of Ludlow built this country house to impress the landed gentry. Lawrence built a magnificent Great Hall where servants and guests gathered on feast days, but the family's private quarters were in the bright, comfortable solar on the first floor. From the outside the castle forms a picturesque grouping of castle, parish church and timber-framed Jacobean gatehouse set in the rolling Shropshire countryside.

Location: OS137 Ref. SO436 817. 7m NW of Ludlow off A49. 1m S of Craven Arms off A49.

Open: 29 Mar - 31 Oct: daily, 10am - 6pm (5pm in Oct). 1 Nov - 31 Mar: Wed - Sun, 10am - 4pm. Closed 1 - 2pm in Winter. Closed 24 - 26 Dec & 1 Jan.

Admission: Adult £4.40, Child £2.20, Conc. £3.30, Family £11. Groups of 11+ 15% discount.

♿ Great Hall & gardens. WC. ⛏ ⌂ **P** ✳ ♿ Tel for details.

Accommodation Index
◁ ◁ ◁   pg 27

WALCOT HALL ⌂

LYDBURY NORTH, Nr BISHOP'S CASTLE, SHROPSHIRE SY7 8AZ

www.walcothall.com

Tel: 01568 610693 **Fax:** 01568 615851 **e-mail:** enquiries@walcothall.com

Owner: C R W Parish   **Contact:** Lesley Higgs, Marketing Manager

Historic home of Lord Clive of India who commissioned Sir William Chambers to redesign it in 1763. It remains a beautiful, Georgian, family home set in spectacular surroundings with a 30 acre arboretum and gardens to the rear and overlooking a mile-long, fishing lake with panoramic views of the Shropshire hills. The Ballroom, Anteroom and Main Hall are available for hire including a secluded courtyard and access to the gardens – an ideal venue for weddings, balls and corporate events. Self-catering holiday apartments for 40 guests are situated within the estate and concerts and plays are staged within the Ballroom and grounds.

Location: OS Ref. SO348 850. 3m SE of Bishop's Castle on B4385. Entrance to drive adjacent to Powis Arms pub in Lydbury North.

Open: Arboretum: 3 May - 28 Oct: Fri - Mon, 12 noon - 5pm. Hall: by appointment only, except 2 - 4 Jun, 2 - 6pm.

Admission: Adult £3, Child (under 15yrs) Free.

ℹ Catering if booked. ⛏ ♿ Partial. ●By arrangement. **P** ⌖In grounds, on leads. ⊞ 6 double, 9 twin, 1 single. ▲ ✳ ♿ Tel for details.

WENLOCK GUILDHALL
Much Wenlock, Shropshire TF13 6AE
Tel: 01952 727509
Owner/Contact: Much Wenlock Town Council
16th century half-timbered building has an open-arcade market area.
Location: OS127 Ref. SJ624 000. In centre of Much Wenlock, next to the church.
Open: 1 Apr - 31 Oct: Mon - Sat, 10.30am - 1pm & 2 - 4pm. Suns: 2 - 4pm.
Admission: Adult 50p, Child Free.

WENLOCK PRIORY ⌗
Much Wenlock, Shropshire TF13 6HS
Tel: 01952 727466
Owner: English Heritage   **Contact:** The Custodian
A prosperous, powerful priory at its peak in the Middle Ages. A great deal of the structure still survives in the form of high, romantic ruined walls and it is the resting place of St Milburga the first Abbess. A monastery was first founded at Wenlock in the 7th century, and little more is known of the site until the time of the Norman Conquest when it became a Cluniac monastery. These majestic ruins of the priory church are set in green lawns and topiary, and there are substantial remains of the early 13th century church and Norman Chapter House.
Location: OS127 Ref. SJ625 001. In Much Wenlock.
Open: 29 Mar - 31 Oct: daily: 10am - 6pm (5pm in Oct). 1 Nov - 31 Mar: Wed - Sun, 10am - 4pm (closed 1 - 2pm in winter). Closed 24 - 26 Dec & 1 Jan.
Admission: Adult £3, Child £1.50, Conc. £2.30, Family £7.50. 15% discount for groups (11+).
P ✳ ♿ Tel for details.

WESTON PARK 🏛
See page 328 for full page entry.

WILDERHOPE MANOR ✿
Longville, Much Wenlock, Shropshire TF13 6EG
Tel: 01694 771363
Owner: The National Trust   **Contact:** The Warden
This limestone house stands on southern slope of Wenlock Edge in remote country with views down to Corvedale. Dating from 1586, it is unaltered but unfurnished. Features include remarkable wooden spiral stairs, unique bow rack and fine plaster ceilings.
Location: OS Ref. SO545 929. 7m SW of Much Wenlock. 7m E of Church Stretton, ½ m S of B4371.
Open: Apr - Sept: Weds & Sats, 2 - 4.30pm. Oct - Mar: Sats only, 2 - 4.30pm.
Admission: £1. No reduction for groups. Steep access to house.

WOLLERTON OLD HALL GARDEN
Wollerton, Market Drayton, Shropshire TF9 3NA
Tel: 01630 685760 **Fax:** 01630 685583
Owner: Mr & Mrs J D Jenkins   **Contact:** Mrs Di Oakes
Three acre plantsman's garden created around a 16th century house (not open).
Location: OS Ref. SJ623 296. 14m NE of Shrewsbury off A53 between Hodnet and Market Drayton.
Open: Easter Good Fri - end Aug: Fris, Suns & BHs (Fris only in Sept), 12 noon - 5pm. Groups (25+) by appointment at other times.
Admission: Adult £3.50, Child £1.

WROXETER ROMAN CITY ⌗
Wroxeter, Shrewsbury, Shropshire SY5 6PH
Tel: 01743 761330
Owner: English Heritage   **Contact:** The Custodian
The part-excavated centre of the fourth largest city in Roman Britain, originally home to some 6,000 men and several hundred houses. Impressive remains of the 2nd century municipal baths. There is a site museum in which many finds are displayed, including those from recent work by Birmingham Field Archaeological Unit.
Location: OS Ref. SJ568 088. At Wroxeter, 5m E of Shrewsbury, on B4380.
Open: 29 Mar - 31 Oct: daily 10am - 6pm (5pm in Oct). 1 Nov - 31 Mar: daily, 10am - 1pm & 2 - 4pm. Closed 24 - 26 Dec & 1 Jan.
Admission: Adult £3.60, Child £1.80, Conc. £2.70, Family £9.
♿ P ✳ ♿ Tel for details.

Right: Wollerton Old Hall Garden

West Midlands - England

British Tourist Authority

SHUGBOROUGH

STAFFORD

www.staffordshire.gov.uk/shugboro/shugpark.htm

Shugborough is the magnificent 900-acre ancestral home of the 5th Earl of Lichfield, who is known world-wide as Patrick Lichfield the leading photographer.

The 18th century mansion house contains a fine collection of ceramics, silver, paintings and French furniture. Part of the house is still lived in by the Earl and his family.

Visitors can enjoy the splendid 18-acre Grade I Historic Garden with its Edwardian Rose Garden and terraces. A unique collection of neo-classical monuments by James Stuart can be found in the parkland which also includes walks and trails.

Other attractions include the County Museum which is housed in the original servants' quarters. The working laundry, kitchens and brewhouse have all been lovingly restored and are staffed by costumed guides who show how the servants lived and worked over 100 years ago.

Shugborough Park Farm is a Georgian working farm which features an agricultural museum, restored working corn mill and is also a rare breeds centre. In the farmhouse kitchen visitors can see bread baked in brick ovens and in the dairy, cheese and butter being made.

Throughout the year a lively collection of themed tours are in operation for the coach market and an award-winning educational programme for schools. From April to December an exciting events programme is in operation.

Shugborough is an ideal venue for weddings, conferences, corporate activity days and product launches.

Owner:
The National Trust

▶ CONTACT

Sales and
Marketing Office
Shugborough
Milford
Stafford ST17 0XB

Tel: 01889 881388
Fax: 01889 881323

e-mail: shugborough.
promotions@
staffordshire.gov.uk

▶ LOCATION
OS Ref. SJ992 225

10mins from M6/J13 on A513 Stafford/
Lichfield Road.

Rail: Stafford 6m.

Taxi: Anthony's
01785 252255

CONFERENCE/FUNCTION

ROOM	SIZE	MAX CAPACITY
Banqueting Hall	15 x 6.5m	65
Saloon	15 x 6m	80
Conference Suite	6 x 6m	35
Granary	5.5 x 9.5m	60
Blue Drawing Rm	6.5 x 8m	20
Tower of the Winds	6.5 x 6.5m	20

▶ OPENING TIMES
Please call 01889 881388
for full details.

▶ ADMISSION
Please call 01889 881388
for full details.

Private and corporate entertainment, conferences, product launches and dinner parties. Filming and event location. Over 900 acres of parkland and gardens available for hire. Themed activities. No photography in house.

Catering for special functions/ conferences.

Visitors may alight at entrance before parking. WCs. Stairclimber to house. Batricars available. Disabled-friendly picnic tables available. Taped tours.

Licensed tearoom/café seating 95, also tearoom at Farm seats 30. Prior notice for large groups.

Tour time 1hr. Themed tours as required. Groups of 15+. Please telephone for details.

Ample car and coach parking. Discounted vouchers for coach drivers' meals available.

Award-winning educational packages. Curriculum-related. Contact Sales & Development Officer.

In grounds, on leads.

Civil Wedding Licence.

Tel for details.

THE ANCIENT HIGH HOUSE

GREENGATE STREET, STAFFORD ST16 2JA

Tel: 01785 619131 **Fax:** 01785 619132 **e-mail:** ahh@staffordbc.gov.uk

Owner: Stafford Borough Council **Contact:** K Stringer

This building is the largest timber-framed town house in England. Built in 1595 by the Dorrington family, this house is still very impressive on Stafford's skyline. It was lived in by Richard Sneyd, a member of one of Staffordshire's greatest families when King Charles I stayed here in 1642. It is now a registered museum with displays set out as period room settings which present aspects of the house's history. The Staffordshire Yeomanry Museum is on the top floor.

Location: OS Ref. SJ922 232. Town centre.

Open: All year: Mon - Sat, 10am - 5pm. Check BHs.

Admission: Please telephone for details.

🖻 ⓑ Unsuitable. 🐕 Guide dogs only. 🌸 🎗 Tel for details.

NTPL / Ian Shaw

BIDDULPH GRANGE GARDEN 🌿

GRANGE ROAD, BIDDULPH, STOKE-ON-TRENT ST8 7SD

Tel: 01782 517999 **Fax:** 01782 510624

Owner: The National Trust **Contact:** The Garden Office

A rare and exciting survival of a High Victorian garden, restored by the National Trust. The garden is divided into a series of themed gardens within a garden, with a Chinese temple, Egyptian court, pinetum, dahlia walk, glen and many other settings. Difficult uneven levels, unsuitable for wheelchairs.

Location: OS Ref. SJ891 592. E of A527, 3½ m SE of Congleton, 8m N of Stoke-on-Trent.

Open: 23 Mar - 3 Nov: Wed - Fri, 12 noon - 5.30pm. Sats, Suns & BH Mons, 11am - 5.30pm or dusk. Closed Good Fri. 11 Nov - 22 Dec: Sats & Suns, 12 noon- 4pm or dusk if earlier.

Admission: Adult £4.50, Child £2.40, Family (2+2) £11.50. Booked guided tours: £6.50. Groups (15+): £3.80. Nov & Dec: Free. Voucher to visit Little Moreton Hall at a reduced fee when purchasing Adult ticket.

🖻 ⓑ Unsuitable for wheelchairs. 🍴 🐕 In car park, on leads.

Dorothy Clive Garden

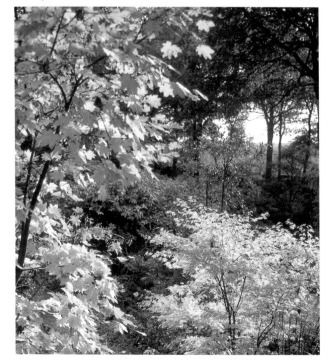

CASTERNE HALL

Ilam Nr Ashbourne, Derbyshire DE6 2BA

Tel: 01335 310489

Owner/Contact: Charles & Susannah Hurt

Manor house in fine location.

Location: OS Ref. SK123 523. Take first turning on left N of Ilam and continue past 'No through Road' sign.

Open: 28 May - 26 June: weekdays only plus May & Aug BH weekends, 10am - 1pm & 2 - 5pm.

Admission: £3.

🎦 Obligatory.

CHILLINGTON HALL 🏛

Codsall Wood, Wolverhampton, Staffordshire WV8 1RE

Tel: 01902 850236 **Fax:** 01902 850768

e-mail: mrsplod@chillingtonhall.co.uk **www**.chillingtonhall.co.uk

Owner/Contact: Mr & Mrs J W Giffard

Georgian red brick house with fine saloon by Soane set in 'Capability' Brown park having one of the largest lakes created by Brown. Extensive woodland walks.

Location: OS Ref. SJ864 067. 2m S of Brewood off A449. 4m NW of M54/J2.

Open: Easter Sun; Suns prior to both May BHs; Jul: Thur & Sun; Aug: Wed - Fri & Sun, 2 - 5pm.

Admission: Adult £4, Child £2. Grounds only: half price.

ⓑ Partial. 🎦 Obligatory. 🅿 🐕 In grounds, on leads.

THE DOROTHY CLIVE GARDEN

WILLOUGHBRIDGE, MARKET DRAYTON, SHROPSHIRE TF9 4EU

www.dorothyclivegarden.co.uk

Tel: 01630 647237 **Fax:** 01630 647902

Owner: Willoughbridge Garden Trust   **Contact:** Mrs M Grime

The Dorothy Clive Garden accommodates a wide range of choice and unusual plants providing year round interest. Features include a quarry with spectacular waterfall, flower borders, a scree and water garden. Tearoom serving home-baked hot and cold snacks throughout the day.

Location: OS Ref. SJ753 400. A51, 2m S of Woore, 3m from Bridgemere.

Open: 1 Apr - 31 Oct: daily, 10am - 5.30pm.

Admission: Adult £3.20, Child (11-16yrs) £1, (under 11yrs Free), OAP £2.70. Groups (20+) £2.70.

▤ ▣ **P** ▣ In grounds on leads.

LICHFIELD CATHEDRAL

CATHEDRAL OFFICE, 19A THE CLOSE, LICHFIELD WS13 7LD

www.lichfield-cathedral.org

Tel: 01543 306240 **Fax:** 01543 306109

e-mail: enquiries@lichfield-cathedral.org **www**.lichfield-cathedral.org

Owner: Dean & Chapter   **Contact:** Canon A N Barnard

The only medieval cathedral with three spires, in the heart of an historic city. Meet a living Christian community, 1300 years old. See the 8th century illuminated 'Lichfield Gospels' manuscript; superb 16th century Flemish glass; sculpture by Chantrey & Epstein, modern silver collection and half-timbered buildings of Vicars' Close.

Location: OS Ref. SK115 097. Approach from A38 and A51, N from M42 and M6. N of city centre.

Open: All year: daily.

Admission: Suggested donation, £3 per adult.

▤ ▣ ▣ ▣Licensed. ƒBy arrangement. **P**None. ■ ▣Guide dogs only. ✴

Open All Year Index
◁ ◁ ◁ pgs 44-48

Open All Year Index ◁ ◁ ◁ pgs 44-48

FORD GREEN HALL

Ford Green Road, Smallthorne, Stoke-on-Trent ST6 1NG

Tel: 01782 233195 **Fax:** 01782 233194

e-mail: fordgreenhall@stoke.gov.uk **www**.stoke.gov.uk/fordgreenhall

Owner: Stoke-on-Trent City Council   **Contact:** Angela Graham

A 17th century house, home to the Ford family for two centuries. The hall has been designated a museum with an outstanding collection of original and reproduction period furniture, ceramics and textiles. There is a Tudor-style garden. The museum has an award-winning education service and regular events. Children's parties available.

Location: OS Ref. SJ887 508. NE of Stoke-on-Trent on B551, signposted from A500.

Open: All year: (closed 25 Dec - 1 Jan), Sun - Thurs, 1 - 5pm.

Admission: Adult £1.50, Conc. £1. Special group packages & packages with other visitor attractions (must book, min 10).

▤ ▣ ▣Partial. WC. ▣ **P** ■ ▣In grounds, on leads. ▲ ✴ ▣Tel for details.

SAMUEL JOHNSON BIRTHPLACE MUSEUM

Breadmarket Street, Lichfield, Staffordshire WS13 6LG

Tel: 01543 264972 **Fax:** 01543 414779

Owner: Lichfield City Council   **Contact:** Annette French

The house where his father had a bookshop is now a museum with many of Johnson's personal belongings.

Location: OS Ref. SK115 094. Breadmarket Street, Lichfield.

Open: Daily: 10.30am - 4.30pm. Closed Suns, Nov - Jan.

Admission: Adult £2, Child/Conc. £1.10, Family £5.40. Groups: £1.10. (2001 prices).

Moseley Old Hall

MOSELEY OLD HALL ✤
FORDHOUSES, WOLVERHAMPTON WV10 7HY

Tel/Fax: 01902 782808

Owner: The National Trust   **Contact:** The Property Manager

An Elizabethan timber-framed house encased in brick in 1870; with original interiors. Charles II hid here after the Battle of Worcester. The bed in which he slept is on view as well as the hiding place he used. An exhibition retells the story of the King's dramatic escape from Cromwell's troops, and there are optional, free guided tours. The garden has been reconstructed in 17th century style with formal box parterre, only 17th century plants are grown. The property is a Sandford Education Award Winner.

Location: OS Ref. SJ932 044. 4m N of Wolverhampton between A449 and A460.

Open: 23 Mar - 3 Nov: Sats, Suns, Weds, BH Mons & following Tues. 10 Nov - 15 Dec: Suns (guided tour only). Times: Mar - end Oct: 1 - 5pm (garden & tearoom from 12 noon). BH Mons: 11am - 5pm. Nov & Dec: 1 - 4pm.
3 Mar: special opening: Garden, ground floor of house, tearoom & shop: 1 - 4pm (tearoom 12 noon - 4pm). Pre-booked groups at other times including evening tours.

Admission: Adult £4.20, Child £2.10, Family £10.50.

Ground floor & grounds. WC. Tearoom in 18th century barn. Guide dogs only.

SANDON HALL
SANDON, STAFFORDSHIRE ST18 0BZ
www.sandonhall.co.uk

Tel/Fax: 01889 508004   **e-mail:** info@sandonhall.co.uk

Owner: The Earl of Harrowby   **Contact:** Michael Bosson

Ancestral seat of the Earls of Harrowby, conveniently located in the heart of Staffordshire. The imposing neo-Jacobean house was rebuilt by William Burn in 1854. Set amidst 400 acres of glorious parkland, Sandon, for all its grandeur and elegance, is first and foremost a home. The family museum which opened in 1994 has received considerable acclaim, and incorporates several of the State Rooms. The 50 acre landscaped gardens feature magnificent trees and are especially beautiful in May and autumn.

Location: OS Ref. SJ957 287. 5m NE of Stafford on the A51, between Stone and Lichfield, easy access from M6/J14.

Open: All year: for events, functions and for pre-booked visits to the museum and gardens. Evening tours by special arrangement. Closed Christmas Day, Boxing Day and New Year's Day.

Admission: Museum: Adult £4, Child £3, OAP £3.50. Gardens: Adult £1.50, Child £1, OAP £1. NB. Max group size 22 or 45 if combined Museum and Gardens.

Grounds. By arrangement. In grounds, on leads.

SHUGBOROUGH ✤   *See page 336 for full page entry.*

Shugborough

West Midlands - England

STAFFORD CASTLE & VISITOR CENTRE
NEWPORT ROAD, STAFFORD ST16 1DJ

Tel/Fax: 01785 257698

Owner: Stafford Borough Council　　　　**Contact:** N Thomas

This impressive site was once a Norman motte and bailey castle. Earl Ralph, a founder member of the Order of the Garter, spent part of his fortune building a stone keep in 1348. During the Civil War, the castle was successfully defended, but eventually demolished. The current building was erected in the early 19th century and fell into ruin through this century. The Visitor Centre displays artefacts found during recent excavations. An imaginative audio-visual presentation describes the castle's mixed fortunes.

Location: OS Ref. SJ904 220. On N side of A518, 1¹/₂ m WSW of town centre.

Open: Apr - Oct: Tue - Sun, 10am - 5pm. Nov - Mar: Tue - Sun, 10am - 4pm.

Admission: Please telephone for details.

[Icons] Grounds. WC. [Icons] In grounds, on leads. [Icons] Tel for details.

IZAAK WALTON'S COTTAGE
WORSTON LANE, SHALLOWFORD, Nr STAFFORD ST15 0PA

Tel/Fax: 01785 760278

Owner: Stafford Borough Council　　　　**Contact:** T Forrester

Thatched, timber-framed cottage in the heart of the Staffordshire countryside. Bequeathed by Izaak Walton, author of *The Compleat Angler*, it has displays on the history of angling. Ground floor rooms are set out in 17th century style.

Location: OS Ref. SJ876 293. Shallowford, nr Great Bridgeford, 6m N of Stafford.

Open: Apr - Oct: Wed - Sun & BHs, 1 - 5pm.

Admission: Please telephone for details.

[Icons] By arrangement. [P] [Icon] Guide dogs only. [Icon] Tel for details.

TAMWORTH CASTLE
The Holloway, Tamworth, Staffordshire B79 7NA

Tel: 01827 709626　**Fax:** 01827 709630　**e-mail:** heritage@tamworth.gov.uk

Owner: Tamworth Borough Council　　　　**Contact:** Mrs Esme Ballard

Dramatic Norman castle with 15 rooms open to the public, spanning 800 years of history.

Location: OS Ref. SK206 038. Town centre off A51.

Open: All year: Mon - Fri, 10am - 5.30pm. Sats & Suns, 12 noon - 5.30pm, last adm. 4.30pm. Please check opening times: 1 Nov - mid Feb.

Admission: Please telephone for 2002 prices.

TUTBURY CASTLE
Tutbury, Staffordshire

Tel: 01283 812129

Owner: The Duchy of Lancaster　　　　**Contact:** Lesley Smith

Remains of a large motte and bailey castle overlooking the Dove Valley. Also recreated Tudor Garden/Herbery. Now possible to go into castle. Often costumed guides.

Location: OS Ref. SK210 291. W side of Tutbury off A50 Tutbury - Barton road.

Open: Apr - Oct: Wed - Suns, 11am - 5pm.

Admission: Adult £3, Child/OAP £2.20.

WALL ROMAN SITE (Letocetum) ⚎ ⚘
Watling Street, Nr Lichfield, Staffordshire WS14 0AW

Tel: 01543 480768

Owner: English Heritage　　　　**Contact:** The Custodian

The remains of a staging post alongside Watling Street. Foundations of an Inn and a Bath House can be seen and there is a display of finds in the site museum.

Location: OS139 Ref. SK099 067. Off A5 at Wall, nr Lichfield.

Open: 29 Mar - 31 Sept: daily, 10am - 6pm. 1 - 30 Oct: daily, 10am - 5pm.

Admission: Adult £2.50, Child £1.30, Conc. £1.90. 15% discount for groups (11+).

[Icon] Tel for details.

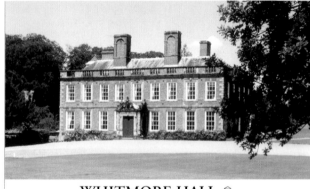

WHITMORE HALL 🏛
WHITMORE, NEWCASTLE-UNDER-LYME ST5 5HW

Tel: 01782 680478　**Fax:** 01782 680906

Owner: Mr Guy Cavenagh-Mainwaring　　**Contact:** Mr Michael Cavenagh-Thornhill

Whitmore Hall is a Grade I listed building, designated as a house of outstanding architectural and historical interest, and is a fine example of a small Carolinian manor house, although parts of the hall date back to a much earlier period. The hall has beautifully proportioned light rooms, curving staircase and landing. There are some good family portraits to be seen with a continuous line, from 1624 to the present day. It has been the family seat, for over 900 years, of the Cavenagh-Mainwarings who are direct descendants of the original Norman owners. The interior of the hall has recently been refurbished and is in fine condition. The grounds include a beautiful home park with a lime avenue leading to the house, as well as landscaped gardens encompassing an early Victorian summer house. One of the outstanding features of Whitmore is the extremely rare example of a late Elizabethan stable block, the ground floor is part cobbled and has nine oak-carved stalls.

Location: OS Ref. SJ811 413. On A53 Newcastle - Market Drayton Road, 3m from M6/J15.

Open: 1 May - 31 Aug: Tues, Weds, 2 - 5pm. Groups of 15+ by arrangement outside normal opening days. (between 1 Apr - 31 Aug). Teas arranged for groups over 15.

Admission: Adult £3, Child 50p.

[Icon] Ground floor & grounds. [P] [Icon]

ARBURY HALL

NUNEATON

Arbury Hall has been the seat of the Newdegate family for over 400 years and is the ancestral home of Viscount Daventry. This Tudor/Elizabethan House was gothicised by Sir Roger Newdegate in the 18th century and is regarded as the 'Gothic Gem' of the Midlands. The Hall contains a fine collection of both oriental and Chelsea porcelain, portraits by Lely, Reynolds, Devis and Romney and furniture by Chippendale and Hepplewhite. The principal rooms, with their soaring fan vaulted ceilings and plunging pendants and filigree tracery, stand as a most breathtaking and complete example of early Gothic Revival architecture and provide a unique and fascinating venue for corporate entertaining, product launches, receptions, fashion shoots and activity days. Exclusive use of this historic Hall, its gardens and parkland is offered to clients. The Hall stands in the middle of beautiful parkland with landscaped gardens of rolling lawns, lakes and winding wooded walks. Spring flowers are profuse and in June rhododendrons, azaleas and giant wisteria provide a beautiful environment for the visitor.

George Eliot, the novelist, was born on the estate and Arbury Hall and Sir Roger Newdegate were immortalised in her book *'Scenes of Clerical Life'*.

Owner:
The Viscount Daventry

▶ CONTACT
Brenda Newell
Arbury Hall
Nuneaton
Warwickshire
CV10 7PT

Tel: 024 7638 2804
Fax: 024 7664 1147

▶ LOCATION
OS Ref. SP335 893

London, M1, M6/J3
(A444 to Nuneaton),
2m SW of Nuneaton.
1m W of A444.

Chester A51, A34, M6
(from J14 to J3),
2¹/2 hrs.
Nuneaton 10 mins.

London 2 hrs,
Birmingham ¹/2 hr,
Coventry 20 mins.

Bus: Nuneaton 3m.

Rail: Nuneaton
Station 3m.

Air: Birmingham
International 17m.

CONFERENCE/FUNCTION

ROOM	SIZE	MAX CAPACITY
Dining Room	35' x 28'	120
Saloon	35' x 30'	70
Long Gallery	48' x 11'	40
Stables Tearooms	31' x 18'	80

Corporate hospitality, film location, small conferences, product launches and promotions, marquee functions, clay pigeon shooting, archery and other sporting activities, grand piano in Saloon, helicopter landing site. No cameras or video recorders.

Exclusive lunches and dinners for corporate parties in dining room, max. 50, buffets 120.

Visitors may alight at the Hall's main entrance. Parking in allocated areas. Ramp access to main hall.

By arrangement for groups.

Obligatory. Tour time: 1hr.

200 cars and 3 coaches 250 yards from house. Follow tourist signs. Approach map available for coach drivers.

Welcome, must book. School room available.

In gardens on leads. Guide dogs only in house.

Tel for details.

▶ OPENING TIMES
All Year

Open all year on Tues, Weds & Thurs only, for corporate events.

Pre-booked visits to the Hall and Gardens for groups of 25+ on Tues, Weds & Thurs (until 4pm) from Easter to the end of September.

Hall & Gardens open 2 - 5pm on BH weekends only (Suns & Mons) Easter - September.

▶ ADMISSION
Summer

Hall & Gardens

Adult £6.00
Child (up to 14 yrs.)... £3.50
Family (2+2) £14.00

Gardens Only

Adult £4.00
Child (up to 14 yrs.)... £2.50

Groups (25+)

Adult £5.00

Special rates for pre-booked groups of 25+.

COUGHTON COURT

ALCESTER

www.coughtoncourt.co.uk

Coughton Court has been the home of the Thockmortons since the 15th century and the family still live here today. The magnificent Tudor gatehouse was built around 1530 with the north and south wings completed 10 or 20 years later. The gables and the first storey of these wings are of typical mid-16th century half-timbered work.

Of particular interest to visitors is the Thockmorton family history from Tudor times to the present generation. On view are family portraits through the centuries with other family memorabilia and recent photographs. Also furniture, tapestries and porcelain.

A long-standing Roman Catholic theme runs through the family history as the Thockmortons have maintained their Catholic religion until the present day. The house has a strong connection with the Gunpowder Plot and also suffered damage during the Civil War. Exhibitions on the Gunpowder Plot as well as Children's Clothes (included in price).

GARDENS

The house stands in 25 acres of gardens and grounds along with two churches (both open to visitors) and a lake. A formal garden was constructed in 1992 with designs based on an Elizabethan knot garden in the courtyard. A new $1^{1}/_{2}$ acre garden was opened in 1996 and is now one of Britain's finest walled gardens. Visitors can also enjoy a specially created walk beside the River Arrow and a new bog garden opened in 1997.

Owner:
Mrs C Throckmorton

▶ CONTACT

Sales Office
Coughton Court
Alcester
Warwickshire B49 5JA

Tel: 01789 400777
Fax: 01789 765544

Visitor Information:
01789 762435

e-mail: sales@
throckmortons.co.uk

▶ LOCATION

OS Ref. SP080 604

Located on A435,
2m N of Alcester,
8m NW of
Stratford-on-Avon.
18m from Birmingham
City Centre.

Rail: Birmingham
International.

Air: Birmingham
International.

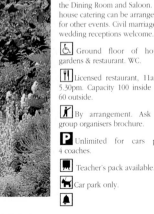

▢ ✳ ⓘ Receptions, special dinners, filming, buffets, business meetings, fairs and company activity days. The excellent acoustics of the Saloon make it ideal for concerts, especially chamber music. Marquees can be erected on the large lawn area, grand piano. No photography or stiletto heels in house.

🍽 Buffet or sit-down meals can be provided by arrangement, in the Dining Room and Saloon. In-house catering can be arranged for other events. Civil marriages & wedding receptions welcome.

♿ Ground floor of house, gardens & restaurant. WC.

🍴 Licensed restaurant, 11am - 5.30pm. Capacity 100 inside and 60 outside.

🚶 By arrangement. Ask for group organisers brochure.

🅿 Unlimited for cars plus 4 coaches.

▨ Teacher's pack available.

🐕 Car park only.

🔔

▶ OPENING TIMES

House
23 March - end September:
Wed - Sun, 11.30am - 5pm
(BH Mons open 11am).

Also open BH Mon & Tue plus Tues in Jul & Aug (Closed Good Fri, Sat 22 Jun & 20 Jul).

October: Sats & Suns (closes 27 Oct for winter).

Gardens, Restaurant, Gift Shop & Plant Centre: 11am - 5.30 on house open days.

Grounds
As house: 11am - 5.30pm.
Walled Garden: 11.30am - 4.45pm.

Last admissions are 30 minutes before closing times.

▶ ADMISSION

House & Gardens
Adult £9.45
Child* (5-15yrs) £4.75
Family (2+4) £29.25
Booked Groups (15+)
Adult £7.60
Child £3.80

Gardens only
Adult £6.95
Child* (5-15yrs) £3.45
Family (2+4) £21.45
Groups (15+)
per person £5.60

*under 5yrs Free.
NT & HHA members & HHA Friends Free admission to house, £2.50 charge to walled garden.

CONFERENCE/FUNCTION

ROOM	SIZE	MAX CAPACITY
Dining Rm	45' x 27'	60
Saloon	60' x 36'	100

The Saloon, which has particularly good acoustics, is often used for music recording.

RAGLEY HALL

ALCESTER

www.ragleyhall.com

Owner:
The Marquess of
Hertford

▶ CONTACT

Sally J Smith
Ragley Hall
Alcester
Warwickshire B49 5NJ

Tel: 01789 762090
Fax: 01789 764791

e-mail:
ragley.hall@
virginnet.co.uk

▶ LOCATION

OS Ref. SP073 555

Off A46/A435 1m
SW of Alcester.
From London 100m,
M40 via Oxford and
Stratford-on-Avon.

Rail: Evesham
Station 9m.

Air: Birmingham
International 20m.

Taxi: 007 Taxi
01789 414007

Ragley Hall, home of the Marquess and Marchioness of Hertford and their family, was designed by Robert Hooke in 1680 and is one of the earliest and loveliest of England's great Palladian houses. The perfect symmetry of its architecture remains unchanged except for the massive portico added by Wyatt in 1780.

In 1750, when Francis Seymour owned Ragley, James Gibbs designed the magnificent baroque plasterwork of the Great Hall. On completion, Francis filled the Hall with French and English furniture and porcelain and had portraits of himself and his sons painted by Sir Joshua

Reynolds. Notable also is the mural, by Graham Rust, in the south Staircase Hall which was completed in 1983.

PARK, GARDENS & GROUNDS

Ragley is a working estate with more than 6000 acres of land, the house is situated in 27 acres of gardens that were designed by 'Capability' Brown, and include the beautiful Rose Garden. Near to the hall are the working stables, housing a carriage collection dating back to 1760 and a display of assorted historical equestrian equipment. For children there is the adventure playground and maze situated by the lake.

CONFERENCE/FUNCTION

ROOM	SIZE	MAX CAPACITY
Great Hall	70' x 40'	150
Red Saloon	30' x 40'	40
Green Drawing Rm	20' x 30'	30
Hertford	45' x 22'	60
Seymour	25' x 23'	30

🖼️ ℹ️ Product launches, dinners and activity days, film and photographic location, park, lake and picnic area, marquee. No photography or camcorders in the house.

🔾 Private and corporate entertainment, wedding receptions, conferences, seminars. Telephone for details.

♿ Visitors may alight at entrance. Parking in allocated areas. WCs. Lifts.

☕ Licensed tearooms 11am - 5pm. Groups must book.

🍴 Licensed.

🧑 By arrangement.

🅿️ Coach drivers admitted free and receive info pack and luncheon voucher. Please advise of group visits.

🎒 Welcome, £2.50 per head. Teachers' packs and work modules on request. Adventure Wood and Woodland Walk.

🐕 In grounds, on leads.

▶ OPENING TIMES

28 March - 29 September
(Closed Good Friday).

House
Thur - Sun,
12 noon - 5pm
(last adm. 4.30pm),
Sat closing times may vary
subject to events and
functions.

Park & Gardens
Thur - Sun only,
10am - 6pm
Plus school holidays:
1 - 5 Apr, 3 - 7 Jun,
22 Jul - 1 Sept.

Tearoom, Gift Shop &
cloakrooms open
11am - 5pm.

▶ ADMISSION

House Park & Garden
Adult £6.00
Child (5-16yrs) £4.50
OAP £5.00
Disabled Badge
Holders £5.00
Family £22.00
Groups* (20-100)
Adult £4.50
Schools £2.50

Park & Garden
Adult £5.00
Child (5-16yrs) £4.00
OAP £4.00
Disabled Badge
Holders £4.00
Family £17.00
Groups* (20-100)
Adult £3.50
Schools £2.50

* Groups of 20+ must book
and confirm in writing
prior to visit.

Season tickets available.

West Midlands - England

Shakespeare's Birthplace

Anne Hathaway's Cottage

THE SHAKESPEARE HOUSES

STRATFORD-UPON-AVON

www.shakespeare.org.uk

Step back in time to enjoy these beautifully preserved Tudor homes connected with William Shakespeare and his family; the architectural character, period furniture, special collections, attractive gardens, grounds and walks and craft displays.

In Town: Shakespeare's Birthplace: Step into the house where William Shakespeare was born in 1564 and re-enter the Tudor World. Newly refurbished, the house now offers visitors a fascinating insight into life as it was when Shakespeare was a child. See the Shakespeare Exhibition which provides an introduction to his life and background and the traditional English garden.

Nash's House and New Place: The site and grounds of Shakespeare's home from 1597 until his death, with its Elizabethan-style garden, is approached through Nash's House adjoining, which contains exceptional furnishings and displays on the history of Stratford.

Hall's Croft: A delightful Elizabethan town house, once the home of Dr Hall, Shakespeare's physician son-in-law. Exceptional furniture and paintings and exhibition on Tudor medicine. Fine walled garden. Meals and refreshments available which can also be served in the beautiful garden.

Out of Town: Anne Hathaway's Cottage: This famous, picturesque thatched cottage was Anne's home before her marriage to Shakespeare. Cottage garden and Shakespeare Tree Garden as well as a garden shop and attractive Shottery Brook and Jubilee Walks. Summer tea garden.

Mary Arden's House and The Shakespeare Countryside Museum: Tudor farmstead, home of Shakespeare's mother, with out-buildings and nearby Palmer's Farm containing exhibits illustrating country life over 400 years. Gypsy caravans, dovecote, duck pond, rare breeds, field walk, and falconry displays. Refreshments and picnic area.

Owner:
The Shakespeare Birthplace Trust

▶ CONTACT

The Shakespeare Birthplace Trust
Henley Street
Stratford-upon-Avon
CV37 6QW

Tel: 01789 204016
(General enquiries)

Tel: 01789 201806/201836 (Group Visits)
01789 201808 (Evening Visits).

Fax: 01789 263138

e-mail: info@shakespeare.org.uk

▶ LOCATION

OS Refs:
Birthplace - SP201 552
New Place - SP201 548
Hall's Croft - SP200 546
Hathaway's - SP185 547
Arden's - SP166 582

Rail: Direct service from London (Paddington)

2 hrs from London
45 mins from Birmingham by car.

4m from M40/J15 and well signed from all approaches.

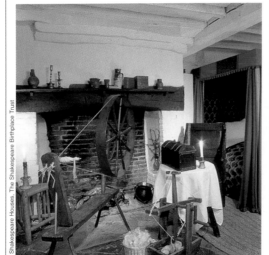

© Shakespeare Houses, The Shakespeare Birthplace Trust

[i] Regular Guide Friday, City Sightseeing guided bus tour service connecting the town houses with Anne Hathaway's Cottage and Mary Arden's House, does not include admission to houses. No photography inside houses.

[shop] Shops at Shakespeare's Birthplace, Hall's Croft, Anne Hathaway's Cottage and Mary Arden's House.

[Y] Available, details upon request.

[WC] WCs. Naturally difficult levels but much for disabled to enjoy at Mary Arden's House, ground floor & gardens accessible. Virtual reality tour at Shakespeare's Birthplace.

[cup] Available on site or close by.

[figure] By special arrangement.

[P] The Trust provides a free coach terminal for delivery and pick-up of groups, maximum stay 30 mins at Shakespeare's Birthplace. Parking at Anne Hathaway's Cottage and Mary Arden's House.

[bed] Available for all houses. For information 01789 201804.

[dog] Guide dogs only. [❄]

▶ OPENING TIMES

Mid-Season: 1 Apr - 31 May & 1 Sept - 31 Oct.

Birthplace & Anne Hathaway's & Mary Arden's House
Mon - Sat: 10am - 5pm.
Suns: 10.30am - 5pm.

Hall's Croft & Nash's House
Daily: 11am - 5pm.

Summer Season:
1 Jun - 31 Aug.

Birthplace & Anne Hathaway's
Mon - Sat: 9am - 5pm.
Suns: 9.30am - 5pm.

Mary Arden's House, Hall's Croft & Nash's House
Mon - Sat: 9.30am - 5pm.
Suns: 10am - 5pm.

Winter Season: 1 Jan - 31 Mar & 1 Nov - 31 Dec.

Birthplace & Anne Hathaway's & Mary Arden's House
Mon - Sat: 10am - 4pm.
Suns: 10.30am - 4pm.

Hall's Croft & Nash's House
Mon - Sat: 11am - 4pm.
Suns: 12 noon - 4pm

Closed 23 - 26 Dec. Early & Evening visits by special arrangement.

▶ ADMISSION

Shakespeare's Birthplace
Adult..........................£6.50
Child..........................£2.50
Conc...........................£5.50
Family (2+3)..............£15.00

New Place/Nash's House or Hall's Croft
Adult..........................£3.50
Child..........................£1.70
Conc...........................£3.00
Family (2+3)...............£8.50

Anne Hathaway's Cottage
Adult..........................£5.00
Child..........................£2.00
Conc...........................£4.00
Family (2+3).............£11.00

Mary Arden's House
Adult..........................£5.50
Child..........................£2.50
Conc...........................£5.00
Family (2+3).............£13.50

3 in-town houses
Adult..........................£8.50
Child..........................£4.20
Conc...........................£7.50
Family (2+3).............£20.00

All five houses
Adult.........................£12.00
Child...........................£6.00
Conc..........................£11.00
Family.......................£29.00
Accompanied groups 20+, 10% discount.

STONELEIGH ABBEY

KENILWORTH

www.stoneleighabbey.org

Owner:
Stoneleigh Abbey Ltd

▶ **CONTACT**

Enquiry Office
Stoneleigh Abbey
Kenilworth
Warwickshire CV8 2LF

Tel: 01926 858535

Fax: 01926 850724

e-mail: enquiries
@stoneleighabbey.org

▶ **LOCATION**
OS Ref. SP318 712

Off A46/B4115,
2m W of Kenilworth.
From London 100m,
M40 to Warwick.

Rail: Coventry station
5m, Leamington Spa
station 5m.

Air: Birmingham
International 20m.

Stoneleigh Abbey was founded in the reign of
Henry II and after the Dissolution was granted to
the Duke of Suffolk. The estate then passed into
the ownership of the Leigh family who remained
for 400 years. The estate is now managed by a
charitable trust.

Visitors will experience a wealth of architectural
styles spanning more than 900 years: the
magnificent state rooms and chapel of the
18th century Baroque West Wing contain original
pieces of furniture including a set of library chairs
made by William Gomm in 1763; a medieval
Gatehouse; the Gothic Revival-style Regency
Stables. Jane Austen was a distant relative of the
Leigh family and in her description of 'Sotherton'
in *Mansfield Park* she recalls her stay at

Stoneleigh Abbey. Parts of *Northanger Abbey* also
use Stoneleigh for inspiration.

The River Avon flows through the estate's 690
acres of grounds and parkland which displays the
influences of Humphry Repton and other major
landscape architects. In June 1858 Queen Victoria
and Prince Albert visited Stoneleigh Abbey.
During their stay Queen Victoria planted an oak
tree and Prince Consort planted a Wellington
Gigantia. While Prince Albert's tree flourished it is
thought that the oak did not survive.

Stoneleigh Abbey has been the subject of a major
restoration programme funded by the Heritage
Lottery Fund, English Heritage and the European
Regional Development Fund.

▶ **OPENING TIMES**

April - October

Tue - Thur, Sun & BHs for
guided tours at 11am,
1pm, 3pm & 4pm.

The parkland is open
throughout the year, apart
from Christmas Day and
during the Royal Show,
dawn - dusk.

Groups also welcome at
other pre-arranged times.
Please telephone.

▶ **ADMISSION**

Adult £5.00
1 child free with each adult

Additional Child £2.50
OAP £3.50

Groups (20-70)
Please telephone for
details.

 Production launches,
dinners, weddings, corporate
entertaining, film and
photographic locations.

 Obligatory.

 In grounds, on leads.

❄ Parkland only.

⛨ Tel for details.

CONFERENCE/FUNCTION

ROOM	SIZE	MAX CAPACITY
Saloon	14 x 10m	120
Gilt Hall	12 x 10m	80
Servants' Hall	14 x 8m	100

© NT Severn/R Charlton

Owner:
The National Trust

▶ **CONTACT**

The Property Manager
Upton House
Banbury
Oxfordshire OX15 6HT

Tel: 01295 670266

Infoline: 01684 855365

e-mail: upton_house
@smtp.ntrust.org.uk

▶ **LOCATION**

**OS151 Ref. SP371
461**

On A422, 7m NW
of Banbury. 12m SE of
Stratford-upon-Avon

Rail: Banbury
Station, 7m.

UPTON HOUSE

BANBURY

www.nationaltrust.org.uk

Upton House stands less than a mile to the south of the battlefield of Edgehill and there has been a house on this site since the Middle Ages. The present house was built at the end of the 17th century and remodelled 1927 - 29 for the 2nd Viscount Bearsted.

He was a great collector of paintings, china and many other valuable works of art, and adapted the building to display them. The paintings include works by El Greco, Bruegel, Bosch, Memling, Guardi, Hogarth and Stubbs. The rooms provide an admirable setting for the china collection which includes Chelsea figures and superb examples of beautifully decorated Sèvres porcelain. The set of 17th century Brussels tapestries depict the Holy Roman Emperor Maximilian I's boar and stag hunts.

Artists and Shell Exhibition of Paintings and Posters commissioned by Shell for use in its publicity 1921 - 1949, while the 2nd Viscount Bearsted was chairman of the company, founded by his father.

GARDEN

The outstanding garden is of interest throughout the season with terraces descending into a deep valley from the main lawn. There are herbaceous borders, the national collection of asters, over an acre of kitchen garden, a water garden laid out in the 1930s and pools stocked with ornamental fish.

A new 80-seat licensed restaurant will open during 2002, replacing the existing 40-seat restaurant which serves light lunches together with teas. Group lunches and dinners available by arrangement.

© NT Severn/R Charlton

▶ **OPENING TIMES**

Summer
23 March - 3 November
Sat - Wed including
BH Mons & Good Fri,
1 - 5pm.

Sat, Sun & BHs: Garden &
Restaurant: 11am - 5pm.
House & Shop: 1 - 5pm.

Mon - Wed: Restaurant
opens 12 noon, Garden
12.30pm, House & Shop
1pm. All close at 5pm.

Last admission &
last teas 4.30pm.

Winter
Garden & Restaurant:
9 Nov - 15 Dec, Sat & Sun,
12 noon - 4pm.

▶ **ADMISSION**

Adult £6.00
Child £3.00
Family £15.00

Garden
Adult £3.00

 Parent & baby room. No indoor photography.

 Wheelchair available. Access to all ground floor rooms. WC. Motorised buggy to/from lower garden.

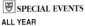 Licensed.

Tour time 1½ - 2hrs. Groups (15+) must pre-book. Evening tours by written appointment (no reduction).

P Coaches in main car park.

▶ **SPECIAL EVENTS**

ALL YEAR
Fine arts study tours, jazz concerts and other events, please send SAE or telephone.

WARWICK CASTLE

WARWICK

Over a thousand years of secrets hide in the shadows of Warwick Castle. Murder, mystery, intrigue and scandal: the Castle has witnessed it all, and now reveals the secret life of England as you have never seen it before.

From the days of William the Conqueror to the reign of Queen Victoria, the Castle has provided a backdrop for many turbulent times.

Here you can join a mediaeval household in our Kingmaker attraction, watching them prepare for the final battle of the Earl of Warwick. Enter the eerie Ghost Tower, where it is said that the unquiet spirit of Sir Fulke Greville, murdered most foully by a manservant, still roams.

Descend into the gloomy depths of the Dungeon and Torture Chamber, then step forward in time and marvel at the grandeur of the Great Hall and in 'Death or Glory', our Armoury attraction, you can feel the weight of a sword and try on a helmet. The 14th century Great Hall lies at the heart of the Castle and here you can see the magnificent Kenilworth Buffet made in 1851.

Witness the perfect manners and hidden indiscretions of Daisy, Countess of Warwick and her friends at the Royal Weekend Party 1898 or stroll through the 60 acres of grounds and gardens, landscaped by 'Capability' Brown, which surround the Castle today.

Besides the secrets, there are a host of special events to enjoy throughout the year, with a unique opportunity to witness mediaeval life at the Mediaeval Festival.

Warwick Castle really is one of the best days out in history.

▶ CONTACT

Sales Office
Warwick Castle
Warwick CV34 4QU

Tel: 0870 442 2000

Fax: 01926 401692

▶ LOCATION

OS Ref. SP284 648

2m from M40/J15.
Birmingham 35 mins
Leeds 2 hrs 5 mins
London, 1 hr 30 mins
Vehicle entrance from
A429 ¹/₂ m SW of town
centre.

Rail: Intercity from
London Euston to
Coventry. Direct
service Chiltern Line
from Marylebone &
Paddington to Warwick.

CONFERENCE/FUNCTION

ROOM	SIZE	MAX CAPACITY
Great Hall	61' x 34'	130
State Dining Room	40' x 25'	32
Undercroft	46' x 26'	120
Coach House	44' x 19'	70
Marquees		2000

[i] Corporate events, receptions, Kingmaker's Feasts and Highwayman's Supper. Guide books available in French, German, Japanese, Spanish and Italian.

Four shops.

Parking spaces in Stables Car Park, free admission for registered blind and visitors in wheelchairs.

Available, ranging from cream teas to three-course hot meals. During the summer there is an open air barbecue and refreshment pavilion in the grounds (weather permitting).

For groups (must be pre-booked). Guides in every room.

[P] Limited free car parking in main car park. Free coach parking, free admission and refreshment voucher for coach driver.

Ideal location, being a superb example of military architecture dating back to the Norman Conquest and with elegant interiors up to Victorian times. Group rates apply. To qualify for group rates, groups must book in advance. Education packs available.

Registered assistance dogs only.

❄ Tel for details.

▶ OPENING TIMES

Summer
April - September
10am - 6pm
Last admission 5.30pm.

Winter
October - March
10am - 5pm
Last admission 4.30pm.

▶ ADMISSION

10 Sept 2001 - 28 Feb 2002

Adult £10.50
Child (4 - 16yrs) ... £6.25
Student £7.80
OAP £7.35
Family (2+2) £29.00
Groups (20+)
Adult £8.25
Child(4 - 16yrs) £5.40
Student £7.25
OAP £6.60

**Call the Warwick Castle
Information Line on:
0870 442 2000
for the latest
admission prices.**

ARBURY HALL 🏛   *See page 341 for full page entry.*

NT Photographic Library: Andreas von Einsiedel

NT Photographic Library: Oliver Benn

BADDESLEY CLINTON ❧

RISING LANE, BADDESLEY CLINTON, KNOWLE, SOLIHULL B93 0DQ

www.nationaltrust.org.uk

Tel: 01564 783294 **Fax:** 01564 782706 **e-mail:** baddesley@smtp.ntrust.org.uk

Owner: The National Trust   **Contact:** The Property Manager

A romantically sited medieval moated manor house, dating from 15th century; little changed since 1634; family portraits, priest holes; garden; ponds and lake walk. Make a day of it! Revised opening times and substantial discounts on joint ticket prices make a combined visit to Baddesley Clinton and Packwood House even more attractive, especially since both properties are only two miles apart.

Location: OS139, Ref. SP199 715. ¾ m W of A4141 Warwick/Birmingham road at Chadwick End.

Open: House: 6 Mar - 3 Nov: Wed - Sun, BH Mons & Jubilee BH Mon & Tue (closed Good Fri). Mar, Apr, Oct & Nov: 1.30 - 5pm; May - end Sept: 1.30 - 5.30pm. Grounds: 6 Mar - 15 Dec: Wed - Sun, Good Fri, BH Mons & Jubilee BH Mon & Tue; Mar, Apr, Oct & 1 - 3 Nov: 12 noon - 5pm; May - end Sept: 12 noon - 5.30pm; 6 Nov - 15 Dec: 12 noon - 4.30pm.

Admission: Adult £5.80, Child £2.90, Family £14.50. Grounds only: Adult £2.90, Child £1.45. Groups: £4.65. Guided tours (out of hours) £9.30.

Combined ticket with Packwood House: Adult £8.50, Child £4.25, Family £21.25. Gardens only: Adult £4.25, Child £2.10. Groups £6.80.

🏛🐕♿ Partial. WC. 🍴 Licensed. 🎫 By arrangement. ⬛ 🦮 Guide dogs only. ♿ Tel for details.

Stoneleigh Abbey

NT Photographic Library

NT Severn SWT / D Sellman

CHARLECOTE PARK

WARWICK CV35 9ER

www.nationaltrust.org.uk

Tel: 01789 470277 **Fax:** 01789 470544 **e-mail:** charlecote@smtp.ntrust.org.uk

Owner: The National Trust **Contact:** The Property Manager

Owned by the Lucy family since 1247, Sir Thomas Lucy built the house in 1558. Now, much altered, it is shown as it would have been a century ago, complete with Victorian kitchen, brewhouse and family carriages in the coach house and two bedrooms, a dressing room and the main staircase. A video of Victorian life can be viewed. The formal gardens and informal parkland lie to the north and west of the house. Jacob Sheep were brought to Charlecote in 1756 by Sir Thomas Lucy. It is reputed that William Shakespeare was apprehended for poaching c1583 and Sir Thomas Lucy is said to be the basis of Justice Shallow in Shakespeare's '*Merry Wives of Windsor*'.

Location: OS151 Ref. SP263 564. 1m W of Wellesbourne, 5m E of Stratford-upon-Avon.

Open: House & Grounds: 23 Mar - 3 Nov: daily except Weds & Thurs. Open Good Fri. House: 12 noon - 5pm. Grounds: 11am - 6pm. Park, Grounds, Restaurant & Shop: 9 Nov - 15 Dec, Sat & Sun, 11am - 4pm; 2 Feb - 17 Mar: Sats & Suns, 11am - 4pm including Brewhouse, Victorian Kitchens & Carriage Collection. Evening guided tours for booked groups: May - Sept, Tue, 7.30 - 9.30pm (min. charge £150).

Admission: Adult £5.80, Child (5-16yrs) £2.90, Family £14.50. Groups: Adult £4.80, Under 5s Free. Grounds only: Adult £3, Child £1.50.

Children's play area. Licensed. For booked groups. Limited for coaches. By arrangement. On leads, in car park. Tel for details.

COUGHTON COURT *See page 342 for full page entry.*

Honington Hall

FARNBOROUGH HALL

BANBURY, OXFORDSHIRE OX17 1DU

www.nationaltrust.org.uk

Tel: 01295 690002

Owner: The National Trust **Contact:** Mr G Holbech

A classical mid-18th century stone house, home of the Holbech family for 300 years; notable plasterwork, the entrance hall, staircase and 2 principal rooms are shown; the grounds contain charming 18th century temples, a $^2/_3$ mile terrace walk and an obelisk.

Location: OS151, Ref. SP430 490. 6m N of Banbury, $^1/_2$ m W of A423.

Open: House & Grounds: Apr - end Sept: Weds & Sats, also 5/6 May, 2 - 6pm. Terrace Walk only: (by arrangement only, please telephone) Thur & Fri, 2 - 6pm. Closed Good Fri. Last admission to house 5.30pm.

Admission: House, grounds & terrace walk: Adult £3.50. Garden & terrace walk: £1.75. Terrace walk only (Thurs & Fris) £1, by prior arrangement only.

House & grounds, but steep terrace walk. In grounds, on leads.

THE HILLER GARDEN

Dunnington Heath Farm, Alcester, Warwickshire B49 5PD

Tel: 01789 490991 **Fax:** 01789 490439

Owner: Mr & Mrs R Beach   **Contact:** Mr David Carvill

2 acre garden of unusual herbaceous plants and over 200 rose varieties.

Location: OS Ref. SP066 539. 1$^{1}/_{2}$ m S of Ragley Hall on B4088 (formerly A435).

Open: All year: daily 10am - 5pm.

Admission: Free.

English Heritage Photo Library

KENILWORTH CASTLE ⌗

KENILWORTH, WARWICKSHIRE CV8 1NE

Tel: 01926 852078

Owner: English Heritage   **Contact:** The Custodian

Kenilworth is the largest castle ruin in England, the former stronghold of great Lords and Kings. Its massive walls of warm red stone tower over the peaceful Warwickshire landscape. The Earl of Leicester entertained Queen Elizabeth I with 'Princely Pleasures' during her 19 day visit. He built a new wing for the Queen to lodge in and organised all manner of lavish and costly festivities. The Great Hall, where Gloriana dined with her courtiers, still stands and John of Gaunt's Hall is second only in width and grandeur to Westminster Hall. Climb to the top of the tower beside the hall and you will be rewarded by fine views over the rolling wooded countryside. Exhibition, interactive castle model and café in Leicester's Barn. Recreated Tudor garden and atmospheric audio tour.

Location: OS140 Ref. SP278 723. In Kenilworth, off A452, W end of town.

Open: 29 Mar - 31 Oct: daily, 10am - 6pm (5pm in Oct). 1 Nov - 31 Mar: daily 10am - 4pm. Closed 24 - 26 Dec & 1 Jan.

Admission: Adult £4.40, Child £2.20, Conc. £3.30, Family £11. 15% discount for groups (11+).

🔲 ▣ ⌂ 🅿 ✳ 🔲Tel for details.

HONINGTON HALL 🏛

SHIPSTON-ON-STOUR, WARWICKSHIRE CV36 5AA

Tel: 01608 661434 **Fax:** 01608 663717

Owner/Contact: Benjamin Wiggin Esq

This fine Caroline manor house was built in the early 1680s for Henry Parker in mellow brickwork, stone quoins and window dressings. Modified in 1751 when an octagonal saloon was inserted. The interior was also lavishly restored around this time and contains exceptional mid-Georgian plasterwork. Set in 15 acres of grounds.

Location: OS Ref. SP261 427. 10m S of Stratford-upon-Avon. 1$^{1}/_{2}$ m N of Shipston-on-Stour. Take A3400 towards Stratford, then signed right to Honington.

Open: Jun - Aug: Weds only. BH Mon, 2.30 - 5pm. Groups at other times by appointment.

Admission: Adult £3.50, Child £1.75.

🔲Unsuitable. 🎫Obligatory. 🔳

LORD LEYCESTER HOSPITAL

HIGH STREET, WARWICK CV34 4BH

Tel/Fax: 01926 491422

Owner: The Governors   **Contact:** The Master

This magnificent range of 14th century half-timbered buildings was adapted into almshouses by Robert Dudley, Earl of Leycester, in 1571. The Hospital still provides homes for ex-servicemen and their wives. The Guildhall, Great Hall, Chapel, Brethren's Kitchen and galleried Courtyard are still in everyday use. The Queen's Own Hussars regimental museum is here. The historic Master's Garden, featured in BBC TV's Gardener's World, has been restored and a new Knot Garden created for the Millennium.

Location: OS Ref. 280 648. 1m N of M40/J15 on the A429 in town centre.

Open: All year: Tue - Sun & BHs, 10am - 5pm (4pm in winter). Garden: Apr - Sept: 10am - 4pm.

Admission: Adult £3.20, Child £2, Conc. £2.70. 5% discount for adult groups (20+).

🔲🎫🔲Partial. ▣ 🎫 🎫By arrangement. 🅿Limited. 🔲 🔳Guide dogs only. ✳

Website Information
◁ ◁ ◁   pg 39

MIDDLETON HALL

Middleton, Tamworth, Staffordshire B78 2AE

Tel: 01827 283095   **Fax:** 01827 285717

Owner: Middleton Hall Trust   **Contact:** Mrs B Ellerslie

Hall (1285 - 1824). Former home of Hugh Willoughby (Tudor explorer), Francis Willughby and John Ray (17th century naturalists).

Location: OS Ref. SP193 982. A4091, S of Tamworth.

Open: Easter - 29 Sept: Suns, 2 - 5pm, BH Mons, 11am - 5pm.

Admission: Adult £2.50, OAP £1.50.

PACKWOOD HOUSE ✤

LAPWORTH, SOLIHULL B94 6AT

www.nationaltrust.org.uk

Tel: 01564 783294   **Fax:** 01564 782706   **e-mail:** baddesley@smtp.ntrust.org.uk

Owner: The National Trust   **Contact:** The Property Manager

Originally a 16th century house, Packwood has been much altered over the years and today is the vision of Graham Baron Ash who recreated a Jacobean house in the 1920s and '30s. A fine collection of 16th century textiles and furniture. Important gardens with renowned herbaceous border and famous yew garden based on the Sermon on the Mount. Make a day of it! Revised opening times and substantial discounts on joint ticket prices make a combined visit to Baddesley Clinton and Packwood House even more attractive, especially since both properties are only two miles apart.

Location: OS139, Ref. 174 722. 2m E of Hockley Heath (on A3400), 11m SE of central Birmingham.

Open: House: 6 Mar 3 Nov: Wed - Sun, Good Fri, BH Mons & Jubilee BH Mon & Tue, 12 noon - 4.30pm. NB: on busy days entry may be by timed ticket. Garden: 6 Mar - 3 Nov: Wed - Sun, Good Fri, BH Mons & Jubilee BH Mon & Tue; Mar, Apr, Oct & Nov: 11am - 4.30pm; May - end Sept: 11am - 5.30pm. Park & Woodland Walks: All year: daily.

Admission: Adult £5.20, Child £2.60, Family £13, Garden only: Adult £2.60, Child £1.30. Groups £4.20. Guided tours (out of hours) £8.40.

Combined ticket with Baddesley Clinton: Adult £8.50, Child £4.25, Family £21.25. Gardens only: Adult £4.25, Child £2.10. Groups £6.80.

▣ ▣ ▣ ▣ Partial. WC. ▣ By arrangement. ▣ ▣ ▣ Guide dogs only. ▣ ▣ Tel for details.

RAGLEY HALL ▣   *See page 343 for full page entry.*

THE SHAKESPEARE HOUSES   *See page 344 for full page entry.*

STONELEIGH ABBEY ▣   *See page 345 for full page entry.*

UPTON HOUSE ✤   *See page 346 for full page entry.*

WARWICK CASTLE ▣   *See page 347 for full page entry.*

Coughton Court

CJB Photography

HAGLEY HALL

HAGLEY

Hagley Hall is set in a 350-acre landscaped park yet is only 25 minutes from Birmingham city centre, the NEC and ICC and close to the motorway network of M5, M6, M40 and M42. The house is available throughout the year on an exclusive basis for conferences, product launches, presentations, lunches, dinners, country sporting days, team building activities, themed evenings, murder mysteries, concerts, filming and wedding receptions. Hagley's high standards of catering are now available at other venues as well as at Hagley Hall. The elegant Palladian house, completed in 1760, contains some of the finest examples of Italian plasterwork. Hagley's rich rococo decoration is a remarkable tribute to the artistic achievement of great 18th century amateurs and is the much loved home of the 11th Viscount Cobham.

Owner:
Viscount Cobham

▶ CONTACT

Miss Lucy Carpenter
Hagley Hall
Hagley
Worcestershire DY9 9LG

Tel: 01562 882408

Fax: 01562 882632

▶ LOCATION
OS Ref. SO920 807

Easily accessible from all areas of the country. ¹/4 m S of A456 at Hagley.

Close to the M42, M40, M6 and only 5m from M5/J3/J4.

Birmingham City Centre 12m.

Rail: Railway Station and the NEC 25 mins.

Air: Birmingham International Airport 25 mins.

▶ OPENING TIMES
House

3 - 27 January,
4 - 24 February,
1 - 8 March,
1 - 9 April (excl. Sats),
and 26 - 29 August

2 - 5pm. Guided tours.

Lunches available during house opening from 12 noon - 2pm.

Please telephone prior to visit to ensure the house is open.

▶ ADMISSION
House

Adult	£3.50
Child (under 14 yrs)	£1.50
Conc.	£2.50
Student	£2.50

ℹ️ Available on an exclusive basis for conferences, presentations, lunches, dinners, product launches, themed evenings, murder mysteries, concerts, wedding receptions. Extensive parkland for country sporting days, team-building activities, off-road driving and filming.

🍽️ As well as in-house catering, Hagley also offers a unique catering service at the venue of your choice.

♿ Visitors may alight at the entrance. No WC.

☕ Teas available during opening times.

🚶 Obligatory. Please book parties in advance, guided tour time of house 1 hr. Colour guide - book.

🅿️ Unlimited for coaches and cars.

📷 By arrangement.

🐕 Guide dogs only.

🔔 ❄️

CONFERENCE/FUNCTION

ROOM	SIZE	MAX CAPACITY
Gallery	85' x 17'	130
Crimson Rm	23' x 31'	40
The Saloon	34' x 27'	70
Westcote	31' x 20'	60

ASTON HALL

TRINITY ROAD, BIRMINGHAM, WEST MIDLANDS B6 6JD

www.bmag.org.uk

Tel: 0121 327 0062   **Fax:** 0121 327 7162

Owner: Birmingham City Council   **Contact:** Curator/Manager

A large Jacobean mansion built 1618 - 1635 from plans by John Thorpe. The Hall is brick-built with a fairytale skyline of gables and turrets. The interior has period rooms from the 17th, 18th and 19th centuries and a splendid long gallery measuring 136ft. A large kitchen and servants' rooms are also on display.

Location: OS139, Ref. SP080 899. 3m NE of Birmingham,¹/₄ m from A38(M).

Open: 29 Mar - 27 Oct: Tue - Fri, 1 - 4pm; Sat & Sun, 12 noon - 5pm. Closed Mons except BH Mons. Parkland open all year round.

Admission: Free.

Ground floor & grounds. Guide dogs only.

BLAKESLEY HALL

BLAKESLEY ROAD, YARDLEY, BIRMINGHAM B25 8RN

www.bmag.org.uk

Tel: 0121 303 1675

Owner: Birmingham City Council   **Contact:** Curator/Manager

Blakesley Hall is a late 16th century farmhouse. Following a major development scheme funded by Birmingham City Council and the Heritage Lottery Fund, the site reopens in 2002, with new displays and facilities.

Location: OS139, Ref. SP130 862. 6m E of Birmingham city centre off A4040 from A45.

Open: 29 Mar - 27 Oct: Tue - Fri, 1 - 4pm, Sat & Sun, 12 noon - 4pm. Closed Mon except BH Mons.

Admission: Free.

Ground floor.

THE BIRMINGHAM BOTANICAL GARDENS AND GLASSHOUSES

WESTBOURNE ROAD, EDGBASTON, BIRMINGHAM B15 3TR

www.birminghambotanicalgardens.org.uk

Tel: 0121 454 1860   **Fax:** 0121 454 7835

e-mail: admin@birminghambotanicalgardens.org.uk

Owner: Birmingham Botanical & Horticultural Society   **Contact:** Mrs H Champion

Tropical, Mediterranean and Arid Glasshouses contain a wide range of exotic and economic flora. 15 acres of beautiful gardens with the finest collection of plants in the Midlands. Home of the National Bonsai Collection. Children's adventure playground, aviaries and gallery.

Location: OS Ref. SP048 855. 2m W of city centre. Follow signs to Edgbaston then brown tourist signs.

Open: Daily: 9am - Dusk (7pm latest except pre-booked groups). Suns opening time 10am. Closed Christmas Day.

Admission: Adult £5 (£5.50 on summer Suns & BHs), Conc. £2.70, Family £13.50 (£14.50, summer Suns & BHs). Groups (10+): Adult £4.20, Conc. £2.40.

Licensed. Guide dogs only. Tel for details.

CASTLE BROMWICH HALL GARDENS

CHESTER ROAD, CASTLE BROMWICH, BIRMINGHAM B36 9BT

www.cbhgt.swinternet.co.uk

Tel/Fax: 0121 749 4100   **e-mail:** enq@cbhgt.swinternet.co.uk

Owner: Castle Bromwich Hall Gardens Trust   **Contact:** The Secretary

A unique example of 17th and 18th century formal garden design within a 10 acre walled area, comprising historic plants, vegetables, herbs and fruit, with a 19th century holly maze. Classical patterned parterres can be seen at the end of the holly walk, together with restored green house and summer house.

Location: OS Ref. SP142 898. Off B4114, 4m E of Birmingham city centre, 1m from M6/J5 (exit northbound only). Southbound M6/J6 and follow A38 & A452.

Open: 31 Mar - end Oct: Tue - Thur, 1.30 - 4.30pm. Sats, Suns & BHs 2 - 6pm. Closed Mons & Fris including Good Fri.

Admission: Adult £3.50, Child £1.50, OAP £2.50.

Daily. Limited for coaches. In grounds, on leads. Tel for details.

COVENTRY CATHEDRAL

7 Priory Row, Coventry CV1 5ES
Tel: 02476 227597 **Fax:** 02476 631448
e-mail: information@coventrycathedral.org **www**.coventrycathedral.org
Owner: Dean & Canons of Coventry Cathedral   **Contact:** The Visits Secretary
The remains of the medieval Cathedral, bombed in 1940, stand beside the new Cathedral by Basil Spence, consecrated in 1962. Modern works of art include a huge tapestry by Graham Sutherland, a stained glass window by John Piper and a bronze sculpture by Epstein. *'Reconciliation'* statue by Josefina de Vasconcellos.
Location: OS Ref. SP336 790. City centre.
Open: Cathedral: Easter - Oct: from 8.30am - 6pm. Nov - Easter: 9.30am - 5pm. Visitors Centre: Easter - Oct: Mon - Sat, 10am - 4pm. Nov - Easter: Mon - Sat, 11am - 3pm.
Admission: Cathedral: £3 donation. Visitor Centre: closed winter 2001/02 for refurbishment. Groups must book in advance.
ℹ️Photo permit required. 📷 ♿Partial.WC. 🖥️ 🍴 👥By arrangement. 🅿️None. 🎧 🦮Guide dogs only. ✳️

HAGLEY HALL 🏛️

See page 352 for full page entry.

HALESOWEN ABBEY ⌗

Halesowen, Birmingham, West Midlands
Tel: 0121 625 6820 (Regional Office)
Owner: English Heritage   **Contact:** The West Midlands Regional Office
Remains of an abbey founded by King John in the 13th century, now incorporated into a 19th century farm. Parts of the church and the monks' infirmary can still be made out.
Location: OS Ref. SO975 828. Off A456 Kidderminster road, 1/2 m W of M5/J3, 6m W of Birmingham city centre.
Open: Heritage Open Days weekend, 10am - 6pm. Please contact Regional Office for dates.
Admission: Free.

MUSEUM OF THE JEWELLERY QUARTER

75 - 79 VYSE STREET, HOCKLEY, BIRMINGHAM B18 6HA

www.bmag.org.uk

Tel: 0121 554 3598 **Fax:** 0121 554 9700
Owner: Birmingham City Council   **Contact:** The Curator
Built around the preserved workshops and offices of Smith and Pepper, a Birmingham jewellery firm. This lively working Museum offers a fascinating insight into the city's historic jewellery trade. Enjoy a tour of the factory with one of our knowledgeable guides and meet skilled jewellers at work. You can also explore the displays which tell the story of the Quarter and the jeweller's craft, practiced in this distinctive part of Birmingham for over 200 years. The museum is available for private evening bookings.
Location: OS Ref. SP060 880. 3/4 m NW of city centre, just within A4540 (ring road).
Open: Mon - Fri, 10am - 4pm. Sats, 11am - 5pm. Closed Suns.
Admission: Adult £2.50, Conc. £2, Family (2+3) £6.50. 10% discount for booked groups (10+).
ℹ️Temporary exhibitions. 📷 ♿ 🖥️ 👥 🅿️On street parking only. 🎧 🦮Guide dogs only. ✳️ 📹Tel for details.

RYTON ORGANIC GARDENS

Ryton-on-Dunsmore, Coventry, West Midlands CV8 3LG
Tel: 024 7630 3517 **Fax:** 024 7663 9229
Owner: HDRA - The Organic Organisation   **Contact:** Sally Furness
Beautiful and informative gardens including herbs, shrubs, flowers, rare and unusual vegetables, all organically grown.
Location: OS Ref. SP400 745. 5m SE of Coventry off A45 on the road to Wolston.
Open: Daily (closed Christmas week): 9am - 5pm.
Admission: Adult £3 (no concessions), accompanied child free. Groups (14+) £2.50 plus 50p for garden tour.

SELLY MANOR

MAPLE ROAD, BOURNVILLE, WEST MIDLANDS B30 2AE

Tel: 0121 472 0199 **Fax:** 0121 471 4101 **e-mail:** sellymanor@bvt.org.uk
Owner: Bournville Village Trust   **Contact:** Gillian Ellis
A beautiful half-timbered manor house in the heart of the famous Bournville village. The house has been lived in since the 14th century and was rescued from demolition by George Cadbury. It houses furniture dating back several centuries and is surrounded by a delightful typical Tudor garden.
Location: OS Ref. SP045 814. N side of Sycamore Road, just E of Linden Road (A4040). 4m SSW of City Centre.
Open: All year: Tue - Fri, 10am - 5pm. Apr - Sept: Sats, Suns & BHs, 2 - 5pm. Closed Mons.
Admission: Adult £2, Child 50p, Conc. £1.50, Family £4.50.
📷 ♿Partial. WC. 👥By arrangement. 🅿️Limited. 🎧 🦮In grounds, on leads. 🔼 ✳️

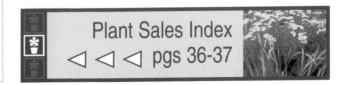

Plant Sales Index
◁ ◁ ◁ pgs 36-37

SOHO HOUSE

SOHO AVENUE, HANDSWORTH, BIRMINGHAM B18 5LB

www.bmag.org.uk

Tel: 0121 554 9122   **Fax:** 0121 554 5929

Owner: Birmingham City Council   **Contact:** Reception

The elegant home of the industrial pioneer Matthew Boulton from 1766 to 1809, Soho House has been carefully restored. Special features include an early 19th century hot air heating system. Period rooms and displays on Boulton's businesses, family and associates as well as the architectural development of the house.

Location: OS Ref. SP054 893. S side of Soho Avenue, just SW of Soho Hill/Soho Road (A41). 2m NW of city centre. Follow signs for Handsworth then brown tourist signs.

Open: Tue - Sat, 10am - 5pm. Suns, 12 noon - 5pm. Closed Mons except BHs.

Admission: Adult £2.50, Conc. £2, Family £6.50. 10% discount for booked groups.

⓵ Meeting room. ▣ ♿ ▣ 𝑓 By arrangement. 🅿 Limited for cars. ▣ 🐕 Guide dogs only. ✳

WIGHTWICK MANOR 🌿

Wightwick Bank, Wolverhampton, West Midlands WV6 8EE

Tel: 01902 761108   **Fax:** 01902 764663

Owner: The National Trust   **Contact:** The Property Manager

Begun in 1887, the house is a notable example of the influence of William Morris, with many original Morris wallpapers and fabrics. Also of interest are pre-Raphaelite pictures, Kempe glass and De Morgan ware. The 17 acre Victorian/Edwardian garden designed by Thomas Mawson has formal beds, pergola, yew hedges, topiary and terraces, woodland and two pools.

Location: OS Ref. SO869 985. 3m W of Wolverhampton, up Wightwick Bank (A454), beside the Mermaid Inn.

Open: 1 Mar - 31 Dec: Thurs & Sats, 1.30 - 5pm (last entry 4.30pm). Admission by timed ticket. Guided groups through ground floor, freeflow upstairs. Min. tour time approx. 1 hr 30 mins. Also open BH Sats, Suns & Mons, 1.30 - 5pm (last entry 4.30pm) - ground floor only, no guided tours. booked groups Weds & Thurs. Garden: Weds & Thurs, 11am - 6pm; Sats, BH Mons, 11am - 6pm.

Admission: Adult £5.60, Child £2.80. Garden only: £2.50, Child Free.

▣ ♿ Ground floor & grounds. ▣ 🅿 400 yds. 🐕 In grounds, on leads.

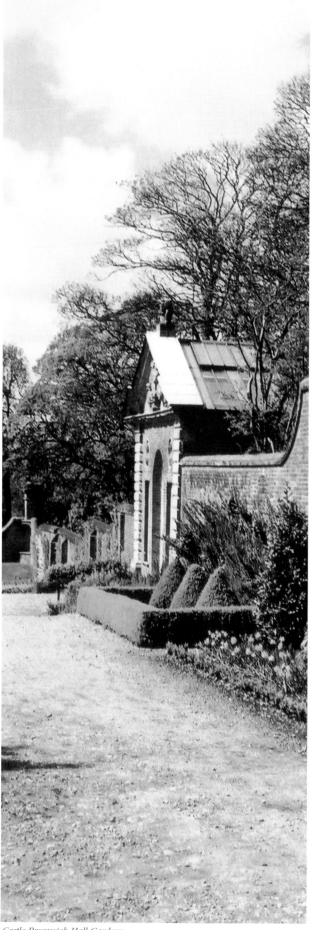

National Trust Photographic Library

Castle Bromwich Hall Gardens

BIRTSMORTON COURT

MALVERN, WORCESTERSHIRE WR13 6JS

www.birtsmortoncourt.com

Tel: 01684 833888   **Fax:** 01684 833837   **e-mail:** birtsmorton@aol.com

Owner: Nigel Dawes   **Contact:** Jenny Glading

Birtsmorton Court, with its mix of history, informality and modern facilities, is a rare medieval moated manor house surrounded by parkland and formal gardens. The original stables have been converted into the Old Motor House, a 150-person capacity conference and function centre. Selected rooms within the main house are also available, such as the Banqueting Hall and the Great Hall, both with adjoining reception rooms. A Civil wedding licence is in place. The terrace, which overlooks the moat and surrounding gardens, can be used to host intimate and magical events and the surrounding lawns and parkland are available for marquees.

Location: OS150, Ref. SO802 355. 1m NW of Sledge Green, off A438 Tewkesbury/Ledbury road.

Open: By appointment only.

Admission: Please telephone for details.

⊤ ⬚ *f* By arrangement. **P** Guide dogs only. ⬚

BROADWAY TOWER COUNTRY PARK

BROADWAY, WORCESTERSHIRE WR12 7LB

Tel: 01386 852390   **Fax:** 01386 858038   **e-mail:** broadway-tower@clara.net

Owner: Broadway Tower Country Park Ltd   **Contact:** Annette Gorton

Broadway Tower is a unique historic building on top of the Cotswold ridge, having been built by the 6th Earl of Coventry in the late 1790s. Its architecture, the fascinating views as well as its exhibitions on famous owners and occupants (including William Morris) make the Tower a "must" for all visitors to the Cotswolds. The Tower is surrounded by 35 acres of parkland with animal enclosures, picnic/BBQ facilities and adventure playground. A complete family day out.

Location: OS Ref. SP115 362. ½ m SW of the A44 Evesham to Oxford Rd. 1½ m E of Broadway.

Open: 1 Apr – 31 Oct: daily, 10.30am - 5pm. Nov - Mar: Sats & Suns (weather permitting), 11am - 3pm.

Admission: Adult £4, Child £2.30, Conc. £3, Family (2+3) £11.50. Group rate on request. Passport Ticket: (free adm. for 1 yr) Adult £12, Child/Conc. £9, Family £34.50. Tower: Adult £3, Child £1.50. (2001 prices.)

⬚ ⊤ Wedding receptions. ⬚ WC. **P** ⬚ ⊤ Licensed. ⬚
⬚ In grounds, on leads. ⬚

THE COMMANDERY

SIDBURY, WORCESTER WR1 2HU

Tel: 01905 361821   **Fax:** 01905 361822

e-mail: thecommandery@cityofworcester.gov.uk

Owner: Worcester City Council   **Contact:** Amanda Lunt

A complex of mainly timber-framed buildings, the Commandery was originally founded as a monastic institution and served as the Royalist headquarters at the Battle of Worcester in 1651. Today it houses fascinating exhibitions including 'Civil War', 'The Commandery Chronicle' and plays host to a varied events programme.

Location: OS Ref. SO853 544. Worcester city centre. 350 yds SE of Cathedral.

Open: All year: Mon - Sat, 10am - 5pm; Suns, 1.30 - 5pm.

Admission: Adult £3.90, Child/Conc. £2.75, Family £9.95. Groups (20-100): Adult £2.90, Child/Conc. £2.25.

⬚ ⊤ ⬚ Partial. ⬚ *f* By arrangement. ⬚ **P** Limited. ⬚ Guide dogs only. ⬚

CROOME PARK ⚘

SEVERN STOKE, WORCESTERSHIRE WR8 9JS

www.nationaltrust.org.uk

Tel: 01905 371006 **Fax:** 01905 371090 **e-mail:** croome@smtp.ntrust.org.uk

Owner: The National Trust   **Contact:** The Property Manager

Croome was 'Capability' Brown's first complete landscape, making his reputation and establishing a new parkland aesthetic which became universally adopted over the next fifty years. The elegant park buildings and other structures are mostly by Robert Adam and James Wyatt. The Trust acquired most of the park in 1996 with substantial grant aid from the Heritage Lottery Fund. The Trust has embarked on a ten year restoration plan, including dredging the water features, clearance and replanting of the gardens and parkland. Royal & SunAlliance is making a major financial contribution towards the cost of this restoration.

Location: OS150 Ref. SO887 452. 8m S of Worcester and E of A38 and M5, 6m W of Pershore and A44.

Open: 24 Mar - 3 Nov: Fri - Mon, BH Mon & Jubilee BH Mon & Tue, 11am - 5pm. Church: as gardens. Open in association with the Churches Conservation Trust, who own the church. Last admission 4.30pm.

Admission: Adult £3.40, Child £1.70, Family £8.50.

HANBURY HALL ⚘

DROITWICH, WORCESTERSHIRE WR9 7EA

www.nationaltrust.org.uk

Tel: 01527 821214 **Fax:** 01527 821251 **e-mail:** hanbury@smtp.ntrust.org.uk

Owner: The National Trust   **Contact:** The Property Manager

In its beautiful setting of Worcestershire parkland, this delightful William and Mary style country house retains its lived in and friendly atmosphere. With its superb staircase murals by Thornhill, and the unique Watney collection of fine porcelain, Hanbury Hall also boasts tranquil 18th century formal gardens including newly reconstructed bowling green and a stunning Orangery and working mushroom house.

Location: OS150, Ref. SO943 637. 4¹/₂ m E of Droitwich, 4m SE M5/J5.

Open: 24 Mar - 30 Oct: Sun - Wed, 1.30- 5.30pm (open Good Fri). Last admission 5pm or dusk if earlier. Gardens, shop & tearoom open at 12 noon.

Admission: House & Garden: Adult £4.60, Child £2.30, Family £11.50. Gardens only: Adult £2.90, Child £1.50. Groups: £4.10.

🖼 ✁ ⊤ ♿ Partial. WC. ☞ 𝑓 For pre-booked groups. 🅿 ✈ Guide dogs only. ▲ ✉ Tel for details.

THE ELGAR BIRTHPLACE MUSEUM

Crown East Lane, Lower Broadheath, Worcester WR2 6RH

Tel: 01905 333224 **Fax:** 01905 333426 **e-mail:** birthplace@elgar.org **www.**elgar.org

Owner: The Elgar Foundation   **Contact:** The Museum Services Manager

A fascinating insight into Elgar's life and music, family and friends. Photographs and memorabilia are displayed in the country cottage where the composer was born. Letters, manuscripts, concert programmes and other treasures from this unique collection feature in the new Elgar Centre's major exhibition, exploring his musical development and inspirations.

Location: OS Ref. SO807 556. 3m W of Worcester, signposted from A44 Worcester/Leominster road.

Open: Daily, 11am - 5pm (last admission 4.15pm). Closed Christmas - end Jan.

Admission: Adult £3.50, Child £1.75, OAP £3, Family £8.75. Booked groups (10+): Adult £3, Child £1.25, OAP £2.50.

ℹ No inside photography. 🖼 ♿ Partial. WC. 🅿 Limited for coaches. ▣ ✈ In grounds, on leads. ✱ ✉ Tel for details.

THE GREYFRIARS ⚘

Worcester WR1 2LZ

Tel: 01905 23571 **e-mail:** greyfriars@smtp.ntrust.org.uk **www.**nationaltrust.org.uk

Owner: The National Trust   **Contact:** The Custodian

Built about 1480 next to a Franciscan friary in the centre of medieval Worcester, this timber-framed house has 17th and late 18th century additions. It was rescued from demolition at the time of the Second World War and was carefully restored. The panelled rooms have noteworthy textiles and interesting furniture. An archway leads through to a delightful walled garden.

Location: OS150, Ref. SO852 546. Friar Street, in centre of Worcester.

Open: 1 Apr - 31 Oct: Weds, Thurs, BH Mons & Jubilee BH Mon & Tue, 2 - 5pm. Also Three Choirs Festival: 17 & 19 - 24 Aug, 11am - 1pm & 2 - 5pm.

Admission: Adult £3, Child £1.50, Family £7.50.

HARTLEBURY CASTLE

HARTLEBURY, NR KIDDERMINSTER DY11 7XZ

Tel: 01299 250416 **Fax:** 01299 251890 **e-mail:** museum@worcestershire.gov.uk

Owner: The Church Commissioners   **Contact:** The County Museum

Hartlebury Castle has been home to the Bishops of Worcester for over a thousand years. The three principal State Rooms – the medieval Great Hall, the Saloon and the unique Hurd Library – contain period furniture, fine plasterwork and episcopal portraits. In the former servants' quarters in the Castle's North Wing, the County Museum brings to life the past inhabitants of the county, from Roman times to the twentieth century. A wide range of temporary exhibitions and events are held each year, and detailed listings are available from the Museum.

Location: OS Ref. SO389 710. N side of B4193, 2m E of Stourport, 4m S of Kidderminster.

Open: 1 Feb - 30 Nov. County Museum: Mon - Thur, 10am - 5pm. Fris & Suns, 2 - 5pm. Closed Good Fri and Sats. Staterooms: Tue - Thur, 10am - 5pm.

Admission: Combined ticket (Museum & State rooms): Adult £2.50, Child/OAP £1.20. Family (2+3) £6.50.

🖼 ♿ Ground floor & grounds. WC. ☞ 𝑓 By arrangement for groups. 🅿 ▣ ✈ Guide dogs only. ✉ Tel for details.

HARVINGTON HALL 🏛

HARVINGTON, KIDDERMINSTER, WORCESTERSHIRE DY104LR

www.harvingtonhall.org.uk

Tel: 01562 777846 **Fax:** 01562 777190 **e-mail:** thehall@harvington.fsbusiness.co.uk

Owner: Roman Catholic Archdiocese of Birmingham

Contact: The Administrator

Harvington Hall is a moated, medieval and Elizabethan manor house. Many of the rooms still have their original Elizabethan wall paintings and the Hall contains the finest series of priest-holes in the country. A full programme of events throughout the year including outdoor plays, craft fairs, living history weekends and a pilgrimage is available.

Location: OS Ref. SO877 745. On minor road, 1/2 m NE of A450/A448 crossroads at Mustow Green. 3m SE of Kidderminster.

Open: Mar & Oct: Sats & Suns; Apr - Sept: Wed - Sun & BH Mons (closed Good Fri), 11.30am - 5pm. Open throughout the year for pre-booked groups and schools. Occasionally the Hall may be closed for a private function.

Admission: Adult £4.20, Child £3, OAP £3.50, Family £12.50. Garden: £1.

📷 ⊤ 🚻 Partial. 🍴 Licensed. 🅿 Limited for coaches. 🏠 🐕 Guide dogs only. ✲ ♿ Tel for details.

HAWFORD DOVECOTE ✄

Hawford, Worcestershire

Tel: 01684 855300 **www.**nationaltrust.org.uk

Owner: The National Trust   **Contact:** Regional Office

A 16th century half-timbered dovecote.

Location: OS Ref. SO846 607. 3m N of Worcester, 1/2 m E of A449.

Open: Apr - 31 Oct: daily 9am - 6pm or sunset if earlier. Closed Good Fri, other times by prior appointment.

Admission: £1.

LEIGH COURT BARN ⌗

Worcester

Tel: 0121 625 6820 - Regional Office

Owner: English Heritage   **Contact:** The West Midlands Regional Office

Magnificent 14th century timber-framed barn built for the monks of Pershore Abbey. It is the largest of its kind in Britain.

Location: OS Ref. SO784 534. 5m W of Worcester on unclassified road off A4103.

Open: 29 Mar - 30 Sept: Thur - Sun, 10am - 6pm.

Admission: Free.

LITTLE MALVERN COURT 🏛

Nr Malvern, Worcestershire WR14 4JN

Tel: 01684 892988 **Fax:** 01684 893057

Owner: Trustees of the late T M Berington   **Contact:** Mrs T M Berington

Prior's Hall, associated rooms and cells, c1480, of former Benedictine Monastery. Formerly attached to, and forming part of the Little Malvern Priory Church which may also be visited. It has an oak-framed roof, 5-bay double-collared roof, with two tiers of cusped windbraces. Library. Collections of religious vestments, embroideries and paintings. Gardens: 10 acres of former monastic grounds with spring bulbs, blossom, old fashioned roses and shrubs.

Location: OS130, Ref. SO769 403. 3m S of Great Malvern on Upton-on-Severn Rd (A4104).

Open: 17 Apr - 18 Jul: Weds & Thurs, 2.15 - 5pm. Last admission 4.30pm.

Admission: House & Garden: Adult £4.80, Child £2.50, Garden only: Adult £3.80, Child £1.50.

🚻 Garden (partial). 🐕

MADRESFIELD COURT

Madresfield, Malvern WR13 5AU

Tel: 01684 573614   **Fax:** 01684 569197   **e-mail:** madresfield@clara.co.uk

Owner: The Trustees of Madresfield Estate   **Contact:** Mr Peter Hughes

Elizabethan and Victorian house with medieval origins. Fine contents. Extensive gardens and arboretum.

Location: OS Ref. SO809 474. 6m SW of Worcester. 1 1/2 m SE of A449. 2m NE of Malvern.

Open: Guided tours between mid-Apr and Jul on specified dates which are available from the Estate Office, Madresfield, Malvern, Worcs WR13 5AH, tel: 01684 573614. All visitors must join a guided tour and pre-booking is advisable to avoid disappointment.

Admission: £6.

🚻 Unsuitable. 🎧 Obligatory. 🐕

SPETCHLEY PARK GARDENS 🏛

SPETCHLEY PARK, WORCESTER WR5 1RS

www.spetchleygardens.co.uk

Tel: 01905 345213/345224   **Fax:** 01453 511915   **e-mail:** hb@spetchleygardens.co.uk

Owner: Spetchley Gardens Charitable Trust   **Contact:** Mr R J Berkeley

This lovely 30 acre private garden contains a large collection of trees, shrubs and plants, many rare or unusual. A garden full of secrets, every corner reveals some new vista, some treasure of the plant world. The exuberant planting and the peaceful walks make this an oasis of beauty, peace and quiet. Deer Park close by.

Location: OS Ref. SO895 540. 2m E of Worcester on A422. Leave M5/J6 or J7.

Open: 29 Mar - 30 Sept: Tue - Fri & BH Mons, 11am - 5pm. Suns, 2 - 5pm. Closed all Sats and all other Mons.

Admission: Adult £3.50, Child £1.80. Groups: Adult £3.30, Child £1.70.

🚻 🍴 🅿 🏠 🐕

THE TUDOR HOUSE

16 Church Street, Upton-on-Severn, Worcestershire WR8 0HT

Tel: 01684 592447/594522

Owner: Mrs Lavender Beard   **Contact:** Mrs Wilkinson

Upton past and present, exhibits of local history.

Location: OS Ref. SO852 406. Centre of Upton-on-Severn, 7m SE of Malvern by B4211.

Open: Apr - Oct: daily, 2 - 5pm (Suns until 4pm). Winter Suns only, 2 - 4pm.

Admission: Adult £1, Conc. 50p, Family £2.

THE WALKER HALL

Market Square, Evesham, Worcestershire WR11 4RW

Tel: 01386 446623 **Fax:** 01386 48215 **e-mail:** wds@ricsonline.org

Owner: Ward & Dale Smith   **Contact:** Peter Rhodes

A 15th century timber-framed jettied building, being a recipient of English Heritage grant aid.

Location: OS Ref. SP037 437. Centre of Evesham.

Open: By prior appointment only.

Admission: Charitable donation.

WICHENFORD DOVECOTE 💥

Wichenford, Worcestershire

Tel: 01684 855300 **www**.nationaltrust.org.uk

Owner: The National Trust   **Contact:** Regional Office

A 17th century half-timbered dovecote.

Location: OS Ref. SO788 598. 5¹/₂ m NW of Worcester, N of B4204. Behind the barns.

Open: Apr - 31 Oct: daily, 9am - 6pm or sunset if earlier. Closed Good Fri, other times by appointment.

Admission: £1.

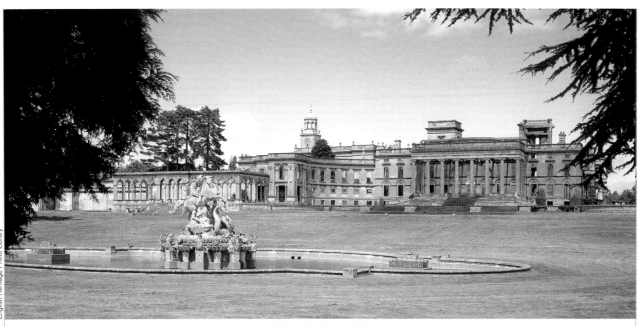

English Heritage Photo Library

WITLEY COURT ⊞

GREAT WITLEY, WORCESTER WR6 6JT

Tel: 01299 896636

Owner: English Heritage   **Contact:** The Custodian

The spectacular ruins of a once great house. An earlier Jacobean manor house, converted in the 19th century into an Italianate mansion, with porticoes by John Nash. The adjoining church, by James Gibbs, has a remarkable 18th century baroque interior. The gardens, William Nesfield's 'Monster Work' were equally elaborate and contained immense fountains, which survive today. The largest is the Perseus and Andromeda Fountain which once sent water 100ft skywards with 'the noise of an express train'. The landscaped grounds, fountains and woodlands are being restored to their former glory. The historic parkland contains the Jerwood Sculpture Park, eventually consisting of 40 modern British sculptures. An atmospheric audio tour leads visitors through the Court.

Location: OS150, Ref. SO769 649. 10m NW of Worcester off A443.

Open: 29 Mar - 31 Oct: daily, 10am - 6pm (5pm in Oct). 1 Nov - 31 Mar: Wed - Sun, 10am - 4pm. Closed 24 - 26 Dec & 1 Jan.

Admission: Adult £4, Child £2, Conc. £3, Family £10. 15% discount for groups of 11+.

ℹ️Visitor welcome point. 📷 ♿Grounds. WC. 🍴 🎧 🅿 ❄ ♿Tel for details.

Little Malvern Court

Jerry Harpur

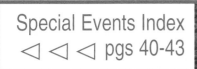

Special Events Index
◁ ◁ ◁ pgs 40-43

Sledmere House

Sir Tatton Sykes

Sledmere House

"Till Sledmere is quite completed, the delight you take in that pretty place, I dare say, will not let you stop your hand, but afford you daily employment and the most delightful amusements till all is completed; I hope all your improvements there answer your most sanguine expectations."

Lord Robert Manners writing to Richard Sykes in 1751

Sir Tatton Sykes

Sir Tatton Sykes

Sir Tatton Sykes

Sir Tatton Sykes

Sir Tatton Sykes

Sir Tatton Sykes

Sledmere House is about six miles from the northern boundary of the Yorkshire Wolds, an area of rolling hills covering about 200,000 acres.

There had been a manor house at Sledmere since medieval times but up until the 17th century it was likely only to have been used as a hunting lodge. It was Richard Sykes who in 1751 demolished the Tudor manor and began building the shell of the house we see today. His nephew Christopher Sykes embarked on further improvements to both the house and grounds.

On inheriting the estate in 1776, Christopher Sykes employed 'Capability' Brown to landscape the 2,000 acre park.Brown's use of the ha-ha near to the house allows the park the appear to reach right up to the house, whilst from the house magnificent views can be seen through great groupings of copper beeches and horse chestnuts.

Once the park was redesigned Sykes turned his attention to the house. Although correspondence exists between him and the architects, John Carr and Samuel Wyatt, it appears that the alterations to the house were in fact made to Sir Christopher's own designs. He refaced the old house with a grey Northamptonshire stone, built a new pediment and added two cross-wings. The exterior was completed by 1786 and in 1787 the interior rooms were decorated with plaster ornament by the famous Joseph Rose.

Visiting Sledmere today one can easily be forgiven for thinking that this is the quintessential Georgian house, but appearances can deceive. In fact, the building that Sir Christopher extended and redecorated in the 1780s and 1790s was gutted by fire in 1911, but the rooms were so carefully restored between 1912 - 1917 that most people still think of Sledmere as a great 18th century house. Miraculously, the way the fire spread gave the staff enough time to save all the contents of the house, including even doors and banisters, and most importantly Joseph Rose's plaster moulds.

This house has some very fine paintings and furniture to enjoy, including a particularly fine painting of Sir Christopher and his wife by George Romney, dated 1793. At the centre of the house the great staircase hall and the drawing room, music room, dining room and library with its great arched ceiling, are on the same grand scale and still have the ability to take the breath away.

Sledmere is perhaps all the more spectacular when the visitor considers that Sir Christopher, on inheriting his estate, described the lands surrounding the house as 'barren waste'. The energy that he applied within his own lifetime to building up the estate continues to be applied by his successors; the gardens, village and the famous stud farm all have a wonderfully well-managed and ordered appearance.

Sledmere may be a grand country house but it does not overwhelm. Enjoy it as one of the very finest Georgian estates in England and appreciate it all the more because it was so beautifully and sympathetically restored over 130 years later. ✛

For further details about *Sledmere House* see entry on page 389.

Sir Tatton Sykes

Sir Tatton Sykes

© English Heritage Photo Library: John Critchley

BRODSWORTH HALL ⬚ & GARDENS

NR DONCASTER

Owner:
English Heritage

▶ **CONTACT**

The Custodian
Brodsworth Hall
Brodsworth
Nr Doncaster
Yorkshire DN5 7XJ

Tel: 01302 722598

Fax: 01302 337165

▶ **LOCATION**
OS Ref. SE507 071

In Brodsworth, 5m NW
of Doncaster off A635.
Use A1(M)/J37.

Rail: Doncaster.

Brodsworth Hall is a rare example of a Victorian country house that has survived largely unaltered with much of its original furnishings and decorations intact. Designed and built in the 1860s it remains an extraordinary time capsule. The now faded grandeur of the reception rooms speaks of an opulent past whilst the cluttered servants wing, with its great kitchen from the age of Mrs Beeton, recalls a vanished way of life. Careful conservation by English Heritage has preserved the patina of time throughout the house to produce an interior that is both fascinating and evocative. The Hall is set within beautifully restored Victorian gardens rich in features which are a delight in any season.

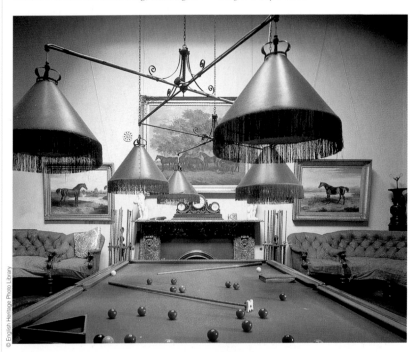

© English Heritage Photo Library

▶ **OPENING TIMES**

Summer
29 March - 27 October
Tue - Sun, & BHs.

House: 1 - 6pm
(last admission 1 hour
before closing).

Gardens: 12 noon - 6pm.

Winter

**Gardens, Shop &
Tearoom only**
10 November - 26 March
Sats & Suns: 11am - 4pm.

▶ **ADMISSION**
Summer

House
Adult	£5.50
Child* (5-15yrs)	£2.80
Conc.	£4.10

Groups (11+) 15% discount

Free admission for tour leaders and coach drivers.

Gardens
Adult	£3.50
Child* (5-15yrs)	£1.80
Conc.	£2.60

Winter Gardens
Adult	£2.00
Child	£1.00
Conc.	£1.50

* Under 5yrs Free

Exhibitions about the family and their love of yachting, the servants and the gardens.

Most of house is accessible. WCs.

Seating for 70.

Groups must book. Booked coach parties: 10am - 1pm.

220 cars and 3 coaches. Free.

Education Centre. Free if booked in advance.

No dogs in gardens.

Tel for details.

Yorkshire & The Humber · England

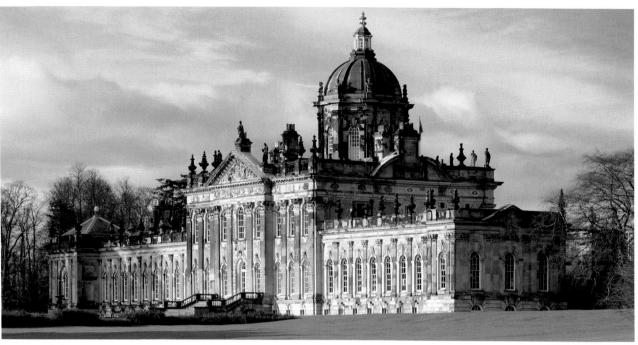

CASTLE HOWARD 🏛

YORK

www.castlehoward.co.uk

In a dramatic setting between two lakes with extensive gardens and impressive fountains, this 18th century Palace was designed by Sir John Vanbrugh in 1699. Undoubtedly the finest private residence in Yorkshire it was built for Charles Howard, 3rd Earl of Carlisle, whose descendants still live here.

With its painted and gilded dome reaching 80ft into the Yorkshire sky, this impressive house has collections of antique furniture, porcelain and sculpture, while its fabulous collection of paintings is dominated by the famous Holbein portraits of Henry VIII and the Duke of Norfolk.

GARDENS

Designed on a heroic scale covering 1,000 acres. The gardens include memorable sights like the Temple of the Four Winds and the Mausoleum, the New River Bridge and the recently restored waterworks of the South Lake, Cascade, Waterfall and Prince of Wales Fountain. The walled garden has collections of old and modern roses.

Ray Wood, acknowledged by the Royal Botanic Collection, Kew, as a "rare botanical jewel" has a unique collection of rare trees, shrubs, rhododendrons, magnolias and azaleas.

Owner:
The Hon Simon Howard

▶ CONTACT

Mrs K Maynard
Castle Howard
York, North Yorks,
YO60 7DA

Tel: 01653 648444
Fax: 01653 648501

e-mail:
house@
castlehoward.co.uk

▶ LOCATION
OS Ref. SE716 701

Approaching from S, A64 to Malton, on entering Malton, take Castle Howard road via Coneysthorpe village. Or from A64 following signs to Castle Howard via the Carrmire Gate 9' wide by 10' high.

York 15m (20 mins), A64. From London: M1/J32, M18 to A1(M) to A64, York/Scarborough Road, 3½ hrs.

Train: London Kings Cross to York 1hr. 50 mins. York to Malton Station 30 mins.

Bus: Service and tour buses from York Station.

CONFERENCE/FUNCTION

ROOM	SIZE	MAX CAPACITY
Long Gallery	197' x 24'	280
Grecian Hall	40' x 40'	160

▶ OPENING TIMES
Summer
15 March - 3 November
Daily, 11am - 4.30pm.

Last admission 4.30pm.

NB. Grounds, Rose Gardens, Plant Centre and Stable Courtyard Complex open 10am.

Winter
November - mid March

Grounds open most days November, December and January - telephone for confirmation.

▶ ADMISSION
Summer

House & Garden
Adult £8.00
Child (4-16yrs)........£5.00
OAP £7.00

Groups (12+)
Adult £6.75
Child (4-16yrs)........£4.25
OAP £6.25

Garden only
Adult £5.00
Child* £3.00

Winter
Grounds only.

Suitable for concerts, craft fairs, fashion shows, clay pigeon shooting, equestrian events, garden parties, filming, product launches. Helicopter landing. Firework displays.

Booked private parties and receptions, min. 25.

Transport equipped for wheelchairs. Chairlift in house to main floor. WCs.

Two cafeterias.

Guides posted throughout house. Private garden tours and lectures by arrangement covering house, history, contents and garden.

400 cars, 20 coaches.

1:10 teacher/pupil ratio required. Special interest: 18th century architecture, art, history, wildlife, horticulture.

FAIRFAX HOUSE 🏛

YORK

www.fairfaxhouse.co.uk

Fairfax House was acquired and fully restored by the York Civic Trust in 1983/84. The house, described as a classic architectural masterpiece of its age and certainly one of the finest townhouses in England, was saved from near collapse after considerable abuse and misuse this century, having been converted into a cinema and dance hall.

The richly decorated interior with its plasterwork, wood and wrought-iron, is now the home for a unique collection of Georgian furniture, clocks, paintings and porcelain.

The Noel Terry Collection, gift of a former treasurer of the York Civic Trust, has been described by Christie's as one of the finest private collections formed this century. It enhances and complements the house and helps to create that special 'lived-in' feeling, providing the basis for a series of set-piece period exhibitions which bring the house to life in a very tangible way.

Owner:
York Civic Trust

▶ CONTACT

Mr Peter Brown
Fairfax House
Castlegate
York YO1 9RN

Tel: 01904 655543

Fax: 01904 652262

▶ LOCATION

OS Ref. SE605 515

In centre of York between Castle Museum and Jorvik Centre.

London 4 hrs by car, 2 hrs by train.

Rail: York Station, 10 mins walk.

Taxi: Station Taxis 01904 623332.

▶ OPENING TIMES

Summer

17 February - 6 January

Mon - Thur: 11am - 5pm.

Fris: Guided tours only at 11am and 2pm.

Sats: 11am - 5pm.

Suns: 1.30 - 5pm.

Last admission 4.30pm.

Winter

Closed
7 January - 16 February
& 24 - 26/31 December.

▶ ADMISSION

Adult	£4.50
Child (5 -16yrs)	£1.50
Conc.	£3.75

Groups*

Adult	£4.00
Child (5 -16yrs)	£1.00
Conc.	£3.25

* Min payment 15 persons.

ℹ️ Suitable for filming. No photography in house. Liveried footmen, musical & dancing performances can be arranged.

🛍

🍽 Max. 28 seated. Groups up to 50: buffet can be provided.

♿ Visitors may alight at entrance prior to parking. No WCs except for functions.

🚶 A guided tour can be arranged at a cost of £5. Evening and daytime guided tours, telephone for details. Available in French and German. Tour time: 1½ hrs.

🅿 300 cars, 50 yds from house. Coach park is ½ m away, parties are dropped off; drivers please telephone for details showing the nearest coach park and approach to the house.

❄️

Mike Williams

FOUNTAINS ABBEY & STUDLEY ROYAL

RIPON

www.fountainsabbey.org.uk

Owner:
The National Trust

▶ **CONTACT**

The National Trust
Fountains Abbey
and Studley Royal
Ripon
North Yorkshire
HG4 3DY

Tel: 01765 608888

Fax: 01765 601002

▶ **LOCATION**
OS Ref. SE275 700

Abbey entrance;
4m W of Ripon off
B6265.
8m W of A1.

One of the most remarkable sites in Europe, sheltered in a secluded valley, Fountains Abbey and Studley Royal, a World Heritage Site, encompasses the spectacular remains of a 12th century Cistercian abbey with one of the finest surviving monastic watermills in Britain, an Elizabethan mansion, and one of the best surviving examples of a Georgian green water garden. Elegant ornamental lakes, avenues, temples and cascades provide a succession of unforgettable eye-catching vistas in an atmosphere of peace and tranquillity. St Mary's Church, built by William Burges in the 19th century, provides a dramatic focal point to the medieval deer park with over 500 deer.

Small museum near to the Abbey. Exhibitions in Fountains Hall, Swanley Grange and the Mill.

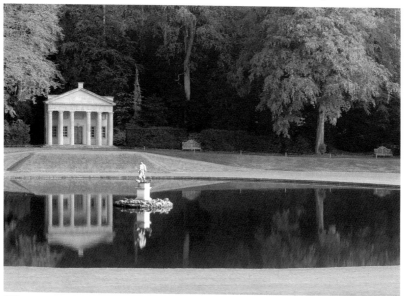

▶ **OPENING TIMES**

April - September
Daily: 10am - 6pm.

January - March &
October - December
Daily: 10am - 4pm.

Closes at 4pm on
12/13 July.

Closed 24/25 December, and Fris in November - January.

▶ **ADMISSION**

Adult £4.80
Child* (5-16yrs)........ £2.50
Family £12.00

Groups (15-30)
Adult £4.20
Child* (5-16yrs)........ £2.30

Groups (31+)
Adult £3.80
Child* (5-16yrs)........ £2.10

*Under 5s Free.

Group discount
applicable only with
prior booking.

Group visits and disabled
visitors, please telephone
in advance, 01765 601005.

The Abbey is maintained
by English Heritage.
St Mary's Church is owned
by English Heritage and
managed by the National
Trust.

ⓘ Events held throughout the year. Exhibitions. Seminar facilities. Outdoor concerts, meetings, activity days, walks.

🛍 Two shops.

♈ Dinners and dances.

♿ Free Batricars & wheelchairs, please book, tel. 01765 601005. 3-wheel Batricars not permitted due to terrain. Tours for visually impaired, please book. WC.

🍴 Groups please book, discounted rates. Licensed.

🍽 Licensed.

👤 Free, but seasonal. Groups, please use Visitor Centre entrance.

🅿 Drivers must book groups. Limited for coaches.

🐕 In grounds, on leads.

❄

🎭 Tel for details.

Harewood House

HAREWOOD HOUSE

LEEDS

www.harewood.org

Designed in 1759 by John Carr, Harewood House is the Yorkshire home of the Queen's cousin, the Earl of Harewood. His mother, HRH Princess Mary, Princess Royal - daughter of King George V - lived at Harewood for 35 years and much of her fascinating Royal memorabilia is still displayed throughout her former rooms.

The House, renowned for its stunning architecture and exquisite Adam interiors, contains a rich collection of Chippendale furniture, fine porcelain and outstanding art collections from Italian Renaissance masterpieces and Turner watercolours to 18th century and 20th century works. Also on permanent display is the opulent Chippendale State Bed - restored to its former glory and previously unseen for 150 years.

In the 1000 acres of parkland, landscaped by 'Capability' Brown are lakeside and woodland walks, magnificent collections of Rhododendron (April - June) and Sir Charles Barry's parterre Terrace which offers excellent views of the surrounding countryside beyond.

The hugely popular Bird Garden is home to around 100 rare and endangered species from Africa, America and Australia, as well as popular favourites - penguins, flamingos and owls.

Throughout the season are a host of special events including open-air concerts, theatre performances, craft festivals, car rallies and much more. The dedicated Watercolour Rooms and Terrace Gallery feature a changing programme of exhibitions from works by JMW Turner to historical and contemporary portraiture.

Owner:
The Earl of Harewood

▶ CONTACT

Harewood House Trust
Moor House
Harewood Estate
Harewood
Leeds
West Yorkshire
LS17 9LQ

Tel: 0113 2181010
Fax: 0113 2181002
e-mail: business@
harewood.org

▶ LOCATION

OS Ref. SE311 446

A1 N or S to Wetherby.

A659 via Collingham, Harewood is on A61 between Harrogate and Leeds. Easily reached from A1, M1, M62 and M18. Half an hour from York,

15 mins from centre of Leeds or Harrogate.

Rail: Leeds Station 7m.

Bus: No. 36 from Leeds or Harrogate.

CONFERENCE/FUNCTION

ROOM	SIZE	MAX CAPACITY
State Dining Rm.		32
Gallery		96
Courtyard Suite		120
Courtyard Marquee	20' x 24'	400

Harewood House

Marquees can be accommodated, concerts and product launches. No photography in the house.

Ideal for corporate entertaining including drinks receptions, buffets and wedding receptions. Specific rooms available for corporate entertaining plus Courtyard Suite for conferences/ product launches.

Visitors may alight at entrance. Parking in allocated areas. Most facilities accessible. Wheelchair available at House and Bird Garden. WC. Special concessions apply to disabled groups. Some steep inclines.

Licensed.   Licensed.

Cars 400 yds from house. 50+ coaches 500 yds from house. Drivers to verify in advance.

By arrangement. Audio tour of house available. Lectures by arrangement.

Dogs on leads in grounds, guide dogs only in house.

Civil Wedding Licence.

▶ OPENING TIMES

Summer
7 Mar - 3 Nov.

House
Daily from 11am - 4.30pm.

Bird Garden & Grounds
Daily from 10am.

Café
10.30am - 4.30pm.

Winter
Weekends Nov - 15 Dec (ring to confirm times). Closed: Nov - Mar.

▶ ADMISSION

All attractions
Adult	£9.00
Child (4-15yrs)	£5.00
OAP	£7.50
Family (2+3)	£30.00

Groups (15+)
Including House, Old Kitchen & Below Stairs
Adult	£8.00
Child	£4.00
OAP	£7.00

Bird Garden, Grounds & Terrace Gallery
Adult	£6.50
Child (4-15yrs)	£4.00
OAP	£5.50
Family (2+3)	£20.00

▶ SPECIAL EVENTS

MAY 24 - 26
Food Lovers Fair.

JUN 1 - 4
Spring Craft Fair.

JUN 16
Classic & Vintage Vehicle Rally.

AUG 11
Rolls Royce Rally.

NEWBY HALL & GARDENS 🏛

RIPON

www.newbyhall.com

Newby Hall, the Yorkshire home of the Compton family, is a late 17th century house built in the style of Sir Christopher Wren. William Weddell, an ancestor of Mr Compton, made the Grand Tour in the 1760s, and amongst the treasures he acquired were magnificent classical statuary and a superb set of Gobelin Tapestries. To house these treasures, Weddell commissioned Robert Adam to create the splendid domed Sculpture Gallery and Tapestry Room that we see today. The Regency dining room and billiard room were added later. There is much fine Chippendale furniture and in recent years Mrs Robin Compton restored the decoration of the house, painstakingly researching colour and decor of the Adam period.

GARDENS

25 acres of glorious gardens contain rare and beautiful shrubs and plants. Newby's famous double herbaceous borders, flanked by great bastions of yew hedges, sweep down to the River Ure. Formal gardens such as the Autumn and Rose Gardens – each with splashing fountains – a Victorian rock garden, the tranquillity of Sylvia's Garden, pergolas and even a tropical garden, make Newby a 'Garden for all Seasons'. Newby holds the National Collection of the Genus Cornus and in 1987 won the Christie's/HHA Garden of the Year Award. The gardens also incorporate an exciting children's adventure garden and miniature railway.

🎬 ♿ ℹ Suitable for filming and for special events, craft and country fairs, vehicle rallies etc, promotions and lectures. No indoor photography. Allow a full day for viewing house and gardens.

🍷 Wedding receptions & special functions.

♿ 5 wheelchairs available. Access to ground floor of house and key areas in gardens. WC.

🍴 Garden restaurant, teas, hot and cold meals. Booked groups in Grantham Room. Menus/rates on request.

🅿 Ample. Hard standing for coaches.

🎒 Welcome. Rates on request. Grantham Room for use as wet weather base subject to availability. Woodland discovery walk, adventure gardens and train rides on 10¹/₄" gauge railway.

🐕 Guide dogs only.

🛡 SPECIAL EVENTS

MAY 12
Spring Plant Fair.

MAY 24 - 26 & SEPT 27 - 29
Rainbow Craft Fair.

JUL 21
Historic Vehicle Rally.

See Special Events Index for full details.

Owner:
Mr Richard Compton

▶ CONTACT

The Opening
Administrator
Newby Hall
Ripon
North Yorkshire
HG4 5AE

Tel: 01423 322583

Fax: 01423 324452

e-mail:
info@newbyhall.com

▶ LOCATION

OS Ref. SE348 675

Midway between London and Edinburgh, 4m W of A1, towards Ripon. S of Skelton 2m NW of (A1) Boroughbridge. 4m SE of Ripon.

Taxi: Ripon Taxi Rank 01765 601283.

Bus: On Ripon - York route.

CONFERENCE/FUNCTION

ROOM	SIZE	MAX CAPACITY
Grantham Room	90' x 20'	200

▶ OPENING TIMES

Summer

House
29 March - end September
Daily except Mons but open BH Mons,
12 noon - 5pm
Last admission 4.30pm.

Garden
29 March - end September
Daily except Mons but open BH Mons.
11am - 5.30pm
Last admission 5pm.

Winter
October - end March
Closed.

▶ ADMISSION

House & Garden

Adult	£7.00
Child (4-16yrs)	£4.50
OAP	£6.00
Disabled	£4.50

Group (15+)

Adult	£5.80
Child (4-16yrs)	£4.00

Garden only

Adult	£5.50
Child (4-16yrs)	£4.00
OAP	£4.50
Disabled	£4.00

Group (15+)

Adult	£4.50
Child (4-16yrs)	£3.50

Additional charge for train.

Yorkshire & The Humber - England

RIPLEY CASTLE

HARROGATE

www.ripleycastle.co.uk

Ripley Castle has been the home of the Ingilby family for twenty-six generations and Sir Thomas and Lady Ingilby together with their five children continue the tradition. The guided tours are amusing and informative, following the lives and loves of one family for over 670 years and how they have been affected by events in English history. The Old Tower dates from 1555 and houses splendid armour, books, panelling and a Priest's Secret Hiding Place, together with fine paintings, china, furnishings and chandeliers collected by the family over the centuries. The extensive Victorian Walled Gardens have been transformed and are a colourful delight through every season. In the Spring you can appreciate 150,000 flowering bulbs which create a blaze of colour through the woodland walks, and also the National Hyacinth Collection whose scent is breathtaking. The restored Hot Houses have an extensive tropical plant collection, and in the Kitchen Gardens you can see an extensive collection of rare vegetables from the Henry Doubleday Research Association.

Ripley village on the Castle's doorstep is a model estate village with individual charming shops, an art gallery, delicatessen and Farmyard Museum.

Owner:
Sir Thomas Ingilby Bt

▶ CONTACT

Tours: Wendy McNae
Meetings/Dinners:
Chloë Drummond
Ripley Castle
Ripley
Harrogate
North Yorkshire
HG3 3AY

Tel: 01423 770152
Fax: 01423 771745
e-mail: enquiries@
ripleycastle.co.uk

▶ LOCATION

OS Ref. SE283 605

W edge of village. Just off A61, 3½ m N of Harrogate, 8m S of Ripon. M1 18m S, M62 20m S.

Rail: London - Leeds/York 2hrs. Leeds/York - Harrogate 30mins.

Taxi: Blueline taxis Harrogate (01423) 503037.

CONFERENCE/FUNCTION

ROOM	SIZE	MAX CAPACITY
Morning Rm	27' x 22'	80
Large Drawing Rm	30' x 22'	80
Library	31 x 19'	75
Tower Rm	33' x 21'	75
Map Rm	19' x 14'	20
Dining Rm	23' x 19'	30

No photography inside castle unless by prior written consent. Parkland for outdoor activities & concerts. Murder mystery weekends.

VIP lunches & dinners (max. 66): unlimited in marquees. Full catering service, wedding receptions, banquets and medieval banquets.

5/7 rooms accessible. Gardens accessible (not Tropical Collection). WCs. Parking 50 yds.

The Castle Tearooms (seats 56) in Castle courtyard. Licensed. Pub lunches or dinner at hotel (100 yds). Groups must book.

Obligatory. Tour time 75 mins.

290 cars - 300 yds from castle entrance. Coach park 50 yds. Free.

Welcome by arrangement, between 10.30am - 7.30pm. Educational Fact Pack.

Guide dogs only.

Boar's Head Hotel (RAC***) 100 yds. Owned and managed by the estate.

Civil Wedding Licence.

Open all year.

▶ OPENING TIMES

Summer
Castle & Gardens
January - May,
September - December:
Tues, Thurs, Sats & Suns:
10.30am - 3pm.

June - August:
Daily: 10.30am - 3pm.

Gardens
Daily, 10am - 5pm.

Winter
December - May &
September - December:
Tues, Thurs, Sats & Suns.

10.30am - last guided tour 3pm.

▶ ADMISSION

All Year
Castle & Gardens

Adult	£5.50
Child (5-16yrs)	£3.00
OAP	£4.50

Groups (15+)

Adult	£4.50
Child (5-16yrs)	£2.50

Gardens only

Adult	£3.00
Child (5-16yrs)	£1.50
OAP	£2.50

Groups (15+)

Adult	£2.50

▶ SPECIAL EVENTS

MAR 15 - 17
Galloway Antiques Fair.

JUN 13 - 16
Homes & Gardens Grand Summer Sale.

AUG 26
'Ripley Revel' – Hog Roast.

SKIPTON CASTLE

SKIPTON

www.skiptoncastle.co.uk

Guardian of the gateway to the Yorkshire Dales for over 900 years, this is one of the most complete and well-preserved medieval castles in England. From 1310 stronghold of the Cliffords, two Lords of Skipton went out from here to die on Roses battlefields. In the Civil War this was the last Royalist bastion in the North, falling after a three year siege.

Every phase of this turbulent history has left its mark, from the Norman entrance arch and gateway towers to the beautiful early Tudor courtyard built in the heart of the castle by 'The Shepherd Lord'; it was there in 1659, that Lady Anne Clifford planted a yew tree (in whose shade you can sit today) to mark the completion of her repairs after the Civil War. Thanks to her, and to Cromwell, who permitted them on condition that the roofs should not be able to support cannon – the castle is still fully roofed,

making a visit well worthwhile at any time of year. A delightful picnic area has been created on the Chapel Terrace with views over the town and woods.

The gatehouse of the castle contains the Shell Room, decorated in 1620 with shells and Jamaican coral said to have been brought home by Lady Anne's father, George Clifford, 3rd Earl of Cumberland, Champion to Queen Elizabeth and one of her Admirals against the Armada; he lies beneath a splendid tomb in Skipton's parish church, a few yards from the castle gates.

On leaving the castle, the visitor is at once in the town's bustling High Street, with its four market days every week (and lots of other good shopping) and a great variety of pubs and restaurants. Close by, the Leeds and Liverpool canal presents a lively scene.

CONTACT

Judith Parker
Skipton Castle
Skipton
North Yorkshire
BD23 1AQ

Tel: 01756 792442

Fax: 01756 796100

e-mail: info@
skiptoncastle.co.uk

LOCATION
OS Ref. SD992 520

In the centre of Skipton, at the N end of High Street.

Skipton is 20m W of Harrogate on the A59 and 26m NW of Leeds on A65.

Rail: Regular services from Leeds & Bradford.

OPENING TIMES
All Year
(closed 25 December)

Mon - Sat: 10am - 6pm
Suns: 12 noon - 6pm
(October - February 4pm)

ADMISSION
Adult £4.60
Child (0 - 4yrs) .... Free

Child (5-17yrs) £2.30
OAP £4.00
Student (with ID) .. £4.00
Family (2+3) £12.50

Groups (15+)
Adult £3.80
Child (0-17yrs) £2.30

Includes illustrated tour sheet in a choice of eight languages, plus free badge for children.

Groups welcome: Guides available for booked groups at no extra charge.

Unsuitable.

Tearoom. Indoor and outdoor picnic areas.

By arrangement.

Large public coach and car park off nearby High Street. Coach drivers' rest room at Castle.

Welcome. Guides available. Teachers free.

In grounds on leads.

Tel for details.

WHITE SCAR CAVE

INGLETON

www.wscave.co.uk

Owner:
White Scar Caves Ltd

▶ CONTACT

John Connaughton
White Scar Cave
Ingleton
North Yorkshire
LA6 3AW

Tel: 01524 241244
Fax: 01524 241700

e-mail: wsb@
oyez.freeserve.co.uk

▶ LOCATION
OS Ref. SD713 745

1¹/₂ m from Ingleton on
B6255 road to Hawes.

White Scar Cave is the longest show cave in Britain. The guided tour covers one mile, and takes about 80 minutes. The highlight of the tour is the impressive 200,000 year old Battlefield Cavern. Over 330 feet long, with its roof soaring in places to 100 feet, this is one of the largest caverns in Britain. It contains thousands of delicate stalactites, which hang from the roof in great clusters.

The tour begins near the original entrance found by Christopher Long, the student who discovered the cave in 1923. The path winds its way past cascading waterfalls, between massive banks of flowstone, and through galleries decorated with cream and carrot-coloured stalactites and stalagmites. Under the steel-grid walkways you can see the stream rushing and foaming on its way. Your guide will show you curious cave formations, including the Devil's Tongue, the Arum Lily and the remarkably lifelike Judge's Head.

There is electric lighting throughout, and the principal features are floodlit. White Scar Cave is part of a Site of Special Scientific Interest. It enjoys a spectacular location in the Yorkshire Dales National Park on the slopes of Ingleborough Hill (2372 ft).

▶ OPENING TIMES
All Year
Daily: 10am
Last tour at 5.30pm.

Closed 25 December.

▶ ADMISSION
Adult	£6.50
Child	£3.60
Family	£18.50
Groups (12+)	
Adult	£5.25
Child	£2.85

 Member of the International Show Caves Association.

 Partial.

 Obligatory.

Fact sheets.

In grounds on leads.

ALDBOROUGH ROMAN TOWN ⌗

High Street, Boroughbridge, North Yorkshire YO5 9ES

Tel: 01423 322768

Owner: English Heritage **Contact:** The Custodian

The principal town of the largest Roman tribe in Britain. The delightfully located remains include Roman defences and two mosaic pavements, a small museum displays finds.

Location: OS99 Ref. SE405 661. Close to Boroughbridge off A1.

Open: 29 Mar - 30 Sept: daily, 10am - 6pm. 1 - 31 Oct: daily, 10am - 5pm. Closed 1 - 2pm.

Admission: Adult £1.80, Child 90p, Conc. £1.40. 15% discount for groups (11+).

◼

ARCHAEOLOGICAL RESOURCE CENTRE

St Saviour's Church, St Saviourgate, York YO1 8NN

Tel: 01904 643211 **Fax:** 01904 627097

e-mail: enquiries@vikingjorvik.com **www**.vikingjorvik.com

Owner: York Archaeological Trust **Contact:** Rachel Court

Housed in the restored medieval church of St Saviour, the ARC offers a glimpse behind the scenes of a leading archaeological unit. Led by experienced archaeologists, visitors take part in hands-on activities with real finds, investigating a section of a layer from an archaeological dig and even examining Viking-Age artefacts.

Location: OS99 Ref. SE606 519. Central York, close to the Shambles.

Open: School holidays: Mon - Sat, 11am - 3pm. Term time (pre-booked groups only): Mon - Fri, 10am - 3.30pm. Closed last two weeks of Dec & first week of Jan.

Admission: £4.50, Conc. £4. Pre-booked groups (15+) £4 (prices valid until 31 Mar 2002).

▢ ♿Partial. ⓕObligatory. Ⓟ None. ◼ 🦮Guide dogs only.

ASKE HALL

See right.

BAGSHAW MUSEUM

Wilton Park, Batley, West Yorkshire WF17 0AS

Tel: 01924 326155 **Fax:** 01924 326164 **e-mail:** bagshawmuseum@kirkleesmc.gov.uk

Owner: Kirklees Cultural Services **Contact:** Melanie Brook

Victorian Gothic House set in Wilton House.

Location: OS Ref. SE235 257. From M62/J27 follow A62 to Huddersfield. At Birstall, follow tourist signs.

Open: Mon - Fri, 11am - 5pm. Sat & Sun, 12 noon - 5pm. Pre-booked groups and school parties welcome.

Admission: Free.

BAYSGARTH HOUSE MUSEUM

Caistor Road, Barton-on-Humber, North Lincolnshire DN18 6AH

Tel: 01652 632318

Owner: North Lincolnshire Council **Contact:** Mr D J Williams

18th century town house and park. Displays of porcelain and local history.

Location: OS Ref. TA035 215. Caistor Road, Barton-on-Humber.

Open: Please contact for details.

Admission: Please contact for details.

Bolling Hall Museum

ASKE HALL

RICHMOND, NORTH YORKSHIRE DL10 5HJ

Tel: 01748 850391 **Fax:** 01748 823252

Owner: The Marquess of Zetland **Contact:** Mhairi Mercer

Nestling in 'Capability' Brown landscaped parkland, Aske has been the family seat of the Dundas family since 1763. This Georgian treasure house boasts exquisite 18th century furniture, paintings and porcelain, including work by Robert Adam, Chippendale, Gainsborough, Raeburn and Meissen.

Aske is an architectural kaleidoscope. There is the original 13th century pele tower and remodelled Jacobean tower. John Carr's stable block, built in 1765, was later converted into a chapel with Italianate interior. A coach house with clock tower houses the family's carriage. There are follies and a lake as well as the new three tier terraced garden.

Patrick Lane

Location: OS Ref. NZ179 035. 2m SW of A1 at Scotch Corner, 1m from the A66, on the Gilling West road (B6274).

Open: All year: for groups (15+) by appointment only.

Admission: House & grounds: Adult £7, Child £4.50.

ⓘConferences. No photography in house. 🚾 ♿Partial. ⓕBy arrangement. Ⓟ ◼ 🦮In grounds on leads. ▲ ✳ ♿Tel for details.

BENINGBROUGH HALL & GARDENS ✤

BENINGBROUGH, NORTH YORKSHIRE YO30 1DD

Tel: 01904 470666 **Fax:** 01904 470002 **e-mail:** ybblmb@smtp.ntrust.org.uk
Owner: The National Trust   **Contact:** The Visitor Services Manager
Imposing 18th century house with over 100 portraits from the National Portrait Gallery. Walled garden, children's playground, Victorian laundry. Herbaceous borders and parkland.
Location: OS Ref. SE516 586. 8m NW of York, 3m W of Shipton, 2m SE of Linton-on-Ouse, follow signposted route.
Open: 23 Mar - 3 Nov: Sat - Wed & Good Fri also Fris in Jul & Aug. House: 12 noon - 5pm. Last admission 4.30pm. Grounds: 11am - 5.30pm.
Admission: House & Garden: Adult £5.20, Child £2.60, Family £13. Garden: Adult £3.60, Child £1.80, Family £9.
🖸 ⬚ Partial. WC. 🍴 ✕ ⬚

BOLTON ABBEY

SKIPTON, NORTH YORKSHIRE BD23 6EX

www.boltonabbey.com

Tel: 01756 718009 **Fax:** 01756 710535 **e-mail:** tourism@boltonabbey.com
Owner: Trustees of the Chatsworth Settlement   **Contact:** Visitor Manager
Wordsworth, Turner and Landseer were inspired by this romantic and varied landscape. The Estate, centred around Bolton Priory (founded 1154), is the Yorkshire home of the Duke and Duchess of Devonshire and provides 80 miles of footpaths to enjoy some of the most spectacular landscape in England.
Location: OS Ref. SE074 542. On B6160, N from the junction with A59 Skipton - Harrogate road, 23m from Leeds.
Open: All year.
Admission: £4 per car, £2 for disabled (car park charge only).
🖸 ⬚ ⬚ ⬚ Licensed. 🍴 Licensed. ⬚ 🅿 ⬚ ⬚ In grounds, on leads.
⬚ Devonshire Arms Country House Hotel & Devonshire Fell Hotel nearby. ⬚ ❀

BISHOPS' HOUSE

Meersbrook Park, Norton Lees Lane, Sheffield, Yorkshire S8 9BE
Tel: 0114 278 2600
Owner: Sheffield Galleries & Museums Trust   **Contact:** S A Potts
A beautiful 16th century timber-framed house, the oldest surviving building of its type in Sheffield.
Location: OS Ref. SK348 843. A61, 2m S of city centre E of the Chesterfield Road.
Open: Sat, 10am - 4.30pm. Sun, 11am - 4.30pm. Mon - Fri: 10am - 3pm for pre-booked groups only.
Admission: Free.

BOLLING HALL MUSEUM

Bowling Hall Road, Bradford, West Yorkshire BD4 7LP
Tel: 01274 723057
Owner: City of Bradford Metropolitan District Council   **Contact:** Anthea Bickley
Medieval tower with 17th century additions.
Location: OS Ref. SE174 315. 1½ m SE of Bradford centre, ¼ m SE of A650.
Open: Wed - Fri, 11am - 4pm. Sat, 10am - 5pm, Sun, 12 noon - 5pm.
Admission: Free.

BOLTON CASTLE

LEYBURN, NORTH YORKSHIRE DL8 4ET

www.boltoncastle.co.uk

Tel: 01969 623981 **Fax:** 01969 623332 **e-mail:** harry@boltoncastle.co.uk
Owner/Contact: Hon Mr & Mrs Harry Orde-Powlett
A fine medieval castle that overlooks beautiful Wensleydale. Bolton Castle celebrated its 600th anniversary in 1999. Set your imagination free as you wander round this fascinating castle, which once held Mary Queen of Scots prisoner for 6 months and succumbed to a bitter Civil War siege. Don't miss the beautiful medieval garden and vineyard.
Location: OS Ref. SE034 918. Approx 6m from Leyburn. 1m NW of Redmire.
Open: All year: daily, 10am - 5pm or dusk. Please telephone to confirm times from 14 Dec - 14 Feb.
Admission: Adult £4, Conc. £3. Groups: Adult £3, Conc. £2.
🖸 ⬚ Wedding receptions. ⬚ Partial. ⬚ 🅿 ⬚ ⬚ In grounds, on leads. ⬚ ❀

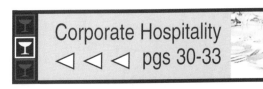

Corporate Hospitality
◁ ◁ ◁ pgs 30-33

BRAMHAM PARK 🏛

WETHERBY, WEST YORKSHIRE LS23 6ND

Tel: 01937 846002   **Fax:** 01937 846001

Owner: George Lane Fox   **Contact:** Lucy Finucane

This Queen Anne house is 5 miles south of Wetherby on the A1, 10 miles from Leeds and 15 miles from York. The grand design of the gardens (66 acres) and pleasure grounds (100) are the only example of a formal, early 18th century landscape in the British Isles. Unexpected views and grand vistas, framed by monumental hedges and trees, delight the visitor, while temples, ornamental ponds and cascades focus the attention. The profusion of spring and summer wild flowers give a constant variety of colour and include many rare species.

Location: OS Ref. SE410 416. Half way from London to Edinburgh, 1m W of A1, 5m S of Wetherby, 10m NE of Leeds, 15m SW of York.

Open: Gardens: 1 Apr - 30 Sept: daily, 10.30am - 5.30pm, last admission 5pm. Closed: week of horse trials (tel. for details). House: by appointment for groups (6+).

Admission: Garden only: Adult £4, Child under 5yrs Free, Child (under 16yrs)/ OAP £2.

🔲 Grounds. WC. ⬛ Guide dogs only. 🔲 Tel for details.

Burton Agnes Manor House

BROCKFIELD HALL 🏛
Warthill, York YO19 5XJ

Tel: 01904 489298

Owner/Contact: Lord Martin Fitzalan Howard

A fine late Georgian house designed by Peter Atkinson, whose father had been assistant to John Carr of York, for Benjamin Agar Esq. Begun in 1804, its outstanding feature is an oval entrance hall with a fine cantilevered stone staircase curving past an impressive Venetian window. It is the happy family home of Lord and Lady Martin Fitzalan Howard. He is the brother of the 17th Duke of Norfolk and son of the late Baroness Beaumont of Carlton Towers, Selby. There are some interesting portraits of her old Roman Catholic family, the Stapletons, and some good furniture.

Location: OS Ref. SE664 550. 5m E of York off A166 or A64.

Open: Aug: daily except Mons (open Aug BH Mon), 1 - 4pm. Other times by appointment.

Admission: Adult £3.50, Child £1.

🔲 Partial. 🔲 Obligatory. 🅿 ⬛ Guide dogs only.

BRODSWORTH HALL ♯ *See page 366 for full page entry.*
& GARDENS

BRONTË PARSONAGE MUSEUM
Church St, Haworth, Keighley, West Yorkshire BD22 8DR

Tel: 01535 642323 **Fax:** 01535 647131 **www**.bronte.org.uk

e-mail: bronte@bronte.prestel.co.uk

Owner: The Brontë Society   **Contact:** The Administrator

Georgian Parsonage, former home of the Brontë family, now a museum with rooms furnished as in the sisters' day and displays of their personal treasures.

Location: OS Ref. SE029 373. 8m W of Bradford, 3m S of Keighley.

Open: Apr - Sept: 10am - 5pm, Oct - Mar: 11am - 4.30pm. Daily except 24 - 27 Dec & 7 Jan - 1 Feb 2001.

Admission: Adult £4.80, Child £1.50 (5-16 inclusive), Conc. £3.50, Family £10.50. Discounts for booked groups.

Patrick Lane

Yorkshire & The Humber - England

BROUGHTON HALL

SKIPTON, NORTH YORKSHIRE BD23 3AE

www.broughtonhall.co.uk   www.ruralsolutions.co.uk

Tel: 01756 799608   **Fax:** 01756 700357

e-mail: tempest@broughtonhall.co.uk   **e-mail:** info@ruralsolutions.co.uk

Owner: The Tempest Family   **Contact:** The Estate Office

The Hall was built in 1597 by the Tempest family and it continues to be their private home which provides it with a very special atmosphere. The building is Grade I listed and set in 3000 acres of parkland and rolling countryside. It is available to groups for tours by prior arrangement throughout the year and also as a prestigious venue for business promotions and functions. The grounds were designed by Nesfield in 1855 including fine Italianate gardens, gazebo, fountains and balustrades. The magnificent conservatory is a particular feature. Filming often takes place at Broughton with its wide diversity of settings and

locations and the owners appreciate and understand production requirements.

Separate from the Hall is the Broughton Hall Business Park formed from Listed estate buildings housing 40 companies employing 500 people in quality office accommodation. The business park is managed by Rural Solutions Ltd who specialise in non-agricultural rural development (01756 799955).

Location: OS Ref. SD943 507. On A59, 3m W of Skipton midway between the Yorkshire and Lancashire centres. Good air and rail links.

Open: Year round tours for groups by arrangement.

Admission: £5.

⛟ T 🅵 By arrangement. 🅿 ✳

BURTON AGNES HALL 🏛

DRIFFIELD, EAST YORKSHIRE YO25 0ND

www.burton-agnes.com

Tel: 01262 490324   **Fax:** 01262 490513

Owner: Burton Agnes Hall Preservation Trust Ltd   **Contact:** Mrs Susan Cunliffe-Lister

A lovely Elizabethan Hall containing treasures collected by the family over four centuries from the original carving and plasterwork to modern and Impressionist paintings. The Hall is surrounded by lawns and topiary yew. The old walled garden contains a maze, potager, jungle garden, campanula collection and colour gardens incorporating giant game boards. Children's corner.

Location: OS Ref. TA103 633. Off A614 between Driffield and Bridlington.

Open: 29 Mar - 31 Oct: daily, 11am - 5pm.

Admission: House & Gardens: Adult £4.80, Child £2.40, OAP £4.30. Gardens only: Adult £2.40, Child £1, OAP £2.20. 10% reduction for groups of 30+.

🔲 🖼 ⛟ Ground floor & grounds. 🍴 Café. Ice-cream parlour.

BURTON AGNES MANOR HOUSE ⌗

Burton Agnes, Bridlington, Humberside

Tel: 01904 601901

Owner: English Heritage   **Contact:** The North Regional Office

A rare example of a Norman house, altered and encased in brick in the 17th & 18th centuries.

Location: OS Ref. TA103 633. Burton Agnes village, 5m SW of Bridlington on A166.

Open: Please telephone for details.

Admission: Free.

View of York Minster (showing Fairfax House in the foreground)

Patrick Lane

BURTON CONSTABLE HALL 🏛

SKIRLAUGH, EAST YORKSHIRE HU11 4LN

www.burtonconstable.com

Tel: 01964 562400 **Fax:** 01964 563229 **e-mail:** enquiries@burtonconstable.com
Owner: Burton Constable Foundation   **Contact:** Mrs Helen Dewson
Built in the 16th century and set in 300 acres of parkland landscaped by
'Capability' Brown, Burton Constable Hall is the magnificent ancestral home of the
Constable family. Superb interiors containing paintings, prints and fine English
furniture. 30 rooms open to view including a unique 'Cabinet of Curiosities', a
fascinating Lamp Room and servants' corridors.
Location: OS Ref. TA193 369. 14m E of Beverley via A165 Bridlington Road,
follow Historic House signs. 7m NE of Hull via B1238 to Sproatley then follow
Historic House signs.
Open: Easter Sun - 31 Oct: Sat - Thur. Grounds & tearoom open 12.30pm. Hall:
1 - 5pm. Last admission 4.15pm.
Admission: Hall & Grounds: Adult £5, Child £2, OAP £4.50, Family £11. Grounds
only: Adult £1, Child 50p. Groups (20+): special rates available. Connoisseur
Study Visits: prices on application.
ℹ️ No photography in house. 🎥 ♿ 🍴 💷 By arrangement. 🅿 ▣
🐾 In grounds on leads. 🛏 Tel for details.

BYLAND ABBEY ⚏
Coxwold, Helmsley, North Yorkshire YO6 4BD
Tel: 01347 868614
Owner: English Heritage   **Contact:** The Custodian
Hauntingly beautiful ruin, set in peaceful meadows in the shadow of the Hambleton
Hills. It illustrates later development of Cistercian churches, including a beautiful
floor of mosaic tiles.
Location: OS100 Ref. SE549 789. 2m S of A170 between Thirsk and Helmsley, NE of
Coxwold village.
Open: 29 Mar - 30 Sept: daily 10am - 6pm. 1 - 31 Oct: daily, 10am - 5pm. Closed 1 - 2pm.
Admission: Adult £1.70, Child 90p, Conc. £1.30. 15% discount for groups (11+).
♿ 🅿 Limited. ▣ 🐾 On leads. 🛏 Tel for details.

CANNON HALL MUSEUM, PARK & GARDENS
Cawthorne, Barnsley, South Yorkshire S75 4AT
Tel: 01226 790270 **Fax:** 01226 792117 **e-mail:** cannonhall@barnsley.gov.uk
Owner: Barnsley Metropolitan Borough Council   **Contact:** The Keeper
Late 17th century house, remodelled in the 1760s by John Carr. Contains decorative
arts collections including fine furniture and paintings. Moorcroft pottery and Glass
galleries. Also *Charge* the Regimental Museum of the 13th/18th Royal Hussars
(QMO). Surrounding 18th century park landscaped by Richard Woods, with Walled
Garden. Events and education programme.
Location: OS Ref. SE272 084. 6m NW of Barnsley of A635.
Open: Nov, Dec & Mar: Sun, 12 noon - 4pm; closed Jan & Feb. Apr - Oct: Tue - Thur,
10.30am - 5pm; Sat & Sun, 12 noon - 5pm. Last admission 4.15pm for 5pm. Closure
in Jan & Feb does not apply to schools.
Admission: Adults £1, Child/Conc. 50p (2001 prices, subject to change). Group
discount (10+).
🎥 🇹 ♿ Partial. WC. 💷 Weekends. 🅿 ▣ 🐾 In grounds, on leads. 🏵
🛏 Tel for details.

CASTLE HOWARD 🏛   *See page 367 for full page entry.*

CAWTHORNE VICTORIA JUBILEE MUSEUM
Taylor Hill, Cawthorne, Barnsley, South Yorkshire S75 4HQ
Tel: 01226 790545/790246
Owner: Cawthorne Village   **Contact:** Mrs Mary Herbert
A quaint and eccentric collection in a half-timbered building. Museum has a ramp and
toilet for disabled visitors. School visits welcome.
Location: OS Ref. SE285 080. 4m W of Barnsley, just off the A635.
Open: Palm Sun - end Oct: Sats, Suns & BH Mons, 2 - 5pm. Groups by appointment
throughout the year.
Admission: Adult 50p, Child 20p.

CLIFFE CASTLE
Keighley, West Yorkshire BD20 6LH
Tel: 01535 618231
Owner: City of Bradford Metropolitan District Council   **Contact:** Alison Armstrong
Typical Victorian manufacturer's mansion of 1878 with tall tower and garden. Now a
museum.
Location: OS Ref. SE057 422. ³/₄ m NW of Keighley off the A629.
Open: Please telephone for details.
Admission: Free.

CLIFFORD'S TOWER ⚏
Clifford Street, York YO1 1SA
Tel: 01904 646940
Owner: English Heritage   **Contact:** The Custodian
A 13th century tower on one of two mottes thrown up by William the Conqueror to
hold York. There are panoramic views of the city from the top of the tower.
Location: OS105 Ref. SE 605 515. York city centre.
Open: 29 Mar - 30 Sept: daily, 10am - 6pm; 17 Jul - 31 Aug: 9.30am - 7pm; 1 - 31 Oct:
daily, 10am - 5pm. 1 Nov - 31 Mar: daily, 10am - 4pm. Closed 24/25 Dec & 1 Jan.
9 - 16 Feb: 10am - 5pm.
Admission: Adult £2.10, Child £1.10, Conc. £1.60. Family ticket £5.30. 15% discount
available for groups (11+).
🎥 ♿ Unsuitable. ▣ 🐾 In grounds, on leads. 🏵

CLIFTON PARK MUSEUM
Clifton Lane, Rotherham, South Yorkshire S65 2AA
Tel: 01709 823635
Owner: Rotherham Metropolitan Borough Council.   **Contact:** Steven Blackbourn
Furnished period rooms and one of the best collections of Rockingham porcelain in
the country in an 18th century house set within a delightful park.
Location: OS Ref. SK435 926.
Open: Mon - Thur & Sats, 10am - 5pm. Suns, 1.30 - 5pm (Apr - Sept) & 1.30 - 4.30pm
(Oct - Mar).
Admission: Free.

CONISBROUGH CASTLE ⚏
Conisbrough, South Yorkshire
Tel: 01709 863329
Owner: English Heritage   **Contact:** The Administrator
The oldest circular keep in England and one of the finest medieval buildings.
Location: OS111 Ref. SK515 989. 4¹/₂ m SW of Doncaster.
Open: 15 Mar - 30 Jun: Tue - Sun, 10am - 5pm. 1 Jul - 31 Aug: daily, 10am - 5pm.
1 Sept - 13 Oct: Tue - Sun, 10am - 5pm. 14 Oct - 14 Mar: Wed - Sun, 10am - 5pm.
Admission: Adults £4.50, Child £2.50, Conc. £3, Family £11.50.

Duncombe Park

CONSTABLE BURTON HALL GARDENS 🏛

LEYBURN, NORTH YORKSHIRE DL8 5LJ

www.constableburtongardens.co.uk

Tel: 01677 450428 **Fax:** 01677 450622

Owner/Contact: M C A Wyvill Esq

A delightful terraced woodland garden of lilies, ferns, hardy shrubs, roses and wild flowers, attached to a beautiful Palladian house designed by John Carr (not open). Garden trails, rockery with an interesting collection of alpines. Stream garden with large architectural plants and reflection ponds. Impressive spring display of daffodils and tulips.

Location: OS Ref. SE164 913. 3m E of Leyburn off the A684.

Open: Garden only: 24 Mar - 14 Oct: daily, 9am - 6pm.

Admission: Adult £2.50, Child (under 16yrs) 50p, OAP £2.

🔯 Tel for details.

The Georgian Theatre Royal

CRAKEHALL WATERMILL

Little Crakehall, Nr Bedale, North Yorkshire DL8 1HU

Tel: 01677 423240

Owner/Contact: Mrs Gill

Site of a mill since 1086, still milling stone-ground wholemeal flour.

Location: OS Ref. SE244 902. ½ m from village centre.

Open: Easter - End September: Closed Mons & Tues. Please telephone for details.

Admission: Adult £1, Child/OAP 60p.

DANBY WATERMILL

Danby, Whitby, North Yorkshire YO21 2JL

Tel: 01287 660330

Owner/Contact: Frank & Brenda Palmer

350 year old watermill restored to working order.

Location: OS Ref. NZ708 082. ½ m S of village.

Open: Please contact for details.

Admission: Please contact for details.

DUNCOMBE PARK 🏛 🏛

HELMSLEY, NORTH YORKSHIRE YO62 5EB

www.duncombepark.com

Tel: 01439 770213 **Fax:** 01439 771114

e-mail: sally@duncombepark.com

Owner/Contact: Lord & Lady Feversham

Lord and Lady Feversham's restored family home in the North York Moors National Park. Built on a virgin plateau overlooking Norman Castle and river valley, it is surrounded by 35 acres of beautiful 18th century landscaped gardens and 400 acres of parkland with national nature reserve and veteran trees.

Location: OS SE604 830. Entrance just off Helmsley Market Square, signed off A170 Thirsk - Scarborough road.

Open: 28 Apr - 27 Oct: Sun - Thur.

Admission: House & Gardens: Adult £6, Child £3, Conc. £5, Family (2+2) £13.50 Groups (15+): £4.50. Gardens & Parkland: Adult £3, Child (10-16yrs) £2. Parkland: Adult £2, Child (10-16yrs) £1. Season ticket (2+2) £20.

ℹ Country walks, nature reserve, orienteering, conferences. 📷 ⚡
🍽 Banqueting facilities. 🔯 Partial. 🔯 Licensed. 🔯 Obligatory. 🅿 🔯
🐕 In park on leads. 🔯 🔯 Tel for details.

EASBY ABBEY ⌗

Nr Richmond, North Yorkshire

Tel: 01904 601901

Owner: English Heritage **Contact:** The Custodian

Substantial remains of the medieval abbey buildings stand by the River Swale near Richmond.

Location: OS92 Ref. NZ185 003. 1m SE of Richmond off B6271.

Open: Any reasonable time.

Admission: Free.

EAST RIDDLESDEN HALL ✼

BRADFORD ROAD, KEIGHLEY, WEST YORKSHIRE BD20 5EL

www.nationaltrust.org.uk

Tel: 01535 607075 **Fax:** 01535 691462 **e-mail:** yorker@smtp.ntrust.org.uk

Owner: The National Trust   **Contact:** Visitor Services Manager

Homely 17th century merchant's house with beautiful embroideries and textiles, Yorkshire carved oak furniture and fine ceilings. Delightful garden with lavender and herbs. Also wild garden with old varieties of apple trees. Magnificent Great Barn with timber structure. Handling collection, children's play area. Live interpretation. Events.

Location: OS104 SE079 421. 1m NE of Keighley on S side of B6265 in Riddlesden. 50yds from Leeds/Liverpool Canal. Bus: Frequent services from Skipton, Bradford and Leeds. Railway station at Keighley 2m.

Open: 23 Mar - 3 Nov: daily except Mons, Thurs & Fris (open Good Fri, BH Mons & Mons in Jul & Aug), 12 noon - 5pm, Sats, 1 - 5pm.

Admission: Adult £3.60, Child £1.80, Family £9.00. Booked groups (15+): Adult £3.20, Child £1.80.

⬚ ⊤ ⬚Partial. ⬛ ⬚By arrangement. ⬛ ⬚Limited for coaches, please book. ⬚In grounds, on leads. ⬛ ⬚Tel for details.

EPWORTH OLD RECTORY

1 Rectory Street, Epworth, Doncaster, South Yorkshire DN9 1HX

Tel: 01427 872268   **e-mail:** epworth@oldrectory63.freeserve.co.uk

Owner: World Methodist Council   **Contact:** A Milson (Curator/Warden)

1709 Queen Anne period house, John and Charles Wesley's boyhood home. Portraits, period furniture, Methodist memorabilia. Garden, picnic facilities, cinematic presentation.

Location: OS Ref. SE785 036. Epworth lies on A161, 3m S M180/J2. 10m N of Gainsborough. When in Epworth follow the Wesley Trail information boards.

Open: 1 Mar - 31 Oct. Mar, Apr & Oct: Mon - Sat, 10am - 12 noon & 2 - 4pm, Suns, 2 - 4pm. May - Sept: Mon - Sat, 10am - 4.30pm, Suns, 2 - 4.30pm.

Admission: Adult £3, Child (6yrs+) £2.50 (under 6yrs) £1, OAP £2, Family £7.

⬚ ⬚Ground floor & grounds. ⬚By arrangement. ⬚Obligatory. ⬚Limited. ⬛ ⬚Guide dogs only. ⬚2 twins.

FAIRFAX HOUSE ⬚   *See page 368 for full page entry.*

FOUNTAINS ABBEY & STUDLEY ROYAL ✼   *See page 369 for entry.*

THE GEORGIAN THEATRE ROYAL & THEATRE MUSEUM

Victoria Road, Richmond, North Yorkshire DL10 4DW

Tel: 01748 823710   Box Office: 01748 823021

Owner: Georgian Theatre Royal Trust   **Contact:** Bill Sellers

A unique example of Georgian theatre with the majority of its original features intact. Built in 1788 by actor/manager, Samuel Butler. Restoration work began in 1960 and the theatre was reopened in 1963 – it today attracts actors and visitors from around the world. The museum houses a unique collection of Georgian theatre artefacts.

Location: OS Ref. NZ174 013. 4m from the A1 (Scotch Corner) on the A6108.

Open: Mid-Feb - Wed prior to Spring BH & Oct - Dec: guided tours every hour, 1.30 - 3.30pm (last tour). Thur prior to Spring BH - end Sept: 10.30am - 3.30pm (last tour). Other times by arrangement. Group tours on Sun by arrangement.

Admission: Charge.

HANDS ON HISTORY

Market Place, Hull HU1 1EP

Tel: 01482 613902   **Fax:** 01482 613710   **e-mail:** museums@hullcc.gov.uk

Owner: Hull City Council   **Contact:** S R Green

Housed in the Old Grammar School this history resource centre offers hands on activities for the public and schools alike.

Location: OS Ref. TA099 285. 50 yds SW of the Church at centre of the Old Town.

Open: School holidays and weekends open to the public. Please phone for details.

Admission: Free.

HAREWOOD HOUSE   *See page 370 for full page entry.*

HELMSLEY CASTLE ⬚

Helmsley, North Yorkshire YO6 5AB

Tel: 014397 70442

Owner: English Heritage   **Contact:** The Custodian

Close to the market square, with a view of the town, is this 12th century castle. Spectacular earthworks surround a great ruined Norman keep. Exhibition and tableau on the castle's history.

Location: OS100 SE611 836. In Helmsley town.

Open: 29 Mar - 30 Sept: daily, 10am - 6pm. 1 - 31 Oct, daily, 10am - 5pm. 1 Nov - 31 Mar: Wed - Sun, 10am - 4pm (closed 1 - 2pm). Closed 24 - 26 Dec & 1 Jan.

Admission: Adult £2.50, Child £1.30, Conc £1.90, Family £6.30. 15% discount for groups (11+).

⬛ ⬚ ⬚Tel for details.

HELMSLEY WALLED GARDEN

Cleveland Way, Helmsley, North Yorkshire YO6 5AH

Tel/Fax: 01439 771427

Owner: Helmsley Walled Garden Ltd   **Contact:** Paul Radcliffe/Lindsay Tait

A 5 acre walled garden under restoration. Orchid house restored. Plant sales area and café conservatory.

Location: OS100 SE611 836. 25m N of York, 15m from Thirsk. In Helmsley follow signs to Cleveland Way.

Open: 1 Apr - 31 Oct: daily, 10.30am - 5pm. Nov - Mar: Sats/Suns, 12 noon - 4pm.

Admission: Adult £2.50, Child Free, Conc. £1.50.

HOVINGHAM HALL

York, North Yorkshire YO62 4LU

Tel: 01653 628206   **Fax:** 01653 628668

Owner: Sir Marcus Worsley   **Contact:** Mrs Lamprey

Location: OS Ref. SE666 756. 18m N of York on Malton/Helmsley Road (B1257).

Open: Due to refurbishment Hovingham Hall will be closed in 2002 but is due to re-open June 2003.

JERVAULX ABBEY

Ripon, North Yorkshire HG4 4PH

Tel: 01677 460226

Owner/Contact: Mr I S Burdon

Extensive ruins of a former Cistercian abbey.

Location: OS100 Ref. SE169 858. Beside the A6108 Ripon - Leyburn road, 5m SE of Leyburn and 5m NW of Masham.

Open: Daily during daylight hours. Tearoom: Mar - 1 Nov (all home baking).

Admission: Adult £2, Child £1.50 in honesty box at Abbey entrance.

Civil Wedding Venues
◁ ◁ ◁ pgs 28-29

KIPLIN HALL 🏛

KIPLIN, Nr SCORTON, RICHMOND, NORTH YORKSHIRE DL10 6AT

www.kiplinhall.co.uk www.herriotdaysout.co.uk

Tel/Fax: 01748 818178 **e-mail:** kiplinhall@hotmail.com

Owner: Kiplin Hall Trustees **Contact:** The Administrator
A Grade I Listed Jacobean house built in 1620 by George Calvert, 1st Lord Baltimore, founder of the State of Maryland, USA, containing paintings and furniture collected by four families over four centuries. Recent major restoration work has brought the Hall back to life as a comfortable Victorian family home.
Location: OS Ref. SE274 976. Signposted from Scorton - Northallerton road (B6271).
Open: Easter weekend, then 2 May - 29 Sept: Thur - Sun & BH Mons, 2 - 5pm. Open at other times of the year by appointment with the Administrator.
Admission: Adult £3.50, Child £1.75, Conc. £2.50. Groups (10-50) by arrangement.
⬜ ⬜Partial. ⬛ 🎥By arrangement. ⬜Limited. ⬛
🐕In grounds, on leads. Guide dogs only in house. ⬜Tel for details.

KIRKHAM PRIORY 🏛

Kirkham, Whitwell-on-the-Hill, North Yorkshire YO6 7JS

Tel: 01653 618768

Owner: English Heritage **Contact:** The Custodian
The ruins of this Augustinian priory include a magnificent carved gatehouse.
Location: OS100 Ref. SE735 657. 5m SW of Malton on minor road off A64.
Open: 29 Mar - 30 Sept: daily, 10am - 6pm. 1 - 31 Oct: daily, 10am - 5pm.
Admission: Adult £1.70, Child 90p, Conc. £1.30. 15% discount for groups (11+).
⬜ ⬜ ⬜Limited. ⬛ 🐕On leads.

KNARESBOROUGH CASTLE

Knaresborough, North Yorkshire HG5 8AS

Tel: 01423 556188 **Fax:** 01423 556130 **e-mail:** lg12@harrogate.gov.uk

Owner: Duchy of Lancaster **Contact:** Ms Vanessa Hirst
Ruins of 14th century castle standing high above the town. Local history museum housed in Tudor Courthouse. Gallery devoted to the Civil War.
Location: OS Ref. SE349 569. 5m E of Harrogate, off A59.
Open: Easter BH - 30 Sept: daily, 10.30am - 5pm.
Admission: Adult £2, Child £1.25, OAP £1.50, Family £5.50, Groups (10+) £1.50.

LEDSTON HALL

Hall Lane, Ledston, Castleford, West Yorkshire WF10 2BB

Tel: 01423 523423 **Fax:** 01423 521373 **e-mail:** james.hare@carterjonas.co.uk

Owner/Contact: James Hare
17th century mansion with some earlier work.
Location: OS Ref. SE437 289. 2m N of Castleford, off A656.
Open: Exterior only: May - Aug, Mon - Fri, 9am - 4pm. Other days by appointment.
Admission: Free.

THE LINDLEY MURRAY SUMMERHOUSE

The Mount School, Dalton Terrace, York YO24 4DD

Tel: 01904 667506

Owner/Contact: The Mount School
Location: OS Ref. SE593 510. Dalton Terrace, York.
Open: By prior arrangement: Mon - Fri, 9am - 4.30pm throughout the year (apart from BHs).
Admission: Free.
⬜ ⬜ 🐕Guide dogs only. ⬛

LING BEECHES GARDEN

Ling Lane, Scarcroft, Leeds, West Yorkshire LS14 3HX

Tel: 0113 2892450

Owner/Contact: Mrs A Rakusen
A 2 acre woodland garden designed by the owner.
Location: OS Ref. SE354 413. Off A58 midway between Leeds & Wetherby. At Scarcroft turn into Ling Lane, signed to Wike on brow of hill.
Open: By appointment, please telephone for details.
Admission: Adult £2.50, Child Free.

LONGLEY OLD HALL

Longley, Huddersfield, West Yorkshire HD5 8LB

Tel: 01484 430852 **e-mail:** robingallagher@debrett.net **www**.longleyoldhall.co.uk

Owner: Christine & Robin Gallagher **Contact:** Christine Gallagher
This timber framed Grade II* manor house dates from the 14th century. It was owned by the Ramsden family, the former Lords of the Manors of Almondbury and Huddersfield, for over 400 years.
Location: OS Ref. SE154 150. 1½ m SE of Huddersfield towards Castle Hill, via Dog Kennel Bank.
Open: 29 Mar - 2 Apr; 31 May - 4 Jun; 23 - 26 Aug; 27 - 31 Dec: Booked guide tours (8+). Available at other times by appointment. Candlelit evenings - contact for details.
Admission: £6.
⬜ ⬜Unsuitable. 🎥Obligatory. ⬜Limited for coaches. ⬛ ⬛

LOTHERTON HALL

Aberford, West Yorkshire LS25 3EB

Tel: 0113 2813259 **Fax:** 0113 2812100

Owner: Leeds City Council **Contact:** Adam White
Late Victorian and Edwardian country house of great charm and character.
Location: OS92 Ref. SE450 360. 2½ m E of M1 J47 on B2177 the Towton Road.
Open: 1 Apr - 31 Oct: Tue - Sat, 10am - 5pm, Suns, 1 - 5pm. 1 Nov - 31 Dec & Mar: Tue - Sat, 10am - 4pm, Suns, 12 noon - 4pm. Closed Jan & Feb.
Admission: Adult £2, Child 50p, Conc. £1. Groups: £1. Parking: £5 includes 1 yrs free admission to house. Day ticket: £2.

MARKENFIELD HALL

Nr Ripon, North Yorkshire HG4 3AD

Tel: 01845 597226 **Fax:** 01845 597023 **www**.markenfield.com

Owner: Lady Deirdre Curteis **Contact:** Strutt & Parker
Fine example of a moated English Manor House (14th and 15th century).
Location: OS Ref. SE294 672. Access from W side of A61, 1½m S of Safeways roundabout, Ripon.
Open: 1 - 14 May & 1 - 14 Jul: daily, 1 - 5pm. Groups at other times by appointment.
Admission: Adult £3, Child (under 16) £1.50. Min. charge for groups out of season £50.

MIDDLEHAM CASTLE 🏛

Middleham, Leyburn, North Yorkshire DL8 4RJ

Tel: 01969 623899

Owner: English Heritage **Contact:** The Custodian
This childhood home of Richard III stands controlling the river that winds through Wensleydale. There is a massive 12th century keep with splendid views of the surrounding countryside from the battlements.
Location: OS99 Ref. SE128 875. At Middleham, 2m S of Leyburn of A6108.
Open: 29 Mar - 30 Sept: daily, 10am - 6pm. 1 - 31 Oct, daily, 10am - 5pm. 1 Nov - 31 Mar: Wed - Sun, 10am - 4pm (closed 1 - 2pm). Closed 24 - 26 Dec & 1 Jan.
Admission: Adult £2.60, Child £1.30, Conc. £2. 15% discount for groups (11+).
ℹ️Exhibition. ⬜ ⬜Grounds. ⬛ 🐕In grounds, on leads. ⬛ ⬜Tel for details.

White Scar Cave

English Heritage Photo Library

MOUNT GRACE PRIORY

SADDLE BRIDGE, NORTH YORKSHIRE DL6 3JG

Tel: 01609 883494

Owner: National Trust   **Managed by:** English Heritage   **Contact:** The Custodian
Hidden in tranquil wooded countryside at the foot of the Cleveland Hills, one of the loveliest settings of any English priory, and the best preserved Carthusian monastery in England. Monks lived as hermits in their cells and one cell, recently restored, is furnished to give a clear picture of their austere routine of work and prayer. Visitors enter through the manor built by Thomas Lascelles in 1654 on the site of the monastery guest house. It was rebuilt at the turn of the century using traditional techniques, typical of the Arts and Crafts movement.

Location: OS Ref. SE449 985. 12m N of Thirsk, 7m NE of Northallerton on A19.

Open: 29 Mar - 30 Sept: daily, 10am - 6pm. 1 - 31 Oct: daily, 10am - 5pm. 1 Nov - 31 Mar: Wed - Sun, 10am - 4pm (closed 1 - 2pm). Closed 24 - 26 Dec & 1 Jan.

Admission: Adult £3, Child £1.50, Conc. £2.30, Family £7.50. 15% discount for groups (11+).

⬚ ♿Ground floor & grounds. 🅿 ◼ ✳ ♿ Tel for details.

NEWBURGH PRIORY

Coxwold, North Yorkshire YO61 4AS

Tel: 01347 868435

Owner/Contact: Sir George Wombwell Bt

Originally 1145 with major alterations in 1568 and 1720, it has been the home of the Earls of Fauconberg and of the Wombwell family since 1538. Tomb of Oliver Cromwell (3rd daughter Mary married Viscount Fauconberg) is in the house. Extensive grounds contain a water garden, walled garden, topiary yews and woodland walks.

Location: OS Ref. SE541 764. 4m E of A19, 18m N of York, ½ m E of Coxwold.

Open: Easter Sun & Mon. 3 Apr - 30 Jun: Wed & Sun only. House: 2.30 - 4.45pm. Garden: 2 - 6pm. Tours every ½ hour, take approximately 50mins. Booked groups by arrangement.

Admission: Gardens only: £2, Child Free. House & Grounds: £4.50, Child £1.50.

ℹ No photography in house. ♿Partial. ☕ 🔦Obligatory.
🅿Limited for coaches. 🐕In grounds, on leads. ▲

THE MUSEUM OF SOUTH YORKSHIRE LIFE

Cusworth Hall, Cusworth Lane, Doncaster, South Yorkshire DN5 7TU

Tel: 01302 782342

Owner: Doncaster Metropolitan Borough Council   **Contact:** Mr F Carpenter, Curator
A magnificent Grade I country house set in a landscaped parkland and built in 1740, with a chapel and other rooms designed by James Paine, the house is now the home of a museum showing the changing home, work and social conditions of the region over the last 250 years. Regular events and activities.

Location: OS Ref. SE547 039. A1(M)/J37, then A635 and right into Cusworth Lane.

Open: Mon - Fri, 10am - 5pm. Sats, 11am - 5pm, Suns, 1 - 5pm. Closes at 4pm Dec & Jan.

Admission: Free.

⬚ ☕ ✳

NATIONAL CENTRE FOR EARLY MUSIC

St Margaret's Church, Walmgate, York YO1 9TL

Tel: 01904 632220   **Fax:** 01904 612631   **e-mail:** info@ncem.co.uk
www.ncem.co.uk

Owner: York Early Music Foundation   **Contact:** Mrs G Baldwin
The National Centre for Early Music is based in the medieval church of St Margaret's York. The church boasts a 12th century Romanesque doorway and a 17th century brick tower of considerable note. The Centre hosts concerts, music education activities, conferences, recordings and events.

Location: OS Ref. SE609 515. Inside Walmgate Bar, within the city walls, on the E side of the city.

Open: Mon - Fri, 10am - 4pm. Also by appointment. Access is necessarily restricted when events are taking place.

Admission: Free, donations welcome.

♿ 🔦By arrangement. 🅿Limited. No coaches. 🐕Guide dogs only. ◼ ✳
♿ Tel for details.

NEWBY HALL & GARDENS 🏛   *See page 371 for full page entry.*

Ripley Castle

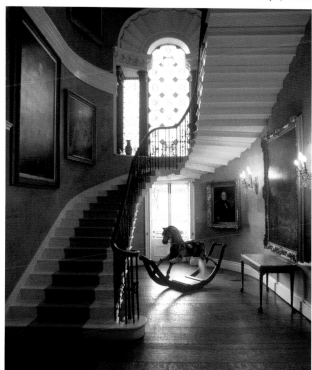

Yorkshire & The Humber · England

NORMANBY HALL

NORMANBY, SCUNTHORPE, NORTH LINCOLNSHIRE DN15 9HU

www.northlincs.gov.uk/normanby

Tel: 01724 720588 **Fax:** 01724 721248 **e-mail:** susan.hopkinson@northlincs.gov.uk

Owner: North Lincolnshire Council   **Contact:** Park Manager

Set in 300 acres of Park, the restored working Victorian Walled Garden has something to captivate and impress at every turn. Victorian varieties of fruit, vegetables and flowers are grown using traditional and organic methods of cultivation, for the Victorian owner's lavish banquets. Complemented by glasshouses displaying a wonderful collection of exotic plants and ferns. Visitors may tour the Regency Mansion, designed by Sir Robert Smirke, discovering re-creations of Regency, Victorian and Edwardian interiors. Unwind with a leisurely meal, then wander through the deer park, follow one of the woodland trails or combine your visit with a themed event.

"Yorkshire in Bloom, 2001 Winner"

Location: OS Ref. SE886 166. 4m N of Scunthorpe off B1430. Follow signs for M181 & Humber Bridge. Tours by arrangement.

Open: Hall & Farming Museum: 25 Mar - 29 Sept: 1 - 5pm. Park & Adventure Playground: daily, 9am - dusk. Walled Garden: daily, 10.30am - 5pm (4pm in winter). Last admission at all venues ½ hour before closing.

Admission: Summer Season: Adult £3.50, Conc. £2.50, Family (2+3) £9.50. Discounts for North Lincolnshire residents. Winter Season: £2.20 per car.

All details correct at time of going to press. For up to date information, please contact Normanby Hall Country Park.

ⓘ 🖼 🎫 🍽 Wedding receptions. ♿Ground floor & grounds. WC. 🎥
🎦By arrangement. 🅿 🖼 🐾 In grounds, on leads. ♨ ❋ 🐕 Tel for details.

NORTON CONYERS 🏠

Nr Ripon, North Yorkshire HG4 5EQ

Tel/Fax: 01765 640333 **e-mail:** norton.conyers@ripon.org

Owner: Sir James and Lady Graham   **Contact:** Lady Graham

Visited by Charlotte Brontë in 1839, Norton Conyers is an original of the 'Thornfield Hall' in 'Jane Eyre' and a family legend was an inspiration for the mad Mrs Rochester. Building is late medieval with Stuart and Georgian additions. Friendly atmosphere, resulting from 378 years of occupation by the same family. 18th century walled garden near house, with orangery and herbaceous borders. Small plant sales area specialising in unusual hardy plants. Pick your own fruit in season.

Location: OS Ref. SF319 763. 4m N of Ripon. $3^1/2$m from the A1.

Open: House & Garden: Easter Sun & Mon. BH Suns & Mons also Jubliee BH. 19 May - 1 Sept: Suns. 8 - 13 Jul: daily. House: 2 - 5pm. Garden 12 noon - 5pm. Last admissions 4.40pm. Garden also open Thurs throughout the year, 10am - 4pm (please check beforehand). Also some Sundays for Charity, tel for details.

Admission: House: Adult £4, Child (10-16yrs)/Conc. £3. Reduced rate for two or more children. Garden: Free (donations welcome), but charges are made at charity openings. Groups: by arrangement.

ⓘNo interior photography. No stilettos in house. 🖼 🎫 ♿Partial. WC.
🍽Only available on Sunday Charity Days, please telephone for dates.
🎦By arrangement. 🅿 🐾In grounds, on leads, guide dogs only in house. 🐕

NOSTELL PRIORY 🦋

DONCASTER ROAD, WAKEFIELD, WEST YORKSHIRE WF4 1QE

www.nationaltrust.org.uk

Tel: 01924 863892 **Fax:** 01924 865282

Owner: The National Trust   **Contact:** The Property Manager

Nostell Priory, one of Yorkshire's finest jewels, is an 18th century architectural masterpiece by James Paine. The State Rooms were later completed by Robert Adam and are amongst the finest examples of his interiors. The Priory houses one of England's finest collections of Chippendale furniture, designed specially for the house.

Location: OS Ref. SE403 175. 6m SE of Wakefield, off A638.

Open: 2 - 17 Mar: Sat & Sun. Grounds, Shop & Tearoom: 11am - 4pm. 23 Mar - 3 Nov: Wed - Sun (open Good Fri & BH Mons incl. 3 Jun), 1 - 5.30pm. Grounds: 11am - 6pm. Shop & Tearoom: 11am - 5.30pm. 9 Nov - 15 Dec: Sat & Sun, 12 noon - 4pm. Grounds, Shop & Tearoom: 11am - 4.30pm.

Admission: House & Gardens: Adult £4.50, Child £2.20, Family £11. Grounds only: Adult £2.50, Child £1.20. Guided tours for booked groups only, outside normal opening times: £250 min charge.

ⓘBaby facilities. 🍽 🖼 ♿Partial. WC. 🎥 🎦By arrangement. 🅿 🖼
🐾In grounds, on leads. ♨ 🐕Send SAE for details.

The National Trust

NUNNINGTON HALL ✻
NUNNINGTON, NORTH YORKSHIRE YO62 5UY

Tel: 01439 748283 **Fax:** 01439 748284

Owner: The National Trust　　　　　**Contact:** The Property Manager

The sheltered walled garden on the bank of the River Rye with its delightful mixed borders, orchards of traditional Ryedale fruit varieties and spring flowering meadows, complements this mellow 17th century manor house. From the magnificent oak-panelled hall, follow three staircases to discover family rooms, the nursery, the haunted room and the attics, with their fascinating Carlisle collection of miniature rooms fully furnished to reflect different periods.

Location: OS Ref. SE670 795. In Ryedale, 4¹/₂ m SE of Helmsley, 1¹/₂ m N of B1257.

Open: Mar, Apr, May, Sept, Oct & Nov: Wed - Sun (open BH Mons); Hall & Shop: 1.30 - 4.30pm (last admission 5pm May & Sept); Tearoom & Garden: open 12.30pm. Jun, Jul & Aug: Tue - Sun (open BH Mons & 3 Jun): Hall & Shop: 1.30 - 5pm (last admission), Tearoom & Garden: open 12.30pm.

Admission: House and Garden: Adult £4.50, Child £2. Family (2+3) £11. Garden only: Adult £2, Child Free. Groups (15+): £4. NT members Free.

🖻 ♿ Ground floor and grounds. WC. 🖼 🐕 Guide dogs only. 📷 Tel for details.

NT/Libby Conway

ORMESBY HALL ✻
LADGATE LANE, ORMESBY, MIDDLESBROUGH TS7 9AS

Tel: 01642 324188 **Fax:** 01642 300937 **e-mail:** yorkor@smtp.ntrust.org.uk

Owner: The National Trust　　　　　**Contact:** The House Manager

A mid 18th century house with opulent decoration inside, including fine plasterwork by contemporary craftsmen. A Jacobean doorway with a carved family crest survives from the earlier house on the site. The stable block, attributed to Carr of York, is a particularly fine mid 18th century building with an attractive courtyard leased to the Mounted Police; also an attractive garden with holly walk.

Location: OS Ref. NZ530 167. 3m SE of Middlesbrough.

Open: 24 Mar- 3 Nov: daily except Mons, Fris & Sats (open Good Fri & BH Mons), 2 - 5pm. Garden tours, last Thur of each month (please enquire for further details).

Admission: House, garden, model railway and exhibitions: Adult £3.50, Child £1.70, Family £8.50. Garden, railway and exhibitions: Adult £2.20, Child £1.

🖻 ♿ Ground floor & grounds. WC. 🖼

OAKWELL HALL COUNTRY PARK
Nutter Lane, Birstall, Batley, West Yorkshire WF17 9LG

Tel: 01924 326240 **Fax:** 01924 326249

Owner: Kirklees Cultural Services

Location: OS99 Ref. SE217 271. On A652 in Birstall. Take J27/A62 towards Huddersfield to Birstall.

Open: All year: Mon - Fri, 11am - 5pm. Sats & Suns, 12 noon - 5pm.

Admission: Adult £1.40, Child 50p, Family £3. Discounts for booked groups. Admission charge seasonal - 2001/2 prices.

OLD SLENINGFORD HALL
Ripon, North Yorkshire HG4 3JD

Tel: 01765 635229 **Fax:** 01765 635485 **e-mail:** james@oldslen.fsnet.co.uk

　　　　　　　　　　　　　　　　　Contact: Mrs Ramsden

Unusual garden with extensive lawns, interesting trees, lake and islands watermill in walled kitchen garden and Victorian fernery.

Location: OS99 Ref. SE265 768. From Ripon on A6108. After North Stainley take 2nd left, follow signs to Mickley for 1m from main road.

Open: Spring BH Sun & Mon, Whit BH Sun & Mon. Also all year by appointment.

Admission: Adult £2.50, Child 50p.

PARCEVALL HALL GARDENS
Skyreholme, Skipton, North Yorkshire BD23 6DE

Tel: 01756 720311　　　　　**Contact:** Phillip Nelson (Head Gardener)

Owner: Walsingham College (Yorkshire Properties) Ltd.

Location: OS Ref. SE068 613. E side of Upper Wharfedale, 1¹/₂ m NE of Appletreewick. 12m NNW of Ilkley by B6160 and via Burnsall.

Open: 1 Apr - 31 Oct: 10am - 6pm.

Admission: £3, Child 50p. (Prices subject to increase in 2002.)

PICKERING CASTLE ⌗
Pickering, North Yorkshire YO18 7AX

Tel: 01751 474989

Owner: English Heritage　　　　　**Contact:** The Custodian

A splendid motte and bailey castle, once a royal ranch. It is well preserved, with much of the original walls, towers and keep, and there are spectacular views over the surrounding countryside. There is an exhibition on the castle's history.

Location: OS100 Ref. SE800 845. In Pickering, 15m SW of Scarborough.

Open: 29 Mar - 30 Sept: daily, 10am - 6pm. 1 - 31 Oct: daily, 10am - 5pm. 1 Nov - 31 Mar: Wed - Sun, 10am - 4pm (closed 1 - 2pm). Closed 24 - 26 Dec & 1 Jan.

Admission: Adult £2.50, Child £1.30, Conc. £1.90, Family £6.30. 15% discount for groups (11+).

🖻 ♿ Partial. 🅿 Limited. ■ 🐕 In grounds, on leads. ❄

PLUMPTON ROCKS
Plumpton, Knaresborough, North Yorkshire HG5 8NA

Tel: 01423 863950

Owner: Edward de Plumpton Hunter　　　**Contact:** Robert de Plumpton Hunter

Grade II* listed garden extending to over 30 acres including an idyllic lake, dramatic millstone grit rock formation, romantic woodland walks winding through bluebells and rhododendrons. Declared by English Heritage to be of outstanding interest. Painted by Turner. Described by Queen Mary as 'Heaven on earth'.

Location: OS Ref. SE355 535. Midway between Harrogate and Wetherby on the A661, 1m SE of A661 junction with the Harrogate southern bypass.

Open: Mar - Oct: Sat, Sun & BHs, 11am - 6pm.

Admission: Adult £1.50, Child/OAP £1, Student £1.50.

♿ Unsuitable. 🅍 By arrangement. 🅿 Limited for coaches. ■ 🐕 In grounds, on leads.

Special Events Index
◁ ◁ ◁ pgs 40-43

© English Heritage Photo Library

RHS HARLOW CARR

CRAG LANE, HARROGATE, NORTH YORKSHIRE HG3 1QB

www.rhs.org.uk

Tel: 01423 565418 **Fax:** 01423 530663 **e-mail:** moiram@harlowcarr.fsnet.co.uk

Owner: Royal Horticultural Society   **Contact:** Property Manager

Fifty eight acres of vegetable, fruit and flower trials, rock, foliage, scented, winter and heather gardens, alpines, herbaceous beds, display houses, streamside, woodland and arboretum. Museum of Gardening, National Collections, Model Village, library and children's play area. Fully licensed café bar, restaurant and The Harlow Carr Plant Centre and Shop.

Location: OS Ref. SE285 543. 1¹/2m W from town centre on B6162.

Open: Daily: 9.30am - 6pm or dusk if earlier.

Admission: Adult £4.50, Child (11-16yrs) £1, Child (under 11yrs) Free, OAPs £3.50. Groups (20+): £3.50.

ℹ️Picnic area. 📷 ⚙️ ♿Partial. WC. 🍴Licensed. 🍴Licensed. 📷By arrangement. ■ 🐕Guide dogs only. ✱ ☎Tel for details.

RICHMOND CASTLE ⌗

RICHMOND, NORTH YORKSHIRE DL10 4QW

Tel: 01748 822493

Owner: English Heritage   **Contact:** The Custodian

A splendid medieval fortress, with a fine 12th century keep and 11th century remains of the curtain wall and domestic buildings. There are magnificent views from the 100 feet high keep. Exciting interactive exhibition brings the history of the site alive. A new contemporary heritage garden opens in a contemplative setting with stunning views.

Location: OS92 Ref. NZ174 006. In Richmond.

Open: 29 Mar - 30 Sept: daily, 10am - 6pm. (17 Jul - 31 Aug: 9.30am - 7pm) 1 - 31 Oct: daily, 10am - 5pm. 1 Nov - 28 Mar: daily, 10am - 1pm & 2 - 4pm (9 - 16 Feb: 10am - 5pm). Closed 24- 26 Dec & 1 Jan.

Admission: Adult £2.90, Child £1.50, Conc. £2.20. 15% discount for groups (11+). ℹ️New interactive exhibition. 📷 ♿Partial. ■ 🐕In grounds, on leads. ✱ ☎Tel for details.

English Heritage Photo Library

RIEVAULX ABBEY ⌗

RIEVAULX, Nr HELMSLEY, NORTH YORKSHIRE YO6 5LB

Tel: 01439 798228

Owner: English Heritage   **Contact:** The Custodian

In a deeply wooded valley by the River Rye you can see some of the most spectacular monastic ruins in England, dating from the 12th century. The church has the earliest large Cistercian nave in Britain. A fascinating exhibition shows how successfully the Cistercians at Rievaulx ran their many businesses and explains the part played by Abbot Ailred, who ruled for twenty years. New interactive museum, exhibition and interactive display.

Location: OS100 Ref. SE577 849. 2¹/4 m W of Helmsley on minor road off B1257.

Open: 29 Mar - 30 Sept: daily, 10am - 6pm (17 Jul - 31 Aug: 9.30am - 6pm). 1 - 31 Oct: daily, 10am - 5pm. 1 Nov - 31 Mar: daily, 10am - 4pm (9 - 16 Feb: 10am - 5pm). Closed 24- 26 Dec & 1 Jan.

Admission: Adult £3.60, Child £1.80, Conc. £2.70. 15% discount for groups (11+). 📷 ♿Partial. 📷 🅿 ■ 🐕On leads. ✱ ☎Tel for details.

The National Trust

RIEVAULX TERRACE & TEMPLES ✂

RIEVAULX, HELMSLEY, NORTH YORKSHIRE YO62 5LJ

Tel: 01439 748283 **Fax:** 01439 748284

Owner: The National Trust　　　**Contact:** The Property Manager

A ¹/₂ m long grass-covered terrace and adjoining woodlands with vistas over Rievaulx Abbey (English Heritage) and Rye valley to Ryedale and the Hambleton Hills. There are two mid-18th century temples: the Ionic Temple has elaborate ceiling paintings and fine 18th century furniture. Note: no access to property Nov - end Mar.

Location: OS Ref. SE579 848. 2¹/₂ m NW of Helmsley on B1257. E of the Abbey.

Open: 23 Mar - 3 Nov: daily, 10.30am - 6pm (5pm Oct & Nov). Last admission 1hr before closing. Ionic Temple closed 1 - 2pm. Events: for details contact Property Secretary at Nunnington Hall, tel. 01439 748283.

Admission: Adult £3.30, Child £1.50, Family (2+3) £8. Groups (15+): £2.80. NT members Free.

🖼 ⬧Grounds. Batricar available. ⬧In grounds, on leads. ☎ Tel for details.

RYEDALE FOLK MUSEUM

Hutton le Hole, York, North Yorkshire YO62 6UA

Tel: 01751 417367

Owner: The Crosland Foundation　　　**Contact:** Martin Watts

13 historic buildings showing the lives of ordinary folk from earliest times to the present day.

Location: OS Ref. SE705 902. Follow signs from Hutton le Hole. 3m N of Kirkbymoorside.

Open: 10 Mar - 3 Nov: 10am - 5.30pm last admission 4.30pm.

Admission: Adult £3.25, Child £1.75, Conc. £2.75, Family (2+2) £8.25 (2001 prices).

ST WILLIAM'S COLLEGE

5 College Street, York YO1 7JF

Tel: 01904 557233 **Fax:** 01904 557234

Owner: The Dean and Chapter of York　　　**Contact:** Sandie Clarke

15th century medieval home of Minster Chantry Priests. Three large medieval halls.

Location: OS Ref. SE605 522. College Street, York. Adjoining E end of York Minster.

Open: 10am - 5pm.

Admission: Adult 60p, Child 30p. For further details please telephone.

SCAMPSTON HALL 🏛

Scampston, Malton, North Yorkshire YO17 8NG

Tel: 01944 758224 **Fax:** 01944 758700

e-mail: info@scampston.co.uk **www**.scampston.co.uk

Owner/Contact: Sir Charles Legard Bt

Opened for the first time in 1997, this country house has remained in the same family since it was built towards the end of the 17th century. The house was extensively remodelled in 1801 by the architect Thomas Leverton and has fine Regency interiors. It houses an important collection of works of art including pictures by Gainsborough, Marlow, Scott and Wilson. The park was laid out under the guidance of 'Capability' Brown and includes 10 acres of lakes and a Palladian bridge. The garden features a recently restored 19th century walk in rock and water garden with a collection of alpines, some of which are available for sale.

Location: OS100 Ref. SE865 755. 5m E of Malton, off A64.

Open: 26 May - 9 Jun & 21 Jul - 4 Aug (closed Sats), 1.30 - 5pm. Last admission 4.30pm.

Admission: House & Garden: £5, Garden £2, no concessions. Groups and coaches by appointment only. Prices for groups by arrangement. Friends of the HHA admitted free.

♿ ⬧Unsuitable. ⬧ 🎫Guided tours only. ✖

RIPLEY CASTLE 🏛

See page 372 for full page entry.

RIPON CATHEDRAL

Ripon, North Yorkshire HG4 1QR

Tel: 01765 604108 (information on tours etc.) **e-mail:** postmaster@riponcathedral.org.uk

　　　Contact: Canon Keith Punshon

One of the oldest crypts in Europe (672). Marvellous choir stalls and misericords (500 years old). Almost every type of architecture. Treasury.

Location: OS Ref. SE314 711. 5m W signposted off A1, 12m N of Harrogate.

Open: All year: 8am - 6pm.

Admission: Donations. £2 per head pre-booked guided tours.

RIPON WORKHOUSE

Allhallowgate, Ripon, North Yorkshire

Tel: 01765 690799　　　**Contact:** Mr D Gowling

The workhouse shows restored vagrants' wards and the treatment of paupers.

Location: OS Ref. SE312 712 Close to Market Square.

Open: 7 Apr - 28 Oct: daily, 11am - 4pm.

Admission: Adult £1.25, Child (6 - 16yrs) 75p, Child under 6yrs Free, Conc./Student £1.

ROCHE ABBEY 🏛

Maltby, Rotherham, South Yorkshire S66 8NW

Tel: 01709 812739

Owner: English Heritage　　　**Contact:** The Custodian

This Cistercian monastery, founded in 1147, lies in a secluded landscaped valley sheltered by limestone cliffs and trees. Some of the walls still stand to their full height and excavation has revealed the complete layout of the abbey.

Location: OS111 Ref. SK544 898. 1m S of Maltby off A634.

Open: 29 Mar - 30 Sept: daily, 10am - 6pm. 1 - 31 Oct: daily, 10am - 5pm.

Admission: Adult £1.70, Child 90p, Conc. £1.30. 15% discount for groups (11+).

⬧Partial. 🅿 Limited. ⬧ ⬧In grounds, on leads. ☎ Tel for details.

English Heritage Photo Library

SCARBOROUGH CASTLE ⊞

CASTLE ROAD, SCARBOROUGH, NORTH YORKSHIRE YO11 1HY

Tel: 01723 372451

Owner: English Heritage　　　**Contact:** The Custodian

Spectacular coastal views from the walls of this enormous 12th century castle. The buttressed castle walls stretch out along the cliff edge and remains of the great rectangular stone keep still stand to over three storeys high. There is also the site of a 4th century Roman signal station. The castle was frequently attacked, but despite being blasted by cannons of the Civil War and bombarded from the sea during World War I, it is still a spectacular place to visit.

Location: OS101, Ref. TA050 893. Castle Road, E of town centre.

Open: 29 Mar - 30 Sept: daily, 10am - 6pm (17 Jul - 31 Aug: 9.30am - 6pm). 1 - 31 Oct: daily, 10am - 5pm. 1 Nov - 31 Mar: daily, 10am - 4pm (closed 1 - 2 pm) (9 - 16 Feb: 10am - 5pm). Closed 24 - 26 Dec & 1 Jan.

Admission: Adult £2.80, Child £1.40, Conc. £2.10, Family £7. 15% discount for groups (11+).

🖼 ⬧Partial. ⬧ 🎫Inclusive. ⬧ ⬧In grounds, on leads. ✱ ☎ Tel for details.

SEWERBY HALL & GARDENS

Church Lane, Sewerby, Bridlington, East Yorkshire YO15 1EA

Tel: 01262 673769 **Fax:** 01262 673090 **e-mail:** sewerbyhall@yahoo.com
www.bridlington.net/sewerby

Owner: East Riding of Yorkshire Council   **Contact:** Customer Service Officer

Sewerby Hall and Gardens, set in 50 acres of parkland, dates back to 1715. The Georgian house contains: 19th century orangery; history/archaeology displays; art galleries and an Amy Johnson Room. The Grounds include: walled gardens, woodland, children's zoo and play area, golf and putting.

Location: OS Ref. TA203 690. 2m N of Bridlington in Sewerby village.

Open: Please telephone for details.

Admission: Please telephone for admission prices.

🖼️ 🛉 🍵 ⏳ 🍽️Licensed. 🅿️ 🍽️ 🦽In grounds, on leads. Guide dogs in hall. 🔺 🛏️Tel for details.

SHIBDEN HALL

Lister's Road, Halifax, West Yorkshire HX3 6XG

Tel: 01422 352246 **Fax:** 01422 348440 **www.**calderdale.gov.uk

Owner: Calderdale MBC   **Contact:** Valerie Stansfield

A half-timbered manor house, the home of Anne Lister set in a landscaped park. Oak furniture, carriages and an array of objects make Shibden an intriguing place to visit.

Location: OS Ref. SE106 257. 1¹/₂ m E of Halifax off A58.

Open: 1 Mar - 30 Nov: Mon - Sat, 10am - 5pm. Suns, 12 noon - 5pm. Last admission 4.30pm. Dec - Feb: Mon - Sat, 10am - 4pm. Suns, 12 noon - 4pm.

Admission: Adult £2.50, Child/Conc. £1.50, Family £6. Prices subject to change Apr 2002.

🖼️ ⏳ Ground floor & grounds. 🍽️ 🅿️ 🍽️ 🦽Guide dogs only. ❄️

SHANDY HALL

COXWOLD, YORK YO61 4AD

www.shandy-hall.org.uk

Tel/Fax: 01347 868465

Owner: The Laurence Sterne Trust   **Contact:** Mrs J Monkman

Here in 1760-1767 the witty and eccentric parson Laurence Sterne wrote *Tristam Shandy* and *A Sentimental Journey*. Shandy Hall was built as a timber-framed open-hall in the 15th century and added to by Sterne in the 18th century. Not a museum but a lived-in house where you are sure of a personal welcome. Surrounded by a walled garden full of old-fashioned roses and cottage garden plants. Also an acre of wild garden in adjoining old quarry. May - Sept: exhibitions; paintings & pots by local artists.

Location: OS Ref. SE531 773. W end of Coxwold village, 4m E of A19 between Easingwold and Thirsk. 20m N of York.

Open: 1 May - 30 Sept: Weds, 2 - 4.30pm. Suns, 2.30 - 4.30pm. Garden: 1 May - 30 Sept: Sun - Fri, 11am - 4.30pm.

Admission: Hall & Garden: Adult £4.50, Child £1.50. Garden only: Adult £2.50, Child £1.

ℹ️No photography in house. 🖼️ 🛉 ⏳Partial. 🍽️In nearby village. 📷Obligatory. 🅿️ 🦽

SION HILL HALL 🏛️

KIRBY WISKE, THIRSK, NORTH YORKSHIRE YO7 4EU

www.sionhillhall.co.uk

Tel: 01845 587206 **Fax:** 01845 587486
e-mail: enquiries.sionhall@virgin.net

Owner: H W Mawer Trust   **Contact:** R M Mallaby

Designed in 1912 by the renowned York architect Walter H Brierley, 'the Lutyens of the North', receiving an award from the Royal Institute of British Architects as being of 'outstanding architectural merit'. Sion Hill contains the H W Mawer collection of fine furniture, porcelain, paintings and clocks in superb settings.

Location: OS Ref. SE373 844. 6m S of Northallerton off A167, signposted. 4m W of Thirsk, 6m E of A1 via A61.

Open: June - Aug: Weds only, 1 - 5pm, last entry 4pm. Also Easter Sun & Mon and all BH Mons. Guided/Connoisseur tours at any time May - Oct by arrangement.

Admission: House: Adult £4.50, Child 12 - 16yrs, £2, Child under 12yrs £1, Conc. £4. Guided tours: £5.75 per person. Connoisseur Tours: £8.50pp. Grounds: £1.50. ⏳Partial. WC. 🅿️

SKIPTON CASTLE   *See page 373 for full page entry.*

Plant Sales Index
◁ ◁ ◁ pgs 36-37

SLEDMERE HOUSE 🏛

SLEDMERE, DRIFFIELD, EAST YORKSHIRE YO25 3XG

Tel: 01377 236637 **Fax:** 01377 236500

Owner: Sir Tatton Sykes Bt   **Contact:** Mrs Anne Hines

Sledmere House is the home of Sir Tatton Sykes, 8th Baronet. There has been a manor house at Sledmere since medieval times. The present house was designed and built by Sir Christopher Sykes, 2nd Baronet, a diary date states "June 17th, 1751 laid the first stone of the new house at Sledmere." Sir Christopher employed a fellow Yorkshireman, Joseph Rose, the most famous English plasterer of his day, to execute the decoration of Sledmere. Rose's magnificent work at Sledmere was unique in his career. A great feature at Sledmere is the 'Capability' Brown parkland and the beautiful 18th century walled rose gardens. Also worthy of note is the recently laid out knot-garden, all accessible by wheelchair.

Location: OS Ref. SE931 648. Off the A166 between York & Bridlington. ¹/₂ hr drive from York, Bridlington & Scarborough.

Open: 29 Mar - 1 Apr & 5 May - 22 Sept: closed Mons & Sats except BHs: 11.30am - 4.30pm. Famous pipe organ played Weds, Fris & Suns.

Admission: House & Gardens: Adult £4.50, Child £2, OAP £4. Gardens & Park: Adult £2, Child £1.

ⓘNo photography in house. 🅿Licensed. 🅕By arrangement. 🅿 In grounds on leads. Guide dogs in house. 🔺

Shibden Hall

Patrick Lane

SPOFFORTH CASTLE ⌗

Harrogate, North Yorkshire

Tel: 01904 601901

Owner: English Heritage   **Contact:** The Northern Regional Office

This manor house has some fascinating features including an undercroft built into the rock. It was once owned by the Percy family.

Location: OS Ref. SE360 511. 3¹/₂ m SE of Harrogate on minor road off A661 at Spofforth.

Open: 29 Mar - 30 Sept: daily, 10am - 6pm. 1 - 31 Oct: daily, 10am - 6pm or dusk if earlier. 1 Nov - 31 Mar: 10am - 4pm. Closed 24 - 26 Dec & 1 Jan.

Admission: Free.

STOCKELD PARK 🏛

WETHERBY, NORTH YORKSHIRE LS22 4AH

Tel: 01937 586101 **Fax:** 01937 580084

Owner: Mr and Mrs P G F Grant   **Contact:** Mrs L A Saunders

Stockeld is a beautifully proportioned Palladian villa designed by James Paine in 1763, featuring a magnificent cantilevered staircase in the central oval hall. Stockeld is still very much a family home, with a fine collection of 18th and 19th century furniture and paintings. The house is surrounded by lovely gardens of lawns, large herbaceous and shrub borders, fringed by woodland, and set in 100 acres of fine parkland in the midst of an extensive farming estate.

Location: OS Ref. SE376 497. York 12m, Harrogate 5m, Leeds 12m.

Open: 18 Apr - 17 Oct: Thurs only, 2 - 5pm. Groups please book.

Admission: Adult £4.50. Group prices on application.

🅖House only. 🅕Obligatory. 🅧

STUDLEY ROYAL: ST MARY'S CHURCH ⌗

Ripon, North Yorkshire

Tel: 01765 608888

Owner: English Heritage   **Contact:** The Custodian

A magnificent Victorian church, designed by William Burges in the 1870s, with a highly decorated interior. Coloured marble, stained glass, gilded and painted figures and a splendid organ.

Location: OS Ref. SE278 703. 2¹/₂ m W of Ripon off B6265, in grounds of Studley Royal estate.

Open: 29 Mar - 30 Sept: daily, 1 - 5pm.

Admission: Free.

Website Information ◁ ◁ ◁ pg 39

SUTTON PARK 🏠

SUTTON-ON-THE-FOREST, NORTH YORKSHIRE YO61 1DP

www.statelyhome.co.uk

Tel: 01347 810249/811239 **Fax:** 01347 811251 **e-mail:** suttonpark@fsbdial.co.uk

Owner: Sir Reginald & Lady Sheffield   **Contact:** Mrs A Wilkinson

The Yorkshire home of Sir Reginald and Lady Sheffield. Charming example of early Georgian architecture. Magnificent plasterwork by Cortese. Rich collection of 18th century furniture, paintings, porcelain, needlework, beadwork. All put together with great style to make a most inviting house. Award winning gardens attract enthusiasts from home and abroad.

Location: OS Ref. SE583 646. 8m N of York on B1363 York - Helmsley Road.

Open: House: Good Friday - Easter Monday, 29 Mar - 1 Apr then Wed & Sun until end Sept, plus all BH Mons. 1.30 - 5pm. Tearoom: as house, 12 noon - 5pm. Teas & buffet suppers for booked groups. Private Groups: Any other day by appointment. House open Oct - Mar for private groups only. Gardens: Easter - end Sept, daily, 11am - 5pm.

Admission: House & Garden: Adult £5, Child £2.50, Conc. £4. Gardens only: Adult £2.50, Child 50p, Conc. £1.50. Coach parties: £4.50. Gardens only £2. Private Groups (15+): £5.50. Caravans: £5 per night. Electric hookup: £6.50 per night.

ℹ️No photography. 🍴Hosted lunches & dinners. ♿Partial. 📷 ⓕObligatory. 🅿️Limited for coaches. ⬚ 🛏️23 double with ensuite bathrooms. 📺Tel for details.

TREASURER'S HOUSE 🌿

MINSTER YARD, YORK, NORTH YORKSHIRE YO1 7JL

Tel: 01904 624247 **Fax:** 01904 647372 **e-mail:** yorkth@smtp.ntrust.org.uk

Owner: The National Trust   **Contact:** The Property Manager

Named after the Treasurer of York Minster and built over a Roman road, the house is not all that it seems! Nestled behind the Minster, the size and splendour and contents of the house are a constant surprise to visitors – as are the famous ghost stories. Free trails for children and free access to the National Trust tearoom.

Location: OS Ref. SE604 523. The N side of York Minster. Entrance on Chapter House St.

Open: 23 Mar - 3 Nov: daily except Fri, 11am - 4.30pm. Last adm. 4.30pm.

Admission: Adult £3.80, Child £2. Family £9.50. Booked groups (15+): Adult £3, Child £1.50.

🍴 ♿Partial. WC. 📷Licensed. 🍴Licensed. 🅿️None. ⬛ 🐕In grounds, on leads. ▲

TEMPLE NEWSAM HOUSE

Leeds LS15 0AE

Tel: 0113 2647321 **Fax:** 0113 2602285

Owner: Leeds City Council   **Contact:** Denise Lawson

A Tudor-Jacobean mansion with over thirty rooms open to the public.

Location: OS Ref. SE358 321. 5m E of city centre, off A63 Selby Road. M1/J46.

Open: House closed to the general public during building repair project. Special groups by appointment, subject to Health & Safety.

Admission: Groups (15+): Adult £1, Child 50p.

THORNTON ABBEY ⛫

Scunthorpe, Humberside

Tel: 01904 601901

Owner: English Heritage   **Contact:** The Yorkshire Regional Office

The magnificent brick gatehouse of this ruined Augustine priory stands three storeys high.

Location: OS Ref. TA115 190. 18m NE of Scunthorpe on minor road N of A180.

Open: 29 Mar - 30 Sept: 1st & 3rd Suns, 12 - 6pm. 1 Oct - 31 Mar: 3rd Suns, 12 - 4pm.

Admission: Free.

THORP PERROW ARBORETUM & 🏠
THE FALCONS OF THORP PERROW

Bedale, North Yorkshire DL8 2PR

Tel/Fax: 01677 425323

e-mail: louise@thorpperrow.freeserve.co.uk **www**.thorpperrow.com

Owner: Sir John Ropner Bt   **Contact:** Louise McNeill

85 acres of woodland walks. One of the largest collections of trees and shrubs in the north of England, including a 16th century medieval spring wood and 19th century pinetum. The Falcons of Thorp Perrow, an additional attraction which opened spring 2000. Various trails available, playground with mini beast station, tearoom and plant centre.

Location: OS Ref. SE258 851. Bedale - Ripon road, S of Bedale, 4m from Leeming Bar on A1.

Open: All year: dawn - dusk.

Admission: Arboretum & Falcons: Adult £5.25, Child £2.75, OAP £4, Family (2+2) £15, (2+4) £19.

ℹ️Picnic area. Children's playground. 📷 ⬚ ♿Partial. 📷Licensed. ⓕBy arrangement. 🅿️Limited for coaches. ⬛ 🐕In grounds, on leads. ❄️ 📺Tel for details.

WAKEFIELD CATHEDRAL

Northgate, Wakefield, West Yorkshire WF1 1HG

Tel: 01924 373923 **Fax:** 01924 215054

Owner: Church of England   **Contact:** Mr F Arnold, Head Verger

Built on the site of a previous Saxon church, this 14th century Parish Church became a cathedral in 1888.

Location: OS Ref. SE333 208. Wakefield city centre. M1/ J39-41, M62/J29W, J30 E.

Open: Mon - Sat: 8am - 5pm. Suns: between services only. For service details contact Cathedral.

Admission: Free admission. Donations welcome.

WENTWORTH CASTLE GARDENS

Lowe Lane, Stainborough, Barnsley, South Yorkshire S75 3ET

Tel: 01226 731269

Owner: Barnsley MBC   **Contact:** Chris Margrave

300 years old, these gardens are the only Grade I listed gardens in South Yorkshire, 28 listed buildings and monuments and the National Collections of rhododendrons, magnolias and williamsii camellias.

Location: OS Ref. SE320 034. 5km W of Barnsley, M1/J36 via Birdwell & Rockley Lane then Lowe Lane.

Open: Mid April - end June, mainly by guided tours. Please telephone 01226 731269 for a recorded message.

Admission: £2.50, Conc. £2.

Open All Year Index
◁ ◁ ◁ pgs 44-48

Yorkshire & The Humber - England

WHITBY ABBEY ⌗

WHITBY, NORTH YORKSHIRE YO22 4JT

Tel: 01947 603568

Owner: English Heritage   **Contact:** The Custodian

An ancient holy place, once a burial place of kings and an inspiration for saints. A religious community was first established at Whitby in 657 by Abbess Hilda and was the home of Caedmon, the first English poet. The remains we can see today are of a Benedictine church built in the 13th and 14th centuries, and include a magnificent three-tiered choir and north transept. It is perched high above the picturesque harbour town of Whitby. A new museum has been created within the 17th century banqueting hall exploring the 1500 year old story of the Abbey and town as never before.

Location: OS94, Ref. NZ904 115. On cliff top E of Whitby.

Open: 29 Mar - 30 Sept: daily 10am - 6pm. 17 Jul - 31 Aug: 9.30am - 6pm. 1 - 31 Oct: daily, 10am - 5pm. 1 Nov - 31 Mar: daily, 10am - 4pm. 9 - 16 Feb: 10am - 5pm. Closed 24 - 26 Dec & 1 Jan.

Admission: Adult £3.60, Child £1.80, Conc. £2.70, Family £9. 15% discounts for groups (11+).

🗑 ♿Ground floor. ■ 🐕In grounds, on leads. ❄ ♨Tel for details.

YORK GATE GARDEN

BACK CHURCH LANE, ADEL, LEEDS, WEST YORKSHIRE LS16 8DW

www.gardeners-grbs.org.uk

Tel: 0113 2678240

Owner/Contact: The Gardeners' Royal Benevolent Society

One acre masterpiece demonstrating the very best of 20th century English garden design. A series of smaller gardens, separated by hedges and walls, are linked by a succession of delightful vistas. Exquisite detail. Rare and interesting plants.

Location: OS Ref. 275 403. 2$^{1}/_{4}$m SE of Bramhope. $^{1}/_{2}$m E of A660.

Open: May - Sept: Thur, Sun & BH Mons, 2 - 5pm.

Admission: Adult £3, Child Free.

ℹ Coach parties must book. ♿Partial. 🚹By arrangement. 🅿Limited. 🐕Guide dogs only.

WHITE SCAR CAVE   *See page 374 for full page entry.*

WILBERFORCE HOUSE

High Street, Hull, East Yorkshire HU1 1NQ

Tel: 01482 613902 **Fax:** 01482 613710

Owner: Hull City Council   **Contact:** S R Green

Built c1660 the house is a museum to the memory of William Wilberforce.

Location: OS Ref. TA102 286. High Street, Hull.

Open: Mon - Sat, 10am - 5pm. Suns, 1.30 - 4.30pm. Closed Good Fri & Christmas Day.

Admission: Free.

WORTLEY HALL

Wortley, Sheffield, South Yorkshire S35 7DB

Tel: 0114 2882100 **Fax:** 0114 2830695

Owner: Labour, Co-operative & Trade Union Movement   **Contact:** John Howard

15 acres of formal Italianate gardens surrounded by 11 acres of informal pleasure grounds.

Location: OS Ref. SK313 995. 10kms S of Barnsley in Wortley on A629.

Open: Gardens: All year except 7 - 14 Aug & 6 - 13 Nov.

Admission: Free. Groups must book for gardeners' tour, £1.50.

YORK MINSTER

Deangate, York YO1 7HH

Tel: 01904 557216 **Fax:** 01904 557218

Owner: Dean and Chapter of York   **Contact:** Dorothy Lee, Visitors' Officer

Large gothic church housing the largest collection of medieval stained glass in England.

Location: OS Ref. SE603 522. Centre of York.

Open: Nov - Mar: 7am - 6pm, Apr: 7am - 6.30pm, May: 7am - 7.30pm, Jun - Aug: 7am - 8.30pm, Sept: 7am - 8pm, Oct: 7am - 7pm, daily. Open afternoons only on Suns.

Admission: By donation. Tour companies £4 per person, Child (6-16yrs) £1.

Hovingham Hall

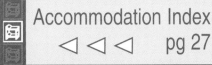

Accommodation Index
◁ ◁ ◁   pg 27

Hutton-in-the-Forest

North **West**

Lord and Lady Inglewood

Hutton-in-the-Forest

"*For me and my family – my wife Cressida and our children Miranda,
Rosa and Henry – Hutton-in-the-Forest is first and foremost our home,
albeit hardly a conventional one.*"

Richard, 2nd Baron Inglewood

Lord and Lady Inglewood

Lord and Lady Inglewood

Lord and Lady Inglewood

Lord and Lady Inglewood

Lord and Lady Inglewood

Lord and Lady Inglewood

Lord and Lady Inglewood

As one commentator aptly put it, in country houses as in everything else fashions change, and nowhere is this more evident than in the architecture of Hutton-in-the-Forest.

Seeing Hutton for the first time it is almost bewildering for its differing styles. These span over five centuries and reflect the contributions of the three families which have been linked with Hutton during this time; the de Huttons who arrived in the late 13th century; the Fletchers, rich merchants from Cockermouth to whom the de Huttons sold the property in 1606; and the Vanes, forebears of the present Lord Inglewood, to whom it passed by descent in about 1720.

The oldest part of the house is the 14th century pele tower, built as a refuge for the de Hutton family from raiders across the border. By the 17th century Cumbria had become a far more peaceful part of England and to the north of the pele tower is a wing of the 1630s built by the Fletcher family, who started the process of converting Hutton from a castle into a country house. It was at this time that the moat was filled in. To the east is a square Baroque front of c1685. Beyond this front is a heavy crenellated sandstone tower remodelled in the medieval style in 1826 by Anthony Salvin then enlarged in the 1870s, which is taller than the rest of the house and stands rather like an exclamation mark over the whole building.

One of the charms of Hutton is that most of the different parts of the building are by local architects and each has its own appeal. The north wing by Alexander Pogmire contains the long gallery which shows the influence of some of the great Elizabethan and Jacobean houses of the south of England. The gallery is, in fact, a rare example to be seen in the north. The swaggering Baroque centre of the main front was designed by Edward Addison, a little-known Cumbrian architect, and is also one of the earliest examples of this style in the north.

The interiors at Hutton may be less spectacular but are nonetheless at least as interesting in their own right. They, like the exterior, are a mixture of styles and periods, the rooms have some very fine English furniture and portraits, together with family mementoes acquired over the years by the Vanes.

However, it is the garden which does so much to make a visit to Hutton-in-the-Forest so memorable and enjoyable. Lord and Lady Inglewood have invested much time and thought into the planting schemes throughout the gardens. The walled garden, which dates from the 1730s is divided into compartments with wide herbaceous borders creating a riot of colour during the summer.

Hutton is a house to enjoy at your leisure and provides a wonderful day out ... visit the Cloistered Tea Room or take your picnic and make the most of not only a magnificent Cumbrian house but the beautiful grounds, walks and countryside that surround it. ✠

For further details about *Hutton-in-the-Forest* see entry on page 415.

Lord and Lady Inglewood

Lord and Lady Inglewood

ADLINGTON HALL

MACCLESFIELD

www.adlingtonhall.com

Owner:
Mrs C J C Legh

▶ **CONTACT**

Corporate Enquiries:
Julian Langlands-Perry
or Tessa Quayle
The Estate Office
Adlington Hall
Macclesfield
Cheshire SK10 4LF

Tel: 01625 829206
Fax: 01625 828756

e-mail: enquiries@
adlingtonhall.com

Hall Tours:
The Guide
Tel: 01625 820875

▶ **LOCATION**

OS Ref. SJ905 804

5m N of
Macclesfield, A523,
13m S of Manchester.
London 178m.

Rail: Macclesfield
& Wilmslow
stations 5m.

Air: Manchester
Airport 8m.

Adlington Hall, the home of the Leghs of Adlington from 1315 to the present day, was built on the site of a Hunting Lodge which stood in the Forest of Macclesfield in 1040. Two oaks, part of the original building, remain with their roots in the ground and support the east end of the Great Hall, which was built between 1480 and 1505.

The Hall is a manor house, quadrangular in shape, and was once surrounded by a moat. Two sides of the Courtyard and the east wing were built in the typical 'Black and White' Cheshire style in 1581. The south front and west wing (containing the Drawing Room and Dining Room) were added between 1749 and 1757 and are built of red brick with a handsome stone portico with four Ionic columns on octagonal pedestals. Between the trees in the Great Hall stands an organ built by

'Father' Bernard Smith (c1670-80). Handel subsequently played on this instrument, and now fully restored, it is the largest 17th century organ in the country.

GARDENS

The gardens were landscaped in the style of 'Capability' Brown in the middle of the 18th century. Visitors may walk round the 'wilderness' area, among the follies to be seen are 'Temple to Diana', a 'Shell Cottage', Chinese bridge and T'ing house. There is a fine yew walk and a lime avenue planted in 1688. Old fashioned rose garden and yew maze recently planted. New in 2000 was a herbaceous border and woodlands area to enhance the North Lodge entrance. A water feature is planned for 2002 in the 'Father Tiber' garden.

Open to the public:
19 June - 4 September
Wed only, 2 - 5pm.

National Garden Scheme
opening: 14 July.

Also by prior arrangement
for groups throughout the
year. Please contact for
details.

▶ **ADMISSION**

Hall & Gardens

Adult	£4.50
Child	£1.75
Student	£1.75
Groups of 20+	£4.00

 Suitable for corporate events, product launches, business meetings, conferences, concerts, fashion shows, garden parties, rallies, clay-pigeon shooting and filming.

The Great Hall and Dining Room are available for corporate entertaining. Catering can be arranged.

Visitors may alight at entrance to Hall. WCs.

 By arrangement.

 For 100 cars and 4 coaches, 100 yds from Hall.

Schools welcome. Guide can be provided.

No dogs.

CONFERENCE/FUNCTION

ROOM	SIZE	MAX CAPACITY
Great Hall	11 x 8m	120
Dining Rm	10.75 x 7m	90
Courtyard	27 x 17m	300

ARLEY HALL & GARDENS

ARLEY

www.arleyestate.zuunet.co.uk

Set in a beautiful park, and surrounded by glorious gardens, Arley Hall is the home of Viscount and Viscountess Ashbrook, direct descendants of the Warburtons who came to Arley in the 15th century. The present house and chapel (designed by Salvin) were built between 1832 and 1845.

The Hall contains fine plasterwork and panelling, and historic furniture, pictures and porcelain. With its essentially family atmosphere it provides the perfect setting for receptions and other events and is licensed for weddings.

The gardens created by the family over the centuries contain a wide variety of design and plantings and rank among the finest in the country. The double herbaceous border laid out in 1846 is perhaps the oldest in England. Other features include the pleached lime avenue, the avenue of Quercus Ilex shaped like giant cylinders, and fine yew hedges as well as a collection of shrub roses, walled gardens and a herb garden. A woodland garden (the Grove) containing a large collection of rhododendrons and azaleas, and other ericaceous shrubs and exotic trees, has been developed over the past twenty years or so.

Arley stages many special events throughout the year including the Arley Garden Festival on 29th and 30th June.

Owner:
Viscount Ashbrook

▶ CONTACT

Estate Secretary
Arley
Nr Northwich
Cheshire CW9 6NA

Tel: 01565 777353/
777284
Fax: 01565 777465
e-mail: enquiries@
arleyestate.zuunet.co.uk

▶ LOCATION

OS Ref. SJ675 809

Knutsford 5m,
NW Northwich 5m,
N M6/J19 & 20 5m
M56/J9 & 10, 5m.

Rail: Intercity
Warrington 9m. Local
Knutsford 5m.

Air: Manchester
Airport 17m.

▶ OPENING TIMES

Gardens & Grounds:
31 March - 29 September:
Tues - Suns & BH Mons
11am - 5pm.
Hall: Tues & Suns only,
12 noon - 4.30pm.

October:
Gardens: weekends only
Hall: Suns only
(times as above).

Arley welcomes disabled
visitors - please telephone
for details.

▶ ADMISSION

**Gardens, Grounds
& Chapel:**

Adult £4.50
Child (5-15yrs) £2.25
OAP £3.90
Family £11.25
Groups (15+)
Adult £3.85
Child (5-15yrs) £2.05
OAP £3.35

Season ticket £19.90
Family ST (2+2) £50.00

Hall & Gardens

Adult £7.00
Child (5-15yrs) £3.50
OAP £5.90
Family £17.75
Groups (15+)
Adult £6.15
Child (5-15yrs) £3.20
OAP £5.15

▦ SPECIAL EVENTS

APR 7
Rare & Unusual Plant Fair.
JUN 13
Arley Celebrity Lecture.
JUN 29-30
Arley Garden Festival.
SEPT 1
Autumn Plant Hunters' Fair
See special events list for
further details.

ℹ Photography in garden only.
☎ Available.
♿ Partial.
☕ ⏹

✍ By arrangement.
🅿 Ample. 🚌
🐕 In grounds, on leads.
🔔

CAPESTHORNE HALL 🏛

MACCLESFIELD

www.capesthorne.com

Owner:
Mr & Mrs
Bromley-Davenport

▶ **CONTACT**

Gwyneth Jones,
Hall Manager
Capesthorne Hall
Siddington
Macclesfield
Cheshire SK11 9JY

Tel: 01625 861221
Fax: 01625 861619
e-mail: info@
capesthorne.com

▶ **LOCATION**

OS Ref. SJ840 727

5m W of Macclesfield.
30 mins S of
Manchester on A34.
Near M6, M63 and M62.

Air: Manchester
International 20 mins.

Rail: Macclesfield 5m
(2 hrs from London).

Taxi: 01625 533464.

Capesthorne Hall, set in 100 acres of picturesque Cheshire parkland, has been touched by nearly 1,000 years of English history - Roman legions passed across it, titled Norman families hunted on it and, during the Civil War, a Royalist ancestress helped Charles II to escape after the Battle of Worcester. The Jacobean-style Hall has a fascinating collection of fine art, marble sculptures, furniture and tapestries. Originally designed by the Smiths of Warwick it was built between 1719 and 1732. It was altered by Blore in 1837 and partially rebuilt by Salvin in 1861 following a disastrous fire.

The present Squire is William Bromley-Davenport, Lord Lieutenant of Cheshire, whose ancestors have owned the estate since Domesday times when they were appointed custodians of the Royal Forest of Macclesfield.

In the grounds near the family Chapel the 18th century Italian Milanese Gates open onto the herbaceous borders and maples which line the beautiful lakeside gardens. But amid the natural spectacle and woodland walks, Capesthorne still offers glimpses of its man-made past... the remains of the Ice House, the Old Boat House and the curious Swallow Hole.

Facilities at the Hall can be hired for corporate occasions and family celebrations including Civil wedding ceremonies.

ℹ️ Available for corporate functions, meetings, product launches, promotions, exhibitions, presentations, seminars, activity days, Civil weddings and receptions, family celebrations, still photography, fishing, clay shooting, car rallies, garden parties, barbecues, firework displays, concerts, antique, craft, country and game fairs. No photography in Hall.

🍽 Catering can be provided for groups (full menus on request). Function rooms available for wedding receptions, corporate hospitality, meetings and other special events. 'The Butler's Pantry' serves tea, coffee and ices.

♿ Compacted paths, ramps. WCs.

🚶 For up to 50. Tours are by staff members or Hall Manager. Tour time 1 hr.

🅿️ 100 cars/20 coaches on hard-standing and unlimited in park, 50 yds from house. Rest room and free refreshment for coach drivers.

🐕 Guide dogs in Hall. Under control in Park.

🔔 Civil Wedding Licence.

CONFERENCE/FUNCTION

ROOM	SIZE	MAX CAPACITY
Theatre	45' x 19'	155
Garden Room	52' x 20'	80
Saloon	40' x 25'	80
Queen Anne Room	34' x 25'	80
Board Room		10

▶ **OPENING TIMES**

Summer
April - October
BHs, Weds & Suns.

**House, Gardens
& Chapel**
Open at 1.30pm
Last admission 3.30pm.

Gardens & Chapel
12 noon - 5pm.

Groups welcome by appointment.

Caravan Park also open Easter - end October.

Corporate enquiries:
March - December.

▶ **ADMISSION**

Sundays & BHs
Hall & Gardens
Adult £6.50
Child (5-18yrs) £3.00
OAP £5.50
Family £15.00

Garden only
Adult £4.00
Child (5-18yrs) £2.00
OAP £3.00

Transfers to Hall
Adult/OAP £3.50
Child (5-18yrs) £1.50
Family £3.50

Wednesdays
House .... Free
Chapel & Gardens
Car (4 people) £5.00
Minibus/People carrier (5+) £10.00
Coach £25.00

Caravans
Up to 2 people £11.50 pn
Over 2 people. £13.50 pn

Groups (25+) tel. for details.

Season Ticket £25.00

The National Trust Photographic Library

Owner:
The National Trust

▶ **CONTACT**

Conferences, exhibitions, weddings etc.
Sheila Hetherington
01625 534406

Party Visits
Janet Gidman
01625 534428

Tatton Park
Knutsford
Cheshire WA16 6QN

Tel: 01625 534400
info line: 534428
Fax: 01625 534403

▶ **LOCATION**

OS Ref. SJ745 815

From M56/J7 follow signs. From M6/J19, signed on A56 & A50.

Rail: Knutsford or Altrincham Station, then taxi.

Air: Manchester Airport 6m.

TATTON PARK 🌿

KNUTSFORD

www.tatton.park.org.uk

Tatton is one of the most splendid historic estates in Europe. The 1000 acres of parkland are home to herds of red and fallow deer and provide the setting for a Georgian Mansion, over 50 acres of Gardens, Tudor Old Hall and a working Farm. These attractions, plus private functions and a superb events programme attract over 700,000 visits each year.

Archaeologists have found evidence of occupation at Tatton since 8000 BC with the discovery of flints in the park. There is also proof of people living here in the Iron Age, Roman times, Anglo-saxon and medieval periods.

The neo-Classical Mansion by Wyatt is the jewel in Tatton's crown and was built in stages from 1780 - 1813. The Egerton family collection of Gillow furniture, Baccarat glass, porcelain and paintings by Italian and Dutch masters is found in the splendid setting of the magnificent staterooms. In stark contrast, the Victorian kitchens and cellars provide fascinating insight

into life as it would have been 'downstairs'. Guided tours are available for a small extra charge at 12 noon and 12.15pm.

The Gardens extend over 50 acres and feature rare species of plants, shrubs and trees, and in fact are considered to be one of the most important gardens within the National Trust. Features include: a conservatory by Wyatt, Fernery by Paxton, Italian terraced garden and recently restored Japanese garden. The rare collection of plants including rhododendrons, tree ferns, bamboo and pines are the result of 200 years of collecting by the Egerton family.

The Home Farm has traditional breeds of animals including rare sheep and cattle, pigs and horses plus estate workshops. The Tudor Old Hall shows visitors how life would have been at Tatton Park over centuries past for the estate workers. Tours start in the smoky 16th century Great Hall lit by flickering candles and end in the 1950s home of an estate employee.

▶ **OPENING TIMES**

Summer
23 March - 29 September

Park: All year, daily 10am - 7pm, last entry 6pm.
Gardens: All year: Tue - Sun, 10.30am - 6pm, last entry 5pm.

Mansion: Apr - Oct:
Tue - Sun
1 - 5pm (last entry 4pm).
(12 noon - 12.15pm guided tours by timed ticket, limited number per tour)

Tudor Old Hall: Guided tours: Tue - Fri, 3pm & 4pm. Sats & Suns, hourly, 12 noon - 4pm.

Restaurant: Daily, 10.30am - 5pm.

Gift, Garden & Housekeeper's Store:
Tue - Sun, 11am - 5pm.

Winter
Special openings in Oct & Dec: Mansion & Farm.

Park: Tue - Sun, 11am - 4pm.

Farm: Suns only.

▶ **ADMISSION**

Any two attractions

	Single	Group*
Adult	£4.60	£3.70
Child**	£2.60	£2.10
Family	£12.80	

Mansion, Gardens, Tudor Old Hall, Farm

Adult	£3.00	£2.40
Child**	£2.00	£1.60
Family	£8.00	

(50% reduction for NT members to Tudor Old Hall & Farm.)

Parking
Per car £3.60
Coaches.................... Free

*Min. 12

** Aged 4 - 15yrs.

OAP rate as Adult

Tours available outside normal openings phone for details.

CONFERENCE/FUNCTION

Room	Size	Max Capacity
Tenants' Hall	125' x 45'	330 - 400
Foyer	23' x 20'	50 - 100
Tenants' Hall Event Wing - total of 8,000 sq.ft. available		
Lord Egerton's Apartment	20' x 16'	16 - 40
	24' x 18'	19 - 40
Stable Block	31' x 20'	80

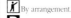 Conferences, trade exhibitions, presentations, product launches, concerts and fashion shows. Special family days. Spotlights, stages, dance floor, PA system. The Tenants' Hall seats up to 400 for presentations.

⊺ Telephone for details. Dinners, dances, weddings.

♿ Upstairs in Mansion, Tudor Old Hall & areas of farm not accessible. Wheelchairs & electric vehicles available. WCs.

☕ 🍴 Self-service. Tuck shop.

🏃 By arrangement.

P 200-300 yds away. Meal vouchers for coach drivers.

▪ Award-winning educational programmes, please book. Environmental days, Orienteering, adventure playground.

🐕 In grounds, on leads.

🔔 Civil Wedding Licence.

ADLINGTON HALL
See page 398 for full page entry.

ARLEY HALL & GARDENS
See page 399 for full page entry.

BEESTON CASTLE ⌗
Beeston, Tarporley, Cheshire CW6 9TX
Tel: 01829 260464
Owner: English Heritage   **Contact:** The Custodian
Standing majestically on sheer, rocky crags which fall sharply away from the castle walls, Beeston has stunning views across 8 counties. (Access by steep paths.) Exhibition on the site's 4,000 year history.
Location: OS117, Ref. SJ537 593. 11m SE of Chester on minor road off A49, or A41. 2m SW of Tarporley.
Open: 29 Mar - 30 Sept: 10am - 6pm. 1 - 31 Oct: daily, 10am - 5pm. 1 Nov - 31 Mar: daily, 10am - 4pm. Closed 24 & 25 Dec.
Admission: Adult £3, Child £1.50, Conc. £2.30. 15% discount for groups (11+).
ⓘExhibition. 🖻 ♿Unsuitable. 🐕In grounds on leads. ✳ ♿Tel for details.

CHOLMONDELEY CASTLE GARDEN 🏛
MALPAS, CHESHIRE SY14 8AH

Tel/Fax: 01829 720383
Owner: The Marchioness of Cholmondeley   **Contact:** The Secretary
Extensive ornamental gardens dominated by romantic Gothic Castle built in 1801 of local sandstone. Beautiful temple water garden, rose garden and many mixed borders. Lakeside picnic area, children's play areas, rare breeds of farm animals, including llamas. Ancient private chapel in the park.
Location: OS Ref. SJ540 515. Off A41 Chester/Whitchurch Rd. & A49 Whitchurch/Tarporley Road. 7m N of Whitchurch.
Open: 29 Mar (Good Fri) - 29 Sept: Weds, Thurs, Suns & BH Mons, 11.30am - 5pm, Groups (25+): other days by prior arrangement at reduced rates.
Admission: Adult £3, Child £1.50.
🖻 ⌷ ⓣ ♿Limited. WCs. 🖼 🐕In grounds on leads only. ✳

BRAMALL HALL 🏛
BRAMHALL PARK, BRAMHALL, STOCKPORT SK7 3NX

Tel: 0161 485 3708   **Fax:** 0161 486 6959   **e-mail:** bramall.hall@stockport.gov.uk
Owner: Stockport MBC   **Contact:** Scott Manton
Surrounded by 70 acres of beautiful parkland, Bramall Hall is a superb example of a Cheshire black and white timber-framed manor house, dating from the 14th century. The house has beautiful Tudor rooms with splendid Victorian additions. Extensive events programme and ideal for weddings.
Location: OS117, Ref. SJ886 863. 4m S of Stockport, off A5102.
Open: Good Fri - 30 Sept: Mon - Sat, 1 - 5pm, Suns & BHs, 11am - 5pm. 1 Oct - 1 Jan: Tue - Sat, 1 - 4pm, Suns & BHs, 11am - 4pm. Closed 25/26 Dec. 2 Jan - 4 Apr: Sats & Suns, 12 noon - 4pm.
Admission: Adult £3.95, Child/Conc. £2.50. Group prices on request.
🖻 ⓣ ♿Partial. 🖼 ⓕBy arrangement. 🅿 Limited for coaches. 🖼
🐕In grounds on leads. ⬛ ✳ ♿Tel for details.

DORFOLD HALL 🏛
ACTON, Nr NANTWICH, CHESHIRE CW5 8LD

Tel: 01270 625245   **Fax:** 01270 628723
Owner/Contact: Richard Roundell
Jacobean country house built in 1616 for Ralph Wilbraham. Family home of Mr & Mrs Richard Roundell. Beautiful plaster ceilings and oak panelling. Attractive woodland gardens and summer herbaceous borders.
Location: OS Ref. SJ634 525. 1m W of Nantwich on the A534 Nantwich - Wrexham road.
Open: Apr - Oct: Tues only and BH Mons, 2 - 5pm.
Admission: Adult £5, Child £3.
ⓕObligatory. 🅿Limited. Narrow gates with low arch prevent coaches.
🐕In grounds on leads.

CAPESTHORNE HALL 🏛
See page 400 for full page entry.

CHESTER ROMAN AMPHITHEATRE ⌗
Vicars Lane, Chester, Cheshire
Tel: 0161 242 1400
Owner: English Heritage   **Contact:** The North West Regional Office
The largest Roman amphitheatre in Britain, partially excavated. Used for entertainment and military training by the 20th Legion, based at the fortress of Deva.
Location: OS Ref. SJ404 660. On Vicars Lane beyond Newgate, Chester.
Open: Any reasonable time.
Admission: Free.

Patrick Lane

DUNHAM MASSEY

ALTRINCHAM, CHESHIRE WA14 4SJ

Tel: 0161 941 1025 **Fax:** 0161 929 7508

Owner: The National Trust   **Contact:** The Property Manager

Originally an early Georgian house, Dunham Massey has sumptuous interiors, with collections of walnut furniture, paintings and magnificent Huguenot silver. The richly planted garden contains waterside plantings, late flowering azaleas, an orangery and Elizabethan mount. The surrounding deer park escaped the attentions of 18th century landscape gardeners and contains some notable specimen trees.

Location: OS Ref. SJ735 874. 3m SW of Altrincham off A56. M56/J7.

Open: House: 23 Mar - 3 Nov: Sat - Wed, 12 noon - 5pm (11am - 5pm BH Sun & Mon; Oct & Nov: 12 noon - 4pm). Garden: 23 Mar - 3 Nov: daily, 11am - 5.30pm (4.30pm in Oct & Nov). Last admission normally ½ hr before closing. Park open daily throughout the year.

Admission: House & Garden: Adult £5.50, Child £2.75, Family £13.75 (2 adults + children). House or Garden only: Adult £3.50, Child £1.75. Car entry: £3 per car. Coach/minibus entry: £5 (free to booked parties). Motorcycle: £1. Booked Groups: £4.40 for 15 or more paying adults.

[i] No photography in house. 🖼 ⬛ 🚻 Partial. WC. Batricars. 🍴 Licensed. 🅵 Optional. No extra charge. 🅿 🚌 🐕 In grounds, on leads. ❋

GAWSWORTH HALL

MACCLESFIELD, CHESHIRE SK11 9RN

www.gawsworthhall.com

Tel: 01260 223456 **Fax:** 01260 223469 **e-mail:** gawsworth@lineone.net

Owner: Mr and Mrs T Richards   **Contact:** Mr T Richards

Fully lived-in Tudor half-timbered manor house with Tilting Ground. Former home of Mary Fitton, Maid of Honour at the Court of Queen Elizabeth I, and the supposed 'Dark Lady' of Shakespeare's sonnets. Pictures, sculpture and furniture. Open air theatre with covered grandstand - June, July and August, please telephone for details. Situated halfway between Macclesfield and Congleton in an idyllic setting close to the lovely medieval church.

Location: OS Ref. SJ892 697. 3m S of Macclesfield on the A536 Congleton to Macclesfield road.

Open: Easter - 6 Oct; 28 Mar - 16 Jun & 29 Aug - 6 Oct: Sun - Wed, 2 - 5pm. 17 June - 28 Aug: daily, 2 - 5pm. Also special events & BH weekends.

Admission: Adult £4.50, Child £2.25.

🖼 🚌 🅿 🐕 Guide dogs in garden only. 🔔 📺 Tel for details.

HARE HILL 🌿

Over Alderley, Macclesfield, Cheshire SK10 4QB

Tel/Fax: 01625 584412

Owner: The National Trust   **Contact:** The Head Gardener

A woodland garden surrounding a walled garden with pergola, rhododendrons and azaleas; parkland.

Location: OS Ref. SJ875 765. Between Alderley Edge and Prestbury, turn N at B5087, Greyhound Road.

Open: 1 Apr - 30 Oct: Weds, Thurs, Sats, Suns & BH Mons, 10am - 5.30pm. 11 - 30 May: daily, 10am - 5.30pm.

Admission: £2.50. Car £1.50 (refundable on entry to garden). Groups by written appointment c/o Garden Lodge at address above.

🅵 Gravel paths - strong companion advisable. 🐕 On leads in park.

LITTLE MORETON HALL 🌿

CONGLETON, CHESHIRE CW12 4SD

Tel: 01260 272018 **Fax:** 01260 292802

Owner: The National Trust   **Contact:** The Property Manager

Begun in 1450 and completed 130 years later, Little Moreton Hall is regarded as the finest example of a timber-framed moated manor house in the country. The drunkenly reeling South Front topped by its Elizabethan Long Gallery opens onto a cobbled courtyard and the main body of the Hall. The Chapel, Great Hall, wall paintings and Knot Garden are of particular interest.

Location: OS Ref. SJ833 589. 4m SW of Congleton on E side of A34.

Open: 23 Mar - 3 Nov: Wed - Sun (includes BH Mons & Good Fri), 11.30am - 5pm. 9 Nov - 22 Dec: weekends only, 11.30am - 4pm or dusk.

Admission: Adult £4.50, Child £2.25, Family £11. Groups: £3.75 (must book). Reduced price joint ticket with Biddulph Grange Garden.

🖼 🚻 🅵 Braille guide, wheelchair & electric vehicle. WCs. 🔔 🐕 Car park only.

NT Photographic Library / Geoff Morgan

LYME PARK

DISLEY, STOCKPORT, CHESHIRE SK12 2NX

Tel: 01663 762023 **Fax:** 01663 765035 **e-mail:** mlyrec@smtp.ntrust.org.uk

Owner: The National Trust **Contact:** The Property Manager

Legh family home for 600 years. Part of the original Elizabethan house survives with 18th and 19th century additions by Giacomo Leoni and Lewis Wyatt. Four centuries of period interiors – Mortlake tapestries, Grinling Gibbons carvings, unique collection of English clocks. Historic gardens with conservatory by Wyatt, a lake and a 'Dutch' garden. A 1,400 acre medieval deer park, home to red and fallow deer. Exterior featured as 'Pemberley' in BBC's *Pride and Prejudice*.

Location: OS Ref. SJ966 843. Off the A6 at Disley. 6½ m SE of Stockport.

Open: Park: 29 Mar - Oct: daily, 8am - 8.30pm; Nov - Mar: 8am - 6pm. Gardens: 29 Mar - 30 Oct: Fri - Tue, 11am - 5pm, Wed & Thur 1 - 5pm. Nov - 18 Dec: Sats & Suns, 12 noon - 3pm. House: 29 Mar - 30 Oct: Fri - Tue, 1 - 5pm (last admission 4.30pm) (BH Mons, 11am - 5pm). Shop & Tearoom: 29 Mar - 30 Oct: daily, 11am - 5pm. Nov - Mar: Sats & Suns, 12 noon - 4pm.

Admission: House & Garden: £5.50, House only: £4, Garden only: £2.50, Park only: car £3.50, motorbike £2, coach/minibus £6 (refundable on purchase of adult house & garden ticket). Combined Family Ticket: £15. Booked coach groups park admission Free. NT members Free.

No photography in house. Partial. WC. Licensed. By arrangement. In park, close control. Guide dogs only in house & garden.

NESS BOTANIC GARDENS

Ness, Neston, Cheshire CH64 4AY

Tel: 01513 530123 **Fax:** 01513 531004 **e-mail:** ejs@liv.ac.uk

Owner: University of Liverpool **Contact:** Dr E J Sharples

Location: OS Ref. SJ302 760 (village centre). Off A540. 10m NW of Chester. 1½ m S of Neston.

Open: 1 Mar - 31 Oct: 9.30am - 5pm. Nov - Feb: 9.30am - 4pm.

Admission: Charge for Adults & Conc. Accompanied child (under 18yrs) Free. 10% discount for groups. Please telephone for details.

NETHER ALDERLEY MILL

Congleton Road, Nether Alderley, Macclesfield, Cheshire SK10 4TW

Tel/Fax: 01625 584412

Owner/Contact: The National Trust

A fascinating overshot tandem wheel watermill, dating from the 15th century, with a stone-tiled low pitched roof. The machinery is in full working order, and grinds flour occasionally for demonstrations.

Location: OS Ref. SJ844 763. 1½ m S of Alderley Edge, on E side of A34.

Open: Apr, May & Oct: Weds, Suns & BH Mons, 1 - 4.30pm. Jun - Sept: daily (except Mons but open BH Mons), 1 - 5pm.

Admission: Adult £2, Child £1. Groups by prior arrangement (max. 20).

Unsuitable. By arrangement.

NORTON PRIORY MUSEUM & GARDENS

Tudor Road, Manor Park, Runcorn, Cheshire WA7 1SX

Tel: 01928 569895 **e-mail:** info@nortonpriory.org **www**.nortonpriory.org

Owner/Contact: The Norton Priory Museum Trust

Site of medieval priory set in beautiful woodland gardens.

Location: OS Ref. SJ545 835. 3m from M56/J11. 2m E of Runcorn.

Open: All year: daily, from 12 noon. Telephone for details.

Admission: Adult £3.95, Child/Conc. £2.75, Family £10, Groups £2.50.

Wheelchairs, braille guide, audio tapes & WC. By arrangement. In grounds, on leads. Tel for details.

MACCLESFIELD MUSEUMS

THE HERITAGE CENTRE, ROE STREET, MACCLESFIELD SK11 6UT

www.silk-macclesfield.org

Tel: 01625 613210 **Fax:** 01625 617880

e-mail: postmaster@silk-macc.u-net.com

Owner: Macclesfield Museums Trust **Contact:** Louanne Collins

Three museums devoted to the silk industry in this historic town. Silk Museum housed in former Georgian Sunday School tells the development of the industry through an award-winning audio visual programme, exhibition, models, costume and textiles. Nearby Paradise Mill houses 26 hand jacquard silk looms demonstrations of weaving by knowledgeable guides. Exciting major extension opens in May 2002 in former Art School.

Location: OS Ref. SJ917 733. Centre of Macclesfield.

Open: All year. Please ring for opening times and admission charges. Groups at any time by prior booking.

Admission: Adult £2.90, Child/Conc. £2, Family £7.60. (2001 prices.)

Partial. Licensed. Licensed. By arrangement. Guide dogs only.

PEOVER HALL

OVER PEOVER, KNUTSFORD WA16 9HN

Tel: 01565 632358

Owner: Randle Brooks **Contact:** I Shepherd

An Elizabethan house dating from 1585. Fine Carolean stables. Mainwaring Chapel, 18th century landscaped park. Large garden with topiary work, also walled and herb gardens.

Location: OS Ref. SJ772 734. 4m S of Knutsford off A50 at Whipping Stocks Inn.

Open: Apr - Oct: House, Stables & Gardens: Mons except BHs, 2 - 5pm. Tours of the House at 2.30 & 3.30pm. Stables & Gardens only: Thurs, 2 - 5pm.

Admission: House, Stables & Gardens: Adult £4.50, Child £3. Stables & Gardens only: Adult £3, Child £2.

Mondays only. Obligatory.

QUARRY BANK MILL & STYAL ESTATE 🌿
Styal, Wilmslow, Cheshire SK9 4LA
Tel: 01625 527468 **Fax:** 01625 539267 **e-mail:** msyrec@smtp.ntrust.org.uk
www.quarrybankmill.org.uk
Owner: The National Trust **Contact:** The Property Manager
Location: OS Ref. SJ835 830. 1¹/₂ m N of Wilmslow off B5166. 2¹/₂ m from M56/J5.
Open: Mill: Apr - end Sept: daily, 10.30am - 5.30pm, last adm. 4pm. Oct - Mar: daily except Mons (open BH Mons), 10.30am - 5pm, last adm. 3.30pm. Apprentice House & garden: daily except Mons,Tue - Fri, 2 - 4pm, Sats, Suns & Aug: 11am - 4.30pm.
Admission: Adult £6.50, Child/Conc. £3.70, Family £16.50. Mill only: Adult £5, Child/Conc. £3.40, Family £14. Advance bookings essential for groups (10+).

RODE HALL 🏛
CHURCH LANE, SCHOLAR GREEN, CHESHIRE ST7 3QP

Tel: 01270 873237 **Fax:** 01270 882962 **e-mail:** rodehall@scholargreen.fsnet.co.uk
Owner/Contact: Sir Richard Baker Wilbraham Bt

The Wilbraham family have lived at Rode since 1669; the present house was constructed in two stages, the earlier two storey wing and stable block around 1705 and the main building was completed in 1752. Later alterations by Lewis Wyatt and Darcy Braddell were undertaken in 1812 and 1927 respectively. The house stands in a Repton landscape and the extensive gardens include a woodland garden, with a terraced rock garden and grotto, which has many species of rhododendrons, azaleas, hellebores and climbing roses following snowdrops and daffodils in the early spring. The formal rose garden was designed by W Nesfield in 1860 and there is a large walled kitchen garden which is at its best from the middle of June. The icehouse in the park has recently been restored.
Location: OS Ref. SJ819 573. 5m SW of Congleton between the A34 and A50. Kidsgrove railway station 2m NW of Kidsgrove.
Open: 1 Apr - 25 Sept: Weds & BHs (closed Good Fri) and by appointment. Garden only: Tues & Thurs, 2 - 5pm. Snowdrop Walk: 6 - 24 Feb: 12 noon - 4pm. NGS: 12 May.
Admission: House, Garden & Kitchen Garden: Adult £4, OAP £2.50. Garden & Kitchen Garden: Adult £2.50, OAP £1.50. Snowdrop Walk: £2.50.
🎭 🍽 Home-made teas. 🐕 On leads.

Arley Hall

TABLEY HOUSE
KNUTSFORD, CHESHIRE WA16 0HB

www.tableyhouse.co.uk

Tel: 01565 750151 **Fax:** 01565 653230 **e-mail:** inquiries@tableyhouse.co.uk
Owner: Victoria University of Manchester **Contact:** The Administrator
The finest Palladian mansion in the North West of England, Grade I, by John Carr of York completed 1767 for the Leicester family who lived at Tabley for over 700 years. The first collection of English paintings ever made, furniture and memorabilia, can be seen in the State Rooms. Private chapel 1678 re-erected due to brine pumping.
Location: OS Ref. SJ725 777. M6/J19, A556 S on to A5033. 2m W of Knutsford.
Open: Apr - end Oct inclusive: Thurs, Fris, Sats, Suns & BHs, 2 - 5pm.
Admission: Adult £4. Child/Student £1.50. Groups by arrangement.
📷 ♿ 🍽 P 🏠 Civil Wedding Licence plus Civil Naming Ceremonies & Re-affirmation of Vows. 🎭 Tel for details.

TATTON PARK 🌿   *See page 401 for full page entry.*

WOODHEY CHAPEL
Faddiley, Nr Nantwich, Cheshire CW5 8JH
Tel: 01270 524215 **Contact:** Mr Robinson, The Curator
Owner: The Trustees of Woodhey Chapel
Small private chapel that has been recently restored.
Location: OS Ref. SJ573 528. Proceeding W from Nantwich on A534, turn left 1m W of the Faddiley - Brindley villages onto narrow lane, keep ahead at next turn, at road end obtain key from farmhouse.
Open: Apr - Oct: Sats & BHs, 2 - 5pm, or apply for key at Woodhey Hall.
Admission: £1.

Accommodation Index
◁ ◁ ◁   pg 27

ABBOT HALL ART GALLERY

KENDAL

www.lakelandartstrust.org.uk

Owner:
Lakeland Arts Trust

▶ **CONTACT**

Sandy Kitching
Abbot Hall Art Gallery
Kendal
Cumbria LA9 5AL

Tel: 01539 722464

Fax: 01539 722494

e-mail: info@
abbothall.org.uk

▶ **LOCATION**
OS Ref. SD516 922

10mins from M6/J36.
Follow brown museum
signs to South Kendal.

Rail: Oxenholme.

Air: Manchester.

Abbot Hall is a jewel of a building in a beautiful setting on the banks of the River Kent, surrounded by a park and overlooked by the ruins of Kendal Castle. This is one of Britain's finest small art galleries and a wonderful place in which to see and enjoy changing exhibitions in the elegantly proportioned rooms of a Grade I Listed Georgian building. The collection includes works by Romney, Ruskin, Turner and Freud. The adjacent Museum of Lakeland Life is a popular family attraction with a Victorian street scene, farmhouse rooms, Arthur Ransome room and displays of Arts and Crafts Movement furniture and fabrics.

▶ **OPENING TIMES**

14 February - 22 December
Mon - Sat, 10.30am - 5pm,
reduced hours in winter.

▶ **ADMISSION**

Adult £3.50

All ages welcome.

ℹ️ No photography. No mobile phones.		🅿️ Ample. Free.	
👜		▮	
♿ Chairlifts in split level galleries. WCs.		🐕 Guide dogs only.	
Licensed.	🚶 By arrangement.	❄️	

Lakeland Arts Trust/Jonathan Lynch

BLACKWELL -
THE ARTS & CRAFTS HOUSE

BOWNESS ON WINDERMERE

www.lakelandartstrust.org.uk

Owner:
Lakeland Arts Trust

▶ **CONTACT**

Sandy Kitching
Blackwell
The Arts & Craft House
Bowness on
Windermere
Cumbria LA23 3JR

Tel: 01539 446139

Fax: 01539 488486

e-mail: info@
blackwell.org.uk

▶ **LOCATION**

OS Ref. SD400 945

1¹/₂ m S of Bowness
just off the A5074 on
the B5360.

Rail: Windermere.

Air: Manchester.

Blackwell is a superb example of an Arts and Crafts Movement house situated in the Lake District. Completed in 1900, it sits in an elevated position overlooking Lake Windermere. Blackwell is the most important, and the largest, surviving early example of work by the architect Mackay Hugh Baillie Scott. Changing exhibitions of the highest quality applied arts and crafts can be seen in the setting of the Arts and Crafts Movement architecture itself.

In this treasure trove of 1890s Arts and Crafts design are fine examples of the decorative arts, drawn from natural forms. Lakeland birds and local wild flowers, trees and berries can be seen in the many original stained glass windows, pristine oak panelling and plasterwork. These rooms were designed for relaxation and everywhere you turn you will find inglenooks and places to sit and enjoy the views and garden terraces.

▶ **OPENING TIMES**

14 February -
22 December 2002
Daily, 10am - 5pm,
reduced hours in winter.

▶ **ADMISSION**

Adult £4.50

All ages welcome.

Lakeland Arts Trust/Jonathan Lynch

Lakeland Arts Trust/Jonathan Lynch

ⓘ No photography. No mobile phones. 📷 🍴 ♿ Ground floor & part of 1st floor. WCs. ☕ Licensed.

🚶 By arrangement. 🅿 Limited for cars and coaches. 🐕 Guide dogs only. ❄

DALEMAIN

PENRITH

www.dalemain.com

Dalemain is a fine mixture of mediaeval, Tudor and early Georgian architecture. The imposing Georgian façade strikes the visitor immediately but in the cobbled courtyard the atmosphere of the north country Tudor manor is secure. The present owner's family have lived at Dalemain since 1679 and have collected china, furniture and family portraits. Visitors can see the grand Drawing Rooms with 18th century Chinese wallpaper and fine oak panelling, also the Nursery and Housekeeper's Room. The Norman pele tower contains the regimental collection of the Westmorland and Cumberland Yeomanry. The house is full of the paraphernalia of a well established family house which is still very much lived in by the family.

The 16th century Great Barn holds a collection of agricultural bygones and a Fell Pony Museum.

Do not miss Mrs Mouse's house on the back stairs or the Nursery with toys from all ages. Something of interest for all the family. Location for ITV's production of *Jane Eyre*.

GARDENS

Delightful and fascinating 5 acre plantsman's gardens set against the picturesque splendour of the Lakeland Fells and Parkland. Richly planted herbaceous borders. Rose Walk with over 100 old-fashioned roses and ancient apple trees of named varieties. Magnificent Abies Cephalonica and Tulip Tree. Tudor Knot Garden. Wild Garden with profusion of flowering shrubs and wild flowers and in early summer the breathtaking display of blue Himalayan Poppies. Glorious woodland walk high above Dacre Beck. The gardens have been featured on *BBC Gardeners' World* and in *Country Life* and *English Garden*.

Owner:
Robert Hasell-McCosh Esq

▶ CONTACT

Bryan McDonald
Administrator
Dalemain Estate Office
Dalemain
Penrith
Cumbria
CA11 0HB

Tel: 017684 86450

Fax: 017684 86223

e-mail:
admin@dalemain.com

▶ LOCATION
OS Ref. NY477 269

On A592 1m S of A66.
4m SW of Penrith.
From London, M1,
M6/J40: 5 hrs.

From Edinburgh,
A73, M74,
M6/J40: 2¹/₂ hrs.

Rail: Penrith 4m.

Taxi: Lakeland Taxis:
Penrith 01768 865722.

[🎭🎯ℹ️] Fashion shows, archery, clay pigeon shooting, garden parties, rallies, filming, caravan rallies, antique fairs and children's camps. Business meetings and conferences. Grand piano available. Deer Park. Lectures on the house, gardens and history by arrangement (max 50). No photography in house. Moorings available on Ullswater.

[T] Corporate events: telephone for details.

[♿] Visitors may drive into the Courtyard and alight near the gift shop. Electric scooter for visiting the gardens. Admission free for visitors in wheelchairs. WCs.

[☕🍴] Licensed (in Mediaeval Hall). Seats 50. Groups must book for lunches/high teas. Free admission.

[👤] 1 hr tours. German and French translations in every room. Garden tour for groups extra.

[P] 50 yds from house. Free.

[🎒] Welcome. Guides can be arranged. Interest includes Military, Country Life, Agricultural and Fell Pony Museums, also country walk past Dacre Castle to St Andrew's Church, Dacre where there is a fine Laurence Whistler window.

[🐕] Guide dogs in house only. Strictly no dogs in garden but allowed in grounds.

[❄️]

▶ OPENING TIMES

Summer
24 March - 13 October
Sunday - Thursday

House:
11am - 4pm.

**Gardens, restaurant,
tearoom, gift shop,
plant sales & museums:**
10.30am - 5pm.

NB. Groups (10+)
please book.

Winter
October - Easter
open by special
arrangement with the
Administrator.

▶ ADMISSION
House & Garden

Adult	£5.50
Child (6-16yrs)	£3.50
Family	£14.50

Gardens only

Adult	£3.50
Child (6-16yrs)	Free

Groups (10+)

Adult	£4.50
Child (6-16yrs)	£3.00

All prices include VAT.

🎭 SPECIAL EVENTS

MAY 18
Fell Pony Society Stallion Show.

MAY 25 - 26
Lilliput Lane Collectors Fair.

JUL 20 - 21
Dalemain Rainbow Craft Fair.

AUG 18
Cumbrian Classic Car Show.

Please telephone for further details.

CONFERENCE/FUNCTION

ROOM	MAX CAPACITY
Dining Room	40
Old Hall	50

North West - England

Nicola Stocken-Jenkins

LEVENS HALL 🏛

KENDAL

www.levenshall.co.uk

Levens Hall is an Elizabethan mansion built around a 13th century pele tower. The much loved home of the Bagot family, visitors comment on the warm and friendly atmosphere. Fine panelling and plasterwork, period furniture, Cordova leather wall coverings, paintings by Rubens, Lely and Cuyp, the earliest English patchwork and Wellingtoniana combine with other beautiful objects to form a fascinating collection.

The world famous Topiary Gardens were laid out by Monsieur Beaumont from 1694 and his design has remained largely unchanged to this day. Over ninety individual pieces of topiary, some over nine metres high, massive beech hedges and colourful seasonal bedding provide a magnificent visual impact. Past winner of the HHA/Christie's Garden of the Year Award. Monty Don wrote in The Observer that the gardens at Levens are *'Considered to be in the top ten UK gardens'.*

On Sundays and Bank Holidays 'Bertha', a full size Showman's Engine, is in steam. Delicious home-made lunches and teas are available, together with the award-winning Levens beer 'Morocco Ale', in the Bellingham Buttery.

Owner: C H Bagot

▶ **CONTACT**

Peter Milner
Levens Hall
Kendal
Cumbria LA8 0PD

Tel: 01539 560321

Fax: 01539 560669

e-mail: email@
levenshall.fsnet.co.uk

▶ **LOCATION**

OS Ref. SD495 851

5m S of Kendal on the A6. Exit M6/J36.

Rail: Oxenholme 5m.

Air: Manchester.

▶ **OPENING TIMES**

Summer

31 March - 10 October
Sun - Thur
(closed Fris & Sats).

House: 12 noon - 5pm
Last admission 4.30pm.

Group tours of Hall
at 10am available by prior arrangement.

Gardens, Plant Centre, Gift Shop & Tearoom:
10am - 5pm.

Winter

Closed.

▶ **ADMISSION**

House & Gardens

Adult	£6.50
Child	£3.20

Groups (20+)

Adult	£5.00
School	£3.00
Family (2+3)	£19.00

Gardens

Adult	£5.00
Child	£2.50

Groups (20+)

Adult	£4.00
School	£2.20
Family (2+3)	£14.50

Evening Tours

House & Garden for groups (20+)
by arrangement £7.50

Gardens only groups (20+) by prior arrangement £5.50

Morning Tours

House tours for groups (20+/min charge £120.)
by arrangement £6.00

Season Tickets

Garden (single) £17.00

No admission charge for gift shop, tearoom and plant centre.

 No indoor photography. Partial. WC. Wheelchair loan - gardens only suitable. Licensed. By arrangement. **P** Guide dogs only.

North West - England

MUNCASTER CASTLE 🏛

GARDENS & OWL CENTRE, RAVENGLASS

www.muncastercastle.co.uk

Owner: Mrs Phyllida
Gordon-Duff-
Pennington

▶ **CONTACT**

Peter Frost-Pennington
Muncaster Castle
Ravenglass
Cumbria CA18 1RQ
Tel: 01229 717614
Fax: 01229 717010

e-mail: info@
muncastercastle.co.uk

▶ **LOCATION**
OS Ref. SD103 965

On the A595 1m S of
Ravenglass, 19m S of
Whitehaven.

From London 6 hrs,
Chester 2½ hrs,
Edinburgh 3½ hrs,
M6/J36, A590,
A595 (from S). M6/J40,
A66, A595 (from E).
Carlisle, A595 (from N).

Rail: Ravenglass
(on Barrow-in-Furness-
Carlisle Line) 1½ m.

Air: Manchester 2½ hrs.

CONFERENCE/FUNCTION

ROOM	MAX CAPACITY
Drawing Rm	120
Dining Rm	50
Family Dining Rm	60
Great Hall	110
Old Laundry	120
Library	40

Muncaster Castle has been owned by the Pennington family since 1208. It has grown from the original pele tower built on Roman foundations to the impressive structure visible today. Outstanding features are the Great Hall and Salvin's Octagonal Library and the Drawing Room with its barrel ceiling.

The haunted castle contains many treasures including beautiful furniture, exquisite needlework panels, tapestries and oriental rugs. The family silver is very fine and is accompanied in the Dining Room by the Ongley Service, the most ornamental set of porcelain ever created by the Derby factory, Florentine 16th century bronzes and an alabaster lady by Giambologna can be seen. The family are actively involved in entertaining their many visitors.

The woodland gardens cover 77 acres and command spectacular views of the Lakeland Fells, with many delightful walks. From mid-March to June the rhododendrons, azaleas, camellias and magnolias are at their best. Muncaster has designated walks and trails to help you explore this wonderful wild wilderness including the new three hour Muncaster Wild Walk which allows visitors into new and exciting areas with superb views not previously accessible to the public.

The Owl Centre boasts a fine collection of owls from all over the world. 'Meet the Birds' occurs daily at 2.30pm (10 Mar to 3 Nov), when a talk is given on the work of the centre. Weather permitting, the birds fly free.

Imagine being a meadow vole - just two and a half inches tall - living in meadowland, where dangers lurk at every turn. It's no picnic. Down at the Meadow Vole Maze the secret world of wildlife makes for a wild experience. Here, where the grass is seven feet tall, you'll find out what life is like for these tiny creatures. Great for kids of all ages! Then revert to size and wander into the real wildflower meadow with glorious views of the Castle.

Badger and Vole

🛍 ❄ ℹ Church. Suitable for fashion shoots, garden parties, film location, clay pigeon shooting. No photography inside the Castle. Home of the World Owl Trust, run by TV naturalist Tony Warburton.

🍸 Wedding receptions. For catering and functions in the castle Tel: 01229 717614.

♿ By prior arrangement visitors alight near Castle. Wheelchairs for loan. WCs. Special audio tour tapes for the partially sighted/those with learning difficulties. Allocated parking.

🍽 Creeping Kate's Kitchen (licensed) (max 80) – full menu. Groups can book: 01229 717614 to qualify for discounts.

🚶 🎧 Individual audio tour (40mins) included in price. Private tours with a personal guide (family member possible) can be arranged at additional fee. Lectures by arrangement.

🅿 500 cars 800 yds from House; coaches may park closer.

📷 Guides available. Historical subjects, horticulture, conservation, owl tours.

🦌 In grounds, on leads.

▶ **OPENING TIMES**

Castle
10 March - 3 November
Daily (closed Sat),
12 noon - 5pm.

Gardens & Owl Centre
All year: daily:
10.30am - 6pm or dusk
if earlier.

'Meet the Birds'
10 March - 3 November
Daily at 2.30pm.

**Watch the wild herons
feeding during the
'Heron Happy Hour'.**
Daily at 4.30pm.

Winter
Castle closed. Open by
appointment for groups.

▶ **ADMISSION**

**Castle, Gardens &
Owl Centre**
Adult £7.50
Child (5-15yrs) £5.00
Under 5yrs .... Free
Family (2+2) £20.00
Groups
Adult £6.50
Child (5-15yrs) £3.50

Season Tickets available

**Gardens & Owl Centre
and Meadow Vole Maze**
Adult £5.50
Child (5-15yrs) £3.50
Under 5yrs .... Free
Family (2+2) £16.50
Groups
Adult £5.00
Child (5-15yrs) £2.50

MUNCASTER CASTLE…

The Library

Drawing Room, Wedgwood pattern barrel ceiling

ABBOT HALL ART GALLERY

See page 406 for full page entry.

BLACKWELL - THE ARTS & CRAFTS HOUSE

See page 407 for full page entry.

Abbot Hall Art Gallery

ACORN BANK GDN & WATERMILL ❧

TEMPLE SOWERBY, PENRITH, CUMBRIA CA10 1SP

Tel: 01768 361893 **e-mail:** racorn@smtp.ntrust.org.uk

Owner: The National Trust   **Contact:** The Custodian

A one hectare garden protected by fine oaks under which grow a vast display of daffodils. Inside the walls there are orchards containing a variety of fruit trees surrounded by mixed borders with shrubs, herbaceous plants and roses, while the impressive herb garden has the largest collection of culinary and medicinal plants in the north. A circular woodland walk runs beside the Crowdundle Beck to Acorn Bank Watermill, which although under restoration, is open to visitors. The house is open only during some events.

Location: Gate: OS Ref. NY612 281. Just N of Temple Sowerby, 6m E of Penrith on A66.

Open: 23 Mar - 3 Nov: daily except Tue, 10am - 5pm. Last admission 4.30pm.

Admission: Adult £2.50, Child £1.20, Family £6.20. Pre-arranged groups £1.80.

🔲 ♿ Grounds only. WCs. ✖

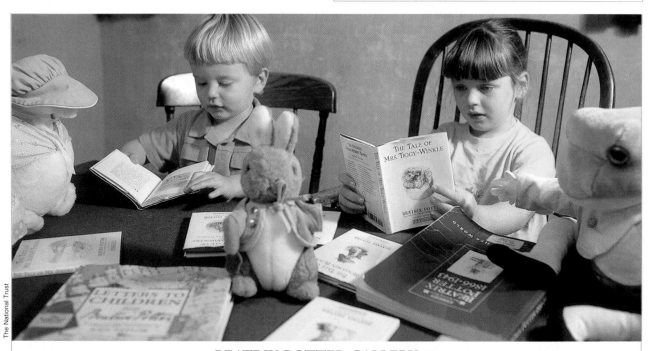

The National Trust

BEATRIX POTTER GALLERY ❧

MAIN STREET, HAWKSHEAD, CUMBRIA LA22 0NS

Tel: 01539 436355 **e-mail:** rhabpg@smtp.ntrust.org.uk

Owner: The National Trust   **Contact:** The Custodian

An annually changing exhibition of original sketches and watercolours painted by Beatrix Potter for her children's stories. Each year the new exhibition delights young and old as they discover the amazing delicacy and charm of her work. One of many historic buildings in this picturesque village, the gallery was once the office of Beatrix Potter's husband, William Heelis, and the interior remains substantially unaltered since his day. The gallery is ideally matched with a visit to Beatrix Potter's house, Hill Top, two miles away, where she wrote and illustrated many of her children's stories.

Location: OS Ref. SD352 982. 5m SSW of Ambleside. In the Square.

Open: 24 Mar - 31 Oct: Sun - Thur (closed Fris & Sats except Good Fri) 10.30am - 4.30pm. Last admission 4pm. Admission is by timed ticket (incl. NT members).

Admission: Adult £3, Child £1.50, Family £7.50. No reduction for groups.

🔲 ✖ Guide dogs only.

BROUGH CASTLE ⌗

Brough, Cumbria
Tel: 0161 242 1400
Owner: English Heritage   **Contact:** The North West Regional Office
This ancient site dates back to Roman times. The 12th century keep replaced an earlier stronghold destroyed by the Scots in 1174.
Location: OS Ref. NY791 141. 8m SE of Appleby S of A66. South part of the village.
Open: Any reasonable time.
Admission: Free.

BROUGHAM CASTLE ⌗

Penrith, Cumbria CA10 2AA
Tel: 01768 862488
Owner: English Heritage   **Contact:** The Custodian
These impressive ruins on the banks of the River Eamont include an early 13th century keep and later buildings. You can climb to the top of the keep and survey the domain of its eccentric one-time owner Lady Anne Clifford. Exhibition about the Roman fort, medieval castle and Lady Anne Clifford.
Location: OS Ref. NY537 290. 1½ m SE of Penrith, between A66 & B6262.
Open: 29 Mar - 30 Sept: daily, 10am - 6pm. 1 - 31 Oct: daily, 10am - 5pm.
Admission: Adult £2.20, Child £1.10, Conc. £1.70. 15% discount for groups (11+).
⬜ ♿Grounds. **P**Limited. ▨ ⬛In grounds, on leads. ▨Tel for details.

CARLISLE CASTLE ⌗

CARLISLE, CUMBRIA CA3 8UR

Tel: 01228 591922
Owner: English Heritage   **Contact:** The Custodian
This impressive medieval castle, where Mary Queen of Scots was once imprisoned, has a long and tortuous history of warfare and family feuds. A portcullis hangs menacingly over the gatehouse passage, there is a maze of passages and chambers, endless staircases to lofty towers and you can walk the high ramparts for stunning views. There is also a medieval manor house in miniature: a suite of medieval rooms furnished as they might have been when used by the castle's former constable. The castle is also the home of the King's Own Royal Border Regimental Museum (included in the admission price). 2002 is the 300th anniversary of the regiment.
Location: OS85 Ref. NY397 563. In Carlisle town, at N end of city centre.
Open: 29 Mar - 30 Sept: daily, 9.30am - 6pm. 1 - 31 Oct: daily, 10am - 5pm. 1 Nov - 31 Mar: daily, 10am - 4pm. Closed 24 - 26 Dec & 1 Jan.
Admission: Adult £3.20, Child £1.60, Conc £2.40. 15% discount for groups (11+).
⬜ ♿Partial, wheelchairs available. ⓕBy arrangement. **P**None. ▨
⬛Dogs on leads. ▨Tel for details.

CARLISLE CATHEDRAL

Carlisle, Cumbria CA3 8TZ
Tel: 01228 548151 **Fax:** 01228 547049
e-mail: office@carlislecathedral.org.uk   **Contact:** Ms C Baines
Fine sandstone Cathedral, founded in 1122. Medieval stained glass.
Location: OS Ref. NY399 559. Carlisle city centre, 2m from M6/J43.
Open: Mon - Sat: 7.45am - 6.15pm, Suns, 7.45 - 5pm. Closes 4pm between Christmas Day & New Year. Sun services: 8am, 10.30am & 3pm. Weekday services: 8am, 5.30pm & a 12.30 service on Weds, Fris and Saints' Days.
Admission: Donation.

CONISHEAD PRIORY & MANJUSHRI BUDDHIST TEMPLE

Ulverston, Cumbria LA12 9QQ
Tel: 01229 584029 **Fax:** 01229 580080 **e-mail:** info@manjushri.org.uk
Owner: Manjushri Mahayana Buddhist Centre   **Contact:** Mr D Coote
A Georgian gothic mansion on site of a medieval Augustinian Priory.
Location: OS Ref. SD300 750. 2m S of Ulverston on Bardsea Coast Rd A5087.
Open: Easter - Oct, w/e & BHs, 2 - 5pm. Closed 25 Jun - 10 Jul & 20 Jul - 19 Aug. Opening times may change, please telephone to confirm.
Admission: Free. House tours and audio visual: Adult £2, Child/Conc £1.

DALEMAIN 🏛   *See page 408 for full page entry.*

DOVE COTTAGE & WORDSWORTH MUSEUM

See full page advertisement on page 23
Grasmere, Cumbria LA22 9SH
Tel: 01539 435544 **Fax:** 01539 435748
e-mail: enquiries@wordsworth.org.uk **www**.wordsworth.org.uk
Owner: Wordsworth Trust   **Contact:** Mark McTigue
Situated in the heart of the English Lake District, Dove Cottage is the beautifully preserved Grasmere home of England's finest poet William Wordsworth. Visitors are offered fascinating guided tours of his world-famous home. The award-winning Museum displays priceless Wordsworth manuscripts and memorabilia. Onsite tearooms and book and gift shop.
Location: OS Ref. NY342 070. Immediately S of Grasmere village on A591. Main car/coach park next to Dove Cottage Tea Rooms.
Open: All year: daily, 9.30am - 5pm. Closed 7 Jan - 3 Feb (inc) & 24 - 26 Dec.
Admission: Adult £5, Child £2.50, Student £4.20, plus family tickets (2001 prices). Pre-arranged groups (15-60): Adult £4.40. Reciprocal discount ticket with Rydal Mount and Wordsworth House.
ⓘNo photography. ⬜ ♿Partial. WC. ▣ ⓕObligatory. **P**Limited. ▨
⬛Guide dogs only. ✱ ▨Tel for details.

FELL FOOT PARK 🌿

Newby Bridge, Ulverston LA12 8NN
Tel: 01539 531273 **Fax:** 01539 530049 **e-mail:** rffoot@smtp.ntrust.org.uk
Owner: The National Trust   **Contact:** The Property Manager
This Victorian park, restored to its former glory, offers substantial access to the lakeshore of Windermere where there are leisure facilities in season. Fine picnic areas and boat hire make this property particularly rewarding for families.
Location: OS96 Ref. SD381 869. At the extreme S end of Lake Windermere on E shore, entrance from A592.
Open: Daily, 9am - 7pm or dusk if earlier. Facilities & Shop: 31 Mar - 4 Nov: daily, 11am - 4.30pm.
Admission: Car park: £2 (up to 2hrs), £5 (all day). Coaches £15 by arrangement.
⬜ ♿Partial. ▣ **P**Charge. ⬛On leads. ✱ ▨Tel for details.

FURNESS ABBEY ⌗

Barrow-in-Furness, Cumbria LH13 0TJ
Tel: 01229 823420
Owner: English Heritage   **Contact:** The Custodian
Hidden in a peaceful green valley are the beautiful red sandstone remains of the wealthy abbey founded in 1123 by Stephen, later King of England. This abbey first belonged to the Order of Savigny and later to the Cistercians. There is a museum and exhibition.
Location: OS96 Ref. SD218 717. 1½ m NE of Barrow-in-Furness.
Open: 29 Mar - 30 Sept: daily, 10am - 6pm. 1 - 31 Oct:, daily, 10am - 5pm. 1 Nov - 31 Mar: Wed - Sun, 10am - 4pm. Closed 1 - 2pm in winter. Closed 24 - 26 Dec & 1 Jan.
Admission: Adult £2.80, Child £1.40, Conc. £2.10. 15% discount for groups (11+).
⬜ ♿Grounds. ⓘInclusive. **P** ▨ ⬛In grounds, on leads. ✱ ▨Tel for details.

HARDKNOTT ROMAN FORT ⌗

Ravenglass, Cumbria
Tel: 0161 242 1400
Owner: English Heritage   **Contact:** The North West Regional Office
This fort, built between AD120 and 138, controlled the road from Ravenglass to Ambleside.
Location: OS Ref. NY219 015. At the head of Eskdale. 9m NE of Ravenglass, at W end of Hardknott Pass.
Open: Any reasonable time. Access may be hazardous in winter.
Admission: Free.

© English Heritage Photo Library

HERON CORN MILL & MUSEUM OF PAPERMAKING

c/o Henry Cooke, Waterhouse Mills, Beetham, Milnthorpe LA7 7AR
Tel: 015395 65027 **Fax:** 015395 65033 **e-mail:** ntstobbs@virgin.net
Owner: Heron Corn Mill Beetham Trust   **Contact:** Mr Neil Stobbs
Location: OS Ref. SD497 800. At Beetham. 1m S of Milnthorpe on the A6.
Open: Easter: 1 Apr - 30 Sept: Tue - Sun & BH Mon, 11am - 5pm.
Admission: Adult £1.50, Child/OAP £1, Family (2+2) £4.50, Coach parties/groups
10% discount if pre-booked.

HILL TOP ⚘

Near Sawrey, Ambleside, Cumbria LA22 0LF
Tel: 01539 436269 **Fax:** 01539 436118 **e-mail:** rpmht@smtp.ntrust.org.uk
Owner: The National Trust   **Contact:** The Property Manager
Beatrix Potter wrote many of her famous children's stories in this little 17th century
house, which contains her furniture and china. There is a traditional cottage garden
attached. 2002 is the 100th anniversary of the commercial publication of 'Peter
Rabbit'. Events to celebrate.
Location: OS Ref. SD370 955. 2m S of Hawkshead, in hamlet of Near Sawrey, behind
the Tower Bank Arms.
Open: 23 Mar - 3 Nov: Sat - Wed, 11am - 4.30pm (June - Aug, 10.30am - 5pm): daily
except Thur & Fri. Last admission 30mins before closing. Please book all visits to
guarantee entry.
Admission: Adult £4.50, Child £1, Family £10. Joint ticket with Beatrix Potter
Gallery: Adult £7, Child £2, Family £16. No reduction for groups.
📺 Tel for details.

HOLEHIRD GARDENS

Patterdale Road, Windermere, Cumbria LA23 1NP
Tel: 01539 446008 **e-mail:** thomas@oldbelfield.freeserve.co.uk
Owner: Lakeland Horticultural Society   **Contact:** The Hon Secretary
Over 10 acres of hillside gardens overlooking Windermere, including a walled garden
and national collection of astilbes, hydrangeas and polystichum ferns. All work in the
gardens is done by volunteers.
Location: OS Ref. NY410 008. On A592, $^3/_4$ m N of junction with A591. $^1/_2$ m N of
Windermere. 1m from Townend.
Open: All year: dawn to dusk.
Admission: Free. Donation appreciated (at least £2 suggested).

Blackwell - The Arts & Crafts House

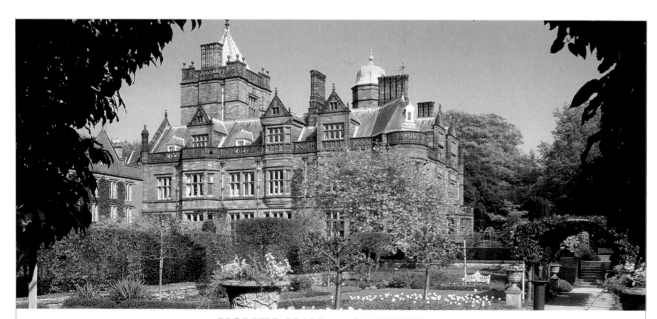

HOLKER HALL & GARDENS 🏛

CARK-IN-CARTMEL, GRANGE-OVER-SANDS, CUMBRIA LA11 7PL

www.holker-hall.co.uk

Tel: 01539 558328 **Fax:** 01539 558378 **e-mail:** publicopening@holker.co.uk
Owner: Lord Cavendish of Furness
Holker Hall, home of Lord and Lady Cavendish, shows the confidence, spaciousness
and prosperity of Victorian style on its grandest scale. The New Wing was designed by
architects Paley and Austin and built by the 7th Duke of Devonshire during 1871-4.
Despite this grand scale, Holker is very much a family home with visitors able to
wander freely throughout the New Wing. Varying in period and style, Louis XV pieces
happily mix with the Victorian, including an early copy of the famous triple portrait of
Charles I by Van Dyck. The award-winning gardens include formal and woodland
areas covering 25 acres. Designated 'amongst the best in the world in terms of design

and content' by the *Good Gardens Guide*. This inspiring garden includes a lime
stone cascade, fountain, the Sunken Garden, the Elliptical and Summer Gardens
and many rare plants and shrubs.
Location: OS Ref. SD359 773. Close to Morecambe Bay, 5m W of Grange-over-
Sands by B5277. From Kendal, A6, A590, B5277, B5278: 16m. Motorway: M6/J36.
Open: Easter - 31 Oct: daily except Sats, 10am - 6pm. Last admission 4.30pm.
Admission: House & Garden: Adult £6.50, Child £3.95. Groups (20-100): Adult
£4.50, Child £3.00, OAP £4.00. Under 6yrs Free.
📷 🚫 ℹ️No photography in house. 🍴 ♿Visitors alight at entrance. WCs.
📹 🍴 🎦By arrangement. 🅿150 yds from Hall. 🔲 🐕In grounds on leads. 📺

HUTTON-IN-THE-FOREST 🏛

PENRITH, CUMBRIA CA11 9TH

Tel: 01768 484449 **Fax:** 01768 484571 **e-mail:** hutton-in-the-forest@talk21.com

Owner: Lord Inglewood   **Contact:** Edward Thompson

The home of Lord Inglewood's family since 1605. Built around a medieval pele tower with 17th, 18th and 19th century additions. Fine collections of furniture, paintings, ceramics and tapestries. Outstanding grounds with terraces, topiary, walled garden, dovecote and woodland walk through magnificent specimen trees.

Location: OS Ref. NY460 358. 6m NW of Penrith & 2 ¹/₂ m from M6/J41 on B5305.

Open: Easter Fri, Sun & Mon. 2 May - 29 Sept: Thur, Fri, Suns & BHs. 12.30 - 4pm (last entry).

Tearoom: As house: 11am - 4.30pm. Grounds: daily except Sats, 11am - 5pm.

Admission: House, Gardens & Grounds: Adult £4.50, Child £2.50, Family £12. Gardens & Grounds: Adult £2.50, Child Free.

ⓘ Picnic area. 🅶 Gift stall. 🆃 By arrangement. 🅴 Partial. ▣
🅵 Obligatory (except Jul/Aug & BHs). ▣

LANERCOST PRIORY ⌗

Brampton, Cumbria CA8 2HQ

Tel: 01697 73030

Owner: English Heritage   **Contact:** The Custodian

This Augustinian priory was founded c1166. The nave of the church, which is intact and in use as the local parish church, contrasts with the ruined chancel, transepts and priory buildings. Free audio tour.

Location: OS86, Ref. NY556 637. 2m NE of Brampton. 1m N of Naworth Castle.

Open: 29 Mar - 30 Sept: daily, 10am - 6pm. 1 - 31 Oct: daily, 10am - 5pm.

Admission: Adult £2.20, Child £1.10, Conc. £1.70. Groups (11+): 15% discount.

🅶 🅴 Ground floor. ⓘ Inclusive. 🅿 Limited. ▣ 🅷 🅶 Tel for details.

LEVENS HALL 🏛   *See page 409 for full page entry.*

MIREHOUSE 🏛

KESWICK, CUMBRIA CA12 4QE

Tel/Fax: 017687 72287   **e-mail:** info@mireho.freeserve.co.uk

Owner: James Fryer-Spedding   **Contact:** Clare Spedding

'The Best Heritage Property for Families in the UK' 1999 NPI Award. Our visitors particularly appreciate the spectacular setting between mountain and lake, the extraordinary literary and artistic connections, varied gardens, walks, natural playgrounds, live classical music and the personal attention of members of the family. The tearoom is known for generous Cumbrian cooking.

Location: OS Ref. NY235 284. Beside A591, 3¹/₂ m N of Keswick. Good bus service.

Open: 1 Apr - 31 Oct: Gardens & Tearoom: daily, 10am - 5.30pm. House: Suns & Weds (also Fris in Aug), 2 - 5pm (4.30pm last entry). At other times for groups by appointment.

Admission: House & Garden: Adult £4, Child £2, Family £11.75. Gardens only: Adult £2, Child £1. 10% discount for groups (20+), booked in advance.

ⓘ No photography in house. 🅴 ▣ 🅵 By arrangement. 🅿 Limited. ▣
🐕 Guide dogs only. ✱ Booked groups only.

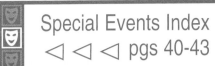

Special Events Index
◁ ◁ ◁ pgs 40-43

MUNCASTER CASTLE  *See pages 410/411 for double page entry.*

MUNCASTER WATER MILL
Ravenglass, Cumbria CA18 1ST
Tel: 01229 717232
Owner: Lake District Estates   **Contact:** E & P Priestly
Working old manorial mill with 13ft overshot wheel and all milling equipment.
Location: OS Ref. SD094 977. 1m N of Ravenglass on A595.
Open: Easter - Oct: daily 10am - 5pm. Nov - Mar: weekends only, 11am - 4pm.
Admission: Adult £2, Child 50p, Family (2+3) £5. Groups by arrangement.

PENRITH CASTLE ⌗
Penrith, Cumbria
Tel: 0161 242 1400
Owner: English Heritage   **Contact:** The North West Regional Office
This 14th century castle, set in a park on the edge of the town, was built to defend Penrith against repeated attacks by Scottish raiders.
Location: OS Ref. NY513 299. Opposite Penrith railway station. W of the town centre. Fully visible from the street.
Open: Park opening hours.
Admission: Free.

THE QUAKER TAPESTRY EXHIBITION CENTRE
Friends Meeting House, Stramongate, Kendal, Cumbria LA9 4BH
Tel/Fax: 01539 722975
e-mail: info@quaker-tapestry.co.uk **www**.quaker-tapestry.co.uk
Owner: Trustees of the Quaker Tapestry   **Contact:** Bridget Guest
This unique exhibition of 77 panels of community embroidery delights visitors of all ages. Explore the Quaker journey from 17th century to the present day as you uncover over 300 years of social history, beautifully illustrated by 4000 men, women and children from 15 countries.
Location: OS Ref. SD517 927. Centre of Kendal, access from either Stramongate or New Road.
Open: Apr - Oct: Mon - Sat, 10am - 5pm, last admission 4.15pm. Nov - Dec: Mon - Fri.
Admission: Adult £3.25, Child £1.25, Conc. £2.75.
ⓘNo indoor photography. Demonstrations. ▣ ♿
▣Tapestry tearooms open Apr 2002. 🎦 By arrangement. ▢ Ⓟ Limited. ▣
♿Guide dogs only.

RYDAL MOUNT & GARDENS 🏛
See full page advertisement on page 23
Ambleside, Cumbria LA22 9LU
Tel: 01539 433002 **Fax:** 01539 431738
e-mail: rydalmount@aol.com **www**.wordsworthlakes.co.uk
Owner: Rydal Mount Trustees   **Contact:** Peter & Marian Elkington
Nestling between the beautiful fells, Lake Windermere and Rydal Water lies the 'most beloved' home of William Wordsworth from 1813 - 1850. Now the home of his direct descendants, visitors can wander through the house and the extensive gardens landscaped by the poet. *'Nowhere on earth have I ever seen a spot of more perfect and enjoyable beauty'* wrote Dr Thomas Arnold.
Location: OS Ref. NY364 063. 1¹/₂ m N of Ambleside on A591 Grasmere Road.
Open: Mar - Oct: Daily, 9.30am - 5pm. Nov - Feb: Daily except Tues, 10am - 4pm.
Admission: Adult £4, Child £1.50, Student £3, OAP £3.25, Family £10. Pre-arranged groups £2.75. Garden only: £1.75. Free parking. Reciprocal discount ticket with Dove Cottage & Wordsworth House.
ⓘNo inside photography. ▣ ♿Partial. 🎦 By arrangement. Ⓟ Limited. ▣
♿In grounds, on leads. Guide dogs only in house. ❄

NT Photographic Library: Alasdair Ogilvie

SIZERGH CASTLE & GARDEN 🌿
Nr KENDAL, CUMBRIA LA8 8AE
Tel: 01539 560070 **Fax:** 01539 561621 **e-mail:** ntrust@sizerghcastle.fsnet.co.uk
Owner: The National Trust   **Contact:** The House Manager
The Strickland family has lived here for more than 750 years. The impressive 14th century tower was extended in Tudor times, with some of the finest Elizabethan carved overmantels in the country. Contents include good English and French furniture and family portraits. A visit culminates in the important and impressive Inlaid Chamber. The castle is surrounded by gardens of beauty and interest, including the Trust's largest limestone rock garden; good autumn colour. Large estate; walks leaflet available in shop.
Location: OS Ref. SD498 878. 3¹/₂ m S of Kendal, NW of the A590/A591 interchange.
Open: Castle: 24 Mar - 31 Oct: Sun - Thur, 1.30 - 5.30pm. Garden: As house: 12.30 - 5.30pm. Last admission 5pm.
Admission: Adult £5, Child £2.50, Family £12.50. Garden only: £2.50. Groups (15+): £4 by arrangement (not on BHs).
▣ ♿Partial. ▣ 🌿

STAGSHAW GARDEN 🌿
Ambleside, Cumbria LA22 0HE
Tel /Fax: 015394 46027 **e-mail:** rwinpm@smtp.ntrust.org.uk
Owner: The National Trust   **Contact:** Windermere & Troutbeck Property Office
This woodland garden was created by the late Cubby Acland, Regional Agent for the National Trust. It contains a fine collection of azaleas and rhododendrons, planted to give good blends of colour under the thinned oaks on the hillside; also many trees and shrubs, including magnolias, camellias and embothriums.
Location: OS Ref 200. NY380 029. ¹/₂ m S of Ambleside on A591.
Open: 1 Apr - end Oct: daily, 10am - 6.30pm. Colours best Apr - Jun.
Admission: £1.50, no reduction for groups.
♿Unsuitable. ⓅNone. ▣

STEAM YACHT GONDOLA 🌿
(NT Gondola Bookings) National Trust Office, The Hollens, Grasmere, LA22 9QZ
Tel: 015394 41288 **Fax:** 015394 35353
Owner: The National Trust   **Contact:** The Manager
The Steam Yacht Gondola, first launched in 1859 and now completely renovated by the Trust, provides a steam-powered passenger service, carrying 86 passengers in opulently upholstered saloons. A superb way to see Coniston's scenery.
Location: OS Ref. SD305 975. Coniston (¹/₂ m to Coniston Pier).
Open: Sails from Coniston Pier daily from 11am, 1 Mar - 31 Oct. The Trust reserves the right to cancel sailings in the event of high winds or lack of demand. Piers at Coniston and Brantwood (not NT).
Admission: Ticket prices & timetable on application and published locally. Family ticket available. No reduction for NT members as Gondola is an enterprise and not held solely for preservation. Groups & private charters by prior arrangement.
♿Unsuitable. ♿Dogs on leads, outside saloons, 50p any journey.

Website Information
◁ ◁ ◁   pg 39

STOTT PARK BOBBIN MILL ⊞

Low Stott Park, Nr Newby Bridge, Cumbria LA12 8AX
Tel: 01539 531087
Owner: English Heritage   **Contact:** The Custodian
When this working mill was built in 1835 it was typical of the many mills in the Lake District which grew up to supply the spinning and weaving industry in Lancashire but have since disappeared. A remarkable opportunity to see a demonstration of the machinery and techniques of the Industrial Revolution. Steam days: Tues - Thurs.
Location: OS96 Ref. SD373 883. Near Newby Bridge on A590.
Open: 29 Mar - 30 Sept: daily, 10am - 6pm. 1 - 31 Oct: daily, 10am - 5pm. Last admission 1hr before closing.
Admission: Adult £3.20, Child £1.60, Conc. £2.40. Groups: discount for groups (11+).
🖻 ⑤ Ground floor. WC. 🏰 Free. 🅿 ▣ ✉

HELENA THOMPSON MUSEUM

Park End Road, Workington, Cumbria CA14 4DE
Tel: 01900 326255   **e-mail:** heritage.arts@allerdale.gov.uk
Owner: Allerdale Borough Council   **Contact:** Heritage & Arts Unit
The museum is housed in a fine listed mid-Georgian building. Displays include pottery, silver, glass, furniture and dress collection.
Location: OS Ref. NY007 286. Corner of A66, Ramsey Brow & Park End Road.
Open: Apr - Sept: Mon - Sat, 10.30am - 4pm. Nov - Mar: Mon - Sat, 11am - 3pm.
Admission: Free.

WORDSWORTH HOUSE ✄

See full page advertisement on page 23
Main Street, Cockermouth, Cumbria CA13 9RX
Tel: 01900 824805   **e-mail:** rwordh@smtp.ntrust.org.uk   **www.**wordsworthlakes.co.uk
Owner: The National Trust   **Contact:** The Custodian
A Georgian town house where William Wordsworth was born in 1770 in the ancient market town of Cockermouth. Several rooms contain some of the poet's personal effects. His childhood garden, with terraced walk attractively restored, with views over the River Derwent referred to in *'The Prelude'*. Kitchen garden under restoration.
Location: OS Ref. NY118 307. Main Street, Cockermouth.
Open: 25 Mar - 1 Nov: weekdays only, plus all BH Sats and Sats in Jun, Jul & Aug, 10.30am - 4.30pm. Last admission 4pm.
Admission: Adult £3.50, Child £1.50, Family £8. Pre-booked groups £2.50. Reciprocal discount ticket with Dove Cottage and Rydal Mount.
🖻 ⑤ By arrangement only. ▣ 🅿 None. ✉

WORKINGTON HALL

Ramsey Brow, Workington, Cumbria
Tel: 01900 326408   **e-mail:** heritage.arts@allerdale.gov.uk
Owner: Allerdale Borough Council   **Contact:** Allerdale Borough Tourism Dept.
Refuge for Mary Queen of Scots during her last night of freedom in May 1568, this was one of the finest Manor houses in the region. Now a ruin.
Location: OS Ref. NY007 288. In public park on N side of A66.
Open: Please telephone for opening times.
Admission: Adult 85p, Conc. 55p, Family (2+2/1+3) £2.25.

Acorn Bank Garden & Watermill

NT Photographic Library: Matthew Antrobus

National Trust Photo Library / Stephen Robson

TOWNEND ✄

TROUTBECK, WINDERMERE, CUMBRIA LA23 1LB

Tel: 01539 432628   **e-mail:** rtown@smtp.ntrust.org.uk
Owner: The National Trust   **Contact:** The Administrator
An exceptional relic of Lake District life during past centuries. Originally a 'statesman' (wealthy yeoman) farmer's house, built about 1626. Townend contains carved woodwork, books, papers, furniture and fascinating implements of the past which were accumulated by the Browne family who lived here from 1626 until 1943. Regular 'Living History' programme - Meet George Browne c1900.
Location: OS Ref. NY407 020. 3m SE of Ambleside at S end of Troutbeck village. 1m from Holehird, 3m N of Windermere.
Open: 2 Apr - 31 Oct: Tue - Fri, Suns & BH Mons, 1 - 5pm or dusk if earlier. Last admission 4.30pm.
Admission: Adult £3, Child £1.50, Family £7.50. No reduction for groups which must be pre-booked. Townend and village unsuitable for coaches; 12 - 15 seater mini-buses are acceptable; permission to take coaches to Townend must be obtained from the Transportation and Highways Dept, Cumbria CC, Carlisle, Cumbria.
⑤ Unsuitable for wheelchairs. Braille guide. ✉ ⑭ Tel for details.

❄ Open All Year Index
◁ ◁ ◁ pgs 44-48

English Life Publication Ltd

LEIGHTON HALL

CARNFORTH

www.leightonhall.co.uk

Owner:

Richard Gillow
Reynolds Esq

▶ CONTACT

Mrs C S Reynolds
Leighton Hall
Carnforth
Lancashire LA5 9ST

Tel: 01524 734474
Fax: 01524 720357

e-mail: info@
leightonhall.co.uk

▶ LOCATION

OS Ref. SD494 744

9m N of Lancaster,
10m S of Kendal,
3m N of Carnforth.
1¹/₂ m W of A6.
3m from M6/A6/J35,
signed from J35A.

Rail: Lancaster
Station 9m.

Air: Manchester
Airport 65m.

Taxi: Carnforth Radio
Taxis, Carnforth
732763.

CONFERENCE/FUNCTION

ROOM	SIZE	MAX CAPACITY
Music Room	24' x 21'6"	80
Dining Rm		30
Other		80

Leighton Hall is one of the most beautifully sited houses in the British Isles, situated in a bowl of parkland, with the whole panorama of the Lakeland Fells rising behind. The hall's neo-gothic façade was superimposed on an 18th century house, which, in turn, had been built on the ruins of the original medieval house. The present owner is descended from Adam d'Avranches who built the first house in 1246.

The whole house is lived in by the Reynolds family and emphasis is put on making visitors feel welcome in a family home.

Connoisseurs of furniture will be particularly interested in the 18th century pieces by Gillow of Lancaster. Mr Reynolds is directly descended from the founder of Gillow and Company, hence the strong Gillow connection with the house. Also on show are some fine pictures, clocks, silver and *objets d'art.*

GARDENS

The main garden has a continuous herbaceous border and rose covered walls, while the Walled Garden contains flowering shrubs, a herb garden, an ornamental vegetable garden and a maze. Beyond is the Woodland Walk, where wild flowers abound from early Spring.

A varied collection of Birds of Prey is on display in the Bird Garden, and flown each afternoon that the hall is open, weather permitting.

Performing Arts

🗄️ ✳️ ℹ️ Product launches, seminars, filming, garden parties, conferences, rallies, overland
driving, archery and clay pigeon shoots, grand piano. No photography in house. Large collection of birds of prey on display in the afternoon, some of which fly at 3.30pm, weather permitting.

🍽️ Buffets, lunches, dinners and wedding receptions.

♿ Partially suitable. WC. Visitors may alight at the entrance.

🍴 Groups must book, menus on request.

🚶 Obligatory. By prior arrangement owner may meet groups, tour time: 45 mins. House and flying display tour time: 2 hrs. Lectures on property, its contents, gardens and history.

🅿️ Ample.

🏫 School programme 10am-2pm daily May-Sept except Mons & Sats. Birds of prey flown for schools at 12pm. Schools Visit Programme won the Sandford Award for Heritage Education in 1983 and in 1989.

🐕 In grounds, on leads.

❄️ For booked groups & functions.

🛡️ Tel for details.

▶ OPENING TIMES

Summer

1 May - 30 September
Daily except Mons & Sats
2 - 5pm. Open BH Mons.

August only:
12.30 - 5pm.

NB. Booked groups (25+) at any time by arrangement.

Winter

1 October - 30 April
Open to booked
groups (25+).

▶ ADMISSION

Summer

House, Garden & Birds

Adult	£4.50
Child (5-12yrs)	£3.00
Student/OAP	£4.00

Groups (Min. payment £80)

Adult	£3.75
Child (5-12yrs)	£2.95
Family (2+3)	£13.50
School	£2.95

Child under 5yrs, Free

Grounds only
(after 4.30pm)

Per person £1.50

Winter

As above but groups by appointment only.

North West - England

ASTLEY HALL
ASTLEY PARK, OFF HALL GATE, CHORLEY PR7 1NP
www.astleyhall.co.uk

Tel: 01257 515555 **Fax:** 01257 515556 **e-mail:** astleyhall@lineone.net

Owner: Chorley Borough Council   **Contact:** Dr Nigel Wright

A charming house, dating back to 1580, with additions in the 1660s and 1820s. Interiors include sumptuous plaster ceilings, fine 17th century oak furniture and tapestries, plus displays of fine and decorative art. Set in parkland.

Location: OS Ref. SD574 183. 2m W of Chorley, off A581 Chorley - Southport road. 5 mins from M61/J8.

Open: Easter - end Oct: Tue - Sun, 12 noon - 5pm. Plus BH Mons. Nov - Easter: weekends only, 12 noon - 4pm. Closed Christmas & New Year.

Admission: Adult £2.95, Child/Conc. £1.95, Family £7.50. Groups: Adult £2.35, Child/Conc. £1.35.

ℹ️No photography. 🏠 🚻 ♿Partial. Braille guide. 🍽️ 📷By arrangement. 🏮 🎁 P 🐕Guide dogs only. ⚓ ✳️

BLACKBURN CATHEDRAL
Cathedral Close, Blackburn, Lancashire BB1 5AA

Tel: 01254 51491 **Fax:** 01254 689666   **Contact:** Mrs Alison Feeney

On an historic Saxon site in town centre. The 1826 Parish Church dedicated as the Cathedral in 1977 with new extensions to give a spacious and light interior. The distinctive 'crowning glory' Lantern Tower was rebuilt in 1998 with 56 panels of newly-designed symbolic stained glass to give a new and unique magnificence by day and night. Other features include a fine Walker organ, 12 peal bells and a 'corona' (crown of thorns) above the central altar.

Location: OS Ref. SD684 280. 9m E of M6/J31, via A59 and A677. City centre.

Open: Daily, 9am - 5pm. Sun services: at 8am, 9.15am, 10.30am and 4pm.

Admission: Free. Donations invited.

♿Wheelchair access. 🍽️Wed & Fri, 10am - 2.30pm or Sats by arrangement. 📷By arrangement. PNearby shopping centre. ✳️

GAWTHORPE HALL 🌿
Padiham, Nr Burnley, Lancashire BB12 8UA

Tel: 01282 771004 **Fax:** 01282 770178 **e-mail:** rpmgaw@smtp.ntrust.org.uk

Owner: The National Trust   **Contact:** The Property Manager

The house was built in 1600-05, and restored by Sir Charles Barry in the 1850s. Barry's designs have been re-created in the principal rooms. Gawthorpe was the home of the Shuttleworth family, and the Rachel Kay-Shuttleworth textile collections are on display in the house, private study by arrangement. Collection of portraits on loan from the National Portrait Gallery.

Location: OS Ref. SD806 340. M65/J8. On E outskirts of Padiham, ³/₄ m to house on N of A671. Signed to Clitheroe, then signed from 2nd set of traffic lights.

Open: Hall: 1 Apr - 31 Oct: daily except Mons & Fris, open Good Fri & BH Mons, 1 - 5pm. Last adm. 4.30pm. Garden: All year: daily, 10am - 6pm.

Admission: Hall: Adult £3, Child £1.30, Conc. £1.50, Family £8 (prices may change). Garden: Free. Groups must book.

♿Prior warning of visit essential. 🍽️ 🐕In grounds on leads. ✳️

HALL I'TH'WOOD
off Green Way, Tonge Moor, Bolton BL1 8UA

Tel: 01204 332370

Owner: Bolton Metropolitan Borough Council   **Contact:** Vicky Geddes

Late medieval manor house with 17/18th century furniture, paintings and decorative art.

Location: OS Ref. SD724 116. 2m NNE of central Bolton. ¹/₄ m N of A58 ring road between A666 and A676 crossroads.

Open: Please contact for details.

Admission: Adult £3, Conc. £1.50.

HOGHTON TOWER 🏛️
HOGHTON, PRESTON, LANCASHIRE PR5 0SH

Tel: 01254 852986 **Fax:** 01254 852109

Owner: Sir Bernard de Hoghton Bt   **Contact:** Office

Hoghton Tower, home of 14th Baronet, is one of the most dramatic looking houses in northern England. Three houses have occupied the hill site since 1100 with the present house re-built by Thomas Hoghton between 1560 - 1565. Rich and varied historical events including the Knighting of the Loin 'Sirloin' by James I in 1617.

Location: OS Ref. SD622 264. M65/J3. Midway between Preston & Blackburn on A675.

Open: Jul, Aug & Sept: Mon - Thur, 11am - 4pm. Suns, 1 - 5pm. BH Suns & Mons excluding Christmas & New Year. Group visits by appointment all year.

Admission: Gardens & House tours: Adult £5, Child £2, Conc. £4, Family £12. Gardens, Shop & Tearoom only: £2. Children under 16 Free. Private tours by arrangement (25 min) £6, OAP £5.

🏠 🚻Conferences, wedding receptions. ♿Unsuitable. 🍽️ 📷Obligatory. P ⚓ ✳️

LEIGHTON HALL 🏛️   *See page 418 for full page entry.*
See page 418 for full page entry.

MANCHESTER CATHEDRAL
Manchester M3 1SX

Tel: 0161 833 2220 **Fax:** 0161 839 6226

In addition to regular worship and daily offices, there are frequent professional concerts, day schools, organ recitals, guided tours and brass-rubbing. The cathedral contains a wealth of beautiful carvings and has the widest medieval nave in Britain. Visitor Centre and restaurant opening early in July.

Location: OS Ref. SJ838 988. Manchester.

Open: Daily.

Admission: Donations welcome.

ℹ️Visitor Centre. 🍴Due to open July 2002.

MARTHOLME
Great Harwood, Blackburn, Lancashire BB6 7UJ

Owner: Mr & Mrs T H Codling   **Contact:** Miss P M Codling

Part of medieval manor house with 17th century additions and Elizabethan gatehouse.

Location: OS Ref. SD753 338. 2m NE of Great Harwood off A680 to Whalley.

Open: Groups (8+) by written appointment only.

Admission: £3.50.

Accommodation Index ◁ ◁ ◁ pg 27

RUFFORD OLD HALL ❧

RUFFORD, Nr ORMSKIRK, LANCASHIRE L40 1SG

Tel: 01704 821254 **e-mail:** rrufoh@smtp.ntrust.org.uk

Owner: The National Trust   **Contact:** The Property Manager

There is a legend that William Shakespeare performed here for the owner Sir Thomas Hesketh in the Great Hall of this, one of the finest 16th century buildings in Lancashire. The playwright would have delighted in the magnificent hall with its intricately carved movable wooden screen. Built in 1530, it established the Hesketh family seat for the next 250 years. In the Carolean Wing, altered in 1821, there are fine collections of 16th and 17th century oak furniture, arms, armour and tapestries.

An audio tour is available to guide visitors around the house. The attractive garden includes sculpture and topiary.

Location: OS Ref. SD463 160. 7m N of Ormskirk, in village of Rufford on E side of A59.

Open: 23 Mar - 30 Oct: Sat - Wed, 1 - 5pm. Garden: as house, 11am - 5.30pm.

Admission: House & Garden: Adult £4, Child £2, Family £10. Garden only: £2. Pre-booked groups £2.75 (no groups on Suns & BH Mons).

⬚ ⬚ Partial. ⬚⬚ ⬚ In grounds, on leads.

SAMLESBURY HALL

Preston New Road, Samlesbury, Preston PR5 0UP

Tel: 01254 812010 **Fax:** 01254 812174

Owner: Samlesbury Hall Trust   **Contact:** Mr David Hornby

Built in 1325, the hall is an attractive black and white timbered manor house set in extensive grounds.

Location: OS Ref. SD623 305. N side of A677, 4m WNW of Blackburn.

Open: All year: daily except Sats & Mons: 11am - 4.30pm. Closed over Christmas and New Year.

Admission: Adult £2.50, Child £1.

SMITHILLS HALL MUSEUM

Smithills Dean Road, Bolton BL1 7NP

Tel: 01204 332377

Owner: Bolton Metropolitan Borough Council   **Contact:** Mr Derek Mills

14th century fortified manor house with Tudor panelling. Stuart furniture. Stained glass.

Location: OS Ref. SD699 119. 2m NW of central Bolton, 1/2 m N of A58 ringroad.

Open: Please contact for details.

Admission: Adult £3, Conc. £1.50.

STONYHURST COLLEGE

Stonyhurst, Clitheroe, Lancashire BB7 9PZ

Tel: 01254 826345 **Fax:** 01254 826732   **Contact:** Miss F Ahearne

The original house dates from the late 16th century. Set in extensive grounds.

Location: OS Ref. SD690 391. 4m SW of Clitheroe off B6243.

Open: House: 15 Jul - 25 Aug: Sat - Thur (including Aug BH Mon), 1 - 5pm. Grounds & Gardens: 1 Jul - 26 Aug: Sat - Thur (including Aug BH Mon), 1 - 5pm.

Admission: House & Grounds: Adult £4.50, Child (4-14yrs)/OAP £3.50. Grounds only £1.

TOWNELEY HALL ART GALLERY & MUSEUMS

Burnley BB11 3RQ

Tel: 01282 424213 **Fax:** 01282 436138 **www.**towneleyhall.org.uk

Owner: Burnley Borough Council   **Contact:** Miss Susan Bourne

House dates from the 14th century with 17th and 19th century modifications. Collections include oak furniture, 18th and 19th century paintings. There is a Museum of Local Crafts and Industries and a Natural History Centre with an aquarium in the grounds.

Location: OS Ref. SD854 309. 1/2 m SE of Burnley on E side of Todmorden Road (A671).

Open: All year: Mon - Fri, 10am - 5pm. Suns, 12 noon - 5pm. Closed Sats. Closed Christmas - New Year. North West Wing closed spring 2002 due to Heritage Lottery Fund refurbishment work - please telephone to confirm opening arrangments.

Admission: Free. Guided tours: Tues, Weds & Thurs afternoons or as booked for groups.

⬚ ⬚ Ground floor & grounds. WC. ⬚ ⬚ ✳ ⬚ Tel for details.

TURTON TOWER

Chapeltown Road, Turton BL7 0HG

Tel: 01204 852203 **Fax:** 01204 853759 **e-mail:** turntontower.lcc@btinternet.com

Owner: Lancashire County Council   **Contact:** Martin Robinson-Dowland

Country house based on a medieval tower, extended in the 16th, 17th and 19th centuries.

Location: OS Ref. SD733 153. On B6391, 4m N of Bolton.

Open: Feb & Nov: Suns, 1 - 4pm. Mar & Oct: Sat - Wed, 1 - 4pm. Apr: Sat - Wed, 2 - 5pm. May - Sept: Mon - Thur, 10am - 12 noon, 1 - 5pm. Sats & Suns 1 - 5pm.

Admission: Adult £3, Child/OAP £1.50, Family £8. Season ticket available.

WARTON OLD RECTORY ⌗

Warton, Carnforth, Lancashire

Tel: 0161 242 1400

Owner: English Heritage   **Contact:** The North West Regional Office

A rare medieval stone house with remains of the hall, chambers and domestic offices.

Location: OS Ref. SD499 723. At Warton, 1m N of Carnforth on minor road off A6.

Open: Any reasonable time.

Admission: Free.

BLUECOAT ARTS CENTRE
School Lane, Liverpool L1 3BX

Tel: 0151 709 5297 **Fax:** 0151 707 0048 **e-mail:** admin@bluecoatartscentre.com
www.bluecoatartscentre.com

Owner: Bluecoat Arts Centre Ltd   **Contact:** Building Manager
Built in 1717, the Bluecoat is of outstanding historical and architectural interest, with Grade I listed building status, and is a popular tourist attraction in the heart of Liverpool. The oldest building in the city centre, and now, arguably the oldest arts centre in Britain, it is one of the most exciting arts venues in the region with an impressive Queen Anne style façade and walled garden. The unique mix of exhibitions and perfomances, café and shops, including local history, books and crafts and collectors' fairs offers visitors an alternative experience in the city.
Location: OS Ref. SJ346 902. ¼ m S of Lime Street station.
Open: Mon - Sat, 9.30am - 6pm (unless there is an evening performance, outside hire or exhibition setting). Gallery closed Suns & Mons.
Admission: Free admission to Building and Gallery, with varying prices for the Performing Arts events.
Partial. WC.

CROXTETH HALL & COUNTRY PARK
Liverpool, Merseyside L12 0HB

Tel: 0151 228 5311 **Fax:** 0151 228 2817 **www**.croxteth.co.uk

Owner: Liverpool City Council   **Contact:** Mrs Irene Vickers
Ancestral home of the Molyneux family. 500 acres country park. Special events and attractions most weekends.
Location: OS Ref. SJ408 943. 5m NE of Liverpool city centre.
Open: Parkland: daily throughout the year. Hall, Farm & Garden: daily, 11am - 5pm during main season. Telephone for exact dates.
Admission: Parkland: Free. Hall, Farm & Garden: prices on application.

LIVERPOOL CATHEDRAL
Liverpool, Merseyside L1 7AZ

Tel: 0151 709 6271 **Fax:** 0151 702 7292

Owner: The Dean and Chapter   **Contact:** Canon Noel Vincent
Sir Giles Gilbert Scott's greatest creation. Built this century from local sandstone with superb glass, stonework and major works of art, it is the largest cathedral in Britain and has a fine musical tradition, a tower offering panoramic views, and an award-winning refectory. There is a unique collection of church embroidery, and SPCK shop with a full range of souvenirs, cards and religious books.
Location: OS Ref. SJ354 893. Central Liverpool, ½ m S of Lime Street Station.
Open: 8am - 6pm. Sun services: 8am, 10.30am, 3pm, 4pm. Weekdays: 8am & 5.30pm. Sats: 8am & 3pm.
Admission: Donation. Lift to Tower and Embroidery Exhibition: £2.
Grounds. WC. Guide dogs only.

LIVERPOOL METROPOLITAN CATHEDRAL OF CHRIST THE KING
Liverpool, Merseyside L3 5TQ

Tel: 0151 709 9222 **Fax:** 0151 708 7274 **e-mail:** met.cathedral@cwcom.net
Owner: Roman Catholic Archdiocese of Liverpool   **Contact:** Rt Rev P Cookson
Modern circular cathedral with spectacular glass by John Piper and numerous modern works of art. Extensive earlier crypt by Lutyens. Grade II* listed.
Location: OS Ref. SJ356 903. Central Liverpool, ½ m E of Lime Street Station.
Open: 8am - 6pm (closes 5pm Suns in Winter). Sun services: 8.30am, 10am, 11am, 3pm & 7pm. Weekday services: 8am, 12.15pm, 5.15pm & 5.45pm. Sats, 9am.
Admission: Donation.
Except crypt. WCs. By arrangement. Ample for cars.
Guide dogs only.

MEOLS HALL
Churchtown, Southport, Merseyside PR9 7LZ

Tel: 01704 228326 **Fax:** 01704 507185 **e-mail:** events@meolshall.com

Owner: Robert Hesketh Esq   **Contact:** Pamela Whelan
17th century house with subsequent additions. Interesting collection of pictures and furniture.
Location: OS Ref. SD365 184. 3m NE of Southport town centre in Churchtown. SE of A565.
Open: 14 Aug - 14 Sept: daily, 2 - 5pm.
Admission: Adult £3, Child £1. Groups £8.50 (inclusive of afternoon tea).

PORT SUNLIGHT VILLAGE & HERITAGE CENTRE
95 Greendale Road, Port Sunlight CH62 4XE

Tel: 0151 6446466 **Fax:** 0151 6458973   **Contact:** The Centre
Port Sunlight is a picturesque 19th century garden village on the Wirral.
Location: OS Ref. SJ340 845. Follow signs from M53/J4 or 5 or follow signs on A41.
Open: All year, 10am - 4pm in summer; 11am - 4pm in winter.
Admission: Adult 70p, Child 30p, Conc. 60p. Group rates on application.

SPEKE HALL GARDEN & ESTATE
The Walk, Liverpool L24 1XD

Tel: 0151 427 7231 **Fax:** 0151 427 9860 **Info Line:** 08457 585702
www.spekehall.org.uk
Owner: The National Trust   **Contact:** Simon Osborne, The Property Manager
One of the most famous half-timbered houses in the country.
Location: OS Ref. SJ419 825. North bank of the Mersey, 6m SE of city centre. Follow signs for Liverpool John Lennon airport.
Open: House: 23 Mar - 29 Oct: daily except Mons & Tues (open BH Mons), 1 - 5.30pm. 4 Nov - 10 Dec: Sats & Suns, 1 - 4.30pm. Woodland & Garden: 28 Mar - 29 Oct: Daily except Mons (open BH Mons) from 12 noon. Nov - Mar 2000: daily except Mons, 12 noon - 4pm. Closed Good Fri, 24/25/26/31 Dec & 1 Jan. Last admission 30 mins before close.
Admission: Estate: £3 per car (refunded when when garden or house ticket purchased). Garden: £2.50pp. House & Garden: £5. Family £14.

Croxteth Hall

Patrick Lane

Chipchase Castle

North East

Mrs P J Torday

Chipchase Castle

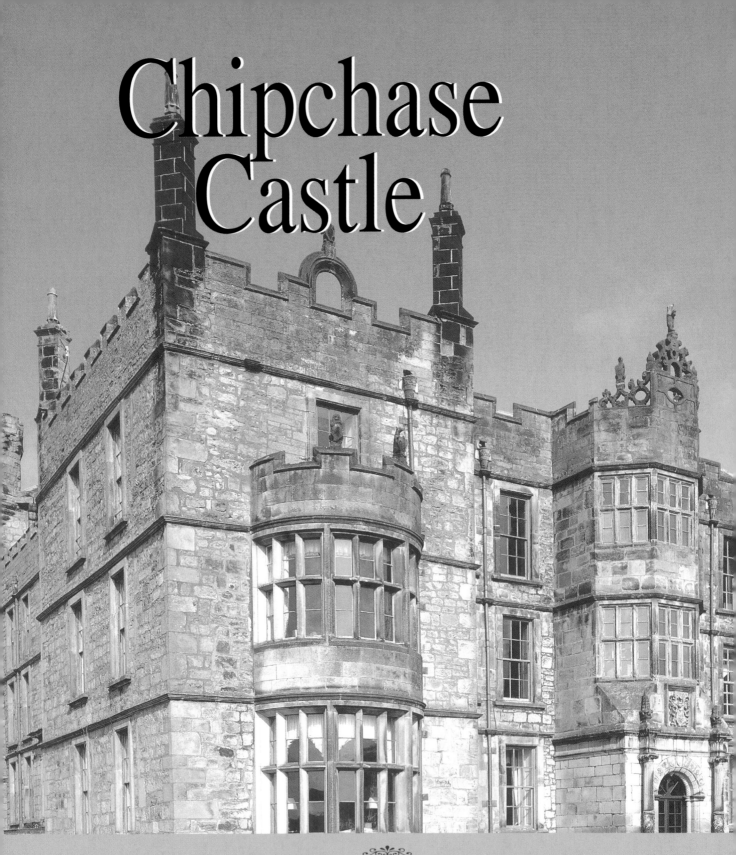

"A fare tower and a manor of stone warke joyned thereunto of thinheytaunce of John Heron of the same, esquier, kepte in good reparacions."

Description of Chipchase Castle – an official view of the Castle, Towers, Barmekyns and Fortresses of the Frontier of the East and Middle Marches drawn up by the Royal Commissioners 1541

Mrs P J Torday

Mrs P J Torday

Mrs P J Torday

Mrs P J Torday

Mrs P J Torday

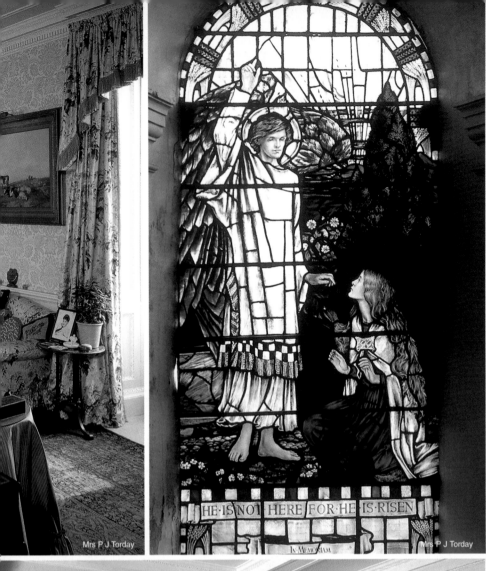

Mrs P J Torday

HE IS NOT HERE FOR HE IS RISEN

IN MEMORIAM

Mrs P J Torday

Mrs P J Torday

Chipchase Castle is to be found some 10 miles north of Hexham in south-west Northumberland. It lies on the east bank of the North Tyne and sits at the centre of a 1,603 acre estate. Records exist as far back as 1261 when Peter de Insula, the owner of Chipchase, obtained a licence from Alexander III, King of the Scots, to strengthen his mill dam on the North Tyne, because the right bank of the river was in the lordship of Tyndale, held by the King of Scots.

Chipchase is truly one of the hidden gems to be found in *Hudson's*. Not as well known as its fellow Northumbrian country house companions – Seaton Delaval Hall; Belsay Hall, Castle and Gardens; or Wallington – its history is no less interesting. Whilst the visitor to Chipchase today can wander through the elegantly comfortable reception rooms of the castle, built in c1621 and extended in 1784, it is the mediaeval heavily fortified pele tower on the east side of the building which really tells the tale of Chipchase's and the region's rugged past.

Legally it was necessary for licence to be obtained from the Crown before any castle could be erected. There are many such licences, called licences to crenellate, recorded in the Patent Rolls between 1267 and 1378 but none relate to Chipchase. However, the great angle bartizans on the pele tower, closely resemble those at neighbouring Belsay. Belsay was not built before 1371 and it may therefore be presumed that Chipchase was erected by Walter Heron between 1370 – 1390.

The 14th century tower is a rectangular structure, with walls over 9 feet thick. The remains of an oaken portcullis is still embedded in the slot above the entrance door. Although this has every appearance of considerable age, there can be little doubt that it replaces an older one of iron. Such stout defences were vital at a time of fierce border wars with Scotland – even now the greyness of these huge stone walls seem to exude the wildness and bleakness of this former time.

Little wonder then that in 1490 John Heron was appointed bailiff of Rededale by the King, under penalty of £500 *'to execute the duties of his office to capture felons and evil-doers and bring them to justice, and to allow no conventicles or privy meetings between English and Scots on the Marches or elsewhere at liberty.'*

The Herons were to own Chipchase until 1749. Over succeeding centuries it has been owned by a number of prominent local families and has mellowed into a wonderfully comfortable family home. Today it is owned by Mrs P J Torday, a descendant of Mr Hugh Taylor who bought the estate in 1862.

Northumbria is an area brimming with a vibrant sense of history, the legacy of the Roman Empire at Hadrian's Wall, the early steps of Christianity at Lindisfarne, and mediaeval border warfare of which Chipchase Castle, like its more famous neighbours, was to play a vital part. There may be bigger and more swaggering tales to tell at other castles in Northumbria but don't miss Chipchase – it has an equally beguiling story to tell and should be part of a great day out.

For further details about *Chipchase* see entry on page 435.

Mrs P J Torday

RABY CASTLE 🏛

DARLINGTON

www.rabycastle.com

Raby is without doubt one of the most impressive lived-in castles in England. Built mainly in the 14th century by the Nevill family on the site of an earlier manor house, it remained in their ownership until 1569. Since 1626 to the present day it has been the home of the Vane family. It was the childhood home of Cicely, Rose of Raby, mother of Kings Edward IV and Richard III, scene of the Plotting of the Rising of the North and a Parliamentary stronghold during the Civil War.

Despite its medieval exterior, Raby houses a fabulous art collection and sumptuous interiors. Treasures include an important collection of Meissen porcelain, tapestries, furniture, furnishings and paintings by De Hooch, Herring, Reynolds, Teniers, and Van Dyck.

Raby Castle is situated amidst a 200-acre Deer Park in the foothills of the North Pennines, where Red and Fallow Deer and Longhorn Cattle graze. Beautiful walled gardens with formal lawns, rose gardens and ornamental pond frame picturesque views of the Castle and valley beyond. The 18th century stable block contains a horse-drawn carriage collection and a Woodland Adventure Playground near the Stable Tearooms and Gift Shop means that Raby has something for everyone to enjoy.

Owner:
The Lord Barnard

▶ CONTACT

Clare Simpson/
Catherine Turnbull
Raby Castle
Staindrop
Darlington
Co. Durham DL2 3AH

Tel: 01833 660202
01833 660207
Fax: 01833 660169

e-mail: admin@
rabycastle.com

▶ LOCATION

OS Ref. NZ129 218

On A688, 1m N of Staindrop. 8m NE of Barnard Castle, 12m WNW of Darlington.

Rail: Darlington Station, 12m.

Air: Teesside Airport, 20m.

▶ OPENING TIMES

Summer

Castle
Easter & BH weekends
Sat - Wed, 1- 5pm.

May & September:
Weds & Suns only, 1 - 5pm.

June, July & August:
Daily except Sats, 1 - 5pm.

Guided tours by arrangement Easter - end September:
Mon - Fri, mornings only.

Park & Gardens
On Castle open days:
11am - 5.30pm.

Tearooms & Giftshop
All year, Sats & Weds.

Winter
October - Easter: Closed.

▶ ADMISSION

Castle, Park & Gardens
Adult £5.00
Child (5-15yrs) £2.00
OAP/Student £4.00
Family (2+3) £12.00
Season
Adult £25.00
Child (5-15yrs) £10.00
OAP/Student £20.00
Groups (20+)
Adult £4.00
Child (5-15yrs). £1.75
OAP/Student £3.50

Guided Tour
(incl. tea/coffee) £7.50

Park & Gardens
Adult £3.00
Child (5-15yrs) £2.00
OAP/Student £2.00
Groups (20+)
Adult £2.00
Child (5-15yrs). £1.75
OAP/Student £1.75

ℹ️ Film locations, product launches, corporate events, fairs & concerts. Raby Estates beef, lamb, venison & game. Soft fruit when in season. Lectures on castle, its contents, gardens & history. No photography or video filming is permitted, slides are on sale.

🏃 By arrangement. Tour time: 1½ hrs. 🅿️

🎒 Up to 60 children. £1.50 per pupil, 1 adult free per 20 pupils.

🐕 Guide dogs welcome, others on leads in park & gardens only.

  ⊤ ♿ Partial. WC. Licensed.

AUCKLAND CASTLE 🏰

BISHOP AUCKLAND, CO. DURHAM DL14 7NR

www.auckland-castle.co.uk

Tel: 01388 601627 **Fax:** 01388 609323 **e-mail:** auckland.castle@zetnet.co.uk

Owner: Church Commissioners **Contact:** The Manager

Principal country residence of the Bishops of Durham since Norman times and now the official residence of the present day Bishops. The Chapel, reputedly one of the largest private chapel in Europe, was originally the 12th century banquet hall. Chapel and State Rooms including the Throne Room, Long Dining Room and King Charles Dining Room are open to the public. Access to the adjacent Bishop's Park with its 18th century Deer House.

Location: OS Ref. NZ214 303. Bishop Auckland, N end of town centre.

Open: 1 Apr - 30 Sept: Mons & Thurs, 12.30 - 5pm. Suns 2 - 5pm. Last admission 4.30pm.

Admission: Adult £3.50, Child/Conc. £2.50. Child (under 8yrs) Free. Special openings for groups (15+).

ⓘExhibitions. No indoor photography. 🄰 ⓉWedding receptions, functions. ♿ 🕊 🅿 🔌 🐕Guide dogs only.

AUCKLAND CASTLE DEER HOUSE ⌗

Bishop Auckland, Durham

Tel: 0191 2691200

Owner: English Heritage **Contact:** The North Regional Office

A charming building erected in 1760 in the Park of the Bishops of Durham so that the deer could shelter and find food.

Location: OS Ref. NZ216 305. In Bishop Auckland Park, just N of town centre on A689. About 500 yds N of the castle.

Open: Park opening times – see Auckland Castle.

Admission: Free.

BARNARD CASTLE ⌗

Barnard Castle, Castle House, Durham DL12 9AT

Tel: 01833 638212

Owner: English Heritage **Contact:** The Custodian

The substantial remains of this large castle stand on a rugged escarpment overlooking the River Tees. Parts of the 14th century Great Hall and the cylindrical 12th century tower, built by the Baliol family can still be seen. Sensory garden.

Location: OS92 Ref. NZ049 165. In Barnard Castle.

Open: 29 Mar - 30 Sept: daily, 10am - 6pm. 1 - 31 Oct: daily, 10am - 5pm. 1 Nov - 31 Mar: Wed - Sun, 10am - 4pm. Closed 24 - 26 Dec & 1 Jan. Closed 1 - 2pm.

Admission: Adult £2.50, Child £1.30, Conc. £1.90. 15% discount for groups (11+).

🄰 ♿Grounds. 🕊Inclusive. 🅿None. 🔌 🐕In grounds, on leads. ✳ 🛏Tel for details.

BINCHESTER ROMAN FORT

Bishop Auckland, Co. Durham

Tel: 0191 3834212 **e-mail:** archaeology@durham.gov.uk

Owner: Durham County Council **Contact:** Niall Hammond

Once the largest Roman fort in Co Durham, the heart of the site has been excavated.

Location: OS92 Ref. NZ210 312. $1^{1}/_{2}$ m N of Bishop Auckland, signposted from A690 Durham - Crook and from A688 Spennymoor - Bishop Auckland roads.

Open: Easter weekend & 1 May - 30 Sept: daily, 11am - 5pm.

Admission: Please contact for details.

THE BOWES MUSEUM

BARNARD CASTLE, CO. DURHAM DL12 8NP

www.bowesmuseum.org.uk

Tel: 01833 690606 **Fax:** 01833 637163 **e-mail:** info@bowesmuseum.org.uk

Owner: The Bowes Museum Ltd

This stunning Grade I listed French-style château houses a designated collection of European fine and decorative art, together with displays of archaeology and local history. A busy programme brings new exhibitions and events including concerts, craft markets, family fun days and theatre. The summer exhibition for 2003 is 600 years of Royal Sugar Sculpture.

Location: OS Ref. NZ055 164. $^{1}/_{4}$ m E of Market Place in Barnard Castle.

Open: All year: Daily, 11am - 5pm. Closed 25/26 Dec & 1 Jan.

Admission: Adult £4, Child/Conc £3, Family £12. Groups (10+): Adult £3.60, Child/Conc. £2.70.

🄰 Ⓣ ♿ 🄳Licensed. 🕊By arrangement. 🎧 🔌 🅿 🐕In grounds. 🄰 ✳ 🛏Tel for details.

CROOK HALL & GARDENS

Sidegate, Durham DH1 5SZ

Tel: 0191 3848028

Owner: Keith & Maggie Bell   **Contact:** Mrs Maggie Bell

Medieval manor house set in rural landscape on the edge of Durham city.

Location: OS Ref. NZ274 432. 1/2 m N of city centre.

Open: Easter weekend, BHs, Suns in May & Sept; Jun, Jul & Aug: daily except Sats, 1 - 5pm.

Admission: Adult £3.80, Child/OAP £3, Family £9.75.

DERWENTCOTE STEEL FURNACE ♯

Newcastle, Durham

Tel: 0191 2691200

Owner: English Heritage   **Contact:** The Custodian

Built in the 18th century it is the earliest and most complete authentic steel making furnace to have survived.

Location: OS Ref. NZ131 566. 10m SW of Newcastle N of the A694 between Rowland's Gill and Hamsterley.

Open: 29 Mar - 30 Sept: Suns, 1 - 5pm.

Admission: Free.

DURHAM CASTLE

Palace Green, Durham DH1 3RW

Tel: 0191 3743863 **Fax:** 0191 3747470   **Contact:** Mrs Julie Marshall

Durham Castle, founded in the 1070s, with the Cathedral is a World Heritage Site.

Location: OS Ref. NZ274 424. City centre, adjacent to cathedral.

Open: Mar - Sept: 10am - 12 noon & 2 - 4.30pm. Oct - Mar: 2 - 4pm.

Admission: Adult £3, Child £2, Family £6.50. Guide book £2.50.

DURHAM CATHEDRAL

Durham DH1 3EH

Tel: 0191 3864266 **Fax:** 0191 3864267 **e-mail:** enquiries@durhamcathedral.co.uk

Contact: Miss A Heywood

A World Heritage Site. Norman architecture. Burial place of St Cuthbert and the Venerable Bede.

Location: OS Ref. NZ274 422. Durham city centre.

Open: Summer: 17 Jun - 8 Sept. 9.30am - 8pm. Open only for worship and private prayer: All year: Mon - Sat, 7.30am - 9.30am and Suns, 7.45am - 12.30pm. The Cathedral is closed to visitors during evening recitals and concerts. Visitors welcome Mon - Sat, 9.30 - 5pm, Suns 12.30 - 3.30pm.

Admission: Cathedral: £3 donation. Tower: Adult £2, Child (under 16) £1, Family £5. Monk's Dormitory: Adult 80p, Child 20p, Family £1.50. AV: Adult 80p, Child 20p, Family £1.50.

EGGLESTONE ABBEY ♯

Durham

Tel: 0191 2691200

Owner: English Heritage   **Contact:** The North Regional Office

Picturesque remains of a 12th century abbey, located in a bend of the River Tees. Substantial parts of the church and abbey buildings remain.

Location: OS Ref. NZ062 151. 1 1/2 m SE of Barnard Castle on minor road off B6277.

Open: Any reasonable time.

Admission: Free.

ESCOMB CHURCH

Escomb, Bishop Auckland DL14 7ST

Owner: Church of England   **Contact:** Mrs E Kitching (01388 662265) or The Vicar (01388 602861)

Saxon church dating from the 7th century built of stone from Binchester Roman Fort.

Location: OS Ref. NZ189 302. 3m W of Bishop Auckland.

Open: Summer: 9am - 8pm. Winter: 9am - 4pm. Key available from 22 Saxon Green, Escomb.

Admission: Free.

FINCHALE PRIORY ♯

Finchdale Priory, Brasside, Newton Hall DH1 5SH

Tel: 0191 3863828

Owner: English Heritage   **Contact:** The Custodian

These beautiful 13th century priory remains are located beside the curving River Wear.

Location: OS85 Ref. NZ297 471. 4 1/2 m NE of Durham.

Open: 29 Mar - 30 Sept: daily, 10am - 6pm.

Admission: Adult £1.40, Child 70p, Conc. £1.10. 15% discount for groups (11+).

PIERCEBRIDGE ROMAN FORT

Piercebridge, Co. Durham

Tel: 01325 460532

Owner: Darlington Borough Council   **Contact:** Heritage Manager

Visible Roman remains include the east gate and defences, courtyard building and Roman road. Also remains of a bridge over the Tees.

Location: OS85 Ref. NZ211 157. Through narrow stile and short walk down lane opposite car park off A67 NE of the village. Bridge via signposted footpath from George Hotel car park.

Open: At all times.

Admission: Free.

RABY CASTLE 🏰   *See page 428 for full page entry.*

ROKEBY PARK 🏰

Nr Barnard Castle, Co Durham DL12 9RZ

Tel: 01833 637334

Owner: Trustees of Mortham Estate   **Contact:** Mrs P I Yeats (Curator)

Rokeby, a fine example of a 18th century Palladian-style country house.

Location: OS Ref. NZ082 142. Between A66 & Barnard Castle.

Open: May BH Mon then each Mon & Tue from Spring BH until the first Tue in Sept. Groups (25+) on other days by appointment.

Admission: Adult £5, Child £2, OAP £4.50. Group prices on request.

THE WEARDALE MUSEUM

Ireshopeburn, Co. Durham DL13 1EY

Tel: 01388 517433 **e-mail:** dtheatherington@argonet.co.uk

Contact: D T Heatherington

Small folk museum in minister's house. Includes 1870 Weardale cottage room, Wesley room and local history displays.

Location: OS Ref. NZ872 385. Adjacent to 18th century Methodist Chapel.

Open: Easter & May - Sept: Wed - Sun & BH, 2 - 5pm. Aug: daily, 2 - 5pm.

Admission: Adult £1, Child 30p.

WHITWORTH HALL COUNTRY PARK

Nr Spennymoor, Durham, Co Durham DL16 7QX

Tel: 01388 811772 **Fax:** 01388 818669 **e-mail:** enquiries@whitworthhall.co.uk **www.**whitworthhall.co.uk

Owner: Whitworth Hall Estates Ltd   **Contact:** Andrew Cummings

Grade II listed building, steeped in regional history, set in 73 acre estate, with ornamental lake, swans, herds of deer, Victorian walled garden and Britain's most northerly vineyard. Whitworth Hall Country Park Hotel offers luxurious accommodation, restaurants, function rooms and civil wedding licence. Shafto's Inn and Restaurant provides informal refreshment.

Location: OS Ref. NZ234 347. From Durham on A690 take 1st left after Brancepeth. Hotel 1m on left. A688 follow signs to Spennymoor town centre. Left at 1st roundabout into Whitworth Terrace then follow heritage signs.

Open: Gardens, Hotel & Shafto's Inn & Restaurant: all year, daily; Mon - Sat, 11am - 11pm, Sun, 11am - 10.30pm.

Admission: Free.

🔲 🔲 Partial. WCs. 🔲 Licensed. 🔲 Licensed. 🅿 🔲 Guide dogs only. 🔲 29 double with ensuite. 🔲 🔲 🔲 Tel for details.

Accommodation Index ◁ ◁ ◁   pg 27

ALNWICK CASTLE 🏛

ALNWICK

www.alnwickcastle.com   www.alnwickgarden.com

Owner:
His Grace the Duke of
Northumberland

▶ **CONTACT**

Alnwick Castle
Estate Office
Alnwick
Northumberland
NE66 1NQ

Tel: 01665 510777
Info: 01665 511100
Fax: 01665 510876

e-mail: enquiries@
alnwickcastle.com

▶ **LOCATION**

OS Ref. NU187 135

In Alnwick 1¹/₂ m
W of A1.

From London 6hrs,
Edinburgh 2hrs,
Chester 4hrs,
Newcastle 40mins
North Sea ferry
terminal 30mins.

Bus: From bus station
in Alnwick.

Rail: Alnmouth
Station 5m.
Kings Cross, London
3¹/₂hrs

Air: Newcastle 40mins.

Set in magnificent 'Capability' Brown landscape, Alnwick Castle is the home of the Duke of Northumberland. Owned by his family, the Percys, since 1309, the castle was a major stronghold during the Scottish wars.

Restorations by the 1st and 4th Dukes have transformed this massive fortress into a comfortable family home. The Italian Renaissance-style State Rooms are filled with fine furniture, porcelain and paintings by Canaletto, Van Dyck and Titian.

Within the grounds are the recently refurbished museums of the Northumberland Fusiliers, Northumberland Archaeology and the Percy Tenantry Volunteers 1798 - 1814. Quizzes and a location for the *Harry Potter* film make it a magical place for the whole family.

The castle's splendid Guest Hall is available for entertaining, concerts, wedding receptions and dinner dances. (Not open to the public.)

The Alnwick Garden. The ambitious 12 acre public garden is being created on the site of the neglected 18th century walled garden. The lines of original earth banks have been adopted by Belgian garden designers, Wirtz International, and the first phase opens in October 2001. By Easter 2002, the spectacular Grand Cascade feature will be complete, together with the Ornamental Garden and the Rose Garden, with 3,000 roses. To become a Friend of The Alnwick Garden, ring 01665 511133, and visit our website.

ℹ️ Conference facilities. Fashion shows, fairs, filming, parkland for hire. No photography inside the castle. No unaccompanied children.

🛍️ 🚻

🍷 Wedding receptions.

♿ Unsuitable.

🚶 By arrangement.

☕ Coffee, light lunches and teas.

🅿️ 200 cars and 6 coaches.

📖 Guidebook and worksheet, special rates for children and teachers.

🐕 Guide dogs only.

❄️ Garden only.

▶ **OPENING TIMES**

Castle
28 March - 25 October
Daily, 11am - 5pm,
last admission 4.15pm.

Private functions by
arrangement.

The Alnwick Garden
Every day except 25
December: 10am - 5pm
(or dusk), last admission
4.15pm.

▶ **ADMISSION**

Castle

Adult £6.95
Child* (16yrs & under).... Free
Conc. £5.95

Pre-booked Groups (14+)
Adult £5.95
Conc. £5.50
Education £1.20

The Alnwick Garden

Adult £4.00
Child...................... Free
Conc. £3.50

Pre-booked Groups (14+)
Adult £3.50
Conc. £3.00
Education £1.20

Joint Admission

Adult £9.50
Child* (16yrs & under).... Free
Conc. £8.50

Pre-booked Groups (14+)
Adult £8.50
Conc. £7.50
Education £2.00

* max. 3 per adult

CONFERENCE/FUNCTION

ROOM	SIZE	MAX CAPACITY
The Guest Hall	100' x 30'	300

Jarrold Colour Publications

BAMBURGH CASTLE

BAMBURGH

www.bamburghcastle.com

Owner:
Trustees Lord Armstrong
dec'd.

▶ **CONTACT**

The Administrator
Bamburgh Castle
Bamburgh
Northumberland
NE69 7DF

Tel: 01668 214515

Fax: 01668 214060

e-mail: bamburghcastle
@aol.com

▶ **LOCATION**
OS Ref. NU184 351

42m N of
Newcastle-upon-Tyne.
20m S of Berwick upon
Tweed. 6m E of Belford
by B1342 from
A1 at Belford.

Bus: Bus service
200 yards.

Rail: Berwick-upon-
Tweed 20m.

Taxi: J Swanston
01289 306124.

Air: Newcastle-upon-
Tyne 45m.

Bamburgh Castle is the home of the Armstrong family. The earliest reference to Bamburgh shows the craggy citadel to have been a royal centre by AD 547. Recent archaeological excavation has revealed that the site has been occupied since prehistoric times.

The Norman Keep has been the stronghold for nearly nine centuries, but the remainder has twice been extensively restored, initially by Lord Crewe in the 1750s and subsequently by the 2nd Lord Armstrong at the beginning of the 20th century. This Castle was the first to succumb to artillery fire – that of Edward IV.

The public rooms contain many exhibits,

including the loan collections of armour from HM Tower of London, the John George Joicey Museum, Newcastle-upon-Tyne and other private sources, which complement the castle's armour. Porcelain, china, jade, furniture from many periods, oils, water-colours and a host of interesting items are all contained within one of the most important buildings of Britain's national heritage.

VIEWS

The views from the ramparts are unsurpassed and take in Holy Island, the Farne Islands, one of Northumberland's finest beaches and, landwards, the Cheviot Hills.

▶ **OPENING TIMES**

16 March - 31 October
Daily, 11am - 5pm.
Last entry 4.30pm.

Tours by arrangement
at any time.

▶ **ADMISSION**

Summer

Adult	£4.50
Child (6 - 16yrs)	£1.50
OAP	£3.50

Groups *

Adult	£3.00
Child (6 - 16yrs)	£1.00
OAP	£2.00

* Min payment £50

Winter
Group rates only quoted.

ℹ️ Filming. No photography in house.

📷

♿ Limited access. WC.

☕ Tearooms for light refreshments. Groups can book.

🚶 By arrangement at any time, min charge out of hours £50.

🅿️ 100 cars, coaches park on tarmac drive at entrance.

🚌 Welcome. Guide provided if requested, educational pack.

🐕 Guide dogs only.

CHILLINGHAM CASTLE

NR ALNWICK

www.chillingham-castle.com

Owner:
Sir Humphry
Wakefield Bt

▶ CONTACT

Adminstrator
Chillingham Castle
Northumberland
NE66 5NJ

Tel: 01668 215359
Fax: 01668 215463

e-mail: enquiries@
chillingham-castle.com

▶ LOCATION

OS Ref. NU062 258

45m N of Newcastle
between A697 & A1.
2m S of B6348
at Chatton.
6m SE of Wooler.

Rail: Alnmouth
or Berwick.

This remarkable castle, the home of Sir Humphry Wakefield Bt, with its alarming dungeons has, since the 1200s, been continuously owned by the family of the Earls Grey and their relations. You will see active restoration of complex masonry, metalwork and ornamental plaster as the great halls and state rooms are gradually brought back to life with antique furniture, tapestries, arms and armour as of old and even a torture chamber.

At first a 12th century stronghold, Chillingham became a fully fortified castle in the 14th century. Wrapped in the nation's history it occupied a strategic position as a fortress during Northumberland's bloody border feuds, often besieged and at many times enjoying the patronage of royal visitors. In Tudor days there were additions but the underlying medieval character has always been retained. The 18th and 19th centuries saw decorative refinements and extravagances including the lake, garden and grounds laid out by Sir Jeffrey Wyatville, fresh from his triumphs at Windsor Castle.

GARDENS

With romantic grounds, the castle commands breathtaking views of the surrounding countryside. As you walk to the lake you will see, according to the season, drifts of snowdrops, daffodils or bluebells and an astonishing display of rhododendrons. This emphasises the restrained formality of the Elizabethan topiary garden, with its intricately clipped hedges of box and yew. Lawns, the formal gardens and woodland walks are all fully open to the public.

▶ OPENING TIMES

Summer

Easter
1 May - 30 September
Daily except Tue & Sat,
12 noon - 5pm.

Winter

October - April: Groups
any time by appointment.
All function activities
available.

▶ ADMISSION

Summer

Adult	£4.50
OAP	£4.00
Child (12+)	£1.00
Child under 12	Free

Groups (10+)

Per person	£3.80
Tour	£25.00

CONFERENCE/FUNCTION

ROOM	MAX CAPACITY
King James I Room	
Great Hall	100
Minstrels' Hall	60
2 x Drawing Room	
Museum	
Tea Room	35
Lower Gallery	
Upper Gallery	

 Corporate entertainment, lunches, drinks, dinners, wedding ceremonies and receptions.

Partial.

Booked meals for up to 100 people.

By arrangement.

 Avoid Lilburn route, coach parties welcome by prior arrangement. Limited for coaches.

 Apartments.

Civil Wedding Licence.

North East - England

ALNWICK CASTLE 🏛

See page 431 for full page entry.

AYDON CASTLE ⚜

Corbridge, Northumberland NE45 5PJ

Tel: 01434 632450

Owner: English Heritage   **Contact:** The Custodian

One of the finest fortified manor houses in England, dating from the late 13th century. Its survival, intact, can be attributed to its conversion to a farmhouse in the 17th century.

Location: OS87 Ref. NZ002 663. 2m NE of Corbridge, on minor road off B6321 or A68.

Open: 29 Mar - 30 Sept: daily, 10am - 6pm. 1- 31 Oct: daily, 10am - 5pm.

Admission: Adult £2.20, Child £1.10, Conc. £1.70. 15% discount for groups (11+).

📷 ♿ Ground floor & grounds. 🎦 🅿 Limited. 🔲 🐕In grounds, on leads.
🎗Tel for details.

BAMBURGH CASTLE 🏛

See page 432 for full page entry.

BELSAY HALL, CASTLE & GARDENS ⚜

See opposite for half page entry.

BERWICK BARRACKS ⚜

The Parade, Berwick-upon-Tweed, Northumberland TD15 1DF

Tel: 01289 304493

Owner: English Heritage   **Contact:** The Custodian

Among the earliest purpose built barracks, these have changed very little since 1717. They house an exhibition 'By Beat of Drum', which recreates scenes such as the barrack room from the life of the British infantryman, the Museum of the King's Own Scottish Borderers and the Borough Museum with fine art, local history exhibition and other collections. Guided tours available.

Location: OS75 Ref. NT994 535. On the Parade, off Church Street, Berwick town centre.

Open: 29 Mar - 30 Sept: daily, 10am - 6pm. 1 - 31 Oct: daily, 10am - 5pm. 1 Nov - 31 Mar: Wed - Sun, 10am - 4pm. Closed 24 - 26 Dec and 1 Jan.

Admission: Adult £2.80, Child £1.40, Conc. £2.10. 15% discount for groups (11+).

📷 ♿ Ground floor & grounds. 🎦 🅿 Limited. 🔲 🐕In grounds, on leads. ✳
🎗Tel for details.

BERWICK RAMPARTS ⚜

Berwick-upon-Tweed, Northumberland

Tel: 0191 269 1200

Owner: English Heritage   **Contact:** The Northern Regional Office

A remarkably complete system of town fortifications consisting of gateways, ramparts and projecting bastions built in the 16th century.

Location: OS Ref. NT994 535. Surrounding Berwick town centre on N bank of River Tweed.

Open: Any reasonable time.

Admission: Free.

BRINKBURN PRIORY ⚜

Long Framlington, Morpeth, Northumberland NE65 8AF

Tel: 01665 570628

Owner: English Heritage   **Contact:** The Custodian

This late 12th century church is a fine example of early gothic architecture, almost perfectly preserved, and is set in a lovely spot beside the River Coquet.

Location: OS81, Ref. NZ116 984. 4¹/2 m SE of Rothbury off B6344 5m W of A1.

Open: 29 Mar - 30 Sept: daily, 10am - 6pm. 1 - 31 Oct, daily, 10am - 5pm. Closed 24 - 26 Dec and 1 Jan.

Admission: Adult £1.70, Child 90p, Conc. £1.30. 15% discount for groups (11+).

♿ Unsuitable. 🅿 🔲 🐕 On leads. 🎗Tel for details.

CAPHEATON HALL

Newcastle-upon-Tyne NE19 2AB

Tel/Fax: 01830 530253

Owner/Contact: J Browne-Swinburne

Built for Sir John Swinburne in 1668 by Robert Trollapp, an architect of great and original talent.

Location: OS Ref. NZ038 805. 17m NW of Newcastle off A696.

Open: By written appointment only.

✳

© English Heritage Photo Library

BELSAY HALL, CASTLE & GARDENS ⚜

BELSAY, Nr PONTELAND, NORTHUMBERLAND NE20 0DX

www.english-heritage.org.uk

Tel: 01661 881636   **Fax:** 01661 881043

Owner: English Heritage   **Contact:** The Custodian

Belsay is one of the most remarkable estates in Northumberland's border country. The buildings, set amidst 30 acres of magnificent landscaped gardens, have been occupied by the same family for nearly 600 years. The gardens, created largely in the 19th century, are a fascinating mix of the formal and the informal with terraced gardens, a rhododendron garden, magnolia garden, mature woodland and even a winter garden. The buildings comprise a 14th century castle, a manor house and Belsay Hall, an internationally famous mansion designed by Sir Charles Monck in the 19th century in the style of classical buildings he had encountered during a tour of Greece.

© English Heritage Photo Library

Location: OS87, Ref. NZ088 785. In Belsay 14m (22.4 km) NW of Newcastle on SW of A696. 7m NW of Ponteland. Nearest airport and station is Newcastle.

Open: 29 Mar - 30 Sept: daily, 10am - 6pm. 1 - 31 Oct: daily, 10am - 5pm. 1 Nov - 31 Mar: daily, 10am - 4pm. Closed 24 - 26 Dec and 1 Jan.

Admission: Adult £4, Child £2, Conc. £3. 15% discount for groups (11+).

📷 🎦 ♿ Partial. WC. 🔲 During summer & weekends Apr - Oct. 🅿 🔲
🐕In grounds, on leads. 🎗Tel for details.

CHERRYBURN – THOMAS BEWICK BIRTHPLACE

Station Bank, Mickley, Stocksfield, Northumberland NE43 7DD

Tel: 01661 843276 **www:** nationaltrust.org.uk

Owner: The National Trust **Contact:** The Administrator

Birthplace of Northumbria's greatest artist, wood engraver and naturalist, Thomas Bewick, b.1753. The Museum explores his famous works and life with occasional demonstrations of wood block printing in the printing house. Farmyard animals, picnic area, garden.

Location: OS Ref. NZ075 627. 11m W of Newcastle on A695 (400yds signed from Mickley Square). 1¹/₂ m W of Prudhoe.

Open: 29 Mar - end Oct: daily except Tues & Weds, 1 - 5.30pm. Last admission 5pm.

Admission: Adult £3. No group rate.

🄐 🄳Some steps. WC. 🄿Morning coffee for booked groups. 🄦Tel for details.

CHESTERS ROMAN FORT & MUSEUM ⌗

CHOLLERFORD, Nr HEXHAM, NORTHUMBERLAND NE46 4EP

Tel: 01434 681379

Owner: English Heritage **Contact:** The Custodian

The best preserved example of a Roman cavalry fort in Britain, including remains of the bath house on the banks of the River North Tyne. The museum houses a fascinating collection of Roman sculpture and inscriptions.

Location: OS87, Ref. NY913 701. 1¹/₂ m from Chollerford on B6318.

Open: 29 Mar - 30 Sept: daily, 9.30am - 6pm. 1 - 31 Oct: daily, 10am - 5pm. 1 Nov - 31 Mar: daily, 10am - 4pm. Closed 24 - 26 Dec and 1 Jan.

Admission: Adult £3, Child £1.50, Conc. £2.30. 15% discount for groups (11+).

🄐 🄳 Grounds. WC. 🄿Summer only. 🄿 🄷In grounds, on leads. ✳
🄦 Tel for details.

CHILLINGHAM CASTLE 🏰

See page 433 for full page entry.

CHIPCHASE CASTLE 🏰

Wark, Hexham, Northumberland NE48 3NT

Tel: 01434 230203 **Fax:** 01434 230740

Owner/Contact: Mrs P J Torday

The castle overlooks the River North Tyne and is set in formal and informal gardens. One walled garden is used as a nursery specialising in unusual perennial plants.

Location: OS Ref. NY882 758. 10m NW of Hexham via A6079 to Chollerton. 2m SE of Wark.

Open: Castle: 1 - 28 Jun: daily 2 - 5pm. Tours by arrangement at other times. Castle Gardens & Nursery: Easter - 31 Jul, Thur - Sun & BH Mons, 10am - 5pm.

Admission: Castle £4, Garden £2, concessions available. Nursery Free.

🄳Unsuitable. 🄵Obligatory. ✳

Special Events Index
◁ ◁ ◁ pgs 40-43

CORBRIDGE ROMAN SITE ⌗

Corbridge, Northumberland NE45 5NT

Tel: 01434 632349

Owner: English Heritage **Contact:** The Custodian

A fascinating series of excavated remains, including foundations of granaries with a grain ventilation system. From artefacts found, which can be seen in the site museum, we know a large settlement developed around this supply depot.

Location: OS87 Ref. NY983 649. ¹/₂ m NW of Corbridge on minor road, signposted for Corbridge Roman Site.

Open: 29 Mar - 30 Sept: daily, 10am - 6pm. 1 - 31 Oct: daily, 10am - 5pm. 1 Nov - 31 Mar: Wed - Sun, 10am - 4pm. Closed 1 - 2pm during winter & 24 - 26 Dec and 1 Jan.

Admission: Adult £2.70, Child £1.40, Conc. £2.60. 15% discount for groups (11+).

🄐 🄳Partial. 🄿Inclusive. 🄿 Limited for coaches. 🄷 🄷In grounds, on leads. ✳
🄦 Tel for details.

Bamburgh Castle

NT Photographic Library: Nigel Shuttleworth

NT Photographic Library

CRAGSIDE

ROTHBURY, MORPETH, NORTHUMBERLAND NE65 7PX

www.nationaltrust.org.uk

Tel: 01669 620150 **Fax:** 01669 620066

Owner: The National Trust   **Contact:** Property Manager

Built for the 19th century's greatest gun-maker and innovator, 1st Lord Armstrong, Cragside became one of the most modern and surprising houses for its time in the country. In the 1880s, the house had hot and cold running water, central heating, telephones, a Turkish bath suite and a passenger lift but - most remarkable of all - it was the first house in the world to be lit by hydro-electricity. No wonder it was described as 'The Palace of a Modern Magician'. Children will love exploring the 1000-acre forest garden, which contains one of Europe's largest rock gardens, a formal garden, lakes and an exciting Play Area. Allow a whole day!

Location: OS Ref. NU073 022. 1/2 m NE of Rothbury on B6341.

Open: House: 23 Mar - 3 Nov: daily except Mons (open BH Mons). House: 23 Mar - 30 Sept: 1 - 5.30pm (last admission 4.30pm); 1 Oct - 3 Nov: 1 - 4.30pm (last admission 3.30pm). Estate & Formal Garden: 10.30am - 7pm (last admission 5pm); 6 Nov - 15 Dec: Wed - Sun, 11am - 4pm. From Sept shop and restaurant possible closure due to refurbishment. Please telephone in advance.

Admission: House, Estate & Gardens: Adult £6.90, Child (5-17yrs) £3.50, Family (2+3) £17.30. Groups (15+) £5.90. Estate & Gardens: Adult £4.40, Child (5-17yrs) £2.20, Family (2+3) £11. Groups (15+) £3.80.

DUNSTANBURGH CASTLE

c/o 14 Queen Street, Alnwick, Northumberland NE66 1RD

Tel: 01665 576231

Owner: The National Trust   **Guardian:** English Heritage   **Contact:** The Custodian

An easy, but bracing, coastal walk leads to the eerie skeleton of this wonderful 14th century castle sited on a basalt crag, rearing up more than 100 feet from the waves crashing on the rocks below. The surviving ruins include the large gatehouse, which later became the keep, and curtain walls.

Location: OS75 Ref. NU258 220. 8m NE of Alnwick.

Open: 29 Mar - 30 Sept: daily, 10am - 6pm. 1 - 31 Oct, daily, 10am - 5pm. 1 Nov - 31 Mar: Wed - Sun, 10am - 4pm. Closed 24 - 26 Dec and 1 Jan.

Admission: Adult £2, Child £1, Conc. £1.50. 15% discount for groups (11+).

Unsuitable. None. In grounds, on leads.

EDLINGHAM CASTLE

Edlingham, Alnwick, Northumberland

Tel: 0191 269 1200

Owner: English Heritage   **Contact:** The Northern Regional Office

Set beside a splendid railway viaduct this complex ruin has defensive features spanning the 13th and 15th centuries.

Location: OS Ref. NU115 092. At E end of Edlingham village, on minor road off B6341 6m SW of Alnwick.

Open: Any reasonable time.

Admission: Free.

ETAL CASTLE

Cornhill-on-Tweed, Northumberland

Tel: 01890 820332

Owner: English Heritage   **Contact:** The Custodian

A 14th century castle located in the picturesque village of Etal. Award-winning exhibition about the castle, Border warfare and the Battle of Flodden.

Location: OS75 Ref. NT925 394. In Etal village, 10m SW of Berwick.

Open: 29 Mar - 30 Sept: daily, 10am - 6pm. 1 - 31 Oct: daily, 10am - 5pm.

Admission: Adult £2.80, Child £1.40, Conc. £2.10. 15% discount for groups (11+).

Partial. WC. Inclusive. Limited. In grounds, on leads. Tel for details.

HERTERTON HOUSE GARDENS

Hartington, Cambo, Morpeth, Northumberland NE61 4BN

Tel: 01670 774278

Owner/Contact: C J "Frank" Lawley

One acre of formal garden in stone walls around a 16th century farmhouse, including a small topiary garden, physic garden, flower garden, fancy garden and gazebo.

Location: OS Ref. NZ022 881. 2m N of Cambo, just off B6342.

Open: 1 Apr - 30 Sept: Mons, Weds, Fri - Sun, 1.30 - 5.30pm.

Admission: Adult £2.50, Child (5-15yrs) £1. Groups by arrangement.

Unsuitable. By arrangement. Limited for coaches. Guided tours for adult students only.

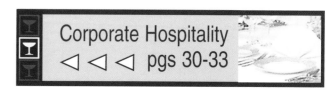

Corporate Hospitality ◁ ◁ ◁ pgs 30-33

English Heritage Photo Library

HOUSESTEADS ROMAN FORT

NR HAYDON BRIDGE, NORTHUMBERLAND NE47 6NN

Tel: 01434 344363

Owner: The National Trust **Guardian:** English Heritage **Contact:** The Custodian

Perched high on a ridge overlooking open moorland, this is the best known part of the Wall. The fort covers five acres and there are remains of many buildings, such as granaries, barrack blocks and gateways. A small exhibition displays altars, inscriptions and models.

Location: OS87 Ref. NY790 687. 2m NE of Bardon Mill.

Open: 29 Mar - 30 Sept: daily, 10am - 6pm. 1 - 31 Oct: daily, 10am - 5pm. 1 Nov - 31 Mar: daily, 10am - 4pm. Closed 24 - 26 Dec and 1 Jan.

Admission: Adult £3, Child £1.50, Conc. £2.30. 15% discount for groups (11+).

Unsuitable. Charge. In grounds, on leads. Tel for details.

HOWICK HALL GARDENS

Howick, Alnwick, Northumberland NE66 3LB

Tel: 01665 577285 **e-mail:** estateoffice@howickuk.com

Owner: Howick Trustees Ltd **Contact:** Mrs D Spark

Romantically landscaped grounds surrounding the house in a little valley, with rare rhododendrons and flowering shrubs and trees.

Location: OS Ref. NU249 175. 6m NE of Alnwick. 1m E of B1339.

Open: Apr - Oct: daily 1 - 6pm.

Admission: Adult £2, Child/OAP £1, Student (up to 16yrs) £1. Season tickets available.

Grounds partial. WC. Limited.

KIRKLEY HALL GARDENS

Ponteland, Northumberland NE20 0AQ

Tel: 01670 841200 **Fax:** 01661 860047 **Contact:** J Guy

Over 9 acres of beautiful gardens incorporating a Victorian walled garden, woodland walks, sunken garden and wildlife areas and ponds.

Location: OS Ref. NZ150 772. 10m from the centre of Newcastle upon Tyne. 2 1/2 m N of Ponteland on byroad to Morpeth.

Open: All year: daily, 10am - 4pm.

Admission: Free.

THE LADY WATERFORD HALL & MURALS

Ford, Berwick-upon-Tweed TD15 2QA

Tel: 01890 820503 Fax: 01890 820384

Owner: Ford & Etal Estates **Contact:** The Caretaker

Commissioned in 1860 the walls of this beautiful building are decorated with beautiful murals depicting Bible stories.

Location: OS Ref. NT945 374. On the B6354, 9m from Berwick-upon-Tweed, midway between Newcastle-upon-Tyne and Edinburgh, close to the A697.

Open: 31 Aug - 3 Nov: daily, 10.30am - 12.30pm & 1.30 - 5.30pm. By arrangement with the caretaker during winter months.

Admission: Adult £1.50, Child Free (over 12yrs 50p), Conc. £1. Groups by arrangement.

LINDISFARNE CASTLE

Holy Island, Berwick-upon-Tweed, Northumberland TD15 2SH

Tel: 01289 389244 **www.**nationaltrust.org.uk

Owner: The National Trust **Contact:** The Administrator

Built in 1550 to protect Holy Island harbour from attack, the castle was restored and converted into a private house for Edward Hudson by Sir Edwin Lutyens in 1903. Small walled garden was designed by Gertrude Jekyll. 19th century lime kilns in field by the castle.

Location: OS Ref. NU136 417. On Holy Island, 3/4 m E of village, 6m E of A1 across causeway. Usable at low tide.

Open: 16 Mar - 3 Nov: daily except Fri (but open Good Fri), 12 noon - 3pm, but earlier or later as the tide allows. Last admission 1/2 hr before close. Admission to garden only when gardener in attendance. Holy Island is cut off by the tide from 2 hours before and 3 1/2 hours after high tide. Visitors are advised to check tide times before visiting.

Admission: £4.20, Family £10.50. No group rate. Groups (15+) must pre-book.

NT Shop (in Main St.) Unsuitable. None. In grounds, on leads.

© English Heritage Photo Library

LINDISFARNE PRIORY

HOLY ISLAND, BERWICK-UPON-TWEED TD15 2RX

Tel: 01289 389200

Owner: English Heritage **Contact:** The Custodian

The site of one of the most important early centres of Christianity in Anglo-Saxon England. St Cuthbert converted pagan Northumbria, and miracles occurring at his shrine established this 11th century priory as a major pilgrimage centre. The evocative ruins, with the decorated 'rainbow' arch curving dramatically across the nave of the church, are still the destination of pilgrims today. The story of Lindisfarne is told in an exhibition which gives an impression of life for the monks, including a reconstruction of a monk's cell.

Location: OS75 Ref. NU126 418. On Holy Island, check tide times.

Open: 29 Mar - 30 Sept: daily, 10am - 6pm. 1 - 31 Oct: daily, 10am - 5pm. 1 Nov - 31 Mar: daily, 10am - 4pm. Closed 24 - 26 Dec and 1 Jan.

Admission: Adult £3, Child £1.50, Conc. £2.30. 15% discount for groups (11+).

Partial. Charge. Restricted. Tel for details.

NORHAM CASTLE

Norham, Northumberland

Tel: 01289 382329

Owner: English Heritage **Contact:** The Custodian

Set on a promontory in a curve of the River Tweed, this was one of the strongest of the Border castles, built c1160.

Location: OS75 Ref. NT907 476. 6m SW of Berwick.

Open: 29 Mar - 30 Sept: daily, 10am - 6pm.

Admission: Adult £1.90, Child £1, Conc. £1.40. 15% discount for groups (11+).

Partial. On leads. Tel for details.

North East - England

PRESTON TOWER

Chathill, Northumberland NE67 5DH

Tel: 01665 589227

Owner/Contact: Major T Baker Cresswell

The Tower was built by Sir Robert Harbottle in 1392 and is one of the few survivors of 78 pele towers listed in 1415. The tunnel vaulted rooms remain unaltered and provide a realistic picture of the grim way of life under the constant threat of "Border Reivers". Two rooms are furnished in contemporary style and there are displays of historic and local information. Visitors are welcome to walk in the grounds which contain a number of interesting trees and shrubs. A woodland walk to the natural spring from which water is now pumped up to the Tower for the house and cottages.

Location: OS Ref. NU185 253. Follow Historic Property signs on A1 7m N of Alnwick.

Open: Daylight hours all year.

Admission: Adult £1, Child/Conc./Groups 50p.

Grounds.

PRUDHOE CASTLE

Prudhoe, Northumberland NE42 6NA

Tel: 01661 833459

Owner: English Heritage **Contact:** The Custodian

Set on a wooded hillside overlooking the River Tyne are the extensive remains of this 12th century castle including a gatehouse, curtain wall and keep. Small exhibition and video presentation.

Location: OS88 Ref. NZ092 634. In Prudhoe, on minor road N from A695.

Open: 29 Mar - 30 Sept: daily, 10am - 6pm. 1 - 31 Oct: daily, 10am - 5pm.

Admission: Adult £1.90, Child £1, Conc. £1.40. 15% discount for groups (11+).

Partial. Limited. In grounds, on leads. Tel for details.

Cragside

NT Photographic Library: Rupert Truman

Website Information ◁ ◁ ◁ pg 39

SEATON DELAVAL HALL

SEATON SLUICE, WHITLEY BAY, NORTHUMBERLAND NE26 4QR

Tel: 0191 2371493/0191 2370786

Owner: Lord Hastings **Contact:** Mrs Mills

The home of Lord and Lady Hastings, half a mile from Seaton Sluice, is the last and most sensational mansion designed by Sir John Vanbrugh, builder of Blenheim Palace and Castle Howard. It was erected 1718 - 1728 and comprises a high turreted block flanked by arcaded wings which form a vast forecourt. The centre block was gutted by fire in 1822, but was partially restored in 1862 and again in 1959 - 1962 and 1999 - 2000. The remarkable staircases are a visual delight, and the two surviving rooms are filled with family pictures and photographs and royal seals spanning three centuries as well as various archives. This building is used frequently for concerts and charitable functions. The East Wing contains immense stables in ashlar stone of breathtaking proportions. Nearby are the Coach House with farm and passenger vehicles, fully documented, and the restored ice house with explanatory sketch and description. There are beautiful gardens with herbaceous borders, rose garden, rhododendrons, azaleas, laburnum walk, statues, and a spectacular parterre by internationally famous Jim Russell, also a unique Norman Church.

Location: OS Ref. NZ322 766. 1/2m from Seaton Sluice on A190, 3m from Whitley Bay.

Open: May & Aug BH Mons; Jun 3/4; Jun - 30 Sept: Weds & Suns, 2 - 6pm.

Admission: Adult £3, Child £1, Conc. £2.50. Groups (20+): Adult £2.50, Child £1, Student £1.

Partial. WC. Free. In grounds, on leads.

North East - England

NTPL

WALLINGTON ✣

CAMBO, MORPETH, NORTHUMBERLAND NE61 4AR

www.nationaltrust.org.uk

Tel: 01670 773600 **e-mail:** nwaplr@smtp.ntrust.org.uk

Owner: The National Trust **Contact:** The Estate Office

A beautiful walled garden, Edwardian conservatory, woodland walks and ornamental ponds make a delightful setting for the Trevelyan's historic home. The house at Wallington dates from 1688 and boasts fine interiors, a superb collection of ceramics and William Bell-Scott's famous paintings of Northumbrian history but still retains the atmosphere of a much loved family home.

Location: OS Ref. NZ030 843. Near Cambo, 6m NW of Belsay (A696).

Open: House: 23 Mar - 30 Sept: daily (except Tues), 1 - 5.30pm (then closed for major works until Spring 2004). Gardens only: daily, 10am - 7pm. Grounds: all year.

Admission: House, Garden & Grounds: Adult £5.70, Child £2.85, Family £14.25, Group: £5.20. Garden & Grounds: Adult £4.10, Child £2.05, Groups £3.60.

ⓘ No photography in house. 🅿 ⚲ ⊤ ⎇ ⊡ ⚲ By arrangement. 🅿 ⬛
🐾 In grounds on leads. ⬛ ❊ ⎘ Tel for details.

English Heritage Photo Library

WARKWORTH CASTLE ⌗

WARKWORTH, MORPETH, NORTHUMBERLAND NE66 0UJ

Tel: 01665 711423

Owner: English Heritage **Contact:** The Custodian

The great towering keep of this 15th century castle, once the home of the mighty Percy family, dominates the town and River Coquet. Warkworth is one of the most outstanding examples of an aristocratic fortified residence. Upstream by boat from the castle lies Warkworth Hermitage, cutting into the rock of the river cliff (separate charge applies).

Location: OS81 Ref. NU247 057. 7m S of Alnwick on A1068.

Open: 29 Mar - 30 Sept: daily, 10am - 6pm. 1 - 31 Oct: daily, 10am - 5pm. 1 Nov - 31 Mar: daily, 10am - 4pm (closed 1 - 2pm). Closed 24 - 26 Dec and 1 Jan.

Admission: Adult £2.60, Child £1.30, Conc. £2. 15% discount for groups (11+).

🅿 ⎇ Grounds. 🅿 ⬛ 🐾 On leads. ❊ ⎘ Tel for details.

WARKWORTH HERMITAGE ⌗

Warkworth, Northumberland

Tel: 01665 711423

Owner: English Heritage **Contact:** The Custodian

Upstream by boat from the castle this curious hermitage cuts into the rock of the river cliff.

Location: OS Ref. NU247 057. 7$^{1}/_{2}$ m SE of Alnwick on A1068.

Open: 29 Mar - 30 Sept: Weds, Suns & BHs, 11am - 5pm.

Admission: Adult £1.60, Child 80p, Conc. £1.20.

Seaton Delaval

Norman Hudson

ARBEIA ROMAN FORT

Baring Street, South Shields, Tyne & Wear NE33 2BB

Tel: 0191 456 1369 **Fax:** 0191 427 6862

Owner: South Tyneside Metropolitan Borough Council **Contact:** The Curator

Managed by: Tyne & Wear Museums

Extensive remains of 2nd century Roman fort, including fort defences, stone granaries, gateways and latrines. Full-scale reconstruction of Roman gateway and museum featuring finds including weapons, jewellery and tombstones. Watch excavations throughout the year.

Location: OS Ref. NZ365 679. Near town centre and Metro Station.

Open: Easter - Oct: Mon - Sat: 10am - 5.30pm, Suns, 1 - 5pm. Open BH Mons. Winter: Mon - Sat, 10am - 4pm. Closed Christmas Day, Boxing Day, New Year's Day, Good Friday.

Admission: Free, except for Time Quest Gallery: Adult £1.50, Child/Conc. 80p.

BEDE'S WORLD MUSEUM

Church Bank, Jarrow, Tyne & Wear NE32 3DY

Tel: 0191 489 2106 **Fax:** 0191 428 2361

Managed by: Jarrow 700AD Ltd **Contact:** Visitor Services

A museum telling the story of the Venerable Bede and Anglo-Saxon Northumbria.

Location: OS Ref. NZ339 652. Just off A19, S end of Tyne Tunnel.

Open: Apr - Oct: Mon - Sat, 10am - 5.30pm, Suns, 12 noon - 5.30pm. Nov - Mar: Mon - Sat, 10am - 4.30pm, Suns, 12 noon - 4.30pm. Also open BH Mons.

Admission: Adult £4.50, Conc. £2.50, Family £9. Groups by arrangement.

BESSIE SURTEES HOUSE

41 - 44 Sandhill, Newcastle, Tyne & Wear

Tel: 0191 269 1200

Owner: English Heritage **Contact:** The Custodian

Two 16th and 17th century merchants' houses stand on the quayside near the Tyne Bridge. One is a rare example of Jacobean domestic architecture. 3 rooms open.

Location: OS Ref. NZ252 639. 41- 44 Sandhill, Newcastle.

Open: Weekdays only: 10am - 4pm. Closed BHs, 24 - 26 Dec and 1 Jan.

Admission: Free.

CATHEDRAL CHURCH OF ST NICHOLAS

Newcastle-upon-Tyne, Tyne & Wear NE1 1PF

Tel: 0191 232 1939 **Fax:** 0191 230 0735 **e-mail:** stnicholas@aol.com

www.newcastle-ang-cathedral-stnicholas.org.uk

Contact: Rev Canon Peter Strange

A cathedral only since 1882, it retains its town parish church character of the 14th - 15th centuries. The striking tower with its arched crown resembling Edinburgh's St Giles is 193 feet high and dominates the entire city; '*an airy confection with a flurry of gilded wind-vanes*' Pevsner. The nine-bay interior has good 14th century arcading, flanked by very wide aisles.

Location: OS Ref. NZ250 640. City centre, 1/2 m from A167 signposted from Swan House roundabout.

Open: Suns: 7am - 12 noon, 4 - 7pm. Mon - Fri: 7am - 6pm. Sats: 8.30am - 4pm. BHs, 8am - 12 noon.

By arrangement. No parking. Guide dogs only.

GIBSIDE

Nr Rowlands Gill, Burnopfield, Newcastle-upon-Tyne NE16 6BG

Tel: 01207 542255 **www.**nationaltrust.org.uk

Owner: The National Trust **Contact:** The Property Manager

Gibside is one of the finest 18th century designed landscapes in the north of England. The Chapel was built to James Paine's design soon after 1760. Outstanding example of Georgian architecture approached along a terrace with an oak avenue. Walk along the River Derwent through woodland.

Location: OS Ref. NZ172 583. 6m SW of Gateshead, 20m NW of Durham. Entrance on B6314 between Burnopfield and Rowlands Gill.

Open: Grounds: 23 Mar - 3 Nov: daily except Mons (open BH Mons), 10am - 6pm. Last admission 4.30pm. 1 Nov - 31 Mar: 10am - sunset. Last admission 1 hour before sunset. Chapel: 23 Mar - 3 Nov: as grounds, otherwise by arrangement.

Admission: Chapel and Grounds: Adult £3, Child half price. Booked groups £2.60.

NEWCASTLE CASTLE KEEP

Castle Keep, Castle Garth, Newcastle-upon-Tyne NE1 1RQ

Tel: 0191 232 7938

Owner: Newcastle City Council **Contact:** Paul MacDonald

The Keep originally dominated the castle bailey. The 'new' castle was founded in 1080.

Location: OS Ref. NZ251 638. City centre between St Nicholas church and the High Level bridge.

Open: All year: daily, 9.30am - 5.30pm (4.30pm winter).

Admission: Adult £1.50, Child/Conc. 50p.

ST PAUL'S MONASTERY

Jarrow, Tyne & Wear

Tel: 0191 489 2106

Owner: English Heritage **Contact:** The Custodian

The home of the Venerable Bede in the 7th and 8th centuries, partly surviving as the chancel of the parish church. It has become one of the best understood Anglo-Saxon monastic sites.

Location: OS Ref. NZ339 652. In Jarrow, on minor road N of A185.

Open: Any reasonable time.

Admission: Free.

SOUTER LIGHTHOUSE

Coast Road, Whitburn, Sunderland, Tyne & Wear SR6 7NH

Tel: 0191 529 3161 **Fax:** 0191 529 0902 **e-mail:** nslhse@smtp.ntrust.org.uk

www.nationaltrust.org.uk

Owner: The National Trust **Contact:** The Property Manager

Dramatic red and white lighthouse tower on rugged coast. Built in 1871, the first to be powered by alternating electric current. New hands-on activities for all ages.

Location: OS Ref. NZ408 641. 21/2 m S of South Shields on A183. 5m N of Sunderland.

Open: 9 - 17 Feb & 23 Mar - 3 Nov: daily except Fris (open Good Fri), 11am - 5pm. Last admission 4.30pm. Open after 3 Nov by arrangement – contact property for details.

Admission: Adult £3, Child £1.50, Family £7.50. Booked Groups: £2.50. NT members Free.

Partial. WCs. By arrangement. In grounds, on leads.

TYNEMOUTH PRIORY & CASTLE

North Pier, Tynemouth, Tyne & Wear NE30 4BZ

Tel: 0191 257 1090

Owner: English Heritage **Contact:** The Custodian

The castle walls and gatehouse enclose the substantial remains of a Benedictine priory founded c1090 on a Saxon monastic site. Their strategic importance has made the castle and priory the target for attack for many centuries. In World War I, coastal batteries in the castle defended the mouth of the Tyne.

Location: OS88 Ref. NZ374 695. In Tynemouth.

Open: 29 Mar - 30 Sept: daily, 10am - 6pm. 1 - 31 Oct: daily, 10am - 5pm. 1 Nov - 31 Mar: Wed - Sun, 10am - 4pm (closed 1 - 2 pm). Closed 24 - 26 Dec & 1 Jan.

Admission: Adult £2.20, Child £1.10, Conc. £1.70, Family £5.50. 15% discount for groups (11+).

Grounds. By arrangement. In grounds, on leads. Tel for details.

WASHINGTON OLD HALL

The Avenue, Washington Village, District 4, Washington, Tyne & Wear NE38 7LE

Tel: 0191 416 6879 **Fax:** 0191 419 2065 **www.**nationaltrust.org.uk

Owner: The National Trust **Contact:** The Property Manager

Jacobean manor house incorporating portions of 12th century house of the Washington family. Displays of George Washington commemoratives and the history of the Old Hall. Small Jacobean knot garden.

Location: OS Ref. NZ312 566. In Washington on E side of The Avenue. 5m W of Sunderland (2m from A1), S of Tyne Tunnel, follow signs for Washington District 4 and then village.

Open: 24 Mar - 30 Oct: Sun - Wed. Closed Thur - Sat (open Good Fri), 11am - 5pm. Last admission 4.30pm.

Admission: Adult £3, Child £1.50. Booked groups (15+): £2.50. NT members Free. Membership available from shop.

Conferences. Ground floor and grounds. By arrangement. Limited. In grounds, on leads.

THE REGIONS OF
SCOTLAND

Scone Palace © The Earl of Mansfield

SCOTLAND

Fyvie Castle

Scotland

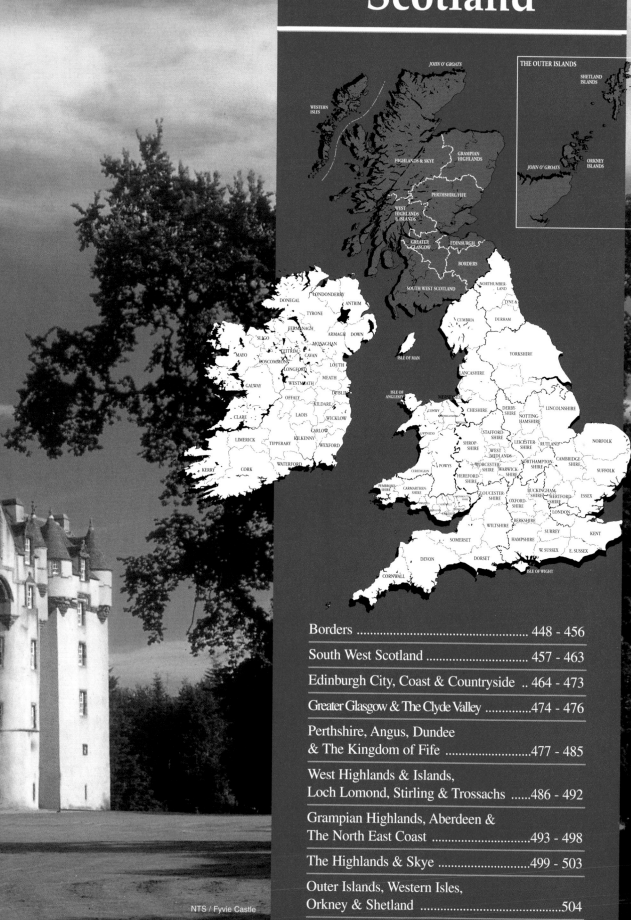

THE OUTER ISLANDS

JOHN O' GROATS

WESTERN ISLES

HIGHLANDS & SKYE

GRAMPIAN HIGHLANDS

PERTHSHIRE/FIFE

WEST HIGHLANDS & ISLANDS

GREATER GLASGOW

EDINBURGH

BORDERS

SOUTH WEST SCOTLAND

SHETLAND ISLANDS

JOHN O' GROATS

ORKNEY ISLANDS

NTS / Fyvie Castle

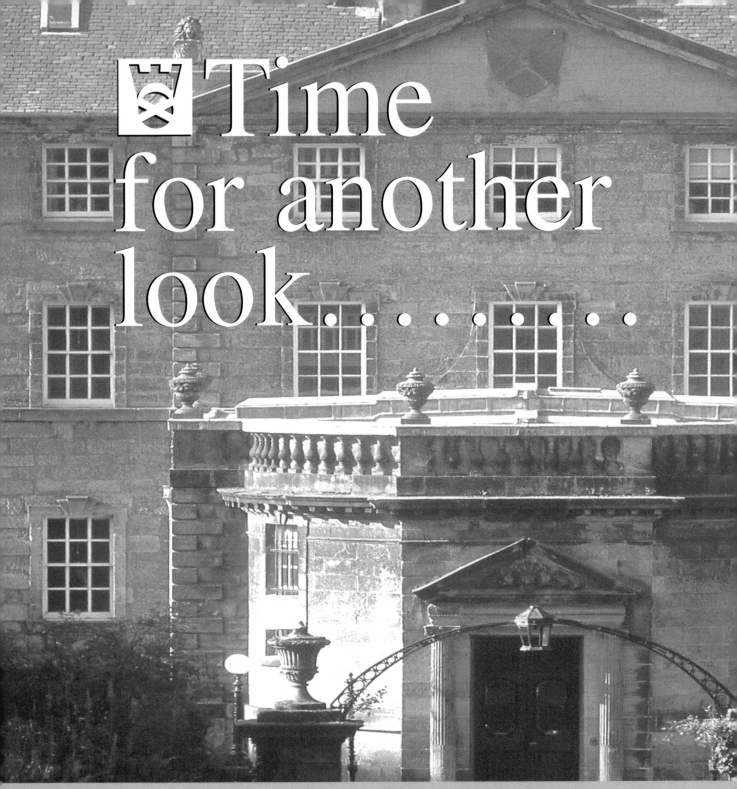

Time for another look.........

The National Trust for Scotland

The range of properties in the National Trust for Scotland's care is enormous – beautiful castles and country houses packed with outstanding fine and decorative art collections, glorious gardens, historic battle sites, romantic islands, areas of open and unspoilt countryside and some intriguing examples of Scotland's industrial heritage

Mrs Stratford Canning
by Romney

Pollok House
NTS Photo Library

The National Trust for Scotland was established as a charity in 1931 to protect places of historic interest and natural beauty in Scotland and to provide public access to them. In those early days the Trust had very few places in its care and only a handful of members for support. Today, more than 120 properties are owned and managed by the Trust and it enjoys the support of some 245,000 members who can count free access among the benefits of membership.

The National Trust for Scotland aims to provide a great visit and its ever-improving catering and retail outlets at properties have become established as popular destinations in their own right, especially so where restaurants and cafés have been awarded the prestigious 'Taste of Scotland' award.

Taking its place among recent developments is the opening of a new Head Office in Edinburgh's Charlotte Square, complete with visitor facilities open to everyone. A gallery with a collection of 20th century Scottish paintings, coffee house, shop and evening restaurant await visitors and this property acts as a good place to take your bearings and plan visits further afield throughout the country. In the west, the Trust has been working in partnership with Glasgow City Council to present Pollok House (in the extensive Pollok Country Park and next to the renowned Burrell Collection), as an Edwardian country home by adding furniture and furnishings to complement the exceptional art collection there.

2002 will also see some significant openings in the north and south. An exciting new visitor centre opens in the spring at Glencoe, to provide improved interpretation of the infamous massacre in 1692 and the natural beauty of the area. It is set to become a 'must see' attraction for travellers who can also discover the village and surrounding areas. Further south, in Musselburgh on the outskirts of Edinburgh, Newhailes will provide a different experience as visitors enjoy the interiors of this country house, which dates from 1686. Newhailes became a centre of the Scottish Enlightenment and played host to many famous figures of the time – now it looks forward to welcoming visitors from summer onwards contact the The National Trust for Scotland's Head Office for further information tel: 0131 243 9300. Smaller developments. too, add up to offer more for visitors – plant centres, special events, costumed interpretation and much more besides.

As well as opening its properties for visitors to enjoy, the Trust has a network of outstanding holiday cottages and flats offering ideal locations for self-catering holidays. New members are always welcome – it is possible to join at any of the properties, or by telephone, or online at www.nts.org.uk before visiting and although a separate organisation from the National Trust, a reciprocal agreement allows free admission to members of both charities north and south of the border. So wherever you travel in Scotland in 2002, take another look at The National Trust for Scotland – you'll be guaranteed a warm welcome and a visit to remember. +

28 Charlotte Square
NTS / Mairi Semple 2000

Still Life with Roses and Mirror
by Samuel John Peploe

The Pink Boy - Sir Joshua Reynolds

BOWHILL HOUSE & 🏛 COUNTRY PARK

SELKIRK

Owner: His Grace the
Duke of Buccleuch &
Queensberry KT

▶ CONTACT

Buccleuch Heritage
Trust
Bowhill House &
Country Park
Bowhill
Selkirk TD7 5ET

Tel/Fax: 01750 22204

e-mail:
bht@buccleuch.com

▶ LOCATION

OS Ref. NT426 278

3m W of Selkirk off
A708 Moffat Road,
A68 from Newcastle,
A7 from Carlisle
or Edinburgh.

Bus: 3m Selkirk.

Taxi: 01750 20354.

Scottish Borders home of the Duke and Duchess
of Buccleuch, dating mainly from 1812 and
christened 'Sweet Bowhill' by Sir Walter Scott in
his *Lay of the Last Minstrel.*

Many of the works of art were collected by
earlier Montagus, Douglases and Scotts or given
by Charles II to his natural son James, Duke of
Monmouth and Buccleuch. Paintings include
Canaletto's *Whitehall*, works by Guardi, Claude,
Ruysdael, Gainsborough, Raeburn, Reynolds, Van
Dyck and Wilkie. Superb French furniture,
Meissen and Sèvres porcelain, silver and
tapestries.

Historical relics include Monmouth's saddle and
execution shirt, Sir Walter Scott's plaid and some

proof editions, Queen Victoria's letters and gifts
to successive Duchesses of Buccleuch, her
Mistresses of the Robes.

There is also a completely restored Victorian
Kitchen, 19th century horse-drawn fire engine,
'Bowhill Little Theatre', a lively centre for the
performing arts and where, prior to touring
the house, visitors can see 'The Quest for
Bowhill', a 20 minute audio-visual presentation by
Dr Colin Thompson.

Conference centre, arts courses, literary lunches,
education service, visitor centre. Shop, tearoom,
adventure playground, woodland walks, nature
trails, picnic areas. Garden and landscape
designed by John Gilpin.

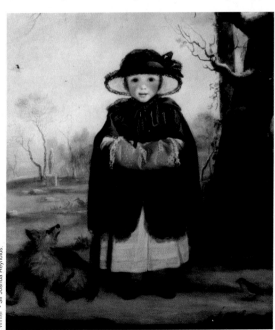

Winter - Sir Joshua Reynolds

Fashion shows, air
displays, archery, clay pigeon
shooting, equestrian events, charity
garden parties, shows, rallies, filming,
lecture theatre. House is open by
appointment outside public hours to
groups led by officials of a
recognised museum, gallery or
educational establishment. No
photography inside house.

Inside caterers normally used
but outside caterers considered.

Visitors may alight at entrance.
WC. Wheelchair visitors free.

Groups can book in advance
(special rates), menus on request.

For groups. Tour time 1¼ hrs.

60 cars and 6 coaches within
50yds of house.

Welcome. Projects in Bowhill
House and Victorian kitchen,
Education Officers (service provided
free of charge), schoolroom,
ranger-led nature walks, adventure
playground. Heritage Education Trust
Sandford Award winner 1993 and
1998.

On leads.

▶ OPENING TIMES

Summer

13 April - 26 August

Country Park
Daily except Fris
(open Fris in July)
12 noon - 5pm.

House
1 - 31 July
Daily: 1 - 4.30pm.

Winter
By appointment only,
for educational groups.

▶ ADMISSION

Summer

House & Country Park
Adult £4.50
Child (5-16yrs)....... £2.00
OAP/Student £4.00
Group (20+) £4.00
Wheelchair visitors . Free

Country Park only
All ages £2.00

Winter

House & Country Park
Adult £6.00
Child (5-16yrs)....... £2.00

Pre-booked educational
groups (20+) welcomed.

CONFERENCE/FUNCTION

ROOM	MAX CAPACITY
Bowhill Little Theatre	72

Skyscan Photo Library

FLOORS CASTLE 🏛

KELSO

www.floorscastle.com

Owner: His Grace the
Duke of Roxburghe

▶ **CONTACT**

Judy Potts
Sales & Marketing
Co-ordinator
Roxburghe Estates
Office
Kelso
Roxburghshire
Scotland TD5 7SF

Tel: 01573 223333

Fax: 01573 226056

e-mail:
jpotts@floorscastle.com

▶ **LOCATION**
OS Ref. NT711 347

From South A68, A698.

From North A68,
A697/9
In Kelso follow signs.

Bus: Kelso Bus Station
1m.

Rail: Berwick 20m.

Floors Castle, home of the Duke and Duchess of Roxburghe, is situated in the heart of the Scottish Border Country. It is reputedly the largest inhabited castle in Scotland. Designed by William Adam, who was both masterbuilder and architect, for the first Duke of Roxburghe, building started in 1721.

It was the present Duke's great-great-grand-father James, the 6th Duke, who embellished the plain Adam features of the building. In about 1849 Playfair, letting his imagination and talent run riot, transformed the castle, creating a multitude of spires and domes.

The apartments now display the outstanding collection of French 17th and 18th century furniture, magnificent tapestries, Chinese and European

porcelain and many other fine works of art. Many of the treasures in the castle today were collected by Duchess May, American wife of the 8th Duke.

The castle has been seen on cinema screens worldwide in the film *Greystoke*, as the home of Tarzan, the Earl of Greystoke.

GARDENS

The extensive parkland and gardens overlooking the Tweed provide a variety of wooded walks. The walled garden contains splendid herbaceous borders and in the outer walled garden a parterre to commemorate the Millennium can be seen. An excellent children's playground and picnic area are very close to the castle.

▶ **OPENING TIMES**

Summer
29 March - 27 October
Daily: 10am - 4.30pm.

Last admission 4pm.

Winter
November - March
Closed to the general public, available for events.

▶ **ADMISSION**

Summer

Adult	£5.50
Child* (5 - 15yrs)	£3.25
OAP/Student	£4.75
Family	£15.00

Groups (20+)

Adult	£4.25
Child* (5 - 15yrs)	£2.75
OAP/Student	£4.00

*Under 5yrs Free.

🎭 **SPECIAL EVENTS**

MAR 31
Easter Eggstravaganza.

MAY 18/19
Floors Castle Horse Trials.

AUG 25
Massed Pipe Bands Family Day.

ℹ️ Gala dinners, conferences, product launches, 4 x 4 driving, incentive groups, highland games and other promotional events. Extensive park, helicopter pad, fishing, clay pigeon and pheasant shooting. No photography inside the castle.

🛍 ✿

🍽 Self-service, licensed, seats 125 opens 10am.

🎬 By arrangement.. Tour time 1¼ hrs.

🅿 Unlimited for cars, 100 yds away, coach park 50 yds. Coaches can be driven to the entrance, waiting area close to restaurant exit. Lunch or tea for coach drivers.

♿ Visitors may alight at the entrance. WC.

🎒 Welcome, guide provided. Playground facilities.

🐕 Guide dogs only.

CONFERENCE/FUNCTION

ROOM	SIZE	MAX CAPACITY
Dining Rm	18m x 7m	150
Ballroom	21m x 8m	150

MANDERSTON 🏛

DUNS

www.manderston.co.uk

Owner:
The Lord Palmer

▶ CONTACT

The Lord or Lady
Palmer
Manderston
Duns
Berwickshire
Scotland TD11 3PP

Tel: 01361 883450
Secretary: 01361 882636
Fax: 01361 882010
e-mail: palmer@
manderston.co.uk

▶ LOCATION

OS Ref. NT810 544

From Edinburgh
47m, 1hr.
1¹/₂ m E of Duns on
A6105.

Bus: 400 yds.
Rail: Berwick
Station 12m.
Taxi: Chirnside 818216.
Airport: Edinburgh or
Newcastle both
60m or 80 mins.

Manderston, together with its magnificent stables, stunning marble dairy and 56 acres of immaculate gardens, forms an ensemble which must be unique in Britain today.

The house was completely rebuilt between 1903 and 1905, with no expense spared.

Visitors are able to see not only the sumptuous State Rooms and bedrooms, decorated in the Adam manner, but also all the original domestic offices, in a truly 'upstairs downstairs' atmosphere. Manderston boasts a unique and recently restored silver staircase.

There is a special museum with a nostalgic display of valuable tins made by Huntley and Palmer from 1868 to the present day. Winner of the AA/NPI Bronze Award UK 1994.

GARDENS

Outside, the magnificence continues and the combination of formal gardens and picturesque landscapes is a major attraction: unique amongst Scottish houses.

The stables, still in use, have been described by *Horse and Hound* as "probably the finest in all the wide world."

🛍 ℹ Corporate & incentives venue. Ideal retreat: business groups, think-tank weekends. Fashion shows, air displays, archery, clay pigeon shooting, equestrian events, garden parties, shows, rallies, filming, product launches and marathons. Two airstrips for light aircraft, approx 5m, grand piano, billiard table, fox-hunting, pheasant shoots, sea angling, salmon fishing, stabling, cricket pitch, tennis court, lake. Nearby: 18-hole golf course, indoor swimming pool, squash court. No photography in house.

🍽 Available. Buffets, lunches and dinners. Wedding receptions.

♿ Special parking available outside the House.

☕ Tearoom (open as house) with waitress service. Can be booked in advance, menus on request.

🚶 Included. Available in French. Guides in rooms. If requested, the owner may meet groups. Tour time 1¹/₄ hrs.

🅿 400 cars 125yds from house, 30 coaches 5yds from house. Appreciated if group fees are paid by one person.

🏫 Welcome. Guide can be provided. Biscuit Tin Museum of particular interest.

🐕 Grounds only, on leads.

🛏 5 twin, 4 double and 1 single.

❄

▶ OPENING TIMES

Summer

Mid-May - end September
Thurs & Suns
2 - 5pm.

BH Mons, late May
& late August
2 - 5pm.

Groups welcome all year
by appointment.

Winter

September - May
Group visits welcome
by appointment.

▶ ADMISSION

(2000 prices -
subject to alteration)

House & Grounds
Adult £6.00
Child £3.00
Groups (20+ on open days)
Per person £5.00

Grounds only
Including Stables &
Marble Dairy
Adult £3.50
Child £1.50

On days when the house is closed to the public, groups viewing by appointment will have personally conducted tours. The Gift Shop will be open. On these occasions reduced party rates (except for school children) will not apply. Group visits (20+) other than open days are £6 (minimum £120).

CONFERENCE/FUNCTION

ROOM	SIZE	MAX CAPACITY
Dining Rm	22' x 35'	100
Ballroom	34' x 21'	150
Hall	22' x 38'	130
Drawing Rm	35' x 21'	150

ABBOTSFORD HOUSE 🏛
Melrose, Roxburghshire TD6 9BQ
Tel: 01896 752043 **Fax:** 01896 752916 **e-mail:** abbotsford@melrose.bordernet.co.uk
Sir Walter Scott purchased the Cartley Hall farmhouse on the banks of the Tweed in 1812. Together with his family and servants he moved into the farm which he renamed Abbotsford. Scott had the old house demolished in 1822 and replaced it with the main block of Abbotsford as it is today. Scott was a passionate collector of historic relics including an impressive collection of armour and weapons and over 9,000 rare volumes in his library.
Location: OS Ref. NT508 343. 35m S of Edinburgh. Melrose 3m, Galashiels 2m. On B6360.
Open: 18 Mar - 31 Oct: Mon - Sat. 9.30am - 5pm. Suns in Jun - Sept: 9.30am - 5pm; Suns in Mar - May & Oct: 2 - 5pm. Other dates by arrangement.
Admission: Adult £4, Child £2. Groups: Adult £3.20 Child £1.60.
🔲 ♿House. WC. 🐾 🐕Guide dogs only.

AYTON CASTLE 🏛
AYTON, EYEMOUTH, BERWICKSHIRE TD14 5RD

Tel: 018907 81212 or 018907 81550
Owner: D I Liddell-Grainger of Ayton   **Contact:** The Curator
Built in 1846 by the Mitchell-Innes family and designed by the architect James Gillespie Graham. Over the last ten years it has been fully restored and is now a family home. It is a unique restoration project and the quality of the original and restored workmanship is outstanding. The castle stands on an escarpment surrounded by mature woodlands containing many interesting trees and has been a film-making venue due to this magnificent setting.
Location: OS Ref. NT920 610. 7m N of Berwick-on-Tweed on Route A1.
Open: 12 May - 15 Sept: Sats and Suns, 2 - 5 pm or by appointment.
Admission: Adult £3, Child (under 15yrs) Free.
🔲 👤Obligatory. 🅿 🐕In grounds, on leads. ❄

BOWHILL HOUSE & 🏛 COUNTRY PARK
See page 448 for full page entry.

Open All Year Index
◁ ◁ ◁ pgs 44-48

DAWYCK BOTANIC GARDEN
Stobo, Peeblesshire EH45 9JU
Tel: 01721 760254 **Fax:** 01721 760214   **Contact:** The Curator
Renowned historic arboretum. Amongst mature specimen trees – some over 40 metres tall – are a variety of flowering trees, shrubs and herbaceous plants. Explore the world's first Cryptogamic Sanctuary and Reserve for 'non-flowering' plants.
Location: NT168 352. 8m SW of Peebles on B712.
Open: Daily. 14 - 28 Feb & 1 - 17 Nov: 10am - 4pm. 1 Mar - 31 Oct: 9.30 am - 6pm
Admission: Adult £3, Child £1, Family £7, Conc. £2.50, Group discounts available.

DRUMLANRIG'S TOWER
Tower Knowe, Hawick TD9 9EN
Tel: 01450 373457 **Fax:** 01450 378506 **e-mail:** hawickmuseum@hotmail.com
Owner: Scottish Borders Council   **Contact:** The Curator
An 18th century town house containing the remains of a fortified tower of the 1550s.
Location: OS Ref. NT502 144. In Hawick town centre at W end of the High Street.
Open: Please contact for details: open all year.
Admission: Adult £2.50, Conc. £1.50 10% group discount. Free for local residents. Free for under 16s if accompanied.

DRYBURGH ABBEY 🛏
St Boswells, Melrose
Tel: 01835 822381
Owner: Historic Scotland   **Contact:** The Steward
Remarkably complete ruins of Dryburgh Abbey.
Location: OS Ref. NT591 317. 5m SE of Melrose off B6356. 1¹/₂ m N of St Boswells.
Open: 1 Apr - 30 Sept: daily, 9.30am - 6.30pm. Last ticket 6pm. 1 Oct - 31 Mar: Mon - Sat, 9.30am - 4.30pm, Suns, 2 - 4.30pm, last ticket 4pm.
Admission: Adult £2.80, Child £1, Conc. £2.

DUNS CASTLE
See page 452 for half page entry.

FERNIEHIRST CASTLE
See page 452 for half page entry.

FLOORS CASTLE 🏛
See page 449 for full page entry.

HALLIWELL'S HOUSE MUSEUM
Halliwell's Close, Market Place, High Street, Selkirk
Tel: 01750 20096 **Fax:** 01750 23282   **e-mail:** museums@scotborders.gov.uk
Owner: Scottish Borders Council   **Contact:** Ian Brown
Re-creation of buildings, formerly used as a house and ironmonger's shop.
Location: OS Ref. NT472 286. In Selkirk town centre.
Open: Easter - 31 Oct: Mon - Sat, 10am - 5pm, Suns, 2 - 4pm. Jul & Aug: Mon - Sat, 10am - 5.30pm, Suns, 2 - 5pm.
Admission: Free.

Monteviot Garden

Patrick Lane

DUNS CASTLE

DUNS, BERWICKSHIRE TD11 3NW

www.dunscastle.co.uk

Tel: 01361 883211   **Fax:** 01361 882015   **e-mail:** aline_hay@lineone.net

Owner: Alexander Hay of Duns   **Contact:** Mrs Aline Hay

This historical 1320 pele tower has been home to the Hay family since 1696, and the current owners Alexander and Aline Hay offer it as a welcoming venue for individuals, groups and corporate guests to enjoy. They have renovated it to produce the highest standards of comfort while retaining all the character of its rich period interiors. Wonderful lakeside and parkland setting.

Location: OS Ref. NT777 544. 10m off A4. Rail: Berwick station 16m. Airports: Newcastle & Edinburgh, 1 hr.

Open: Not open to the public except by arrangement and for individuals, groups and companies for day or residential stays. Available all year.

Admission: Rates for private and corporate visits, wedding receptions, filming on application.

⊞ 4 x 4-poster, 3 x double, 3 x twin (all with bathrooms), 2 single. ✻

FERNIEHIRST CASTLE

JEDBURGH, ROXBURGHSHIRE TD8 6NX

Tel: 01835 862201 **Fax:** 01835 863992

Owner: The Ferniehirst Trust

Contact: Mrs J Fraser

Ferniehirst Castle – Scotland's Frontier Fortress. Ancestral home of the Kerr family. Restored (1984/1987) by the 12th Marquess of Lothian. Unrivalled 16th century Border architecture. Grand Apartment and Turret Library. A 16th century Chamber Oratory. The Kerr Chamber – Museum of Family History. A special tribute to Jedburgh's Protector to Mary Queen of Scots – Sir Thomas Kerr. Riverside walk by Jed Water. Archery Field opposite the Chapel where sheep of Viking origin still graze as they did four centuries ago.

Location: OS Ref. NT653 181. 2m S of Jedburgh on the A68.

Open: Jul: Tue - Sun (closed Mons), 11am - 4pm.

Admission: Adult £3, Child £1.50. Groups (max. 50) by prior arrangement (01835 862201).

⬚ ♿ Partial. WCs.
🎫 Guided tours only, groups by arrangement.
🅿 Ample for cars and coaches.
🐕 In grounds, on leads.

HARMONY GARDEN

St Mary's Road, Melrose TD6 9LJ

Tel: 01721 722502 **Fax:** 01721 724700 **www**.nts.org.uk/harmony.html

Owner: The National Trust for Scotland   **Contact:** Head Gardener

A tranquil garden offering herbaceous and mixed borders, lawns, vegetable and fruit areas. Fine views of Melrose Abbey and the Eildon Hills. Garden set around 19th century house (not open to visitors).

Location: OS Ref. NT549 342. In Melrose, opposite the Abbey.

Open: 25 Mar - 27 Oct: Mon - Sat, 10am - 6pm, Suns, 1 - 5pm.

Admission: £2 (honesty box).

🅿 No parking. ✖

HERMITAGE CASTLE

Liddesdale, Newcastleton

Tel: 01387 376222

Owner: In the care of Historic Scotland   **Contact:** The Steward

Eerie fortress at the heart of the bloodiest events in the history of the Borders. Mary Queen of Scots made her famous ride here to visit her future husband.

Location: OS Ref. NY497 961. In Liddesdale 5^1/$_2$ m NE of Newcastleton, B6399.

Open: 1 Apr - 30 Sept: daily, 9.30am - 6.30pm, last ticket 6pm.

Admission: Adult £2, Child 75p, Conc. £1.50.

THE HIRSEL GARDENS, COUNTRY PARK & HOMESTEAD MUSEUM

Coldstream, Berwickshire TD12 4LP

Tel/Fax: 01573 224144   **e-mail:** rogerdodd@btconnect.com

www.hirselcountrypark.co.uk

Owner: Lord Home of the Hirsel   **Contact:** Roger G Dodd

Wonderful spring flowers and rhododendrons. Homestead museum and crafts centre. The Cottage Tearoom. Displays of estate life and adaptation to modern farming.

Location: OS Ref. NT838 393. Immediately W of Coldstream off A697.

Open: All year during daylight hours.

Admission: £2 per car, coaches by appointment.

👁 ✳

Historic Scotland

JEDBURGH ABBEY

4/5 ABBEY BRIDGEND, JEDBURGH TD8 6JQ

Tel: 01835 863925

Owner: In the care of Historic Scotland   **Contact:** The Steward

Founded by David I c1138 for Augustinian Canons. The church is mostly in the Romanesque and early Gothic styles and is remarkably complete. The award-winning visitor centre contains the priceless 12th century 'Jedburgh Comb' and other artefacts found during archaeological excavations.

Location: OS Ref. NT650 205. In Jedburgh on the A68.

Open: Apr - Sept: daily, 9.30am - 6.30pm. Oct - Mar: Mon - Sat, 9.30am - 4.30pm, Suns, 2 - 4.30pm. Last ticket 30 mins before closing. 10% discount for groups (10+).

Admission: Adult £3.30, Child £1.20, Conc. £2.50.

ℹ Picnic area. 📷 👥 Partial. WC. 🅿 🍴 Free when booked. 🦮 Guide dogs only. ✳

MANDERSTON

See page 450 for full page entry.

MARY QUEEN OF SCOTS' VISITOR CENTRE

Jedburgh, Roxburghshire

Tel/Fax: 01835 863331   **e-mail:** hawickmuseum@hotmail.com

Owner: Scottish Borders Council   **Contact:** The Curator

16th century fortified L-shaped house. Telling the story 'Scotland's tragic Queen'.

Location: OS Ref. NT652 206. In Queen Street between High Street and A68.

Open: Mar - Nov: Mon - Sat, 10am - 4.30pm, Sun, 12 noon - 4.30pm. Jun - Aug: Suns, 10am - 4.30pm.

Admission: Adult £2.50, Accompanied child (under 16yrs) Free, Conc. £1.50. 10% group discount. Free for Scottish Borders residents.

MELLERSTAIN HOUSE

MELLERSTAIN, GORDON, BERWICKSHIRE TD3 6LG

http://www.mellerstain.com

Tel: 01573 410225 **Fax:** 01573 410636 **e-mail:** mellerstain.house@virgin.net

Owner: The Earl of Haddington   **Contact:** Mr A Ashby

One of Scotland's great Georgian houses and a unique example of the work of the Adam family; the two wings built in 1725 by William Adam, the large central block by his son, Robert 1770-78. Rooms contain fine plasterwork, colourful ceilings and marble fireplaces. The library is considered to be Robert Adam's finest creation. Many fine paintings and period furniture.

Location: OS Ref. NT648 392. From Edinburgh A68 to Earlston, turn left 5m, signed.

Open: Easter weekend (4 days), 1 May - 30 Sept: daily except Sats, 12.30 - 5pm. Groups at other times by appointment. Last admission 4.30pm. Tearoom & shops: daily, except Sats, 11.30am - 5.30pm.

Admission: Adult £5.50, Child £3, Conc. £5. Groups (20+) £5. Grounds only: £3.

ℹ No photography or video cameras. 📷 👥 🍴 👥 Partial. 🍴 Licensed. 🍴 Licensed. 🎭 By arrangement. 🅿

🦮 In grounds, on leads. Guide dogs only in house. 👥 Tel for details.

Abbotsford House

Patrick Lane

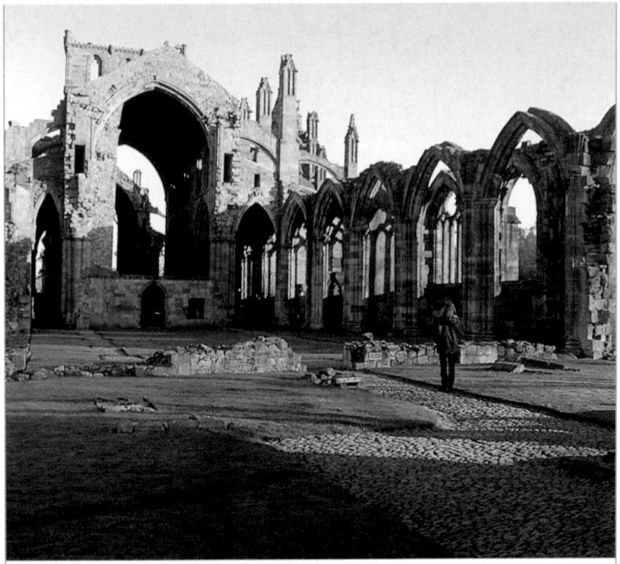

MELROSE ABBEY

MELROSE, ROXBURGHSHIRE TD6 9LG

Tel: 01896 822562

Owner: Historic Scotland **Contact:** The Steward

The Abbey was founded about 1136 by David I as a Cistercian Abbey and at one time was probably the richest in Scotland. Richard II's English army largely destroyed it in 1385 but it was rebuilt and the surviving remains are mostly 14th century. Burial place of Robert the Bruce's heart. Local history displays.

Location: OS Ref. NT549 342. In the centre of Melrose off the A68 or A7.

Open: Apr - Sept: daily, 9.30am - 6.30pm. Oct - Mar: Mon - Sat, 9.30am - 4.30pm, Suns, 2 - 4.30pm. Last ticket 30 mins before closing.

Admission: Adult £3.30, Child £1.20, Conc. £2.50. 10% discount for groups (10+).

Picnic area. Tape for visitors with learning difficulties.

Pre-booked visits free. Guide dogs only.

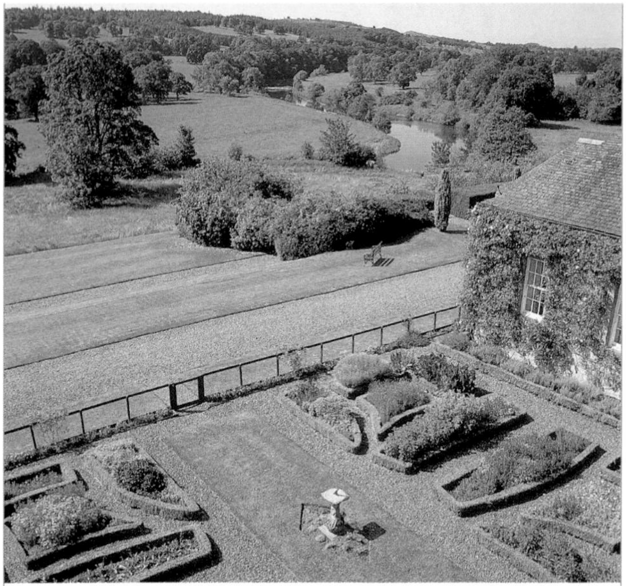

MONTEVIOT HOUSE GARDEN

JEDBURGH, ROXBURGHSHIRE TD8 6UQ

Tel: 01835 830380 (mornings only) **Fax:** 01835 830288

Owner: The Earl of Ancram **Contact:** The Administrator

The river garden planted with herbaceous shrub borders, has a beautiful view of the River Teviot. A semi-enclosed rose garden with a collection of hybrid teas, floribunda and shrub roses. The pinetum is full of unusual trees and nearby a water garden of islands is linked by bridges.

Location: OS Ref. NT648 247. 3m N of Jedburgh. S side of B6400 (to Nisbet). 1m E of A68.

Open: Apr - Oct: daily, 12 noon - 5pm. Coach parties by prior arrangement.

Admission: Adult £2, Child (under 16yrs) Free.

Partial. Parking & WCs. By arrangement. In grounds, on leads.

MERTOUN GARDENS

St Boswells, Melrose, Roxburghshire TD6 0EA

Tel: 01835 823236 **Fax:** 01835 822474

Owner: His Grace the Duke of Sutherland **Contact:** Mrs Barnsley

26 acres of beautiful grounds. Walled garden and well-preserved circular dovecote.

Location: OS Ref. NT617 318. Entrance off B6404 2m NE of St Boswells.

Open: Apr - Sept: weekends & Public Holiday Mons only, 2 - 6pm. Last admission 5.30pm.

Admission: Adult £2, Child 50p, OAP £1.50. Groups by arrangement: 10% reduction.

By arrangement.

Ayton Castle

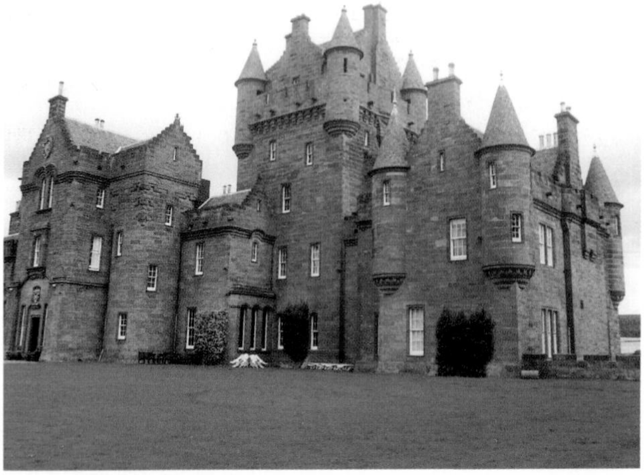

Patrick Lane

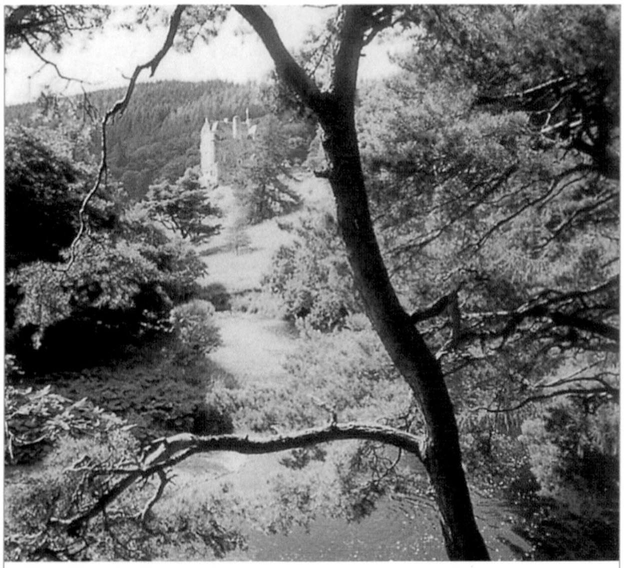

NEIDPATH CASTLE

PEEBLES, SCOTTISH BORDERS EH45 8NW

Tel/Fax: 01721 720333

Owner: Wemyss and March Estates **Contact:** The Custodian

Authentic 14th century castle converted to tower house (17th century) home of Fraser, Hay and Douglas families. Pit prison, Laigh Hall with displays, Great Hall with 'Life of Mary Stuart - Queen of Scots' in Batik wall hangings. Wonderful setting in wooded gorge of River Tweed. Popular film location (7 to date).

Location: OS Ref. NT237 405. In Tweeddale 1m W of Peebles on A72.

Open: Easter week. May BH: Fri - Mon. 22 Jun - 31 Aug: Mon - Sat, 10.30am - 4.30pm, Suns, 12.30 - 4.30pm. Group bookings available outside listed opening hours.

Admission: Adult £3, Child £1, Conc. £2.50, Family (2+3) £7.50. 10% discount for groups in season (20+). School rate available, 1 teacher free for every 10 children.

Ground floor & grounds. In grounds, on leads.

OLD GALA HOUSE
Scot Crescent, Galashiels TD1 3J
Tel: 01750 20096   **Fax:** 01750 23282   **e-mail:** museums@scotborders.gov.uk
Owner: Scottish Borders Council
Dating from 1583, the former house of the Lairds of Gala. Particularly memorable is the painted ceiling dated 1635.
Location: OS Ref. NT492 357. S of town centre, signed from A7.
Open: Apr - Sept: Tue - Sat, 10am - 4pm. Jun - Aug: Mon - Sat, 10am - 4pm, Suns, 2 - 4pm. Oct: Tue - Sat, 1 - 4pm.
Admission: Free.

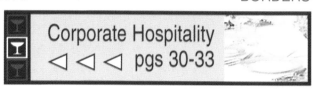

Corporate Hospitality
◁ ◁ ◁ pgs 30-33

PAXTON HOUSE & COUNTRY PARK
BERWICK-UPON-TWEED TD15 1SZ
www.paxtonhouse.com

Tel: 01289 386291   **Fax:** 01289 386660   **e-mail:** info@paxtonhouse.com
Owner: The Paxton Trust   **Contact:** Jacky Miller
Award-winning country house and country park built from 1758-62 to the design of John and James Adam for Patrick Home, Laird of Wedderburn. The house boasts the pre-eminent collection of Chippendale furniture in Scotland, the largest picture gallery in a Scottish country house built by Robert Reid in 1814, now acting as the first outstation of the National Galleries of Scotland, and a fine collection of regency furniture by William Trotter of Edinburgh. The estate has woodland trails, riverside walks, gardens, park land, red squirrel hide, highland cattle and croquet. There are shops, a stables tearoom, a function suite and a temporary exhibition programme.
Location: OS Ref. NT931 520. 3m off the A1 Berwick-upon-Tweed on B6461.
Open: 1 Apr - 31 Oct: Grounds: 10am - sunset. House: 11am - 5pm. Last house tour 4.15pm. Open to groups/schools all year by appointment.
Admission: Adult £5, Child £2.50, OAP £4.75, Student £4. Groups (pre-arranged, 12+). Adult £4, Child £1.50, OAP £4. Grounds only: Adult £2.25, Child £1.
ℹ No photography. 🅾 👕 🇹 Conferences, wedding receptions. ♿ Partial.
🍴 ‖ Licensed. 🎫 Obligatory. 🅿 ▣ 🐕 In grounds, on leads. ❄ 📺 Tel for details.

ROBERT SMAIL'S PRINTING WORKS
High Street, Innerleithen EH44 6HA
Tel: 01896 830206   www.nts.org.uk/robertsmail.html
Owner: The National Trust for Scotland   **Contact:** Edward Nicol
A printing time-capsule featuring a completely restored Victorian printing works. Visitors can experience the almost forgotten craft of hand typesetting. They will discover the secrets of the printing works from the archive-based posters and see the fully restored machines in action. The buildings also contain the Victorian office with its acid-etched windows, reconstructed waterwheel and many historic items which provide an insight into the history of the Border town of Innerleithen.
Location: OS Ref. NT333 366. In High Street, Innerleithen, 30m S of Edinburgh.
Open: 25 Mar - 28 Jun & 2 Sept - 27 Oct: Thur - Mon, 12 noon - 5pm (Sun, 1 - 5pm); 29 Jun - 1 Sept: Thur - Mon, 10am - 6pm (Sun, 1 - 5pm).
Admission: Adult £3.50, Conc. £2.60, Family £9.50. Groups: Adult £2.80, Child/School £1.
🅾 ♿ Ground floor. 🅿 None. 🐕

PRIORWOOD GARDEN & DRIED FLOWER SHOP
Melrose TD6 9PX
Tel: 01896 822493   www.nts.org.uk/priorwood.html
Owner: The National Trust for Scotland   **Contact:** Mrs Cathy Ross
Overlooked by the Abbey's 15th century ruins is this unique garden, where most of the plants are suitable for drying. With the aid of volunteers, Priorwood Garden markets a wide variety of dried flower arrangements through its own dried flower shop.
Location: OS Ref. NT549 341. In the Border town of Melrose, beside the Abbey.
Open: 25 Mar - 28 Jun: daily, 10am - 5pm. 29 Jun - 1 Sept: daily, 10am - 6pm. 2 Sept - 27 Oct: daily, 10am - 5pm.
Admission: Honesty box £2.
🅾 ♿ Grounds. WC. 🅿 No parking. 🐕 Guide dogs only.

SMAILHOLM TOWER
Smailholm, Kelso
Tel: 01573 460365
Owner: In the care of Historic Scotland   **Contact:** The Steward
Set on a high rocky knoll this well preserved 16th century tower houses an exhibition of tapestries and costume dolls depicting characters from Sir Walter Scott's Minstrelsy of the Scottish Borders.
Location: OS Ref. NT638 347. Nr Smailholm Village, 6m W of Kelso on B6937.
Open: 1 Apr - 30 Sept: daily, 9.30am - 6.30pm. Last tickets 1/2 hour before closing.
Admission: Adult £2, Child 75p, Conc. £1.50.

THIRLESTANE CASTLE 🏛

LAUDER, BERWICKSHIRE TD2 6R

www.thirlestanecastle.co.uk

Tel: 01578 722430   **Fax:** 01578 722761   **e-mail:** admin@thirlestanecastle.co.uk

Owner: Thirlestane Castle Trust   **Contact:** Peter Jarvis

One of the seven 'Great Houses of Scotland', Thirlestane Castle was the ancient seat of the Earls and Duke of Lauderdale and is still home to the Maitlands. Standing in beautiful Border countryside, Thirlestane has exquisite 17th century plasterwork ceilings, a fine portrait collection, historic toys, kitchens and country life exhibitions. Facilities include free parking, audio visual display, gift shop, café, adventure playground, woodland picnic tables, and dungeon display. Four star STB award; Registered Museum.

The state rooms are available for banquets, dinners and receptions. Non-destructive events can be held in the grounds which overlook the Leader Valley and Lammermuir Hills.

Location: OS Ref. NT540 473. Off A68 at Lauder, 28m S of Edinburgh.

Open: 29 Mar - 31 Oct: daily except Sats, 10.30am - 4.15pm (last admission).

Admission: Adult £5.30, Child £3, Family £13.50. Groups (30+): Adult £4.50, Child £3.

▢ 🅣 ♿ Unsuitable. ▣ ⓕ By arrangement. 🅿 ■ 🐾 In grounds, on leads.

TRAQUAIR 🏛

INNERLEITHEN, PEEBLESSHIRE EH44 6PW

www.traquair.co.uk

Tel: 01896 830323   **Fax:** 01896 830639   **e-mail:** enquiries@traquair.co.uk

       Contact: Ms C Maxwell Stuart

Traquair, situated amidst beautiful scenery and close by the River Tweed, is the oldest inhabited house in Scotland - visited by twenty-seven kings. Originally a Royal hunting lodge, it was owned by the Scottish Crown until 1478 when it passed to a branch of the Royal Stuart family whose descendants still live in the house today. Nearly ten centuries of Scottish political and domestic life can be traced from the collection of treasures in the house. It is particularly rich in associations with the Catholic Church in Scotland, Mary Queen of Scots and the Jacobite Risings.

There is an 18th century working brewery in one of the wings of the house where the famous Traquair House Ales are produced. Maze, Craft Workshops, Children's Adventure Playground.

Location: OS Ref. NY330 354. On B709 near junction with A72. Edinburgh 1hr, Glasgow 1¹/₂ hrs, Carlisle 1¹/₂ hrs, Newcastle 1¹/₂ hrs.

Open: 30 Mar - 31 Oct: daily, 12.30 - 5.30pm. Jun - Aug: 10.30am - 5.30pm. Last admission 5pm. Oct: 12.30 - 4.30pm. Grounds: daily 10.30am - 5.30pm. Guided tours outside normal opening times by arrangement.

Admission: House & Grounds: Adult £5.50, Child (under 15yrs) £3, OAP £5.20, Family (2+3) £16. Grounds only: Adult £2.50, Child (under 15yrs) £1. Groups (20+): Adult £5, Child £2.50. Guided tours: £6 (min. rate £120). Guidebook £3.50. Receptions in the High Drawing Room: £3.75pp, with canapés £5pp.

▢ ⓘ No photography in house. 🅣 ♿ ▣ Licensed, self-service. ⓕ Outside opening hours. 🅿 Coaches please book. 🐾 In grounds on leads. 🛏 2 four-poster suites, B&B. ▣

Christine Ottewill

BLAIRQUHAN CASTLE

MAYBOLE

www.blairquhan.co.uk

Blairquhan is the home of James Hunter Blair, the great-great-grandson of Sir David Hunter Blair, 3rd Baronet for whom it was designed by William Burn and built in 1821-24.

All the Regency furniture bought for the house remains, and the house has not been altered except discreetly to bring it up-to-date. There are ten double bedrooms including four four-poster beds, with en-suite bathrooms, five singles, and many public rooms which can be used for conferences and every sort of occasion.

The castle is approached by a 3 mile private drive along the River Girvan and is situated in one of the most charming parts of south west Scotland. There is a well-known collection of pictures. It is particularly suitable for conferences because the house is entirely at your disposal.

A five minute walk from the Castle are the walled gardens, laid out around the 1800s and recently replanned and replanted.

Blairquhan is only 50 miles from Glasgow. It is within about half an hour's drive of the world-famous golf courses of Prestwick, Troon and Turnberry, the last two of which are venues for the British Open Golf Championships.

Owner:
James Hunter Blair

▶ CONTACT

James Hunter Blair
Blairquhan Castle
Maybole
Ayrshire   KA19 7LZ

Tel: 01655 770239
Fax: 01655 770278
e-mail: enquiries@
blairquhan.co.uk

▶ LOCATION

OS Ref. NS366 055

From London M6 to Carlisle, A75 to Crocketford, A712 to A713 nr New Galloway, B741 to Straiton, B7045 to Ayr. Turn left ¼ m beyond village. 6m SE of Maybole off B7045.

Rail: Maybole 7m.

Air: Prestwick Airport, 15m. Direct flights to London, Dublin, Paris, Frankfurt & Brussels. Executive Travel: contact 01655 882666.

CONFERENCE/FUNCTION

ROOM	SIZE	MAX CAPACITY
Drawing Rms	1200 sq ft	100
Dining Rm	750 sq ft	100
Library	400 sq ft	25
Saloon	600 sq ft	100
Meeting Rm	255 sq ft	50

Christine Ottewill

▶ OPENING TIMES

Summer
13 July - 11 August
Daily (except Mons)
1.30 - 4.15pm
(Last admission).

Open at all other times by appointment.

Winter
Open by appointment.

▶ ADMISSION

House & Garden
Adult £5.00
Child (6-16yrs) £3.00
Conc £4.00

Groups*
Negotiable

* Minimum payment £20.

Tree trail, fashion shows, shooting, equestrian events, garden parties, shows, rallies, filming, grand piano, snooker, fishing. Slide projector, overhead projector, screen, and secretarial assistance for meetings. No photography in castle.

Wedding receptions.

Two main floors suitable. WC.

Teas, lunches, buffets and dinners. Groups can book in advance, special rates for groups.

By arrangement. Also available in French.

Unlimited.

Guide and schoolroom provided, cost negotiable.

10 doubles (4x4-posters) with bathrooms en-suite, 5 singles. The Dower House at Milton has 10 doubles, 1 single, 6 bathrooms. 7 holiday cottages on the Estate.

In grounds on leads.

🎭 SPECIAL EVENTS

EVENTS EVERY WEEKEND INCLUDING:
Model aeroplane flying
Battle re-enactments
Kite-flying
Highland Dancing
Music

NTS / Brian Chapple

BRODICK CASTLE & COUNTRY PARK

ISLE OF ARRAN

www.nts.org.uk/brodick.html

Owner:
The National Trust
for Scotland

▶ **CONTACT**
Administrator
Isle of Arran
KA27 8HY

Tel: 01770 302202

Fax: 01770 302312

This is a castle you will never forget! The tall, stately building beckons you with the glow of its warm red sandstone. The setting is staggering, fronted by the sea, bedecked with gardens and overlooked by the majestic mountain of Goatfell.

The castle was built on the site of a Viking fortress and dates from the 13th century. The contents are magnificent and include superb silver, porcelain, paintings and sporting trophies. The woodland garden ranks as one of Europe's finest.

▶ **LOCATION**
OS Ref. NS010 360

Isle of Arran. Ferries
from Ardrossan &
Claonaig and Kintyre.
Ferry enquiries:
01475 650100.

NTS / D MacGregor

▶ **OPENING TIMES**

Castle
25 Mar - 27 Oct: daily,
10am - 5pm.
Visitor facilities also
open weekends:
28 Oct - 24 Dec:
10am - 5pm.

Country Park
All year.

▶ **ADMISSION**
Combined Ticket
Adult £7.00
Conc £5.25
Family £19.00

Groups
Adult £5.60
Child/School £1.00

Garden & Country Park
Adult £3.50
Conc. £2.60
Family £9.50

Groups
Adult £2.80
Child/School.......... £1.00

Licensed. In grounds on leads.

NTS Photo Library

CULZEAN CASTLE & COUNTRY PARK

MAYBOLE

www.nts.org.uk/culzean.html

Owner: The National Trust for Scotland

▶ **CONTACT**

Jonathan Cardale
Culzean Castle &
Country Park
Maybole
KA19 8LE

Tel: 01655 884455

Fax: 01655 884503

e-mail: culzean@
nts.org.uk

▶ **LOCATION**

OS Ref. NS240 100

12m SW of Ayr, on
A719, 4m W
of Maybole.

One of Scotland's major attractions – a perfect day out for all the family. Robert Adam's romantic 18th century masterpiece – a real 'castle in the air' – is perched on a cliff high above the the Firth of Clyde. The interior, with its spectacular oval staircase and circular saloon, has been restored to the original elegant colour scheme. Gifted to the Trust by the 5th Marquess of Ailsa and the Kennedy family in 1945, the top floor was given to General Eisenhower as a Scottish holiday home. Today the Eisenhower Apartments offer country house style accommodation for that special occasion.

Culzean was Scotland's first country park and has been described as 'the most magnificent in Britain'. The 560 acres include 5km of coastline, woodland walks, ponds, a deer park, gardens, picnic areas and a new children's playground. Fascinating restored buildings include the Gas House, Ruined Arch and Viaduct, Ice House, Camellia House and unique Pagoda. The Victorian Vinery has recently been rebuilt in the Walled Garden. A new exhibition in the Visitor Centre tells the history of the castle and estate and 50 years of the Trust's conservation work. Three exciting shops offer an exclusive range of gifts and souvenirs and the self-service restaurant provides snacks and full meals.

▶ **OPENING TIMES**

Castle

25 Mar - 27 Oct: daily,
10am - 6pm. Visitor
facilities also open
weekends: 28 Oct - 24 Dec
& 20 Jan - 24 Mar:
10am - 6pm.

Country Park

All year.

▶ **ADMISSION**

Combined Ticket

Adult	£8.50
Conc.	£6.40
Family	£23.00

Groups

Adult	£6.80
Child/School	£1.00

Castle & Country Park only

Adult	£4.50
Conc.	£3.40
Family	£12.50

Groups

Adult	£3.60
Child/School	£1.00

NTS Photo Library/ Douglas MacGregor

Licensed.

By arrangement.

In grounds on leads.

Contact for details.

Tel for details.

DRUMLANRIG CASTLE

THORNHILL

www.drumlanrigcastle.org.uk

Drumlanrig Castle, Gardens and Country Park, the home of the Duke of Buccleuch and Queensberry KT was built between 1679 and 1691 by William Douglas, 1st Duke of Queensberry. Drumlanrig is rightly recognised as one of the first and most important buildings in the grand manner in Scottish domestic architecture. James Smith, who made the conversion from a 15th century castle, made a comparable transformation at Dalkeith a decade later.

The castle, of local pink sandstone, offers superb views across Nithsdale. It houses a renowned art collection, including work by Leonardo, Holbein,

and Rembrandt, as well as cabinets made for Louis XIV's Versailles, relics of Bonnie Prince Charlie and a 300 year old silver chandelier.

The story of Sir James Douglas, killed in Spain while carrying out the last wish of Robert Bruce, pervades the castle in the emblem of a winged heart. Douglas family historical exhibition. Working forge. The gardens, now being restored to the plan of 1738, add to the overall effect. The fascination of Drumlanrig as a centre of art, beauty and history is complemented by its role in the Queensberry Estate, a model of dynamic and enlightened land management.

Owner: His Grace the Duke of Buccleuch & Queensberry KT

▶ CONTACT

Claire Fisher
Drumlanrig Castle
Thornhill
Dumfriesshire
DG3 4AQ

Tel: 01848 330248
Fax: 01848 331682

Countryside Service:
01848 331555

e-mail: bre@
drumlanrigcastle.org.uk

▶ LOCATION
OS Ref. NX851 992

18m N of Dumfries,
3m NW of Thornhill
off A76.
16m from M74 at
Elvanfoot.
Approx. 1¹/₂ hrs
by road from
Edinburgh, Glasgow
and Carlisle.

🚫📷ℹ️ No photography inside the castle.

♿ Suitable. WC. Please enquire about facilities before visit.

🍽 Licensed.

🍴 Snacks, lunches and teas during opening hours.

🅿️ Adjacent to the castle.

Children's quiz and worksheets. Ranger-led activities, including woodlands and forestry. Adventure playground. School groups welcome throughout the year by arrangement.

In grounds on leads.

CONFERENCE/FUNCTION

ROOM	SIZE	MAX CAPACITY
Visitors' Centre	6m x 13m	50

▶ OPENING TIMES

Summer

Castle
27 April - 11 August
24 August - 8 September
Weekdays: 11am - 4pm,
Suns, 12 noon - 4pm.

9 - 30 September groups
by appointment only.

**Country Park, Gardens
& Adventure Woodland**
27 April - 30 September:
daily, 11am - 5pm.

Winter
By appointment only.

▶ ADMISSION

Castle and Country Park
Adult £6.00
Child £2.00
OAP/Student £4.00
Family (2+4) £14.00
Disabled in
   wheelchairs .... Free
Pre-booked groups (20+)
Adult £4.00
Child £2.00
Outside normal
opening times £8.00

Country Park only
Adult £3.00
Child £2.00
Family (2+4) £8.00

ARDWELL GARDENS

Ardwell, Nr Stranraer, Dumfries and Galloway DG9 9LY

Tel: 01776 860227

Owner: Mr Francis Brewis   **Contact:** Mrs Terry Brewis

The gardens include a formal garden, wild garden and woodland.

Location: OS Ref. NX102 455. A716 10m S of Stranraer.

Open: 1 Apr - 30 Sept: daily, 10am - 5pm.

Admission: Adult £2, Child/Conc. £1.

AUCHINLECK HOUSE

Ochilltree, Ayrshire

Tel: 01628 825920 or 825925   **Fax:** 01628 825417

e-mail: bookings@landmarktrust.co.uk **www**.landmarktrust.co.uk

Owner/Contact: The Landmark Trust

One of the finest examples of an 18th century Scottish country house, the importance of which is further enhanced by its association with James Boswell, author of *The Life of Samuel Johnson*. The restoration of the house was completed in 2001 by the Landmark Trust.

Location: OS Ref. NS507 230. Ochilltree, Ayrshire.

Open: Parts of the house will be open to the public on certain days throughout the year. Contact for details. Grounds: dawn - dusk in the Spring & Summer season.

Admission: Please contact for details.

In grounds, on leads. Up to 13 people, self-catering.

BACHELORS' CLUB

Sandgate Street, Tarbolton KA5 5RB

Tel: 01292 541940   **www**.nts.org.uk/bachelor.html

Owner: The National Trust for Scotland   **Contact:** The Manager

17th century thatched house in which poet Robert Burns and friends formed a debating society in 1780. Burns' mementos and relics, period furnishings.

Location: OS Ref. NS430 270. In Tarbolton, B744, 7$^{1}/_{2}$ m NE of Ayr, off B743.

Open: 25 Mar - 27 Oct: daily, 1 - 5pm.

Admission: Adult £2.50, Conc. £1.90, Family £7. Groups: £2.

Ground floor.

BARGANY GARDENS

Girvan, Ayrshire KA26 9QL

Tel: 01465 871249   **Fax:** 01465 871282

Owner/Contact: Mr John Dalrymple Hamilton

Lily pond, rock garden and a fine collection of hard and softwood trees.

Location: OS Ref. NS250 001. 4m ENE of Girvan by B734. After 2$^{1}/_{2}$ m keep ahead on to minor road to Old Dailly.

Open: Weekends & Mons in May only, 10am - 5pm.

Admission: £2 per head, Child Free. Buses by arrangement.

BLAIRQUHAN CASTLE

See page 457 for full page entry.

BROUGHTON HOUSE & GARDEN

High Street, Kirkcudbright DG6 4JX

Tel/Fax: 01557 330437   **www**.nts.org.uk/broughton.html

Owner: The National Trust for Scotland   **Contact:** Frances Scott

This fascinating 18th century house in the pleasant coastal town of Kirkcudbright was the home and studio from 1901 - 1933 of the artist E A Hornel, one of the 'Glasgow Boys'. It contains many of his works, along with paintings by other contemporary artists, and an extensive collection of rare Scottish books, including valuable editions of Burns' works.

Location: OS Ref. NX684 509. Off A711 / A755, in Kirkcudbright, at 12 High St.

Open: House & Garden: 25 Mar - 28 Jun: daily, 12 noon - 5pm. 29 Jun - 1 Sept: daily, 10am - 6pm. 2 Sept - 27 Oct: Mon - Sat, 12 noon - 5pm, Sun, 1 - 5pm.

Admission: Adult £3.50, Conc. £2.60, Family £9.50. Groups: £2.80.

Unsuitable. By arrangement. Limited.

BRODICK CASTLE & COUNTRY PARK

See page 458 for full page entry.

BURNS' COTTAGE

Alloway, Ayrshire KA7 4PY

Tel: 01292 441215   **Contact:** J Manson

Thatched cottage, birthplace of Robert Burns in 1759, with adjacent museum.

Location: OS Ref. NS335 190. 2m SW of Ayr. Two separate sites, 600yds apart.

Open: Apr - Oct: daily, 9am - 6pm. Nov - Mar: daily, 10am - 4pm (Suns, 12 noon - 4pm).

Admission: Adult £2.80, Child/OAP £1.40. Please telephone for 2002 charges.

CAERLAVEROCK CASTLE

GLENCAPLE, DUMFRIES DG1 4RU

Tel: 01387 770244

Owner: In the care of Historic Scotland   **Contact:** The Steward

One of the finest castles in Scotland on a triangular site surrounded by moats. Its most remarkable features are the twin-towered gatehouse and the Renaissance Nithsdale lodging. The site of two famous sieges. Children's park, replica siege engines and nature trail to site of earlier castle.

Location: OS84 NY025 656. 8m S of Dumfries on the B725.

Open: Apr - Sept: daily, 9.30am - 6.30pm. Oct - Mar: Mon - Sat, 9.30am - 4.30pm, Suns, 2 - 4.30pm. Last ticket sold 30 mins before closing.

Admission: Adult £2.80, Child £1, Conc. £2. 10% discount for groups (10+).

Partial. WCs. Limited for coaches. Free if pre-booked.

In grounds, on leads.

CARDONESS CASTLE

Gatehouse of Fleet

Tel: 01557 814427

Owner: In the care of Historic Scotland   **Contact:** The Steward

Well preserved ruin of a four storey tower house of 15th century standing on a rocky platform above the Water of Fleet. Ancient home of the McCullochs. Very fine fireplaces.

Location: OS Ref. NX591 553. 1m SW of Gatehouse of Fleet, beside the A75.

Open: 1 Apr - 30 Sept: daily, 9.30am - 6.30pm. Last ticket 6pm. 1 Oct - 31 Mar: Sats, 9.30am - 4.30pm, Suns, 2 - 4.30pm. Last ticket 4pm.

Admission: Adult £2.20, Child 75p, Conc. £1.60.

THOMAS CARLYLE'S BIRTHPLACE

Ecclefechan, Dumfriesshire DG11 3DG

Tel: 01576 300666   **www**.nts.org.uk/carlyles.html

Owner: The National Trust for Scotland   **Contact:** The Manager

Thomas Carlyle was born here in The Arched House in 1795, the year before Burns died. Carlyle was a brilliant essayist, historian, social reformer, visionary and literary giant. When he was 14 he walked the 84 miles to Edinburgh University - taking three days. Upstairs is the bedroom in which Carlyle was born. There is also a little museum with a notable collection of photographs, manuscripts and other documents.

Location: OS Ref. NY193 745. Off M74, 6m SE of Lockerbie. In Ecclefechan village.

Open: 1 May to 29 Sept: daily (except Tues & Weds), 1 - 5pm.

Admission: Adult £3.50, Conc. £2.60, Family £9.50. Groups: £2.80.

Unsuitable. By arrangement. Limited.

CASTLE KENNEDY GARDENS

Stair Estates, Rephad, Stranraer, Dumfries and Galloway DG9 8BX

Tel: 01776 702024 **Fax:** 01776 706248 **e-mail:** ckg@stair-estates.sol.co.uk

Owner: The Earl & Countess of Stair   **Contact:** The Earl of Stair

75 acres of gardens, originally laid out in 1730, includes rhododendrons, pinetum, walled garden and circular lily pond.

Location: OS Ref. NX109 610. 3m E of Stranraer on A75.

Open: Apr - Sept: daily.

Admission: Adult £3, Child £1, OAP £2 (2001 prices).

CRAIGDARROCH HOUSE
Moniaive, Dumfriesshire DG3 4JB
Tel: 01848 200202
Owner/Contact: Mr Alexander Sykes
Location: OS Ref. NX741 909. S side of B729, 2m W of Moniaive, 19m WNW of Dumfries.
Open: Jul: daily, 2 - 4pm. Please note: no WCs.
Admission: £2.

CRAIGIEBURN GARDEN
Craigieburn House, Nr Moffat, Dumfriesshire DG10 9LF
Tel: 01683 221250 **e-mail:** ajmw1@aol.com
Owner/Contact: Janet Wheatcroft
A plantsman's garden with a huge range of rare and unusual plants surrounded by natural woodland.
Location: OS Ref. NT117 053. NW side of A708 to Yarrow & Selkirk, 2¹/₂ m E of Moffat.
Open: May - Sept: Sats & Suns (open for charity).
Admission: Adult £2, Child Free.

CROSSRAGUEL ABBEY 🏛
Maybole, Strathclyde
Tel: 01655 883113
Owner: In the care of Historic Scotland **Contact:** The Steward
Founded in the early 13th century by the Earl of Carrick. Remarkably complete remains include church, cloister, chapter house and much of the domestic premises.
Location: OS Ref. NS275 083. 2m S of Maybole on the A77.
Open: 1 Apr - 30 Sept: daily, 9.30am - 6.30m. Last ticket 6pm.
Admission: Adult £2, Child 75p, Conc. £1.50.

CULZEAN CASTLE & COUNTRY PARK 🏰
See page 459 for full page entry.

DALGARVEN MILL MUSEUM
Dalry Road, Kilwinning, Ayrshire K13 6PL
Tel: 01294 552448
Owner: Dalgarven Mill Trust **Contact:** The Administrator
Water-driven flour mill and Ayrshire country life & costume museum.
Location: OS Ref. NS295 460. On A737 2m from Kilwinning.
Open: All year: Summer: Easter - end Oct: Tue - Sat, 10am - 5pm. Suns, 11am - 5pm. Winter: Tue - Sat, 10am - 4pm. Suns, 11am - 5pm. Closed Mons.
Admission: Charges.

DEAN CASTLE COUNTRY PARK
Dean Road, Kilmarnock, East Ayrshire KA3 1XB
Tel: 01563 522702 **Fax:** 01563 572552
Owner: East Ayrshire Council **Contact:** Andrew Scott-Martin
Set in 200 acres of Country Park. Visits to castle by guided tour only.
Location: OS Ref. NS437 395. Off A77. 1¹/₄ m NNE of town centre.
Open: Country Park & Visitor Centre: All year. Castle: Easter - end Oct: daily, 12 noon - 5pm (last tour 4.15pm). Oct - Easter: weekends only, 12 noon - 4pm (last tour 3.15pm).
Admission: Free (group charge on application). Conducted tours.

DRUMLANRIG CASTLE 🏰
See page 460 for full page entry.

DUNDRENNAN ABBEY 🏛
Kirkcudbright
Tel: 01557 500262
Owner: Historic Scotland **Contact:** The Steward
Mary Queen of Scots spent her last night on Scottish soil in this 12th century Cistercian Abbey founded by David I. The Abbey stands in a small and secluded valley.
Location: OS Ref. NX749 475. 6¹/₂ m SE of Kirkcudbright on the A711.
Open: 1 Apr - 30 Sept: daily, 9.30am - 6.30pm. Last ticket 6pm. 1 Oct - 31 Mar: Sats, 9.30am - 4.30pm, Suns, 2 - 4.30pm.
Admission: Adult £1.80, Child 75p, Conc. £1.30.

GALLOWAY HOUSE GARDENS
Garlieston, Newton Stewart, Wigtownshire DG8 8HF
Tel: 01988 600680
Owner: Galloway House Gardens Trust **Contact:** D Marshall
Created in 1740 by Lord Garlies, currently under restoration.
Location: OS Ref. NX478 453. 15m S of Newton Stewart on B7004.
Open: 1 Mar - 31 Oct: 9am - 5pm.
Admission: £1 per person.

GILNOCKIE'S TOWER
Hollows, Canonbie, Dumfriesshire
Tel: 01387 371876
Owner/Contact: Edward Armstrong
16th century tower house, occupied by the Clan Armstrong Centre.
Location: OS Ref. NY383 787. 2m N of Canonbie on minor road E of A7 just N of Hollows.
Open: Summer months by guided tour: 2.30pm sharp (closed 11.45am - 2pm). Winter months open by appointment. Tours to be booked in advance by telephone.
Admission: Adult £3, Child (under 14yrs) £1.50.

GLENLUCE ABBEY 🏛
Glenluce
Tel: 01581 300541
Owner/Contact: In the care of Historic Scotland
A Cistercian Abbey founded in 1190. Remains include a 16th century Chapter House.
Location: OS Ref. NX185 587. 2m NW of Glenluce village off the A75.
Open: 1 Apr - 30 Sept: daily 9.30am - 6.30pm. Last ticket 6pm. 1 Oct - 31 Mar: Sats, 9.30am - 4.30pm, Suns, 2 - 4.30pm. Last ticket 4pm.
Admission: Adult £1.80, Child 75p, Conc. £1.30.

GLENWHAN GARDENS
Dunragit, Stranraer, Wigtownshire DG9 8PH
Tel: 01581 400222 **Fax:** 01581 400222/400361 **Contact:** Tessa Knott
Beautiful 12 acre garden overlooking Luce Bay and the Mull of Galloway.
Location: OS Ref. NX150 580. N side of A75, 6m E of Stranraer.
Open: 1 Apr - 30 Sept: daily, 10am - 5pm or by appointment at other times.
Admission: Adult £3, Child £1, Conc. £2.50.

KELBURN 🏰
Fairlie, Nr Largs, Ayrshire KA29 0BE
Tel: 01475 568685/568204
Owner/Contact: The Earl of Glasgow
The home of the Boyle family, later the Earls of Glasgow since the 13th century.
Location: OS Ref NS210 580. A78 to Largs, 2m S of Largs.
Open: Castle: Jul & Aug and first week in Sept.
Admission: Castle: Adult: £1.50, Student £1.20, plus entrance fee to Country Centre: Adult £ 4.50, Child £3, Groups (12+): Adult: £3, Child/OAPs £2, Family (2+3) £13.00.

LOGAN BOTANIC GARDEN
Port Logan, Stranraer, Wigtownshire DG9 9ND
Tel: 01776 860231 **Fax:** 01776 860333
Owner: Royal Botanic Garden Edinburgh **Contact:** The Curator
Scotland's most exotic garden. Take a trip to the south west of Scotland and experience the southern hemisphere!
Location: OS Ref. NX097 430. 14m S of Stranraer on B7065, off A716.
Open: 1 Mar - 31 Oct: daily, 9.30am - 6pm.
Admission: Adult £3, Child £1, Conc. £2.50, Family £7. Group discount available.

MACLELLAN'S CASTLE 🏛
Kirkcudbright
Tel: 01557 331856
Owner: In the care of Historic Scotland **Contact:** The Steward
Castellated mansion, built in 1577 using stone from an adjoining ruined monastery by the then Provost. Elaborately planned with fine architectural details, it has been a ruin since 1752.
Location: OS Ref. NX683 511. Centre of Kirkcudbright on the A711.
Open: 1 Apr - 30 Sept: daily, 9.30am - 6.30pm. Last ticket 6pm.
Admission: Adult £2, Child 75p, Conc. £1.50.

Burns' Birthplace

Patrick Lane

NEW ABBEY CORN MILL

New Abbey Village

Tel: 01387 850260

Owner: Historic Scotland   **Contact:** The Custodian

This carefully renovated 18th century water-powered oatmeal mill is in full working order and regular demonstrations are given for visitors in the summer.

Location: OS Ref. NX962 663. 8m S of Dumfries on the A710. Close to Sweetheart Abbey.

Open: 1 Apr - 30 Sept: daily, 9.30am - 6.30pm. Last ticket 6pm. 1 Oct - 31 Mar: Mon - Wed & Sat, 9.30am - 4.30pm, Thurs, 9.30am - 12 noon, Fris closed, Suns, 2 - 4.30pm. Last ticket 4pm.

Admission: Adult £1.80, Child 75p, Conc. £1.30. Joint entry ticket with Sweetheart Abbey: Adult £3.50, Child £1.20, Conc. £1.60.

RAMMERSCALES

Lockerbie, Dumfriesshire DG11 1LD

Tel: 01387 810229   **Fax:** 01387 810940   **e-mail:** estate@rammerscales.co.uk

Owner/Contact: Mr M A Bell Macdonald

Georgian house.

Location: OS Ref. NY080 780. W side of B7020, 3m S of Lochmoben.

Open: Last week in Jul, 1st three weeks in Aug: daily (excluding Sats), 2 - 5pm.

Admission: Adult £5, Conc. £2.50.

SHAMBELLIE HOUSE MUSEUM OF COSTUME

New Abbey, Dumfries DG2 8HQ

Tel: 01387 850375   **Fax:** 01387 850461

Owner: National Museums of Scotland   **Contact:** Sheila Watt

Shambellie House is a modest country house designed by David Bryce in 1856 for William Stewart. It is set in woodland just outside the village of New Abbey. Shambellie offers visitors the chance to see period clothes in appropriate room settings, with accessories, furniture and decorative art.

Location: OS Ref. NX960 665. On A710, 7m outside Dumfries on Solway coast road.

Open: 1 Apr - 31 Oct: daily, 11am - 5pm.

Admission: Please telephone for details.

📷 ℹ️ No photography in house. 🚻 ♿ Unsuitable. 📹 🅘 By arrangement. 🅿️ Limited. 🔲 🐕 In grounds, on leads.

SORN CASTLE

Ayrshire KA5 6HR

Tel: 01290 551555

Owner/Contact: Mrs R G McIntyre

14th century castle. Enlarged several times, most recently in 1908.

Location: OS Ref. NS555 265. 4m E of Mauchline on B743.

Open: 13 Jul - 10 Aug: daily, 2 - 4pm and by appointment.

Admission: Adult £3.50.

SOUTER JOHNNIE'S COTTAGE

Main Road, Kirkoswald KA19 8HY

Tel: 01655 760603   www.nts.org.uk

Owner: The National Trust for Scotland   **Contact:** Ms Jan Gibson

The home of John Davidson, original 'Souter' (cobbler) of Robert Burns' famous narrative poem *Tam O' Shanter*. Burns mementos and restored cobbler's workshop. Life-sized stone figures in adjacent 'ale-house'.

Location: OS Ref. NS240 070. On A77, in Kirkoswald village, 4m SW of Maybole.

Open: 25 Mar - 27 Oct: daily, 11.30am - 5pm.

Admission: Adult £2.50, Conc. £1.90, Family £7. Groups: £2.

♿ House. 🅿️ Limited. 🐕

STRANRAER CASTLE

Stranraer, Galloway

Tel: 01776 705088   **Fax:** 01776 705835

Owner: Dumfries & Galloway Council   **Contact:** John Pickin

Also referred to as the Castle of St John. A much altered 16th century L-plan tower house, now a museum.

Location: OS Ref. NX061 608. In Stranraer, towards centre, 1/4 m short of the harbour.

Open: Easter - mid-Sept: Mon - Sat, 10am - 1pm & 2 - 5pm.

Admission: Adult £1.20, Conc. 60p, Family £3.

SWEETHEART ABBEY

New Abbey Village

Tel: 01387 850397

Owner: In the care of Historic Scotland   **Contact:** The Steward

Cistercian abbey founded in 1273 by Devorgilla, in memory of her husband John Balliol. A principal feature is the well-preserved precinct wall enclosing 30 acres.

Location: OS Ref. NX965 663. In New Abbey Village, on A710 8m S of Dumfries.

Open: 1 Apr - 30 Sept: daily, 9.30am - 6.30pm. Last ticket 6pm. 1 Oct - 31 Mar: Mon - Wed & Sat, 9.30am - 4.30pm, Thurs, 9.30am - 12 noon, Fris closed, Suns, 2 - 4.30pm. Last ticket 4pm.

Admission: Adult £1.80, Child 75p, Conc. £1.30. Joint entry ticket with New Abbey Corn Mill: Adult £3, Child £1.20, Conc. £2.25.

THREAVE CASTLE

Castle Douglas

Tel: 01831 168512

Owner: The National Trust for Scotland   **Contact:** Historic Scotland

Built by Archibald the Grim in the late 14th century, early stronghold of the Black Douglases. Around its base is an artillery fortification built before 1455 when the castle was besieged by James II. Ring the bell and the custodian will come to ferry you over. Long walk to property. Owned by The National Trust for Scotland but under the guardianship of Historic Scotland.

Location: OS Ref. NX739 623. 2m W of Castle Douglas on the A75.

Open: 1 Apr - 30 Sept: daily, 9.30am - 6.30pm. Last ticket 6pm.

Admission: Adult £2.20, Child 75p, Conc. £1.60. Charges include ferry trip.

THREAVE GARDEN & ESTATE

CASTLE DOUGLAS DG7 1RX

Tel: 01556 502575   **Tel:** 01556 502683   www.nts.org.uk/threave.html

Owner: The National Trust for Scotland   **Contact:** Trevor Jones

The garden has a wide range of features and a good collection of plants. There are peat and woodland garden plants and a colourful rock garden. Summer months bring a superb show from the herbaceous beds and borders. The heather gardens give a splash of colour, along with bright berries in the autumn. Truly a garden for all seasons.

Location: OS Ref. NX752 605. Off A75, 1m SW of Castle Douglas.

Open: Estate & garden: 1 Mar- 24 Mar: daily, 10am - 4pm. 25 Mar - 27 Oct: daily, 9.30am - 5.30pm. 28 Oct - 23 Dec: daily, 10am - 4pm.

Admission: Adult £5, Conc. £3.75, Family £13.50. Groups: £4.

📷 ♿ Grounds. WC. 🍴 🐕

WHITHORN PRIORY

Whithorn

Tel: 01988 500700

Owner: In the care of Historic Scotland   **Contact:** The Project Manager

The site of the first Christian church in Scotland. Founded as 'Candida Casa' by St Ninian in the early 5th century it later became the cathedral church of Galloway.

Location: OS Ref. NX445 403. At Whithorn on the A746. 18m S of Newton Stewart.

Open: Please telephone for details.

Admission: Joint ticket gives entry to Priory, Priory Museum and archaeological dig.

Open All Year Index
◁ ◁ ◁ pgs 44-48

DALMENY HOUSE

SOUTH QUEENSFERRY

www.dalmeny.co.uk

Owner:
The Earl of Rosebery

▶ **CONTACT**

The Administrator
Dalmeny House
South Queensferry
Edinburgh
EH30 9TQ

Tel: 0131 331 1888
Fax: 0131 331 1788

e-mail: events@
dalmeny.co.uk

▶ **LOCATION**

OS Ref. NT167 779

From Edinburgh A90,
B924, 7m N, A90 ¹/₂ m.

On south shore
of Firth of Forth.

Bus: From St Andrew
Square to Chapel Gate
1m from House.

Rail: Dalmeny
station 3m.

Taxi: Queensferry Fare
Radio Cabs
0131 331 1041.

Dalmeny House rejoices in one of the most beautiful and unspoilt settings in Great Britain, yet it is only seven miles from Scotland's capital, Edinburgh, fifteen minutes from Edinburgh airport and less than an hour's drive from Glasgow. It is an eminently suitable venue for group visits, business functions, meetings and special events, including product launches. Outdoor activities such as off-road driving, also feature strongly.

Dalmeny Estate, the family home of the Earls of Rosebery for over 300 years, boasts superb collections of porcelain and tapestries, fine paintings by Gainsborough, Raeburn, Reynolds and Lawrence, together with the exquisite Mentmore Rothschild collection of 18th century French furniture. There is also the Napoleonic collection, assembled by the 5th Earl of Rosebery, Prime Minister, historian and owner of three Derby winners.

The Hall, Library and Dining Room will lend a memorable sense of occasion to corporate receptions, luncheons and dinners. A wide range of entertainment can also be provided, from piano recitals to a floodlit pipe band Beating the Retreat.

▶ **OPENING TIMES**

Summer
July and August
Sun - Tue, 2 - 5.30pm.
Last admission 4.30pm.

Winter
Open at other times by
appointment only.

▶ **ADMISSION**

Summer
Adult £4.00
Child (10-16yrs) £2.00
OAP £3.50
Student £3.00
Groups (20+) £3.00

i Fashion shows, product launches, archery, clay pigeon shooting, equestrian events, shows, filming, background photography, small meetings and special events. Lectures on House, contents and family history. Screen and projector. Helicopter landing area. House is centre of a 4¹/₂ m shore walk from Forth Rail Bridge to small foot passenger ferry at Cramond (ferry 9am - 1pm, 2 - 7pm in summer, 2 - 4pm winter, closed Fri). No fires, picnics or photography.

T Conferences and functions, buffets, lunches, dinners.

♿ Partially suitable. Visitors may alight at entrance. WC.

☕ Teas and lunches, groups can book in advance.

🚶 Obligatory. Special interest tours can be arranged outside normal opening hours.

P 60 cars, 3 coaches. Parking for functions in front of house.

THE GEORGIAN HOUSE

EDINBURGH

www.nts.org.uk/georgian.html

The north side of Charlotte Square is Robert Adam's masterpiece of urban architecture - a splendid example of the neo-classical 'palace front'. The three floors of No.7, The Georgian House, are delightfully furnished as they would have been around 1796. There is a fascinating array of china and silver, pictures and furniture, gadgets and utensils from the decorative to the purely functional. On the south side of Charlotte Square, The National Trust for Scotland has opened a gallery, coffee house and shop (pictured above).

Owner:
The National Trust for Scotland

▶ **CONTACT**
Jacqueline Wright
7 Charlotte Square
Edinburgh EH2 4DR

Tel/Fax: 0131 226 3318

▶ **LOCATION**
OS Ref. NT247 740

In Edinburgh's city centre, NW of Princes St.

▶ **OPENING TIMES**

20 Jan - 24 Mar
daily 12 noon - 5pm

25 Mar - 27 Oct
daily 10am - 6pm.

28 Oct - 24 Dec
daily 12 noon - 5pm.

Shop
As house.

▶ **ADMISSION**
Adult....................£5.00
Conc. £3.75
Family £13.50
Groups (20+).........£4.00

Inclusive in price.

 No parking.

Edinburgh City, Coast & Countryside

HARBURN HOUSE

NR LIVINGSTON

www.harburnhouse.com

Owner: Humphrey & Rozi Spurway

▶ **CONTACT**

Rozi Spurway
Harburn House
Harburn
West Calder
West Lothian
EH55 8RN

Tel: 01506 461818

Fax: 01506 416591

e-mail: information@
harburnhouse.com

▶ **LOCATION**
OS Ref. NT045 608

Off B7008, 2½ m S of
A71. 2m N of A70. 20m
SW of Edinburgh.
Almost equidistant
between Glasgow and
Edinburgh, within 1hr
of Perth, Stirling,
Dundee and the
Border country.

Harburn House offers its guests the perfect alternative to a first class hotel. This privately owned Georgian mansion, surrounded by its own 3000 acre sporting and leisure estate, is ideally situated offering unparalleled accessibility.

Harburn is essentially small and very personal. It is therefore frequently taken over exclusively for conferences, incentive travel, training seminars and product launches, etc. In this way guests may enjoy the luxury of a five star hotel, combined with the comfort and privacy of their own home.

The policies and lawns of Harburn are ideal for larger events and these can be complemented by

our own fully lined and floored marquee.

A stay at Harburn is a very relaxed and informal affair. The staff are first class and the atmosphere is one of a private house party.

The estate provides the full range of sporting and leisure activities including, golf, game shooting, fishing, clay pigeon shooting, tennis, riding and archery to name but a few.

The complete privacy and outstanding scenery, so accessible to the major cities and beauty spots, makes Harburn the ultimate choice for the discerning event or conference organiser.

▶ **OPENING TIMES**

All year by appointment for exclusive use of house and grounds.

▶ **ADMISSION**

The exclusive use of House and Grounds for activity days (without accommodation).

Per day from £700.00

Accommodation Rates
On application

Day Delegate Rate
Per person £48.00

24 hour rate
Per person £140.00

VAT is not included in the above rates.

ROOM	SIZE	MAX CAPACITY
Conference Room	30' x 18'	60
Drawing Rm	30' x 18'	40
Dining Rm	30' x 18'	50
Library	14' x 12'	15
Morning Rm	16' x 15'	20
Whole house		80
Marquee	120' x 40'	200

CONFERENCE/FUNCTION

ⓘ Filming, conferences, activity days, product launches, golf, riding, fishing, archery, buggies, game shooting, falconry, etc. Golf and Country Club nearby.

▮ High quality in-house catering by our own top chef and fully trained staff. Prices and menus on request. Wedding receptions.

♿ Ground floor bedroom, dining room and drawing room.

🅿 Parking for 300 cars and 10 coaches in summer, 100+/10 in winter. Follow one way system and 20 mph speed limit, vehicles should not park on grass verges.

🐕 On leads.

🛏 20 bedrooms, all with their own bathrooms, exclusive to one group at a time.

HOPETOUN HOUSE 🏛
Edinburgh

www.hopetounhouse.com

Owner:
Hopetoun House
Preservation Trust

▶ **CONTACT**

Lois Bayne Jardine
Hopetoun House
South Queensferry
Edinburgh
West Lothian
EH30 9SL

Tel: 0131 331 2451
Fax: 0131 319 1885

▶ **LOCATION**
OS Ref. NT089 790

2¹/₂ m W of Forth Road
Bridge.

12m W of Edinburgh
(25 mins. drive).

34m E of Glasgow
(50 mins. drive).

Hopetoun House is a unique gem of Europe's architectural heritage and undoubtedly 'Scotland's Finest Stately Home'. Situated on the shores of the Firth of Forth, it is one of the most splendid examples of the work of Scottish architects Sir William Bruce and William Adam. The interior of the house, with opulent gilding and classical motifs, reflects the aristocratic grandeur of the early 18th century, whilst its magnificent parkland has fine views across the Forth to the hills of Fife. The house is approached from the Royal Drive, used only by members of the Royal Family, notably King George IV in 1822 and Her Majesty Queen Elizabeth II in 1988.

Hopetoun is really two houses in one, the oldest part of the house was designed by Sir William Bruce and built between 1699 and 1707. It shows some of the finest examples in Scotland of carving, wainscotting and ceiling painting. In 1721 William Adam started enlarging the house by adding the magnificent façade, colonnades and grand State apartments which were the focus for social life and entertainment in the 18th century.

The house is set in 100 acres of rolling parkland including fine woodland walks, the red deer park, the spring garden with a profusion of wild flowers, and numerous picturesque picnic spots.

Hopetoun has been home of the Earls of Hopetoun, later created Marquesses of Linlithgow, since it was built in 1699 and in 1974 a charitable trust was created to preserve the house with its historic contents and surrounding landscape for the benefit of the public for all time.

▶ **OPENING TIMES**

Summer
29 March - 30 September:
daily, 10am - 5.30pm.
Last admission 4.30pm.

1 - 27 October:
11am - 4pm.
Last admission 3.30pm.

Winter
By appointment only
for groups of 15+.

▶ **ADMISSION**

Adult £5.30
Child (5-16yrs)........ £2.70
Conc £4.70
Groups
Adult £4.70

Under 5yrs Free.

Winter prices on request.

Admission to Shop &
Adam Stables Restaurant
Free.

🛍 ℹ Private functions, special events, antiques fairs, concerts, Scottish gala evenings, conferences, wedding ceremonies and receptions, grand piano, boules (petanque) piste, croquet lawn, helicopter landing. No smoking or flash photography in house.

🍽 Receptions, gala dinners.

♿ Restaurant and exhibitions on ground floor. WC.

🍴 Licensed. Groups (up to 250) can book in advance, menus on request tel: 0131 331 4305.

🚶 By arrangement. Foreign language guides are usually available.

🅿 Close to the house for cars and coaches. Book if possible, allow 1-2hrs for visit (min).

📖 Holders of 2 Sandford Awards for Heritage Education. Special tours of house and/or grounds for different age/interest groups. Teachers' information pack.

🐕 No dogs in house, on leads in grounds.

❄

CONFERENCE/FUNCTION

ROOM	SIZE	MAX CAPACITY
Ballroom	92' x 35'	300
Tapestry Rm	37' x 24'	100
Red Drawing Rm	44' x 24'	100
State Dining Rm	39' x 23'	20

AMISFIELD MAINS

Nr Haddington, East Lothian EH41 3SA

Tel: 01875 870201 **Fax:** 01875 870620

Owner: Wemyss and March Estates Management Co Ltd   **Contact:** M Andrews

Georgian farmhouse with gothick barn and cottage.

Location: OS Ref. NT526 755. Between Haddington and East Linton on A1 Edinburgh-Dunbar Road.

Open: Exterior only: By appointment, Wemyss and March Estates Office, Longniddry, East Lothian EH32 0PY.

Admission: Please contact for details.

ARNISTON HOUSE 🏠

GOREBRIDGE, MIDLOTHIAN EH23 4RY

www.arniston-house.co.uk

Tel/Fax: 01875 830515 **e-mail:** henrietta.d.bekker2@btinternet.com

Owner: Mrs A Dundas-Bekker   **Contact:** Miss H Dundas-Bekker

Magnificent William Adam mansion started in 1726. Fine plasterwork, Scottish portraiture, period furniture and other fascinating contents. Beautiful country setting beloved by Sir Walter Scott.

Location: OS Ref. NT326 595. Off B6372, 1m from A7, Temple direction.

Open: Apr, May & Jun: Tue & Wed; 1 Jul - 15 Sept: Mon - Fri & Sun, guided tours at 2pm & 3.30pm. Pre-arranged groups (10-50) accepted throughout the rest of the year.

Admission: Adult £5, Child £2, Conc. £4.

ℹ️No inside photography. ♿WC. 👥Obligatory. 🅿️ 🐕In grounds, on leads. ❄️

BEANSTON

Nr Haddington, East Lothian EH41 3SB

Tel: 01875 870201 **Fax:** 01875 870620

Owner: Wemyss and March Estates Management Co. Ltd   **Contact:** M Andrews

Georgian farmhouse with Georgian orangery.

Location: OS Ref. NT546 763. Between Haddington and East Linton on A1 Edinburgh-Dunbar Road.

Open: Exterior only: By appointment, Wemyss and March Estates Office, Longniddry, East Lothian EH32 0PY.

Admission: Please contact for details.

BIEL 🏠

Dunbar, East Lothian EH42 1SY

Tel: 01620 860355

Owner/Contact: C G Spence

Originally a fortified tower, considerably added to over time.

Location: OS Ref. NT635 759. 5m from Dunbar on the A1 towards Edinburgh.

Open: By appointment.

Admission: Contribution to charity.

BLACKNESS CASTLE 🏛️

Blackness

Tel: 01506 834807

Owner: In the care of Historic Scotland   **Contact:** The Steward

One of Scotland's most important strongholds. Built in the 14th century and massively strengthened in the 16th century as an artillery fortress, it has been a Royal castle and a prison armaments depot and film location for *Hamlet*. It was restored by the Office of Works in the 1920s. It stands on a promontory in the Firth of Forth.

Location: OS Ref. NT055 803. 4m NE of Linlithgow on the Firth of Forth, off the A904.

Open: 1 Apr - 30 Sept: daily, 9.30am - 6.30pm, last ticket 6pm. 1 Oct - 31 Mar: Mon - Sat, 9.30am - 4.30pm, last ticket 4pm. Closed Thur pm, Fri & Sun in winter.

Admission: Adult £2.20, Child 75p, Conc. £1.60.

CRAIGMILLAR CASTLE 🏛️

Edinburgh

Tel: 0131 661 4445

Owner: In the care of Historic Scotland   **Contact:** The Steward

Mary Queen of Scots fled to Craigmillar after the murder of Rizzio and it was here that the plot was hatched for the murder of her husband Lord Darnley. This handsome structure with courtyard and gardens covers an area of one and a quarter acres. Built around an L-plan tower house of the early 15th century including a range of private rooms linked to the hall of the old tower.

Location: OS Ref. NT285 710. 2 1/2 m SE of Edinburgh off the A68.

Open: 1 Apr - 30 Sept: daily, 9.30am - 6.30pm, last ticket 6pm. 1 Oct - 31 Mar: Mon - Sat, 9.30am - 4.30pm, Suns, 2 - 4.30pm, last ticket 4pm. Closed Thur pm & Fri in winter.

Admission: Adult £2.20, Child 75p, Conc. £1.60.

CRICHTON CASTLE 🏛️

Pathhead

Tel: 01875 320017

Owner: In the care of Historic Scotland   **Contact:** The Steward

A large and sophisticated castle with a spectacular façade of faceted stonework in an Italian style added by the Earl of Bothwell between 1581 and 1591 following a visit to Italy. Mary Queen of Scots attended a wedding here.

Location: OS Ref. NT380 612. 2 1/2 m SSW of Pathhead off the A68.

Open: 1 Apr - 30 Sept: daily, 9.30am - 6.30pm, last ticket 6pm.

Admission: Adult £2, Child 75p, Conc. £1.50.

DALKEITH COUNTRY PARK

Dalkeith, Midlothian EH22 2NJ

Tel: 0131 663 5684 **e-mail:** cmanson@buccleuch.com

Contact: J C Manson

Extensive grounds of Dalkeith Palace. 18th century bridge and orangery. Interpretation area.

Location: OS Ref. NT333 679. 7m SE of Edinburgh.

Open: Mar - Oct: 10am - 6pm.

Admission: Adult/Child £2, Family £7, Groups £1.50.

DALMENY HOUSE 🏠   *See page 464 for full page entry.*

Newliston

Patrick Lane

DIRLETON CASTLE & GARDEN

DIRLETON, EAST LOTHIAN EH39 5ER

Tel: 01620 850330

Owner: In the care of Historic Scotland   **Contact:** The Steward

The oldest part of this romantic castle dates from the 13th century, when it was built by the De Vaux family. The renowned gardens, first laid out in the 16th century, now include a magnificent Arts and Crafts herbaceous border (the longest in the world) and a re-created Victorian Garden. In the picturesque village of Dirleton.

Location: OS Ref. NT516 839. In Dirleton, 2m W of North Berwick on the A198.

Open: Apr - Sept: daily, 9.30am - 6.30pm. Oct - Mar: Mon - Sat, 9.30am - 4.30pm, Suns, 2 - 4.30pm. Last ticket 30 mins before closing.

Admission: Adult £2.80, Child £1, Conc. £2. 10% discount for groups (10+).

🔲 🕭 Partially. 🅿 ◼ Free if booked. 🐕 Guide dogs only. ✳

DUNDAS CASTLE

SOUTH QUEENSFERRY, EDINBURGH EH30 9SP

www.dundascastle.co.uk

Tel: 0131 319 2039 **Fax:** 0131 319 2068 **e-mail:** sales@dundascastle.co.uk

Owner: Sir Jack Stewart-Clark   **Contact:** David Adams – Manager

One of Scotland's most romantic castles overlooking the River Forth yet only 20 minutes from Edinburgh centre. The 15th century auld Keep and magnificent main house, built 1818 by William Burn, offer the perfect location for exclusive weddings, incentive and corporate events of up to 250 guests. Further marquee site for 1500. 1000 acre of wooded parklands for outdoor events including golf, clay shooting, archery, falconry, off-roading, quadbikes, riding and team building programmes. Golf course, squash court, riding stable, billiard room.

Location: OS Ref. NT117 767. 5m Edinburgh airport. 8m Edinburgh City. S of Forth Bridge, Southqueensferry. On the A8000 off A90. By train: 5 mins Dalmeny Station, 15 mins via Edinburgh Waverly Station.

Open: All year for exclusive bookings.

Admission: Prices on application for group bookings (20-2000).

🔲 🕭 🕭 🍽 By appointment. 🅿 🐕 On leads.
🛏 10+ luxury king-size twin rooms with ensuite. ✳ 📺 Tel for details.

DUNGLASS COLLEGIATE CHURCH 🔔

Cockburnspath

Tel: 0131 668 8800

Owner: In the care of Historic Scotland

Founded in 1450 for a college of canons by Sir Alexander Hume. A handsome cross-shaped building with vaulted nave, choir and transepts.

Location: OS Ref. 67 NT766 718. 1m NW of Cockburnspath. SW of A1.

Open: All year.

Admission: Free.

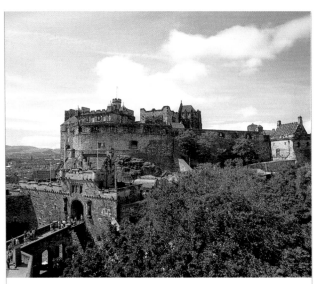

EDINBURGH CASTLE 🔔

CASTLEHILL, EDINBURGH EH1 2NG

Tel: 0131 225 9846 **Fax:** 0131 220 4733

Owner: Historic Scotland   **Contact:** Barbara Smith

Scotland's most famous castle, dominating the capital's skyline and giving stunning views of the city and countryside. Home to the Scottish crown jewels, the Stone of Destiny and Mons Meg. Other highlights include St Margaret's Chapel, the Great Hall and the Scottish National War Memorial.

Location: OS Ref. NT252 736. At the top of the Royal Mile in Edinburgh.

Open: Apr - Sept: daily, 9.30am - 6pm. Oct - Mar: daily, 9.30am - 5pm. Last ticket 45 mins before closing.

Admission: Adult £8, Child £2, Conc. £6. Pre-booked school visits available free, except May - Aug.

🔲 📺 Private evening hire. 🕭 Partial. WCs. Courtesy vehicle. 🍽 Licensed. 📷 🕱
🔊 In 6 languages. 🅿 Ample (except Jun-Oct). ◼ 🐕 Guide dogs. ✳

The Georgian House

Douglas MacGregor

THE GEORGIAN HOUSE ☘   *See page 465 for full page entry.*

GLADSTONE'S LAND ☘

477b Lawnmarket, Royal Mile, Edinburgh EH1 2NT

Tel: 0131 226 5856 **Fax:** 0131 226 4851 www.nts.org.uk/gladstone.html

Owner: The National Trust for Scotland   **Contact:** Pat Wigston

Gladstone's Land was the home of a prosperous Edinburgh merchant in the 17th century. On the Royal Mile, near the Castle, it is decorated and furnished with great authenticity to give visitors an impression of life in Edinburgh's Old Town some 300 years ago. Features of the 6-storey building are the painted ceilings and the reconstructed shop both complete with replicas of 17th century goods.

Location: OS Ref. NT255 736. In Edinburgh's Royal Mile, near the castle.

Open: House & Shop: 25 Mar - 27 Oct: Mon - Sat, 10am - 5pm, Suns, 1 - 5pm.

Admission: Adult £5, Conc. £3.75, Family £13.50. Groups: Adult £4. Group visits must be booked.

🖸 ⓰ Ground floor. 🅿 None. ✈

GOSFORD HOUSE 🏛

LONGNIDDRY, EAST LOTHIAN EH32 0PX

Tel: 01875 870201   **Owner/Contact:** The Earl of Wemyss

Though the core of the house is Robert Adam, the family home is in the South Wing built by William Young in 1890. This contains the celebrated Marble Hall and a fine collection of paintings and works of art. The house is set in extensive policies with an 18th century Pleasure Garden and Ponds. Greylag geese and swans abound.

Location: OS Ref. NT453 786. Off A198 2m NE of Longniddry.

Open: 26 Jun - 28 Jul (inclusive): Wed - Sun, 2 - 5pm.

Admission: Adult £5, Child £1.

🅿 ✈ In grounds, on leads.

Amisfield Mains

GREYWALLS 🏛

MUIRFIELD, GULLANE, EAST LOTHIAN EH31 2EG

www.greywalls.co.uk

Tel: 01620 842144 **Fax:** 01620 842241 **e-mail:** hotel@greywalls.co.uk

Owner: Giles Weaver   **Contact:** Mrs Sue Prime

Stunning Edwardian Country House Hotel only 30 minutes from the centre of Edinburgh. Close to wonderful golf courses and beaches. Designed by Sir Edwin Lutyens with secluded walled gardens attributed to Gertrude Jekyll. Greywalls offers the delights of an award-winning menu and an excellent wine list in this charming and relaxed environment. There is a welcome whether you stay or simply spend a peaceful few hours in this oasis of calm.

Location: OS Ref. NT490 835. Off A198, 5m W of North Berwick, 30 mins from Edinburgh.

Open: Apr - Oct.

🔟 ⑪ 🖾

HAILES CASTLE ⚑

East Linton

Tel: 0131 668 8800

Owner: In the care of Historic Scotland

Beautifully-sited ruin incorporating a fortified manor of the 13th century. It was extended in the 14th and 15th centuries. There are two vaulted pit prisons.

Location: OS Ref. NT575 758. 1¹/₂ m SW of East Linton. 4m E of Haddington. S of A1.

Open: All year.

Admission: Free.

HARBURN HOUSE   *See page 466 for full page entry.*

HARELAW FARMHOUSE

Nr Longniddry, East Lothian EH32 0PH

Tel: 01875 870201 **Fax:** 01875 870620

Owner: Wemyss and March Estates Management Co Ltd   **Contact:** M Andrew

Early 19th century 2-storey farmhouse built as an integral part of the steading. Dovecote over entrance arch.

Location: OS Ref. NT450 766. Between Longniddry and Drem on B1377.

Open: Exteriors only: By appointment, Wemyss and March Estates Office, Longniddry, East Lothian EH32 0PY.

Admission: Please contact for details.

HOPETOUN HOUSE 🏛   *See page 467 for full page entry.*

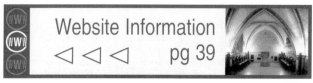

Website Information
◁ ◁ ◁   pg 39

Patrick Lane

HOUSE OF THE BINNS

Linlithgow, West Lothian EH49 7NA

Tel: 01506 834255 **www.**nts.org.uk/binns.html

Owner: The National Trust for Scotland   **Contact:** Tam & Kathleen Dalyell

A 17th century house, the home of the Dalyells, one of Scotland's great families, since 1612. Here in 1681, General Tam Dalyell raised the Royal Scots Greys Regiment, named after the colour of their uniforms. The house contains fine Italian-style plasterwork and an outstanding collection of family paintings.

Location: OS Ref. NT051 786. Off A904, 15m W of Edinburgh. 3m E of Linlithgow

Open: House: 1 May - 29 Sept: daily (except Fris), 1 - 5pm.

Admission: House & Parkland: Adult £5, Conc. £3.75, Family £13.50. Groups: Adult £4, Child/School £1. Group visits must be booked. Members of the Royal Scots Dragoon Guards admitted Free.

Partial. WCs. Limited. Obligatory. Guide dogs only.

INVERESK LODGE GARDEN

24 Inveresk Village, Musselburgh, East Lothian EH21 7TE

Tel: 01721 722502 **Fax:** 01721 724700 **www.**nts.org.uk/inveresk.html

Owner: The National Trust for Scotland   **Contact:** Head Gardener

Small garden in grounds of 17th century house, with large selection of plants. House closed.

Location: OS Ref. NT348 718. A6124, S of Musselburgh, 6m E of Edinburgh.

Open: All year: 10am - 6pm (except Sats, 1 Nov - 24 Mar)

Admission: £2 (honesty box).

Grounds. Limited. No dogs in garden. Park cars by garden wall only.

LAURISTON CASTLE

Cramond Road South, Edinburgh EH4 5QD

Tel: 0131 336 2060 **Fax:** 0131 312 7165

Owner: City of Edinburgh Council   **Contact:** Robin Barnes

A beautiful house overlooking the Firth of Forth. The oldest part is a 16th century tower house.

Location: OS Ref. NT203 761. Between Davidsons Mains and Cramond, NW Edinburgh.

Open: 1 Apr - 31 Oct: daily except Fri. Guided tours at: 11.20am, 12.20pm, 2.20pm, 3.20pm, 4.20pm. 1 Nov - 31 Mar: Sats & Suns, guided tours at 2.20 and 3.20pm. Admission by guided tour only. Booking only required for groups of 10+.

Admission: Adult £4.50, Conc. £3.

LENNOXLOVE HOUSE

HADDINGTON, EAST LOTHIAN EH41 4NZ

www.lennoxlove.org

Tel: 01620 823720 **Fax:** 01620 825112 **e-mail:** lennoxlove@compuserve.com

Owner: Lennoxlove House Ltd   **Contact:** House Administrator

Home of the Duke of Hamilton. The 14th century keep houses a death mask said to be that of Mary Queen of Scots, a silver casket which once contained incriminating letters that helped send Mary to her death, and a sapphire ring given to her by Lord John Hamilton. The 17th century part of the house contains the Hamilton Palace collection of pictures, furniture and porcelain arranged in classic stately home style.

Location: OS Ref. NT515 721. 20m E of Edinburgh, near Haddington.

Open: Easter - end Oct: Wed, Thur, Sat & Sun, 2 - 4.30pm. Guided tours. Please check if house is open on a Sat before arriving.

Admission: Adult £4, Child £2. Group charges on application.

No photography in house. Weddings, gala dinners. Obligatory.

LIBERTON HOUSE

73 Liberton Drive, Edinburgh EH16 6NP

Tel: 0131 467 7777 **Fax:** 0131 467 7774

e-mail: mail@nicholas-groves-raines-architects.co.uk

Owner/Contact: Nicholas Groves-Raines

Built around 1600 for the Littles of Liberton, this harled L-plan house has been carefully restored by the current architect owner using original detailing and extensive restoration of the principal structure. Public access restricted to the Great Hall and Old Kitchen. The restored garden layout suggests the original and there is a late 17th century lectern doocot by the entrance drive.

Location: OS Ref. NT267 694. 73 Liberton Drive, Edinburgh.

Open: 1 Mar - 31 Oct: 10am - 4.30pm, by prior appointment only.

Admission: Free.

Unsuitable. Limited.

Historic Scotland: Crown Copyright

LINLITHGOW PALACE

LINLITHGOW, WEST LOTHIAN EH49 7AL

Tel: 01506 842896

Owner: Historic Scotland   **Contact:** The Steward

The magnificent remains of a great royal palace set in its own park and beside Linlithgow Loch. A favoured residence of the Stewart monarchs, James V and his daughter Mary Queen of Scots were born here. Bonnie Prince Charlie stayed here during his bid to regain the British crown.

Location: OS Ref. NT003 774. In the centre of Linlithgow off the M9.

Open: Apr - Sept: daily, 9.30am - 6.30pm. Oct - Mar: Mon - Sat, 9.30am - 4.30pm, Suns, 2 - 4.30pm. Last ticket 30 mins before closing.

Admission: Adult £2.80, Child £1, Conc. £2. 10% discount for groups (10+).

Picnic area. Private evening hire. Partial. By arrangement. Cars only. Free if booked. In grounds, off leads.

NEWLISTON

Kirkliston, West Lothian EH29 9EB

Tel: 0131 333 3231 **Fax:** 0131 335 3596

Owner/Contact: Mrs Caroline Maclachlan

Late Robert Adam house. Costumes on display. 18th century designed landscape, rhododendrons, azaleas and water features. On Sundays tea is in the Edinburgh Cookery School in the William Adam Coach House. Also on Sundays there is a ride-on steam model railway from 2 - 5pm. An inventory of chattels not on public display can be inspected and such chattels can be viewed by request when the house is open to the public.

Location: OS Ref. NT110 735. 8m W of Edinburgh, 3m S of Forth Road Bridge, off B800.

Open: 1 May - 2 Jun: Wed - Sun, 2 - 6pm. Also by appointment.

Admission: Adult £1.50, Child/OAP 50p, Student £1.

Grounds. In grounds, on leads.

Edinburgh City, Coast & Countryside

THE PALACE OF HOLYROODHOUSE
EDINBURGH EH8 8DX
www.the-royal-collection.org.uk

Tel: 0131 556 1096 **Fax:** 0131 557 5256

Owner: HM The Queen   **Contact:** The Superintendent

The Palace of Holyroodhouse, the official residence in Scotland of Her Majesty The Queen, stands at the end of Edinburgh's Royal Mile against the spectacular backdrop of Arthur's Seat. This fine baroque palace is closely associated with Scotland's rich history. Today the Royal Apartments are used regularly by The Queen for State ceremonies and official entertaining. They are finely decorated with magnificent works of art from the Royal Collection.

The Palace is perhaps best known as the home of Mary, Queen of Scots, and was the setting for many dramatic episodes in her short and turbulent reign. Mary,

Queen of Scots chambers are housed in the Palace's west corner tower. The suite of rooms includes her Bed Chamber, described as the most famous room in Scotland. The Queen's Gallery, Edinburgh will open on 30 Nov 2002 with an exhibition of drawings from the Print Room at Windsor Castle.

Location: OS Ref. NT269 739. Central Edinburgh, E end of Royal Mile.

Open: Apr - Oct: daily, 9.30am - 5.15pm. Nov - Mar: daily, 9.30am - 3.45pm. Closed 25 - 26 Dec & 29 Mar and during Royal visits. Opening arrangements may change at short notice.

Admission: Adult £6.50, Child (up to 17yrs) £3.30, Over 60yrs £5, Family (2+2) £16.30.

Guide dogs only.

PARLIAMENT HOUSE
Parliament Square, Royal Mile, Edinburgh

Tel: 0131 225 2595   **Contact:** Reception Desk at Door 11
Supreme Court for Scotland, adjacent exhibition detailing the history of Parliament House and its important features.

Location: OS Ref. NT258 736. In the centre of Edinburgh's Royal Mile.

Open: All year: Mon - Fri, 10am - 4pm.

Admission: Free.

PRESTON MILL
East Linton, East Lothian EH40 3DS

Tel: 01620 860426 **www.nts.org.uk/preston.html**

Owner: The National Trust for Scotland   **Contact:** Property Manager
For centuries there has been a mill on this site and the present one operated commercially until 1957.

Location: OS Ref. NT590 770. Off the A1, in East Linton, 23m E of Edinburgh.

Open: 25 Mar - 27 Oct: daily (except Tues/Wed) 12 noon - 5pm, Sun 1 - 5pm.

Admission: Adult £3.50, Conc. £2.60, Family £9.50. Group: Adult £2.80, Child/School £1. Group visits must book.

Grounds. WC. Limited. Guide dogs only.

RED ROW
Aberlady, East Lothian

Tel: 01875 870201 **Fax:** 01875 870620

Owner: Wemyss & March Estates Management Co Ltd   **Contact:** M Andrews
Terraced Cottages.

Location: OS Ref. NT464 798. Main Street, Aberlady, East Lothian.

Open: Exterior only. By appointment, Wemyss & March Estates Office, Longniddry, East Lothian EH32 0PY.

Admission: Please contact for details.

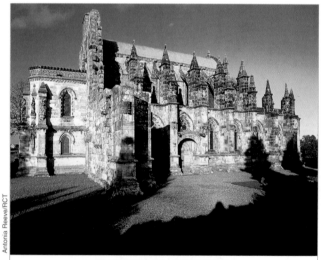

ROSSLYN CHAPEL
ROSLIN, MIDLOTHIAN EH25 9PU
www.rosslynchapel.org.uk

Tel: 0131 440 2159 **Fax:** 0131 440 1979 **e-mail:** rosslynch@aol.com

Owner: The Earl of Rosslyn   **Contact:** Stuart Beattie

This most remarkable of churches was founded in 1446 by William St Clair, Prince of Orkney. Set in the woods of Roslin Glen and overlooking the River Esk, the Chapel is renowned for its richly carved interior and world famous apprentice pillar. Visitors to the chapel can enjoy a walk in some of Scotland's most romantic scenery. As Sir Walter Scott wrote, 'A morning of leisure can scarcely be anywhere more delightfully spent than in the woods of Rosslyn'. The chapel is available for weddings throughout the year.

Location: OS Ref. NT275 630. 6m S of Edinburgh off A701. Follow B7006.

Open: All year: Mon - Sat, 10am - 5pm, Suns, 12 noon - 4.45pm.

Admission: Adult £4, Child £1, Conc. £3.50. 10% discount for groups (20-40).

Chapel. Grounds. WC. Limited for coaches.

ROYAL BOTANIC GARDEN EDINBURGH
20A Inverleith Row, Edinburgh EH3 5LR

Tel: 0131 552 7171   **Fax:** 0131 248 2901   **Contact:** Press Office
Scotland's premier garden. Discover the wonders of the plant kingdom in over 70 acres of beautifully landscaped grounds.
Location: OS Ref. NT249 751. Off A902, 1m N of city centre.
Open: Daily (except 25 Dec & 1 Jan): open from 9.30am. Closing: Feb 5pm; Mar 6pm; Apr - Aug 7pm; Sept 6pm; Oct 5pm; Nov - Jan 4pm.
Admission: Free. Donations welcome.

ST GILES' CATHEDRAL
Royal Mile, Edinburgh EH1 1RE

Tel: 0131 225 9442   **Fax:** 0131 225 9576   **e-mail:** stgiles@hotmail.com

Owner: St Giles' Cathedral   **Contact:** Jan-Andrew Henderson
St Giles' Cathedral dates from the 12th century and is central to Scotland's turbulent history. This beautiful building was the church of John Knox during the Reformation.
Location: OS Ref. NT258 736. In the centre of Edinburgh's Royal Mile.
Open: Easter - Mid Sept: Mon - Fri, 9am -7pm, Sats, 9am - 5pm, Suns, 1 - 5pm. Mid Sept - Easter: Mon - Sat, 9am - 5pm, Suns, 1 - 5pm.
Admission: Admission free - donation of £1 per head suggested.

ST MARY'S CATHEDRAL
Palmerston Place, Edinburgh EH12 5AW

Tel: 0131 225 6293   **Fax:** 0131 225 3181

e-mail: office@cathedral.net   **Contact:** Cathedral Secretary
Neo-gothic grandeur in the classical new town. Designed by G Gilbert Scott.
Location: OS Ref. NT241 735. ¹/₂ m W of west end of Princes Street.
Open: Mon - Fri, 7.30am - 6pm; Sat & Sun, 7.30am - 5pm. Sun services: 8am, 10.30am and 3.30pm. Weekday services: 7.30am, 1.05pm and 5.30pm. Sat service: 7.30am.
Admission: Free.

SCOTTISH NATIONAL PORTRAIT GALLERY
1 Queen Street, Edinburgh EH2 1JD

Tel: 0131 624 6200   **e-mail:** enquiries@natgalscot.ac.uk   **Contact:** Michael Gormley
Unique visual history of Scotland.
Location: OS Ref. NT256 742. At E end of Queen Street, 300yds N of Princes Street.
Open: All year: Mon - Fri, 10am - 5pm. Suns, 12 noon - 5pm. Closed 25 & 26 Dec.
Admission: Free

WINTON HOUSE
PENCAITLAND, TRANENT, EAST LOTHIAN EH34 5AT

www.wintonhouse.co.uk

Tel: 01620 824986   **Fax:** 01620 823961   **e-mail:** enquiries@wintonhouse.co.uk
Owner: The Winton Trust   **Contact:** Robert Steadman
A masterpiece of the Scottish Renaissance with famous stone twisted chimneys and magnificent plaster ceilings. A family home, still after 500 years with many treasures inside, including paintings by some of Scotland's most notable artists, and fine furniture. New Loch. Specimen trees and terraced gardens.
Location: OS Ref. NT439 695. 14m E of Edinburgh off the A1 at Tranent. Lodge gates S of New Winton (B6355) and in Pencaitland (A6093).
Open: 1/2 Jun; 6/7 Jul; 3/4 Aug: 12.30 - 4.30pm. Other times by prior arrangement.
Admission: Adult £4.50, Child £2, Conc. £3.80, Family £11.50. Groups should book (10+).
ⓘ Filming, product launches, conferences. Pottery. ⏹ ♿ WCs. ▣
🎬 Obligatory. ℗ ⛺ In grounds, on leads. ⑂ ❋ ☎ Tel for details.

Crown Copyright

TANTALLON CASTLE 🏛
BY NORTH BERWICK, EAST LOTHIAN EH39 5PN

Tel: 01620 892727

Owner: In the care of Historic Scotland   **Contact:** The Steward
Set on the edge of the cliffs, looking out to the Bass Rock, this formidable castle was a stronghold of the powerful Douglas family. The castle has earthwork defences and a massive 80-foot high 14th century curtain wall. Interpretive displays include a replica gun.
Location: OS67 Ref. NT595 850. 3m E of North Berwick off the A198.
Open: Apr - Sept: daily, 9.30am - 6.30pm. Oct - Mar: Mon - Sat, 9.30am - 6.30pm (but closed Thur pm & all day Fri), Suns, 2 - 4.30pm.
Admission: Adult £2.80, Child £1, Conc. £2. 10% discount for groups (10+).
ⓘ Picnic area. ⏹ ♿ Partial. ℗ ■ Booked school visits free.
⛺ In grounds, on leads. ❋

Harelaw Farmhouse

Patrick Lane

NTS / Douglas MacGregor

POLLOK HOUSE

GLASGOW

www.nts.org.uk/pollok.html

The Maxwell family have lived at Pollok since the 13th century. Three earlier castles here were replaced by the present house (c1740) after consultation with William Adam. The house now contains an internationally famed collection of paintings as well as porcelain and furnishings appropriate to an Edwardian house. Favourite features also include the popular restaurant, which is ideal for morning coffee, lunch or afternoon tea, and shop.

Owner:
Glasgow City Council
(Managed by The
National Trust for
Scotland)

▶ **CONTACT**

The Property Manager
Pollok Country Park,
Pollokshaws Road,
Glasgow G43 1AT

Tel: 0141 616 6410

▶ **LOCATION**
OS Ref. NS550 616

In Pollok Country Park,
off M77/J1, follow signs
for Burrell Collection.

▶ **OPENING TIMES**
**House, Shop &
Restaurant**
All year
daily 10am - 5pm
(closed 25/26 Dec,
1 & 2 Jan)

▶ **ADMISSION**
Summer

Adult	£5.00
Conc.	£3.75
Family	£13.50

Groups (20+)

Adult	£4.00
School	£1.00

1 Nov - 31 Mar .... Free

NTS / Douglas MacGregor

 No in-house photography.

 Partial.

BURRELL COLLECTION

Pollok Country Park, 2060 Pollokshaws Road, Glasgow G43 1AT

Tel: 0141 287 2550 **Fax:** 0141 287 2597

Owner: Glasgow Museums

An internationally renowned, outstanding collection of art.

Location: OS Ref. NS555 622. In Pollok Country Park W of B769.

Open: All year: Mon - Thur & Sats, 10am - 5pm. Fri & Sun, 11am - 5pm. Closed Christmas Day, Boxing Day & 1 & 2 Jan.

Admission: Free.

COLZIUM HOUSE & WALLED GARDEN

Colzium-Lennox Estate, off Stirling Road, Kilsyth G65 0RZ

Tel/Fax: 01236 828156

Owner: North Lanarkshire Council   **Contact:** Charlie Whyte

A walled garden with an extensive collection of conifers, rare shrubs and trees. Kilsyth Heritage Museum, curling pond, picnic tables, woodland walks.

Location: OS Ref. NS722 786. Off A803 Banknock to Kirkintilloch Road. ¹/₂ m E of Kilsyth.

Open: House: All year, daily, 9am - 4pm (closed 25 Dec & 1 Jan). Walled garden: Apr - Sept: daily, 12 noon - 7pm; Oct - Mar: Sats & Suns, 12 noon - 4pm.

Admission: Free.

COREHOUSE

Lanark ML11 9TQ

Tel: 01555 663126 or 0131 667 1514

Owner: The Trustees of the late Lt Col A J E Cranstoun MC   **Contact:** Estate Office

Designed by Sir Edward Blore and built in the 1820s, Corehouse is a pioneering example of the Tudor Architectural Revival in Scotland.

Location: OS Ref. NS882 416. On S bank of the Clyde above the village of Kirkfieldbank.

Open: 14 Aug - 15 Sept: Wed - Sun; Guided tours. Weekdays: 1 & 2pm, Weekends: 12 noon & 4pm. Closed Mons & Tues.

Admission: Adult £4, Child (under 14yrs)/OAP £2.

CRAIGNETHAN CASTLE

Lanark, Strathclyde

Tel: 01555 860364

Owner: Historic Scotland   **Contact:** The Steward

In a picturesque setting overlooking the River Nethan and defended by a wide and deep ditch with an unusual caponier, a stone vaulted artillery chamber, unique in Britain.

Location: OS Ref. NS815 463. 5¹/₂ m WNW of Lanark off the A72. ¹/₂ m footpath to W.

Open: 1 Apr - 30 Sept: daily, 9.30am - 6.30pm.

Admission: Adult £2.20, Child 75p, Conc. £1.60.

GLASGOW CATHEDRAL

Glasgow

Tel: 0141 552 6891

Owner: Historic Scotland   **Contact:** The Steward

The only Scottish mainland medieval cathedral to have survived the Reformation complete. Built over the tomb of St Kentigern. Notable features in this splendid building are the elaborately vaulted crypt, the stone screen of the early 15th century and the unfinished Blackadder Aisle.

Location: OS Ref. NS603 656. E end of city centre. In central Glasgow.

Admission: Free.

GREENBANK GARDEN

Clarkston, Glasgow G76 8RB

Tel: 0141 639 3281 **www.**nts.org.uk/greenbank.html

Owner: The National Trust for Scotland   **Contact:** Mr Jim May

Be allured by the beautiful bronze water nymph 'Foam' whose exquisite form complements the circular pool and surrounding greenery. There are several small gardens including a parterre layout illustrating different aspects of gardening. The larger borders contain a wide range of shrub roses and perennial and annual flowers.

Location: OS Ref. NS563 566. Flenders Road, off Mearns Road, Clarkston. Off M77 and A726, 6m S of Glasgow city centre.

Open: Garden: All year: 10am - sunset. Visitor facilities: 25 Mar - 27 Oct: 11am - 5pm.

Admission: Adult £3.50, Conc. £2.60, Family £9.50. Groups: £2.80.

Grounds. WC. In grounds, on leads. No dogs in garden.

HOLMWOOD HOUSE

61 NETHERLEE ROAD, CATHCART, GLASGOW G44 3YG

www.nts.org.uk/holmwood.html

Tel: 0141 637 2129

Owner: The National Trust for Scotland   **Contact:** The Property Manager

This unique villa has been described as Alexander 'Greek' Thomson's finest domestic design. It was built in 1857-8 for James Couper who owned Millholm Paper Mills. The architectural style of the house is classical Greek and many rooms are richly ornamented in wood, plaster and marble. Conservation work continuing to reveal this decoration.

Location: OS Ref. NS580 593. Netherlee Road, off Clarkston road (off A77 and B767).

Open: 25 Mar - 27 Oct: daily 1 - 5pm. Groups must book.

Admission: Adult £3.50, Conc. £2.60, Family £9.50. Groups: £2.80.

No photography in house. Limited for coaches.

HUTCHESONS' HALL

158 Ingram Street, Glasgow G1 1EJ

Tel: 0141 552 8391 **Fax:** 0141 552 7031 **www.**nts.org.uk/hutchesons.html

Owner: The National Trust for Scotland   **Contact:** Carla Sparrow

Described as one of Glasgow city centre's most elegant buildings, the Hall by David Hamilton, replaced the earlier 1641 hospice founded by George and Thomas Hutcheson. Reconstructed in 1876, the building is now 'A-Listed' as being of national importance. New 'Glasgow Style' exhibition & shop now open.

Location: OS Ref NS594 652. Glasgow city centre, near SE corner of George Square.

Open: Gallery, Shop & Hall: 20 Jan - 24 Dec: Mon - Sat, 10am - 5pm.

Admission: Free.

Conferences. Up to 120. Stairlift. WC. By arrangement.

DAVID LIVINGSTONE CENTRE

165 Station Road, Blantyre, Glasgow G72 9BT

Tel: 01698 823140 **www.**nts.org.uk

Owner: The National Trust for Scotland   **Contact:** Karen Carruthers

Scotland's most famous explorer and missionary was born here in 1813 and today the Centre commemorates his life and work. Livingstone's childhood home - consisting of just one room - remains much as it would have done in his day and gives a fascinating insight into the living conditions endured by industrial workers in the 19th century. The museum contains a wide range of his personal belongings and travel aids.

Location: OS Ref NS690 575. In Blantyre town centre, at N end of Station Road.

Open: Museum & Shop: 25 Mar - 24 Dec: daily, 10am - 5pm (Sun, 12.30 - 5pm).

Admission: Adult £3.50, Conc. £2.60, Family £9.50. Group: £2.80.

MOTHERWELL HERITAGE CENTRE

High Road, Motherwell ML1 3HU

Tel: 01698 251000

Owner: North Lanarkshire Council   **Contact:** The Manager

Multimedia exhibition and other displays of local history. STB 4-Star attraction.

Location: OS Ref. NS750 570. In High Road, 200 yds N of A723 (Hamilton Road).

Open: Wed - Sat, 10am - 5pm. Suns, 12 noon - 5pm. (closed 25/26 Dec & 1 Jan). Closed Mons & Tues.

Admission: Free.

MUSEUM OF SCOTTISH COUNTRY LIFE ♛

Wester Kittochside, off Stewartfield Way, East Kilbride G76 9HR

Tel: 01355 224181 **Fax:** 01355 571290 **e-mail:** kittochside@nms.ac.uk

www.nms.ac.uk/countrylife

Owner: National Museum of Scotland & The National Trust for Scotland

Contact: Mr Duncan Dornan

This new museum, built on a 170 acre farm, consists of a new state-of-the-art exhibition building, which houses the National Collection of Country Life exhibits, an outdoor events area and the original Georgian farmhouse and steading. The farmhouse has been magnificently restored to its original 1950s style.

Location: OS Ref NS607 558. 3m from East Kilbride, off A725/A749/A726, S of Glasgow.

Open: Daily, 10am - 5pm. Closed Christmas & New Year.

Admission: Adult £3, Child (under 18) Free, Conc. £1.50. Discounts available for groups.

◻ ⊤ ⅃ Partial. WC. ▣ 🄵 By arrangement. 🅿 ▣ 🅱 In grounds, on leads. ✳
♛ Tel for details.

NEW LANARK

NEW LANARK MILLS, LANARK, S. LANARKSHIRE ML11 9DB

www.newlanark.org

Tel: 01555 661345 **Fax:** 01555 665738 **e-mail:** visit@newlanark.org

Owner: New Lanark Conservation Trust **Contact:** Richard Evans

Surrounded by native woodlands and close to the famous Falls of Clyde, this cotton mill village was founded in 1785 and became famous as the site of Robert Owen's radical reforms. Now beautifully restored as both a living community and attraction, the fascinating history of the village is interpreted in an award-winning Visitor Centre. Accommodation is available in the New Lanark Mill Hotel and Waterhouses, a stunning conversion from an original 18th century mill. New Lanark is now a nominated World Heritage Site.

Location: OS Ref. NS880 426. 1m S of Lanark.

Open: All year: daily, 11am - 5pm (closed 25 Dec & 1 Jan).

Admission: Visitor Centre: Adult £4.75, Child/Conc. £3.25. Groups: 1 free/10 booked.

ℹ Conference facilities. ◻ ⊤ ⅃ Partial. WC. Visitor Centre wheelchair friendly.
🍴 🄵 By arrangement. 🅿 5 min walk. 🅱 In grounds, on leads. ▣ ✳

NEWARK CASTLE 🏰

Port Glasgow, Strathclyde

Tel: 01475 741858

Owner: In the care of Historic Scotland **Contact:** The Steward

The oldest part of the castle is a tower built soon after 1478 with a detached gatehouse, by George Maxwell. The main part was added in 1597 - 99 in a most elegant style. Enlarged in the 16th century by his descendent, the wicked Patrick Maxwell who murdered two of his neighbours.

Location: OS Ref. NS329 744. In Port Glasgow on the A8.

Open: 1 Apr - 30 Sept: daily, 9.30am - 6.30pm. Last ticket 6pm.

Admission: Adult £2.20, Child 75p, Conc. £1.60.

POLLOCK HOUSE ♛ *See page 474 for full page entry.*

ST MARY'S EPISCOPAL CATHEDRAL

300 Great Western Road, Glasgow G4 9JB

Tel: 0141 339 6691 **Fax:** 0141 334 5669 **e-mail:** cathedral@glasgow.anglican.org

Contact: Very Rev Griff Dines

Newly restored, fine Gothic Revival church by Sir George Gilbert Scott, with outstanding contemporary murals by Gwyneth Leech. Regular concerts and exhibitions.

Location: OS Ref. NS578 669. ¼ m after the Dumbarton A82 exit from M8 motorway.

Open: Daily, 9.30am - 10.30am, 4 - 5pm and at other service times. Please telephone for details of services.

SUMMERLEE HERITAGE PARK

Heritage Way, Coatbridge, North Lanarkshire ML5 1QD

Tel: 01236 431261

Owner: North Lanarkshire Council **Contact:** The Manager

STB 4-star attraction. 22 acres of industrial heritage including Scotland's only remaining electric tramway; a re-created addit mine and mine workers' cottages.

Location: OS Ref. NS729 655. 600yds NW of Coatbridge town centre.

Open: All year. Summer, 10am - 5pm. Winter: 10am - 4pm (closed 25/26 Dec & 1/2 Jan).

Admission: Free. Tram ride: Adult 70p, Child 35p.

THE TENEMENT HOUSE ♛

145 Buccleuch Street, Glasgow G3 6QN

Tel: 0141 333 0183 www.nts.org.uk/tenement.html

Owner: The National Trust for Scotland **Contact:** Miss Lorna Hepburn

A typical Victorian tenement flat of 1892, and fascinating time capsule of the first half of the 20th century. It was the home of an ordinary Glasgow shorthand typist, who lived up this 'wally close' for more than 50 years. It is exceptional as the gaslit flat retains many of its original fittings and items such as her mother's sewing machine.

Location: OS Ref. NS583 662. Garnethill (three streets N of Sauchiehall Street, near Charing Cross), Glasgow.

Open: 1 Mar - 27 Oct; daily, 2 - 5pm.

Admission: Adult £3.50, Conc. £2.60, Family £9.50. Groups: £2.80.

⅃ Unsuitable. 🅿 Very restricted.

THE TOWER OF HALLBAR

Braidwood Road, Braidwood, Lanarkshire

Tel: 0845 090 0194 **Fax:** 0845 090 0174 **e-mail:** emily@vivat.demon.org.uk

www.vivat.org.uk

Owner: The Vivat Trust **Contact:** Miss Emily Abrams

A 16th century defensive tower and Bothy set in ancient orchards and meadowland. Converted into self-catering holiday accommodation and furnished and decorated in keeping with its history, by The Vivat Trust. Hallbar sleeps up to seven people, including facilities for a disabled person and their carer.

Location: OS Ref. NS842 471. S side of B7056 between Crossford Bridge & Braidwood.

Open: All year: Sats afternoon only, 2 - 3pm, by appointment. Also four open days a year.

Admission: Free.

⅃ Partial. 🄵 By arrangement. 🅿 Limited. 🅱 In grounds, on leads.
🛏 3 single, 1 twin & 1 double. ✳

WEAVER'S COTTAGE ♛

Shuttle Street, Kilbarchan, Renfrew PA10 2JG

Tel: 01505 705588 www.nts.org.uk/weaver.html

Owner: The National Trust for Scotland **Contact:** Grace Murray

Typical cottage of an 18th century handloom weaver contains looms, weaving equipment and domestic utensils. Attractive cottage garden. Regular weaving demonstrations.

Location: OS Ref. NS402 633. Off A740 (off M8) and A737, at The Cross, Kilbarchan, (nr Johnstone, Paisley) 12m SW of Glasgow.

Open: 25 Mar - 27 Oct: daily, 1 - 5pm.

Admission: Adult £3.50, Conc. £2.60, Family £9.50. Groups: £2.80.

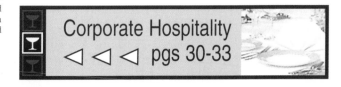

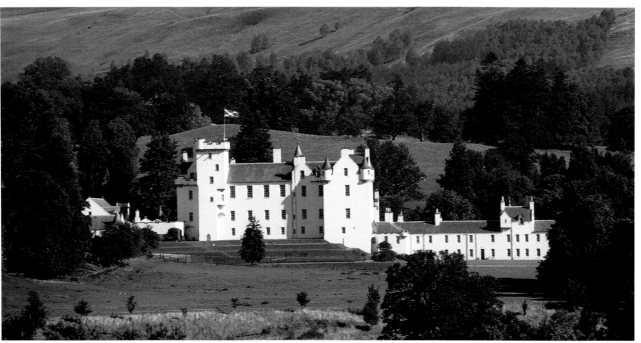

Perthshire, Angus & Dundee and The Kingdom of Fife

BLAIR CASTLE

PITLOCHRY

www.blair-castle.co.uk   www.blaircastleshop.co.uk

Blair Castle has been the ancient home and fortress of the Earls and Dukes of Atholl for over 725 years. Its central location makes it easily accessible from all major Scottish centres in less than two hours.

The castle has known the splendour of Royal visitations, submitted to occupation by opposing forces on no less than four occasions, suffered siege and changed its architectural appearance to suit the taste of successive generations.

Today 30 rooms of infinite variety display beautiful furniture, fine collections of paintings, arms, armour, china, costumes, lace and embroidery, Jacobite relics and other unique treasures giving a stirring picture of Scottish life from the 16th to 20th centuries.

The Duke of Atholl has the unique distinction of having the only remaining private army in Europe - The Atholl Highlanders.

GARDENS

Blair Castle is set in extensive grounds. Near the car and coach parks, there is a picnic area, a deer park and a unique two acre plantation of large trees known as 'Diana's Grove.' It has been said that *"it is unlikely that any other two acres in the world contain such a number of different conifers of such heights and of such small age."* A restored 18th century garden re-opened to visitors in 1996.

Owner: Blair Castle Charitable Trust

▶ CONTACT

Administration Office
Blair Castle
Blair Atholl
Pitlochry
Perthshire PH18 5TL

Tel: 01796 481207
Fax: 01796 481487
e-mail: office@
blair-castle.co.uk

▶ LOCATION

OS Ref. NN880 660

From Edinburgh 80m, M90 to Perth, A9, follow signs for Blair Castle, 1½ hrs. Trunk Road A9 2m.

Bus: Bus stop 1m in Blair Atholl.

Train: 1m, Blair Atholl Euston-Inverness line.

Taxi: Elizabeth Yule, 01796 472290.

▶ OPENING TIMES

Summer

28 March - 25 October
Daily, 10am - 6pm
Last admission 5pm.
(Jul & Aug: opens 9.30am).

At other times by special arrangement.

Winter

Access by arrangement.

▶ ADMISSION

House & Grounds

Adult	£6.25
Child (5-16yrs)	£4.00
OAP/Student	£5.25
Family	£18.00
Disabled	£2.00

Groups (12-40) (Please book)

Adult	£5.00
Child (5-16yrs)	£4.00
Primary School	£3.00
OAP	£4.50
Student	£4.00
Disabled	£2.00

Grounds only

Adult	£2.00
Child	£1.00
OAP/Student	£2.00
Family	£5.00
Disabled	Free

▶ SPECIAL EVENTS

APR 12 - 14
Needlework & Lace Exhibition.

MAY 1 - 7
Quilt Exhibition.

MAY 25
Atholl Highlanders' Parade.

MAY 26
Atholl Gathering & Highland Games.

JUL 4
Charity Day in aid of Macmillan Cancer Research.

AUG 22 - 25
Bowmore Blair Castle Int'l Horse Trials & Country Fair.

OCT 26 - 27
Glenfiddich Piping & Fiddling Championships.

FUNCTION

ROOM	SIZE	MAX CAPACITY
Ballroom	88' x 36'	400
State Dining Rm	36' x 25'	200
Exhibition Hall	55' x 27'	90

ℹ️ Fashion shows, equestrian events, shows, rallies, filming, highland and charity balls, piping championships, grand piano, helicopter pad, cannon firing by Atholl Highlanders, resident piper, needlework displays. No smoking.

🍽️ Buffets, dinners, wedding receptions and banquets.

♿ Visitors may alight entrance. WC & wheelchair facilities.

🚭 Non-smoking. Seats up to 125.

In English, German and French at no extra cost. Max group size 25, tour time 1½ hrs (max).

🅿️ 200 cars, 20 coaches. Coach drivers/couriers free, plus free meal and shop voucher, information pack.

Nature walks, deer park, ranger service & pony trekking, children's play area.

 Grounds only. ❄️

NTS / Harvey Woods

Owner: The National Trust for Scotland

▶ **CONTACT**

Mrs Margaret Marshall
Falkland KY15 7BU

Tel: 01337 857397

Fax: 01337 857980

▶ **LOCATION**

OS Ref. NO253 075

A912, 11m N of Kirkcaldy.

FALKLAND PALACE ♛

FALKLAND

www.nts.org.uk/falkland.html

The Royal Palace of Falkland, set in the heart of a unique medieval village, was the country residence and hunting lodge of eight Stuart monarchs, including Mary Queen of Scots. Built between 1502 and 1541, the Palace is an extremely fine example of Renaissance architecture. It includes the exceptionally beautiful Chapel Royal, and is surrounded by internationally known gardens, laid out in the 1950s. The Royal Tennis Court, reputedly the world's oldest, is still used today.

▶ **OPENING TIMES**

Palace & Garden

1 Mar to 27 Oct,
Mon - Sat, 10am - 6am,
Sun, 1 - 5pm.

▶ **ADMISSION**

Palace & Grounds

Adult	£7.00
Conc.	£5.25
Family	£19.00

Groups	
Adult	£5.60
Child/School	£1.00

Garden only

Adult	£3.00
Conc.	£1.70
Family	£7.00

Groups	
Adult	£2.00
Child/School	£1.00

Member of Scots Guard's Association Free.

NTS / Douglas MacGregor

 Grounds.

GLAMIS CASTLE 🏛

BY FORFAR

www.glamis-castle.co.uk

Owner: The Earl of Strathmore & Kinghorne

▶ CONTACT

Mr Stuart Gill
Castle Administrator
Estates Office
Glamis Castle
Glamis
by Forfar
Angus DD8 1RJ

Tel: 01307 840393
Fax: 01307 840733

e-mail: admin@
glamis-castle.co.uk

▶ LOCATION
OS Ref. NO386 480

From Edinburgh M90,
A94, 81m.
From Forfar A94, 6m.
From Glasgow 93m.
Motorway: M90.
Rail: Dundee
Station 12m.
Air: Dundee
Airport 12m.
Taxi: K Cabs
01575 573744.

Glamis Castle is the family home of the Earls of Strathmore and Kinghorne and has been a royal residence since 1372. It is the childhood home of Her Majesty Queen Elizabeth The Queen Mother, the birthplace of Her Royal Highness The Princess Margaret and the legendary setting of Shakespeare's play Macbeth. Although the castle is open to visitors it remains a family home lived in and loved by the Strathmore family.

The castle, a five-storey 'L' shaped tower block, was originally a royal hunting lodge. It was remodelled in the 17th century and is built of pink sandstone. It contains the Great Hall, with its

magnificent plasterwork ceiling dated 1621, a beautiful family Chapel constructed inside the Castle in 1688, an 18th century billiard room housing what is left of the extensive library once at Glamis, a 19th century dining room containing family portraits and the Royal Apartments which have been used by Her Majesty Queen Elizabeth The Queen Mother.

The castle stands in an extensive park, landscaped towards the end of the 18th century, and contains the beautiful Italian Garden and the Pinetum which reflect the peace and serenity of the castle and grounds.

▶ OPENING TIMES

29 March - 27 October
Daily, 10.30am - 5.30pm.

(July - August
opens 10am).

Last admission 4.45pm.

Groups welcome by
appointment at other times.

Winter
By arrangement.

▶ ADMISSION

Summer
House & Grounds

Adult	£6.50
Child* (5-16yrs)	£3.20
OAP/Student	£4.80
Family	£18.00

Groups (20+)

Adult	£5.50
Child* (5-16yrs)	£3.00
OAP/Student	£4.30

**Grounds only
ticket available.**

CONFERENCE/FUNCTION

ROOM	SIZE	MAX CAPACITY
Dining Rm	84 sq.m	120
Restaurant	140 sq.m	100
16th century Kitchens		50

ℹ️ Fashion shoots, archery, equestrian events, shows, rallies, filming, product launches, highland games, new cricket pavilion, grand piano. No photography in the castle.

🛍 Shopping complex. ✱

🍽 The State Rooms are available for grand dinners, lunches and wedding receptions.

♿ Disabled visitors may alight at entrance. Those in wheelchairs will be unable to tour the castle but may visit the two exhibitions. WC.

🍴 Morning coffees, light lunches, afternoon teas. Self-service, licensed restaurant.

🚶 All visits are guided, tour time 50 - 60 mins. Tours leave every 10 - 15 mins. Tours in French, German, Italian and Spanish by appointment at no additional cost. Three exhibitions.

🅿 500 cars and 20 coaches 200 yds from castle. Coach drivers and couriers admitted free. Beware narrow gates; they are wide enough to take buses (10ft wide).

🎓 One teacher free for every 10 children. Nature trail, family exhibition rooms, dolls' house, play park. Glamis Heritage Education Centre in Glamis village. Education pack. Winner of Sandford Award in 1997.

🐕 In grounds, on leads. ✱ Tel for details.

SCONE PALACE & GROUNDS

PERTH

www.scone-palace.co.uk

Owner: The Earl of Mansfield

▶ CONTACT

The Administrator
Scone Palace
Perth   PH2 6BD

Tel: 01738 552300
Fax: 01738 552588

e-mail: visits@
scone-palace.co.uk

▶ LOCATION

OS Ref. NO114 266

From Edinburgh
Forth Bridge M90,
A93 1hr.

Bus: Regular buses
from Perth.

Rail: Perth Station 3m.

Motorway: M90 from
Edinburgh.

Taxi: 01738 636777.

Scone Palace, on the outskirts of Perth, sits on one of Scotland's most historic sites. The crowning place of Scottish kings including Macbeth and Robert the Bruce, and until its infamous removal by Edward I, home of the Stone of Destiny on the Moot Hill.

The Palace was built on the ruins of the old Abbey and Bishop's Palace which were destroyed in the Reformation. After a brief spell under the Gowrie family, in 1600 Scone passed to the Murray family who continue to own and live in it. Extensively rebuilt by the 3rd Earl around 1804, Scone now houses unique collections of Vernis Martin, French furniture, clocks, 16th century needlework (including pieces by Mary Queen of Scots), ivories, *objets d'art* and one of the country's finest porcelain collections.

Winner of a 2000 Sandford Award from the Heritage Education Trust for education services.

GARDENS

The grounds of the Palace house magnificent collections of shrubs, with woodland walks through the pinetum containing David Douglas' original fir and the unique Murray Star Maze. There are Highland cattle and peacocks to admire and an adventure play area for children. The 100 acres of mature Policy Parks, flanked by the River Tay, are available for a variety of events, including corporate and private entertaining.

▶ OPENING TIMES

Summer

31 March - 31 October
Daily: 9.30am - 5.15pm.

Last admission 4.45pm.

Evening tours by appointment.

Winter

By appointment only.

Grounds only: Fri,
11am - 4pm.

▶ ADMISSION

Summer

Palace & Grounds

Adult	£6.20
Child (5-16yrs)	£3.60
Conc	£5.30
Family	£20.00

Groups (20+)

Adult	£5.30
Child (5-16yrs)	£3.10
Conc	£4.60

Grounds only

Adult	£3.10
Child (5-16yrs)	£1.70
Conc.	£2.50

Under 5s Free
Private Tour £35
supplement.

Winter

On application.

SPECIAL EVENTS

MAY - SEPT (MONTHLY):
Horse Trials.

APR - SEPT
Perth Races (01738 551597).

Receptions, fashion shows, war games, archery, clay pigeon shooting, equestrian events, garden parties, shows, rallies, filming, shooting, fishing, floodlit tattoos, product launches, highland games, parkland, cricket pitch, helicopter landing, croquet, racecourse, polo field, firework displays, adventure playground.

Grand dinners in state rooms, buffets, receptions, wedding receptions, cocktail parties.

All state rooms on one level, wheelchair access to restaurants. Visitors may alight at entrance. WC.

Licensed. Teas, lunches & dinners, can be booked, menus upon request, special rates for groups.

By arrangement. Guides in rooms, tour time 45 mins. French and German guides available by appointment.

Welcome.

300 cars and 15 coaches, groups please book, couriers and coach drivers free meal and admittance.

In grounds on leads.

CONFERENCE/FUNCTION		
ROOM	SIZE	MAX CAPACITY
Long Gallery	140' x 20'	200
Queen Victoria's Rm	20' x 20'	20
Drawing Rm	48' x 25'	80

ABERDOUR CASTLE

Aberdour, Fife

Tel: 01383 860519

Owner: In the care of Historic Scotland   **Contact:** The Steward

A 14th century castle built by the Douglas family. The gallery on the first floor gives an idea of how it was furnished at the time. The castle has a 14th century tower extended in the 16th and 17th centuries, a delightful walled garden and a circular dovecote.

Location: OS Ref. NT193 854. In Aberdour 5m E of the Forth Bridge on the A921.

Open: 1 Apr - 30 Sept: daily, 9.30am - 6.30pm, last ticket 6pm. 1 Oct - 31 Mar: Mon - Sat, 9.30am - 4.30pm, Suns, 2 - 4.30pm, last ticket 4pm. Closed Thur pm & Fris in winter.

Admission: Adult £2.20, Child 75p, Conc. £1.60.

ANGUS FOLK MUSEUM

Kirkwynd, Glamis, Forfar, Angus DD8 1RT

Tel: 01307 840288   **Fax:** 01307 840233   **www.nts.org.uk/angus.html**

Owner: The National Trust for Scotland   **Contact:** The Manager

Where will you find cruisie lamps, pirn winders, cloutie rugs, bannock spades and a thrawcrook? All these fascinating items, and many more, are to be found in the Angus Folk Museum, one of Scotland's finest. The domestic section is housed in six charming 18th century cottages in Kirkwynd, and the agricultural collection is in the farmsteading opposite. The displays inside the building explain and illustrate changes in the Angus countryside in the last 200 years.

Location: OS Ref. NO385 467. Off A94, in Glamis, 5m SW of Forfar.

Open: 25 Mar- 27 Oct, daily (not Thur/Fri) 12 noon - 5pm.

Admission: Adult £3.50, Conc. £2.60, Family £9.50. Groups: £2.80.

⬜ ♿ Partial. WC. 🅿 Limited. ✖

ARBROATH ABBEY

Arbroath, Tayside

Tel: 01241 878756

Owner: In the care of Historic Scotland   **Contact:** The Steward

The substantial ruins of a Tironensian monastery, notably the gate house range and the abbot's house. Arbroath Abbey holds a very special place in Scottish history. Scotland's nobles swore their independence from England in the famous 'Declaration of Arbroath' in 1320. New visitor centre.

Location: OS Ref. NO644 414. In Arbroath town centre on the A92.

Open: 1 Apr - 30 Sept: daily 9.30am - 6.30pm, last ticket 6pm. 1 Oct - 31 Mar: Mon - Sat, 9.30am - 4.30 pm, Suns, 2 - 4.30pm, last ticket 4pm.

Admission: Adult £2.50, Child 75p, Conc. £1.90. Prices will change when visitor centre opens.

BALCARRES

Colinsburgh, Fife KY9 1HL

Tel: 01333 340206

Owner: Balcarres Trust   **Contact:** The Earl of Crawford

16th century tower house with 19th century additions by Burn and Bryce. Woodland and terraced gardens

Location: OS Ref. NO475 044. $^1/_2$ m N of Colinsburgh.

Open: Woodland & Gardens: 4 - 20 Feb & 1 Apr - 15 Jun, 2 - 5pm. House not open except by written appointment and 15 - 30 Apr.

Admission: Adult £5. Garden only: £2.50.

ⓕ By arrangement.

BALGONIE CASTLE

Markinch, Fife KY7 6HQ

Tel: 01592 750119   **Fax:** 01592 753103

Owner/Contact: The Laird of Balgonie

14th century tower, additions to the building up to 1702. Still lived in by the family. 14th century chapel for weddings.

Location: OS Ref. NO313 006. $^1/_2$ m S of A911 Glenrothes - Leven road at Milton of Balgonie on to B921.

Open: All year: daily, 10am - 5pm.

Admission: Adult £3, Child £1.50, OAP £2.

BALHOUSIE CASTLE (BLACK WATCH MUSEUM)

Hay Street, North Inch Park, Perth PH1 5HR

Tel: 0131 310 8530

Owner: MOD   **Contact:** Major Proctor

Regimental museum housed in the castle.

Location: OS Ref. NO115 244. $^1/_2$ m N of town centre, E of A9 road to Dunkeld.

Open: May - Sept: Mon - Sat, 10am - 4.30pm. Oct - Apr: Mon - Fri, 10am - 3.30pm. Closed 23 Dec - 5 Jan & last Sat in Jun.

Admission: Free.

J M BARRIE'S BIRTHPLACE

9 Brechin Road, Kirriemuir, Angus DD8 4BX

Tel: 01575 572646   **www.nts.org.uk/barrie.html**

Owner: The National Trust for Scotland   **Contact:** Karen Gilmour/Mrs Sheila Philip

'Do you believe in fairies?' The creator of the eternal magic of Peter Pan, J M Barrie, was born here in 1860. He was the ninth of ten children born to David Barrie, a handloom weaver and his wife Margaret Ogilvy. See the imaginative exhibition about this famous novelist and dramatist with life-size figures, miniature stage sets, dioramas, theatre posters and stage costumes, while a darting light, 'Tinkerbell', moves around the room!

Location: OS Ref. NO388 542. On A926/B957, in Kirriemuir, 6m NW of Forfar.

Open: 25 Mar to 27 Oct daily (not Tues/Wed) 12 noon - 5pm.

Admission: Adult £5, Conc. £3.75, Family £13.50. Groups: £4. Includes admission to Camera Obscura.

♿ Stairlift. 🔳 🅿 None. ✖

BARRY MILL

Barry, Carnoustie, Angus DD7 7RJ

Tel: 01241 856761   **www.nts.org.uk/barry.html**

Owner: The National Trust for Scotland   **Contact:** Peter Ellis

19th century meal mill. Demonstrations and displays. Waymarked walks. Picnic area.

Location: OS Ref. NO533 349. N of village between A92 & A930, 2m W of Carnoustie.

Open: 25 Mar to 27 Oct, daily (not Thurs/Fri) 12 noon - 5pm.

Admission: Adult £3.50, Conc £2.60, Family £9.50. Groups: £2.80.

BLAIR CASTLE

See page 477 for full page entry.

BOLFRACKS GARDEN

Aberfeldy, Perthshire PH15 2EX

Tel: 01887 820344   **Fax:** 01887 829522

Owner/Contact: Mr R A Price

A garden of approximately 4 acres with splendid views over the River Tay to the hills beyond. A walled garden contains a wide collection of trees, shrubs and perennials. Also a burn garden with rhododendrons, azaleas, meconopsis, primulas etc. with peat wall arrangements. Lots of bulbs and good autumn colour.

Location: OS Ref. NN822 481. 2m W of Aberfeldy on A827 towards Kenmore.

Open: 1 Apr - 31 Oct: daily, 10am - 6pm.

Admission: Adult £2.50, Child (under 16 yrs) Free.

✖

BRANKLYN GARDEN

Dundee Road, Perth PH2 7BB

Tel: 01738 625535   **www.nts.org.uk/branklyn.html**

Owner: The National Trust for Scotland   **Contact:** Steve McNamara

Small but magnificent garden with an impressive collection of rare and unusual plants. Among the most breathtaking is the Himalayan blue poppy, Meconopsis x sheldonii. There is a rock garden with purple maple and the rare golden Cedrus. Seasonal highlights are in May and June are the alpines and rhododendrons and in autumn the fiery red Acer palmatum.

Location: OS Ref. NO125 225. On A85 at 116 Dundee Road, Perth.

Open: All year: daily, 10am - 6pm.

Admission: Adult £3.50, Conc. £2.60, Family £9.50. Groups: £2.80.

⬜ ♿ ♿ Grounds, but limited access. ✖

CAMBO GARDENS

Cambo Estate, Kingsbarns, St Andrews, Fife KY16 8QD

Tel: 01333 450054   **Fax:** 01333 450987   **e-mail:** cambohouse@cs.com **www.camboestate.com**

Owner: Mr & Mrs T P N Erskine   **Contact:** Catherine Erskine

Enchanting Victorian walled garden designed around the Cambo Burn. Snowdrops, lilac and roses are specialities. Ornamental potager, autumn borders. Garden supplies mansion house (not open) with fruit, vegetables and flowers. Woodland walks to sandy beach.

Location: OS Ref. NO603 114. 3m N of Crail. 7m SE of St Andrews on A917.

Open: All year: daily except Christmas and New Year, 10am - dusk.

Admission: Adult £2.50, Child Free.

ⓘ Conferences. ♿ Mail order snowdrops in the green. 🔲 ♿ 🅿 Limited for coaches. 🐕 In grounds, on leads. 🛏 2 doubles & self-catering apartments/cottages. ✲

CASTLE CAMPBELL

Dollar Glen, Central District

Tel: 01259 742408

Owner: The National Trust for Scotland   **Contact:** Historic Scotland

Known as 'Castle Gloom' this spectacularly sited 15th century fortress was the lowland stronghold of the Campbells. Stunning views from the parapet walk.

Location: OS Ref. NS961 993. At head of Dollar Glen, 10m E of Stirling on the A91.

Open: 1 Apr - 30 Sept: daily, 9.30am - 6.30pm, last ticket 6pm. 1 Oct - 31 Mar: Mon - Sat, 9.30am - 4.30pm (closed Thurs pm & Fris all day) Suns, 2 - 4.30pm, last ticket 4pm.

Admission: Adult £2.80, Child £1, Conc. £2.

CASTLE MENZIES
Weem, Aberfeldy, Perth PH15 2JD

Tel: 01887 820982 **e-mail:** menziesclan@tesco.net

Owner: Menzies Charitable Trust   **Contact:** The Administrator

Magnificent example of a 16th century 'Z' plan fortified tower house, seat of the Chiefs of Clan Menzies for over 400 years. 'Bonnie Prince Charlie' was given hospitality here in 1746. Visitors can explore the whole building, together with part of 19th century addition. Small clan museum and gift shop.

Location: OS Ref. NN838 497. 1½ m from Aberfeldy on B846.

Open: 31 Mar - 13 Oct: Mon - Sat, 10.30am - 5pm, Suns, 2 - 5pm, last entry 4.30pm.

Admission: Adult £3.50, Child £2, Conc. £3, Groups (20+): Adult £3.

Ground floor. WC. Guide dogs only.

CHARLETON HOUSE
Colinsburgh, Leven, Fife KY9 1HG

Tel: 01333 340249 **Fax:** 01333 340583

Location: OS Ref. NO464 036. Off A917. 1m NW of Colinsburgh. 3m NW of Elie.

Open: Sept: 12 noon - 3pm. Admission every ½ hr with guided tours only.

Admission: £8.

Obligatory.

CORTACHY ESTATE
Cortachy, Kirriemuir, Angus DD8 4LX

Tel: 01575 540223 **Fax:** 01575 540400

e-mail: cortachyoffice@airlieestates.u-net.com

Owner: Trustees of Airlie Estates   **Contact:** Estate Office

Countryside walks including access through woodlands to Airlie Monument on Tulloch Hill with spectacular views of the Angus Glens and Vale of Strathmore. Footpaths are waymarked and colour coded.

Location: OS Ref. NO394 596. Off the B955 Glens Road from Kirriemuir.

Open: Woodland Walks: all year. Gardens: 29 Mar - 1 Apr; 6 May; 13 May - 2 Jun; 5 & 26 Aug: 10am - 4pm, last admission 3.30pm. Castle not open.

Admission: Please contact for details.

Not suitable. Limited.

CULROSS PALACE
Culross, Fife KY12 8JH

Tel: 01383 880359 **Fax:** 01383 882675 **www.**nts.org.uk/culross.html

Owner: The National Trust for Scotland   **Contact:** Property Manager

Relive the domestic life of the 16th and 17th centuries at this Royal Burgh fringed by the River Forth. Here the old buildings and cobbled streets create a time warp for visitors as they explore the old town. Enjoy too the Palace, dating from 1597 and the medieval garden.

Location: OS Ref. NS985 860. Off A985. 12m W of Forth Road Bridge and 4m E of Kincardine Bridge, Fife.

Open: Palace, Study & Town House: 25 Mar to 27 Oct, daily 12 noon - 5pm. Groups at other times by appointment.

Admission: Combined ticket: Adult £5, Conc. £3.75, Family £13.50. Groups: £4.

WC. By arrangement.

DRUMMOND CASTLE GARDENS
See below.

DUNFERMLINE ABBEY & PALACE
Dunfermline, Fife

Tel: 01383 739026

Owner: In the care of Historic Scotland   **Contact:** The Steward

The remains of the Benedictine abbey founded by Queen Margaret in the 11th century. The foundations of her church are under the 12th century Romanesque-style nave. Robert the Bruce was buried in the choir. Substantial parts of the Abbey buildings remain, including the vast refectory.

Location: OS Ref. NY090 873. In Dunfermline off the M90.

Open: 1 Apr - 30 Sept: daily, 9.30am - 6.30pm, last ticket 6pm. 1 Oct - 31 Mar: Mon - Sat, 9.30am - 4.30pm, Suns, 2 - 4.30pm, last ticket 4pm. Closed Thur pm and Fris in winter.

Admission: Adult £2.20, Child 75p, Conc. £1.60.

DRUMMOND CASTLE GARDENS
MUTHILL, CRIEFF, PERTHSHIRE PH5 2AA

Tel: 01764 681257 **Fax:** 01764 681550 Weekends: 01764 681433

e-mail: the gardens@drummondcastle.sol.co.uk

Owner: Grimsthorpe & Drummond Castle Trust   **Contact:** Pat Keith

Scotland's most important formal gardens, among the finest in Europe. A mile of beech-lined avenue leads to a formidable ridge top tower house. Enter through the woven iron yett to the terraces and suddenly revealed is a magnificent Italianate parterre, celebrating the saltire and family heraldry, surrounding the famous multiplex sundial by John Milne, master mason to Charles I. First laid out in the early 17th century by John Drummond, the 2nd Earl of Perth and renewed in the early 1950s by Phyllis Astor, Countess of Ancaster.

Location: OS Ref. NN844 181. 2m S of Crieff off the A822.

Open: Easter weekend, then 1 May - 31 Oct: 2 - 6pm, last entry 5pm.

Admission: Adult £3.50, Child £1.50, OAP £2.50. 10% discount for groups (20+).

Partial. WC. By arrangement. In grounds, on leads.

DUNNINALD

Montrose, Angus DD10 9TD

Tel: 01674 674842 **Fax:** 01674 674860

Owner/Contact: J Stansfeld

This house, the third Dunninald built on the estate, was designed by James Gillespie Graham in the gothic Revival style, and was completed for Peter Arkley in 1824. It has a superb walled garden and is set in a planned landscape dating from 1740. It is a family home.

Location: OS Ref. NO705 543 2m S of Montrose, between A92 and the sea.

Open: 29 Jun - 28 Jul: Tue - Sun, 1 - 5pm. Garden: from 12 noon.

Admission: Adult £4, Child £2.50, Conc. £2.50. Garden only: £2.

ⓘ No photography in house. Unsuitable. Obligatory. P

In grounds, on leads.

EDZELL CASTLE AND GARDEN

Edzell, Angus

Tel: 01356 648631

Owner: In the care of Historic Scotland **Contact:** The Steward

The beautiful walled garden at Edzell is one of Scotland's unique sights, created by Sir David Lindsay in 1604. The 'Pleasance' is a delightful formal garden with walls decorated with sculptured stone panels, flower boxes and niches for nesting birds. The fine tower house, now ruined, dates from the last years of the 15th century. Mary Queen of Scots held a council meeting in the castle in 1562 on her way north as her army marched against the Gordons.

Location: OS Ref. NO585 691. At Edzell, 6m N of Brechin on B966. 1m W of village.

Open: 1 Apr - 30 Sept: daily, 9.30am - 6.30pm, last ticket 6pm. 1 Oct - 31 Mar: Mon - Sat, 9.30am - 4.30pm, Suns, 2 - 4.30pm, last ticket 4pm. Closed Thur pm and Fris in winter.

Admission: Adult £2.80, Child £1, Conc. £2.

ELCHO CASTLE

Perth

Tel: 01738 639998

Owner: In the care of Historic Scotland

This handsome and complete fortified mansion of 16th century date has four projecting towers. The original wrought-iron grilles to protect the windows are still in place.

Location: OS Ref. NO164 211. On the Tay, 3m SE of Perth.

Open: 1 Apr - 30 Sept: daily, 9.30am - 6.30pm, last ticket 6pm.

Admission: Adult £2, Child 75p, Conc. £1.50.

FALKLAND PALACE

See page 478 for full page entry.

GLAMIS CASTLE

See page 479 for full page entry.

GLENEAGLES

Auchterarder, Perthshire PH3 1PJ

Tel: 01764 682388

Owner: Gleneagles 1996 Trust **Contact:** J Martin Haldane of Gleneagles

Gleneagles has been the home of the Haldane family since the 12th century. The 18th century pavilion is open to the public by written appointment.

Location: OS Ref. NS931 088. Auchterarder.

Open: By written appointment only.

HILL OF TARVIT MANSION HOUSE

Cupar, Fife KY15 5PB

Tel/Fax: 01334 653127 **www.nts.org.uk/hill.html**

Owner: The National Trust for Scotland **Contact:** The Manager

This fine house was rebuilt in 1906 by Sir Robert Lorimer, the renowned Scottish architect, for a Dundee industrialist, Mr F B Sharp. The house still presents a perfect setting for Mr Sharp's notable collection of superb French, Chippendale and vernacular furniture. Fine paintings by Raeburn and Ramsay and a number of eminent Dutch artists are on view together with Chinese porcelain and bronzes. Don't miss the restored Edwardian laundry behind the house which is set in the midst of a delightful garden.

Location: OS Ref. NO379 118. Off A916, 2½ m S of Cupar, Fife.

Open: 25 Mar to 27 Oct, daily 12 noon - 5pm.

Admission: House & Garden: Adult £5, Conc. £3.75, Family £13.50. Groups: £4.

Ground floor & grounds. WC. By arrangement. P

HOUSE OF DUN

MONTROSE, ANGUS DD10 9LQ

www.nts.org.uk/dun.html

Tel: 01674 810264 **Fax:** 01674 810722

Owner: The National Trust for Scotland **Contact:** The Manager

This beautiful Georgian house, overlooking the Montrose Basin, was designed by William Adam and built in 1730 for David Erskine, Lord Dun. Lady Augusta Kennedy-Erskine was the natural daughter of William IV and Mrs Jordan and House of Dun contains many royal mementos. The house features superb plasterwork by Joseph Enzer.

Location: OS Ref. NO670 599. 3m W Montrose on A935.

Open: 25 Mar - 27 Oct: Fri - Tue, 12 noon - 5pm.

Admission: House & Gardens: Adult £7, Conc. £5.25, Family £19. Groups: Adult £5.60.

ⓘ Conferences. Ground floor & basement. WC. In grounds, on leads. Special dog walk.

HUNTINGTOWER CASTLE

Perth

Tel: 01738 627231

Owner: In the care of Historic Scotland **Contact:** The Steward

The splendid painted ceilings are especially noteworthy in this castle, once owned by the Ruthven family. Scene of a famous leap between two towers by a daughter of the house who was nearly caught in her lover's room. The two towers are still complete, one of 15th - 16th century date, the other of 16th century origin. Now linked by a 17th century range.

Location: OS Ref. NO084 252. 3m NW of Perth off the A85.

Open: 1 Apr - 30 Sept: daily, 9.30am - 6.30pm, last ticket 6pm. 1 Oct - 31 Mar: Mon - Sat, 9.30am - 4.30pm, Suns, 2 - 4.30pm, last ticket 4pm. Closed Thur pm & Fris in winter.

Admission: Adult £2.20, Child 75p, Conc. £1.60.

INCHCOLM ABBEY

Inchcolm, Fife

Tel: 01383 823332

Owner: In the care of Historic Scotland **Contact:** The Steward

Known as the 'Iona of the East'. This is the best preserved group of monastic buildings in Scotland, founded in 1123. Includes a 13th century octagonal chapter house.

Location: OS Ref. NT190 826. On Inchcolm in the Firth of Forth. Reached by ferry from South Queensferry (30 mins).

Open: 1 Apr - 30 Sept: daily, 9.30am - 6.30pm, last ticket 6pm.

Admission: Adult £2.80, Child £1, Conc. £2. Additional charge for ferries.

Accommodation Index ◁ ◁ ◁ pg 27

Perthshire, Angus & Dundee and The Kingdom of Fife

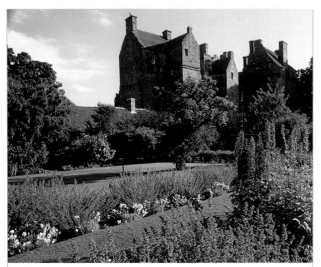

KELLIE CASTLE & GARDEN ♥
PITTENWEEM, FIFE KY10 2RF
www.nts.org.uk/kellie.html

Tel: 01333 720271 **Fax:** 01333 720326

Owner: The National Trust for Scotland   **Contact:** The Property Manager

This very fine example of domestic architecture in Lowland Scotland dates from the 14th century and was sympathetically restored by the Lorimer family in the late 19th century. The castle contains magnificent plaster ceilings and painted panelling as well as fine furniture designed by Sir Robert Lorimer. Of particular interest are the Victorian nursery and the old kitchen. The late Victorian garden features a fine collection of old-fashioned roses and herbaceous plants which are cultivated organically.

Location: OS Ref. NO519 051. On B9171, 3m NW of Pittenweem, Fife.

Open: Castle: 25 Mar - 29 Sep: daily (except Tues/ Wed) 12 noon - 5pm.

Admission: House & Garden: Adult £5, Conc. £3.75, Family £13.50. Groups: £4.

🏠 ♿ Ground floor & grounds. ▦ ⛔ ✳

National Trust for Scotland

KILLIECRANKIE ♥
PITLOCHRY, PERTH & KINROSS PH16 5LG

Tel: 01796 473233

Owner: The National Trust for Scotland   **Contact:** The Administrator

The first shots in the Jacobite cause were fired in 1689 at the Battle of Killiecrankie about one mile from the Trust's property. Although the Highland army was victorious over the troops of King William, Jacobite resistance later collapsed as a result of the mortal wounding in the battle of their leader, John Graham of Claverhouse, Viscount Dundee. One Government soldier evaded capture by making a spectacular jump across the river Garry at Soldier's Leap. The wooded gorge was admired by Queen Victoria. The exhibition in the Visitor Centre features the battle, natural history and ranger services.

Location: OS Ref. NN915 620. B8079 (old A9), 3m N of Pitlochry.

Open: 25 Mar - 23 Dec: daily, 10am - 6pm.

LOCH LEVEN CASTLE 🏛
Loch Leven, Kinross

Tel: 0388 040483

Owner: In the care of Historic Scotland   **Contact:** The Steward

Mary Queen of Scots endured nearly a year of imprisonment in this 14th century tower before her dramatic escape in May 1568. During the First War of Independence it was held by the English, stormed by Wallace and visited by Bruce.

Location: OS Ref. NO138 018. On island in Loch Leven reached by ferry from Kinross off the M90.

Open: 1 Apr - 30 Sept: daily, 9.30am - 6.30pm, last ticket 6pm.

Admission: Adult £3.30, Child £1.20, Conc. £2.50. Prices include ferry trip.

MEGGINCH CASTLE GARDENS
Errol, Perthshire PH2 7SW

Tel: 01821 642222 **Fax:** 01821 642708

Owner: Captain Drummond of Megginch and Lady Strange

15th century castle, 1,000 year old yews, flowered parterre, double walled kitchen garden, topiary, astrological garden, pagoda dovecote in courtyard. Part used as a location for the film *Rob Roy*.

Location: OS Ref. NO241 245. 8m E of Perth on A90.

Open: Apr - Oct: Weds. Aug: daily, 2.30 - 6pm. (2000 details.)

Admission: Adult £3, Child £1.

⊤ ♿ Partial. 🐕 By arrangement. 🅿 Limited for coaches. 🐕 In grounds, on leads.

MEIGLE SCULPTURED STONE MUSEUM 🏛
Meigle

Tel: 01828 640612

Owner: In the care of Historic Scotland

A remarkable collection of 25 sculptured monuments of the Celtic Christian period. This is one of the finest collections of Dark Age sculpture in Western Europe.

Location: OS Ref. NO287 446. In Meigle on the A94.

Open: 1 Apr - 30 Sept: daily, 9.30am - 6.30pm, last ticket 6pm.

Admission: Adult £2, Child 75p, Conc. £1.50.

MONZIE CASTLE
Crieff, Perthshire PH7 4HD

Tel: 01764 653110

Owner/Contact: Mrs C M M Crichton

Built in 1791. Destroyed by fire in 1908 and rebuilt and furnished by Sir Robert Lorimer.

Location: OS Ref. NN873 244. 2m NE of Crieff.

Open: 18 May - 16 Jun: daily, 2 - 5pm. By appointment at other times.

Admission: Adult £3, Child £1. Groups: Adult £2.50.

✳

PITTENCRIEFF HOUSE MUSEUM
Dunfermline, Fife

Tel: 01383 313838/722935

Owner: Fife Council   **Contact:** Museum Co-ordinator

A temporary exhibition programme.

Location: OS Ref. NN087 873. In Dunfermline, S of A994 in Pittencrieff Park. 5mins walk W from Abbey.

Open: 16 Mar - 29 Sept: 11am - 5pm. 30 Sept - 31 Dec: 11am - 4pm. Closed 13 Jan - 15 Mar.

Admission: Free.

Elcho Castle

Patrick Lane

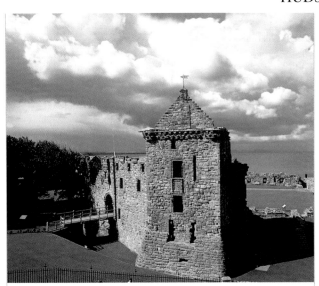

ST ANDREWS CASTLE

The Scores, St Andrews, KY16 9AR

Tel: 01334 477196

Owner: Historic Scotland   **Contact:** The Steward

This was the castle of the Bishops of St Andrews and has a fascinating mine and counter-mine, rare examples of medieval siege techniques. There is also a bottle dungeon hollowed out of solid rock. Cardinal Beaton was murdered here and John Knox was sent to the galleys when the ensuing siege was lifted.

Location: OS Ref. NO513 169. In St Andrews on the A91.

Open: Apr - Sept: daily, 9.30am - 6.30pm. Oct - Mar: Daily, 9.30am - 4.30pm. Last ticket 30 mins before closing. Joint ticket with St Andrews Cathedral available.

Admission: Adult £2.80, Child £1, Conc. £2. 10% discount for groups (10+). Free pre-booked school visits.

Visitor centre. Private evening hire. Partial. WCs. By arrangement. On street. Free if booked. Guide dogs.

STOBHALL GARDENS & CHAPEL

Stobhall, Guildtown, Perthshire PH2 6DR

Tel: 01821 640332

Owner: The Earl of Perth   **Contact:** J Stormonth-Darling

Dramatic shrub gardens surround this unusual and charming cluster of historic buildings in a magnificent situation overlooking the River Tay. Access to 14th century chapel with its unique painted ceiling (1630).

Location: OS Ref. NO132 343. 8m N of Perth on A93.

Open: 25 May - 23 Jun: 1 - 5pm. Also 20 & 27 Oct: 2 - 5pm.

Admission: Adult £2, Child £1.

Partial. WC. Limited. Welcome if accompanied. No education programme. Guide dogs only.

STRATHTYRUM HOUSE & GARDENS

St Andrews, Fife

Tel: 01334 475126

Owner: The Strathtyrum Trust   **Contact:** Max Stewart – Caretaker

Location: OS Ref: NO490 172. Entrance from the St Andrews/Guardbridge Road which is signposted when open.

Open: 1 May - 30 Sept: Wed & every other Sun, 2 - 4pm, last admission 3.45pm.

Admission: Adult £5, Child £2.50. Cars Free.

ST ANDREWS CATHEDRAL

St Andrews, Fife

Tel: 01334 472563

Owner: Historic Scotland   **Contact:** The Administrator

The remains still give a vivid impression of the scale of what was once the largest cathedral in Scotland along with the associated domestic ranges of the priory.

Location: OS Ref: NO514 167. In St Andrews.

Open: 1 Apr - 30 Sept: daily, 9.30am - 6.30pm, last ticket 6pm. 1 Oct - 31 Mar: Mon - Sat, 9.30am - 4.30pm, Suns, 2 - 4.30pm, last ticket 4pm.

Admission: Adult £2, Child 75p, Conc. £1.50. Joint entry ticket available with St Andrews Castle: Adult £3.75, Child £1.25, Conc. £2.80.

SCONE PALACE & GROUNDS

See page 480 for full page entry.

Bolfracks Garden

Patrick Lane

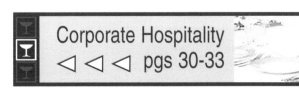

Corporate Hospitality
◁ ◁ ◁ pgs 30-33

West Highlands & Islands, Loch Lomond, Stirling and Trossachs

Historic Scotland

ARGYLL'S LODGING

STIRLING

This attractive townhouse, sitting at the foot of Stirling Castle, is decorated as it would have been during the 9th Earl of Argyll's occupation around 1680. Before coming into Historic Scotland's care the building was a youth hostel, but restoration revealed hidden secrets from the Lodging's past. Perhaps the best of these was a section of 17th century *trompe l'oeil* panelling in the dining room, created by painter David McBeath.

Visitors to Argyll's Lodging might wonder at the highly decorated walls and rich materials and colours used but the restoration relied on a household inventory of 1680 found among the then Duchess's papers. But no matter how rich the decoration, it cannot match the colourful lives of Argyll Lodging's inhabitants.

The 9th Earl, Archibald Campbell, was sentenced to death for treason and imprisoned in Edinburgh Castle. However he escaped when his stepdaughter smuggled him out dressed as her page. Archibald escaped to Holland, but his stepdaughter was arrested and placed in public stocks – a major humiliation. He didn't cheat death a second time, however. Joining plots over the succession following Charles II's death, he was captured and beheaded in 1685.

An earlier inhabitant of Argyll's Lodging, Sir William Alexander, was tutor to James VI's son, Prince Henry and in 1621 he attempted to colonise Nova Scotia in Canada. Great wealth eluded him all his life, however, and he died a bankrupt in 1640, leading to the town council taking over the lodging and selling it to the Earl of Argyll in the 1660s.

Owner: Historic Scotland

▶ CONTACT

Neil Young
Argyll's Lodging
Castle Wynd
Stirling FK8 1EJ

Tel: 01786 431319

Fax: 01786 448194

▶ LOCATION

OS Ref. NS793 938

At the top and on E side of Castle Wynd in Stirling. One way route from town centre from Albert Street.

Rail: Stirling.

Air: Edinburgh or Glasgow.

▶ OPENING TIMES

April - September:
Daily: 9.30am - 6pm.

October - March:
Daily: 9.30am - 5pm.

▶ ADMISSION

Adult	£3.00
Child*	£1.20
Conc	£2.25

*up to 16 years

FUNCTION

ROOM	SIZE	MAX CAPACITY
Laigh Hall reception	11 x 6m	60 fo
High Dining Room	11 x 6m	26 for dinner
Both rooms: 120 for receptions		

📷ℹ️ Interpretation scheme includes computer animations; joint ticket with Stirling Castle available.

🍽️ Evening receptions/dinners.

♿ Partial. No wheelchair access to upper floor.

🅿️ Ample parking for coaches and cars on Stirling Castle Esplanade.

🏫 Free pre-booked school visits scheme.

🐕 Guide dogs only. ❄️

INVERARAY CASTLE

INVERARAY

www.inveraray-castle.com

The Duke of Argyll's family have lived in Inveraray since the early 15th century. The present Castle was built between 1745 and 1790.

The ancient Royal Burgh of Inveraray lies about 60 miles north west of Glasgow by Loch Fyne in an area of spectacular natural beauty combining the ruggedness of highland scenery with the sheltered tidal loch 90 miles from the open sea.

The Castle is the home of the Duke of Argyll. Its fairytale exterior belies the grandeur of its gracious interior. The building was designed by Roger Morris and decorated by Robert Mylne, the clerk of works being William Adam, father of Robert and John, who did much of the laying out of the present Royal Burgh, an unrivalled example of an early planned town.

Visitors may see the famous Armoury Hall containing some 1300 pieces, French tapestries made especially for the Castle, fine examples of Scottish, English and French furniture together with a wealth of other works of art including china, silver and family artifacts, all of which form a unique collection spanning the generations which are identified by a magnificent genealogical display in the Clan Room.

Owner:
Duke of Argyll

▶ **CONTACT**

The Factor
Dept HHD
Argyll Estates Office
Cherry Park
Inveraray
Argyll PA32 8XE

Tel: 01499 302203
Fax: 01499 302421

e-mail: enquiries@
inveraray-castle.com

▶ **LOCATION**
OS Ref. NN100 090

From Edinburgh
2¹/₂ - 3 hrs via
Glasgow.

Just NE of Inveraray
on A83. W shore
of Loch Fyne.

Bus: Bus route
stopping point within
¹/₂ m.

▶ **OPENING TIMES**

Summer

30 March - 27 October

March, April, May, June,
September & October:
Mon -Thur & Sats:
10am - 1pm & 2 - 5.45pm
Fris: Closed
Suns: 1 - 5.45pm.

July & August
Daily: 10am - 5.45pm
(including Friday)
Suns: 1 - 5.45pm.

Last admissions
12.30 & 5pm.

Winter
Closed.

▶ **ADMISSION**
House only

Adult	£5.50
Child (under 16yrs)	£3.50
OAP/Student	£4.50
Family (2+2)	£14.00

Groups of
(20+) .... 20% discount

No photography. Guide books in French, Italian, Japanese and German translations.

Visitors may alight at the entrance. 2 wheelchair ramps to castle. All main public rooms suitable but two long flights of stairs to the smaller rooms upstairs. WCs.

Seats up to 50. Licensed. Menus available on request. Groups book in advance. Tel: 01786 813317.

Available for up to 100 people at no additional cost. Groups please book. Tour time: 1 hr.

100 cars. Separate coach park close to Castle

£1.50 per child. A guide can be provided. Areas of interest include a nature walk.

In grounds, on leads. Guide dogs only inside Castle.

West Highlands & Islands, Loch Lomond, Stirling and Trossachs

ACHAMORE GARDENS

Isle of Gigha, Argyll PA41 7AD

Tel: 01583 505254/505267

Owner: Mr & Mrs Derek Holt   **Contact:** Mr William Howden

Gardens only open. Sub-tropical gardens created by Sir James Horlick who bought Gigha in 1944.

Location: OS Ref. NR650 500. Off the Mull of Kintyre. Ferry from Tayinloan.

Open: Dawn until dusk every day.

Admission: Adult £2, Child £1.

ALLOA TOWER ♥

Alloa Park, Alloa, Clackmannanshire FK10 1PP

Tel: 01259 211701

Owner: The National Trust for Scotland   **Contact:** The Manager

Alloa Tower is a beautifully restored and furnished 14th century Tower House with an unusual 18th century interior. It contains several rare medieval features including the original oak-beamed roof, groin vaulting and interior well. Alloa Tower was the ancestral home of the Erskines, Earls of Mar, and contains a superb collection of family portraits, including works on loan from the present Earl.

Location: OS Ref. NS886 925. On A907, in Alloa.

Open: 25 Mar-27 Oct, daily 1 - 5pm.

Admission: Adult £3.50, Conc. £2.60, Family £9.50. Groups: £2.80. 25% discount to Clackmannanshire residents.

⟨⟩ Partial. WC.

ANGUS'S GARDEN

Barguillean, Taynuilt, Argyll, West Highlands PA35 1HY

Tel: 01866 822375   **Fax:** 01866 822048

Contact: Mr Sam MacDonald

Memorial garden of peace, tranquillity and reconciliation.

Location: OS Ref. NM978 289. 4m SW on Glen Lonan road from A85.

Open: All year: daily, 9am - 5pm.

Admission: £2.

ARDENCRAIG GARDENS

Ardencraig, Rothesay, Isle of Bute, West Highlands PA20 9BP

Tel: 01700 504225   **Fax:** 01700 504225

Owner: Argyll and Bute Council   **Contact:** Allan Macdonald

Walled garden, greenhouses, aviaries.

Location: OS Ref. NS105 645. 2m from Rothesay.

Open: May - Sept: Mon - Fri, 10am - 4.30pm, Sats & Suns, 1 - 4.30pm.

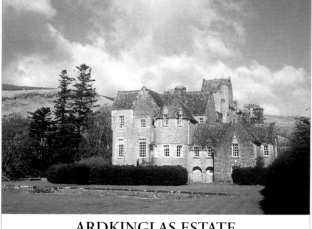

ARDKINGLAS ESTATE

CAIRNDOW, ARGYLL PA26 8BH

www.ardkinglas.com

Tel: 01499 600261   **Fax:** 01499 600241   **e-mail:** ardkinglas@btinternet.com

Owner: S J Noble   **Contact:** The Estate Manager

Ardkinglas House, a superb neo-baronial house near the head of Loch Fyne was built by Sir Robert Lorimer in 1907. Although not open to the public, the house is available for corporate days or as a film location. The Woodland Gardens, which are open to the public, are part of a designed landscape and are of outstanding horticultural and scenic significance. The Gardens include fine champion trees, gazebo containing unique scriptorium and a newly opened area containing a 17th century ruined mill.

Location: OS Ref. NN179 106. Head of Loch Fyne, just off the A83 at Cairndow, 10m W of Arrochar. About 1hr from Glasgow.

Open: Woodland Garden & woodland trails: All year, dawn - dusk.

Admission: Garden admission charge for adults.

⊡ Tree shop. ▣ ⊤ ⟨⟩ Partial. ▣ ⊤ ⟨ℐ⟩ By arrangement. ▣ Limited. ▣ In grounds, on leads. ✺

Harvey Wood

ARDUAINE GARDEN ♥

ARDUAINE, BY OBAN, ARGYLL PA34 4XQ

www.nts.org.uk/arduaine.html

Tel/Fax: 01852 200366

Owner: The National Trust for Scotland   **Contact:** Maurice Wilkins

A haven of tranquillity nestling on the west coast, Arduaine Garden is most spectacular in the late spring and early summer when the rhododendrons and azaleas are at their glorious best. With informal perennial borders giving a delightful display of colour throughout the season, the garden offers pleasant surroundings for a relaxing walk through the woodland garden to the coastal viewpoint, or simply an opportunity to sit and enjoy the peaceful atmosphere of the water garden.

Location: OS Ref. NM798 105. On A816, 20m S of Oban and 17m N of Lochgilphead.

Open: All year: daily, 10am - 6pm.

Admission: Adult £3.50, Conc. £2.60, Family £9.50. Groups: £2.80.

⟨ℐ⟩ By arrangement. ▣ ▣ Guide dogs only. ✺

Bonawe Iron Furnace

Patrick Lane

ARGYLL'S LODGING

See page 486 for full page entry.

AUCHINDRAIN TOWNSHIP

Auchindrain, Inveraray, Argyll PA32 8XN

Tel: 01499 500235

Owner: Auchindrain Trust   **Contact:** Curator

Open-air museum of an original West Highland township.

Location: OS Ref. NN050 050. On A83, 6m SW of Inveraray.

Open: Apr - Sept: daily, 10am - 5pm.

Admission: Please contact for details.

BALLOCH CASTLE COUNTRY PARK

Balloch, Dunbartonshire G83 8LX

Tel: 01389 722600   **Fax:** 01389 720922

                    Contact: Loch Lomond & The Trossachs Interim Committee

A 200 acre country park on the banks of Loch Lomond.

Location: OS Ref. NS390 830. SE shore of Loch Lomond, off A82 for Balloch or A811 for Stirling.

Open: Visitor Centre: Easter - Oct: daily, 10am - 5.30pm. Country Park: All year: dawn - dusk.

Admission: Free for both Visitor Centre and Country Park.

NTS / Kathy Collins

BANNOCKBURN HERITAGE CENTRE

Glasgow Road, Stirling FK7 0IJ

Tel: 01786 812664   **Fax:** 01786 810892   www.nts.org.uk/bannockburn.html

Owner: The National Trust for Scotland   **Contact:** Judith Fairley

In 1314 from this battlefield the Scots 'sent them homeward to think again', when Edward II's English army was soundly defeated by King Robert the Bruce. Inside the Heritage Centre there is a life-size statue of William Wallace, Bruce on his throne, a display enriched with replicas, vignettes of Scottish life and a panorama of historical characters.

Location: OS Ref. NS810 910. Off M80 & M9/J9, 2m S of Stirling.

Open: 20 Jan - 24 Mar: daily, 10.30am - 4pm. 25 Mar - 27 Oct: daily, 10am - 6pm. 28 Oct - 24 Dec: daily, 10.30am - 4pm.

Admission: Adult £3.50, Conc. £2.60, Family £9.50. Groups: £2.80.

In grounds, on leads.

BENMORE BOTANIC GARDEN

Dunoon, Argyll PA23 8QU

Tel: 01369 706261   **Fax:** 01369 706369   **Contact:** The Curator

A botanical paradise. Enter the magnificent avenue of giant redwoods and follow trails through the Formal Garden and hillside woodlands with its spectacular outlook over the Holy Loch and the Eachaig Valley.

Location: OS Ref. NS150 850. 7m N of Dunoon on A815.

Open: 1 Mar - 31 Oct: daily, 9.30am - 6pm.

Admission: Adult £3, Child £1, Conc. £2.50, Family £7. Group discounts available.

BONAWE IRON FURNACE

Taynuilt, Argyll

Tel: 01866 822432

Owner: In the care of Historic Scotland   **Contact:** The Steward

Founded in 1753 by Cumbrian iron masters this is the most complete remaining charcoal fuelled ironworks in Britain. Displays show how iron was once made here.

Location: OS Ref. NN005 310. By the village of Taynuilt off the A85.

Open: 1 Apr - 30 Sept: daily, 9.30am - 6.30pm, last ticket 6pm.

Admission: Adult £2.80, Child £1, Conc. £2.

CASTLE STALKER

Portnacroish, Appin, Argyll PA38 4BA

Tel: 01883 622768   **Fax:** 01883 626238   www.castlestalker.com

Owner: Mrs M Allward   **Contact:** Messrs R & A Allward

Early 15th century tower house and ancient seat of the Stewarts of Appin. Picturesquely set on a rocky islet approx 400 yds off the mainland on the shore of Loch Linnhe. Reputed to have been used by James IV as a hunting lodge. Garrisoned by Government troops during the 1745 rising. Restored from a ruin by the late Lt Col Stewart Allward following acquisition in 1965 and now retained by his family.

Location: OS Ref. NM930 480. Approx. 20m N of Oban on the A828. On islet ¼ m offshore.

Open: Apr - Sept for 25 days. Telephone for details. Times variable depending on tides and weather.

Admission: Adult £6, Child £3.

Not suitable for coach parties. Unsuitable.

DOUNE CASTLE

Doune

Tel: 01786 841742

Owner: Earl of Moray (leased to Historic Scotland)   **Contact:** The Steward

A formidable 14th century courtyard castle, built for the Regent Albany. The striking keep-gatehouse combines domestic quarters including the splendid Lord's Hall with its carved oak screen, musicians' gallery and double fireplace.

Location: OS Ref. NN720 020. In Doune, 8m S of Callendar on the A84.

Open: 1 Apr - 30 Sept: daily, 9.30am - 6.30pm. 1 Oct - 31 Mar: Mon - Wed & Sats, 9.30am - 4.30pm, Thurs, 9.30am - 12 noon, Fris, closed, Suns, 2 - 4.30pm, last admission ½ hr before closing.

Admission: Adult £2.80, Child £1, Conc. £1.90.

DUART CASTLE

ISLE OF MULL, ARGYLL PA64 6AP

www.duartcastle.com

Tel: 01680 812309 or 01577 830311   **e-mail:** duartguide@isle-of-mull.demon.co.uk

Owner/Contact: Sir Lachlan Maclean Bt

Duart Castle has been a Maclean stronghold since the 12th century. The keep was built by Lachlan Lubanach, 5th Chief, in 1360. Burnt by the English in 1758, the castle was restored in 1912 and today is still the home of the Chief of the Clan Maclean. It has a spectacular position overlooking the Sound of Mull.

Location: OS Ref. NM750 350. Off A849 on the east point of the Isle of Mull.

Open: 1 - 30 Apr: Sun - Fri, 11am - 4pm. 1 May - 13 Oct: daily, 10.30am - 6pm.

Admission: Adult £4, Child £2, Conc. £3.50, Family £9.50.

Unsuitable. By arrangement. In grounds, on leads.

West Highlands & Islands, Loch Lomond, Stirling and Trossachs

DUMBARTON CASTLE 🏛

Dumbarton, Strathclyde

Tel: 01389 732167

Owner: Historic Scotland   **Contact:** The Steward

Location: OS Ref. NS401 744. 600yds S of A84 at E end of Dumbarton.

Open: 1 Apr - 30 Sept: daily, 9.30am - 6.30pm, last ticket 6pm. 1 Oct - 31 Mar: Mon - Wed & Sats, 9.30am - 4.30pm, Thurs, 9.30am - 12 noon, Fris closed, Suns, 2 - 4.30pm, last ticket 4pm.

Admission: Adult £2.20, Child 75p, Conc £1.60.

DUNBLANE CATHEDRAL 🏛

Dunblane

Tel: 01786 823388

Owner: Historic Scotland   **Contact:** The Steward

One of Scotland's noblest medieval churches. The lower part of the tower is Romanesque but the larger part of the building is of the 13th century. It was restored in 1889 - 93 by Sir Rowand Anderson.

Location: OS Ref. NN782 015. In Dunblane.

Open: All year.

Admission: Free.

Open All Year Index ◁ ◁ ◁ pgs 44-48

Crown Copyright

DUNSTAFFNAGE CASTLE 🏛

BY OBAN, ARGYLL PA37 1PZ

Tel: 01631 562465

Owner: In the care of Historic Scotland   **Contact:** The Steward

A very fine 13th century castle built on a rock with a great curtain wall. The castle's colourful history stretches across the Wars of Independence to the 1745 rising. The castle was briefly the prison of Flora Macdonald. Marvellous views from the top of the curtain wall. Close by are the remains of a chapel with beautiful architectural detail.

Location: OS49 NM882 344. 3¹/₂ m NE of Oban off A85.

Open: Apr - Sept: daily, 9.30am - 6.30pm, last ticket ¹/₂ hr before closing. Oct - Mar: Mon - Sat, 9.30am - 4.30pm; Suns, 2 - 4.30pm.

Admission: Adult £2.20, Child 75p, Conc. £1.60. 10% discount for groups (10+).

🖻 🖿 Partial. 🎦 By arrangement. 🅿 🖿 Free pre-booked school visits. 🖿 In grounds, on leads. ❄

NTS / Kathy Collins

GLENCOE 🌳

BALLACHULISH, ARGYLL PA39 4HX

Tel: 01855 811307/811729 (during closed season) **Fax:** 01855 811772

www.nts.org.uk/glencoe.html

Owner: The National Trust for Scotland   **Contact:** Derrick Warner

This is a breathtaking, dramatic glen with jagged peaks incised on either side by cascading water. In 1692 many of the MacDonald clan were massacred by soldiers of King William's army, to whom they had given hospitality. Wildlife abounds and herds of red deer, wildcat and golden eagle enjoy this wilderness area.

Location: OS Ref. NN100 590. Off A82, 17m S of Fort William.

Open: New Visitor Centre: 1 May - 27 Oct: daily, 10am - 6pm.

Admission: Adult £3.50, Conc. £2.60, Family £9.50. Groups: £2.80.

🖻 🖿 Ground floor. WC. 🖿 🖿 Guide dogs only.

THE HILL HOUSE 🌳

Upper Colquhoun Street, Helensburgh G84 9AJ

Tel: 01436 673900 **Fax:** 01436 674685 www.nts.org.uk/hill.html

Owner: The National Trust for Scotland   **Contact:** Mrs Anne Ellis

Certainly the finest domestic creation of the famous Scottish architect and artist, Charles Rennie Mackintosh. He set this 20th century masterpiece high on a hillside overlooking the Firth of Clyde. Mackintosh also designed furniture, fittings and decorative schemes to complement the house, and suggested a layout for the garden which has been renovated by the Trust.

Location: OS Ref. NS300 820. Off B832, between A82 & A814, 23m NW of Glasgow.

Open: 25 Mar - 27 Oct: daily, 1.30 - 5.30pm. Access may be restricted at peak times and at the discretion of the Property Manager. Groups must book.

Admission: Adult £7, Conc. £5.25, Family £19.

🖻 🖿

INCHMAHOME PRIORY 🏛

Port of Menteith

Tel: 01877 385294

Owner: In the care of Historic Scotland   **Contact:** The Steward

A beautifully situated Augustinian priory on an island in the Lake of Menteith founded in 1238 with much of the building surviving. The five year old Mary Queen of Scots was sent here for safety in 1547.

Location: OS Ref. NN574 005. On an island in Lake of Menteith. Reached by ferry from Port of Menteith, 4m E of Aberfoyle off A81.

Open: 1 Apr - 30 Sept: daily, 9.30am - 6.30pm, last ticket 6pm.

Admission: Adult £3.30, Child £1.20, Conc. £2.50. Charge includes ferry trip.

INVERARAY CASTLE 🏛   *See page 487 for full page entry.*

INVERARAY JAIL

Church Square, Inveraray, Argyll PA32 8TX

Tel: 01499 302381 **Fax:** 01499 302195 **e-mail:** inverarayjail@btclick.com

Owner: Visitor Centres Ltd   **Contact:** J Linley

A living 19th century prison! Uniformed prisoners and warders, life-like figures, imaginative exhibitions, sounds, smells and trials in progress, bring the 1820 courtroom and former county prison back to life. See the 'In Prison Today' exhibition.

Location: OS Ref. NN100 090. Church Square, Inveraray, Argyll.

Open: Apr - Oct: 9.30am - 6pm, last adm. 5pm. Nov - Mar: 10am - 5pm, last adm. 4pm.

Admission: Adult £4.95, Child £2.50, OAP £3.20, Family £13.65. Groups (10+): £3.95, OAP £2.60 (from 1 Apr 2002).

IONA ABBEY & NUNNERY

Iona, West Highlands

Tel/Fax: 01681 700512 **e-mail:** hs.ionaabbey@scotland.gov.uk
www.historic-scotland.gov.uk

Owner: In the care of Historic Scotland   **Contact:** Chris Calvert

One of Scotland's most historic and venerated sites, Iona Abbey is a celebrated Christian centre and the burial place for many Scottish kings. The abbey and nunnery grounds house one of the most comprehensive collections of Christian carved stones in Scotland, dating from 600AD to the 1600s. Includes the Columba Centre, Fionnphort exhibition and giftshop.

Location: OS Ref. NM270 240. Ferry service from Fionnphort, Mull.

Open: All year, daily.

Admission: Adult £2.80, Child (under 16) £1.20, Conc. £2. Columba Centre, exhibition & giftshop: Free.

KILCHURN CASTLE

Loch Awe, Dalmally, Argyll

Tel: 01786 431323

Owner: In the care of Historic Scotland   **Contact:** The Steward

A square tower, built by Sir Colin Campbell of Glenorchy c1550, it was much enlarged in 1693 to give the building, now a ruin, its present picturesque outline. Spectacular views of Loch Awe.

Location: OS Ref. NN133 276. At the NE end of Loch Awe, 2¹/₂ m W of Dalmally.

Open: Ferry service operates in the summer. Tel: 01838 200440 for times & prices.

Admission: Please telephone for details.

ROTHESAY CASTLE

Rothesay, Isle of Bute

Tel: 01700 502691

Owner: In the care of Historic Scotland   **Contact:** The Steward

A favourite residence of the Stuart Kings, this is a wonderful example of a 13th century circular castle of enclosure with 16th century forework containing the Great Hall. Attacked by Vikings in its earlier days.

Location: OS Ref. NS088 646. In Rothesay, Isle of Bute. Ferry from Wemyss Bay on the A78.

Open: 1 Apr - 30 Sept: daily, 9.30am - 6.30pm, last ticket 6pm. 1 Oct - 31 Mar: Mon - Wed & Sats, 9.30am - 4.30pm, Thurs 9.30am - 12 noon, Fris closed, Suns, 2 - 4.30pm, last ticket 4pm.

Admission: Adult £2.20, Child 75p, Conc. £1.60.

ST BLANE'S CHURCH

Kingarth, Isle of Bute

Tel: 0131 668 8800

Owner: In the care of Historic Scotland

This 12th century Romanesque chapel stands on the site of a 12th century Celtic monastery.

Location: OS Ref. NS090 570. At the S end of the Isle of Bute.

Open: All year: daily.

Admission: Free.

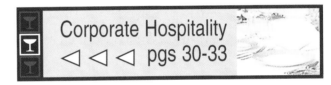
Corporate Hospitality
◁ ◁ ◁ pgs 30-33

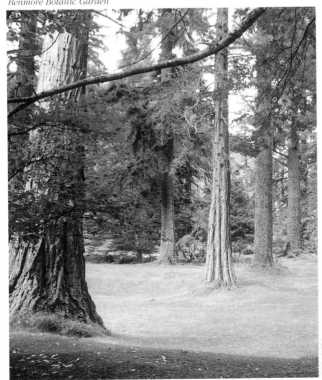

Benmore Botanic Garden

Patrick Lane

Historic Scotland

STIRLING CASTLE

CASTLE WYND, STIRLING FK8 1EJ

Tel: 01786 450000 **Fax:** 01786 464678

Owner: Historic Scotland   **Contact:** Neil Young

Stirling Castle has played a key role in Scottish history, dominating the North–South and East–West routes through Scotland. The battles of Stirling Bridge and Bannockburn were fought in its shadow and Mary Queen of Scots lived here as a child. Marvellous Renaissance architecture and restored Great Hall.

Location: OS Ref. NS790 941. At the top of Castle Wynd in Stirling.

Open: Apr - Sept: 9.30am - 6pm. Oct - Mar: 9.30am - 5pm, last ticket 45 mins before closing.

Admission: Adult £7, Child £2, Conc. £5. 10% discount for groups (10+). Free booked school visits, except May - August.

ℹ️ Picnic area. Joint ticket with Argyll's Lodging. Private hire.
Partial. WC. Licensed. Guide dogs.

TOROSAY CASTLE & GARDENS

CRAIGNURE, ISLE OF MULL PA65 6AY

www.holidaymull.org/members/torosay

Tel: 01680 812421   **Fax:** 01680 812470   **e-mail:** torosay@aol.com

Owner/Contact: Mr Chris James

Torosay Castle and Gardens set on the magnificent Island of Mull, was completed in 1858 by the eminent architect David Bryce in the Scottish baronial style, and is surrounded by 12 acres of spectacular gardens which offer a dramatic contrast between formal terraces, impressive statue walk and informal woodland, also rhododendron collection, alpine, walled, bog and oriental gardens. The house offers family history, portraits, scrapbooks and antiques in an informal and relaxed atmosphere.

Location: OS Ref. NM730 350. 1½ m SE of Craignure by A849.

Open: House: Easter - mid-Oct: daily, 10.30am - 5pm. Gardens: All year: daily, 9am - 7pm or daylight hours in winter.

Admission: Adult £5, Child £1.75, Conc. £4, Family £12.

Grounds. WC. In grounds, on leads.

Website Information ◁ ◁ ◁ pg 39

Inveraray Jail - Courtroom with waxwork figures

Patrick Lane

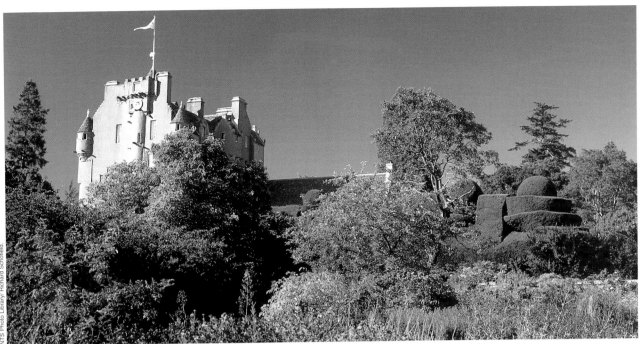

NTS Photo Library/ Richard Schofield

CRATHES CASTLE & GARDEN

BANCHORY

www.nts.org.uk/crathes.html

Owner: The National Trust for Scotland

▶ **CONTACT**

The Property
Administrator
Crathes Castle
Banchory   AB31 3QJ

Tel: 01330 844525
Fax: 01330 844797

e-mail:
crathes@nts.org.uk

▶ **LOCATION**
OS Ref. NO733 969

On A93, 3m E of
Banchory and 15m W
of Aberdeen.

Part of Aberdeenshire's Castle Trail: fairytale-like turrets, gargoyles of fantastic design, superb painted ceilings and the ancient Horn of Leys given in 1323 to Alexander Burnett by King Robert the Bruce, are just a few of the exciting features at this most picturesque castle. The building of the castle began in 1553 and took 40 years to complete. Just over 300 years later, Sir James and Lady Burnett began developing the walled garden and created not just one but eight superb gardens which now provide a riot of colour throughout the summer.

▶ **OPENING TIMES**

Castle, Visitor Centre & Shop
20 Jan - 24 Mar: daily
(except Mon/Tue),
10am - 5.30pm.

25 Mar - 27 Oct:
daily, 10am - 5.30pm.

28 Oct - 23 Dec:
10am - 5.30pm.

Other times by
appointment.

To help you to enjoy your
visit, admission to the
Castle is by timed ticket
and entry may be delayed.

Garden & Grounds
All year: daily,
9am - sunset.
Grounds may be closed at
short notice on very busy
days due to the limited
capacity for car parking.

▶ **ADMISSION**

Castle & Garden
Adult £8.50
Conc. £6.40
Family £23.00
Groups
Adult £6.80
Child/School £1.00

Car Park £1.00

**Castle or Walled
Garden only**
Adult £5.00
Conc. £3.75

NTS Photo Library

    Partial. Licensed.   Tel for details.

ARBUTHNOTT HOUSE

Arbuthnott, Laurencekirk AB30 1PA

Tel: 01561 361226 **Fax:** 01561 320476 **e-mail:** keith@arbuthnott.co.uk
www.arbuthnott.co.uk

Owner: The Viscount of Arbuthnott   **Contact:** The Master of Arbuthnott
Arbuthnott family home for 800 years with formal 17th century walled garden on unusually steep south facing slope. Well maintained grass terraces, herbaceous borders, shrubs and greenhouses.

Location: OS Ref. NO796 751. Off B967 between A90 and A92, 25m S of Aberdeen.

Open: House: 31 Mar; 1 Apr, 5/6 & 26/27 May; 4/5 & 25/26 Aug. Guided tours: 2 - 5pm. Garden: All year: 9am - 5pm.

Admission: House: £3.50. Garden: £2.

🔲 Ground floor. 🎦 Obligatory. 🅿 ⬚ ✳

BALFLUIG CASTLE

Alford, Aberdeenshire AB33 8EJ

Tel: 020 7624 3200

Owner/Contact: Mark Tennant of Balfluig
Small 16th century tower house in farmland, restored in 1967.

Location: OS Ref. NJ586 151. Alford, Aberdeenshire.

Open: Please write to M I Tennant Esq, 30 Abbey Gardens, London NW8 9AT. Occasionally let by the week for holidays. Scottish Tourist Board ***.

🔲 Unsuitable. ⬚ 🛏 1 single, 4 double. ✳

BALMORAL CASTLE (GROUNDS & EXHIBITIONS)

Balmoral, Ballater, Aberdeenshire AB35 5TB

Tel: 013397 42334/42335 **Fax:** 013397 42034 **e-mail:** info@balmoralcastle.com

Owner: Her Majesty The Queen   **Contact:** Captain Roger Wilson
Holiday home of The Royal Family, bought by Prince Albert in 1852. Grounds, gardens and exhibition of paintings and works of art in the Ballroom. Exhibition of royal heraldry, commemorative china and a display of native wildlife in their natural habitat in the Carriage Hall. Display of carriages and Upper Deeside Art Society exhibition on view in the Stables.

Location: OS Ref. NO256 951. Off A93 between Ballater and Braemar. 50m W of Aberdeen.

Open: 28 Mar - 31 Jul: daily, 10am - 5pm (last recommended admission 4pm).

Admission: Adult £4.50, Child (5-16yrs) £1, OAP £3.50.

BALVENIE CASTLE 🏛

Dufftown

Tel: 01340 820121

Owner: In the care of Historic Scotland   **Contact:** The Steward
Picturesque ruins of 13th century moated stronghold originally owned by the Comyns. Visited by Edward I in 1304 and by Mary Queen of Scots in 1562. Occupied by Cumberland in 1746.

Location: OS Ref. NJ326 408. At Dufftown on A941.

Open: 1 Apr - 30 Sept: daily, 9.30am - 6.30pm, last ticket 6pm.

Admission: Adult £1.50, Child 50p, Conc. £1.10.

BRODIE CASTLE ♥

FORRES, MORAY IV36 0TE

www.nts.org.uk/brodie.html

Tel: 01309 641371 **Fax:** 01309 641600

Owner: The National Trust for Scotland   **Contact:** Dr Stephanie Blackden
This imposing Castle stands in rich Morayshire parkland. The lime harled building is a typical 'Z' plan tower house with ornate corbelled battlements and bartizans, with 17th & 19th century additions. The interior has unusual plaster ceilings, a major art collection, porcelain and fine furniture. There is a woodland walk by a large pond with access to wildlife observation hides. In springtime the grounds are carpeted with many varieties of daffodils for which Brodie Castle is rightly famous.

Location: OS Ref. NH980 577. Off A96 4½ m W of Forres and 24m E of Inverness.

Open: Castle & Shop: 25 Mar - 29 Sep: daily (except Tues & Weds) 11am - 6pm. Other times by appointment. Grounds: All year: daily, 9.30am - sunset.

Admission: Adult £5, Conc. £3.75, Family £13.50. Groups: Adult £4, Child/Schools £1. Grounds only: £1 honesty box.

🔲 🔲 ⬛ 🛏 In grounds, on leads. ✳

CANDACRAIG GARDEN & GALLERY

Candacraig Gardens, Strathdon AB36 8XT

Tel: 01975 651226 **Fax:** 01975 651391

Owner/Contact: Harry Young
1820s B listed walled display garden, art gallery and specialist plant nursery.

Location: OS Ref. NJ339 110. On A944 1½ m SW of Strathdon, 20m from Alford.

Open: 1 May - 30 Sept: daily, 10am - 6pm.

Admission: Donation box. Pre-arranged groups: Adult £1, Child Free.

Delgatie Castle

CASTLE FRASER & GARDEN ✿

SAUCHEN, INVERURIE AB51 7LD

www.nts.org.uk/fraser.html

Tel: 01330 833463

Owner: The National Trust for Scotland   **Contact:** The Manager

Over 400 years of history could be told if the stout walls of Castle Fraser could speak. Begun in 1575 by the 6th Laird, Michael Fraser, the two low wings contribute to the scale and magnificence of the towers rising above them, combining to make this the largest and most elaborate of the Scottish castles built on the 'Z' plan. The stunning simplicity of the Great Hall, which occupies the entire first floor of the main block, with its striking fireplace, almost 3 metres wide, immediately creates for the visitor the atmosphere of past centuries.

Location: OS Ref. NJ723 125. Off A944, 4m N of Dunecht & 16m W of Aberdeen.

Open: Castle: 25 Mar - 28 Jun, daily (except Tue/Wed), 12 noon - 5pm. 29 Jun - 1 Sept, daily 10am - 6pm. 2 Sept - 27 Oct: daily (except Tue/Wed), 12 noon - 5pm Grounds: All year: daily, 9.30am - sunset.

Admission: Castle & Garden: Adult £7, Conc. £5.25, Family £19. Groups: Adult £5.60. Child/School £1.

🅿️ 🎫 ♿ 🍽️ ❄️

CORGARFF CASTLE ⚖️

Strathdon

Tel: 013398 83635

Owner: In the care of Historic Scotland   **Contact:** The Steward

A 16th century tower house converted into a barracks for Hanoverian troops in 1748.

Location: OS Ref. NJ255 086. 8m W of Strathdon on A939. 14m NW of Ballater.

Open: 1 Apr - 30 Sept: daily, 9.30am - 6.30pm. 1 Oct - 31 Mar: Sats, 9.30am - 4.30pm. Suns, 2 - 4.30pm, last admission ½ hr before closing.

Admission: Adult £2.80, Child £1, Conc. £2.

CRATHES CASTLE & GARDEN ✿   *See page 493 for full page entry.*

CRAIGSTON CASTLE

Turriff, Aberdeenshire AB53 5PX

Tel: 01888 551228/551640

Owner: William Pratesi Urquhart   **Contact:** Mrs Fiona Morrison

Built in 1607 to John Urquhart Tutor of Cromarty's individualistic plan. An arch and ornate sculptured balcony joins two towers, one noticeably wider than the other, to accommodate the Laird's private apartments. The largely unchanged interior, still lived in by the Urquhart family, includes carved portraits of the Scottish Kings.

Location: OS Ref. NJ762 550. On B9105, 4½ m NE of Turriff.

Open: 26 Jul - 11 Aug: daily (closed Mons & Tues), 24 Aug - 8 Sept: daily (closed Mons & Tues), 10am - 4pm. Groups throughout the year by appointment.

Admission: Adult £3.50, Child £1, OAP £3, Student £1.50.

♿ Unsuitable. 🎫 Obligatory. 🅿️ 🐕 In grounds on leads. ❄️

CRUICKSHANK BOTANIC GARDEN

St Machar Drive, Aberdeen AB24 3UU

Tel: 01224 272704   **Fax:** 01224 272703

Owner: University of Aberdeen   **Contact:** R B Rutherford

Extensive collection of shrubs, herbaceous and alpine plants and trees. Rock and water gardens.

Location: OS Ref. NJ938 084. In old Aberdeen.

Open: All year: Mon - Fri, 9am - 4.30pm. May - Sept: Sats & Suns, 2 - 5pm.

Admission: Free.

DALLAS DHU DISTILLERY ⚖️

Forres

Tel: 01309 676548

Owner: In the care of Historic Scotland   **Contact:** The Steward

A completely preserved time capsule of the distiller's craft. Wander at will through this fine old Victorian distillery then enjoy a dram. Visitor centre, shop and audio-visual theatre.

Location: OS Ref. NJ035 566. 1m S of Forres off the A940.

Open: 1 Apr - 30 Sept: daily, 9.30am - 6.30pm, last ticket 6pm. 1 Oct - 31 Mar: Mon - Sat, 9.30am - 4.30pm, Suns, 2 - 4.30pm, last ticket 4pm. Closed Thurs pm and Fris in winter.

Admission: Adult £3.30, Child £1, Conc. £2.50.

DELGATIE CASTLE

TURRIFF, ABERDEENSHIRE AB53 5TD

www.delgatiecastle.com

Tel/Fax: 01888 563479   **e-mail:** jjohnson@delgatie-castle.freeserve.co.uk

Owner: Delgatie Castle Trust   **Contact:** Mrs Joan Johnson

Dating from 1030 the Castle is steeped in Scottish history yet still has the atmosphere of a lived in home. It has some of the finest painted ceilings, Mary Queen of Scots' bed-chamber and armour, Victorian clothes, fine furniture and paintings are displayed. Widest turnpike stair of its kind in Scotland. Clan Hay Centre.

Location: OS Ref. NJ754 506. Off A947 Aberdeen to Banff Road.

Open: 2 Apr - 25 Oct: 10am - 5pm.

Admission: Adult £3, Conc. £2. Groups (10+): £2.

ℹ️ No photography. 🅿️ 📺 ♿ Ground floor. WC. 🍴 Home-baking. 🍽️ 🎫 By arrangement. 🅿️ 🚌 🐕 Guide dogs only. 🏠 Self catering apartments.

Website Information ◁ ◁ ◁   pg 39

Grampian Highlands, Aberdeen and North East Coast

DRUM CASTLE

Drumoak, by Banchory AB31 3EY

Tel: 01330 811204 **www.nts.org.uk**

Owner: The National Trust for Scotland   **Contact:** The Property Manager

The combination over the years of a 13th century square tower, a very fine Jacobean mansion house and the additions of the Victorian lairds make Drum Castle unique among Scottish castles. Owned for 653 years by one family, the Irvines, every stone and every room is steeped in history. Superb furniture and paintings provide a visual feast for visitors. In the 16th century chapel, the stained glass windows, the font copied from the Saxon one in Winchester Cathedral and the Augsburg silver Madonna, all add immense interest for visitors.

Location: OS Ref. NJ796 004. Off A93, 3m W of Peterculter and 10m W of Aberdeen.

Open: Castle: 25 Mar - 28 June: daily, 12 noon - 5pm. 29 Jun - 1 Sep: daily, 10am - 6pm; 2 Sep - 27 Oct: 12 noon - 5pm.

Admission: Castle & Garden: Adult £7, Conc. £5.25, Family £19. Groups: Adult £5.60, Child/ School £1. Garden & Grounds only: £1.

DRUMMUIR CASTLE

Drummuir, by Keith, Banffshire AB55 5JE

Tel: 01542 810332 **Fax:** 01542 810302

Owner: The Gordon-Duff Family   **Contact:** Joy James

Castellated Victorian Gothic-style castle built in 1847 by Admiral Duff. 60ft high lantern tower with fine plasterwork. Family portraits, interesting artefacts and other paintings. Organic walled garden and plant sales.

Location: OS Ref. NO881 839. Midway between Keith (5m) and Dufftown, off the B9014.

Open: 23/24 & 30 Aug, 31 Aug & 3 - 24 Sept: Tours at 2pm & 3pm.

Admission: Adult £2, Child £1.50. Pre-arranged groups: Adult £2, Child £1.50.
Obligatory. In grounds on leads.

DUNNOTTAR CASTLE

Dunnottar Castle Lodge, Dunnottar, Stonehaven AB39 2TL

Tel: 01569 762173   **Contact:** P McKenzie

Spectacular ruin. Impregnable fortress to the Earls Marischals of Scotland.

Location: OS Ref. NO881 839. Just off A92. 1 1/2 m SE of Stonehaven.

Open: Easter weekend - 28 Oct: Mon - Sat, 9am - 6pm. Suns, 2 - 5pm. 29 Oct - Easter weekend: Fri - Mon, 9am - dusk. Closed Tue - Thur. Last admission: 30 mins before closing.

Admission: Please telephone for details.

DUTHIE PARK & WINTER GARDENS

Polmuir Road, Aberdeen, Grampian Highlands AB11 7TH

Tel: 01224 585310 **Fax:** 01224 210532 **e-mail:** wintergardens@aberdeen.nct.uk
www.aberdeencity.gov.uk

Owner: Aberdeen City Council   **Contact:** Alan Findlay

45 acres of parkland and gardens. Glasshouses.

Location: OS Ref. NJ97 044. Just N of River Dee, 1m S of city centre.

Open: All year: daily from 9.30pm.

Admission: Free.

ELGIN CATHEDRAL

Elgin

Tel: 01343 547171

Owner: Historic Scotland   **Contact:** The Steward

When entire this was perhaps the most beautiful of Scottish cathedrals, known as the Lantern of the North. 13th century, much modified after almost being destroyed in 1390 by Alexander Stewart, the infamous 'Wolf of Badenoch'. The octagonal chapterhouse is the finest in Scotland. You can see the Bishop's home at Spynie Palace, 2m north of the town.

Location: OS Ref. NJ223 630. In Elgin on the A96.

Open: 1 Apr - 30 Sept: daily, 9.30am - 6.30pm, last ticket 6pm. 1 Oct - 31 Mar: Mon - Sat, 9.30am - 4.30pm, Suns, 2 - 4.30pm, last ticket 4pm. Closed Thurs pm & Fris in winter.

Admission: Adult £2.80, Child £1, Conc. £2. Joint entry ticket with Spynie Palace: Adult £3.30, Child £1.20, Conc. £2.50.

DUFF HOUSE

BANFF, AB45 3SX

www.duffhouse.com

Tel: 01261 818181 **Fax:** 01261 818900   **Contact:** The Chamberlain

One of the most imposing and palatial houses in Scotland, with a strong classical façade and a grand staircase leading to the main entrance. It remained in the hands of the Duffs, Dukes of Fife until 1906 when the family presented the estate to Banff and Macduff, consigning its contents to the saleroom. Duff House opened to the public as an outstation of the National Galleries of Scotland in 1995.

Location: OS Ref. NJ691 634. Banff. 47m NW of Aberdeen on A947.

Open: 1 Apr - 31 Oct: daily, 11am - 5pm. 1 Nov - 31 Mar: Thur - Sun, 11am - 4pm.

Admission: Adult £4, Conc. £3, Family £9. Groups (10+): £3. Free admission to shop, tearoom, grounds & woodland walks.

Coaches to book.

FASQUE

FETTERCAIRN, LAURENCEKIRK, KINCARDINESHIRE AB30 1DN

Tel/Fax: 01561 340569

Owner: Charles Gladstone   **Contact:** Scott Traynor MBE

Fasque is a spectacular example of a Victorian 'Upstairs-Downstairs' stately home. Bought by Sir John Gladstone in 1829, it was home to William Gladstone, four times Prime Minister, for much of his life. In front of the house red deer roam in the park, and behind the hills rise dramatically towards the Highlands. Inside very little has changed since Sir John's days. Fasque is not a museum, but rather an unspoilt old family home.

Location: OS Ref. NO648 755. On the B974, 1m N of Fettercairn, 4m from A90. Aberdeen/ Dundee 35m.

Open: 1 Jul - 31 Aug: daily, 11am - 5.30pm, last admission 4.30pm. Groups (10+) all year by arrangement..

Admission: Adult £4, Child £1.50, OAP £3.

By arrangement. Tel for details.

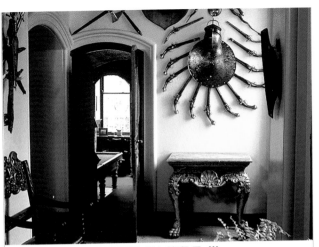

FYVIE CASTLE ♛

TURRIFF, ABERDEENSHIRE AB53 8JS

www.nts.org.uk/fyvie.html

Tel: 01651 891266   **Fax:** 01651 891107

Owner: The National Trust for Scotland   **Contact:** The Property Manager

The south front of this magnificent building employs a plethora of crow-stepped gables, turrets, sculpted dormers and finials in the form of musicians, to create a marvellous façade. The five towers of the castle bear witness to the five families who have owned it. Fyvie Castle boasts the finest wheel stair in Scotland and there is a superb collection of arms and armour and paintings, including works by Batoni, Raeburn, Romney, Gainsborough, Opie and Hoppner.

Location: OS Ref. NJ763 393. Off A947, 8m SE of Turriff, and 25m N of Aberdeen.

Open: Castle: 25 Mar - 28 Jun: Sat - Wed, 10am - 5pm; 29 Jun - 1 Sept: daily, 10am - 6pm; 2 Sept - 27 Oct: Sat - Wed, 10am - 5pm. Tearoom & Shop: open at 12.30pm when Castle opens at 1.30pm. Grounds: All year, daily, 9.30am - sunset.

Admission: Adult £7, Conc. £5.25, Family £19. Groups: Adult £5.60, Child/School £1.

HADDO HOUSE ♛

TARVES, ELLON, ABERDEENSHIRE AB41 0ER

www.nts.org.uk/haddo.html

Tel: 01651 851440   **Fax:** 01651 851888

Owner: The National Trust for Scotland   **Contact:** Craig Ferguson

This appealing house was designed by William Adam in 1731 for William, 2nd Earl of Aberdeen. Much of the splendid interior is 'Adam Revival' carried out about 1880 for John, 7th Earl and 1st Marquess of Aberdeen and his Countess, Ishbel. It is arguably the most elegant house in the north east, a classic English-style stately home transplanted to Scotland. Features of the house include the Italianate sweeping twin staircases at the front of the house, the atmospheric library and the subtlety of the great curving corridor.

Location: OS Ref. NJ868 348. Off B999, 4m N of Pitmedden, 10m NW of Ellon.

Open: House: 29 June - 1 Sep: daily, 10am - 5pm.

Admission: Adult £7, Conc. £5.25, Family £19. Groups: Adult £5.60, Child/School £1.

HUNTLY CASTLE ⚲

Huntly

Tel: 01466 793191

Owner: In the care of Historic Scotland   **Contact:** The Steward

Known also as Strathbogie Castle, this glorious ruin stands in a beautiful setting on the banks of the River Deveron. Famed for its fine heraldic sculpture and inscribed stone friezes.

Location: OS Ref. NJ532 407. In Huntly on the A96. N side of the town.

Open: 1 Apr - 30 Sept: daily, 9.30am - 6.30pm, last ticket 6pm. 1 Oct - 31 Mar: Mon - Sat, 9.30am - 4.30pm, Suns, 2 - 4.30pm, last ticket 4pm. Closed Thur pm & Fris in winter.

Admission: Adult £3, Child £1, Conc. £2.

KILDRUMMY CASTLE ⚲

Alford, Aberdeenshire

Tel: 01975 571331

Owner: In the care of Historic Scotland   **Contact:** The Steward

Though ruined, the best example in Scotland of a 13th century castle with a curtain wall, four round towers, hall and chapel of that date. The seat of the Earls of Mar, it was dismantled after the first Jacobite rising in 1715.

Location: OS Ref. NJ455 164. 10m W of Alford on the A97. 16m SSW of Huntley.

Open: 1 Apr - 30 Sept: daily, 9.30am - 6.30pm, last ticket 6pm.

Admission: Adult £2, Child 75p, Conc. £1.50.

KILDRUMMY CASTLE GARDEN

Kildrummy, Aberdeenshire

Tel: 01975 571203 / 571277   **Contact:** Alastair J Laing

Ancient quarry, shrub and alpine gardens renowned for their interest and variety. Water gardens below ruined castle.

Location: OS Ref. NJ455 164. On A97 off A944 10m SW of Alford. 16m SSW of Huntley.

Open: Apr - Oct: daily, 10am - 5pm.

Admission: Adult £2.50, Child Free.

LEITH HALL ♛

Huntly, Aberdeenshire AB54 4NQ

Tel: 01464 831216   **Fax:** 01464 831594   www.nts.org.uk/leith.htm

Owner: The National Trust for Scotland   **Contact:** The Property Manager

This mansion house is built around a courtyard and was the home of the Leith family for almost 400 years. With an enviable family record of military service over the centuries, the house contains a unique collection of military memorabilia displayed in an exhibition 'For Crown and Country'. The graciously furnished rooms are a delight to wander through and present a fine impression of the lifestyle of the Leith family.

Location: OS Ref. NJ541 298. B9002, 1m W of Kennethmont, 7m S of Huntley.

Open: House & tearoom: 25 Mar-27 Oct: daily (except Mons & Tues) 12 noon - 5pm.

Admission: Adult £7, Conc. £5.25, Family £19. Groups: Adult £5.60, Child/School £1. Gardens & grounds only: Adult £2, Conc. £1.30, Family £6. Groups: Adult £1.60, Child/School £1.

⚬ Partial. WC. ▣

LICKLEYHEAD CASTLE

Auchleven, Insch, Aberdeenshire AB52 6PN

Tel: 01464 820200

Owner: The Leslie family   **Contact:** Mrs Cruden

A beautifully restored Laird's Castle, Lickleyhead was built by the Leslies c1450 and extensively renovated in 1629 by John Forbes of Leslie, whose initials are carved above the entrance. It is an almost unspoilt example of the transformation from 'Chateau-fort' to 'Chateau-maison' and boasts many interesting architectural features.

Location: OS Ref. NJ628 237. Auchleven is 2m S of Insch on B992. Twin pillars of castle entrance on left at foot of village.

Open: 1 Jun - 21 Sept: Tue & Sat by appointment only.

Admission: Free.

⚬ Unsuitable. ▣ Limited. No coaches. ⚬ In grounds, on leads.

MONYMUSK WALLED GARDEN

Home Farm, Monymusk, Aberdeen AB51 7HL

Tel: 01467 651543

Owner/Contact: Robbie McGregor

Mainly herbaceous plants in walled garden setting.

Location: OS Ref. NJ692 152. N side of B993, ½ m E of Monymusk village.

Open: Nov - Mar: Mon - Sat, 10am - 3pm, Suns, 12 noon - 3pm. Apr - Oct: Mon - Fri, 10am - 5pm, Sat & Sun, 11am - 5pm.

Admission: Free.

Grampian Highlands, Aberdeen and North East Coast

Doug Westland

PITMEDDEN GARDEN

ELLON, ABERDEENSHIRE AB41 0PD

www.nts.org.uk/pitmedden.html

Tel: 01651 842352 **Fax:** 01651 843188

Owner: The National Trust for Scotland **Contact:** The Property Manager

The centrepiece of this property is the Great Garden which was originally laid out in 1675 by Sir Alexander Seton, 1st Baronet of Pitmedden. The elaborate designs, inspired by the garden at the Palace of Holyroodhouse in Edinburgh, have been painstakingly recreated for the enjoyment of visitors. The 100 acre estate contains the very fine Museum of Farming Life, which presents a vivid picture of the lives and times of bygone days when the horse was the power in front of the plough and farm machinery was less complicated than it is today.

Location: OS Ref. NJ885 280. On A920 1m W of Pitmedden village and 14m N of Aberdeen.

Open: Garden, Visitor Centre, museum & tearoom: 1 May - 1 Sep: daily, 10am - 5pm.

Admission: Adult: £5, Conc. £3.75, Family £13.50. Groups: Adult £4, Child/School £1.

PROVOST SKENE'S HOUSE

45 GUEST ROW, OFF BROAD STREET, ABERDEEN AB10 1AS

www.aagm.co.uk

Tel: 01224 641086 **Fax:** 01224 632133

Owner: Aberdeen City Council **Contact:** Christine Rew

Built in the 16th century, Provost Skene's House is one of Aberdeen's few remaining examples of early burgh architecture. Splendid room settings include a suite of Georgian rooms, an Edwardian nursery, magnificent 17th century plaster ceilings and wood panelling. Costume gallery features changing displays of historic dress. The painted gallery houses the most important cycle of religious painting in North East Scotland.

Location: OS Ref. NJ943 064. Aberdeen city centre, off Broad Street.

Open: All year: Mon - Sat, 10am - 5pm, Suns, 1 - 4pm (closed 25/26/31 Dec & 1/2 Jan).

Admission: Free.

No photography in house. Small functions. Unsuitable. By arrangement. Nearby. Guide dogs only.

PLUSCARDEN ABBEY

Nr Elgin, Moray IV30 8UA

Tel: 01343 890257 **Fax:** 01343 890258

e-mail: monks@pluscardenabbey.org **Contact:** Father Giles

Valliscaulian, founded 1230.

Location: OS Ref. NJ142 576. On a minor road 6m SW of Elgin. Follow B9010 for first mile.

Open: All year: 4.45am - 8.30pm. Shop open 8.30am - 5pm.

Admission: Free.

ST MACHAR'S CATHEDRAL TRANSEPTS

Old Aberdeen

Tel: 0131 668 8800

Owner: In the care of Historic Scotland

The nave and towers of the Cathedral remain in use as a church, and the ruined transepts are in care. In the south transept is the fine altar tomb of Bishop Dunbar (1514 - 32).

Location: OS Ref. NJ939 088. In old Aberdeen. 1/2 m N of King's College.

Admission: Free.

SPYNIE PALACE

Elgin

Tel: 01343 546358

Owner: In the care of Historic Scotland **Contact:** The Steward

Spynie Palace was the residence of the Bishops of Moray from the 14th century to 1686. The site is dominated by the massive tower built by Bishop David Stewart (1461-77) and affords spectacular views across Spynie Loch.

Location: OS Ref. NJ231 659. 2m N of Elgin off the A941.

Open: 1 Apr - 30 Sept: daily, 9.30am - 6.30pm. 1 Oct - 31 Mar: Sats, 9.30am - 4.30pm, Suns, 2 - 4.30pm. Last ticket 30 mins before closing.

Admission: Adult £2, Child 75p, Conc. £1.50. Joint entry ticket with Elgin Cathedral: Adult £3.30, Child £1.20, Conc. £2.50.

TOLQUHON CASTLE

Aberdeenshire

Tel: 01651 851286

Owner: In the care of Historic Scotland **Contact:** The Steward

Tolquhon was built for the Forbes family. The early 15th century tower was enlarged between 1584 and 1589 with a large mansion around the courtyard. Noted for its highly ornamented gatehouse and pleasance.

Location: OS Ref. NJ874 286. 15m N of Aberdeen on the A920. 6m N of Ellon.

Open: 1 Apr - 30 Sept: daily, 9.30am - 6.30pm. 1 Oct - 31 Mar: Sats, 9.30am - 4.30pm, Suns, 2 - 4.30pm. Last ticket 30 mins before closing.

Admission: Adult £2, Child 75p, Conc. £1.50.

Special Events Index
◁ ◁ ◁ pgs 40-43

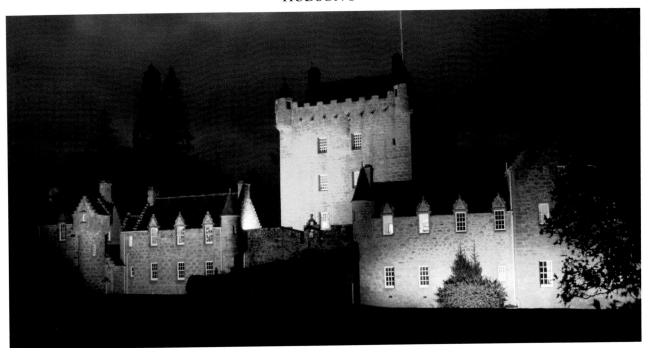

CAWDOR CASTLE 🏛

NAIRN

www.cawdorcastle.com

This splendid romantic castle dating from the late 14th century was built as a private fortress by the Thanes of Cawdor, and remains the home of the Cawdor family to this day. The ancient medieval tower was built around the legendary holly tree.

Although the house has evolved over 600 years, later additions mainly of the 17th century were all built in the Scottish vernacular style with slated roofs over walls and crow-stepped gables of mellow local stone. This style gives Cawdor a strong sense of unity, and the massive, severe exterior belies an intimate interior that gives the place a surprisingly personal, friendly atmosphere.

Good furniture, fine portraits and pictures, interesting objects and outstanding tapestries are arranged to please the family rather than to echo fashion or impress. Memories of Shakespeare's *Macbeth* give Cawdor an elusive, evocative quality that delights visitors.

GARDENS

The flower garden also has a family feel to it, where plants are chosen out of affection rather than affectation. This is a lovely spot between spring and late summer. The walled garden has been restored with a holly maze, paradise garden, knot garden and thistle garden. The wild garden beside its stream leads into beautiful trails through a spectacular mature mixed woodland, through which paths are helpfully marked and colour-coded.

Owner: The Dowager Countess Cawdor

▶ CONTACT

The Secretary
Cawdor Castle
Nairn
Scotland IV12 5RD

Tel: 01667 404615

Fax: 01667 404674

e-mail: info@ cawdorcastle.com

▶ LOCATION

OS Ref. NH850 500

From Edinburgh A9, 3½ hrs, Inverness 20 mins, Nairn 10 mins. Main road: A9, 14m.

Rail: Nairn Station 5m.

Bus: Inverness to Nairn bus route 200 yds.

Taxi: Cawdor Taxis 01667 404315.

Air: Inverness Airport 5m.

CONFERENCE/FUNCTION

ROOM	MAX CAPACITY
Cawdor Hall	40

ℹ️ 9 hole golf course, putting green, golf clubs for hire, Conferences, whisky tasting, musical entertainments, specialised garden visits. No photography, video taping or tripods inside.

📷 Gift, book and wool shops.

🍸 Lunches, sherry or champagne receptions.

♿ Visitors may alight at the entrance. WC. Only ground floor accessible.

☕ Licensed buttery, May-Oct, groups should book.

🅿️ 250 cars and 25 coaches. Two weeks' notice for group catering, coach drivers/couriers free.

👤 £2.60 per child. Room notes, quiz and answer sheet can be provided. Ranger service and nature trails.

🐕 Guide dogs only.

▶ OPENING TIMES

Summer
1 May - 13 October
Daily: 10am - 5.30pm.

Last admission 5pm.

Winter
14 October - 30 April
Closed.

▶ ADMISSION

Summer
House & Garden

Adult	£6.10
Child (5-15yrs)	£3.30
OAP/Student	£5.10
Family (2+5)	£18.00

Groups (20+)

Adult	£5.30
Child (5-15yrs)	£2.60
OAP/Student	£5.10

Garden only

Per person	£3.20

🎭 SPECIAL EVENTS

JUN 1 - 2
Special Gardens Weekend: Guided tours of gardens and Cawdor Big Wood.

DUNVEGAN CASTLE 🏛

ISLE OF SKYE

www.dunvegancastle.com

Owner: John Macleod of Macleod

▶ **CONTACT**

The Administrator
Dunvegan Castle
Isle of Skye
Scotland   IV55 8WF

Tel: 01470 521206
Fax: 01470 521205
Seal Tel: 01470 521500

e-mail: info@
dunvegancastle.com

▶ **LOCATION**

OS Ref. NG250 480

1m N of village. NW corner of Skye.

From Inverness A82 to Invermoriston, A887 to Kyle of Lochalsh 82m. From Fort William A82 to Invergarry, A87 to Kyle of Lochalsh 76m.

Kyle of Lochalsh to Dunvegan 45m via Skye Bridge (toll).

Ferry: To the Isle of Skye, 'roll-on, roll-off', 30 minute crossing.

Rail: Inverness to Kyle of Lochalsh 3 - 4 trains per day - 45m.

Bus: Portree 25m, Kyle of Lochalsh 45m.

Dunvegan is unique. It is the only Great House in the Western Isles of Scotland to have retained its family and its roof. It is the oldest home in the whole of Scotland continuously inhabited by the same family – the Chiefs of the Clan Macleod. A Castle placed on a rock by the sea - the curtain wall is dated before 1200 AD – its superb location recalls the Norse Empire of the Vikings, the ancestors of the Chiefs.

Dunvegan's continuing importance as a custodian of the Clan spirit is epitomised by the famous Fairy Flag, whose origins are shrouded in mystery but whose ability to protect both Chief and Clan is unquestioned. To enter Dunvegan is to arrive at a place whose history combines with legend to make a living reality.

GARDENS

The gardens and grounds extend over some ten acres of woodland walks, peaceful formal lawns and a water garden dominated by two spectacular natural waterfalls. The temperate climate aids in producing a fine show of rhododendrons and azaleas, the chief glory of the garden in spring. One is always aware of the proximity of the sea and many garden walks finish at the Castle Jetty, from where traditional boats make regular trips to view the delightful Seal Colony.

ℹ️ Gift and craft shop. Boat trips to seal colony. Pedigree Highland cattle. No photography in castle.

♿ Visitors may alight at entrance. WC.

🍴 Licensed restaurant, (cap. 70) special rates for groups, menus upon request. Tel: 01470 521310. Open late peak season for evening meals.

🧍 By appointment in English or Gaelic at no extra charge. If requested owner may meet groups, tour time 45mins.

🅿 120 cars and 10 coaches. Do not attempt to take passengers to Castle Jetty (long walk). If possible please book. Seal boat trip dependent upon weather.

Welcome by arrangement. Guide available on request.

🐕 In grounds only, on lead.

4 self-catering units, 3 of which sleep 6 and 1 of which sleeps 7.

▶ **OPENING TIMES**

Summer
25 March - 31 October
Daily: 10am - 5.30pm.
Last admission 5pm.

Winter
November - March
Daily: 11am - 4pm.
Last admission 3.30pm.

Closed Christmas Day, Boxing Day, New Year's Day and 2 January.

▶ **ADMISSION**

2000 prices
Summer

Castle & Gardens
Adult £6.00
Child* (5 -15yrs) £3.50
OAP/Student £5.50

Groups (10+) £5.50

Gardens only
Adult £4.00
Child* (5 -15yrs) £2.50

Seal Boats
Adult £4.00
Child* (5 -15yrs) £2.50

*Child under 5yrs Free.

Winter
11am - 4pm.
No boat trips.

ARMADALE CASTLE GARDENS & MUSEUM OF THE ISLES

ARMADALE, SLEAT, ISLE OF SKYE IV45 8RS

www.cland.demon.co.uk

Tel: 01471 844305 **Fax:** 01471 844275 **e-mail:** office@cland.demon.co.uk

Owner/Contact: Clan Donald Lands Trust

40 acre gardens with sea views to Knoydart across the Sound of Sleat. Sheltered and due to the warming effect of the gulf stream allowing exotic trees, shrubs and flowers to grow. Enjoy a complete experience to Armadale by visiting the Museum of the Isles within the gardens.

Location: OS Ref. NG630 020. 1m from Armadale – Mallaig ferry terminal and approximately 21m S of Skye Bridge.

Open: Apr - Oct: 9.30am - 5.30pm.

Admission: Adult £4, Child/Conc. £3. Booked Groups (min 8): £2.60.

🗖 🕎 🍴 🕭 🌳Licensed. 🍴Licensed. 🎦 By arrangement. 🅿 🔲 🐕In grounds, on leads. 🏠Self-catering cottages.

BALLINDALLOCH CASTLE 🏛

GRANTOWN-ON-SPEY, BANFFSHIRE AB37 9AX

www.ballindallochcastle.co.uk

Tel: 01807 500206 **Fax:** 01807 500210 **e-mail:** enquiries@ballindallochcastle.co.uk

Owner: Mr & Mrs Russell **Contact:** Mrs Clare Russell

Ballindalloch is a much loved family home and one of the few castles lived in continuously by its original owners, the Macpherson-Grants, since 1546. Filled with family memorabilia and a magnificent collection of 17th century Spanish paintings, it is home to the famous breed of Aberdeen Angus cattle. Beautiful rock and rose garden, river walks.

Location: OS Ref. NJ178 366. 14m NE of Grantown-on-Spey on A95, 22m S of Elgin on A95.

Open: Good Fri - 30 Sept: 10.30am - 5.30pm, closed Sats. Coaches all year by appointment.

Admission: House & Grounds: Adult £4.50, Child (6-16) £2, Conc. £4, Family (2+3) £10. Grounds only: Free. Groups: (20+) Adult £4, Child £2. Car park ticket £1.

🗖 🕭Ground floor & grounds. WC. 🔲 🅿 🎦 Audio-visual. 🐕In grounds, on leads in dog walking area.

Geoff Wilkinson

ATTADALE GARDENS

BY STRATHCARRON, ROSS-SHIRE IV54 8YX

www.attadale.com

Tel: 01520 722217 **Fax:** 01520 722546 **e-mail:** info@attadale.com

Owner/Contact: Mr & Mrs Ewen Macpherson

Old rhododendron and woodland gardens surrounding one of the prettiest houses on the West Coast. Outstanding water gardens planted with almost tropical profusion – giant gunnera, iris, bamboo, meconopsis and a large collection of primulas from China and the Himalayas. Sunken formal garden and restored Victorian kitchen and herb garden. Unusual damp loving plants for sale.

Location: OS Ref. NG920 400. On A890 between Strathcarron and South Strome. 12m N of A87.

Open: 1 Apr - 31 Oct: Mon - Sat, 10am - 5.30pm. Closed Suns.

Admission: Adult £3, Child £1. Coaches/guided tours by prior arrangement.

🕎 🍴Nearby.

CASTLE LEOD

Strathpeffer IV14 9AA

Tel/Fax: 01997 421264

Owner: The Earl of Cromartie **Contact:** The Secretary

An interesting L-plan 5 storey tower house, built in early 15th century and modified by Sir Roderick Mackenzie of Coigach about 1610, now set amongst some of the finest trees in Scotland. Seat of the Clan Mackenzie. Still occupied by the Mackenzie Earls of Cromartie. A Jacobite stronghold.

Location: OS Ref. NH485 593. 1km E of Strathpeffer on the A834 Strathpeffer to Dingwall road.

Open: 9 - 12 & 23 - 26 May; 6 - 9 & 20 - 23 Jun; 22 - 25 Aug; 11 - 15 Sept: 1 - 5pm (last admission 4pm).

Admission: Adult £4, Child £2.

ℹNo coaches. 🕭Unsuitable for wheelchairs. 🅿¹/₄ m.

CAWDOR CASTLE 🏛

See page 499 for full page entry.

CROMARTY COURTHOUSE

Church Street, Cromarty IV11 8XA

Tel/Fax: 01381 600418 **e-mail:** courthouse@mail.cali.co.uk **Contact:** David Alston

18th century town courthouse, visitor centre and museum.

Location: OS Ref. NH790 680. 25m N of Inverness.

Open: Apr - Oct: 10am - 5pm. Nov, Dec & Mar: 12 noon - 4pm.

Admission: Adult £3, Conc. £2, Family (2+4) £8.

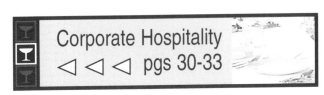

Corporate Hospitality ◁ ◁ ◁ pgs 30-33

Harvey Woods / NTS

CULLODEN

Culloden Moor, Inverness IV1 2ED

Tel: 01463 790607   **Fax:** 01463 794294   **www.**nts.org.uk/culloden.html

Owner: The National Trust for Scotland   **Contact:** Ross Mackenzie

No name in Scottish history evokes more emotion than that of Culloden, the bleak moor which in 1746 saw the hopes of the young Prince Charles Edward Stuart crushed, and the end of the Jacobite Rising, the 'Forty-Five'. The Prince's forces, greatly outnumbered by those of the brutal Duke of Cumberland, nevertheless went into battle with a courage which has passed into legend.

Location: OS Ref. NH745 450. On B9006, 5m E of Inverness.

Open: Site: 20 Jan - 24 Mar: daily, 10am - 4pm. 25 Mar - 27 Oct: daily, 9am - 6pm. 28 Oct - 24 Dec: daily, 10am - 4pm.

Admission: Visitor Centre & Old Leanach Cottage: Adult £5, Conc. £3.75, Family £13.50. Groups: £4.

ⓘ Visitor centre. ⬜ ⬜ ⬜ ⬜ Audio-visual. ⬜ In dog walking area only. ✳

DUNROBIN CASTLE 🏛

GOLSPIE, SUTHERLAND KW10 6SF

www.highlandescape.com

Tel: 01408 633177   **Fax:** 01408 634081   **e-mail:** dunrobin.est@btinternet.com

Owner: The Sutherland Trust   **Contact:** Keith Jones, Curator

Dates from the 13th century with additions in the 17th, 18th and 19th centuries. Wonderful furniture, paintings, library, ceremonial robes and memorabilia. Victorian museum in grounds with a fascinating collection including Pictish stones. Set in fine woodlands overlooking the sea. Magnificent formal gardens, one of few remaining French/Scottish formal parterres. Falconry display.

Location: OS Ref. NC850 010. 50m N of Inverness on A9. 1m NE of Golspie.

Open: 1 Apr - 31 May & 1 - 15 Oct: Mon - Sat, 10.30am - 4.30pm. Suns, 12 noon - 4.30pm. 1 Jun - 30 Sept: Mon - Sat, 10.30am - 5.30pm. Suns, 12 noon - 5.30pm (Jul & Aug: Suns, opens at 10.30am).

Admission: Adult £6.25, Child/Conc. £5. Booked groups: Adult £5.50, Child/Conc £4.50. Family (2+2) £17.

⬜ ⬜ ⬜ Unsuitable for wheelchairs. ⬜ ⬜ ⬜ By arrangement. ℙ ⬜

DOCHFOUR GARDENS

Dochgarroch, Inverness IV3 6JY

Tel: 01463 861218   **Fax:** 01463 861366

Owner: Dochfour Estate   **Contact:** Miss J Taylor

Victorian terraced garden near Inverness with panoramic views over Loch Dochfour. Magnificent specimen trees, naturalised daffodils, rhododendrons, water garden, yew topiary.

Location: OS Ref. NH620 610. 6m SW of Inverness on A82 to Fort William.

Open: Gardens: Apr - Sept, Mon - Fri, 10am - 4pm. House not open.

Admission: Garden walk - £1.50.

THE DOUNE OF ROTHIEMURCHUS 🏛

By Aviemore PH22 1QH

Tel: 01479 812345   **www.**rothiemurchus.net

Owner: J P Grant of Rothiemurchus   **Contact:** Rothiemurchus Visitor Centre

The family home of the Grants of Rothiemurchus was nearly lost as a ruin and has been under an ambitious repair programme since 1975. This exciting project may be visited on selected Mondays throughout the season. Book with the Visitor Centre for a longer 2hr 'Highland Lady' tour which explores the haunts of Elizabeth Grant of Rothiemurchus, born 1797, author of *Memoirs of a Highland Lady*, who vividly described the Doune and its surroundings from the memories of her childhood.

Location: OS Ref. NH900 100. 2m S of Aviemore on E bank of Spey river.

Open: House: selected Mons. Grounds: May - Aug: Mon, 10am - 12.30pm & 2 - 4.30pm, also 1st Mon in the month during winter.

Admission: House only £1. Tour (booking essential, min 4) £5.

ⓘ Visitor Centre. ⬜ ⬜ Obligatory. ℙ Limited. ⬜ In grounds, on leads.

DUNVEGAN CASTLE 🏛

See page 500 for full page entry.

Attadale Gardens

Mr & Mrs Ewen Macpherson

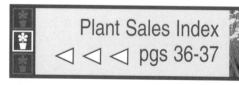

Plant Sales Index
◁ ◁ ◁ pgs 36-37

EILEAN DONAN CASTLE

Dornie, Kyle of Lochalsh, Wester IV40 8DX
Tel: 01599 555202 **Fax:** 01599 555262 **e-mail:** info@donan.f9.co.uk
www.eileandonancastle.com **Contact:** Rod Stenson – Castle Keeper
Location: OS Ref. NG880 260. On A87 8m E of Skye Bridge.
Open: Mar & Nov: 10am - 3.30pm. Apr - Oct: 10am - 5.30pm.
Admission: Adult £4, Conc. £3.20.

Historic Scotland

INVEREWE GARDEN 🌺

POOLEWE, ROSS & CROMARTY IV22 2LQ

www.nts.org.uk/inverewe.html

Tel: 01445 781200 **Fax:** 01445 781497
Owner: The National Trust for Scotland **Contact:** Keith Gordon
Where in Scotland will you see the tallest Australian gum trees in Britain, sweetly scented Chinese rhododendrons, exotic trees from Chile and Blue Nile lilies from South Africa, all growing on a latitude more northerly than Moscow? The answer is Inverewe: you are in Wester Ross, you are also in a sheltered garden, blessed by the North Atlantic Drift. In a spectacular lochside setting among pinewoods, Osgood Mackenzie's Victorian dreams have produced a glorious 50 acre mecca for garden lovers.
Location: OS Ref. NG860 820. On A832, by Poolewe, 6m NE of Gairloch, Highland.
Open: Garden: 25 Mar - 27 Oct. Visitor centre: 9.30am - 5.30pm. Garden: 9am - 9pm.
Admission: Adult £7, Conc. £5.25, Family £19. Groups: £5.60.
ℹ️Visitor centre. 📷 ♿Grounds. WC. 🍴 Licensed. 🅿 No shade for dogs.
🐕 Guide dogs only. ❄️

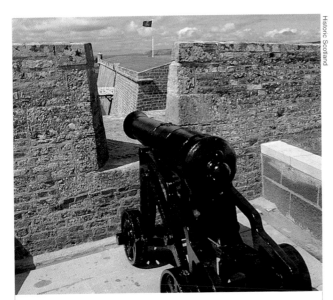

FORT GEORGE ⚔️

Ardersier by Inverness IV1 2TD

Owner: In the care of Historic Scotland **Contact:** Brian Ford
Tel: 01667 462777 **Fax:** 01667 462698
Built following the Battle of Culloden to subdue the Highlands, Fort George never saw a shot fired in anger. One of the most outstanding artillery fortifications in Europe with reconstructed barrack room displays. The Queen's Own Highlanders' Museum.
Location: OS Ref. NH762 567. 11m NE of Inverness off the A96 by Ardersier.
Open: Apr - Sept: daily, 9.30am - 6.30pm. Oct - Mar: Mon - Sat, 9.30am - 4.30pm; Suns, 2 - 4.30pm. Last ticket sold 45 mins before closing.
Admission: Adult £5, Child £1.50, Conc. £3.50. 10% discount for groups (10+).
ℹ️Picnic tables. 📷 🎭Private evening hire. ♿Wheelchairs available. WCs.
🍴In summer. 🅿 ■Free if pre-booked. 🐕In grounds, on leads. ❄️

Crown copyright Reserved Historic Scotland

GLENFINNAN MONUMENT 🌺

Inverness-shire PH37 4LT

Tel/**Fax:** 01397 722250 **www.**nts.org.uk/glenfinnan.html
Owner: The National Trust for Scotland **Contact:** Mrs Lillias Grant
The monument, situated on the scenic road to the Isles, is set amid superb Highland scenery at the head of Loch Shiel. It was erected in 1815 in tribute to the clansmen who fought and died in the Jacobite cause. Prince Charles Edward Stuart's standard was raised near here in 1745. Despite its inspired beginnings, the campaign came to a grim conclusion on the Culloden battlefield in 1746.
Location: OS Ref. NM906 805. On A830, 18m W of Fort William, Lochaber.
Open: Site: All year: daily. Monument & Visitor Centre: 25 Mar - 27 Oct: daily, 10am - 6pm.
Admission: Adult £2, Conc. £1.50, Family £5.50. Groups: £1.60.
ℹ️Visitor centre. 📷 ♿Grounds. WC. ■ 🅿 🐕In grounds, on leads. ❄️
🛏️Tel for details.

HUGH MILLER'S COTTAGE 🌺

Cromarty IV11 8XA
Tel: 01381 600245 **www.**nts.org.uk/hugh.html
Owner: The National Trust for Scotland **Contact:** Ms Frieda Gostwick
Furnished thatched cottage of c1698, birthplace of eminent geologist and writer Hugh Miller. Exhibition and video.
Location: OS Ref. NH790 680. Via Kessock Bridge & A832, in Cromarty, 22m NE of Inverness.
Open: 1 May - 29 Sep: daily, 12 noon - 5pm.
Admission: Adult £5, Conc. £3.75, Family £13.50. Groups: £4.
♿Unsuitable. 🅿 Public parking at shore. 🐕 Guide dogs only.

URQUHART CASTLE ⚔️

DRUMNADROCHIT, LOCH NESS

Tel: 01456 450551
Owner: In the care of Historic Scotland **Contact:** The Steward
The remains of one of the largest castles in Scotland dominate a rocky promontory on Loch Ness. Most of the existing buildings date from the 16th century. New visitor centre with original artefacts, audio-visual presentation, shop and café.
Location: OS Ref. NH531 286. On Loch Ness, 1¹/2m S of Drumnadrochit on A82.
Open: 1 Apr - 30 Sept: daily, 9.30am - 6.30pm, last ticket 5.45pm. 1 Oct - 31 Mar: daily, 9.30am - 4.30pm, last ticket 3.45pm.
Admission: Adult £5, Child £1.20, Conc. £3.75.
📷 ♿Partial. WCs. ■ 🅿 📷 ■Free if pre-booked. 🐕Guide dogs only. ❄️

BALFOUR CASTLE

Shapinsay, Orkney Islands KW17 2DY

Tel: 01856 711282 **Fax:** 01856 711283 **e-mail:** balfourcastle@btinternet.com

Owner/Contact: Mrs Lidderdale

Built in 1848.

Location: OS Ref. HY475 164 on Shapinsay Island, 3^1/2 m NNE of Kirkwall.

Open: Mid-May – mid-Sept: Weds, 2.30 - 5.30pm.

Admission: £16 including boat fare, guided tour, gardens & afternoon tea. Child £7.50.

BISHOP'S & EARL'S PALACES

Kirkwall, Orkney

Tel: 01856 875461

Owner: In the care of Historic Scotland   **Contact:** The Steward

The Bishop's Palace is a 12th century hall-house with a round tower built by Bishop Reid in 1541-48. The adjacent Earl's Palace built in 1607 has been described as the most mature and accomplished piece of Renaissance architecture left in Scotland.

Location: Bishop's Palace: OS Ref. HY447 108. Earl's Palace: OS Ref. HY448 108. In Kirkwall on A960.

Open: 1 Apr - 30 Sept: daily, 9.30am - 6.30pm, last ticket 6pm.

Admission: Adult £2, Child 75p, Conc. £1.50. Joint entry ticket available for all the Orkney monuments: Adult £11, Child £3.50, Conc. £8.

BLACK HOUSE

Arnol, Isle of Lewis

Tel: 01851 710395

Owner: In the care of Historic Scotland   **Contact:** The Steward

A traditional Lewis thatched house, fully furnished, complete with attached barn, byre and stockyard. A peat fire burns in the open hearth. New visitor centre open and restored 1920s croft house.

Location: OS Ref. NB320 500. In Arnol village, 11m NW of Stornoway on A858.

Open: 1 Apr - 30 Sept: Mon - Sat, 9.30am - 6.30pm, last ticket 6pm. 1 Oct - 31 Mar: Mon - Thur & Sat, 9.30am - 4.30pm, last ticket 4pm.

Admission: Adult £2.80, Child £1, Conc. £2.

BROCH OF GURNESS

Aikerness, Orkney

Tel: 01831 579478

Owner: In the care of Historic Scotland   **Contact:** The Steward

Protected by three lines of ditch and rampart, the base of the broch is surrounded by a warren of Iron Age buildings.

Location: OS Ref. HY383 268. At Aikerness, about 14m NW of Kirkwall on A966.

Open: 1 Apr - 30 Sept: daily, 9.30am - 6.30pm, last ticket 6pm.

Admission: Adult £2.80, Child £1, Conc. £2. Joint entry ticket available for all Orkney monuments: Adult £11, Child £3.50, Conc. £8.

CARRICK HOUSE

Carrick, Eday, Orkney KW17 2AB

Tel: 01857 622260

Owner: Mr & Mrs Joy   **Contact:** Mrs Rosemary Joy

17th century house of 3 storeys, built by John Stewart, Lord Kinclaven Earl of Carrick younger brother of Patrick, 2nd Earl of Orkney in 1633.

Location: OS Ref. NT227 773. N of island of Eday on minor roads W of B9063 just W of the shore of Calf Sound. Regular ferry service.

Open: Mid-Jun - mid-Sept: Sun afternoons, also guided tours of the house, 2pm onwards. Other times by arrangement.

Admission: Adult £2, Child £1.

🛈 ✳

JARLSHOF PREHISTORIC & NORSE SETTLEMENT

Shetland

Tel: 01950 460112

Owner: In the care of Historic Scotland   **Contact:** The Steward

Over 3 acres of remains spanning 3,000 years from the Stone Age. Oval-shaped Bronze Age houses, Iron Age broch and wheel houses. Viking Long Houses, medieval farmstead and 16th century laird's house.

Location: OS Ref. HY401 096. At Sumburgh Head, 22m S of Lerwick on the A970.

Open: 1 Apr - 30 Sept: daily, 9.30am - 6.30pm. Last adm. ^{1}/2 hr before closing.

Admission: Adult £3, Child £1, Conc. £2.20.

MAES HOWE

Orkney

Tel: 01856 761606

Owner: In the care of Historic Scotland   **Contact:** The Steward

This world-famous tomb was built in Neolithic times, before 2700 BC. The large mound covers a stone-built passage and a burial chamber with cells in the walls. Runic inscriptions tell of how it was plundered of its treasures by Vikings.

Location: OS Ref. NY318 128. 9m W of Kirkwall on the A965.

Open: 1 Apr - 30 Sept: daily, 9.30am - 6.30pm. 1 Oct - 31 Mar: daily, 9.30am - 5pm except Thurs pm, Fris and Suns am.

Admission: Adult £2.80, Child £1, Conc. £2. Joint entry ticket available for all Orkney monuments: Adult £11, Child £3.50, Conc. £8. Admission, shop and refreshments at nearby Tormiston Mill.

RING OF BRODGAR STONE CIRCLE & HENGE

Stromness, Orkney

Tel: 0131 668 8800

Owner/Contact: In the care of Historic Scotland

A magnificent circle of upright stones with an enclosing ditch spanned by causeways. Of late Neolithic date.

Location: OS Ref. HY294 134. 5m NE of Stromness.

Open: Any reasonable time.

Admission: Free.

Historic Scotland

SKARA BRAE & SKAILL HOUSE

SANDWICK, ORKNEY

Tel: 01856 841815

Owner: Historic Scotland/Major M R S Macrae   **Contact:** The Steward

Skara Brae is one of the best preserved groups of Stone Age houses in Western Europe. Built before the Pyramids, the houses contain stone furniture, hearths and drains. New visitor centre and replica house with joint admission with Skaill House – 17th century home of the Laird who excavated Skara Brae.

Location: OS6 HY231 188. 19m NW of Kirkwall on the B9056.

Open: Apr - Sept: daily, 9.30am - 6.30pm. Oct - Mar: Mon - Sat, 9.30am - 4.30pm, Suns, 2 - 4.30pm.

Admission: Apr - Sept: Adult £4.50, Child £1.30, Conc. £3.30. Oct - Mar: Adult £3.50, Child £1.20, Conc. £2.60. 10% discount for groups (10+). Joint ticket with other Orkney sites available.

🛈 Visitor centre. ▣ ♿ Partial. WCs. ▣ Licensed. 🅿
▣ Free school visits when booked. 🐕 Guide dogs only. ✳

TANKERNESS HOUSE

Broad Street, Kirkwall, Orkney

Tel: 01856 873191 **Fax:** 01856 871560

Owner: Orkney Islands Council   **Contact:** Bryce S Wilson

A fine vernacular 16th century town house contains The Orkney Museum.

Location: OS Ref. HY446 109. In Kirkwall opposite W end of cathedral.

Open: Oct - Apr: Mon - Sat, 10.30am - 12.30pm & 1.30 - 5pm. May - Sept: Mon - Sat, 10.30am - 5pm, Suns, 2 - 5pm. Gardens always open.

Admission: Free.

THE REGIONS OF
WALES

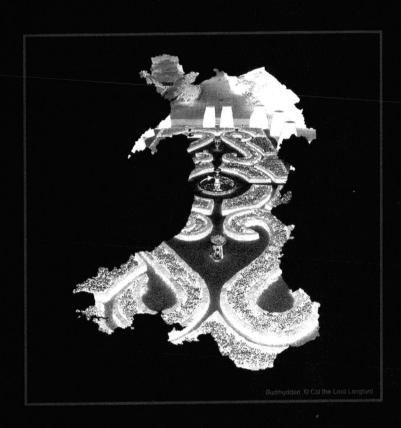

Bodrhyddan © Col the Lord Langford

WALES

Wales

WESTERN
ISLES

HIGHLANDS & SKYE

GRAMPIAN
HIGHLANDS

PERTHSHIRE/FIFE

WEST
HIGHLANDS
ISLANDS

GREATER
GLASGOW

EDINBURGH

BORDERS

SOUTH WEST SCOTLAND

NORTHUMBER-
LAND

CUMBRIA

DURHAM

TYNE & WEAR

DONEGAL

LONDONDERRY

TYRONE

ANTRIM

FERMANAGH

ARMAGH

DOWN

SLIGO

MONAGHAN

LEITRIM

CAVAN

MAYO

ROSCOMMON

LONGFORD

LOUTH

ISLE OF MAN

YORKSHIRE

LANCASHIRE

GALWAY

WESTMEATH

MEATH

OFFALY

KILDARE

DUBLIN

ISLE OF
ANGLESEY

MERSEYSIDE

CHESHIRE

DERBY-
SHIRE

NOTTING-
HAMSHIRE

LINCOLNSHIRE

CLARE

LAOIS

WICKLOW

CONWY

GWYNEDD

STAFFORD-
SHIRE

LEICESTER-
SHIRE

RUTLAND

NORFOLK

CARLOW

SHROP-
SHIRE

WEST
MIDLANDS

NORTHAMPTON-
SHIRE

CAMBRIDGE-
SHIRE

LIMERICK

KILKENNY

TIPPERARY

WEXFORD

POWYS

WORCESTER-
SHIRE

WARWICK-
SHIRE

SUFFOLK

KERRY

WATERFORD

CORK

CEREDIGION

HEREFORD-
SHIRE

BEDFORDSHIRE

PEMBROKE-
SHIRE

CARMARTHEN-
SHIRE

GLOUCESTER-
SHIRE

BUCKINGHAM-
SHIRE

HERTFORD-
SHIRE

ESSEX

SWANSEA

CARDIFF

OXFORD-
SHIRE

LONDON

CARDIFF

BERKSHIRE

WILTSHIRE

SURREY

KENT

SOMERSET

HAMPSHIRE

W. SUSSEX

E. SUSSEX

DEVON

DORSET

ISLE OF WIGHT

CORNWALL

Aberglasney Restoration Trust

Aberglasney Gardens

"He has a proud hall,
A fortress made bright with whitewash,
And encompassing it all around
Nine green gardens.
Orchard trees and crooked vines,
Young oaks reaching up to the sky."

Lewis Glyn Cothi, Ode to Rhydderch ap Rhys 1477
(trans. Dafydd Johnston)

Jonn Dyer (1699 - 1757)

Mr Thomas Phillips

Aberglasney Restoraton Trust

The story of Aberglasney is a wonderful and beguiling tale of one beautiful house and garden's changing fortunes over many centuries. Much of its past is shadowy but enough is bewitchingly intriguing to make the work of the Aberglasney Restoration Trust over the last four years so rewarding and fruitful.

Records going back about 500 years, just before Henry Tudor became Henry VII, mention *'nine green gardens'* in the parish of Llangathen, and it is thought that the poet Cothi's words refer to the medieval gardens at Aberglasney in Carmarthenshire. The property only became known as Aberglasney in the mid-1600s, having been acquired by Bishop Rudd in c1600. It is Rudd, Bishop of St Davids and a high-flying cleric, who built the house. With his son Sir Rice Rudd, a favourite of James I, who took over the property in 1614, he obviously had ideas of turning the estate into a private palace. The Gatehouse and recently restored Jacobean Cloister Garden date from this period and are what make Aberglasney so remarkable today.

The Cloister Garden is truly an extraordinary feature and a rare piece of garden history. To the west of the existing house stands a three-sided vast parapet walkway. The house itself is a little apart at the fourth side, creating the final side of a loose rectangle. This type of long parapet walkway is understood to have been very fashionable around the end of the reign of Elizabeth I. No other examples now exist, many having been destroyed in the Civil War or were swept away by the Landscape Movement of the 18th century.

The Pool Garden may not be unique, but is formal rectangular shape is in keeping with Jacobean garden fashion. Step back in time and let your imagination fly, and you can visualise the Bishop and his wife in courtly dress walking in the Cloisters on a summer's evening – the picture is idyllic.

However, Aberglasney's fortunes have not always been so prosperous. It is an estate which has gone from splendid heights at one moment to plunging depths of decay at another. The Restoration Trust has done a magnificent job in a short space of time to return Aberglasney to its former glory.

Amongst other treasures to be enjoyed at Aberglasney is a Yew Tunnel, again unique in the UK. A masterful job has been done by Penelope Hobhouse to meld together the formal areas of the garden – the Cloister Walk, Upper Walled Garden, Kitchen Garden and Pool Garden. These new plantings are cleverly complemented by the natural parts of the garden such as the Stream Garden, Pigeon House Wood and Bishop Rudd's Walk.

As with all projects of this kind, Aberglasney will be a wonderful place to visit over the years – a place to watch and learn how this *'garden lost in time'* develops in the 21st century. It is sure not to disappoint. ⌁

For further details about *Aberglasney Gardens* see entry on page 519.

Aberglasney Restoraton Trust

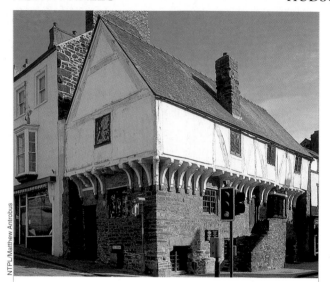

ABERCONWY HOUSE ✤

CASTLE STREET, CONWY LL32 8AY

Tel: 01492 592246 **Fax:** 01492 585153

Owner: The National Trust   **Contact:** The Custodian

Dating from the 14th century, this is the only medieval merchant's house in Conwy to have survived the turbulent history of this walled town for nearly six centuries. Furnished rooms and an audio-visual presentation show daily life from different periods in its history.

Location: OS Ref. SH781 777. At junction of Castle Street and High Street.

Open: 23 Mar - 3 Nov: daily except Tues, 11am - 5pm. Last adm. 30 mins before close.

Admission: Adult £2, Child £1, Family (2+2) £5. Pre-booked groups (15+) £1.60. National Trust members Free.

ℹ️No indoor photography. 📷All year. ✈️By arrangement. 🎧
🅿️In town car parks only. ■ ♿Guide dogs only.

BEAUMARIS CASTLE ✤

BEAUMARIS, ANGLESEY LL58 8AP

www.cadw.wales.gov.uk

Tel: 01248 810361

Owner: In the care of Cadw   **Contact:** The Custodian

The most technically perfect medieval castle in Britain, standing midway between Caernarfon and Conwy, commanding the old ferry crossing to Anglesey. A World Heritage Listed Site.

Location: OS Ref. SH608 762. 5m NE of Menai Bridge (A5) by A545. 7m from Bangor.

Open: 27 Mar - 26 May: 9.30am - 5pm. 27 May - 1 Oct: 9.30am - 6pm. 2 - 29 Oct: 9.30am - 5pm. 30 Oct - 31 Mar: Mon - Sat, 9.30am - 4pm, Suns, 11am - 4pm. Closed 24 - 26 Dec & 1 Jan. Opening times & prices subject to review Mar 2002.

Admission: Adult £2.50, Child/Conc. £2, Family £7.

📷 ♿ ✈️ 🅿️ ♿Guide dogs only. ❋

BODELWYDDAN CASTLE

BODELWYDDAN, DENBIGHSHIRE LL18 5YA

www.bodelwyddan-castle.co.uk

Tel: 01745 584060 **Fax:** 01745 584563 **e-mail:** enquiries@bodelwyddan-castle.co.uk

Owner: Bodelwyddan Castle Trust   **Contact:** Kevin Mason

Set against the Clwydian Hills, Bodelwyddan Castle is the Welsh home of the National Portrait Gallery. The sequence of rooms range from the early to late 19th century including period furniture from the Victoria and Albert Museum and sculpture from the Royal Academy of Arts. Free audio tour. Victorian games gallery. Terrace café and courtyard. An ideal wedding venue.

Location: OS Ref. SH999 749. Follow signs off A55 expressway. 2m W of St Asaph, opposite Marble Church.

Open: Nov - Apr: daily except Mon & Fri; May, Jun, Sept & Oct: daily except Fri: 10.30am - 5pm (4pm in Winter).

Admission: Adult £4, Child (under 16yrs) £2.50 (under 5yrs Free), OAP £3.50, Family (2+2) £10. Discounts for schools, groups & disabled. Season ticket available.

📷 🚻 ♿Partial. WCs. ■ ✈️By arrangement. 🎧 🅿️ ■ ♿Guide dogs only. ❋ 🔔

BODNANT GARDEN ❧
TAL-Y-CAFN, COLWYN BAY LL28 5RE

www.sissons.demon.co.uk/bodnant.htm

Tel: 01492 650460 **Fax:** 01492 650448

Owner: The National Trust   **Contact:** General Manager & Head Gardener

Bodnant Garden is one of the finest gardens in the country not only for its magnificent collections of rhododendrons, camellias and magnolias but also for its idyllic setting above the River Conwy with extensive views of the Snowdonia range. Visit in early Spring and be rewarded by the sight of masses of golden daffodils and other spring bulbs, as well as the beautiful blooms of the magnolias, camellias and flowering cherries. The spectacular rhododendrons and azaleas will delight from mid-April until late May, whilst the famous original Laburnum Arch is an overwhelming mass of yellow bloom from mid-May to mid-June. The herbaceous borders, roses, hydrangeas, clematis and water lilies flower from the middle of June until September. This 32-ha garden has many interesting features including the Lily Terrace, pergola, Canal Terrace, Pin Mill and the Dell Garden.

Location: OS Ref. SH801 723. 8 miles S of Llandudno and Colwyn Bay, off A470. Signposted from A55.

Open: 16 Mar - 3 Nov: daily, 10am - 5pm.

Admission: Adult £5.20, Child £2.60. Groups (20+) £4.70. Refreshment Pavilion: Daily from 11am (Entrance fee does not have to be paid for the Pavilion).

◻ ⊞ ⧉ Partial. WCs. ▣ **P** ⊠ Guide dogs only.

CAERNARFON CASTLE ✚
CASTLE DITCH, CAERNARFON LL55 2AY

www.cadw.wales.gov.uk

Tel: 01286 677617

Owner: In the care of Cadw   **Contact:** The Custodian

The most famous, and perhaps the most impressive castle in Wales. Taking nearly 50 years to build, it proved the costliest of Edward I's castles. A World Heritage Listed Site.

Location: OS Ref. SH477 626. In Caernarfon, just W of town centre.

Open: 27 Mar - 26 May: 9.30am - 5pm. 27 May - 1 Oct: 9.30am - 6pm. 2 - 29 Oct: 9.30am - 5pm. 30.Oct - 31 Mar: Mon - Sat, 9.30am - 4pm, Suns, 11am - 4pm. Closed 24 - 26 Dec & 1 Jan. Opening/admission details subject to review Mar 2002.

Admission: Adult £4.20, Child/Conc. £3.20, Family £11.60.

◻ ⧉ **P** ⊠ Guide dogs only. ❄

BODRHYDDAN
Rhuddlan, Clwyd LL18 5SB

Tel: 01745 590414 **www:** bodrhyddan.co.uk

Owner/Contact: Colonel The Lord Langford OBE DL

The home of Lord Langford and his family, Bodrhyddan is basically a 17th century house with 19th century additions by the famous architect, William Eden Nesfield, although traces of an earlier building exist. The house has been in the hands of the same family since it was built over 500 years ago. There are notable pieces of armour, pictures, period furniture, a 3,000 year old mummy, a formal parterre, a woodland garden and attractive picnic areas. Bodrhyddan is a Grade I listing, making it one of few in Wales to remain in private hands.

Location: OS Ref. SJ045 788. On the A5151 midway between Dyserth and Rhuddlan, 4m SE of Rhyl.

Open: Jun - Sept inclusive: Tues & Thurs, 2 - 5.30pm.

Admission: House & Gardens: Adult £4, Child £2. Gardens only: Adult £2, Child £1.

⊤ Receptions by special arrangement. ⧉ Partial. ▣ ⒡ Obligatory. **P**

BRYN BRAS CASTLE
Llanrug, Caernarfon, Gwynedd LL55 4RE

Tel/Fax: 01286 870210 **e-mail:** holidays@brynbrascastle.co.uk

www.brynbrascastle.co.uk

Owner: Mr & Mrs N E Gray-Parry   **Contact:** Marita Gray-Parry

Built in the Neo-Romanesque style in 1830, on an earlier structure and probably designed by Thomas Hopper. Elegantly romantic family home with fine stained-glass, panelling, interesting ceilings and richly carved furniture. The castle stands in the beautiful Snowdonian range and the extensive gardens include herbaceous borders, walled knot garden, woodland walks, stream and pools, 1/4 m mountain walk with superb views of Snowdon, Anglesey and the sea. Picnic area.

Location: OS Ref. SH543 625. 1/2 m off A4086 at Llanrug, 4 1/2 m E of Caernarfon.

Open: Only for groups by appointment.

Admission: By arrangement. No young children please.

▣ ⊠ ⊞ Self-catering apartments for twos within castle. ❄

CHIRK CASTLE ❧
CHIRK LL14 5AF

Tel: 01691 777701 **Fax:** 01691 774706

Owner: The National Trust   **Contact:** The Property Manager

700 year old Chirk Castle, a magnificent marcher fortress, commands fine views over the surrounding countryside. Rectangular with a massive drum tower at each corner, the castle has beautiful formal gardens with clipped yews, roses and a variety of flowering shrubs. Voted best National Trust garden in 1999. The dramatic dungeon is a reminder of the castle's turbulent history, whilst later occupants have left elegant state rooms, furniture, tapestries and portraits. The castle was sold for five thousand pounds to Sir Thomas Myddelton in 1595, and his descendants continue to live in part of the castle today.

Location: OS Ref. SJ275 388. 8m S of Wrexham off A483, 2m from Chirk village.

Open: 23 Mar - 3 Nov: daily (except Mons & Tues) & BHs throughout the season. Castle: Mar - Sept: 12 noon - 5pm. Oct: 12 noon - 4pm. Last admission 1/2 hr before close. Garden: Mar - Sept: 11am - 6pm. Oct: 11am - 5pm. Last admission 1hr before closing.

Admission: Adult £5.60, Child £2.80, Family (2+3) £14. Pre-booked groups (15+) £4.50. Garden only: Adults £3.40, Child £1.70.

ⓘ No indoor photography. ◻ ⧉ ▣ Licensed. ⒡ By arrangement. **P** ▣ ⊠ Guide dogs only.

North Wales

COCHWILLAN OLD HALL
Talybont, Bangor, Gwynedd LL57 3AZ

Tel: 01248 355853

Owner: R C H Douglas Pennant   **Contact:** Mrs G Lloyd

A fine example of medieval architecture with the present house dating from about 1450. It was probably built by William Gryffydd who fought for Henry VII at Bosworth. Once owned in the 17th century by John Williams who became Archbishop of York. The house was restored from a barn in 1971.

Location: OS Ref. SH606 695. $3^1/2$ m SE of Bangor. 1m SE of Talybont off A55.

Open: By appointment.

Admission: Please telephone for details.

❄

DENBIGH CASTLE ✠
Denbigh, Clwyd

Tel: 01745 813385   www.cadw.wales.gov.uk

Owner: In the care of Cadw   **Contact:** The Custodian

Crowning the summit of a prominent outcrop dominating the Vale of Clwyd, the principal feature of this spectacular site is the great gatehouse dating back to the 11th century. Some of the walls can still be walked by visitors.

Location: OS Ref. SJ052 658. Denbigh via A525, A543 or B5382.

Open: Early Apr - late Oct: Mon - Fri, 10am - 5.30pm. Sats & Suns, 9.30am - 5.30pm. Winter: open site. Opening/admission details subject to review Mar 2002.

Admission: Castle: Adult £2, Child/Conc. £1.50, Family £5.50.

📷 🅿 🖼 Guide dogs only. ❄

DOLWYDDELAN CASTLE ✠
Blaenau Ffestiniog, Gwynedd

Tel: 01690 750366   www.cadw.wales.gov.uk

Owner: In the care of Cadw   **Contact:** The Custodian

Standing proudly on a ridge, this stern building remains remarkably intact and visitors cannot fail to be impressed with the great solitary square tower, built by Llewelyn the Great in the early 13th century.

Location: OS Ref. SH722 522. A470(T) Blaenau Ffestiniog to Betws-y-Coed, 1m W of Dolwyddelan.

Open: Early Apr - late Oct: daily, 9.30am - 6.30pm. Late Oct - late Mar: Mon - Sat, 9.30am - 4pm, Suns, 11am - 4pm. Closed 24 - 26 Dec & 1 Jan. Opening/admission details subject to review Mar 2002.

Admission: Adult £2, Child/Conc. £1.50, Family £5.50.

🔲 🅿 🖼 Guide dogs only. ❄

Cadw: Welsh Historic Monuments. Crown Copyright

CONWY CASTLE ✠
CONWY LL32 8AY
www.cadw.wales.gov.uk

Tel: 01492 592358

Owner: In the care of Cadw   **Contact:** The Custodian

Taken together the castle and town walls are the most impressive of the fortresses built by Edward I, and remain the finest and most impressive in Britain. A World Heritage Listed Site.

Location: OS Ref. SH783 774. Conwy by A55 or B5106.

Open: 27 Mar - 26 May: 9.30am - 5pm. 27 May - 1 Oct: 9.30am - 6pm. 2 - 29 Oct: 9.30am - 5pm. 30 Oct - 31 Mar: Mon - Sat, 9.30am - 4pm, Suns, 11am - 4pm. Closed 24 - 26 Dec & 1 Jan. Opening/admission details subject to review Mar 2002.

Admission: Adult £3.60, Child/OAP £2.60, Family £9.80.

📷 ♿ 🎫 By arrangement. 🅿 🖼 Guide dogs only. ❄

NT Photographic Library / Andreas Van Einsiedel

ERDDIG ❀
Nr WREXHAM LL13 0YT

Tel: 01978 355314   **Fax:** 01978 313333   **Info Line:** 01978 315151

Owner: The National Trust   **Contact:** Jamie Watson

One of the most fascinating houses in Britain, not least because of the unusually close relationship that existed between the family of the house and their servants. The beautiful and evocative range of outbuildings includes kitchen, laundry, bakehouse, stables, sawmill, smithy and joiner's shop, while the stunning state rooms display most of their original 18th & 19th century furniture and furnishings, including some exquisite Chinese wallpaper. The large walled garden has been restored to its 18th century format design with Victorian parterre and yew walk, and also contains the National Ivy Collection. There is an extensive park with woodland walks.

Location: OS Ref. SJ326 482. 2m S of Wrexham.

Open: 23 Mar - 3 Nov: daily except Thurs & Fris, open Good Fri. House: 12 noon - 5pm. Garden: 11am - 6pm (10am - 6pm during Jul & Aug). From 1 Oct: House: 12 noon - 4pm, Garden: 11am - 5pm. Last admission 1 hr before closing.

Admission: All-inclusive ticket: Adult £6.60, Child £3.30, Family (2+3) £16.50. Pre-booked group (15+) £5.30. Outbuildings & Garden: Adult £3.40, Child £1.70, Family (2+3) £8.50, Pre-booked groups (15+) £2.70. NT members Free.

📷 ❄ ♿ Partial. WCs. 🎫 Licensed. 📹 AV presentation. 🅿 🖼 Guide dogs only.

CRICCIETH CASTLE ✠
Castle Street, Criccieth, Gwynedd LL52 0DP

Tel: 01766 522227   www.cadw.wales.gov.uk

Owner: In the care of Cadw   **Contact:** The Custodian

Overlooking Cardigan Bay, Criccieth Castle is the most striking of the fortresses built by the native Welsh Princes. Its inner defences are dominated by a powerful twin-towered gatehouse.

Location: OS Ref. SH500 378. A497 to Criccieth from Porthmadog or Pwllheli.

Open: 1 Apr - 26 May: 10am - 5pm. 27 May - 24 Sept: 10am - 6pm. Opening/admission details subject to review Mar 2002. Winter: open site.

Admission: Adult £2.50, Child/Conc. £2, Family £7.

📷 🅿 🖼 Guide dogs only. ❄

FFERM

Pontblyddyn, Mold, Flintshire

Tel/Fax: 01352 770217

Owner/Contact: Dr M Jones-Mortimer

17th century farmhouse. Viewing is limited to 7 persons at any one time. Prior booking is recommended. No toilets or refreshments.

Location: OS Ref. SJ279 603. Access from A541 in Pontblyddyn, 3$\frac{1}{2}$ m SE of Mold.

Open: 2nd Wed in every month, 2 - 5pm. Pre-booking is recommended.

Admission: £4.

GLANSEVERN HALL GARDENS

Berriew, Welshpool, Powys SY21 8AH

Tel: 01686 640200 **Fax:** 01686 640829

Owner: Mr G and Miss M Thomas **Contact:** Mr & Mrs R N Thomas

A classic Greek revival house romantically positioned on banks of River Severn. Over 18 acres of mature gardens notable for variety of unusual tree species. Also much new planting. Lakeside and woodland walks, water and rock gardens, grotto, walled rose garden.

Location: OS Ref. SJ195 001. On A483, 5m S of Welshpool, 1m SE of Berriew.

Open: May - Sept: Fris, Sats and BH Mons, 12 noon - 6pm. Groups by appointment on other days.

Admission: Adult £3, Child (under 16) Free.

Grounds. In grounds, on leads.

GWYDIR CASTLE

LLANRWST, GWYNEDD LL26 0PN

www.gwydircastle.co.uk

Tel/Fax: 01492 641687 **e-mail:** info@gwydircastle.co.uk

Owner/Contact: Mr & Mrs Welford

Gwydir Castle is situated in the beautiful Conwy Valley and is set within a Grade I listed, 10 acre garden. Built by the illustrious Wynn family c1500, Gwydir is a fine example of a Tudor courtyard house, incorporating re-used medieval material from the dissolved Abbey of Maenan. Further additions date from c1600 and c1826. The important 1640s panelled Dining Room has now been reinstated, following its repatriation from the New York Metropolitan Museum.

Location: OS Ref. SH795 610. $\frac{1}{2}$ m W of Llanrwst on A5106.

Open: 1 Mar - 31 Oct: daily, 10am - 5pm. Limited openings at other times. Occasional weddings on Sats.

Admission: Adult £3, Child £1.50. Group discount 10%.

Partial. By arrangement. By arrangement. 2 doubles.

GYRN CASTLE

Llanasa, Holywell, Flintshire CH8 9BG

Tel/Fax: 01745 853500

Owner/Contact: Sir Geoffrey Bates BT

Dating, in part, from 1700, castellated 1820. Large picture gallery, panelled entrance hall. Pleasant woodland walks and fantastic views to the River Mersey and the Lake District.

Location: OS Ref. SJ111 815. 26m W of Chester, off A55, 4$\frac{1}{2}$ m SE of Prestatyn.

Open: All year by appointment.

Admission: £4. Discount for groups.

Grounds. By arrangement. Obligatory. Limited for coaches. On leads.

HARLECH CASTLE ✿

HARLECH LL46 2YH

www.cadw.wales.gov.uk

Tel: 01766 780552

Owner: In the care of Cadw **Contact:** The Custodian

Set on a towering rock above Tremadog Bay, this seemingly impregnable fortress is the most dramatically sited of all the castles of Edward I. A World Heritage Listed Site.

Location: OS Ref. SH581 312. Harlech, Gwynedd on A496 coast road.

Open: 27 Mar - 26 May: 9.30 - 5pm. 27 May - 1 Oct: 9.30am - 6pm. 2 - 29 Oct: 9.30am - 5pm. 30 Oct - 31 Mar: Mon - Sat, 9.30am - 4pm, Suns, 11am - 4pm. Closed 24 - 26 Dec & 1 Jan. Opening/admission details subject to review Mar 2002.

Admission: Adult £3, Child/OAP £2, Family £8.

Guide dogs only.

HARTSHEATH

Pontblyddyn, Mold, Flintshire

Tel/Fax: 01352 770217

Owner/Contact: Dr M Jones-Mortimer

18th and 19th century house set in parkland. Viewing is limited to 7 persons at any one time. Prior booking is recommended. No toilets or refreshments.

Location: OS Ref. SJ287 602. Access from A5104, 3$\frac{1}{2}$ m SE of Mold between Pontblyddyn and Penyffordd.

Open: 1st, 3rd & 5th Wed in every month, 2 - 5pm.

Admission: £4.

ISCOYD PARK

Nr Whitchurch, Shropshire SY13 3AT

Owner/Contact: Mr P C Godsal

18th century Grade II* listed redbrick house in park.

Location: OS Ref. SJ504 421. 2m W of Whitchurch on A525.

Open: By written appointment only.

Special Events Index
◁ ◁ ◁ pgs 40-43

PENRHYN CASTLE ❧

BANGOR LL57 4HN

Tel: 01248 353084   **Infoline:** 01248 371337   **Fax:** 01248 371281

Owner: The National Trust   **Contact:** The Property Manager

This dramatic neo-Norman fantasy castle sits between Snowdonia and the Menai Strait. Built by Thomas Hopper between 1820 and 1845 for the wealthy Pennant family, who made their fortune from Jamaican sugar and Welsh slate. The castle is crammed with fascinating things such as a 1-ton slate bed made for Queen Victoria, elaborate carvings, mock-Norman furniture and an outstanding collection of paintings and offers a fascinating insight into domestic life in its recently restored Victorian kitchens and servants' quarters. With a countryside exhibition, industrial railway and railway model museums and a superb doll museum. Its grounds include parkland, an extensive exotic tree and shrub collection and a Victorian walled garden.

Location: OS Ref. SH602 720. 1m E of Bangor, at Llandygai (J11, A55).

Open: 23 Mar - 3 Nov: daily except Tues but open BHs throughout the season. Castle: 12 noon - 5pm (Jul & Aug: 11am - 5pm). Grounds: 11am - 5pm (Jul & Aug: 10am - 5.30pm). Last audio tour 4pm. Last admission 4.30pm.

Admission: All inclusive ticket: Adult £6, Child £3, Family (2+2) £15. Pre-booked groups (15+) £5. Garden & Stableblock Exhibitions only: Adult £4, Child £2. Audio tour: £1 (including NT members). NT members Free.

⬚ ▣ Licensed. ▣ ▣

PLAS MAWR ✚

HIGH STREET, CONWY LL32 8EF

www.cadw.wales.gov.uk

Tel: 01492 580167

Owner: In the care of Cadw   **Contact:** The Custodian

The best preserved Elizabethan town house in Britain, the house reflects the status of its builder Robert Wynn. A fascinating and unique place allowing visitors to sample the lives of the Tudor gentry and their servants, Plas Mawr is famous for the quality and quantity of its decorative plasterwork.

Location: OS Ref. SH781 776. Conwy by A55 or B5106 or A547.

Open: 1 Apr - 26 May: 9.30am - 5pm. 27 May - 3 Sept: 9.30am - 6pm. 4 Sept - 1 Oct: 9.30am - 5pm. 2 - 29 Oct: 9.30am - 4pm. Closed on Mons except BHs. Last admission 1 hour before closing.

Admission: Adult £4.10, Child/OAP £3.10, Family £11.30. Opening/admission details subject to review Mar 2002.

⬚ ⓟLimited. ▣ ▣ Guide dogs only.

PLAS BRONDANW GARDENS

Plas Brondanw, Llanfrothen, Gwynedd LL48 6SW

Tel: 07880 766741 (day time) / 07787 926793

Owner: Trustees of the Second Portmeirion Foundation

Italianate gardens with topiary.

Location: OS Ref. SH618 423. 3m N of Penrhyndeudraeth off A4085, on Croesor Road.

Open: All year: daily 9am - 5pm. No group bookings.

Admission: Adult £1.50, Child 25p.

Brushing Room at Penrhyn Castle

PLAS NEWYDD ❧

LLANFAIRPWLL, ANGLESEY LL61 6DQ

Tel: 01248 714795   **Fax:** 01248 713673   **e-mail:** ppnmsn@smtp.ntrust.org.uk

Owner: The National Trust   **Contact:** The Property Manager

Set amidst breathtaking beautiful scenery and with spectacular views of Snowdonia. Fine spring garden and Australasian arboretum with an understorey of shrubs and wildflowers. Summer terrace, and , later, massed hydrangeas and Autumn colour. A woodland walk gives access to a marine walk on the Menai Strait. Rhododendron garden open April - early June only. Elegant 18th century house by James Wyatt, famous for its association with Rex Whistler whose largest painting is here. Military museum contains relics of 1st Marquess of Anglesey and Battle of Waterloo. A historic cruise, a boat trip on the Menai Strait operates from the property weather and tides permitting (additional charge). 5 seater buggy to rhododendron garden and woodland walk.

Location: OS Ref. SH521 696. 2m S of Llanfairpwll and A5.

Open: 23 Mar - 3 Nov: Sat - Wed (open Good Fri). House: 12 noon - 5pm. Garden: 11am - 5.30pm. Last admission ½ hr before closing.

Admission: House & Garden: Adult £4.60, Child £2.30 (under 5s Free), Family (2+3) £11.50. Groups (15+) £3.70. Garden only: Adult £2.60, Child £1.30.

ⓘNo indoor photography. ⬚ ▣ Partial. WCs. Minibus from car park to house. ▣ Licensed. Award winning. ▣ By arrangement. ⓟ ▣ ▣Tel for details.

NTPL/Joe Cornish

PLAS YN RHIW ✹
RHIW, PWLLHELI LL53 8AB

Tel/Fax: 01758 780219

Owner: The National Trust   **Contact:** The Custodian

A small manor house, with garden and woodlands, overlooking the west shore of Porth Neigwl (Hell's Mouth Bay) on the Llyn Peninsula. The house is part medieval, with Tudor and Georgian additions, and the ornamental gardens have flowering trees and shrubs, divided by box hedges and grass paths, rising behind to the snowdrop wood.

Location: OS Ref. SH237 282. 16m SW of Pwllheli, 3m S of the B4413 to Aberdaron. No access for coaches.

Open: 23 Mar - 13 May: daily except Tue & Wed. 15 May - 30 Sept: daily except Tue. 1 - 31 Oct: Sat & Sun only, 12 noon - 5pm (21 - 25 Oct: daily). Open all BHs.

Admission: Adult £3.20, Child £1.60, Family (2+3) £8. Guided tour for pre-booked groups additional £1.40 (including NT members). Gardens only: Adult £2, Child £1, Family (2+3) £5. Garden & snowdrop wood (Jan & Feb only): £2.50.

⬚ 🚻 ♿Partial. WCs. 🅕By arrangement. 🅿Limited. 🐕Guide dogs only.

NTPL/Andreas von Einsiedel

POWIS CASTLE & GARDEN ✹
Nr WELSHPOOL SY21 8RF

Tel: 01938 551920   **Infoline:** 01938 551944   **Fax:** 01938 554336
e-mail: gpcajw@smtp.ntrust.org.uk

Owner: The National Trust   **Contact:** Amanda Whitmore

The world-famous garden, overhung with enormous clipped yew trees, shelters rare and tender plants in colourful herbaceous borders. Laid out under the influence of Italian and French styles, the garden retains its original lead statues and, an orangery on the terraces. Perched on a rock above the garden terraces, the medieval castle contains one of the finest collections of paintings and furniture in Wales.

Location: OS Ref. SJ216 064. 1m W of Welshpool, 1m SE of Berriew, car access on A483.

Open: Castle & Museum: 23 Mar - 3 Nov: daily except Mons & Tues (Jul & Aug: daily except Mons), but open BHs throughout the season, 1 - 5pm. Garden: as Castle, 11am - 6pm. Shop & Tearoom: Also open 8 Nov - 15 Dec, Fri - Sun, 11am - 4pm.

Admission: All inclusive: Adult £7.50, Child £3.75, Family £18.75. Groups: (15+ booked): £6.50. Garden only: Adult £5, Child £2.50, Family £12.50. Groups (15+ booked): £4. No groups rates on Suns or BHs. NT members & under 5s Free.

ℹ️No indoor photography. ⬚ 🚻 ♿Partial. ◼Licensed. 🅕By arrangement. 🅿 Limited for coaches. 🐕 Guide dogs only.

PORTMEIRION
Portmeirion, Gwynedd LL48 6ET

Tel: 01766 770000   **Fax:** 01766 771331   **e-mail:** info@portmeirion-village.com

Owner: The Portmeirion Foundation   **Contact:** Mr R Llywelyn

Built by Clough Williams-Ellis as an 'unashamedly romantic' village resort.

Location: OS Ref. SH590 371. Off A487 at Minffordd between Penrhyndeudraeth and Porthmadog.

Open: All year (except Christmas Day): daily, 9.30am - 5.30pm.

Admission: Adult £5.30, Child £2.60, OAP £4.20, Family (2+2) £12.60.

Bodnant Garden

NTPL / Ian Shaw

RHUDDLAN CASTLE ✤
Castle Gate, Castle Street, Rhuddlan LL18 5AD

Tel: 01745 590777   www.cadw.wales.gov.uk

Owner: In the care of Cadw   **Contact:** The Custodian

Guarding the ancient ford of the River Clwyd, Rhuddlan was the strongest of Edward I's castles in North-East Wales. Linked to the sea by an astonishing deep water channel nearly 3 miles long, it still proclaims the innovative genius of its architect.

Location: OS Ref. SJ025 779. SW end of Rhuddlan via A525 or A547.

Open: Apr - Sept: daily, 10am - 5pm. Opening/admission details subject to review Mar 2002.

Admission: Adult £2, Child/OAP £1.50, Family £5.50.

⬚ 🅿 🐕Guide dogs only.

RUG CHAPEL & LLANGAR CHURCH ✤
c/o Coronation Cottage, Rug, Corwen LL21 9BT

Tel: 01490 412025   www.cadw.wales.gov.uk

Owner: In the care of Cadw   **Contact:** The Custodian

Prettily set in a wooded landscape, Rug Chapel's exterior gives little hint of the wonders within. Nearby the attractive medieval Llangar Church still retains its charming early Georgian furnishings.

Location: Rug Chapel: OS Ref. SJ065 439. Off A494, 1m N of Corwen. Llangar Church: OS Ref. SJ064 423. Off B4401, 1m S of Corwen (obtain key at Rug).

Open: Rug Chapel: 21 Apr - 24 Sept:10am - 5pm. Closed Mons & Tues except BHs. Llangar Church: Interior access between 2 - 3pm, Apr - Sept through the Custodian at Rug Chapel. Both sites closed in winter. Opening/admission details subject to review Mar 2002.

Admission: Adult £2, Child/Conc. £1.50, Family £5.50.

♿ 🅕By arrangement. 🅿 ◼ 🐕Guide dogs only.

ST ASAPH CATHEDRAL
St Asaph, Denbighshire LL17 0RL

Tel: 01745 583429   **Contact:** Chapter Office

Britain's smallest ancient cathedral founded in 560AD by Kentigern, a religious community enclosed in a 'llan', hence Llanelwy

Location: OS Ref. SJ039 743. In St Asaph, S of A55.

Open: Summer: 8am - 6.30pm. Winter: 8am - dusk. Sun services: 8am, 11am, 3.30pm.

TOWER 🏛

Nercwys, Mold, Flintshire CH7 4EW

Tel: 01352 700220

Owner/Contact: Charles Wynne-Eyton

This Grade I listed building is steeped in Welsh history and bears witness to the continuous warfare of the time. A fascinating place to visit or for overnight stays.

Location: OS Ref. SJ240 620. 1m S of Mold.

Open: Summer: BHs plus other dates. Please telephone for exact dates and times. Groups welcome at other times by appointment.

Admission: Adult £3, Child £2.

TREBINSHWN

Nr Brecon, Powys LD3 7PX

Tel: 01874 730653   **Fax:** 01874 730843

Owner/Contact: R Watson

16th century mid-sized manor house. Extensively rebuilt 1780. Fine courtyard and walled garden.

Location: OS Ref. SO136 242. 1½m NW of Bwlch.

Open: Easter - 31 Aug: Mon - Tue, 10am - 4.30pm.

Admission: £1.

🅿

TŶ MAWR WYBRNANT 🌿

Penmachno, Betws-y-Coed, Gwynedd LL25 0HJ

Tel: 01690 760213

Owner: The National Trust   **Contact:** The Custodian

Situated in the beautiful and secluded Wybrnant Valley, Tŷ Mawr was the birthplace of Bishop William Morgan, first translator of the entire Bible into Welsh. The house has been restored to its probable 16th-17th century appearance and houses a display of Welsh Bibles. A footpath leads from the house through woodland and the surrounding fields, which are traditionally managed.

Location: OS Ref. SH770 524. From A5 3m S of Betws-y-Coed, take B4406 to Penmachno. House is 2½m NW of Penmachno by forest road.

Open: 23 Mar - 30 Sept: Thur - Sun (open BHs throughout the season), 12 noon - 5pm; Oct - 3 Nov: Thur, Fri & Sun, 12 noon - 4pm.

Admission: Adult £2, Child £1, Family £5. Booked groups (15+): £1.60. NT members Free.

♿Ground floor. 🅿 🐕Guide dogs only. ✳

VALLE CRUCIS ABBEY ♣

Llangollen, Clwyd

Tel: 01978 860326   **www.cadw.wales.gov.uk**

Owner: In the care of Cadw   **Contact:** The Custodian

Set in a beautiful valley location, Valle Crucis Abbey is the best preserved medieval monastery in North Wales, enhanced by the only surviving monastic fish pond in Wales.

Location: OS Ref. SJ205 442. B5103 from A5, 2m NW of Llangollen, or A542 from Ruthin.

Open: 21 Apr - 24 Sept: 10am - 5pm. Winter: open site. Opening/admission details subject to review Mar 2002.

Admission: Adult £2, Child/Conc. £1.50. Family £5.50.

🔲 ♿ 🅿 🐕 Guide dogs only. ✳

WERN ISAF

Penmaen Park, Llanfairfechan LL33 0RN

Tel: 01248 680437

Owner/Contact: Mrs P J Phillips

This Arts and Crafts house was built in 1900 by the architect H L North as his family home and it contains much of the original furniture and William Morris fabrics. It is situated in a woodland garden and is at its best in the Spring. It has extensive views over the Menai Straits and Conwy Bay. One of the most exceptional houses of its date and style in Wales.

Location: OS Ref. SH685 752.

Open: 2 - 30 Mar: daily except Mons, 12 noon - 4pm. Please telephone for details.

Admission: £1

The Servants' Hall, Chirk Castle

ABERCAMLAIS

Brecon, Powys LD3 8EY

Tel: 01874 636206 **Fax:** 01874 636964 **e-mail:** susan.ballance@virgin.net
www.abercamlais.co.uk

Owner/Contact: Mrs S Ballance

Splendid Grade II* mansion dating from middle ages, altered extensively in early 18th century with 19th century additions, in extensive grounds beside the river Usk. Still in same family ownership and occupation since medieval times. Exceptional octagonal pigeon house, formerly a privy.

Location: OS Ref. SN965 290. 5m W of Brecon on A40.

Open: Apr - Oct: by appointment.

Admission: Adult £5, Child Free.

🔓 ⓘ Obligatory. 🅿 🖼

ABERDULAIS FALLS 🌿

Aberdulais, Vale of Neath SA10 8EU

Tel: 01639 636674 **Fax:** 01639 645069

Owner: The National Trust   **Contact:** The Property Warden

For over 300 years this famous waterfall has provided the energy to drive the wheels of industry, from the first manufacture of copper in 1584 to present day remains of the tinplate works. It has also been visited by famous artists such as J M W Turner in 1796. The site today houses a unique hydro-electrical scheme which has been developed to harness the waters of the Dulais river.

Location: OS Ref. SS772 995. On A4109, 3m NE of Neath. 4m from M4/J43, then A465.

Open: 1 - 22 Mar: Sats & Suns only, 11am - 4pm. 23 Mar - 3 Nov: Mon - Fri, 10am - 5pm, Sats, Suns & BHs 11am - 6pm. Shop: as property. 8 Nov - 22 Dec: Fri - Sun, 11am - 4pm & open 23 Dec (Mon).

Admission: Adult £3, Child £1.50, Family £7.50. Groups (15+): Adult £2.40, Child £1.20. National Trust members Free.

🔲 ⬛ Light refreshments (summer only). 🅿 Limited. 🔳

The Drawing Room, Castell Coch

ABERGLASNEY GARDENS

LLANGATHEN, CARMARTHENSHIRE SA32 8QH

www.aberglasney.org.uk

Tel/Fax: 01558 668998 **e-mail:** info@aberglasney.org.uk

Owner: Aberglasney Restoration Trust   **Contact:** Booking Department

Aberglasney is one of the most remarkable restoration projects of recent years. When acquired in 1995 the Mansion and grounds were so derelict they were considered by most to be beyond restoration. It was not until the undergrowth was cleared and extensive archaeological surveys undertaken, that the importance of this historical garden was realised. The parapet walkway, dating from 1600, is the only example that survives in the United Kingdom. The nine acre garden is already planted with many rare and unusual plants, giving interest throughout the year. Aberglasney is destined to become one of the most fascinating gardens in the country.

Location: OS Ref. SN581 221. 4m W of Llandeilo. Follow signs from A40.

Open: 1 Apr - 31 Oct: daily, 10am - 6pm (last entry 5pm). Please telephone for winter opening times.

Admission: Adult £5, Child £2.50, OAP £4. Booked groups (10+): Adult £4, Child £2, OAP £3.

🔲 🚻 🔓 ⬛ Licensed. ⓘ Daily: 11.30am & 2.30pm. 🅿 Limited for coaches. 🔳 🐕 Guide dogs only. ✳

BIG PIT NATIONAL MINING MUSEUM OF WALES

BLAENAFON, TORFAEN NP4 9XP

www.nmgw.ac.uk

Tel: 01495 790311 **Fax:** 01495 792618 **e-mail:** kathryn.stowers@nmgw.ac.uk
Owner: National Museums & Galleries of Wales
Contact: Kathryn Stowers (Marketing Officer)

Big Pit, the National Mining Museum of Wales, is a unique attraction offering tours 300ft below ground. Journey down in the pit cage with an ex-miner as your guide. Explore underground roadways, air-doors and the pit stables before travelling back up to the surface to view the original colliery buildings. See the winding engine house, the blacksmith workshop and pit head baths and much, much more. Take a well earned rest in the licensed cafeteria and buy a souvenir of your visit in our well stocked Welsh craft shop. The museum is sited in Blaenafon which has been designated as a World Heritage Site, and it is free to visit. A truly unique attraction.

Location: OS Ref. SO238 088. 1m W of Blaenafon (A4043), 5m SW of Abergavenny.
Open: Mar - Nov: daily, 9.30am - 5pm. Tours: 10am - 3.30pm.
Admission: Free.

[i]No photography underground. ⬚ 🔲 🖥 🍴Licensed. 🎟Obligatory. 🅿 🔲
🦮In grounds, on leads. 🔺

BLAENAVON IRONWORKS ✚

Nr Brecon Beacons National Park, Blaenavon, Gwent

Tel: 01495 792615 **Winter Bookings:** 01633 648082 **www.cadw.wales.gov.uk**

Owner: In the care of Cadw **Contact:** The Custodian

The famous ironworks at Blaenavon were a milestone in the history of the Industrial Revolution. Visitors can view much of the ongoing conservation work as well as 'Stack Square' - a rare survival of housing built for pioneer ironworkers. Part of a World Heritage Site.

Location: OS Ref. SO248 092. Via A4043 follow signs to Big Pit Mining Museum and Blaenavon Ironworks. Abergavenny 8m. Pontypool 8m. From carpark, cross road, then path to entrance gate.

Open: Easter - end Oct: 9.30am - 4.30pm. For opening times outside this period call the above number or 029 2050 0200. Opening/admission details subject to review Mar 2002.

Admission: Adult £2, Child/Conc. £1.50, Family £5.50.
⬚ 🔲Partial. 🎟By arrangement. 🅿 🦮Guide dogs only.

CAE HIR GARDENS

Cae Hir, Cribyn, Lampeter, Cardiganshire SA48 7NG

Tel: 01570 470839

Owner/Contact: Mr W Akkermans

This transformed 19th century smallholding offers a succession of pleasant surprises and shows a quite different approach to gardening.

Location: OS Ref. SN521 520. W on A482 from Lampeter, after 5m turn S on B4337. Cae Hir is 2m on left.

Open: Daily, excluding Mons (open BH Mons), 1 - 6pm.

Admission: Adult £2.50, Child 50p, OAP £2. Groups: (20+) £2.

CAERLEON ROMAN BATHS & AMPHITHEATRE ✚

High Street, Caerleon NP6 1AE

Tel: 01633 422518 **www.cadw.wales.gov.uk**

Owner: In the care of Cadw **Contact:** The Custodian

Caerleon is the most varied and fascinating Roman site in Britain – incorporating fortress and baths, well-preserved amphitheatre and a row of barrack blocks, the only examples currently visible in Europe.

Location: OS Ref. ST340 905. 4m ENE of Newport by B4596 to Caerleon, M4/J25 (westbound), M4/J26 (eastbound).

Open: 27 Mar - 29 Oct: 9.30am - 5pm. 30 Oct - 31 Mar: Mon - Sat, 9.30am - 5pm, Suns, 1 - 5pm. Closed 24 - 26 Dec & 1 Jan. Opening/admission details subject to review Mar 2002.

Admission: Adult £2, Child/Conc. £1.50, Family £5.50.
⬚ 🔲 🅿 🦮Guide dogs only. ✳

Civil Wedding Venues
◁ ◁ ◁ pgs 28-29

CADW: Welsh Historic Monuments, Crown Copyright

CAERPHILLY CASTLE ✠
Caerphilly CF8 1JL
www.cadw.wales.gov.uk

Tel: 029 2088 3143

Owner: In the care of Cadw **Contact:** The Custodian

Often threatened, never taken, this vastly impressive castle is much the biggest in Wales. 'Red Gilbert' de Clare, Anglo-Norman Lord of Glamorgan, flooded a valley to create the 30 acre lake, setting his fortress on 3 artificial islands. Famous for its leaning tower, its fortifications are scarcely rivalled in Europe.

Location: OS Ref. ST156 871. Centre of Caerphilly, A468 from Newport, A470, A469 from Cardiff.

Open: 27 Mar - 26 May: 9.30am - 5pm. 27 May - 1 Oct: 9.30am - 6pm. 2 - 29 Oct: 9.30am - 5pm. 30 Oct - 31 Mar: Mon - Sat, 9.30am - 4pm, Suns, 11am - 4pm. Closed 24 - 26 Dec & 1 Jan. Opening/admission details subject to review Mar 2002.

Admission: Adult £2.50, Child/Conc. £2, Family £7.

🖥 🗐 🅿Limited. ▣ ♿Guide dogs only. ▲ ✳

CADW: Welsh Historic Monuments, Crown Copyright

CASTELL COCH ✠
TONGWYNLAIS, CARDIFF CF4 7JS
www.cadw.wales.gov.uk

Tel: 029 2081 0101

Owner: In the care of Cadw **Contact:** The Custodian

A fairytale castle in the woods, Castell Coch embodies a glorious Victorian dream of the Middle Ages. Designed by William Burges as a country retreat for the 3rd Lord Bute, every room and furnishing is brilliantly eccentric, including paintings of Aesop's fables on the drawing room walls.

Location: OS Ref. ST131 826. M4/J32, A470 then signposted. 5m NW of Cardiff city centre.

Open: 27 Mar - 26 May: 9.30am - 5pm. 27 May - 1 Oct: 9.30am - 6pm. 2 - 29 Oct: 9.30am - 5pm. 30 Oct - 31 Mar: Mon - Sat, 9.30am - 4pm, Suns, 11am - 4pm. Closed 24 - 26 Dec & 1 Jan. Teashop: Summer: daily. Winter: weekends. Opening/admission details subject to review Mar 2002.

Admission: Adult £2.50, Child/Conc. £2, Family £7.

🖥 ☕ ♿ 🖥 🗐 🅿 ♿Guide dogs only. ▲ ✳

CARDIFF CASTLE
Castle Street, Cardiff CF10 3RB

Tel: 029 2087 8100 **Fax:** 029 2023 1417

Owner: City and County of Cardiff **Contact:** Booking Office

2000 years of history, including Roman Walls, Norman Keep and Victorian interiors.

Location: OS Ref. ST181 765. Cardiff city centre, signposted from M4.

Open: 1 Mar - 30 Oct: daily, 9.30am - 6pm, last entry 5pm. Nov - Feb: daily, 9.30am - 4.30pm, last entry 3.15pm. Closed 25/26 Dec & 1 Jan.

Admission: Adult £5.25, Child/OAP £3.15 (2001 prices).

CAREW CASTLE & TIDAL MILL
Tenby, Pembrokeshire SA70 8SL

Tel/Fax: 01646 651782 **e-mail:** enquiries@carewcastle.com

www.carewcastle.com

Owner: Pembrokeshire Coast National Park **Contact:** Mr G M Candler

A magnificent Norman castle which later became an Elizabethan country house. Royal links with Henry Tudor and the setting for the Great Tournament of 1507. The Mill is one of only four restored tidal mills in Britain. Introductory slide programme, automatic 'talking points' and special exhibition on 'The Story of Milling'.

Location: OS Ref. SN046 037. 1/2 m N of A477, 5m E of Pembroke.

Open: Easter - end Oct: daily, 10am - 5pm.

Admission: Adult £2.80, Child/OAP £1.90, Family £7.50 (prices under review).

🖥 ♿Partial. WC. ⓘ By arrangement. 🅿 ▣ ♿In grounds on leads. 🎥 Tel for details.

CARREG CENNEN CASTLE ✠
Tir-y-Castell Farm, Llandeilo

Tel: 01558 822291 **www.cadw.wales.gov.uk**

Owner: In the care of Cadw **Contact:** The Custodian

Spectacularly crowning a remote crag 300 feet above the River Cennen, the castle is unmatched as a wildly romantic fortress sought out by artists and visitors alike. The climb from Rare Breeds Farm is rewarded by breathtaking views and the chance to explore intriguing caves beneath.

Location: OS Ref. SN668 190. Minor roads from A483(T) to Trapp village. 5m SE of A40 at Llandeilo.

Open: early Apr - late Oct: 9.30am - 7.30pm. Late Oct - late Mar: 9.30am - dusk. Closed 25 Dec. Opening/admission details subject to review March 2002.

Admission: Adult £2.50, Child/Conc. £2, Family £7.

🖥 ▣ 🗐 🅿 ♿Guide dogs only. ✳

CHEPSTOW CASTLE ✠
Chepstow, Gwent

Tel: 01291 624065 **www.cadw.wales.gov.uk**

Owner: In the care of Cadw **Contact:** The Custodian

This mighty fortress has guarded the route from England to South Wales for more than nine centuries. So powerful was this castle that it continued in use until 1690, being finally adapted for cannon and musket after an epic civil war siege. This huge, complex, grandiosely sited castle deserves a lengthy visit.

Location: OS Ref. ST533 941. Chepstow via A466, B4235 or A48. 1 1/2 m N of M4/J22.

Open: 27 Mar - 26 May: 9.30am - 5pm. 27 May - 1 Oct: 9.30am - 6pm. 2 - 29 Oct: 9.30am - 5pm. 30 Oct - 31 Mar: Mon - Sat: 9.30am - 4pm, Suns, 11am - 4pm. Closed 24 - 26 Dec & 1 Jan. Opening/admission details subject to review Mar 2002.

Admission: Adult £3, Child/OAP £2, Family £8.

🖥 ♿Partial. 🅿 ♿Guide dogs only. ✳

CILGERRAN CASTLE ✠ ♦
Cardigan, Dyfed

Tel: 01239 615007 **www.cadw.wales.gov.uk**

Owner: In the care of Cadw **Contact:** The Custodian

Perched high up on a rugged spur above the River Teifi, Cilgerran Castle is one of the most spectacularly sited fortresses in Wales. It dates from the 11th - 13th centuries.

Location: OS Ref. SN195 431. Main roads to Cilgerran from A478 and A484. 3 1/2 m SSE of Cardigan.

Open: Late Mar - late Oct: 9.30am - 6.30pm. Late Oct - late Mar: 9.30am - 4pm. Closed 24 - 26 Dec & 1 Jan. Opening/admission details subject to review Mar 2002.

Admission: Adult £2, Child/OAP £1.50, Family £5.50.

🖥 🅿 ♿Guide dogs only. ✳

CLYNE GARDENS
Mill Lane, Blackpill, Swansea SA3 5BD

Tel: 01792 401737

Owner: City and County of Swansea **Contact:** Steve Hopkins

50 acre spring garden, large rhododendron collection, 4 national collections, extensive bog garden, native woodland.

Location: OS Ref. SS614 906. S side of Mill Lane, 500yds W of A4067 Mumbles Road, 3m SW of Swansea.

Open: All year: daily.

Admission: Free.

South Wales

NTPL/Andrew Butler

COLBY WOODLAND GARDEN 🌿
AMROTH, NARBETH, PEMBROKESHIRE SA67 8PP

Tel: 01834 811885 **Fax:** 01834 831766

Owner: The National Trust   **Contact:** The Centre Manager

An attractive woodland garden. There are walks through secluded valleys along open woodland pathways. Nearby is the coastal resort of Amroth.

Location: OS Ref. SN155 080. 1/2m inland from Amroth beside Carmarthen Bay. Signs from A477.

Open: 23 Mar - 3 Nov: daily, 10am - 5pm. Walled Garden: 1 Apr - 31 Oct: 11am - 5pm.

Admission: Adult £2.80, Child £1.40, Family £7. Groups: by arrangement (15+): Adult £2.30, Child £1.15. National Trust members Free.

ℹ️ Gallery events. 🖼️ 💺

CRESSELLY
Kilgetty, Pembrokeshire SA68 0SP

Fax: 01646 687045

Owner/Contact: H D R Harrison-Allen Esq MFH

Home of the Allen family for 250 years. The house is of 1770 with matching wings of 1869 and contains good plasterwork and fittings of both periods. The Allens are of particular interest for their close association with the Wedgwood family of Etruria and a long tradition of foxhunting.

Location: OS Ref. SN065 065. W of the A4075.

Open: 1 - 30 May: 10am - 4pm. Closed 4/5 May. Guided tours on the hour.

Admission: Adult £3.50, no children under 12.

♿ Ground floor only. 🎫 Obligatory. 🅿️ Coaches by arrangement. 💺

CYFARTHFA CASTLE MUSEUM
Brecon Road, Merthyr Tydfil, Mid Glamorgan CF47 8RE

Tel/Fax: 01685 723112

Owner: Merthyr Tydfil County Borough Council   **Contact:** Scott Reid

Castle originates from 1824/1825, now a museum and school.

Location: OS Ref. SO041 074. NE side of A470 to Brecon, 1/2 m NW of town centre.

Open: 1 Apr - 30 Sept: Mon - Sun, 10am - 5.30pm. Winter: Tue - Fri, 10am - 4pm, Sat & Sun, 12 noon - 4pm.

Admission: Free.

❄️ Open All Year Index
◁ ◁ ◁ pgs 44-48

DINEFWR 🌿
Llandeilo SA19 6RT

Tel: 01558 825912 **Fax:** 01558 822036 **e-mail:** gdroff@smtp.ntrust.org.uk

Owner: The National Trust   **Contact:** The House Manager

A deeply historic site with particular connections to the medieval Princes of Wales. An 18th century part 'naturalistic', part designed landscape parkland, with deer herd and White Park cattle, surrounds a 17th century mansion. Access to Dinefwr Castle (Cadw).

Location: OS Ref. SN625 225. On outskirts of Llandeilo. M4 from Swansea to Pont Abraham. A48 to Cross Hands and A476 to Llandeilo. Entrance by police station (A40).

Open: House, Garden, Deer Park: 23 Mar - 3 Nov: daily except Tues & Weds, open BHs throughout the season, 11am - 5pm. Parkland: All year: 11am - 5pm (Nov - Mar: daily during daylight hours).

Admission: House & Park: Adult £3.20, Child £1.60, Family £8. Groups: (pre-booked 15+) £3. Park only (charges apply between 1 Apr - 29 Oct): Adult £2.20, Child £1.10, Family £5.50. National Trust members Free.

♿ 💺 ℹ️ By arrangement. 🅿️ Limited for coaches. 🔲 🐕 In grounds on leads. ❄️

THE DINGLE
Dingle Lane, Crundale, Haverfordwest, Pembrokeshire SA62 4DJ

Tel: 01437 764370 **Fax:** 01437 768844

Owner/Contact: Andrew Barton

18th century country gentleman's home, surrounded by gardens. Gardens only open.

Location: OS Ref. SM973 175. 2m NE of Haverfordwest 600yds SE of B4329.

Open: 10am - 6pm.

Admission: Gardens: Adult £2, Child Free. Nursery & tearooms Free.

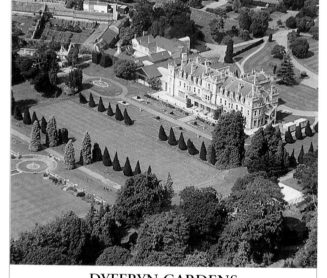

DYFFRYN GARDENS
ST NICHOLAS, CARDIFF CF5 6SU
www.dyffryngardens.org.uk

Tel: 029 2059 3328 **Fax:** 029 2059 1966

Owner: The Vale of Glamorgan Council   **Contact:** Ms G Donovan

Dyffryn Gardens is a delightful Edwardian garden set in the heart of the Vale of Glamorgan and currently being restored with the aid of a Heritage Lottery Grant. Many themed Garden Rooms, an Italianate design, floral bedding displays, herbaceous borders and a well stocked arboretum.

Location: OS Ref. ST095 723. 3m NW of Barry, J33/M4. 1 1/2 m S of St Nicholas on A48.

Open: Visitor Centre: Apr - Oct.

Admission: Adult £3. Please telephone for details of concessions and tours.

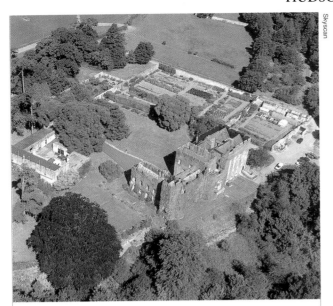

Skyscan

FONMON CASTLE 🏰

RHOOSE, BARRY, SOUTH GLAMORGAN CF62 3ZN

Tel: 01446 710206 **Fax:** 01446 711687 **e-mail:** sophie@fonmoncastle.fsnet.co.uk
Owner: Sir Brooke Boothby Bt   **Contact:** Sophie Katzi
Occupied as a home since the 13th century, this medieval castle has the most stunning Georgian interiors and is surrounded by extensive gardens. Available for weddings, concerts, corporate entertainment and multi-activity days.
Location: OS Ref. ST047 681. 15m W of Cardiff, 1m W of Cardiff airport.
Open: 1 Apr - 30 Sept: Tues & Weds, 2 - 5pm (last tour 4pm). Other times by appointment. Groups: by appointment.
Admission: Adult £4, Child Free.
ⓘConferences. 🍽By arrangement (up to 120). ♿Partial. WC. 🅿
🐕Guide dogs only. 🔺 ✳

Alex Ramsay

THE JUDGE'S LODGING

BROAD STREET, PRESTEIGNE, POWYS LD8 2AD

www.judgeslodging.org.uk

Tel: 01544 260650 **Fax:** 01544 260652 **e-mail:** info@judgeslodging.org.uk
Owner: Powys County Council   **Contact:** Gabrielle Rivers
Explore the fascinating world of the Victorian judges, their servants and felonious guests at this award-winning, totally hands-on historic house. From the stunning restored judge's apartments to the gas lit servants' quarters below. Follow an 'eavesdropping' audio tour featuring actor Robert Hardy. Damp cells, vast courtroom and local history rooms included.
Location: OS Ref. SO314 644. In town centre, off A44 and A4113. Easy reach from Herefordshire and mid-Wales.
Open: 1 Mar - 31 Oct: daily, 10am - 6pm. 1 Nov - 22 Dec: Wed - Sun, 10am - 4pm. Bookings by arrangement accepted all year.
Admission: Adult £3.75, Child/Conc. £2.75. Groups (10-80): Adult £3,Child/Conc. £2.25, Family £11.
⬛ ♿Partial (access via lift). 🅵By arrangement. ⬛ 🅿In town. 📷
🐕Guide dogs only. ✳

KIDWELLY CASTLE ♣

Kidwelly, West Glamorgan SA17 5BG

Tel: 01554 890104 **www.cadw.wales.gov.uk**
Owner: In the care of Cadw   **Contact:** The Custodian
A chronicle in stone of medieval fortress technology this strong and splendid castle developed during more than three centuries of Anglo-Welsh warfare. The half-moon shape stems from the original 12th century stockaded fortress, defended by the River Gwendraeth on one side and a deep crescent-shaped ditch on the other.
Location: OS Ref. SN409 070. Kidwelly via A484. Kidwelly Rail Station 1m.
Open: 27 Mar - 26 May: 9.30am - 5pm. 27 May - 1 Oct: 9.30am - 6pm. 2 - 29 Oct: 9.30am - 5pm. 30 Oct - 31 Mar: Mon - Sat, 9.30am - 4pm, Suns, 11am - 4pm. Closed 24 - 26 Dec & 1 Jan. Opening/admission details subject to review Mar 2002.
Admission: Adult £2.50, Child/OAP £2, Family £7.
⬛ ♿ 🅵By arrangement. ⬛ 🅿 🐕Guide dogs only. ✳

LAMPHEY BISHOP'S PALACE ♣

Lamphey, Dyfed

Tel: 01646 672224 **www.cadw.wales.gov.uk**
Owner: In the care of Cadw   **Contact:** The Custodian
Lamphey marks the place of the spectacular Bishop's Palace but it reached its height of greatness under Bishop Henry de Gower who raised the new Great Hall. Today the ruins of this comfortable retreat reflect the power enjoyed by the medieval bishops.
Location: OS Ref. SN018 009. A4139 from Pembroke or Tenby. N of village (A4139).
Open: Daily, 10am - 5pm. Closed 25 Dec. Opening/admission details subject to review Mar 2002.
Admission: Adult £2, Child/Conc. £1.50, Family £5.50.
⬛ ⬛ 🅿 🐕Guide dogs only. ✳

LAUGHARNE CASTLE ♣

King Street, Laugharne SA33 4SA

Tel: 01994 427906 **www.cadw.wales.gov.uk**
Owner: In the care of Cadw   **Contact:** The Custodian
Picturesque Laugharne Castle stands on a low ridge overlooking the wide Taf estuary, one of a string of fortresses controlling the ancient route along the South Wales coast.
Location: OS Ref. SN303 107. 4m S of A48 at St Clears via A4066.
Open: Apr - Sept: daily, 10am - 5pm. Winter: closed. Opening/admission details subject to review Mar 2002.
Admission: Adult £2, Child/Conc. £1.50, Family £5.50.
⬛ 🅿 🐕Guide dogs only.

LLANCAIACH FAWR MANOR

Nelson, Treharris CF46 6ER

Tel: 01443 412248 **Fax:** 01443 412688
Owner: Caerphilly County Borough Council   **Contact:** The Administrator
Tudor fortified manor dating from 1530 with Stuart additions.
Location: OS Ref. ST114 967. S side of B4254, 1m N of A472 at Nelson.
Open: All year: weekdays, 10am - 5pm. weekends, 10am - 6pm. Last admission 1¹/₂ hours before closing. Nov - Feb: closed Mons. Closed Christmas week.
Admission: Adult £4.50, Child/Conc. £3, Family £12.

LLANDAFF CATHEDRAL

Llandaff, Cardiff, Glamorgan CF5 2YF

Tel: 029 2056 4554 **Fax:** 029 203897 **e-mail:** office@llandaffcathedral
Contact: The Cathedral Office
Oldest cathedral in the British Isles. Epstein's 'Christ in Majesty' and Rosetti's 'Seed of David'.
Location: OS Ref. ST155 781. 2¹/₂ m NW of city centre, ¹/₄ m W of A48 ring road.
Open: Daily: 7am - 7pm. Sun services: 8am, 9am, 11am, 12.15pm (Holy Eucharist), 3.30pm Choral Evensong and 6.30pm Parish Evensong. Weekday evening service: 6pm, (Wed 5.30pm).
Admission: Donation.

LLANERCHAERON ✤

Aberaeron, Ceredigion SA48 8DG

Tel: 01545 570200 **Infoline:** 01558 825147 **Fax:** 01545 571759
Owner: The National Trust   **Contact:** The Property Manager
A small 18th century Welsh gentry estate which survived virtually unaltered into the 20th century. The house was designed and built by John Nash in 1794-96. Llanerchaeron was a self sufficient estate – evident in the dairy, laundry, brewery and salting house of the service courtyard as well as the home farm buildings from the stables to the threshing barn. Llanerchaeron today is a working organic farm and the two restored walled gardens also produce organically grown fruit and herbs. There are extensive walks around the estate and pleasure grounds. The house and servants' quarters will open to visitors for the first time in June 2002 following extensive restoration.
Location: OS Ref. SN480 602. 2¹/₂m E of Aberaeron off A482.
Open: Home Farm, Gardens & Grounds: 31 Mar - 4 Nov: Thur - Sun (open BH Mons) 11am - 5pm. Jul & Aug: thur, 2pm guided tours of garden & home farm. Parklands: All year, dawn - dusk.
Admission: Adult £4, Child £2, Family £10.
✳

MARGAM PARK 🏛

Port Talbot, Glamorgan SA13 2TJ

Tel: 01639 881635   **Fax:** 01639 895897

Owner: Neathport Talbot County Borough Council   **Contact:** Mr Ray Butt

Margam Orangery is the largest of its kind in Britain. Castle and Abbey ruins, 850 acres of parkland and forest, with waymarked signs.

Location: OS Ref. SS804 865. NE side of A48, 1m SE of M4/J38, 4m SE of Port Talbot.

Open: Summer: daily, 10am - 5pm, last entry 4pm. Winter: Wed - Sun, 10am - 5pm, last entry 3pm.

Admission: Please contact property for details.

MUSEUM OF WELSH LIFE

St Fagans, Cardiff CF5 6XB

Tel: 029 2057 3500   **Fax:** 029 2057 3490

St Fagans Castle, a 16th century building built within the walls of a 13th century castle.

Location: OS Ref. ST118 772. 4m W of city centre, 1¹/₂ m N of A48, 2m S of M4/J33 off A4232.

Open: All year: daily, 10am - 5pm.

Admission: Free.

THE NATIONAL BOTANIC GARDEN OF WALES

Llanarthney, Carmarthenshire SA32 8HG

Tel: 01558 668768/667134   **Fax:** 01558 667138

Owner: The National Botanic Garden of Wales   **Contact:** Ben Thomas

The first national botanic garden to be created in the United Kingdom for more than two hundred years.

Location: OS159 Ref. SN518 175. ¹/₂ m off A48 (M4), 4¹/₂ m NW Cross Hands.

Open: Please contact property for details.

Admission: Please contact property for details.

OXWICH CASTLE ✚

c/o Oxwich Castle Farm, Oxwich SA3 1NG

Tel: 01792 390359   **www.cadw.wales.gov.uk**

Owner: In the care of Cadw   **Contact:** The Custodian

Beautifully sited in the lovely Gower peninsula, Oxwich Castle is a striking testament to the pride and ambitions of the Mansel dynasty of Welsh gentry.

Location: OS159 Ref. SS497 864. A4118, 11m SW of Swansea, in Oxwich village.

Open: Apr - Sept: daily, 10am - 5pm. Winter: closed. Opening/admission details subject to review Mar 2002.

Admission: Adult £2, Child/OAP £1.50, Family £5.50.

📷 ♿ 🅿 🦮 Guide dogs only.

PEMBROKE CASTLE

Pembroke, Dyfed SA71 4LA

Tel: 01646 681510   **Fax:** 01646 622260   **e-mail:** pembroke.castle@talk21.com
www.pembrokecastle.co.uk

Owner: Trustees of Pembroke Castle   **Contact:** I B Ramsden

Explore from the top of its many lofty towers to the bottom of the vast cavern beneath. This early Norman castle, birthplace of the first Tudor King, houses many fascinating displays and exhibitions. It makes an exhilarating visit for all ages. Enjoy a picnic in the beautifully kept grounds, or on the roof of St Anne's Bastion and take in the views along the estuary.

Location: OS Ref. SM983 016. W end of the main street in Pembroke.

Open: 1 Apr - Sept: daily, 9.30am - 6pm. Mar & Oct: daily, 10am - 5pm. Nov - Feb: daily, 10am - 4pm. Closed 24 - 26 Dec & 1 Jan. Brass rubbing centre open Summer months & all year by arrangement.

Admission: Adult £3, Child/Conc. £2. Groups (20+): Adult £2.60, OAP £1.70.

📷 ♿ 🎥 Summer only. 🎫 By arrangement. 🍴 🦮 In grounds on leads. ✱

PENHOW CASTLE 🏛

Nr NEWPORT, GWENT NP26 3AD

www.penhowcastle.com

Tel: 01633 400800   **Fax:** 01633 400990   **e-mail:** admin@penhowcastle.com

Owner: Stephen Weeks Esq   **Contact:** The Administrator

Wales' oldest lived-in Castle, the first home in Britain of the Seymour family. Now lovingly restored by the present owner, visitors explore the varied period rooms from battlements to kitchens. Discover the Norman bedchamber, 15th century Great Hall with minstrels' gallery, elegant panelled Carolean dining room, guided by the acclaimed 'Time Machine' audio tours included in the admission; also in French and German. Penhow holds 8 awards for careful restoration and imaginative interpretation. Exciting children's tours and school visits.

Location: OS Ref. ST423 908. Midway between Chepstow and Newport on the A48. Use M4/J24.

Open: Summer: Good Fri - 30 Sept: Wed - Sun & BHs. Aug: daily, 10am - 5.15pm (last adm.) Winter: Weds, 10am - 4pm. Selected Suns, 1 - 4pm. Evening Candlelit Tours all year by arrangement. Christmas Tours: 15 Nov - 5 Jan.

Admission: Adult £3.85, Child £2.60, Family (2+2) £10.50. Groups: by arrangement all year, 10% discount for 20+.

📷 ♿ Partial. 📹 📷 🎫 By arrangement. 🅿 Limited. 🍴 🦮 Guide dogs only. 🛏 1 double. ✱

PICTON CASTLE 🏛

HAVERFORDWEST, PEMBROKESHIRE SA62 4AS

www.pictoncastle.co.uk

Tel/Fax: 01437 751326   **e-mail:** pct@pictoncastle.freeserve.co.uk

Owner: Picton Castle Trust   **Contact:** D Pryse Lloyd

Built in the 13th century by Sir John Wogan, his direct descendants still use the castle as their family home, carrying the family name of Philipps. Retaining its external appearance, the castle was remodelled inside, above the undercroft in the 1750s and extended around 1800. The woodland and walled gardens cover 40 acres and are part of The Royal Horticultural Society access scheme for beautiful gardens. There is a unique collection of rhododendrons and azaleas, mature trees, unusual shrubs, wild flowers and a large collection of herbs as featured on television. The Picton Gallery is used for nationally acclaimed exhibitions. Events include spring and autumn plant sales.

Location: OS Ref. SN011 135. 4m E of Haverfordwest, 2m S of A40.

Open: Castle: Apr - Sept. Closed Mon & Sat except BHs, open all other afternoons for guided tours. Garden & Gallery: Apr - Oct: Tue - Sun, 10.30am - 5pm.

Admission: Castle, Garden & Gallery: Adult £4.95, Child £1.95, OAP £4.75. Garden & Gallery: Adult £3.95, Child £1.95, OAP £3.75. Groups (20+): reduced prices by prior arrangement.

ℹ No indoor photography. 📷 🎥 🚃 ♿ 🍴 Licensed. 🎫 Obligatory. 🅿 🦮 In grounds, on leads. 🔔 📞 Tel for details.

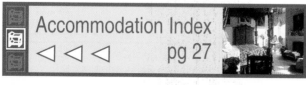

Accommodation Index ◁ ◁ ◁   **pg 27**

RAGLAN CASTLE ✠
Raglan NP5 2BT
Tel: 01291 690228   www.cadw.wales.gov.uk
Owner: In the care of Cadw   **Contact:** The Custodian
Undoubtedly the finest late medieval fortress-palace in Britain, it was begun in the 1430s by Sir William ap Thomas who built the mighty 'Yellow Tower'. His son William Lord Herbert added a palatial mansion defended by a gatehouse and many towered walls. The high quality is still obvious today.
Location: OS Ref. SO415 084. Raglan, NE of Raglan village off A40 (eastbound) and signposted.
Open: 27 Mar - 26 May: 9.30am - 5pm. 27 May - 1 Oct: 9.30am - 6pm. 2 - 29 Oct: 9.30am - 5pm. 30 Oct - 31 Mar: Mon - Sat, 9.30am - 4pm, Suns, 11am - 4pm. Closed 24 - 26 Dec & 1 Jan. Opening/admission details subject to review Mar 2002.
Admission: Adult £2.50, Child/Conc. £2, Family £7.

ST DAVIDS BISHOP'S PALACE ✠
St Davids, SA62 6PE
Tel: 01437 720517   www.cadw.wales.gov.uk
Owner: In the care of Cadw   **Contact:** The Custodian
The city of St Davids boasts not only one of Britain's finest cathedrals but also the most impressive medieval palace in Wales. Built in the elaborate 'decorated' style of gothic architecture, the palace is lavishly encrusted with fine carving.
Location: OS Ref. SM750 254. A487 to St Davids, minor road past the Cathedral.
Open: 27 Mar - 26 May: 9.30am - 5pm. 27 May - 1 Oct: 9.30am - 6pm. 2 - 29 Oct: 9.30am - 5pm. 30 Oct - 31 Mar, Mon - Sat, 9.30am - 4pm, Suns, 11am - 4pm. Closed 24 - 26 Dec & 1 Jan. Opening/admission details subject to review Mar 2002.
Admission: Adult £2, Child/Conc. £1.50, Family £5.50.

ST DAVIDS CATHEDRAL
St Davids, Dyfed SA62 6QW
Tel: 01437 720691 **Fax:** 01437 721885   **Contact:** Mr R G Tarr
Over eight centuries old. Many unique and 'odd' features.
Location: OS Ref. SM751 254. 5-10mins walk from car/coach parks: signs for pedestrians.
Open: Daily: 7.30am - 6.30pm. Suns: 12.30 - 5.30pm, may be closed for services in progress. Sun services: 8am, 9.30am, 11.15am & 6pm. Weekday services: 8am & 6pm. Weds extra service: 10am.
Admission: Donations. Guided tours (Adult £3, Child £1.20) must be booked.

STRATA FLORIDA ABBEY ✠
Ystrad Meurig, Pontrhydfendigaid SY25 6BT
Tel: 01974 831261   www.cadw.wales.gov.uk
Owner: In the care of Cadw   **Contact:** The Custodian
Remotely set in the green, kite-haunted Teifi Valley with the lonely Cambrian mountains as a backdrop, the ruined abbey has a wonderful doorway with Celtic spiral motifs and preserves a wealth of beautiful medieval tiles.
Location: OS Ref. SN746 658. Minor road from Pontrhydfendigaid 14m SE of Aberystwyth by the B4340.
Open: 21 Apr - 24 Sept: daily, 10am - 5pm. Winter: open site. Opening/admission details subject to review Mar 2002.
Admission: Adult £2, Child/Conc. £1.50, Family £5.50.

TINTERN ABBEY ✠
Tintern NP6 6SE
Tel: 01291 689251   www.cadw.wales.gov.uk
Owner: In the care of Cadw   **Contact:** The Custodian
Tintern is the best preserved abbey in Wales and ranks among Britain's most beautiful historic sites. Elaborately decorated in 'gothic' architecture style this church stands almost complete to roof level. Turner sketched and painted here, while Wordsworth drew inspiration from the surroundings.
Location: OS Ref. SO533 000. Tintern via A466, from M4/J23. Chepstow 6m.
Open: 27 Mar - 26 May: 9.30am - 5pm. 27 May - 1 Oct: 9.30am - 6pm. 2 - 29 Oct 9.30am - 5pm. 30 Oct - 31 Mar: Mon - Sat, 9.30am - 4pm, Suns, 11am - 4pm. Closed 24 - 26 Dec & 1 Jan. Opening/admission details subject to review Mar 2002.
Admission: Adult £2.50, Child/Conc. £2, Family £7.

Dyffryn Gardens

The Vale of Glamorgan Council

TREDEGAR HOUSE & PARK 🏛
NEWPORT, SOUTH WALES NP1 9YW
Tel: 01633 815880 **Fax:** 01633 815895 **e-mail:** tredegar.house@newport.gov.uk
Owner: Newport County Borough Council   **Contact:** The Manager
South Wales' finest country house, ancestral home of the Morgan family. Parts of a medieval house remain, but Tredegar owes its reputation to lavish rebuilding in the 17th century. Visitors have a lively and entertaining tour through 30 rooms, including glittering State Rooms and 'below stairs'. Set in 90 acres of parkland with formal gardens. Winner of Best Public Park and Garden in Great Britain 1997. Craft workshops.
Location: OS Ref. ST290 852. M4/J28 signposted. From London 2½ hrs, from Cardiff 20 mins. 2m SW of Newport town centre.
Open: Easter - Sept: Wed - Sun & BHs, 11.30am - 4pm. Evening tours & groups by appointment. Oct - Mar: Groups only by appointment.
Admission: Adult £4.95, Child £2.25, Conc. £3.65, Family £12.95. Special discounts for Newport residents (2001 prices).
ℹ Conferences. No photography in house. Partial. WC.
Obligatory. In grounds, on leads. Tel for details.

TREOWEN

Wonastow, Nr Monmouth NP25 4DL

Tel/Fax: 01600 712031   **e-mail:** john.wheelock@virgin.net

http://freespace.virginnet.co.uk/treowen.com

Owner: R A & J P Wheelock   **Contact:** John Wheelock

Early 17th century mansion built to double pile plan with magnificent well-stair to four storeys.

Location: OS Ref. SO461 111. 3m WSW of Monmouth.

Open: 11/12 & 18/19 May and 14/15, 21/22 & 28/29 Sept: 10am - 4pm.

Admission: £5 (£3 if appointment made). Groups by appointment only.

Ⓣ 🅱 Entire house let, self-catering. Sleeps 24+. ▲

TRETOWER COURT & CASTLE ♣

Tretower, Crickhowell NP8 2RF

Tel: 01874 730279   www.cadw.wales.gov.uk

Owner: In the care of Cadw   **Contact:** The Custodian

A fine fortress and an outstanding medieval manor house, Tretower Court and Castle range around a galleried courtyard, now further enhanced by a beautiful recreated medieval garden.

Location: OS Ref. SO187 212. Signposted in Tretower Village, off A479, 3m NW of Crickhowell.

Open: 1 - 26 Mar: 10am - 4pm. 27 Mar - 26 May: 10am - 5pm. 27 May - 3 Sept: 10am - 6pm. 4 Sept - 29 Oct: 10am - 5pm. Winter: closed. Opening/admission details subject to review Mar 2002.

Admission: Adult £2.50, Child/Conc. £2, Family £7.

🔲 🅱 🔲 🅿 🖼 Guide dogs only.

TYTHEGSTON COURT

Tythegston, Bridgend CF32 0NE

e-mail: cknight@tythegston.com   www.tythegston.com

Owner/Contact: C Knight

Mansion house, originally built in the 14th century, owned throughout by the Knight family and their ancestors. Substantially altered in 1776 by Colonel Knight of the Glamorgan Militia. Georgian entrance hall with contemporary portraits, Adam style wall frieze and ceilings.

Location: OS Ref. SS857 789. 2m E of Porthcawl on Glamorgan coast.

Open: By written appointment.

Admission: Adult £10, Child £2.50, Conc. £5.

Ⓣ 🅱 Partial. 🎦 Obligatory. 🅿 Limited. No coaches. 🖼 Guide dogs only.

USK CASTLE

The Castle House, Usk, Monmouthshire NP15 1SD

Tel: 01291 672563   www.castlewales.com/usk

Owner/Contact: J H L Humphreys

Romantic, ruined castle overlooking the picturesque town of Usk. Inner and outer baileys, towers and earthwork defences. Surrounded by enchanting gardens (open under NGS) incorporating The Castle House, the former medieval gatehouse.

Location: OS Ref. SO376 011. Up narrow lane off Monmouth road in Usk, opposite fire station.

Open: Castle ruins: daily, 11am - 5pm. Groups by appointment. Gardens: private visits welcome & groups by arrangement. House: Jun & BHs: 2 - 5pm (except 22/23 Jun), small groups & guided tours only.

Admission: Castle ruins: Adult £2, Child Free. Gardens: Adult £2. House: Adult £5, Child £2.

Ⓣ 🅱 Partial. 🎦 By arrangement. 🔲 🅿 No coaches. 🖼 In grounds, on leads. ❄

WEOBLEY CASTLE ♣

Weobley Castle Farm, Llanrhidian SA3 1HB

Tel: 01792 390012   www.cadw.wales.gov.uk

Owner: In the care of Cadw   **Contact:** The Custodian

Perched above the wild northern coast of the beautiful Gower peninsula, Weobley Castle was the home of the Knightly de Bere family. Its rooms include a fine hall and private chamber as well as numerous 'garderobes' or toilets and an early Tudor porch block.

Location: OS Ref. SN477 928. B4271 or B4295 to Llanrhidian Village, then minor road for 1¹/₂ m.

Open: Apr - early Oct: 9.30am - 6pm. Oct - late Mar: 9.30am - 4pm. Closed 24 - 26 Dec & 1 Jan. Opening/admission details subject to review Mar 2002.

Admission: Adult £2, Child/Conc. £1.50, Family £5.50.

🔲 🅿 🖼 Guide dogs only. ❄

WHITE CASTLE ♣

Llantillio Crossenny, Gwent

Tel: 01600 780380   www.cadw.wales.gov.uk

Owner: In the care of Cadw   **Contact:** The Custodian

With its high walls and round towers reflected in the still waters of its moat, White Castle is the ideal medieval fortress. It was rebuilt in the mid-13th century by the future King Edward I to counter a threat from Prince Llywelyn the Last.

Location: OS Ref. SO380 167. By minor road 2m NW from B4233 at A7 Llantilio Crossenny. 8m ENE of Abergavenny.

Open: 21 Apr - 24 Sept: 10am - 5pm. Winter: Open site. Opening/admission details subject to review Mar 2002.

Admission: Adult £2, Conc. £1.50, Family £5.50.

🔲 🅿 🖼 Guide dogs only. ❄

NTPL/Erik Pelham

TUDOR MERCHANT'S HOUSE ✤

QUAY HILL, TENBY SA70 7BX

Tel/Fax: 01834 842279

Owner: The National Trust   **Contact:** The Custodian

A late 15th century town house, characteristic of the building tradition of south west Wales. The ground-floor chimney at the rear of the house is a fine vernacular example, and the original scarfed roof-trusses survive. The remains of early frescoes can be seen on three interior walls. Access to small herb garden, weather permitting. Furniture and fittings re-create the atmosphere from the time when a Tudor family was in residence.

Location: OS Ref. SN135 004. Tenby. W of alley from NE corner of town centre square.

Open: 23 Mar - 30 Sept: daily except Weds, 10am - 5pm; Suns, 1 - 5pm. 1 Oct - 3 Nov: daily except Weds & Sats, 10am - 3pm; Suns, 12 noon - 3pm.

Admission: Adult £2, Child £1. Groups: Adult £1.60, Child 80p. NT members Free.

ⓘ No indoor photography. 🅿 No parking. 🔲 🖼 Guide dogs only.

Colby Woodland Garden

NT Photographic Library: Andrew Butler

THE REGIONS OF
IRELAND

Kylemore Abbey © Benedictine Nuns

IRELAND

Mount Stewart

Ireland

WESTERN
ISLES

HIGHLANDS & SKYE

GRAMPIAN
HIGHLANDS

PERTHSHIRE/FIFE

WEST
HIGHLANDS
ISLANDS

GREATER
GLASGOW

EDINBURGH

BORDERS

SOUTH WEST SCOTLAND

NORTHUMBER-
LAND

TYNE & WEAR

CUMBRIA

DURHAM

ISLE OF MAN

YORKSHIRE

LANCASHIRE

DONEGAL

LONDONDERRY

TYRONE

ANTRIM

FERMANAGH

ARMAGH

DOWN

SLIGO

MONAGHAN

LEITRIM

CAVAN

MAYO

ROSCOMMON

LONGFORD

LOUTH

WESTMEATH

MEATH

GALWAY

OFFALY

DUBLIN

KILDARE

LAOIS

WICKLOW

CLARE

CARLOW

LIMERICK

TIPPERARY

KILKENNY

WEXFORD

KERRY

CORK

WATERFORD

ISLE OF
ANGLESEY

MERSEYSIDE

CONWY

CHESHIRE

DERBY-
SHIRE

NOTTING-
HAMSHIRE

LINCOLNSHIRE

GWYNEDD

STAFFORD-
SHIRE

LEICESTER-
SHIRE

RUTLAND

NORFOLK

SHROP-
SHIRE

WEST
MIDLANDS

NORTHAMPTON-
SHIRE

CAMBRIDGE-
SHIRE

SUFFOLK

POWYS

CEREDIGION

WORCESTER-
SHIRE

WARWICK-
SHIRE

HEREFORD-
SHIRE

BEDFORDSHIRE

PEMBROKE-
SHIRE

CARMARTHEN-
SHIRE

GLOUCESTER-
SHIRE

BUCKINGHAM-
SHIRE

HERTFORD-
SHIRE

ESSEX

OXFORD-
SHIRE

LONDON

BERKSHIRE

WILTSHIRE

SURREY

KENT

HAMPSHIRE

W. SUSSEX

E. SUSSEX

SOMERSET

DEVON

DORSET

ISLE OF WIGHT

CORNWALL

Mount Stewart

"Mount Stewart's gardens ..... blend classical proportions and Celtic whimsy; they mix pavilions, topiary, statuary and dovecotes. They are a scrapbook of Edith Lady Londonderry's life and loves, and they are blessed by the temperate climate of the Ards peninsula, sitting between Strangford Lough and the Irish Sea."

Lyn Gallagher

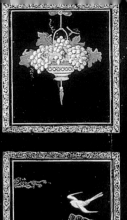

NTPL / Peter Aprahamiam

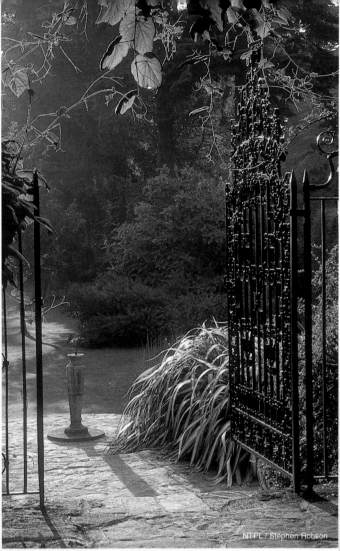

NTPL / Stephen Robson

Mount Stewart Gardens in Northern Ireland are one of the jewels in the crown of the National Trust and should not be missed. They have recently been nominated by the Government for World Heritage status.

The charm of Mount Stewart is that, more than any other National Trust property in Northern Ireland, it is a family creation for when Alexander Stewart bought the estate in 1744 it was the beginning of a process in which each generation of the family applied their own ideas, tastes and enthusiasms to both the house and the garden. However it was when Edith, wife of the 7th Marquess of Londonderry, came to Mount Stewart in the 1920s that a new era dawned for the house and garden, and the seeds of the full glory we all enjoy today were planted.

The 7th Marquess had inherited Mount Stewart in 1915 but the family came to settle at the house only in 1921 when Lord Londonderry took up the post of Minister of Education in the first Ulster Parliament. When Lady Londonderry had visited Mount Stewart some years before she described it as *'the dampest, darkest and saddest place I have ever stayed in'*.

However, Lady Londonderry was obviously not a woman to be easily deterred. Everywhere you look in the house and garden today you feel her elegant touch and humorous spirit. The power of these gardens stems from Lady Londonderry's obvious talent as a plantswoman and her remarkable ability to collect specimen plants and take advice. For this she turned to renowned gardeners Sir John Ross of Rostrevor in Co Down and Sir Herbert Maxwell of Monreith in Scotland. From these two men she learned the art of mixing sub-tropical plants who enjoyed the warm, humid climate provided by the nearby Irish Sea and the Gulf Stream, with their native partners. Walk through the garden long enough and you will have seen bay trees in pots said to be the largest in Europe, olive trees grown from seed from the Mount of Olives, and purple Japanese Maples.

Part of the garden is divided into a series of 'compartments'. Some, like the Sunken Garden to the north west of the house are formal plantings; others, like the Shamrock Garden designed in the shape of Ireland's emblem, are idiosyncratic, with the red Hand of Ulster blazing in scarlet begonias and the Irish topiary harp acting as the centrepiece. The Mairi Garden derives its name from the youngest daughter of Lady Londonderry who was placed here in her pram everyday – the fountain represents the *'Mairi, Mairi, quite contrary'* of the nursery rhyme. These are only a few of the formal gardens which the visitor can enjoy.

There is also a myriad of informal areas. The acres of spring flowering rhododendrons and magnificent magnolias are breathtaking. The Lake Walk, the Jubilee Avenue Walk and the Rock Walk – as with other parts of the garden – should be seen several times during the year to fully appreciate the skill and sheer brilliance of the colour of the plantings. If, though, you can only visit this beautiful garden once, it will still guarantee to be an unforgettable experience.

For further details about *Mount Stewart* see entry on page 539.

NTPL / Jerry Harpur

Elizabeth Frances Charlotte, Viscountess Castlereagh

ANNES GROVE GARDENS
Castletownroche, Co Cork

Tel: +353 22 26145

Owner/Contact: Mr P Annesley

The gardens around the 18th century house contain magnolias, eucryphias and hoherias of unusual size. Winding paths and riverside walks.

Location: 1.6 km N of Castletownroche.

Open: 17 Mar - 30 Sept: Mon - Sat, 10am - 5pm; Suns, 1 - 6pm. Other times by arrangement.

Admission: Adult €4, Child €1, Conc. €3.

ANTRIM CASTLE GARDENS
Randalstown Road, Antrim BT41 4LH

Tel: 028 9442 8000   **Fax:** 028 9446 0360   **e-mail:** clotworthyartscentre@hotmail.com

Owner: Antrim Borough Council   **Contact:** Philip Magennis

Situated adjacent to Antrim Town, the Sixmilewater River and Lough Neagh's shore, these recently restored, 17th century Anglo-Dutch water gardens are maintained in a manner authentic to the period. The gardens comprise of ornamental canals, round pond, ancient motte and a parterre garden planted with 17th century plants - many with culinary or medicinal uses. An interpretative display introducing the history of the gardens and the process of their restoration, along with a scale model of former Antrim Castle is located in the reception of Clotworthy Arts Centre.

Location: Outside Antrim town centre off A26 on A6.

Open: All year: Mon - Fri, 9.30am - 9.30pm (dusk if earlier). Sats, 10am - 5pm. Jul & Aug: also open Suns, 2 - 5pm.

Admission: Free. Charge for guided group tours (by arrangement only).

🛈 ❋

ARDRESS HOUSE & FARMYARD ❧
64 Ardress Road, Portadown, Co Armagh BT62 1SQ

Tel/Fax: 028 3885 1236   **e-mail:** uagest@smtp.ntrust.org.uk

Owner: The National Trust   **Contact:** The Custodian

A 17th century farmhouse with elegant 18th century additions by owner-architect George Ensor. Includes a display of antique farming implements in the farmyard. House tours include the Adam-style drawing room, fine furniture and pictures. Also an attractive garden with woodland and riverside walks amid apple orchards.

Location: On B28, 5m from Moy, 5m from Portadown, 3m from M1/J13.

Open: 16 Mar - May: weekends & BH/PHs; Jun - Aug: daily (except Tue unless BH/PH Tue); Sept: weekends; 2 - 6pm.

Admission: House tour: Adult £2.70, Child £1.35, Family £6.75. Groups £2.20.

🚻 Ground floor. WC. 🛈 Obligatory. 🅿

THE ARGORY ❧
Moy, Dungannon, Co Tyrone BT71 6NA

Tel: 028 8778 4753   **Fax:** 028 8778 9598   **e-mail:** uagest@smtp.ntrust.org.uk

Owner: The National Trust   **Contact:** The Property Manager

The Argory is a handsome 19th century Victorian house furnished as it was in 1900, providing an excellent illustration of Victorian/Edwardian interior taste and interests. Includes the 1824 Bishop's barrel organ, still in working order. Imposing stableyard with horse carriages, harness room, acetylene gas plant, laundry and children's playground. It is set in 130 hectares of wooded countryside overlooking the River Blackwater. Variety of garden, woodland or riverside walks suitable for all ages.

Location: On Derrycaw road, 4m from Moy, 3m from M1/J13 or J14 (coaches J13).

Open: House: 16 Mar - May; weekends & BH/PHs; Jun - Aug: daily, 12 noon - 6pm (open 1pm Jun weekdays); Sept: weekends. Grounds: Oct - Apr: daily, 10am - 4pm. May - Sept: daily, 10am - 8pm.

Admission: House tour: Adult £4, Child £2, Family £10. Groups: Adult £3.25, Child £1.65. Car park: £2 (refunded on purchase of house ticket).

📷 🚻 Ground floor. WC. 📺 🛈 Obligatory. 🅿 🔼

BALLINDOOLIN HOUSE & GARDEN
Carbury, Co Kildare

Tel: +353 405 31430   **Fax:** +353 405 32377   **e-mail:** sundial@iol.ie   **www.**ballindoolin.com

Owner: R Molony   **Contact:** Esther Molony

Large country house and farmyards surrounded by extensive gardens, including a 2 acre working walled garden. Also ³/₄hr heritage and nature trail.

Location: 5.6km N of Edenderry on the R401 to Kinnegad.

Open: 1 May - 30 Sept: Tue - Sun, 12 noon - 6pm. Tyrrells Restaurant: All year, tel. +353 405 32400.

Admission: House: €3.50. Garden: Adult €5, Child €2.50. Under 5s Free. Concessions for booked groups (20+).

🛈 No photography in house. 📷 🚼 🇹 🚻 Partial. WC. 🍽 🛈 Obligatory for house. 🅿 ▪ 🦮 Guide dogs only. ❋ Restaurant only.

BALLINLOUGH CASTLE GARDENS
Ballinlough Castle, Clonmellon, Co Westmeath

Tel: +353 46 33135   **Fax:** +353 46 33331

Owner: Sir John & Lady Nugent   **Contact:** Sir John Nugent

Set in the lakeland county of Westmeath the gardens comprise of herbaceous borders, roses, fruit and much more.

Location: On N52 half-way between Clonmellon and Delvin. Signed from Athboy.

Open: 1 May - 30 Sept: Thur - Sat, 12 noon - 6pm. Suns & BHs, 2 - 6pm. Gardens: closed 1st two weeks in Aug.

Admission: Adult £4, Child £1, Conc. £3. Groups (20+): £3.50.

BALLYWALTER PARK 🏛
Nr Newtownards, Co Down BT22 2PP

Tel: 028 4275 8264   **Fax:** 028 4275 8818

e-mail: enquiries@dunleath-estates.co.uk   **www.**dunleath-estates.co.uk

Owner: Lord Dunleath   **Contact:** The Secretary, The Estate Office

Victorian mansion, situated in 40 acres of landscaped grounds, built in the mid-19th century by Charles Lanyon, with Edwardian additions by W J Fennell. Currently undergoing major restoration works. Self-catered (4 star) listed gatelodge overlooking beach available for holiday lets (sleeps four).

Location: 1km S of Ballywalter village.

Open: Please telephone for access, due to major restoration work.

Admission: House or Gardens: Adult £4, Child/Conc. £3. House and gardens: Adult £7, Conc. £5.50. Groups (Max. 50): Adult £4, Child/Conc. £2.

🛈 No photography indoors. 📷 Pick-your-own, Jun - Aug. 🛈 Obligatory. 🅿 🔼

Shaw Birthplace

BANTRY HOUSE
BANTRY, Co CORK
www.bantryhouse.ie

Tel: +353 27 50047 **Fax:** +353 27 50795 **e-mail:** info@bantryhouse.ie

Owner/Contact: Mr & Mrs E Shelswell-White

Overlooking Bantry Bay, with views to the Cork-Kerry mountains, the house and gardens enjoy one of the most spectacular views in Ireland. Bantry House, home to the White family since 1739, is one of the finest stately homes in Ireland, containing a unique collection of tapestries, furniture, carpets and art treasures, collected mainly by the 2nd Earl in the 19th century. The magnificent gardens and grounds (under restoration) are home to many sub-tropical plants and shrubs – reflecting the best European design and style. Other features within the 45 acre grounds include the renowned 100-steps 'Stairway to the Sky', the Italian Garden and the largest wisteria circle in the country. Bantry House and Gardens is a member of the Houses, Castles & Gardens of Ireland Scheme and Hidden Ireland.

Location: E outskirts of Bantry town on the main Cork – Killarney coast road (N71).

Open: 1 Mar - end Oct: daily, 9am - 5pm (last admission).

Admission: House, Gardens & Exhibition: Adult €9.50, Child Free, Conc. €8. Groups (20+): €6. Gardens & Exhibition: Adult €4, Child Free.

⬛ ⬛ ⬛ Partial. ⬛ ⬛ ⬛ In grounds, on leads. ⬛ 8 doubles.

BARONS COURT
Newtownstewart, Omagh, Co Tyrone BT78 4EZ

Tel: 028 8166 1683 **Fax:** 028 8166 2059   **Contact:** The Agent

The home of the Duke and Duchess of Abercorn, Barons Court was built between 1779 and 1782, and subsequently extensively remodelled by John Soane (1791), William and Richard Morrison (1819-1841), Sir Albert Richardson (1947-49) and David Hicks (1975-76).

Location: 5km SW of Newtownstewart.

Open: By appointment only.

Admission: Adult £4.50, Conc. £3. Groups max. 50.

⬛ Partial. WCs. ⬛ By arrangement. ⬛ ⬛ ⬛ ⬛

BENVARDEN GARDEN
Dervock, Ballymoney, Co Antrim

Tel: 028 2074 1331 **Fax:** 028 2074 1955 **e-mail:** benvarden@onetel.net.uk

Owner/Contact: Mr H J Montgomery

Beautiful walled gardens with woodland walks on the banks of the River Bush.

Location: 10km from Giants' Causeway on B67 Coleraine – Ballycastle road, then follow brown tourist signs.

Open: 1 Jun - 31 Aug: daily (except Mons), 1.30 - 5pm. Other times by arrangement.

Admission: Adult £2.50, Child £1. Group rates on request.

⬛ Small museum. ⬛ ⬛ ⬛ ⬛ By arrangement. ⬛

BIRR CASTLE DEMESNE
Birr, Co Offaly

Tel: +353 509 20336 **Fax:** +353 509 21583

e-mail: info@birrcastle.com **www**.birrcastle.com   **Contact:** P Hynes

Discover the largest telescope for over 70 years; constructed here at Birr Castle in the 1840s by the 3rd Earl of Rosse. The telescope looks and moves just as it did over 150 years ago. Magnificent award-winning gardens which feature collections of rare trees, imaginative planting, the tallest box hedges in the world, beautiful landscapes with lake, rivers and waterfalls. At the science centre discover many pioneering achievements of the Parsons family and of other great Irish scientists in the fields of astronomy, photography, engineering, botany and horticulture.

Location: In town of Birr. 130km from Dublin; 90km from Shannon via Limerick.

Open: All year: 9am - 6pm or dusk if earlier. Science Centre: As gardens.

Admission: Adult €7, Child €3.50, Family (2+2) €20. Groups (20+): Adult €5.70, Child €3.50.

⬛ ⬛ ⬛ Partial. WC. ⬛ ⬛ By arrangement. ⬛ ⬛ Limited for coaches. ⬛ In grounds, on leads. ⬛

BLARNEY CASTLE & ROCK CLOSE
Co Cork

Tel: +353 21 438 5252 **Fax:** +353 21 438 1518 **e-mail:** info@blarneycastle.ie

Owner: Sir Richard La T Colthurst Bart   **Contact:** Mervyn Johnston Esq

Site of the Blarney Stone.

Location: 8km from Cork city, off N20.

Open: May: Mon - Sat, 9am - 6.30pm. Jun - Aug: Mon - Sat, 9am - 7pm. Sept: Mon - Sat, 9am - 6.30pm. Oct - Apr: Mon - Sat, 9am - 5pm or sundown. Summer Suns: 9.30am - 5.30pm. Winter Suns: 9.30am - sundown. Closed 24 & 25 Dec.

Admission: Adult €5.50, Child €2, Student/OAP €4, Family (2+2) €11.50.

CARRIGGLAS MANOR
Longford

Tel: +353 43 45165 **Fax:** +353 43 42882

Owner: Mr J G Lefroy   **Contact:** Mrs J G Lefroy or Miss Flynn

A romantic Tudor Gothic house. Family occupied. Robinsonia garden.

Location: 4.8km from Longford town on T15/R194.

Open: Please telephone for details.

Admission: Teashop & Shop: Free. Gardens & museum: Adult £4, Child (under 7yrs) Free, Conc. £2. House: £3 extra. Pre-booked groups (12+) welcome throughout the year.

CASTLE COOLE ❧
ENNISKILLEN, Co FERMANAGH BT74 6JY

Tel: 028 6632 2690 **Fax:** 028 6632 5665 **e-mail:** ucasco@smtp.ntrust.org.uk
Owner: The National Trust **Contact:** The Property Manager
Castle Coole is one of the finest neo-classical houses in Ireland, built by James Wyatt in the late 18th century, and sited in a rolling landscape park right on the edge of Enniskillen. Features opulent Regency interior decoration, furnishings and furniture. Guided tour includes ornate state bedroom prepared for George IV in 1821. Also includes stables, Belmore private coach, servants' tunnel, laundry house, dairy and icehouse. The surrounding parkland is ideal for long walks and picnics and includes a children's play area. Tea-room in Tallow House for light refreshments.
Location: On A4, 1m from Enniskillen on A4, Belfast - Enniskillen road.
Open: House: 16 Mar - May: weekends & BH/PHs (including 29 Mar); Jun: daily (except Tue unless BH/PH Tue); Jul - Aug: daily; Sept: weekends: 12 noon - 6pm. Grounds: Oct - Apr: 10am - 4pm. May - Sept: 10am - 8pm.
Admission: House tour: Adult £3.50, Child £1.75, Family £8.50. Groups: £3. Grounds charge (applies Mar - Sept): Car £2 (refunded on purchase of house tour).

CASTLE WARD ❧
STRANGFORD, DOWNPATRICK, Co DOWN BT30 7LS

Tel: 028 4488 1204 **Fax:** 028 4488 1729 **e-mail:** ucwest@smtp.ntrust.org.uk
Owner: The National Trust **Contact:** The Property Manager
Castle Ward is a beautiful 750 acre walled estate in a stunning location overlooking Strangford Lough. The mid-Georgian mansion is one of the architectural curios of its time, built inside and out in two distinct architectural styles. Due to a difference of opinion between its 18th century owners, Bernard and Anne Ward, the house features Classical styling on one side and Gothic on the other. The picturesque estate also includes a Victorian laundry and children's playroom, water-driven cornmill demonstrations, a disused leadmine and sawmill, which provide a fascinating insight into how the house and estate worked. Paths and horse trails wind their way throughout the estate. Also formal gardens, the Old Castle Ward tower house from 1610, the Temple Water (a man-made lake) and the Strangford Lough Wildlife Centre. Stableyard includes tearoom and a large Trust shop.
Location: On A25, 7m from Downpatrick and 1½ m from Strangford.
Open: House & Wildlife Centre: 16 - 18, 23/24 & 29 Mar; Apr: weekends & BH/PH: May: daily (except Tue). Jun - Aug: daily; Sept - Oct: weekends. All 12 noon - 6pm. (May & Jun open 1pm). Grounds: Oct - Apr: 10am - 4pm. May - Sept: 10am - 8pm.
Admission: House tour: Adult £4.50, Child £1.75, Family £9.50. Groups: £3.50 (after hours £4.50). Grounds: £3 per car. Coach £15. Horsebox £5. Car park charge refunded on purchase of house ticket.

CASTLE LESLIE
Glaslough, Co Monaghan
Tel: +353 47 88109 **Fax:** +353 47 88256 **e-mail:** info@castleleslie.com
Owner/Contact: Samantha Leslie
The present castle was built in 1878. Contains Italian and Spanish furniture, tapestries and carpets. The family home of the Leslies.
Location: 6 km N of Monaghan at Glaslough village.
Open: Open for accommodation and dining throughout the year.

CLONALIS HOUSE
Castlerea, Co Rosscommon
Tel: +353 907 20014
Owner: P O'Conor Nash Esq
Ancestral home of the O'Conors of Connaught, descendants of the last High Kings of Ireland.
Location: W of Castlerea town on N60.
Open: 1 Jun - 15 Sept: daily (except Suns), 11am - 5pm. Open all year to groups by arrangement.
Admission: Adult £4, Child £2, Conc. £3.

CRATLOE WOODS HOUSE
Cratloe, Co Clare
Tel: +353 61 327028 **Fax:** +353 61 327031
Owner/Contact: Mr & Mrs G Brickenden
House dates from the 17th century and is the only example of the Irish longhouse which is still a home.
Location: 8 km from Limerick and 16 km from Shannon airport on N7 westbound carriageway. Enter at Red Gate Lodge.
Open: 1 Jun - mid Sept: Mon - Sat, 2 - 6pm. Open other times by arrangement.
Admission: Adult £3, Child £1.50, Conc. £2.50. Special rate for guided tour in morning with lunch, for groups of 20 - 40.

Bantry House

CROM ESTATE

Newtownbutler, Co Fermanagh BT92 8AP

Tel/Fax: 028 6773 8118 (Visitor Centre) 028 6773 8174 (Estate)

e-mail: ucromw@smtp.ntrust.org.uk

Owner: The National Trust   **Contact:** The Visitor Facilities Manager

Crom is one of Ireland's most important nature conservation areas. It is set in 770 hectares of romantic and tranquil islands, woodland and ruins on the shores of Upper Lough Erne. Things to look out for include the spotted flycatcher, curlew, purple hairstreak butterfly, pine marten and fallow deer. Lots of well-maintained nature trails take in the Old Castle, boathouse and summer house. Wildlife exhibition, information point and tearoom for light snacks in visitor centre. Further facilities include jetty for boats, boat hire, award-winning holiday cottages, coarse angling, pike fishing, overnight woodland hide, lecture and conference facilities. The 19th century castle within the estate is private.

Location: 3m from A34, well signposted from Newtownbutler. Jetty at Visitor Centre.

Open: 17 Mar - Jun: daily, 10am - 6pm; Jul & Aug: daily, 10am - 8pm; Sept: daily,10am - 6pm Suns: open 12 noon.

Admission: Grounds & Visitor Centre: Car or Boat £4. Minibus £12, Coach £25.

⊤ ⊕ P ⊞ Holiday cottages. ▲

CURRAGHMORE

Portlaw, Co Waterford

Tel: +353 51 387 101 **Fax:** +353 51 387 481

Owner/Contact: Lord Waterford

Magnificent home of the Marquis of Waterford and his ancestors since 1170.

Location: 14m from Waterford. 8m from Kilmacthomas.

Open: Jan: Mon - Fri, 9am - 1pm. May - Jun & 1 - 15 Jul: Mon - Sat, 9am - 1pm.

Admission: House £4. Grounds & Shell House: £3

DERRYMORE HOUSE

Bessbrook, Newry, Co Armagh BT35 7EF

Tel: 028 3083 8361

Owner: The National Trust

An elegant late 18th century thatched cottage, built by Isaac Corry, who represented Newry in the Irish House of Commons. Good walks in picturesque park laid out in the style of 'Capability' Brown. Good attraction to break journey between Belfast and Dublin.

Location: On A25, 2m from Newry on road to Camlough.

Open: 30 Mar & 1 - 2 Apr; May - Aug: Thur - Sat, 2pm - 5.30pm. Grounds: Oct - Apr: 10am - 4pm. May - Sept: 10am - 8pm.

Admission: House tour: Adult £2.25, Child £1, Family £4.50. Groups: £1.30.

P ⊞ On leads.

DRIMNAGH CASTLE

Longmile Road, Drimnagh, Dublin 12

Tel: +353 450 2530 **Fax:** +353 450 8927

Medieval castle with a flooded moat and boasts a barrel-vaulted undercroft.

Location: 5 km SW of Dublin. Buses: 18, 56, 77.

Open: 1 Apr - 31 Sept: Wed, Sat & Sun, 12 noon - 5pm. 1 Oct - 31 Mar: Sun, 2 - 5pm, Wed, 12 noon - 5pm. Last tour 4.15pm. Other times by appointment.

Admission: Adult €3.17, Child €1.27, Student/OAP/Groups €2.54.

DUBLIN WRITERS MUSEUM

18 Parnell Square, Dublin 1

Tel: +353 1 8722077 **Fax:** +353 1 8722231 **e-mail:** writers@dublintourism.ie

Owner: Dublin Tourism Enterprises   **Contact:** Eilish Rafferty

The museum features the lives and works of Dublin's literary celebrities over the past 300 years.

Location: City Centre, N of O'Connell Street.

Open: Jan - Dec: Mon - Sat, 10am - 5pm. Suns & Public Hols, 11am - 5pm. Jun - Aug: late opening Mon - Fri, 10am - 6pm.

Admission: Adult £4, Child (3-11yrs) £2, Conc. £3, Student £3.60, Family £11.

DUNKATHEL

Glanmire, Co Cork

Tel: +353 21 482 1014 **Fax:** +353 21 482 1023

Owner: The Russell Family   **Contact:** Mr John Russell

House dates from c1790. Contains splendid bifurcated staircase of Bath stone.

Location: 5 km from Cork off N25.

Open: 1 May - mid Oct: Wed - Sun, 2 - 6pm.

Admission: Adult £2, Child £1, Conc. £1.50. Special group rate.

DUNLOE CASTLE HOTEL GARDENS

Beaufort, Killarney, Co Kerry

Tel: +353 64 44111 **Fax:** +353 64 44583

Owner: The Liebherr Family   **Contact:** Michael Brennan

Collection of trees, shrubs and plants from around the world.

Location: 13 km from Killarney.

Open: May - Oct: Groups and tours by appointment.

Admission: Free. Catalogue £1.

FLORENCE COURT

ENNISKILLEN, Co FERMANAGH BT92 1DB

Tel: 028 6634 8249 **Fax:** 028 6634 8873 **e-mail:** ufcest@smtp.ntrust.org.uk

Owner: The National Trust   **Contact:** The Property Manager

Florence Court is a fine mid-18th century house and estate set against the stunning backdrop of the Cuilcagh Mountains. It was the home of the Earls of Enniskillen and is one of the most important houses in Ulster. It is now a popular attraction for all the family. Exquisite rococo ceilings and panels, fine Irish furniture. Original paintings, furniture and artefacts returned in 1998 and 1999. House tour includes service quarters popular with all ages. Water-powered sawmill; ice-house; summer house; beautiful walled garden and lots of walks in grounds. Morning coffee, lunches and afternoon teas in Stables Restaurant, gift shop. Also children's playground and holiday cottage.

Location: 8m SW of Enniskillen via A4 then A32 to Swanlinbar.

Open: House: 17, 24, 29 - 31 Mar; Apr & May: weekends & BH/PHs; Jun - Aug: daily (open 1pm Jun weekdays); Sept: weekends: 12 noon - 6pm. Grounds: Oct - Apr: 10am - 4pm. May - Sept: 10am - 8pm.

Admission: House tour: Adult £3.50, Child £1.75, Family £8.50. Groups: £3. Grounds (charged Mar - Sept): Car £2.50 (refundable on purchase of house tour).

□ ♿ Ground floor. WC. ⊕ 🎫 Obligatory. P ⊞ In grounds, on leads. ⊞ Holiday cottage. ▲

THE FRY MODEL RAILWAY

Malahide Castle Demesne, Malahide, Co Dublin

Tel: +353 1 846 3779 **Fax:** +353 1 846 3723

Owner: Dublin Tourism Attractions   **Contact:** John Dunne

The Fry Model Railway is a unique collection of handmade models of Irish trains from the beginning of travel to modern times.

Location: 10m N of Dublin.

Open: Apr - Sept: Mon - Sat, 10am - 5pm, Suns & BHs 2 - 6pm. Closed 1 - 2pm daily all year.

Admission: Adult £5.50, Child (3-11yrs) £3, Conc. £5, Family (2+4) £15.

GLIN CASTLE

Glin, Co Limerick

Tel: +353 68 34173 **Fax:** +353 68 34364 **e-mail:** knight@iol.ie

Owner: The Knight of Glin   **Contact:** Bob Duff

Glin Castle, one of Ireland's most historic properties and home to the FitzGerald family, hereditary Knights of Glin. The castle, with its superb interiors, decorative plasterwork and collections of Irish furniture and paintings stands on the banks of the River Shannon.

Location: Co Limerick.

Open: Tours by appointment only.

Admission: Adult £5.

GRAY'S PRINTING PRESS

49 Main Street, Strabane, Co Tyrone BT82 8AU

Tel: 028 7188 4094

Owner: The National Trust   **Contact:** The Administrator

Historic printworks, featuring 18th century printing press and 19th century hand-printing machines. John Dunlap, printer of the American Declaration of Independence, and James Wilson, grandfather of President Woodrow Wilson, are said to have learned their trade here. Tour includes audio-visual presentation, check in advance for compositor demonstrations. Strabane District Council local history museum in the same building.

Location: In the centre of Strabane.

Open: Apr - Sept: Tue - Sat, 2 - 5pm.

Admission: Tour price: Adult £2.50, Child £1.50, Family £5.50. Group £1.75.

🎫 🎧

HAMWOOD HOUSE
Dunboyne, Co Meath
Tel: +353 44 8255210
Owner: Major and Mrs Hamilton   **Contact:** Mrs Hamilton
Palladian-style house, built in 1779, contains a fine collection of 18th century furniture.
Location: 2m from Dunboyne on Maynooth Rd.
Open: 1 Feb - 31 Mar: Mon - Fri, 10am - 2pm. 1 Apr - 31 Aug: Mon - Fri. 2 - 6pm. 3rd Sun of each month, 2 - 6pm.
Admission: House: Adult £3. Garden: Adult £3. Groups by arrangement.

HEZLETT HOUSE ✤
107 Sea Road, Castlerock, Coleraine, Co Londonderry BT51 4TW
Tel/Fax: 028 7084 8567 **e-mail:** undpmx@smtp.ntrust.org.uk
Owner: The National Trust   **Contact:** The Custodian
Charming 17th century thatched house with 19th century furnishings. Interesting cruck-truss roof construction viewed from specially exposed attic. One of only a few pre-18th century Irish buildings still surviving. Excellent attraction for visitors en-route from Causeway to Londonderry.
Location: 5m W of Coleraine on Coleraine - Downhill coast road, A2.
Open: 16 Mar - May: weekends & BH/PHs; Jun - Aug: daily except Tue (unless BH/PH Tue); Sept: weekends: 12 noon - 5pm.
Admission: Adult £2.50, Child £1.25, Family £6. Groups £2 (outside hours £3). Ground floor. Obligatory. In grounds, on leads.

HILTON PARK
Hilton Park, Clones, Co Monaghan
Tel: +353 47 56007 **Fax:** +353 47 56033 **e-mail:** jm@hiltonpark.ie
Owner/Contact: Mr John Madden
Lakeside pleasure grounds, herb garden, parterre and herbaceous border in rolling parkland.
Location: 3m due S of Clones on L46, Ballyhaise Rd.
Open: By appointment.
Admission: Adult £3.

THE IRISH MUSEUM OF MODERN ART
Royal Hospital, Military Rd, Kilmainham, Dublin 8
Tel: + 353 1 612 9900 **Fax:** +353 1 612 9999
e-mail: info@modernart.ie **www.**modernart.ie
Owner: Irish Museum of Modern Art   **Contact:** Monica Cullinane
The Irish Museum of Modern Art opened in 1991 in the magnificently restored Royal Hospital building and grounds, which include a formal garden, meadow and medieval burial grounds as well as a series of other historic buildings. The museum presents, through its permanent collection and temporary exhibitions, an exciting and innovative range of Irish and international art of the 20th century, alongside strong education and community, national and artists' residency programmes.
Location: Near Heuston Station, 2km from city centre. Buses: 69, 78A, 79, 90.
Open: Tue - Sat, 10am - 5.30pm. Suns, 12 noon - 5.30pm. Guided tours of exhibitions: Weds & Fris at 2.30pm, Suns at 12.15pm. Closed Mons. Summer Heritage Season with guided tours from 5 Jun - 9 Sept.
Admission: Exhibitions: Free. Guided Heritage Tours: Adult £2.50/€3.17, Conc. £1.50/€1.90, Family £6/€7.61.
No inside photography. On leads in grounds.

JAMES JOYCE MUSEUM
Joyce Tower, Sandycove, Co Dublin
Tel/Fax: +353 1 280 9265 **e-mail:** joycetower@dublintourism.ie
Owner: Dublin Tourism Enterprises   **Contact:** Robert Nicholson
A martello tower containing a museum devoted to the life and works of James Joyce.
Location: Dun Laoghaire, 8m S of Dublin.
Open: Apr - Oct: Mon - Sat, 10am - 5pm. Closed 1 - 2pm. Suns & BHs, 2 - 6pm.
Admission: Adult €5.50, Child (3 - 11yrs) €3, Conc. €5, Family €15. Group rates on request.

JAPANESE GARDENS & ST FIACHRA GARDEN
Tully, Kildare Town, Co Kildare
Tel: +353 45 521617 **Fax:** +353 45 522964 **e-mail:** stud@irish-national-stud.ie
Owner: Irish National Stud   **Contact:** Freda O'Connell
Location: 1m from Kildare Town. 30m from Dublin off M/N7.
Open: 12 Feb - 12 Nov: daily 9.30am - 6pm.
Admission: Adult €8.50, Child (under 12yrs) €4.50, Conc. €6.50, Family (2+4) €18. One ticket includes National Stud, Japanese Garden & St Fiachra's Garden.

Admission prices for properties in Northern Ireland are given in £ Sterling.
Admission prices for properties in the Republic of Ireland are given in Euros.

KILLYLEAGH CASTLE
Killyleagh, Downpatrick, Co Down BT30 9QA
Tel/Fax: 028 4482 8261 **e-mail:** rowanhamilton.killyleaghcastle@virgin.net
www.fjiordlands.org/strngfrd/kilapts.htm
Owner/Contact: Mrs G Rowan-Hamilton
Oldest occupied castle in Ireland. Self-catering towers available to sleep 4-15. Swimming pool and tennis court available. Access to garden.
Location: At the end of the High Street.
Open: By arrangement. Groups (30-50): by appointment.
Admission: Adult £3.50, Child £2. Groups: Adult £2.50, Child £1.50.
No photography in house. Wedding receptions. Unsuitable. Obligatory.

KING HOUSE
Boyle, Co Roscommon
Tel: +353 79 63242 **Fax:** +353 79 63243 **e-mail:** kinghouseboyle@hotmail.com
Owner: Roscommon County Council   **Contact:** The Manager
Magnificently restored Georgian mansion dating from the early 18th century.
Location: In the centre of Boyle.
Open: Apr & late Oct: weekends, 10am - 6pm. May - mid Oct: daily, 10am - 6pm. Last admission 5pm.
Admission: Adult €4, Child €2.50, Conc. €3.50, Family (2+4) €10. Group rates on request.

KYLEMORE ABBEY & GARDEN
CONNEMARA, CO GALWAY
www.kylemoreabbey.com
Tel: +353 95 41146 **Fax:** +353 95 41145 **e-mail:** info@kylemoreabbey.ie
Owner: Benedictine Nuns   **Contact:** Sister Magdalena OSB
Set in the heart of the Connemara mountains. Kylemore is a premier tourist attraction, international girls' boarding school, a magnificent gothic church, superb restaurant and one of the finest craft shops in Ireland. Victorian Walled Garden, currently undergoing restoration. The walls stretch for up to half a mile to enclose: the kitchen garden, flower or pleasure garden, gardener's cottage, bothy and the glass (hot) house complex. The Benedictine Nuns at Kylemore continue to restore the estate and open it to the education and enjoyment of all who visit.
Location: Between Reccess & Letterfrack, West of Ireland.
Open: Abbey, exhibition, church, lake walk, video & tearoom: All year (closed Good Fri & Christmas week), 9am - 5.30pm. Craftshop: mid Mar - mid Nov. Garden, woodland walk, shop, tea house & exhibition: Easter - Oct: 10.30am - 4.30pm.
Admission: Abbey: Adult €5, Conc. €3.50, Family €11. Groups (10+): €3.50. Gardens: Adult €6.50, Conc. €4, Family €14. Groups (10+): €4. Joint ticket: Adult €10, Conc. €6.50, Family €20. Groups (10+): €6.50.
Ground floor & grounds. WC.

LISNAVAGH GARDENS
Lisnavagh, Rathvilly, Co Carlow, Ireland
Tel: +353 503 61104 **Fax:** +353 503 61148
Owner/Contact: Lord and Lady Rathdonnell
Ten acres of outstanding trees and shrubs, mixed borders, rock garden and cruciform yew walk, with panoramic views of the Wicklow Hills and Mount Leinster.
Location: Situated 2m S of Rathvilly. Signposted.
Open: Open occasionally strictly by appointment. Please telephone.
Admission: Adult €4, Child €2.50, Family €15.

James Joyce Museum, Joyce Tower

NT Photographic Library: Joe Cornish

MOUNT STEWART
NEWTOWNARDS, Co DOWN BT22 2AD

Tel: 028 4278 8387 **Fax:** 028 4278 8569 **e-mail:** umsest@smtp.ntrust.org.uk

Owner: The National Trust   **Contact:** The Property Manager

Home of the Londonderry family since the early 18th century, Mount Stewart was Lord Castlereagh's house and played host to many prominent political figures. The magnificent gardens planted in the 1920s have made Mount Stewart famous and earned it a World Heritage Site nomination. They feature a series of formal outdoor 'rooms', vibrant parterres, and formal and informal vistas, some with Strangford Lough views. Many rare and unusual plants thrive in the mild climate of the Ards, including eucalyptus, beschorneria, mimosa, and cordyline. The garden is also home to national collections of phormium and libertia. The house includes the famous painting 'Hambletonian', as well as the full set of chairs used at Congress of Vienna. The Temple of the Winds, a 1785 banqueting hall, is in the grounds. Much improved visitor facilities will open at the beginning of 2002, including a new bistro restaurant, shop and exhibition areas.

Location: On A20, 5m from Newtownards on the Portaferry road.

Open: House: 16 - 18, 23 - 24, 29 - 31 Mar; Apr: weekends & BH/PHs (inc 3 - 5 Apr); May & Sept: daily except Tue; Jun - Aug: daily; Oct: weekends: 12 noon - 6pm. Formal Gardens: Mar: as house; Apr - Sept: daily; Oct - Dec: weekends (11am - 5pm). Lakeside Gardens & Walks: Oct - Apr: 10am - 4pm. May - Sept: 10am - 8pm.

Admission: House tour, Gardens & Temple: Adult £4.75, Child £2.25, Family £9.75. Group: Adult £4, Child £2. Garden only: Adult £3.75, Child £2, Family £8.50. Group: Adult £3.50, Child £1.75.

New bistro restaurant. Obligatory. In grounds, on leads.

LISSADELL HOUSE
Ballinfull, Co Sligo

Tel/Fax: +353 71 63150

House built in the 1830s by Sir Robert Gore-Booth, and still the family home.

Location: 13km NW of Sligo.

Open: 1 Jun - mid Sept: (except Suns), 10.30am - 1pm & 2 - 5pm. Last admission 12.15pm & 4.15pm. Guided tours.

Admission: Adult €5, Child €2.50. Group: (20+) €4.

MUSSENDEN TEMPLE
Castlerock, Co. Londonderry

Tel/Fax: 028 7084 8728 **e-mail:** undpmx@smtp.ntrust.org.uk

Owner: The National Trust

Set on a stunning and wild headland with fabulous views over Ireland's north coast is the landscaped estate of Downhill, laid out in the late 18th century by the eccentric Earl and Bishop, Frederick Hervey.

Location: 1m W of Castlerock.

Open: Downhill Estate: All year: dawn - dusk. Mussenden Temple: 17 Mar - May: weekends & BH/Public Hols. Jun - Aug: daily. Sept: weekends, 11am - 6pm.

Admission: Car park charge at Lion's Gate during Temple opening: Car £3, Minibus £8, Coach £15, Motorbike £1.50.

On leads.

LODGE PARK WALLED GARDENS & STEAM MUSEUM
STRAFFAN, CO KILDARE
www.steam-museum.ie

Tel: +353 1 6273155 **Fax:** +353 1 6273477 **e-mail:** garden@steam-museum.ie

Owner: Mr R Guinness

Lodge Park Walled Garden with brick lined north wall of 18th century origin is a plantsman's delight. From the axis of the long walk it features garden rooms extending to a long rosarie. The Steam Museum building incorporates the roof, windows and other architectural features taken from the c1865 Great Southern & Western Railway Church of St Jude (attributed to the architect Sancton Wood) Inchicore, Dublin. Taken down in 1988 it was rebuilt here, under the consultant architect Mr Percy Le Clerc, and opened by the President of Ireland in 1992 as the Steam Museum. The Richard Guinness model hall displays his collection of historic prototype locomotive models. The Power Hall displays restored stationary engines working in steam. Interactive area for educational use. Memorabilia gallery.

Location: 16m from Dublin, signposted off the N7 road at Kill junction traffic lights.

Open: Easter Sun - May: Suns & BHs, 2.30 - 5.15pm. Jun - Aug: Tue - Sun & BHs, 2 - 5.45pm. Sept: Suns & BHs 2.30 - 5.15pm.

Admission: Steam Museum: €4, Garden: €4. Steam Museum & Garden: €7. Groups (10+) less 10%. Conc. €3, Family €13.

By arrangement.

NEWMAN HOUSE
85/86 St Stephen's Green, Dublin

Tel: +353 1 706 7422 **Fax:** +353 1 706 7211

Owner: University College, Dublin   **Contact:** Ruth Ferguson, Curator

Two Georgian houses containing examples of Dublin's finest 18th century plasterwork.

Location: Central Dublin.

Open: Jun, Jul & Aug only. Tue - Fri, 12 noon - 5pm. Sats, 2 - 5pm.

Admission: Adult €4, Conc. €3.

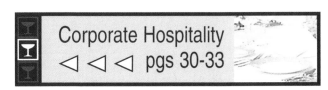

NUMBER TWENTY-NINE
Lower Fitzwilliam Street, Dublin 2
Tel: +353 1 702 6165   **Fax:** +353 1 702 7796
Owner: Electricity Supply Board & National Museum of Ireland   **Contact:** K Burns
Restored middle-class house of the late 18th century.
Location: Lower Fitzwilliam Street, adjacent Merrion Square.
Open: Tue - Sat, 10am - 5pm. Suns, 2 - 5pm. Closed Mons & 2 weeks before Xmas.
Admission: Adult £2.50, Conc. £1. Subject to review in 2002.

PALM HOUSE BOTANIC GARDENS
Belfast City
Tel: 028 9032 4902   **e-mail:** maxwellr@belfastcity.gov.uk
Owner: Belfast City Council   **Contact:** Mr Reg Maxwell
Built by Richard Turner who later built the Great Palm House at Kew.
Location: Between Botanic Avenue & Stranmillis Road, South Belfast.
Open: Palm House & Tropical Ravine: Apr - Sept: Mon - Fri, 10am - 12 noon &
1 - 5pm; Sats & Suns, 1 - 5pm. Oct - Mar: Mon - Fri, 10am - 12 noon & 1 - 4pm; Sats
& Suns, 1 - 4pm. BHs as Sats & Suns. Park: 8am - sunset.
Admission: Free.

PATTERSON'S SPADE MILL ❧
Templepatrick, Co Antrim BT39 0AP
Tel/Fax: 028 9443 3619
Owner: The National Trust
Founded in 1919, this is the last surviving water-driven spade mill in Ireland. The
original equipment is working for visitors to see, complete with hammers, a turbine and
a press. An authentic workshop setting, complete with the smell of oil, metal and wood
shavings. Guided tour includes traditional spade-making demonstration, and the
history and culture of the humble turf and garden spade. Excellent exhibition in the
reception. Good outing from Belfast, or as a stop-off from the M2. Garden spades made
in the mill are for sale and make a popular gift. Spades are available by mail order.
Location: On A6 (between Sandyknowes roundabout and Templepatrick roundabout),
M2/J4. 1st left at Templepatrick roundabout after exiting motorway.
Open: 17/18, 23/24 & 29 Mar; Apr - May: weekends & BH/PHs, Jun - Aug: daily; Sept:
weekends; 2 - 6pm.
Admission: Mill Tour: Adult £3.25, Child £1.50, Family £8.50, Groups £2 (outside
normal hours £4).

♿ 🚻 🅿

POWERSCOURT ESTATE
ENNISKERRY, Co WICKLOW
www.powerscourt.ie
Tel: +353 1 204 6000   **Fax:** +353 1 204 6900   **e-mail:** gardens@powerscourt.ie
Owner: The Slazenger Family   **Contact:** The Estate Office
One of the world's great gardens, situated in the foothills of the Wicklow
Mountains. It is a sublime blend of formal gardens, sweeping terraces, statuary
and ornamental lakes together with secret hollows, rambling walks, walled
gardens and over 200 varieties of trees and shrubs. Powerscourt House
incorporates an exhibition on the history of the estate, a terrace café overlooking
the gardens and speciality shops, including Interiors Gallery and Garden Pavilion.
5km from the gardens is Powerscourt Waterfall, the highest in Ireland. Waterfall
playground, sand and water play and unique 'space net'.
Location: 12m S of Dublin City centre, off N11 adjacent to Enniskerry village.
Open: Summer: daily, 9.30am - 5.30pm. Winter: daily, 9.30am - dusk. Open all year
except 25/26 Dec.
Admission: House Exhibition & Gardens: Adult €8, Child €4, Conc. €6.50.
Groups (20+): Adult €6.50, Child €4, Conc. €5.50. Please tel. for other prices.
🖥 🚻 ♿Partial. WCs. 🍽 🅿 🐕Guide dogs only. ❋

Bantry House

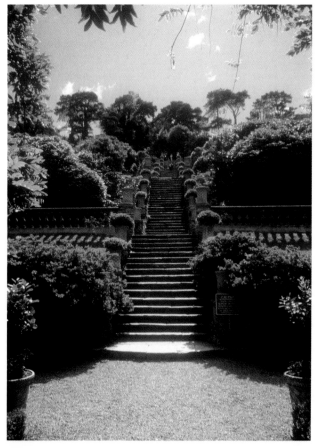

POWERSCOURT TOWN HOUSE
South William St, Dublin 2
Tel: +353 1 679 4144   **Fax:** +353 1 671 7505
Owner: Clarendon Properties
Built for the 4th Viscount Powerscourt between 1771 and 1774.
Location: Central Dublin.
Open: All year: Mon - Sat, 10am - 6pm. Suns, 12 noon - 6pm.
Admission: Free.

RAM HOUSE GARDEN
Ram House, Coolgreany, Gorey, Co Wexford
Tel/Fax: +353 402 37238
Owner: Godfrey & Lolo Stevens   **Contact:** Mrs Lolo Stevens
A two acre romantic scented garden. Twice shown on TV and judged 'Best in Co
Wexford' in the last Shamrock National Gardens Competition. There are gravel and
woodland areas, terraces, pergola, gazebo, mixed borders in soft colours, ponds,
lavish planting around a little stream and over 70 varieties of clematis.
Location: In Coolgreany village, 3km off N11 between Arklow and Gorey.
Open: May - Aug: Fri - Sun & BHs, 2.30 - 6pm. Other times and groups by
appointment.
Admission: Adult €4, Child €2.
ℹ️Garden plan & plant list. ♿Unsuitable. 🍽 🅿Limited. 🐕Guide dogs only. ❋

RIVERSTOWN HOUSE
Glanmire, Co Cork
Tel: +353 21 4821205
Owner: Mr & Mrs D Dooley   **Contact:** Mrs D Dooley
Georgian House. Plasterwork by Lafrancini Bros.
Location: 1m from Glanmire Village, turn right at Riverstown Cross.
Open: May - mid Sept: Wed - Sat, 2 - 6pm. Other times by appointment.
Admission: €5.

ROTHE HOUSE
Parliament St, Kilkenny
Tel/Fax: +353 56 22893
Owner: Kilkenny Archaeological Society   **Contact:** Mary Flood
Built 1594. Various exhibitions. Also houses the County Genealogical Research Service.
Location: Parliament Street, in Kilkenny City.
Open: All year: Mon - Sat, 10.30am - 5pm. Suns, 3 - 5pm.
Admission: Adult €3, Child €1, Conc. €2. Groups (20+): Adult €2.

ROWALLANE GARDEN
Saintfield, Ballynahinch, Co Down BT24 7LH
Tel: 028 9751 0131 **Fax:** 028 9751 1242 **e-mail:** uroest@smtp.ntrust.org.uk
Owner: The National Trust   **Contact:** The Property Manager
Rowallane is a natural landscape of some 21 hectares, planted with an outstanding collection of trees, shrubs and other plants from many parts of the world, creating a beautiful display of form and colour throughout the year. The garden was established in the 1860s by the Rev John Moore, and carried on by his plant-collecting nephew in the early 1900s. Planting and collecting continue today. In spring the garden features a magnificent display of rhododendrons, azaleas, bulbs, flowering trees and shrubs. Summer brings hypericum, viburnum, shrub roses and fuschias in the walled garden; primulas and heathers in the rock garden and wild flower meadows rich with orchids. The scarlet and gold foliage of autumn gives way to winter, when Rowallane's plentiful supplies of fruit and berries attracts an array of interesting birds.
Location: On A7, 1m from Saintfield on road to Downpatrick.
Open: Oct - Apr: 10am - 4pm (closed 24 Dec - 1 Jan). May - Sept: 10am - 8pm.
Admission: 16 Mar - Oct: Adult £3, Child £1.25, Family £7. Groups £2.
Grounds. WC. Apr - Aug. In grounds, on leads.

RUSSBOROUGH
Blessington, Co Wicklow
Tel: + 353 45 865239 **Fax:** +353 45 865054   **Contact:** The Administrator
A beautifully maintained 18th century house housing the Beit collection, fine furniture, tapestries, carpets, porcelain, silver and bronzes.
Location: 30km from Dublin on N81. 3km S of Blessington.
Open: Apr & Oct: Suns & BH, 10.30am - 5.30pm. May - Sept: daily, 10.30am - 5.30pm. Last admission 5pm.
Admission: Main rooms: Adult €6, Child €3. Upstairs: €3.50

SEAFORDE GARDENS
Seaforde, Co Down BT30 8PG
Tel: 028 44811 225 **Fax:** 028 44811 370 **www**.seafordegardens.com
Owner/Contact: Patrick Forde
18th century walled garden and adjoining pleasure grounds, containing many rare and beautiful trees and shrubs; many of them tender. There are huge rhododendrons and the National Collection of Eucryphias. The oldest maze in Ireland is in the centre of the walled garden, which can be viewed from the Mogul Tower. The tropical butterfly house contains hundreds of beautiful highly coloured butterflies; also a collection of parrots, insects and reptiles. The nursery garden contains many interesting plants for sale.
Location: 20m S of Belfast on the main road to Newcastle.
Open: Easter - end Sept: Mon - Sat, 10am - 5pm; Suns, 1 - 6pm. Gardens only: Oct - Mar: Mon - Fri, 10am - 5pm.
Admission: Butterfly House or Gardens: Adult £2.50, Child £1.50. Groups (10+): Adult £2. Child groups: £1.30. Butterfly House & Gardens: Adult £4.30, Child £2.50. Groups: Adult £3.50, Child £2, Family (2+2) £12.
By arrangement.

SHAW BIRTHPLACE
33 Synge Street, Dublin 8
Tel: + 353 1 4750854 **Fax:** +353 1 8722231
Owner: Dublin Tourism Enterprises   **Contact:** Eilish Rafferty
The first home of the Shaw family and the renowned playwright, George Bernard Shaw.
Location: 10 mins from City centre.
Open: Contact property for details.
Admission: Contact property for details.

SPRINGHILL
20 Springhill Road, Moneymore, Co Londonderry BT45 7NQ
Tel/Fax: 028 8674 8210 **e-mail:** uspest@smtp.ntrust.org.uk
Owner: The National Trust   **Contact:** The Property Manager
A charming and atmospheric 17th century 'plantation' house, said by many to be one of the prettiest houses in Ulster. It was home to ten generations of the Conyngham family, originally from Ayr. 50 minutes drive from Belfast or Londonderry, 35 minutes from Coleraine. House tour takes in exceptional library, gun room, nursery, and includes the story of resident ghost. Colourful costume collection, with some Irish 17th century pieces. Beautiful walks in walled gardens and way-marked paths in estate. Excellent tearoom, small shop and children's play area.
Location: 1m from Moneymore on B18 to Coagh, 5m from Cookstown.
Open: 16 Mar - Jun: weekends & BH/PHs; Jul & Aug: daily; Sept: weekends: 12 noon - 6pm.
Admission: House & Costume Collection tour: Adult £3.50, Child £1.75, Family £7.25, Group £2.75 (outside hours £4).
Partial. WC. P In grounds, on leads.

STROKESTOWN PARK HOUSE
Strokestown, Co Roscommon
Tel: +353 78 33013 **Fax:** +353 78 33712 **e-mail:** info@strokestownpark.ie
Owner: Westward Group   **Contact:** John O'Driscoll
The Palladian-style house is complete with its original contents. Houses the National Famine Museum. Recently restored Georgian fruit and vegetable garden.
Location: 114 km from Dublin on N5.
Open: 1 Apr - 31 Oct: daily, 11am - 5.30pm. Tours, other times by appointment.
Admission: €5 for one attraction. €8.50 for 2 attractions. €12 for 3 attractions.

TULLYNALLY CASTLE & GARDENS
Castlepollard, Co. Westmeath
Tel: +353 44 61159 **Fax:** +353 44 61856 **e-mail:** pakenham@eircom.net
Owner: Thomas & Valerie Pakenham   **Contact:** Valerie Pakenham
Romantic woodland and walled gardens laid out in the early 19th century, with follies, grotto and ornamental lakes. The present owners have added a Chinese garden complete with pagoda and a Tibetan garden of waterfalls and streams, and a local sculptor has carved fantastic shapes from existing trees. The Gothick Revival castle forms a splendid backdrop.
Location: 1m from Castlepollard on Granard Road off N52, or N4 via Mullingar.
Open: Gardens: 1 May - 31 Aug: 2 - 6pm. Castle: 15 Jun - 30 Jul:, 2 - 6pm. Open to groups at other times by appointment. Tearoom: daily, 2 - 6pm.
Admission: Castle & Gardens: Adult €8, Child €4. Groups: Adult €7. Gardens only: Adult €5, Child €2.
Obligatory. In grounds, on leads.

WELLBROOK BEETLING MILL
20 Wellbrook Road, Corkhill, Co. Tyrone BT80 9RY
Tel: 028 8674 8210/8675 1735 **e-mail:** uspest@smtp.ntrust.org.uk
Owner: The National Trust   **Contact:** The Custodian
Wellbrook is an 18th century water-powered beetling mill with the only working beetling engines on show in Northern Ireland. Costumed guides lead visitors through hands-on demonstration of the linen process, from the flax growing next to the car park to watching the beetles pound rolls of linen. Includes new exhibition on the history of linen and its importance to Ireland. Set in picturesque wooded glen with good paths.
Location: 4m from Cookstown, following signs from A505 Cookstown - Omagh road.
Open: 16 Mar - Jun: weekends & BH/PHs; Jul - Aug: daily; Sept: weekends: 12 noon - 6pm.
Admission: Mill tour: Adult £2.50, Child £1.25, Family £5.50. Group: £2 (outside hours £3).
P

Dublin Writers Museum

WESTPORT HOUSE & COUNTRY PARK

WESTPORT, CO. MAYO

www.westporthouse.ie

Tel: +353 98 27766/25430   **Fax:** +353 98 25206   **e-mail:** info@westporthouse.ie
Owner: Marquess of Sligo & Family   **Contact:** Karen Browne

Westport House and Country Park is generally regarded as one of Ireland's most beautiful and historic homes, in a magnificent setting. It is located on the shores of Clew Bay between Westport Town, Westport Quay and Westport Golf Course. The original house was built in 1685 by Col. John Browne and his wife Maud Bourke, ancestors of the present family. The house then had no lake or dam and the tide rose and fell against the walls. In 1730 the East Front as it is today was built by the famous German architect Cassels who also built Carton, Hazelwood, Russborough and Leinster House. The house was completed by James Wyatt in 1778 and his large dining room at Westport House is generally regarded as one of Ireland's most beautiful rooms.

Location: 3.2km from Westport Town on the main Westport Louisburgh Road R335 turn right at Westport Quay.

Open: Easter Weekend, Suns in May; 1 Jul - 25 Aug: weekdays, 11.30am - 5.30pm; Sat & Sun, 1.30 - 5.30pm; 26 Aug - 1 Sept: daily, 1 - 5pm. Jun & Sept: tel. for details.

Admission: House & Gardens: Adult €9, Child €5, Conc. €6. Groups rates available and special family ticket for house and attractions.

🖼 ♿ Partial. 📷 Groups only. 🅿 🚻 ✖

Admission prices for properties in Northern Ireland are given in £ Sterling.

Admission prices for properties in the Republic of Ireland are given in Euros.

Mount Stewart

NT Photographic Library

Opening Arrangements at Properties grant-aided by English Heritage

ENGLISH HERITAGE

ENGLISH HERITAGE

23 Savile Row, London W1S 2ET

I am very pleased to introduce this year's list of opening arrangements at properties grant-aided by English Heritage. The list has been expanded to make it even more useful to potential visitors. It now includes buildings such as theatres and railway stations, which are open to the public by virtue of their use and grant-aided gardens and landscapes with a current public access condition. Over half the properties are open free, but we give details of admission charges where appropriate. There is also a brief description of each property, information on parking and access for people with disabilities.

The extent of public access varies from one property to another. The building's size, nature and function are all taken into account. Some buildings, such as town halls, museums or railway stations, are of course open regularly. For other properties, especially those which are family homes or work places, access may need to be arranged in a way which also recognises the vulnerability of the building or the needs of those who live or work in it. Usually this will mean opening by appointment or on an agreed number of days each year. This is made clear by each entry.

Some properties are open by written appointment only. In most cases you should still be able to make initial contact by telephone, but you will be asked to confirm your visit in writing. This is to confirm the seriousness of the visitor's interest as you would for example with a hotel booking. It also provides a form of identification, enabling owners to feel more secure about inviting strangers into their house.

It has always been a condition of grant-aid from English Heritage that the public should have a right to see the buildings to whose repair they have contributed. We therefore welcome feedback from visitors on the quality of their visit to grant-aided properties. In particular, please let us know if you are unable to gain access to any of the buildings on the list on the days or at the times specified, or if you have difficulty in making an appointment to visit and do not receive a satisfactory explanation from the owner. Please contact English Heritage Customer Services at PO Box 569, Swindon SN2 2YP (telephone: 0870 3331181; e-mail: customers@english-heritage.org.uk).

Information about public access is also included on our website (www.english-heritage.org.uk). The website is regularly updated to include new properties, any subsequent changes which have been notified to us or any corrections. We suggest that you consult our website for up to date information before visiting. If long journeys or special requirements are involved, we recommend that you telephone the properties in advance, even if no appointment is required.

Finally, may I use this introduction to thank all those owners with whom we work. Their support for the access arrangements has been hugely encouraging. That the public can enjoy a visit to a grant-aided property is not only good in itself, it demonstrates that the historic environment is in a very real sense a common wealth, part of the richness and diversity that makes the English landscape – both urban and rural – so special. It also illustrates how important the private owner is in maintaining that quality and distinctiveness.

I hope you will enjoy the sites and properties you find in this list – from the famous to the many lesser-known treasures. They are all worth a visit – I hope we have helped you to find, and enjoy, them.

Neil Cossons.

Sir Neil Cossons
Chairman

BERKSHIRE

Welford Park
Welford, Newbury, Berkshire RG20 8HU
Red brick country house c1652 and remodelled in 1702, when a third storey was added and the front façade was decorated with Ionic columns. Other alterations were made in the Victorian period.
Grant Recipient/Owner: Mr J H L Puxley
Access contact: Mr J H L Puxley
Tel: 01488 608203 **Fax:** 01488 608853
Open: 2 - 28 June, 26 Aug: 11am - 5pm. Interior of house (4 principal rooms) by arrangement only.
Heritage Open Days: No
P Spaces: 40
♿ Yes. No disabled WC. Guide Dogs: Yes
£ Charge for house. Free entry to garden and grounds. **Adult:** £3.50 **Child:** £2 **Other:** £2

BUCKINGHAMSHIRE

Abbey Farmhouse
Church Street, Great Missenden, Buckinghamshire HP16 0AZ
Thought to have been the gatehouse to Missenden Abbey. The major part was built in the early 15th century and was converted to a farmhouse probably in the mid 16th century with further 19th century alterations.
Grant Recipient/Owner: Mr N F Pearce
Access contact: Mr N F Pearce
Tel: 01494 862767
Open: By arrangement (written appointments preferred). A few days notice will usually be sufficient.
Heritage Open Days: No
P Spaces: 2
♿ Partial. Wheelchair access to ground floor only. No disabled WC. Guide Dogs: Yes £ No

Chilton House
Chilton, Aylesbury, Buckinghamshire HP18 9LR
Country house, built in the 16th century and remodelled c1740 for Chief Justice Carter based on William Winde's Buckingham House of c1705 in London.
www.chiltonhouse.co.uk
Grant Recipient/Owner: Chilton House Ltd
Access contact: Lady Aubrey-Fletcher
Tel: 01844 265200 **Fax:** 01844 265202
Email: chiltonhouse@farming.co.uk
Open: By arrangement any day 11am - 5pm.
Heritage Open Days: No
P Spaces: 50 ♿ Yes. Disabled WC. Guide Dogs: Yes
£ No

Claydon House
Middle Claydon, nr. Buckingham, Buckinghamshire MK18 2EY
18th century house with fine rococo decoration. A series of great rooms have wood carvings in Chinese and gothic styles, and tall windows overlook parkland and a lake. In continuous occupation by the Verney family for over 350 years.
www.nationaltrust.org.uk
Grant Recipient/Owner: The National Trust
Access contact: The Custodian
Tel: 01296 730349 **Fax:** 01296 738511
Open: 23 Mar - 3 Nov: open daily except Thursdays and Fridays: House 1 - 5pm; Grounds 12 noon - 6pm. House closes at 4pm on event days.
Heritage Open Days: No
P Spaces: 30
♿ Partial. Wheelchair access to ground floor and all of garden. Disabled WC. Guide Dogs: Yes
£ **Adult:** £4.40 **Child:** £2.20 **Other:** £11(family), £3.60 (groups 15+ Sats, Mons-Weds)

Cliveden Mansion & Clock Tower
Cliveden, Taplow, Maidenhead, Buckinghamshire SL6 0JA
Built by Charles Barry in 1851, once inhabited by Lady Astor now let as an hotel. Series of gardens, each with its own character, featuring roses, topiary, water gardens, a formal parterre, informal vistas, woodland and riverside walks.
www.nationaltrust.org.uk
Grant Recipient/Owner: The National Trust
Access contact: Property Manager
Tel: 01628 605069 **Fax:** 01628 669461
Open: House (three rooms) and Octagon Temple: Apr - Oct, Thurs and Suns 3 - 5.30pm. Estate and garden: 13 Mar - 31 Dec, daily 11am - 6pm (closes at 4pm from 1 Nov). Woodlands car park: open all year, daily 11am - 5.30pm (closes at 4pm Nov - Mar).
Heritage Open Days: No
P Spaces: 300
♿ Partial. Wheelchair access to house (some steps in house) and much of garden. Disabled WC. Guide Dogs: Yes
£ **Adult:** £1 (house), £6 (grounds), £3 (woodlands car park) **Child:** 50p (house), £3 (grounds), £1.50 (woodlands car park) **Other:** £15 (family: grounds), £7.50 (family: woodlands car park)

Hughenden Manor Disraeli Monument
High Wycombe, Buckinghamshire HP14 4LA
The home of Prime Minister Benjamin Disraeli from 1848-1881. Hughenden has a red brick 'gothic' exterior. Much of his furniture, books and paintings remain. The garden has been recreated in the spirit of his wife, Mary Anne, with colourful designs. Park and woodland walks.
www.nationaltrust.org.uk
Grant Recipient/Owner: The National Trust
Access contact: Property Manager
Tel: 01494 755573
Open: House: 2 - 31 Mar, Sat and Sun 1 - 5pm; 3 Apr - 3 Nov, Wed - Sun (open BH Mons, closed Good Fri), 1 - 5pm. Gardens: as house 12 noon - 5pm. Park and woodlands all year. Note: long and steep walk to house entrance if arriving by public transport.
Heritage Open Days: No
P Spaces: 100
♿ Partial. Wheelchair access to ground floor of house and terrace only. Disabled WC. Guide Dogs: Yes
£ **Adult:** £4.40, £1.50 (garden only) **Child:** £2.20, 75p (garden only) **Other:** £11 (family). Parks & woods free

Old Amersham Market Hall
Market Square, Old Amersham, Buckinghamshire HP7 0DJ
17th century market hall.
Grant Recipient/Owner: Amersham Town Council
Access contact: The Town Clerk, Amersham Town Council
Tel: 01494 586892 **Fax:** 01494 586890
Email: amershamtowncouncil@supanet.com
Open: Available for hire throughout the year.
Heritage Open Days: Yes
P On-street parking available. ♿ No £ No

Princes Risborough Market House
Market Square, Princes Risborough, Buckinghamshire HA27 0AS
17th/18th century brick building, with slate roof, built on wooden stilts. Originally used to store grain, straw and hay. The market was held under the store room. Now used as a meeting room by town council.
Grant Recipient/Owner: Princes Risborough Town Council
Access contact: Mr D J Phillips
Tel: 01844 273934
Email: dennisphillips@tinyworld.co.uk
Open: Weekdays by telephone or written arrangement to Mr D J Phillips, Town Clerk, Princes Risborough Town Council, 3 Barn Rd, Longwick, Princes Risborough, Buckinghamshire HP27 9RW (tel.01844 273934).
Heritage Open Days: Yes
P Short term parking in High Street public car park, within 100 yards (next to parish church). Spaces: 10
♿ No £ No

Stowe House
Buckingham, Buckinghamshire MK18 5EH
Mansion built 1680 and greatly altered and enlarged in the 18th century, surrounded by important 18th century gardens. House and gardens variously worked on by Vanbrugh, Gibbs, Kent and Leoni. Many of the greatest alterations carried out for Viscount Cobham, one of Marlborough's Generals, between 1715 and 1749. Gardens cover 325 acres and contain 6 lakes and 32 garden temples. Kent designed the Elysian Fields in the 1730s, one of the first experiments in 'natural' landscaping, and 'Capability' Brown worked here for 10 years as head gardener and was married in the church in the grounds in 1744. The House is now occupied by the Preservation Trust's tenant, Stowe School. The Gardens are owned by the National Trust.
www.stowe.co.uk
Grant Recipient/Owner: The Stowe House Preservation Trust
Access contact: Ms Christine Shaw
Tel: 01280 818282 **Fax:** 01280 818186
Email: sses@stowe.co.uk
Open: 21 Mar - 14 Apr: Wed - Sun 12 - 5pm; 10 July - 6 Sept: Wed - Sun 12 - 5pm; 30 Oct - 3 Nov: Wed - Sun 11am - 3pm; 18 Dec - 22 Dec: Wed - Sun 11am - 3pm. It may be necessary to close the house on Fridays, Saturdays or Sundays due to functions. Please phone prior to your visit to check if the house is open (01280 818282).
Heritage Open Days: Yes
P Spaces: 30 ♿ Yes. Disabled WC. Guide Dogs: Yes
£ No

West Wycombe Park (West Portico)
West Wycombe, Buckinghamshire HP14 3AJ
House built early 18th century, extensively remodelled between 1750 and 1780 by Sir Francis Dashwood (creator of the Hell-Fire Club). Porticos were added to the east and west fronts by Nicholas Revett (his work is relatively rare), and on the south, linking the wings, John Donovell added a two storey colonnade. Although the latter is based on Renaissance prototypes, it too is a rare feature. Frescoes were painted on the ceiling of the west Portico by one of the Borgnis.
www.nationaltrust.org.uk
Grant Recipient/Owner: The National Trust
Access contact: The National Trust
Tel: 01494 528051 **Fax:** 01494 463310
Open: Grounds only: 1 Apr - 31 May, Sun - Thurs & BHs 2 - 6pm. House & Grounds: 1 June - 31 Aug, daily 2 - 6pm except Fri & Sat. Weekdays: entry by guided tour every 20 minutes (approx). Last admission 5.15pm.
Heritage Open Days: No
P On site. ♿ No
£ **Adult:** £4.80, £2.60 (grounds only) **Child:** £2.40, **Other:** £12 (family)

Widmere Farm Chapel
Widmere, nr. Marlow, Buckinghamshire SL7 3DF
Chapel attached to farmhouse, early 13th century with traces of 14th century windows and later alterations, Grade II*. 11th or 12th century crypt and medieval roof.
Grant Recipient/Owner: Mr G J White
Access contact: Mr G J White
Tel: 01628 484204
Open: By arrangement.
Heritage Open Days: No
P On site. ♿ No £ No

CAMBRIDGESHIRE

The Almonry
High Street, Ely, Cambridgeshire CB7 4JU
The Almonry (now a restaurant) is part of a long range of buildings which back onto the High Street on the north side of the Cathedral. Originally built by Alan of Walsingham soon after he became Sacrist in 1322, but mainly rebuilt in the 19th century.
www.cathedral.ely.anglican.org
Grant Recipient/Owner: The Dean & Chapter of Ely Cathedral
Access contact: The Events Manager
Tel: 01353 667735 **Fax:** 01353 665658
Email: events.manager@cathedral.ely.anglican.org
Open: Daily 10am - 4.30pm.
Heritage Open Days: Yes
P In town centre car parks. Parking for disabled in Cathedral car park by arrangement. Spaces: 5
♿ Partial. Wheelchair access to ground floor only. Disabled WC in Cathedral. Guide Dogs: Yes
£ No

The Black Hostelry
The College, Ely, Cambridgeshire CB7 4DL
Built c1291-2 of Carr stone rubble with Barnack, or similar, stone dressings, upper storey is timber-framed and plastered on the south and east sides with stone on the west side. Has early 13th century undercroft with ribbed vaults, 13-14th century King Post roof, and 15th century red brick chimney and doorway. Constructed to accommodate visiting monks from other Benedictine monasteries.
www.cathedral.ely.anglican.org
Grant Recipient/Owner: The Dean & Chapter of Ely Cathedral
Access contact: The Events Manager
Tel: 01353 667735 **Fax:** 01353 665658
Email: events.manager@cathedral.ely.anglican.org
Open: By written arrangement with the Events Manager, Chapter House, The College, Ely, Cambs CB7 4DL.
Heritage Open Days: Yes
P In town centre car parks. Parking for disabled in Cathedral car park by arrangement Spaces: 5
♿ Partial. Wheelchair access to ground floor only. Disabled WC in Cathedral. Guide Dogs: Yes £ No

Buckden Towers
High Street, Buckden, Cambridgeshire PE18 9TA
Victorian house set in 15 acres of gardens and grounds, which include a Grade I gatehouse built in 1480.
www.claretcentre.fsnet.co.uk
Grant Recipient/Owner: Claretian Missionaries
Access contact: Ms Jill Davies
Tel: 01480 810344
Open: By arrangement. Tea shop open on Sat and Sun afternoons in summer.
Heritage Open Days: No
P Spaces: 50 ♿ Yes. Disabled WC. Guide Dogs: Yes
£ No

Canonry House
The College, Ely, Cambridgeshire CB7 4DL
Probably originally 11th/12th century, the ground floor has massive walls and a Norman barrel vault. Much of the medieval building was demolished in 1770 when the current dwelling was built. Contains part of the 12th century Infirmary.
Grant Recipient/Owner: The Dean & Chapter of Ely Cathedral
Access contact: The Assistant Bursar
Tel: 01353 660700 **Fax:** 01353 662187
Email: nigelc@kings-ely.cambs.sch.uk
Open: By written arrangement with the Assistant Bursar, King's School, Ely, Cambs CB7 4DN.
Heritage Open Days: Yes
P In town centre car parks. Parking for disabled in Cathedral car park by arrangement. Spaces: 5
♿ Partial. Wheelchair access to ground floor only. Disabled WC in Cathedral. Guide Dogs: Yes £ No

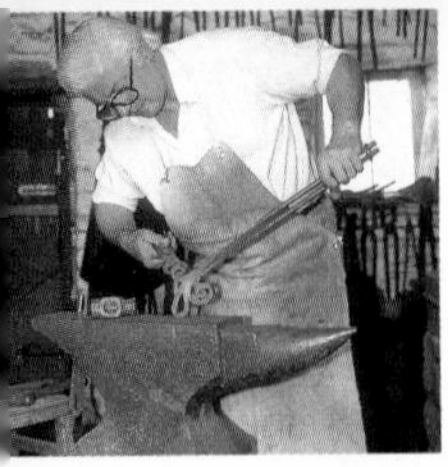

The Chapter House

The College, Ely, Cambridgeshire CB7 4DL

Originally part of the chapel of the Infirmary, now the remains of this house the Deanery. Contains part of the arch, ribbed vaulting and arcade of the 12th century chancel.

www.cathedral.ely.anglican.org

Grant Recipient/Owner: The Dean & Chapter of Ely Cathedral

Access contact: The Events Manager

Tel: 01353 667735 **Fax:** 01353 665658

Email: events.manager@cathedral.ely.anglican.org

Open: By written arrangement with the Events Manager, Chapter House, The College, Ely, Cambs CB7 4DL.

Heritage Open Days: Yes

P In town centre car parks. Parking for disabled in Cathedral car park by arrangement. Spaces: 5

♿ Partial. Wheelchair access to ground floor only. Disabled WC in Cathedral. Guide Dogs: Yes £ No

Elton Hall

Elton, nr. Peterborough, Cambridgeshire PE8 6SH

Grade I historic building and country house. Late 15th century gatehouse and chapel built by Sapcote family. Main entrance façade built by Sir Thomas Proby in the 16th century and remodelled by Henry Ashton for 3rd Earl of Carysfort in the 19th century. South Garden façade built between 1789 and 1812 in gothic style.

Grant Recipient/Owner: Mr William Proby

Access contact: Mr W H Proby

Tel: 01832 280468 **Fax:** 01832 280584

Email: whp@eltonhall.com

Open: 27/28 May; Weds in June; Weds, Thurs and Suns in July and Aug, plus Aug BH Mon 2 - 5pm. Private groups by arrangement on weekdays Apr - Sept.

Heritage Open Days: No

P Parking 300 metres from the Hall. Spaces: 500

♿ Partial. Wheelchair and guide dog access to garden only. No disabled WC. Guide Dogs: Yes

£ **Adult:** £5 (house), £3 (garden) **Child:** Free if accompanied

Madingley Post Mill

Mill Farm, Madingley Road, Coton, Cambridgeshire CB3 7PH

Historic post mill with machinery intact.

Grant Recipient/Owner: Mr Matthew Mortlock

Access contact: Mr Matthew Mortlock

Tel: 01954 211047 **Fax:** 01954 210752

Open: Weekdays and Sats 11am - 4pm by telephone arrangement.

Heritage Open Days: No

P Parking available in car park of American Cemetery (next door).

♿ Partial. Wheelchair access around base of Windmill only. No disabled WC. Guide Dogs: Yes £ No

The Manor

Hemingford Grey, Huntingdon, Cambridgeshire PE28 9BN

Built c1130 and reputedly the oldest continuously inhabited house in Britain. Made famous as Green Knowe by the author Lucy Boston. Her patchwork collection is also shown. Four acre garden with topiary, old roses and herbaceous borders.

www.greenknowe.co.uk

Grant Recipient/Owner: Mrs Diana Boston

Access contact: Mrs Diana Boston

Tel: 01480 463134 **Fax:** 01480 465026

Email: diana_boston@hotmail.com

Open: House: all year (except May) to individuals or groups by arrangement May: guided tours at 11am and 2pm (booking is advisable). Garden: all year, daily 10am - 6pm (4pm in winter).

Heritage Open Days: No

P Parking for disabled only.

♿ Partial. Wheelchair access to garden and dining room only. No disabled WC. Guide Dogs: Yes

£ **Adult:** £4, £2 (garden only) **Child:** £1.50, 50p (garden only) **Other:** £3.50

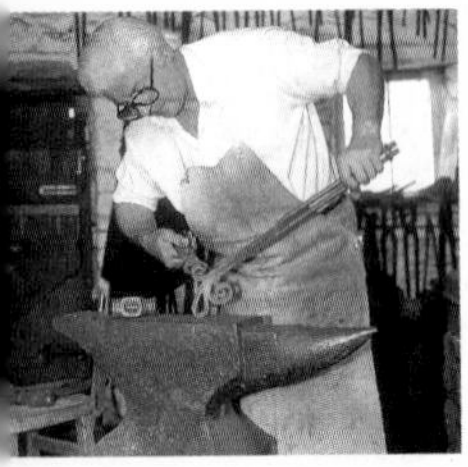

The Old Palace

Sue Ryder Care, Palace Green, Ely, Cambridgeshire CB7 4EW

Grade I building formerly a Bishop's Palace opposite cathedral, with an Elizabethan promenading gallery, bishops chapel and monks room. 2 acre garden contains the oldest plane tree in Europe. Used as a neurological centre for the physically disabled.

Grant Recipient/Owner: The Sue Ryder Care

Access contact: Mrs Mavis Garner

Tel: 01353 667686 **Fax:** 01353 669425

Email: suerely@dialstart.net

Open: By arrangement for access to the Long Gallery and Chapel. Gardens open: 6 May and 9 June. Events held all year, contact Mrs Garner for details.

Heritage Open Days: No

P Nearest car park: St Mary's Street.

♿ Partial. Disabled WC. Guide Dogs: Yes

£ No charge on garden open days. **Adult** £3 - £1 **Child** 50p

Prior Crauden's Chapel

The College, Ely, Cambridgeshire CB7 4DL

Private chapel built by Prior Crauden in 1524-5 of Barnack stone ashlar with clunch carved interior, over a 13th century vaulted undercroft. Has windows in the "Decorated" style, octagonal entrance and tower with spiral staircase, richly carved interior and a 14th century mosaic tile floor.

www.cathedral.ely.anglican.org

Grant Recipient/Owner: The Dean & Chapter of Ely Cathedral

Access contact: The Events Manager

Tel: 01353 667735 **Fax:** 01353 665658

Email: events.manager@cathedral.ely.anglican.org

Open: By written arrangement with Events Manager, Chapter House, The College, Ely, Cambs CB7 4DL.

Heritage Open Days: Yes

P In town centre car parks. Parking for disabled in Cathedral car park by arrangement. Spaces: 5

♿ Partial. Wheelchair access to the undercroft only. Disabled WC in Cathedral. Guide Dogs: Yes £ No

Priory House

Ely, Cambridgeshire CB7 4DL

Rebuilt early 14th century by Prior Crauden (1321-1341) of mainly Carr stone rubble with Barnack stone dressings and a considerable amount of brick. Has 12th century undercroft with groined vaults and transverse arches, 14th century pointed arched windows with "Decorated" tracery and early 14th century fireplace.

Grant Recipient/Owner: The Dean & Chapter of Ely Cathedral

Access contact: The Assistant Bursar

Tel: 01353 660700 **Fax:** 01353 662187

Email: nigelc@kings-ely.cambs.sch.uk

Open: By written arrangement with the Assistant Bursar, The King's School, Ely, Cambs CB7 4DN.

Heritage Open Days: Yes

P In town centre car parks. Parking for disabled in Cathedral car park by arrangement. Spaces: 5

♿ Partial. Wheelchair access to ground floor only. Disabled WC in Cathedral. Guide Dogs: Yes £ No

Queen's Hall

The Gallery, Ely, Cambridgeshire CB7 4DL

Built by Prior Crauden c1330 of Carr stone rubble with Barnack, or similar, stone dressings and much brick patching. Has original undercroft with ribbed vaulting, 14th century pointed arched windows with curvilinear tracery and corbels carved in the shape of crouching figures. Reputedly constructed for entertaining Queen Philippa, wife of Edward III.

Grant Recipient/Owner: The Dean & Chapter of Ely Cathedral

Access contact: The Assistant Bursar

Tel: 01353 660700 **Fax:** 01353 662187

Email: nigelc@kings-ely.cambs.sch.uk

Open: By written arrangement with the Assistant Bursar, The King's School, Ely, Cambs CB7 4DN.

Heritage Open Days: Yes

P In town centre car parks. Parking for disabled in Cathedral car park by arrangement. Spaces: 5

♿ Partial. Wheelchair access to ground floor only. Disabled WC in Cathedral. Guide Dogs: Yes £ No

Sacrewell Watermill

Sacrewell Farm & Country Centre, Sacrewell, Thornhaugh, Peterborough, Cambridgeshire PE8 6HJ

18th century pitch back wheel watermill and millers house, with range of 18th century buildings housing various bygones (domestic, farming and country life).

www.sacrewell.org.uk

Grant Recipient/Owner: William Scott Abbott Trust

Access contact: Mr M Armitage

Tel: 01780 782254 **Fax:** 01780 782254

Email: wsatrust@supanet.com

Open: Daily (except Christmas Day, Boxing Day and New Year's Day) 9.30am - 4pm (winter), 9.30am - 5pm (summer). Refreshments available.

Heritage Open Days: No

P Spaces: 300

♿ Partial. Wheelchair access to ground floor only. Disabled WC. Guide Dogs: Yes

£ **Adult:** £3 **Child:** £1.50 **Senior Citizens:** £2

Sir John Jacob's Almshouses' Chapel

Church Street, Gamlingay, Cambridgeshire SG19 3JH

Built 1745 of Flemish bond red brick with plain tiled roof, in keeping with adjoining terrace of 10 almshouses constructed 80 years before. Now used as parish council offices.

Grant Recipient/Owner: The Trustees of Sir John Jacob's Almshouses

Access contact: Mrs L Mayne

Tel: 01767 650310 **Fax:** 01767 650310

Email: gamlingaypc@lineone.net

Open: Mon and Fri mornings and Wed afternoons.

Heritage Open Days: Yes

P On-street parking.

♿ Yes. Disabled WC. Guide Dogs: Yes £ No

Stoker's Cottage at Stretham Old Engine

Ely, Cambridgeshire

Four-roomed bungalow constructed about 1835 as a Toll Keeper's Cottage. Subsequently used to house the stoker of Stretham Old Engine, which it adjoins.

Grant Recipient/Owner: The Trustees of the Stretham Engine Preservation Trust

Access contact: Mr E Langford

Tel: 01353 649210

Open: Second Sun in each month and BHs from Good Fri to Aug, 1.30 - 5pm. Otherwise by arrangement.

Heritage Open Days: No

P Limited parking in layby in front of Old Engine.

♿ No. Guide Dogs: Yes

£ Old Engine complex & displays

Adult: £2 **Child/Other:** £1

Thomas à Becket Chapel (Becket's Restaurant & Gift shop)

The Song School, Minster Precincts, Peterborough, Cambridgeshire PE1 1XX

The Chapel was originally built by Abbot Benedict, c1180, along with the Norman Arch giving access to Cathedral precincts from Cathedral Square. Houses restaurant and shop alongside Tourist Information Office.

Grant Recipient/Owner: The Dean & Chapter of Peterborough Cathedral

Access contact: The Dean & Chapter of Peterborough Cathedral

Tel: 01733 343342 **Fax:** 01733 552465

Email: bk@peterborough-cathedral.org.uk

Open: Mon - Sat from 9.30am - 5pm all year round.

Heritage Open Days: Yes

P No ♿ Yes. Disabled WC. Guide Dogs: No £ No

Thorpe Hall

Sue Ryder Care, Longthorpe, Peterborough, Cambridgeshire PE3 6LW

Built in the 1650s by Peter Mills for Oliver St John, Oliver Cromwell's Lord Chief Justice. Ground floor retains many original features.

Grant Recipient/Owner: Sue Ryder Care

Access contact: Mr Bruce Wringe

Tel: 01733 330060 **Fax:** 01733 269078

Email: carole.srcth@virgin.net

Open: Access to the Hall by arrangement. Gardens: open all year.

Heritage Open Days: Yes

P Spaces: 30 ♿ Yes. Disabled WC. Guide Dogs: Yes

£ Donations welcome

The Verger's House & The Old Sacristy

High Street, Ely, Cambridgeshire CB7 4JU

The Sacristy is part of a long range of buildings which back onto the High Street on the north side. Originally built by Alan of Walsingham soon after he became sacrist in 1322, but mainly rebuilt in the 19th century.

www.cathedral.ely.anglican.org

Grant Recipient/Owner: The Dean & Chapter of Ely Cathedral

Access contact: The Events Manager

Tel: 01353 667735 **Fax:** 01353 665658

Email: events.manager@cathedral.ely.anglican.org

Open: By written arrangement with Events Manager, The Chapter House, The College, Ely, Cambs CB7 4DL.

Heritage Open Days: Yes

P In town centre car parks. Parking for disabled in Cathedral car park by arrangement. Spaces: 5

♿ Partial. Wheelchair access to ground floor only. Disabled WC in Cathedral. Guide Dogs: Yes £ No

Walsingham House

The College, Ely, Cambridgeshire CB7 4DL

Originally a 14th century Hall built by the Sacrist, Alan of Walsingham, adjoining the monastic infirmary. Famed for its "painted chamber", a first floor decorated hall used for entertaining guests of the monastery. Now houses the Cathedral choristers.

Grant Recipient/Owner: The Dean & Chapter of Ely Cathedral

Access contact: The Assistant Bursar

Tel: 01353 660700 **Fax:** 01353 622187

Email: nigelc@kings-ely.cambs.sch.uk

Open: By written arrangement with the Assistant Bursar, The King's School, Ely, Cambs CB7 4DN.

Heritage Open Days: Yes

P In town centre car parks. Parking for disabled in Cathedral car park by arrangement Spaces: 5

♿ Partial. Wheelchair access to ground floor only. Disabled WC in Cathedral. Guide Dogs: Yes £ No

Wicken Windmill

High Street, Wicken, Cambridgeshire CB7 5XR

Late 18th or early 19th century 12-sided smock mill. Much of the original machinery, including the wind and main shafts, is in place and now being returned to working order.

www.geocities.com/wickenmill

Grant Recipient/Owner: Wicken Windmill Partnership

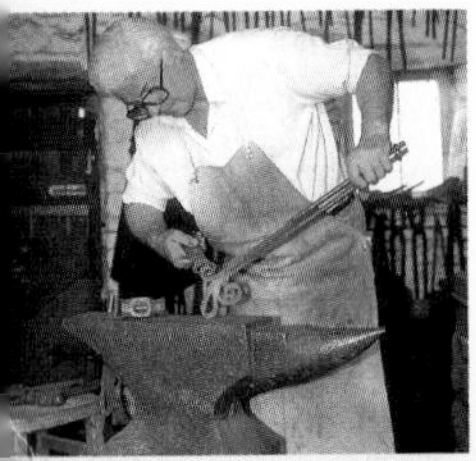

Access contact: Mr D L Pearce
Tel: 01664 822751
Email: dave@pearce52.freeserve.co.uk
Open: 10.30am - 5.30pm on the following days: 5 Jan; 2 Feb; 2 & 3 Mar; 1, 6 & 7 Apr; 4 - 12 May; 1 - 4 June; 6 & 7 July; 3, 4 & 18 - 26 Aug; 7 & 8 Sept, 5 & 6 Oct; 2 & 3 Nov, 7 Dec. In addition the Windmill is open on other occasions when the sails are turning.
Heritage Open Days: Yes
[P] Spaces: 7
♿ Partial. Wheelchair and guide dog access to ground floor only. No disabled WC. Guide Dogs: Yes
[£] Donations towards repair and maintenance gratefully received

Wimpole Estate
Arrington, Royston, Cambridgeshire SG8 0BW
18th century house set in extensive wooded park. Interior features work by Gibbs, Flitcroft and Soane. The park was landscaped by Bridgeman, Brown and Repton featuring a grand folly, Chinese bridge and lake. Walled garden restored to a working vegetable garden - best seen from June to Aug.
www.nationaltrust.org.uk/eastanglia
Grant Recipient/Owner: The National Trust
Access contact: Property Manager
Tel: 01223 207257 **Fax:** 01223 207838
Email: aweusr@smtp.ntrust.org.uk
Open: Hall: 23 Mar - 31 July and 2 Sept - 4 Nov: daily except Mon and Fri (but open Good Fri and BH Mons); Aug: daily except Mon (but open BH Mon); 10, 17 and 24 Nov: Suns only. Times: 1 - 5pm (BH Mons 11am - 5pm, closes 4pm after 27 Oct). Garden: 23 Mar - 30 June, 3 Sept - 3 Nov: daily except Mons and Fris (but open Good Fri and BH Mons); July and Aug: daily except Mons (but open BH Mons); Nov - Mar 2003 Sat and Sun (open Feb Half Term week). Times: 23 Mar - 3 Nov 10.30am - 5pm; 5 Nov - Mar 2003 11am - 4pm.
Heritage Open Days: No
[P] Charged. NT members free. Spaces: 500
♿ Partial. Wheelchair access to garden (gravel paths) and restaurant. Disabled visitors may be set down near Hall. Telephone in advance for details. Disabled WC. Guide Dogs: Yes
[£] **Adult:** £6.50, £2.90 (garden only) **Child:** £2.80 **Other:** £9.00 (joint ticket with Wimpole Home Farm, adult, £4.50 child, £22 family), £5.20 (group rate. No group rates on Suns and BHs)

CHESHIRE

Bache House Farm
Chester Road, Hurleston, Nantwich, Cheshire CW5 6BO
A timber-framed house with slate roof dating from 17th century with 18th century extension. The house is a four square house with two gables at the rear. The interior shows timbers in the house walls and an oak staircase.
Grant Recipient/Owner: P R Posnett
Access contact: Mr & Mrs R J Posnett
Tel: 01829 260251
Open: By arrangement at all reasonable times.
Heritage Open Days: No
[P] Spaces: 10 ♿ No [£] No

Belmont Hall
Warrington Road, Great Budworth, Northwich, Cheshire CW9 6HN
Country house, built 1755, initial design by James Gibbs, with fine plasterwork interiors. Set in parkland. Now a private day school with family appartments in the East Wing. Also accessible is surrounding farmland, woods and medieval moat.
Grant Recipient/Owner: The Trustees of Belmont Hall
Access contact: Mr R C Leigh
Tel: 01606 891235 **Fax:** 01606 892349
Open: Free guided tours by arrangement with the Estate Manager. Please note: the property and adjacent area are also open by way of a Countryside Access Educational Agreement.
Heritage Open Days: No
[P] Unlimited, free parking on site. ♿ No [£] No

Bramall Hall
Bramhall Park, Stockport, Cheshire SK7 3NX
Black and white timber-framed manor house dating back to 14th century, with subsequently several renovations (many during the Victorian period). Contains 14th century wallpaintings, an Elizabethan plaster ceiling and Victorian kitchen and servants quarters.
Grant Recipient/Owner: Stockport Metropolitan Borough Council
Access contact: Ms Caroline Egan
Tel: 0161 485 3708 **Fax:** 0161 486 6959
Email: bramall.hall@stockport.gov.uk
Open: Good Fri - end Sept: Mon - Sat 1 - 5pm. Suns and BHs 11am - 5pm. Oct - 1 Jan: Tues - Sat 1 - 4pm. Sun and BHs 11am - 4pm. 2 Jan - Easter: w/ends only 1 - 4pm.
Heritage Open Days: No
[P] Pay parking. Spaces: 60
♿ Partial. Wheelchair access to ground floor only. Disabled WC. Guide Dogs: Yes
[£] **Adult:** £3.95 **Child:** £2.50 **Other:** £2.5

Capesthorne Hall
Macclesfield, Cheshire SK11 9JY
Jacobean style hall with a collection of fine art, sculpture, furniture, tapestry and antiques from Europe, America and the Far East. The Hall dates from 1719 when it was originally designed by the Smith's of Warwick. Altered in 1837 by Blore and rebuilt by Salvin in 1861 following a disastrous fire.
www.capesthorne.com
Grant Recipient/Owner: Mr William Arthur Bromley-Davenport
Access contact: Mrs Gwyneth Jones
Tel: 01625 861221 **Fax:** 01625 861619
Email: info@capesthorpe.com
Open: Apr - Oct: Sun, Wed and BHs (except Christmas and New Year). Gardens and Chapel from 12 noon to 5.30pm, Hall from 1.30pm (last adm. 3.30pm). Parties on other days by arrangement.
Heritage Open Days: No
[P] Spaces: 2000
♿ Partial. Wheelchair access to ground floor and butler's pantry. Disabled WC. Guide Dogs: Yes
[£] **Adult:** £6.50 (Sun & BHs) **Child:** £3 **Other:** £5.50 (senior citizen), £15 (family). Weds only: £5 (Car: 4 people) £10 (minibus) £25 (coach)

Chester Town Hall
Northgate Street, Chester, Cheshire CH1 2HS
Victorian town hall situated in centre of city, home to the Chester Tapestry, portraits of the Grosvenor family, and World War I memorial dedicated to Chester citizens. Also a memorial to the Polish air force. One of many stained glass windows shows the Common Seal of the city.
Website: chestercc.gov.uk
Grant Recipient/Owner: Chester City Council
Access contact: Ms Rebecca Pinfold
Tel: 01244 402320 **Fax:** 01244 341965
Email: b.pinfold@chestercc.gov.uk
Open: Mon - Fri, 8.30am - 7pm. Saturdays by arrangement.
Heritage Open Days: No
[P] Parking in Princess Street.
♿ Yes. Disabled WC. Guide Dogs: Yes [£] No

Gawsworth Hall
Gawsworth, Cheshire SK11 9RN
Fully lived-in Tudor half-timbered manor house with Tiliting Ground. Former home of Mary Fitton, Maid of Honour at the Court of Queen Elizabeth I, and the supposed 'Dark Lady' of Shakespeare's sonnets. Pictures, sculpture and furniture. Open air theatre with covered grandstand.
www.gawsworthhall.com
Grant Recipient/Owner: Mr T Richards
Access contact: Mr T Richards
Tel: 01260 223456 **Fax:** 01260 223469
Email: gawsworth@lineone.net
Open: Easter - mid June: Sun - Wed 2 - 5pm; mid June - end Aug: daily 2-5pm; end Aug - early Oct: Sun - Wed 2 - 5pm.
Heritage Open Days: No
[P] Parking for disabled near house. Spaces: 600
♿ Partial. Wheelchair and guide dog access to garden only. Disabled WC. Guide Dogs: No
[£] **Adult:** £4.50 **Child:** £2.25 **Groups:** £3.50 (20+)

Highfields
Audlem, nr. Crewe, Cheshire CW3 0DT
Small half-timbered manor house dating back to c1600.
Grant Recipient/Owner: Mr J B Baker
Access contact: Mrs Susan Baker
Tel: 01630 655479
Open: Guided tour of hall, drawing room, dining room, parlour, bedrooms and gardens by written arrangement.
Heritage Open Days: No
[P] Spaces: 20
♿ Partial. Wheelchair access to ground floor only, disabled WC with assistance (down 2 steps). Guide Dogs: Yes [£] **Adult:** £4 **Child:** £2

Lightshaw Hall Farm
Lightshaw Lane, Golborne, Warrington, Cheshire WA3 3UJ
16th century timber-framed farmhouse largely rebuilt in the 18th and 19th centuries. Historical evidence suggests there was an estate and probably a house on the site by the end of the 13th century if not before. The west range is supposed to represent the solar apartments of an early post-medieval house. External walls were replaced by bricks in the 18th and 19th centuries. Timber trusses and main roof timbers survive.
Grant Recipient/Owner: Mrs J Hewitt
Access contact: Mrs J Hewitt
Tel: 01942 717429
Open: All year round by telephone arrangement.
Heritage Open Days: No
[P] Spaces: 20
♿ Partial. Access for wheelchair users to the ground floor only. Video and photographs available for those unable to climb stairs. No disabled WC. Guide Dogs: Yes [£] No

Lyme Park
Disley, Stockport, Cheshire SK12 2NX
Home to the Legh family for 600 years, Lyme Park comprises a 1400 acre medieval deer park, a 17 acre Victorian garden and a Tudor hall which was transformed into an Italianate palace in the 18th century. Location for *'Pemberley'* in the BBC TV's production of *Pride and Prejudice*.
www.nationaltrust.org.uk
Grant Recipient/Owner: Stockport Metropolitan Borough Council
Access contact: Mr Philip Burt
Tel: 01663 762023 **Fax:** 01663 765035
Email: mlyrec@smtp.ntrust.org.uk
Open: Hall: 29 Mar - 30 Oct, daily except Weds and Thurs 1 - 5pm. Garden: 29 Mar - 30 Oct, Fri - Tues 11am - 5pm, Wed & Thurs 1 - 5pm; Nov - 15 Dec, w/ends 12 - 3pm. Park: Apr - Oct, daily 8am - 8.30pm; Nov - Mar, daily 8am - 6pm.
Heritage Open Days: No
[P] Spaces: 1500
♿ Partial. Wheelchair access to garden, first floor of house, parts of park, shop and restaurant. Disabled WC. Guide Dogs: Yes
[£] **Adult:** £5.50 **Child:** £2.50 **Other:** NT members free

Quarry Bank Mill
Styal, Cheshire SK9 4LA
Georgian cotton mill, now a museum and the only water powered cotton mill in the world. Working demonstrations of cotton processing, a giant iron water wheel and two mill engines steaming daily. Restored Apprentice House once housed child workers.
www.quarrybankmill.org.uk
Grant Recipient/Owner: The National Trust
Access contact: Ms Josselin Hill
Tel: 01625 527468 **Fax:** 01625 539267
Email: enquiries@quarrybankmill.org.uk
Open: Mill: Apr - Sept, daily 11am - 6pm (last adm. 4.30pm); Oct - Mar (closed Mons) 11am - 5pm (last adm. 3.30pm). Apprentice House and Garden: Easter and daily during Aug as Mill, w/ends throughout the year as Mill and Tues - Fridays all year 2pm - Mill closing time.
Heritage Open Days: No
[P] Spaces: 350
♿ Partial. Wheelchair access to ground and lower ground floors only. Disabled WC. Guide Dogs: Yes
[£] **Adult:** £6 **Child/Other:** £3.70

Rode Hall
Church Lane, Scholar Green, Cheshire ST7 3QP
Country house built early - mid 18th century, with later alterations. Set in a parkland designed by Repton. Home to the Wilbraham family since 1669.
Grant Recipient/Owner: Sir Richard Baker Wilbraham Bt
Access contact: Sir Richard Baker Wilbraham Bt
Tel: 01270 873237 **Fax:** 01270 882962
Email: rodehall@scholargreen.fsnet.co.uk
Open: Hall and Gardens: 1 Apr - 25 Sept, Weds and Bank Holidays (closed Good Fri) 2 - 5pm; Gardens only: Tues and Thurs 2 - 5pm.
Heritage Open Days: No
[P] Yes. Parking for disabled available adjacent to entrance by arrangement. Spaces: 200
♿ Partial. Wheelchair access with assistance to ground floor. No disabled WC. Guide Dogs: Yes
[£] **Adult:** £4 (house & garden), £2.50 (garden only). **Child:** £2.50 (house & garden), £1.50 (garden only). **Other:** £2.50 (senior citizens, house & garden), £1.50 (garden only)

St Chad's Church Tower
Wybunbury, Nantwich, Cheshire CW5 7LS
Grade II* listed 15th or 16th century church tower, rest of Church demolished in 1977. 96ft high and containing six restored bells, spiral staircase, charity boards, monuments and affords panoramic views over the South Cheshire plain.
Grant Recipient/Owner: Mrs D Lockhart
Access contact: Mrs D Lockhart
Tel: 01270 841481 **Fax:** 01270 842659
Open: Sat 25 May 2 - 5pm. **Heritage Open Days:** 11am - 4pm. At other times by arrangement with Mrs D Lockhart, Wybunbury Tower Preservation Trust, Hawthorn House, 1 Main Road, Wybunbury, Nantwich, Cheshire CW5 7NA (tel. 01270 841481) or Mr Sam Wood (tel. 01270 841188).
Heritage Open Days: Yes
[P] Spaces: 20
♿ Partial. Wheelchair access to ground floor only. No disabled WC. Guide Dogs: Yes
[£] **Adult:** £1 **Child:** 50p

Tatton Park Fernery
Knutsford, Cheshire WA16 6QN
Designed by Joseph Paxton in the 1850s to house the Egerton family's collection of New Zealand ferns and is situated adjacent to a conservatory by Lewis Wyatt.
www.tattonpark.org.uk
Grant Recipient/Owner: Cheshire County Council/ National Trust
Access contact: Mr B Flanagan
Tel: 01625 534400 **Fax:** 01625 534403

Email: tattonpark@cheshire.gov.uk
Open: Fernery daily except Mons and Christmas Day (but open BHs), 10.30am - 4pm in summer, 11am - 3pm in winter.
Heritage Open Days: No
P Spaces: 1000 Yes. Disabled WC. Guide Dogs: Yes
£ Adult: £3 Child: £2 Other: £3.50 (car entry)

CLEVELAND

Former Holy Trinity Church

Yarn Lane, Stockton-on-Tees, Cleveland
Built 1837-8 by John & Benjamin Green, chancel enlarged 1906. Wide 4-bay nave, 2-bay chancel. Spire removed in 1957, interior gutted by fire in 1991.
Grant Recipient/Owner: Stockton-on-Tees Borough Council
Access contact: Mr Bryan Harris
Tel: 01642 391286 **Fax:** 01642 391282
Email: bryan.harris@stockton.gov.uk
Open: Exterior only at all times.
Heritage Open Days: No
P On-street parking available. No £ No

CO DURHAM

9 & 10 The College

Durham, DH1 3EH
Independent preparatory school housed in part of the Cathedral Close at Durham. 18th and 19th century buildings, mainly local sandstone with some brickwork. Medieval basement rooms.
Grant Recipient/Owner: The Dean & Chapter of Durham Cathedral
Access contact: Mr C S S Drew
Tel: 0191 3842935 **Fax:** 0191 3839261
Email: head@choristers.durham.sch.uk
Open: During Sept for 28 days by arrangement only.
Heritage Open Days: No
P No No £ No

Barnard Castle Market Cross

Barnard Castle, Co. Durham
Two-storey building dating from 1747 with a colonnaded ground floor and enclosed upper storey. Two slate roofs crowned by a bell tower and gilded weather vane with two bullet holes from 1804. Formerly used as Town Hall, butter market, lock-up, Court room and fire station.
Grant Recipient/Owner: Teesdale District Council
Access contact: Director of Development
Tel: 01833 696282 **Fax:** 01833 637269
Email: business@teesdale.gov.uk
Open: Colonnaded area (ground floor) open to the public at all times. First floor only accessible through organised tours with keys available from Teesdale House, Galgate, Barnard Castle by special arrangement.
Heritage Open Days: No
P On-street parking. No £ No

Christ Church

(Hartlepool Art Gallery & Tourist Info Centre)
Church Square, Hartlepool, Co. Durham TS24 7EQ
Built as the parish church for the new town of West Hartlepool in 1854 to a design by E.B. Lamb, Christ Church closed as a church in 1971 due to population movement in the town centre. Converted in the 1990s into a new art gallery, café and tourist information centre complete with a new staircase giving tower access to a viewing platform.
www.thisishartlepool.com
Grant Recipient/Owner: Hartlepool Borough Council
Access contact: The Arts & Museums Officer
Tel: 01429 523441 **Fax:** 01429 523477
Email: arts-museums@hartlepool.gov.uk
Open: Open Tues - Sat 10am - 5pm; Sun 2 - 4.30pm. Closed on Mondays and Christmas Day, Boxing Day and New Year's Day.
Heritage Open Days: No
P Public parking 200m. Parking for disabled adjacent. Spaces: 200
 Partial. Wheelchair access to all areas except Tower. Disabled WC. Guide Dogs: Yes
£ Tower Adult: 50p Child: 30p

Croxdale Hall

Durham, County Durham DH6 5JP
18th century re-casing of an earlier Tudor building, containing comfortably furnished mid-Georgian rooms with Rococo ceilings. There is also a private chapel in the north elevation, walled gardens, a quarter-of-a-mile long terrace, an orangery and lakes which date from the mid-18th century.
Grant Recipient/Owner: Captain G M Salvin
Access contact: Mr W H T Salvin
Tel: 01833 690100 **Fax:** 01833 637004
Email: williamsalvin@compuserve.com
Open: By arrangement on Tues and Weds from the first Tues in May to the second Wed in July, 11am - 1pm.
Heritage Open Days: No
P Spaces: 20 Yes. Disabled WC. Guide Dogs: No
£ £5

Durham Castle

Palace Green, Durham,
County Durham DH1 3RW
Dating from 1072, the Castle was the seat of the Prince Bishops until 1832. Together with the Cathedral, the Castle is a World Heritage Site. Now houses University College, the Foundation College of Durham University, and is a conference, banqueting and holiday centre in vacations.
www.durhamcastle.com
Grant Recipient/Owner: University of Durham
Access contact: Bursar
Tel: 0191 374 3800 **Fax:** 0191 374 7470
Email: e.a.gibson@dur.ac.uk
Open: Easter - end of Sept: guided tours daily from 10am - 4pm; 1 Oct - Easter Mon: Weds, Fri, Sat and Sun (afternoons only). (Tours may not take place when the Castle is being used for functions).
Heritage Open Days: No
P Parking in city car parks.
 Access for wheelchair users to courtyard only.
No disabled WC. Guide Dogs: Yes
£ Adult: £3 Child: £2 Other: £6.50 (family)

Former Stockton & Darlington Railway Booking Office

48 Bridge Road, Stockton-on-Tees,
Co. Durham TS18 3AX
Original booking office of the Stockton and Darlington Railway. Cottage of plain brick with slate roof facing railway line. A bronze tablet on the gable ends "Martin 1825 the Stockton and Darlington Company booked first passenger, thus marking an epoch in the history of mankind". The first rail of the Railway was laid outside the building. Now used as an administration office and accommodation for single homeless men.
Grant Recipient/Owner: Stockton Church Mission
Access contact: Ms Margaret McCarthy
Tel: 01642 800322 **Fax:** 01642 800322
Open: Mon - Fri, 9am - 3pm.
Heritage Open Days: No
P On-street parking.
 Partial. Full wheelchair access to exterior of site.
No disabled WC. Guide Dogs: Yes £ No

Kepier Farm Hospital

Kepier Lane, Durham, Co. Durham
Ruins of Kepier Hospital which was the wealthiest of the county's medieval hospitals. Refounded c1180 after the original hospital was destroyed in 1144. As well as caring for the sick and elderly it provided accommodation for pilgrims to the shrine of St Cuthbert. At the Reformation the hospital was dissolved and a new house, with a fashionable rennaisance loggia, was built after 1588. The loggia survives within the medieval hospital enclosure.
Grant Recipient/Owner: Mrs R A Watson
Access contact: R A Wilson
Tel: 0191 3842761
Open: W/ends by arrangement (tel. 0191 3842761).
Heritage Open Days: Yes
P Available. No £ No

Low Butterby Farmhouse

Croxdale & Hett, Co. Durham DH6 5JN
Stone built farmhouse constructed on medieval site incorporating elements of 17th, 18th and 19th century phases of development.
Grant Recipient/Owner: Mr W H T Salvin
Access contact: Mr W H T Salvin
Tel: 01833 690100 **Fax:** 01833 637004
Email: williamsalvin@compuserve.com
Open: By written or telephone arrangement with Mr W H T Salvin, The Estate Office, Egglestone Abbey, Barnard Castle, Co. Durham DL12 9TN.
Heritage Open Days: No
P Spaces: 2
 Partial. Limited wheelchair access with assistance (some changes in floor level). No disabled WC. Guide Dogs: No
£ No

The Priest's House

Croxdale Hall, Croxdale, Co. Durham DH6 5JP
18th century stone built cottage with 19th century extension adjacent to and ancillary to the Old Church and Croxdale Hall.
Grant Recipient/Owner: Mr W H T Salvin
Access contact: Mr W H T Salvin
Tel: 01833 690100 **Fax:** 01833 637004
Email: williamsalvin@compuserve.com
Open: By written or telephone arrangement with Mr W H T Salvin, The Estate Office, Egglestone Abbey, Barnard Castle, Co. Durham DL12 9TN (tel 01833 690100).
Heritage Open Days: No
P Spaces: 2
 Partial. Wheelchair access to ground floor only.
No disabled WC. Guide Dogs: Yes £ No

Raby Castle

PO Box 50, Staindrop, Darlington,
County Durham DL2 3AY
Medieval castle, once the seat of the Nevills, has been home to Lord Barnard's family since 1626. Contains a collection of art and highly decorated interiors. Surrounded by 200-acre Deer Park and walled gardens.
www.rabycastle.com
Grant Recipient/Owner: Lord Barnard TD
Access contact: Miss Catherine Turnbull
Tel: 01833 660207 **Fax:** 01833 660835
Email: rabyestate@rabycastle.com
Open: Easter and BH w/ends: Sat - Wed. May and Sept: Wed and Sun. June, July and Aug: daily except Sat. Castle open 1 - 5pm. Garden and Park 11am - 5.30pm. Guided tours weekday mornings from Easter to end Sept.
Heritage Open Days: No
P Spaces: 500
 Partial. Limited wheelchair access to lower floor with assistance (3 steps to entrance and some internal steps to be negotiated). Disabled WC. Guide Dogs: Yes
£ Adult: £5 (Castle, Park & Gdns), £3 (Park & Gdns) Child: £2 (Castle, Park & Gdns), £2 (Park & Gdns) Other: £4 (Castle, Park & Gdns), £2 (Park & Gdns), £12 (family), £7.50 (guided tour), £12 & £25 (Adult season ticket for Castle, Park & Gdns)

Rokeby Hall

Barnard Castle, County Durham DL12 9RZ
Early 18th century Palladian country house with fine needlework pictures.
Grant Recipient/Owner: Executors of R A Morrit
Access contact: Mr W H T Salvin
Tel: 01833 690100 **Fax:** 01833 637004
Email: williamsalvin@compuserve.com
Open: May BH Mon and Spring BH Mon and Tues, then Mon and Tues until the second Tues in Sept, 2 - 5pm (last adm. 4.30pm).
Heritage Open Days: No
P Spaces: 15
 Partial. Wheelchair access to ground floor only.
No disabled WC. Guide Dogs: No £ Adult: £5

Windlestone Hall Clock Tower

Rushyford, Chilton, Ferryhill,
Co. Durham DL17 0LX
Windlestone Hall was the seat of the Edens and birthplace of former Prime Minister, Sir Anthony Eden. The Hall was rebuilt in 1835 and is now a residential school run by Durham Lea. The clock tower is not working at the present time and access to the interior is unsafe. Visitors are welcome to view the exterior.
Grant Recipient/Owner: Durham County Council
Access contact: Ms Trish Sharkey
Tel: 01388 720337 **Fax:** 01388 724904
Open: The Clock Tower is unavailable for viewing during school term time. For access during the school holidays contact Trish Sharkey (01388 720337).
Heritage Open Days: No
P Spaces: 50
 Partial. Wheelchair access to exterior of clock tower. No disabled WC. Guide Dogs: Yes £ No

CORNWALL

Caerhays Castle & Gardens

Gorran, St Austell, Cornwall PL26 6LY
Built by John Nash in 1808. Set in 60 acres of informal woodland gardens created by J C Williams, who sponsored plant hunting expeditions to China at the turn of the 19th century.
www.caerhays.co.uk
Grant Recipient/Owner: Mr F J Williams
Access contact: Miss A B Mayes
Tel: 01872 501144/501312 **Fax:** 01872 501870
Email: estateoffice@caerhays.co.uk
Open: Gardens: 11 Mar - 31 May: daily, 10am to 5.30pm (last entry 4.30pm), plus charity openings on Easter Sun, 14 Apr and 6 May. House: 18 Mar - 26 Apr: Mon - Fri, 1 - 4pm. Tours every 45 minutes.
Heritage Open Days: No
P Spaces: 500
 Partial. Limited wheelchair access to gardens (area around House). Access to ground floor with assistance, please telephone to check. No disabled WC. Guide Dogs: Yes
£ Adult: £4.50 (House or garden only), £8 (combined ticket), £2.50 (charity openings) Child: £1.50 (under 16s, gardens), Free entry on charity openings Other: £5.50 (groups 15+, garden tour), £3.50 (groups, gardens), £4 (groups, House)

Cotehele

St Dominick, Saltash, Cornwall PL12 6TA
Cotehele, situated on the west bank of the River Tamar, was built mainly between 1485-1627. Home of the Edgcumbe family for centuries. Its granite and slatestone walls contain intimate chambers adorned with tapestries, original furniture and armour.
www.nationaltrust.org.uk

Grant Recipient/Owner: The National Trust
Access contact: Lewis Enyon
Tel: 01579 351346 **Fax:** 01579 351222
Email: cctlce@smtp.ntrust.org.uk
Open: House and restaurant: 23 Mar - 3 Nov daily except Fridays (open Good Fri) 11am - 5pm; Oct and Nov 11am - 4.30pm. Mill: 23 Mar - 30 June and 1 Sept - 3 Nov daily except Fridays (open Good Fri), July and Aug daily; Mar, June and Sept: 1 - 5.30pm, July and Aug: 1- 6pm, Oct and Nov: 1 - 4.30pm. Garden: all year, daily 10.30am until dusk. Gallery and tea-room on quay: 23 Mar - 3 Nov daily 11am - 5pm; gallery 12 - 5pm or dusk; Nov and Dec Christmas opening tel 01579 351346.
Heritage Open Days: Yes
P Parking space available for coaches. Spaces: 100
♿ Partial. Wheelchair access to house (hall and kitchen only), garden, area around house, restaurant and shop. Ramps available. Woodland walks: some paths accessible. Disabled WC. Guide Dogs: Yes
£ **Adult:** £6.40 (house, garden & mill). £3.60 (garden & mill) **Child:** £3.20 (house, garden & mill). £1.80 (garden & mill) **Other:** £16 (family: house, garden & mill). £5.40 (booked groups). £9 (family: garden & mill)

Cullacott Farmhouse

Werrington, Launceston, Cornwall PL15 8NH
Grade I medieval hall house, built in the 1480s as a long house, and extended 1579. Contains wall paintings of fictive tapestry, Tudor arms, St James of Compostella and remains of representation of St George and the Dragon. Extensively restored 1995-7 but still retains many original features. Now holiday accommodation.
Grant Recipient/Owner: Mr & Mrs J Cole
Access contact: Mr & Mrs J Cole
Tel: 01566 772631
Open: By arrangement.
Heritage Open Days: No
P Spaces: 20
♿ Partial. Wheelchair access to Great Hall, through passage and disabled toilet. Guide Dogs: Yes
£ **Adult:** £2 **Child:** Free

Godolphin House

Godolphin Cross, Helston, Cornwall, TR13 9RE
Tudor-Stuart mansion of granite round a courtyard. For many generations seat of the Godolphin family who were courtiers from the 16th to the 18th century, the 1st Earl (who was born here) rose to be Queen Anne's Lord Treasurer. Has late Elizabethan stables with wagon collection and a large medieval and other gardens.
Grant Recipient/Owner: Mrs S E Schofield
Access contact: Mrs Joanne Schofield
Tel: 01736 763194 **Fax:** 01736 763194
Email: godo@euphony.net
Open: May - June & Sept: Thursdays & Fridays 10am - 5pm, Sun 2 - 5pm. July - Aug: Tues, Thurs & Fri 10am - 5pm, Sun 2 - 5pm. BH Mons (except Christmas) 10am - 5pm. Groups all year by arrangement
Heritage Open Days: No
P Parking for 3 coaches. Spaces: 100
♿ Partial. Wheelchair access to whole house except one room, access to stables and gardens may be difficult. Disabled WC. Guide Dogs: Yes
£ **Adult:** £4 (house & gardens) **Child:** £1 **Other:** £2 (gardens only)

Mount Edgcumbe House & Country Park

Cremyll, Torpoint, Cornwall PL10 1HZ
Grade II former home of the Earls of Mount Edgcumbe in Grade I registered landscape park of 850 acres. Includes 52 Listed buildings and 16 acres of formal gardens. 16th - 18th centuries. Spectacular setting above River Tamar and Plymouth Sound. Landscape noted by Horace Walpole and Alexander Pope in 18th century. Used as starting point for D-Day landings by American troops in 1944.
Grant Recipient/Owner: Mount Edgcumbe Country Park Joint Committee
Access contact: The Manager
Tel: 01752 822236 **Fax:** 01752 822199
Open: Country Park (with listed structures): all year, dawn to dusk. Mount Edgcumbe House and Earls Garden: 4 Apr - 30 Sept, Wed - Sun and BHs 11am - 4.30pm.
Heritage Open Days: No
P Spaces: 120
♿ Partial. Wheelchair access to flat areas of garden and most of house. Disabled WC. Guide Dogs: Yes
£ **Adult:** £4.50 (house only) **Child:** £2.25 **Other:** £3.50 (concessions & groups)

Porth-en-Alls Lodge

Prussia Cove, St Hilary, Cornwall TR20 9BA
Originally a chauffeur's lodge, built c1910-1914 and designed by Philip Tilden. The Lodge is built into the cliff and sits in close proximity to the main house. The chauffeur's lodge is one of a number of historic houses on the Porth-en-Alls Estate.
Grant Recipient/Owner: Trustees of Porth-en-Alls Estate
Access contact: Mr P Tunstall-Behrens
Tel: 01736 762 014 **Fax:** 01736 762 014
Email: penapc@dial.pipex.com
Open: Available as self-catering holiday lets throughout the year. Members of the public may view the property by appointment, but only if it is unoccupied at the time.
Heritage Open Days: No
P Public car park approximately 1/2 mile from the Lodge, off the A394 (near Rosudgeon village).
♿ Partial. No disabled WC. Guide Dogs: Yes £ No

Prideaux Place

Padstow, Cornwall PL28 8RP
Elizabethan mansion, with various subsequent alterations and additions, built by and still lived in by the Prideaux family. Remodelled in Gothic style in late 18th or early 19th century. Has formal garden, Temple, Gothic dairy and exhibition areas in the stables.
Grant Recipient/Owner: Mr Peter Prideaux-Brune
Access contact: Mr Peter Prideaux-Brune
Tel: 01841 532411 **Fax:** 01841 532945
Email: office@prideauxplace.fsnet.co.uk
Open: Easter Sun - 11 Apr and 12 May - 3 Oct: Sun - Thurs. Tea room and grounds 12.30 - 5pm; house 1.30 - 4pm (last tour). Coach groups all year by arrangement.
Heritage Open Days: No
P Spaces: 40
♿ Partial. Wheelchair access to ground floor, tea room and gardens. No disabled WC. Guide Dogs: Yes
£ **Adult:** £6 **Child:** £2 **Other:** £4 (groups, £5 Fri & Sat)

Southgate Arch

Southgate Street, Launceston, Cornwall PL15 7AR
Only remaining gateway of the three original entrances to the old walled town. Main arch part of original 12th century town wall. Used as a jail for many years, now houses art gallery.
Grant Recipient/Owner: Launceston Town Council
Access contact: Mr P J Freestone
Tel: 01566 773693 **Fax:** 01566 773693
Email: ltc@talk21.com
Open: 1 Apr - 25 Dec: Mon, Tues, Wed, Fri and Sat 10am - 4.30pm.
Heritage Open Days: No
P No ♿ No. Guide Dogs: Yes £ No

Tintagel Old Post Office

Tintagel, Cornwall PL34 0DB
Small 14th century manor house is furnished with local oak pieces. One room used in the 19th century as the letter-receiving office for the district is now restored to that period and function.
www.nationaltrust.org.uk
Grant Recipient/Owner: The National Trust
Access contact: Sandy Chadwick
Tel: 01840 770024
Open: 23 Mar - 3 Nov: daily 11am - 5.30pm; Oct - 3 Nov 11am - 4pm.
Heritage Open Days: Yes
P Private car park directly opposite (with lavatories). National Trust car park 1/4 mile from house.
♿ Partial. Wheelchair access to ground floor only. Garden accessible with help (no ramps), staff will assist. Disabled WC. Guide Dogs: Yes
£ **Adult:** £2.30 **Child:** £1.15 **Other:** £5.70 (family). £1.80 (booked groups)

Tregithew

Manaccan, Helston, Cornwall TR12 6HX
18th century farmhouse, barn and buildings, and horse engine house. Some parts of the property may date back to the 16th century. Panelled parlour, original windows and fireplaces, barrel ceiling in one bedroom and 3 leaded windows.
Grant Recipient/Owner: Mrs B Faull
Access contact: Mrs B Faull
Tel: 01326 231382
Open: By written arrangement June - Sept.
Heritage Open Days: No
P Spaces: 2 ♿ No £ No

Tresco Abbey Gardens

Tresco Estate, Isles of Scilly, Cornwall TR24 0QQ
25 acre garden with plants mainly from the Mediterranean region. Plant groups include protea, aloe from South Africa, succulents from Canary Isles and palms from Mexico. All grown outside all year round. Unique, frost-free climate.
www.tresco.co.uk
Grant Recipient/Owner: Mr Michael Nelhams
Access contact: Mr Michael Nelhams
Tel: 01720 424105 **Fax:** 01720 424105
Email: mikenelhams@tresco.co.uk
Open: Daily 10am - 4pm.
Heritage Open Days: No
P No
♿ Partial. Wheelchair access to all garden areas but some gravel slopes which may be difficult. No disabled WC. Guide Dogs: No
£ **Adult:** £7.50 **Child:** Free (under 14) **Other:** £12 (weekly ticket)

CUMBRIA

23-26 Lowther Village

Penrith, Cumbria CA10 2HG
Dwelling houses in a model village built 1766-73 by Robert Adam as estate houses for Sir James Lowther, part of a model village which was never completed.
Grant Recipient/Owner: Lowther and District Housing Association Ltd
Access contact: Lowther & District Housing Association Ltd
Tel: 01931 712577 **Fax:** 01931 712087
Email: jn.ldha@talk21.com
Open: Access to exterior at all times.
Heritage Open Days: Yes
P Available. ♿ No £ No

Brantwood

Coniston, Cumbria LA21 8AD
Brantwood, situated on Coniston Water, was the former home of Victorian writer and artist, John Ruskin, from 1872 to 1900. Displays a collection of paintings by Ruskin and his circle, his furniture, books and personal items. Video, bookshop, craft gallery and restaurant on site. Gardens include the Harbour Walk and Professor's Garden where Ruskin experimented with native flowers and fruit.
www.brantwood.org.uk
Grant Recipient/Owner: Brantwood Education Trust Ltd
Access contact: Mr Howard Hull
Tel: 015394 41396 **Fax:** 015394 41263
Email: enquiries@brantwood.org.uk
Open: All year: 11 Mar - 11 Nov, daily 11am - 5.30pm; 13 Nov - 12 Mar, Wed - Sun 11am - 4.30pm (closed Christmas and Boxing Day).
Heritage Open Days: No
P Spaces: 50
♿ Partial. Wheelchair access to house, toilets and restaurant only. Disabled WC. Guide Dogs: Yes
£ **Adult:** £4.50 **Child:** £1 **Other:** £3 (student)

Church Brow Cottage

Ruskin's View, Kirkby Lonsdale, Cumbria LA6 2BB
An early 19th century picturesque garden pavilion built in the romantic gothic style, perched high on the steep west bank of the River Lune. Coarsed rubble, 2 storey building with spectacular views out across the valley to the fells beyond.
www.vivat.org.uk
Grant Recipient/Owner: The Vivat Trust Ltd
Access contact: Mrs F Lloyd
Tel: 020 7930 2212 **Fax:** 020 7930 2295
Email: enquiries@vivat.demon.co.uk
Open: 14 - 15 June, 10am - 5pm. At other times by arrangement with The Vivat Trust.
Heritage Open Days: No
P Public parking 3 minutes walk. ♿ No £ No

Coop House

Netherby, nr. Carlisle, Cumbria CA6 5PX
Stands on the bank of the River Esk where 'coops' or traps were set to catch salmon. This summerhouse was built c1765 by Dr Robert Graham as an ornament in the landscape around Netherby Hall and as a place to enjoy the river. By 1980 it was completely derelict.
www.landmarktrust.co.uk
Grant Recipient/Owner: The Landmark Trust
Access contact: Ms Victoria Piggott
Tel: 01628 825920 **Fax:** 01628 825417
Email: vpiggott@landmarktrust.co.uk
Open: The Landmark Trust is an independent charity, which rescues small buildings of historic or architectural importance from decay or unsympathetic improvement. Landmark's aim is to promote the enjoyment of these historic buildings by making them available to stay in for holidays. These buildings can be rented by anyone, at all times of the year, for periods ranging from a weekend to three weeks. Bookings can be made by telephoning the Booking Office on 01628 825925. As the building is in full-time use for holiday accommodation, it is not normally open to the public. However the public can view the building by arrangement by telephoning the access contact (Victoria Piggott on 01628 825920) to make an appointment. Potential visitors will be asked to write to confirm the details.
Heritage Open Days: No
P No ♿ No. Guide Dogs: Yes £ No

Crown & Nisi Prius Court

The Courts, English Street, Carlisle, Cumbria CA3 8NA
Former Crown Court in Carlisle situated at southern entrance to the city. One of a pair of sandstone towers built in the early 19th century as replicas of the medieval bastion. The towers were built to house the civil and criminal courts, used until the 1980s.
Grant Recipient/Owner: Cumbria Crown Court
Access contact: Mr Mike Telfer
Tel: 01228 606116
Open: By arrangement with Mr Mike Telfer, Office

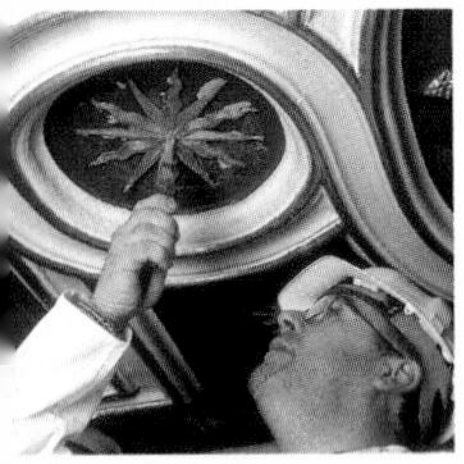
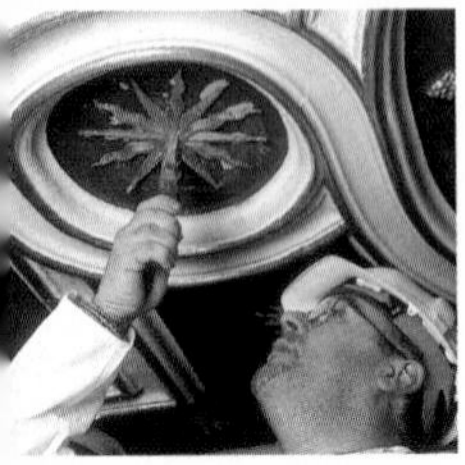

Superintendent, The Courts, English Street, Carlisle, Cumbria CA3 8NA (tel.01228 606116).
Heritage Open Days: No
P No ♿ No. Guide Dogs: Yes £ No

Dean Tait's Lane Arch

Carlisle, Cumbria CA3 8TZ
16th century stone arch across the Dean Tait Lane pedestrian footpath and adjoining the Prior Slee Gatehouse.
Grant Recipient/Owner: The Chapter of Carlisle Cathedral
Access contact: Mr E T Amos
Tel: 01228 548151 **Fax:** 01228 547049
Email: office@carlislecathedral.org.uk
Open: Exterior visible at all times - the arch spans a public footpath.
Heritage Open Days: No
P No ♿ Yes. No disabled WC. Guide Dogs: Yes £ No

Devonshire Buildings

Michaelson Road, Barrow Island, Cumbria
Red sandstone tenements, 1870s, of 4 storey height with cellars and slate roof. Two blocks of 9 closes and 5 closes. The buildings represent a good example of late-Victorian tenements based on similar tenement blocks from Glasgow.
Grant Recipient/Owner: Holker Estate Trust
Access contact: Mr D P R Knight
Tel: 015395 58313 **Fax:** 015395 58966
Open: Access to exterior at all times. Interior all year by arrangement with Mr D P R Knight, Holker Estate Trust, Cark-in-Cartmel, Grange-over-Sands, Cumbria LA11 7PH.
Heritage Open Days: No
P On-street parking nearby. ♿ No £ No

Kirkby Hall Wallpaintings

Kirkby-in-Furness, Cumbria LA17 7UX
Chapel in west wing, accessible only from trap door in dairy passage. Wallpaintings in red ochre and black consisting of panels with stylised trees, animals and birds with texts above of the Lord's Prayer, Creed, Ten Commandments and Galations 5, 16-21 from the Great Bible of 1541.
Grant Recipient/Owner: Holker Estates Co. Ltd
Access contact: Mr D P R Knight
Tel: 015395 58313 **Fax:** 015395 58966
Email: estateoffice@holker.co.uk
Open: By written arrangement with the Holker Estate Office, Cark-in-Cartmel, Grange-over-Sands, Cumbria LA11 7PH
Heritage Open Days: No
P Spaces: 3 ♿ No £ No

Muncaster Castle

Ravenglass, Cumbria CA18 1RQ
Large house incorporating medieval fortified tower, remodelled by Anthony Salvin for 4th Lord Muncaster in 1862-66. Ancestral home of the Pennington family for 800 years containing a panelled Hall and octagonal library. Headquarters of the World Owl Trust. Woodland garden, Lakeland setting. World-famous rhododendrons, camellias and magnolias with terrace walk along the edge of the Esk valley.
www.muncastercastle.co.uk
Grant Recipient/Owner: Mrs P R Gordon-Duff-Pennington
Access contact: Mrs Iona Frost-Pennington
Tel: 01229 717614 **Fax:** 01229 717010
Email: info@muncastercastle.co.uk
Open: 10 Mar - 3 Nov: Castle open daily Sun - Fri (closed Saturdays) 12 noon - 5pm; Gardens, Owl Centre and Maze 10.30am - 6pm. Refreshments available.
Heritage Open Days: No
P Spaces: 150
♿ Partial. Wheelchair access to ground floor of Castle only but other attractions and facilities accessible. The hilly nature of the site can create access difficulties, ask for further information on arrival. Disabled WC. Guide Dogs: Yes
£ **Adult:** £7.50 (Castle, Gardens, Owls & Maze), £5.50 (Gardens, Owls & Maze) **Child:** £4.50 (Castle, Gardens, Owls & Maze), £3.50 (Gardens, Owls & Maze) **Other:** £20 (family: Castle, Gardens, Owls & Maze), £17 (family: Gardens, Owls & Maze)

Orthwaite Hall Barn

Uldale, Wigton, Cumbria CA7 1HL
Grade II* listed agricultural barn. Former house adjoining later Hall, probably late 16th or early 17th century, now used for storage and housing animals.
Grant Recipient/Owner: Mrs S Hope
Access contact: Mr Jonathan Hope
Tel: 016973 71344
Open: By telephone arrangement.
Heritage Open Days: No
P Spaces: 3 ♿ No. Guide Dogs: Yes £ No

Prior Slee Gatehouse

Carlisle Cathedral, Carlisle, Cumbria CA3 8TZ
Dated 1528, the Gatehouse would have replaced an earlier one. It has a large chamber over the gate, with two Tudor fireplaces. Graffiti carved in the stonework is believed to include merchants' marks. One of two integral lodges survives on the north-east side of the building. Now used as residential accommodation.
Grant Recipient/Owner: The Chapter of Carlisle Cathedral
Access contact: Mr E T Amos
Tel: 01228 548151 **Fax:** 01228 547049
Email: office@carlislecathedral.org.uk
Open: By arrangement with Mr E T Amos, The Chapter of Carlisle Cathedral, 7 The Abbey, Carlisle, Cumbria CA3 8TZ.
Heritage Open Days: No
P Parking in nearby City centre car parks. 2 disabled parking spaces in Cathedral grounds.
♿ No. Guide Dogs: Yes £ No

Prior's Tower

The Abbey, Carlisle, Cumbria CA3 8TZ
This Grade I three storey pele tower type building was constructed c1500. It formed part of the Prior's Lodgings and until relatively recently was part of the Deanery. Of special interest is the magnificent ceiling of 45 hand-painted panels dating from c1510 and associated with Prior Senhouse.
Grant Recipient/Owner: The Chapter of Carlisle Cathedral
Access contact: Mr E T Amos
Tel: 01228 548151 **Fax:** 01228 547049
Email: office@carlislecathedral.org.uk
Open: By arrangement with Mr E T Amos, The Chapter of Carlisle Cathedral, 7 The Abbey, Carlisle, Cumbria CA3 8TZ.
Heritage Open Days: Yes
P Parking in nearby City centre car parks. 2 disabled parking spaces in Cathedral grounds.
♿ No. Guide Dogs: Yes £ No

Sizergh Castle

nr. Kendal, Cumbria LA8 8AE
Sizergh Castle has been the home of the Strickland family for over 760 years. Its core is the 14th century pele tower, later extended and containing some fine Elizabethan carved wooden chimney-pieces and inlaid chamber. The Castle is surrounded by gardens, including a rock garden.
www.nationaltrust.org.uk
Grant Recipient/Owner: The National Trust
Access contact: Property Manager
Tel: 015395 60951 **Fax:** 015395 60951
Email: rsizpm@smtp.ntrust.org.uk
Open: Castle: 24 Mar - 31 Oct: daily except Fridays and Saturdays 1.30 - 5.30pm. Garden: 24 Mar - 31 Oct: daily except Fridays and Saturdays 12.30 - 5.30pm.
Heritage Open Days: No
P Parking for disabled visitors available near the house. Spaces: 250
♿ Partial. Wheelchair access to Castle Lower Hall and garden gravel paths only. Disabled WC. Guide Dogs: Yes
£ **Adult:** £5. £2.50 (garden only). **Child:** £2.50 **Other:** £12.50 (family) £4 per person (booked groups 15+)

St Anne's Hospital

Boroughgate, Appleby, Cumbria
17th century almshouses. There are 13 dwellings and a chapel set round a cobbled courtyard. Founded by Lady Anne Clifford in 1653.
Grant Recipient/Owner: The Trustees of St Anne's Hospital
Access contact: Lord Hothfield
Open: All year, daily 9am - 5pm.
Heritage Open Days: No
P On-street parking. ♿ No. Guide Dogs: Yes £ No

Strickland Hall

Little Strickland, Penrith, Cumbria CA10 3EG
Elizabethan farmhouse, with 17th century alterations. Most notable feature is the Elizabethan plasterwork ceiling in the Lord's Parlour.
Grant Recipient/Owner: W H O'Connor
Access contact: W H O'Connor
Tel: 01931 716 780 **Fax:** 01931 716 985
Open: Access to Lord's Parlour by written arrangement. House not open for public viewing.
Heritage Open Days: No
P Spaces: 3
♿ Partial. Wheelchair access with assistance (one 25cm high step at entrance). No disabled WC. Guide Dogs: Yes
£ No

Wray Castle

Low Wray, Ambleside, Cumbria
A large Gothic mock castle and arboretum. Built in the 1840s over looking western shore of Lake Windermere.
www.nationaltrust.org.uk
Grant Recipient/Owner: The National Trust
Access contact: Property Manager
Tel: 015394 47997 **Fax:** 015394 47997
Open: Castle (entrance hall only): July and Aug, weekdays 2 - 4 pm. Gardens and grounds all year. Telephone the Property Manager for further details.
Heritage Open Days: No
P Spaces: 20 ♿ No £ No

DERBYSHIRE

Assembly Rooms

The Crescent, Buxton, Derbyshire SK17 6BH
The Crescent was designed by John Carr of York and built by the 5th Duke of Devonshire between 1780- 89. It provided hotels, lodgings and a suite of elaborately decorated Assembly Rooms. The front elevation of three storeys is dominated by Doric pillasters over a continuous rusticated ground floor arcade.
Grant Recipient/Owner: Derbyshire County Council
Access contact: Mr Allan Morrison
Tel: 01629 580000 **Fax:** 01629 585114
Email: allan.morrison@derbyshire.gov.uk
Open: Exterior accessible from public highway. No interior access until refurbishment works completed.
Heritage Open Days: No
P On-street parking available. ♿ No £ No

Barlborough Hall

Barlborough, Chesterfield, Derbyshire S43 4TL
Built by Sir Francis Rhodes in 1580s, the Hall is square in plan and stands on a high basement with a small internal courtyard to provide light. Contains Great Chamber, now a chapel, bearing a date of 1584 on the overmantel whilst the porch is dated 1583. Now a private school.
Grant Recipient/Owner: The Governors of Barlborough Hall School
Access contact: C F A Bogie
Tel: 01246 435138 **Fax:** 01246 435090
Open: By arrangement. Further access to the building is under review at time of going to print, please check the English Heritage website or with C.F.A. Bogie, Mount St Mary's Cottage, Spinkmill, Derbyshire SZ1 3YL for current information. Grounds open all year.
Heritage Open Days: No
P Spaces: 50 ♿ No. Guide Dogs: Yes £ No

Buxton Opera House

Water Street, Buxton, Derbyshire SK17 6XN
The Buxton Opera House was designed by Frank Matcham and opened in 1903. Its baroque guilded plasterwork and painted ceiling panels by De Jong were restored in Spring 2001 following extensive research into the original colour scheme.
www.buxton-opera.co.uk
Grant Recipient/Owner: Richard Tuffrey
Access contact: Mr Andrew Aughton
Tel: 01298 72050 **Fax:** 01298 27563
Email: director.boh@virgin.net
Open: The theatre is open all year for performances (mostly evenings), exact schedule varies. Theatre tours offered most Sat mornings. Box Office and Foyer open Mon - Sat 10am - 6pm (or 8pm) and some Sundays.
Heritage Open Days: No
P Limited on-street parking.
♿ Partial. Wheelchair access to stalls only. Disabled WC. Guide Dogs: Yes
£ Tours **Adult:** £2 **Child:** Free

Calke Abbey

Ticknall, Derbyshire DE73 1LE
Baroque mansion, built 1701-3 for Sir John Harpur and set in a landscaped park. Little restored, Calke is preserved by a programme of conservation as a graphic illustration of the English house in decline. It contains the natural history collection of the Harpur Crewe family, an 18th century state bed and interiors that are essentially unchanged since the 1880s.
www.nationaltrust.org.uk
Grant Recipient/Owner: The National Trust
Access contact: Property Manager
Tel: 01332 863822 **Fax:** 01332 865272
Email: eckxxx@smtp.ntrust.org.uk
Open: House, garden and Church: 23 Mar - 3 Nov: daily except Thurs and Fridays. House: 1 - 5.30pm (ticket office opens at 11am). Garden and Church: 11am - 5.30pm. Park: most days until 9pm or dusk if earlier. Timed ticket system is in operation. All visitors (inc. NT members) require a ticket from the ticket office.
Heritage Open Days: No
P Spaces: 75
♿ Partial. Wheelchair access to ground floor, stables, shop and restaurant. Garden and park partly accessible. Disabled WC. Guide Dogs: Yes
£ **Adult:** £5.40 **Child:** £2.70 **Other:** £13.50 (family), £3 (garden only)

Caudwell's Mill Trust Ltd

Rowsley, Matlock, Derbyshire DE4 2EB
Victorian (1874) Grade II*, complete, 'automatic', water-turbine powered roller flour mill and provender mill. Four floors with a collection of early original milling machinery illustrating the changes over the years in the milling process. Exhibitions, displays and 'hands-on' models. Craftspeople around Stable Courtyard.
www.caudwellsmill.museum.com
Grant Recipient/Owner: The Manager
Access contact: The Manager

Tel: 01629 734374 Fax: 01629 734374
Email: raymarjoram@compuserve.com
Open: Mill Building: 1 Mar - 31 Oct daily 10am - 5.30pm; rest of year w/ends 10am - 4.30pm, closed Christmas. Rest of site and shops: daily except 24-26 Dec and weekdays in Jan. Introductory film to mill available.
Heritage Open Days: No
[P] Parking for disabled in the mill yard. Spaces: 50
♿ Partial. Wheelchair access to some buildings. Disabled WC. Guide Dogs: Yes
[£] Adult: £3 Child: £1.50 Senior Citizen: £2.50

Cromford Mill

Mill Lane, Cromford, nr. Matlock, Derbyshire DE4 3RQ

Grade I listed mill complex established in 1771 by Sir Richard Arkwright and where the "Spinning Jenny" was first used to manufacture cotton goods. Semi-fortified buildings, designed to resist rioters. Now contains shops and a restaurant.
www.cromfordmill.co.uk
Grant Recipient/Owner: The Arkwright Society
Access contact: Mr Jon Charlton
Tel: 01629 823256 Fax: 01629 824297
Open: Daily 9am - 5pm, closed on Christmas Day. Free entry to main site, charges for guided tours.
Heritage Open Days: Yes
[P] Spaces: 100
♿ Partial. Wheelchair access to shops, lavatories and restaurant. Disabled WC. Guide Dogs: Yes
[£] Guided tour Adult: £2 Child/Other: £1.50

Dale Abbey Windmill

Cat & Fiddle Lane, Dale Abbey, Ilkeston, Derbyshire DE7 6HD

A four-sailed Mill, built c1788, known as a Post Mill. Circular gritstone base reinforced by four later buttresses. The Mill ceased to operate in 1952 and is a rare surviving example of a Midlands-type Mill.
Grant Recipient/Owner: Mr M Richardson
Access contact: Mr M Richardson
Tel: 01159 301585 Fax: 01159 443368
Email: mrichardson@ilkestoncontractors.freeserve.co.uk
Open: Arrangements under review at time of going to print, please check the English Heritage website or with Mr Richardson, 19 Henshaw Place, Cotmanhay, Ilkeston, Derbyshire (tel.01159 301585) for current information.
Heritage Open Days: No
[P] Spaces: 5 ♿ No [£] No

Hardwick Hall

Doe Lea, Chesterfield, Derbyshire S44 5QJ

A late 16th century 'prodigy house' designed by Robert Smythson for Bess of Hardwick. Contains an outstanding collection of 16th century furniture, tapestries and needlework. Walled courtyards enclose gardens, orchards and herb garden.
www.nationaltrust.org.uk
Grant Recipient/Owner: The National Trust
Access contact: Property Manager
Tel: 01246 850430 Fax: 01246 854200
Email: ehwxxx@smtp.ntrust.org.uk
Open: 27 Mar - 27 Oct: daily except Mon, Tues and Fri (but open BH Mondays, Good Fri and Tues 4 June), 12.30 - 5pm (12.30 - 4pm in Oct). Garden: daily except Tues, 11 - 5.30pm. Parkland: daily.
Heritage Open Days: No
[P] Spaces: 200
♿ Partial. Wheelchair access to Great Kitchen, shop, garden and ground floor by ramped entrance. Illustrated booklet of upper floors. Disabled WC. Guide Dogs: Yes
[£] Adult: £6.40 Child: £3.20 Other: £16 (family), £3.40 (garden only), £8.50 (joint ticket with Hardwick Old Hall, EH property)

Kedleston Hall

Derby, Derbyshire DE22 5JH

A classical Palladian mansion built 1759-65 for the Curzon family and little altered since. Robert Adam interior with state rooms retaining their collection of paintings and original furniture. The Eastern museum houses a range of objects collected by Lord Curzon when Viceroy of India (1899-1905). Set in 800 acres of parkland and 18th century pleasure ground, garden and woodland walks.
www.nationaltrust.org.uk
Grant Recipient/Owner: The National Trust
Access contact: Property Manager
Tel: 01332 842191 Fax: 01332 841972
Email: ekdxxx@smtp.ntrust.org.uk
Open: House: 23 Mar - 3 Nov: daily except Thurs and Fri 12 noon - 4.30pm. Garden: as house 10am - 6pm. Park: 23 Mar - 22 Dec daily 10am - 6pm; 5 Jan - 17 Mar 2003 Sat and Sun 10am - 4pm.
Heritage Open Days: No
[P] Please note £2 charge for use of car park on Thurs and Fri. Spaces: 60
♿ Partial. Wheelchair access to ground floor of house via stairclimber, garden, restaurant and shop. Disabled WC. Guide Dogs: Yes
[£] Adult: £5.30 Child: £2.60 Other: £13.20 (family), £2.40 (park & garden only)

Masson Mills

Derby Road, Matlock Bath, Derbyshire DE4 3PY

Built 1783 as the showpiece mills of Sir Richard Arkwright, they are the oldest continuously occupied mills in the world. Now a working textile museum producing cloth on old looms. Originally water-powered by the River Derwent the water turbines are still in use.
www.massonmills.co.uk
Grant Recipient/Owner: Mara Securities Ltd
Access contact: The Co-ordinator
Tel: 01629 581001 Fax: 01629 582403
Open: All year except Christmas Day and Easter Day: Mon - Fri 10am - 4pm, Sat 11am - 5pm and Sun 11am - 4pm.
Heritage Open Days: No
[P] Spaces: 200
♿ Partial. Wheelchair access to most areas. Disabled WC. Guide Dogs: No
[£] Adult: £2.50 Child: £1.50 Other: £2

Melbourne Hall & Gardens

Church Square, Melbourne, Derbyshire DE73 1EN

Historic house and formal 18th century garden with yew tunnel and wrought iron arbour by Bakewell. House once home of Victorian Prime Minister William Lamb, who as Viscount Melbourne named the Australian city. A family home since 1628, the hall is lived in by Lord Ralph Kerr (a descendant of the original owner Sir John Coke) and his family.
Grant Recipient/Owner: Trustees of the Melbourne Garden Charity
Access contact: Mrs Gill Weston
Tel: 01332 862502 Fax: 01332 862263
Email: melbhall@globalnet.co.uk
Open: Hall: daily during Aug (except first three Mondays) 2 - 5pm. Gardens: Apr - Sept, Wed, Sat, Sun and BH Mondays 1.30 - 5.30pm.
Heritage Open Days: No
[P] Limited and none reserved just for Hall and Garden visitors. Spaces: 6
♿ Partial. Wheelchair access to Hall tours may be limited on busy days. No specially designed disabled WC but one cubicle is larger than others with handrail. Guide Dogs: Yes
[£] Adult: £3 (Hall), £3 (gardens), £5 (combined)
Child: £1.50 (Hall), £2 (gardens), £3 (combined)
Other: £2.50 (Hall), £2 (gardens), £4 (combined)

St Ann's Hotel

The Crescent, Buxton, Derbyshire SK17 6BH

The Crescent was designed by John Carr of York and built by the Fifth Duke of Devonshire between 1780-89. It provided hotels, lodgings and a suite of elaborately decorated Assembly Rooms. The front elevation of three storeys is dominated by Doric pillasters over a continuous rusticated ground floor arcade.
Grant Recipient/Owner: High Peak Borough Council
Access contact: Mr Richard Tuffrey
Tel: 01457 851653 Fax: 01457 860290
Email: richard.tuffrey@highpeak.gov.uk
Open: Exterior accessible from public highway. No interior access until refurbishment works completed.
Heritage Open Days: No
[P] On-street parking available. ♿ No [£] No

Sudbury Hall

Sudbury, Ashbourne, Derbyshire DE6 5HT

17th century house with rich interior decoration including wood carvings by Laguerre. The Great Staircase (c1676) with white-painted balustrade with luxuriantly carved foliage by Edward Pierce, is one of the finest staircases of its date in an English house. 19th century service wing houses the National Trust Museum of Childhood.
www.nationaltrust.org.uk
Grant Recipient/Owner: The National Trust
Access contact: Property Manager
Tel: 01283 585305 Fax: 01283 585139
Email: esuxxx@smtp.ntrust.org.uk
Open: Hall: 16 Mar - 3 Nov: daily except Mon and Tues (but open BH Mondays and Good Fri) 1 - 5pm. Grounds: as Hall 10am - 5pm.
Heritage Open Days: No
[P] Car park is a short distance from the Hall; six-seater volunteer driven buggy available. Spaces: 100
♿ Partial. Wheelchair access to lake, tearoom and shop. Access to Hall difficult - please contact the Property Manager in advance. Disabled WC. Guide Dogs: Yes
[£] Hall & Museum Adult: £3.90, £6.30 Child: £2, £3.10
Other: £9.80 (family), £15.60

DEVON

Broomham Farm

King's Nympton, Devon EX37 9TS

Late medieval Grade II* Devon long-house of stone and cob construction with thatched roof. Contains a smoking room. Currently undergoing renovation.
Grant Recipient/Owner: Mr Clements
Access contact: Miss J Clements
Tel: 01769 572322
Open: By telephone arrangement.
Heritage Open Days: No
[P] Spaces: 3 ♿ No [£] No

Canonsleigh Abbey Gatehouse

Burlescombe, Devon EX16 7JF

15th century Auginian priory gatehouse built of local stone. Large double gateway with chamber over a stone spiral staircase. Much contemporary decoration.
Grant Recipient/Owner: Mr Burroughs
Access contact: Mr Burroughs
Open: By written arrangement any day from 1 Apr - 1 Oct, at least 10 days notice is required.
Heritage Open Days: No
[P] Spaces: 5
♿ Partial. Wheelchair access to ground floor only. No disabled WC. Guide Dogs: Yes [£] No

Coldharbour Mill

Uffculme, Devon EX15 3EE

Woollen mill, earliest reference 1707, rebuilt as a grist mill after a flood. Now a working textile mill museum with demonstrations of textile machinery. Picnic area, café, waterside walks and shop. Also houses the New World Tapestry.
Grant Recipient/Owner: Ms Jill Taylor
Access contact: Mr Keith Taylor
Tel: 01884 840960 Fax: 01884 840858
Email: info@coldharbourmill.org.uk
Open: Easter - end Oct: daily 10.30am - 5pm. Nov - Mar: Mon - Fri 10.30am - 5pm.
Heritage Open Days: Yes
[P] Spaces: 100
♿ Partial. Wheelchair access to all areas except café. Disabled WC. Guide Dogs: Yes
[£] Provisional Adult: £3.50 Child: £2.50
Other: £15.00 (family)

Colleton Manor Chapel

Chulmleigh, Devon EX18 7JS

Small chapel over gatehouse, possibly one mentioned in licence of 1381. Stone walls, slate roof, west wall recently rebuilt in stone and cob. Plain interior with Edwardian matchboard panelling and exposed timbers. Still used as a chapel.
Grant Recipient/Owner: Mr Phillips
Access contact: Mr Phillips
Tel: 01769 580240
Open: By telephone arrangement with Mr Phillips at Colleton Manor.
Heritage Open Days: No
[P] Spaces: 3 ♿ No
[£] Voluntary donation requested towards chapel maintenance

Cookworthy Museum of Rural Life in South Devon

The Old Grammar School, 108 Fore Street, Kingsbridge, Devon TQ7 1AW

17th century schoolroom with 19th century annex in Tudor style. Original entrance arch. Now local museum with Victorian kitchen, Edwardian pharmacy and walled garden.
www.devonmuseums.net
Grant Recipient/Owner: William Cookworthy Museum Society
Access contact: Mr Clifford Peach
Tel: 01548 853235
Email: wcookworthy@talk21.com
Open: 25 Mar - 31 Oct: Mon - Sat 10am - 5pm (Oct 10am - 4pm). Pre-booked groups all year. Local History Resource Centre open all year.
Heritage Open Days: No
[P] Public car park on Fore Street, 100 metres from Museum. Spaces: 100
♿ Partial. Wheelchair access with assistance to Victorian kitchen, photographic display, Farm Gallery, walled garden and shop. Disabled WC. Guide Dogs: Yes
[£] Adult: £2 Child: 90p Seniors: £1.50, £5 (family)

Dartington Hall

Dartington, Totnes, Devon TQ9 6EL

Medieval mansion and courtyard built 1388-1399 by John Holland, Earl of Huntingdon and later Duke of Exeter, half brother to Richard II. Set in a landscaped garden and surrounded by a 1200 acre estate. The Champernowne family owned Dartington for 400 years before selling the estate to Leonard and Dorothy Elhurst who founded the Dartington Hall Trust.
www.dartington.v-net.com
Grant Recipient/Owner: The Dartington Hall Trust
Access contact: Ms Carol Richards
Tel: 01803 847012 Fax: 01803 847007
Open: All year for courses, events and activities. The Hall, courtyard and gardens are accessible for external viewing all year. Access to the interior by arrangement.
Heritage Open Days: No
[P] Spaces: 250
♿ Partial. Wheelchair access to Great Hall, courtyard and top garden paths. Disabled WC. Guide Dogs: Yes
[£] No

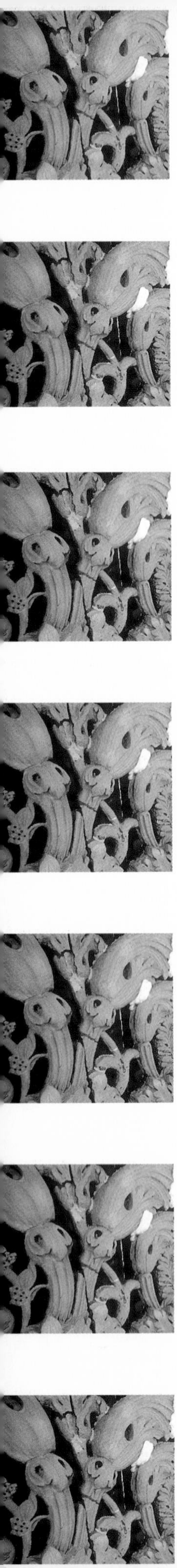

The Devon & Exeter Institution Library & Reading Room

7 Cathedral Close, Exeter, Devon EX1 1EZ

Building housing the Library and Reading Rooms of the Devon and Exeter Institution since 1813 but was formerly the town house of the Courtenay family and one time home of the Parliamentary General, Sir William Waller. Part of the Tudor house remains at the rear and also the gatehouse range which fronts The Close. In the early 19th century the two lofty libraries were built on the site of the old hall and kitchen.

Grant Recipient/Owner: The Devon & Exeter Institution Library & Reading Rooms

Access contact: Mrs M M Rowe

Tel: 01392 274727

Open: Mon - Fri 9am - 5pm. Closed for a week at Easter and Christmas.

Heritage Open Days: No

P No ♿ Yes. Disabled WC. Guide Dogs: Yes £ No

Dunkeswell Abbey

nr. Honiton, Devon EX14 4RP

Ruins of Cistercian abbey.

Grant Recipient/Owner: Dunkeswell Abbey Preservation Fund

Access contact: Reverend N J Wall

Tel: 01404 891243

Open: At all times.

Heritage Open Days: No

P Roadside parking.

♿ Yes. No disabled WC. Guide Dogs: Yes £ No

Eastleigh Manor

Eastleigh, Bideford, Devon EX39 4PA

Late 15th or early 16th century manor house, remodelled in late 16th or early 17th century and c1800. Contains interesting features from each stage of its building history, including a medieval ceiling in one room.

Grant Recipient/Owner: Mr D Grigg

Access contact: Mr D Grigg

Tel: 01271 860418

Open: By written arrangement between Oct and Mar.

Heritage Open Days: No

P Spaces: 5 ♿ No £ No

Endsleigh House and Gardens

Milton Abbot, Tavistock, Devon PL19 0PQ

Built 1811-14 by 6th Duke of Bedford to the designs of Sir Jeffry Wyatville, the grounds were laid out by Humphry Repton. Cottage Orne house overlooking the River Tamar, ornamental gardens with grottos and waterworks, terraced walks and extensive historic arboretum.

Grant Recipient/Owner: Endsleigh Charitable Trust

Access contact: Lt Col R D Hourahane

Tel: 01822 870248 **Fax:** 01822 870502

Open: House: Apr - Sept: daily 11am - 5pm. Gardens: daily 11am - 5pm.

Heritage Open Days: No

P Spaces: 40 ♿ Yes. Disabled WC. Guide Dogs: Yes

£ **Adult:** £3

Finch Foundry

Sticklepath, Okehampton, Devon EX20 2NW

19th century water-powered forge, which produced agricultural and mining hand tools. Still in working order with regular demonstrations. Foundry has three water-wheels driving the huge tilt hammer and grindstone.

www.nationaltrust.org.uk

Grant Recipient/Owner: The National Trust, Devon Regional Office

Access contact: Mr Alex Raeder

Tel: 01392 881691 **Fax:** 01392 881954

Email: dlaarx@smtp.ntrust.org.uk

Open: 31 Mar - 4 Nov: daily except Tues 11am - 5.30pm.

Heritage Open Days: Yes

P Access to car park is narrow and unsuitable for coaches and wide vehicles. Spaces: 50

♿ Partial. Wheelchair access to museum and workshop is difficult, Foundry can be viewed through shop window. No disabled WC. Guide Dogs: Yes

£ **Adult:** £3 **Child:** £1.50 (5-16 yrs), Free (under 5s)

Higher Thornham

Romansleigh, South Molton, Devon EX36 4JS

16th century through passage house, remodelled in the 17th century. Built of stone and cob, with thatched roof. Beamed ceilings on ground floor and one moulded door frame. Recently renovated using traditional materials.

Grant Recipient/Owner: Mr S W Chudley

Access contact: Mr S W Chudley

Open: By written arrangement 1 May - end of Sept: Mondays or Fridays 2 - 4.30pm. Dogs not allowed and children must be accompanied by an adult. No photography. Guide dog access to ground floor only.

Heritage Open Days: No

P Spaces: 2 ♿ No. Guide Dogs: Yes

£ **Adult:** £4 **Child:** £1.50

Lawrence Castle Haldon Belvedere

Higher Ashton, nr. Dunchideock, Exeter, Devon EX6 7QY

Grade II* building built in 1788 as the centrepiece to a 11,600 acre estate. Stands 800ft above sea level overlooking the cathedral city of Exeter, the Exe estuary and the surrounding countryside. Contains a spiral staircase and miniature ballroom.

www.haldonbelvedere.co.uk

Grant Recipient/Owner: Devon Historic Buildings Trust

Access contact: Mr Ian Turner

Tel: 01392 833668 **Fax:** 01392 833668

Email: turner@haldonbelvedere.co.uk

Open: Feb - Oct: Suns and BHs 2 - 5pm. At other times by arrangement.

Heritage Open Days: No

P Parking for disabled adjacent to building. Spaces: 15

♿ Partial. Wheelchair access to ground floor only. No disabled WC. Guide Dogs: Yes

£ **Adult:** £1.50 **Child:** 75p

Prysten House

Catherine Street, Plymouth, Devon PL1 2AD

15th century merchant's house, extended during the 17th century and restored in the 1920s. An excellent example of a large late medieval merchant's house, typically built to a courtyard plan. Includes the Door of Unity, a memorial to two American Naval Officers who died in 1813, and the Plymouth Tapestry.

www.standrewschurch.org.uk

Grant Recipient/Owner: Abbey Hall Charity

Access contact: Mrs Carol Springett

Tel: 01752 661414 **Fax:** 01752 661414

Email: prystenhouse@standrewschurch.org.uk

Open: Apr - Oct: Mon - Fri 10am - 3.30pm, Sun 10am - 12.30pm. Prysten House is normally kept locked for security purposes. Please contact the church office (tel. 01752 661414) for a guided tour.

Heritage Open Days: No

P Public car park within 2 minutes walk.

♿ No £ **Adult:** £1 **Child:** 50p

Saltram House

Plympton, Plymouth, Devon PL7 1UH

A remarkable survival of a George II mansion, complete with its original contents and set in landscaped park. Robert Adam worked here on two occasions to create the state rooms. Three rooms are decorated with the original Chinese wallpaper. 18th century gardens.

www.nationaltrust.org.uk

Grant Recipient/Owner: The National Trust

Access contact: Alex Raeder

Tel: 01392 881691 **Fax:** 01392 881954

Email: dlaarx@smtp.ntrust.org.uk

Open: 1 Apr - 4 Nov: daily except Fri and Sat (but open Good Fri) at the following times: 1 Apr - 30 Sept 12 - 5pm (last adm. 4.15pm); 1 Oct - 4 Nov 12 - 4pm (last adm. 3.15pm, due to poor light). Garden: 1 Feb - 31 Mar: Sat and Sun only 11am - 4pm; 1 Apr - 4 Nov, as for house 10.30am - 5.30pm

Heritage Open Days: No

P Parking 500 metres from house, 30 marked spaces on tarmac, remainder on grass. Spaces: 250

♿ Wheelchair access to first floor via lift (66cm wide by 86.5cm deep), restaurant, tearoom, ticket offices over cobbles. Wheelchairs available at house. Disabled WC. Guide Dogs: Yes

£ **Adult:** £6 (House & garden), £3 (garden) **Child:** Under 5s Free. 5-16 yrs half-price **Other:** Discount for booked groups, rates on application

Ugbrooke Park

Chudleigh, Devon TQ13 0AD

House and Chapel built c1200 and redesigned by Robert Adam in the 1760s for the 4th Lord Clifford. Chapel and library wing in Adam's characteristic castle style. Set in 'Capability' Brown landscaped park with lakes and 18th century Orangery. Home of the Lords Clifford of Chudleigh for 400 years.

www.historichouses.co.uk

Grant Recipient/Owner: Clifford Estate Co. Ltd

Access contact: Mrs Lee Martin

Tel: 01626 852179 **Fax:** 01626 853322

Email: leececo@netscape.co.uk

Open: 14 July - 5 Sept: Tues, Weds, Thursdays, Sundays and Aug BH Mon 1.30 - 5.30pm. Group tours and private functions by arrangement.

Heritage Open Days: No

P Spaces: 200

♿ Yes. Disabled WC. Guide Dogs: Yes

£ **Adult:** £5 **Child:** £2 **Other:** £4.70 (senior citizens & groups)

DORSET

Blandford Forum Town Hall & Corn Exchange

Market Place, Blandford Forum, Dorset DT1 7PY

Town hall dated 1734. The ground floor has 3 semi-circular arches leading to an open portico, formerly a market. The mid-Victorian Corn Exchange is to the rear of the entrance.

Grant Recipient/Owner: Blandford Forum Town Council

Access contact: The Town Clerk

Tel: 01258 454500 **Fax:** 01258 454432

Email: admin@blandford-tc.co.uk

Open: All year for markets, civic functions and other events. Other times by telephone arrangement with Town Clerk, Mon - Fri 9.30am -12.30pm.

Heritage Open Days: No

P On-street meter parking.

♿ Partial. Wheelchair access to ground floor. Disabled WC. Guide Dogs: Yes £ No

The Chantry

128 South Street, Bridport, Dorset DT6 3PA

14th or 15th century two-storey stone rubble house, originally situated on a promontory of the River Brit. At one time known as the "Prior's House", more probably the house of a chantry priest. Interesting internal details including fragments of 17th century domestic wall paintings.

www.vivat.org.uk

Grant Recipient/Owner: The Vivat Trust Ltd

Access contact: Mrs F Lloyd

Tel: 020 7930 2212 **Fax:** 020 7930 2295

Email: enquiries@vivat.demon.co.uk

Heritage Open Days:, 14 - 15 Sept 10am - 5pm. Open at other times by arrangement with The Vivat Trust (tel. 020 7930 2212, fax. 020 7930 2295, email. enquiries@vivat.demon.co.uk).

P Additional on-street parking. Spaces: 1

♿ No. Guide Dogs: Yes £ No

Highcliffe Castle

Rothesay Drive, Highcliffe-on-Sea, Christchurch, Dorset BH23 4LE

Cliff-top mansion built in the 1830s by Charles Stuart. Constructed in the romantic, picturesque style, much of its stonework is medieval coming from France. Exterior has been restored, interior houses changing exhibitions and the 16th century stained glass Jesse window. Gift shop and tea rooms on site with 14 acre cliff-top park.

www.highcliffecastle.co.uk

Grant Recipient/Owner: Christchurch Borough Council

Access contact: Mr Mike Allen

Tel: 01425 278807 **Fax:** 01425 280423

Email: m.allen@christchurch.gov.uk

Open: 30 Mar - 27 Oct: daily 11am - 5pm. 11 Nov - 22 Dec: daily 11am - 4pm. Also w/ends in March for Special Events. Closed in Jan and Feb. Tea Rooms all year 10am - late afternoon; grounds all year from 7am.

Heritage Open Days: Yes

P Charged parking in Council car park. Spaces: 108

♿ Although there is currently no wheelchair access to the building, there are toilet facilities for the disabled at the site. Guide Dogs: Yes

£ **Adult:** £1.50 **Child:** Free **Other:** HHA/Season Ticket holders free

EAST RIDING OF YORKSHIRE

Church of Our Lady & St Everilda

Everingham, East Riding of Yorkshire YO42 4JA

Roman Catholic parish church for Everingham, built between 1836 and 1839 to the designs of Agostino Giorgiola. Interior has columned walls and a barrelled ceiling with a semi-dome above the high altar. Also of note are the altar, font and statues and the 1839 organ by William Allen.

Grant Recipient/Owner: The Herries Charitable Trust

Access contact: Mr N J M Turton

Tel: 01759 304105 **Fax:** 01759 304105

Email: nturton@btinternet.com

Open: Key available during reasonable hours by telephoning 01430 861443 or 01759 302226.

Heritage Open Days: No

P Spaces: 12 ♿ No. Guide Dogs: Yes £ No

Maister House

160 High Street, Kingston-upon-Hull, East Riding of Yorkshire HU1 1NL

Rebuilt in 1743 during Hull's heyday as an affluent trading centre, this house is a typical but rare survivor of a contemporary merchant's residence. The restrained exterior belies the spectacular plasterwork staircase inside. The house is now let as offices.

www.nationaltrust.org.uk

Grant Recipient/Owner: The National Trust

Access contact: The National Trust

Tel: 01904 702021 **Fax:** 01904 771970

Open: Daily except Sat and Sun (closed Good Fri and all BHs) 10am - 4pm. Access is to entrance hall and staircase only. Unsuitable for groups. No WC.

Heritage Open Days: No

P No ♿ No. Guide Dogs: Yes £ 80p

Old Lighthouse

Flamborough, nr. Bridlington, East Riding of Yorkshire

Grade II* light tower, built in 1674. 24 metres high, designed for a coal and brushwood fire to have been burnt

on top although it is uncertain whether it was ever lit. The octagonal tower has four floors, several windows and a fireplace so it was possibly built to be lived in.
Grant Recipient/Owner: East Riding of Yorkshire Council
Access contact: Mr Richard Baines
Tel: 01482 395208
Open: Access to interior by arrangement with Richard Baines, Countryside Officer.
Heritage Open Days: No
P Public parking at Flamborough headland, 1/4 mile.
No £ No

Stamford Bridge Viaduct
Stamford Bridge, East Riding of Yorkshire
Built 1847 for the York & North Midland Railway Company, East Riding lines. Mainly red brick with 10 unadorned round brick arches. The railway line was closed in the mid 1960s and is now repaired as part of a circular pedestrian walkway around the village.
Grant Recipient/Owner: East Riding of Yorkshire Council
Access contact: Mr Cameron Costello
Tel: 01482 887700
Open: The site is open permanently for informal access (walking).
Heritage Open Days: No
P Informal parking for approximately 20 cars near sports hall. No £ No

EAST SUSSEX

Becks Garage Building
Riverside, Cliffe Bridge, Lewes, East Sussex BN7 2AD
Two-storey, timber-framed building with classical façade. Originally constructed as coal warehouse in late 18th century. Now small shopping centre and brasserie.
Grant Recipient/Owner: Riverside (Lewes) Ltd
Access contact: Mr J Giles
Tel: 020 7253 9692 **Fax:** 020 7253 0846
Email: jonathan.giles@cornish-architects.co.uk
Open: Daily except Sun and BHs, 9am - 5pm.
Heritage Open Days: No
P Public parking. Spaces: 100
Yes. Disabled WC. Guide Dogs: Yes £ No

Brickwall House
Northiam, Rye, East Sussex TN31 6NL
Jacobean manor house containing a front hall, drawing room and chamber room with leather panels. Previously home of the Frewen family, now a school for dyslexic boys aged 9-17.
Grant Recipient/Owner: Frewen Educational Trust
Access contact: Mr Peter Mould
Tel: 01797 253388 **Fax:** 01797 252567
Email: post@frewcoll.demon.co.uk
Open: Mar 26, 27, 31; Apr 2, 3, 9, 10; May 6 (BH); June 3, 4, 30; July 9, 10, 16, 17, 21, 23, 24, 30, 31; Aug 6, 7, 13, 14, 18, 20, 21, 26, 27, 28; afternoons. Public access arrangements and opening times are under review at time of going to print, please check the English Heritage website or with Mr Peter Mould for current information.
Heritage Open Days: No
P Spaces: 40 Yes. Disabled WC. Guide Dogs: Yes
£ **Adult:** £4.50

De La Warr Pavilion
The Marina, Bexhill-on-Sea, East Sussex
The "People's Palace" built in 1935 by architects Erich Mendholson and Serge Chermayeff was the first steel-framed building in this country. Its circular staircase and sweeping seaviews make it unique.
www.dlwp.com
Grant Recipient/Owner: Rother District Council
Access contact: Mr Alan Haydon
Tel: 01424 787900 **Fax:** 01424 787940
Email: dlwp@rother.gov.uk
Open: Jan - Mar: daily 10am - 6pm; May - Oct: daily 10am - 11pm; Oct - Jan: daily 10am - 6pm.
Heritage Open Days: Yes
P Pay car park.
Yes. Disabled WC. Guide Dogs: Yes £ No

The Flushing Inn
4 Market Street, Rye, East Sussex TN31 7LA
15th century timber-framed building with large recently restored 16th century wallpainting, now a restaurant.
Grant Recipient/Owner: Mr Flynn
Access contact: Mr Flynn
Tel: 01797 223292
Open: Restaurant Wed - Sun for lunches and dinners, Mondays lunch only and Tues closed. Closed first 2 weeks in Jan and Oct. Unless dining, visiting to view the Fresco is restricted to 10.30 - noon.
Heritage Open Days: No
P Parking on-street but restricted to 1 hour, otherwise public parking elsewhere in Rye.
Partial. Wheelchair access to Fresco with assistance (entrance steps to be negotiated). No disabled WC. Guide Dogs: Yes £ No

Lamb House
(Coromandel Lacquer Panels), 3 Chapel Hill, Lewes, East Sussex BN7 2BB
The incised lacquer panels in the study of Lamb House are a unique surviving example of imported late 17th century Chinese lacquer work that remains as decorative wall panelling. Recently restored.
Grant Recipient/Owner: Prof. Paul Benjamin
Access contact: Prof. Paul Benjamin
Tel: 01273 475657
Open: W/ends only by telephone arrangement.
Heritage Open Days: No
P On-street parking.
Partial. Wheelchair access to ground floor only. No disabled WC. Guide Dogs: No £ No

The Royal Pavilion
Brighton, East Sussex BN1 1EE
Former seaside residence of George IV in Indian style with Chinese-inspired interiors. Originally a neo-classical villa by Henry Holland was built on the site in 1787, but this was subsequently replaced by the current John Nash building constructed between 1815-23.
www.royalpavilion.brighton.co.uk
Grant Recipient/Owner: Brighton & Hove City Council
Access contact: Ms Cara Bowen
Tel: 01273 292810 **Fax:** 01273 292871
Email: cara.bowen@brighton-hove.gov.uk
Open: 1 Oct - 31 May: daily 10am - 5pm (closed Christmas and Boxing Day); 1 June - 30 Sept: daily 10am - 6pm. Admission charges are valid until 31 Mar 2002, for rates after that date please check with the Royal Pavilion.
Heritage Open Days: No
P Parking for disabled is available in the grounds of the Pavilion by arrangement.
Partial. Wheelchair access to ground floor only. Currently no admission charge for wheelchair users but this is under review, please check with the Royal Pavilion. Disabled WC. Guide Dogs: Yes
£ **Adult:** £5.20 (see above), £2.10 (local residents, Oct - Feb only). **Child:** £3.20 under 16 (Oct - Feb, local residents free with paying adult). **Other:** £3.75 (seniors/students/unemployed). £13.60 (family of 2 adults, 4 children), £8.40 (1 adult, 4 children)

St Mary-in-the-Castle
Pelham Crescent, Hastings, East Sussex TN34 3AF
Built in 1828, architect Joseph Kay, it forms an integral part of the design of Pelham Crescent. The Church has a horseshoe-shaped auditorium with gallery and is now used as an arts centre.
www.1066.net/maryinthecastle
Grant Recipient/Owner: Friends of St Mary in the Castle
Access contact: Ms Judith A Clark
Tel: 01424 781635/01424 781624 **Fax:** 01424 781625
Email: maryinthecastle@1066.net
Open: Monthly open days with guided tours; 'Open House' every BH except Tues 4 June; guided tours Tues - Sat by arrangement. Arts activities run throughout the year. Contact the Box Office (01424 781624) or check the website for further information.
Heritage Open Days: Yes
P Pay & Display parking opposite. Spaces: 400
Yes. Disabled WC. Guide Dogs: Yes
£ **Adult:** £1 (guided tours). **Other:** 'Open House' free but collection taken. Events individually priced

West Pier
Kings Road, Brighton, East Sussex BN1 2FL
The only Grade I listed pier, built 1865-6. Derelict since 1975 but recipient of a major Heritage Lottery Fund grant. Restoration due to begin in 2002.
www.westpier.co.uk
Grant Recipient/Owner: Dr Geoff Lockwood
Access contact: Dr Geoff Lockwood
Tel: 01273 321499 **Fax:** 01273 726070
Email: westpier@westpier-trust.demon.co.uk
Open: At the time of publication, arrangements are unconfirmed due to physical state of pier and the uncertain start date of the restoration work. The Trust hope to run guided tours at w/ends Jan - Apr 2002 and daily tours from May. Check with the Trust in advance.
Heritage Open Days: No
P No No
£ **Adult:** £10 **Child:** n/a **Other:** £7.50 (concessions & discounts for groups 10+)

ESSEX

150 High Street
Kelvedon, nr. Colchester, Essex CO5 9JD
A timber framed building with 14th/15th century origins. May have once been an Inn but now a private dwelling. The house has a front range comprising former hall and crosswing with a long addition with several unique features - a rare assemblage for structures in Essex.
Grant Recipient/Owner: Mr J Loy
Access contact: Mr & Mrs J Loy
Tel: 01376 570200
Email: jorolo@cwcom.net
Open: By telephone arrangement.
Heritage Open Days: No
P On-street parking (restricted 10-11am).
Partial. Wheelchair access with assistance to ground floor of front and rear range. No disabled WC. Guide Dogs: Yes
£ **Adult:** £1.50 (donation to charity requested)

The Great Dunmow Maltings
Mill Lane, Great Dunmow, Essex CM6 1BD
Grade II* maltings complex (listed as Boyes Croft Maltings, White Street), early 16th century and later, timber-framed and plastered, part weatherboarding and brick. Fully restored, the building houses the Great Dunmow Museum Society on the ground floor with displays of local history. The first floor is available for community use.
Grant Recipient/Owner: David A Westcott
Access contact: Mr David A Westcott
Tel: 01371 873958 **Fax:** 01371 873958
Email: david.westcott2@btinternet.com
Open: All year: Sat, Sun and BHs 11am - 4pm. In addition, from Easter - end Oct: Tues 11am - 4pm. Groups at any reasonable time by arrangement. Closed over Christmas/New Year holiday week.
Heritage Open Days: Yes
P Public car park nearby. Spaces: 100
Yes. Disabled WC. Guide Dogs: Yes
£ **Adult:** £1 **Child/Other:** 50p

Harwich Redoubt Fort
behind 29 Main Road, Harwich, Essex CO12 3LT
180ft diameter circular fort commanding the harbour entrance built in 1808 to defend the port against a Napoleonic invasion. Surrounded by a dry moat, there are 11 guns on the battlements. 18 casements which originally sheltered 300 troops in seige conditions now house a series of small museums.
www.harwich-society.com
Grant Recipient/Owner: Harwich Society
Access contact: Mr A Rutter
Tel: 01255 503429 **Fax:** 01255 503429
Email: theharwichsociety@quista.net
Open: 1 May - 31 Aug: daily 10am - 5pm. Rest of year: Sundays only 10am - 4pm.
Heritage Open Days: Yes
P No No. Guide Dogs: Yes
£ **Adult:** £1 **Child:** Free

Hylands House
Hylands Park, London Road, Widford, Chelmsford, Essex CM2 8WQ
Grade II* building, surrounded by 600 acres of landscaped parkland, partly designed by Humphrey Repton. Built c1730, the original house was a red brick Queen Anne style mansion, subsequent owners set about enlarging the property, which produced a neo-classical style house. Internal inspection of the house reveals its Georgian and Victorian features.
www.hylandshouse.org.uk
Grant Recipient/Owner: Chelmsford Borough Council
Access contact: Ms Linda Pittom
Tel: 01245 606396 **Fax:** 01245 250783
Email: linda.pittom@chelmsford.gov.uk
Open: Sun, Mon and BHs (except Christmas Day) throughout the year 11am - 6pm. Tea Room: Sun 11am - 4.30pm. Group visits by arrangement with Mrs Ceri Lowen, Assistant Hylands House Manager, Leisure Services, Chelmsford Borough Council, Civic Centre, Duke Street, Chelmsford, Essex CM1 1JE (tel.01245 606812). Events programme. Please note that restoration work may commence in Oct 2001 and access to House may be affected, please telephone in advance to check.
Heritage Open Days: Yes
P Yes. 4 disabled parking spaces, coaches by arrangement. Spaces: 54
Yes. Disabled WC. Guide Dogs: Yes
£ **Adult:** £3 **Child:** Free (under 12) **Other:** £2

John Webb's Windmill
Fishmarket Street, Thaxted, Essex CM6 2PG
Brick tower mill built in 1804 consisting of five floors. Has been fully restored as a working mill. On two floors there is a museum of rural and domestic bygones. There is also a small picture gallery of early photographs of the mill and the surrounding countryside.
Grant Recipient/Owner: Thaxted Parish Council
Access contact: Mr L A Farren
Tel: 01371 830285 **Fax:** 01371 830285
Open: At the time of publication the Mill is closed for major repair work, scheduled for completion during 2002. For further information please contact Mr L A Farren, Borough Hill, Bolford Street, Thaxted, Essex CM6 2PY.
Heritage Open Days: Yes
P Public parking in Thaxted.
Partial. Wheelchair access to ground floor only. No disabled WC. Guide Dogs: Yes
£ **Adult:** £1 (provisional) **Child:** Free (when accompanied by paying adult, provisional)

Maldon Moot Hall

High Street, Maldon, Essex CM9 4RL

15th century listed building which once housed a police station and still has the exercise yard, a brickbuilt spiral staircase with brick handrail, courtroom and council chamber. Access to the roof gives good views of the Blackwater estuary and surrounding district.

Grant Recipient/Owner: The Town Clerk, Maldon Town Council

Access contact: The Town Clerk

Tel: 01621 857373 **Fax:** 01621 850793

Email: maldontowncouncil@u.genie.co.uk

Open: By telephone arrangement with the Town Clerk of Maldon Town Council. Otherwise open Mar - end of Oct, Sat afternoons for visits at 2 and 3.30pm. (This may be extended).

Heritage Open Days: Yes

P No

Partial. Wheelchair access to ground floor only

No disabled WC. Guide Dogs: Yes

£ **Adult:** £1 **Child:** 50p **Senior Citizen:** 50p

Monks Barn

Netteswellbury, Harlow, Essex CM20 1UU

A medieval tithe barn built around 1440, now housing Harlow Study Centre. Schoolchildren and visitors can learn how the new town was designed and plans for the future. Many original features are visible.

Grant Recipient/Owner: Harlow District Council

Access contact: Ms Sandra Farrington

Tel: 01279 446745 **Fax:** 01279 421945

Email: sandra.farrington@harlow.gov.uk

Open: By arrangement.

Heritage Open Days: No

P Spaces: 16

Yes. Full wheelchair access but cobbled flooring may prove uncomfortable. Disabled WC. Guide Dogs: Yes

£ No

Old Friends Meeting House

High Street, Stebbing, Essex CM6 3SG

The Stebbing Meeting House is the earliest Quaker meeting House in Essex. Built circa 1674 it is a particularly fine and complete example of an early Quaker meeting house and its historical importance is recognised by its Grade II* listing.

Grant Recipient/Owner: The Trustees of the Old Friends Meeting House

Access contact: Mr J B Newbrook

Tel: 01371 856464 **Fax:** 01371 856464

Email: jnewbrook@aol.com

Open: By telephone or written arrangement with Mr J B Newbrook, 7 Oakfield, Stebbing, Essex CM6 3SX.

Heritage Open Days: Yes

P Spaces: 10 Yes. Disabled WC. Guide Dogs: Yes £ No

Rainham Hall

The Broadway, Rainham, Essex RM13 9YN

Georgian house built in 1729 to a symmetrical plan and with fine wrought iron gates, carved porch and interior panelling plasterwork.

www.nationaltrust.org.uk

Grant Recipient/Owner: The National Trust

Access contact: Thames & Chilterns Regional Office

Tel: 01494 528051 **Fax:** 01494 463310

Open: Apr - end Oct: Weds and BH Mondays 2 - 6pm. Saturdays by written arrangement (Thames & Chilterns Regional Office, Hughenden Manor, High Wycombe, Bucks HP14 4LA).

Heritage Open Days: No

P On-street pay-and-display parking nearby.

Partial. Wheelchair access to ground floor only. Guide dogs by arrangement. Disabled WC.

£ **Adult:** £2.10 **Other:** No group reduction

St Mary

Mundon, Essex

Listed Grade I church, now redundant and owned by the Friends of Friendless Churches since 1975. Two-tier timber-framed weatherboarded tower of the 16th century and roughly contemporary north porch. The nave is partly 14th century and retains a complete set of 18th century box pews. Chancel is also Georgian but with simple 19th century fittings. Naïve baroque *trompe l'oeil* painting of murals on the east wall.

www.friendsoffriendlesschurches.org.uk

Grant Recipient/Owner: Friends of Friendless Churches

Access contact: Mr Matthew Saunders

Tel: 020 7236 3934 **Fax:** 020 7329 3677

Email: office@ancientmonumentssociety.org.uk

Open: At all reasonable times.

Heritage Open Days: Yes

P No Partial. No disabled WC. Guide Dogs: Yes £ No

Stansted Windmill

Millside, Stansted Mountfitchet, Essex CM24 8BL

Brick tower mill, built 1787 and a scheduled ancient monument. Ceased working in 1910 but most of the original machinery remains *in situ*. Given in trust to the village by Lord Blyth in 1935.

Grant Recipient/Owner: Stansted Mountfitchet Council

Access contact: Mrs D P Honour

Tel: 01279 647213 **Fax:** 01279 813160

Open: Apr - Oct: first Sun of each month 2 - 6pm; plus BH Suns and Mons. Parties at any reasonable time of the year by arrangement with Mrs D P Honour, 59 Blythwood Gardens, Stansted, Essex CM24 8HH. For school groups contact Mrs Minshull (01279 812230). Children must be accompanied. Small souvenir shop.

Heritage Open Days: No

P No No

£ **Adult:** 50p **Child:** 25p **Other:** £2 (for group guided tour up to approx. 30 in number)

Stock Windmill

Mill Lane, Stock, Ingatesone, Essex CM4 9RY

Early 19th century tower mill, modernised in the late 1890s. Five floors, all of which may be visited. The mill has patent sails driving three pairs of French Burr millstones. The mill is in working order and occasionally grinds flour.

Grant Recipient/Owner: Essex County Council

Access contact: Mr Geoff Wood

Tel: 01245 437663 **Fax:** 01245 258353

Email: geoffwood@essexcc.gov.uk

Open: Apr - Sept: second Sun of each month 2 - 5pm, plus any reasonable time by arrangement with Geoff Wood, Mill Support Officer, Essex County Council, County Hall, Chelmsford, Essex CM1 1QH mobile. 07887 662177). Charge for guided group visit only.

Heritage Open Days: Yes

P Spaces: 6 No. Guide Dogs: Yes

£ Guided **Adult:** £2 **Child:** £1.50

Thorrington Tide Mill

Brightlingsea Road, Thorrington, Colchester, Essex CO7 8JJ

Weatherboarded watermill built in 1831 on a creek off the River Colne. The breastshot water wheel is external and drives two pairs of French Burr millstones, a sack hoist and a reel separator. There is provision for a drive from an external portable engine. The mill has been restored and is in working order.

Grant Recipient/Owner: Essex County Council

Access contact: Mr Geoff Wood

Tel: 01245 437663 **Fax:** 01245 258353

Email: geoffwood@essexcc.gov.uk

Open: Mar - Sept: last Sun of each month and BH Mondays 2 - 5pm, plus guided group visits at other times by arrangement with Geoff Wood, Mill Support Officer, Essex County Council, County Hall, Chelmsford, Essex CM1 1QH (mobile: 07887 662177). Charge for group guided visits only.

Heritage Open Days: Yes

P Parking not adjacent to the property but disabled people may be dropped off at the mill door. Spaces: 8

Partial. Wheelchair access to ground floor with assistance, there is always someone available to help when mill is open. No disabled WC. Guide Dogs: Yes

£ Guided **Adult:** £2 **Child:** £1.50

Valentines Mansion

Emerson Road, Ilford, Essex IG1 4XA

Valentines Mansion is a late 17th century house, largely Georgian in appearance with Regency additions. Of particular interest is the unusual curved late 18th century porte cochere. The exterior was extensively repaired and restored in 2000, now used as an arts centre.

Grant Recipient/Owner: London Borough of Redbridge

Access contact: Mr Nigel Burch

Tel: 020 8708 3619 **Fax:** 020 8708 3178

Email: nigel.burch@redbridge.gov.uk

Open: Open to the public by virtue of use as an arts centre. Also on 11 May for annual May Fair and for London Open House w/end, 21 - 22 Sept. Other times by arrangement with Nigel Burch, Chief Leisure Officer, London Borough of Redbridge, Lynton House, 255/259 High Road, Ilford, Essex IG1 1NY.

Heritage Open Days: See above

P No

Partial. Wheelchair access to ground floor only. No disabled WC. Guide Dogs: Yes £ No

GLOUCESTERSHIRE

Abbey Gatehouse

Tewkesbury, Glos

The gatehouse dates from 1500 and restored in 1849. Only one very fine room on the first floor. Steep staircase.

www.landmarktrust.co.uk

Grant Recipient/Owner: The Landmark Trust

Access contact: Ms Victoria Piggott

Tel: 01628 825920 **Fax:** 01628 825417

Email: vpiggott@landmarktrust.co.uk

Open: For details of opening arrangements at Landmark Trust properties please see the entry for Coop House, Netherby, Cumbria (page 549).

Heritage Open Days: No

P Yes. Spaces: 1 No £ No

Acton Court

Latteridge Road, Iron Acton, Glos BS37 9TJ

Seat of the Poyntzes, an influential courtier family who occupied the house until 1680 when it was converted into a farm house. A Tudor range, constructed in 1535 to accommodate King Henry VIII and Queen Anne Boleyn survives along with part of the North range. The rooms are unfurnished but contain important traces of original decoration.

Grant Recipient/Owner: Rosehill Corporation

Access contact: Ms Lisa Kopper

Tel: 01454 228224 **Fax:** 01454 227256

Email: actonct@dircon.co.uk

Open: Guided tours 30 Mar - 21 Apr and 3 Aug - 8 Sept. Pre-booking essential. Ring information line for details 01454 228224.

Heritage Open Days: No

P Spaces: 40

Partial. Wheelchair access to ground floor only. Disabled WC. Guide Dogs: Yes

£ **Adult:** £5 **Child:** £3.50 **Other:** £3.50 (senior citizens & disabled), £4 (groups 20+)

Beach Hall Gazebo

Witcombe Park, Great Witcombe, Glos

Summerhouse, dated 1697, interior altered in the 19th century. Formerly stood at corner of walled garden.

Grant Recipient/Owner: Mrs Diana Hicks-Beach

Access contact: Mrs M Hicks-Beach

Tel: 01452 863591

Open: By arrangement with Mrs M Hicks-Beach, Witcombe Farm, Great Witcombe, Glos..

Heritage Open Days: No

P Spaces: 20

Partial. The interior of the summerhouse can be seen fully from the outside but access inside for wheelchair users is difficult (4 steps to entrance). No disabled WC. Guide Dogs: Yes

£ Donation requested for St Mary's Church

Chastleton House

Chastleton, Moreton-in-Marsh, Glos GL56 0SU

Jacobean house filled with a mixture of rare and everyday objects, furniture and textiles collected since 1612. Continually occupied for 400 years by the same family. Emphasis lies on conservation rather than restoration.

www.nationaltrust.org.uk

Grant Recipient/Owner: The National Trust

Access contact: The Custodian

Tel: 01608 674355 **Fax:** 01608 674355

Open: 23 Mar - 2 Nov: Wed - Sat. Times: Apr - Sept, 1 - 5pm (last adm. 4pm); Oct & Nov 1 - 4pm (last adm. 3pm). Booking essential at all times (tel. 01494 755585 between 9.30am - 4pm, Mon - Fri). Groups by written arrangement with Custodian.

Heritage Open Days: No

P Spaces: 50

Partial. Wheelchair access to ground floor and parts of garden only. Disabled WC. Guide Dogs: Yes

£ **Adult:** £5.40 **Child:** £2.70 **Family:** £13.50

Chavenage

Tetbury, Glos GL8 8XP

Elizabethan Manor House (c1576), contains tapestry rooms, furniture and relics from the Cromwellian Period. Has been the home of only two families since the time of Elizabeth I. Television and film location.

www.chavenage.com

Grant Recipient/Owner: Trustees of the Chavenage Settlement

Access contact: Miss Caroline Lowsley-Williams

Tel: 01666 502329 **Fax:** 01453 836778

Email: info@chavenage.com

Open: May - Sept: Thursdays, Sundays and BHs 2 - 5pm; plus Easter Sun and Mon. Groups at other times by arrangement.

Heritage Open Days: No

P Spaces: 40

Partial. Access for wheelchair users to ground floor only. Disabled WC. Guide Dogs: Yes

£ **Adult:** £5 **Child:** £2.50

Court Farm Dovecote

Quenington, Cirencester, Glos GL7 5BN

Reputed to be dovecote mentioned in 1338, belonging to the Knights Hospitallers, but possibly 17th century. Small round structure of rubble stone with conical stone slate roof with retractable lantern "lid". Contains 600 dove holes stacked at an angle one above another inside wall, above rat rail around which moves revolving ladder on central wooden pin.

Grant Recipient/Owner: Mrs B Gollins

Access contact: Mrs B Gollins

Tel: 01285 750371 **Fax:** 01285 750322

Open: By arrangement with Mrs B Gollins.

Heritage Open Days: No

P Spaces: 5

Yes. No disabled WC. Guide Dogs: Yes £ No

East Banqueting House

Calf Lane, Chipping Campden, Glos

The East Banqueting House stands opposite the West Banqueting House across a broad terrace that ran in front of Sir Baptist Hick's mansion, which was deliberately destroyed by the Royalists in 1645 only 30 years after it had been built. It is elaborately decorated with spiral chimney stacks, finials and ebullient strapwork parapets. Steep staircases.

www.landmarktrust.co.uk

Grant Recipient/Owner: The Landmark Trust

Access contact: Ms Victoria Piggott

Tel: 01628 825920 **Fax:** 01628 825417

Email: vpiggott@landmarktrust.co.uk

Open: For details of opening arrangements at Landmark Trust properties please see the entry for Coop House, Netherby, Cumbria (page 549)

Heritage Open Days: No

P Parking available in town only. ♿ No **£** No

Ebley Mill

Westward Road, Stroud, Glos GL5 4UB

19th century riverside textile mill, now restored and converted into offices occupied by Stroud District Council. Has Gothic-style clock tower and block designed by George Bodley.

www.stroud.gov.uk

Grant Recipient/Owner: Stroud District Council

Access contact: Mr D Marshall

Tel: 01453 754646 **Fax:** 01453 754934

Email: information@stroud.gov.uk

Open: Mon - Thurs 8.45am - 5pm; Fridays 8.45am - 4.30pm. Closed BHs. Tours by arrangement.

Heritage Open Days: No

P Spaces: 30 ♿ Yes. Disabled WC. Guide Dogs: Yes

£ No

Great House Farm

Hasfield, Glos GL19 4LQ

16th, 17th and 19th century former manor house of stone, timber-frame and brick construction.

Grant Recipient/Owner: Hasfield Estate Trust

Access contact: Mr D Banwell

Tel: 01452 780206 **Fax:** 01452 780784

Email: d.j.barnwell@aol.com

Open: By arrangement Apr - Sept.

Heritage Open Days: No

P Spaces: 6 ♿ Yes. No disabled WC. Guide Dogs: Yes

£ No

The Malt House

High Street, Chipping Campden, Glos GL55 6AH

18th century malt house converted to a dwelling in 1905. Now part of a hotel and used as a conference room.

www.seymourhousehotel.com

Grant Recipient/Owner: Seymour House Hotel Ltd

Access contact: The Director

Tel: 01386 840429 **Fax:** 01386 840369

Email: enquiry@seymourhousehotel.com

Open: At all times except when in use for functions.

Heritage Open Days: Yes

P Spaces: 30 ♿ No. Guide Dogs: Yes **£** No

Newark Park

Ozleworth, nr. Wotton-under-Edge, Glos GL12 7PZ

Tudor hunting lodge converted into a castellated county house by James Wyatt and retaining many original features. Of special architectural interest and set in spectacular countryside.

www.ntrustsevern.org.uk

Grant Recipient/Owner: The National Trust

Access contact: South Glos Office

Tel: 01452 814213

Open: Provisional: Apr - May, Wed and Thurs; June - Sept, Wed, Thurs, Sat and Sun, 11am - 5pm (last entry 4.30pm). Open BH Mondays but not Easter BH. Contact South Glos Office for confirmation.

Heritage Open Days: No

P Spaces: 10 ♿ No. Guide Dogs: Yes

£ **Adult:** £3 **Child:** £1.50

St Mary Magdalene Chapel

Hillfield Gardens, London Road, Glos

Chancel of former church serving the inmates of St Mary Magdalene Hospital, originally a leper hospital, then later almshouses. Medieval graffiti visible on exterior, perhaps mementos of visiting pilgrims. Interior contains south and west doorways rebuilt after church demolished in 1861 and tomb of 13th century lady, removed from St Kyneburgh's Chapel nr the South Gate in 1550.

Grant Recipient/Owner: Gloucester Historic Buildings Trust Ltd

Access contact: Mr Malcolm J Watkins

Tel: 01452 396620 **Fax:** 01452 396622

Email: culture@gloucester.gov.uk

Open: By arrangement with Mr Malcolm J Watkins, Heritage Manager, Cultural Services, Gloucester City Council, Herbert Warehouse, The Docks, Glos GL1 2EQ, plus part of the Heritage Open Days w/end. Exterior accessible at all times in public park.

Heritage Open Days: Yes

P No

♿ Partial. Wheelchair access to exterior and to interior with assistance (entrance steps to be negotiated). No disabled WC. Guide Dogs: Yes **£** No

Stancombe Park Temple

Dursley, Glos GL11 6AU

One in a series of buildings built in the folly gardens at Stancombe Park, in the form of a Greek temple.

Grant Recipient/Owner: Mr N D Barlow

Access contact: Mrs G T Barlow

Tel: 01453 542815

Email: nic@diginic.uk.com

Open: All year by telephone arrangement.

Heritage Open Days: No

P Spaces: 50 ♿ No. Guide Dogs: Yes **£** No

Stanley Mill

KIngs Stanley, Stonehouse, Glos GL10 3HQ

Built 1813, with large addition c1825, of Flemish bond red brick with ashlar dressings and Welsh slate roof. Early example of fireproof construction (which survived a major fire in 1884).

Grant Recipient/Owner: Stanley Mills Ltd

Access contact: Mr Mark Griffiths

Tel: 01453 824444

Open: By written arrangement.

Heritage Open Days: No

P Parking available by arrangement. ♿ No **£** No

Stanway House (Kitchen Court)

Stanway, Cheltenham, Glos GL54 5PQ

Kitchen Courtyard surrounded by domestic buildings including 18th century brewhouse and servants quarters, and 19th century kitchen range. Adjoins Jacobean manor house.

Grant Recipient/Owner: The Trustees of the Lord Wemyss Trust

Access contact: Lord Neidpath

Tel: 01386 584469 **Fax:** 01386 584688

Email: neidpath@btinternet.com

Open: To the exterior: 24 Mar, 12 May, 3 June, 17 June - 30 Aug (weekdays only) and 13 and 20 July. Interior by arrangement.

Heritage Open Days: No

P Spaces: 10 ♿ No. Guide Dogs: Yes

£ **Adult:** £1 **Child:** Free **Other:** £1

Wick Court

Overton Lane, Arlingham, Glos GL2 7JJ

Medieval, 16th and 17th century Grade II* manor house with a range of farm buildings enclosed by a moat. The house is now a Farms for City Children centre.

Grant Recipient/Owner: Farms for City Children

Access contact: Ms Heather Tarplee

Tel: 01452 741023 **Fax:** 01452 741023

Open: By arrangement.

Heritage Open Days: No

P Spaces: 20

♿ Partial. Wheelchair access to ground floor of manor house only. Disabled WC. Guide Dogs: Yes

£ **Adult:** £2.50 (guided tour)

Woodchester Park Mansion

Nympsfield, Stonehouse, Glos GL10 3TS

Grade I Victorian mansion, abandoned incomplete in 1870. One of the most remarkable houses of its period and uniquely exhibiting its construction process. Set in a large landscaped park (possibly by Capability Brown). The building is also an SSSI housing 2 nationally important populations of endangered bats.

www.the-mansion.co.uk

Grant Recipient/Owner: Mr M Hill

Access contact: Mr David Price

Tel: 01453 750455 **Fax:** 01453 750457

Email: office@the-mansion.co.uk

Open: Easter - Oct: every Sun, 1st w/end in month (Sat & Sun) and BH w/ends (Sat/Sun/Mon) 11am - 4pm. Groups and private visits welcome by arrangement.

Heritage Open Days: No

P Parking is 1 mile from Mansion, access via woodland walk. Minibus service. Spaces: 60

♿ No. Guide Dogs: Yes

£ **Adult:** £4 **Child/Student:** £2

GREATER MANCHESTER

1830 Warehouse

The Museum of Science & Industry in Manchester, Liverpool Road, Castlefield, Manchester, Greater Manchester M3 4FP

Former railway warehouse, c1830, originally part of the Liverpool Road Railway Station (the oldest surviving passenger railway station in the world) which was the terminus of the Liverpool and Manchester Railway built by George Stephenson and his son Robert. Now part of The Museum of Science and Industry in Manchester.

www.msim.org.uk

Grant Recipient/Owner: The Museum of Science & Industry in Manchester

Access contact: Miss Val Smith

Tel: 0161 832 2244 **Fax:** 0161 833 1471

Email: marketing@msim.org.uk

Open: Daily (except 24/25/26 Dec) 10am - 5pm.

Heritage Open Days: No

P Spaces: 50

♿ Yes. Disabled WC. Guide Dogs: Yes

£ **Adult:** Free entry to all to main museum building from 1 Dec 2001. Charge for special exhibitions.

Albion Warehouse

Penny Meadow, Ashton-under-Lyne, Greater Manchester OL6 6HG

School, now warehouse. Built 1861-2 by Paull and Ayliffe in Italianate style.

Grant Recipient/Owner: G A Armstrong Ltd

Access contact: Mr David Armstrong

Tel: 0161 339 5353 **Fax:** 0161 339 5353

Open: Mon - Sat 9am - 5pm. Closed Sundays, BHs, Christmas Day and New Year's Day.

Heritage Open Days: No

P No ♿ No. Guide Dogs: Yes **£** No

George Street Independent Methodist Chapel

George Street, Oldham, Greater Manchester OL1 1LS

Methodist chapel built 1815. Said to be the oldest place of worship in Oldham for Methodists.

Grant Recipient/Owner: Ms Paula-Jane Rothermel

Access contact: Ms Paula-Jane Rothermel

Email: p.j.rothermel@btinternet.com

Open: By written arrangement to Ms Rothermel at the Chapel.

Heritage Open Days: No

P On street pay and display parking.

♿ Partial. Ground floor. Disabled WC. Guide Dogs: Yes

£ No

Heaton Hall

Heaton Park, Prestwich, Greater Manchester M25 2SW

18th century country house designed by James Wyatt in 1772, containing scrolling plasterwork, wall and ceiling paintings, furniture and paintings. Set in 650 acres of parkland.

Grant Recipient/Owner: Manchester City Council

Access contact: Ms Ruth Shrigley

Tel: 0161 235 8888 **Fax:** 0161 235 8805

Email: r.shrigley@notes.manchester.gov.uk

Open: Easter - end Oct: Wed - Sun 10am - 5.30pm (arrangements correct at time of going to print but may change, contact Manchester City Art Galleries, Room 1025, Lloyd Street, Manchester M60 2LA, tel. 0161 234 1456, for current details).

Heritage Open Days: No

P Spaces: 200

♿ Partial. Independent wheelchair access to ground floor rooms only. No disabled WC. Guide Dogs: Yes

£ No

Manchester Jewish Museum

190 Cheetham Hill Road, Manchester M8 8LW

Grade II* building located in the premises of the former Spanish and Portuguese Synagogue, completed in 1874 in Moorish style containing stained-glass windows and distinctive cast-iron fitments.

www.manchesterjewishmuseum.com

Grant Recipient/Owner: Trustees of Manchester Jewish Museum

Access contact: Mr Don Rainger

Tel: 0161 834 9879 **Fax:** 0161 834 9801

Email: info@manchesterjewishmuseum.com

Open: Mon - Thurs 10.30am - 4pm, Sun 10.30am - 5pm and Fridays by arrangement. Closed: 1 Jan; 28 Mar; 3 - 4 Apr; 8, 16, 22, 29 Sept; 24 - 26, 31 Dec. Early closing (1pm) 27 Mar & 15 Sept. May participate in Heritage Open Days w/end on the Sun, please contact Museum for current information. Groups only by arrangement.

Heritage Open Days: Yes

P On-street parking immediately outside museum.

♿ Partial. Wheelchair access to ground floor only. No disabled WC. Guide Dogs: Yes

£ **Adult:** £3.50 **Child:** £2.60 **Family:** £8.50

Manchester Law Library

14 Kennedy Street, Manchester M2 4BY

Built in Venetian Gothic style in 1885 to a design by Manchester architect, Thomas Hartas. Has stained glass windows by Evans of Birmingham.

www.manchester-law-library.co.uk

Grant Recipient/Owner: The Manchester Incorporated Law Library Society

Access contact: Mrs Julia Bragg

Tel: 0161 236 6312 **Fax:** 0161 236 6119

Email: librarian@manchester-law-library.co.uk

Open: By telephone or written arrangement.

Heritage Open Days: Yes

P No ♿ No. Guide Dogs: Yes **£** No

Old Grammar School
Boarshaw Road, Middleton, Greater Manchester M24 6BR
Endowed by Elizabeth I in 1572, completed 1584 with house added 1830s. Restored 1998. A Grade II* building with fine original oak beams and items of historical and local interest. An important early example of a building type for which there was little architectural precedent.
www.mwmsites.com/oldgrammarschool
Grant Recipient/Owner: The Old Grammar School Trust
Access contact: Revd Canon N J Feist
Tel: 0161 643 2693 **Fax:** 0161 643 2693
Email: nickjfeist@ntlworld.com
Open: All year except Christmas/New Year period: Tues, Weds & Thurs 2 - 4pm. Parties by arrangement on 0161 643 7442 or 0161 643 2693. Regular programme of events and use by community groups.
Heritage Open Days: Yes
P Spaces: 9 ♿ Yes. Disabled WC. Guide Dogs: Yes
£ £1 (donation per person requested)

Ordsall Hall
Ordsall Lane, Salford, Greater Manchester
Ordsall Hall is a Grade I early 16th century timber-framed house, extended in brick and incorporating the remains of the original 14th century house. Once an important manor house and home to the wealthy and influential Radclyffe family.
www.ordsallhall.org.uk
Grant Recipient/Owner: Salford City Council
Access contact: The Director of Technical Services
Tel: 0161 793 3770
Open: Mon - Fri 10am - 4pm; Sun 1 - 4pm. Closed on Sats, Christmas Day and New Year's Day. For further information contact the Director of Technical Services at Salford City Council or Ordsall Hall (tel. 0161 872 0251, fax. 0161 872 4951).
Heritage Open Days: Yes
P Yes. Free parking in grounds. Spaces: 40
♿ No. Guide Dogs: Yes £ No

Portico Library
57 Mosley Street, Manchester, Greater Manchester M2 3HY
19th century subscription library with Reading Room and Gallery, situated in Manchester city centre. 25,000 volumes, mainly 19th century. Particularly valuable for Victorian studies. Gallery shows mainly art exhibitions of new and established artists' work - local, national and international. Occasionally literary/local history exhibitions also shown.
www.theportico.org.uk
Grant Recipient/Owner: The Trustees of the Portico Library
Access contact: Emma Marigliano
Tel: 0161 236 6785 **Fax:** 0161 236 6803
Open: Mon - Fri and 3rd Sun of each month: 9.30am - 4.30pm. Closed Christmas period (usually 22 Dec - 2 Jan) and BHs.
Heritage Open Days: No
P No ♿ No. Guide Dogs: Yes £ No

Victoria Baths
Hathersage Road, Manchester, Greater Manchester M13 0FE
Swimming pool complex built 1906, with 2 pools, Turkish and Russian Bath suite, Aerotone and extensive stained glass and tilework.
Grant Recipient/Owner: The Manchester Victoria Baths Trust
Access contact: Ms Gill Wright
Tel: 0161 224 2020 **Fax:** 0161 224 0707
Email: victoriabaths@aol.com
Open: Afternoons of Heritage Open Days plus other events during the year and at other times by arrangement with Ms Gill Wright of the Manchester Victoria Baths Trust, 3 Birch Polygon, Rusholme, Manchester M14 5HX (tel.0161 224 2020/8437).
Heritage Open Days: Yes
P On-street parking during the week. Use of large adjacent car park at w/ends by arrangement. Spaces: 5
♿ Partial. Wheelchair access to ground floor with assistance. No disabled WC. Guide Dogs: Yes £ No

HAMPSHIRE

Avington Park
Winchester, Hampshire S021 1DB
Palladian mansion dating back to the 11th century, enlarged in 1670 by the addition of two wings and a classical Portico surmounted by three statues. Visited by Charles II and George IV. Highly decorated State rooms and Georgian church in the grounds.
www.avingtonpark.co.uk
Grant Recipient/Owner: Mrs Sarah Bullen
Access contact: Mrs Sarah Bullen
Tel: 01962 779260 **Fax:** 01962 779864
Email: sarah@avingtonpark.co.uk
Open: May - Sept: Sundays and BHs 2.30 - 5.30pm. At other times by arrangement.
Heritage Open Days: Yes
P Spaces: 150 ♿ Yes. Disabled WC. Guide Dogs: Yes
£ **Adult:** £3.75 **Child:** £1.75

Breach Farm Barn
Sherfield-on-Loddon, Hampshire RG27 0EU
15th century barn. Timber frame of 5 bays on a masonry base, with central entrances (projecting slightly on the east side). Cruck construction. Weather-boarded walls. Listed Grade II*.
Grant Recipient/Owner: Mr D Mitchell
Access contact: Mr D Mitchell
Tel: 01962 734275
Open: By telephone arrangement any reasonable time.
Heritage Open Days: No
P Spaces: 20
♿ Yes. No disabled WC. Guide Dogs: Yes £ No

Breamore Home Farm Tithe Barn
Breamore, nr. Fordingbridge, Hampshire SP6 2DD
Late 16th century tithe barn with dwarf walls supporting a timber-frame and external cladding under a tiled roof with massive timber aisle posts, double doors in the centre of each side and an area of threshing boards.
Grant Recipient/Owner: Breamore Ancient Buildings Conservation Trust
Access contact: Mr Michael Hulse
Tel: 01725 512858 **Fax:** 01725 512858
Open: Weekdays by arrangement with Mr Michael Hulse of Breamore House.
Heritage Open Days: Yes
P Spaces: 10
♿ Yes. No disabled WC. Guide Dogs: Yes £ No

Calshot
(Activities Main Hanger, Games Hanger & FFF Hanger), Calshot, Fawley, Hampshire SO45 1BR
Part of the most outstanding group of early aircraft structures of this type in Britain and the largest hanger built for fixed-wing aircraft during World War I. Now an activities centre.
Grant Recipient/Owner: Hampshire County Council
Access contact: Mr Peter Davies
Tel: 01962 841841 **Fax:** 01962 841326
Email: arccpd@pbrs.hants.gov.uk
Open: Daily except Christmas, Boxing and New Year's Day.
Heritage Open Days: No
P Ample free parking on-site.
♿ Yes. Disabled WC. Guide Dogs: Yes £ No

The Deanery
The Close, Winchester, Hampshire SO23 9LS
Earliest remains are late 12th or early 13th century, fragments visible in a stairwell cupboard of the Prior's Hall. The hall itself is probably 13th century in origin. Until 1539 the Prior's House, now home of the Dean of Winchester.
www.winchester-cathedral.org.uk
Grant Recipient/Owner: The Chapter of Winchester
Access contact: Ms Kathryn Vere
Tel: 01962 857225 **Fax:** 01962 857201
Email: cathedral.office@winchester-cathedral.org.uk
Open: By written arrangement with Cathedral Office, 1 The Close, Winchester, Hampshire SO23 9LS.
Heritage Open Days: Yes. 2 - 4pm.
P No ♿ No
£ **Adult:** £2.50 **Child:** £1 **Booked Groups:** £2pp

Highclere Castle & Park
Highclere, Newbury, Berkshire RG20 9RN
Early Victorian mansion rebuilt by Sir Charles Barry in 1842, surrounded by 'Capability' Brown parkland with numerous listed follies. Family home of the Earl and Countess of Carnarvon.
www.highclerecastle.co.uk
Grant Recipient/Owner: Earl of Carnarvon & Lord Porchester
Access contact: H W Dean & Son
Tel: 01223 351421 **Fax:** 01223 324554
Email: agent@hwdean.co.uk
Open: 1 July - 2 Sept: daily. Access enquiries may be made direct to the Castle (01635 253210). Admission charges are provisional, please check with H W Dean & Son, 57 Regent Street, Cambridge CB2 1AQ (01223 351421) for current details.
Heritage Open Days: No
P Unlimited.
♿ Partial. Wheelchair access to ground floor only. Disabled WC. Guide Dogs: Yes
£ **Adult:** £6.50 **Child:** £3 **Senior Citizens:** £5

Manor Farmhouse
Hambledon, Hampshire PO7 4RW
12th century stone built house with later medieval wing. 17th and 18th century re-fronting of part and minor renovation.
Grant Recipient/Owner: Mr Stuart Mason
Access contact: Mr Stuart Mason
Tel: 023 92632433
Open: By arrangement only.
Heritage Open Days: No
P Spaces: 2
♿ Yes. No disabled WC. Guide Dogs: Yes £ No

St Michael's Abbey
Farnborough, Hampshire GI14 7NQ
Grade I church and Imperial Mausoleum crypt of Napoleon III and his family. Abbey Church also built for the Empress Eugenie so the monks could act as custodians of the tombs. Now a Benedictine priory, raised to Abbey status in 1903.
www.farnboroughabbey.org
Grant Recipient/Owner: Empress Eugenie Memorial Trust
Access contact: Fr Magnus Wilson
Tel: 01252 546105 **Fax:** 01252 372822
Email: prior@farnboroughabbey.org
Open: Saturdays and Public Holidays at 3.30pm. Contact Fr Magnus Wilson, Bursar, or Fr D C Brogan, Prior, for further information.
Heritage Open Days: No
P No ♿ No £ No

The Vyne
Sherborne St John, Basingstoke, Hampshire RG24 9HL
Built in the early 16th century for Henry VIII's Lord Chamberlain. The house acquired a classical portico mid 17th century (the first of its kind in England). Tudor chapel with Renaissance glass, Palladian staircase, old panelling and fine furniture. Grounds, containing wild garden, lakes and woodland walks.
www.nationaltrust.org.uk
Grant Recipient/Owner: The National Trust
Access contact: The Property Manager
Tel: 01256 883858 **Fax:** 01256 881720
Email: svgen@smtp.ntrust.org.uk
Open: House: 23 Mar - 3 Nov: daily except Thurs and Fri (open Good Fri) 11am - 5pm (last entry 4.30pm). Grounds: w/ends in Feb and Mar 11am - 5pm; 31 Mar - 4 Nov: daily except Thurs and Fri (open Good Fri) 11am - 5pm.
Heritage Open Days: No
P New car park (140 cars and 3 coaches) 450 metres from house (buggy service if volunteers available). Disabled drivers able to park by house. Spaces: 70
♿ Partial. Wheelchair access to ground floor only. Disabled WC. Guide Dogs: Yes
£ **Adult:** £6.50 **Child:** £3.25 **Other:** £16.25 (family), £5 (group rate per head Mon, Tues & Wed only)

Whitchurch Silk Mill
28 Winchester Street, Whitchurch, Hampshire RG28 7AL
Grade II* watermill built c1800 and has been in continuous use as a silk weaving mill since the 1820s. Now a working museum, the winding, warping and weaving machinery installed between 1890 and 1927 produces traditional silks for theatrical costume, historic houses, fashion and artworks.
www.whitchurchsilkmill.org.uk
Grant Recipient/Owner: Hampshire Buildings Preservation Trust
Access contact: General Manager
Tel: 01256 892065 **Fax:** 01256 893882
Email: silkmill@btinternet.com
Open: Mill and shop: Tues - Sun 10.30am - 5pm (last adm. 4.15pm). Mill and shop closed Mondays (except BHs) and between Christmas and New Year.
Heritage Open Days: No
P Free parking next to Mill, 2 disabled spaces next to shop. Spaces: 20
♿ Partial. Wheelchair access to ground floor of Mill, shop and gardens. Disabled WC. Guide Dogs: Yes
£ **Adult:** £3.50 **Child:** £1.75 **Other:** £3

HEREFORDSHIRE

Chandos Manor
Rushall, Ledbury, Herefordshire HR8 2PA
Farmhouse, probably late 16th century with 18th century extensions. Timber-frame, partly rendered.
Grant Recipient/Owner: Mr Richard White
Access contact: Mr Richard White
Tel: 01531 660208
Open: Easter - Sept: Sundays by arrangement.
Heritage Open Days: No
P Spaces: 12 ♿ No. Guide Dogs: Yes
£ Donations to charity

Chapel Farm
Wigmore, nr. Leominster, Herefordshire HR6 9UQ
Timber-framed farmhouse c1400 of rectangular plan, originally a hall-house with first floor inserted in the 16th century. Contains an open roof with foliate carved windbraces, ornate post-heads and late Elizabethan wall painting. Associated with the Lollards around 1400.
Grant Recipient/Owner: Mr M Pollitt
Access contact: Mr M Pollitt
Open: By written arrangement Mondays (except BHs) May - Sept 2 - 4.30pm. Max 2 persons per visit. No children under 16 and no animals.
Heritage Open Days: No
P Parking available. ♿ No £ No

College of the Vicars Choral

Cathedral Close, Hereford, Herefordshire HR1 2NG

College, c1473, of coursed sandstone rubble with a Welsh slate roof and 7 stepped buttress stacks with ashlar chimneys.

Grant Recipient/Owner: Dean & Chapter of Hereford Cathedral
Access contact: Andrew Eames
Tel: 01432 359880 **Fax:** 01432 374220
Email: office@herefordcathedral.co.uk
Open: Sundays (except Palm Sun, Easter Day and Christmas Day) 11am - 12.30pm and on other days by arrangement with the Chapter Clerk, Cathedral Office, 5 College Cloisters, Cathedral Close, Hereford HR1 2NG (tel.01432 374200).
Heritage Open Days: No
[P] No ♿ Yes. Disabled WC. Guide Dogs: Yes [£] No

Croft Castle

nr. Leominster, Herefordshire HR6 9PW

Home of Croft family since Domesday (with break of 170 years from 1750). Walls and corner towers date from 14th and 15th centuries interior mainly 18th century. The park contains an avenue of 350 year old Spanish chestnuts. The walled garden is independently maintained by the Croft Trust and contains various historic fruit trees and plants.
www.ntrustsevern.org.uk
Grant Recipient/Owner: The National Trust
Access contact: Mr David Atkins
Tel: 01568 780246 **Fax:** 01568 780462
Email: croft@smtp.ntrust.org.uk
Open: Castle will be closed for major structural works. Gardens and grounds will remain open: 23 Mar - 3 Nov: daily except Mondays and Tues (open BH Mondays and Jubilee Mon and Tues) 11am - 5pm (last entry 4.30pm).
Heritage Open Days: No
[P] Spaces: 300
♿ Yes. Disabled WC. Guide Dogs: Yes
[£] Gardens **Adult:** £3 **Child:** £1.50 **Parking:** £2

Eastnor Castle

nr. Ledbury, Herefordshire HR8 1RL

Norman-style castellated mansion set in the western slopes of the Malvern Hills. Constructed 1812 - 1820, designed by Sir Robert Smirke, the Castle has 15 state and other rooms fully-furnished and open to visitors. The decoration includes tapestries, paintings, armour and a drawing room by Augus Pugin.
www.eastnorcastle.com
Grant Recipient/Owner: Mr J Hervey-Bathurst
Access contact: Mr S Foster
Tel: 01531 633160 **Fax:** 01531 631776
Email: enquiries@eastnorcastle.com
Open: Easter - end Sept: Suns and BH Mondays, plus every day in July and Aug except Sat, 11am - 5pm.
Heritage Open Days: No
[P] Spaces: 150
♿ Partial. Wheelchair access to grounds, tea room and ground floor with assistance (always available). Disabled WC. Guide Dogs: Yes
[£] **Adult:** £5.50 **Child:** £3 **Senior Citizen:** £4.75

Hergest Court

Kington, Herefordshire HR5 3EG

House dates back to 1267 and was the ancestral home of the Clanvowe and Vaughan families. An unusual example of fortified manor in the Welsh Marches. Literary associations with Sir John Clanvowe and Lewis Glyn Cothi.
Grant Recipient/Owner: Mr W L Banks
Access contact: Mr W L Banks
Tel: 01544 230160 **Fax:** 01544 230160
Email: banks@hergest.kc3.co.uk
Open: By arrangement with Hergest Estate Office, Kington, Herefordshire HR5 3EG. Bookings by phone or fax with five days' notice.
Heritage Open Days: No
[P] Spaces: 5
♿ Partial. Wheelchair access to ground floor only. No disabled WC. Guide Dogs: Yes
[£] **Adult:** £4 **Child:** Free **Other:** £3.50 (groups)

Lower Brockhampton

Brockhampton-by-Bromyard, Herefordshire WR6 5UH

A late 14th century moated manor house with a detached half-timbered 15th century gatehouse. Also, the ruins of a 12th century chapel. Woodland walks.
www.ntrustsevern.org.uk
Grant Recipient/Owner: The National Trust
Access contact: Mr Les Rogers
Tel: 01885 488099 **Fax:** 01885 482151
Email: brockhampton@smtp.ntrust.org.uk
Open: House: 3 Apr - 3 Nov: daily except Mon and Tues (but open BH Mondays and Jubilee Mon/Tues). Apr - Nov: 12 - 5pm (closes at 4pm in Oct and Nov).
Heritage Open Days: No
[P] Yes. Parking for disabled near house. Spaces: 60
♿ Partial. Wheelchair access to ground floor of house, chapel and estate. No disabled WC. Guide Dogs: Yes
[£] **Adult:** £3 **Other:** £7.50 (family). £2 (car park). Estate free to pedestrians.

The Painted Room

Town Council Offices, Church Street, Ledbury, Herefordshire HR8 1DH

The wall paintings, discovered in 1989, are a unique example of domestic wall painting dating from the Tudor period. They are clearly the work of a commoner, created to imitate the rich tapestries or hangings that would have been found in the homes of the gentry.
Grant Recipient/Owner: Ledbury Town Council
Access contact: Mrs J McQuaid
Tel: 01531 632306 **Fax:** 01531 631193
Email: ledburytowncouncil@ledbury.org.uk
Open: Easter - end Sept: guided tours Mon - Fri 11.30am - 3pm. Rest of year: Mon, Tues, Wed and Fri, if staff available. Tours may be arranged out of hours at a cost of £1 per adult (min £10). Childrens' groups are free.
Heritage Open Days: No
[P] Town centre car parks nearby.
♿ No. Guide Dogs: Yes
[£] **Adult:** £1 (out of normal hours)

St Katharine's Hall and Chapel

High Street, Ledbury, Herefordshire HR8 1DZ

Part of Hospital founded in 1232 by Bishop Hugh Foliot, the Hall and Chapel were built c1330-40 of local stone rubble with a tiled gabled roof.
Grant Recipient/Owner: The Trustees of St Katharine's Hospital Charity
Access contact: Clerk to the Trustees of St Katharine's Hospital Charity
Tel: 01432 374200 **Fax:** 01432 374220
Email: office@herefordcathedral.co.uk
Open: Hall normally open during the week. Access to Chapel is by arrangement with the Clerk to the Trustees of St Katharine's Hospital Charity, Cathedral Office, 5 College Cloisters, Hereford HR1 2NG.
Heritage Open Days: No
[P] No ♿ Yes. No disabled WC. Guide Dogs: Yes [£] No

HERTFORDSHIRE

Berkhamsted Town Hall

196 High Street, Berkhamsted, Herts HP4 3AP

Berkhamsted Town Hall and Market House, built in 1859, also housed the Mechanics' Institute. It has a gothic façade and retains much of the original stonework. There are 3 rooms: the Great Hall, Clock Room, Sessions Hall. In the Great Hall many of the original features have been preserved, including the fireplace and barrel vaulted ceiling.
Grant Recipient/Owner: Berkhamsted Town Hall Trust
Access contact: Ms Janet Fen
Tel: 01442 862288
Email: janet_fen@lineone.net
Open: Mon - Fri 10am - 1pm. At other times the Town Hall is let for functions. Additional opening by arrangement with the Town Hall Manager, Janet Fen.
Heritage Open Days: Yes
[P] Parking in nearby public car parks.
♿ Yes. Disabled WC. Guide Dogs: Yes [£] No

Bishop Seth Ward's Almshouses

Market Hill, High Street, Buntingford, Herts SG9 9AB

Almshouses c1684 (possibly by Robert Hooke) for Seth Ward, Bishop of Exeter and Salisbury, mathematician and astronomer and friend of Wren.
Grant Recipient/Owner: Mr R C Woods
Access contact: Mr R C Woods
Tel: 01763 271974 **Fax:** 01763 271974
Open: The exterior and gardens by arrangement with Mr R C Woods, Chairman of the Trustees, Bishop Seth Ward's Almshouse Trust, 58 Hare Street Road, Buntingford, Herts SG9 9HN.
Heritage Open Days: No
[P] No ♿ No [£] No

Bridgewater Monument

Aldbury, Herts HP4 1LT

The monument was erected in 1832 to commemorate the Duke of Bridgewater. The focal point of Ashridge Estate which runs across the borders of Herts and Buckinghamshire along the main ridge of the Chilterns.
www.nationaltrust.org.uk
Grant Recipient/Owner: The National Trust
Access contact: Property Manager
Tel: 01442 851227 **Fax:** 01442 842062
Open: Estate: all year. Visitor Centre: 29 Mar - 3 Nov, daily except Fridays (open Good Fri), Mon - Thurs & Good Fri 2 - 5pm; Sat, Sun, BH Mondays & Tues 4 June 12 noon - 5pm. Monument: Sat, Sun, BH Mondays & Tues 4 June 12 noon - 5pm; Mon - Thurs by arrangement, weather permitting.
Heritage Open Days: No
[P] Spaces: 100 ♿ Yes. Disabled WC. Guide Dogs: Yes
[£] **Adult:** £1 **Child:** 50p

Cromer Windmill

Ardeley, Stevenage, Herts SG2 7QA

Grade II* postmill dated 1674, last surviving postmill in Herts. Restored to working order (but not actually working). Houses displays about Herts's lost windmills, television and video display on the history of Cromer Mill and audio sound effects of a working mill.
www.hertsmuseums.org.uk
Grant Recipient/Owner: Herts Building Preservation Trust
Access contact: Ms Cristina Harrison
Tel: 01279 843301/07944 928552 **Fax:** 01279 841295
Email: cristinaharrison@hotmail.com
Open: Sat before National Mill Day, ie. second Sun in May. Then Sundays and BHs, and second and fourth Saturdays, until Heritage Open Days, 2.30 - 5pm. 30 minute video available for schools and groups. Guided tours. Special groups by arrangement with Ms Cristina Harrison, The Forge Museum, High Street, Much Hadham, Herts SG10 6BS. Refreshments available.
Heritage Open Days: Yes
[P] Spaces: 20
♿ Partial. Wheelchair access to ground floor only but video of upper floors showing all the time. No disabled WC. Guide Dogs: Yes
[£] **Adult:** £1.50 **Child:** 25p

Ducklake House Wallpainting

Springhead, Ashwell, Baldock, Herts SG7 5LL

16th century wall painting, located on the ground floor, containing classical grotesques holding cartouches.
Grant Recipient/Owner: Mr P W H Saxton
Access contact: Mr P W H Saxton
Open: By written arrangement to view the wall painting only.
Heritage Open Days: No
[P] Spaces: 1 ♿ No [£] No

Knebworth House

Knebworth, nr. Stevenage, Herts SG3 6PY

Originally Tudor manor house, rebuilt in gothic style 1843. Contains rooms in various styles, including a Jacobean banqueting hall. Set in 250 acres of parkland. 25 acres of formal gardens. Home of Lytton family since 1490.
www.knebworthhouse.com
Grant Recipient/Owner: Knebworth House Education & Preservation Trust
Access contact: Miss Jacky Wilson
Tel: 01438 812661 **Fax:** 01438 811908
Email: info@knebworthhouse.com
Open: 23 Mar - 7 Apr, 1 - 9 June, 6 July - 3 Sept: daily. 13 Apr - 26 May, 15 - 30 June, 7 - 29 Sept: w/ends and BHs only. Gardens, Park and Playground: 11am - 5.30pm. House: 12 noon - 5pm (last adm. 4.15pm). Groups (20+) all year by arrangement.
Heritage Open Days: No
[P] 50-75 parking spaces on gravel; unlimited on grass.
♿ Partial. Wheelchair access to ground floor of House only. Gravel paths around gardens and House but level route from car park to House entrance. Disabled WC. Guide Dogs: Yes
[£] **Adult:** £7 (£6 group) **Child/Other:** £6.50 (£5.50 group)

Old Palace

23 Kneeworth Street, Royston, Herts SG8 5AB

Built 1610 by James I, much altered (half of original building has subsequently been demolished). Georgian façade to the rear, the street frontage is in fact the dividing wall of the original building which has been left exposed following demolition of part of the building.
Grant Recipient/Owner: Mr Peter Franks
Access contact: Mr Peter Franks
Tel: 01763 245331
Open: By written arrangement.
Heritage Open Days: No
[P] Spaces: 1 ♿ No. Guide Dogs: Yes [£] No

Redbournbury Mill

Redbournbury Lane, Redbourn Road, St. Albans, Herts AL3 6RS

18th century watermill in full working order after 10 year restoration programme following 1987 fire. Supplementary power from Crossley oil engine.
Grant Recipient/Owner: Mr J T James
Access contact: Mrs A L James
Tel: 01582 792874
Email: redbrymill@aol.com
Open: 21 Mar - 3 Oct: Suns 2.30 - 5pm, plus Easter, late May and Aug BHs. National Mills W/end, Heritage Open Days and New Year's Day open all day. Special events all year. Private groups by arrangement. Refreshments available. Milling demonstrations. Organic flour and bread for sale.
Heritage Open Days: Yes
[P] Spaces: 30
♿ Partial. Wheelchair access to ground floor only. No disabled WC. Guide Dogs: No
[£] **Adult:** £1.50 **Child/Other:** 80p

The Old Clockhouse

Cappell Lane, Stanstead Abbots, Herts SG12 8BU

Grammar school, now private residence, c1636 also used for Sunday services in 17th century.

Grant Recipient/Owner: Mr Michael Hannon
Access contact: Mr Michael Hannon
Open: Access to exterior at all times; Bell Tower can only be viewed from High Street.
Heritage Open Days: No
[P] Public car park in Stansted Abbots High Street.
[♿] No [£] No

Torilla

11 Wilkins Green Lane, Nast Hyde, Hatfield, Herts AL10 9RT

'Torilla' (house at Nast Hyde) was built by F R S Yorke in 1935 in the international style and features a flat roof, 2 balconies and a large double height living room. Constructed of concrete with large steel framed windows. F R S Yorke was a key figure in the evolution of modern architecture in Britain.

Grant Recipient/Owner: Mr Alan Charlton
Access contact: Mr Alan Charlton
Tel: 01707 259582
Open: By arrangement (written or telephone) 11am - 5pm on Sun 19 May and Sun 18 Aug. At other times by written arrangement.
Heritage Open Days: No
[P] Spaces: 5
[♿] Partial. Wheelchair access to ground floor only. No disabled WC. Guide Dogs: Yes [£] No

Woodhall Park

Watton-at-Stone, Herts SG14 3NF

Country house, now school. Designed and built by Thomas Leverton in 1785 in neo-Classical style. Normally associated with London houses, this is one of his few country houses. Highly decorated interiors which include the Print Room with walls covered in engraved paper, reproductions of paintings with frames, ribbons, chains, busts, candelabra and piers with vases.

Grant Recipient/Owner: Trustees of R M Abel Smith 1991 Settlement
Access contact: The Trustees of R M Abel Smith 1991 Settlement
Tel: 01920 830286 **Fax:** 01920 830162
Email: woodhallest@dial.pipex.com
Open: At all reasonable times, preferably school holidays, by arrangement with the Trustees.
Heritage Open Days: No
[P] Limited to 10 spaces in school terms. Spaces: 30
[♿] Partial. Wheelchair access to ground floor only. No disabled WC. Guide Dogs: Yes [£] No

KENT

The Archbishops' Palace

Mill Street, Maidstone, Kent ME15 6YE

14th century Palace built by the Archbishops of Canterbury. Much altered and extended over the centuries. The interior contains 16th century panelling and fine wood or stone fireplaces. Now Kent County Council's Register Office and a conference venue.

Grant Recipient/Owner: Maidstone Borough Council
Access contact: Ms Claire Mason
Tel: 01622 754497 **Fax:** 01622 685022
Open: Function rooms open when not in use. Solar Restaurant open daily 10.30am - 5pm (closes 4.30pm from Sept). From Sept 2002 please tel. for availability.
Heritage Open Days: Yes
[P] Public parking in town centre car parks.
[♿] No. Guide Dogs: Yes [£] No

Chiddingstone Castle

Chiddingstone, nr. Edenbridge, Kent TN8 7AD

Tudor mansion subsequently twice remodelled by the Streatfeilds whose seat it was. William Atkinson "Master of the picturesque" is responsible for the romantic design, c1805, of the building as it is today. Rescued from dereliction by Denys Bower in the 20th century, now managed by a charitable trust.

Grant Recipient/Owner: Trustees of the Denys Eyre Bower Bequest
Access contact: Miss M R Eldridge
Tel: 01892 870347
Open: Easter and Spring BHs, June - Sept: Wed, Thurs, Fri and Sun; 2 - 5.30pm weekdays; 11.30am - 5.30pm (last adm. 5pm) Sundays and BHs. Groups (20+) during winter by arrangement. School groups when Castle is normally closed by arrangement. No mobile phones.
Heritage Open Days: No
[P] Spaces: 50
[♿] Partial. Wheelchair access to ground floor (includes everything except the Egyptian collection) and tea room. Disabled WC. Guide Dogs: Yes
[£] **Adult:** £4 **Child:** £2 (5-15, under 5 free but must be accompanied by an adult)

Church House

72 High Street, Edenbridge, Kent TN8 5AR

Late 14th century timber-framed farmhouse, Tudor additions include fireplace and 18th century brick frontage. Now houses the Eden Valley Museum which illustrates economic and social changes during the 14th to 20th centuries.

Grant Recipient/Owner: Mr M Downing
Access contact: Ms Elizabeth Wright
Tel: 01732 868102 **Fax:** 01732 867866
Email: ewright.edenvalley@virgin.net
Open: Oct - Mar: Tues and Wed 2 - 4.30pm; Thurs and Sat 10am - 4.30pm. Apr - Sept: Tues, Wed, Sun 2 - 4.30pm; Thurs and Sat 10am - 4.30 pm. Private/educational groups by arrangement.
Heritage Open Days: Yes
[P] Free parking in town centre car park, 200 yards from House. Spaces: 150
[♿] Partial. Wheelchair access to ground floor only (visual computer link to upstairs). Disabled WC. Guide Dogs: Yes
[£] **Adult:** £1.75 **Child:** 75p **Other:** 75p (disabled)

Cobham Hall and Dairy

Cobham, Kent DA12 3BL

Gothic-style dairy in grounds of Cobham Hall, built by James Wyatt c1790.

Grant Recipient/Owner: Cobham Hall Heritage Trust
Access contact: Mr N G Powell
Tel: 01474 823371 **Fax:** 01474 825904
Open: Easter - end Aug: Hall Wednesdays and Sundays 2 - 5pm (last tour 4.30pm). Tel. to check times. Other times (and coach groups) by arrangement. Self-guided tour of Gardens and Parkland (historical/conservation tour by arrangement). Special events.
Heritage Open Days: No
[P] Spaces: 100
[♿] Partial. Wheelchair access to ground floor only. Disabled WC. Guide Dogs: Yes
[£] **Adult:** £3.50 **Child/Other** (seniors/groups): £2.75

Crabble Corn Mill

Lower Road, River, nr. Dover, Kent CT17 0UY

Georgian watermill with millpond, cottages and gardens. Guided and non-guided tours and demonstrations of milling techniques. Flour produced and sold on site. Cafeteria and art gallery. Available for group tours, functions and events.

Grant Recipient/Owner: Crabble Corn Mill Trust
Access contact: Mr Alan Davis
Tel: 01304 823292
Email: miller@ccmt.freeserve.co.uk
Open: Feb - Apr: Sundays 11am - 5pm. Apr - Sept: Daily 11am - 5pm. Open to group visits all year by arrangement (contact Alan Davis, Tony Staveley or Anne Collins.)
Heritage Open Days: Yes
[P] In recreation ground opposite site. Spaces: 32
[♿] Partial. Wheelchair access to ground and first floor, art gallery, cafeteria and milling floor. No disabled WC. Guide Dogs: Yes
[£] **Adult:** £2 (mill tour) **Child:** £1 (5-15 years, mill tour) **Other:** £1.50 (seniors & students, mill tour), £5 (family, mill tour)

Foord Almshouses

Priestfields, Rochester, Kent ME1 3AF

Main Hall of almshouses built in 1926 of English bond red brick with stone dressings and old tile roof in neo-vernacular style of the 17th century with Baroque reference.

Grant Recipient/Owner: Trustees of the Foord Almshouses
Access contact: Mr David Hubbard
Tel: 01634 844138
Open: By arrangement.
Heritage Open Days: No
[P] Spaces: 10 [♿] Yes. Disabled WC. Guide Dogs: Yes
[£] No

Gad's Hill Place

Higham-by-Rochester, Kent ME3 7PA

Former home of Charles Dickens, who lived here from 1856 until his death in 1870 whilst writing The Mystery of Edwin Drood. Built c1780 with Dickensian additions, now an Independent School standing in 11 acres of meadowland and gardens.

Grant Recipient/Owner: Gad's Hill School
Access contact: Mrs Jean Wardrop
Tel: 01474 822366 **Fax:** 01474 822977
Email: info@gadshill.org
Open: Easter onwards: first Sun of each month plus BH Sundays 2 - 5pm. Summer and Christmas Dickens Festivals 11am - 4.30pm. Guided tours at other times by arrangement. Refreshments available.
Heritage Open Days: Yes
[P] Spaces: 40
[♿] Partial. Access for certain types of wheelchair only, please check with Place for details. Disabled WC. Guide Dogs: Yes
[£] **Adult:** £3.50 **Child:** £1.50

Herne Windmill

Mill Lane, Herne Bay, Kent CT6 7DR

Kentish smock mill built 1789, worked by wind until 1952 and then by electricity until 1980. Bought by Kent County Council in 1985, which carried out some restoration. Now managed by Friends of Herne Mill on behalf of the County Council. Much of the original machinery is in place, some is run for demonstration and the sails used when the wind conditions permit.

www.kentwindmills.co.uk
Grant Recipient/Owner: Kent County Council
Access contact: Mr Ken Cole
Tel: 01227 361326
Open: Easter - end Sept: Sundays and BHs, plus Thursdays in July and Aug, 2 - 5pm. National Mills Day, 11am - 5pm. For further information contact Ken Cole, Secretary, Friends of Herne Mill or Bill Martin (tel.01227 374539).
Heritage Open Days: Yes
[P] Limited in Mill grounds. Free on-street parking.
[♿] Partial. Wheelchair and guide dog access to ground floor of Mill and meeting room. Disabled WC. Guide Dogs: Yes
[£] **Adult:** £1 **Child:** 25p (accompanied by adult)

Ightham Mote

Ivy Hatch, Sevenoaks, Kent TN15 0NT

Moated manor house covering 650 years of history from medieval times to 1960s. Extended visitor route includes the newly refurbished north-west quarter with Tudor Chapel, Billiards Room and Drawing Room. Interpretation displays and special exhibition featuring conservation in action.

www.nationaltrust.org.uk/regions/kentesussex
Grant Recipient/Owner: The National Trust
Access contact: The Property Manager
Tel: 01732 810378 **Fax:** 01732 811029
Email: kimxxx@smtp.ntrust.org.uk
Open: 24 Mar - 3 Nov: daily except Tues and Sat, 11am - 5.30pm. Last admission 5pm.
Heritage Open Days: No
[P] Spaces: 420
[♿] Partial. Wheelchair access to ground floor and part of the exterior only. Disabled WC. Guide Dogs: Yes
[£] **Adult:** £5.40 **Child:** £2.70 **Other:** £13.50 (family), £4.70 (groups), NT members free

Littlebourne Tithe Barn

Church Road, Littlebourne, nr. Canterbury, Kent CT3 1TU

Early 14th century timber-framed aisled barn of 7 and a half bays. Aisled on all four sides with crown-post roof construction, has oak-riven boarding to walls and now thatched in water reed (formerly long straw). The two hipped roof entrances date from 1961.

Grant Recipient/Owner: Canterbury City Council
Access contact: Secretary, Conservation Section
Tel: 01227 862190 **Fax:** 01227 862020
Email: conservation@canterbury.gov.uk
Open: For events during the year, and at other times by arrangement For details please contact the Conservation Section at Canterbury City Council, Military Road, Canterbury, Kent CT1 1TW.
Heritage Open Days: Yes
[P] Spaces: 15 [♿] Yes. Disabled WC. Guide Dogs: Yes
[£] No

Penshurst Place Park

Tonbridge, Kent TN11 8DG

Open parkland, formerly a medieval deer park, c80 hectares. Scattered mature trees, lake with a small island and Lime Avenue originally planted in 1730s.

www.penshurstplace.com
Grant Recipient/Owner: Lord De L'Isle
Access contact: Mr Ian R Scott
Tel: 01892 870307 **Fax:** 01892 870866
Email: ianscott@penshurstplace.com
Open: Footpaths through parkland open all year.
Heritage Open Days: No
[P] Parking available. [♿] No. Guide Dogs: Yes [£] No

Sissinghurst Tower

Sissinghurst, Cranbrook, Kent TN17 2AB

Red-brick prospect tower and walls - surviving part of an Elizabethan mansion. Surrounded by a world-famous garden. The study where Vita Sackville-West worked and Long Library are open to the public.

www.nationaltrust.org.uk/regions/kentesussex
Grant Recipient/Owner: The National Trust
Access contact: Ms Sarah Cook
Tel: 01580 710700 **Fax:** 01580 710702
Email: ksisdc@smtp.ntrust.org.uk
Open: 23 Mar - 3 Nov: Daily, except Wed and Thurs, 11am - 6.30pm. Sat, Sun and Good Fri 10am - 6.30pm. Last admission 1 hour before closing.
Heritage Open Days: No
[P] Spaces: 610
[♿] Partial. Wheelchair access to garden but some narrow paths and steps. For further details contact the Property Manager (01580 710700). Disabled WC. Guide Dogs: Yes
[£] **Adult:** £6.50 **Child:** £3 **Other:** £16.00 (family)

Somerhill
Tonbridge, Kent TN11 0NJ
Grade I Jacobean mansion with Victorian addition set in 150 acres of parkland. Now a school, but original ceilings, panelling and stables have been retained.
Grant Recipient/Owner: Somerhill Charitable Trust Ltd
Access contact: Diane M Huntingford
Tel: 01732 352124 **Fax:** 01732 363381
Open: By written or telephone arrangement with Diane Huntingford, Administrator, plus the Sunday of Heritage Open Days weekend.
Heritage Open Days: Yes
P Spaces: 170
♿ Partial. Wheelchair access to ground floor only. No disabled WC. Guide Dogs: Yes £ No

Willesborough Windmill
Willesborough, Ashford, Kent, TN24 0GQ
Grade II* windmill built in 1869 and coaching barn. 1911 Hornsby 14HP gas oil engine now installed to give auxiliary power. The barn is now enclosed and houses a heritage museum.
Grant Recipient/Owner: Ashford Borough Council
Access contact: Willesborough Windmill Trust
Tel: 01233 661866
Open: Apr - end Sept: Sat, Sun and BH Mondays 2 -5pm
Heritage Open Days: No
P Spaces: 30
♿ Partial. Wheelchair access to ground floor of mill and all of barn. Disabled WC. Guide Dogs: Yes
£ **Adult:** £1 **Child:** 50p **Seniors:** 50p

LANCASHIRE

Accrington Town Hall
Blackburn Road, Accrington, Lancashire BB5 1LA
Town Hall, built in the classical style as Peel Institution 1857-8, by J. Green and T. Birtwhistle. Renamed the Town Hall when Accrington received its charter of incorporation in 1878. Now used by two council departments and for events, festivals and public hire.
Grant Recipient/Owner: Hyndburn Borough Council
Access contact: Mr Peter Baron
Tel: 01254 380296 **Fax:** 01254 380291
Email: leisure@hyndburnbc.gov.uk
Open: At all reasonable times. Information Centre open Mon - Sat 9am - 5pm. Wed 9am - 4pm.
Heritage Open Days: No
P Free throughout town centre. Parking for disabled adjacent to town hall.
♿ Yes. Disabled WC. Guide Dogs: Yes £ No

Gawthorpe Hall
Padiham, nr. Burnley, Lancashire BB12 8UA
An Elizabethan property in the heart of industrial Lancashire. Restored and refurbished in the mid 19th century by Sir Charles Barry. Many notable paintings on display loaned to the National Trust by the National Portrait Gallery, and a collection of needlework, assembled by the last family member to live there, Rachel Kay- Shuttleworth.
www.nationaltrust.org.uk
Grant Recipient/Owner: The National Trust
Access contact: Property Manager
Tel: 01282 770353 **Fax:** 01282 770353
Email: rpmgaw@smtp.ntrust.org.uk
Open: Hall: 1 Apr - 31 Oct daily except Mondays and Fridays (but open Good Fri and BH Mondays) 1 - 5pm. Garden: all year 10am - 6pm.
Heritage Open Days: No
P Spaces: 50
♿ Partial. Wheelchair access to garden only. Disabled WC. Guide Dogs: Yes
£ **Adult:** £3 **Child:** £1.30 **Other:** £8 (family), garden free

Grand Theatre
33 Church Street, Blackpool, Lancashire FY1 1HT
Grade II* 1200-seat theatre designed by Frank Matcham, 1894. Major restoration due for completion, Jan 2002.
www.blackpoolgrand.co.uk
Grant Recipient/Owner: Blackpool Grand Theatre Trust Ltd
Access contact: Mr David Fletcher
Tel: 01253 290111 **Fax:** 01253 751767
Email: info@blackpoolgrand.co.uk
Open: Daily. Tours on a semi-regular basis. Shows in the auditorium once or twice a day. Contact David Fletcher for more information.
Heritage Open Days: No
P West Street car park (2 minute walk). Spaces: 200
♿ Partial. Wheelchair access to stalls and bar. Disabled WC. Guide Dogs: Yes
£ Yes, Varies depending on show.

Harris Museum & Art Gallery
Market Square, Preston, Lancashire PR1 2PP
The Harris is a Grade I Greek Revival style building opened in 1893, designed by James Hibbert. Collections of paintings, sculpture, textiles, costume, glass and ceramics and a permanent local history gallery, The Story of Preston. Temporary exhibitions.
www.preston.gov.uk
Grant Recipient/Owner: Preston Borough Council
Access contact: Ms Alexandra Walker
Tel: 01772 258248 **Fax:** 01772 886764
Email: harris.museum@preston.gov.uk
Open: All year Mon - Sat 10am - 5pm. Closed on Sundays and BHs.
Heritage Open Days: Yes
P Public parking in Bus Station car park. Parking for disabled by museum entrance.Spaces: 1000
♿ Partial. Wheelchair access to all areas except Egyptian Balcony. Disabled WC. Guide Dogs: Yes £ No

Hoghton Tower
Hoghton, Preston, Lancashire PR5 0SH
16th century fortified manor house, ancestral home of the de Hoghton family since William the Conqueror. Associated with many kings and queens (the Banqueting Hall is where James I knighted the Loin of Beef 'Sirloin') and William Shakespeare. Various staterooms open to the public, as well as a Tudor horse-drawn well, dungeons and underground passages.
Grant Recipient/Owner: Hoghton Tower Preservation Trust
Access contact: Ms Carol Chalmers
Tel: 01254 852986 **Fax:** 01254 852109
Open: July - Sept: Mon - Thurs, 11am - 4pm (Sun 1 - 5pm). Guided tours: BH Sundays/Mondays (excl. Christmas and New Year); private tours all year by arrangement.
Heritage Open Days: No
P Spaces: 250 ♿ No. Guide Dogs: Yes
£ **Adult:** £5 **Child:** £4 **Senior Citizen/Student:** £4, £8 (family)

Judges Lodgings
Church Street, Lancaster, Lancashire LA1 1YS
Home of Thomas Covell, Keeper of the Castle at the time of the Lancashire witch trials in 1612. For two centuries a Judges' Lodgings, now a museum with Regency period rooms, Gillow furniture, portraits by Wright of Derby, Romney and Lawrence. Museum of Childhood with historic doll collection.
www.lancashire.com/lcc/museums
Grant Recipient/Owner: Lancashire County Council
Access contact: Lancashire County Council
Open: Good Fri - 30 June: Mon - Sat 2 - 5pm. 1 July - 30 Sept: Mon - Sat 10.30am - 1pm and 2 - 5pm. Oct: Mon - Sat 2 - 5pm. Closed on Sun but open on BH w/ends.
Heritage Open Days: Yes
P Public car parking nearby.
♿ Partial. Wheelchair access to ground floor only via side entrance. Please telephone in advance. No disabled WC. Guide Dogs: Yes
£ **Adult:** £2 **Child/Other:** £1

Leighton Hall
Carnforth, Lancashire LA5 9ST
Country House, 1765, probably by J Hird, with earlier remains. Gothic south-east front early 19th century, possibly by Thomas Harrison. Tower at west end of façade 1870 by Paley and Austin. Gillow family ancestral home with fine furniture, paintings and *objets d'art*.
www.leightonhall.co.uk
Grant Recipient/Owner: Mr Richard Reynolds
Access contact: Mr & Mrs Richard Reynolds
Tel: 01524 734474 **Fax:** 01524 720357
Email: leightonhall@yahoo.co.uk
Open: 1 May - end of Sept: daily (except Sat and non-BH Mondays), 2 - 5pm (12.30 - 5pm in Aug). Groups all year by arrangement. The owner reserves the right to close or restrict access to Hall and grounds for special events (dates to be confirmed). Refreshments available.
Heritage Open Days: No
P Spaces: 100
♿ Partial. Wheelchair access to ground floor, shop and tea rooms. Disabled WC. Guide Dogs: Yes
£ **Adult:** £4.50 **Child:** £3 **Other:** £4 (senior citizens)

Lytham Hall
Fylde, Lancashire FY8 4LE
18th century manor house incorporating elements of early 17th century predecessor. Many fine original features and decoration. Recently bought by Lytham Town Trust and leased to Heritage Trust for the North West.
Grant Recipient/Owner: Heritage Trust for the North West
Access contact: Heritage Trust for the North West
Tel: 01253 736652 **Fax:** 01253 737656
Open: At the time of going to print the Hall is closed for refurbishment works. It is hoped to reopen Easter 2002 and remain open each Sun until the end of Oct. The Trust aims to open the building more regularly in the future as the project develops. Please check the English Heritage website or with the Trust (tel.01253 736652) for current information.
Heritage Open Days: No
P Spaces: 200 ♿ No
£ **Adult:** £3 **Child:** £1.50 **Other:** £1.5

Rufford Old Hall
Rufford, nr. Ormskirk, Lancashire L40 1SG
Fine 16th century building with intricately carved movable wooden screen and hammerbeam roof. Owned by Hesketh family for 400 years. House contains collections of 16th and 17th century oak furniture, arms, armour and tapestries.
www.nationaltrust.org.uk
Grant Recipient/Owner: The National Trust
Access contact: Property Manager
Tel: 01704 821254 **Fax:** 01704 821254
Email: rrufoh@smtp.ntrust.org.uk
Open: House: 23 Mar - 30 Oct, daily except Thursdays and Fridays (but open Good Fri) 1 - 5pm. Garden: as house 11.30am - 5.30pm.
Heritage Open Days: No
P Spaces: 130
♿ Partial. Wheelchair access to ground floor, restaurant, shop and garden. Disabled WC. Guide Dogs: Yes
£ **Adult:** £4 **Child:** £2 **Other:** £10 (family).£2 (garden only), £2.75 (pp for booked groups)

Samlesbury Hall
Preston New Road, Samlesbury, Preston, Lancs PR5 0UP
Built in 1325, the hall is an attractive black and white timbered manor house set in extensive grounds. Independently owned and administered since 1925 by The Samlesbury Hall Trust whose primary aim is to maintain and preserve the property for the enjoyment and pleasure of the public.
www.samlesburyhall.co.uk
Grant Recipient/Owner: Samlesbury Hall Trust
Access contact: Samlesbury Hall Trust
Tel: 01254 812010 **Fax:** 01254 812174
Email: samlesburyhall@btconnect.com
Open: Tues - Fri and Sun 11am - 4.30pm. Closed Sat, Mon and 2 weeks at Christmas (please contact the Hall for details).
Heritage Open Days: No
P Yes. Additional parking for 100 cars in overflow car park. Spaces: 70
♿ Partial. Wheelchair access to ground floors of historical part of Hall. Disabled WC. Guide Dogs: Yes
£ **Adult:** £2.50 **Child:** £1 (4-16 years)

Smithills Hall
Smithills Dean Road, Bolton, Lancashire BL3 3FE
Grade I Hall, some parts of which date back to the medieval period. The early East Wing contains collection of mainly 17th century oak furniture. The largely Victorian West Wing has been recently conserved and includes Victorian period rooms, a shop, toilets and refreshments. Also a Grade II garden.
www.smithills.org.uk
Grant Recipient/Owner: Bolton Metropolitan Borough Council
Access contact: Mr David Mills
Tel: 01204 332377
Email: smithills_hall@hotmail.com
Open: Easter - end Sept: Tues - Sat 11am - 5pm, plus Sun 2 - 5pm. Oct - Easter: Winter: please telephone for details. Groups at other times by arrangement with Administration, Smithills Hall and Park Trust, Smithills Hall, Smithills Dean Road, Bolton, Lancs BL3 3FE.
Heritage Open Days: Yes
P Spaces: 40
♿ Partial. Wheelchair access to lower floor only. Disabled WC. Guide Dogs: Yes
£ **Adult:** £3 **Child:** £1.75 **Other:** £1.7

Stonyhurst College
Stonyhurst, Clitheroe, Lancashire BB7 9PZ
16th century manor house, now home to a Catholic independent co-education boarding and day school. Contains dormitories, library, chapels, school-rooms and historical apartments.
www.stonyhurst.ac.uk
Grant Recipient/Owner: Stonyhurst College
Access contact: Miss Frances Ahearne
Tel: 01254 826345 **Fax:** 01254 826732
Email: domestic-bursar@stonyhurst.ac.uk
Open: House: 15 July - 26 Aug daily (except Fri), plus Aug BH Mon, 1 - 5pm; Gardens: 1 July - 26 Aug daily (except Fri), plus Aug BH Mon, 1 - 5pm. Coach groups by arrangement.
Heritage Open Days: No
P Spaces: 20
♿ Partial. Limited wheelchair access. Assistance available by arrangement. Disabled WC Guide Dogs: Yes
£ **Adult:** £4.50 **Child/Other:** £3.50

Todmorden Unitarian Church
Honey Hole Road, Todmorden, Lancashire OL14 6LE
Grade I church with a large wooded burial ground and ornamental gardens designed by John Gibson, 1865-69. Victorian Gothic style with tall tower and spire. Detached smaller burial ground nearby and listed lodge in churchyard.

www.hct.org.uk
Grant Recipient/Owner: Historic Chapels Trust
Access contact: Mr Rob Goldthorpe
Tel: 01706 815648
Email: rob.goldthorpe@btinternet.com
Open: At all reasonable times by application to keyholder, Mr Rob Goldthorpe, 14 Honey Hole Close, Todmorden, Lancashire OL14 6LH or by calling at caretaker's house, Todmorden Lodge, at the entrance to the churchyard.
Heritage Open Days: Yes
P Spaces: 10
Yes. Disabled WC. Guide Dogs: Yes £ No

Towneley Hall Art Gallery & Museum

Todmorden Road, Burnley, Lancashire BB11 3RQ
Former home of the Towneley family on outskirts of Burnley, Towneley Hall has been the town's art gallery and museum since 1903. Earliest part of the building dates from c1450. 16th century chapel and Long Gallery, baroque entrance hall and two reception rooms by Jeffry Wyat c1820.
www.towneleyhall.org.uk
Grant Recipient/Owner: Burnley Borough Council
Access contact: Jackie Sims
Tel: 01282 424213 **Fax:** 01282 436138
Email: towneleyhall@burnley.gov.uk
Open: Mon - Fri 10am - 5pm, Sun 12 - 5pm (Sat closed). Also open BHs but closed for approx. one week over Christmas and New Year. Some rooms closed from Jan to June for installation of new facilities and displays. Refreshments available.
Heritage Open Days: Yes
P Free parking for cars and coaches. Spaces: 50
Partial. Wheelchair access to the ground floor of all buildings and level, lightly gravelled tarmac paths in the park. Please ask for assistance. Disabled WC. Guide Dogs: Yes £ Donations welcome

Whalley Abbey

Whalley, Clitheroe, Lancashire BB7 9SS
14th century Cistercian abbey ruins. Exhibition centre on site. Gardens, woodland trail and riverside walk.
Grant Recipient/Owner: Blackburn Diocesan Board of Finance
Access contact: Mr John Wilson
Tel: 01254 828400 **Fax:** 01254 828401
Open: Ruins and Gardens: Easter - Oct, daily 11am - 5pm; Nov - Easter, daily 11am - 4pm. 17th century Retreat House: Open Days and by arrangement Refreshments available.
Heritage Open Days: Yes
P Spaces: 25
Partial. Wheelchair access to most of ruins, coffee shop and exhibition centre. Chairlift in Retreat House. Disabled WC. Guide Dogs: Yes
£ **Adult:** £2 **Child:** 50p **Senior/Student:** £1.25, **Family:** £4.50, £1 (coach 40+)

LEICESTERSHIRE

Leicester Guildhall

Guildhall Lane, Leicester, Leicestershire LE1 5FQ
14th century medieval Great Hall with Lord Mayor's Parlour, Old Town Library and Victorian police cells. Now a museum.
www.leicestermuseums.ac.uk
Grant Recipient/Owner: Leicester City Council
Access contact: The Head of Museums & Heritage Services
Tel: 0116 252 8912 **Fax:** 0116 255 6048
Email: levisool@leicester.gov.uk
Open: Apr - Sept: Mon - Sat 10am - 5pm, Sun 1 - 5pm. Oct - Mar: Mon - Sat 10am - 4pm, Sun 1 - 4pm. Contact Guildhall for Christmas/New Year opening times.
Heritage Open Days: Yes
P Public car parks in City centre.
Partial. Wheelchair access to ground floor only. Disabled WC. Guide Dogs: No £ No

Stanford Hall

Lutterworth, Leicestershire LE17 6DH
William and Mary house, built by the Smiths of Warwick (begun 1697), for Sir Roger Cave, ancestor of present owner whose family home it is. Visitors see every room on the ground floor (except modern kitchen), the "flying staircase" and two bedrooms. Contents include collection of Royal Stuart paintings.
Grant Recipient/Owner: Lady Braye
Access contact: Lt-Col EHL Aubrey-Fletcher
Tel: 01788 860250 **Fax:** 01788 860870
Email: enquiries@stanfordhall.co.uk
Open: 30 Mar - 29 Sept: Saturdays, Sundays, BH Mondays and following Tues, 1.30 - 5.30pm (last adm. 5pm). Groups by arrangement any day or evening during this period. Special events. On BH Mondays and Event days grounds open 12 noon. Closed Oct - Easter, except for corporate events in Oct.
Heritage Open Days: No
P Spaces: 1500
Partial. Wheelchair access to the Park, the Gardens, the Motorcycle Museum, the 1898 Flying Machine and the ground floor of the Hall if entrance steps can be negotiated.
Disabled WC. Guide Dogs: Yes
£ **Adult:** £4.50 (house & grounds), £2.50 (grounds only) **Child:** £2 (house & grounds), £1 (grounds only) **Groups (20+):** £4.20 adult, £1.80 child

LINCOLNSHIRE

12 Minster Yard

Lincoln, Lincolnshire LN2 1PJ
House of early 14th, late 17th and 19th centuries.
Grant Recipient/Owner: Dean & Chapter of Lincoln Cathedral
Access contact: Mr William Roberts
Tel: 01522 527637 **Fax:** 01522 575 688
Email: clerkoftheworks@lincolncathedral.com
Open: By written arrangement with the Clerk of Works, Lincoln Cathedral, 28 Eastgate, Lincoln LN2 4AA.
Heritage Open Days: No
P No No. Guide Dogs: Yes £ No

13/13a Minster Yard

Lincoln, Lincolnshire LN2 1PW
Houses, mid-18th century, with late 18th and 19th century alterations.
Grant Recipient/Owner: Dean & Chapter of Lincoln Cathedral
Access contact: Mr William Roberts
Tel: 01522 527637 **Fax:** 01522 575 688
Email: clerkoftheworks@lincolncathedral.com
Open: By written arrangement with the Clerk of Works, Lincoln Cathedral, 28 Eastgate, Lincoln LN2 4AA.
Heritage Open Days: No
P No No. Guide Dogs: Yes £ No

17 Minster Yard

Lincoln, Lincolnshire LN2 1PX
13th and 14th century building with 15th century additions. Sacked in 1644, restored 1671-94 and 1704-32 with internal alterations, c1813, by William Fowler. Further additions to building made late 19th century.
Grant Recipient/Owner: Dean & Chapter of Lincoln Cathedral
Access contact: Mr William Roberts
Tel: 01522 527637 **Fax:** 01522 575 688
Email: clerkoftheworks@lincolncathedral.com
Open: By written arrangement with the Clerk of Works, Lincoln Cathedral, 28 Eastgate, Lincoln LN2 4AA.
Heritage Open Days: No
P No No. Guide Dogs: Yes £ No

18/18a Minster Yard

Lincoln, Lincolnshire LN2 1PX
13th and 14th century building with 17th century additions. Remodelled and extended in 1827 and refronted 1873 by J L Pearson.
Grant Recipient/Owner: Dean & Chapter of Lincoln Cathedral
Access contact: Mr William Roberts
Tel: 01522 527637 **Fax:** 01522 575 688
Email: clerkoftheworks@lincolncathedral.com
Open: By written arrangement with the Clerk of Works, Lincoln Cathedral, 28 Eastgate, Lincoln LN2 4AA.
Heritage Open Days: No
P No No. Guide Dogs: Yes £ No

2/2a Exchequergate

Lincoln, Lincolnshire LN2 1PZ
Late 15th century house, rebuilt 1834-48.
Grant Recipient/Owner: Dean & Chapter of Lincoln Cathedral
Access contact: Mr William Roberts
Tel: 01522 527637 **Fax:** 01522 575 688
Email: clerkoftheworks@lincolncathedral.com
Open: By written arrangement with the Clerk of Works, Lincoln Cathedral, 28 Eastgate, Lincoln LN2 4AA.
Heritage Open Days: No
P No No. Guide Dogs: Yes £ No

22 Minster Yard

Lincoln, Lincolnshire LN2 1PX
Early 18th century house, altered early 19th and divided mid-19th century.
Grant Recipient/Owner: Dean & Chapter of Lincoln Cathedral
Access contact: Mr William Roberts
Tel: 01522 527637 **Fax:** 01522 575688
Email: clerkoftheworks@lincolncathedral.com
Open: By written arrangement with the Clerk of Works, Lincoln Cathedral, 28 Eastgate, Lincoln LN2 4AA.
Heritage Open Days: No
P No No. Guide Dogs: Yes £ No

3/3a Pottergate

Lincoln, Lincolnshire LN2 1PH
17th century house, now 2 houses, incorporating medieval walling. Remodelled in early 18th century with late 18th and 19th century alterations.
Grant Recipient/Owner: Dean & Chapter of Lincoln Cathedral
Access contact: Mr William Roberts
Tel: 01522 527637
Email: clerkoftheworks@lincoln.cathedral.com
Open: By written arrangement with the Clerk of Works, Lincoln Cathedral, 28 Eastgate, Lincoln LN2 4AA.
Heritage Open Days: Yes
P Public parking in local authority car parks.
No £ No

3/3a Vicars Court

Lincoln, Lincolnshire LN2 1PT
Former priests' vicars lodgings, now 2 houses. Begun late 13th century by Bishop Sutton, completed c1309. Altered 15th century, re-roofed and altered late 16th, 17th, 18th and 19th centuries.
Grant Recipient/Owner: Dean & Chapter of Lincoln Cathedral
Access contact: Mr William Roberts
Tel: 01522 527637 **Fax:** 01522 575688
Email: clerkoftheworks@lincolncathedral.com
Open: By written arrangement with the Clerk of Works, Lincoln Cathedral, 28 Eastgate, Lincoln LN2 4AA.
Heritage Open Days: No
P No No. Guide Dogs: Yes £ No

4 Pottergate

Lincoln, Lincolnshire LN2 1PH
14th and 15th century house, with mid-17th century additions. Altered c.1760 and in the 19th century.
Grant Recipient/Owner: Dean & Chapter of Lincoln Cathedral
Access contact: Mr William Roberts
Tel: 01522 527637 **Fax:** 01522 575688
Email: clerkoftheworks@lincolncathedral.com
Open: By written arrangement with the Clerk of the Works, Lincoln Cathedral, 28 Eastgate, Lincoln LN2 4AA.
Heritage Open Days: No
P No No. Guide Dogs: Yes £ No

46 & 47 Steep Hill & 1 Christ's Hospital Terrace

Lincoln, Lincolnshire LN2
Grade I house c1170 with late 18th and 19th century additions. Restored 1878 and during the 20th century. Dressed stone and brick with pantile roof and wooden gutter in iron brackets, two storeys with basements and garrets. Important example of 12th century domestic architecture, now a private house and two shops.
Grant Recipient/Owner: Lincoln City Council
Access contact: Mr Arthur Ward
Tel: 01522 873479 **Fax:** 01522 567934
Email: arthur.ward@lincoln.gov.uk
Open: Shops open during business hours. Access to non-public areas by arrangement with Arthur Ward, Head of Heritage, Lincoln City Council, City Hall, Beaumont Fee, Lincoln, Lincs LN1 1DF.
Heritage Open Days: No
P Parking in Castle Square/Westgate public car parks.
No. Guide Dogs: Yes £ No

Arabella Aufrere Temple

Brocklesby Park, Grimsby, Lincolnshire DN41 8PN
Garden Temple of ashlar and red brick with coupled doric columns either side of a central arch leading to a rear chamber. Built c1787 and attributed to James Wyatt. Inscription above inner door: "Dedicated by veneration and affection to the memory of Arabella Aufrere."
Grant Recipient/Owner: The Earl of Yarborough
Access contact: Mr H A Rayment
Tel: 01469 560214
Open: 1 Apr - 31 Aug: viewable from permissive paths through Mausoleum Woods at all reasonable times.
Heritage Open Days: No
P Free parking in village or walks car park, 1/4 mile from site. Spaces: 10
No £ No

Brocklesby Mausoleum

Brocklesby Park, N E Lincolnshire DN41 8PN
Family Mausoleum designed by James Wyatt, built 1787 - 1794 by Charles Anderson Pelham, who subsequently became Lord Yarborough, as a memorial to his wife Sophia who died at 33. The classical design is based on the Temples of Vesta at Rome and Tivoli.
Grant Recipient/Owner: The Earl of Yarborough
Access contact: Mr H A Rayment
Tel: 01469 560214
Open: Exterior: 1 Apr - 31 Aug: viewable from permissive paths through Mausoleum Woods at all reasonable times. Interior (excluding private crypt) by arrangement with the Estate Office. Admission charge for interior.
Heritage Open Days: No
P Free parking in village or walks car park, 5 minutes from site. Spaces: 10
No. Guide Dogs: Yes £ See above: £2

Burghley House

Stamford, Lincolnshire PE9 3JY
Large country house built by William Cecil, Lord High Treasurer of England, 1565 - 1587, and still lived in by descendants of his family. Eighteen State Rooms, many decorated by Antonio Verrio in the 17th century, housing collection of artworks including 17th century Italian paintings, Japanese ceramics, European porcelain and wood carvings by Grinling Gibbons and his followers. There are four State Beds, English and continental furniture, and tapestries and textiles. 'Capability' Brown parkland.
www.burghley.co.uk
Grant Recipient/Owner: Burghley House Preservation Trust Ltd
Access contact: Mr David Parratt
Tel: 01780 752451 **Fax:** 01780 480125
Email: burghley@burghley.co.uk
Open: 29 Mar - 27 Oct: daily (except 31 Aug) 11am - 4.30pm. Guided tours only apart from Sat and Sun afternoons when there are guides in each room.
Heritage Open Days: No
P Parking for disabled available close to visitors' entrance. Spaces: 500
♿ Yes. Please telephone the Property Manager for information on wheelchair access. Disabled WC. Guide Dogs: Yes
£ **Adult:** £7.10 **Child:** £3.50, (1 child 5-12 free with each paying adult) **Other:** £6.35 (senior), £6.20 (pp for groups 20+), £3.20 (school groups up to 14)

Doddington Hall

Lincoln LN6 4RU
Late Elizabethan mansion with original garden walls, gatehouse and outbuildings. Contents, including furniture, textiles, porcelain and pictures, reflect 400 years of domestic use.
www.doddingtonhall.free-online.co.uk
Grant Recipient/Owner: Mr Antony Jarvis
Access contact: Mr Antony Jarvis
Tel: 01522 694308 **Fax:** 01522 685259
Email: estateoffice@doddingtonhall.free-online.co.uk
Open: House & Gardens: May - Sept, Wed, Sun and BH Mondays 2 - 6pm; Gardens only: Feb - Apr, Suns 2 - 6pm. Check with Mr Antony Jarvis or Miss Fiona Cairns-Watson at the Hall for additonal information.
Heritage Open Days: No
P Spaces: 250
♿ Partial. Wheelchair access to gardens and ground floor of Hall only. Disabled WC. Guide Dogs: Yes
£ **Adult:** £4.50 (£3 garden only) **Child:** £2.25 (£1.50 garden only) **Family:** £12.50

Harding House

48-54 Steep Hill, Lincoln, Lincolnshire LN2
Grade II 16th century house, remodelled in the 18th and restored in the 20th century. Built of coursed rubble and brick with pantile roof, now houses a craft studio.
Grant Recipient/Owner: The Chief Executive, Lincoln City Council
Access contact: Mr Mark Wheater
Tel: 01522 873464 **Fax:** 01522 560049
Email: mark.wheater@lincoln.gov.uk
Open: During normal shop opening hours.
Heritage Open Days: No
P No ♿ No. Guide Dogs: Yes £ No

Heggy's Cottage

Hall Road, Haconby, nr. Bourne, Lincolnshire PE10 0UY
Built c1500 of mud and stud construction, a good example of early conversion to two storeys. Restored to its original state in 1995.
Grant Recipient/Owner: J E Atkinson & Son
Access contact: Mrs J F Atkinson
Tel: 01778 570790
Open: By written arrangement with Mrs J F Atkinson, Haconby Hall, nr. Bourne, Lincolnshire PE10 0UY.
Heritage Open Days: No
P Spaces: 1 ♿ No £ No

Jews Court

(the Society for Lincolnshire History & Archaeology), 2/3 Steep Hill, Lincoln, Lincolnshire LN2 1LS
Grade I two storey stone building, c12th century, with cellar and attic. Traditionally the medieval synagogue. Now used by the Society for Lincolnshire History & Archaeology and for worship.
Grant Recipient/Owner: Jews' Court Trust
Access contact: Ms Pearl Wheatley
Tel: 01522 521337 **Fax:** 01522 521337
Open: Daily except Sundays, 10am - 4pm. Closed over the Christmas period.
Heritage Open Days: No
P Ample public parking within 50 yards.
♿ No. Guide Dogs: Yes £ No

Kyme Tower

Manor Farm, South Kyme, Lincoln, Lincolnshire LN4 4JN
23.5m high tower with four storeys and a stair turret. Remainder of a fortified medieval manor house, built on the site of an Augustinian priory, itself built on an Anglo-Saxon religious establishment. There are also visible earthworks of the former moat and fishponds.
Grant Recipient/Owner: The Crown Estate Commissioners
Access contact: Mr W B Lamyman
Tel: 01526 860603
Open: By telephone arrangement with Mr W B Lamyman. At least one week's notice required.
Heritage Open Days: No
P Spaces: 3 ♿ No £ No

Lincoln Castle

Castle Hill, Lincoln, Lincolnshire LN1 3AA
Lincoln Castle was begun by William the Conqueror in 1068. For 900 years the castle has been used as a court and prison. Many original features still stand and the wall walks provide magnificent views of the cathedral, city and surrounding countryside.
Grant Recipient/Owner: Lincolnshire County Council
Access contact: Mr Peter Allen
Tel: 01522 511068 **Fax:** 01522 512150
Email: allenp@lincolnshire.gov.uk
Open: Mon - Sat: 9.30am - 5.30pm, Sun 11am - 5.30pm. Winter closes 4pm. Closed 24 - 26 Dec, 31 Dec and 1 Jan.
Heritage Open Days: No
P Yes. Additional parking spaces nearby. Spaces: 30
♿ Partial. Wheelchair access to grounds, Magna Carta exhibition, audio visual presentation and café. Disabled WC. Guide Dogs: Yes
£ **Adult:** £2.50 **Child:** £1 **Other:** £1.50 (under 5s free), £6.50 (family)

Tattershall Castle

Tattershall, Lincoln, Lincolnshire LN4 4LR
Vast fortified and moated red-brick tower, built c1440 for Ralph Cromwell, Treasurer of England. The building rescued from becoming derelict by Lord Curzon 1911-14 and contains 4 great chambers with enormous Gothic fireplaces, tapestries and brick vaulting. Gatehouse with museum room.
www.nationaltrust.org.uk
Grant Recipient/Owner: The National Trust
Access contact: The Custodian
Tel: 01526 342543 **Fax:** 01526 342543
Email: etcxxx@smtp.ntrust.org.uk
Open: 23 Mar - 3 Nov: daily except Thurs and Fri 11am - 5.30pm (11am - 4pm in Oct). 9 Nov - 15 Dec: Sat and Sun 12 noon - 4pm. Ground floor may occasionally be closed for functions or events.
Heritage Open Days: No
P Spaces: 40
♿ Partial. Wheelchair access to ground floor via ramp. Photograph album of inaccessible parts of Castle. Disabled WC. Guide Dogs: Yes
£ **Adult:** £3.20 **Child:** £1.60 **Family:** £8

Uffington Manor Gatepiers

Main Street, Uffington, nr. Stamford, Lincolnshire
Pair of Grade II* gate piers, possibly by John Lumley c1700, surmounted by urns with wrought iron entrance gates with a coat of arms over of later 19th century date.
Grant Recipient/Owner: Mr David Pike
Access contact: Mr David Pike
Tel: 01780 751944 **Fax:** 01780 764256
Open: Can be viewed from public roadway, otherwise by written arrangement.
Heritage Open Days: No
P Spaces: 2 ♿ No. Guide Dogs: Yes £ No

Waltham Windmill

Brigsley Road, Waltham, Grimsby, Lincolnshire DN37 0JZ
Grade II six-sailed tower mill, one of only three in the country. Built 1880 by John Sanderson of Louth, 90ft high with 6 publicly accessible floors. At the centre of a 2 acre site, now home to a museum of rural life. There is also a wild flower area and a children's play area.
Grant Recipient/Owner: Waltham Windmill Trust
Access contact: Mrs M A Stennett
Tel: 01472 822236
Open: Easter - Sept: Sat, Sun and BH Mondays 10am - 4pm. Open Tues - Fri in half-term week. Whitsun - Sept: daily except Mondays 10am - 4pm. For group visits contact Mrs M Stennett.
Heritage Open Days: Yes
P Spaces: 30
♿ Partial. Wheelchair and guide dog access to ground floor of mill and site. Disabled WC. Guide Dogs: Yes
£ **Adult:** £1 **Child:** 50p

LONDON

Bruce Castle

Lordship Lane, London N17 8NU
Originally built in the 16th century, altered extensively in the 17th, 18th and 19th centuries. Now a museum with displays about the building and local district, and an archive.
www.brucecastlemuseum.org.uk
Grant Recipient/Owner: London Borough of Haringey
Access contact: Ms Sian Harrington
Tel: 020 8808 8772 **Fax:** 020 8808 4118
Email: museum.services@haringey.gov.uk
Open: Wed - Sun 1 - 5pm plus Easter Mon, May Day, late May BH and Aug BH. Closed Good Fri, Christmas, Boxing and New Year's Day. Groups at other times by arrangement. Archive open by arrangement.
Heritage Open Days: Yes
P Spaces: 15 ♿ Yes. Disabled WC. Guide Dogs: Yes
£ No

Charlton House Gateway

Charlton Road, London SE7 8RE
On the front lawn of Charlton House, the arch (previously known as the Gateway) marks the original front boundary to the House. The House is a Grade I Jacobean mansion, built 1607-1612 by Sir Adam Newton with later additions.
www.greenwich.gov.uk
Grant Recipient/Owner: London Borough of Greenwich
Access contact: Mrs Sue Brown
Tel: 020 8856 3951 **Fax:** 020 8856 4162
Email: sue.brown@greenwich.co.uk
Open: All year: Mon - Fri 9am - 10pm; Sat 10am - 5pm. Closed on Sundays.
Heritage Open Days: No
P Spaces: 25 ♿ Yes. Disabled WC. Guide Dogs: Yes
£ No

College of Arms

Queen Victoria Street, London EC4V 4BT
Built in 1670s/1680s to the design of Francis Sandford and Morris Emmett to house the Heralds' offices, on the site of their earlier building, Derby Place, destroyed in the Great Fire of 1666. The principal room is Earl Marshal's Court which is two floors high with gallery, panelling and throne. New record room added 1842 and portico and terrace in 1867.
www.college-of-arms.gov.uk
Grant Recipient/Owner: College of Arms
Access contact: Officer in Waiting
Tel: 020 7248 2762 **Fax:** 020 7248 6448
Email: enquiries@college-of-arms.gov.uk
Open: Earl Marshal's Court only: all year (except Public Holidays and State and Special Occasions), Mon - Fri 10am - 4pm. Group visits (up to 10) by arrangement with the Officer in Waiting. Group tours of Record Room (up to 20) also by arrangement.
Heritage Open Days: Yes
P No ♿ No. Guide Dogs: Yes £ No

Countess of Derby's Almshouses

Church Hill, Harefield, London UB9 6DU
16th century range, established in 1636 for the poor women in the Parish of Harefield, known as the Countess of Derby Almshouses. Four stacks of paired or tripled diagonal brick chimney stacks. Originally housed six tenants.
Grant Recipient/Owner: Mrs Joyce Willis
Access contact: Mrs Joyce Willis
Tel: 01895 822657
Open: Access to the exterior from the main road, Church Hill, Harefield.
Heritage Open Days: No
P On-street parking. ♿ No £ No

Dissenters' Chapel

Kensal Green Cemetery, Harrow Road, London W10 4RA
Grade II* building within Grade II* cemetery. Cemetery dates from 1832 and is London's oldest. The Chapel was designed in Greek Revival style by John Griffith in 1834. It is now used by the Friends of Kensal Green Cemetery as a headquarters, exhibition space and art gallery.
www.hct.org.uk or www.kensalgreen.co.uk
Grant Recipient/Owner: Historic Chapels Trust
Access contact: Mr Henry Vivian-Neal
Tel: 020 8960 1030
Open: Cemetery: daily; Dissenters' Chapel: w/ends and other times by arrangement. Guided tours of chapels and cemetery for modest charge.
Heritage Open Days: Yes
P Parking in adjacent streets, parking for disabled in cemetery.
♿ Yes. Disabled WC. Guide Dogs: Yes
£ **Adult:** £4 (donation requested for guided tours)

Dulwich College

College Road, Dulwich, London SE21 7LD
Dulwich College founded in 1619; main buildings date from 1866-70 by the younger Charles Barry and listed Grade II*. 3 blocks lined by arcades in ornate Northern Italian

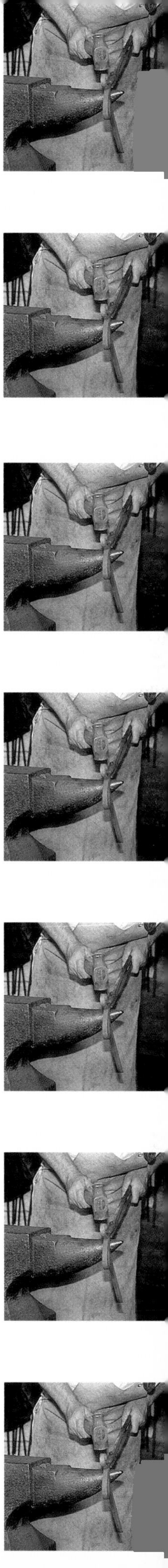

Renaissance style. Close to Dulwich Village.
Grant Recipient/Owner: Dulwich College
Access contact: Ms Julia Field
Tel: 020 8693 3737 **Fax:** 020 8693 6319
Email: skinneraw@dulwich.org.uk
Open: Exterior visible from South Circular. Interior by arrangement with the Bursar.
Heritage Open Days: Yes
P Spaces: 50. Plus 200 spaces during school holidays.
♿ Partial. Wheelchair access with assistance (a few steps at entrance). Disabled WC. Guide Dogs: Yes £ £3

Fulham Palace Stableyard Wall

Bishop's Avenue, London SW6
Home to the Bishops of London for over a thousand years to 1973. The two storey medieval west court is red brick with terracotta roof tiles. The mainly three storey Georgian east court is brown and yellow brick with parapets and slate roofs. Set in riverside gardens.
Grant Recipient/Owner: London Borough of Hammersmith & Fulham
Access contact: Ms Stella Washington
Tel: 020 8753 4960
Email: stella.washington@lbhf.gov.uk
Open: Palace grounds daily all year in daylight hours, admission free. Museum of Fulham Palace: Mar - Oct: Wed - Sun 2 - 5pm; Nov - Feb: Thurs - Sun 1 - 4pm. Tours of principal rooms and gardens every 2nd and 4th Sun.
Heritage Open Days: Yes
P On-street meter parking. Spaces: 50
♿ Partial. Notice required for wheelchair users wishing to visit the ground floor rooms for ramp to be installed. Gardens accessible. Disabled WC. Guide Dogs: Yes
£ Museum **Adult:** £1 **Child/Other:** 50p

Garrick's Temple

Hampton Court Road, Richmond-upon-Thames, London TW12 2EJ
The actor-manager David Garrick built the Temple in 1756 to celebrate the genius of William Shakespeare. Temple was restored 1997-1999 and now houses an exhibition of Garrick's acting career and life at Hampton. Grounds landscaped to echo their original 18th century layout.
www.hampton.online.co.uk
Grant Recipient/Owner: London Borough of Richmond-upon-Thames
Access contact: The Curator
Tel: 020 8892 0221 **Fax:** 020 8744 0501
Email: r.tranter@richmond.gov.uk
Open: Temple: Sundays: first Sun in Apr to last Sun in Sept 2 - 5pm. London Open House w/end Sat and Sun 10am - 5pm. Booked visits for small groups all year. Lawn: All year 7.30am - dusk.
Heritage Open Days: Yes
P No
♿ Partial. Wheelchair access to lawn gardens only. No disabled WC. Guide Dogs: Yes £ No

Great Stanmore Old Church

Church Road, Stanmore, Middlesex HA7 4AQ
Early all red brick church attributed to Nicholas Stone, consecrated in 1632 by William Laud, later Archbishop of Canterbury. Used until partial demolition in 1851. Contains the tombs of the 4th Earl of Aberdeen, Victorian Prime Minister, and the Marquess of Abercorn.
Grant Recipient/Owner: Dr Frederick Hicks
Access contact: Dr Frederick Hicks
Tel: 020 8954 1677
Open: Apr - Sept: Saturdays 2.30 - 4.30pm. At other times by arrangement with Dr Frederick Hicks, 30 Elm Park, Stanmore, Middlesex HA7 4BJ (tel.020 8954 1677).
Heritage Open Days: Yes
P Spaces: 10
♿ Wheelchair access may be difficult as there is some 50 metres of grass from car park to church.
No disabled WC. Guide Dogs: Yes £ No

Gunnersbury Park Temple

Gunnersbury Park, London W3 8LQ
Grade II* temple. Built pre 1760. Red brick with stone Doric portico. Situated in Gunnersbury Park, the estate of Princess Amelia in the 18th century. The 185 acre park became a public park in 1926.
Grant Recipient/Owner: London Borough of Hounslow
Access contact: Buildings Manager
Tel: 020 8992 1612
Open: Park daily 7.30am - dusk. The Temple is used for events all year and is available for hire.
Heritage Open Days: No
P Spaces: 120
♿ Partial. Wheelchair access to the exterior only. Disabled WC. Guide Dogs: Yes £ No

Hackney Empire

291 Mare Street, London E8 1EJ
Hackney Empire, designed and built by Frank Matcham 1901. One of the finest surviving variety theatres in Britain. Now undergoing restoration and renovation, due to reopen autumn 2002, providing modern facilities and access for all.
www.hackneyempire.co.uk
Grant Recipient/Owner: Mr S Thomsett
Access contact: Mr S Thomsett
Tel: 020 8510 4500 **Fax:** 020 8510 4530
Email: info@hackneyempire.co.uk
Open: Sept 2002: Scheduled opening after refurb-ishment. Likely to be partial opening ie. 50% capacity.
Heritage Open Days: Yes
P On-street parking.
♿ Yes. Disabled WC. Guide Dogs: Yes
£ Varies depending on performance. Free tours planned after reopening.

Highgate Cemetery

Swain's Lane, London N6 6PJ
Western, older cemetery, opened 1839, has good examples of Victorian funerary architecture. The Grade I Egyptian Avenue and Circle of Lebanon formed part of the original cemetery layout. Eastern cemetery opened 1854. Some 168,000 persons are buried in the cemetery including many notables. The cemetery is still in use.
Grant Recipient/Owner: Friends of Highgate Cemetery Ltd
Access contact: Mrs J A Pateman
Tel: 020 8340 1834
Open: Western cemetery: Mar - Nov daily tours at 12 noon, 2 & 4pm, w/end tours hourly 11am - 3pm (winter) and 11am - 4pm (summer). Eastern cemetery: daily (unescorted) weekdays 10am - 3.45pm (winter) and 10am - 4.45pm (summer), w/ends always. Both cemeteries closed 25 & 26 Dec, plus during funerals.
Heritage Open Days: No
P Some on-street parking.
♿ Partial. Wheelchair access to Eastern cemetery only. No disabled WC. Guide Dogs: Yes
£ **Adult:** £3 (tour of West, £1 small cameras), £2 (East, £1 small cameras) **Child:** £1 (9-15, tour of West), Free for East but donations welcome

Highpoint

North Hill, Highgate, London N6
Two blocks of flats built in 1935 and 1938 by Lubetkin and Tecton. Constructed of reinforced concrete with decorative features.
Grant Recipient/Owner: Mantra Ltd
Access contact: Mr Stephen Ellman
Tel: 020 7554 5800 **Fax:** 020 7554 5801
Email: smc@grossfine.com
Open: By arrangement with Mr Stephen Ellman of Gross Fine, 14/16 Stephenson Way, London NW1 2HD.
Heritage Open Days: No
P No ♿ No. Guide Dogs: Yes £ No

The House Mill

Three Mill Lane, Bromley-by-Bow, London E3 3DU
Industrial water mill, originally built 1776 as part of a distillery. Contains 4 floors with remains of unrestored machinery, 4 water wheels and gearing. Originally had 12 pairs of millstones and has unique survival of Fairbairn-style "silent millstone machinery".
Grant Recipient/Owner: River Lea Tidal Mill Trust
Access contact: Ms Patricia Wilkinson
Tel: 020 8980 4626
Open: Sun of National Mills Week, Heritage Open Days: & first Sun of each month Apr - Dec: 11am - 4pm. Other Sundays May - Oct: 2 - 4pm. Groups by arrangement with Ms Patricia Wilkinson, 1B Forest Drive East, Leytonstone, London E11 1JX. For further information ring 020 8980 4626. Note future arrangements and admission charges under review.
Heritage Open Days: Yes
P Car park nearby.
♿ Yes. Disabled WC. Guide Dogs: Yes
£ **Adult:** £2 **Child:** Free **Other:** £1

Kew Bridge Steam Museum

Kew Bridge Pumping Station, Green Dragon Lane, Brentford, London TW8 0EN
19th century Victorian waterworks with original steam pumping engines which operate every weekend. "Water for Life" gallery exploring 2000 years of London's water.
www.kbsm.org
Grant Recipient/Owner: Kew Bridge Engines Trust & Water Supply Museum Ltd
Access contact: Kew Bridge Engines Trust & Water Supply Museum Ltd
Tel: 020 8568 4757 **Fax:** 020 8569 9978
Email: info@kbsm.org
Open: Daily 11am - 5pm. Closed Good Fri and the week before Christmas. Note admission prices will increase for 2002, contact Museum for details.
Heritage Open Days: No
P Spaces: 45
♿ Partial. Wheelchair access to 80% of the museum. Two wheelchairs available for use by visitors. Disabled WC. Guide Dogs: Yes
£ See above **Adult:** £4 **Child:** £2 **Other:** £3

Orleans House Gallery

Riverside, Twickenham, London TW1 3DJ
Orleans House Gallery comprises the Octagon Room with its fine Roman baroque interior, and the surviving wing/stable block of the 18th century Orleans House, the rest having been demolished in 1927. Overlooking the Thames and residing in preserved natural woodland, the Gallery presents a programme of temporary exhibitions, organises educational projects/activities and is responsible for the Richmond Borough art collection.
www.richmond.gov.uk
Grant Recipient/Owner: London Borough of Richmond-upon-Thames
Access contact: Ms Rachel Tranter
Tel: 020 8892 0221 **Fax:** 020 8744 0501
Email: r.tranter@richmond.gov.uk
Open: All year: Tues - Sat 1 - 5.30pm; Sundays and BHs 2 - 5.30pm. Oct - Mar: closes 4.30pm. Grounds open daily from 9am until dusk.
Heritage Open Days: Yes
P Spaces: 60
♿ Partial. Wheelchair access to ground floor only. Disabled WC. Guide Dogs: Yes £ No

Paddington Station

Praed Street, London W2 1HA
Railway station for Great Western Railway. Built 1852-4 by Isambard Kingdom Brunel and Sir Matthew Digby Wyatt. Wrought iron arches with decorative work in sections on cast iron bolted on to the ribs. Originally 3 parallel train sheds, with 4th train shed added to the north in the same style in 1914-16. Platform One War Memorial with bronze figure by Charles Sargeant Jagger.
Grant Recipient/Owner: British Railways
Access contact: Station Manager
Tel: 020 7313 0408 **Fax:** 020 7313 1324
Open: During hours of train services. Group tours by arrangement
Heritage Open Days: No
P Pay and display car park at Country end of the Station off Bishops Bridge Road. Spaces: 100
♿ Partial. Wheelchair access to concourse & platforms from street level. Disabled WC. Guide Dogs: Yes
£ No

Pitshanger Manor

Walpole Park, Ealing Green, London W5
Pitshanger Manor is set in Walpole Park, Ealing and was owned and rebuilt by architect and surveyor Sir John Soane (1753-1837). Much of the house has been restored to its early 19th century style and a Victorian wing houses a collection of Martinware Pottery (1877-1923). Pitshanger Manor Gallery opened in 1996 is a 1940s extension and shows a wide range of contemporary art.
www.ealing.gov.uk/pitshanger
Grant Recipient/Owner: London Borough of Ealing
Access contact: Ms Neena Sonal
Tel: 020 8758 5096/020 8567 1227
Fax: 020 8567 0596
Email: pitshanger@ealing.gov.uk
Open: Tues - Sat 11am - 6pm. May - Sept Sun opening 1 - 5pm. Closed BHs, Christmas and Easter.
Heritage Open Days: No
P For orange badge holders. Parking meters. Spaces: 2
♿ Partial. Access for some types of wheelchair only with assistance (domestic lift and some steps), please phone for details. Disabled WC. Guide Dogs: Yes £ No

Prendergast School Murals

Hilly Fields, Adelaide Avenue, London SE4 1LE
Painted in the school hall in the 1930s by students of the Royal College of Art, the murals depict classical tales and incorporate local features.
Grant Recipient/Owner: Governors of Prendergast School
Access contact: Miss E Pienaar
Tel: 020 8690 3710 **Fax:** 020 8690 3155
Email: ericapienaar@yahoo.com
Open: By written arrangement during school hours in term-time.
Heritage Open Days: Yes
P No ♿ Yes. No disabled WC. Guide Dogs: Yes
£ No

The Queen's Chapel of the Savoy

Savoy Hill, Strand, London WC2R 0DA
Originally part of hospital founded 1512 by Henry VII. Rebuilt by Robert Smirke after fire (1864), from which time the ceiling, covered with heraldic emblems, dates. Recently restored.
Grant Recipient/Owner: Duchy of Lancaster
Access contact: John Robson
Tel: 020 7836 7221 **Fax:** 020 7379 8088
Open: All year except Aug and Sept: Tues - Fri 10.30am - 3.30pm; Sundays for Morning Service only. Closed week after Christmas Day and the week after Easter Day.
Heritage Open Days: No
P Parking on meters in adjoining streets.
♿ No. Guide Dogs: Yes £ No

Richmond Theatre

The Green, Richmond-upon-Thames, London TW9 1QJ
A Frank Matcham designed theatre, 1899, with original moulding restored in 1989. Seating 840 on 3 levels with

3 licensed bars, new toilets and air conditioning.
www.theambassadors.com/richmond
Grant Recipient/Owner: Ms Sally Green
Access contact: Ms Karin Gartzke
Tel: 020 8940 0220 **Fax:** 020 8948 3601
Email: richmondtheatre@theambassadors.com
Open: Foyer Mon - Sat 10am - 8pm for theatre bookings. 10am - 6pm for public access to the building by arrangement. Public access for 46 performing weeks in year: 2 afternoons per week (Wed, Sat), 6 evenings per week (Mon-Sat).
Heritage Open Days: No
P Paid parking to 6.30pm, then free. Parking for disabled in front of Theatre, 3-5 spaces. Spaces: 400
♿ Partial. Wheelchair access to stalls, stalls bar and an adapted toilet. Disabled WC. Guide Dogs: Yes
£ Admission charge for performances

Richmond Weir & Lock

Riverside, Richmond-upon-Thames, London
The lock and weir are important examples in the history of hydraulic engineering. Constructed in 1894 to control river levels between Richmond and Teddington at half-tide level, the weir was engineered to ensure that the river remained navigable at all times. Operated and maintained by the Port of London Authority since its establishment in 1909, the machinery was designed and built by Ransomes & Rapier.
Grant Recipient/Owner: Port of London Authority
Access contact: Mr James Trimmer
Tel: 020 7743 7900 **Fax:** 020 7743 7998
Email: james.trimmer@pola.co.uk
Open: Lock and weir at all times for passage by river except for 3 weeks Nov/Dec for major maintenance by the Port of London Authority. Footbridge over lock is currently open at all times but this is under review due to sustained vandalism. Other works/facilities open as part of London Open House w/end.
Heritage Open Days: Yes
P On-street parking. Please note this area is liable to flooding at high spring tides. Spaces: 50 ♿ No £ No

The Round Chapel

(Clapton Park United Reformed Church), 1d Glenarm Road, London E5 0LY
Grade II* United Reformed Church, 1871. Horseshoe-shaped plan with roof and gallery supported by iron pillars. Detailed columns form a continuous iron arcade at roof level with latticework effects. Contemporary pulpit with double flight of stairs, organ and organ case.
Grant Recipient/Owner: Mr Patrick Hammill
Access contact: Mr Patrick Hammill
Tel: 020 7249 0834
Open: Available for public to hire for private events, otherwise by arrangement with The Round Chapel (Mon - Fri 10am - 2pm, tel. 020 8986 0029, email. roundchapel@pop3.poptel.org.uk)
Heritage Open Days: Yes
P Spaces: 3
♿ Partial. Wheelchair access to ground floor only. Disabled WC. Guide Dogs: Yes £ No

The Roundhouse

Chalk Farm Road, London NW1 8EH
The Roundhouse is a Grade II* engine maintenance and turning shed built in 1846 for the London and North Western railway. By the 1860s engines had become too long to be turned and stored there so it was leased to W&A Gilbey Ltd as a liquor store until its conversion into a theatre in the 1960s.
www.roundhouse.org.uk
Grant Recipient/Owner: The Roundhouse Trust
Access contact: The Roundhouse Trust
Tel: 020 7424 9991 **Fax:** 020 7424 9992
Email: info@roundhouse.org.uk
Open: Open day with free tours of the building to be arranged for 2002, contact The Roundhouse for further information.
Heritage Open Days: No
P Adjacent parking for disabled visitors only.
♿ Partial. Wheelchair access to undercroft and main floor. Disabled WC. Guide Dogs: Yes
£ No, but charges for performances vary

Royal Geographical Society

(with the Institute of British Geographers), Lowther Lodge, 1 Kensington Gore, London SW7 2AR
Norman Shaw building in the Queen Anne style, built in the 1870s as a private house with a 2 acre garden for the Lowthers. Owned by the Royal Geographical Society since 1912 and houses a large collection of geographical material, which comprises archives, books, maps and pictures, dating from the 15th century to the present day. The Lecture Theatre extension was built in 1930 in order to mark the Society's centenary and has been refurbished in 2001 and renamed the Ondaatje Theatre.
www.rgs.org
Grant Recipient/Owner: Royal Geographical Society
Access contact: Ms Denise Prior
Tel: 020 7591 3090 **Fax:** 020 7591 3091
Email: d.prior@rgs.org
Open: Weekdays (except BHs) 9.30am - 5.30pm. Closed between Christmas and New Year. Use of collections, library, map room and picture library by arrangement only: Mon - Fri 11am - 5pm; archives Thursdays and Fridays 11am - 5pm. Charges for use of collections.
Heritage Open Days: No
P Space subject to availability and by arrangement with the House Manager. Spaces: 1
♿ Partial. Wheelchair access to all areas except Council Room and Ondaatje Theatre balcony. Disabled WC. Guide Dogs: Yes £ No

The Royal Institution of Great Britain

21 Albemarle Street, London W1X 4BS
Houses the Michael Faraday Museum and a 200 year old lecture theatre. Regular public lectures on scientific themes.
www.ri.ac.uk
Grant Recipient/Owner: Royal Institution of Great Britain
Access contact: Mr Alan Winter
Tel: 020 7409 2992 **Fax:** 020 2670 2920
Email: alanw@ri.ac.uk
Open: Mon - Fri 9am - 5pm. Public lectures/events on various days of the week, usually starting at 6.30pm or 7.30pm. Lecture lists published on RI website (www.ri.ac.uk). Entry charge for Faraday Museum only.
Heritage Open Days: Yes
P No ♿ Yes. Disabled WC. Guide Dogs: Yes
£ **Adult:** £1 (museum), £5 (lecture). **Child:** £1 (museum), £3 (lecture), Schools free

St Alban

(now the Landmark Arts Centre), Ferry Road, Teddington, Middlesex TW11 9NN
Grade II* church, 1889, in French-Gothic style by architect William Niven. Flying buttresses to nave never fully completed. Redundant as a church in 1977. Following renovation now used as an Arts Centre with a variety of arts events, classes and private events.
www.landmarkartscentre.org
Grant Recipient/Owner: London Diocesan Fund
Access contact: Mr Graham Watson
Tel: 020 8614 8036 **Fax:** 020 8614 8080
Open: Normally Mon - Fri 10am - 5pm (shorter hours at w/ends when public events are held), visitors advised to contact Zoe Lovell at the Landmark Arts Centre (tel. 020 8977 7558, fax. 020 8977 4830, email. landmarkinfo@ash.com) to check. Other times by arrangement with Zoe Lovell, subject to staff availability. Admission charges for some public events.
Heritage Open Days: Yes
P Additional on-street parking nearby. Spaces: 4
♿ Wheelchair access to all areas except toilets. No disabled WC at time of publication but planned for late-2002, funds permitting. Guide Dogs: Yes
£ No

St Matthias Old Church

113 Poplar High Street, Poplar, London E14 0AE
Built 1650-54 by the East India Company, St Matthias Old Church is the oldest building in Docklands. Declared redundant in 1977, the building became derelict. In 1990 the building was restored and is now used as a community arts/cultural centre.
Grant Recipient/Owner: London Diocesan Fund
Access contact: Mrs Kathleen Haley
Tel: 020 7987 0459 **Fax:** 020 7531 9973
Open: Mon: 11am - 1pm.
Heritage Open Days: Yes
P No ♿ Yes. Disabled WC. Guide Dogs: Yes £ No

St Pancras Chambers

Euston Road, London NW1 2QR
Grade I Gothic-style building fronting St Pancras Station. Built as Midland Grand Hotel 1868 - 1876 to designs by Sir George Gilbert Scott. Key features are its impressive grand gothic façade and sweeping 'fairytale' staircase.
www.lcrproperties.co.uk
Grant Recipient/Owner: British Railways Board/ London & Continental Stations & Property Ltd
Access contact: Ms Anne Evans
Tel: 020 7304 3927 **Fax:** 020 7304 3901
Email: aevans@lcsp.co.uk
Open: Front entrance and former ground floor coffee lounge generally open each weekday 11.30am - 3.30pm free (except during filming and events). Tel. for information on guided tours of remainder of the building.. Tours (min 15, max 25) conducted by experienced guides with a unique understanding of the building and its history. Note tours involve climbing several flights of stairs and that there are no working lifts or other facilities for disabled visitors.
Heritage Open Days: No
P No ♿ No
£ **Adult:** £9 **Child:** Free (if accompanied by a paying adult)

Salisbury House

Bury Street, West Edmonton, London N9
Late 16th or early 17th century, timber-framed with modern 2-storey addition. The main features are the original painted panelling, beams and fresco fireplace.
Grant Recipient/Owner: Mr John McDonagh
Access contact: Ms Madelaine Wright
Tel: 020 8360 7779 **Fax:** 020 8360 7779
Open: For courses all year. Open House w/end in Apr (contact Ms Madelaine Wright for details). W/end of Sept Heritage open days: Sat and Sun 10am - 4pm.
Heritage Open Days: Yes
P Available. ♿ No £ No

Victoria Embankment Gardens

Whitehall Court, Westminster, London
Part of Victoria Embankment Gardens which run along the side of the Embankment from Westminster to Temple tube. The gardens are formal and have a wide range of monuments. The Whitehall section has been restored to the original design and retains many original trees and specimens of note.
Grant Recipient/Owner: Westminster City Council
Access contact: Mr Colin Buttery
Tel: 020 7641 2693 **Fax:** 020 7641 2959
Email: cbuttery@westminster.gov.uk
Open: Daily from 7.30am - dusk throughout the year.
Heritage Open Days: No
P Limited on-street parking at meters.
♿ Yes. Disabled WC. Guide Dogs: Yes £ No

Walpole's House

St Mary's College, Strawberry Hill, Waldegrave Road, Twickenham, London TW1 4SX
Bought by Horace Walpole 1749 and over the next half century converted into his vision of a 'gothic' fantasy with 14 rooms open to the public containing chimneypieces based on medieval tombs and collection of 16th century painted glass roundels. Reputedly the first substantial building of the Gothic Revival.
Grant Recipient/Owner: St Mary's, Strawberry Hill
Access contact: Conference Officer
Tel: 020 8240 4114/4044 **Fax:** 020 8255 6174
Email: rodrigum@smuc.ac.uk
Open: Easter - mid-Oct: Sun 2 - 3.30pm. Booked guided group tours (min 10 people) any day except Sat.
Heritage Open Days: Yes
P Spaces: 60
♿ Partial. Wheelchair access to ground floor and grounds with difficulty - doorways are small. Disabled WC. Guide Dogs: Yes
£ **Adult:** £5 **Other:** £4.20

Wapping Hydraulic Power Pumping Station

Wapping Wall, London E1W 3ST
Wapping Hydraulic Power Station was built by the London Hydraulic Power Company in 1890. One of the five London Stations of its kind, it harnessed Thames water to provide power throughout the central London area. The showcase building of the LHPC, it was used as a model for power stations in Argentina, Australia, New York and Europe.
www.wapping-wpt.com
Grant Recipient/Owner: Women's Playhouse Trust
Access contact: Women's Playhouse Trust
Tel: 020 7680 2080 **Fax:** 020 7680 2081
Email: info@wapping-wpt.com
Open: Mon - Fri: 12.00 noon - Midnight. Sat 10am - Midnight, Sun 10.00am - 6pm. All year, except Christmas and New Year BHs.
Heritage Open Days: No
P Spaces: 30 ♿ Yes. Disabled WC. Guide Dogs: Yes
£ No

MERSEYSIDE

Bluecoat Chambers

School Lane, Liverpool, Merseyside L1 3BX
Queen Anne building dated 1716 housing contemporary art gallery, café bar, crafts centre and shops. Reputedly the oldest arts centre in the country.
Grant Recipient/Owner: Bluecoat Arts Centre Ltd
Access contact: Mr A Hurley
Tel: 0151 709 5297 **Fax:** 0151 707 0048
Email: admin@bluecoatartscentre.com.uk
Open: All year (except Sundays and BHs) Mon - Sat 9am - 5.30pm.
Heritage Open Days: No
P No
♿ Partial. Wheelchair access to ground floor only. Disabled WC. Guide Dogs: Yes £ No

Broughton Hall Conservatory

Convent of Mercy, Yew Tree Lane, West Derby, Liverpool, Merseyside L12 9HH
Victorian conservatory of rectangular shape with entrance porch at one end and access bay to main building, at the other. The cast iron structure is mounted on a stone plinth. The elevations are divided into a series of panels with decorated cast iron circular columns. From the capitols spring semi-circular arches. These form the bases of the frieze moulding which runs round the periphery of the building. Quarry tiles flooring.
Grant Recipient/Owner: The Institute of Our Lady of Mercy

Access contact: Sister Superior
Tel: 0151 228 9232 **Fax:** 0151 259 0677
Open: By written arrangement only, Mon - Sat 10am - 4pm. No access on Sundays or BHs.
Heritage Open Days: No
P Spaces: 4 ♿ Yes. Disabled WC. Guide Dogs: Yes
£ No

Ince Blundell Hall & Garden Temple

Hightown, Liverpool, Merseyside L38 6JN
New Hall built c1720-50 with 19th century additions. Brick with stone dressings in nine bays with central Corinthian pilasters and demi-columns. Domed Pantheon added 1802. Rococo stucco ceiling in Drawing Room c1750 and Dining Room decoration by Crace. Garden Temple c1780 by William Everard of Liverpool with Tuscan columns and antique reliefs.
Grant Recipient/Owner: Augustinian Nursing Sisters of the Mercy of Jesus
Access contact: Augustinian Nursing Sisters of the Mercy of Jesus
Tel: 0151 929 2596 **Fax:** 0151 929 2188
Open: By telephone or written arrangement with the Augustinian Sisters.
Heritage Open Days: Yes
P Spaces: 10 ♿ No £ No

Liverpool Collegiate Apartments

Shaw Street, Liverpool, Merseyside L6
Grade II* former school built 1843 of red sandstone in Tudor Gothic style, gutted by fire and now converted into residential block.
www.urbansplash.co.uk
Grant Recipient/Owner: Mr Bill Maynard
Access contact: Mr Bill Maynard
Tel: 0151 707 1493 **Fax:** 0151 708 0479
Email: design@urbansplash.co.uk
Open: Exterior only, visible from Shaw Street.
Heritage Open Days: No
P No ♿ No £ No

Sefton Park

Liverpool, Merseyside L18 3JD
108 hectare public park, designed in 1867, the first to introduce French influence to parks design through designer Edouard André who had worked on the design of major Parisian parks. Sefton Park is Grade II* registered and contains several listed statues and other features. The Grade II* Palm House, 1896 by Mackenzie and Moncur, is an octagonal iron frame structure which appears as 3 domed roofs, one above the other.
www.palmhouse.org.uk
Grant Recipient/Owner: Liverpool City Council
Access contact: Ms Elizabeth-Anne Williams
Tel: 0151 726 9304 **Fax:** 0151 726 2419
Email: info@palmhouse.org.uk
Open: Park at all times. Palm House: Jan - 31 Mar: Mon - Sun 10.30am - 4pm, may be closed Tues and Thurs for events; 1 Apr - 31 Dec: Mon - Sat 10.30am - 5pm, Sun 10.30am - 4pm, may be closed Tues and Thurs from 4pm for events. The Trust reserves the right to shut the Palm House on other occasions and will endeavour to give as much notice as possible on the website and information line (tel.0151 726 2415).
Heritage Open Days: No
P On-street parking available on edge of park.
♿ Yes. No disabled WC. Guide Dogs: Yes £ No

Speke Hall

The Walk, Liverpool, Merseyside L24 1XD
One of the most important timber framed manor houses in the country, dating from 1490. The interior spans many periods: the Great Hall and priest holes evoke Tudor times, the Oak Parlour and smaller rooms, some with William Morris wallpapers, show the Victorian desire for privacy and comfort. There is some Jacobean plasterwork and intricately carved furniture. Restored garden and woodland walks.
www.nationaltrust.org.uk
Grant Recipient/Owner: The National Trust
Access contact: Simon Osborne
Tel: 0151 427 7231 **Fax:** 0151 427 9860
Open: House: 23 Mar - end Oct: Wed - Sun (open Bank Holidays); Nov and Dec: Sat and Sun only. Times: Mar - mid Oct 1 - 5.30pm; mid Oct - Dec 1 - 4.30pm. Woodland and garden: daily all year except Mondays (open BHs), closed 24-26 and 31 Dec, 1 Jan. Times: Mar - mid Oct 11am - 5.30pm; mid Oct - end Mar 2002 11am - 4pm.
Heritage Open Days: No
P Car park 500 yards from property. Courtsey shuttle service available. Spaces: 400
♿ Partial. Wheelchair access to ground floor of house. Disabled WC. Guide Dogs: Yes
£ **Adult:** £5 **Child:** £3

NORFOLK

All Saints

Rackheath, Norwich, Norfolk NR13
Early 14th century church with quatrefoil clerestory windows. Internal arcading with several interesting memorials. Stands alone separate from habitation.
Grant Recipient/Owner: Norfolk Churches Trust
Access contact: Mr Malcolm Fisher
Tel: 01603 767576
Open: At all reasonable times.
Heritage Open Days: Yes
P Spaces: 4 ♿ No £ No

All Saints Ruins

Oxwick, Colkirk, nr. Fakenham, Norfolk
Ruins of a pre-Reformation church which has changed in shape over the centuries. Most of the walls remain at full height though little else remains. The Ruin stands in a wooded churchyard.
Grant Recipient/Owner: Colkirk Parochial Church Council
Access contact: Reverend Paul Inman
Tel: 01328 863890
Open: Always open for pedestrian access. No locked gates or doors.
Heritage Open Days: No
P On-street parking. Spaces: 6
♿ No. Guide Dogs: Yes £ No

Billingford Cornmill

Scole, Norfolk IP21 4HL
Built in 1860. One pair of stones have been repaired to full working order and are run occasionally.
www.norfolkwindmills.co.uk
Grant Recipient/Owner: Norfolk Windmills Trust
Access contact: Mrs A L Rix
Tel: 01603 222708 **Fax:** 01603 224413
Email: amanda.jaques.pt@norfolk.gov.uk
Open: Sat and Sun: 11am - dusk; Weds and Thurs 11am - 5pm, Mon, Tues and Fri by arrangement with Mrs Linda Joslin, The Old Post Office, Lower Street, Billingford, Diss, Norfolk, 1T21 4HL (tel. 01379 740743).
Heritage Open Days: No
P Spaces: 2 ♿ No
£ **Adult:** £1.50 (£2 on milling days) **Child:** 75p

The Deanery

56 The Close, Norwich, Norfolk NR1 4EG
13th century with later additions, originally the Prior's lodgings. It remains the residence of the Dean of Norwich. The interior is closed to the public.
www.cathedral.org.uk
Grant Recipient/Owner: The Dean & Chapter of Norwich Cathedral
Access contact: Mr Tim Cawkwell
Tel: 01603 218300 **Fax:** 01603 766032
Email: steward@cathedral.org.uk
Open: Exterior visible from The Close which is open to visitors during daylight hours throughout the year.
Heritage Open Days: No
P No ♿ Yes. No disabled WC. Guide Dogs: No
£ No

Denver Windmill

Sluice Road, Denver, Downham Market, Norfolk PE38 0EG
Working windmill on edge of the fens, built in 1835 and recently restored.
www.denvermill.co.uk
Grant Recipient/Owner: The Norfolk Windmills Trust
Access contact: Mr Richard Townsley
Tel: 01366 384009 **Fax:** 01366 384009
Open: 1 Apr - end of Oct: Mon - Sat 10am - 5pm, Sun 12 - 5pm; 1 Nov - end of Mar: Mon - Sat 10am - 4pm, Sun 12 - 4pm.
Heritage Open Days: No
P Spaces: 50
♿ Partial. Wheelchair access to ground floor only, there is a video of mill in the new visitor facilities, accessible to wheelchair users. Disabled WC. Guide Dogs: Yes
£ **Adult:** £2.75 **Child:** £1.50 **Other:** £2.50 **Family:** £7

Dragon Hall

115-123 King Street, Norwich, Norfolk NR1 1QE
Medieval timber-framed merchant's hall. The 15th century great hall has a crown post roof with an intricately carved and painted dragon.
www.http://freespace.virgin.net/dragon.hall/index.htm
Grant Recipient/Owner: Norfolk & Norwich Heritage Trust
Access contact: Mr Neil Sigsworth
Tel: 01603 663922 **Fax:** 01603 663922
Email: dragon.hall@virgin.net
Open: 1 Nov - 31 Mar: Mon - Fri 10am - 4pm; 1 Apr - 31 Oct: Mon - Sat 10am - 4pm; closed BHs and 22 Dec - New Year's Day.
Heritage Open Days: Yes
P Spaces: 6
♿ Partial. Wheelchair access to Great Hall, ground floor rooms but not cellars. No disabled WC. Guide Dogs: Yes
£ **Adult:** £2.50 **Child:** £1 **Other:** £2

Felbrigg Hall

Felbrigg, Norwich, Norfolk NR11 8PR
17th century house containing its original 18th century furniture and paintings. The walled garden has been restored and features a working dovecote, small orchard and the national collection of Colchicum. The park is renowned for its fine and aged trees.
www.nationaltrust.org.uk/eastanglia
Grant Recipient/Owner: The National Trust
Access contact: Property Manager
Tel: 01263 837444 **Fax:** 01263 837032
Email: atgusr@smtp.ntrust.org.uk
Open: House: 23 Mar to 3 Nov: daily except Thurs and Fri. 1 - 5pm, BH Sun and BH Mondays 11am - 5pm. House closes 4pm on and after 27 Oct. Garden: 23 Mar to 3 Nov: daily except Thurs and Fri. Times: 11am to 5.30pm. Estate walks: daily, dawn to dusk.
Heritage Open Days: No
P Charges apply. NT members free. Visitors with disabilities may be set down at Visitor Reception by arrangement. Spaces: 200
♿ Partial. Wheelchair access to ground floor, photograph album of first floor. Garden, shop and bookshop (ramp), tea room and restaurant accessible. Disabled WC. Guide Dogs: Yes
£ **Adult:** £5.90 **Child:** £2.90 **Other:** £14.70 (family), £2.30 (gardens only)

Hales Hall Barn

Loddon, Norfolk NR14 6QW
Late 15th century brick and thatch barn 180ft long, built by James Hobart, Henry VII's Attorney General. Queen post roof, and crown post roof to living accommodation, and richly patterned brickwork. The Barn and similar sized gatehouse, ranged around defended courtyards, are all that remains of the house that stood on this site.
Grant Recipient/Owner: Mr & Mrs Terence Read
Access contact: Mr & Mrs Terence Read
Tel: 01508 548395 **Fax:** 01508 548040
Open: All year: Tues - Sat 10am - 5pm (dusk if earlier); plus Easter - Oct: Sun afternoons and BH Mons 11am - 4pm. Closed 25 Dec - 5 Jan and Good Fri. Garden with yew and box topiary included in admission charge. Parties and guided tours by arrangement with Mr or Mrs Terence Read.
Heritage Open Days: No
P Spaces: 40
♿ Yes. No disabled WC. Guide Dogs: Yes
£ **Adult:** £1.50 **Child:** Free **Other:** £1.50, £2.50 (guided tours by arrangement)

King's Lynn Custom House

Purfleet Quay, King's Lynn, Norfolk PE30 1HP
Built 1683 as a merchants exchange, became official Custom House in 1703. Building purchased by the Crown 1717 for £800 and used by HM Customs until 1989. The Borough Council of King's Lynn and West Norfolk obtained a lease of the building in 1995 and restored it.
Grant Recipient/Owner: King's Lynn & West Norfolk Council
Access contact: Mr Tim Hall
Tel: 01553 774297 **Fax:** 01553 772361
Email: gaolhouse@west-norfolk.gov.uk
Open: Easter - end Oct: Mon - Sat 9.15am - 5pm, Sun 10am - 4pm; Nov - Mar: daily 10.30am - 4pm.
Heritage Open Days: Yes
P Parking in public car parks.
♿ Partial. Wheelchair access to ground floor only. No disabled WC. Guide Dogs: Yes £ No

Old Buckenham Cornmill

Green Lane, Old Buckenham, Norfolk NR17
Mill with the largest diameter tower in England, which had five sets of stones when it was working. Once owned by the Colmans of Norwich and Prince Duleep Singh. Built by John Burlingham in 1818.
www.norfolkwindmills.co.uk
Grant Recipient/Owner: Norfolk Windmills Trust
Access contact: Mrs A L Rix
Tel: 01603 222708 **Fax:** 01603 224413
Email: amanda.jaques.pt@norfolk.gov.uk
Open: Apr - Sept: second Sun of each month 2 - 5pm. Groups at other times by arrangement with Mrs A L Rix, Conservation Officer, Building Conservation Section, Dept of Planning & Transportation, Norfolk County Council, County Hall, Martineau Lane, Norwich, Norfolk NR1 2SG.
Heritage Open Days: No
P Spaces: 6 ♿ No £ **Adult:** 70p **Child:** 30p

Old Hall

Norwich Road, South Burlingham, Norfolk NR13 4EY
Small Elizabethan manor house with a painted stucco fireplace, painted stucco mermaids and scrollwork on the front porch, and a long gallery of hunting scenes in grisaille, c1600.
Grant Recipient/Owner: Mr P Scupham
Access contact: Mr P Scupham
Tel: 01493 750804 **Fax:** 01493 750804
Email: goodman@dircon.co.uk
Open: By telephone arrangement with Mr P Scupham or Ms M E Steward. No access for guide dogs to the Long Gallery.
Heritage Open Days: Yes
P Spaces: 8
♿ Partial. Wheelchair access to ground floor and garden. Painted gallery inaccessible. No disabled WC. Guide Dogs: Yes
£ No

Old Meeting House/Congregational Church

Colegate, Norwich, Norfolk NR3 1BW

Built 1693 in brick with classical dressings and black glazed pantile roof. Unusual sun dial with date of building on front elevation, which is a feature of Free Church buildings. Contains tiered pews to a gallery on three sides and an organ in working order dating from 1650. External paving mirrors the Dutch influence.

Grant Recipient/Owner: Norwich City Council
Access contact: Mr G F D Eve
Tel: 01603 212343 **Fax:** 01603 212345
Email: property@norwich.gov.uk
Open: Apr - Sept: Weds 12.30 - 4pm. Other times by arrangement with Mr G F D Eve, Property Services, St Giles House, St Giles Street, Norwich NR2 1UZ.
Heritage Open Days: Yes
P Spaces: 2
♿ Partial. Wheelchair access to ground floor only. Disabled WC. Guide Dogs: Yes £ No

Oulton Congregational Chapel

Hall Road, Oulton, Norfolk NR11 6NU

Early 18th century non-conformist chapel, Grade II*. Symmetrical plan with two entrance lobbies, each with staircase leading to gallery supported on wooden Doric and slender iron columns.

Grant Recipient/Owner: Norfolk Historic Buildings Trust
Access contact: Norfolk Historic Buildings Trust
Tel: 01603 222705 **Fax:** 01603 224413
Open: Arrangements under review at time of going to print, check the English Heritage website or with the Norfolk Historic Buildings Trust (tel.01603 222705/Trust Office tel.01603 629048) for current information. May be hired for private events.
Heritage Open Days: No
P Spaces: 30
♿ Partial. Wheelchair access to ground floor of Chapel only with assistance (a few steps at entrance). Disabled WC. Guide Dogs: Yes £ No

Oxburgh Hall

Oxborough, King's Lynn, Norfolk PE33 9PS

Moated manor house with tudor gatehouse, was built in 1482 by the Bedingfeld family who still live there. The rooms show the development from medieval austerity to Victorian comfort, and include a display of embroidery done by Mary, Queen of Scots and Bess of Hardwick. Gardens include a French Parterre and woodland walks, as well as a Catholic chapel.

www.nationaltrust.org.uk/eastanglia
Grant Recipient/Owner: The National Trust
Access contact: Property Manager
Tel: 01366 328258 **Fax:** 01366 328066
Email: aohusr@smtp.ntrust.org.uk
Open: House: 23 Mar - 3 Nov: daily except Thurs and Fri. Times: 1 - 5pm, BHs 11am - 5pm (last adm. 4.30pm). Garden: 2 - 17 Mar: Sats and Suns; 23 Mar - 3 Nov: daily except Thurs and Fri; Aug: daily. Times: Mar 11am - 4pm, 23 Mar - 3 Nov 11am - 5.30pm.
Heritage Open Days: No
P Spaces: 100
♿ Partial. Wheelchair access to 4 ground floor rooms (shallow ramp), difficult stairs to upper floors. Garden largely accessible, restaurant and shop accessible. Disabled WC. Guide Dogs: Yes
£ **Adult:** £5.50 **Child:** £2.80 **Other:** £14.50 (family), £2.80 (garden & estate only)

Ruined Church of St Mary the Virgin

Houghton-on-the-Hill, Norfolk PE37 8DP

Ancient church at least 900 years old. Many original features remain including double splay windows, keyhole chancel, arch built with Roman brick, 12th century North door and early wall paintings. All areas open.

Grant Recipient/Owner: Norfolk County Council
Access contact: R Davey
Tel: 01760 440470
Open: All year at any reasonable time.
Heritage Open Days: Yes
P Spaces: 40
♿ Yes. No disabled WC. Guide Dogs: Yes £ No

Ruined Church of St Peter

Wiggenhall St Peter with Wigge, Norfolk

Former parish church, largely 15th century, now ruined. South aisle was demolished in 1840.

Grant Recipient/Owner: Wiggenhall St Peter PCC
Access contact: Norfolk County Council
Tel: 01603 222706 **Fax:** 01603 224413
Email: caroline.davison.pt@norfolk.gov.uk
Open: At all times.
Heritage Open Days: No
P Spaces: 2 ♿ No £ No

Shotesham Park Dairy Farm Barn

Newton Flotman, Norfolk NR15 1XA

Built c1500 with later additions, part weather-boarded and part-rendered 5-bay timber framed barn with double queen post thatched roof.

Grant Recipient/Owner: Norfolk Historic Buildings Trust/ Mr Christopher Bailey
Access contact: Mr John Nott
Tel: 01508 470113
Open: All year by arrangement with either Mr John Nott (tel.01508 470113) or Mr Christopher Bailey (tel.01508 499285).
Heritage Open Days: No
P The Barn is in a busy farmyard but parking can usually be found (apart from at harvest time) for at least two cars by arrangement. Spaces: 2
♿ Partial. Wheelchair access with assistance, rough surface outside Barn. Disabled WC. Guide Dogs: Yes £ No

St Andrew's Hall

St Andrew's Plain, Norwich, Norfolk NR3 1AU

Remains of medieval friary, including the nave (St Andrew's Hall), choir (Blackfriars Hall), crypt, cloisters, private chapel (Beckets) and chapter house. Hammerbeam roof in nave, medieval bosses in choir and a 15th century 7 light East Window. A civic hall in use since 1540.

www.norwich.gov.uk
Grant Recipient/Owner: Norwich City Council
Access contact: Mr Tim Aldous
Tel: 01603 628477 **Fax:** 01603 762182
Email: timaldous@norwich.gov.uk
Open: Mon - Sat 9am - 5pm. Subject to events.
Heritage Open Days: No
P Multi-storey car park in city centre. Blue Badge on site, Orange Badge if space is available.
♿ Partial. Wheelchair access to ground floor only. Disabled WC. Guide Dogs: Yes £ No

St Lawrence

The Street, South Walsham, Norfolk NR13 6DQ

Former parish church used for worship until c.1890, now redundant. Medieval church destroyed by fire and rebuilt in 1832. Now St Lawrence Centre for Training and the Arts. Access to Sacristans Garden.

Grant Recipient/Owner: South Walsham Parochial Church Council
Access contact: Ms Veronica Dewing
Tel: 01603 270271 **Fax:** 01603 270017
Email: vdewing@freenet.com
Open: Daily 9am - 6pm.
Heritage Open Days: No
P Spaces: 8 ♿ Yes. Disabled WC. Guide Dogs: Yes £ No

St Mary's Abbey

West Dereham, Norfolk

The present six bay house is the remains of the service block of Sir Thomas Dereham's Renaissance-style mansion, which he built after 1689 incorporating the surviving parts of Premonstratensian Abbey founded 1188 by Hubert Walter. Became a ruin and only recently restored, the building re-roofed, re-fenestrated and a first floor and stair tower added. Now a private residence.

Grant Recipient/Owner: Mr G Shropshire
Access contact: Mrs Ann King
Tel: 01353 727200 **Fax:** 01353 727325
Open: By arrangement with Mrs Ann King, G's Marketing Ltd, Barway, Ely, Cambridgeshire CB7 5TZ, Mon-Fri only). Toilet facilities for the disabled are available on request, although they are not specifically designed for such use.
Heritage Open Days: No
P Spaces: 20 ♿ Yes. Disabled WC. Guide Dogs: Yes
£ No

St Mary's Ruins

Saxlingham Thorpe, Norfolk

Ruined church of Saxlingham Thorpe. Dated from 11th to 14th centuries.

Grant Recipient/Owner: Saxlingham Nethergate plc
Access contact: Saxlingham Nethergate Parochial Church Council
Email: blythgj@waitrose.com
Open: At all times.
Heritage Open: Days: No
P Spaces: 6 ♿ No £ No

St Peter

Dunton, Norfolk NR21 7PG

Grade II* redundant medieval church built of flint with stone dressings. Victorian stained glass, rebuilt porch of 1896, 15th century tower, 14th century nave and remains of previous building. Occasionally used for services.

Grant Recipient/Owner: Norfolk Churches Trust
Access contact: Mr Malcolm Fisher
Tel: 01603 767576 **Fax:** 01986 798776
Open: At any reasonable time.
Heritage Open Days: No
P Spaces: 3 ♿ Yes. No disabled WC. Guide Dogs: Yes
£ No

Thornage Hall Dovecote

Thornage, Holt, Norfolk NR25 7QH

Square dovecote, dated 1728, built of red brick in English bond with hipped roof in red black and black glazed pantiles terminating in square wooden glover. Contains 20 tiers of holes on all 4 sides and on brick spokes projecting from each corner toward the centre.

Grant Recipient/Owner: Norfolk Dovecote Trust/ Camphill Communities East Anglia
Access contact: Ms A Gimelli
Tel: 01263 860305
Open: For village fete in July, plus first Sun in Sept, 2 - 5pm. At other times by written arrangement with Ms A Gimelli at Thornage Hall.
Heritage Open Days: No
P Spaces: 50 ♿ No. Guide Dogs: Yes £ No

Waxham Great Barn

Sea Palling, Norfolk NR1 2DH

Grade I listed barn, 1570s-80s, with later additions. Flint with ashlar dressings and thatched roof. Much of its fabric is reused from dissolved monasteries.

Grant Recipient/Owner: Norfolk County Council
Access contact: Caroline Davison
Tel: 01603 222706 **Fax:** 01603 224413
Email: caroline.davison.pt@norfolk.gov.uk
Open: By arrangement with Caroline Davison until building works commence (planned for Apr 2002).
Heritage Open Days: No
P Yes. Free parking. Spaces: 100
♿ Partial. Wheelchair access with assistance (gravel path from car park to Barn). No disabled WC. Guide Dogs: Yes
£ No

NORTH YORKSHIRE

Aiskew Water Cornmill

Bedale, North Yorkshire DL8 1AW

Grade II* watermill, late 18th and early 19th century. Sold in 1918 in a major dispersal of estate properties. Roof and main structure restored. Restoration of interior with original wooden machinery is planned.

Grant Recipient/Owner: David Clark
Access contact: Jared and Duncan Clark
Tel: 01677 422125 **Fax:** 01677 425205
Email: oakwood.ent@btinternet.com
Open: Guided tours by arrangement Apr - Oct. Please note that the condition of the interior floors may make access unsafe but restoration work is planned, telephone Jared or Duncan Clark for further details.
Heritage Open Days: No
P Yes. Free parking. Spaces: 40
♿ Partial. Wheelchair access to middle floor only. No disabled WC. Guide Dogs: Yes but not on farm tour
£ Charge for guided tours when Mill fully restored

Beningbrough Hall

Shipton-by-Beningbrough, North Yorkshire YO30 1DD

Country house, 1716, contains an impressive baroque interior. A very high standard of craftsmanship is displayed throughout, most of the original work surviving with extremely fine woodcarvings and unusual central corridor running the full length of the house. Over 100 pictures on loan from the National Portrait Gallery on display. Fully equipped Victorian laundry and walled garden.

www.nationaltrust.org.uk
Grant Recipient/Owner: The National Trust
Access contact: Property Manager
Tel: 01904 470666 **Fax:** 01904 470002
Email: ybbrgh@smtp.ntrust.org.uk
Open: 23 Mar - 30 June & 1 Sept - 3 Nov: House daily except Thurs & Fri (open Good Fri); July and Aug: daily except Thurs 12 - 5pm (last adm.4.30pm). Grounds open as above 11am - 5.30pm.
Heritage Open Days: No
P Spaces: 250
♿ Partial. Wheelchair access (ramped) to ground floor only. Disabled WC. Guide Dogs: Yes
£ **Adult:** £5.30 (house), £3.60 (garden & exhibition) **Child:** £2.60 (house), £1.80 (garden & exhibition) **Other:** £13 (family, house), £9 (family, garden & exhibition). Discount for cyclists

Braithwaite Hall

East Witton, Leyburn, North Yorkshire DL8 4SY

17th century stone farmhouse with fine original features including fireplaces, panelling and oak staircase.

www.nationaltrust.org.uk
Grant Recipient/Owner: The National Trust
Access contact: Mrs David Duffus
Tel: 01969 640287
Open: By arrangement with tenant, Mrs David Duffus. No WC.
Heritage Open Days: No
P Yes. No access for coaches. Spaces: 10
♿ No. Guide Dogs: Yes £ £1 (including leaflet)

Castle Howard

York, North Yorkshire YO60 7DA

Large stately home dating from the beginning of the 18th century and designed by Sir John Vanbrugh. Situated in 1000 acres of landscaped grounds which includes numerous monuments.

www.castlehoward.co.uk
Grant Recipient/Owner: The Hon. Simon Howard
Access contact: Mr D N Peake

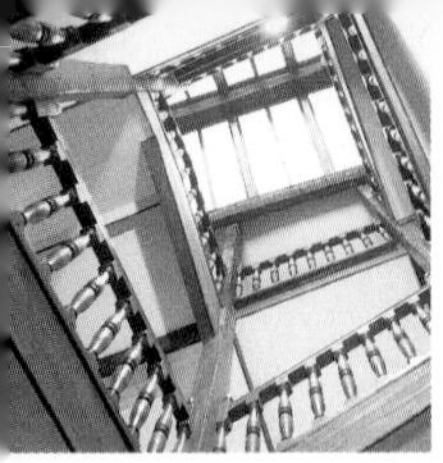

Tel: 01653 648444 **Fax:** 01653 648529
Email: estatemanager@castlehoward.co.uk
Open: 15 Mar - 3 Nov: daily 11am - 4.45pm (Grounds only from 10am); Nov - mid-Mar: grounds open most days but tel. for confirmation in Nov, Dec and Jan.
Heritage Open Days: No
P Spaces: 300
♿ Partial. Wheelchair access to all but chapel and first floor of exhibition wing. Disabled WC. Guide Dogs: Yes
£ **Adult:** £8 **Child:** £5 **Other:** £7

Cawood Castle

nr. Selby, North Yorkshire
This decorated gatehouse, and wing to one side, is all that remains of the castle, once a stronghold of the Archbishops of York. Visitors have included Thomas Wolsey, Henry III, Edward I, and Henry VIII. In the 18th century it was used as a courtroom eventually ending up in domestic use. Extremely steep spiral staircase.
www.landmarktrust.co.uk
Grant Recipient/Owner: The Landmark Trust
Access contact: Ms Victoria Piggott
Tel: 01628 825920 **Fax:** 01628 825417
Email: vpiggott@landmarktrust.co.uk
Open: For details of opening arrangements at Landmark Trust properties please see the entry for Coop House, Netherby, Cumbria (page 549)
Heritage Open Days: No
P Spaces: 1 ♿ No £ No

Duncombe Park

Helmsley, York, North Yorkshire YO62 5EB
Recently restored family home of Lord and Lady Feversham. Originally built in 1713 and rebuilt after a fire in 1879 largely to the original design. Early 18th century gardens.
www.duncombepark.com
Grant Recipient/Owner: Lord Feversham
Access contact: The Agent
Tel: 01439 770213 **Fax:** 01439 771114
Email: sally@duncombepark.com
Open: 28 Apr - 27 Oct, Sun - Thurs: House & Garden 12 noon - 5.30pm (tours on the hour 12.30pm - 3.30pm lasting 1 1/2 hours, last adm. gardens and parkland 4.30pm). Parkland Centre Tearoom, shop & parkland walks 11am - 5.30pm (last orders in tearoom 5.15pm). Special Events all year. Duncome Park reserve the right to alter opening details without notice - tel. to check.
Heritage Open Days: No
P Spaces: 200
♿ Partial. Wheelchair access to ground floor only. Disabled WC. Guide Dogs: Yes
£ **Adult:** £6 (house & gardens), £3 (gardens & parkland), £2 (parkland) **Child:** £3 (10-16, house & garden), £2 (10-16, gardens & parkland), £1 (10-16, parkland) **Other:** £5 (concessions, house & garden), £13.50 (family, house & garden), £4.50 (groups, house & garden), £20.00 (family season ticket)

Farnley Hall

Farnley, Otley, North Yorkshire LS21 2QF
Grade I building, older part of the house (generally referred to as the Manor House) dates from mid-17th century. Jacobeanized in the 1840s, recently renovated and modernised and is now let as a separate assured shorthold. Chief visitor interest lies in the Reception Wing added in 1785, designed and built by John Carr of York. The Carr Wing houses a collection of gouache drawings by J M W Turner depicting the Hall itself and the surrounding countryside. Collections of 18th and early 19th century furniture.
Grant Recipient/Owner: Mr G N Le G Horton-Fawkes
Access contact: Mr Michael Blacknell
Tel: 01943 467905 **Fax:** 01943 463031
Email: farnley.hall@farming.co.uk
Open: May - Aug by written arrangement. Flexible times (visits for mornings or late evenings). Final acceptance confirmed by letter from the Farnley Estate Office.
Heritage Open Days: No
P Spaces: 20
♿ Partial. Some help may be required for wheelchair users at certain points, please check with the Farnley Hall Estate Office. Disabled WC. Guide Dogs: Yes
£ **Adult:** £5

Filey Railway Station

Filey, North Yorkshire
Grade II* railway station, 1846, with later alterations. Red brick with slate roof.
Grant Recipient/Owner: British Rail
Access contact: Mr Barry Casterton
Open: Open as a working station, Mon - Sat 7am - 7pm. Sundays same times until Sept. Underside of roof can be viewed from platforms only, east side elevation viewed from car park. No other viewings on Railtrack property.
Heritage Open Days: No
P Station car park.
♿ Yes. No disabled WC. Guide Dogs: Yes
£ No

Fountains Hall

Studley Royal, Ripon, North Yorkshire HG4 3DY
Elizabethan mansion, built between 1589 and 1604 for Stephen Proctor. Two rooms; the Stone Hall and the Arkell Room, both unfurnished, are open. During summer 2001 a third room, the Great Chamber, was opened to guided tours. This upper room features an ornate chimney piece depicting the Biblical story of the Judgement of Solomon.
www.fountainsabbey.org.uk
Grant Recipient/Owner: The National Trust
Access contact: Sarah Kay
Tel: 01765 608888 **Fax:** 01765 601002
Email: yfnsak@smtp.ntrust.org.uk
Open: As part of Fountain's Abbey and Studley Royal estate. Jan - Mar: 10am - 4pm; Apr - Sept: 10am - 6pm (closed 4pm 12/13 July); Oct - Dec: 10am - 4pm. Estate closed 24, 25 Dec and Fridays in Jan, Nov and Dec.
Heritage Open Days: No
P Spaces: 500 ♿ Yes. Disabled WC. Guide Dogs: Yes
£ **Adult:** £4.80 **Child:** £2.50 **Other:** £12 (family)

Friends Meeting House

off Bolton Road, Addingham, nr. Ilkley, West Yorkshire LS29
Land for burial ground purchased in 1666, followed by construction of Meeting House in 1669. A simple single cell building with rubblestone walls, mullioned windows, stone-slated roof and stone-flagged floor. Contains loose benches and an oak minister's stand of an unusual panelled design with turned balusters.
www.hct.org.uk
Grant Recipient/Owner: Historic Chapels Trust
Access contact: John Spencer
Tel: 01756 710225
Open: At all reasonable times by application to keyholders Mr & Mrs John Spencer, who live opposite the Meeting House at Cook's Cottage, 3 Farfield Cottages, Bolton Road, Addingham, nr. Ilkley, West Yorks LS29 0RQ.
Heritage Open Days: No
P Spaces: 2 ♿ No. Guide Dogs: Yes £ No

Giggleswick School Chapel

Giggleswick, Settle, North Yorkshire BD24 0DE
Built 1897-1901 by T G Jackson for Walter Morrison as a gift to the school to commemorate the Diamond Jubilee of Queen Victoria. Constructed of Gothic Banded rockfaced millstone grit sandstone and limestone, with copper hipped roof to nave and copper covered terracotta dome to chancel. Contains Italian sgrafitto work throughout.
www.giggleswick.n-yorks.sch.uk/chapel
Grant Recipient/Owner: The Governors of Giggleswick School
Access contact: The Bursar and Clerk to the Governors
Tel: 01729 893000/893012 **Fax:** 01729 893150
Email: bursar@giggleswick.n.yorks.sch.uk
Open: Arrangements under review at time of going to print, check the English Heritage website or with the School (tel. 01729 893000 or 01729 893012) for current information.
Heritage Open Days: No
P Spaces: 25 ♿ Partial. No disabled WC. Guide Dogs: Yes
£ No

Hackfall

Grewelthorpe, North Yorkshire
Developed as a wild gothic woodland landscape in the 18th century and remains of a number of man-made features can still be seen. The woodland is known to have existed since at least 1600 and the ground flora is characteristic of ancient woodland. Beech, oak, ash and wild cherry can also be seen together with spindle, an unusual tree found in chalk and limestone. Site is very steep and paths can be narrow and difficult to negotiate.
www.woodland-trust.org.uk
Grant Recipient/Owner: The Woodland Trust
Access contact: Ms Shani Lambert
Tel: 01476 581146 **Fax:** 01476 590808
Email: shanilambert@woodland-trust.org.uk
Open: At all times. For further information contact Shani Lambert or Alistair Nash.
Heritage Open Days: No
P Yes. Parking on opposite side of road. Spaces: 6
♿ No £ No

Jervaulx Abbey

Ripon, Yorkshire HG4 4PH
Ruins of Cistercian Abbey moved to this site in 1156, built of sandstone ashlar in Early English style. Remains of nave, transepts and choir, with a cloister on the south side of the nave, flanked by a chapter house to the east and a kitchen and dorter to the south.
Grant Recipient/Owner: Mr Ian Burdon
Access contact: Mr Ian Burdon
Tel: 01677 460391/01677 460226
Open: At any reasonable time.
Heritage Open Days: No
P Spaces: 55
♿ Partial. Wheelchair access to church, infirmary, frater and cloisters. Uneven terrain and steps on other parts of site. Disabled WC. Guide Dogs: Yes
£ Honesty Box **Adult:** £2 **Child:** £1.50

Kiplin Hall

Scorton, Richmond, North Yorkshire DL10 6AT
Grade I Jacobean house with 19th century additions. Built in 1620 by George Calvert, 1st Lord Baltimore, founder of the State of Maryland, USA. Hall contains fine paintings and furniture collected by four families over four centuries. Recent restoration work has brought the Hall back to life as a comfortable Victorian family home.
www.kiplinhall.co.uk
Grant Recipient/Owner: Kiplin Hall Trust
Access contact: Ms Dawn Webster
Tel: 01748 818178 **Fax:** 01748 818178
Email: kiplinhall@hotmail.com
Open: Easter w/end: daily, 2 - 5pm. 2 May - 29 Sept: Thurs - Sun, 2 - 5pm; BH Mondays, 2 - 5pm. Special events, contact the Hall for further details.
Heritage Open Days: Yes
P Free parking a short walk along drive to Hall, overflow into coach area. Disabled parking adjacent to Hall, 12 spaces.
♿ Partial. Wheelchair access to ground floor and tea room only. No disabled WC. Guide Dogs: Yes
£ **Adult:** £3.50 **Child:** £1.75 **Other:** £2.50

The Mount School Lindley Murray Summerhouse

Dalton Terrace, York, North Yorkshire YO24 4DD
Grade II* summerhouse built c1774, formerly situated in the grounds of Holgate House, York. Octagonal timber structure on raised stepped circular base with lead ogee roof and decorated with Doric columns. Restored 1997.
www.mount.n-yorks.sch.uk
Grant Recipient/Owner: The Mount School
Access contact: Ms Anne Bolton
Tel: 01904 667506 **Fax:** 01904 667524
Email: bursar@themount.fsbusiness.co.uk
Open: By arrangement Mon - Fri all year (except BHs) 9am - 4.30pm.
Heritage Open Days: No
P Spaces: 3 ♿ Yes. Disabled WC. Guide Dogs: Yes
£ No but donations welcome

Newburgh Priory

Coxwold, York, North Yorkshire YO6 4AS
Priory originally built in 1145 with alterations in Tudor, Jacobean and Georgian periods. Tomb of Oliver Cromwell in the House, extensive grounds, walled garden and walks with views across the lake to the White Horse. Tea rooms.
Grant Recipient/Owner: Sir George Wombwell Bt
Access contact: Sir George Wombwell Bt
Tel: 01347 868372
Open: Apr, May and June: Weds and Sun, Easter Sun and BH Mon and May BH Mondays. Guided tours only every 30 mins from 2.30pm, last tour 4.30pm. Grounds: 2 - 6pm. Coach groups and groups by arrangement.
Heritage Open Days: No
P Spaces: 200
♿ Partial. Wheelchair access to ground floor of house and parts of garden. No disabled WC. Guide Dogs: Yes
£ **Adult:** £2.50 (house) £2 (grounds) **Child:** £1.50 (house) Free (grounds)

Norton Conyers Hall

nr. Ripon, North Yorkshire HG4 5EQ
Medieval house with Stuart and Georgian additions. 18th century walled garden nearby. Family pictures, furniture and costumes. Visited by Charlotte Bronte in 1839, a family legend of a mad woman confined in an attic room inspired the mad Mrs Rochester in *'Jane Eyre'* and the Hall was the model for *'Thornfield Hall'*.
Grant Recipient/Owner: Sir James Graham Bt
Access contact: Sir James Graham Bt
Tel: 01765 640333 **Fax:** 01765 640333
Email: norton.conyers@ripon.org
Open: House & Garden: Easter Sun & Mon, BHs (inc. Jubilee BH, Tues 4 June) & Sun 19 May - 1 Sept; 8 - 13 July daily. House: 2 - 5pm (last adm. 4.40pm). Garden: 12 noon - 5pm. Garden also open on Thurs all year 10am - 4pm but please check beforehand.
Heritage Open Days: No
P Spaces: 60
♿ Partial. Wheelchair access to ground floor of house only. Some gravelled paths in garden may be difficult. Disabled WC. Guide Dogs: Yes
£ **Adult:** £4 **Child:** £3 (10-16, reduced rate for 2 or more children) **Senior Citizens:** £3 Admission to garden only is free but donations are welcome; a charge is made when the garden is open for charity.

Ormesby Hall

Church Lane, Ormesby, Middlesbrough TS7 9AS
A mid-18th century Palladian mansion, notable for fine plasterwork and carved wood decoration. The Victorian laundry and kitchen with scullery and game larder are interesting. 18th century stable block, attributed to Carr of York, is leased to the Cleveland Mounted Police. Large model railway and garden with holly walk.
www.nationaltrust.org.uk
Grant Recipient/Owner: The National Trust

Access contact: Property Manager
Tel: 01642 324188 **Fax:** 01642 300937
Email: yorkor@smtp.ntrust.org.uk
Open: 23 Mar - 3 Nov: daily except Mon, Fri and Sat (but open Good Fri and BH Mons) 2 - 5pm.
Heritage Open Days: No
P Yes. Car park 100 metres from House. Spaces: 100
♿ Partial. Wheelchair access to ground floor (shallow step at entrance), shop, tea room and garden. Disabled WC. Guide Dogs: Yes
£ **Adult:** £3.70, £2.50 (garden, railway and exhibition only) **Child:** £1.80, £1 (garden, railway and exhibition only) **Family:** £9

Ribblehead Viaduct

Ribblehead, North Yorkshire
Railway viaduct, 1870-74, rockfaced stone and brick. 104 feet high at highest point. Largest and most impressive of the viaducts of Settle - Carlisle line of Midland Railway.
Grant Recipient/Owner: British Rail
Access contact: Mr Barry Casterton
Open: Viewing from ground level only. Strictly no access from Railtrack property.
Heritage Open Days: No
P On-street parking in Cave. ♿ No £ No

Scampston Hall

Scampston, Malton, North Yorkshire, YO17 8NG
Late 17th century country house, extensively remodelled 1801 by Thomas Leverton. Contains Regency interiors and art collection. Set in parkland designed by 'Capability' Brown, 10 acres of lakes and Palladian bridge.
www.scampston.co.uk
Grant Recipient/Owner: Sir Charles Legard Bt
Access contact: Sir Charles Legard Bt
Tel: 01944 758224 **Fax:** 01944 758700
Email: legard@scampton.co.uk
Open: 26 May - 9 June and 21 July - 4 Aug (closed Sats), 1.30 - 5pm. Groups at other times by arrangement.
Heritage Open Days: No
P Spaces: 50
♿ Partial. Wheelchair access to ground floor only. Disabled WC. Guide Dogs: Yes
£ **Adult:** £5 (house, garden & park)

St Paulinus

Brough Park, Richmond, North Yorkshire DL10 7PJ
Catholic neo-Gothic chapel designed by Bonomi with priest's accommodation and school room in undercroft.
Grant Recipient/Owner: Mr Greville Worthington
Access contact: Mr Greville Worthington
Tel: 01748 812127 **Fax:**
Email: tote@grev.demon.co.uk
Open: By arrangement.
Heritage Open Days: No
P Spaces: 2 ♿ No. Guide Dogs: Yes £ No

St Saviour's Church

(Archaeological Resource Centre),
St Saviourgate, York, North Yorkshire YO1 8NN
Church on site by late 11th century, present building dates from the 15th and extensively remodelled in 1845. Now houses the Archaeological Resource Centre which contains an archaeological collection excavated by the York Archaeological Trust and promotes access to archaeological material through hands-on displays.
www.yorkarchaeology.co.uk
Grant Recipient/Owner: Dr R A Hall
Access contact: Miss Christine McDonnell
Tel: 01904 654324 **Fax:** 01904 627097
Email: cmcdonnell@yorkarchaeology.co.uk
Open: School holidays: Mon - Sat 10am - 3.30pm; booked groups during school term. 24-hr information line (01904 643211); advance bookings (01904 543403). Visitors who only want to view building may look round free, otherwise charge for entrance to Archaeological Resource Centre, £4.50 adults, £4 children, £15 family ticket (carers/enablers free if helping disabled person). Sensory garden on architectural theme.
Heritage Open Days: No
P Disabled on-street parking outside entrance; public car parks nearby.
♿ Full wheelchair access for exhibition areas but no access to offices on mezzanine floor. Disabled WC. Guide Dogs: Yes
£ See above.

St William's College

5 College Street, York, North Yorkshire YO1 7JF
St William's College is one of the most important timber framed buildings in York. Named after St William, Archbishop of York in 1154. Founded 1461 as home for the Chantry Priests of the Minster until the Reformation. Also used to house a printing press and mint for King Charles I in 1642 as well as being the home of the Earls of Carlisle in 1719 (builders of Castle Howard). Now used as York Minster's Conference & Banqueting Centre.
Grant Recipient/Owner: The Trustees of St William's College
Access contact: Mr A S Clarke
Tel: 01904 557233 **Fax:** 01904 557234
Email: info@yorkminster.org
Open: Daily 9am - 5pm, subject to functions - check with Mr A S Clarke, The Trustees of St William's College. Closed: Good Fri, Christmas Day, Boxing Day.
Heritage Open Days: No
P Public car parks in York City centre. ♿ No
£ **Adult:** £1 **Child:** 50p

Temple of Victory

Allerton Park, nr. Knaresborough, North Yorkshire HG5 0SE
Attributed to Henry Holland, architect for the Duke of York, but possibly by James Payne. Late 18th century octagon tower in the Grecian style. The entrance is by a double flight of steps secured by iron palisades.
Grant Recipient/Owner: The Gerald Arthur Rolph Foundation for Historic Preservation & Education
Access contact: The Gerald Arthur Rolph Foundation for Historic Preservation & Education
Tel: 01423 330927 **Fax:** 01423 330 632
Open: Easter Sun - end Sept: Sun and BH Mons 1 - 5pm.
Heritage Open Days: No
P Parking 1/2 mile away. Spaces: 30 ♿ No £ No

Thompson Mausoleum

Little Ouseburn Churchyard, Little Ouseburn, North Yorkshire YO26 9TS
18th century Mausoleum in magnesian limestone. Rotunda encircled by 13 Tuscan columns, above which a frieze and cornice support a plain drum and ribbed domed roof. Listed Grade II*. Built for the Thompson family of Kirby Hall.
Grant Recipient/Owner: Little Ouseburn Mausoleum Ltd
Access contact: Mr H Hibbs
Tel: 01423 330414
Email: helier@clara.net
Open: Always available to view from outside but no access to interior at present as still awaiting repair, anticipated during Spring 2002. Following repair the interior will be visible through a replica of the original wrought iron gate. Contact Mr Hibbs, Friends of Ouseburn Mausoleum Ltd, Hilltop Cottage, Little Ouseburn, North Yorks YO26 9TD for details..
Heritage Open Days: No
P Spaces: 4
♿ Partial. Wheelchair access with assistance (gravel path and grass). No disabled WC. Guide Dogs: Yes £ No

NORTHAMPTONSHIRE

Hall Farmhouse

Hall Yard, Kings Cliffe, Peterborough, Northamptonshire PE8 6XQ
Former medieval open hall. Music room, c1795, with coved and ornamented ceiling. Home of William Law 1740-61.
Grant Recipient/Owner: Mr J A R Grove
Access contact: Mr J A R Grove
Tel: 01780 470748
Open: By arrangement.
Heritage Open Days: No
P Spaces: 3 ♿ No. Guide Dogs: Yes £ No

Laxton Hall

Corby, Northamptonshire NN17 3AU
Stone built 18th century manor house, enlarged and modified in 19th century and set in 60 acres of parkland. Stable block by Repton. Formerly a boys school, now a residential home for elderly Poles.
Grant Recipient/Owner: Polish Benevolent Housing Association Ltd
Access contact: Mr Z F Fleszar
Tel: 020 7359 8863 **Fax:** 020 7226 7677
Email: pbt.pmk@ukonlinke.co.uk
Open: By written arrangement with Mr Z Fleszar, PBF Housing Association, 2 Devonia Road, London N1 8JJ, in the early afternoon of the first Monday of each month (except during Religious Festivals).
Heritage Open Days: No
P Spaces: 10
♿ Partial. Wheelchair access to ground floor only. Disabled WC. Guide Dogs: Yes £ No

The Manor House

Hardwick, Wellingborough, Northamptonshire NN9 5AL
Manor house dating back to the 12th century. The exterior of the building has been restored including a fine example of a Collyweston roof. Now part of a modern working farm.
Grant Recipient/Owner: Mr Siddons
Access contact: Mr Siddons
Tel: 01933 678785 **Fax:** 01933 678166
Email: siddons@siddons.fsbusiness.co.uk
Open: By arrangement with Mr Siddons.
Heritage Open Days: No
P Spaces: 4 ♿ No £ No

Nunnery Cottages

1/2 The Maltings, Desborough Road, Rothwell, Northamptonshire NN14 6JZ
Farmhouse, now two houses, built 1660 (part may be earlier, mid-16th century) of ironstone with limestone and brick dressings, plain tile and thatched roofs.
Grant Recipient/Owner: Rothwell Preservation Trust
Access contact: Mrs C E Mackay
Tel: 01536 713252/711086
Open: By written arrangement with Mrs C E Mackay, Secretary of the Rothwell Preservation Trust, 23 High Street, Rothwell, Northamptonshire NN14 6AD.
Heritage Open Days: No
P No ♿ No £ No

NORTHUMBERLAND

Barmoor Castle

Lowick, Berwick-upon-Tweed, Northumberland TD15 2TR
Country house, largely 1801 by James Patterson of Edinburgh, incorporating earlier masonry with building continuing throughout the 19th century.
Grant Recipient/Owner: Mr W H Lamb
Access contact: Mr W H Lamb
Tel: 01289 388376 **Fax:** 01289 388376
Open: Exterior only 9 Mar - 24 Dec: 9am - 6pm. The interior is unsafe at the present time.
Heritage Open Days: No
P Available. ♿ No £ No

Belford Hall

Belford, Northumberland NE70 7EY
Country house, 1754-56 by James Paine, wings and rear entrance added 1818 by John Dobson. The property stood derelict for 40 years until it was restored (1984-87) by the North East Civic Trust and the Monument Trust.
Grant Recipient/Owner: North East Civic Trust
Access contact: Ms Sheila Fairbairn
Tel: 01668 213794
Open: Interior: any day 9am - 5pm, by arrangement with Ms Fairburn or Mrs Harrison (tel.01668 213810), excluding Christmas and Easter. Exterior: any day 9am - 5pm (3pm in winter months), excluding Christmas and Easter. No public toilets.
Heritage Open Days: Yes
P Spaces: 8
♿ Partial. Wheelchair access to ground floor with assistance (three steps to main entrance). No disabled WC. Guide Dogs: Yes £ No

Brinkburn Mill

Longframlington, Rothbury, Northumberland NE65 8AR
Brinkburn Priory was founded c1135 within a loop of the River Coquet. The Mill was built c1800 near the site of its medieval predecessor, but dressed up later to improve the view from the house. Wheel and grinding stones are still in place, although long unused.
www.landmarktrust.co.uk
Grant Recipient/Owner: The Landmark Trust
Access contact: Ms Victoria Piggott
Tel: 01628 825920 **Fax:** 01628 825417
Email: vpiggott@landmarktrust.co.uk
Open: For details of opening arrangements at Landmark Trust properties please see the entry for Coop House, Netherby, Cumbria (page 549)
Heritage Open Days: No
P Spaces: 1 ♿ No. Guide Dogs: Yes £ No

Chillingham Castle

Chillingham, Northumberland NE66 5NJ
Medieval castle owned by the same family for 800 years, housing collection of antiques and artefacts from all over the world and a museum. Set in grounds designed by Sir Jeffrey Wyatville. Due to its strategic position close to Scottish border the Castle was often besieged and visited many times by royalty.
www.chillingham-castle.com
Grant Recipient/Owner: Sir Humphry Wakefield Bt
Access contact: Ms Margaret Smith
Tel: 01668 215359 **Fax:** 01668 215463
Email: enquiries@chillingham-castle.com
Open: May - Sept: daily 12 noon - 5pm. Closed Saturdays in May, June and Sept.
Heritage Open Days: No
P Spaces: 50
♿ Partial. Limited wheelchair access to parts of the ground floor only due to varying floor levels, steep and spiral staircases. Disabled WC. Guide Dogs: Yes
£ **Adult:** £4.50 **Child:** Free **Other:** £4 (senior citizens), £3.80 (groups)

Cragside

Rothbury, Morpeth, Northumberland NE65 7PX
High Victorian mansion by Norman Shaw, with original furniture and fittings including William Morris's stained glass and earliest wallpapers. Built for inventor-industrialist and armaments manufacturer, Lord Armstrong, who installed the world's first hydro-electric lighting. Mansion is set in 1,000-acre wooded estate, with rock garden, formal garden, man-made lakes and hydro-electric machinery.
www.nationaltrust.org.uk
Grant Recipient/Owner: The National Trust
Access contact: Mr John O'Brien
Tel: 01669 620333 ext. 101 **Fax:** 01669 620066
Email: nrcjob@smtp.ntrust.org.uk

Open: 23 Mar - 3 Nov: Tues - Sun (& BH Mondays). House: 23 Mar - 30 Sept 1 - 5.30pm (last adm. 4.30pm); 1 Oct - 3 Nov 1 - 4.30pm (last adm. 3.30pm). Estate and formal gardens as House 10.30am - 7pm (last adm. 5pm). Also 6 Nov - 15 Dec, daily except Mon and Tues 11am - 4pm.
Heritage Open Days: No
P Spaces: 400
♿ Partial. Wheelchair access to ground floor of house and one landing area on first floor. Disabled WC. Guide Dogs: Yes
£ **Adult:** £6.90 (house & garden), £4.40 (estate only) **Child:** £3.45 (house & garden), £2.20 (estate only) **Other:** £17.30 (family, house & garden), £11.00 (family, estate only), £5.90 (booked groups, house & garden), £3.80 (booked groups, estate only)

Hexham Moot Hall
Market Place, Hexham, Northumberland NE46 3NH
Built c1400, used as a home, office and court for the Archbishop of York's bailiff who administered Hexhamshire from the Hall. The former stores on ground floor are now an art gallery. First floor courtroom houses Border Library and the second floor hall is used for community activities.
Grant Recipient/Owner: Tynedale District Council
Access contact: Ms Janet Goodridge
Tel: 01434 652351 **Fax:** 01434 652425
Email: museum@tynedale.gov.uk
Open: Mon, Tues, Thurs and Fri 10am - 12.30pm and 1.30 - 3pm. Closed Christmas to New Year.
Heritage Open Days: Yes
P No ♿ No. Guide Dogs: Yes £ No

High Staward Farm
Langley-on-Tyne, Hexham, Northumberland NE47 5NS
Georgian farmhouse standing inside a walled garden surrounded by the farm steading. Has a ging gang, threshing machine, pigstys with stone troughs and a blacksmiths shop. Most of the house and buildings are of dressed stone and the house has flagged floors, ceiling hooks, cheeseboard and rail, large pantry and servants staircase. Still a working hill farm.
Grant Recipient/Owner: Mr R J Coulson
Access contact: Mr R J Coulson
Tel: 01434 683619
Open: By arrangement.
Heritage Open Days: No
P Spaces: 2 ♿ No. Guide Dogs: Yes £ No

Lady's Well
Holystone, Harbottle, Northumberland
The Lady's Holy Well is considered to be of Roman origin and is located on a halting place along the Roman road. The main feature of the well today is a rectangular stone tank which is fed by a natural spring.
www.nationaltrust.org.uk
Grant Recipient/Owner: The National Trust
Access contact: Mr John O'Brien
Tel: 01669 620333 ext. 101 **Fax:** 01669 620066
Email: ncrjob@smtp.ntrust.org.uk
Open: Open at all times.
Heritage Open Days: No
P No ♿ No. Guide Dogs: Yes £ No

Lambley Viaduct
Lambley, Tynedale, Northumberland
17 arch stone viaduct, 100ft high and 1650ft long, spanning the South Tyne river. Originally carried single track, now used as a footpath.
www.npht.com
Grant Recipient/Owner: British Rail Property Board/North Pennines Heritage Trust
Access contact: Mr David Flush
Tel: 01434 382045 **Fax:** 01434 382294
Email: np.ht@virgin.net
Open: At all times as part of the South Tyne Trail between Featherstone Park and Alston.
Heritage Open Days: No
P Spaces: 30
♿ Wheelchair access from Coanwood End. No disabled WC. Guide Dogs: Yes £ No

Lindisfarne Castle
Holy Island, Berwick-upon-Tweed, Northumberland TD15 2SH
Built in 1550 to protect Holy Island harbour from attack, the castle was converted into a private house for Edward Hudson by Sir Edwin Luytens in 1903. Small walled garden was designed by Gertrude Jekyll. 19th century lime kilns in field by the castle.
www.nationaltrust.org.uk
Grant Recipient/Owner: The National Trust
Access contact: Property Manager
Tel: 01289 389244 **Fax:** 01289 389349
Open: 16 Mar - 3 Nov: daily except Fri (but open Good Fri). For 4 1/4 hours, which always includes 12 noon - 3pm (last adm. always 30 mins before closing), sometimes earlier or later depending on the tide.
Heritage Open Days: No
P Local authority car park 1 mile from site.
♿ No. Guide Dogs: Yes
£ **Adult:** £4.20 **Child:** £2.10 **Family:** £10.50, NT members free

Little Harle Tower
Kirkwhelpington, Newcastle-upon-Tyne, Northumberland NE19 2PD
Medieval tower with 17th century range and a Victorian wing which contains a recently restored 1740s drawing room. It has been one family's home since 1830 though part is now let.
Grant Recipient/Owner: Mr J P P Anderson
Access contact: Mr John Clark
Tel: 01434 320363 **Fax:** 01434 320675
Email: post.haltwhistle@csh.co.uk
Open: By arrangement (at least 2 weeks notice required) with Mr John Clark of Clark Scott Harden, Market Place, Haltwhistle, Northumberland NE49 0BP.
Heritage Open Days: No
P Spaces: 6
♿ Partial. Wheelchair access to ground floor only. No disabled WC. Guide Dogs: Yes
£ Donations to the church requested

Mitford Hall Camellia House
Morpeth, Northumberland NE61 3PZ
East wing and conservatory of country house built c1820 by John Dobson, detached from main house by demolition of north-east wing in 20th century.
Grant Recipient/Owner: Shepherd Offshore plc
Access contact: Mr B Shepherd
Open: By written arrangement during the summer.
Heritage Open Days: No
P Spaces: 3
♿ Wheelchair access by arrangement. Ordinary toilet on site may be accessible for some disabled persons, please contact Hall for further information. Disabled WC. Guide Dogs: Yes £ No

Netherwitton Hall
Morpeth, Northumberland NE61 4NW
Grade I mansion house built c1685 by Robert Trollope for Sir Nicholas Thurston. Access to main ground floor rooms and external elevations. Built as a family home and remains the current family home.
Grant Recipient/Owner: Mr J C R Trevelyan
Access contact: Mr J C R Trevelyan
Tel: 01670 772 219 **Fax:** 01670 772 332
Open: By written arrangement.
Heritage Open Days: No
P Yes. Free parking. Spaces: 20
♿ No wheelchair access - steps up to the property and to get around the front of the house. No disabled WC. Guide Dogs: Yes
£ **Adult:** £3 **Child:** Free

St Cuthbert's Chapel
Farne Islands, Northumberland
St Cuthbert's Chapel was completed 1370. By early 19th century it was in a ruinous condition. Restored 1840 by Archdeacon Thorp it includes some fine 17th century woodwork from Durham Cathedral and a memorial to Grace Darling. Remains of an original window.
www.nationaltrust.org.uk
Grant Recipient/Owner: The National Trust
Access contact: Mr John Walton
Tel: 01665 720651 **Fax:** 01665 720651
Email: john.walton@ntrust.org.uk
Open: 29 Mar, Apr & 1 Aug - 30 Sept: daily 10.30am - 6pm. 1 May - 31 July (breeding season) daily Staple Island 10.30am - 1.30pm, Inner Farne 1.30 - 5pm.
Heritage Open Days: No
P Public parking in Seahouses (nearest mainland village).
♿ Partial. Inner Farne is accessible for wheelchairs (telephone the Property Manager in advance). Staple Island not accessible. Disabled WC on Inner Farne. Guide dogs allowed on boat but not on islands. Disabled WC. Guide Dogs: No
£ **Adult:** £4.40 (breeding season), £3.60 (outside breeding season) **Child:** £2.20 (breeding season), £1.80 (outside breeding season) **Other:** £2.20 (booked school groups, breeding season, per island), £1.90 (outside breeding season, per island)

The Shambles
Market Place, Hexham, Northumberland NE46 1XQ
Covered market erected by Sir Walter Blackett 1766 with stone columns to front. Wooden rear columns. 9 x 3 bays. Moulded cast iron gutter and shallow doubled pitched slate roof. Listed Grade II* and a Scheduled Ancient Monument.
Grant Recipient/Owner: Tynedale Council
Access contact: Mr Keith Murray
Tel: 01434 652200 **Fax:** 01434 652421
Open: Open at all times.
Heritage Open Days: No
P Spaces: 20 ♿ No £ No

The Tower
Elsdon, Northumberland NE19 1AA
14th century Tower House, residence of the Rector until 1961 and originally used as a refuge against Border raids.
Grant Recipient/Owner: J F Wollaston
Access contact: J F Wollaston
Fax: 01830 520904
Open: By arranged guided tour, w/ends only, 1 Apr - 30 Oct.
Heritage Open Days: No
P Spaces: 30 ♿ No. Guide Dogs: Yes £ **Adult:** £3

Vindolanda Roman Fort
Bardon Mill, Hexham, Northumberland, NE47 7NJ
Roman Fort and civilian settlement in central sector of Hadrian's Wall with active excavation and education programmes. The site is owned and administered by the Vindolanda Charitable Trust and has a superb on-site museum, with full visitor services, reconstructed Roman buildings and charming gardens.
www.vindolanda.com
Grant Recipient/Owner: Mrs Patricia Birley
Access contact: Mrs Patricia Birley
Tel: 01434 344277 **Fax:** 01434 344060
Email: info@vindolanda.com
Open: 1 - 6 Jan, 10am - 4pm. Closed 7 - 25 Jan. Daily 26 Jan - mid-Nov from 10am. Closing times: Jan, Feb & Nov 4pm; Mar & Oct 5pm; Apr & Sept 5.30pm; May & June 6pm; July & Aug 6.30pm.
Heritage Open Days: No
P Yes. Coach parking available on-site. Spaces: 60
♿ Partial. Wheelchair access to parts of the archaeological site and all museums, gardens and open-air museum. Disabled WC. Guide Dogs: Yes
£ **Adult:** £3.90 (10% reduction for EH members) **Child:** £2.80 (10% reduction for EH members) **Other:** £3.30 (10% reduction for EH members)

Wallington Hall & Clock Tower
Cambo, Morpeth, Northumberland NE61 4AP
House built in 1688 on site of a former pele tower for Sir Walter Blackett, a wealthy Newcastle-upon-Tyne merchant. It served as a shooting box until Sir Walter's grandson, Sir Walter Calverley Blackett decorated the interiors and erected Clock Tower and stable buildings.
www.nationaltrust.org.uk
Grant Recipient/Owner: The National Trust
Access contact: Property Manager
Tel: 01670 774283 **Fax:** 01670 774420
Email: nwabmp@smtp.ntrust.org.uk
Open: House: 23 Mar - 30 Sept, daily except Tues 1 - 5.30pm. Walled Garden open daily: Apr - end Sept 10am - 7pm; Oct 10am - 6pm; Nov - Mar 2003 10am - 4pm or dusk if earlier. Grounds: open daily in daylight.
Heritage Open Days: No
P Spaces: 500
♿ Partial. Wheelchair access to ground floor of house only. Disabled WC. Guide Dogs: Yes
£ **Adult:** £5.70 (house, garden & grounds), £4.10 (garden & grounds) **Child:** £2.85 (house, garden & grounds), £2 (garden & grounds) **Other:** £14.25 (family: house, garden & grounds), £5.20 (booked groups: house, garden & grounds), £3.60 (groups: gardens & grounds)

NOTTINGHAMSHIRE

Kiln Warehouse
Mather Road, Newark, Nottinghamshire NG24 1FB
Grade II* former warehouse. Early example of the use of massed concrete construction. Interior completely destroyed by fire in the early 1990s, the exterior walls restored and warehouse converted into offices.
Grant Recipient/Owner: The Regional Director
Access contact: Miss E A Blackhurst
Tel: 0115 950 7577 **Fax:** 0115 950 7688
Email: liz@fhp.co.uk
Open: Exterior walls for which the property is notable can be viewed without arrangement. Access to internal courtyard is by arrangement with Elizabeth Blackhurst of Fisher Hargreaves Proctor, Chartered Surveyors, 10 Oxford Street, Nottingham NG1 5BG.
Heritage Open Days: No
P Parking is available on adjacent land.
♿ Yes. Disabled WC. Guide Dogs: Yes £ No

Newdigate House
Castle Gate, Nottingham, Nottinghamshire NG1 6AF
House, c1675, built for Thomas Newdigate. Stucco with ashlar dressings, hipped slate roof, sash windows, panelled rooms and Adam-style plasterwork. Crested wrought-iron railings, central gateway and overthrow, probably by Francis Foulgham, to the exterior. Marshal Tallard was held prisoner here after the battle of Blenheim. The ground floor is now a restaurant.
Grant Recipient/Owner: Nottingham and Nottinghamshire United Sevices Club
Access contact: Mr Ashley Walters
Tel: 0115 8475587 **Fax:** 0115 8475584
Email: enquiries@worldservicerestaurant.com
Open: Daily 11am - 6pm, preferably by arrangement.
Heritage Open Days: No
P No
♿ Partial. Some assistance may be required for wheelchair access, please check with Mr Walters. Disabled WC. Guide Dogs: Yes £ No

North Leverton Windmill

North Leverton, Retford, Nottinghamshire DN22 0BA
Grade II* working windmill built in 1813 and in excellent condition.
Grant Recipient/Owner: Mr P Atkinson
Access contact: Mr P Atkinson
Open: For viewing at any time, all year round. Access to the inside of the Mill is usually possible but it is advisable to telephone either Keith Barlow, Miller (01427 880573) or Lyn & Dennis Leighton, Cottage Tenants (01427 880662) in advance.
Heritage Open Days: No
P Available. ♿ No £ No

Upton Hall

(the British Horological Institute)
Upton, Newark, Nottinghamshire NG23 5TE
Grade II* house in Greek revival style, 1832, incorporating earlier 17th century house. Large addition and interior remodelled in 1895. During World War II the house was a school for partially-sighted children. Now houses the British Horological Institute watch and clock museum featuring clocks from the 17th - 20th centuries.
Grant Recipient/Owner: Alan Midleton
Access contact: British Horological Institute
Tel: 01636 813795 **Fax:** 01636 812258
Email: clocks@bhi.co.uk
Open: Apr - Nov: Tues - Sat 11am - 5pm; Sun 2 - 5pm; BHs 11am - 5pm. Closed on Mon. Nov - Apr: Tues - Fri 1.30 - 4.30pm. Closed on Mon, Sat and Sun.
Heritage Open Days: Yes
P Spaces: 50
♿ Partial. No disabled WC. Guide Dogs: Yes
£ **Adult:** £3.50 **Child:** £2 (under 10s free)
Seniors: £3, £10 (family)

OXFORDSHIRE

Aston Martin Owners Club

Drayton St Leonard, Wallington, Oxfordshire OX10 7BG
15th century tithe barn, 6 bays. Constructed of Elm with hipped roof. Listed Grade II*.
Grant Recipient/Owner: Aston Martin Owners Club
Access contact: Ms Christine Sharrock
Tel: 01865 400400 **Fax:** 01865 400200
Email: hqstaff@amoc.org
Open: Wed: 2 - 4pm. Other times by arrangement.
Heritage Open Days: No
P Spaces: 40 ♿ No Disabled WC. Guide Dogs: Yes
£ No

Blenheim Palace & Park

Woodstock, Oxfordshire OX20 1PX
Ancestral home of the Dukes of Marlborough and birthplace of Winston Churchill. Built between 1705-22 for John Churchill, the 1st Duke, in recognition of his victory at the Battle of Blenheim in 1704. Designed by Sir John Vanbrugh, the house contains in its many state rooms a collection of paintings, furniture, bronzes and the Marlborough Victories tapestries. A five-room Churchill Exhibition includes his birth room. 'Capability' Brown park and gardens.
www.blenheimpalace.com
Grant Recipient/Owner: Duke of Marlborough
Access contact: Mr N Day
Tel: 01993 811325/811091 **Fax:** 01993 813527
Email: nickday@blenheimpalace.com
Open: Palace: 11 Mar - end of Oct, daily 10.30am - 5.30pm (last adm. 4.45pm). Park: daily (except Christmas Day) 9am - 6pm (last adm. 4.45pm). High Lodge may be visited by written arrangement with the Estate Office. Charges provisional at time of going to press, check with Estate Office for up-to-date information.
Heritage Open Days: No
P Spaces: 10000 ♿ Yes. Disabled WC. Guide Dogs: Yes
£ **Adult:** £9.50 **Child:** £4.50 **Seniors:** £7.50

Broughton Castle

Banbury, Oxfordshire OX15 5EB
Originally built c1300, the Castle stands on an island site surrounded by a 3 acre moat. Greatly enlarged 1550 and decorated with plaster ceilings, panelling and fireplaces. Ancestral home of the Lords Saye and Sele since 1450.
www.broughtoncastle.demon.co.uk
Grant Recipient/Owner: Lord Saye and Sele
Access contact: Lord Saye and Sele
Tel: 01295 262624 **Fax:** 01295 276070
Open: 19 May - 11 Sept: Wed and Sun, plus Thurs in July and Aug and BH Sundays and Mondays (inc. Easter) 2 - 5pm. Groups any time all year by arrangement.
Heritage Open Days: Yes
P Spaces: 150
♿ Partial. Wheelchair access to ground floor only. Disabled WC. Guide Dogs: Yes
£ **Adult:** £5 **Child:** £2 (5-15) **Senior/Student:** £4

Clattercote Priory Farm

Claydon, Banbury, Oxfordshire OX17 1QB
Founded c1150, the Priory is now a family house - part farmhouse, part tenanted. A rare example of a Gilbertine Priory with cellars and 'chapel', probably medieval.
Grant Recipient/Owner: Mr Adrian Taylor
Access contact: Mr Adrian Taylor
Tel: 01295 690476 **Fax:** 01295 690476
Email: clattercote1@aol.com
Open: By written arrangement.
Heritage Open Days: No
P Spaces: 4 ♿ No. Guide Dogs: Yes
£ **Adult:** £5 (to cancer charity)

Cornbury Park

Charlbury, Oxford, Oxon OX7 3EH
400 acre deer park adjacent to Wychwood Forest containing newly restored/replanted beech avenues, ancient English oak trees and several ancient monuments.
www.cornburypark.co.uk
Grant Recipient/Owner: The Lord Rotherwick
Access contact: Helen Spearman & Richard Watkins
Tel: 01608 811276 **Fax:** 01608 811252
Email: estate@cpark.co.uk
Open: 1 Mar - 31 Oct: Tues and Thurs 10am - 4pm. Please note permit required for access to the Park and must be applied for in advance. Organised educational access walks for groups by arrangement.
Heritage Open Days: No
P Spaces: 20 ♿ No £ No

Farnborough Hall

Farnborough, Banbury, Oxfordshire OX17 1DU
Mid-18th century honey-coloured stone built home of the Holbech family for over 300 years, contains impressive plasterwork. Set in grounds with 18th century temples, a terrace walk and an obelisk.
www.ntrustsevern.org.uk
Grant Recipient/Owner: The National Trust
Access contact: Mr & Mrs G Holbech
Tel: 01295 690002
Open: Apr - end Sept: House and grounds: Weds and Sats 2 - 6pm, also 5/6 May 2 - 6pm. Terrace walk: Apr - end Sept by arrangement, Thurs and Fris 2 - 6pm (closed Good Fri).
Heritage Open Days: No
P Spaces: 10
♿ Partial. Wheelchair access to ground floor of house and garden. Terrace walk may be difficult as it is very steep. No disabled WC. Guide Dogs: Yes
£ **Adult:** £3.50, £1.75 (garden), £1 (Terrace walk only).
Child: £1.75

Freeman Mausoleum

St Mary's Churchyard, Fawley,
nr Henley-on-Thames, Oxon RG9 6HZ
Built in 1752 for the Freeman family who owned the Fawley Estate. Design by John Freeman based on the mausoleum of Cecilia Metella on the Appian Way in Rome, which he visited while on his Grand Tour. It contains 30 coffin slots with 12 being filled by the Freemans before they sold the Estate in 1850.
Grant Recipient/Owner: St Mary's Parochial Church Council
Access contact: Mr R A Sykes
Tel: 01491 573778 **Fax:** 01491 411406
Open: Mausoleum permanently open. For further information please telephone Mr R A Sykes.
Heritage Open Days: No
P On-street parking adjacent to church. Spaces: 10
♿ Yes. No disabled WC. Guide Dogs: Yes £ No

The Old Rectory Dovecote

Mill Street, Kidlington,
Oxford, Oxfordshire OX5 2EE
Large round medieval dovecote.
Grant Recipient/Owner: Ms Felicity Duncan
Access contact: Ms Felicity Duncan
Open: Daily, 10am - 5.30pm.
Heritage Open Days: No
P No ♿ No £ No

Shotover Park

Wheatley, Oxfordshire OX33 1QS
Early 18th century garden follies. The Gothic Temple (designer unknown) lies east of the house at the end of a long canal vista. Has a battlemented gable with a central pinnacle and a rose-window, below which is an open loggia of three pointed arches. The other Temple west of the house, designed by William Kent, is of a domed octagonal construction.
Grant Recipient/Owner: Sir John Miller
Access contact: Sir John Miller
Tel: 01865 872450 or 874095
Open: Access to Temples at all reasonable times (lie close to public rights of way). Parking for a few cars at Gothic Temple, other arrangements can be made with Sir John Miller (tel above) or Mrs Price on 01865 874095.
Heritage Open Days: No
P Spaces: 50
♿ Partial. Wheelchair access to the Gothic Temple with assistance. No disabled WC. Guide Dogs: Yes £ No

Swalcliffe Tithe Barn

Shipston Road, Swalcliffe,
nr. Banbury, Oxfordshire OX15 5DR
15th century barn built by New College, Oxford, for estates in north Oxfordshire. Built for Rectorial Manor of Swalcliffe by New College, who owned the Manor. Constructed 1400 - 1409, much of the medieval timber half-cruck roof remains intact. Now a museum.
Grant Recipient/Owner: Oxfordshire Building Trust Ltd
Access contact: Mr Martyn Brown
Tel: 01993 814114 **Fax:** 01993 813239
Email: martyn.brown@oxfordshire.gov.uk
Open: Easter - end of Sept: Suns and BHs, 2 - 5pm.Wed, Thurs and Fri for Aug. At other times by arrangement (contact Jeff Demmar tel.01295 788278).
Heritage Open Days: Yes
P Spaces: 10 ♿ Yes. Disabled WC. Guide Dogs: Yes
£ No

Tirrold House

(formerly The Cottage), Aston Street, Aston Tirrold, Oxfordshire OX11 9DQ
House dates to 1286, with later 16th and 17th century alterations and additions. Timber-framed with water reed thatched roof. 13th century west wing is one of very few known domestic timber-framed buildings of this date in which aisled construction is not used.
Grant Recipient/Owner: Mr B C Bateman
Access contact: Mr B C Bateman
Tel: 01235 850351 **Fax:** 01235 850351
Email: bateman5@supanet.com
Open: By written arrangement.
Heritage Open Days: No
P No ♿ No. Guide Dogs: Yes £ No

Tudor House

East Hagbourne, Oxfordshire OX11 9LR
Early 17th century barn constructed for cattle with thatched roof and queenpost construction. Three bays and an aisle on one side. Original wattle and daub infill at ends only. The house was painted by Helen Allingham c.1901 when she stayed here whilst the artist Robert Anning Bell was in residence.
Grant Recipient/Owner: Mr IC Barfoot and Mrs PJ Kisby
Access contact: Mr I C Barfoot
Tel: 01235 818968 **Fax:** 01235 818968
Open: By arrangement.
Heritage Open Days: No
P On-street parking.
♿ Yes. No disabled WC. Guide Dogs: Yes £ No

SHROPSHIRE

2/3 Milk Street

Shrewsbury, Shropshire SY1 1SZ
Timber-framed two and a half storey building dating from 15th century with later alterations and additions. Medieval shop front to rear. Still a shop.
Grant Recipient/Owner: Mr M J Cockle
Access contact: Mr H Carter
Tel: 01743 236789 **Fax:** 01743 242140
Email: htc@pooks.co.uk
Open: Ground floor shop 6 days a week all year. Mon - Sat 9.30am - 5.30pm. Upper floor flats can be visited only by arrangement with Mr H Carter, Pooks, 26 Claremont Hill, Shrewsbury, Shropshire SY1 1RE.
Heritage Open Days: No
P No
♿ Partial. Wheelchair access to ground floor only. No disabled WC. Guide Dogs: Yes £ No

Attingham Park

Atcham, Shrewsbury, Shropshire SY4 4TP
Built 1785 by George Steuart for the 1st Lord Berwick, with a picture gallery by John Nash. Contains Regency interiors, Italian neo-classical furniture and Grand Tour paintings. Park landscaped by Repton in 1797.
www.nationaltrust.org.uk
Grant Recipient/Owner: The National Trust
Access contact: The Property Manager
Tel: 01743 708162 **Fax:** 01743 708175
Email: matsec@smtp.ntrust.org.uk
Open: House: 23 Mar - 3 Nov: daily except Wed and Thurs 1 - 4.30pm (last adm. 4pm). Park: all year except Christmas Day, Mar - end Oct 9am - 8pm, Nov - Feb 9am - 5pm.
Heritage Open Days: No
P Spaces: 150
♿ Yes. Disabled WC. Guide Dogs: Yes
£ **Adult:** £4.60, £2.20 (park & grounds) **Child:** £2.30
Other: £11.50 (family), £4 (booked groups 15+)

Benthall Hall

Broseley, Shropshire TF12 5RX
16th century stone house situated on a plateau above the gorge of the River Severn, with mullioned and transomed windows, carved oak staircase, decorated plaster ceilings and oak panelling. Restored plantsman's garden, old kitchen garden and a Restoration church.

www.nationaltrust.org.uk
Grant Recipient/Owner: The National Trust
Access contact: The Custodian
Tel: 01952 882159
Open: 31 Mar - 29 Sept: Wed, Sun and BH Mondays 1.30 - 5.30pm. Groups by arrangement with the Custodian (Wed and Sun only).
Heritage Open Days: No
P Spaces: 50
♿ Partial. Wheelchair access to ground floor of Hall and part of garden only. No disabled WC. Guide Dogs: Yes
£ **Adult:** £3.60 **Child:** £1.80 **Other:** £2.30 (garden)

Blodwell Summerhouse

Blodwell Hall, Llanyblodwell, Oswestry, Shropshire SY10 8LT
Square red brick summerhouse with ashlar dressings and slate roof, built 1718, at end of terrace in a restored formal garden.
Grant Recipient/Owner: Trustees of Bradford Estate
Access contact: Mr R J Taylor
Tel: 07977 239955
Open: By arrangement.
Heritage Open Days: No
P Spaces: 2 ♿ Yes. No disabled WC. Guide Dogs: Yes
£ No

Bromfield Priory Gatehouse

nr. Ludlow, Shropshire SY8 2JN
The Benedictine monks of Bromfield Priory added new stone gatehouse pre 1400. After the Dissolution a timber-framed upper storey was added. The main room over the arch was used for the manorial court; then as the village school, ending up as parish recreational room.
www.landmarktrust.co.uk
Grant Recipient/Owner: The Landmark Trust
Access contact: Ms Victoria Piggott
Tel: 01628 825920 **Fax:** 01628 825417
Email: vpiggott@landmarktrust.co.uk
Open: For details of opening arrangements at Landmark Trust properties please see the entry for Coop House, Netherby, Cumbria (page 549)
Heritage Open Days: No
P Spaces: 1 ♿ No. Guide Dogs: Yes £ No

Dudmaston

Quatt, Bridgnorth, Shropshire WV15 6QN
Queen Anne mansion of red brick with stone dressings, set in parkland overlooking the Severn. Contains furniture, Dutch flower paintings, contemporary paintings and sculpture. Gardens, wooded valley and estate walks starting from Hampton Loade.
www.nationaltrust.org.uk
Grant Recipient/Owner: The National Trust
Access contact: The Administrator
Tel: 01746 780866 **Fax:** 01746 780744
Email: mduefe@smtp.ntrust.org.uk
Open: 31 Mar - 29 Sept: House & Garden: Tues, Wed, Sun & BH Mon 2 - 5.30pm. Garden: Mon, Tues, Wed & Sun 12 noon - 6pm. Groups by arrangement Mon afternoons only. Tea Room same days as garden, 11.30am - 5.30pm. Shop same days as garden, 1 - 5.30pm.
Heritage Open Days: No
P Spaces: 150
♿ Partial. Wheelchair access main and inner halls, Library, oak room, No 1 and Derby galleries, old kitchen, garden and grounds (some estate walks), shop and tearoom. Disabled WC. Guide Dogs: Yes
£ **Adult:** £3.95 **Child:** £2 **Other:** £9.00 (family), £2.90 (garden only), £3.30 (booked groups of 15+)

Hawkstone Hall

Marchamley, Shrewsbury, Shropshire SY4 5LG
Grade I Georgian mansion and restored gardens set in spacious parkland. Ancestral home of the Hill family from 1556-1906.
Grant Recipient/Owner: Rector & Trustees of Hawkstone Hall/ Redemptorists
Access contact: Guest Mistress
Tel: 01630 685242 **Fax:** 01630 685565
Open: Spring BH and 5 - 31 Aug: 2 - 5pm.
Heritage Open Days: No
P Spaces: 40
♿ Partial. Wheelchair access via ramp at side door to principal rooms on ground floor. No disabled WC. Guide Dogs: Yes
£ **Adult:** £4 **Child:** £1

Hospital of the Undivided Trinity

Hospital Lane, Clun, Shropshire SY7 8LE
Founded 1607 by Henry Howard, Earl of Northampton and built in 1618 with alterations of 1857. Dwellings and other rooms arranged around a square courtyard. A well preserved example of a courtyard-plan almshouses.
Grant Recipient/Owner: The Trustees of Trinity Hospital
Access contact: Mr B Corley
Tel: 01588 640830
Open: By arrangement with the Warden, Mr Corley. Gardens and chapel open daily except Christmas Day.
Heritage Open Days: No
P Spaces: 70 ♿ Yes. No disabled WC. Guide Dogs: Yes
£ No

John Rose Building

High Street, Coalport, Telford, Shropshire TF8 7HT
China decorating workshop, part of the Coalport Chinaworks, built c1792. John Rose started his chinaworks at Jackfield about 1790, and moved to Coalport in about 1792. Repaired and adapted to Youth Hostel with conference rooms, workshops and café.
www.yha.org.uk
Grant Recipient/Owner: Ironbridge Gorge Museum Trust
Access contact: Ironbridge Gorge Museum Trust
Tel: 0952 433522
Open: All year except Jan. Café: 10am - 5pm daily. Workshops: 11am - 5pm Mon - Fri.
Heritage Open Days: No
P Museum car park.
♿ Partial. No wheelchair access to second floor. Disabled WC. Guide Dogs: Yes £ No

Langley Gatehouse

Acton Burnell, Shropshire SY5 7PE
Gatehouse has two quite different faces: one is of plain dressed stone; the other, which once looked inwards to long demolished Langley Hall, is timber-framed. It was probably used for the Steward or important guests. It was rescued from a point of near collapse and shows repair work of an exemplary quality.
www.landmarktrust.co.uk
Grant Recipient/Owner: The Landmark Trust
Access contact: Ms Victoria Piggott
Tel: 01628 825920 **Fax:** 01628 825417
Email: vpiggott@landmarktrust.co.uk
Open: For details of opening arrangements at Landmark Trust properties please see the entry for Coop House, Netherby, Cumbria (page 550)
Heritage Open Days: No
P Spaces: 2 ♿ No. Guide Dogs: Yes £ No

Lord Hill Column

Abbey Foregate, Shrewsbury, Shropshire
Giant fluted Greek Doric column surmounted by statue of Lord Hill (1772-1842). Erected 1814-1816, designed by Edward Haycock of Shrewsbury and Thomas Harrison of Chester, the monument stands 132 feet, 6 inches high. Built by public subscription to honour Lord Hill's achievements during the Napoleonic Wars as a Lieutenant-General under Wellington.
Grant Recipient/Owner: Shropshire County Council
Access contact: Shirehall Services Manager
Tel: 01743 252896
Open: Monument closed for repair until Feb 2002. Once works completed, the monument can be viewed from exterior at all times, access to interior by arrangement.
Heritage Open Days: Yes
P Free parking (150 metres). Spaces: 100 ♿ No £ No

The Lyth

Ellesmere, Shropshire SY12 0HR
Grade II* small country house, 1819, with minor later additions and alterations. Glass canopied cast-iron verandah with trellised supports.
Grant Recipient/Owner: Mr L R Jebb
Access contact: Mr Richard Jebb
Tel: 01691 622339 **Fax:** 01691 624134
Open: Suns: 14 Apr, 2 June, 15 Sept, 13 Oct, 2 - 6pm. At other times by arrangement with Mr Lionel Jebb.
Heritage Open Days: No
P Spaces: 40 ♿ Yes. No disabled WC. Guide Dogs: Yes
£ Charity donation for visits to garden **Adult:** £2
Child: £1

Newport Guildhall

High Street, Newport, Shropshire TF10 7TX
15th century timber framed Guildhall now used as town council offices.
Grant Recipient/Owner: Newport Town Council
Access contact: Miss Dee Halliday
Tel: 01952 814338 **Fax:** 01952 825353
Email: townclark@newportsaloptowncouncil.co.uk
Open: Mon - Fri 9am - 1pm (closed BHs). Special Open Day on Fri 12 July 9am - 4pm.
Heritage Open Days: No
P Spaces: 5
♿ Partial. Wheelchair access via chair lift to first floor. No disabled WC. Guide Dogs: Yes £ No

The Old Mansion

St Mary's Street, Shrewsbury, Shropshire SY1 1UQ
Early 17th century house with original staircase. The building was renovated in 1997 and now provides 4 bedroom suites for the Prince Rupert Hotel.
www.prince-rupert-hotel.co.uk
Grant Recipient/Owner: Mr A Humphreys
Access contact: Mr A Humphreys
Tel: 01291 672 563
Open: By arrangement.
Heritage Open Days: No
P Public car park in town centre. ♿ No £ No

Weston Park

Weston-under-Lizard, Shifnal, Shropshire TF11 8LE
Stately home, built 1671, designed by Lady Wilbraham. Houses collection of paintings by Van Dyck, Gainsborough, Lely and Stubbs, and surrounded by 1000 acres of 'Capability' Brown parkland and formal gardens. Formerly home to the Earls of Bradford, now held in trust for the nation by The Weston Park Foundation.
www.weston-park.com
Grant Recipient/Owner: Weston Park Foundation
Access contact: Mr Colin Sweeney
Tel: 01952 852100 **Fax:** 01952 850430
Email: enquiries@weston-park.com
Open: Easter 30 Mar - 1 Apr, then every w/end in Apr, May and June; July & Aug: daily; 1 - 15 Sept: w/ends only. House 1 - 5pm. Park 11am - 7pm.
Heritage Open Days: No
P Spaces: 300
♿ Partial. Wheelchair access all areas except open parkland and some formal gardens. Disabled WC. Guide Dogs: Yes
£ **Adult:** £2 (house), £2.50 (park) **Child:** £1 (house), £1.50 (park) **Other:** £1.50 (house), £2 (park)

Yeaton Peverey Hall

Yeaton Peverey, Shrewsbury, Shropshire SY4 3AT
Mock Jacobean country house, 1890-2 by Aston Webb. Previously a school, now reinstated as a family home. Principal rooms on the ground floor open to visitors.
Grant Recipient/Owner: Mr Martin Ebelis
Access contact: Mr Martin Ebelis
Tel: 01743 851185
Open: 19/20 Mar, 17/18 Apr, 13/14 May, 7 June: 12 noon - 5pm. When family in residence by arrangement with written confirmation or introduction through known contact. Open for local charity events (see local press).
Heritage Open Days: No
P Parking adjacent to the property for disabled. Spaces: 6
♿ Yes. Disabled WC. Guide Dogs: No
£ Admission charges under review at time of going to print, please contact Mr Ebelis or check the English Heritage website for details

SOMERSET

Bath Assembly Rooms

Bennett Street, Bath, Somerset BA1 2QH
Built in 1771 by John Wood the Younger, now owned by the National Trust and administered by Bath and North East Somerset District Council. Each of the rooms has a complete set of original chandeliers. The Museum of Costume is located on the lower ground floor.
www.museumofcostume.co.uk
Grant Recipient/Owner: Bath City Council/National Trust
Access contact: Mrs P C Ruddock
Tel: 01225 477752 **Fax:** 01225 444793
Email: penny_ruddock@bathnes.gov.uk
Open: Daily 10am - 5pm when not in use for booked functions. Tel. (01225 477789) to check availability. No booked functions during the day during Aug. Closed Christmas Day and Boxing Day.
Heritage Open Days: No
P On street car parking (pay and display).
♿ Yes. Disabled WC. Guide Dogs: Yes
£ No but charge for Museum of Costume

British Empire and Commonwealth Museum

Clock Tower Yard, Temple Meads, Bristol BS1 6QH
Museum housed in world's earliest surviving railway terminus, completed 1840 and originally part of the Great Western Railway designed by I.K. Brunel. Over 220ft long with timber and iron roof spans of 72ft, this Grade I building has been nominated as a World Heritage Site. Contains the Passenger shed and the adjoining former Engine and Carriage shed, the latter currently holds the Museum's temporary exhibitions until a permanent gallery opens in 2002.
www.empiremuseum.co.uk
Grant Recipient/Owner: Empire Museum Ltd
Access contact: Mr Simon Boice
Tel: 0117 925 4980 **Fax:** 0117 925 4983
Email: shop@empiremuseum.co.uk
Open: Daily 9am - 5pm. Unrestricted access to exterior.
Heritage Open Days: Yes
P Parking in station car park. Spaces: 25
♿ Yes. Disabled WC. Guide Dogs: Yes
£ Prices subject to change. **Adult:** £3 **Child/Other:** £1.50

Dovecote adjacent to Church Memorial Garden

Priory Green, Dunster, Somerset TA24 6RY
Scheduled medieval circular tower dovecote 8.5 metres high with internal diameter of 4.5 metres. Probably 13-14th century part of the monastic estate of the Benedictine Priory of Dunster, a cell of Bath Priory, sent to build the church of St George in 1150. Contains over 500 nest sites lining the

4' thick round stone wall, which was served by a revolving ladder from a central vertical ash post with two alighting platforms for feeding the birds when enclosed.
Grant Recipient/Owner: Dunster Parish Council
Access contact: Reverend M P Grantham
Tel: 01643 821812
Open: Interior can be viewed all year from barred doorway, otherwise access by arrangement with the Reverend M P Grantham, The Rectory, St George's Street, Dunster, Somerset TA24 6RS (tel.01643 821812) or the Churchwarden (tel.01643 708056).
Heritage Open Days: No
P Spaces: 6 ♿ No. Guide Dogs: Yes £ No

Dovery Manor

Porlock, Somerset, TA24 8LG
A mid-15th century dower house consisting of hall and solar wing with access by narrow stair to upper chamber and cross chamber. The hall and main upper chamber house a museum dedicated to local history and artefacts.
Grant Recipient/Owner: Porlock Parish Council
Access contact: Mr D Corner
Tel: 01643 862645
Open: 1 May - 30 Sept: Mon - Fri 10am - 1pm, 2 - 5pm; Sat 10am - 12 noon, 2.30 - 4.30pm. Closed on Sundays. Open during Easter Week, check details with Mr Corner.
Heritage Open Days: No
P Pay and display car park opposite property (50 spaces).
♿ No £ No

Englishcombe Tithe Barn

Rectory Farmhouse, Englishcombe, Bath, Somerset BA2 9DU
Early 14th century cruck framed tithe barn. Recently restored with new crucks, masonry and straw lining to the roof, and filigree windows unblocked. There are masons and other markings on the walls. Now used as a venue, principally for wedding receptions.
www.barnhire.com
Grant Recipient/Owner: Mrs Jennie Walker
Access contact: Mrs Jennie Walker
Tel: 01225 425073
Email: jennie@barnhire.com
Open: BHs 2 - 6pm; all other times by arrangement with Mrs Walker. Closed 21 Dec 2002 - 7 Jan 2003.
Heritage Open Days: Yes
P Spaces: 34
♿ Yes. Disabled WC. Guide Dogs: Yes
£ Free, but £1 a head donation requested from groups

Eyre Mortuary Chapel

Perrymead Cemetery, Bath, Somerset BA2 4NW
Mid-19th century Gothic Revival Catholic building, built as a mortuary chapel for the Eyre family. Constructed of Bath stone from the designs of Charles Hanson. The interior has recessed arches supported on columns of Devonshire marble, a screen of hammered ironwork and an elaborate marble altar with a Minton tile floor.
Grant Recipient/Owner: Trustees of the Eyre Mortuary Chapel
Access contact: Mrs B Carruthers
Tel: 01684 292600 **Fax:** 01684 292042
Open: By arrangement with Mrs B Carruthers, Walton Cardiff Manor, nr. Tewkesbury, Glos GL20 7BL.
Heritage Open Days: No
P Bath City centre. Rail: Bath Spa. Spaces: 4
♿ No. Guide Dogs: Yes £ Donation requested

Forde Abbey

Chard, Somerset TA20 4LU
Cistercian monastery founded in 1140 and dissolved in 1539 when church was demolished. The monks quarters were converted in 1640 into an Italian style "palazzo" by Sir Edmund Prideaux. Interior has plaster ceilings and Mortlake tapestries.
www.fordeabbey.co.uk
Grant Recipient/Owner: Trustees of the Roper Settlement
Access contact: Mrs Clay
Tel: 01460 220231
Email: forde.abbey@virgin.net
Open: Gardens: daily 10am - 4.30pm. House: Apr - Oct; Tues - Fri, Sun and BHs 1 - 4.30pm
Heritage Open Days: No
P Spaces: 500 ♿ No. Disabled WC. Guide Dogs: No
£ **Adult:** £5.40 (house & garden), £4.20 (gardens) **Child:** Free **Other:** £5.10 (seniors house & garden), £3.95 (seniors garden)

Gants Mill

Gants Mill Lane, Bruton, Somerset BA10 0DB
Working watermill with deeds dating back to owner John le Gaunt in 1290. Documents were saved for posterity by the model for "Tom Jones's" Sophia Weston. Corn grinding demonstrations, historical displays and timeline of a millennium of milling - corn, wool and silk.
www.gantsmill.co.uk
Grant Recipient/Owner: Mr Brian Shingler
Access contact: Brian & Alison Shingler
Tel: 01749 812393
Email: shingler@gantsmill.co.uk
Open: Mill: Easter - end of May, Thurs and BH Mondays; Mill & Garden: June - end of Sept, Sun, Thurs and BH Mondays 2 - 5pm. Groups by arrangement. Refreshments available.
Heritage Open Days: No
P Spaces: 20
♿ Partial. Gardens accessible by wheelchair. No disabled WC. Guide Dogs: Yes
£ **Adult:** £3.50 **Child:** £1 **Other:** Group reductions by arrangement.

Goldney Hall Hercules Statue

Lower Clifton Hill, Bristol, Somerset BS8 1BH
Grade II* lead statue of Hercules. Erected 1758. Part of notable and well-preserved mid-18th century garden layout. Located approximately 100 metres south of Goldney Hall.
Grant Recipient/Owner: University of Bristol
Access contact: Mrs Ann Longney
Tel: 0117 903 4873/0117 954 4792
Open: Goldney Hall open day: 28 Apr 2 - 6pm; charity open days: 19 May, 23 June, 4 Aug 2 - 5.30pm. Group tours other times by arrangement with Mrs Ann Longney. Events held all year. Goldney Hall available for hire during the summer vacation.
Heritage Open Days: No
P On site during University vacations. Spaces: 22
♿ Yes. Wheelchair access to the statue and grounds. No disabled WC. Guide Dogs: Yes
£ On open days. **Adult:** £2 **Child/Other:** £1

Great House Farm

Theale, Wedmore, Somerset BS28 4SJ
17th century farmhouse with Welsh slate roof, oak doors and some original diamond paned windows. Inside is a carved well staircase with two murals on the walls. There are 4 servants rooms at the top, 3 of which are dark and occupied by Lesser Horseshoe bats.
Grant Recipient/Owner: Mr A R Millard
Access contact: Mr A R Millard
Tel: 01934 713133
Open: Apr - Aug: Tues and Thurs 2 - 6pm by telephone arrangement.
Heritage Open Days: No
P Spaces: 6 ♿ No. Guide Dogs: Yes
£ **Adult:** £2 **Child:** Free

Gurney Manor

Cannington, Somerset TA5 2MW
Late medieval house built around a courtyard. Used as a tenant farm before converted into flats in the 1940s, now restored to its original undivided state.
www.landmarktrust.co.uk
Grant Recipient/Owner: The Landmark Trust
Access contact: Ms Victoria Piggott
Tel: 01628 825920 **Fax:** 01628 825417
Email: vpiggott@landmarktrust.co.uk
Open: For details of opening arrangements at Landmark Trust properties please see the entry for Coop House, Netherby, Cumbria (page 549)
Heritage Open Days: No
P Spaces: 3 ♿ No. Guide Dogs: Yes £ No

Hall Farm High Barn

Stogumber, Taunton, Somerset TA4 3TQ
17th century Grade II* building with 7 bays of red local sandstone rubble with jointed cruck roof. South wall supported by 4 buttresses but there are none on the North wall. There are blocked windows on the South wall and 2 stub walls extend north. Lines of joist holes were provided for internal flooring and the 2 main entrances were to the north and south.
Grant Recipient/Owner: Mr G R Hayes
Access contact: Mr G R Hayes
Tel: 01984 656321
Open: By arrangement with Mr G R Hayes at Hall Farm.
Heritage Open Days: No
P Spaces: 4 ♿ Yes. No disabled WC. Guide Dogs: Yes
£ No

Hestercombe

Cheddon Fitzpaine, Taunton, Somerset TA2 8LG
Formal gardens, featuring terraces, rills and an orangery, designed by Sir Edwin Lutyens and Gertrude Jekyll. The newly restored Landscape Garden was designed by Bampfylde in 1750 and comprises 40 acre pleasure grounds with classical temples and a Great Cascade.
www.hestercombegardens.com
Grant Recipient/Owner: Somerset County Council
Access contact: Mrs J Manning
Tel: 01823 413923 **Fax:** 01823 413747
Email: info@hestercombegardens.com
Open: Daily, inc. Christmas Day, 10am - 5pm (last adm.).
Heritage Open Days: No
P Spaces: 100
♿ Partial. Limited wheelchair access to Gardens. Full access to tea room. Disabled WC. Guide Dogs: Yes
£ **Adult:** £4 **Child:** £1 (5-15yrs) **Seniors:** £3.80, £3.50 (groups 20+)

Merefield House Gazebo

East Street, Crewkerne, Somerset TA18 7AB
18th century garden house/gazebo, set in walled terraced town garden, approached by flight of steps. The stucco faced cube building has steep Dutch gable, supporting large lead eagle and sundial to the front. Virtually complete 18th century interior with hemispherical dome in the centre with vine leaves and grapes, set in a square moulded frame, with views over Crewkerne and the Dorset Hills.
Grant Recipient/Owner: Mr Roger Rousell
Access contact: Mr Roger Rousell
Tel: 01460 73222
Open: By arrangement with Mr Rousell.
Heritage Open Days: Yes
P No ♿ No. Guide Dogs: Yes £ No

The Old Manse

14 Bath Road, Beckington, Somerset BA11 6SW
Late 16th/early 17th century gabled stone built dwelling with mullioned windows with transoms to front elevation and stone tiled roof. Contains 2 large Plantagenet/Tudor fireplaces, 16th century oak staircase, strapwork ceilings and transitional rococo fireplaces. Gallery of attic rooms reveal an unusual roof structure.
Grant Recipient/Owner: Mr J Evans
Access contact: Mr J Evans
Tel: 01373 831401 **Fax:** 01373 831401
Email: jennie@stackridge.com
Open: By arrangement.
Heritage Open Days: No
P On-street parking. ♿ No. Guide Dogs: Yes
£ No

Orchard Wyndham

Williton, Somerset TA4 4HH
Manor house, originally medieval with many subsequent alterations and additions. Family home of the Wyndhams and their ancestors, the Orchards and Sydenhams, for 700 years.
Grant Recipient/Owner: Wyndham Estate
Access contact: Dr K S H Wyndham
Tel: 01984 632309 **Fax:** 01984 633526
Email: wyndhamest@talk21.com
Open: Aug: Thurs and Fridays 2 - 5pm, BH 11am - 5pm, by guided tour (groups, max 8, last tour 4pm). Other times by arrangement (min 2 weeks notice requested).
Heritage Open Days: No
P Spaces: 25
♿ Partial. Wheelchair access to ground floor and gardens only. No disabled WC. Guide Dogs: Yes
£ **Adult:** £5 **Child:** £1 (under 12)

Priest's House

Muchelney, Langport, Somerset TA10 0DQ
A late medieval hall house, built by Muchelney Abbey in 1308 for the parish priest and little altered since the hall was divided in the early 17th century. Interesting features include the Gothic doorway, beautiful tracery windows and a massive 15th century stone fireplace. The house is occupied and furnished by tenants.
www.nationaltrust.org.uk
Grant Recipient/Owner: The National Trust
Access contact: Sir Anthony Denny
Tel: 01458 252621
Open: 24 Mar - 30 Sept: Sundays and Mondays 2.30 - 5.30pm (last adm. 5.15pm).
Heritage Open Days: No
P On-street parking. Unsuitable for coaches and trailer caravans.
♿ No. Guide Dogs: Yes
£ £2

Prior Park College Chapel Mansion & Old Gymnasium,

Ralph Allen Drive, Bath, Somerset BA2 5AH
Built for Ralph Allen in mid-18th century as an early and successful demonstration of the quality of Bath stone. Chapel and Old Gymnasium are part of mid-19th century additions to adapt property as a Catholic seminary for Bishop Baines. Now boarding and day school.
www.park.co.uk
Grant Recipient/Owner: Governors of Prior Park College
Access contact: C J Freeman
Tel: 01225 837491 **Fax:** 01225 835753
Email: bursar@park.co.uk
Open: Chapel: Sundays all year for public worship, plus 17 June (to be confirmed), 2 - 5pm, or by arrangement. Mansion: some Sundays Mar - July 11.30am - 6pm, tel. or e-mail for details, plus 16 June (to be confirmed) 2 - 5pm; limited number of group tours July and Aug by arrangement Old Gymnasium: 8 July - 16 Aug, Mondays - Fridays 10am - 4pm but please tel in advance.
Heritage Open Days: No
P Spaces: 50
♿ Partial. Wheelchair access to ground floor of Mansion via wooden ramp and to Chapel. No access to upper floors of Mansion or Old Gymnasium. No disabled WC. Guide Dogs: Yes
£ £2.50

Opening arrangements at properties grant-aided by English Heritage

Robin Hood's Hut

Halswell Park, Goathurst, nr. Bridgwater, Somerset TA5 2DH

Thatched banqueting house, built in the 1760s to designs probably by Henry Keene, Surveyor of the Fabric at Westminster Abbey. Designed to look like a hermit's hut from the South, its Northern Italianate loggia has views over the Bristol Channel.

Grant Recipient/Owner: Somerset Building Preservation Trust Ltd

Access contact: Mrs Erica Adams

Tel: 01823 669022

Open: Access to the exterior of the building and umbrello at all times. Access to interior by arrangement with Mr D R Miller, Somerset Building Preservation Trust, Acacia House, 37 Station Road, Ilminster, Somerset TA19 9BG (tel.01460 52604) or The Landmark Trust, Shottesbrooke, Maidenhead, Berkshire SL6 3SW (tel. Victoria Piggott on 01628 825920). Partipating in Heritage Open Days: via Halswell Park Trust, contact Mr M Humphreys on 01823 443955 for details. One mile country walk with stiles.

Heritage Open Days: Yes

[P] No [♿] No. Guide Dogs: Yes [£] No

Rowes Leadworks

('Wildscreen at Bristol' and Firehouse restaurant), Harbourside, Bristol BS1 5DB

Former leadworks built in the 19th century. One of a few surviving structures associated with the industrial character of this area with goods station and nearby warehouses. Now transformed into restaurant/bar, The Firehouse Rotisseries. Attached is a modern canopied, large open structure, the entrance to 'Wildscreen at Bristol' featuring imagery and interactive exhibits of the natural world. Includes Imax cinema and living botanical house.

www.at-bristol.org.uk

Grant Recipient/Owner: Bristol City Council

Access contact: Mr John Durant

Tel: 0117 9092000 **Fax:** 0117 9157202

Email: john.durant@at-bristol.org.uk

Open: All venues: daily 10am - 6pm. Possible late openings for Aug (please ring for confirmation).

Heritage Open Days: No

[P] Pay parking operated by Bristol City Council. Spaces: 500

[♿] Yes. Disabled WC. Guide Dogs: Yes

[£] Charges for access to 'Wildscreen at Bristol

Rowlands Mill

Rowlands, Ilminster, Somerset TA19 9LE

Grade II* stone and brick 3-storey millhouse and machinery, c1620, with a mill pond, mill race, overshooting wheel and waterfall. The millhouse is now a holiday let but the machinery has separate access and is in working condition.

Grant Recipient/Owner: Mr P G H Speke

Access contact: Mr P G H Speke

Tel: 01460 52623 **Fax:** 01460 52623

Open: Millhouse Fridays and machinery Mon - Fri 10am - 4pm by written arrangement (at least 1 week's notice required). Heritage Open Days: machinery only unless a Friday, then whole building.

Heritage Open Days: Yes

[P] Spaces: 7

[♿] Partial. Wheelchair access to ground floor only. No disabled WC. Guide Dogs: Yes

[£] **Adult:** £3 **Child/Conc:** Free

Temple of Harmony

Halswell Park, Goathurst, nr. Bridgwater, Somerset TA5 2DH

18th century folly, a copy of the Temple of Verilis, forms part of the 18th century Pleasure Gardens at Halswell House. Restored in 1994.

www.somersite.co.uk/temple.htm

Grant Recipient/Owner: Somerset Buildings Preservation Trust

Access contact: Mr H M Humphreys

Tel: 01823 443955 **Email:** mick@somersite.co.uk

Open: 1 June - end Sept: Sats and Suns 2 - 5pm, plus Easter W/end and May Day BH. Other days by arrangement with Mr H M Humphreys, Hon Secretary, The Halswell Park Trust, Creech Barn, Creech St Michael, Taunton, Somerset TA3 5PP.

Heritage Open Days: Yes

[P] Spaces: 4 [♿] No. Guide Dogs: Yes

[£] **Adult:** £1 **Child/Conc:** 50p

Wells Old Almshouses

Chamberlain Street, Wells, Somerset BA5 2PJ

Comprises 4 unchanged almshouses, the oldest dating from 1435, with a Guild Room, chapel and gardens.

Grant Recipient/Owner: Wells Old Almshouses Trust

Access contact: Mr John Warne

Tel: 01749 671286 **Fax:** 01749 677399

Email: johnwarne@roza.freeserve.co.uk

Heritage Open Days:: Sat and Sun 11am - 4pm. At other times by arrangement with the Secretary, Wells Old Almshouses Trust, 16 Carlton Mews, Wells, Somerset BA5 1SG.

[P] No [♿] Yes. No disabled WC. Guide Dogs: Yes [£] No

SOUTH YORKSHIRE

Cusworth Hall

Museum of South Yorkshire Life, Cusworth Lane, Doncaster, South Yorkshire DN5 7TU

Grade I listed 18th century country house designed by George Platt with additions by James Paine, set in a landscaped park designed by Richard Woods. Home of the Battie-Wrightson family until 1952, now converted into a museum of South Yorkshire life.

Grant Recipient/Owner: Doncaster Metropolitan Borough Council

Access contact: Mr F Carpenter

Tel: 01302 782342 **Fax:** 01302 782342

Email: museum@doncaster.gov.uk

Open: Mon - Fri 10am - 5pm, Sat 11am- 5pm, Sun 1 - 5pm. Early closing 4pm Dec and Jan. Closed Christmas Day, Boxing Day and Good Fri. Refreshments available.

Heritage Open Days: No

[P] Spaces: 150

[♿] Partial. Wheelchair access to ground floor, tea room, shop and Great Kitchen. Disabled WC. Guide Dogs: Yes

[£] No

Hickleton Hall

Hickleton, South Yorkshire DN5 7BB

Georgian Mansion, Grade II*, built in 1740s to a design by James Paine with later additions. The interior is noted for its plasterwork ceilings. Set in 15 acres of formal gardens laid out in the early 1900s, the Hall is now a residential care home.

Grant Recipient/Owner: Sue Ryder Care

Access contact: Mrs A J Towriss

Tel: 01709 892070 **Fax:** 01709 890140

Open: By appointment with Mrs Towriss at Sue Ryder Care, Mon - Fri 2 - 4pm.

Heritage Open Days: No

[P] Parking available.

[♿] Partial. Wheelchair access to House only; no access to gardens. Disabled WC. Guide Dogs: Yes [£] No

The Lyceum Theatre

Tudor Square, Sheffield, South Yorkshire S1 1DA

Grade II* theatre built 1897. Only surviving example of the work of WGR Sprague outside London. Its special features include a domed corner tower, a lavish Rococo auditorium (1097 seats) and a proscenium arch with a rare open-work valance in gilded plasterwork. A notable example of a theatre of the period, with a largely unaltered interior.

www.sheffieldtheatres.co.uk

Grant Recipient/Owner: The Lyceum Theatre Trust

Access contact: Box Office

Tel: 0114 249 5999/ 6000 **Fax:** 0114 249 6003

Email: grahame@sheffieldtheatres.co.uk

Open: For performances all year. 21 scheduled backstage tours per year. Tours start 10.30am. Group guided tours by arrangement. Contact Box Office (0114 249 6000) or check the website for further information.

Heritage Open Days: No

[P] National Car Park adjacent to the theatre.

[♿] Partial. Disabled WC. Guide Dogs: Yes

[£] **Adult:** £2.50 (backstage tour). Admission charge for performances.

The Mansion House

High Street, Doncaster, South Yorkshire DN1 1DG

One of only 3 Mansion Houses in the country, the others being in London and York. Originally built as a residence for the Mayor in the late 1740s, now used as a meeting place for the local authority. Contains ballroom with many paintings of local dignitaries, a banqueting room which is now used as the Council Chamber, the Peace Window at the top of the main staircase depicting local history and the coat of arms, and a kitchen with many original fitings.

Grant Recipient/Owner: The Chief Executive

Access contact: Mr Horace Shillito

Tel: 01302 734032 **Fax:** 01302 734040

Email: irene.raw@doncaster.gov.uk

Open: By arrangement only Mon - Fri 8.30am - 5pm and evenings, contact Doncaster Metropolitan Borough Council, 2 Priory Place, Doncaster, South Yorkshire DN1 1BN. The Mayor hosts an annual open day to the public each summer (free entry). Confirmation of dates available each Spring .

Heritage Open Days: No

[P] In town centre car parks during the day, street parking in evening. Parking for disabled adjacent to property day and night.

[♿] Partial. Wheelchair access to upper floors restricted by small lift which will not accommodate large wheelchairs, for further information please check with the Council. No disabled WC. Guide Dogs: Yes

[£] **Adult:** £2 (evenings only)

Moated Site & Chapel

Thorpe Lane, Thorpe-in-Balne, nr. Doncaster, South Yorkshire DN6 ODY

Medieval chapel, moated site and fishponds. Built 12th century with 13th, 14th, 15th and 19th century alterations. Restored and re-roofed in 1994/5. In 1452 the chapel was the scene of the forcible abduction of Joan, wife of Charles Nowel, by Edward Lancaster of Skipton in Craven, which resulted in the passing of an Act of Parliament for the redress of grievance and the better protection of females.

Grant Recipient/Owner: Mr Attey

Access contact: Mrs Attey

Tel: 01302 883160

Open: By arrangement with Mrs Attey at the Manor House, Thorpe Lane, Thorpe-in-Balne, nr. Doncaster, South Yorks DN6 0DY.

Heritage Open Days: No

[P] Spaces: 10 [♿] No. Guide Dogs: Yes

[£] **Adult:** Donations for charity welcomed

STAFFORDSHIRE

2-5 The Close

Lichfield, Staffordshire WS13 7LD

External steps and handrails to (mainly) early 18th century houses in the Cathedral Close.

Grant Recipient/Owner: The Dean & Chapter of Lichfield Cathedral

Access contact: The Dean & Chapter of Lichfield Cathedral

Tel: 01543 306100 **Fax:** 01543 306109

Email: enquiries@lichfield-cathedral.org

Open: At all reasonable times (exterior only).

Heritage Open Days: No

[P] Public car parks nearby.

[♿] Yes. Disabled WC. Guide Dogs: Yes [£] No

10 The Close

Lichfield, Staffordshire WS13 7LD

Early 15th century timber-framed house, originally one-up one-down and part of a five-dwelling range in the Vicar's Close. Notable doors and solid tread staircase remains in attic. Currently residence of assistant cathedral organist.

Grant Recipient/Owner: Dean & Chapter of Lichfield Cathedral

Access contact: Mr Robert Sharpe

Tel: 01543 306201 **Fax:** 01543 306201

Open: By written arrangement.

Heritage Open Days: No

[P] Public car parks nearby. [♿] No. Guide Dogs: Yes

[£] No

Barlaston Hall

Barlaston, nr. Stoke-on-Trent, Staffordshire ST12 9AT

Mid-18th century Palladian villa attributed to Sir Robert Taylor, with public rooms containing some fine examples of 18th century plasterwork. Extensively restored during the 1990s.

Grant Recipient/Owner: Mr James Hall

Access contact: Mr James Hall

Fax: 01782 372391

Open: 5 Mar - 10 Sept: Tues 2 - 5pm. No groups.

Heritage Open Days: No

[P] Spaces: 6 [♿] No

[£] **Adult:** £2.50 **Child:** £1.50 No charge for Historic Houses Association members.

Biddulph Grange Garden

Biddulph, Stoke-on-Trent, Staffordshire ST8 7SD

Garden with series of connected apartments designed to display specimens from James Bateman's extensive and wide ranging plant collection. Visitors are taken on a miniature tour of the world featuring the Egyptian court, China, a Scottish glen, a pinetum and rock areas.

www.nationaltrust.org.uk

Grant Recipient/Owner:

Access contact: Christine Belford/ Andrew Humphris

Tel: 01782 517999 **Fax:** 01782 510624

Email: mbgwxm@smtp.ntrust.org.uk

Open: 23 Mar - 3 Nov: Wed - Fri 12 noon - 5.30pm, Sat and Sun 11am - 5.30pm (High Season). 11 Nov - 22 Dec: Sat and Sun 12 noon - 4pm (Low Season).

Heritage Open Days: No

[P] Spaces: 100

[♿] Partial. Wheelchair access to Lime Avenue, Lake, Pinetum, Cheshire Cottage, Egypt and East Terrace. No disabled WC. Guide Dogs: Yes

[£] **Adult:** £4.50 (High Season), Free (Low Season) **Child:** £2.40 (High Season), Free (Low Season) **Other:** £11.50 (family, High Season)

Cannock Chase Technical College

"The White House", The Green, Cannock, Staffordshire WS11 1UE

Grade II three-storey 19th century manor house built of rendered brick with pitched slate roof.

Grant Recipient/Owner: Staffordshire County Council

Access contact: Cannock Chase Technical College

Tel: 01543 462200 **Fax:** 01543 574223

Open: During College term times: 8.30am - 9.30pm. Out of term: 9.30am - 5pm. Closed public holidays.

Heritage Open Days: No

[P] On-site parking by arrangement.

[♿] Partial. Wheelchair access ground floor only. Disabled WC in adjacent main building. Guide Dogs: Yes

[£] No

Cheddleton Flint Mill

Cheddleton, Leek, nr. Stoke-on-Trent, Staffordshire ST13 7HL

18th century complex for grinding flint comprising 2 working watermills. South Mill modified in 19th century, now contains displays relating to the pottery industry.

Grant Recipient/Owner: R Copeland
Access contact: E E Royle, MBE
Tel: 01782 502907
Email: eroyle.carol@cwctv
Open: Daily 10am - 5pm.
Heritage Open Days: Yes
P Spaces: 12
♿ Partial. Wheelchair access to ground floor only. No disabled WC. Guide Dogs: No £ No

Claymills Pumping Engines

The Victorian Pumping Station, The Sewage Works, Meadow Lane, Stretton, Burton-on-Trent, Staffordshire DE13 0BA

Large Victorian steam-operated sewage pumping station built 1885. Four beam engines housed in two Italianate engine houses, one operational on steaming w/ends. Boiler house with range of five Lancashire boilers, large Victorian steam-operated workshop with blacksmith's forge, steam hammer, and steam driven machinery. 1930s dynamo house with very early D.C. generating equipment, earliest dynamo 1889 (all operational).

Grant Recipient/Owner: Severn Trent Water Ltd
Access contact: Mr Roy Barratt
Tel: 01283 534960
Email: roybarratt@yahoo.co.uk
Open: Every Thurs and Sat for static viewing. Steaming w/ends: 31 Dec 2001 - 1 Jan 2002, 31 Mar/1 Apr, 5/6 May, 15/16 June, 25/26 Aug, 21/22 Sept, 19/20 Oct, 28/29 Dec. Charge for steaming w/ends, donations requested on other open days. Refreshments available.
Heritage Open Days: No
P Parking for disabled adjacent to site. Parking available for 6 coaches. Spaces: 100
♿ Partial. Wheelchair access to ground floor only (boiler house, workshop, refreshment area, engine house). Disabled WC. Guide Dogs: Yes
£ **Adult:** £3 **Child:** £2 **Other:** £2 (seniors), £7 (family)

Ingestre Pavilion

Tixall, nr. Stafford, Staffordshire ST18 0XT

The pavilion was built in 1752 as part of a formal garden layout subsequently altered by 'Capability' Brown. The façade is a powerful and distinguished one, although the architect is not known. The building behind it had been demolished by 1802 and so there are now new ones including an octagonal saloon.
www.landmarktrust.co.uk

Grant Recipient/Owner: The Landmark Trust
Access contact: Ms Victoria Piggott
Tel: 01628 825920 **Fax:** 01628 825417
Email: vpiggott@landmarktrust.co.uk
Open: For details of opening arrangements at Landmark Trust properties please see the entry for Coop House, Netherby, Cumbria (page 549)
Heritage Open Days: No
P Spaces: 2 ♿ No. Guide Dogs: Yes £ No

Kinver Edge (Hill Fort)

nr. Stourbridge, Staffordshire

Sandstone ridge covered in woodland and heath with Iron Age hill fort with views across surrounding countryside. Famous Holy Austin Rock Houses, inhabited until 1950s, have been restored and parts are open to visitors at selected times.
www.nationaltrust.org.uk

Grant Recipient/Owner: The National Trust
Access contact: The Warden
Tel: 01384 872418
Open: Kinver Edge open at all times free. Holy Austin Rock House grounds: daily, Apr - Sept 9am - 7pm, Oct - Mar 9am - 4pm. Upper Terrace: Wed, Sat and Sun, Apr - Sept 2 - 5pm, Oct - Mar 2 - 4pm. Lower Rock Houses: Sats only 2 - 4pm. Other times for guided tours by arrangement with Custodian (tel.01384 842553).
Heritage Open Days: No
P Spaces: 100 ♿ No. Guide Dogs: Yes
£ Lower Rock Houses only **Adult:** 40p **Child:** 20p

Shugborough

Milford, Stafford, Staffordshire ST17 0XB

The present house was begun c1695. Between 1760 and 1770 it was enlarged and again partly remodelled by Samuel Wyatt at end of 18th century. The interior is particularly notable for its plaster work and other decorations. Ancestral home of the Earls of Lichfield. Houses the Staffordshire County Museum, Georgian working farm and Rare Livestock Breed project.
www.staffordshire.gov.uk

Grant Recipient/Owner: The National Trust
Access contact: Staffordshire County Council
Tel: 01889 881388
Open: 30 Mar to 29 Sept: House, county museum, farm and gardens: daily except Mondays (but open BH Mondays); Oct first three Suns only; 11am - 5pm (last adm. 4.15pm). Times may vary, tel. to check. Tours for booked groups daily from 10.30am. Evening tours also available.
Heritage Open Days: No
P Spaces: 600
♿ Partial. Wheelchair access to ground floor of house and museum only. Disabled WC. Guide Dogs: Yes
£ **Adult:** £4.50 (per site), £9.00 (to all sites) **Child:** £3 (per site), £6 (to all sites) **Other:** £12.00 (per site), £22.00 (to all sites)

Sinai House

Branston, Shobnall, Staffordshire DE14 2BB

Timber-framed E-shaped house, two-thirds derelict, on moated hill-top site, dating from 13th century. House built variously during 15th, 16th and 17th centuries with later additions, including wall paintings and carpenters marks. 18th century bridge and plunge pool in grounds.

Grant Recipient/Owner: Ms C A Newton
Access contact: Ms C A Newton
Tel: 01283 544161/01889 567777 **Fax:** 01889 563258
Email: knewton@brookes-vernons.co.uk
Open: By arrangement only.
Heritage Open Days: No
P No ♿ No. Guide Dogs: Yes £ No

South Fortification Wall

The Close, Lichfield, Staffordshire WS13 7LD

External wall comprising remaining part of medieval building. Set in grounds next to Cathedral Visitors' Centre.

Grant Recipient/Owner: The Dean & Chapter of Lichfield Cathedral
Access contact: The Dean & Chapter of Lichfield Cathedral
Tel: 01543 306100
Open: Grounds open daily 9am - 5pm.
Heritage Open Days: No
P Public car parks nearby.
♿ Yes. Disabled WC. Guide Dogs: Yes £ No

Speedwell Castle

Bargate Street, Brewood, Staffordshire ST19 9BB

Grade I listed. Mid 18th century, red brick designed in the manner of Strawberry Hill. Reputed to have been built by William Rock (d.1753) from the proceeds of betting on the racehorse Speedwell.

Grant Recipient/Owner: Penk Holdings Ltd
Access contact: Mr A S Monckton
Tel: 01902 850214 **Fax:** 01902 850354
Open: The façade can be viewed from Bargate Street and Stafford Street.
Heritage Open Days: No
P No ♿ No. Guide Dogs: Yes £ No

St Mary's

(Lichfield Heritage Centre), Market Square, Lichfield, Staffordshire WS13 6LG

Grade II* medieval guild church, rebuilt 1868-70 by James Fowler. Many original features are preserved and the building is a prominent city landmark. Houses a Community Centre comprising a Heritage Centre, Social Centre for senior citizens, coffee and craft shops, continues to function as the parish church.
www.lichfieldheritage.org.uk

Grant Recipient/Owner: The Guild of St Mary's Centre
Access contact: The Guild of St Mary's Centre
Tel: 01543 256611 **Fax:** 01543 414749
Email: smc@lichfieldheritage.org.uk
Open: Lichfield Heritage Centre: daily 10am - 5pm (last adm. 4.15pm).
Heritage Open Days: Yes
P Pay-and-display parking nearby.
♿ Yes. Disabled WC. Guide Dogs: Yes
£ **Adult:** £2 **Child:** £1.50 (& concessions) **Family:** £6

SUFFOLK

Aldeburgh Moot Hall

Aldeburgh, Suffolk IP15 5DS

Grade I 16th century woodframed building, still in use as a Town Hall. Houses the Moot Hall Museum with collections of local historical interest, including objects from the Snape Ship Burial.

Grant Recipient/Owner: Aldeburgh Town Council
Access contact: Aldeburgh Town Council
Open: Town Hall: Mon and Fri 9.30am - 12.30pm, Weds 2.30 - 4.30pm. Museum: Apr and May: Sat and Sun 2.30 - 5pm; June, Sept and Oct: daily 2.30 - 5pm; July and Aug: daily 10.30am - 12.30pm and 2.30 - 5pm. School groups and tours by arrangement (tel.01728 452158).
Heritage Open Days: Yes
P Public parking alongside building.
♿ No. Guide Dogs: Yes
£ Museum **Adult:** 80p **Child:** Free **Other:** 10% discount on museum entry for group

Christchurch Mansion

Christchurch Park, Soane Street, Ipswich, Suffolk IP4 2BD

16th century red brick mansion with some blue brick diapering, set in fine parkland in the centre of town. The Mansion and its collections trace the lives of the three wealthy families who made it their home. Paintings, English domestic furniture, kitchen and servants' area.
www.ipswich.gov.uk

Grant Recipient/Owner: Ipswich Borough Council
Access contact: Mr Tim Heyburn
Tel: 01473 433543 **Fax:** 01473 433558
Email: tim.heyburn@ipswich.gov.uk
Open: 28 Oct 2001 - 6 Feb 2002: Tues - Sat 10am - 4pm, Sun 2.30 - 4pm. 7 Feb - 27 Sept: Tues - Sat 10am - 5pm, Sun 2.30 - 4.30pm.
Heritage Open Days: Yes
P Public parking within 400 metres. Spaces: 1200
♿ Partial. Wheelchair access to most of ground floor and Wolsey Art Gallery. Disabled WC. Guide Dogs: No
£ No

Culford School Iron Bridge

Culford, Bury St Edmunds, Suffolk IP28 6TX

Constructed for 2nd Marquis Cornwallis in late 1790s by Samuel Wyatt, brother of James, to design patented by Wyatt. The bridge, in Culford Park, is one of the earliest surviving bridges with an unmodified cast iron structure, being the earliest known example with hollow ribs.

Grant Recipient/Owner: Mr J W Beaty
Access contact: Michael Woolley
Tel: 01284 729318 **Fax:** 01284 729077
Email: bursar@culford.co.uk
Open: Access to Iron Bridge and Culford Park is available at any time all year.
Heritage Open Days: No
P Spaces: 100
♿ Partial. Disabled access may be difficult as over grass and rough track. Toilet facilities are only available when Culford School is open and ramps in place. Disabled WC. Guide Dogs: Yes
£ No

Elms Farm Wallpaintings

Old Station Road, Mendlesham, Suffolk IP14 5RS

Wealden hall house dating from 1480, wallpaintings consist of 16th century floral design and Biblical texts in the upper hall and solar and 17th century armorial patterning in the parlour.

Grant Recipient/Owner: Mrs Pamela Gilmour
Access contact: Mrs Pamela Gilmour
Open: By written arrangement.
Heritage Open Days: No
P Spaces: 10 ♿ No £ No

Flatford Mill

Willy Lott's House and Flatford Bridge Cottage, Flatford, East Bergholt, Colchester, Suffolk CO7 6OL

Flatford watermill, 1733 datestone, incorporating possibly earlier but altered former granary range to rear and further 19th Century range adjoining granary. Later alterations. The mill was in the possession of the Constable family from the mid 18th Century. Willy Lott's farmhouse, late 16th-17th Century. Grade I listing of both buildings reflects their significance in the life and work of John Constable. Both buildings leased by the National Trust to Field Studies Council. Flatford Bridge Cottage 16th century thatched cottage, upstream from Flatford Mill houses an exhibition on John Constable.
www.nationaltrust.org.uk/eastanglia

Grant Recipient/Owner: The National Trust
Access contact: Property Manager
Tel: 01206 298260 **Fax:** 01206 299193
Email: atdcykx@smtp.ntrust.org.uk
Open: Flatford Mill and Willy Lott's House owned by the National Trust and leased to Field Studies Council which runs arts-based courses for all ages (for information on courses tel: 01206 298283). No general public access to interior of buildings, but the Field Studies Council will arrange tours for groups. Flatford Bridge Cottage is open Mar and Apr daily except Mondays and Tues 11am - 5.30pm; May to end Sept daily 10am - 5.30pm; Oct daily 11am - 5.30pm; Nov and Dec daily except Mondays and Tues 11am - 3.30pm. Closed Christmas and New Year. For further information contact the Property Manager.
Heritage Open Days: No
P Car park 200 metres from Flatford Bridge Cottage. Parking near the Cottage available for disabled visitors. Spaces: 2000
♿ Partial. Wheelchair access to tea-garden and shop. Lavatory for disabled available in car park owned by Babergh DC, 23 metres from Cottage. Guide Dogs: Yes
£ No

Hall Farm Barn

Withersfield, Suffolk CB9 7RY

100ft long by 30ft wide thatched barn built c1400, with later alterations. Floor is split into 3 levels with the east wall having been bricked-in between the timbers and the west

wall still consisting of horsehair, lathe and plaster. Situated in working farmyard.
Grant Recipient/Owner: Mr C R W Bradford
Access contact: Mr T Mytton-Mills
Tel: 01440 702146 **Fax:** 01440 702552
Email: tom@hall-farm.fsnet.co.uk
Open: By telephone arrangement.
Heritage Open Days: No
P Spaces: 12 ♿ Yes. Disabled WC. Guide Dogs: Yes
£ No

Horseman's House

Boundary Farm, Framsden, Suffolk IP14 6LH
Mid 17th century brick stable. Gable ended with brick pinnacles along upper edge with panels of diaper work in dark headers below round vents/owl holes. Original three bay, two storey structure housed horseman above his charges in unusually ornate accommodation for all. Now horse and rider holiday accommodation.
Grant Recipient/Owner: Mr Bacon
Access contact: Mr Bacon
Tel: 01728 860370 **Fax:** 01728 860370
Email: info@boundaryfarm.co.uk
Open: By arrangement with Mr Bacon, Saturdays 10am - 3pm. It may be possible occasionally to visit until 4pm.
Heritage Open Days: No
P Spaces: 4
♿ Partial. Wheelchair access to ground floor stable and outside of building. Disabled WC. Guide Dogs: Yes
£ No

Ickworth House

Horringer, Bury St Edmunds, Suffolk IP29 5QE
The Earl of Bristol created this eccentric house, with its central rotunda and curved corridors, in 1795 to display his collections including paintings by Titian, Gainsborough and Velasquez and a Georgian silver collection. The house is surrounded by an Italianate garden in a 'Capability' Brown park, woodland walks, Deer enclosure, vineyard, Georgian summerhouse and lake.
www.nationaltrust.org.uk/eastanglia
Grant Recipient/Owner: The National Trust
Access contact: Property Manager
Tel: 01284 735270 **Fax:** 01284 735175
Email: arore@smtp.ntrust.org.uk
Open: House: 23 Mar - 3 Nov: daily except Mons and Thursdays (but open BH Mondays) 1 - 5pm (last adm. 4.30pm). Closes 4.30pm in Oct. Garden: 23 Mar - 3 Nov: daily 10am - 5pm (last adm. 4.30pm); 4 Nov - 21 Dec: daily except Saturdays and Sundays 10am - 4pm. Park open daily 7am - 7pm but closed Christmas Day.
Heritage Open Days: No
P Spaces: 2000
♿ Partial. Wheelchair access to House: ramped access (restricted access in House for large powered vehicles/chairs); lift to first floor; stairlift to basement (shop and restaurant) suitable for wheelchair users able to transfer; wheelchair on each floor. Garden largely accessible, some changes of level, gravel drive and paths. Disabled WC. Guide Dogs: Yes
£ **Adult:** £5.95, £2.70 (park & garden only) **Child:** £2.60, 80p (park & garden only) **Other:** £4.95 (group rate). No group rates Suns & BH Mons. Family discounts

Long Shop Steam Museum

Main Street, Leiston, Suffolk IP16 4ES
Museum housed in the original Richard Garrett & Sons Ltd buildings including the Long Shop, built 1852 as the first purpose-built flow line for the production of portable steam engines. 4 exhibition halls and education/resource centre.
www.longshop.care4free.net
Grant Recipient/Owner: Mr J R G Perrett
Access contact: Mr J R G Perrett
Tel: 01728 832189 **Fax:** 01728 832189
Email: longshop@care4free.net
Open: 1 Apr - 31 Oct: Mon - Sat 10am - 5pm, Sun 11am - 5pm.
Heritage Open Days: No
P Spaces: 40
♿ Partial. Wheelchair access to 95% of site. Disabled WC. Guide Dogs: Yes
£ **Adult:** £3 **Child:** 75p (under 5s free) **Senior Citizen:** £2.50

Nowton Hall

Nowton, Bury St Edmunds, Suffolk IP29 5NA
Former farmhouse dating from 1595. The main point of interest is the parlour chamber which contains painted 'ceiling work'.
Grant Recipient/Owner: Mr Wentworth Waites
Access contact: Mr Wentworth Waites
Open: By arrangement with Mr Wentworth Waites, (address details above). Two weeks' notice required.
Heritage Open Days: No
P Spaces: 1 ♿ No £ No

Somerleyton Hall & Gardens

Somerleyton, Lowestoft, Suffolk NR32 5QQ
Early Victorian stately home, built in Anglo-Italian style for Sir Morton Peto by John Thomas upon former Jacobean mansion. Contains carved stonework and state rooms. Twelve acres of gardens with a yew hedge maze.
www.somerleyton.co.uk
Grant Recipient/Owner: The Rt Hon Lord Somerleyton GCVO
Access contact: Mr Ian Pollard
Tel: 01502 730224 **Fax:** 01502 732143
Email: enquiries@somerleyton.co.uk
Open: Easter Sun - end of Sept: Thursdays, Sundays and BHs, plus Tues and Weds in July and Aug, 12.30 - 5.30pm. Charges provisional at time of going to print, please check with Hall for current rates.
Heritage Open Days: No
P Spaces: 200 ♿ Yes. Disabled WC. Guide Dogs: Yes
£ Provisional **Adult:** £5.20 **Child:** £2.60
Seniors: £5 **Family:** £14.60

St John Lateran

Hengrave Hall, Hengrave,
Bury St Edmunds, Suffolk IP28 6LZ.
Grade I parish church dedicated to St John Lateran. Circular tower in coursed flint, possibly pre-Conquest. 13th century chancel with later additions. Noted for several of its monuments. Now known as Church of Reconciliation, it reflects the present ecumenical vision of Hengrave Hall as a Christian retreat and conference centre and home of Hengrave Community of Reconciliation.
www.hengravehallcentre.org.uk
Grant Recipient/Owner: Hengrave Hall Centre
Access contact: Mr J H Crowe
Tel: 01284 701561 **Fax:** 01284 702950
Email: administrator@hengravehallcentre.org.uk
Open: Church open all year, although the Hall is closed to visitors 24 - 27 Dec. Tours of the Hall by arrangement with the Administrator.
Heritage Open Days: Yes
P Free, 50 metres from Church, 25 metres from Hall. Overflow car park near Church. Spaces: 100
♿ Partial. Wheelchair access to Church and ground floor of Hall only. No disabled WC. Guide Dogs: Yes
£ No but donations to Church welcome

St Lawrence

Dial Lane, Ipswich, Suffolk IP1 1DL
15th century aisleless church with a 97 foot west tower, enlarged in the 19th century and recently restored. Declared redundant in 1975.
Grant Recipient/Owner: Ipswich Historic Churches Trust
Access contact: Mr J S Hall
Tel: 01473 232300 **Fax:** 01473 230524
Email: james-hall@birketts.co.uk
Open: By arrangement with Mr Hall, office hours and weekdays only. At least 24 hours notice required. At other times and days subject to longer notice.
Heritage Open Days: No
P In town centre car parks (10 minute walk).
♿ No £ No

St Peter

College Street, Ipswich, Suffolk IP4 1DD
Large medieval church near the docks, owned by Ipswich Borough Council and redundant since the 1970s. Noted for a Tournai font and adjacent to Thomas Wolsey's gateway. Empty and unused.
Grant Recipient/Owner: Ipswich Historic Churches Trust
Access contact: Mr J S Hall
Tel: 01473 232300 **Fax:** 01473 230524
Email: james-hall@birketts.co.uk
Open: By arrangement with Mr Hall (tel.01473 232300), office hours, weekdays only. 24 hours notice required. Open at other times and days subject to longer notice.
Heritage Open Days: No
P No
♿ Partial. Wheelchair access to all of church apart from the vestry and parts of the chancel. No disabled WC. Guide Dogs: Yes £ No

Steeple Bumpstead Moot Hall

Steeple Bumpstead, nr. Haverhill,
Suffolk CB9 7DQ
Elizabethan two-storey timber-framed building with jettied upper hall, hipped tiled roof supported by crown post and surmounted by mutilated stone lion at the apex. Originally considered to have been a guildhall but subsequently housed a school founded in 1592. Currently used for meetings and public library.
Grant Recipient/Owner: The Moot Hall (Old School) Trustees
Access contact: Mr P E Bruty
Tel: 01440 730558
Open: Thurs 2 - 4pm, other times by written arrangement with Mr P E Bruty of The Moot Hall Charity, 5 Blois Road, Steeple Bumpstead, nr. Haverhill, Suffolk CB9 7BN.
Heritage Open Days: No
P On-street parking (unrestricted).
♿ Partial. Wheelchair and guide dog access to ground floor only. No disabled WC. Guide Dogs: Yes
£ No

Theatre Royal

Westgate Street, Bury St Edmunds, Suffolk IP33 1QR
A rare example of a late Georgian playhouse. Built 1819, later used as a warehouse but restored and re-opened as a theatre in 1965. Constructed of white brick and stucco with a slate roof.
www.theatreroyal.org
Grant Recipient/Owner: The National Trust
Access contact: The Administrator
Tel: 01284 755127 **Fax:** 01284 706035
Email: admin@theatreroyal.org
Open: May - end of Sept: Tues and Thurs 11am - 1pm and 2 - 4pm (tours at 11.30am and 2.30pm); Sats 11am - 1pm (tour at 11.30am). Open all year for performances.
Heritage Open Days: Yes
P Limited parking in Westgate Street.
♿ Partial. Disabled WC. Guide Dogs: Yes
£ No but admission charge for performances

Woodbridge Lodge

Rendlesham, nr. Woodbridge, Suffolk IP12 2RA
Late 18th century small gothic folly. Originally a gatehouse to Rendlesham Hall, now part of a dwelling house.
Grant Recipient/Owner: Dr C P Cooper
Access contact: Dr C P Cooper
Tel: 01394 460642
Open: Exterior only by prior arrangment
Heritage Open Days: No
P Spaces: 3 ♿ No £ No

SURREY

Beddington Park Dovecote

Church Road, Beddington, Wallington,
Surrey SM6 7NH
Early 18th century large octagonal brick dovecote with c1200 interior nesting boxes and original potence (circular ladder).
www.sutton.gov.uk/lfl/heritage
Grant Recipient/Owner: London Borough of Sutton
Access contact: Ms Valary Murphy
Tel: 020 8770 4781 **Fax:** 020 8770 4777
Email: valary.murphy@sutton.gov.uk
Open: Sundays: 12 May, 30 June, 6 Oct, 2 - 5pm. Guided tours of Carew Manor at 2pm and 3.30pm. Groups at other times by arrangement with Valary Murphy, The Heritage Service, Central Library, St Nicholas Way, Sutton, Surrey SM1 1EA.
Heritage Open Days: No
P Spaces: 30 ♿ No. Guide Dogs: Yes
£ Free for Dovecote; charge for guided tours of Carew Manor

Carshalton Water Tower

West Street, Carshalton, Surrey SM5
18th century garden building with an Orangery, Saloon, plunge-bath lined with Delft tiles, part-restored water wheel and stone pump chamber. Built 1721 for Sir John Fellowes, sub-Governor of the South Sea Company.
www.sutton.gov.uk/lfl/heritage/watertower
Grant Recipient/Owner: Carshalton Water Tower Trust
Access contact: Mrs Julia Gertz
Tel: 020 8647 0984
Open: First Sun in Apr - last Sun in Sept 2.30 - 5pm, plus local and national Heritage Open Days:. Private tours by arrangement with Friends of Carshalton Water Tower, 136 West Street, Carshalton, Surrey SM5 2NR.
Heritage Open Days: Yes
P Parking available by arrangement.
♿ Yes. Disabled WC. Guide Dogs: Yes
£ **Adult:** 75p **Child:** 25p

Clandon Park

West Clandon, Guildford, Surrey GU4 7RQ
Palladian mansion, built c1730 by Venetian architect Giacomo Leoni. Two-storeyed Marble Hall, collection of 18th century furniture, porcelain, textiles, carpets, the Ivo Forde Meissen collection of Italian comedy figures and a series of Mortlake tapestries. Grounds contain grotto, sunken Dutch garden, Maori Meeting House and Museum of the Queen's Royal Surrey Regiment.
www.clandonpark.co.uk
Grant Recipient/Owner: The National Trust
Access contact: Mr David Brock-Doyle
Tel: 01483 222482 **Fax:** 01483 223479
Email: sclsea@smtp.ntrust.org.uk
Open: House: 24 Mar - 3 Nov: daily except Mon, Fri and Sat (but open Good Fri, Easter Sat and BH Mondays) 11am - 5pm (last adm. 4.30pm). Museum: as for house 12 noon - 5pm. Garden: all year as house 11am - 5pm.
Heritage Open Days: No
P Spaces: 200
♿ Partial. Wheelchair access to lower ground floor and 5 steps to ground floor. Disabled WC. Guide Dogs: Yes
£ **Adult:** £6 **Child:** £3 **Other:** £15 (family), £5 (group rate, per head Tues, Weds & Thurs only)

Claremont House

Claremont Drive, Esher, Surrey KT10 9LY

Built 1772 in Palladian style by 'Capability' Brown for Clive of India. Henry Holland and John Soane were responsible for the interior decoration. For over a century it was a royal residence, home to Charlotte, Princess of Wales, the young Queen Victoria, and the Duke and Duchess of Albany.
www.claremont-school.co.uk
Grant Recipient/Owner: Claremont Fan Court Foundation Ltd
Access contact: Mr J H Farrar
Tel: 01372 467841 **Fax:** 01372 471109
Email: jhfarrar@claremont69.freeserve.co.uk
Open: Guided tours by arrangement.
Heritage Open Days: No
P Spaces: 100
♿ Partial. Wheelchair access by arrangement. No disabled WC. Guide Dogs: Yes
£ **Adult:** £3 **Child:** £1.50 **Other:** £2

Englefield Green Cemetery

St Jude's Road, Englefield Green, Egham, Surrey TW20 0BZ

Pair of mausolea, c1860 by E B Lamb who designed the adjacent church of St Simon, for Fitzroy Somerset family. Grade II* in limestone and banded red brick.
Grant Recipient/Owner: Englefield Borough Council
Access contact: Mr R W Greenland
Tel: 01932 838383 **Fax:** 01932 855135
Open: Cemetery open at all times.
Heritage Open Days: No
P Parking on-site.
♿ Full wheelchair access to mausolea, remainder of cemetery partially accessible with assistance (some grass paths). No disabled WC. Guide Dogs: Yes £ No

Great Fosters

Stroude Road, Egham, Surrey TW20 9UR

Grade II* garden. Laid out 1918 by WH Romaine-Walker in partnership with GH Jenkins, incorporating earlier features. Site covers 50 acres and is associated with a late 17th century country house, converted to an hotel in 1927. Main formal garden is surrounded on three sides by a moat thought to be of medieval origin and modelled on the pattern of a Persian carpet. Garden also includes a sunken rose garden and avenue of lime trees.
www.greatfosters.co.uk
Grant Recipient/Owner:
Access contact: Mr Richard Young
Tel: 01784 433822 **Fax:** 01784 472455
Email: enquiries@greatfosters.co.uk
Open: At any time all year.
Heritage Open Days: No
P Spaces: 200 ♿ Partial. Disabled WC. Guide Dogs: Yes
£ No

Great Hall

Virginia Park, Christchurch Road, Virginia Water, Surrey GU25 4BM

By W H Crossland for Charas Holloway and opened 1884. Built of red brick with Portland stone dressings and slate roofs in Franco-Flemish Gothic style. Formerly part of the Royal Holloway Sanatorium.
Grant Recipient/Owner: Octagon Virginia Ltd
Access contact: Mr John Ellams
Tel: 01344 845276 **Fax:** 01344 842428
Email: virginiapark@btinternet.com
Open: Entrance Hall, Staircase and Great Hall of former Sanatorium open the following Weds and Sundays 10am - 4pm: Feb 20 & 24, Mar 27 & 31, Apr 17, 24 & 28, May 15, 22 & 26, June 19, 26 & 30, July 17, 24 & 28, Aug 14, 21 & 25, Sept 18, 25 & 29, Oct 16, 23 & 27, Nov 20 , 27 & 24. Other times by tel. arrangement with Estate Office.
Heritage Open Days: No
P Public car park nearby.
♿ Partial. Wheelchair access with assistance (steps into building to be negotiated). Downstairs entrance Hall but not the Great Hall (no lift). Disabled WC. Guide Dogs: Yes
£ £3

Kingston Grammar School Lovekyn Chapel

70 London Road, Kingston-upon-Thames, Surrey KT2 6PY

Chapel of St Mary Magdalene, known as the Lovekyn Chantry Chapel, consecrated in 1310 and one of the oldest buildings in Kingston. Built by Edward Lovekyn in 1299 and restored and re-endowed 1352 by his son John, twice Lord Mayor of London. In 1561 Queen Elizabeth established her grammar school in the Chapel. The school continues to use it for a wide variety of activities and public use.
www.kingston-grammar.surrey.sch.uk
Grant Recipient/Owner: Governors of Kingston Grammar School
Access contact: Mr A G Howard-Harwood
Tel: 020 8939 8825 **Fax:** 020 8974 5177
Email: bursar@kingston-grammar.surrey.sch.uk
Open: By written arrangement with Mr A G Howard-Harwood, Bursar & Clerk to the Governors at the school.
Heritage Open Days: Yes
P Public car park nearby.
♿ Yes. Disabled WC. Guide Dogs: Yes £ No

The Old Mill

Outwood Common, nr. Redhill, Surrey RH1 5PW

England's oldest working windmill, built in 1665. Museum of bygones.
www.outwoodwindmill.co.uk
Grant Recipient/Owner: Mrs Sheila Thomas
Access contact: Mrs Sheila Thomas
Tel: 01342 843644 & answerphone
Fax: 01342 843458
Email: sheila@outwoodwindmill.co.uk
Open: Easter - Oct: Sundays and BHs 2 - 6pm, plus groups by arrangement.
Heritage Open Days: No
P Spaces: 12
♿ Partial. Wheelchair access to ground floor of the mill and museum only. Disabled WC. Guide Dogs: Yes
£ **Adult:** £2 **Child:** £1

Oxenford Farm

Milford Road, Elstead, Godalming, Surrey GU8 6LA

1840 Gothic-style stone barn by Pugin with cowsheds and gatehouse. Working farm with livestock.
Grant Recipient/Owner: Mr C F Baker
Access contact: Mr A C Baker
Tel: 01252 702109 **Fax:** 01252 702109
Open: 1 - 24 Dec: daily 9am - 5pm. Other times by written arrangement.
Heritage Open Days: No
P Spaces: 10
♿ Partial. Wheelchair access to barn and cowsheds. No disabled WC. Guide Dogs: Yes
£ No

Painshill Park

Portsmouth Road, Cobham, Surrey KT11 1JE

Restored Grade I 18th century landscape garden of 150 acres, designed by Charles Hamilton between 1738 and 1773. Contains a Gothic temple, Chinese bridge, ruined abbey, Turkish tent, grotto and 14 acre serpentine lake fed by a large waterwheel.
www.brainsys.com/cobham/painshill
Grant Recipient/Owner: Painshill Park Trust Ltd
Access contact: Mrs Deborah Goodwin
Tel: 01932 868113 **Fax:** 01932 868001
Email: enquiries@painshill.fsbusiness.co.uk
Open: Apr - Oct: Tues - Sun and BHs 10.30am - 6pm (last adm. 4.30pm); Nov - Mar (except Christmas Day and Boxing Day): Tues - Thurs, Sat, Sun and BHs 11am - 4pm or dusk if earlier (last adm. 3pm). Guided tours for groups (10+) by arrangement.
Heritage Open Days: No
P Yes. Parking for 8 coaches. Spaces: 400
♿ Partial. Wheelchair access to most of site, apart from the grotto and Alpine Valley. Wheelchairs and electric buggies available on request. Book one week in advance. Disabled WC. Guide Dogs: Yes
£ **Adult:** £4.50 **Child:** £2 (free under 5) **Other:** £4

Red House

Frith Hill Road, Godalming, Surrey GU7 2DZ

Built by Lutyens 1897-9 for Revd Evans. Irregular mass built into steep hill with Jekyll garden. Each façade contrasting: North, street entrance low Georgian; West, English vernacular; East, romantic; South, keep-like with two bays accentuating the elevation, similar to the later Castle Drogo. Wide top-lit ramp-like staircase with rooms to each façade on 3 split levels. Drawing room and dining room fireplaces are also contrasting features, with the former baroque and the latter neo-Georgian.
Grant Recipient/Owner: Mr H A Laws
Access contact: Mrs Shula Laws
Tel: 01483 429284 **Fax:** 01483 429284
Open: By written arrangement (at least 4 weeks in advance) in Apr, May, June, July and Sept (excluding Weds, Thurs and Sundays).
Heritage Open Days: Yes
P Yes. Additional street parking. Spaces: 2
♿ No. Guide Dogs: Yes £ No

TYNE & WEAR

21-23 Leazes Terrace

Newcastle-upon-Tyne, Tyne & Wear NE1 4LY

Elongated square of houses built 1829-34 in classical style. Now owned by the University of Newcastle and used as halls of residence.
Grant Recipient/Owner: University of Newcastle
Access contact: Miss Helen Stonebank
Tel: 0191 222 7565
Open: Exterior accessible at all times, only one room of the interior can be viewed when the room is not occupied (Room 21F, in near original condition) by arrangement with Miss Helen Stonebank, Accommodation Manager, 10 Leazes Terrace, Newcastle-upon-Tyne.
Heritage Open Days: No
P Metered parking around the Terrace. ♿ No £ No

Gibside Chapel & Column of Liberty

Gibside, nr. Rowlands Gill, Burnopfield, Tyne & Wear NE16 6BG

Palladian Chapel 1760-69; completed 1812 designed by James Paine for George Bowes, MP and coal owner, and Column of Liberty 1750-57 by Daniel Garrett until 1753; then James Paine, situated in extensive landscape. Much of the landscape is an SSSI embracing many miles of riverside and forest walks. A forest garden under restoration. Estate is former home of the Queen Mother's family, the Bowes-Lyons.
www.nationaltrust.org.uk
Grant Recipient/Owner: Regional Director
Access contact: Visitor Services Manager
Tel: 01207 542255
Email: joan.gardner@ntrust.org.uk
Open: Grounds: 23 Mar - 3 Nov, daily except Mondays (open BH Mondays), 10am - 6pm (last adm. 4.30pm). 4 Nov - end Mar 2003, daily except Mondays (open BH Mondays), 10am - 4pm (last adm. 1 hour before sunset). Chapel: 23 Mar - 3 Nov, 11am - 4.30pm. Winter by arrangement only.
Heritage Open Days: No
P Spaces: 1000 Parking for disabled near the site.
♿ Partial. Wheelchair access to tea room, shop, toilets and part of the grounds. Wheelchair access is difficult to Chapel and the Avenue. Staff very happy to assist. Telephone the Visitor Services Manager (01207 542255) in advance. Disabled WC. Guide Dogs: Yes
£ **Adult:** £3 **Child:** £1.50 **Family:** £8 (2+4), £5 (1+3)

High Level Bridge

Gateshead, Tyne & Wear

Grade I listed railway and road bridge of ashlar and cast iron, 1849, designed by Robert Stephenson. One of the finest pieces of architectural iron work in the world.
Grant Recipient/Owner: British Rail
Access contact: Mr Barry Casterton
Open: Open to the public at all times. Best viewed from adjacent riverbanks or via access road/footpath under bridge. No access from Railtrack property.
Heritage Open Days: No
P On-street parking. ♿ No £ No

Literary & Philosophical Society

23 Westgate Road, Newcastle-upon-Tyne, Tyne & Wear NE1 1SE

Grade II* 1825 private library and society rooms designed by John Green in Greek revival style. Extended in late 19th century. Interior shows classical stucco ornament on friezes, wrought-iron balconies and spiral stair to library gallery. The library contains over 140,000 books, many of which are old and rare.
Grant Recipient/Owner: Literary & Philosophical Society
Access contact: Ms Kay Easson
Tel: 0191 232 0192 **Fax:** 0191 261 4494
Email: library@litandphil.org.uk
Open: Mon, Wed, Thurs & Fri: 9.30am - 7pm. Tues 9.30am - 8pm. Sat 9.30am - 1pm. The Society is closed on public and BHs. Visitors welcome to view the building free of charge. Annual subscription is charged for use of the private library.
Heritage Open Days: Yes
P On-street parking on Westgate Road. Spaces: 10
♿ Partial. Stairlift inside building allows wheelchair access, but no exterior ramp. No disabled WC. Guide Dogs: No
£ No

Old Town Hall

Market Place, South Shields, Tyne & Wear NE33 1AG

Built 1768 by the Dean and Chapter of Durham in the centre of the Market Place. Square two-storey building with an open arcaded ground floor and a central pillar on steps supporting what may have been a former market cross. Upper floor reached by a symmetrical, double branch stone staircase. Restored 1977.
Grant Recipient/Owner: South Tyneside Metropolitan Borough Council
Access contact: Director of Community Services
Tel: 0191 427 1717 **Fax:** 0191 427 0469
Open: Access to ground floor at all reasonable times, first floor by arrangement with the Director of Community Services, South Tyneside Metropolitan Borough Council, Central Library Building, Prince George Square, South Shields, Tyne & Wear NE33 2PE.
Heritage Open Days: No
P Pay parking locally with parking for disabled close to site. Spaces: 450
♿ Partial. Wheelchair and guide dog access to ground floor only. 24 hour automatic WC less than 200 metres from the site. No disabled WC. Guide Dogs: Yes £ No

River Derwent Bridge

Sands Lane, Swalwell, Gateshead, Tyne & Wear

Grade II* road bridge, built 1779 over the River Derwent on the Gateshead to Hexham Turnpike. Consists of three arches of coursed, squared sandstone with rusticated voussoirs.

Grant Recipient/Owner: Gateshead Metropolitan Borough Council
Access contact: Mr Ian McCaffery
Tel: 0191 433 3432   **Fax:** 0191 478 3491
Email: ianmccaffery@gateshead.gov.uk
Open: Open at all times - on a public highway.
Heritage Open Days: No
P Spaces: 10 ♿ Yes. No disabled WC. Guide Dogs: Yes
£ No

Theatre Royal

**Grey Street, Newcastle-upon-Tyne,
Tyne & Wear NE1 6BR**
Victorian theatre opened in 1837, rebuilt in 1899 by Frank Matcham in a richly-ornamented style. Classical façade with rare Hanoverian coat of arms.
www.theatre-royal-newcastle.co.uk
Grant Recipient/Owner: The Theatre Royal Trust
Access contact: Mr Malcolm Potts
Tel: 0191 244 2514   **Fax:** 0191 261 1906
Email: malcolm.potts@newcastle.gov.uk
Open: Free tours available Mon - Sat most weeks depending on production schedule.
Heritage Open Days: No
P Public car parks in City centre. ♿ No £ No

Washington Old Hall

**The Avenue, Washington Village, District 4,
Washington, Tyne & Wear NE38 7LE**
17th century manor house, incorporating 12th century remains of the home of George Washington's ancestors. Recreated 17th century interiors and displays of 'Washingtonabilia' celebrating the close connection with the USA. Permanent exhibition on the recent tenement period of the property. Jacobean knot-garden.
www.nationaltrust.org.uk
Grant Recipient/Owner: The National Trust
Access contact: Property Manager
Tel: 0191 4166879   **Fax:** 0191 4192065
Open: 24 Mar - 30 Oct: Sun - Wed & Good Fri 11am - 5pm.
Heritage Open Days: No
P Spaces: 10
♿ Partial. Wheelchair access to ground floor of house and upper garden. Disabled WC. Guide Dogs: Yes
£ **Adult:** £3 **Child:** £1.50 **Other:** £2.50 (groups by arrangement)

WARWICKSHIRE

The Bath House

Walton, Stratford-upon-Avon, Warwickshire LE17 5RG
Designed in 1748 by the architect Sanderson Miller. The upper room, where the bathers recovered, is decorated with dripping icicles and festoons of sea shells - the work of Mrs Delaney, better known for her flower pictures. Narrow steep staircases.
www.landmarktrust.co.uk
Grant Recipient/Owner: The Landmark Trust
Access contact: Ms Victoria Piggott
Tel: 01628 825920   **Fax:** 01628 825417
Email: www.landmarktrust.co.uk
Open: For details of opening arrangements at Landmark Trust properties please see the entry for Coop House, Netherby, Cumbria (page 549)
Heritage Open Days: No
P Spaces: 1 ♿ No £ No

Charlecote Park

**Wellesbourne, Warwick,
Warwickshire CV35 9ER**
Owned by the Lucy family since 1247, Sir Thomas built the house in 1558. Now much altered, it is shown as it would have been a century ago. The balustraded formal garden gives onto a deer park landscaped by 'Capability' Brown.
www.ntrustsevern.org.uk
Grant Recipient/Owner: The National Trust
Access contact: Property Manager
Tel: 01789 470277   **Fax:** 01789 470544
Email: charlecote@smtp.ntrust.org.uk
Open: House and Garden: 23 Mar - 3 Nov: daily except Weds and Thurs (open Good Fri). House: 12 - 5pm; grounds: 11am - 6pm. Grounds, restaurant and shop: 2 Feb - 17 Mar and 9 Nov - 15 Dec, Sat / Sun 11am - 4pm.
Heritage Open Days: No
P Spaces: 200
♿ Partial. Wheelchair access to ground floor of house, restaurant and shop. Disabled WC. Guide Dogs: Yes
£ **Adult:** £5.80 (house & grounds) **Child:** £2.90 (house & grounds) **Other:** £14.50 (family), £4.80 (group rate, max 40)

Lord Leycester Hospital

High Street, Warwick, Warwickshire CV34 4BH
14th century chantry chapel, Great Hall, galleried courtyard and Guildhall. Acquired by Robert Dudley, Earl of Leicester in 1571 as a home for his old soldiers. Still operating as a home for ex-servicemen.
Grant Recipient/Owner: Patron & Governors of Lord Leycester Hospital

---

Access contact: D I Rhodes
Tel: 01926 491422   **Fax:** 01926 491422
Open: Tues - Sun 10am - 4pm (winter), 10am - 5pm (summer), plus BH Mondays. Closed Good Fri and Christmas Day.
Heritage Open Days: No
P Spaces: 15
♿ Partial. Wheelchair access to ground floor only. No disabled WC. Guide Dogs: Yes
£ **Adult:** £3.20 **Child:** £2.20 **Other:** £2.70

Nicholas Chamberlaine's Almshouses' Pump House

**All Saints Square, Bedworth, Nuneaton,
Warwickshire CV12 8NR**
Built 1840 of English bond brick with sandstone dressings and stone pyramid roof in Tudor Gothic style. Contains original cast iron pump. Stands in front of the almshouses and originally provided water for the residents, illuminated at night.
Grant Recipient/Owner: Nicholas Chamberlaine's Hospital Charity
Access contact: Mr David Dumbleton
Tel: 024 76227531   **Fax:** 024 76221293
Email: j.russell@rotherham-solicitors.co.uk
Open: Two sessions Sat and Sun of Heritage Open Days: w/end and other times by arrangement with Mr David Dumbleton, Clerk to the Governors, Nicholas Chamberlaine's Hospital Charity, Rotherhams and Co, 8/9 The Quadrant, Coventry, Warwickshire CV1 2EG. Exterior visible from All Saints Square at all times.
Heritage Open Days: Yes
P Parking at public car parks nearby
♿ Yes. Disabled WC. Guide Dogs: Yes £ No

Packwood House

Lapworth, Solihull, Warwickshire B94 6AT
Originally a 16th century house, Packwood has been much altered over the years and today is a vision of Graham Baron Ash who recreated a Jacobean house in the 1920s and 30s. Collection of 16th century textiles and furniture. Yew garden based on Sermon on the Mount.
www.ntrustsevern.org.uk
Grant Recipient/Owner: The National Trust
Access contact: Mr Alan Langstaff
Tel: 01564 782024   **Fax:** 01564 782912
Email: badelesey@smtp.ntrust.org.uk
Open: House: 6 Mar - 3 Nov: daily except Mon and Tues (but open BHs and Good Fri), 12 - 4.30pm. Gardens: 6 Mar - 3 Nov: daily except Mon and Tues (but open BHs and Good Fri); Mar, Apr, Oct and Nov 11am - 4.30pm; May - Sept 11am - 5.30pm. Park and woodland walks all year, daily.
Heritage Open Days: No
P Spaces: 140
♿ Partial. Wheelchair access to ground floor. Garden largely accessible. Disabled WC. Guide Dogs: Yes
£ **Adult:** £5.20 (house & garden), £2.60 (grounds) **Child:** £2.60 (house & garden), £1.30 (grounds) **Other:** £13 (family), discount for combined ticket to Packwood House and Baddesley Hall

Polesworth Nunnery Gateway

**22-24 High Street, Polesworth, nr. Tamworth,
Warwickshire B78 1DU**
Abbey gatehouse, late 14th century with later alterations. Upper floors now in residential use.
Grant Recipient/Owner: Mr W E Thompson
Access contact: Mr W E Thompson
Tel: 01827 706861
Open: Exterior at all reasonable times, ground floor interior by arrangement with Mr W E Thompson, 46 Kiln Way, Polesworth, nr Tamworth, Warwickshire B78 1JE
Heritage Open Days: No
P Parking in Abbey driveway
♿ Partial. Wheelchair access to ground floor only. No disabled WC. Guide Dogs: Yes £ No

Ragley Hall

Alcester, Warwickshire B49 5NJ
Family home of the Marquess and Marchioness of Hertford. Built 1680 to a design by Robert Hooke in the Palladian style, with portico added by Wyatt 1780. Contents include baroque plasterwork by James Gibb, family portraits by Sir Joshua Reynolds and a mural by Graham Rust completed in 1983. Surrounding gardens designed by 'Capability' Brown.
www.ragleyhall.com
Grant Recipient/Owner: Marquess of Hertford & Earl of Yarmouth
Access contact: Mr Alan Grainger
Tel: 01789 762090   **Fax:** 01789 764791
Email: ragley.hall@virginnet.co.uk
Open: 28 Mar - 29 Sept: House: Thurs - Sun 12 noon - 5pm (last adm. 4.30pm). Sat closing times may vary due to functions. Park and gardens: Thurs - Sun 10am - 6pm, plus daily in main school holidays.
Heritage Open Days: No
P Spaces: 4000
♿ Wheelchair access via lift to first floor. Disabled WC. Guide Dogs: Yes
£ **Adult:** £6 (house & garden), £5 (garden only)

Child: £4.50 (house & garden), £4 (garden only)
Seniors & Orange Badge: £5 (house & garden), £4 (garden only), **Family:** £22 (house & garden), £17 (garden only)

St Peter & St Paul

**The Presbytery, Friars Lane, Lower Brailes,
Warwickshire OX15 5HU**
Roman Catholic chapel built 1726 on first floor of old malthouse. Contains Victorian stained glass, an 18th century crucifixion painting over the altar and original altar rails and pews.
Grant Recipient/Owner: St Philip's Presbytery
Access contact: Anthony Sims
Tel: 01608 682241
Open: Chapel open daily 9am - 6pm.
Heritage Open Days: No
P Spaces: 30 ♿ No. Guide Dogs: Yes £ No

WEST MIDLANDS

Castle Bromwich Hall Garden

**Chester Road, Castle Bromwich,
West Midlands B36 9BT**
18th century formal walled gardens set within 10 acres. Period plants and unusual historic vegetables, fruits and herbs, both culinary and medicinal. 19th century holly maze. Classical parterres with restored summerhouse and greenhouse along holly walk. Refreshments, gifts and plants for sale.
www.cbhgt.swinternet.co.uk
Grant Recipient/Owner: Castle Bromwich Hall Gardens Trust
Access contact: Mr R J Easton
Tel: 0121 749 4100   **Fax:** 0121 749 4100
Email: enq@cbhgt.swinternet.co.uk
Open: 31 Mar - 31 Oct: Tues - Thurs 1.30 - 4.30pm. Sat, Sun and BH Mondays 2 - 6pm. Closed Mon and Fri.
Heritage Open Days: Yes
P Spaces: 200
♿ Yes. Disabled WC. Guide Dogs: Yes
£ **Adult:** £3.50 **Child:** £1.50 **Other:** £2.50

Soho House Museum

**Soho Avenue, Handsworth, Birmingham,
West Midlands B18 5LB**
Soho House Museum is the former home of Matthew Boulton, Birmingham industrialist, entrepreneur and partner of James Watt. Designed by James and Samuel Wyatt, the house was once a meeting place of the Lunar Society and contains period rooms and displays on Boulton's manufacturing activities. The visitor centre houses a temporary exhibition gallery.
www.bmag.org.uk
Grant Recipient/Owner: Birmingham Museums & Art Gallery
Access contact: Ms Val Loggie
Tel: 0121 554 5929   **Fax:** 0121 554 5929
Email: val_loggie@birmingham.gov.uk
Open: All year: Tues - Sat 10am - 5pm; Sun 12 noon - 5pm. Also BH Mondays. Charge to museum, but free access to visitor centre and garden.
Heritage Open Days: Yes
P Spaces: 23
♿ Yes. Disabled WC. Guide Dogs: Yes
£ **Adult:** £2.50 **Child/Other:** £2 **Family:** £6.50

St James

**Great Packington, Meriden, nr. Coventry,
West Midlands CV7 7HF**
Red brick building with four domes topped by finials in neo-classical style. Built to celebrate the return to sanity of King George III. The organ was designed by Handel for his librettist, Charles Jennens, who was the cousin of the 4th Earl of Aylesford, who built the church.
Grant Recipient/Owner: St James Great Packington Trust
Access contact: Packington Estate Office
Tel: 01676 522020   **Fax:** 01676 523399
Open: Mon - Fri 9am - 5pm: key can be obtained from Estate Office at Packington Hall, preferably by phoning in advance. At other times by arrangement with Lord Guernsey (tel.01676 522274).
Heritage Open Days: No
P Spaces: 10
♿ Wheelchair access with assistance (entrance steps and heavy door). No disabled WC. Guide Dogs: Yes
£ No but donations towards restoration welcomed

St Mary's Convent

**Hunters Road, Handsworth, Birmingham,
West Midlands B19 1EB**
Highly original and carefully detailed Tudor-Gothic style building. 1840-41 by A W N Pugin. The cloister to the rear has simple exposed timber truss roof and tiled floors. The original chapel was destroyed in the war. The convent is contemporary with a group of Pugin's innovatory rationally designed religious houses.
Grant Recipient/Owner: Sr Evelyn Gallagher

Access contact: Kyran Rigney/Mary Leonard
Tel: 0121 554 3271
Open: By written or telephone arrangement only.
Heritage Open Days: No
P On-street parking only. ♿ No £ No

Wightwick Manor

Wightwick Bank, Wolverhampton, West Midlands WV6 8EE

Built 1887, the house is a notable surviving example of the Arts and Crafts Movement. Contains original William Morris wallpapers and fabrics, Pre-Raphaelite paintings, Kempe glass and de Morgan ware. 17acre Victorian/Edwardian garden designed by Thomas Mawson.
www.nationaltrust.org.uk
Grant Recipient/Owner: The National Trust
Access contact: The Property Manager
Tel: 01902 761400 **Fax:** 01902 764663
Email: mwtman@smtp.ntrust.org.uk
Open: By guided tour only 1 Mar - 31 Dec: Thurs and Sats (and BH Sun and Mon to ground floor only) 1.30 - 4.30pm. Family open days Weds in Aug 1.30 - 5pm. Admission by timed ticket issued from 11am at Visitor Reception. Other days by arrangement. Garden: Weds, Thursdays, Saturdays and BH Sun and Mon 11am - 6pm.
Heritage Open Days: No
P Yes. For coach parking please telephone 01902 761400. Spaces: 50
♿ Partial. Wheelchair access to ground floor only. No disabled WC. Guide Dogs: Yes
£ **Adult:** £5.60, £2.50 (garden only) **Child:** £2.80 (children/students, children free for garden only)
Family: £13

WEST SUSSEX

High Beeches Gardens Conservation Trust

High Beeches, Handcross, West Sussex RH17 6HQ

20 acre garden with woodland, open glades, natural wildflower meadows and water gardens. Many rare plants to be seen in all seasons. Tree trails. Tea Room in restored Victorian farm.
www.highbeeches.com
Grant Recipient/Owner: Mrs Boscawen
Access contact: Mrs Boscawen
Tel: 01444 400589 **Fax:** 01444 401543
Email: office@highbeeches.com
Open: 28 Mar - 30 June and 1 Sept - 31 Oct: Thurs - Tues 1 - 5pm (last adm. 5pm). July and Aug: open Sun - Tues 1 - 5pm. All coaches and Guided Tours by arrangement.
Heritage Open Days: No
P Spaces: 100
♿ No. Disabled WC. Guide Dogs: Yes
£ **Adult:** £4.50 **Child:** Free. Concessions for groups.

Ouse Valley Viaduct

Balcombe, West Sussex

The most important surviving architectural feature of the original layout of the London - Brighton railway, the Grade II* Ouse Valley Viaduct has 37 circular arches, is 492 yards long and 92 feet high. Designed by John Rastrick with stonework accredited to David Mocatta, it is known for its pierced piers, ornate limestone parapets and pavilions. Built 1839-1841.
Grant Recipient/Owner: Railtrack plc
Access contact: Railtrack plc
Tel: 020 7922 2450
Open: Public access at all times on the footpath running underneath the viaduct.
Heritage Open Days: No
P Limited on-street parking. ♿ No £ No

Parham House

Parham Park, nr. Pulborough, West Sussex RH20 4HS

Granted to the Palmer family 1540 by Henry VIII, the foundation stone of this grey-stone Elizabethan house was laid 1577. From the panelled Great Hall to the Long Gallery running the length of the roof-space, house contains a collection of paintings, furniture and needlework.
www.parhaminsussex.co.uk
Grant Recipient/Owner: Parham Park Ltd
Access contact: Ms Patricia Kennedy
Tel: 01903 742021 **Fax:** 01903 746557
Email: pat@parhaminsussex.co.uk
Open: 31 Mar - 31 Oct: Wed, Thurs, Sun and BH Mondays (also Sat 18 May, 13 July and 7 Sept). Gardens open at 12 noon, House at 2pm, last entry at 5pm. Charges provisional at time of going to print, check with House for current rates.
Heritage Open Days: No
P Parking for disabled close to house. Spaces: 300
♿ Partial. Wheelchair access to ground floor only by arrangement, there is a reduced admission charge for wheelchair users and free loan of recorded tour tape. Disabled WC. Guide Dogs: Yes
£ **Adult:** £5.50 (see above) **Child:** £1 (5-15)
Seniors: £4.50

Petworth House

Petworth, West Sussex GU28 0AE

Late 17th century mansion in 'Capability' Brown parkland. The house contains the Trust's largest collection of pictures including Turners and Van Dycks. Sculptures, furniture and Grinling Gibbons carvings. Servants' quarters including interesting kitchens and other service rooms. Extra rooms open at weekends by kind permission of Lord and Lady Egremont. Major Turner exhibition 6 July - 29 Sept 2002.
www.nationaltrust.org.uk
Grant Recipient/Owner: The National Trust
Access contact: The Property Manager
Tel: 01798 342207 **Fax:** 01798 342963
Email: spegen@smtp.ntrust.org.uk
Open: House and Servants' Quarters: 23 Mar - 3 Nov: daily except Thurs & Fri (but open Good Fri). Extra rooms shown weekdays (not BH Mondays) as follows: Mons - White and Gold Room and White Library; Tues and Weds - 3 bedrooms on first floor. 11am - 5.30pm. Last adm. to house 4.30pm, Servants' Quarters 5pm.
Heritage Open Days: No
P Car park for house and park on A283. Spaces: 150
♿ Partial. Wheelchair access to ground floor of house, shop and tea room. Disabled WC. Guide Dogs: Yes
£ **Adult:** £7 **Child:** £3.50 **Other:** £18 (family), (booked groups of 15+, £6.50 per head)

St Hugh's Charterhouse

Henfield Road, Partridge Green, Horsham, West Sussex RH13 8EB

Large monastery covering 10 acres. One large cloister of over 100 square yards comprising 34 four-room hermitages where the monks live. The fore part is a smaller cloister about 200ft square containing the cells of the Brothers and their work places. There is also a large church, library, refectory, Brothers Chapel and other monastic buildings. The large quad encloses a cemetery. The spire is 203ft high and has a five-bell chime.
www.parkminster.org.uk
Grant Recipient/Owner: St Hugh's Charterhouse
Access contact: Fr John Babeau
Tel: 01403 864231 **Fax:** 01403 864231
Open: By arrangement, with due respect for the rules of the Charterhouse monastery. For further details please contact the monastery.
Heritage Open Days: No
P Spaces: 20 ♿ No. Guide Dogs: Yes £ No

Sackville College

East Grinstead, West Sussex RH19 3AZ

Early Jacobean almshouse with original furniture, hall, chapel, common room, John Mason Neale study and library. Built with Sussex sandstone around a quadrangle. Founded 1609 and still in use, providing 15 flats for elderly people together with Warden's lodging.
Grant Recipient/Owner: The Warden & Trustees of Sackville College
Access contact: Mr David Russell
Tel: 01342 326561 **Fax:** 01342 326561
Open: June, July and Aug: Wed - Sun 2 - 5pm. Groups by arrangement Apr - Oct.
Heritage Open Days: Yes
P Free parking, additional parking at 'Chequer Head' 50 yards away. Spaces: 4
♿ Yes. Disabled WC. Guide Dogs: No
£ **Adult:** £2.50 **Child:** £1 **Other:** £2.50

The Shell House

Goodwood House, Chichester, West Sussex PO18 0PX

One-room Shell House dating from 1740s. Walls and ceiling decorated with hundreds of thousands of shells in classical design, with coffering, niches and cornucopia. Floor with inset horses teeth.
www.goodwood.co.uk
Grant Recipient/Owner: Goodwood Estate Company Ltd
Access contact: Mrs Rosemary Baird
Tel: 01243 755018 **Fax:** 01243 755005
Email: rb@goodwood.co.uk
Open: By written arrangement, usually on set Connoisseurs' Days (21 & 28 May; also one day in July, Sept and Oct) or Sun mornings Apr - Sept. Two weeks' notice preferred. Bookings can be made with Rosemary Baird, or Kathryn Bellamy (tel.01243 755048, email: kathryn@goodwood.co.uk).
Heritage Open Days: No
P Car park 30 metres from house and steps between car park and house. Spaces: 4
♿ No. Lavatory for disabled available only when Goodwood House open to the public. Guide Dogs: No
£ **Adult:** £3.50 (Connoisseurs' Day as part of House visit), £5 (other days) **Child:** £2 (under 12s, accompanied)

WEST YORKSHIRE

Bolling Hall Museum

Bowling Hall Road, Bradford, West Yorkshire BD4 7LP

Furnished house, mainly 17th and 18th centuries with some earlier parts. Large stained glass window with armorial glass, fine collection of 16th century oak furniture. Now a free public museum.
www.bradford.gov.uk
Grant Recipient/Owner: Bradford Metropolitan District Council
Access contact: Ms Anthea Bickley
Tel: 01274 723057 **Fax:** 01274 726220
Email: abickley@legend.co.uk
Open: All year: Wed, Thurs and Fri 11am - 4pm; Sat 10am - 5pm; Sun 12 noon - 5pm. Closed Mondays (except BHs) Christmas and Boxing Days and Good Fri.
Heritage Open Days: Yes
P Free parking 100 metres from Museum. Spaces: 75
♿ Partial. Wheelchair access to ground floor only. Disabled WC. Guide Dogs: Yes £ No

Bramham Park Lead Lads Temple

Wetherby, West Yorkshire LS23 6ND

18th century open temple in the classical style in Bramham Park (approx 1 mile from the house in woodland called Black Fen, close to a public footpath).
Grant Recipient/Owner: Mr G F Lane Fox
Access contact: Mr G F Lane Fox
Tel: 01937 846004 **Fax:** 01937 846001
Email: lucy.finucane@bramhampark.co.uk
Open: Accessible at all times, close to a public footpath.
Heritage Open Days: No
P No ♿ No £ No

City Varieties Music Hall

Swan Street, Leeds, West Yorkshire LS1 6LW

Music hall built in 1865. Grade II*. Used as the location for BBC TV's "*Good Old Days*".
www.cityvarieties.co.uk
Grant Recipient/Owner: Leeds Grand Theatre & Opera House Ltd
Access contact: Mr Peter Sandeman
Tel: 0113 3917777 **Fax:** 0113 2341800
Heritage Open Days:: organised tours. Other times by arrangement. Admission fees for performances.
P No ♿ No. Guide Dogs: Yes
£ No but charges for performances

Crossley Pavilion

The People's Park, King Cross Road, Halifax, West Yorkshire HX1 1EB

Grade II* building, designed by Sir Joseph Paxton and constructed 1857. Contains seating and a statue of the park's benefactor, Sir Francis Crossley (1860), by Joseph Durham. 4 gargoyle fountains supply pools flanking each side of the pavilion, set on formal terrace, balustrades and steps.
Grant Recipient/Owner: Calderdale Metropolitan Borough Council
Access contact: Miss Deborah Comyn-Platt
Tel: 01422 359454 **Fax:** 01422 348301
Email: d.a.comyn-platt@calderdale.gov.uk
Open: Park: 8am until dusk. Pavilion: By arrangement with Calderdale Metropolitan Borough Council Leisure Services, Wellesey Park, Halifax, West Yorkshire. Public toilets open during park hours. Information Centre open by arrangement as above.
Heritage Open Days: Yes
P On-street parking in Park Road. Limited spaces in adjacent college.
♿ Yes. Disabled WC. Guide Dogs: Yes £ No

Harewood House

Harewood, Leeds, West Yorkshire LS17 9LQ

Designed in neo-classical style by John Carr and completed in 1772. Contains Adam interiors, Chippendale furniture and art collection. Home of the Earl and Countess of Harewood.
www.harewood.org
Grant Recipient/Owner: The Trustees of Harewood House Ltd
Access contact: Mr Terence Suthers
Tel: 0113 218 1010 **Fax:** 0113 218 1002
Email: business@harewood.org
Open: Daily 14 Mar - 4 Nov: Grounds & Bird Garden 10am - 4.30pm (last adm. 4pm); House and Terrace Gallery 11am - 4.30pm (last adm. 4pm). Grounds close at 6pm. Grounds and Bird Garden open w/ends 10 Nov - 17 Dec. Guide dogs not allowed in the Bird Garden but a free sound guide is available for the partially sighted visitor and a babysitter for the dog.
Heritage Open Days: No
P Yes. Unlimited overflow parking on grass. Spaces: 200
♿ Yes. Disabled WC. Guide Dogs: Yes
£ **Adult:** £7.50 **Child:** £5 **Other:** £6.75 (senior), £26.00 (family). Annual season tickets and concessions for disabled groups also available.

Holdsworth House Gazebo

Holdsworth, Halifax, West Yorkshire HX2 9TG

Gazebo, probably built c1633 at about the same time as the house, at the corner of the sunken garden. It was either built simply as a summerhouse, a gatekeeper's house or as an oratory (small private chapel).
www.holdsworthhouse.co.uk
Grant Recipient/Owner: The Cavalier County Club
Access contact: Mr Peter Phillips
Tel: 01422 240024 **Fax:** 01422 245174
Email: info@holdsworthhouse.co.uk

Open: Hotel open all year (except Christmas).
Heritage Open Days: No
P Spaces: 40 ♿ No. Guide Dogs: Yes £ No

Huddersfield Station

St George's Square, Huddersfield, West Yorkshire HD1 1JF

Designed by J P Pritchett of York using local ashlar sandstone, the Grade I station opened for passengers on 3 Aug 1850. The grandeur of the station is the result of it having been built at the joint expense of Huddersfield & Manchester Rail & Canal Co. and the Manchester & Leeds Railway Co.
Grant Recipient/Owner: Kirkless Metropolitan Council
Access contact: Head of Estates Property & Markets
Open: Operational building open every day except Christmas Day and Boxing Day. Please note the building may also be closed on other days as may be specified by Railtrack plc or other railway operators.
Heritage Open Days: No
P One hour stay maximum in station car park. Spaces: 20
♿ Partial. Full wheelchair access to main buildings. Access with assistance to inner platforms. No disabled WC. Guide Dogs: Yes £ No

Ledston Hall

Hall Lane, Ledston, Castleford, West Yorkshire WF10 2BB

17th century mansion with some earlier work.
Grant Recipient/Owner: Mr G H H Wheler
Access contact: Mr J F T Hare
Tel: 01423 523423 **Fax:** 01423 521373
Email: james.hare@carterjonas.co.uk
Open: May - Aug: Mon - Fri 9am - 4pm. Other times by arrangement with Mr J F T Hare, Carter Jonas, Regent House, 13/15 Albert St, Harrogate, West Yorks HG1 1JF..
Heritage Open Days: Yes
P Spaces: 5
♿ Partial. Wheelchair access to majority of garden. No disabled WC. Guide Dogs: Yes £ No

Marlborough Hall

Crossley Street, Halifax, West Yorkshire HX1 1UG

Built in 1857 as a Mechanics Institute, which it remained until 1932. From 1917 to 1922 it doubled as the Gem Cinema, the first permanent cinema in Halifax. Contains four floors with many meeting rooms and an auditorium. The frontage hall and stairways have many original features.
Grant Recipient/Owner: Halifax & District YMCA
Access contact: Mr C F Love
Tel: 01422 353626
Email: admin@halifax.ymca.co.uk
Open: Daily 10am - 4pm (except BHs and w/ends).
Heritage Open Days: No
P No
♿ Partial. Wheelchair access to ground floor and lower ground floor only. Disabled WC. Guide Dogs: Yes £ No

Marshall Mill

Marshall Street, Leeds, West Yorkshire LS11 9YJ

Textile mill built c1800 and now converted to offices containing lobby, external and common areas.
Grant Recipient/Owner: Marshall Mill Ltd
Access contact: Mr John Wright
Tel: 0113 245 3324 **Fax:** 0113 245 3317
Open: By arrangement
Heritage Open Days: No
P No ♿ Yes. Disabled WC. Guide Dogs: Yes £ No

Nostell Priory

Doncaster Road, Nostell, Wakefield, West Yorkshire WF4 1QE

Country house, 1736-1750, by James Paine for Sir Rowland Winn 4th Baronet. Later Robert Adam was commissioned to complete the State Rooms. Collection of Chippendale furniture on display, designed especially for house, an art collection with works by Pieter Breughel the Younger and Angelica Kauffmann, and an 18th century dolls house, complete with original fittings and Chippendale furniture. Lakeside walks.
www.nationaltrust.org.uk
Grant Recipient/Owner: The National Trust
Access contact: Property Manager
Tel: 01924 863892 **Fax:** 01924 865282
Email: yorknp@smtp.ntrust.org.uk
Open: 2 - 17 Mar: House closed. Grounds, shop and tearoom open w/ends only 11am - 4pm. 23 Mar - 3 Nov: open daily except Mon and Tues (open Good Fri and BHs including 3 June). House: 1 - 5.30pm; grounds: 11am - 6pm; shop and tearoom: 11am - 5.30pm. 9 Nov - 15 Dec: Saturdays and Sundays only. House: 12 noon - 4pm; grounds, shop and tearoom: 11am - 4.30pm.
Heritage Open Days: No
P Spaces: 120
♿ Partial. Wheelchair access to ground floor of house, lift to first floor, tea room, children's playground and shop. No disabled WC. Guide Dogs: Yes
£ **Adult:** £4.50, £2.50 (grounds only) **Child:** £2.20, £1.20 (grounds only) **Family:** £11 (no family ticket for grounds only).

The Roundhouse

Wellington Road, Leeds, West Yorkshire LS12 1DR

Grade II* railway roundhouse built in 1847 for the Leeds and Thirsk Railway by Thomas Granger. In full use by the North-Eastern Railway until 1904, now home to Leeds Commercial Van and Truck Hire.
www.leedscommercial.co.uk
Grant Recipient/Owner: Wellbridge Properties Ltd
Access contact: Mr J D Miller
Tel: 0113 243 5964 **Fax:** 0113 246 1142
Email: sales@leedscommercial.co.uk
Open: By written arrangement with Leeds Commercial, who manage property as a working garage.
Heritage Open Days: Yes
P Free parking. Spaces: 100
♿ Yes. Disabled WC. Guide Dogs: Yes £ No

Theatre Royal & Opera House

Drury Lane, Wakefield, West Yorkshire WF1 2TE

A 500-seat Victorian Theatre designed by Frank Matcham. Notable for the quality of decoration in auditorium.Provides a year-round programme of events.
www.wakefieldtheatres.co.uk
Grant Recipient/Owner: Wakefield Theatre Royal & Opera House
Access contact: Mr Murray Edwards
Tel: 01924 215531 **Fax:** 01924 215525
Email: murray@wakefieldtheatres.co.uk
Open: Programme of events published in Feb, July and Nov. Guided tours once a month on Saturdays, groups on weekdays by arrangement, contact the Box Office 01924 211311 for further information.
Heritage Open Days: Yes
P Spaces: 150
♿ Partial. Wheelchair access to stalls area only. Disabled WC. Guide Dogs: Yes
£ No but admission charge for performances

WILTSHIRE

Avoncliffe Aqueduct

Kennet & Avon Canal, Westwood, Wiltshire

19th century limestone aqueduct carrying the Kennet and Avon Canal over the River Avon and the railway line. The canal towpath crosses alongside the canal providing a foot link to Bradford-on-Avon or Bath.
www.britishwaterways.co.uk
Grant Recipient/Owner: British Waterways
Access contact: Mr Tim Yeomans
Tel: 01923 208762 **Fax:** 01923 208787
Email: tim.yeomans@britishwaterways.co.uk
Open: At all times.
Heritage Open Days: No
P Spaces: 12 ♿ No £ No

Dyrham Park

nr. Chippenham, Wiltshire SN14 8ER

17th century house set within an ancient deer park, woodlands and formal garden. The house was furnished in the Dutch style and still has many original contents including paintings, ceramics, furniture and 17th century tapestries. The Victorian domestic rooms include the kitchen, larder, bakehouse, dairy and tenants' hall.
www.nationaltrust.org.uk
Grant Recipient/Owner: The National Trust
Access contact: The Property Manager
Tel: 01179 372501 **Fax:** 01179 372501
Email: wdymxa@smtp.ntrust.og.uk
Open: House: 23 Mar - 3 Nov: daily except Wed and Thurs 12 - 5.30pm (last adm. to house 4.45pm). Garden: as house 11am - 5.30pm, dusk if earlier. Winter opening Domestic Rooms: 9 Nov - 15 Dec: Sat and Sun 12 - 4pm. Note: property closed 5 - 8 July for concerts.
Heritage Open Days: No
P Free shuttle bus from car park to house. Spaces: 250
♿ Partial. Wheelchair access to all but four upstairs rooms. A photograph album of these rooms is available. Disabled WC. Guide Dogs: Yes
£ **Adult:** £7.90, £3 (grounds only), £2 (Park only when house & garden closed), £4 (Winter: Park & Domestic Rooms) **Child:** £3.90, £1.50 (grounds only), £1 (Park only when house & garden closed), £2 (Winter: Park & Domestic Rooms) **Other:** £19.50 (family: house & grounds), £7.00 (family: grounds only)

Fonthill Underground Bath House

Fonthill Bishop, Salisbury, Wiltshire SP3 5SH

18th century boathouse or water temple of aisled 'basilica' plan with transepts and apsidal west end, the wet dock being the 'nave' and 'crossing' and the walkways the 'aisles'. Constructed of limestone ashlar with vaulted roof covered in earth.
Grant Recipient/Owner: Lord Margadale
Access contact: Resident Agent
Tel: 01747 820246
Open: 1 Mar - 31 July: by written arrangement with Estate Office, Fonthill Bishop, Salisbury, Wiltshire SP3 5SH. Wellington boots will be required by visitors.
Heritage Open Days: No
P No ♿ No £ **Adult:** £2.50 **Child/Other:** Free

Lacock Abbey

Lacock, nr. Chippenham, Wiltshire SN15 2LG

Founded in 1232 and converted into a country house c1540, the fine medieval Cloisters, Sacristy, Chapter house and monastic rooms of the Abbey have survived largely intact. 16th century stable courtyard has half timbered gables, a clock house, brewery and bakehouse. Victorian woodland garden. Former residents include William Fox Talbot 'the father of modern photography'.
www.nationaltrust.org.uk
Grant Recipient/Owner: The National Trust
Access contact: Property Manager
Tel: 01249 730141 **Fax:** 01249 730501
Open: Abbey: 30 Mar - 3 Nov: daily 1 - 5.30pm (closed Tues and Good Fri). Museum, cloisters and garden: 16 Mar - 3 Nov: daily 11am - 5.30pm (closed Good Fri). Museum open winter w/ends, (closed 21 - 29 Dec), telephone Property Manager for details.
Heritage Open Days: No
P Spaces: 300
♿ Partial. Wheelchair access to Abbey is difficult as 4 sets of stairs. Garden, cloisters and museum accessible (non-wheelchair stairlift in museum). Limited parking in Abbey courtyard by arrangement. Disabled WC. Guide Dogs: Yes
£ **Adult:** £6.20 (Abbey, museum, cloisters & garden), £5 (Abbey & garden), £4 (garden, cloisters & museum) **Child:** £3.40 (Abbey, museum, cloisters & garden), £2.80 (Abbey & garden), £2.40 (garden, cloisters & museum) **Other:** £16.80 (family: Abbey, museum, cloisters & garden), £12.70 (family: Abbey & garden), £11.30 (family: garden, cloisters & museum). Group rates

Larmer Tree Gardens

Tollard Royal, nr Salisbury, Wiltshire SP5 5PY

The Larmer Tree Grounds are set high on the Cranbourne Chase, providing exceptional views of the surrounding countryside. One of the most unusual gardens in England containing an extraordinary collection of colonial and oriental buildings, a Roman Temple and an Open Air Theatre.
www.rushmore-estate.co.uk
Grant Recipient/Owner: Mr Pitt Rivers (dec'd)
Access contact: The Personal Representatives of the late MALF Pitt-Rivers
Tel: 01725 516228 **Fax:** 01725 516449
Email: larmer.tree@rushmore-estate.co.uk
Open: 1 Apr - 31 Oct: Wed, Thurs, Fri and Sun, 11am - 6pm (last adm. 5pm). Outside these dates Mon - Fri, excluding BHs, on an "honesty box" system.
Heritage Open Days: No
P Spaces: 4500
♿ Yes. No disabled WC. Guide Dogs: Yes
£ **Adult:** £3.75 **Child/Other:** £2.75 (under 5s free)

Lydiard Park

Lydiard Tregoze, Swindon, Wiltshire SN5 9PA

Ancestral home of the Bolingbrokes, the restored Palladian mansion contains family furnishings and portraits, plasterwork, rare 17th century painted window and room dedicated to 18th century society artist Lady Diana Spencer.
Grant Recipient/Owner: Swindon Borough Council
Access contact: Mrs Sarah Finch-Crisp
Tel: 01793 770401 **Fax:** 01793 877909
Open: House: Mon - Fri 10am - 1pm & 2 - 5pm, Saturdays and school summer holidays 10am - 5pm, Sundays 2 - 5pm. Nov - Feb early closing at 4pm. Grounds all day, closing at dusk. Admission prices may increase, please check with the House.
Heritage Open Days: Yes
P Spaces: 400
♿ Yes. Disabled WC. Guide Dogs: Yes
£ Provisional **Adult:** £1.40 **Child:** 70p

Merchant's House

132 High Street, Marlborough, Wiltshire SN8 1HN

17th century town house built by the Bayly family, mercers 1653 - c1700. Situated prominently in the High Street it contains a unique stripe-painted dining room c1665, painted balustrading to the oak staircase and panelled chamber of the Commonwealth period.
www.themerchantshouse.co.uk
Grant Recipient/Owner: Merchant's House (Marlborough) Trust
Access contact: Mr Michael Gray
Tel: 01672 511491 **Fax:** 01672 511491
Email: manager@themerchantshouse.co.uk
Open: Easter - end Sept: Sats 11am - 4pm. Other times by arrangement with the Secretary at Merchant's House.
Heritage Open Days: Yes
P Parking for disabled outside the building. Public parking in High Street.
♿ No. Guide Dogs: Yes £ **Adult:** £1.50 **Child:** 50p

Old Bishop's Palace

Salisbury Cathedral School, 1 The Close, Salisbury, Wiltshire SP1 2EQ

13th century building, much altered over the centuries, with 13th century undercroft, Georgian drawing room and a chapel.

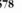

Grant Recipient/Owner: Salisbury Diocesan Board of Finance
Access contact: A J Craigie
Tel: 01722 555300 **Fax:** 01722 410910
Email: aspire@salisbury.enterprise-plc.com
Open: Guided tours 10 days in July/Aug. Details can be obtained from the Visitors' Office at Salisbury Cathedral (tel: Alun Williams: 01722 555121).
Heritage Open Days: No
[P] No
[♿] No. WC for disabled people in the Cloister (100 yards). Guide Dogs: No [£] **Adult:** £2

Sarum College

19 The Close, Salisbury, Wiltshire SP1 2EE
Grade I house, c1677, attributed to Sir Christopher Wren. In the 1870s collegiate buildings were added, designed by William Butterfield. The college is an ecumenical education, training and conference centre.
www.sarum.ac.uk
Grant Recipient/Owner: Trustees of Salisbury & Wells Theological College/Sarum College
Access contact: Mrs Linda Cooper
Tel: 01722 424800 **Fax:** 01722 338508
Email: admin@sarum.ac.uk
Open: Daily in term-time, please check with college for details.
Heritage Open Days: No
[P] Spaces: 37
[♿] Partial. Wheelchair access to ground floor only. Disabled WC. Guide Dogs: Yes [£] No

Stourhead

nr. Warminster, Wiltshire BA12 6QH
Country house, built 1721-24 for Henry Hoare by Colen Campbell. Following fire in 1902, central block was rebuilt between 1902-06. Set in landscaped parkland and with the fine Stourhead Gardens to the west. Landscape garden laid out between 1741 and 1780. Classical temples including the Pantheon and Temple of Apollo are set around the lake. King Alfred's tower is an intriguing red-brick folly. Woodlands with collection of exotic trees.
www.nationaltrust.org.uk
Grant Recipient/Owner: The National Trust
Access contact: Property Manager
Tel: 01747 841152 **Fax:** 01747 841152
Email: wstest@smtp.ntrust.org.uk
Open: House: 23 Mar - 3 Nov: daily (except Thurs and Fri) 12 - 5.30pm. Garden: daily 9am - 7pm or sunset if earlier. King Alfred's Tower: 23 Mar - 3 Nov: daily except Mon (but open BH Mondays): Tues - Fri 2 - 5.30pm; Sat, Sun and BH Mondays 11.30am - 5.30pm or dusk if earlier.
Heritage Open Days: No
[P] Parking close to house for Orange Badge holders. Volunteer-driven vehicle in peak season from car park to garden and house entrances. Spaces: 200
[♿] Partial. Wheelchair access to house with use of stairclimber (must be booked in advance) and to 1½mile path around lakes, steep in places. Wheelchairs and 2-seater self-drive vehicle for garden available. Disabled WC. Guide Dogs: Yes
[£] **Adult:** £8.70 (house & garden), £4.90 (house), £4.90-£3.80 (garden), £1.65 (King Alfred's Tower) **Child:** £4.10 (house & garden), £2.70 (house), £2.70-£1.85 (garden), 85p (King Alfred's Tower) **Other:** £20.50 (family: house & garden), £12.30 (family: house), £12.30-£9.20 (family: garden), £4.10 (family: King Alfred's Tower). Group rates

The Cloisters

Iford Manor, Bradford-on-Avon, Wiltshire BA15 2BA
Small stone-built cloister in gardens of Manor, completed 1914 by Harold Peto and based on 13th century Italian style. Interesting early contents.
www.ifordmanor.co.uk
Grant Recipient/Owner: Mrs E Cartwright-Hignett
Access contact: Mrs E Cartwright-Hignett
Tel: 01225 863146 **Fax:** 01225 862364
Email: iford.manor@which.net
Open: Gardens only: Apr - Oct, Sundays and Easter Mon 2 - 5pm; May - Sept, daily (except Mondays and Fridays), 2 - 5pm. Children under 10 not admitted at w/ends. Coaches and groups by arrangement only.
Heritage Open Days: No
[P] Spaces: 100
[♿] Partial. Wheelchair access by arrangement to Cloisters and part of the gardens. Disabled WC. Guide Dogs: Yes
[£] **Adult:** £3 **Child/Other:** £2.50 (10-16, under 10 free)

Tottenham House

Savernake Forest, Marlborough, Wiltshire SN8 3HP
Great house built of Bath stone in 1820 by Thomas Cundy for the 1st Marquess of Ailesbury. Most of the house is unfurnished, and it is currently leased to the Amber Foundation, a charity for homeless/jobless young people.
Grant Recipient/Owner: Trustees of the Savernake Estate
Access contact: Earl of Cardigan
Tel: 01672 512161 **Fax:** 01672 512105
Open: By arrangement with Savernake Estate Office.
Heritage Open Days: No
[P] Spaces: 30
[♿] Partial. Wheelchair access with assistance (entrance steps to be negotiated). No disabled WC. Guide Dogs: Yes
[£] No

Wilton House

Wilton, Salisbury, Wiltshire SP2 0BJ
Ancestral home of the Earls of Pembroke for over 450 years, rebuilt by Inigo Jones and John Webb in Palladian style with further alterations by James Wyatt c1801. Contains 17th century state rooms and an art collection including works by Van Dyck, Rubens, Joshua Reynolds and Brueghel. Surrounded by landscaped parkland.
www.wiltonhouse.com
Grant Recipient/Owner: Wilton House Charitable Trust
Access contact: Mr Ray Stedman
Tel: 01722 746720 **Fax:** 01722 744447
Email: tourism@wiltonhouse.com
Open: 27 Mar - 27 Oct: 10.30am - 5.30pm (last adm. 4.30pm).
Heritage Open Days: No
[P] Spaces: 200 [♿] Yes. Disabled WC. Guide Dogs: Yes
[£] **Adult:** £9.25 **Child:** £5 **Seniors:** £7.50

Wilton Windmill

East Grafton, Wiltshire SN8 3SS
Built 1821. Only working windmill in Wiltshire, standing on a chalk ridge 550ft high.
www.wiltonwindmill.com
Grant Recipient/Owner: Wiltshire County Council
Access contact: Mr John Talbot
Tel: 01672 870072
Email: jctalbot@waitrose.com
Open: Site is open at all times. Mill: guided tours Easter - end Sept, Suns and BHs 2 - 5pm.
Heritage Open Days: No
[P] Spaces: 8 [♿] No. Guide Dogs: Yes
[£] **Adult:** £2 **Child:** 50p **Senior:** £1.50 **Family:** £4

WORCESTERSHIRE

Abbey Gateway

(formerly Priory Gateway), Abbey Road, Malvern, Worcestershire WR14 3ES
15th century gatehouse of the Benedictine Monastery in Malvern. Extended and restored, notably during 16th and 19th centuries. Now houses the Malvern Museum, an independent voluntary-run local museum.
Access contact: The Curator
Tel: 01684 567811
Open: Easter - end Oct: daily 10.30am - 5pm. Closed Weds in term time. (Opening hours always subject to the availability of volunteers).
Heritage Open Days: No
[P] On-street parking.
[♿] No [£] **Adult:** £1 **Child:** 50p

Detton Hall

Neen Savage, Cleobury Mortimer, Kidderminster, Worcestershire DY14 8LW
Large farmhouse built between the late 16th and early 18th centuries. Part half-timbered, part local stone and with roofs of clay tiles. There are 4 tall Tudor star chimney stacks and the main stairs have fretted panels. Extensively restored by local craftsmen 1991 - 2001.
Grant Recipient/Owner: Mr E C Ratcliff
Access contact: Mr E C Ratcliff
Tel: 01299 270387
Open: By guided tour only by telephone or written arrangement with Mr E C or Mr E B Ratcliff. Admission charge includes light refreshment if required.
Heritage Open Days: Yes
[P] Spaces: 10
[♿] Partial. Wheelchair access to ground floor only with assistance (2 steps). Disabled WC. Guide Dogs: Yes
[£] **Adult:** £5 **Child:** £3

Edgar Tower

College Green, Worcester, Worcestershire WR1 2LH
Gateway dates from mid-14th century and consists of a central block containing a larger arched opening for vehicular access to the precinct and a smaller pedestrian doorway. Blocks to north and south provided accommodation while the corner turrets contained stairs, garderobes, etc.
Grant Recipient/Owner: Dean & Chapter of Worcester Cathedral
Access contact: Cathedral Steward
Tel: 01905 28854 **Fax:** 01905 611139
Email: worcestercathedral@compuserve.com
Open: The Tower is one of the entrances through which visitors pass when approaching the Cathedral from the south. Visits to the interior (King's School Library) during school holidays by written arrangement with Cathedral Steward, Chapter Office, 10a College Green, Worcester WR1 2LH. Note visits to the Tower can by physically demanding as the stairway is steep and narrow.
Heritage Open Days: Yes
[P] No [♿] No [£] No

Hanbury Hall

Hanbury, Droitwich, Worcestershire WR9 7EA
Built in 1701, this William and Mary-style house contains painted ceilings and staircase. It has an orangery, ice house and Moorish gazebos. The re-created 18th century garden is surrounded by parkland and has a parterre, wilderness, fruit garden, open grove and bowling green pavilions.
www.ntrustsevern.org.uk
Grant Recipient/Owner: The National Trust
Access contact: Mr Stewart Alcock
Tel: 01527 821214 **Fax:** 01527 821251
Email: hanbury@smtp.ntrust.org.uk
Open: 24 Mar - 30 Oct: Sun - Wed 1.30 - 5.30pm (but open Good Fri), last adm. 5pm or dusk if earlier. Gardens open at 12 noon.
Heritage Open Days: No
[P] Car parking 200 metres from house. Parking for disabled near house. Spaces: 80
[♿] Yes. Disabled WC. Guide Dogs: Yes
[£] **Adult:** £4.60 **Child:** £2.30 **Other:** £11.50 (family)

Harvington Hall

Harvington, nr. Kidderminster, Worcestershire DY10 4LR
An Elizabethan moated manor house, partly demolished and remodelled c.1701. Contains one of the best known series of priests' hides in the country and extensive traces of an ambitious scheme of wall paintings of late 16th or early 17th century.
www.harvingtonhall.org.uk
Grant Recipient/Owner: Roman Catholic Diocese of Birmingham
Access contact: Mrs S Breeden
Tel: 01562 777846 **Fax:** 01562 777190
Email: thehall@harvington.fsbusiness.co.uk
Open: Mar - Oct: Saturdays and Sundays 11.30am - 5pm; Apr - Sept: Wed - Sun 11.30am - 5pm. Groups and schools by arrangement at any time.
Heritage Open Days: No
[P] Spaces: 100
[♿] Partial. Wheelchair access to ground floor, gardens, tea room and shop. Video of upper floors available. Disabled WC. Guide Dogs: Yes
[£] **Adult:** £4.20 **Child:** £3 **Other:** £3.50 (senior citizens), £12.50 (family), £1 (garden only)

Hopton Court Conservatory

Cleobury Mortimer, Kidderminster, Worcestershire DY14 0EF
Grade II* conservatory, c1830, of cast iron with a rounded archway leading to a rear room roofed with curved glass. Two rooms either side, one housing the boiler beneath to supply heat by way of cast iron grilles running around the floor of the interior.
www.hoptoncourt.co.uk
Grant Recipient/Owner: Mr C R D Woodward
Access contact: Mr Christopher Woodward
Tel: 01299 270734 **Fax:** 01299 271132
Email: hoptoncourt@hotmail.com
Open: W/ends of 1/2 and 22/23 June, please ring for times. At other times by arrangement.
Heritage Open Days: No
[P] Spaces: 150 [♿] Yes. Disabled WC. Guide Dogs: Yes
[£] **Adult:** £3.50

Walker Hall

Evesham, Worcestershire WR11 4RW
16th century timber-framed building adjoining Norman gateway, much altered. In the late 19th century the floor was removed and it became an open hall. In 1999 it was repaired and refitted to form offices (first floor) and a retail unit (ground floor).
Grant Recipient/Owner: Saggers & Rhodes
Access contact: Saggers & Rhodes
Open: Access to interior by arrangement only.
Heritage Open Days: No
[P] In town centre car parks. Spaces: 500
[♿] Partial. Wheelchair access to ground floor only. Disabled WC opposite car park in Oat Street. No disabled WC. Guide Dogs: No
[£] Charitable donation only

[P] Parking information.
[♿] Disabled access.
[£] Admission prices.

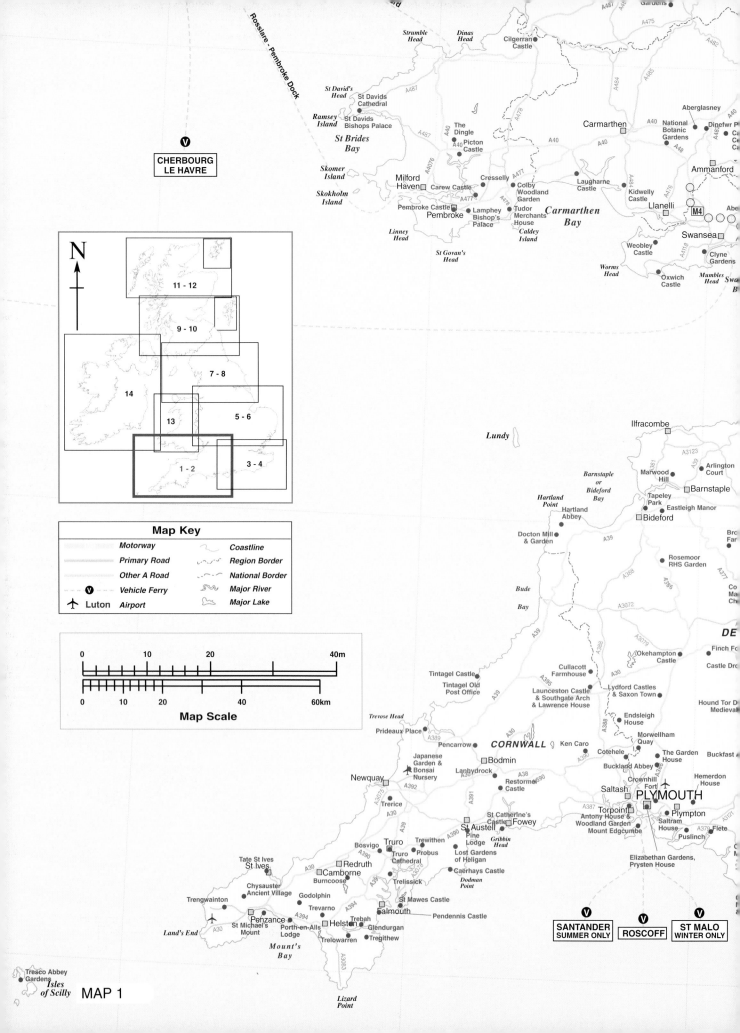

MAP 1

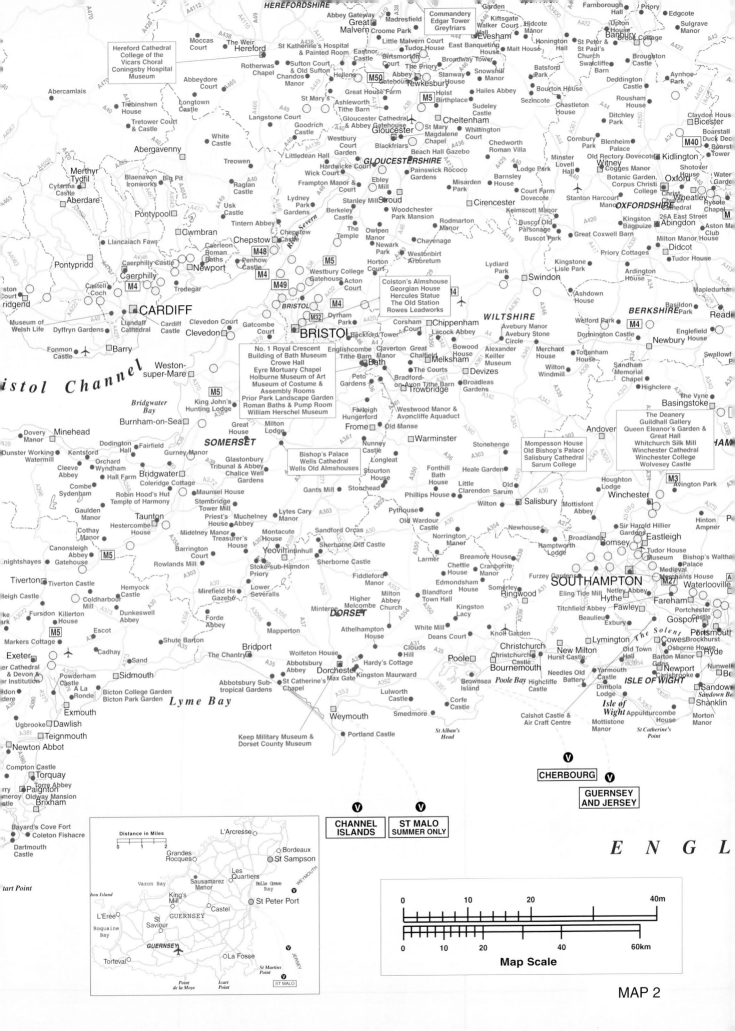

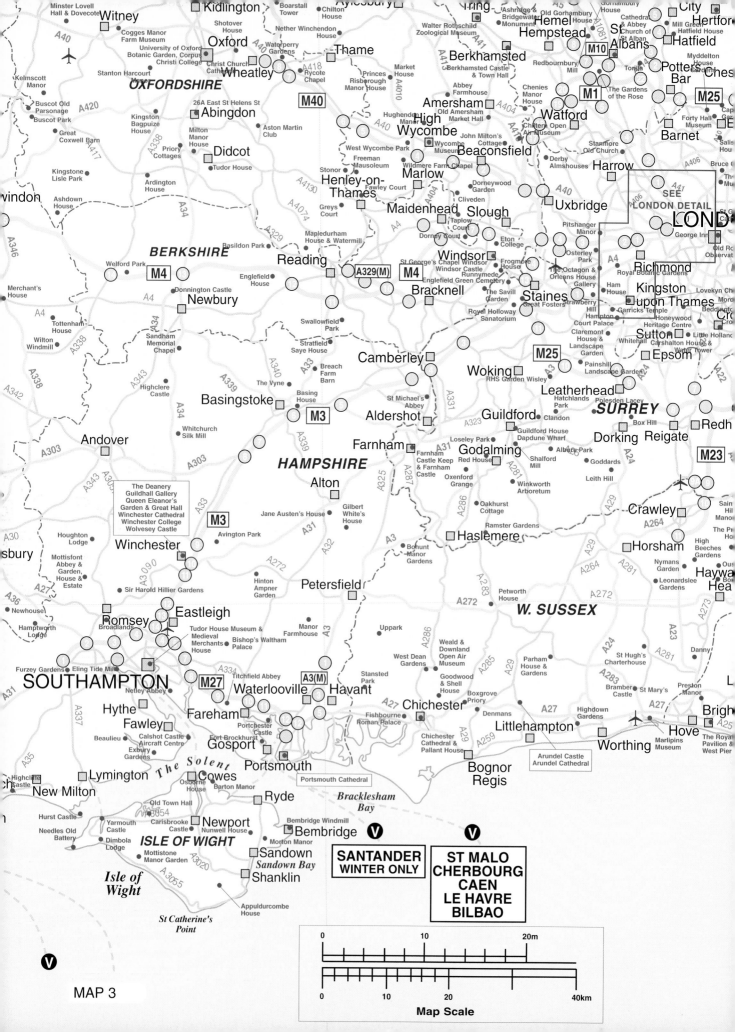

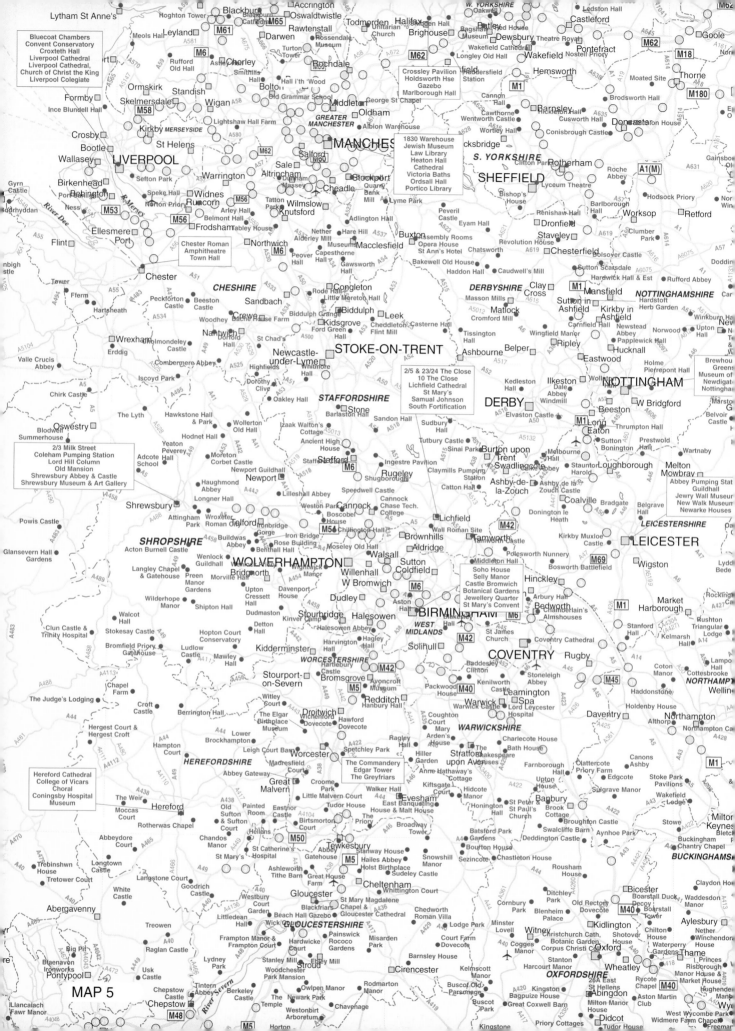

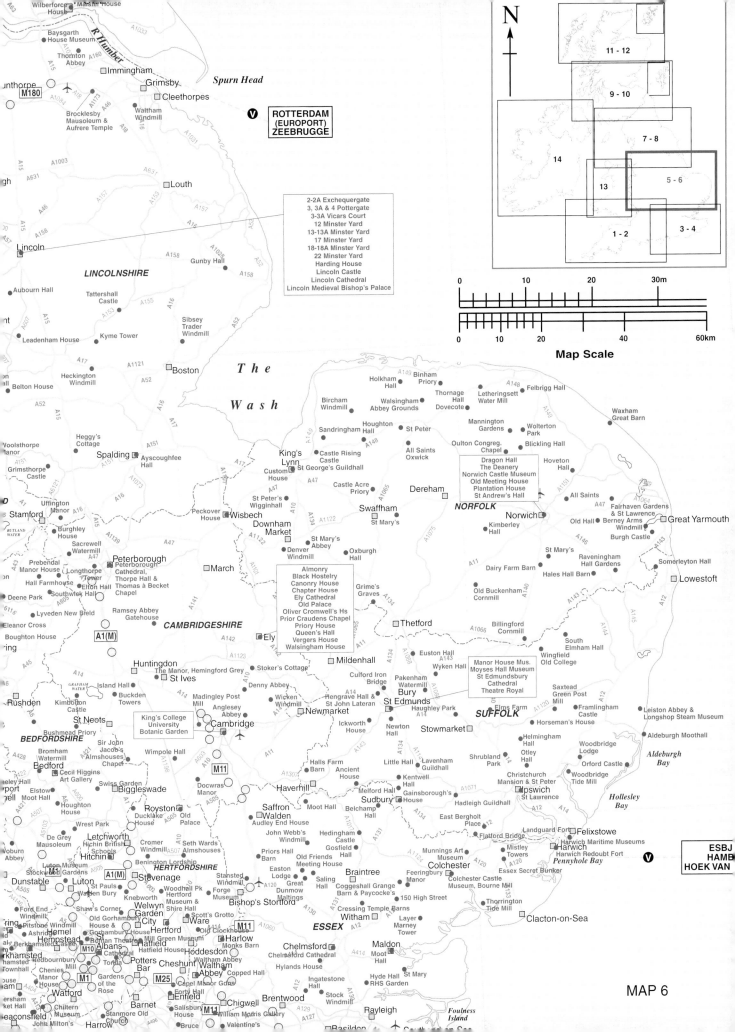

MAP 6

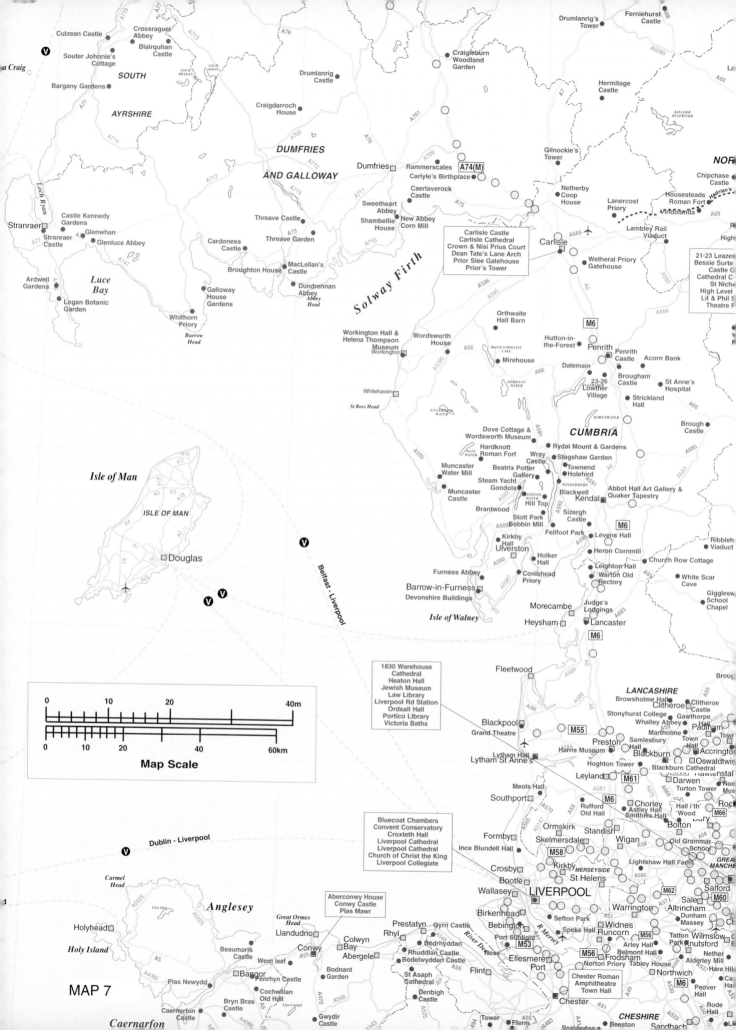

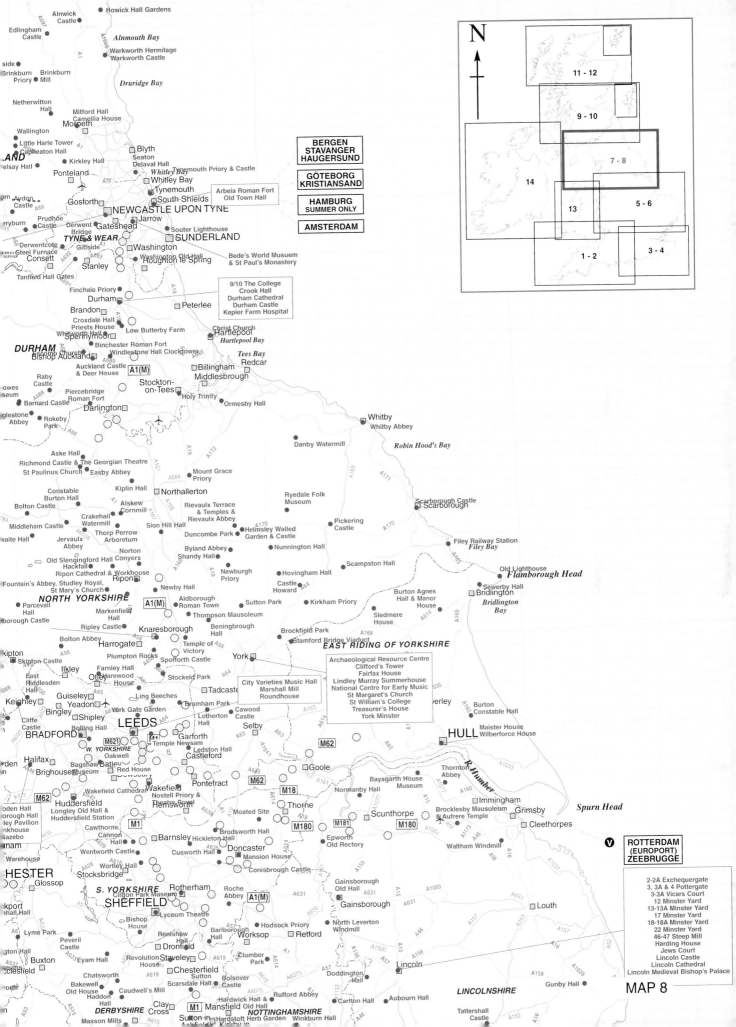

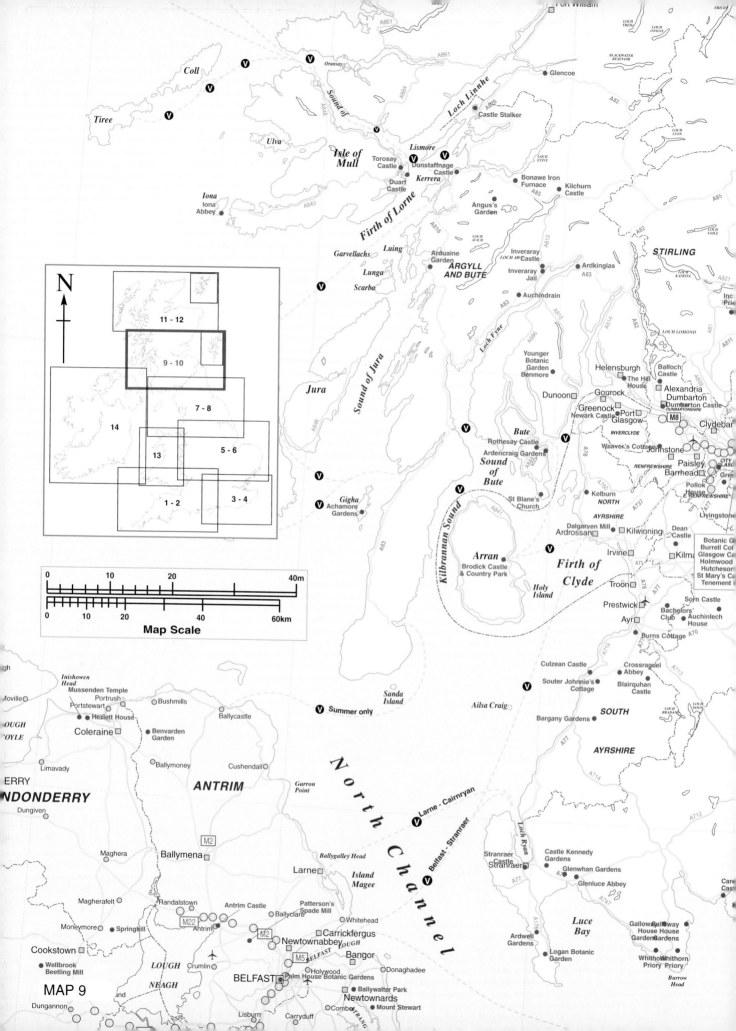

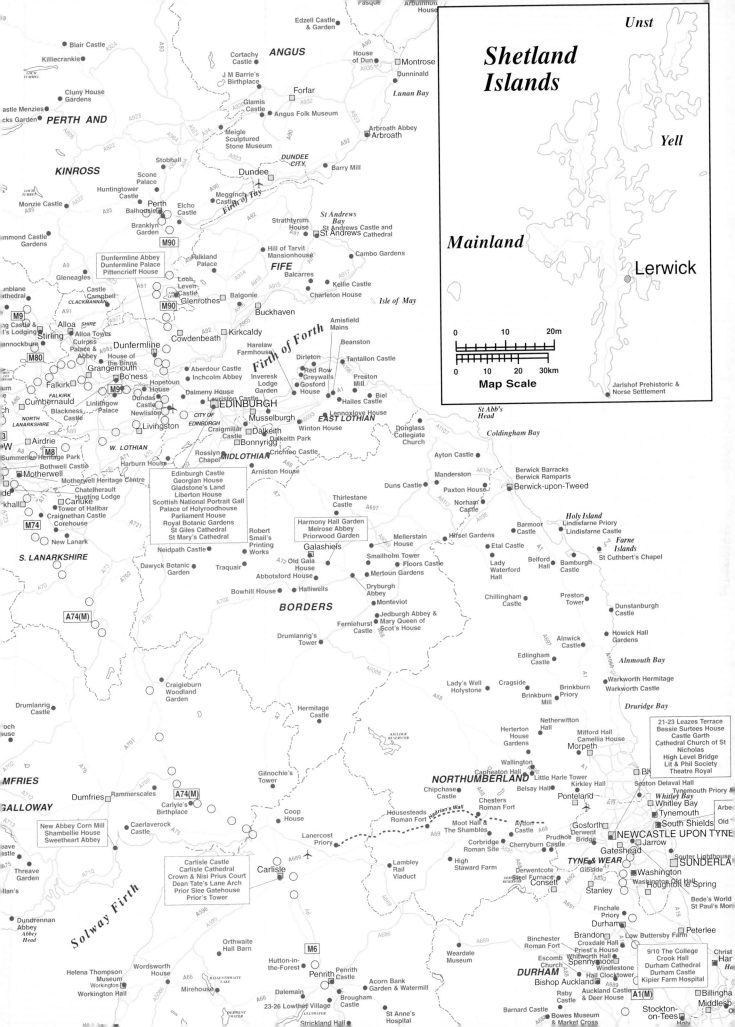

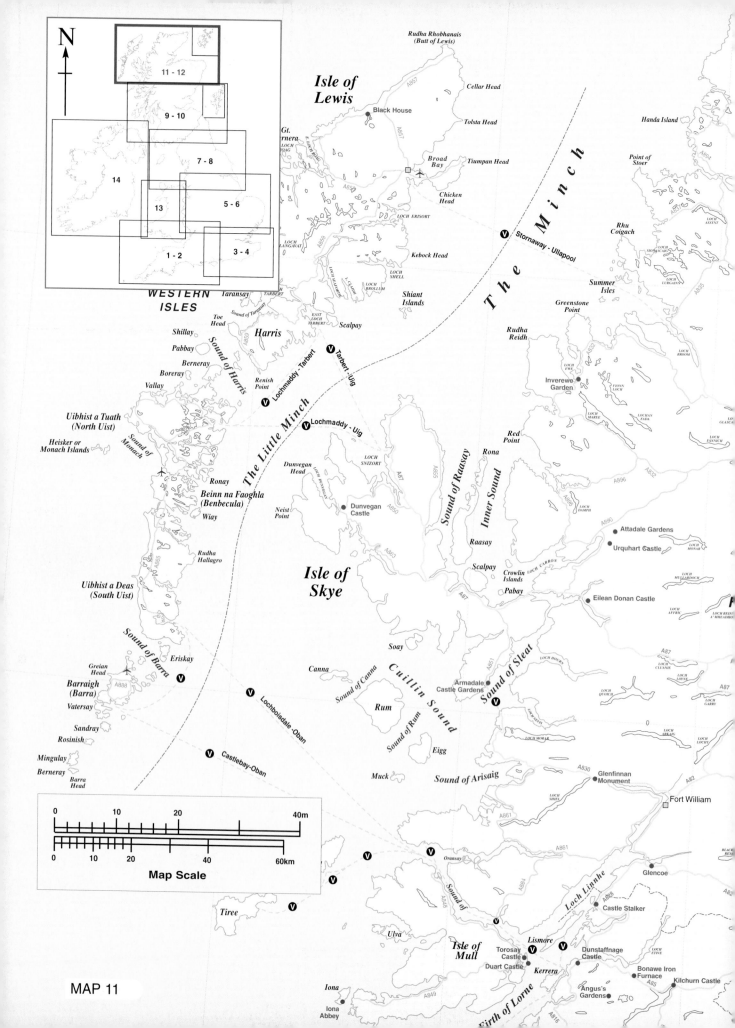

MAP 11

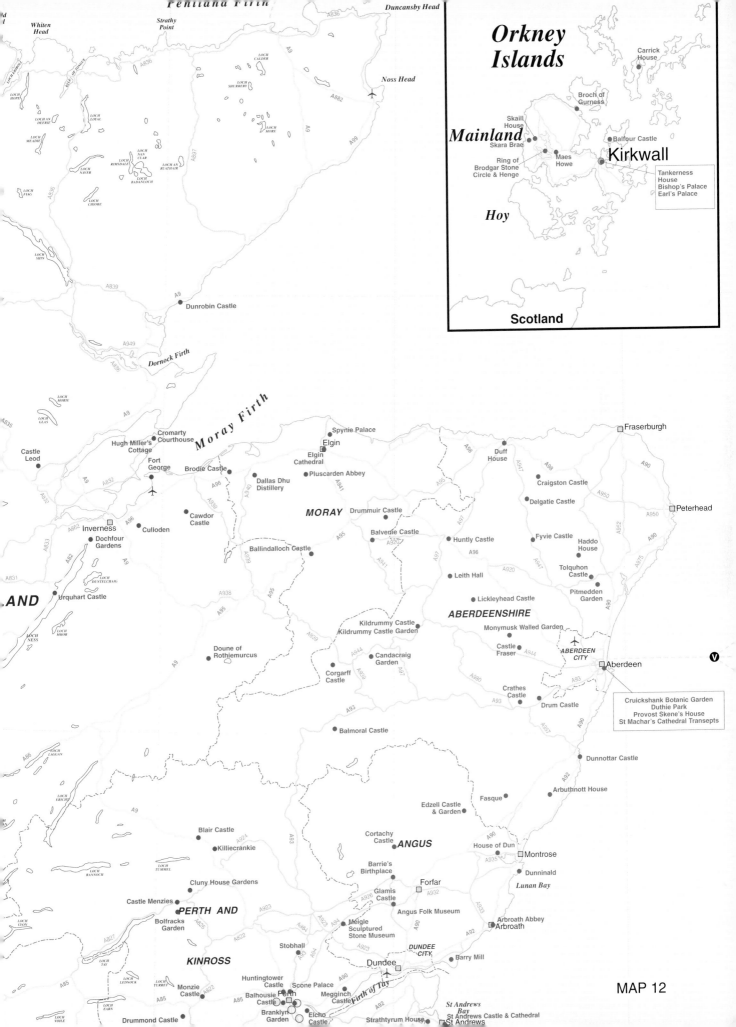

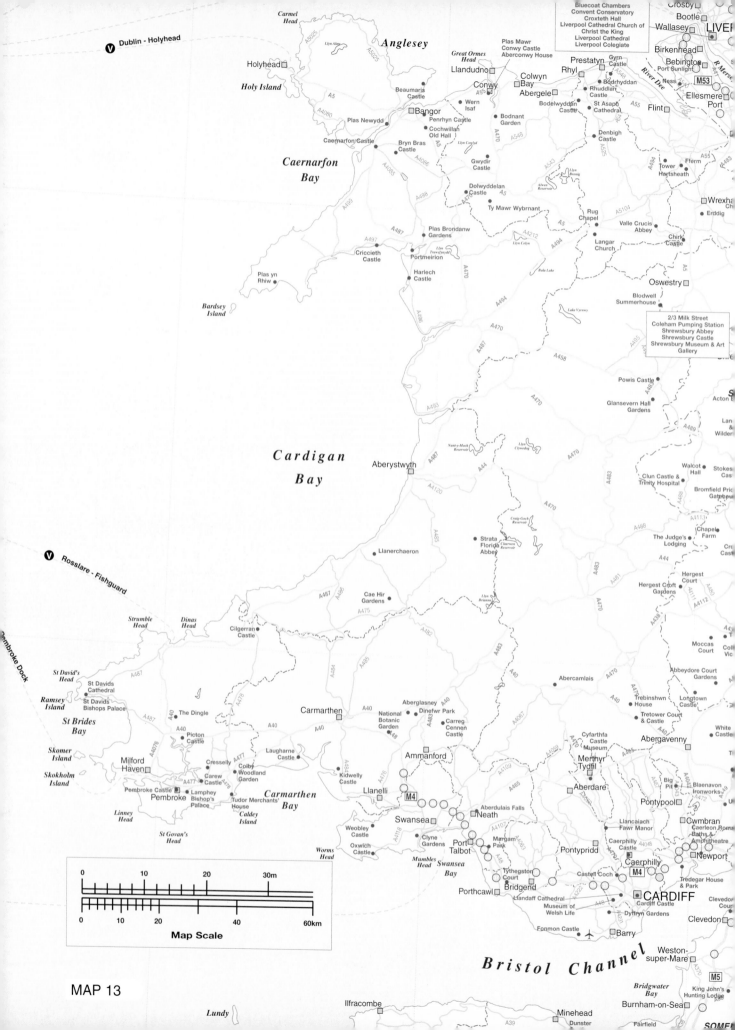

Map Scale

MAP 14

LONDON DETAIL

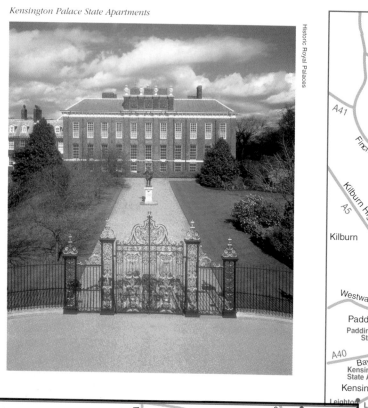

Kensington Palace State Apartments

Historic Royal Palaces

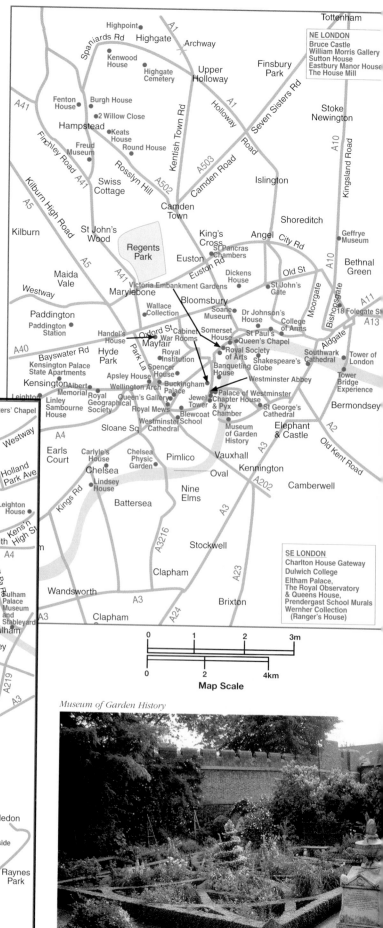

NE LONDON
Bruce Castle
William Morris Gallery
Sutton House
Eastbury Manor House
The House Mill

Tottenham
Highpoint
Spaniards Rd   Highgate   Archway
Kenwood House
Highgate Cemetery   Upper Holloway   Finsbury Park
Fenton House   Burgh House   Stoke Newington
2 Willow Close
Hampstead   Keats House   Kilburn High Road
Freud Museum   Round House   Islington   Shoreditch
Swiss Cottage   Camden Town   Geffrye Museum
Kilburn   St John's Wood   King's Cross   Angel   City Rd   Bethnal Green
Regents Park   Euston   St Pancras Chambers
Maida Vale   Euston Rd   Dickens House   St John's Gate   Moorgate   Folegate St
Westway   Victoria Embankment Gardens   Bloomsbury
Marylebone   Wallace Collection   Soane Museum   Dr Johnson's House   College of Arms   Aldgate
Paddington   Handel's House   Cabinet War Rooms   Somerset House   St Paul's   Queen's Chapel
Paddington Station   Oxford St   Mayfair   Royal Institution   Royal Society of Arts   Shakespeare's Globe   Southwark Cathedral   Tower of London
Bayswater Rd   Hyde Park   Spencer House   Banqueting House   Tower Bridge Experience
Kensington Palace State Apartments   Apsley House   Buckingham Palace   Westminster Abbey
Kensington   Albert Memorial   Wellington Arch   Queen's Gallery   Jewel Tower   Palace of Westminster   Bermondsey
Leighton   Linley Sambourne House   Royal Geographical Society   Royal Mews   Chapter House & Pyx Chamber   St George's Cathedral
Westminster Cathedral   Blewcoat School   Museum of Garden History   Elephant & Castle
Sloane Sq   Carlyle's House   Chelsea Physic Garden   Pimlico   Vauxhall
Earls Court   Chelsea   Lindsey House   Oval   Kennington   Camberwell
Kings Rd   Battersea   Nine Elms   Stockwell
Wandsworth   Clapham   Brixton   Old Kent Road
Clapham

SE LONDON
Charlton House Gateway
Dulwich College
Eltham Palace,
The Royal Observatory
& Queens House,
Prendergast School Murals
Wernher Collection
(Ranger's House)

0   1   2   3m
0   2   4km
Map Scale

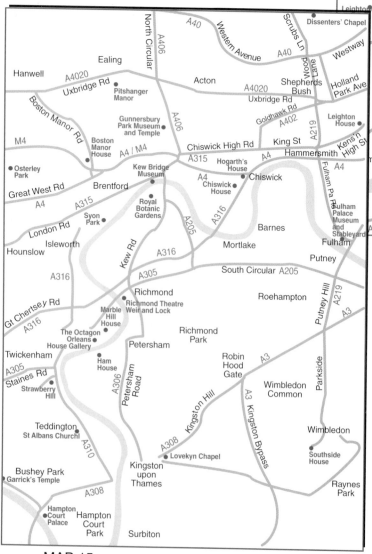

North Circular   A40   Western Avenue   Scrubs Ln   Dissenters' Chapel
Ealing   Acton   Shepherds Bush   Westway
Hanwell   Uxbridge Rd   Holland Park Ave
Pitshanger Manor   Uxbridge Rd   Goldhawk Rd   Leighton House
Boston Manor Rd   Gunnersbury Park Museum and Temple   King St   Leighton House
M4   Boston Manor House   Chiswick High Rd   Hammersmith   Kens'n High St
Osterley Park   Kew Bridge Museum   Hogarth's House   Fulham Palace Museum and Stableyard
Great West Rd   Brentford   Royal Botanic Gardens   Chiswick House   Chiswick   Fulham
London Rd   Syon Park   Barnes   Putney
Isleworth   Mortlake
Hounslow   South Circular   A205   Putney Hill
Richmond   Roehampton
Gt Chertsey Rd   Richmond Theatre Weir and Lock   Robin Hood Gate   Parkside
Marble Hill House   Richmond Park   Wimbledon Common
The Octagon Orleans House Gallery   Petersham
Twickenham   Ham House   Petersham Road   Kingston Hill   Kingston Bypass
Staines Rd   Strawberry Hill   Wimbledon
Teddington   St Albans Church   Southside House
Bushey Park   Lovekyn Chapel   Raynes Park
Garrick's Temple   Kingston upon Thames
Hampton Court Palace   Hampton Court Park   Surbiton

Museum of Garden History

MAP 15

EDINBURGH & YORK DETAIL

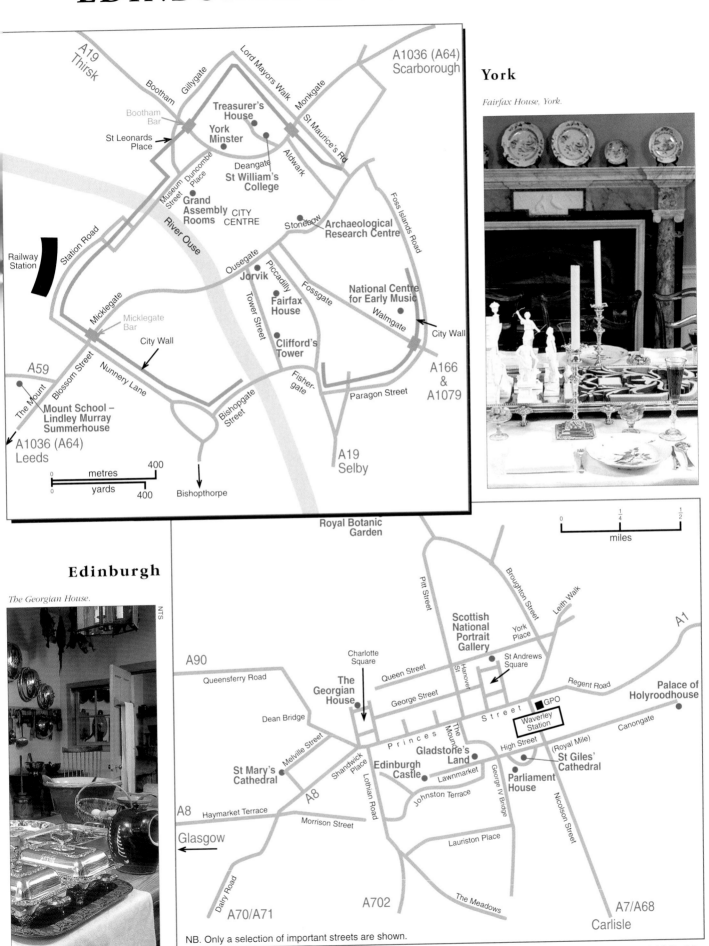

York

Fairfax House, York.

York map labels:

A19 Thirsk
Bootham
Gillygate
Lord Mayors Walk
Monkgate
A1036 (A64) Scarborough
Bootham Bar
Treasurer's House
York Minster
St Maurice's Rd
St Leonards Place
Deangate
Aldwark
St William's College
Museum Street
Duncombe Place
Grand Assembly Rooms
CITY CENTRE
Station Road
River Ouse
Stonebow
Archaeological Research Centre
Foss Islands Road
Railway Station
Micklegate
Ousegate
Piccadilly
Jorvik
Fairfax House
Fossgate
National Centre for Early Music
Walmgate
City Wall
A166 & A1079
Micklegate Bar
City Wall
Tower Street
Clifford's Tower
A59
Blossom Street
Nunnery Lane
Fisher-gate
Bishopgate Street
Paragon Street
The Mount
Mount School – Lindley Murray Summerhouse
A1036 (A64) Leeds
A19 Selby

metres 0 400
yards 0 400

Bishopthorpe

Edinburgh

The Georgian House.

NTS

Edinburgh map labels:

Royal Botanic Garden
A90
Queensferry Road
Charlotte Square
Pitt Street
Broughton Street
Leith Walk
Scottish National Portrait Gallery
York Place
St Andrews Square
A1
Regent Road
Palace of Holyroodhouse
Queen Street
Hanover St
The Georgian House
George Street
Dean Bridge
Street
GPO
Waverley Station
Canongate
Melville Street
Princes
The Mound
High Street
(Royal Mile)
Shandwick Place
Gladstone's Land
St Giles' Cathedral
St Mary's Cathedral
Lothian Road
Edinburgh Castle
Lawnmarket
Parliament House
A8
Johnston Terrace
George IV Bridge
Nicolson Street
A8
Haymarket Terrace
Morrison Street
Glasgow
Lauriston Place
Dalry Road
A70/A71
A702
The Meadows
A7/A68
Carlisle

0 1/4 1/2
miles

NB. Only a selection of important streets are shown.

MAP 16

Heritage Bookshop
DIRECT

Historic houses, interiors, architecture, gardens and antiques are all topics of interest to readers of *Hudson's*. Books covering all these subjects are being brought together in a new specialist mail-order catalogue to be launched in Spring 2002.

Hudson's Heritage Bookshop will offer quality publications – those that are authoritative and well reviewed. Here is a taster of some of those books that will be on offer.

If you would like to receive a copy of Hudson's Heritage Bookshop mail-order catalogue, please complete the order form below (photocopies acceptable) quoting '**HHD Offer**' and you will benefit from a 10% discount on your first order.

The National Trust Guide
Lydia Greeves and Michael Trinick

A fully comprehensive and lavishly illustrated guide giving detailed information on National Trust properties, from the world famous garden of Sissinghurst, to the lesser known oddities in the care of the Trust, such as the last water-driven spade mill in Ireland and a sixteen-sided house in Devon.

Hardback £24.99 432pp
Full colour illustrations 16 maps

Tea-time Recipes
Jane Pettigrew

A mouthwatering selection of regional recipes for cakes, biscuits and breads from National Trust properties. Dishes make use of local ingredients: Old Peculier Fruit Cake from Yorkshire, Bara Brith, the traditional Welsh tea bread, and Irish potato cakes.

Hardback £12.99 164pp
April 2001 Full colour illustrations

A Book of Historical Recipes
Sara Paston-Williams

Provides not only an important insight into social history, but an authentic taste of the past. Based on The Art of Dining, this book contains a brief text to explain the dishes that were eaten at different periods and why certain foods enjoyed favour in their day. Over 50 historical recipes with modern adaptations, using easily acquired ingredients accompany the text.

Paperback £8.50 60pp Full colour illustrations

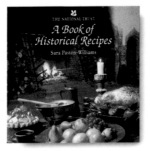

Recipes from the Dairy
Robin Weir and Caroline Liddell with Peter Brears

This informative illustrated guide combines a short history of the country house dairy with traditional dishes adapted to modern tastes. Each recipe is easy to use, requiring neither complicated equipment nor awkward ingredients. Perfect for anyone who loves ice cream in particular or cooking in general.

192pp Full colour illustrations
B&W drawings Hardback £12.99

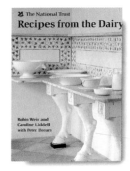

Gardens of the National Trust
Stephen Lacey

The definitive guide to over 130 parks and gardens in England, Wales and Northern Ireland. Stephen Lacey explores each garden horticulturally, describing its beauty and diversity and placing it within the context of garden history. Sponsored by Land Rover.

Hardback £29.99
Full colour illustrations

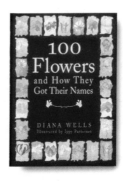

100 Flowers and How They Got Their Names
Ippy Patterson

From abelia to zinnia every flower tells a story. Diana Wells delved deep into horticultural history and uncovered myths, legends and stories of intrepid botanists worldwide search for new and unusual flowers. Illustrations by award-winning

Hardback 234pp

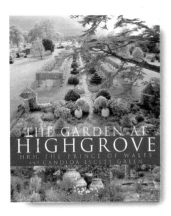

The Garden at Highgrove

HRH The Prince of Wales & Candida Lycett Green

Breathtakingly beautiful photographs of a breathtakingly beautiful garden. With help from some of Britain s finest designers The Prince of Wales has created highly individual gardens. He describes his thinking behind each separate garden, his mistakes and triumphs and his plans for the future. Lavishly illustrated. Will delight and inspire gardeners and horticulturalists at every level.

PB   176pp   £16.99

The Art of Dining:

A History of Cooking

and Eating

Sara Paston-Williams

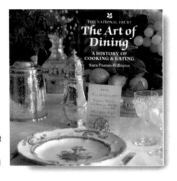

Sara Paston-Williams has used the great wealth of National Trust houses and records to produce a fascinating guide to all the arts of dining. She tackles the huge subject chronologically, from the cavernous kitchens and great halls of medieval houses like Cotehele in Cornwall to the ingenious technology of Victorian service areas like Cragside in Northumberland, producing food for ornate dining rooms and intimate parlours. Each chapter includes historical recipes, together with modern adaptations.

PB   £19.99   320 pages   F/C & B/W illustrations

Historic Interiors

Margaret Willes photographs by Andreas von Einsiedel and Nadia Mackenzie

A grand tour of the National Trust s finest houses. Historic Interiors takes you through the state and family rooms from the great hall to the bedchambers. These superb photographs by two leading interior photographers show how the use of the rooms has changed over the centuries, and in doing so highlight the medieval charms of Little Moreton Hall in Cheshire, the baroque glories of Petworth in Sussex, the Georgian austerity of Kedleston Hall in Derbyshire, the Victorian extravagance of Lanhydrock in Cornwall and many more.

Hardback   144 pp   £17.99   F/C photographs

National Trust Recipes

Sarah Edington

All over the country National Trust cooks are providing good home-cooking for visitors. National Trust Recipes features mouth-watering recipes supplied by cooks from 28 National Trust restaurants and tearooms. Treats include Welsh Lamb and Leek casserole from Erddig, Suffolk Country Crumble from Flatford Mill and Killerton s Chocolate Pot. Of interest to the practical cook, this cookery book will also highlight the gastronomic delights that are on offer in some of the most beautiful places in England, Wales and Northern Ireland.

H/B   £9.99   160pp   B/W drawings

Jackson's Hallmarks

(pocket edition)

Edited by Ian Pickford

Extremely compact but at the same time packed with information and marks. This book has been described as the ideal travelling and buying companion . It is the most accurate and up-to-date guide of its kind in the market.

PB   172pp
Over 1,000 marks   £6.95

Pictorial Dictionary of British 18th Century Furniture Design

compiled by Elizabeth White

Published pattern books regulated the basic proportions and styles throughout the Georgian period. This comprehensive guide includes virtually all known designs published in the 18th century, many of which have not appeared in print since. An invaluable reference work for dating and attributing furniture.

700pp   24 colour plates
over 3,000 B&W designs   £49.50

The Royal School of Needlework 'Art of Embroidery – A History of Style and Technique'

Lanto Synge

The story of embroidery and needlework as discussed within the context of history of fabrics, of decorative costume, of interior decoration, of furniture and pastimes. The book is rich in the art historical background of a fascinating subject.

368pp   320 colour
30 B&W illustrations   £45.00

A Collector's History of British Porcelain,

John and Margaret Cushion

A comprehensive overview of the manufacture of porcelain in Britain from the mid-18th century to the present day enables the collector to easily identify the differences which characterise the individual factories.

448pp   135 colour, 641 B&W illustrations   £45.00

The Dictionary of Portrait Painters in Britain up to 1920
Brian Stewart and Mervyn Cutten

A seemingly unquenchable thirst for portraits of individuals, families and friends has meant that for over 400 years native born portrait artists have been joined by their foreign born colleagues, attracted by the vast number of commissions available. This lists over 5,000 portraitists working in Britain from the early 16th to the early 20th century.

504pp Over 5,000 entries
66 f/c, 370 b/w illus. £49.50

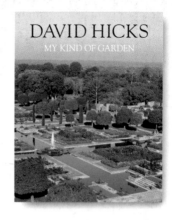

My Kind of Garden
David Hicks

David Hicks was a leading 20th century designer and presented his characteristically idiosyncratic and personal choice of gardens in this, his last book. His approach is dictatorial and uncompromising. What he seeks to impart is style as he personally envisaged it. His view of garden beauty is superbly captured in the extensive colour photographs.

304pp
Illustrations in colour throughout
£29.50

English Country Furniture 1500 – 1900
David Knell

This study of humbler pieces of furniture used in ordinary homes covers regional variations, dating assessments and construction techniques. Each example illustrated is accompanied by a detailed caption, with details of local characteristics, finish, distinctive decorative features and manufacturing methods.

400pp 32 f/c, 625 b/w illus. £45.00

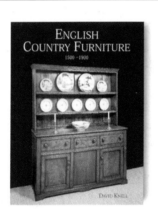

Plant Partners

Magical planting suggestions from today s most compelling garden writer. Herbaceous perennials are the star performers in the garden but to create maximum impact they need the right partners, bulbs and annuals that no garden should be without. Knowing which plant to put with which is an art that often eludes even the most knowledgeable gardener. Now all gardeners, whatever their level ofexpertise, can be inspired to fill a small gap, transform an awkward corner or start a new border from scratch.

HB 240pp £16.99

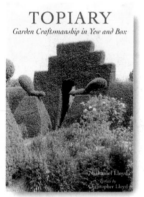

Topiary – Garden Craftmanship in Yew and Box
Nathaniel Lloyd

This is a reprint of a much sought after practical work based on personal experience in establishing Yew and Box topiary and hedging at the famous gardens at Great Dixter. Topiary and Box are now enjoying a revival in our gardens and this is a most useful book.

170pp 56 b/w illus. £14.95

Garden Ornament
Gertrude Jekyll

Design in relation to architecture — gates, steps, balustrades, urns, pergolas, canals and walled gardens. This heavily illustrated book is a mine of contemporary photographic reference of ornamental features both large and small. A vivid and nostalgic picture of garden ornamentation up to the end of the First World War.

476pp 608 illus. £35.00

- ✂

Return this form to get 10% discount off your first order Fax to 01295 750800 or post to:
Hudson's, Heritage Bookshop Direct, High Wardington House, Banbury Oxon OX17 1SP

Please send me a copy of *Hudson's Heritage Bookshop* catalogue.

Name: _____

Address: _____

_____

Postcode: _____

tel: _____ e-mail: _____